BLAKE BOOKS

ANONYMOUS PORTRAIT OF WILLIAM BLAKE (1802?)
aged about 45

From the Collection of Professor Robert N. Essick

This monochrome watercolour was first discovered and identified as
a portrait of Blake in 1974. The extraordinarily hypnotic eyes are
unmistakable

G. E. BENTLEY, Jr.

BLAKE BOOKS

Annotated Catalogues of

WILLIAM BLAKE'S WRITINGS

in Illuminated Printing, in Conventional Typography

and in Manuscript

and Reprints thereof

Reproductions of his Designs

Books with his Engravings

Catalogues

Books he owned

and Scholarly and Critical Works about him

OXFORD · AT THE CLARENDON PRESS
1977

Oxford University Press, Walton Street, Oxford OX2 6DP

OXFORD LONDON GLASGOW NEW YORK
TORONTO MELBOURNE WELLINGTON CAPE TOWN
IBADAN NAIROBI DAR ES SALAAM LUSAKA ADDIS ABABA
KUALA LUMPUR SINGAPORE JAKARTA HONG KONG TOKYO
DELHI BOMBAY CALCUTTA MADRAS KARACHI

ISBN 0 19 818151 5

© *Oxford University Press 1977*

This work is a revised edition of *A Blake Bibliography* by
G. E. Bentley, Jr. & M. K. Nurmi (1964)

*Printed in Great Britain
at the University Press, Oxford
by Vivian Ridler
Printer to the University*

To

BETH

SARAH

JULIA

travellers and scholars

CONTENTS

TABLE OF SYMBOLS

* An entry marked with an asterisk (*) contains one or more illustrations. If there are more than 19 illustrations, the number is specified. If they form a complete series, such as the designs for *Comus*, the series is identified.

§ A section mark (§) indicates a work reported on distant authority (such as an unpublished bibliography) which has not been located for description here.

ABBREVIATIONS

Blake Records (1969)	G. E. Bentley, Jr., *Blake Records* (1969)
BM	British Museum Library of Printed Books, London (now the British Library)
BMPR	British Museum Print Room (i.e. Department of Prints and Drawings)
BNYPL	*Bulletin of the New York Public Library*
Bodley	The Bodleian Library, Oxford University
DA, DAI	*Dissertation Abstracts* (1952–69) and its successor *Dissertation Abstracts International* (1969 ff.)
DS	Mr. David Stamm
DVE	Dr. David V. Erdman
E&S	*Essays and Studies by Members of the English Association*
ELH	*ELH* is the *title* of the periodical; it stands for English Literary History
Fitzwilliam	The Fitzwilliam Museum, Cambridge University
g.e.	gilt edges
GEB	G. E. Bentley, Jr.
HK	Professor Hisao Kodama
HLQ	*Huntington Library Quarterly*
Huntington	The Henry E. Huntington Library and Art Gallery, San Marino, California
JAAC	*Journal of Aesthetics and Art Criticism*
JEGP	*Journal of English and Germanic Philology*
JWCI	*Journal of the Warburg and Courtauld Institutes*
Keynes	The collection of Sir Geoffrey Keynes
Keynes (1921)	Geoffrey Keynes, *A Bibliography of William Blake* (1921)
Keynes & Wolf	Geoffrey Keynes & Edwin Wolf 2nd, *William Blake's Illuminated Books: A Census* (1953)
KP	Mr. Kerrison Preston
LC	The Library of Congress, Washington, D.C.
MKN	Professor M. K. Nurmi
MLN	*Modern Language Notes*
MLQ	*Modern Language Quarterly*
MLR	*Modern Language Review*
Morgan	The Pierpont Morgan Library, New York
MP	*Modern Philology*
N&Q	*Notes and Queries*
NYP	The New York Public Library
PMLA	*PMLA* is the *title* of the periodical; it stands for Publications of the Modern Language Association of America

PQ	*Philological Quarterly*
RES	*Review of English Studies*
RG	Professor Robert Gleckner
RN	Ruth Nurmi
Rosenwald Collection	The Collection of Mr. Lessing J. Rosenwald, Alverthorpe Gallery, Jenkintown, Pennsylvania, given to the Library of Congress and the National Gallery
SB	*Studies in Bibliography*
SP	*Studies in Philology*
t.e.g.	top edge gilt
TLS	*Times Literary Supplement*
V & A	Victoria and Albert Museum, London
vMKN	Entries ending (v . . .), e.g. '(vMKN)', have been verified by the kind assistant whose initials or names follow

ACKNOWLEDGEMENTS

WORK on *A Blake Bibliography* began, as I recall, in 1957, when M. K. Nurmi and I, having undertaken a different collaborative work, which required as a first step a survey of Blake scholarship, discovered that we were uncertain of the exact extent and accomplishment of works about Blake. We exchanged lists of Blake studies, discovered that the overlap was distressingly small, sent similar lists to our friends with similar results, and decided that our first step must be to compile *A Blake Bibliography*.[1]

In general, Professor Nurmi was to be responsible for periodicals after 1831, while I dealt with all books and with periodicals before 1831. Much of my preliminary work was completed in London in the autumn of 1958, when I was supported by the Guggenheim Foundation primarily for work on *Blake Records*. My serious work for *Blake Books* was largely done with the assistance of the Canada Council in the summers from 1962 onwards and in Oxford in 1963–4 and 1970–1. My work with original Blake materials was directed first at the preparation of *William Blake's Writings*, the Bibliographical Notes for which are extended here.

The generous and extensive assistance which M. K. Nurmi and I were given gladly by the Blake fraternity around the world is acknowledged in general terms in *A Blake Bibliography* (1964), xiii–xiv, and is identified here with the initials of the friends who verified individual entries below.[2] The libraries providing original Blake materials are gratefully acknowledged in the Table of Collections here (pp. 57–66). Most of the books and periodicals were in fact seen in the British Museum, Bodley, Toronto, Princeton, and the Diet Library (Tokyo). To the resources and resourcefulness of these and many other libraries and their staffs I am profoundly grateful for generous assistance, both scholarly and personal.

The most extensive assistance with *Blake Books* is, of course, that provided by Professor M. K. Nurmi, whose work has taken him in other directions since we collaborated on *A Blake Bibliography*. His contribution to *Blake Books* is not limited to the many entries bearing his initials, for he was often the intermediary who arranged for others

---

[1] The work for which *A Blake Bibliography* was merely a first step has never got beyond the planning stage.

[2] I should like to thank in addition Miss Phoebe Allen, Professor Robert Essick (particularly for permission to reproduce the newly discovered portrait of Blake as the frontispiece here), Joan Burton (*née* Joan Linnell Ivimy), Sir Geoffrey Keynes, Mr. J. H. Macphail, and Mr. Michael Tolley for divers vital kindnesses.

to check periodical articles for us. I am grateful to him for many forms of assistance.

I have worked happily on *Blake Books* in Canada, Britain, the United States, New Zealand, Australia, Japan, Taiwan, Hong Kong, India, Algeria, and France (more in some than in others); the most satisfying places to work were:

Dutch Boys Landing	Cité des Asphodèles	Bridge House
Mears, Michigan	El Biar, Algeria	Wootton, Oxfordshire

My work on Blake has led me to many lands, homes, and friends. It is my fortune that my work is my pleasure. I wish such pleasure to others.

G. E. B.

Montigny les Arsures
Jura, France
6 August 1971

The last stages of work on *Blake Books* were completed during our peacock year in Poona in 1975–6 where we were sustained by the friendship particularly of the Marathes, Dr. Nagarajan, and the Leclercqs, and where we lived under the protection of Ganesh, a god of knowledge and laughter.

Department of English
University College
University of Toronto
9 July 1976

INTRODUCTION

Blake Books describes the writings of William Blake in original, facsimile, and typographic editions; collected reproductions of his designs; books for which he designed or engraved illustrations; bibliographies, and catalogues of exhibitions or important sales of his work; books which he owned or annotated; and books and articles which discuss him.

I have listed everything I could find concerning Blake published before 1863, when modern interest in him began with the publication of Alexander Gilchrist's *Pictor Ignotus*. After 1863 I have been somewhat more selective, excluding reprints and translations of individual poems which appeared in collections not focused on Blake; reviews that have no independent value or that have not been thought important enough to reprint; reproductions of single pictures in non-Blake books; and most very brief biographical and critical accounts appearing in books. Of these shorter pieces appearing in books, I have in general excluded those less than five pages long; casual references, unless there were a great many of them; and chapters in literary histories in which Blake's name does not appear in the title. Of course, brief accounts of unusual intrinsic value are included. I have tried to include all periodical articles which mention Blake in the title, except for reviews.

The growth of writings about Blake in the last fifty years has been enormous, and *Blake Books* lists many hundreds of items published since Keynes's *Bibliography* of 1921. This has posed special problems, for the languages of Blake scholarship have grown from English, French, Japanese, and German in 1921 to include Italian, Bulgarian, Spanish, Russian,[1] Portuguese, Swedish, Norwegian, Icelandic, Georgian, Chinese, and probably others. In the face of such prodigious growth among proliferating languages and scripts, it may be some comfort to Blake scholars to learn that I have found no Blake materials at all in bibliographies of Arabic; Aramaic; Armenian; Assamese; Bengali; Burmese; Cambodian; Gujarati; Hebrew; Hindi, Panjabi, Sindhi, Pushta; Indonesian; Iranian; Kannada, Badaga, Kurg; Kashmiri; Korean; Kurdish; Maithili; Marathi; Mongol; Oriya; Sanskrit, Pali, and Prakrit; Sinhalese; Syriac; Tamil; Telegu; Tocharian; Turkish; Urdu; and Vietnamese.

There is also the problem of whether or how to deal with various

---

[1] Most of the Russian or other Slavic works in this bibliography derive from A List of Translations and Criticisms of Blake (English excepted) in the M. E. Saltykov-Shchedrin State Public Library, Leningrad, prepared for me in late 1973 by M. V. Brestkina (Bibliographer of the Library).

modes of 'publication' which are not normally considered in bibliographies but which might reasonably be of interest to Blake students.
I have from time to time run across references to Blake as the subject of:

Motion Pictures. I know of two, one of which is 'The Vision of William Blake'
by The Blake Film Trust, in association with The British Film Institute,
music by Vaughan Williams (1958), recorded on Desto DC 6482;

Ballet. Geoffrey Keynes & Gwendolen Raverat, *Job A Masque for Dancing*,
Founded on Blake's Illustrations to the Book of Job, Music by R. Vaughan
Williams, Pianoforte arrangements by Vally Lasker (?1931); first performed at the Norwich Festival in 1930 and now a regular part of the
repertoire of the Royal Ballet;

Microfilms. Most libraries will, of course, supply individual microfilms of works
in their collections. The only organization I know which does so commer-
cially is the EP Group of Companies [formerly Micro Methods] (East
Ardsley, Wakefield, Yorkshire), which supplies coloured microfilms primarily of the Fitzwilliam Blake books and of the *Night Thoughts* drawings
in the BMPR;

Abstracts. It is increasingly common for scholarly journals such as *PMLA*
to give abstracts of the articles they print, a practice which has not been
separately noted below except where the article is in Japanese and the
abstract in English. Many of the abstracts are collected annually in
MLA Abstracts (1970 ff.);[1]

Music, both settings and records. These are described in M. K. Nurmi's
'Note on Musical Settings', *A Blake Bibliography* (1964), 363–5. Two recent
records are 'Songs of Innocence and Experience', 'Tuned by Allan
Ginsberg', with Peter Orlovsky, MGM 'Verbe' FTS–3083, and Benjamin
Britten, Songs, London OS 26099;

Stamps. The Blake stamp is Rumania no. 1219, issued in 1958 as part of an
annual writers' set—see no. 872;

Postcards. Most libraries and museums with Blake collections sell postcard-
sized reproductions of Blake's works. Probably the most extensive collection
of such reproductions is that published by the British Museum;

Poems. For the period before 1863 I have recorded all poems about Blake
that I have discovered; thereafter I have simply ignored them, whether
written by Dante Gabriel Rossetti, James Thomson, Amy Lowell, John
Gould Fletcher, William Rose Benet, or Ezra Pound (Canto XVI);

Broadcasts. These include Désirée Hirst, 'The Grandeur of Inspiration', BBC,
1958; 'As a Man Is—So He Sees', a BBC2 TV essay by Adrian Malone on
Blake, 1969; a dramatization of *Jerusalem* introduced by Sir Geoffrey

---

[1] An example of the danger posed by abstracts to credulous academics is provided by the
digest (*1972 MLA Abstracts*, i [1974], 72) of Patrick M. Brantlinger's short story 'Classic and
Romantic: An Augury of Innocence', *College English*, xxxiii (1972), 702–11, which naughtily
summarizes the story as if it were a scholarly study soberly warning that 'Blake can have
nothing but a deleterious [*i.e.* anti-establishmentarian] effect upon the tender imaginations
of the young'.

Keynes, BBC, spring 1970; Allen Ginsberg reading from *Songs of Innocence and of Experience*, Channel 13 (N.Y.), 28 Oct. 1970; Dr. Melvin Hill talking about Blake's politics, CBC (Toronto), 23 Feb. 1972; 'William Blake: Innocence and Experience' and 'William Blake: Prophet', produced and directed for ABC–TV's Directions by Aram Boyajian and telecast 16, 23 Jan. 1972;[1]

Tape Recordings. Benjamin Demott, 'Blake and Manchild' (N.Y.: McGraw-Hill, 1968), witheringly reviewed by Morris Eaves, *Blake Newsletter*, vi, l (1972), 25–6.

Videotapes. 'Holy Thursday' by George F. Hood & Richard Blakelee, 1969;[1] *America*, script by Janet Warner & John Sutherland for Glendon College (York University, Toronto), 1970; *Visions of the Daughters of Albion*, script by Janet Warner & John Sutherland for Glendon College (York University, Toronto), 1971;

Filmstrips. 'History of the Graphic Arts. Set 33. William Blake. Budek Films and Slides of California, 1969';

Theatre. Dramatization of *The Marriage* in Chicago, May 1970; Jack Lindsay, 'William Blake and Our World', Mermaid Theatre, London, 15 Nov. 1970; Adrian Mitchell, 'Tyger', a 'celebration' opening in London in July 1971; Michael Fischetti, director, 'Blake's Songs of Innocence and Experience', Part III of *Three Pieces in Multi Media* performed by the Dance and Drama Theatre of New York City, January 1972.[1]

My information about such works was so incomplete, and the difficulties of collection so unfamiliar and formidable that I have made no effort to do more than record my chance findings.

Most of the great Blake collections have been formed in the past forty years and given to public institutions, until today twice as many of the illuminated works are in public collections as in private. The best collection of Blake's art is in the Tate Gallery, London, but the majority of the works in Illuminated Printing have come to the United States. The most important repositories of Blake's Illuminated Books are the British Museum and the Library of Congress (exclusively through the munificence of Mr. Lessing J. Rosenwald), followed by Harvard, the Fitzwilliam Museum, the Pierpont Morgan Library, the Huntington Library, Yale, the New York Public Library, and Princeton.

METHODS

Blake Books is divided into six parts: I. Editions of Blake's Writings; II. Reproductions of Drawings and Paintings; III. Engravings; IV. Catalogues and Bibliographies; V. Books Owned by Blake; and VI. Biography and Criticism. With the exception of IV, each part is

---

[1] *Blake Newsletter*, v (1972), 219.

organized alphabetically, by author or (in Parts I–II) by title. Part IV is arranged chronologically, by the year of publication.

Successive editions or printings of books and articles are given immediately after the original entry. In these multiple printings, the first edition is indicated by an A after the number, and successive editions are differentiated from it by B, C, D, and so on. (However, in Part I, Section A, *contemporary* copies of Blake's writings use such capital letters merely to identify separate copies and not to indicate separate editions.)

In listing works published after 1831, I give in italics the short title—that part of the work which would be given in an accurate footnote, for instance—followed in roman type by the sub-title, the place of publication, and the date. For works published before 1831, I normally try to give rather more information, particularly for books with Blake's writings or engravings (Parts I and III). In the discussions which follow the title-pages of early works, the points mentioned are merely the data I have found necessary to distinguish this particular title from others like it, except for original editions of Blake's own writings, where my intention is to give exhaustive information.

LOCATION OF COPIES. (1) For Blake's own writings, I record all copies of which I have evidence, including copies not now locatable. (2) For Blake's engravings, I record copies I happen to know about in public collections. This list is never exhaustive. Normally the copy examined for description here was the one in the British Museum. (3) For other works published before 1831, I have normally recorded only the copy I happen to have examined. (4) All but a very few items have been verified. The few exceptions are indicated by a section mark (§). Naturally, I have less confidence in such descriptions than in those for works actually seen. Despite diligent efforts to exclude errors, however, no doubt some have crept in. I should be grateful to anyone who will take the trouble to call my attention to them gently.

ORGANIZATION OF THE PARTS

PART I. EDITIONS OF BLAKE'S WRITINGS. Blake's writings are listed in alphabetical *order of title*. Various editions of a given work are listed in chronological order, except that all translations are grouped together after the English editions. Part I is divided into two sections. The first section consists of reprints of texts as Blake issued them. Thus *Songs of Innocence*, *Poetical Sketches*, *Jerusalem*, and other individual works will be found in Part I, Section A. I have tried to give exhaustive information about all traceable contemporary copies of Blake's writings. Editions after 1827 are described in a perfunctory manner.

Works in conventional typography are set out conventionally. Facts about works in Illuminated Printing are given in much fuller detail, because each copy differs significantly and intentionally from almost every other. For each Illuminated Work, there is a table giving, for each copy: (1) The *Location* (Huntington); (2) A *letter designation* (copy C); (3) Whether Blake *coloured* it; (4) The *plates* found in it; (5) The total number of *leaves* and, when there are more plates than leaves, an indication of which plates are printed back-to-back; (6) The *watermark*, plate by plate; (7) Blake's manuscript *numeration*; (8) The *order* in which it is bound; (9) The presence of *offsets*; (10) The *leaf-size* in centimetres; (11) Whether it has been *trimmed and gilt*; and (12) The *colour of the printing-ink*. This table is followed by brief discussions about the date, the publication, the colouring, catchwords, order of plates, variants, and errata.

Identification of Copies. Sir Geoffrey Keynes has assigned a letter to each copy of every original printed work by Blake,[1] to make it possible to distinguish easily between one copy and another. These letters are referred to throughout the pages that follow (e.g. '*Jerusalem*[E]'). Keynes assigns letters to copies in what he takes to be their chronological order, A (the earliest copy) to, say, N. I designate copies by the Keynes letters, but I often give reasons for believing that the copies were produced in a different order.

Identification of Plates. Since Blake often altered the order of plates in his works in Illuminated Printing, it is necessary to establish a theoretical plate-order and to refer consistently to the plates by the plate-numbers assigned to them in this order. Sir Geoffrey Keynes established these plate-orders in his *Bibliography of William Blake* (1921), and I have followed these orders.

An inconsistency appears, however, in Sir Geoffrey's designation of preliminaries such as frontispieces, title-pages, and introductory poems; sometimes, as in *Thel* (1789), *Visions* (1793), and *Europe* (1794) he refers to these preliminaries by roman numerals (i–iii), and sometimes, as in *Innocence* (1789), *Marriage* (?1790–3), and *Urizen* (1794), he refers to the preliminaries by the arabic numerals (1–3) which identify the rest of the plates.[2] For the sake of simplicity and consistency, I have imposed the arabic system on all works, so that pl. 1 is always the first plate of a work (frontispiece, title-page, or incipit).

Identification of Watermarks. When the leaves of a given work bear fragmentary watermarks which are unmistakable (e.g. 'TMAN / 804')

---

[1] For Blake's works in Illuminated Printing, the identifications are made in the Keynes & Edwin Wolf 2nd, *William Blake's Illuminated Books: A Census* (1953) (modifying Keynes's *Bibliography of William Blake* [1921]); for *Poetical Sketches* and *Descriptive Catalogue* in his *Blake Studies* (1949, 1971); for separate plates ('The Accusers', 'Albion Rose', 'The Ancient of Days', 'Joseph of Arimathea', 'Laocoon', 'Mirth') in his *Engravings by William Blake: The Separate Plates* (1956); for *For Children* and *For the Sexes* in his *Gates of Paradise* (1968).

[2] Sir Geoffrey sometimes uses one system in his *Bibliography* (1921) and the *Census* (1953) and another system in his editions of Blake's writings (1925–72), as in *Milton*.

or which are mutually consistent (e.g. 'TMAN / 804' plus 'J WHAT / 180'),
the whole of the presumed watermark is reported without reservation.
After the watermark, the pages on which it appears are given in parentheses, e.g. 'J WHATMAN / 1804 (4, 12, 17)'. When a crucial fragment
of the watermark is missing, the vital part of the absent portion is
identified, e.g. 'J WHATMAN / 180[ ]'.

Identification of Blake's Numeration. The manuscript numbers I take to
be Blake's are normally written in old Brown ink, or in the colour in
which the text was printed, above the top right corner of the plate-
mark. Blake added such numbers fairly consistently after about 1805.
So far as I can tell, Blake never numbered his pages in pencil, and pencil
page-numbers are ignored here as bearing no likely authority, probably
having been added by binders or later owners. The rare printed
numbers are, of course, identified.

Significance of Offsets. Sometimes the images of heavily coloured prints
have been offset on to facing leaves. Since these offsets may provide
a valuable indication of the order in which the leaves were once
arranged, the presence of identifiable offsets is reported. However, only
when the order indicated by the offsets differs from the present binding-
order is the offset-order reported in detail.

Measurement of Leaf- and Plate-size. Leaf-sizes and plate-sizes are given
in centimetres, width before height. The leaf-size and plate-size is often
somewhat irregular. The measurement was ordinarily made in the
bottom and right-hand margins.

Publication. For each of Blake's published works there is a brief essay
on publication. These ordinarily include discussions of when copies
were drafted, etched, printed, coloured, and sold, the changes in price
of the work, indications of contemporary reactions to the work, if any
are known, and the identity of contemporary buyers of the work.

Catchwords. Catchwords are reported because they confirm the order
or, as in the case of *Jerusalem*, indicate an alternate order in which the
plates were numbered or bound.

Order. In some of his works Blake's intentions about the page-order
are obscure or contradictory. In manuscript works this may be because
the pages have been rebound, as in the *Notebook*, or because the pages
were loose when rediscovered, as in *Vala*. In Illuminated Works it is
likely to be because copies survive in more than one order; the plates
of *Innocence*, for example, are arranged in over thirty different ways.
Therefore, for each work there is a section discussing the evidence for
the order(s) in which Blake intended the work to be arranged, the dates
of the changes if more than one order appears to be authoritative, and
the reasons for choosing the order used in the present text.

Variants. There are several kinds of variants in Blake's printed works.

He never coloured two copies uniformly;[1] he sometimes altered the etched lines on the copperplates (as in *For Children*), sometimes removed lines by masking the plate (as in *America*) or by wiping off ink in printing, and sometimes added words (as in *Poetical Sketches*) or designs to printed copies. As a consequence, it is necessary for an editor to examine every copy of a given work before speaking confidently about it.

I have examined every original copy of Blake's works which could be located, in some ninety collections ranging from Edinburgh to Auckland. I compared each original with a master photocopy which I carried with me, so that all variants from this master copy could be noted.

In hand-produced works such as Blake's, there are of course many accidental variants which seem scarcely worth reporting. The shade of ink may differ very slightly from plate to plate, or even on different parts of the same plate. An insignificant part of the design, say a leaf, may not be inked at all in one copy, or elsewhere there may be a deforming blob. A branch or cloud outline may alter in a minor way, and facial features may be sharper in one copy than in another, particularly when they have been clarified in ink. In the colouring, a Blue sky will give an effect different from an uncoloured sky (may even identify it positively as sky), and light Green leaves may connote something different from dark Green ones. All these variants have, however, ordinarily been suppressed in the notes below.

The definition of 'Significant Variants' is, of course, partly subjective. A few kinds of variant I have reported regularly. Any verbal change, of word or of letter, has been noted, and the colouring of clothing is reported. I have tried to give all large changes in design, such as the omission or addition of a figure, and all deliberate minor ones, such as the addition of haloes. There is, of course, an undefined limbo between these extremes, where conscientious practice may differ. I have suppressed the colour of brindled cows and sun-tanned flesh but recorded sunrises and dead-Grey bodies. In such details, I expect that readers will more often find themselves surfeited than starved.

Errata. Conspicuous errata in Blake's text are reported, chiefly in the matters of omitted letters ('the' for 'thee'), mis-spellings ('here' for 'hear'), and disagreement of verb and subject ('was' for 'were'). Variant orthography common in the eighteenth century ('tyger'), contractions ('wood' for 'wooed'), and Blake's habitual orthographical irregularities ('recieve') are not ordinarily remarked, nor are vagaries of punctuation reported.

All works which include either more or less than a complete book as Blake issued it, such as *Songs of Innocence and Other Poems*, or *Eight*

---

[1] With the possible exception of *No Natural Religion*.

Songs of William Blake, are listed separately in alphabetical order by title under Part I, Section B, Collections and Selections. I have ignored anthologies including Blake that were published after 1863.

PART II. REPRODUCTIONS OF DRAWINGS AND PAINTINGS. Books which consist chiefly of reproductions of Blake's art are organized in two sections analogous to those in Part I. Blake's illustrations for a given author, say Milton or Gray, are listed under the name of the author in Section A. Illustrations of more than one author, such as *The Paintings of William Blake*, are listed alphabetically by title in Section B.

PART III. COMMERCIAL BOOK ENGRAVINGS. The works for which Blake designed or executed engravings are listed alphabetically by author, or, in the case of periodicals, by title, in Section A. (Only books and periodicals are listed here. I have made no attempt to trace independently issued engravings; information about these is collected in Sir Geoffrey Keynes, *Engravings by William Blake:* The Separate Plates [1956].) In Section B of this Part will be found a few books with collections of his engravings, listed alphabetically by title.

PART IV: CATALOGUES AND BIBLIOGRAPHIES. Since most of the works in this part were issued anonymously, and since the reader is unlikely to remember the precise wording of the title in most cases, I have organized this part by date. I have tried to be exhaustive for works by Blake exhibited or sold before 1831; liberally selective up to 1863; and highly selective after 1863. Catalogues issued within the last hundred years are included only when Blake is mentioned in the title, or when a significant number (say five) of his works in Illuminated Printing were included. I have simply ignored most 'bibliographies' perfunctorily appended to books about Blake.

PART V: BOOKS OWNED BY BLAKE. This Part, organized alphabetically by author, describes the works which Blake owned or annotated and gives the information which associates them with Blake. It also describes a few works with his names on them which did *not* belong to the poet.

PART VI: BIOGRAPHY AND CRITICISM. Part VI, organized alphabetically by author, includes all books or articles I have found with the poet's name in the title, except for reviews; all works published before 1863 which refer to Blake at all, except catalogues—see above; all books which have important discussions of Blake even though they do not have Blake's name in the title.

Dozens, scores, even hundreds of these articles and books, especially those under 'Anon.', are hardly worth the trouble to look up. Indeed, a great many would only cause distress to a serious reader. To save the user time and possibly pain, I have summarized hundreds of articles and books, particularly when the titles are obscure. These comments are normally descriptive rather than evaluative.[1]

BLAKE BOOKS

I became so dissatisfied with the publisher of *A Blake Bibliography* (1964) at an early stage that work on a second edition was undertaken actively during the years that it struggled through the press. Work on revision has, then, been going on for over ten years. The chief differences between *A Blake Bibliography* (1964) and *Blake Books* are as follows:

1. The perfunctory descriptions of contemporary copies of Blake's works in Part I are entirely replaced by the results of work on the originals themselves;

2. All the works with Blake's commercial engravings in Part III are described afresh, in somewhat more detail, with a few new titles and new editions of previously known titles;

3. I have omitted scores of entries which appear in *A Blake Bibliography* (1964), normally because closer inspection proved them either to be reviews or to be substantially irrelevant to Blake;

4. I have omitted as well the 'Table of Type-Printed References to Blake before 1863' (1964, pp. xvii–xviii), largely because the important ones are printed in *Blake Records* (1969); the essay on 'Blake's Chronology' (1964, pp. 33–8), because each work has a discussion of date below; and M. K. Nurmi's 'Note on Musical Settings' (1964, pp. 363–5), chiefly because I am not competent to bring it up to date;

5. Several hundred Japanese items unknown to me in 1964 are now included;

6. Several hundred pre-1960 entries have been incorporated, often from collections of periodical clippings such as that in the Rosenwald Collection;

7. Hundreds of entries were revised for fact or comment, chiefly among periodicals;

8. Hundreds of entries were added for works printed since 1960, when *A Blake Bibliography* was sent to press;

9. In *A Blake Bibliography* (1964), editors and authors in Parts I–V were cross-referenced in Part VI so that all the works about Blake by a given scholar (say Sir Geoffrey Keynes) could be found at a glance; in *Blake Books*, this system of cross-referencing is abandoned, and all such matter is now given in the Index.

The recent proliferation of Blake scholarship and rubbish is startling.

---

[1] The Preface thus far is substantially a revision of the one which appeared in *A Blake Bibliography* (1964).

A Blake Bibliography (1964) contained some 2,200 entries, while *Blake Books*, despite the purges noted in no. 3 above, has over 3,000 entries, a growth of 37 per cent, and even so the multiplication of reprints is concealed. This springtide growth of weeds and grain means that it is scarcely possible for even a responsible scholar to reap all the fruit of Blake writing. I have therefore attempted to separate the wheat from the tares in the essay on 'Blake's Reputation and Interpreters' below.

BLAKE BIBLIOGRAPHIES

The first Blake 'bibliography' was a list of five works by Blake in *A Biographical Dictionary of the Living Authors of Great Britain and Ireland* (1816). W. M. Rossetti extended this list in Gilchrist's *Life of William Blake* (1863, 1880), but the earliest attempt to compile a comprehensive bibliography of works by and about Blake was in Sir Geoffrey Keynes's great *Bibliography of William Blake*, announced in 1912, published in 1921, and reprinted photolithographically in 1969. Excluding such necessarily abbreviated lists as that in the *Cambridge Bibliography of English Literature* (1940, 1957, 1971), the next serious attempt to deal extensively with Blake books was in G. E. Bentley, Jr. & M. K. Nurmi, *A Blake Bibliography* (1964). The compilers endeavoured to list all works of scholarship and appreciation of Blake (excluding reviews) and to describe books with commercial engravings by him in somewhat more detail; information on Blake's writings was largely summarized from various works by Sir Geoffrey Keynes. The present *Blake Books* is an expansion and revision of *A Blake Bibliography* (1964) with a scope similar to Keynes's *Bibliography of William Blake* (1921), except that it is extended to include several thousand publications which have appeared within the last half-century.

The mid twentieth-century Blake bibliographer has the enormous advantage over his predecessors that most of the territory is fully mapped, and all he can well hope to do, besides keeping up to date, is to record a neglected cul-de-sac here or name an overlooked mountain peak there. On the other hand, he faces some problems not familiar to previous generations.

REPRINTS

The problem of reprints has been especially exasperating in the last fifteen years. (*a*) For one thing, the same work is often published in the same year with slightly different title-pages on either side of the Atlantic. I have reported such duplications when I was aware of them (the publishers are strikingly silent about it), but I am not much concerned about such omissions, which ordinarily affect only the place and publisher and leave the texts identical. (*b*) More troublingly, books are now frequently reprinted photolithographically,[1] and such publications, often circularized primarily to new university libraries, may not come to the attention of reviewers and scholars except accidentally. Further, even responsible new editions of old titles burst from the presses so frequently that I am not confident of keeping track of them. (*c*) Articles about Blake are reprinted more and more frequently in Blakean anthologies, which are fairly accessible, in festschrifts, and in collections of the author's writings (e.g. Northrop Frye, T. S. Eliot, Middleton Murry) which are likely to come to the attention of Blake scholars in less predictable ways. The largest lacunae in *Blake Books*, apart from incidental newspaper pieces, are probably among reprints.

JAPANESE BOOKS

Works on Blake in Japanese present rather special difficulties. In the first place, the problems are formidable in size, for there seem to be more books and articles on Blake in Japanese than in all other non-English languages combined. This bulk, combined with the intricacy of the problems and the paucity of Japanese books outside Japan, made it necessary for me to go to Japan[2] in the summer of 1970 to try to see as many as possible of the Japanese works myself. While there, I was given extraordinarily generous assistance by many, particularly by Professor James Hisao Kodama, who made almost all the arrangements for my work; by Professor Narumi Umetsu, who gave me a Xerox copy of his typescript chronological list of references to Blake in Japanese; by Miss Nobuko Yamazaki, who worked beside me and who supplied me with most of the transliterations and translations below; and by my wife, who now knows much more about how to use a Japanese library than I do.

In the second place, there are two systems of transliterating Japanese into Roman characters: the standard (Hepburn) system, used in *A Blake Bibliography* (1964), and the Official System, used in the National Diet Library and here in *Blake Books*.[3] For example, the old standard system

---

[1] For example, in 1973 there were FIVE photolithographic editions in print of Basil de Selincourt's indifferent *William Blake* (1909).

[2] One motive was to heed the injunction of Bunsho Jugaku ('William Blake and Japan', *Eigo Seinen: The Rising Generation*, ciii [1957], 518–19): 'The day will come before long when, I believe, every Western student of Blake will have to learn the Japanese language if he does not wish to remain ignorant of the fruitful works of Japanese scholarship in the field of Blakean literature . . .'. Another motive was to approach the beauty of Japan, where the artificial lakes are in the shape of the Chinese character for 'spirit'.

[3] A further puzzle for the Western scholar is that some Japanese books, generally the older ones, order the pages from right to left, while others arrange them as we do, from left to right, and a few number from both ends toward the middle. Also, in old books the characters plummet in columns down the page, while in newer ones they move 'like a flight of wild geese' (as one Haiku expresses it) horizontally across the page, as ours do.

transliterated Japanese sounds, as in 'Bu-re-i-ku ko Ho-i-tsu-to-man', while the Official system restores such Roman names to their Roman origins, viz.: 'Blake ko Whitman'.

In the third place, proper names, written in Chinese ideographs, can often be pronounced and transliterated in different ways. Thus the name of the most formidable Japanese Blake scholar is sometimes spelled 'Zyugaku', though he himself gives it as 'Jugaku', and the given name of Mr. Yanagi can be read as either 'Mune' or 'Soetsu'. Such variants are likely to create ghosts for the Roman-writing bibliographer (and did once or twice in the *Blake Bibliography* [1964]) and are particularly troublesome in an alphabetical listing. Furthermore, the same set of Japanese characters can have a bewildering range of meanings; for example, the characters meaning 'Blake', or rather 'Bu-re-i-ku', can also mean 'Floating Soul Poems'.

As a consequence, since the only Japanese characters I know are those for 'Blake' (ブレイク), I have had to depend absolutely on the transliterations of Miss Yamazaki and others who have generously assisted me.[1] The inconsistencies, inaccuracies, and omissions in the Japanese books listed below must be due to my own misunderstanding of their patient explanations.

CHINESE BOOKS

My visits to Taipeh and Hong Kong in search of Chinese books about Blake proved almost totally fruitless, and most of the information here about works in Chinese derives from the generosity of Mr. A. D. Hyder of the Oriental Institute Library, Oxford.

POSTSCRIPT

added in Proof

The body of the text (with references complete up to the end of 1970) was completed in the summer of 1971; the last thorough revision of the essay on 'Blake's Reputation and Interpreters' was completed at the end of 1972; and most important works published by June 1974 (with a few even later) have been added as *Blake Books* passed through the press. Where proof additions could be made without serious dislocation of type, they have been added in the text itself. In other cases, they have been added in the section of Addenda (pp. 951–1001, below).

---

[1] In the circumstances, it was not possible to include details of contents, editorial matter, and the like, with Japanese books, and, partially to compensate for this awkward omission, I have instead indicated the number of pages (omitting preliminary matter and index) and plates to give an idea of the bulk involved.

BLAKE'S REPUTATION AND
INTERPRETERS[1]

DURING Blake's lifetime,[2] his reputation was fitful and erratic, wavering from heights of admiration in friendly patrons to depths of mis-understanding in the curious public. Blake's friends generously introduced him to middle-class patrons, but his honest indignation ('the voice of God') often alienated them from him. Except for his last peaceful years among The Ancients, his course is littered with damaged friendships and alarmed criticisms of his personality and work. Unhappily, the preponderance of praise was private, while the denunciations were painfully public.

'A GENIUS WITH A SCREW LOOSE': 1757–1863

Blake's reputation among his contemporaries was based, of course, upon his successes or idiosyncrasies as an artisan and an artist. During his lifetime of seventy years, he produced only about 200 copies of his own poems (judging from surviving copies), and probably these were often bought more for their illuminations than for their literary qualities. No one praised any of his writings apart from the *Poetical Sketches* and *Songs of Innocence and of Experience* until three decades after his death. In the public mind, Blake was an eccentric artist-engraver.

The years of his early manhood were promising enough within a small circle of friends. When his apprenticeship as an engraver was dutifully completed in 1779, Blake embarked vigorously upon his professional career as an engraver, especially for Joseph Johnson. At the same time he was making influential friends. By 1780 he knew Stothard, who designed many of the plates he engraved during these years, and through Stothard he met the ambitious young sculptor John Flaxman. From this time on, Flaxman advertised the talent and originality of his friend. One of his earliest acts of friendship was to introduce Blake to the bluestocking coterie of Harriet Mathew, the wife of the Reverend A. S. Mathew, where Gothick art and Italian music were the subjects of the conversaziones. Apparently Flaxman and A. S. Mathew paid in 1783 for the printing of Blake's *Poetical Sketches*, an unbound sheaf of sheets which attracted no public attention until twenty-three years later.

---

[1] This essay was originally written by G. E. Bentley, Jr. in, I believe, 1958; the section dealing with 1920 to the present was revised by Professor M. K. Nurmi for the 1964 *Blake Bibliography*; I have now revised the whole, sometimes restoring the section after 1920 to its earlier state, and bringing it down to the end of 1972, with a few references to books published after 1972.

[2] Biographical details throughout this essay are silently derived from *Blake Records* (1969).

During these years Blake was also climbing the recognized path to artistic fortune. He became a student at the Royal Academy, and in 1780, 1784, and 1785 he exhibited seven drawings there and saw them praised in print. Further, he formed a partnership with a competent journeyman engraver named James Parker to engrave and sell their own prints. Though only two plates were issued with their imprint, in 1784, the partners may have done well enough for themselves selling prints by others. The print-selling business and Blake's work for the booksellers were sufficiently successful to enable him to marry on 18 August 1782 and to set up house for himself. These must have been years of vaulting hopes and splendid prospects. About 1783 there even seemed to be a chance that he would get to study in Rome, with the support of a subscription, but the subscription never materialized.

Within a few months the partnership with Parker and the patronage of the Mathews had ended, perhaps because Blake had acquired a taste for being his own master. Like William Godwin some years later, he perceived that independence in the book trade was the prerogative of the bookseller, and he determined to turn publisher himself. About 1788 he began etching and selling his own writings in Illuminated Printing. Though his sales were far less than Godwin's, his expenses were far less too, and, unlike Godwin, his publishing ambitions never brought bailiffs down on the family. About the same time he was given more ambitious commercial engraving work. In 1791 he was engraving allegorical subjects after his new friend Fuseli for Erasmus Darwin's learned and loquacious *Botanic Garden* and designing his own plates for Mary Wollstonecraft's *Original Stories*; about 1793 he was given many plates, notably the brutal ones, for his friend Captain Stedman's adventure story, *Narrative, of a five years' expedition, against the Revolted Negroes of Surinam*; and in 1795 he was teaching engraving to his friend George Cumberland and engraving eight of the plates for his ambitious *Thoughts on Outline*. All this brought his name and talents before a wider public.

About 1795 Richard Edwards conceived for Blake the most grandiose engraving project of his lifetime. He commissioned Blake to make an enormous number of drawings, many of which he was later to engrave for a sumptuous folio edition of Young's *Night Thoughts*, to be issued in several parts. The scale of the project was alone enough to rouse comment, and Royal Academicians were full of praise, blame, and gossip about it. Four out of nine Nights appeared, but made, apparently, no immediate impression upon the public whatever, unless it was to 'startle the pious' with unexpectedly 'naked groupes'.[1] The result was catastrophic for Blake. His 537 drawings plus the 43 engravings must

---

[1] M. Pilkington, *A General Dictionary of Painters*, rev. Allan Cunningham (1840), 52.

have occupied most of his time for the better part of two years, and, since he had counted on fame rather than riches, his loss was complete. The scope of the loss may be estimated by the facts that the 43 engravings represent about 20 per cent of the total number he is known to have made for the booksellers during his entire life, and about half as many as he had signed his name to in the previous busy eighteen years.

Fortunately, shortly before this time he had acquired a faithful and patient patron in Thomas Butts, who probably provided a major part of Blake's support until about 1811. For some fifteen years, Butts humoured Blake's idiosyncrasies, bought his pictures at the rate of about one a week, and provided cash when all other sources proved unreliable. In all, he may have bought almost half the separate pictures Blake painted. He was a remarkably dependable and generous patron.

From his experience with the *Night Thoughts* of 1797, Blake discovered that booksellers, or their patrons, were not reliable supports for an artistic career. Certainly the first public mention of his talents which has been noticed (apart from friends' or publishers' puffs) must have been damping. In September 1796 an anonymous reviewer of Bürger's *Leonora* in *The British Critic* took

this opportunity of execrating that detestable taste, founded on the depraved fancy of one man of genius, which substitutes deformity and extravagance for force of expression, and draws men and women without skins, with their joints all dislocated; or imaginary beings, which neither can nor ought to exist.

Blake was shortly rescued from the booksellers through the good offices of his friend Flaxman, and befriended, patronized, and supported for three years by William Hayley, the author of 'some of the quaintest human bosh in the world'.[1] During Blake's sojourn by the sea from 1800 to 1803, Hayley commissioned engravings and drawings, recommended him warmly to his wealthy friends, and defended his eccentricities. These were profitable and on the whole peaceful years for Blake, but his association with Hayley did not mend his reputation with the public. Hayley's facile poetry was occasionally thought to be all too fittingly illustrated by Blake's designs. In *The Annual Review* for 1806 Southey was unkind enough to remark that Hayley's volume of *Ballads*

is so incomparably absurd that no merit within his reach could have amused us half so much . . . . The poet has had the singular good fortune to meet with a painter capable of doing full justice to his conceptions; and, in fact, . . .

---

[1] *Letters of Dante Gabriel Rossetti to William Allingham 1854–1870*, ed. G. B. Hill (1897),159. According to Caroline Bowles (*The Correspondence of Robert Southey with Caroline Bowles*, ed. E. Dowden [1881], ii. 64), 'Hayley wrote epitaphs upon his dearest friends before their eyes were well closed—a sort of poetical carrion crow!'

we know not whether most to admire the genius of Mr. William Blake or of Mr. William Hayley.

While living at Felpham, Blake was charged, perhaps falsely, with having said 'Damn the King'. The subsequent trials for sedition (1803, 1804) roused a little local interest around Chichester and were reported in the newspapers. Some of Hayley's friends rejoiced in Blake's acquittal, while for others, like Lady Hesketh (31 July 1805), the incident confirmed the worst they had suspected of Blake: 'My hair stands on end to think that Hayley & Blake are as dear friends as ever! . . . I don't doubt he will poison him in his Turret or set fire to all his papers, & poor Hayley will consume in his own Fires.'

After his return from Felpham in 1803, Blake evidently met a schoolmaster named Benjamin Heath Malkin, who became the first man to praise in print his genius as a poet. Little is known about their relationship, but Malkin was clearly a man of great perception and enthusiasm. In the introductory letter to his *Father's Memoirs of His Child* (1806), Malkin digressed for twenty-four pages upon the manifold merits of the poet-artist who had designed the frontispiece for his book. He must have known Blake well, for he preserved many stories of his early manhood which are not to be found elsewhere. Further, by praising and quoting Blake's lyrics at length, he made his poetry known for the first time to a wider circle than that composed of Blake's friends. Malkin's appreciation is of great importance in understanding Blake. Not only are his facts reliable and original, but the aspects of Blake which he singled out for praise are indicative of what sympathetic contemporaries were willing to approve in Blake's work.

The reviews of Malkin's *Memoirs* suggest that his contemporaries were willing to tolerate Blake as a Michelangelesque artist but not as a religious poet. *The Monthly Magazine* dismissed Blake with the statement that his poetry 'does not rise above mediocrity; as an artist he appears to more advantage'. *The Monthly Review* was more acid and precise, remarking that the poems 'of Mr. William Blake the artist . . . are highly extolled: but if "Watts seldom rose above the level of a mere versifier," in what class must we place Mr. Blake, who is certainly very inferior to Dr. Watts?'

Two events of the years 1805–10 established even more clearly the stereotyped image of Blake for the next half century as an artist of highly erratic genius. The first event was the publication by R. H. Cromek of Blair's *Grave* with designs by Blake. Cromek had promised that he would publish *twenty* designs *engraved* by Blake but, in fact, there were only twelve designs, engraved by the fashionable Schiavonetti. Blake's indignation at this duplicity blossomed in his *Notebook* in excoriating little verses about that 'petty Sneaking Knave' Cromek.

The book was launched with the endorsement of a group of influential Royal Academicians and went through five printings dated 1808, 1813, and 1826. Blair's *Grave* with Blake's designs was a great success of its kind. William Bell Scott's father, for example, was impressed 'in the profoundest way: the breath of the spirit blown through the judgment trump on the title-page seemed to have roused him as well as the skeleton there represented . . . Indeed nearly every one of the prints he looked upon as almost sacred, and we all followed him in this.'[1] Others, however, objected to the nudity of the figures. James Montgomery, for instance, felt that he had to sell his copy, 'as several of the plates were hardly of such a nature as to render the book proper to lie on a parlour table for general inspection'.[2] Blake's name was inseparably linked with Blair's *Grave* throughout the nineteenth century, and what general fame he had as an artist was associated with it.

The second event which helped to form the public image of Blake was his exhibition of pictures in his brother's house and, more important, the *Descriptive Catalogue* (1809) of the exhibition. Blake's praise for his own pictures in this *Catalogue* and his attacks on the pretensions of his rivals aroused amusement or even alarm. The public was prepared to treat him as a journeyman engraver and a talented if erratic designer, but they were frankly incredulous of his self-portrait of a 'Mental Prince', to be associated with Raphael and Michelangelo. Leigh Hunt's brother Robert drew public attention to the exhibition in *The Examiner* in the cruellest terms, identifying Blake as 'an unfortunate lunatic, whose personal inoffensiveness secures him from confinement', and ungenerously adding that 'The praises which these gentlemen [*of the Royal Academy*] bestowed last year on this unfortunate man's illustrations of *Blair's Grave*, have, in feeding his vanity, stimulated him to publish his madness more largely, and thus again exposed him, if not to the derision, at least to the pity of the public.' In an age whose curse was madness, this was enough to keep away all but the bravest—or the most curious.

Among the most curious was Crabb Robinson, who came for the eccentricity, if not for the art. He was fascinated by the outlandishness of the catalogue, and, when he was asked to write on some characteristically English subject for a German periodical, he chose not his friend Wordsworth but Blake. Robinson was a thorough and energetic man, and he gathered much important information for his article in the *Vaterländisches Museum* (1811). Like Malkin, he dwelt especially

[1] *Autobiographical Notes of the Life of William Bell Scott*, ed. W. Minto (1892), i. 22.
[2] J. Holland & J. Everett, *Memoirs of the Life and Writings of James Montgomery* (1854), i. 38. *The Antijacobin Review*, on the other hand, said that Blake's designs were 'absurd effusions' which had 'totally failed', and that 'his friends would do well to restrain his wanderings by the strait waistcoat' when he attempted poetry.

upon Blake's genius as a poet and he quoted from Blake's lyrics at some length. Robinson had never seen Blake and thought him mad. His essay apparently reached no English readers, and had little perceptible effect in Germany, but it is a sane and patient contemporary judgement of Blake.

Little is known of Blake's life from 1805 until the failure of his exhibition. Scarcely anything is known about him from 1810 until 1818, when he met John Linnell and became the father-confessor and inspiration of an enthusiastic group of very young men who called themselves 'The Ancients' and Blake 'The Interpreter'. Though money and public recognition were as scant as ever for Blake, The Ancients made his last years warm and productive. The most helpful to Blake was John Linnell, who half-supported him, commissioned his magisterial illustrations to Job and Dante, made possible his Virgil woodcuts, and preserved his manuscripts and memory. This last was looked upon as a sacred trust by all The Ancients, most of whom were young enough to survive Blake by half a century. Samuel Palmer helped Gilchrist patiently and defended Blake in print; Frederick Tatham provided a home for Blake's widow and distributed his drawings (carefully authenticated, and for a price); George Richmond talked of Blake with reverent enthusiasm to anyone who would listen (such as Ruskin); and they all echoed Blake's genius in their own work. Edward Calvert said 'that after Blake had died, and before it was known that information regarding him would be so sought for, it was proposed that each one of the brethren should on his own account put down what was then fresh in the memory concerning Blake's life.'[1] Unfortunately, they did not do so.

So far as the public image of Blake was concerned, however, the most important figure among Blake's young friends was John Varley. Artist, boxer, debtor, astrologer, he was a man of immense enthusiasms. Once, when hounded on all sides by bailiffs, he told a friend: 'all these troubles are necessary to me . . . . If it were not for my troubles, I should burst with joy!'[2] One of his bonds with Blake was their common interest in things of the spirit. Varley, however, took as literal truth what Blake, in other contexts at least, meant as metaphor. Varley lived by the stars and Blake among them; they often spoke the same language but with different meanings. The visions that Blake saw in his imagination, Varley looked for across the room. He persuaded Blake to paint literally what he saw, and the result was the midnight 'Visionary Heads'. There is no reasonable doubt that Blake saw, and knew he saw, these visions in his own mind; there is also no doubt that Varley

[1] [S. Calvert] *A Memoir of Edward Calvert Artist* (1893), 19.
[2] A. T. Story, *The Life of John Linnell* (1892), i. 168.

thought Blake saw them as external realities. Varley was not a man to find terrestrial sense when a supernatural one would do—and it may well be that Blake egged him on. Certainly Varley believed, and widely reported, that Blake had actually seen The Man Who Built the Pyramids and The Ghost of a Flea in the same sense that Hamlet saw the ghost and Macbeth met the witches. What perhaps began as a private joke to Blake had a far-reaching effect upon his reputation for the next half-century and beyond. Vision-seers always attract attention, and the audience which had ignored *The Marriage of Heaven and Hell* and *The Book of Job* illustrations was entranced. Some account of Blake's visions of the illustrious dead formed part of every notice of him and appeared in the most unlikely and irrelevant places—in Jane Porter's novel about Highland chiefs and W. C. Dendy's *Philosophy of Mystery*. These visions form the basis of most arguments about Blake's madness or mysticism (terms which were often interchangeable in early discussions of Blake). Everyone who knows anything of Blake knows that he drew a portrait of the ghost of a flea. If only one could be certain on which side the joke lay!

Crabb Robinson finally met Blake at a dinner party in 1825 and was fascinated by his speculative and eccentric conversation. For a time he called on Blake regularly and endeavoured to collect his opinions, particularly those on religion and genius. Robinson talked about Blake with many of his friends such as Wordsworth, Flaxman, Coleridge, Hazlitt, and Lamb, and introduced a visiting German to him, who reported that Blake was the greatest man he had seen in England. More important, Robinson carefully recorded his conversations with Blake in his diary, though he occasionally found it necessary to transcribe such things as Blake's heterodox views of marriage in discreet German. Later he reworked his daily notes into an expanded journal, parts of which were published by Gilchrist and others.

Crabb Robinson's reminiscences of Blake are of the very first importance; in many ways they are the best contemporary record we have of Blake. In their very lack of connective and directing purposes, they seem to give us Blake as he appeared from day to day and from idea to idea. Robinson was a good reporter, because he combined a matter-of-fact strain with an appreciation, even an understanding, of mysticism and the imagination. What he records of Blake tallies remarkably well with what we know of him from his Prophecies and his *Notebook* and gives us an understanding of his public manner and attitudes well beyond anything that has been found elsewhere. Crabb Robinson's diaries are crucially important in helping us to see his life in the perspective of his own times.

But when this is said, it must be remembered that Robinson was not a youthful disciple, that he shied violently away from some of Blake's ideas, and that he often could not supply the connective in what he regarded as mere rambling. Frequently the image of Blake which Robinson gives is clearly coloured by his own views and personality. We must yet weigh Robinson's evidence carefully before accepting it.

During Blake's last years, Linnell saw to it that he met many interesting people, that he went to plays, exhibitions, and dinners, but his reputation did not alter greatly, and his obscurity increased. In 1824 Charles Lamb did not even know whether he was alive. When he died in August 1827, the world of art and letters scarcely noticed that a giant had vanished. Obituaries appeared in a few journals, but only The Ancients followed him to his grave in Bunhill Fields. In death as in life, his admirers were artists and personal friends.

Considering the achievements of the man who had died—an equal of the greatest of his contemporaries in poetry, engraving, and painting —and considering his reputation today, the contemporary response to his death was pitiable, a judgement on the age. But in the light of his lifelong reputation, the magnitude of the first response is surprising. Within a year of his death, John Thomas Smith, an acquaintance from his early manhood, had not only included a thirty-five-page biography of Blake with his account of the sculptor *Nollekens and his Times*, but had thought it worth while to mention Blake on the title-page. Two years later, Blake was included by Allan Cunningham as one of the *Most Eminent British Painters, Sculptors, and Architects* (1830), and within the year the biography was considerably enlarged for the second edition. The two biographical accounts by Cunningham and J. T. Smith are the last of major importance published by Blake's contemporaries.

Both Smith's and Cunningham's accounts are heavily anecdotal, but they are biographical in a way that Malkin and Crabb Robinson had not attempted to be. Smith's life of Blake is remarkable for being longer than the notices he gave of most of Blake's contemporaries, and one of its chief virtues is the information it gives about Blake's early life. It was Smith who had heard Blake sing his songs to tunes of his own composition, who knew him when he was working in partnership with Parker, who remembered (as no one else did) the bluestocking coterie which sponsored him and his *Poetical Sketches*. His account of this period is first-hand, and of the first importance in being so. An artist himself, Smith saw chiefly Blake's art, and thought of his poetry as primarily a vehicle for his illustrations. He printed three short poems, but he thought that *Songs of Innocence* showed 'no great degree of elegance or excellence', and of the rest the best he could say was that 'his later poetry, if it may be so called, attached to his plates, . . . was not always wholly uninteresting'. His comments on Blake's art are far more impressive. Much of the information which he provides is both important and unverifiable, but continuing research indicates that his biographical generalizations are reliable even when his minute particulars are dubious.

Allan Cunningham's biography is a much more polished and ambitious work, remarkable for its anecdotal vigour and wit. It was widely read, and for the next thirty years most of those who knew something of Blake appear to have learned of him through Cunningham. As one of the first reviews perceived, however, there is great cause to complain 'of the stealing, borrowing, or copying a considerable portion of the life from [*J. T. Smith's*] Nollekens's Own Times'.[1] Much of the part that was original with Cunningham is remarkable for its imbalance. He saw Blake as a kind of Jekyll-and-Hyde, sanely engraving for the booksellers by day and madly writing *Urizen* by night. At first he thought of Blake's poems merely as an excuse for the designs, and he wrote of the plates as 'seasoned with verse'. In his first edition, where he was most influenced by J. T. Smith, he found the bulk of Blake's poetry 'utterly wild and mad', and the emphasis upon madness is strong. In the far more important second edition, however, Cunningham had largely ceased to see through Smith's eyes, and he judged as the poet he was. The early opinions were allowed to stand, but he added six new poems, some new biographical material, and a most moving conclusion. Cunningham's biography is chiefly important for its rhetorical effect upon generations of readers.

After 1830 the great silence set in. There were still, of course, the curious such as Caroline Bowles and Edward FitzGerald, and the enthusiasts, such as Ruskin and Dante Gabriel Rossetti, but very little emerged into print. At least four men intended to publish Blake's poems, but only two books appeared. In 1838 the first of the projectors, Richard Monckton Milnes, wrote to Aubrey de Vere: 'Have you ever seen any of Blake's poetry? I think of publishing some selections from him which will astonish those who are astoundable by anything of this kind.'[2] Milnes never astounded his friends, perhaps because James John

---

[1] Anon., 'The Inventions of William Blake, Painter and Poet', *London University Magazine*, ii (1830), 318. This review-essay is of the first importance for its clear perception of the real merits of Blake's poetry. In most respects it is the most important criticism of Blake's poetry to appear before the 1860s.

It may profitably be compared with the equally extensive maunderings of Anon., 'The Last of the Supernaturalists', *Fraser's Magazine*, ii (1830), 217–35, which defends a largely imaginary Blake from imaginary attacks.

Tatham's important but somewhat unreliable 'Life of Blake' (?1832) scarcely influenced his contemporaries, for it was not published until 1906.

[2] T. W. Reid, *The Life, Letters, and Friendships of Richard Monckton Milnes, First Lord Houghton* (1890), i. 220–1.

Garth Wilkinson published anonymously his edition of *Songs of Innocence and of Experience* in 1839. Wilkinson, however, was unwilling to
shock his friends, and he prudishly cancelled 'The Little Vagabond',
despite the counterweight of an enthusiastic Swedenborgian preface.
A few years later, about 1843, Wilkinson's friend C. A. Tulk printed
twelve copies of Blake's *Songs*, with space left so that the friends to
whom he distributed them could copy in the designs if they chose.
And in the summer of 1849 William Allingham found a willing
publisher for Blake's poems but was perhaps discouraged because the
collections in the British Museum 'seem to have nothing of his',[1] and he
abandoned the project.

Beyond these undertakings, there was little but gossip about Blake.
FitzGerald's attitude toward Blake was probably characteristic of the
more perceptive critics of the time; in 1833 he wrote that Blake 'was
quite mad, but of a madness that was really the elements of great genius
ill-sorted; in fact, a genius with a screw loose, as we used to say'.[2] And
so, for thirty years, Blake's reputation was moribund; he was remembered chiefly for his ingenious madness.

THE ACHIEVEMENT OF PUBLIC STATURE: 1863–1893

About 1855, Alexander Gilchrist began to cast about for information
for a book on Blake, to follow his successful life of Etty. He was a most
industrious researcher and was soon in touch with many of the men
who had known Blake best; Linnell, Tatham, Palmer, Richmond,
Crabb Robinson. Unlike the preceding biographers of Blake, Gilchrist
was moved by a passion for accuracy and by a love for his subject. He
wrote to Linnell that 'The first virtue of Biography is entire veracity',
and that it was most important to collect materials about 'so remarkable
& lovable a man: a man who attracts the more of my sympathy, the
better I understand him. It is fullness of *detail* which to Biography im-
parts life & reality.'[3] Six years elapsed before his book was anything
like finished, and then, suddenly in 1861, Gilchrist died, with most of
the book written and a few chapters in print. His widow Anne, an
intelligent, ambitious, and capable person, determined that the book
should be issued as a monument to her husband's memory. She was
helped by a kind of syndicate of the Pre-Raphaelite Brotherhood,
headed by William Michael and Dante Gabriel Rossetti, and in 1863
the book was finally published as *Life of William Blake*, '*Pictor Ignotus*'.

---

[1] *William Allingham: A Diary*, ed. H. Allingham & D. Radford (1907), 53.
[2] *Letters and Literary Remains of Edward FitzGerald*, ed. W. A. Wright (1889), i. 25.
[3] Quoted from letters of 23 and 25 April 1855, the first transcribed in a notebook by A. H.
Palmer (Linnell's grandson), and the second surviving in its original form (both now in the
possession of Joan Linnell Ivimy Burton).

Its effect was thunderous. Never has an important literary reputation been posthumously established so instantaneously and effectively. Enthusiastic reviews appeared in all the major journals, and at a length that hardly seems possible to our own day. Reviewers considered their words carefully, sometimes for years. James Smetham's review in the *London Quarterly Review*, for instance, did not appear until 1869, occupied forty-six pages, and was thought important enough to be published with the second edition of the *Life* in 1880. Gilchrist's title, '*Pictor Ignotus*', had not been mere showmanship. Blake *had* been unknown, and Gilchrist's *Life* made him sensationally well known. From 1863 on Blake at last took his place in literary and artistic history as one of the great figures of the Romantic Movement.

Gilchrist's biography is still, in many respects, the best biography of Blake, though one reason for its indispensability is a defect. Unfortunately, 'It was a tradition in the [*Gilchrist*] family to avoid notes, to recast the text rather than to use them.'[1] Alexander and Anne Gilchrist and William Michael and Dante Gabriel Rossetti are known to have had close contacts with a large number of people who had known Blake well. The information which these people supplied was oral, was not specified by Gilchrist, and is often now not traceable. As a consequence, we must depend absolutely upon Gilchrist for many otherwise unverifiable facts, without even knowing who his oral authorities were. Happily, Gilchrist and his collaborators were careful and responsible, and generally they treated their sources with respect and accuracy. An example may illustrate their fidelity. On 6 December 1860 Thomas Woolner sent Dante Gabriel Rossetti some information for Gilchrist's biography:

There were some very choice copies of some of Blake's smaller Poems at the party where I met the lady [*whose name he couldn't remember*] and which belonged to her I believe, but whether they were such as are not accessible at the B. Museum and elsewhere I am unable to say.

The anecdote as I remember it was this:—*the Lady was thought very [extremely] beautiful when a child, and was taken to an evening party and there presented to Blake, he looked at her very kindly for a long while without speaking, and then stroking her head and long ringlets said 'May God make this world to you, my child, as beautiful as it has been to me'. She thought it strange at the time, she said, [—vain little darling of fortune!—] that such a poor old man, dressed in such shabby clothes, could imagine [that] the world had ever been so beautiful to him as it must be to her, nursed in all the elegancies and luxury of wealth; but in after years she understood well [plainly] enough what he meant and treasured the few words he had spoken to her.*[2]

---

[1] *Anne Gilchrist: Her Life and Writings*, ed. H. H. Gilchrist (1887), 258.
[2] Quoted from the MS in the Library of Congress and printed by Gilchrist, *Life of William Blake*, '*Pictor Ignotus*' (1863), i. 310–11.

Except for the punctuation and the words in brackets which Gilchrist himself supplied, the section between the asterisks appears word for word in Gilchrist's biography. Such corroborating manuscripts are rarely traceable, but a few such specimens are sufficient to give us great confidence in Gilchrist's accuracy. Blake's friends, at least, were convinced of Gilchrist's faithfulness; fifteen years after the book was published, John Linnell told a friend: 'the life contains all that can be said about Blake or me'.[1]

This is not to say, of course, that Gilchrist's *Life* is impeccable. For one thing, many facts, poems, and paintings unknowable to him have since come to light and need to be placed in their proper perspective in Blake's life. These omissions have been largely supplied in Ruthven Todd's editions of Gilchrist (1943, 1945), which meticulously supply and correct an enormous number of details. The standard biography of Blake is Gilchrist's, as verified and emended by Todd.[2]

The second major reservation about Gilchrist's biography is that it is, inevitably for a pioneering work, somewhat dated. The book opens with an apology for choosing such a subject, and Gilchrist found it necessary to cite the previous praise of such men as Wordsworth, Flaxman, and Fuseli, and the prices Blake's works were fetching, to justify his choice. Naturally much of the emphasis of the book was intended to convert the uninterested or the hostile critic, and today such an emphasis is largely irrelevant.

But more important, Gilchrist wrote when Queen Victoria still had forty years left to reign, and his book is heavily influenced by the governing spirit of the time, a spirit largely alien both to Blake and to modern readers. Many aspects of Blake he did not understand and was not prepared to discuss. He found great and just praise for Blake as a lyric poet, as a master engraver, as a painter of originality and power; but he almost ignored the Prophecies, and Blake's profound heterodoxy he treated rather lightly and unsubstantially. Gilchrist had to devote a whole chapter to the question, now largely irrelevant, of whether Blake was 'Mad or Not Mad?'—and such problems as Blake's sources, his mysticism, and his system, which exercise twentieth-century scholars, were scarcely approached. Much of this, of course, is due to Gilchrist's position as a pioneer, but as a consequence, now that the new-found-

---

[1] The letter from Linnell to William Dixon of 23 Aug. 1878 was transcribed by A. H. Palmer in a notebook now among the Ivimy MSS of Mrs. Burton.

[2] The claim of second-hand book-dealers that the edition of 1880 is the 'best edition' is simply nonsense. The editions of 1863 and 1880 have, nevertheless, a major and little-recognized importance in that they contain sixteen plates made from electrotypes of Blake's *Songs*. These virtually perfect electrotype prints are as close to Blake's originals as most readers or collectors are likely to get.

land is heavily populated, the balance of the book seems somewhat curious and inappropriate.

These remarks about Gilchrist's book all apply to the first volume which contains the biography. The second volume, the work of William Michael and Dante Gabriel Rossetti, was equally heroic but of far more limited value in modern terms. The *catalogue raisonné* of Blake's writings and paintings by W. M. Rossetti was of enormous value, and contains many items which have still not been located, but, of course, the works catalogued have long since found new homes, and most of them have been described with greater detail and accuracy. The selections from Blake edited by D. G. Rossetti included everything that had been previously republished, and a good deal that was new, notably from the 'Rossetti Manuscript', but the verse had been vigorously shaken up, and the text today is of little use to anyone who wants to see Blake's poetry as Blake left it. In 1880 a great mass of new material was added in appendices, but this too may be safely ignored by all but the most omnivorous Blake readers. There were also changes in the biography in 1880, chiefly in the addition of new Blake letters, and this text of the biography is the standard one (emended by Todd); but everything in Volume II, with the exception of the catalogue, is of very little interest now.

Gilchrist's biography elicited many other studies and appreciations of Blake in the next thirty years, of which the most influential was Swinburne's *William Blake*, a Critical Essay (1868). This began as an essay for Gilchrist's book and grew, with time and enthusiasm and knowledge, into a work of importance in its own right. Swinburne had sources of information which Gilchrist had not tapped (notably Seymour Kirkup), but the chief importance of his book is as an appreciation. Swinburne's infectious superlatives swirled and bubbled around Blake and his works, lifting him to a pinnacle of praise. The *Poetical Sketches*, for instance, were 'not simply better than any man could do then; better than all except the greatest have done since; [*but*] better than some still ranked among the greatest ever managed to do'. The *Marriage of Heaven and Hell* ranks 'as about the greatest [*work*] produced by the eighteenth century in the line of high poetry and spiritual speculation'. Swinburne's book is valuable for an overflowing enthusiasm, and for many critical insights of real value and originality. It is, however, a work of its author and time. 'Art for art's sake' is premissed as 'the real point of view taken during life by Blake', and Blake's theoretical sexual heterodoxy is isolated as one of his most glorious achievements. Swinburne was not fastidious in his standards of scholarship; of Rossetti's edition of Blake he wrote that 'as far as one can see it could not have been done better'. The essay is interesting

as a rhapsodical eulogy of Blake, but many of the giants of prejudice
and ignorance with whom Swinburne tilted now seem mere wind-
mills, and in his estimate of Blake's Prophetic Books, Swinburne
spoke for his own time but not for ours: 'If any one would realize
to himself for ever a material notion of chaos, let him take a blind
header into the midst of the whirling foam and rolling weed of this
sea of words.'[1]

The most effective proponent of this last point, and indeed probably
the most important denigrator of Blake, is H. A. Hewlett, in his essay
on Blake's 'Imperfect Genius' in the *Contemporary Review* in 1879. Here
Blake's Prophecies are taken apart and displayed as ill-made imitations
of Ossian and Chatterton, with little control and less meaning. Hewlett
deliberately overstated his case to outrage Blake's blind adulators, but
there is a kernel of real importance in his argument.

Of the masses of appreciation which appeared for thirty years after
1863, mostly by well-meaning but ill-informed gentlemanly amateurs,
none is worth singling out for special attention. Indeed, the only three
books of real importance to Blake studies are not primarily about Blake
at all: A. T. Story's *Life of John Linnell* (1892), A. H. Palmer's *Life and
Letters of Samuel Palmer* (1892), and Samuel Calvert's *Memoir of Edward
Calvert Artist* (1893). All three are heavily based upon family memories
and papers of their subjects which have since disappeared, and all
include, often incidentally, considerable information about Blake in
his last years that is almost first-hand. They provide valuable and
rewarding supplements to Gilchrist on Blake's life among The Ancients.

The period of the resurrection of Blake's reputation provided, most
significantly, a great body of biographical information. It introduced
Blake to a mass audience for the very first time, both as an artist and
as a poet. One of the most important results of Gilchrist's *Life* was the
number of exhibitions devoted largely or exclusively to Blake on both
sides of the Atlantic. The most impressive of these was that at the
Burlington Fine Arts Club in 1876, where a total of 333 items relating
to Blake was shown. In this way interest in Blake's art work was stimulated along with enthusiasm for his poetry.

The increased interest in Blake not only multiplied the prices of his
works, but it encouraged the publication of facsimiles. Of these, the
most ambitious, and the most conspicuously successful, were those in
'The Edition of the Works of Wm. Blake' produced at 'The Blake Press
at Edmonton' by William Muir and his family and friends.[2] Twelve

[1] A. C. Swinburne, *William Blake* (1925), 8, 203, 91, 93, 108, 186. This essay was the longest
and most elaborate prose work which Swinburne published.
[2] Seven titles were previously reproduced without colouring in the *Works by William Blake*
(1876).

works in Illuminated Printing were issued between 1884 and 1890, printed and coloured by hand at great trouble and with considerable success. These works have, on occasion, been accidentally sold as originals. The size of the editions was small, but their influence was appreciable, and their scope has only been equalled in recent times by the facsimiles of the Blake Trust.

Such works naturally demanded high standards of devotion. The years from 1863 to 1893 were years of discovery and enthusiasm for Blake students. A myth was established which the succeeding generation felt it must controvert and replace.

THE UNREAL BLAKE: 1893–1920

By the 1890s Blake's reputation was safely established, and since that date, if works about him are any criterion, it has grown steadily. By the last decade of the nineteenth century, enthusiasts no longer needed to apologize for Blake, and some even tried to present him as he really was, as he had tried to present himself. It was two Irishmen, Edwin John Ellis & William Butler Yeats, who took up the task with most vigour. The very title of their work indicates the originality and extent of their claims: *The Works of William Blake, Poetic, Symbolic, and Critical,* With Lithographs of the Illustrated 'Prophetic Books', and a Memoir and Interpretation (1893). Previous to this, no one had even thought of issuing all Blake's 'Works',[1] much less of treating them all with such seriousness and at such length. The explanation of 'The Symbolic System' occupied 185 pages, and the 'Interpretation and Paraphrased Commentary' another 300. And here, directed at a comparatively wide audience, were not only transcripts of the Prophetic Books but facsimiles of them as well. Clearly this was a whole new Blake for the enthusiasts to absorb.

Ellis & Yeats produced a work of great and imaginative originality, but, unfortunately, much of the originality was not Blake's. Their originality took three forms: interpreting the system, editing the texts, and rearranging Blake's life. Each was a labour of love, and the result was a new man and a new myth, more mysterious, supernatural, and Celtic than anything Blake's friends would have recognized.

To begin with the myth: Ellis & Yeats postulated that there was a secret system which would explain all Blake. Ellis & Yeats happened to be fascinated by nineteenth-century spiritualism, by table-rapping and thought transference, and by Celtic folklore. For some good and

---

[1] Ellis & Yeats evidently conceived the undertaking in rather different terms originally, for it was reported in *The Critic*, N.S., xvi (1 Aug. 1891), 60, to be planned in only two volumes, with a 'key to Blake's system' in Vol. I and a transcript of *Vala* and 'over one hundred fifty pages of facsimiles from poems engraved by Blake' in Vol. II.

many not-so-good reasons, a number of similarities could be found
between Blake's myths and those of the medium and the Irish peasant.
Blake's system, therefore, was conceived as a stable if enormous whole
which could be valuably illuminated by reference to Irish myth and
to a body of secret cosmological knowledge, to the Kabbala and the
Illuminati. There were many insights of importance scattered through
their work, but the total effect, in simplifying and at the same time
mystifying what Blake was trying to say, was misguided and mis-
guiding.

Ellis & Yeats were further handicapped because they themselves
used the texts which they presented to the public. Of these, the newest
and most important was *Vala*, none which had ever been published
before, although it forms almost a seventh of the bulk of Blake's
surviving writings. Their transcription of this and of other original
works by Blake was astonishingly bad, even according to the indifferent
standards of accuracy then applied. The editors' aim seems to have
been, like Rossetti's, to supply Blake's meaning where Blake himself
had not been able to do so. Similarly the lithographs were frequently
grossly distorted. On many of the *Vala* plates, for instance, though the
design is clear, the text is absolutely and hopelessly illegible. Consequently, when Ellis & Yeats depended upon their own transcription,
their interpretation was necessarily distorted. Though important in
generating interest, their texts and facsimiles of Blake's poetry are often
worse than useless today.

Perhaps the crowning indignity to Blake, however, was in the re-
arrangement of his ancestry. Not content with the decent ignorance
which still obscures Blake's family, Ellis & Yeats found it necessary to
invent an adventurous lineage for him. Blake's father, it seems, was the
bastard son of an Irish renegade called John O'Neill, who, to evade
political and financial difficulties, married and took the name of an
Irish woman named Ellen Blake. Together they settled in London,
where they nourished their family on Irish legends and bravado. It is
a fine story, but it has nothing to do with the engraver who wrote the
Songs of Innocence. That there are no verifiable facts to support it has not
prevented the story from reappearing in recent times.[1] Ellis's independent biography of *The Real Blake* (1906) reaffirmed the legend and
coloured the thinking of the credulous for a generation.

Ellis & Yeats were clearly learned about occult mysteries and secret
societies, but their enthusiasm outran their knowledge, and their works
should not be approached without a carefully digested understanding
of the less speculative if less inspired Blake books.

[1] See W. P. Witcutt, *Blake*: A Psychological Study (1946) and the wonderful articles of
Elizabeth O'Higgins (1950–6).

The consistent trend from 1893 to 1920 was to produce popular biographies and lyrical appreciations of Blake, to gush over his pretty songs and marvel at his mysticism. Editors of popular series rushed to include Blake, and the resulting volumes in 'Great Lives' or 'The Popular Library of Art' showed unmistakable signs of hasty cooking. With many other books of the time, the desire to appreciate Blake was genuine but ill-informed.

The spread of enthusiasm for Blake meant that a growing public was eager to know his works with as little editorial intervention as possible. The most important response to this demand was John Sampson's edition of *The Poetical Works*, which was published in 1905 and in various editions has been in print ever since. Considering the standards in general prevalent, and the treatment Blake had received in particular, this work was an astonishing achievement. It is careful, scrupulously accurate, meticulously detailed, well informed, and thoroughly intelligent. It can be relied upon with great confidence, and indeed there are only two reasons why Sampson's edition is not 'Standard' for Blake's works. The first is that it includes only poetry, and the second is that since 1905 there have appeared a great deal of information and a certain number of texts—*Vala*, for instance, did not enter a public collection until 1918. Fortunately, Sampson's chief virtues have been incorporated in the serious treatments of Blake's texts which have appeared since that time.

A. G. B. Russell's catalogue and extensive reproduction of *The Engravings of William Blake* (1912) performed a similar service for his engravings. Except for the brief and not impeccable descriptions by W. M. Rossetti for Gilchrist's *Life*, nothing like it had been attempted before. Russell's thoroughness and factual accuracy made his book one of the primary sources of information about Blake's engravings, and his summaries and analyses of doubtful points are of independent importance.

Russell also did important work in publishing in 1906 the *Letters* to and from Blake and Tatham's 'Life of Blake'. Unfortunately, Russell's standards in this volume were not so meticulous, for many letters are imprecisely transcribed, no sources for the letters are given, and the documenting of facts and dates is minimal. The book was important, however, in making some letters and Tatham's 'Life' available for the first time. All the letters have since been published with greater accuracy and detail.

A similar venture was made by Arthur Symons in his *William Blake* (1907). His biography added some useful new facts about Blake's family from parish registers, but of more interest were the contemporary accounts of Blake which he printed in the same volume. Once again, the editorial apparatus and technique are far from what they might be—Symons used the first and considerably shorter version of Cunningham's life, for instance—but the book was useful for the important biographical source-material conveniently gathered together.

The most important critical work of the period is Joseph Wicksteed's study of *Blake's Vision of the Book of Job* (1910, extensively improved in the 1924 edition). Though the *Job* illustrations had been widely admired and reproduced before, they had not been studied in such detail as works of art in their own right. Blake's illustrations are generally accepted as being among his most impressive and important performances, ranking with the greatest masterpieces of engraving, but the very range of Blake's achievements made a thorough consideration of each aspect difficult and rare. Wicksteed's study was the first to demonstrate the consistency and unity of the series, and his work is particularly valuable for the interpretation of Blake's pictorial symbolism. His best-known and most important conclusion about Blake's pictures is the association of the left side (chiefly in hands or feet) with the material, and the right side with the spiritual. It is characteristic of Wicksteed that he occasionally pushes his ideas too far, but his *Job* work is original and of lasting importance.[1]

The period from 1893 to 1920 was a time of consolidation of Blake's reputation and of a few careful editions and studies of his work. The most conspicuous authors of the period, however, are Ellis & Yeats, who, in spite of enthusiasm, energy, and good intentions, went far toward obscuring and mystifying 'The Real Blake'.

A BIBLIOGRAPHY, A TEXT, AND SOURCE STUDIES: 1921–1946

The first half-century of writing about Blake after his rediscovery in 1863 was characterized by great energy and art, in authors such as Swinburne, Ellis & Yeats, and Wicksteed, but by precious little science. The only Blake books of the time which will withstand close scholarly scrutiny are the editions of John Sampson. Happily, his influence was vital in forming the most prolific Blake scholar of the past half-century.

Geoffrey Keynes sent the manuscript of his *Bibliography* to Sampson for advice and received it in heaping measure; he followed the advice, revised the book, and sent it to Oxford, who forwarded it to Sampson for an opinion; Keynes revised it again and sent it to Cambridge, who forwarded it to Sampson for an opinion. This long labour brought to birth in 1921 one of the greatest works of scholarship concerned with Blake or any other literary author in this century: *A Biblio-*

---

[1] Wicksteed's *Blake's Innocence and Experience*: A Study of the Songs and Manuscripts (1928) is useful for the reproduction of the MSS and etchings, but the critical text is often simplistic.

graphy of William Blake. In it, Keynes recorded the history of every traceable contemporary copy of Blake's works, gave the results of rough collation of them (often by mail), established the chronological order of copies printed over perhaps thirty-five years and the sequential order of the plates (which vary from copy to copy), described the hundreds of illustrations in Blake's writings, and traced books with Blake's marginalia; he listed every work which discussed Blake and reprinted many of the short early accounts; and he reproduced many of Blake's most important designs, including for the first time all of *All Religions Are One*. Considering that no previous book had even listed the titles of all Blake's writings, this was an astonishing achievement. The *Bibliography* was not only extensive, but it has proved satisfyingly solid as well. Naturally new copies of Blake's books have turned up since 1921, as well as new letters and new marginalia, but the bibliographical outlines of our knowledge of Blake are those which Keynes established. Such changes as have proved necessary have often been made by Keynes himself, as in his Census of *William Blake's Illuminated Books* (1953). Blake's poetry and designs are so unusual that a solid grounding in fact is absolutely necessary to keep his critics in close touch with his ideas. This solid grounding in Blake books Keynes provided. His *Bibliography* has been an indispensable asset to Blake students for fifty years.[1]

On the foundation of the *Bibliography*, Keynes built the even more influential edifice of his *Writings of William Blake* In Three Volumes (1925). This is the first edition to attempt true comprehensiveness, including letters, marginalia, *The French Revolution*, and *Vala*; no previous edition had included more than one of these. The notes and text had unique authority, for Keynes had examined more copies of Blake's works than any preceding editor. For thirty years, the *Writings* was the only authoritative edition of Blake's works, and then it was only superseded by another edition by Keynes, *The Complete Writings of William Blake* with All the Variant Readings (1957 ff.). This later work is as handsome as the earlier one, though only a fraction of its girth, and the 1957 work included the scholarship of the intervening years. It is still the most comprehensive edition of Blake, though Erdman's texts (1965 ff.) are superior in some respects.

From 1927 to 1957, the edition of Blake which served most scholars was Keynes's popular one-volume condensation of the three 1925 volumes, called *Poetry and Prose of William Blake* (1927 ff., reset in 1939).

---

[1] I have not attempted to survey here the proliferating works on Blake in Japanese, but I should remark that the most productive Japanese Blake scholar is Bunsho Jugaku, whose *William Blake Shoshi* (1929) is an adaptation and extension of Keynes's *Bibliography* (1921), and whose *Bibliographical Study of William Blake's Note-Book* (1953) is carefully based on the Keynes facsimile (1935).

It lacked the notes, the variants, and the sophistication of the earlier work, but it was available, portable, and sufficiently reliable to serve the rather simple textual purposes for which it was needed. Most of the Blake criticism of this century has been based upon the Keynes texts.

Keynes has been a prolific publisher of Blake reproductions. Among the most important of these is his facsimile of the *Notebook* (1935), which made the complexities of that central work available for the first time.

The only other edition of much textual significance for the next thirty years was the *Prophetic Writings* in two volumes edited by D. J. Sloss & J. P. R. Wallis (1926), published as a supplement to Sampson's editions. Their accurate texts provided useful supplements or alternatives to those of Keynes, their annotations were full, and their independent transcriptions of *Tiriel* and *Vala* were particularly valuable. With the edition they included an enormous index of Blake's symbols, which is informed by the assumption that Blake's myth is consistent and unchanging. This oversimplification frequently vitiates the value of their critical conclusions about Blake's symbols.

Interest in Blake's art was stimulated by exhibitions, particularly the great migrant show in 1913-14 (London, Manchester, Nottingham, Edinburgh), the Burlington Fine Arts Club *Centenary Exhibition* (1927), and the Philadelphia exhibition (1939). The most valuable indirect result of these exhibitions was the publication of many of Blake's designs which had not previously been publicly visible. These included those for Gray (ed. H. J. C. Grierson), Dante (1922), *The Heads of the Poets* (ed. T. Wright, 1925), Milton (ed. G. Keynes, 1926), *Job* (ed. L. Binyon & G. Keynes, 1935; ed. P. Hofer, 1937), Virgil (ed. G. Keynes, 1937), and Bunyan (ed. G. Keynes, 1941), the *Pencil Drawings* (ed. G. Keynes, 1927; Second Series, 1956; 1971), the *Drawings and Engravings* (ed. L. Binyon, 1922), *The Paintings* (ed. D. Figgis, 1925), and *The Engraved Designs* (ed. L. Binyon, 1926). Among these, the *Job* edition is the only one with text of major importance; not only does it reproduce sketches, water-colours, proofs, and finished plates, but the essays by Keynes & Binyon are original and of lasting importance. Another important work on Blake's art was the catalogue of the Huntington collection by C. H. C. Baker (1938, admirably revised by R. R. Wark, 1957), with reproductions of many of the designs, and a careful display of the relevant facts.

A similar concern for factual precision is exhibited in Mona Wilson's *Life of William Blake* (1927).[1] Her work is careful, intelligent, and thorough, with a wide use of published source-materials and the easy flow of narrative of the professional writer of popular lives. Her bio-

---

[1] The book was published to range with the Keynes edition of Blake's *Writings* (1925), was purged of notes and republished in a popular form (1932), had the notes restored and expanded (1948), and was revised and expanded once again, this time by Geoffrey Keynes (1971).

graphy is not better than Gilchrist's, but it is better balanced, and her sources are more clearly indicated. Since 1927, no one has attempted a biography on the same scale. Two other authors of the time, however, usefully brought forward new biographical facts. Herbert Jenkins's essays, collected in his *William Blake* (1925), are sound in fact though less reliable in generalizations. Thomas Wright's *Life of William Blake* (1929) also presents useful information, often derived from the manuscripts of Blake's contemporaries, but his use of the historical present tense and of reconstructed dialogue often leaves the reader baffled as to what is fact and what hypothesis.

The most important critical work of the period 1921–46 is S. Foster Damon's *William Blake*, His Philosophy and Symbols (1924). The construction of the book is well suited for a work of reference, for it considers each poem in a separate chapter, and at the end there is a further paraphrase of Blake's entire work. Damon had seen and read more of Blake—including the unpublished *Night Thoughts* drawings and the badly published *Vala*—than the vast majority of his predecessors, and he was learned in those aspects of mysticism and the occult which are likely to have appealed to Blake. Many of his parallels to Blake's thought found in earlier writings are analogies rather than sources, but this does not eliminate the usefulness and expansion of meaning which his technique makes possible. His analyses of Blake's symbolism were considerably enriched by this consideration of other literatures and traditions, and his book remains, with some reservations for its simplification of problems, one of the half-dozen most important works of Blake criticism.[1]

A consistent strain running through most considerations of Blake in the 1920s and 1930s is the importance of his 'mysticism'. Damon posits on his first page the crucial significance of Blake's mysticism and finds it to be the basis and *raison d'être* of most of what Blake wrote; and many others adopted this view. The most thorough study of the subject is Helen C. White's *The Mysticism of William Blake* (1927). After a careful comparison of Blake with other mystics, she concludes that 'he is not a great mystic in any sense that means anything' (p. 245). Whether one rejoices or repines (as Miss White seems to do) at such a conclusion, it has been widely accepted by the most influential post-Second-World-War critics such as Mark Schorer, Northrop Frye, and D. V. Erdman. 'Mysticism' is now generally taken to be a term irrelevant or inapplicable to Blake.

Two books introducing Blake to contemporaries proved very popular.

[1] For many years, T. S. Eliot's short essay on Blake in *The Sacred Wood* (1920) was surprisingly influential, but since 1960 relatively few critics have paid much attention to his view of Blake as 'a wild pet for the supercultivated' who 'approached everything with a mind unclouded by current opinions'.

Max Plowman's *Introduction to the Study of Blake* (1927) is lucid and infectiously enthusiastic, though it makes few claims to originality. Middleton Murry's *William Blake* (1933), on the other hand, is often thought-provoking and original, though few subsequent critics have taken up his challenging statements that Blake was simultaneously a 'Christian' and 'a great Communist'. Murry used 'only his [*Blake's*] written works as evidence', but the few facts he finds relevant receive careful treatment.

The contribution to Blake studies of the French critic Denis Saurat is far-ranging, speculative, and prolific, in *Blake and Milton* (1920), *Blake & Modern Thought* (1929), and *William Blake* (1954); the second of these is the best. In it, Saurat's concern is with Blake and eighteenth-century thought, and he goes far to document his challenging statement that 'there was not one absurdity in Europe at the end of the eighteenth century that Blake did not know' (p. 59). His studies of the influence of Druidism,[1] Kabbalistic lore, and Hindu mythology on Blake are stimulating and useful, and, when he chose, his scholarship and accuracy are commendable.

The interests of Milton O. Percival in *William Blake's Circle of Destiny* (1938) are similar to Saurat's, but his approach and conclusions are more reliable. Percival concentrates on Blake's use of tradition in the construction of his myth and is most illuminating in finding parallels and possible sources in the writings of the alchemists, the Kabbalists, and in Biblical scholarship of all kinds. Unfortunately, he took 'the prophetic writings as a single entity' (p. 12) rather than a developing idea; it is therefore safest to accept his evidence as reliable but to draw one's own conclusions on its relevance to Blake.[2]

General agreement as to Blake's importance and context made possible studies of smaller works and problems. One of the most fruitful of these was Margaret Ruth Lowery's *Windows of the Morning*: A Critical Study of William Blake's *Poetical Sketches* (1940). Her most important conclusion is 'that, contrary to all previous comment on Blake, the influence of the [*eighteenth*] century is more extensive than that of the Elizabethan period' (p. 60). In particular, her analyses of the effect and importance of Chatterton, Ossian, Thomson, and Percy's *Reliques* are of lasting significance.

One of the best introductions to Blake in his own time is Jacob

---

[1] The best work on the subject is A. L. Owen, *The Famous Druids* (1962), 224–40. Much remains to be done on the subject of Blake and Milton.

[2] Important contributions in the same field were made in E. B. Hungerford, *Shores of Darkness* (1941) and Ruthven Todd, *Tracks in the Snow* (1947), who deal with the intricate subject of the influence of the eighteenth-century mythologists. On the other hand, Emily Hamblen's *On the Minor Prophecies of William Blake* (1930) and *Interpretation of William Blake's Job* (c. 1939) are wonderfully credulous. She treats astrology and its influence on Blake with profound seriousness and was aided in her researches by visits from the dead.

Bronowski's *William Blake 1757–1827: A Man Without a Mask* (1945),[1] which surveys the economic and political background of the late eighteenth century and how it directed and thwarted Blake's work. Bronowski has a very wide range of relevant and little-used information which he applies deftly and convincingly.

On the heels of Bronowski's work came Mark Schorer's *William Blake: The Politics of Vision* (1946), which examines a similar area in greater detail and at considerably greater length. Schorer's main concentration, and his greatest achievement, is in his discussion of the radical circle around Joseph Johnson and its influence upon Blake.[2]

The period from 1921 to 1946 saw the appearance of the *Bibliography* (1921) upon which all subsequent Blake studies have been based, the establishment of the text of all Blake's *Writings* (1925), a wide range of reproductions of his drawings and engravings, and a number of important critical works, the most valuable of which is that by S. Foster Damon (1924).

A MAN FOR OUR TIME: 1947–1974

Since 1946, it has been generally assumed that the essence, or at least the most interesting part, of Blake's genius, is effable and eluctable, and that the most rewarding areas for study are his myth, his immediate background, his designs, and his books. The period has seen a general and commendable approach towards accuracy and reliability, and the advance in knowledge and understanding of Blake is remarkable. There is now a wide consensus that Blake is a major Romantic poet who drew his intellectual sustenance from contemporary sources different from those which nourished most authors of his time. There is also a growing recognition of the greatness of Blake's achievement as an artist, an engraver, and an illustrator. He is now an established figure in the literary and academic pantheon; paradoxically he is both part of the literary establishment and the subject of a sub-cultural fad, with television programmes and popular plays about him, excerpts from his works used as novel-titles and graffiti—'The tygers of wrath are wiser than the horses of instruction'. More people know and care about Blake today than ever before. On the crest of the post-Second-World-War tidal wave of publication of all kinds is a little Blake wave sufficient to sweep

---

[1] The work was issued in Penguin paperback in 1954. In the 1964 edition of this *Bibliography* we 'regretted the book's economy and . . . wished for more detail' (p. 25). The work was revised, extended, and republished as *William Blake and Revolution* (1969), but the new details seem to add little of importance.

[2] Schorer's book shows significant signs of its previous forms as a dissertation and as separate articles. It was immediately accepted as a major work in North America, while abroad it was largely ignored. Erdman's magisterial treatment of the same subjects in 1954 cast Schorer's work in shadow.

away all but the sturdiest and most uncritical readers. Because Blake
has become a growth-industry, the areas of growth have had to be
treated separately below.

FACSIMILES. One great advance of the period since 1946 has been in
the production of reliable facsimiles of Blake's writings in Illuminated
Printing and in manuscript. The chief agency in this welcome development has been the William Blake Trust, founded through the initiative
of Geoffrey Keynes who has written Bibliographical Statements to
accompany most of its publications. The chief products of the Blake
Trust, mostly printed with stencils over collotype, are *Jerusalem* copy E
in colour (1951), copy C in black-and-white (1952, 1955),[1] copy B in
colour (1974), *Innocence* copy B (1954), *Songs* copy Z (1955),[2] *Urizen*
copy G[3] (1958), *Visions* copy C (1959), *Marriage* copy D[3] (1960),
America copy M (1963), *Thel* copy O (1965), *Milton* copy D (1967), *For
Children* copy D and *For the Sexes* copy F (1968), *Europe* plates from copies
B, G, K (1969), *All Religions Are One* copy A (1970), *No Natural Religion*
plates from copies C, F–G, L (1971), the illustrations to Gray (1972),
and *Ahania* copy A (1973), and *Job* is in hand. These beautiful and expensive facsimiles are remarkably faithful to Blake's originals,[4] and two
of them are also important for the accompanying text. The notes for *The
Gates of Paradise: For Children, For the Sexes* bring up to date and extend
the information concerning numbers of copies, their provenance, and so
on, which had not been attempted since the 1921 *Bibliography*. Further,
the accompanying text for *No Natural Religion* not only performs a
similar function for that work but reanalyses the information to establish
authoritatively a new order of the plates in this enigmatic work. Both
editions are thus also important contributions to Blake bibliography.[5]

   Blake's manuscripts have also been examined and reproduced with

---

   [1] Joseph Wicksteed, *William Blake's Jerusalem* [1954], an idiosyncratic book reading Blake's
poem as autobiography, was written to accompany the *Jerusalem* facsimiles. A study which
concentrates with greater success on one book is M. K. Nurmi's *Blake's Marriage of Heaven
and Hell: A Critical Study* (1957).

   [2] A facsimile of the same copy 'printed in 6 and 8-colour offset' (1967) is perhaps the most
widely accessible satisfactory Blake facsimile today.

   [3] The Blake Trust colour-facsimiles of *Urizen* and the *Marriage* were in turn reproduced in
black-and-white, edited by C. Emery (1966, 1963), which have the advantage at least of
being cheap.

   [4] They must not, of course, be used as substitutes for the originals, for there are minor
differences both deliberate and accidental. The even-numbered plate-numbers for *Jerusalem*
C have been moved from the right to the left side; Blake's name appears in two or three
different places on the different reproductions of the title-page for Blake's Gray illustrations
(in the catalogue to the 1972 exhibition); and the colours for *All Religions Are One*, which,
unlike most of the facsimiles, was made from photographs rather than from the originals, are
apparently unreliable (see the review by K. P. Easson in *Blake Studies*, v [1972], 168–75).

   [5] A similar kind of contribution was attempted in Nancy Bogen's edition of *Thel* (1971),
which records a minor but novel and bibliographically significant textual variant.

an unwonted pertinacity within the last twenty years. H. M. Margoliouth's edition of *Vala* (1956) attempted valiantly but not altogether
successfully to disentangle the first version of that perplexed work
(*Vala*) from the last one (*The Four Zoas*). A complete facsimile of the
illuminated manuscript of *Vala or The Four Zoas* was made in 1963, with
a transcript of the poem and an extensive analysis of the attendant
problems.[1] A similar reproduction of *Tiriel* (1967) made some of the
illustrations to that poem available for the first time. And the recent
facsimile of the unillustrated fair-copy of *The Pickering Manuscript* presented by Charles Ryskamp (1972) virtually completes the list of Blake's
extensive manuscripts.[2]

The number and quality of good Blake facsimiles which have
appeared since 1951 far exceeds those from all previous periods. As
a consequence, critics are increasingly dissatisfied with analyses which
do not explicitly comprehend Blake's designs as well as his text.

TYPOGRAPHICAL EDITIONS. Blake has been as well served by typographical editions. Sir Geoffrey Keynes's texts of Blake's *Letters* (1956,
1968) presented all the apparatus of addresses and provenances dear
to the hearts of modern scholars, as well as a few letters not previously
printed. His revision of his editions of Blake as *The Complete Writings*
(1957, 1966, 1967, 1969, 1971) filled a long-felt need and provided
serious students with a text which is likely to be widely used for many
years.[3]

The only serious rival to Keynes's *Complete Writings* is the edition of
Poetry and Prose (1965 ff.), edited by D. V. Erdman. The Erdman text
differs in three important ways from that of Keynes: in the first place,
it attempts to present Blake's punctuation exactly as Blake left it,
without the consistent (and largely silent) editorial emendation which
characterized the text of Keynes and of almost all previous editors; in
the second place, it was based upon a very extensive re-examination of
Blake's books and manuscripts by a team of collaborators (assembled
for the very important *Concordance* [1967]), which enabled Erdman to
make many minor verbal corrections to Keynes's text; and in the third
place, it contains a 'Commentary' by Harold Bloom (pp. 807–89) on
some of Blake's knottier works which many readers find illuminating.

[1] For another discussion of some of the problems, see D. V. Erdman, 'The Binding (et
cetera) of *Vala*', *Library*, xix (1968), 116–29.

[2] The chief exceptions are the unillustrated *Island in the Moon*, 'then She bore Pale desire',
and 'Woe cried the muse', the last two of which were transcribed with minute fidelity by
D. V. Erdman in *BNYPL* (1958). Geoffrey Keynes had reproduced Blake's letters to Butts in
1926 and the *Notebook* in 1935, and an admirable facsimile edition of the *Notebook* edited
by D. V. Erdman was published in 1973.

[3] It is the basis for the excellent *Concordance* of Blake by Erdman *et al.* (1967), which contains corrections to the Keynes text in appendices.

It also contains excellent textual notes by Erdman. One drawback of the edition is that it is not quite complete, but it is yet one which many scholars prefer to use, and it is in turn spawning other editions based upon it, such as W. H. Stevenson's *Poems* (1971).[1] Blake students are very fortunate to be thus served by editors as patient and energetic as Dr. Erdman and Sir Geoffrey Keynes.

BLAKE'S ART. Blake's designs have not yet received nearly so much attention as literary students tend to think they deserve, but an extensive range of them has appeared since 1946. So far as mere reproductions are concerned, the most noteworthy are Geoffrey Keynes's extensive collection of *William Blake's Engravings* (1950), the *Blake–Varley Sketchbook of 1819*, ed. Martin Butlin (Blake Trust, 1969), and the magnificent illustrations to Gray (Blake Trust, 1972). This last was preceded by an exhibition whose catalogue reproduced all the designs (1971–2), as did Irene Tayler's important study of *Blake's Illustrations to the Poems of Thomas Gray* (1971).

Most writers on Blake's art, such as Irene Tayler and Jean Hagstrum (below), derive the bulk of their experience from literature rather than from art. The exceptions to this statement are few but notable. A. S. Roe's study and reproduction of *Blake's Illustrations to the Divine Comedy* (1953) makes extensive use of Blake's myth in analysing Blake's drawings but soundly emphasizes their artistic qualities. Perhaps the best study of Blake's artistic career as a whole is in Sir Anthony Blunt's *Art of William Blake* (1959), a series of lectures (with references and proofs checked by a secretary) which incorporates most of the merits of his excellent articles on Blake. In particular, his work demonstrates the fascination to be found in tracing Blake's pictorial sources and traditions. George Wingfield Digby, *Symbol and Image in William Blake* (1957) was also a series of lectures; they apply modern psychological distinctions particularly to the *Gates of Paradise* and the Arlington Court Picture, often with success. Jean Hagstrum's *William Blake, Poet and Painter*: An Introduction to the Illuminated Verse (1964) is the first work to attempt to relate text and design comprehensively; it pretends to be little more than an 'Introduction', but more detailed studies of the subject in future are likely to begin where Hagstrum leaves off. The books called *Blake's Job* by S. Foster Damon (1966) and by Andrew Wright (1972) are useful if amateur (i.e. largely literary) analyses. They are put into distant perspective by Dr. Bo Lindberg's *William Blake's Illustrations to the Book of Job* (1973), one of the most impressive books on Blake's art, which brings together the training of an art

---

[1] Professor Stevenson decided, however, to 'modernize' the spelling, punctuation, and capitalization and to alter the Erdman order in *Vala*. Stevenson's voluminous annotations are very helpful.

historian, the eye of a painter, and the energy and patience of a meticulous scholar to illuminate most rewardingly all Blake's Job designs. Damon's study and reproduction of *Blake's Grave*: A Prophetic Book . . . arranged as Blake directed (1963), is altogether a more quixotic affair, for Blake never applied the term 'Prophecy' to designs without text, and the evidence that 'Blake directed' that the designs should be arranged as Damon gives them is all inferential. *William Blake's 'Heads of the Poets'* by William Wells (1969) carefully traces the pictorial origins of Blake's portraits for Hayley's house in a way which carries satisfactory conviction. All these are serious attempts to advance knowledge.

Kathleen Raine's book on his art called *William Blake* (1970) is lavishly if poorly illustrated, and the text is enthusiastic but perfunctory. Similarly disappointing is Ruthven Todd's *William Blake The Artist* (1971), a mechanical chronological assemblage of events in Blake's life and art, generously illustrated with small, unfamiliar designs; one suspects that the publisher has not done justice to Todd, who has shown himself elsewhere to be an important Blake scholar.

With such assistance, it is possible to see and understand more of Blake's art than had previously been easily available.

CATALOGUES. One of the difficulties in studying Blake's graphic work has been the absence of a *catalogue raisonné*; we just do not know sufficiently clearly what designs Blake made, or how many copies he made of some of them. This lack has been met partially by catalogues first of particular subjects and second of individual collections.

Probably the most important catalogues of the first kind are Geoffrey Keynes's *Engravings by William Blake*: The Separate Plates (1956) and his *William Blake's Illustrations to the Bible* (1957).[1] The former is not only an important catalogue but, as well, an edition (as it were) of the plates designed by Blake, reproduced often in more than one state. All work concerning the separately issued plates, such as 'Glad Day' or 'Chaucer's Canterbury Pilgrims', must begin with Keynes's book. The Bible work is much less ambitious as to text, but it reproduces some 174 designs (mostly in very reduced size) and describes the rest which cannot be traced.

A general list of books connected with Blake was attempted in the first edition of the present work (*A Blake Bibliography* [1964]), particularly with respect to Blake's commercial book-engravings. This area was the focus of Charles Ryskamp's enterprising *William Blake Engraver*: A Descriptive Catalogue of an Exhibition [in] Princeton (1969) and of the important book by R. R. Easson & R. N. Essick, *William*

[1] See also Geoffrey Keynes, *The Tempera Paintings of William Blake*: A Critical Catalogue (1951).

Blake Book Illustrator: A Bibliography and Catalogue of the Commercial Engravings (Vol. I: 1972). This last is more elaborate than anything else which has appeared on the subject, is particularly valuable in its description of states and variants of plates, and is likely to remain for long the standard description of the subject.[1] A more comprehensive work is Robert Essick's very useful 'finding list of reproductions of blake's art', *Blake Newsletter*, v (1971), 1–160, which contains a vast amount of carefully digested information though, of course, it does not pretend to be exhaustive.

Responsible catalogues of individual collections are appearing with gratifying frequency. The most extensive private collection to be thus described is Sir Geoffrey Keynes's *Bibliotheca Bibliographici* (1964); the Blakes (no. 467–783, now largely promised to the Fitzwilliam) are described with a good deal of information not available elsewhere. The most extensive private collection of Blake's art in recent times was that made by Graham Robertson; it was largely sold at Christie's, 22 July 1949, and somewhat casually described in *The Blake Collection of W. Graham Robertson*, ed. Kerrison Preston (1952). G. E. Bentley, Jr., *The Blake Collection of Mrs. Landon K. Thorne* (1971) is a full-dress catalogue of one of the last great private collections of Blake books and pictures, most of which have now been given to the Pierpont Morgan Library. Martin Butlin's 'The Blake Collection of Mrs. William T. Tonner', *Bulletin Philadelphia Museum of Art*, lxvii (1972), 5–31, is not, strictly speaking, a catalogue, but since it describes and reproduces each of her drawings (mostly given to the Philadelphia Museum), it serves a similar purpose. It is striking that three of these private Blake collections have entered, or are entering, public institutions more or less *en bloc*.

The most important collection of Blake's art is that in the Tate Gallery, London, and its catalogue is therefore similarly important. Fortunately, Martin Butlin's book (1957) revised as *William Blake: a complete catalogue of the works in the Tate Gallery* (1971), is fully worthy of such a collection, with reproductions of the works described. A similarly elaborate and reliable treatment is accorded to *William Blake*: Catalogue of the Collection in the Fitzwilliam Museum Cambridge, ed. David Bindman (1970), one of the three most important collections in Britain. The greatest gathering of Blake's literary works anywhere is in the British Museum, but [P. Morgan], 'A Handlist of Works by William Blake in The Department of Prints & Drawings of The British Museum', ed. G. E. Bentley, Jr., *Blake Newsletter*, v (1972),

---

[1] It is considerably more detailed than the present work as to kinds of information given (format, contents, detailed description of states of plates) but is based on examination of relatively few (chiefly U.S.) copies. Often *Blake Books* and *William Blake Book Illustrator* will be found to supplement each other in their descriptions of Blake's commercial engravings.

223–58, is a much humbler affair, though still a considerable improvement on what was previously available either in print or in the British Museum itself.[1] In general, Blake has been well served by cataloguers and bibliographers, but a great deal remains to be done, particularly with catalogues of individual collections.

BIOGRAPHY. The outlines of Blake's life were clearly set out by Gilchrist (1863) and rebalanced by Mona Wilson (1927). Since then, no ambitious, full-scale life has been attempted, but smaller, useful studies have appeared. H. M. Margoliouth's little *William Blake* (1951) is a general account embodying some of the virtues of his excellent articles. *Blake's Hayley* by Morchard Bishop [Oliver Stoner] (1951) is a much more ambitious and useful work, a life of Hayley with particular reference to Blake's small part in it, based largely on Hayley's voluminous manuscripts. The most extensive biographical work of the time is G. E. Bentley, Jr., *Blake Records* (1969), which attempts to locate, verify, and reprint every account of Blake (including those by Malkin, Crabb Robinson, J. T. Smith, Allan Cunningham, and Frederick Tatham), and of his family from the earliest-known record (the apprenticeship of his father in 1737) to the latest (the death of his wife in 1831), with appendices on Blake's residences, financial accounts, and engravings. There is a connective narrative linking the facts, but little attempt is made to digest their significance. *Blake Records* is probably the most convenient place to find the facts of Blake's life, carefully evaluated. A somewhat similar work is Deborah Dorfman's *Blake in the Nineteenth Century*: His Reputation as a Poet From Gilchrist to Yeats (1969), which is perhaps chiefly valuable for its demonstration of the way in which Carlyle's *On Heroes, Hero-Worship and the Heroic* influenced Gilchrist's *Life*.[2] It seems likely that almost all the biographical facts concerning Blake in the eighteenth and nineteenth centuries are now available and reliably displayed.

SOURCES AND INFLUENCES. With an author as independent and heterodox as Blake, the problem of whence he derived his ideas is important and difficult. In the period 1921–46 there was a good deal of speculation, and some sound argument, on the subject, but scholars have now largely turned their attention elsewhere. There have, how-

---

[1] The account of the Blake books in *The Rosenwald Collection* (1954), 186–96, 993–1055, is partial (omitting pictures) and perfunctory, but in this case most of the information is available in fuller form elsewhere.

[2] The facts concerning Blake's reputation between 1831 (the terminus of *Blake Records*) and 1863 (the beginning of *Blake in the Nineteenth Century*) are presented in 'Forgotten Years: References to William Blake 1831–1862' as an appendix to G. E. Bentley, Jr., *Blake*: The Critical Heritage (published 1975); see also S. R. Hoover, 'William Blake in the Wilderness: A Closer Look at his Reputation 1827–1863', pp. 310–48 of *William Blake*: Essays in honour of Sir Geoffrey Keynes, ed. M. D. Paley & M. Phillips (1973).

ever, been a few books worth recording. The question of the influence of Boehme and Swedenborg was usefully explored in Jacques Roos, *Aspects littéraires du mysticisme philosophique et l'influence de Boehme et de Swedenborg au début du romanticisme: William Blake, Novalis, Ballanche* (1951), 25–194, and developed with more depth and greater learning in Désirée Hirst, *Hidden Riches*: Traditional Symbolism from the Renaissance to Blake (1964). Both are on firm ground, for Blake spoke warmly of Boehme and Paracelsus and was, at least briefly, a founder-member of the Swedenborgian New Jerusalem Church (1789). An attractive but much more speculative thesis is put forward in A. L. Morton's brief book *The Everlasting Gospel*: A study in the sources of William Blake (1958), dealing with such extreme seventeenth-century dissenters as the Muggletonians.[1]

A more difficult subject is the question of Blake's Platonism or neo-Platonism, which has exercised George Harper and Kathleen Raine in a series of articles culminating in books, his *The Neoplatonism of William Blake* (1961) and her *Blake and Tradition* (1968). The crux is that, while Blake's Idealism is clearly analogical to Plato's and his myth occasionally parallel to neo-Platonism, Blake strongly condemned Plato and the Greeks during most of his literary life, and there was no unmistakable evidence that Blake knew either the books or the person of Thomas Taylor,[2] the chief transmitter of neo-Platonism in Blake's time and the central figure in both books. Further, in each book far more was alleged than was proved, and most scholars have concluded that the sources and nature of Blake's neo-Platonism have yet to be conclusively demonstrated.

A more attractive work, because quite frankly speculative, is Martha England's 'Apprenticeship at the Haymarket?' (appearing in various incarnations in 1969), which suggests that the *Island in the Moon* echoes, perhaps was deliberately modelled on, Foote's entertainments at the Haymarket Theatre; certainly she has displayed with great learning many intriguing parallels, though most scholarly jurymen are likely to bring in a Scottish verdict of 'not proven'.[3]

Blake's influence on his successors has exercised scholars of Rossetti,[4] Shaw,[4] James Joyce, D. H. Lawrence, Joyce Cary, and others, but the

---

[1] The arguments on similar subjects of F. E. Pierce (1924–31) rarely carry conviction. The earnest essays of Elizabeth O'Higgins (1950–6), asserting that Blake composed in Gaelic and translated his poems into English, are entrancing exercises which scarcely challenge the reader's credulity.

[2] James King has now demonstrated, in 'The Meredith Family, Thomas Taylor, and William Blake', *Studies in Romanticism*, xi (1972), 153–7, that not only were Blake and Taylor acquainted, but that 'Taylor gave Blake lessons in geometry', and the connection is confirmed in *The Reminiscences of Alexander Dyce*, ed. R. J. Schrader (1972), 134–5.

[3] Her exploration of parallels between Blake's *Songs* and Methodist hymns in *Hymns Unbidden* (1966) is also very fruitful.

[4] Irving Fiske, *Bernard Shaw's Debt to William Blake*, with Foreword and Notes by G. B. S.

only one to receive very extensive attention is W. B. Yeats. Margaret Rudd, *Divided Image*: A Study of William Blake and W. B. Yeats (1953) explores the ground tentatively, and Virginia Moore's account of 'Blake as a Major Doctrinal Influence' on Yeats in *The Unicorn* (1954) is similarly unconvincing about each side of the relationship; Blake's influence was more satisfactorily defined in Hazard Adams, *Blake and Yeats*: The Contrary Vision (1955), with a confident grasp of the ideas, significance, and relationship of the two men.

Studies of the sources and influence of Blake have thus tentatively surveyed some of the most obvious ground, but later scholars are likely to feel that much remains to be done, even in the areas already explored.

CRITICISM AND APPRECIATION. The critical figure who dominates, and indeed defines, this period of Blake studies is Northrop Frye, whose *Fearful Symmetry*: A Study of William Blake (1947) is probably the most comprehensive, learned, illuminating, and profound book on Blake of this or any other era. The orientation of the work is critical—indeed, it is the foundation of the most influential critical system of our time—but it makes full use of the best books and information which had preceded it. All Blake's literary achievements are synthesized into a work which has itself a gigantic and fearful symmetry. Blake's development is lucidly and wittily analysed, and the forces and influences which governed his work are displayed confidently and clearly; in particular, Frye finds that Blake was working in a tradition of archetypal symbolism, for instance in the Orc Cycle. As in any really compelling discussion of a work of art, the terms and arguments are complex in themselves, and the criticism is not unlike the original in density and profundity. The enormous merit of the book is the way in which vastly diverse details are subsumed into a directing purpose and understanding. *Fearful Symmetry* is a truly magisterial work.[1]

The only Blake scholar-critic of the period worthy to be named after Northrop Frye is D. V. Erdman, who in *Blake Prophet Against Empire*: A Poet's Interpretation of the History of His Own Times (1954)[2] attempted with great success 'to trace through nearly all of his works

(1951), is brief but intriguing; Kerrison Preston, *Blake and Rossetti* (1944) is lengthy and laboured.

[1] The only persistent criticism of the book of which I am aware is that Frye tends to see each Blake work as part of one gigantic myth, as opposed to abortive attempts at diverse myths or as quite distinct complementary myths (e.g. Blake's private myth and the public Christian myth). Frye's essays on Blake are frequently as compelling as the book itself.

[2] *Blake Prophet Against Empire* was extensively revised in the 1969 edition, incorporating the scholarship of the 15 intervening years (largely in footnotes). Only occasionally do the new facts, such as those about *Vala*, require much alteration; in some cases, Erdman has attempted to let the text stand and make corrections in footnotes only.

a more or less clearly discernible thread of historical reference' (p. viii). Time after time, Erdman relates previously unknown or ignored facts to Blake in a way which illuminates both his life and his works. Floods of light are thrown upon a great many aspects of Blake's history, art, and writings. Throughout, Erdman's facts are judiciously selected and carefully used and may be depended upon with great confidence. Some readers have not been convinced of the consistency of the radical political motifs which Erdman traces, and all readers must remember that the book concerns primarily one aspect of Blake's work and is, therefore, necessarily a partial and unbalanced work. With such reservations, *Blake Prophet Against Empire* must be acknowledged as one of the monuments of Blake scholarship, a work of great learning, care, intelligence, and usefulness. When detailed studies are made in future of Blake's immediate environment, they will have to be measured against Erdman.

Erdman has also made other major contributions to Blake studies, in his editions of the *Poetry and Prose* (1965), *The Notebook* (1973), and *The Illuminated Blake* (1974), in the *Concordance* (1967), and in many articles, the most important of which is 'The Suppressed and Altered Passages in Blake's *Jerusalem*', *Studies in Bibliography*, xvii (1964), 1–54, which applies enormous patience and ingenuity and some new techniques to bibliographical problems in Blake's longest finished Prophecy.

Many books of the period deal with Blake's literary work in general. The most original and controversial portion of Bernard Blackstone's *English Blake* (1949) is his analysis of the contemporary sources and significance of the *Island in the Moon*, but the title and emphasis are directed against authors such as Ellis & Yeats and towards fitting Blake into his own English setting. Peter F. Fisher, *The Valley of Vision*: Blake as Prophet and Revolutionary (1961) is a highly abstract, unfinished study of Blake's context, of which Frye thought well enough to complete it sufficiently for publication after the author's premature death. Another follower of Frye is Harold Bloom who in *The Visionary Company* (1961), 1–119, *Blake's Apocalypse* (1963), and the notes to Erdman's edition of the *Poetry and Prose* (1965), 807–89, analyses Blake's more difficult poems in a sophisticated, allusive way which many readers find rewarding. S. Foster Damon, in *A Blake Dictionary* (1965), attempted to combine an alphabetical encyclopedia of Blake's works, ideas, myth, and even biography, with an independant critical analysis of them; the former purpose is fulfilled with some success, but the latter is occasionally simply quixotic,[1] and the very considerable usefulness of

---

[1] The two purposes are not always entirely distinct, interpretation sometimes appearing as fact. Damon says repeatedly, for example, that in *Jerusalem* Blake alludes to the death of Shelley, though Shelley died (1822) after *Jerusalem* was completed, in print, and on sale (1820).

the whole is significantly vitiated by the lack of an index. Raymond Lister, *William Blake*: An Introduction to the Man and to His Work (1968) is an unpretentious little book whose chief asset is its author's familiarity as a practising artist with Blake's artistic techniques and accomplishments. John Beer's *Blake's Humanism* (1968) and *Blake's Visionary Universe* (1969) often relate the poet usefully to his literary background in an attempt to survey all Blake's writings. Morton Paley, *Energy and The Imagination*: A Study of the Development of Blake's Thought (1970) presents a soundly argued analysis of the decreasing importance in Blake's myth of Orc (Energy) and the parallel rise to centrality of Los (Imagination). Perhaps the most successful of these general works is Alicia Ostriker, *Vision and Verse in William Blake* (1965), because she has limited her attention to Blake's poetic techniques and illuminated them with great sensitivity.

Considering the bulk and diversity of Blake's writings, it is natural that a number of critics have restricted their attentions to his lyric poetry. Probably the most successful of these is Robert Gleckner in *The Piper & The Bard*: a study of William Blake (1959), which deals carefully with the poetry from *Innocence* through the *Visions*, stressing narrative point of view in the *Songs*. Stanley Gardner's slim *Infinity on the Anvil*: A Critical Study of Blake's Poetry (1954) and *Blake* (1968) are straightforward, sensitive analyses of dramatic conflicts in the lyric poetry before 1794 (the later Prophecies 'are barren of poetry'). Hazard Adams is more ambitious and successful (and lengthy) in *William Blake*: A Reading of the Shorter Poems (1963), which is much indebted to Frye; it consistently relates the short poems to the Prophecies, and there is an extensive and helpful annotated list, poem by poem, of criticism of Blake's lyrics. E. D. Hirsch, Jr., has been enterprising in *Innocence & Experience*: An Introduction to Blake (1964) in attempting to trace autobiographical elements in Blake's poems, chiefly the *Songs*, but he is often betrayed by the biographical and bibliographical facts. D. H. Gillham, *Blake's Contrary States* (1966) is a somewhat pedestrian attempt to examine the *Songs* on the basis only of 'a patient reading of the poems themselves' (p. 1), with predictable results. On the other hand, John Holloway, in his little book *Blake*: The Lyric Poet (1968), has been able to illuminate Blake surprisingly frequently by a sensitive intimacy with Blake's literary context, though without a parallel familiarity with Blake scholarship. In general, these books focusing on Blake's lyrics seem more concerned to appeal to a wide audience— some of them are in series designed for the purpose—than to provide novel illumination on his poetry, though Adams and Gleckner prove satisfying exceptions to this conclusion.

Blake's religious ideas are obviously at the centre of much of his poetry, but, though they have been examined repeatedly, no one has succeeded in defining them very persuasively. J. G. Davies, *The Theology of William Blake* (1948) attempts valiantly to prove that Blake was (or perhaps meant to be) an orthodox[1] Anglican Christian; the most useful part of his book, sweeping away the claims that Blake grew up a Swedenborgian, was confirmed by D. V. Erdman in 'Blake's Early Swedenborgianism: A Twentieth Century Legend', *Comparative Literature*, v (1953). H. N. Fairchild, on the other hand, stresses without timidity Blake's religious heterodoxy in his *Religious Trends in English Poetry* (1949), iii. 66–137, and this conclusion is joyously extended by T. T. J. Altizer, *The New Apocalypse*: The Radical Christian Vision of William Blake (1967): 'Blake was the first Christian atheist' (p. xi). A. A. Ansari, *Arrows of Intellect*: A Study in William Blake's Gospel of the Imagination (1965),[2] despite the title, is largely an attempt to set forth Blake's philosophical ideas, with special emphasis on Locke and Wordsworth.

Considering the quality of what has been achieved, there have been mercifully few attempts to study Blake's psychology. The first work devoted entirely to the subject was W. P. Witcutt's *Blake*: A Psychological Study (1946), which argued that Blake was an Irish Jungian introvert whose philosophy 'We can safely disregard' (p. 26). Similarly disregardable is Margaret Rudd, *Organiz'd Innocence*: The Story of Blake's Prophetic Books (1956), which concludes that the 'one long narrative' formed by *Vala, Milton*, and *Jerusalem* is 'Blake's own psychological drama' (p. x), which she paraphrases. Finally, June K. Singer, *The Unholy Bible*: A Psychological Interpretation of William Blake (1970) by a Jungian analyst discusses Blake's sexual life (as deduced from his writings) in wonderful detail, and consistently misrepresents the plainest facts. In Blake studies, at least, there is an unfortunate connection between an inclination to make psychological interpretations and scholarly incompetence.

COLLECTIONS OF ESSAYS. The visible plethora of writings on Blake of all kinds and values has fostered the publication not only of collections of articles in book form but of whole journals devoted largely or exclusively to Blake. *Blake ko Whitman* (1931–2) must have been influential in introducing Blake's writings and ideas to Japanese readers. Special issues of the *Bulletin of the New York Public Library* (1957, 1960) and of other journals have occasionally been devoted to Blake.

---

[1] Margaret Bottrall, *The Divine Image*: A Study of Blake's Interpretation of Christianity (1950) agrees that 'Blake's Christianity was essentially and soundly Christian' (p. 7).

[2] Kathryn Kremen, *The Imagination of the Resurrection*: The Poetic Continuity of a Religious Motif in Donne, Blake, and Yeats (1972), 129–259, is a reading of the theological passages in Blake's poetry.

Professor Morton Paley founded the *Blake Newsletter* in 1967 to keep Blake students abreast of recent developments, and it has performed this function very usefully; recently it has also published important reference works (Essick's catalogue of reproductions of Blake and the Handlist of Blakes in the British Museum), as well as reviews and critical quarrels. In imitation of it, Professors Kay and Roger Easson established the semi-annual *Blake Studies* in 1968. Unlike Sir Geoffrey Keynes's book (1949, 1971), from which the title is borrowed, *Blake Studies* has thus far been largely concerned with appreciations and readings, sometimes of a rather ephemeral kind.

Similar vehicles for new Blake essays are to be found in *The Divine Vision*: Studies in the Poetry and Art of William Blake, ed. Vivian de Sola Pinto (1957), with a profitable essay by Frye on *Milton*; in *William Blake*: Essays for S. Foster Damon, ed. A. H. Rosenfeld (1969), with important essays by Martin Butlin on the great colour prints and by Paul Miner on 'Blake's Biblical Symbolism'; in *Blake's Visionary Forms Dramatic*, ed. D. V. Erdman & John E. Grant (1970), which is full of critical cult-phrases such as 'vicarious palinodes', 'torques of genesis', and 'nodes of verbal imagery'; in *Blake's Sublime Allegory*: Essays on *The Four Zoas, Milton, Jerusalem*, ed. Stuart Curran & Joseph Anthony Wittreich, Jr. (1973), with a fruitful essay by Morton Paley on Blake's garment imagery; and in *William Blake*: Essays in honour of Sir Geoffrey Keynes, ed. Morton D. Paley & Michael Phillips (1973), with an evaluation and checklist of Sir Geoffrey's Blake work, and especially rewarding essays by David Bindman on Blake's history paintings and by Morton Paley on Blake, Richard Brothers, and Joanna Southcott. There have also been more than enough volumes reprinting earlier essays. Of these, virtually the only one of intrinsic importance is Geoffrey Keynes's *Blake Studies* (1949, much extended in 1971), which contains in its revisions of articles a great deal of information that is both important and not elsewhere available. Other such collections include *Discussions of William Blake*, ed. John E. Grant (1961), *Twentieth Century Interpretations of Songs of Innocence and of Experience*, ed. Morton D. Paley (1969), *The Tyger*, ed. Winston Weathers (1969), *Songs of Innocence and Experience* [*sic*], ed. Margaret Bottrall (1970), *Critics on Blake*, ed. Judith O'Neill (1970), and *The Visionary Hand*: Essays for the Study of William Blake's Art and Aesthetics, ed. Robert N. Essick (1973). Doubtless there will be more.

The period from 1947 to 1974 in Blake studies has seen the publication of two magisterial critical works, by Northrop Frye and D. V. Erdman, the appearance of important editions such as Keynes's *Complete Writings* (1957), Erdman's *Poetry and Prose* (1965) and his *Notebook* (1973), and *Vala* (1956, 1963) considerably superior to anything that had previously been available, the advent of a *Concordance* (1967), the establishment of a reliable series of facsimiles sponsored by the Blake Trust, a host of minor critical and scholarly works, and legions of essays,[1] notes, readings, and appreciations of Blake. Blake studies have made great strides in the last twenty-five years, but much yet remains to be done. Fortunately, some of the desiderata are now in hand.

WORK IN PROGRESS. Of the studies of Blake presently in hand, the most important is the *catalogue raisonné* of Blake's art on which Martin Butlin has been working for a number of years. Michael Tolley, John E. Grant, and E. J. Rose, in association with D. V. Erdman, are preparing an edition of all the *Night Thoughts* drawings. An edition of Blake's *Writings*, with reproductions of all the major designs to literary texts, designed to range with *Blake Books*, is forthcoming. The Blake Trust has announced its intention to publish facsimiles of *The Song of Los* and *Job*, and the American Blake Foundation intends to publish facsimiles of *America* (E), *Europe* (H), *The Song of Los* (E), *Visions of the Daughters of Albion* (F), *An Island in the Moon*, and The Genesis Manuscript.

WORK NEEDED. Despite the tidal wave of articles and even books about Blake in the last twenty-five years, there still remain important lacunae, for most appreciations and criticisms of Blake simply pace over the same well-known ground. We need facsimiles of books previously unreproduced, such as *The French Revolution* and the *Descriptive Catalogue*, and of unfamiliar copies of familiar works, such as the plates in *A Small Book of Designs* or the set of large colour prints. Blake's designs in series, such as those for Bunyan and the Bible, call for detailed scrutiny. We need authoritative catalogues of the great Blake collections, such as those at Harvard (Houghton, Widener, and the Fogg), at Yale, Princeton, the Pierpont Morgan Library, the Victoria & Albert Museum, and even for the British Museum and the Library of Congress (i.e. The Rosenwald Collection) for which little more than handlists exist.

A magisterial biography would be most welcome. Ideally, such a work would be preceded by studies of some of Blake's most important friends and contemporaries such as John Flaxman, George Cumberland, Henry Fuseli, Thomas Stothard, and Joseph Johnson. A similarly magisterial work is needed to assess the relationship of Blake and the mythographers of his time such as Stukeley, Jacob Bryant, and Edward Davies. The nature of Blake's religious background and development should be sufficiently defined, with thorough treatment of Baptists,

---

[1] One of the best of these is John Sutherland, 'Blake's "Mental Traveller"', *ELH*, xxii (1955).

Methodists, and Swedenborgians. And the significance and importance of alchemy (chiefly Boehme and Paracelsus), of the Kabbala, of Milton, and of the neo-Platonic traditions have yet to be reliably and definitively evaluated. Such studies, soundly accomplished, would go far toward answering the outstanding questions concerning Blake's work and life. There seems to be no lack of enthusiastic authors writing about Blake, and certainly the important and intriguing tasks remaining to be done are manifold.

31 December 1972

PART I

EDITIONS OF BLAKE'S WRITINGS

Section A

INDIVIDUAL WORKS

ORGANIZATION. Blake's works are listed in alphabetical order of title. Various editions of a given work (like *Jerusalem*) are listed in chronological order, except that translations are grouped together chronologically after the English editions. All works which include either more or less than a complete book as Blake issued it (say *Songs of Innocence and Other Poems*, or *Eight Songs of William Blake*) are listed separately in Section B in alphabetical order by title under Collections and Selections.

HISTORIES

The information about individual contemporary copies of Blake's writings in the following Histories derives chiefly from ownership marks in the copies themselves, descriptions in sales and exhibition catalogues, and casual references in contemporary books and manuscripts. The Histories have previously been set out systematically in Geoffrey Keynes, *A Bibliography of William Blake* (1921) (books and MSS), M. R. Lowery, 'A Census of William Blake's *Poetical Sketches*, 1783', *Library*, 4th Ser., XVII (1936), 354–60, Geoffrey Keynes, *Blake Studies* (1949, 1971) (*Poetical Sketches* and *Descriptive Catalogue*), Geoffrey Keynes & Edwin Wolf 2nd,[1] *William Blake's Illuminated Books*: A Census (1953), Geoffrey Keynes, *Engravings by William Blake*: The Separate Plates (1956), and *Letters of William Blake*, ed. Geoffrey Keynes (1956, 1968). These works have provided vitally important guides, though occasionally the Histories below supplement or attempt to correct their predecessors. In addition, the Histories of the drawings which bear inscriptions are often based upon information collected by Mr. Martin Butlin for his *catalogue raisonné* of Blake's art.

The bindings described in sale and exhibition catalogues are apparently identical with those at present on the works unless otherwise specified. The earlier catalogues rarely mention bindings.

---

[1] In particular, Mr. Edwin Wolf 2nd searched the Rosenbach records and summarized those relevant to Blake in the *Census*; I have relied throughout the following Histories on his summaries.

Information as to when and from whom a permanent collection (such as the Fitzwilliam) acquired a work by Blake derives from the accession records or curators of the collections. Records of exhibition of individual copies are given here chiefly to establish ownership. Consequently, records of exhibition are generally ignored after a copy entered a public collection, or, in some cases, a collection which became public *en bloc*, such as those of Huntington (the Huntington Library), Morgan (the Pierpont Morgan Library), Mr. Rosenwald (the Library of Congress), and Mr. Mellon (Yale). Similarly, I omit pressmarks, book-plates, numbers, etc., which were added when the copies reached public collections, as well as dealers' marks which I cannot understand such as '£cnt . . . £ce.x.x' in *Song of Los* (F).

Dealers are only given a separate entry in the Histories when they catalogued a book or kept it for an appreciable length of time. When they seem to act only as agents, they are not treated as separate owners.

Buyers and prices of copies listed in the auction catalogues derive chiefly from *Book Prices Current* (1887 ff.) and from marked copies of the catalogues; for Sotheby's, ordinarily the file copies now in the British Museum, for Christie's the file copies with the Christie firm.

The identification of a copy described in a catalogue is sometimes made possible only by a process of elimination. Thus a catalogue of 1904 may refer to a copy printed in Blue, which must be copy D, because copy D is the only one printed in Blue whose ownership is not known for 1904. Sometimes the catalogue could refer to an otherwise unknown copy. In the nineteenth century, it is unusual for a catalogue to mention an owner whose book-plate is still with the volume.

COPPERPLATES

Tatham said that Mrs. Blake 'bequeathed' to him in 1831 'a very great number of Copper Plates'.[1] However, almost all of these were, 'it is believed, . . . stolen after Blake's death, and sold for old metal'.[2] The only survivors as far as 1861 were some of the plates of the *Songs* (of which electrotype copies were made before they too disappeared), and a fragment of a rejected plate for *America* which had been used for another purpose. No copperplate survives for the Illuminated Works which Blake published.[3]

BINDINGS

The patterns of stab holes in contemporary copies of Blake's works reported here suggest that Blake usually issued his works stabbed in wrappers, as in surviving copies of *Descriptive Catalogue* (C, G), *Europe* (F), *For the Sexes* (F), *French Revolution*, *Poetical Sketches* (B, V), *Innocence* (E), *Songs* (H), and *Tiriel*. The History of *Songs* (K, O, e and pl. 7, 10, 33) suggests that occasionally, at any rate, Blake stabbed and numbered the plates before colouring them.

---

[1] *Blake Records* (1969), 533.
[2] A. Gilchrist, *Life of William Blake*, '*Pictor Ignotus*' (1863), i. 267.
[3] However, we do have copperplates for *Job*, for Dante, and for a number of other engravings with little or no text, largely because they came through the hands of Linnell rather than those of Tatham.

In copies printed by Blake which do not now exhibit stab holes, perhaps the inner margins were trimmed, removing this evidence. Copies printed after Blake's death, such as *America* (P, Q), *Europe* (L, M), *Jerusalem* (H–J), *Songs* (a–o) do not show these stab holes.

Information about former bindings is generally taken from the History of the volume. Information quoted about present bindings, e.g. 'BOUND BY BEDFORD', is taken from stamps or tickets on the covers or, occasionally, on the fly-leaves. Information about lettering or patterns gilt on the spine or boards, or about fly-leaves or interleaving, is ordinarily omitted except in the case of contemporary bindings ('contemporary' being taken to mean up to about 1835). The leaves may be presumed to be of slightly irregular size unless described as trimmed, gilt, or marbled. *N.B.* Most of the Blake works in the British Museum Print Room were rebound in the summer of 1968.

TABLE OF STAB HOLES[1]

Two Holes

4·8   *Visions* (O)
11·7   *America* (M)

Three Holes

1·0, 1·9	*Songs* pl. 9–10	4·2, 4·7	*Songs* (W)
2·6, 2·8	*Songs* (K, O, e)	4·3, 3·5	*Innocence* (E)
2·6, 3·5	*Innocence* (R)	4·4, 3·5	*For the Sexes* (F)
2·8, 2·8	*Innocence* (S)	4·5, 4·5	*For the Sexes* (J)
3·2, 3·9	*Songs* (E)	4·5, 4·6	Pickering MS
3·2, 2·9	*Poetical Sketches* (D)	4·6, 4·6	*Milton* (B)
3·2, 4·0	*Marriage* (B)	4·8, 4·4	*Innocence* (Q)
3·3, 4·0	*Songs* (L)	4·8, 4·8	*For the Sexes* (H)
3·4, 3·4	*Songs* (I)	4·8, 4·9	*Innocence* (I)
3·4, 4·0	*Songs* (Q)	4·9, 6·4	*Innocence* (D)
3·4, 4·3	Small Book of Designs (B)	5·0, 5·0	*Tiriel*
3·5, 3·4	*Songs* (E)	5·1, 6·3	*Book of Los* (A)
3·5, 4·2	*Milton* (A)	5·3, 5·3	*Songs* (V)
3·6, 3·6	*For the Sexes* (D)	5·3, 6·0	*Urizen* (D)
3·7, 6·0	*Songs* (H)	5·4, 6·9	*Songs* (O)
3·8, 3·9	*Innocence* (X)	5·5, 6·5	*Songs* (B)
3·9, 3·8	*For Children* (A)	5·6, 6·7	*Songs* (T²)
3·9, 4·2	*Innocence* (S)	5·7, 5·9	*Innocence* (F)
4·0, 3·6	*Innocence* (L), *No Natural Religion* (F)	5·7, 6·8	*Songs* (G)
		6·0, 6·0	*Thel* (J)
4·0, 3·7	*Songs* (Q)	6·5, 7·7	*America* (B), *Europe* (C)
4·0, 4·0	*Urizen* (G)	6·8, 7·6	*Innocence* (A)
4·1, 3·7	*Songs* (T¹)	7·0, 7·0	*Thel* (F)
4·1, 5·0	*Jerusalem* (D)	7·2, 8·4	*America* (G)
4·2, 4·3	*Jerusalem* (B)	7·2, 8·8	Small Book of Designs (A)
4·2, 4·6	*Songs* (G)	7·3, 5·8	*Europe* (I)

[1] The stab-hole measurements are given in centimetres from top to bottom. When the distance of the top hole from the top of the leaf varies from plate to plate, this measurement is omitted in the accounts of individual bindings below. Occasionally the stab holes are rather large, as much as 0·3 cm in diameter, and this of course makes the accuracy of such measurements somewhat approximate, since in practice one must guess the effective centre of the hole.

Three Holes (cont.)

7·3, 8·1	Songs (A)	9·0, 9·2	Europe (B)
7·5, 7·3	America (C), Visions (C)	9·4, 7·2	Visions (F)
7·5, 8·1	Thel (K)	9·6, 8·0	Europe (F)
7·6, 8·0	Visions (F)	9·6, 10·3	Song of Los (C)
7·7, 6·7	Urizen (B)	9·7, 9·6	America (D)
7·8, 6·4	America (N)	10·4, 10·4	Song of Los (E), 'Albion
7·9, 10·0	Visions (K)		Rose' (D)
8·2, 8·2	Visions (D)	10·7, 12·9	America (B)
8·3, 8·3	Innocence (P)	10·9, 9·7	Thel (L)
8·5, 10·0	Song of Los (A)		Descriptive Catalogue (A)
8·6, 7·6	Thel (M)		Poetical Sketches (B)
8·9, 7·0	Europe (A)		

Four Holes

1·5, 4·0, 2·3	'Everlasting Gospel'
4·5, 2·0, 6·0	Songs (A)
5·6, 6·5, 6·4	Thel (E)
5·8, 6·0, 9·0	Visions (H)

Five Holes

5·8, 2·1, 3·1, 2·1	Jerusalem pl. (5, 53)
5·7, 2·2, 3·1, 2·1	Jerusalem pl. (9, 11)
10·2, 6·6, 6·8, 6·8	Europe (a)
	Milton (C), Thel (R)

Six Holes

1·2, 4·2, 3·8, 2·9, 5·2	Marriage (D)
4·1, 3·9, 4·5, 4·5, 4·5	Thel (O), Milton (D)

Eight Holes

4·2, 3·7, 2·6, 5·8, 5·7, 5·9, 3·8	Europe (F)

TABLE OF COLLECTIONS OF
CONTEMPORARY COPIES OF BLAKE'S WRITINGS

† Means that I have not seen the original and have worked from a reproduction. Footnotes record those who have generously sent me vital information. Public collections are indicated in SMALL CAPITALS, private collections in *italics*.

Anonymous	ILLUMINATED WORKS: *Thel* (A), *For Children* (C), *Innocence* (J, M), *Jerusalem* pl. 4, 18–19, 28, 35, 37, *Songs* (P, X) MS: ALS, 12 March 1804
ASHMOLEAN MUSEUM, Oxford	Dante design no. 86
AUCKLAND PUBLIC LIBRARY, New Zealand	*America* (N), *Europe* (I)
Barrett, Mr. *Roger W.*, Chicago	ALS: 18 Jan. 1808 (A)
Baskin, Mr. *Leonard*, Northampton, Massachusetts	*Europe* (c, pl. 1^b, 4^a, 5^a)
Bentley, G. E., Jr., Toronto	ILLUMINATED WORKS: *Songs* electrotypes, plus (copy o, pl. 39), pl. 22, 28, 30, 40, 44–6, 48^{a-b} MS: 'Riddle MS'
Berg Collection: see NEW YORK PUBLIC LIBRARY	
BIRMINGHAM CITY MUSEUM & ART GALLERY	Dante design no. 3
Blunt, Sir *Anthony*, London	*Songs* (J), pl. 28
BODLEIAN LIBRARY, Oxford	ILLUMINATED WORKS: 'The Accusers' (B); *Thel* (I); *Marriage* (B); *Innocence* (L) TYPE-PRINTED WORKS: *Descriptive Catalogue* (H), 'Exhibition' (B)
BOSTON MUSEUM OF FINE ARTS	'The Accusers' (D)
BOSTON PUBLIC LIBRARY[1]	ALS: 14 Oct. 1807†

[1] Ellen M. Oldham (Curator of Classical Literature).

BRITISH MUSEUM[1]
(Department of Printed
Books)

ILLUMINATED WORKS: *For the Sexes* (C), *No Natural Religion* (H), *Songs* (a)

TYPE-PRINTED WORKS: *Descriptive Catalogue* (A); *Poetical Sketches* (A, B)
MSS: MARGINALIA: Reynolds, *Works* (1798); Swedenborg, *Divine Love and Divine Wisdom* (1788)

(Department of Prints
and Drawings)

ILLUMINATED WORKS: 'The Accusers' (C, G); 'Albion Rose' (A, C); *America* (F, H), pl. d; *Book of Los* (A); *Thel* (D), pl. 2, 4, 6–7; *Europe* (a, D), pl. 10; *Urizen* (D), pl. 1–3, 5, 7–8, 10–12, 14, 17, 19, 21, 23–4, 27; *For Children* (B); *For the Sexes* (C), pl. 15; 'The Chaining of Orc' [see *America* pl. 3]; *Jerusalem* (A), pl. 5, 53; 'Joseph of Arimathea' (B, C); *Marriage* pl. 11, 14, 16, 20; *Milton* (A); 'Mirth' (A); *Song of Los* (A, D); *Songs* electrotypes plus (A, B, T); *No Natural Religion* (A), pl. a8; *Visions* (A, B, O), pl. 1, 3, 7, 10
TYPE-PRINTED WORKS: 'Blake's Chaucer: An Original Engraving' (A); 'Blake's Chaucer: The Canterbury Pilgrims' (A); *Descriptive Catalogue* (B)
MSS: Dante no. 101; MS title-page; *Tiriel* drawing no. 4; INSCRIPTIONS: 'Is all joy', 'How I pity', 'Visions of Eternity', *America* pl. 2, 'Behold your King', 'Journey of Life' [see *Jerusalem* pl. 97], 'To the Queen', 'The Spirit of Nelson' [see *Descriptive Catalogue* ¶6], 'Return Alpheus'

(Department of
Manuscripts)

MSS: *Notebook*; *Tiriel*; *Vala* or *The Four Zoas*; ALS: 6 Dec. 1795; 23 Dec. 1796; 16, 23, 26 Aug. 1799; 23 Feb. 1804; 19 Dec. 1808; *To Blake*: 18 Dec. 1808

BUFFALO, STATE UNIVER-
SITY OF NEW YORK AT

Europe pl. 18

BUFFALO AND ERIE
COUNTY PUBLIC LIBRARY

Europe pl. 4

Burton, Mrs. Joan
Linnell (née Ivimy)

ALS: *to Blake*: 4 Nov. 1826; *To Mrs. Blake*: 25 Nov. 1827

CINCINNATI ART
MUSEUM

ILLUMINATED WORKS: *Thel* (N); *Innocence* (S); *Songs* (S)
TYPE-PRINTED WORKS: *Poetical Sketches* (D)

---

[1] So far as books and MSS (but not prints and drawings) are concerned, The British Museum has changed its name to The British Library, though the collections are still, and are likely long to remain, in the same building. I have not, however, attempted to alter the references to The British Museum in *Blake Books* to reflect this bureaucratic reorganization. The books and MSS of The British Library are still, after all, housed in The British Museum.

CORNELL UNIVERSITY, Ithaca, N.Y.	MS, MARGINALIA: Wordsworth, *Poems* (1815)
Crawford and Balcarres, Earl of, Colinsburgh, Scotland	*Europe* pl. 2; *Jerusalem* pl. 24; *Songs* (H)
Cunliffe, Lord, London	ILLUMINATED WORKS: *America* (G); *Europe* (B); *Jerusalem* (B); *Songs* (i); *Visions* (C) MS, ALS: Feb. 1808 (C)
Dennis, Mrs. Seth, New York	*Songs* (Q)
DOHENY MEMORIAL LIBRARY: see ST. JOHN'S SEMINARY	
Drysdale, Mrs. William, Radley, Berkshire	*Songs* (c)
Egremont, Lord,[1] Petworth, Sussex	ALS: 18 Jan. 1808 (B)†
Essick, Professor *Robert N.,* Pasadena, California	*Tiriel* drawing no. 6†
FITZWILLIAM MUSEUM, Cambridge, England (The bulk of the Keynes Collection is promised to the Fitzwilliam)	ILLUMINATED WORKS: *America* (O, P); *Thel* (G); *Europe* (K, M); *Jerusalem* (H); *Marriage* (H, I, K); *Songs* (R, AA), electrotypes; *Visions* (P) TYPE-PRINTED WORKS: *Descriptive Catalogue* (G) MSS: *An Island in the Moon*; INSCRIPTION: List of Apostles; ALS: 15 March, 12 April 1827; *To Blake:* 7 Oct. 1801 *Tiriel* drawing no. 2
FOGG MUSEUM,[2] Cambridge, Massachusetts: see also HARVARD	MS: Dante no. 7†, 17
FOLGER SHAKESPEARE LIBRARY, Washington, D.C.	ALS: 31 July 1801
GLASGOW UNIVERSITY LIBRARY	*Descriptive Catalogue* (O)
Goyder, Mr. George, Netherfield Greys, Berkshire	'Ancient of Days' (E)
Greenberg, Mrs. Jack	*Jerusalem* pl. 6

[1] Mr. Francis W. Steer of the Sussex County Record Office.
[2] Mrs. Carol C. Gillham (Drawing Department).

Hanley, Mr. *T.E.*, Bradford, Pennsylvania	*Tiriel* drawing no. 12†
HARVARD COLLEGE, Cambridge, Massachusetts	ILLUMINATED WORKS: *Thel* (J); *Europe* (C, H); *Urizen* (F); *Jerusalem* (D); *Marriage* (A, G); *Innocence* (F, U); *Songs* (O, b), pl. 6–7, 29–30, 37; *No Natural Religion* (D, G); *Visions* (D, G) TYPE-PRINTED WORKS: 'Blake's Chaucer: An Original Engraving' (C); *Descriptive Catalogue* (I) MSS, ALS: 6 May 1800; 14, 27 Jan., 7 April 1804; 22 March, 27 Nov. 1805; MARGINALIA: Swedenborg, *Heaven and Hell* (1784)
HARVARD UNIVERSITY (Widener Collection): see also FOGG MUSEUM	*Songs* (I)
Harvey, Mrs. *Ramsey*	*Jerusalem* (C), pl. 28; *Marriage* (L); *Milton* pl. 38; *No Natural Religion* (E)
HAVERFORD COLLEGE,[1] Haverford, Pennsylvania	ALS: 19 Jan. 1805†
Hilles, Professor *F. W.*,[2] New Haven, Connecticut	ALS: 16 July 1804†
Hofer, Mr. *Phillip*, Cambridge, Massachusetts	*America* (C); *Visions* (M)
Holland, Mr. *Joseph*,[2] Los Angeles	*Urizen* pl. 22†; *Songs* pl. a†
Houghton, Mr. *Arthur A.*, New York	*Songs* (D)
HUNTINGTON (Henry E) LIBRARY and Art Gallery, San Marino, California	ILLUMINATED WORKS: 'Albion Rose' (D); *All Religions are One* (A, pl. 2–10); *America* (I), pl. 3; *Thel* (L); *Europe* (L); *For the Sexes* (F), pl. 12; *The Ghost of Abel* (C); *Milton* (B); *Song of Los* (E); *Innocence* (I); *Songs* (E, N); *No Natural Religion* pl. al; *Visions* (E) TYPE-PRINTED WORKS: *Descriptive Catalogue* (D); 'Exhibition' (A); *The French Revolution*; *Poetical Sketches* (C, S) MSS INSCRIPTIONS: Blair's *Grave* title-page; Illuminated Genesis MS; ALS: [Oct. 1791]; 16 Sept.

[1] Mrs. Elizabeth B. Tritle (Secretary to the Curator, Quaker Collection).
[2] The collector himself has generously assisted me by correspondence.

1800; May 1809 (address only); [March 1825]; [7 June 1825]; 11 Oct., 10 Nov. 1825; 31 Jan., [5 Feb.], 19 May, 5, 16, 29 July, 1 Aug., 1826; 27 Jan., [Feb.], 25 April, 3 July 1827; *To Blake*: 17 Oct. 1791; MARGINALIA: Lavater, *Aphorisms* (1788); Thornton, *Lord's Prayer* (1827); Watson, *Apology for the Bible* (1798)

Hyde, Mrs. Donald F.,   ALS: 7 Oct. 1803
Somerville, New Jersey

Ivimy, Miss Joan; see
Mrs. Burton

Juel-Jensen, Dr. B.,[1]   *Songs* pl. 7, 10, 33, 44†
Oxford

Kain, Mrs. Louise Y.,   *Tiriel* drawing no. 10†
Louisville, Kentucky

Keynes, Sir *Geoffrey,*[1]   ILLUMINATED WORKS: 'The Accusers' (E); *All*
Brinkley, Suffolk   *Religions are One* pl. 1; *America* pl. 3, 6, 10; *Ahania*
(Mostly promised to the   (Ba); 'Ancient of Days' (C); *Europe* pl. 1, 2, 4–7,
Fitzwilliam[2])   10, 12; *Urizen* pl. 1, 3, 25; *For the Sexes* (L), pl. 3,
6–7; *The Ghost of Abel* (B); *Jerusalem* pl. 1, 37, 51,
100; 'Joseph of Arimathea' (A, D, E); 'Laocoon'
(A); *Marriage* pl. 3–4, (E); 'Mirth' (B); *On Homer*
(B); *Innocence* (R); *Songs* (G, pl. 30–2, 37–8, 42–3,
47, 50–1, b, k, l, m), pl. 9–10, 51; *No Natural*
Religion (L[2]); *Visions* pl. 6, 10
TYPE-PRINTED WORKS: 'Blake's Chaucer: An
Original Engraving' (B); *Descriptive Catalogue* (C)
MSS: 'For Children The Gates of Hell'; ALS:
11 Dec. 1805; *To Blake*: 17 April 1800; MARGINA-
LIA: Bacon, *Essays* (1798); Dante, *Inferno* (1785);
Swedenborg, *Divine Providence* (1790)
Tiriel drawings no. 8, 11

KING'S COLLEGE,   *Songs* (W)
Cambridge, England

LIBRARY OF CONGRESS   ILLUMINATED WORKS: 'The Accusers' (F, H);
(Rosenwald Collection)   'Albion Rose' (B); *America* (a, E), copperplate,
pl. d; *Ahania* (A); *Thel* (F, H, O); *Europe* (c, pl. 2,
5[b], 9[a], 10, 11[a], 12, E), pl. 18[a–b]; *Urizen* (G); *For*
Children (A, D); *For the Sexes* (K); *The Ghost of Abel*
(A); *Jerusalem* (I), pl. 8–9, 19–20, 38[a–b], 48, 50,

---

[1] The collector himself has generously assisted me by correspondence.
[2] Sir Geoffrey has 'promised to bequeath' to the Fitzwilliam Museum all these works
except *Ahania* (Ba); 'Ancient of Days' (C); *Descriptive Catalogue* (C); *Ghost* (B); 'Laocoon';
Marriage (E); 'Mirth' (B); *On Homer* (B); *Songs* pl. b, according to *William Blake*: Catalogue
of the Collection in the Fitzwilliam Museum, Cambridge, ed. David Bindman (1970), 60.

	58, 78; 'Joseph of Arimathea' (F); *Marriage* (D), pl. 14; *Milton* (D); *On Homer* (A); *Song of Los* (B); *Innocence* (B); *Songs* (C, Z, g²), pl. 11, 30–2, 37, 40, 44, 47, 50; *No Natural Religion* (C, F); *Visions* (J, a) TYPE-PRINTED WORKS: *Descriptive Catalogue* (K, L); *Poetical Sketches* (T) MSS: 'A Fairy leapt'; the 'Order' of the *Songs*; INSCRIPTION: 'Father & Mother'; ALS: 2 July 1800; 30 Jan. 1803; 28 Sept. 1804; [4 Aug. 1824]; [Feb. 1827]
(Manuscripts Division)[1]	ALS: 4 Dec. 1804†
Lister, Mr. *Raymond*, Linton, Cambridgeshire	*America* pl. 1; *Innocence* (X); *Songs* (G) pl. 40
LIVERPOOL PUBLIC LIBRARY	*Poetical Sketches* (U)
MAINE HISTORICAL SOCIETY,[2] Portland, Maine	ALS: 13 Dec. 1803†
Martin, Mr. *Bradley*, New York	*Poetical Sketches* (E)
McKell, Dr. *David McC., Jr.*, Saratoga, California	*Innocence* (A)
MELBOURNE: see NATIONAL GALLERY OF VICTORIA	
Mellon, Mr. *Paul*, Upperville, Virginia (All apparently promised to Yale)	ILLUMINATED WORKS: *America* (M); *Thel* (B, R); *Europe* (A), pl. 1; *Urizen* (A, C); *For Children* (E); *For the Sexes* (I); *Jerusalem* (E), pl. 28, 30, 35; *Innocence* (G); *Songs* (F, L), imitation; *No Natural Religion* (B); *Visions* (I) TYPE-PRINTED WORKS: *Descriptive Catalogue* (J) MSS: Gray Designs *Tiriel* drawing no. 1†
METROPOLITAN MUSEUM OF ART, New York	*Jerusalem* pl. 1; *Songs* (Y)
MORGAN (J. Pierpont), LIBRARY, New York	ILLUMINATED WORKS: *America* (A–B), pl. 4; *Ahania* (Bc); *Book of Los* (B); *Thel* (a, C); *Europe* (b); *Urizen* (B, I), pl. 12; *For the Sexes* (D, G); *Jerusalem* (F), pl. 28, 45, 56, 74; *Marriage* (C, F); *On Homer*

(F); *Song of Los* (C); *Innocence* (D); *Songs* (K, V, e, n); *No Natural Religion* (G$^{1-2}$, I, L^1), pl. al; *Visions* (F)

TYPE-PRINTED WORKS: *Descriptive Catalogue* (N, P); *Poetical Sketches* (X)

MSS: *L'Allegro* and *Il Penseroso* descriptions; ALS: 12, 14 Sept. 1800; 19 Oct. 1801; 16 March, 27 April, 22 June 1804; 31 March, 14 July 1826; 'Ballads (Pickering) MS'

Moss, H.,
NATIONAL GALLERY OF
ART, Canberra,
Australia; see Preston

NATIONAL GALLERY OF   *Songs* T$^{1-2}$ pl. 29–31, 38, 41, 43, 46–7, 49–51
CANADA, Ottawa

NATIONAL GALLERY OF   ILLUMINATED WORKS: *Europe* pl. 11; *Urizen* pl. 21;
VICTORIA, Melbourne,   *Jerusalem* pl. 51
Australia   MSS: Dante no. 15–16, 36, 51, 56, 90, 99

NEWBERRY LIBRARY,   *Europe* (c, pl. 4^b, 9^b, 11^b, 16, 17^{a-b})
Chicago

Newton, Miss Caroline,   *America* (D); *Urizen* pl. 9; *For the Sexes* (J); *Marriage*
Daylesford, Pennsyl-   pl. 11; *Songs* (j) (bequeathed to Princeton)
vania

NEW YORK PUBLIC   *Milton* (C)
LIBRARY

(Berg Collection)   ILLUMINATED WORKS: *America* (L); *Thel* (M); *Europe* (F); *Innocence* (E); *Visions* (K)
MSS: 'then She bore Pale desire'; 'Woe cried the muse'; Upcott's Autograph Album; ALS: 18 March 1827

NEW YORK UNIVERSITY   *Europe* (c, pl. 6–7, 15^a); *On Homer* (E)

PENNSYLVANIA HISTORI-   ALS: 21 March, 28 Dec. 1804†
CAL SOCIETY,[1] Philadelphia

PFORZHEIMER (The Carl   ILLUMINATED WORK: *Innocence* (K)
and Lily) FOUNDATION,   TYPE-PRINTED WORK: *Poetical Sketches* (H)
Room 815, 41 East
42nd Street, New York

Preston, Mr. Kerrison;[2] see   *Europe* pl. 1^{a-b}, 2^{a-b}; *Jerusalem* pl. 25, 32, 41, 47
also WESTMINSTER
PUBLIC LIBRARY

---

[1] Mr. R. N. Williams (Director).

[2] Mr. Preston's prints were dispersed while *Blake Books* was in the press to H. Moss and The National Gallery of Australia, but the repeated references in the text below to Preston copies have not been correspondingly altered.

PRINCETON UNIVERSITY, Princeton, New Jersey: see also *R. H. Taylor* and *C. Newton*	ILLUMINATED WORKS: *America* (Q); *Songs* (U,g¹); *Visions* (L) TYPE-PRINTED WORKS: *Poetical Sketches* (I) MSS: Genesis MS (Tasso translation); 'I asked a thief'
Radcliffe, Lady Antonia, London	ALS: 1 April 1800 (on deposit in the BM)
ROSENBACH (A. S. W. & Philip) FOUNDATION, Philadelphia	ILLUMINATED WORKS: *America* pl. 1; 'Ancient of Days' (A); *Urizen* pl. 1; *For the Sexes* (E); *Visions* (H) TYPE-PRINTED WORKS: *Descriptive Catalogue* (M); *Poetical Sketches* (R) MSS: 'The Everlasting Gospel' sheet; ALS: 9 June 1818
*Rosenbloom, Mr. Charles J.,*¹ Pittsburgh	*Urizen* (H)†; *Jerusalem* (J); 'Laocoon'(B)†; *No Natural Religion* (K)
ROSENWALD, LESSING J.: see LIBRARY OF CONGRESS	
Ryskamp, Mr. Charles, Princeton, New Jersey	*Europe* (c, pl. 11ᶜ, 17ᶜ)
ST. JOHN'S SEMINARY, Camarillo, California	ILLUMINATED WORK: *Innocence* (N) MS, ALS: 2 July 1826
SAN FRANCISCO PUBLIC LIBRARY	*Thel* pl. 2, 6
at SYRACUSE, UNIVERSITY OF, Syracuse, New York	*Innocence* (Q, on deposit)
TATE GALLERY, London	ILLUMINATED WORKS: *Europe* pl. 6–7; *Urizen* pl. 2; *Songs* pl. 3ᵃ⁻ᵇ, 22, 48ᵃ⁻ᵇ; *Visions* pl. 1, 7 MSS: 'Epitome of Hervey'; 'The Spiritual Form of Pitt' [see *Descriptive Catalogue* ¶8]; Dante designs no. 4, 14
Taylor, Mr. Robert H., Princeton, New Jersey (Destined for and housed in Princeton)	ILLUMINATED WORK: *Innocence* (T) TYPE-PRINTED WORK: *Descriptive Catalogue* (S)
TEXAS CHRISTIAN UNIVERSITY,² Fort Worth, Texas	*Poetical Sketches* (V)†

---

¹ The collector himself has generously assisted me by correspondence.

² C. G. Sparks (Librarian), Dr. Lyle Kendall (Department of English, Texas Christian University).

TEXAS, UNIVERSITY OF,[1] Austin, Texas	ILLUMINATED WORKS: *Urizen* pl. 5†; *Innocence* (O) TYPE-PRINTED WORK: *Poetical Sketches* (O) MSS, ALS: 11 Oct. 1819; 29 Dec. 1826
Thorne, Mrs. Landon K., New York	*Europe* (G)
TORONTO, UNIVERSITY OF	*Poetical Sketches* (K)
TRINITY COLLEGE, Cambridge	TYPE-PRINTED WORK: *Poetical Sketches* (L) MS, MARGINALIA: Berkeley, *Siris* (1744)
TRINITY COLLEGE, Hartford, Connecticut	ILLUMINATED WORKS: *Europe* pl. 2, 18; *For the Sexes* pl. 14; *The Ghost of Abel* (D); 'Joseph of Arimathea' (H); *On Homer* (D); *No Natural Religion* (J) MSS: Blake's Memorandum; ALS: 31 March 1804; May 1809 (message only)
TURNBULL (Alexander) LIBRARY, Wellington, New Zealand	TYPE-PRINTED WORK: *Poetical Sketches* (F) MS: 'Songs by Shepherds'
UNIVERSITY COLLEGE, London	*Poetical Sketches* (W)
Vanderhoef, Mr. F. Bailey, Ojai, California	MS: 'All Genius varies'
VICTORIA & ALBERT MUSEUM, London	ILLUMINATED WORKS: *All Religions are One* pl. 1; *Jerusalem* pl. 9, 11; *Songs* electrotypes; *No Natural Religion* (M) TYPE-PRINTED WORK: *Descriptive Catalogue* (E) MS: 'Theotormon woven' [see *Vala* p. 100]; 'The Fall of Man' *Tiriel* drawing no. 7
VIVIAN (Glynn) ART GALLERY, Swansea, Wales	*America* pl. 2, 5, 15; *Europe* pl. 6–7, 12; *Jerusalem* pl. 35
WEDGWOOD MUSEUM, Barlaston, Stoke-on-Trent, Staffordshire	ALS: 8 Sept. 1815; *to Blake*: 29 July 1815 (copy)
WELLESLEY COLLEGE, Wellesley, Massachusetts	ILLUMINATED WORK: *Innocence* (C) TYPE-PRINTED WORK: *Poetical Sketches* (G)

[1] Mr. William A. Robinson (Research Associate, Iconography Collection, Humanities Research Center).

WESTMINSTER PUBLIC LIBRARY, 35 St. Martin's St., London (Kerrison Preston Collection)

TYPE-PRINTED WORK: *Poetical Sketches* (Q)
MSS, ALS: 22 Sept, 2 Oct. 1800; 10 May, 11 Sept. 1801; 10 Jan., 22 Nov. 1802; 25 April, 6 July, 16 Aug. 1803; *to Blake*: [25–30 Sept. 1800]

WHITWORTH ART GALLERY, University of Manchester

'Ancient of Days' (F); 'The Accusers' (I)

WILLIAMS'S (DR.) LIBRARY, London

MARGINALIA: Wordsworth, *Excursion* (1814), Blake's transcript

YALE UNIVERSITY, New Haven, Connecticut (See also P. Mellon)

ILLUMINATED WORKS: *America* (K); *Ahania* (Bb); *Thel* (E, K); *Urizen* pl. 5, 10; *For the Sexes* (H); *Innocence* (P); *Songs* (M)
TYPE-PRINTED WORKS: *Descriptive Catalogue* (E); *Poetical Sketches* (N)
MSS, ALS: 21 Sept. 1800; 25 March 1823; [April 1826]

UNTRACED

ILLUMINATED WORKS: 'The Accusers' (A, D); *All Religions are One* pl. 1; 'Ancient of Days' (B, D); *America* (R); *Thel* (P, Q); *Europe* (c pl. 1ª, 4ᶜ, 9ᶜ, 13–14, 15ᵇ), pl. 18; *Urizen* (E), pl. 9; *For the Sexes* (A, B); *Jerusalem* (G), pl. 50, 51, 99; 'Joseph of Arimathea' (G); *Marriage* (M–N), pl. 5–6; *On Homer* (C); Prospectus; *Innocence* (H, V, W); *Songs* (G pl. 33, 40–1, 46, 49, BB, d, h, o), pl. 24–5, 31, 37, 42ᵃ⁻ᵇ, 47, 51; *Visions* (N, Q)
TYPE-PRINTED WORKS: *Descriptive Catalogue* (S); *Poetical Sketches* (M, P)
MSS INSCRIPTIONS: 'The Bible of Hell', 'The Spirit of Nelson' [see *Descriptive Catalogue* ¶ 6]; ALS: [Oct. 1791], 18 Feb., 26 Nov. 1800; [1800?]; [1802?]; [Nov. 1802]; 19 Sept., 26 Oct. 1803; 2 April, 4, 28 May, 7, 9 Aug., 23 Oct., 18 Dec. 1804; 22 Jan., 17 May, 4 June 1805; [June 1806]; *to Blake*: [Oct., Nov. 1794, Jan., Feb., May 1796]; May 1807; 29 July 1815; 4 Nov. 1826; 5 March 1827; DOCUMENT: 25 March 1823; MARGINALIA: Spurzheim, *Insanity* (1817); Ceninni, *Trattato* (1820); Wordsworth, *Excursion* (1814); 'Nelson' drawing
Tiriel drawings no. 3, 5, 9

TABLE OF PLATE-SIZES

The dimensions in the following Table, arranged by size, record the indentations of the copperplates measured in centimetres at the bottom and right sides, or, where the dimness of the impression made this impossible, as near to the bottom and right sides as possible.

Variations. Dimensions of the plate-marks vary from copy to copy by about 0·1 cm because the paper has shrunk or stretched in the last century and a half.[1] Therefore virtually every copy of every print was measured, and the figures below are the averages of these measurements.

The plate-marks in posthumous copies (*America* [P], *Songs* [a–o], *Europe* [M], *Jerusalem* [H, I]) are regularly about 0·2 cm larger than in contemporary copies. A most striking illustration of this fact may be seen in *Songs* (e), in which the plates identifiable from other evidence as being from a contemporary printing are regularly of average size, whereas posthumous pulls are larger. The reason for the variation may be that Blake and his wife dampened the paper when printing to get the best possible impressions, and it subsequently shrank, while Tatham did not dampen his posthumous pulls.

All Religions are One (?1788)

1] 3·6 × 5·2	2] 3·7 × 4·6	3] 3·0 × 4·9	4] 3·8 × 5·4	5] 4·1 × 5·0
6] 4·0 × 5·9	7] 3·1 × 5·2	8] 3·8 × 5·7	9] 3·6 × 5·4	10] 3·5 × 5·5

There is No Natural Religion (?1788)

a1] 4·5 × 5·3	a2] 4·3 × 5·2	a3] 4·3 × 5·0	a4] 4·2 × 5·2	a5] 3·9 × 5·0
a6] 3·7 × 5·0	a7] 3·9 × 4·7	a8] 3·5 × 4·7	a9] 4·3 × 5·4	b1] 3·7 × 5·2
	b3] 4·0 × 5·9	b4] 4·2 × 5·6		b6] 4·4 × 6·1
b7] 4·2 × 5·9	b8] 4·2 × 5·7	b9] 4·3 × 5·7	b10] 4·0 × 5·5	b11] invisible
b12] 4·6 × 6·1				

For Children [For the Sexes:] The Gates of Paradise (1793, ?*1818*)

1] 6·3 × 9·4	2] 4·2 × 6·8	3] 6·4 × 7·8	4] 7·3 × 8·2	5] 7·4 × 8·2
6] 7·2 × 8·2	7] 7·3 × 9·1	8] 5·0 × 6·1	9] 5·0 × 7·5	10] 6·3 × 9·3
11] 4·8 × 7·1	12] 5·0 × 6·7	13] 6·3 × 7·1	14] 6·1 × 6·4	15] 7·2 × 8·1
16] 4·6 × 6·7	17] 5·2 × 7·2	18] 5·2 × 6·4	19] *6·8 × 10·5*	20] *6·8 × 10·4*
21] *6·3 × 9·5*				

[1] An analogy to this variation may be found by comparing the dimensions of copies of Blake's prints for Blair's *Grave* (1808) with the surviving copperplates in the Rosenwald Collection. The variation observed is of the same kind as in Blake's etched writings.

Another reason for variations in the records of plate-mark size is that the plates are often not quite rectangular. Therefore if, because of the faintness of the impression, one has to measure, say, the top rather than the bottom dimension, the results may be marginally different.

Songs of Innocence and of Experience (1789, 1794)

1] 7·0×11·2	2] 7·0×11·0	3] 7·4×12·0	4] 7·9×11·9[1]	5] 6·9×11·1
6] 7·0×11·0	7] 6·8×10·9	8] 7·7×11·9	9] 6·9×11·1	10] 6·7×11·1
11] 7·1×11·0	12] 7·3×11·2	13] 7·2×11·8	14] 7·2×11·7	15] 6·7×11·1
16] 7·2×11·3	17] 7·0×11·1	18] 7·0×11·2	19] 7·7×11·4	20] 6·9×11·1
21] 6·8×11·0	22] 7·7×11·6	23] 7·7×10·5	24] 7·8×11·5	25] 6·8×11·1
26] 7·6×12·3	27] 7·1×11·2	28] 7·0×11·0	29] 7·2×12·4	30] 7·2×12·4
31] 7·2×11·7	32] 7·3×11·3	33] 7·3×11·3	34] 6·6×11·2	35] 6·8×11·1
36] 6·9×11·1	37] 6·8×11·0	38] 6·9×11·1	39] 6·8×11·1	40] 7·3×11·8
41] 6·8×11·1	42] 6·3×11·0	43] 7·0×11·0	44] 6·8×11·1	45] 6·6×11·1
46] 6·9×11·1	47] 6·6×11·2	48] 7·0×11·1	49] 6·8×11·1	50] 6·8×11·0
51] 7·3×12·0	52] 7·2×11·4	53] 6·9×11·1	54] 6·3×11·0	
a] 5·2×6·3	b] 7·0×11·2			

The Book of Ahania (1795)

1] 9·8×13·6	2] 9·8×13·6	3] 9·8×13·6	4] 9·9×13·5	5] 9·8×13·6
6] 10·0×13·7				

The Book of Los (1795)

1] 9·9×13·7	2] 9·8×13·5	3] 9·8×13·7	4] 9·9×13·7	5] 9·9×13·6

'Joseph of Arimathea' (1773)

10·7×7·6

On Homers Poetry [&] On Virgil (?1821)

10·6×13·0

The Marriage of Heaven and Hell (?1790–3)

1] 10·3×15·2	2] 10·3×15·1	3] 11·0×15·4	4] 10·1×13·6	5] 10·7×15·0
6] 10·1×15·1	7] 10·3×15·0	8] 10·4×14·9	9] 10·1×15·1	10] 10·2×15·0
11] 9·9×15·0	12] 10·4×15·4	13] 10·6×14·9	14] 10·1×14·9	15] 10·2×14·9
16] 10·2×16·6	17] 10·1×16·5	18] 10·3×16·4	19] 10·2×16·4	20] 10·4×14·5
21] 10·8×15·3	22] 10·8×14·9	23] 10·0×15·1	24] 9·8×14·8	25] 10·4×14·8
26] 10·3×14·8	27] 10·4×15·2			

The First Book of Urizen (1794)

1] 10·3×14·9	2] 10·3×16·8	3] 10·0×14·8	4] 10·2×15·0	5] 10·5×14·9
6] 11·7×14·2	7] 10·5×14·9	8] 10·1×15·0	9] 10·4×14·8	10] 9·9×14·7
11] 10·9×15·2	12] 10·2×15·4	13] 10·2×16·5	14] 10·4×14·5	15] 10·9×14·8
16] 10·5×15·2	17] 9·1×14·8	18] 10·9×15·0	19] 10·4×15·8	20] 10·1×15·2
21] 10·2×16·6	22] 10·1×15·6	23] 10·2×15·0	24] 10·4×15·0	25] 10·3×16·3
26] 9·2×14·9	27] 10·4×15·5	28] 10·3×15·1		

[1] In seventeen copies (*Innocence* [A, F, G, I, J, K, L, M, P, Q, U], *Songs* [B, C, E, F, a, g]), the height appears to be 11·3 cm. The explanation seems to be that in the larger copies Blake added a stream at the bottom, which makes the design-size larger.

The Book of Thel (1789)

1] 10·1 × 6·1   2] 10·7 × 15·5   3] 11·0 × 15·4   4] 10·9 × 15·3   5] 10·7 × 15·3
6] 10·8 × 15·3   7] 10·6 × 15·4   8] 10·9 × 14·1

Milton (1804–?8)

1] 11·2 × 16·0   2] 10·4 × 14·9   3] 10·4 × 14·9   4] 9·5 × 15·7   5] 10·5 × 15·4
6] 10·4 × 14·9   7] 10·5 × 15·3   8] 11·3 × 16·8   9] 10·4 × 13·6   10] 10·8 × 14·3
11] 10·8 × 14·2   12] 10·5 × 15·4   13] 11·1 × 16·0   14] 10·6 × 15·3   15] 11·0 × 16·9
16] 9·6 × 15·7   17] 11·5 × 16·0   18] 12·0 × 16·0   19] 12·0 × 16·0   20] 12·0 × 16·0
21] 11·1 × 16·0   22] 11·9 × 16·0   23] 12·0 × 16·0   24] 12·0 × 16·0   25] 12·0 × 16·2
26] 10·6 × 14·3   27] 11·8 × 16·0   28] 12·0 × 16·0   29] 11·2 × 16·0   30] 10·3 × 14·4
31] 12·1 × 16·0   32] 11·4 × 16·9   33] 11·3 × 16·9   34] 10·8 × 14·0   35] 10·8 × 16·8
36] 10·2 × 14·1   37] 11·3 × 16·9   38] 10·5 × 13·6   39] 11·3 × 16·9   40] 11·3 × 16·8
41] 11·5 × 16·0   42] 10·7 × 14·3   43] 10·3 × 14·4   44] 10·8 × 13·9   45] 10·2 × 14·0
a] 11·3 × 16·1   b] 11·0 × 14·5   c] 9·9 × 15·3   d] 11·0 × 15·5   e] 11·1 × 14·4
f] 10·0 × 13·5

Visions of the Daughters of Albion (1793)

1] 11·9 × 17·1   2] 12·9 × 16·3   3] 11·2 × 14·2   4] 11·7 × 17·0   5] 11·7 × 17·1
6] 11·6 × 16·8   7] 11·5 × 17·0   8] 11·7 × 17·2   9] 11·7 × 15·9   10] 12·0 × 16·9
11] 11·8 × 16·9

The Ghost of Abel (1822)

1] 12·4 × 16·7   2] 12·4 × 16·7

'The Accusers' (1793)

12·0 × 21·7

Jerusalem (1804–?20)

1] 16·2 × 22·3   2] 16·2 × 22·5   3] 16·4 × 22·5   4] 16·3 × 22·5   5] 16·3 × 22·5
6] 16·4 × 22·5   7] 16·3 × 22·4   8] 16·2 × 22·2   9] 16·4 × 22·5   10] 15·0 × 22·5
11] 16·4 × 22·5   12] 16·4 × 22·5   13] 16·3 × 22·3   14] 16·4 × 22·5   15] 15·1 × 21·3
16] 14·7 × 22·3   17] 15·0 × 21·3   18] 16·4 × 22·5   19] 16·3 × 22·5   20] 16·3 × 22·6
21] 15·2 × 21·4   22] 15·2 × 21·3   23] 16·3 × 22·6   24] 16·5 × 22·6   25] 16·3 × 22·2
26] 16·4 × 22·5   27] 16·2 × 22·3   28] 16·3 × 22·5   29] 16·2 × 22·3   30] 15·2 × 21·3
31] 16·3 × 22·3   32] 16·3 × 22·3   33] 14·8 × 22·5   34] 15·0 × 21·2   35] 16·5 × 22·5
36] 15·0 × 21·2   37] 16·3 × 22·6   38] 16·2 × 22·5   39] 16·0 × 22·4   40] 16·3 × 22·5
41] 16·2 × 22·4   42] 16·3 × 22·5   43] 16·2 × 22·3   44] 15·1 × 21·3   45] 16·3 × 22·6
46] 16·3 × 22·5   47] 16·1 × 21·1   48] 16·4 × 22·4   49] 15·2 × 21·4   50] 16·3 × 22·6
51] 16·1 × 22·5   52] 16·3 × 22·6   53] 16·4 × 22·3   54] 14·9 × 21·1   55] 14·9 × 21·1
56] 13·8 × 20·1   57] 14·9 × 21·0   58] 14·9 × 21·1   59] 14·6 × 22·4   60] 14·9 × 21·1
61] 14·4 × 22·5   62] 14·9 × 21·0   63] 14·9 × 22·5   64] 14·5 × 20·4   65] 16·2 × 22·3
66] 16·2 × 22·3   67] 15·1 × 21·3   68] 14·9 × 21·1   69] 15·0 × 21·2   70] 16·1 × 22·2
71] 17·1 × 22·1   72] 15·0 × 22·5   73] 14·8 × 22·5   74] 16·5 × 22·6   75] 16·4 × 22·7
76] 16·3 × 22·4   77] 17·0 × 22·1   78] 16·1 × 21·0   79] 16·1 × 22·0   80] 16·1 × 22·1
81] 14·9 × 21·1   82] 16·1 × 22·2   83] 16·3 × 22·2   84] 15·0 × 21·1   85] 14·9 × 21·1
86] 15·1 × 20·9   87] 15·1 × 20·9   88] 15·0 × 20·9   89] 14·5 × 20·2   90] 15·1 × 21·1
91] 15·1 × 21·3   92] 14·6 × 20·3   93] 15·1 × 21·1   94] 15·2 × 21·2   95] 14·0 × 20·1
96] 14·4 × 20·3   97] 14·9 × 21·0   98] 14·9 × 21·0   99] 15·4 × 22·7   100] 14·8 × 22·4

'The Ancient of Days' (?1794)

16·8×23·2

The Song of Los (1795)

1] 17·3×23·4	2] 17·2×24·3	3] 13·9×21·5	4] 13·6×21·5	5] 17·5×23·2
6] 13·6×23·2	7] 13·5×22·3	8] 17·5×23·5		

America (1793)

1] 16·9×23·4	2] 16·7×23·5	3] 16·3×23·1	4] 16·6×23·8	5] 16·7×23·7
6] 16·4×23·2	7] 16·6×23·3	8] 16·7×23 4	9] 16·8×23·5	10] 16·7×23·5
11] 16·9×23·4	12] 16·9×23·5	13] 17·2×23·7	14] 17·3×23·5	15] 17·4×23·6
16] 17·2×23·6	17] 17·0×23·7	18] 17·1×23·8	a] 16·1×22·8[1]	b] 16·1×22·8?
c] 17·0×24·5	d] 17·0×11·3	e] 8·0× 2·4		

Europe (1794)

1] 16·9×23·4	2] 17·3×23·9	3] 13·4× 9·6	4] 17·1×23·6	5] 17·3×23·6
6] 16·7×23·6	7] 16·4×23·1	8] 17·2×23·6	9] 17·1×23·7	10] 17·0×23·4
11] 16·7×23·6	12] 16·6×23·4	13] 16·7×23·4	14] 16·9×23·4	15] 17·3×23·4
16] 16·9×23·3	17] 16·5×23·3	18] 16·6×23·4		

'Mirth' (?1820)

17·5×13·8

'Albion Rose' (?1796)

20·1×27·2

'Laocoon' (?1820)

22·8×27·6

[1] The surviving copperplate, cut down, measures 5·8×8·2 cm.

TABLE OF WATERMARKS

1800 Sept. 16	Dates are for Blake's letters.
*B	Asterisks are for copies in which more than one watermark is found.

This Table comprehends only the letters and numbers in watermarks. It omits chain lines, crests, arms, and all non-literal symbols.

In his Prospectus of 10 Oct. 1793 (p. 450), Blake stresses that he has used 'the most beautiful wove paper that could be procured'.

179[ ]
1800 Sept. 16

1794¹
Thel (*F)
Urizen (1 pl.)
'Accusers' (G)

1797
Tasso MS

1798²
1800 Sept. 14, Oct. 2

1802
List of Apostles

180[2?]
1807 Oct. 14

1807 AP
'Blake's Chaucer: The
  Canterbury Pilgrims'
Descriptive Catalogue

[18]11
No Natural Religion (H–J)

1818
'Everlasting Gospel' MS
[1825 March]

1821
On Homer (C)

19[?]
Songs (*j)

1832³
Songs (*b)

[. . .]TH
1795 Dec. 6

AP
Descriptive Catalogue

C BALL
Marriage (L)

A B[LACKWELL?]
1803 Oct. 7

A BLACKWELL
1798⁴
1802 Jan. 10
1803 April 25,
  July 6,
  Dec. 13
1804 Jan. 14,
  27

BUTTANSHAW
Songs (3 pl.)

BUTTANSHAW
18[ ]
1801 Oct. 19

BUTTANSHAW
1802
Innocence (?O)
Songs (P, *Q)

CURTEIS & SON
1791 Oct. 18

W DA[CI]E
1803
1805 March 25

W D[AC]IE & CO.
1804
1804 Dec. 4

E & P
Innocence (*E, F, I, J, M)
Marriage (A, F)
Visions (J, K, M)
America (C–E, G–K)
Europe (H)
Songs (C–D, F, 2 pl.)
?Vala

E & P
1802
Innocence (*P)

EDMEADS & [PINE]
Innocence (*Q)
Jerusalem (1 pl.)

EDMEADS & PINE 1802
Innocence (*Q)
Jerusalem (3 pl.)

W ELGAR
1796
Dante Designs (6)

G R
Island
Tiriel

¹ See 1794 / I TAYLOR and 1794 / J WHATMAN.
² See A BLACKWELL / 1798.
³ See J WHATMAN / 1832.
⁴ See 1798.

F HAYES
1798

1801 Sept. 11
1802 Nov. 22
1803 Aug. 16

HAYES & WISE
1799

America (M)

N HENDON[?]
1802

'Exhibition of Paintings'

IVY MILL
1806

1808 Jan. 18   (A–C)

M & J LAY
1816

Milton designs

[LE]PARD
Vala

MA[FRIN]S

For Children (A)

[. . .]R¹
Vala

R & T

Europe (*I)

RUSE & TURNERS
1810

1826 Jan. 31, July 16
?1826 [Feb. 5], March 31,
  May 19, July 2, 5, 29,
  Aug. 1
?1827 Jan. 27, March 15,
  18, April 25, July 3
1827 April 12

RUSE & TURNERS
1812

America (N)
Europe (*I)

RUSE & TURNERS
1815

Thel (N, O)
Marriage (G)
Visions (N, O, P)
Songs (U, ?T, 3 pl.)
Urizen (G)
Milton (D)

S[. . .]

No Natural Religion (F)

SMITH & ALLNUTT
1815

1826 July 14

T STAINS

America (*Q)
Europe (*L)

T STAINS
1813

America (*Q)
Europe (*L)

I TAYLOR

No Natural Religion (B, L¹)
All Religions Are One (*A)
Thel (F)
Marriage (*D)
Songs (A, *C, R)
Europe (B, *C, D–G, C)
Urizen (A, *B)

1794
I TAYLOR

All Religions Are One (*A)
Marriage (*D)
Urizen (B)

J WHATMAN

Thel (a)
Innocence (C, *E, G, U, W)
Marriage (C)
Visions (B–E, H)
Songs (*C, E, H, 1 pl.)
Urizen (*D, E)

J WHATMAN
[   ]

Innocence (*P)
Songs (e, 3 pl.)

1794
J WHATMAN²

Visions (F, G)
America (A, B)
Europe (A, *C)
Urizen (*B, *D, 1 pl.)
Vala
'Albion Rose' (D)
Gray Designs

J WHATMAN
1804

Innocence (*Q, *?T)
Songs (*Q)

J WHATMAN
1808

Innocence (S)
Songs (*R, S)
Milton (A–C)

J WHATMAN
1815

Marriage (I)

J WHATMAN
1818

America (O)
Songs (V, *W)
Europe (*K)
For the Sexes (B)
Jerusalem (*A, B, *C, 1 pl.)

J WHATMAN
1819

Europe (*K)
Jerusalem (*A, *C)

J WHATMAN
1820

America (*O)
Europe (*K)
Jerusalem (*A, *C, D, E)
Ghost of Abel (D)

J WHATMAN
1821

Ghost of Abel (A)
Illuminated Genesis MS

---

  ¹ Perhaps I TAYLOR.
  ² 1794 / J WHATMAN paper was made from 1794 to 1800 (Keynes & Wolf, xviii). Richard
Edwards apparently gave Blake 900 leaves of 1794 / J WHATMAN paper for his drawings and
proofs for Edwards's edition of Young's *Night Thoughts* (1797) (*Blake Records*, 52).

J WHATMAN
1824

Jerusalem (*F)

J WHATMAN
1825

'Joseph of Arimathea' (E)
Songs (*W, X, Y, Z, AA*)
For the Sexes (C, D)

J WHATMAN
1826

For the Sexes (F, H–*J)
Jerusalem (*F)
Illuminated Genesis MS

J WHATMAN
1831

Songs (*a, b–d, ?e, f, g, h, i,
*j, k, m, ?n, *o, 2 pl.*)
Jerusalem (*H, *I, J, 1 pl.*)

J WHATMAN
1832

America (P)
Europe (b, ?M)
Songs (*a, h*)
Jerusalem (*H, *I, 1 pl.*)

J W[HATMAN]
TURKE[Y MILL]
18[ ]

Songs (1 pl.)

H WILLMOTT
1810

'Blake's Chaucer: An
Original Engraving'

TABLE OF BLAKE'S POETRY REPRINTED IN
CONVENTIONAL TYPOGRAPHY BEFORE 1863[1]

America	Robinson (1811) no. 2538
Book of Thel	*London University Magazine* (1830) no. 965
Europe	Robinson (1811) no. 2538
Jerusalem	
'I give you the end of a golden string'	J. T. Smith (1828) no. 2723
'A tear is an intellectual thing'	J. T. Smith (1828) no. 2723
Poetical Sketches	
'Gwin King of Norway'	Cunningham (1830) no. 1433B
'How sweet I roam'd'	Malkin (1806) no. 482; J. T. Smith (1828) no. 2723; Tatham (MS, ?1832) no. 2823; no. 321 (1848)
'I love the jocund dance'	Malkin (1806) no. 482; *Annual Review* (1807); Cunningham (1830), no. 1433B
'King Edward III'	Cunningham (1830) no. 1433B; Pichot (1833) no. 2392A; no. 803 (1849)
'Love and harmony combine'	no. 321 (1848)
'Mad Song'	no. 2731 (1847)
'My silks and fine array'	no. 321 (1848); no. 342 (1857)
'To Autumn'	no. 344 (1848)
'To Morning'	no. 321 (1848)
'To Spring'	no. 344 (1848)
'To Summer'	no. 344 (1848)
'To the Evening Star'	no. 321 (1848)
'To the Muses'	Robinson (1811) no. 2538; Cunningham (1830) no. 1433A; no. 803 (1848)
'To Winter'	no. 344 (1849)
'The Blossom'	no. 264 (1860)
Songs of Innocence	
'The Chimney Sweeper'?	*Chimney Sweeper's Friend* (1824), no. 238; Cunningham (1830) no. 1433B; Pichot (1833) no. 2392A; no. 352B (1858)
'Cradle Song'	*London University Magazine* (1830) no. 965; Tatham (MS, ?1832) no. 2823; no. 242 (?1843)
'The Divine Image'	Malkin (1806) no. 482; *London University Magazine* (1830) no. 965
'The Ecchoing Green'	no. 248 (1854)
'Holy Thursday'	Malkin (1806) no. 482; Robinson (1811) no. 2538; *City Scenes* (1818) no. 260; Cunningham (1830) no. 1433; Pichot (1833) no. 2392A; no. 1028 (1853)

[1] Omitting reprints of the same text, e.g. Cunningham, and collected poetry such as the 1839 *Songs*.

'Introduction'   Robinson (1811) no. 2538; Cunningham (1830) no. 1433A;
                          no. 1083 (1847); no. 1440 (1848); no. 803 (1849);
                          no. 264 (1860); no. 281 (1861); no. 340 (1862)
'The Lamb'   Cunningham (1830) no. 1433B; Tatham (MS, ?1832)
                          no. 2823; Pichot (1833) no. 2392A; no. 268 (1842)
'Laughing Song'   Malkin (1806) no. 482; Cunningham (1830) no. 1433B
'The Little Black   no. 280 (1843); no. 347 (1847); no. 342 (1857)
    Boy'
'The Little Boy   no. 273 (1845)
    Lost'
'The Little Boy   no. 273 (1845)
    Found'
'Night'   no. 280 (1843)
'On Another's   no. 280 (1843); no. 279 (1846); no. 342 (1857)
    Sorrow'
'The Angel'   no. 264 (1860)
Songs of Experience
'The Garden of   Robinson (1811) no. 2538; *London University Magazine*
    Love'   (1830) no. 965; no. 342 (1857)
'Introduction'   *London University Magazine* (1830) no. 965
'The Little Vaga-   no. 1948 (1849)
    bond'
'The Poison Tree'   *London University Magazine* (1830) no. 965
'The Tyger'   Malkin (1806) no. 482; Robinson (1811) no. 2538;
                          Cunningham (1830) no. 1433B; Pichot (1833)
                          no. 2932A; no. 341 (1847); no. 1044 (1850);
                          no. 342 (1857); no. 264 (1860); no. 340 (1862)

1. 'The Accusers' (1793; 1793; ?1810)

BIBLIOGRAPHICAL INTRODUCTION

TABLE

Copy		State	Watermark	Size in cm	Printing Colour
I	*UNTRACED*[1]	I	—		
B	BODLEY	2	—	15·0 × 23·5	pale Green
C	BMPR	3		21·6 × 34·7	
D	BOSTON MUSEUM OF FINE ARTS	3			
E	*Keynes*	3	—		
F	LC	3	—	11·9 × 21·8	Black
G[2]	BMPR		1794		*Colour-printed*
H[2]	LC		—	24·0 × 32·0	*Colour-printed*
I	WHITWORTH[3]	3	—	13·2 × 22·4	Black

DATE: State 1: 1793; State 2: 1793; State 3: ?1810

State 1 is inscribed, like the second and third states, '*Published June 5 1793 by W Blake Lambeth*', and presumably it may be assigned to June 1793.

State 2 was printed integrally (in the only known copy) with *Marriage* (B) which was offered for sale in the Prospectus of 10 Oct. 1793 and must therefore have been completed within a few months of State 1.

State 3 is datable largely on the basis of its inscription, which is similar to the reference in the 'Vision of the Last Judgment' (1810) to 'Satan the Accuser'.

PUBLICATION: Blake clearly kept the plate by him for many years, but only nine copies have survived, and no contemporary reference to the work is known.

DESIGN: Three men hemmed in by giant flames (in State 3) stand close together staring in horror to our left. The man on the left ('Theft') has a handlebar moustache, a thigh-length skirt, a fish-scale shirt of armour and seems to hold the spear visible to the right; the one in the middle ('Adultery') is wearing knee-length transparent clothing, a cloak, and a crown and holds his hands to his cheeks; the one on the right ('Murder') has transparent calf-length clothing and a victor's wreath (in State 3) and is holding a sword upright. (The design derives from that for *Tiriel* [?1789] called 'Tiriel Denouncing his Sons'.)

COPY A: BINDING: Loose.

HISTORY: (1) Lent by E. W. Hooper to the Boston Museum of Fine Arts Exhibition (1891), no. 111; (2) UNTRACED.

---

[1] Copy A is known only from the exhibition catalogue of the Boston Museum of Fine Arts (1891), no. 111.

[2] In copies G–H, the inscriptions are colour-printed out.

[3] Copy I is ill printed, and much of the bottom inscription is illegible.

COPY B: BINDING: Printed integrally with *Marriage* (B).

HISTORY: For its History, see *Marriage* (B), p. 298; it is reproduced in Keynes, *Separate Plates* (1956), pl. 12.

COPY C: BINDING: Loose.

HISTORY: (1) Sold with the Linnell Collection at Christie's, 15 March 1918, lot 190 (with other works) for £54. 12*s*. to Martin for (2) THE BRITISH MUSEUM PRINT ROOM.

COPY D: BINDING: Loose.

HISTORY: (1) Probably this is the copy lent by Horace E. Scudder to the Boston Museum of Fine Arts exhibition (1891), no. 119; (2) Acquired through the Frederick Keppel Bequest in October 1913 by the BOSTON MUSEUM OF FINE ARTS.

COPY E: BINDING: Loose.

HISTORY: (1) Perhaps this is the copy lent by H. H. Gilchrist to the Pennsylvania exhibition (1892), no. 152; (2) Lent by W. E. Moss to the exhibition at Manchester (1914), no. 87 and sold at Sotheby's, 2 March 1937, lot 85, for £6. 10*s*. to Morgan; (3) Acquired by *Geoffrey Keynes*, reproduced in his *Separate Plates* (1956), pl. 13.

COPY F. BINDING: Inlaid to 23·4 × 31·1 cm and bound about 1853 with many leaves of Blakeana including the 'Order' of the *Songs* (see p. 337); separated after 1924 and now loose.

HISTORY: For its History, see the 'Order' of the *Songs*.

COPY G: BINDING: See the Large Book of Designs (A) (p. 269).

HISTORY: For its History as part of the Large Book of Designs (A) see the Small Book of Designs (A) (p. 236); it is reproduced in Keynes, *Separate Plates* (1956), pl. 14.

COPY H: BINDING: (1) Perhaps once bound as part of the Large Book of Designs; (2) then bound 'somewhat irregularly' with *America* (A) and pl. d, *Song of Los* (B), *Visions* (F) pl. 1, *Europe* (A) pl. 1–2, 4–6, and 'Joseph of Arimathea Preaching' (F),[1] but (3) disbound in 1904 and now loose.

HISTORY: (1) Perhaps once part of the Large Book of Designs (B); (2) Probably acquired by Isaac D'Israeli or his son (see *Europe* [A], p. 156); (3) for a time it was 'bound up somewhat irregularly in a cloth case' with *America* (A) and pl. d, *Song of Los* (B), *Visions* (F) pl. 1, *Europe* (A) pl. 1–2, 4–6, and 'Joseph of Arimathea Preaching' (F), before it was disbound and sold separately at an anonymous Hodgson sale, 14 Jan. 1904, lot 227, for £15. 10*s*. to Quaritch; (4) Acquired by W. A. White, who lent it to the exhibition of the Grolier Club (1905), no. 39, perhaps to that of 1919, no. 21 (anonymously), and to the Fogg (1924), and sold it posthumously through Rosenbach on 5 May 1929 to (5) Mr. LESSING J. ROSENWALD.

COPY I: BINDING: Loose.

HISTORY: (1) It was presented by Mr. Thomas Murgatroyd (of the John

---

[1] Pencil numbers (2–11) indicate that part of the order was: *Song of Los* pl. 1, 'The Accusers', *Song of Los* pl. 2, 'Joseph of Arimathea Preaching', *Song of Los* pl. 4–6, *America* pl. 2, *Song of Los* pl. 7–8.

Rylands Library) in 1927 to (2) The WHITWORTH ART GALLERY (now University of Manchester).

2. 'Albion Rose' (?1796)

BIBLIOGRAPHICAL INTRODUCTION

TABLE

Copy		Watermark	Leaf-size in cm	Printing Colour
A¹	BMPR	*invisible*	18·9 × 25·4	
B	LC		inlaid to 23·2 × 31·0	
C²	BM	*invisible*	24·2 × 34·6	*Colour-printed*
D²	HUNTINGTON	1794 / J WHATMAN	26·3 × 36·7	*Colour-printed*

DATE: ?1796

The 'W B inv 1780' on Copies A–B presumably refers to the invention of the design.

The engraving as inscribed and colour-printed may be tentatively assigned to about 1796. For one thing, the colour-printing was apparently done about 1796, and other prints from the Books of Design (one of which included 'Albion Rose' [C]) are dated '1796'. For another, the political sentiment invested in the inscription must relate to the agitation connected with the French Revolution and come from after 1789.[3] And finally, Albion as a Giant Figure (rather than simply as England) does not appear in Blake's myth before the revisions of *Vala* (?1796–?1807).

PUBLICATION: Only four copies are known, and perhaps no more were printed. No contemporary is known to have commented on or bought it.

DESIGN: A naked young man whose head gives off brilliant light dances towards the viewer with outspread arms, like the dawn 'when the Sun dances upon the mountains' (*Vala* [?1796–?1807] p. 129, l. 26); between his ankles is a huge moth, and by his left foot is a worm (both obscured in C–D). (A sketch for 'Albion Rose' in the V & A is reproduced in *Pencil Drawings*, ed. G. Keynes [1927] pl. 1; on the verso is the same figure seen from the back for *Jerusalem* [1804–?20] pl. 76.)

COPY A: BINDING: Loose.

HISTORY: (1) Lent by Mrs. Gilchrist to the Boston Exhibition (1880), no. 114; (2) Lent by her son, H. H. Gilchrist, to the Pennsylvania Academy Exhibition (1892), no. 178, and sold with other works for £150 on 12 June 1894 to THE BRITISH MUSEUM PRINT ROOM, reproduced in G. Keynes (1921).

---

[1] In copy A, the inscription is almost entirely cut off.

[2] In copies C–D, the area with the inscription is heavily coloured, and no words are visible.

[3] Cf. *America* (1793) pl. 8, l. 6 for 'the slave grinding at the mill'. The 'dance of death' is also in *Milton* (1804–?8) pl. 23, l. 62, and in *Jerusalem* (1804–?20) pl. 63, l. 10. Erdman, p. 804, guesses 1790–1 on the basis of the rightward, conventional terminal 'g' in 'Giving'.

COPY B: BINDING: (1) Bound about 1853 with many leaves of Blakeana including the 'Order' of the *Songs*; (2) Separated after 1924 and now loose.

HISTORY: For the History, see the 'Order' of the *Songs* (p. 337); it is reproduced in Keynes, *Separate Plates* (1956).

COPY C: BINDING: See the Large Book of Designs (A) (p. 269)

HISTORY: For its History as part of the Large Book of Designs (A), see the Small Book of Designs (A) (p. 236); it is reproduced in Keynes, *Separate Plates* (1956), pl. 5.

COPY D: BINDING: (1) Perhaps once part of the Large Book of Designs (B); (2) Stabbed and later bound with *Song of Los* (E),¹ but (3) Disbound by 1953 and now loose.

HISTORY: For its History, see *Song of Los* (E) with which it was bound (p. 362).

3. *All Religions are One* (?1788)

All Religions are One and *There is No Natural Religion* (?1788) are so similar in size, method, intention, and history, that it is convenient to treat them together here. In bibliographical terms, they are the most mysterious of Blake's surviving printed works. Neither Blake nor his contemporaries referred to them by name, one (hypothetical) plate does not survive at all, and, so far as we can tell, no copy has ever had all the known plates.

BIBLIOGRAPHICAL INTRODUCTION

See Table on pp. 80–1

TITLES: THERE / is NO / NATURAL / RELIGION
ALL / RELIGIONS / are / ONE

DATE OF ETCHING: ?1788.

Neither work is dated, and our sparse information implies one date for the etching and another for the printing. Both books show signs of being early and experimental, in their very modest dimensions, in their simple and somewhat hesitant technique,² and in the fact that Blake apparently never published them. In all these respects, they seem to precede *Innocence* (1789) and *Thel* (1789), his earliest dated works in Illuminated Printing. And if they are Blake's earliest works in relief-etching, they must be referred to in the colophon of *The Ghost of Abel* (1822): 'W Blakes Original Stereotype was 1788'. *No Natural Religion* and *All Religions are One* appear, then, to have been etched in 1788. However, no surviving copy seems to have been printed this early.

---

¹ Pencil numbers (2–9), plus an offset on a loose fly-leaf, indicate that 'Albion Rose' was bound at the end of *Song of Los*.

² Note, for example, that on *No Natural Religion* pl. a1 Blake apparently forgot to reverse

[*Footnote 2 continued on p. 82*

TABLE

There is No Natural Religion (?1788)

Copy	Plates	Leaves	Watermarks	Blake numbers	Binding-order	Leaf-size in cm	Printing colour
#A BMPR	a1, 3–9, b3–4, 12	11	—	—	a3, b3, a5–9, b4, 12, a1	10·7×13·7* *irregular*	*Olive*
#B Mellon	a1, 3–9, b3–4, 12	11	TAYLOR (b12)	—	†a1, 3–9, b12, 3–4**1	10·5×13·4*1	*Brown*
#C LC	a1–6, 8–9, b3–4, 12	11	—	—	‡a2, 1, 3–5, b4, 12, 3, a6, 8–9	10·6×13·4* plus 7·7×9·5 .a2	*Brown* plus *Black* (a2) *Green* (a5–6)
#D HARVARD	a1–2, 5–9, b3, 12	9	—	—	‡*Loose*	10·9×13·9 plus 10·1×13·2 (a5) c. 10·7×13·4 (a6–9)	*Green* plus *Black* (a1–2) *Brown* (a7)
#E Harvey	a1, 3–4, 8–9, b3–4, 12	8	—	—		11·5×14·0 *irregular*	*Brown*
#F LC	a1, 3–4, 7–9, b3–4, 12	9	S[. .] (b4)	—	‡*Loose*	11·0×13·3	*Brown*
#G1 MORGAN	a1–2, 3a–c, 4a–c, 5a, 6a–c, 7–8, 9a–b, b3a–d, 4, 12a–c	24	—	—	*Loose*	c. 10·8×13·7 plus 10·9×15·0 (a3a) c. 10·0×13·7 (a6c, b4) 11·6×13·7 (a4b)	*Brown*
#G2 MORGAN	a5, a6d	2	—	—	*Loose*	11·1×13·9	*Brown*
#G3 MORGAN	a3d, 4d	2	—	—	*Loose*	c. 10·9×13·7	*Brown*
#H BM	a1–5, 8–9, b3–4, 12	10	[18]11 (b12)	—	a2, 1, 3–4, b4, 12, 3, a8–9, 5**	c. 11·1×13·9	*Brown*
#I MORGAN	a1, 3–4, 8–9a–b, b3–4, 12	10	[1]811 (a1, b3a, 12a)	—	*Loose*	11·1×13·9 plus 10·3×13·5 (a9b, b12b)	*Brown*
#J TRINITY COLLEGE	a1, 3–4, 8–9, b3–4, 12	8	[1]811 (a4, b3)	—	a3, 1, b12, a8, 4, 9, b4, 3²	10·6×13·5 plus 11·1×13·5 (a1) 10·7×13·c (a4)	*Brown*

Copy	Plates	Leaves	Inscription	Binding	Dimensions	Colour
‡K *Rosenbloom*	a1, 3–4, 8–9, b3–4, 12	8	—	a3, 1, b12, a8, 4, 9, b4, 3²	c. 9·8×11·9 (a1, 3, 9) 10·5×12·8 (a4, b4) c. 9·9×12·8 (a8, b3, 12)	*Brown*
‡L¹ MORGAN	a2, b2–4, 6–10, 12	10	I TAYLOR (b3, 6, 9)	a2, b1, 3–4, 11, 6–9, 12	c. 22·0×30·3 plus 22·0×29·0 (a2, b1, 11)	*Green*
‡L² *Keynes*	a3–4, 8, b10	4	—	Loose	23·2×29·5 *irregular*	*Green*
‡M VICTORIA & ALBERT	a1–6, 8–9, b4, 12	10	—	Loose⁴	c. 10·8×13·5	*Brown*
HUNTINGTON	a2	1	—	Loose	24·7×34·7	*Black*
MORGAN	a2	1	—	Loose	24·5×34·8	*Black*
‡BMPR	a8	1	*invisible*	Loose	11·0×13·6	*Brown*

All Religions are One (?1788)

Copy	Plates	Leaves	Inscription	Binding	Dimensions	Colour
‡A HUNTINGTON	2–10	9	1794 I TAYLOR (6)	Loose	26·6×37·4 *irregular*	*Green*
‡A *Keynes*	1	1	I TAYLOR	*Loose*³	23·2×29·5	*Green*
‡B VICTORIA & ALBERT	1	1	—	*Loose*⁴	10·8×13·5	*Brown*

‡ The plates are coloured.
‡‡ The frontispiece faces the title-page.
** The offsets confirm the present binding-order.
* The leaves are trimmed and gilt.
Brown The plates are colour-printed.

¹ In *No Natural Religion* (B), only the top edges are gilt.
² *No Natural Religion* (J–K) are bound in the same order in extra-illustrated sets of Gilchrist's *Life of William Blake* (1863), at ii. 3, 6, 36, 94, 112, 162, 168, 184.
³ The old ink numbers (56–7, 60, 64) on *No Natural Religion* (L²) pl. a3–4, 8 and *All Religions are One* (A) pl. 1 were added when they were bound about 1853.
⁴ The leaves of *No Natural Religion* (M) and *All Religions are One* (B) are mounted on a single sheet.

DATES OF PRINTING: ?1794, ?1815.

Only one copy of *All Religions are One* (A) and one of *No Natural Religion* (L) are anything like complete. *All Religions are One* (A) has all but pl. 1; *No Natural Religion* (L) has all known plates but pl. a1, 5–7, 9; and sixteen of their twenty-three plates are unique. The two copies are like each other, and different from almost all other pulls, in watermarks,[1] leaf-size, and printing colour, and these congruities suggest that they were produced together. The watermark of 1794 and the tentative colour printing (see Colouring, below) imply that these two copies were printed about 1794. There is no evidence that any other copies as complete as these were ever made.

The other pulls seem to have been produced in a very haphazard fashion. There are, in all, eight plates which survive in twelve to sixteen pulls (*No Natural Religion* pl. a1, 3–4, 8–9, b3–4, 12); four plates which survive in five to nine pulls (*No Natural Religion* pl. a2, 5–7); seventeen plates which survive in unique copies (*All Religions are One* pl. 2–10, *No Natural Religion* pl. b2, 6–11) or in duplicate (*All Religions are One* pl. 1); and one hypothetical plate (*No Natural Religion* pl. b5) which does not survive at all.

All pulls after 1794 are colour printed (chiefly in *Brown*) on paper of about the same size ($11 \cdot 0 \times 13 \cdot 9$ cm)[2] which is either unwatermarked or watermarked S, TAYLOR, or [1]811.[3] The general uniformity suggests that they were all printed at the same time, and the watermark date, if it has been correctly read, must indicate that they were printed in or after 1811. Since Blake is not known to have done any printing from 1809 to 1814, it seems likely that the *All Religions are One* and *No Natural Religion* prints on smaller paper were pulled experimentally between 1815 and 1827.

DISTRIBUTION: There is no evidence that Blake ever disposed of copies of the two works,[4] and on Blake's death in 1827 they probably passed as a pile of 161 leaves (or more) to Catherine, and on her death in 1831 to Frederick

the letters, so that they are in mirror-writing when printed. Also, in *All Religions are One* words are sometimes curiously divided ('meth / od' on pl. 3, 'natu / re' on pl. 9); on pl. 10 'variouS' ends with a capital; and pl. 7 in particular is almost illegible. The letters in *No Natural Religion* Series b are larger and more clearly formed than in Series a. In pl. a3, b12, the letters are joined, as in handwriting. In sophistication, and perhaps in order of etching, the order would seem to be: (1) *All Religions are One*, (2) *No Natural Religion* Series b, and (3) *No Natural Religion* Series a.

[1] The I TAYLOR in *No Natural Religion* (L) may be the same as the 1794 I TAYLOR in *All Religions are One* (A), with the date cut off. Perhaps the same size loose monotone pulls of *No Natural Religion* pl. a2 in the Huntington and Morgan were made at the same time.

[2] *No Natural Religion* (A–C) are trimmed slightly smaller, and K and a sprinkling of leaves in other copies seem to have been originally somewhat smaller.

[3] The watermark of 1811 at first seems alarming, for it is found in *No Natural Religion* (H–J) and, as J WHATMAN / 1811, in the facsimile (1886) made by William Muir; moreover, copy H belonged to the forger T. J. Wise and copy L to Muir. However, we need not doubt the genuineness of Blake's plates, for they are clearly distinguishable from the facsimile, in which the lines are distinctly sharper and narrower. The 1811 watermark is not found elsewhere in Blake, and the fact that it was used in copies H–J and in the 1886 facsimile is just coincidence.

[4] *No Natural Religion* (M) and *All Religions are One* pl. 1 (which Mrs. Tulk lent to an exhibition in 1876) may have belonged to C. A. Tulk (1786-1849), and *All Religions are One* (A)

Tatham, who acquired all the rest of Blake's property from her. The incomplete copies known today began to appear heterogeneously in the middle of the nineteenth century,[1] and some at least came from Tatham. In particular, *No Natural Religion* (F) pl. a7 is inscribed: 'given me by Mr Tatham'. Probably all copies came from Tatham when he discovered a market with mid-Victorian enthusiasts such as Locker-Lampson and Monkton Milnes.

CATCHWORDS: None in either work.

ORDER: *All Religions are One*: pl. 2, 1, 3–10.

The sequence of frontispiece, title-page, 'The Argument', and seven numbered 'PRINCIPLES' gives an indubitable order of pl. 2, 1, 3–10. There can be no doubt that the separate title-page of *All Religions are One* belongs with pl. 2–10, for pl. 10 concludes that 'The true Man is the source' of 'All Religions'.

ORDER: *No Natural Religion*: pl. a1–9, b1, a2, b3–4, 6–12.

There are two sets of numbered propositions: a negative Series a, I–VI (pl. a4–9), preceded by a negative 'Argument' (pl. a3); and a positive Series b, I–II, IV–VII (pl. b3–4, 6–9), the latter carefully echoing the former. The logical sequence of numbered propositions is careful, and their order and relationship are scarcely in doubt.

The fact that the plates were never bound or even, so far as we can easily tell, collated by Blake has made for some difficulty in determining whether the small plates of *All Religions are One* and *There is No Natural Religion* form one series or two or three. Even when *All Religions are One* has been disentangled from *No Natural Religion* and the numbered propositions in Series a from those in Series b, important problems remain, for with them must be merged an 'Application' (pl. b10), a 'Conclusion' (pl. b11), and a summary ('Therefore God becomes as we are . . .', pl. b12).

Arguing chiefly from internal evidence, Keynes (1921) and Keynes & Wolf (1953) established an order and numbers for the plates; this order has had to be modified because of bibliographical evidence which appeared in 1953 in copy L. This evidence is that copy L seems to be a virtually complete set of Series b, the only one known: it is the only set on large paper (about twice the dimensions of any other set), and each plate has a border of four, or five (pl. b1), framing-lines. Previously it had been assumed that pl. b11 ('Conclusion') belonged in Series a. Because of its presence in copy L, on

pl. 2–10 (which were sold by the Linnell Trustees in 1918) may have been acquired from Blake by Linnell. However, it seems unlikely that Blake would have supplied defective copies to his friends, and I suspect that Tatham was the source in each case.

[1] No copy has been traced earlier than about 1853, when *No Natural Religion* (L) pl. a1 and *All Religions are One* pl. 1 were bound with other fragments of Blakeana. *No Natural Religion* (A–B, G) were sold as a pile of 50 loose leaves in 1862, probably by Tatham; copies E–F, I were sold as a similar pile of 26 loose leaves 'many years' before 1921; *No Natural Religion* pl. a1 was offered (with other works from Tatham) in the Harvey catalogue of *c.* 1864; another copy of pl. a1 was bound with *Thel* (a) by 1866; and *No Natural Religion* (J–K) were bound identically with sets of Gilchrist (1863).

large paper and with four framing-lines, it now seems to belong in Series b, and it has therefore been renumbered to fit it with Series b. At the same time, the frontispieces (pl. a1, b1), which in Keynes (1921) and Keynes & Wolf (1953) oddly *followed* the title-page (pl. a2), have been placed in a more conventional position as the first plate in each Series.[1]

Of the two frontispieces, it is natural to find the one with Christ and the regenerate man (pl. b1) preceding the positive propositions (Series b), and the other frontispiece (pl. a1) is appropriate for Series a, because it bears the imprint which should come at the very beginning. The general title-page, *There is No Natural Religion* (pl. a2), seems by its negative emphasis to be appropriate for the negative Series a, but it clearly belongs also with Series b, as the framing-lines in copy L show. Pl. a2 then serves as the title-page for both Series a and Series b.

The large paper and framing-lines demonstrate that pl. b10–12 in copy L all belong with the rest of Series b. The order of the 'Application' (pl. b10), 'Conclusion' (pl. b11), and summary (pl. b12) derives from internal logical evidence.

COLOURING: The colour printing in both works is very tentative, consisting primarily of outlines of different colours (Brown or orangish-Brown on people) rather than of solid masses of different colours as in other colour-printed works. Perhaps these are Blake's earliest experiments with colour printing, as they seem to be of relief-etching. Since colour printing is thought, from other evidence, to have been practised about 1795, the evidence of the colour printing in *All Religions are One* (A) and *No Natural Religion* (L) seems to confirm the watermark date of 1794.

In *All Religions are One*, some details are picked out in ink, but the only water-colouring is a little in the Victoria & Albert pl. 1.

In *No Natural Religion*, the dark Browns, Greens, and Blacks are printed, and the rest, chiefly Pink, Blue, and Yellow, is in water-colour. The text is never coloured. Copies A–B, I, L are scarcely water-coloured; copy E has more water-colouring than most, and copies J–K are very similar to each other.

VARIANTS: None significant in either work.

ERRATUM: 'univers[e]' (*No Natural Religion* pl. b6).

---

[1] In all Blake's works with frontispieces, the frontispiece precedes and normally faces the title-page, as it does in copies B–D, F here.

The relationship between, on the one hand, the old order of Keynes (1921) and of Keynes & Wolf (1953) and, on the other, the new order used here and in the Keynes facsimile (1971) is as follows:

New Order: used here and in the 1971 facsimile	a1—a2—a3–a9; b1, a2, b3–b10—b11—b12
Old Order: of Keynes (1921) and Keynes & Wolf (1953)	a2, a1, a3–a9; b2, [?a1], b3–b10, a10, b11

All Religions are One

Pl. 1. DESIGN: Above the text, most of the page is a design of a naked seated youth with a cloth on his knees pointing to the right with both hands in a gesture associated with John the Baptist.

Pl. 2. INCIPIT: 'The Voice of one . . .' DESIGN: The title is inscribed on what appears to be a double tombstone (like the one on pl. 9 which seems to represent 'The Jewish & Christian Testaments'); to the right sits a long-bearded old man holding an open book on his knees as he looks upward; and behind stands an angel with spread wings with his right hand on the stone and his left on the old man's shoulder. (An analogous design is in *Urizen* [1794] pl. 1.)

Pl. 3. INCIPIT: 'The Argument'. DESIGN: Beneath the text, a tiny man lies in tall grass resting his head on his right hand. (His position is similar to that of the figures, reversed, on *No Natural Religion* [?1788] pl. a9 and *Songs* [1794] pl. 43.)

Pl. 4. INCIPIT: 'PRINCIPLE 1ˢᵗ'. DESIGN: At the top, on a cloud which envelops 'PRINCIPLE', sits an old man with outstretched arms (identical in position to the one in *America* [1793] pl. 10 and in *Job* [1826] pl. 14).

Pl. 5. INCIPIT: 'PRINCIPLE 2ᵈ'. DESIGN: Above the text, a naked man sits on the ground leaning on his right hand, while from his ribs appears a person (?the birth of Eve; cf. *Jerusalem* [1804–?20] pl. 35). Up the left margin grows a flourishing plant, and below the text are grazing sheep, and a ?palm-tree.

Pl. 6. INCIPIT: 'PRINCIPLE 3ᵈ'. DESIGN: Above the text, a man with a long beard sits on a chair apparently writing in a book on his lap, and beside him sits another person evidently reading a book.

Pl. 7. INCIPIT: 'PRINCIPLE 4'. DESIGN: Above the text is a walking traveller (very like that in *For Children* [1793] pl. 16).

Pl. 8. INCIPIT: 'PRINCIPLE 5'. DESIGN: Above the text in a ?tent are six tiny children at the knees of a seated woman (a similar scene, reversed, is in *Songs* [1789] pl. 3), while below the text a naked man ?playing a harp runs left with huge strides.

Pl. 9. INCIPIT: 'PRINCIPLE 6'. DESIGN: Above the text is a double tombstone (as on pl. 2) evidently representing 'The Jewish & Christian Testaments', while below it is a person in a long dress apparently groping through a dark wood, perhaps representing 'the confined nature of bodily sensation'.

Pl. 10. INCIPIT: 'PRINCIPLE 7ᵗʰ'. DESIGN: Above the text is a person with raised arms between two naked prone figures, while below the text there seems to be a bird flying over water.

COPY A: BINDING: pl. 1: (1) Bound about 1853 with many leaves of Blakeana including the 'Order' of the *Songs* (see p. 337); (2) separated by 1886, and now loose.

   pl. 2–10: Loose; 4 or 5 framing-lines round the plates.

HISTORY: pl. 1: For its History see the 'Order' of the *Songs* (p. 337).

pl. 2–10: (1) Sold with the Linnell Collection at Christie's, 15 March 1918, lot 203 (unbound, with *No Natural Religion* pl. a1) for £84 to G. D. Smith for (2) The HUNTINGTON LIBRARY; reproduced in Keynes (1921) and (with pl. 1) in the Blake Trust facsimile (1970).

pl. 1: BINDING: Mounted on a sheet with *No Natural Religion* (M).

HISTORY: For its History see *No Natural Religion* (M) (p. 446).

For the HISTORIES, etc., of *There is No Natural Religion,* see below, pp. 441–7.

4.

*_All Religions are One._ London, 1926.
A Frederick Hollyer facsimile.

5.

*_All Religions are One_ [A]. London, 1970. The William Blake Trust.
'Description and Bibliographical Statement' by Geoffrey Keynes is 5 pp.

6. *America* (1793)

BIBLIOGRAPHICAL INTRODUCTION

See Table on pp. 88–9

TITLE: AMERICA / a / PROPHECY / LAMBETH / *Printed by William Blake in the year 1793*

DATE: 1793. There seems to be no sound reason not to accept the date of '1793' on the title-page.[1]

PUBLICATION: More kinds of evidence about the stages of *America* survive than for any other work by Blake. There are sketches on *Notebook* pp. 75 (top right), 77 (bottom), and 17 related to designs on pl. 7, 11, 14.[2] Three or four pages of rejected proofs (pl. a[3]–d) show Blake making both small and large alterations in his work.[4]

[1] I see little validity in D. V. Erdman's suggestion (*Poetry and Prose* [1966], 724, on the basis of the tone of pl. 4, ll. 37–41) of '1794 or 1795 as the date of etching', or in that of Sir Geoffrey Keynes (ed., *America* [1963]) that the watermarks indicate they were not 'printed before 1794'. Copies C–L have no dated watermark and could, so far as paper is concerned, much antedate 1794, and the work was advertised in 1793.

[2] The fact that the top lines of text on pl. 7 are curtailed by the design suggests that here at least the design was etched before the text.

[3] About 1805, pl. a was cut down and the blank verso used for an engraving by Thomas Butts. It is the only surviving copperplate from Blake's works in Illuminated Printing.

[4] Another indication of change is the fragment, apparently of a deleted line, on pl. 16. 'The copperplate maker's stamp [*which*] can be seen on the title-page' of copy Q by Keynes & Wolf is invisible to me, but Michael Tolley reports (in a letter) the discovery of the plate-maker's mark in the New Zealand copy (N) of pl. 6, suggesting that the recto of this plate was originally used for another purpose.

Blake made a number of alterations in the process of printing *America*. First, he wiped clean the margins of the copperplates, so that only the parts integral to the design or text should print; therefore the heavy margins visible in copies N, P, Q are strong indications that they were posthumously printed by someone who did not know Blake's methods.[1]

Second, after he had printed copies E[2]–G, I–L, he reduced to one the multiplicity of serpent tails on the copperplate of pl. 13, so that in copies A–D, H, M–Q (including the posthumous copies) there is no ambiguity. The printing-order can therefore be established partly on the basis of early, three-tailed copies and late, one-tailed copies.

Third, Blake decided to remove the last four lines on pl. 4, and in printing copies B–F, H–M, R, a, and the Morgan pull he masked them, probably putting a sheet of paper across the bottom of the plate.[3]

If we assume, somewhat hesitantly, that Blake was fairly consistent in printing copies of *America* with ten or eighteen leaves, with or without pl. e and the last lines on pl. 4, etc., the order in which he printed copies may have been:

Copy	Approximate date	Serpent tails	Leaves	Pl. e present	Pl. 4 masked	Watermark	Printing colour
G	1793	3	10	yes	*erased*	E & P	greenish-Black
E–F, I–L	1794	3	10[1]	yes	yes	E & P *or* —	greenish-Black
C–D, H	1796	1	10	yes	yes	E & P	greenish-Black, Blue, bluish-Blue
R	1797		18	yes	yes		Green
M	1799	1	18	no	yes	HAYES & WISE / 1799	Brown, Blue, greenish-Black
B	1799	1	18	no	yes	1794 / J WHATMAN	dark Brown
A	1800?	1	18	no	no	1794 / J WHATMAN	brownish-Black
O	1821	1	18	no	no	J WHATMAN / 1818	orangish-Red
N, Q	1833?	1	18	no	no	RUSE & TURNERS / 1812 *or* T STAINS / 1813	Black
P	1833	1	18	no	no	J WHATMAN / 1832	reddish-Brown

[1] In copy F, there are indications that pl. e, 5, 7, 11 were printed after the other plates on these leaves.

The fact that copy G was printed with the last four lines on pl. 4, and that these were then erased, suggests that it was the first copy printed, before

[1] Copy P is on paper watermarked 1832, after both Blake and his wife were dead, and copies N and Q (watermarked RUSE & TURNERS / 1812 and T STAINS / 1813) make use of paper found elsewhere in Blake's works only in the copies of *Europe* with which N and Q were bound. Copy Q is rather carelessly printed; for example, on pl. 14 a syllable at the end of l. 132 ('scep-') did not print, and in all three copies there is no sign of the partial cloud-line at the top left of pl. 2 which shows in all other copies.

[2] In copy E, the area of the tail is smudged, and it is not clear how many there were.

[3] In the copies printed without the four lines, the masking has obscured the plate 0·4 cm *above* the toe of the man in the design (copy a) or varying distances *below* the toe: 0·3 cm (C, F), 0·4 (H, L), 0·5 (B, Morgan pull), 0·6 (D, E, K), 0·7 (M), and 1·0 cm (I)—see the reproductions in 'The Printing of Blake's *America*', *Studies in Romanticism*, vi (1966), 49–52. In copy G, the lines are erased from the paper, not masked.

TABLE

Copy	Plates	Leaves	Watermarks	Blake numbers	Binding-order	Leaf-size in cm.	Printing colour
‡A MORGAN	1–18	18	1794 / J WHATMAN (4, 12, 16–17)	1–16[1]	Loose	23·9 × 23·0	brownish-Black
B MORGAN[2]	1–18	18	1794 / J WHATMAN (1, 5, 8, 11, 18)	—	‡1–18	26·1 × 36·6*	dark Brown
C Hofer[2]	1–18, e	10[3]	E & P (2, [17–18])	—	‡1–18***[4]	25·1 × 38·6*[5]	bluish-Black (1–9, 11, 13, 15, 17), greenish-Black (10, 12, 14, 16, 18)
D Newton[2]	1–18, e	10[3]	E & P ([9–10])	—	‡1–8, 10, 9,[6] 11–18**	26·0 × 36·7*	bluish-Black (1–11, 13, 15, 17), greenish-Black (12, 14, 16, 18)
E LC[2]	1–18, e	10[3]	E & P ([13–14], [17–18])	—	‡1–18**	26·5 × 37·5[7]	greenish-Black
F BMPR[2]	1–18, e	10[3]	—	—	‡1–18**	25·3 × 36·2*	greenish-Black
G Cunliffe[8]	1–18, e	10[3]	E & P (1, [3–4], [7–8])	—	‡1–8**[9]	26·7 × 37·2	greenish-Black
H BMPR[2]	1–18, e	10[3]	E & P ([7–8], [11–12])	—	‡1–18**	25·0 × 34·7*	bluish-Black (1–2, 6, 10, 14, 18), Blue (3–5, 7–9, 11–13, 15–17)
I HUNTINGTON[2]	1–18, e	10[3]	E & P ([3–4], [5–6], [13–14])	—	‡1–18**	25·8 × 36·5*	greenish-Black
[There is no J]							
‡K YALE[2]	1–18, e	10[3]	E & P ([3–4])	—	‡Loose[10]	26·8 × 37·3 (1) 27·3 × 37·8 (2–18)	greenish-Black
L NY[2]	1–18, e	10[3]	—	—	1–18**	26·5 × 38·0	greenish-Black
‡M Mellon[2]	1–18[11]	18	HAYES & WISE / 1799 (2, 6, 8, 11, 13)	1–16[1]	‡Loose**[10]	26·7 × 37·3	Brown (1), Blue (2–7, 9, 12–13, 17–18), greenish-Black (8, 10–11, 14–16)

N AUCKLAND	18	1–18	R & T (1–2, 7, 11–13, 16–17) RUSE & TURNERS / 1812 (3–6, 8–10, 14–15, 18)	—[12]	‡1–9, 11, 12, 10, 13–18**	23·6 × 32·6*[13]	Black
#O FITZWILLIAM	18	1–18	J WHATMAN / 1818 (7) J WHATMAN / 1820 (4–5, 8)	1–18	1–18	24·3 × 30·3	orangish-Red
P FITZWILLIAM	18	1–18	J WHATMAN / 1832 (5–8, 11, 13, 15)	—	2, 1, 3–18	22·8 × 28·0*	reddish-Brown
Q PRINCETON	18	1–18	T STAINS (1–15, 17–18) T STAINS / 1813 (16)	—[12]	1–14, 16–17, 15, 18**	22·0 × 29·0*[14]	Black
#R *UNTRACED*[15]	18	1–18, e,		—	‡1–18	c. 28·0 × 38·7	Green
a LC	6[17]	1, 4, 11, 12, 15[a-b], a,[16] b–c	—	—[18]	1, 4, [a, b], [11–12], [c, 15[a]], 15[b]	174 × 24·0 (1, a–c, 15[a]) *irregular* 23·5 × 31·2 (4, 11–12) 23·5 × 29·3 (15[b])	Blue dark Blue (1, 4) brownish-Black (a–b) greenish-Black (11–12) Black (c) Brown (15[a]) reddish-Brown (15[b])
#ROSENBACH	1	1	—	—	Loose	23·3 × 28·9	Blue
Lister	1	1	—	—	Loose	18·5 × 25·3	dark Green
VIVIAN GALLERY	3	2, 5, 15	J WHATMAN / 1831 (5)	—	Loose	22·7 × 28·8 (2) 23·5 × 28·8 (5) 21·3 × 28·0 (15)	reddish-Brown
Keynes	3	3, 6, 10	—	—	Loose	19·1 × 26·0 (3) 16·8 × 21·7 (6) 17·0 × 24·2 (10)	bluish-Black (3) greyish-Black (6) orangish-Brown (10)
HUNTINGTON	3	3	—	—		18·4 × 24·7	Blue
MORGAN[2]	4	4	—	—		26·9 × 38·0	greenish-Black
UNTRACED[19]		15 + two	—		Loose		
#LC	d		—	9[20]	Loose	23·8 × 21·2	*Colour-printed*
#BMPR	d		*invisible*	—	Loose	24·8 × 34·7	*Colour-printed*

\# Water-coloured by Blake or by his wife.   ‡ Pl. 1 faces pl. 2.   ** The identifiable offsets confirm the order.

1–18 An italicized binding-order indicates that the binding appears to date from before 1835.   * The leaves are trimmed and gilt.

pl. e Pl. e is the small plate from which the word 'Preludium' was printed on pl. 3.

Notes to Table on p. 90.

Blake had begun masking the plate. Similarly, the fact that copy M was printed without pl. e but that the 'PRELUDIUM' was lettered in by hand on pl. 3 where pl. e was normally printed may imply that it was the last copy in which Blake supplied this heading.[1]

America was clearly thought of as a companion to *Europe* (1794), to which it is very similar in size and style, and the two works were often bound together, though *America* is rarely coloured and *Europe* usually is. This accounts for eight of the twelve known copies of *Europe*. Further, it is clear that some of these pairs were carefully produced as companion-copies, for copy O is just like *Europe* (K) in printing colour, framing-lines, and leaf-size, and the two were originally stitched and sold together. From similar evidence, it is clear that the posthumous copy P and *Europe* (M) were made together.

[1] Its watermark demonstrates that it cannot have been the first copy in the process.

Notes to Table on pp. 88–9

[1] Copies A and M are numbered 1–16 on pl. 3–18.

[2] In copies B–F, H–M and the loose copy (Morgan), the last four lines of pl. 4 were masked when the plate was printed.

[3] In copies C–L, pl. [3–4] [5–6] [7–8] [9–10] [11–12] [13–14] [15–16] [17–18] are printed back-to-back.

[4] In copy C, the legible offsets (2–3, 8–9, 12–13, 14–15, 16?–17, 5–18, 16–18) indicate that the last plate (18) at different times followed pl. 5 and pl. 16.

[5] In copy C, the edges are trimmed and dappled.

[6] In copy D, stab holes in the outer margin of the leaf with pl. [10–9] and clear offsets on pl. 8–11 indicate that the leaf with pl. [10–9] has been accidentally bound in backwards.

[7] When copy E was exhibited, untrimmed, at the Grolier Club (1905, no. 19), its dimensions were 27·6 × 38·1 cm.

[8] In copy G, the last four lines of pl. 4 were erased from the paper, leaving some words (e.g. 'enrag'd') still faintly visible.

[9] In copy G, the order was pl. 1–18 (according to Keynes & Wolf) before the work was disbound in 1966; stab holes in the left margin of pl. 1 show that it faced pl. 2.

[10] In copies K and M, stab holes in the right margin of pl. 1 indicate that pl. 1 faced pl. 2 when bound.

[11] In copy M, the word 'Preludium' is lettered by hand in blue at the top of pl. 3, not printed from pl. e as in copies C–L.

[12] Copies N and Q are numbered (probably posthumously) in ink 1–18 in the top right corner in the present mistaken order.

[13] In copy N, the edges seem to be trimmed, but they are not gilt.

[14] According to Keynes & Wolf, when copy Q was coloured in 1913, the size was cut down from 22·5 × 33·5 to 22·5 × 26·5 cm.

[15] If copy R was correctly described, it has not been traced since Quaritch offered it in his *General Catalogue* (1887); most of the details about copy R here and below, especially concerning colouring, derive from the 1887 Muir facsimile of it (BM copy).

[16] All known pulls (LC, Cleveland) from the fragment of the surviving copperplate of pl. a (LC) have been made since the copperplate entered the Rosenwald Collection.

[17] In copy a, pl. [a–b], [11–12], [c, 15ᵃ] are printed back-to-back.

[18] The numbers in copy a (15–17, 19, 96 on pl. a, 15ᵇ, c, 4, 1) were apparently added when the leaves were bound with other Blakeana including the 'Order' of the *Songs*.

[19] These untraced plates are known only from the exhibition catalogues of the Burlington Fine Arts Club (1876), no. 282 (pl. 15), Boston Museum (1880), no. 1 (pl. 15), and Pennsylvania Academy of the Fine Arts (1892), nos. 149–50, 187 (pl. 15 plus two 'page[s]' from *America*).

[20] The '9' on pl. d indicates its position when it was bound with the *Song of Los* (D) (see p. 362).

America was bound with	*Europe*	*America* was bound with	*Europe*
copy	copy	copy	copy
A	A	N	I
B?	C	O	K
F	C	P	M
G	B	Q	L
H	D		

America was advertised in the Prospectus of 10 Oct. 1793 as 'America, a Prophecy, in Illuminated Printing. Folio, with 18 designs, price 10s. 6d.' In his letter of 9 June 1818, Blake described it as 18 folio prints selling for £5. 5s., while in his letter of 12 April 1827 the price is given as £6. 6s. Copies are known to have belonged to Blake's contemporaries Isaac D'Israeli (A), C. H. Tatham (B, acquired in 1799), H. C. Robinson (D, acquired after Dec. 1825), George Cumberland (F, sold in 1835 to Butts), P. A. Hanrott (G), Ozias Humphry (H and pl. d, inherited in 1810 by his son William Upcott), John Linnell (O, bought in 1821), and Samuel Boddington (P).[1]

COLOURING: *America* is essentially an uncoloured work. Only copies A, K, M, O, and R are coloured,[2] and all seem to have been coloured rather late; in particular, the text is coloured in copies A, K,[3] O, and R (suggesting a date after 1805) and copy O was not coloured until after 1821. The colouring is often remarkably brilliant. In A it is sombre and intense, in M some of the colours seem to have been applied rather hastily, and in O, in which gold was used, they are vivid. In copy O, the text and the figures are regularly coloured bluish-Grey, and the plates are outlined in Red.

CATCHWORDS: None.

ORDER: Pl. 1–18, with the frontispiece facing the title-page.
    This is the order of almost all the copies issued by Blake himself; copies B–I,[4] L, O, R were so bound, and copies A, M, O so numbered by Blake. The leaves of copy K are now loose. Of the copies which present slight variants in plate order,[5] P is certainly posthumous, and N and Q are probably so; these exceptions then have little authority. There is no good reason for thinking that Blake ever changed his mind about the order of the plates of *America*.

SIGNIFICANT VARIANTS: Pl. 2: The printed cloud-line in copies A–M is absent in copies N–Q. The corpse is clad in chain-mail in copy O.
    Pl. 3: Pl. e ('PRELUDIUM') is present only in copies C–L, R; in M it has been replaced in water-colour wash.

---

[1] *Pace* Keynes & Wolf (and others), there is no good evidence that copy K belonged to Benjamin West.
[2] I ignore the posthumous colouring of copy Q, the almost random pale Grey washes in copy N (probably posthumous), and the occasional Grey wash on pl. 2 (e.g. copies B, F).
[3] It seems likely that copies A and K were coloured some time after they were printed. We know that this was the case with copy O, for it was sold to Linnell in 1821 when it was still 'not finished' (*Blake Records* [1969], 585).
[4] Copy D was originally bound with the plates in this order (1–18), but the leaf with pl. 9–10 was accidentally misplaced when the book was last bound.
[5] One plate is out of place in copies N (pl. 10), P (pl. 1), and Q (pl. 15).

Pl. 4: ll. 38–41 were masked (copies B–F, H–M, R, a, and the Morgan pull) or erased (G) in all copies except A, N–Q. A sunrise is added in the coloured copies.

Pl. 5 evidently was first etched as pl. a. A butterfly was added in copy B.

Pl. 6: The scales on the wyvern are obscured in copy O.

Pl. 8: In copy O, Blake's colouring has moved the man's left foot so that it partly covers his penis. In copy F, 'The Slave delivered' is written below the design (cf. *Visions* [B]—pp. 469–72).

Pl. 9: The sun rises behind the ram (A, K, M, N, R?).

Pl. 12: The man's right knee is drawn in (N, O), showing his foot under his buttock (O).

Pl. 13: The serpent has three etched tails in copies E–G, I–L, but only one in copies A–D, H, M–Q.

Pl. 14: There seems to be a coiled serpent inside the door in copy O.

Pl. 18: 'FINIS' is coloured out in copy M.

ERRATA: pl. 8 'op[p]ressors'.

Pl. 1. DESIGN: At the left, a huge, heavy-winged, naked figure sits with its head resting on its knees and its manacled hands on the ground. To the right is seated a nude woman with her arms round two small naked children. In the bottom left corner is the barrel of a cannon (especially clear in O), at the woman's feet is a dark cross which appears to be the hilt of a broken sword (invisible in M), and looming over her is a broken wall in a gap of which the angel sits. (A similar broken wall is seen in 'A Breach in a City, the Morning after the Battle' [1784]—reproduced in *Blake's Visionary Forms Dramatic*, ed. D. V. Erdman & J. E. Grant [1970], pl. 23.) Above the angel, there are two openings in the heavy clouds.

COLOURING: The ANGEL'S WINGS are Yellow (A, R), greyish-Pink (M), or Brown (O). The HAIR of the figures is Yellow (M) or Brown (O, R). The SKY is Black (A, M, R) and Brown (Rosenbach), and the CLOUDS Purple (A, K), Red (O), Black (R), or Brown (Rosenbach).

VARIANTS: A shadow is cast across the scene from the middle left (K). The texture of the rock is almost obscured (M, O), and the sword hilt, the cloud outlines, and the plant at bottom right are coloured out (M). The plate is badly printed in copy a.

Pl. 2. DESIGN: 'AMERICA / a / *PROPHECY*' is over clouds; to the left of the 'a' a seated woman in a long dress bends over a book on her knees at which a child is looking, while another child (?naked) is sitting propped against her. To the right of 'a' is seated a man in a long robe bending over a book, while a nude (?female) figure (repeated in *Visions* [1793] pl. 3) flies from before him to the top right corner, and a naked man leaning against his back points toward the top left corner.

Below the clouds but above the imprint, a clothed woman kneels to kiss a stiff corpse with a sword in his hand; under his feet lies another corpse. (A similar armed corpse and mourning woman are visible in 'A Breach in a City' [op. cit.], and a related couple, the man reversed, is in 'Pestilence'

[1805]—reproduced in G. Keynes, *William Blake's Illustrations to the Bible* [1957], no. 39.) A faint shape may represent another corpse under his head. (A sketch perhaps related to these bottom figures is on *Notebook* p. 29 and another, reversed, is in the BMPR. Another, quite different draft for the title-page is also in the BMPR [26·3 × 38·0 cm; watermark: crown without letters, reproduced in *Blake Newsletter*, v [1972], 227]. At the top may be the very vague, large letters of 'AMERICA' while to the left and right are rising naked figures with trumpets. Between their legs is:

Angels to be very small⌊,⌋ / as small as the letters / that they may not / interfere with the / subject at bottom / which is to be a / stormy sky & rain / separated from the angels / by Clouds⌊.⌋

On the verso of this sketch is a finished water-colour vignette, evidently for a fan.)

COLOURING: The CLOTHES of the PEOPLE at the top are, from left to right: (1) Yellow (A, R.), Blue (K), brownish-Pink (M), bluish-Grey (O); (2) Yellow (A, R), pale Raspberry (K), Pink (M), bluish-Grey (O); (3) Blue (A), Purple (K, M, R), bluish-Grey (O). The bottom WOMAN is in Blue (A), yellowish-Green (K), Grey (M), or Purple (R), and the CORPSES are Grey in all copies. The HAIR of the figures is chiefly Brown (A), Black, White, Orange (K), or Auburn (M). The MAN under the 'R' is Black (A), and the TITLE Gold (O). The SKY is Black (A, K, R), Grey at the top left (B, D, F), or Blue (A, M [dark]), and the CLOUD is Pink (A, R), pinkish-Purple (K), Brown (K, M), or greyish-Green (R). The BOTTOM is bluish-Green (A), Grey (B, M), or greyish-Purple (K).

VARIANTS: A line representing the edge of the cloud at the top left is visible in all copies except N, P, Q, though in N it has been drawn in ink. The corpse being kissed seems to be wearing chain-mail in copy O.

Pl. 3. INCIPIT: 'Preludium / The shadowy Daughter . . .'. DESIGN: Above the text, a huge tree arches over a naked youth (Orc) whose spread arms and legs are manacled to the earth, while before him a nude woman (Enitharmon) stands with her hands to her head, and a naked man (Los) stands with his hands raised in the air.

(A sketch related to the two males is on *Notebook* p. 49, and a water-colour of *c*. 1793 showing only the two males, reversed, is in the Tate [reproduced in M. Butlin, *William Blake* (1971), 30]; an almost identical separately engraved design is known as 'The Chaining of Orc' inscribed 'Type by W Blake 1812' [reproduced in *Engravings by William Blake: The Separate Plates*, ed. G. Keynes (1956)]; and a similar one is in *Vala* [?1796–?1807], p. 62. Another related design [BMPR: 12·7 × 16·6 cm; watermark invisible] is entitled in pencil: 'Chaining of orc'. In the bottom left is a dome with a cross [London], and in the bottom right is a Gothic cathedral [Jerusalem; cf. *Jerusalem* (1804–?20) pl. 32, 57, 84]. The BMPR drawing post-dates *America*, for it is on p. 9 of Hayley's *Designs to a Series of Ballads* [1802].)

The roots of the tree extend down the left margin, ending in what may be a naked old man clasped between the legs of a nude woman (they are obscured in A). Below the roots is a naked man seated with his arms round his ankles. Below the text, a worm loops across the page.

On this and the following plates, there are small branches, leaves, birds, and little figures between the stanzas, at the ends of lines, and on flourishing letters.

COLOURING: The colouring is conventional in all copies.

Pl. 4. INCIPIT: 'Silent as despairing love...'. DESIGN: Between ll. 37 and 38, a naked man looks upward as he lifts himself from a hole in the earth. To the left, a curious tree with large leaves and a soaring tendril reaches up the margin.

COLOURING: The SUN (visible in A) rises at the bottom right (A, K, R) or behind the man's head (M) and throws Pink (A, R), Orange (K), Blue (R), and Yellow (R) rays across the design (A, K, M, R).

VARIANTS: Ll. 38–41 were masked (copies B–F, H–M, R, a) or erased (G) in all copies but A, N–Q.

Pl. 5. INCIPIT: 'A / PROPHECY / The Guardian Prince of Albion...'. DESIGN: In the top left corner, beside the 'A', rises a naked man bearing broken chains. 'A / PROPHECY' is sprouting in grain and leaves, and round the words fly six birds. Between ll. 5 and 6 is a naked flying man blowing a serpent-mouthed trumpet from which flames extend to the left margin. Similar flames rise between l. 12 and l. 13 and extend to the margin and to the bottom left corner, where two naked adults and a child flee from them. (The top man and the bottom woman appear, reversed, on an unwatermarked leaf of sketches in the collection of Professor Charles Ryskamp, reproduced in *Drawings* [1970], no. 16; and the top man, without chains, is on a leaf of *America* sketches [see pl. 2, 6–7] in the BMPR.)

COLOURING: The text is Grey to Pink (A, R) or Orange (K), Brown (R), and Yellow (R).

VARIANTS: There is a cloud-line from 'A' to the 'P' of 'PROPHECY' (A), and a Pink cloud has been added by 'A' (K). Flames rise to the 'P' of 'PROPHECY' in A, and a butterfly has been added in ink by the bird at the top right (B).

Pl. 6. INCIPIT: 'Appear to the Americans...'. DESIGN: Between ll. 18 and 19, a heavy-winged, serpent-tailed, scaled, human-handed wyvern pursues with lightning a bearded man in a trailing robe who plunges down the left margin holding an arrow or sceptre before him. (He may be holding an enormous book against his back.) Heavy clouds separate. ll. 28 and 29 and envelop the bottom of the page, where two naked men, one holding a child, cower among rocks and look upward. A large, curious object in the bottom left could be either a horizontal tree or a monstrous animal. (The falling man is sketched with wings and with an arrow fitted to a bow and without books, on a leaf of *America* sketches [see pl. 2, 5, 7] in the BMPR. A very similar design is in pl. b).

COLOURING: The WYVERN is Green in all coloured copies, his tongue Red (A), and the diving MAN is White, Grey, pale Yellow (R) or uncoloured in all copies. Behind the diver is greyish-Purple (M). The CLOUDS are Pink and Grey (K), or Blue (R).

VARIANTS: The scales on the wyvern are obscured (O).

Pl. 7. INCIPIT: 'Albions Angel stood . . .'. DESIGN: All the figures are naked. In the top right (and curtailing ll. 30–1), a long-haired woman carries by the blade a huge, flaming sword. In the top centre, a man bends under the weight of an apparently bound man whom he bears on his shoulders. In the top left, a flying man holds a balance, the right side of which stretches down the left margin almost to a man who is floating in air and clutching his head. Below the text, a huge, coiling, open-mouthed serpent with a forked tongue forms a question mark around a man (apparently sketched on *Notebook* p. 75) falling headlong towards flames which reach up round the serpent from the bottom of the page. (A bust of the top left figure, the man in the serpent coils, and the bottom left figure are on a leaf of *America* sketches [see pl. 2, 5–6] in the BMPR. A naked figure with balances [reversed] at the left and another naked figure [back view] *sheathing* a sword appear in the unused title-page design [1806] for Blair's *Grave* in the BMPR.)

COLOURING: The SNAKE is Blue (A [greenish-], R), flame-Orange (M), its head Yellow (M), its tongue Red (M). The HAIR of the figures is Brown (M). The CLOUD is Yellow (A, R) or shades of Purple and Grey (K, R), and some of the flames are Green (R).

VARIANTS: The serpent's mouth is coloured shut (M). Crudely applied grey wash makes it appear as if the sword carried by the woman at the top right entered her head (N).

Pl. 8. INCIPIT: 'The morning comes . . .'. DESIGN: At the top of the page, a naked man with legs splayed gazes upward. (A very similar figure appears in *Marriage* [?1790–3] pl. 21, the top of the design [1805] called 'Death's Door' for Blair's *Grave* [1808], and the Unnamed Print of about 1805 [G. Keynes, *Engravings by William Blake*: The Separate Plates (1956), no. XIV].) By his right hand on the earth is a human skull. Plants trail down both margins, and below the text are a lizard, a frog, a small snake, a thistle, and other plants.

COLOURING: The SKULL is Yellow (A), the CLOUDS Green (A [greyish-], R [pale]), orangish-Brown (K) or Brown (M, R), the SKY is dark Grey (R), and the GROUND Yellow and Green (M).

VARIANTS: The man's left foot has been extended so as partly to obscure his penis in O. At the bottom in pencil (?in Blake's hand) is 'The Slave delivered' in F.

Pl. 9. INCIPIT: 'In thunders ends the voice . . .'. DESIGN: In the left margin grows a slim birch or willow whose branches gracefully overarch the text and support three exotic birds; three other birds and a butterfly fly beneath its branches. Below the text sleeps a large ram on which one naked boy is sleeping, while beside it another nude, long-haired child stretches out in sleep. By the ram's head is a foot apparently belonging to the boy on the ram, though it is considerably too far from its owner. (In copy M, the foot is not coloured, as if to disguise it.)

COLOURING: The RAM is pale orangish-Brown (M). A SUNRISE behind the ram (A, K, M, N) sends rays through the text (K, M, R). The SKY is Pink and Yellow (A, K, M), or Orange (M) and the SUN Buff (A). The two left sitting BIRDS are Orange (A, M), Ochre (K), Yellow (M), or Red (R), and the left flying bird Raspberry (M).

VARIANTS: The bird at the right is uncoloured and therefore almost invisible in M. A stream was added across the bottom in R. The sun rises behind the ram in coloured copies (A, K, M–N, R).

Pl. 10. INCIPIT: 'The Terror answerd . . .'. DESIGN: At the top of the page, a heavily bearded man in a long robe sits with outstretched arms on a massive cloud which surrounds the text. (His position mirrors that of the young man on pl. 12 and is identical to that of the old man in *All Religions Are One* [?1788], pl. 4.) Below the text are dark waves.

COLOURING: The man's CLOTHES are Grey and White (A, M), White (K, R), or uncoloured (O). His HAIR and beard are touched with Yellow (K). The CLOUDS are Blue (A, M, R), Purple (K, M, O), or Grey (R), the SEA Black (A, M, O, R), and the SKY is Black (A, R), or Orange (K). The TEXT is Grey (K) or Blue (R).

Pl. 11. INCIPIT: 'Sound! sound! my loud war-trumpets . . .'. DESIGN: Below and to the left of the text, a corn-field swirls round the corpse of a rigid, naked child. (A sketch for the child, reversed, is on *Notebook* p. 77, and an almost identical baby is on *Europe* [1794] pl. 9.)

COLOURING: The BABY is uncoloured (M, O), and the WHEAT is Yellow in all coloured copies (greenish in M, a sickly shade in O). The TEXT is Grey (A, M, R), or Blue (K), and the left margin is greenish-Grey (R).

VARIANTS: There are shafts of light in the middle of A.

Pl. 12. INCIPIT: 'Thus wept the Angel voice . . .'. DESIGN: Below the text, a naked, kneeling man with outspread arms is engulfed by flames which reach up the right margin, separate ll. 106 and 107, and fill the gaps at the ends of the lines. (The man's position mirrors that of the old man on pl. 10.)

COLOURING: The man's HAIR is Yellow (A), the FLAMES vary from Pink to Red, Blue (M), Orange, and Brown, and the BACKGROUND is Purple (K).

VARIANTS: The flame-shapes are altered by the colouring in A and M and go over the man in A, K, and R. The man's right knee is drawn in (N, O), showing his foot under his buttock (O).

Pl. 13. INCIPIT: 'Fiery the Angels rose . . .'. DESIGN: Between ll. 117 and 118, a naked man looks backwards as a huge bridled swan carries him to the right, where there are four smaller birds. Clouds and starlit sky fill the margins. Below the text is a huge bridled serpent with forked tongue carrying three naked children to the right. (The serpent and children are repeated almost exactly, reversed, from *Thel* [1789] pl. 8.) Above them are a waning sickle-moon, a bat, and a bird.

COLOURING: The SERPENT is Blue with Yellow and Red spots (A, R), Purple, Pink, and Brown mottled (K), pinkish-Purple (M), and golden-Brown (O). The middle CHILD is Red (A). The SWAN is always uncoloured or White. The right BIRD is Blue (A, R) or Raspberry (K), and the CLOUDS are Buff (A, K, M, R) or Grey (K, O).

VARIANTS: The serpent has three etched tails in copies E–G, I–L, but only one in copies A–D, H, M–Q. The top left star is coloured over in A.

Pl. 14. INCIPIT: 'So cried he . . .'. DESIGN: Below the text, an aged, bearded man on a crutch, with flying hair and billowing robe, seems to be blown into a heavy open stone doorway. (There are related designs on *Notebook* p. 17 and *Jerusalem* [1804–?20] pl. 1, and an almost identical scene appears in the designs called 'Death's Door' in *For Children* [1793], pl. 17, and Blair's *Grave* [1808].) In the left margin, a tree grows from the rough-hewn stones and spreads over the text.

COLOURING: The MAN is uncoloured (A), Purple (K), Grey (M), bluish-Grey (O), or White (R). The STONES are Yellow (A, K) or Brown (M, O, R), and the TREE Green (A) or Yellow (K). The SKY is Lavender (M) or Black (R), and the CLOUDS deep Raspberry (O) or pale Blue (R). The top right and bottom background are Black in A, the bottom right Black and Purple in K. The text is light Blue (A, R [greyish-]).

VARIANTS: There seems to be a coiled snake inside the door in O. In l. 132 'scep-' did not print in Q.

Pl. 15. INCIPIT: 'What time the thirteen Governors . . .'. DESIGN: Above the text, an eagle with outspread wings seems to devour the midriff of a nude woman washed up at the edge of the sea; her right arm hangs down the left margin. (A related scene appears in *Visions* [1793], pl. 6; see also *Jerusalem* [1804–?20], pl. 37.) Below the text a naked man lying beside a seashell and small sea-creatures is enwrapped by an eel, while three open-mouthed fish and an eel approach him from above. Tendrils reach up the left margin, and between ll. 143 and 144 are flourishes, foliage, a worm, and a naked figure.

COLOURING: The top BODY is yellowish-Grey (A), livid whitish-Purple (K), or pale Brown (M), and the EAGLE, which is ordinarily Brown (e.g. in A, R), is Yellow in O. The bottom BODY is greenish-Grey (A), livid whitish-Purple (K), pale Grey (M, O), or Blue and Pink (R), and the right-hand FISH is Red (A), Blue (M), or Pink (R). The CLOUDS are Grey (O [reddish-] R), the top right SKY Black (A) or very pale Pink (M), and the TEXT greyish-Green (A), Green (K), or greyish-Blue (R).

Pl. 16. INCIPIT: 'In the flames stood . . .'. DESIGN: Between ll. 165 and 166 is a huge tree at the right, near which sits a nude (?female) figure from whose head depends a cloth and between whose legs appears a large serpent with a forked tongue. The figure gestures toward a boy whose hands are joined as if in prayer and who is reclining on a pile of what may be books. A branch of the tree arches over the two figures, another extends up the right margin, and roots descend down the right margin. Below the text, a stubby serpent belches flames towards the left margin. Above the text are tiny isolated flowers, birds, and human figures, and between ll. 172 and 173 is a flying bird.

COLOURING: The BOY's CLOTHES are Green (A, R), Blue (K [strong], O [Pale]), or Purple (M), and the BOOKS on which he is leaning Orange (M). The SYBIL's CLOAK is Red (K), and the bottom SNAKE is Purple (A, M), Blue (K), with some Gold (O), or Red (R). The FLAMES are Red or Orange and Green (A, R), Blue and Brown (K), with some Gold (O), the SKY is Black (A, M), and the CLOUDS Purple (K) or Raspberry (O). The TEXT is pale Green (R) and pale Blue (R).

VARIANTS: Below l. 165, above the design, are marks which may be the remains of one line, or perhaps two lines, deleted from the copperplate (visible in copies F, H, I [most clearly], L, M, O).

Pl. 17. INCIPIT: 'On Albions Angels . . .'. DESIGN: Below the text, flames in the centre envelop a nude woman who is clasping two younger nude women. To their right, a seated nude woman wraps her arms round her head. To the left is a large vine leaf above grapes, and in the bottom left corner a nude woman seems to rise on the flames up the margin toward a nude [?female] figure and a small child climbing, or perhaps turning into, a tree, on a branch of which sits a tiny bowed figure. In the top section of the left margin is a bowed figure in a long robe, beneath an almost leafless tree, on the top branches of which is a large bird. (Similar figures appear in *Visions* [1793], pl. 2, 10.) Almost every gap in the text is filled with flying birds, leaves, and tiny people.

COLOURING: The FLAMES are once an odd purplish-Orange and Yellow (M). The top left FIGURES are, from top to bottom, Blue (A, R), Grey (A), Green (A, R), or uncoloured (K). The GRAPES are Purple (O), or Green (R), and the TEXT greyish-Pink (A, R).

Pl. 18. INCIPIT: 'Over the hills . . .'. DESIGN: At the top of the page crouches a kneeling, robed figure with hands clasped in front of head and with long hair which seems to turn to water falling down the right margin. On this large figure's head and by its feet there appear to be two embracing couples (in A it is clear that the naked man by the large figure's feet is raising the skirt of a woman), on its back are a standing figure carrying a large book and another kneeling and stretching upward, while on its thigh a tiny man in a flat-brimmed hat playing a flute (similar to the one who appears, reversed, on *Songs* [1789], pl. 3) leans against what appears to be a palm-tree. Behind it, to the left are bare trees in oddly human shapes. Below the text flourishes an odd, spiky flowering plant on which are two tiny human figures and a forked-tongued serpent on whose body appears the word 'FINIS'.

COLOURING: The large KNEELER is Grey (A, O, R), Tan (K), or greyish-Green (M); its blue HAIR turns into a waterfall (A, K, R). The small FIGURES on its head are Blue (A, K, R), uncoloured (M), or Grey (O). The MAN kneeling by its foot is nude-Pink (A, R), Blue (K), uncoloured (M), or Grey (O), and the WOMAN before him is Yellow (A, R), Raspberry (K), Pink (M), or Grey (O). The STANDING MAN on its back is Raspberry (K), uncoloured (M, R), or Grey (O). The TREES are flesh-Pink (A), the SKY is Grey to Black (A, R), or greyish-Pink (R), and the FLOWERS Red (K, M), or Yellow(R).

VARIANTS: 'FINIS' is coloured out in M.

Pl. a. INCIPIT: 'A PROPHECY / The Guardian Prince of Albion . . .'. DESIGN: The design is very similar to that on pl. 5, except that the chained figure at the top is reversed; there are no birds above or below the 'Y' of 'PROPHECY'; and in the left margin is a figure with a banner.

TEXT: l. 1: Pl. a is evidently a first draft of pl. 5, with slight alterations in the word order in ll. 4, 7, and 'fiery' and 'fierce' instead of 'wrathful' and 'red' in ll. 14 and 16.

l. 6: The only surviving copperplate from Blake's works in Illuminated Printing is a fragment from the top right corner of this rejected plate for *America*. The text seems to have been partly cancelled, ll. 4–5 by heavy pounding. In l. 6, only the tops of the letters are visible, but they are clearly the same as on pl. a. The text reads:

> burns in his [nightly tent; *del*]
> [g]low to America's shore.
> , who rise in silent night
> [*word del*] Gates, Franklin, & Green;
> [*word del*] from Albions fiery Prince.   [5]
> [*Ameri*]ca, look over the A[*tlantic sea*]   [6]

In l. 3 here, the 'w' of 'who' is deleted. These deletions do not seem to be related to the engraving on the verso.

Pl. b. INCIPIT: 'Reveal the dragon . . .'. DESIGN: The design is very similar to that on pl. 6, though many minor details are altered.

Pl. c. INCIPIT: 'Then Albions Angel rose . . .'. DESIGN: All the designs are in the left margin, except for leaves, birds, tiny figures, and flourishes between the lines. In the top left corner, a small naked figure dives towards l. 3 and two birds by l. 4. All the other figures are much larger but, like him, naked. By ll. 5–10 is a man with spread legs resting his heads on his arms on a cloud. Beneath him a man plunges downward with a long trumpet held to his lips. (He is very similar to the trumpeter on the title-pages of *Vala* [?1796–?1807] and Blair's *Grave* [1808].) At the bottom, a man with his back to us seems to have his hands on a woman with her arms raised and her head back as if in despair.

Pl. d. INCIPIT: 'As when a dream of Thiralatha flies . . .'. DESIGN: In the centre, a woman clad only in a skirt sits with her head on her knees, while over her bends a tree trunk. At the left, a nude woman kisses a naked baby who seems to be flying down to her. (The baby is repeated in *Urizen* [1794], pl. 20.)

COLOURING: The woman's SKIRT is dark Green (LC) or Black (BMPR). The SKY is Black at the top right (LC) to Blue and Pink (BMPR).

NOTE: Pl. d is known only from the use of the design in the Large Book of Designs, where the text is heavily covered with pigment in both known copies; it has only been read from the impress of the letters on the verso. There can be no certainty that it belongs with the *America* proofs, but its reference to the fading 'British Colonies' and its similarity in size to the *America* plates makes the hypothesis plausible. (Its width [17·0 cm] is like the *America* plates, but its height [11·3 cm] can be accounted for only by supposing that the *America* proof was cut down or was masked in printing.) If it was intended for *America*, there must have been text or design cut off at the bottom.

Pl. e is a small plate bearing the word 'PRELUDIUM' printed at the top of the page bearing pl. 3.

COPY A: BINDING: (1) Bound 'somewhat irregularly in a cloth case' with *America* pl. d, *Song of Los* (B), *Visions* (F) pl. 1, *Europe* (A) pl. 1–2, 4–6, 'The Accusers' (H), 'Joseph of Arimathea Preaching' (F); (2) Disbound by 1904, the leaves mounted separately after 1909.

HISTORY: (1) Probably acquired by Isaac D'Israeli (see *Europe* [A], p. 156); (2) For a time it was 'bound up somewhat irregularly in a cloth case' with *America* pl. d, *Song of Los* (B), *Visions* (F) pl. 1, *Europe* (A) pl. 1–2, 4–6, 'The Accusers' (H) and 'Joseph of Arimathea Preaching' (F), before it was disbound and sold separately at an anonymous Hodgson sale, 14 Jan. 1904, lot 222, for £207 to Quaritch; (3) Offered in Quaritch's catalogues (1904) lot 1602, (March 1909) lot 287, both for £260; sold by Quaritch on 6 May 1909 to (4) The PIERPONT MORGAN LIBRARY. *N.B.* The extra pl. 4 described with the work in Keynes & Wolf came with *Thel* (a) and had no previous connection with *America* (A).

COPY B: BINDING: (1) Stabbed once (perhaps with *Europe* [C]) through three holes, 6·5 and 7·7 cm apart; (2) Stabbed again through three holes 10·7, 12·9 cm apart; (3) 'BOUND BY F. BEDFORD' in Citron morocco, inlaid with Red leather on the spine and panels ('to a Lyonnese design', according to Keynes & Wolf), g.e.; there are sketches on the versos of pl. 2, 8, 17.

HISTORY: (1) It passed 'From the author / to C. H. Tatham Oct! 7 / 1799'[1] (according to the inscription—not in Blake's hand—on the verso of the title-page), who may have made the tiny sketches on pl. 2, 8, and 17; (2) Below this inscription in old Brown ink is 'Mary[?] Taylor London';[2] (3) This may be the copy sold by 'Sotheby, 1855, 2*l.* 7*s.*';[3] (4) Sold in 1874 for £18 (according to the 1878 catalogue below); (5) Sold with the Library of A. G. Dew-Smith at Sotheby's, 29 Jan. 1878, lot 247, for £16. 5*s.* to Pearson; (6) Acquired by Thomas Gaisford, who added his book-plate, and sold it at Sotheby's, 23 April 1890, lot 189, for £61 to Quaritch, for whom it was described on a fly-leaf as 'Collated & perfect / Ap! 24 90 / J. T'; (7) Acquired by B. B. Macgeorge, described in his catalogues (1892, 1906), lent to the exhibitions in the National Gallery (1913), no. 95, Manchester (1914), no. 162, Nottingham (1914), no. 118, and the National Gallery of Scotland (1914), Case B, no. 4, and sold posthumously at Sotheby's, 1 July 1924, lot 114, for £215 to Maggs; (8) Acquired by George C. Smith, Jr., described in his anonymous catalogue (1927), no. 9, lent to the Fogg exhibition (1930), and sold posthumously at Parke-Bernet, 2 Nov. 1938, lot 22, for $2,600 to Rosenbach; (9) Acquired by Mrs. Landon K. Thorne, who lent it to the Philadelphia exhibition (1939), no. 6, in whose catalogue (1971), it was described (no. 6), and who gave it in 1973 to (10) The PIERPONT MORGAN LIBRARY.

---

[1] Tatham's acquisition of *America* in 1799 may be connected with the fact that 'Mr. William Blake' subscribed to Tatham's *Etchings, Representing the Best Examples of Ancient Ornamental Architecture* (1799–1800). *America* may have been sewn, either earlier or later, with *Europe* (C), which was separate by 1821.

[2] The 'mary[?] Jane / merry[?]' and the pinpricked 'S' on the verso of pl. 2 may be signs of this owner or of a later one.

[3] W. T. Lowndes, *The Bibliographer's Manual of English Literature* (1857), i. 215; the copy referred to could alternatively be copies C, E, I, or L.

COPY C: BINDING: (**1**) Originally stabbed (perhaps with *Visions* [C]) through three holes, 11·0 cm from the top, 7·5, 7·3 cm apart; (**2**) Bound by 1847 in half Maroon morocco over marbled boards, the edges trimmed and dappled (not 'g.e.' as in Keynes & Wolf).

HISTORY: (**1**) *America* (C) may have been sewn with *Visions* (C) and then separated; (**2**) It is probably the copy offered by Henry G. Bohn (1847), i ('hf. bd.', 18 plates) for £3. 3s.;[1] (**3**) Sold anonymously at Sotheby's, 28 July 1919, lot 221 for £100 to Sabin; (**4**) Sold by 'a Prominent Pennsylvania Collector' (Col. Henry D. Hughes, according to Keynes & Wolf) at American Art Association, 22 April 1924, lot 63, for $950 to G. Wells; (**5**) Offered in Dulau & Co. Catalogue 149 (May 1927) for £200 (according to Keynes & Wolf); (**6**) 'This copy [*was*] bot of Jas. F. Drake ca. 1934 by Rosenbach' (according to a note on the front endpaper by the present owner); (**7**) Acquired by Mr. *Philip Hofer*, who added his book-plate and that of 'Frances Hofer', wrote 'I bot of Rosenbach, March. 1936', and lent it to the Philadelphia exhibition (1939), no. 63, and apparently to that of the Fogg (1947), p. 16.

COPY D: BINDING: (**1**) Originally stabbed through three holes, 9·2 cm from the top, 9·7, 9·6 cm apart; it was still sewn and uncut in 1888; the edges were gilt by 1905; (**2**) Bound in half dark Green morocco by 1911; (**3**) Bound (by Riviere, according to the 1938 catalogue) in dark Blue crushed levant morocco (Jansen style) by 1938.

HISTORY: (**1**) 'It was presented by Blake to his friend, Crabb Robinson [*after 10 Dec. 1825 when Blake met Robinson*[2]], who gave it to [(**2**)] the gentleman [?*Edwin W. Field*[2] (*1804–71*)] from whom we purchased it', according to (**3**) John Pearson Catalogues 62 (?1886), lot 70 (£52), and 67 (?1888), lot 64 (£45), describing it as 'sewed and UNCUT'; (**4**) Sold anonymously at Sotheby's, 19 March 1888, lot 154 (sewn and uncut) for £23 to Barnes; (**5**) Acquired 'in 1891' (according to Keynes & Wolf) by W. A. White, who lent it anonymously to the Grolier Club exhibition (1905), no. 18 (trimmed to its present size, g.e.), and sold it anonymously at Anderson's, 27 Oct. 1911, lot 18 for $625; (**6**) Rebound in full Blue morocco and acquired by Cortlandt Bishop, who perhaps lent it anonymously to the Grolier Club exhibition (1919), no. 11, added his book-plate, and sold it at American Art Association, 5 April 1938, lot 281; (**7**) In 1964 it was in the possession of John Fleming, who sold it by 1965 to (**8**) *Miss Caroline Newton*, who lent it to the Princeton exhibitions of 1967 and 1969 (no. 41).

COPY E: BINDING: (**1**) Unbound in 1905; (**2**) Bound for W. A. White at the 'CLUB BINDERY 1908' in Brown levant morocco.

HISTORY: (**1**) Bought by 'W A W[*hite*] / 21 Dec '96 / [*from*] Pearson / [*for*] £33' (according to a note on the verso of pl. 1), lent (anonymously and

---

[1] This corresponds, except in binding, to copy R.

[2] In a letter to Mrs. E. W. Field of 11 Nov. [1863], Robinson speaks of the copy of *America* which he 'read . . . some years since' (and 'thought it Sheer Madness') and which he has 'set apart for Il marito [*E. W. Field*]' (quoted from a Xerox copy of the MS in the Osborn Collection, Yale University Library).

unbound) to the Grolier Club exhibition (1905), no. 19, and to that in the Fogg (1924), and sold posthumously through Rosenbach on 1 May 1929 to (2) Mr. LESSING J. ROSENWALD.

COPY F: BINDING: (1) Bound with *Visions* (B), *Europe* (C), *Song of Los* (D) until 1852, when *Europe* was abstracted; (2) The other works were rebound together after July 1859 in the British Museum in Yellow morocco, stamped and gilt with the Royal Arms, g.e.; (3) They were remounted in heavy paper 'windows' and bound in Red morocco in 1969.

HISTORY: (1) Acquired (probably from Blake) by George Cumberland,[1] 'bound together' with *Visions* (B), *Europe* (C), *Song of Los* (D), and sold at Christie's, 6 May 1835, lot 60 (with Blair's *Grave* [1808]) for £3. 18s. to Butts;[1] (2) The composite volume was sold anonymously (by the son of Thomas Butts—see *Songs* [E], p. 414) at Sotheby's, 26 March 1852, lot 54, for £11 to 'M', probably R. M. Milnes (see *Europe* [C], p. 158); (3) Milnes evidently extracted and retained *Europe* and sold the other three works, still stitched together, to 'F. T. Palgrave / 1852', who put his name and the date on the third fly-leaf and the verso of *America* pl. 1; and sold the three works 'In one volume' for £10 in July 1859 to (4) The BRITISH MUSEUM, where they were rebound; *America* was probably used for the facsimile of Pearson (1876), and 'Transferred to the Department of Prints and Drawings [*according to the note on the third* AMERICA *fly-leaf by*] C. B. Oldman / 1 Jan. 1953'.

COPY G: BINDING: (1) Originally stabbed through three holes, 10·6 cm from the top, 7·2, 8·4 cm apart; (2) Bound about 1821 (the date on three fly-leaves) in a Roxburghe binding with *Europe* (B), *Jerusalem* (B) (which have quite different patterns of stab-marks), the spine gilt with 'AMERICA / – / EUROPE / – / JERUSALEM / – / BY / BLAKE'; (3) Disbound in June 1966.

HISTORY: (1) Bound about 1821 with *Europe* (B) and *Jerusalem* (B) and sold with the Library of P. A. Hanrott[2] by Evans, 19 July 1833, lot 642, for £4 to French; (2) Dealers' marks of '13/5/–', 'hf/hf/=', and 'gh.h.–' on the fly-leaves suggest that it went through several hands before it was bought from C. J. 'Toovey [*for*] 10. 10. 0' (according to the pencil inscription on the first fly-leaf) by (3) Henry Cunliffe, who added his book-plate ('Henrici Cvnliffe'); (4) 'Bequeathed by him to his great-nephew, the present [*1953*] Lord Cunliffe' (according to Keynes & Wolf), who bequeathed them in 1963 to (5) The present *Lord Cunliffe*, who had the works disbound in June 1966 for the Blake Trust facsimile of *Europe* (1969), and lent *America* and *Europe* anonymously to the National Library of Scotland exhibition (1969), no. 43, 48.

COPY H: BINDING: (1) Bound with *Europe* (D) and the Large Book of

---

[1] Not 'Originally bought from Blake by Thomas Butts', as in Keynes & Wolf.
[2] Hanrott listed them together ('3 [*volumes*] in 1') in his acquisition catalogue Vol. IV (dated at the start May 1831), p. 8, with a code price ('m m –') and a comment ('Very curious, and very Rare'), according to the Xerox of the Blake page kindly sent me by Mr. A. N. L. Munby, who owns the MS Hanrott catalogues Vol. III–IV.

Designs (A) from 1827 to 1846; (2) *America* was separately bound in the British Museum after Feb. 1856 in half dark Green morocco, g.e., sewn with old Brown thread; evidently later interleaves were sewn in with new White thread; (3) The leaves were remounted in heavy paper 'windows' and bound in Red morocco in 1969.

HISTORY: (1) Probably acquired from Blake by Ozias Humphry and bequeathed by him at his death in 1810 to his natural son (2) William Upcott, who lent it to H. C. Robinson who quoted it in 1811, and to Richard Thomson about 1827 who described it for J. T. Smith's life of Blake (*Blake Records* [1969], 446, 470–3), and for whom it was sold posthumously by Messrs. Evans, 15 June 1846, lot 277 (with *Europe* [D] and the Large [A] and Small [A] Books of Designs) for £7. 2s. 6d. to Evans; (3) Messrs. Evans separated *Europe* (D), and sold *America* (H) with *Songs* (T), *Thel* (D), *Song of Los* (A), and the Large (A) and Small (A) Books of Designs on 9 Feb. 1856 to (4) The BRITISH MUSEUM PRINT ROOM, where *America* was bound.

COPY I: BINDING: 'BOUND BY F. BEDFORD' in Green levant morocco, g.e., probably for Frederick Locker.

HISTORY: (1) Acquired by Frederick Locker, who probably had it bound by Bedford (see *Songs* [E], p. 414), added his book-plate, lent it to the Burlington Fine Arts Club exhibition (1876), no. 317, and in whose *Rowfant Library* (1886) it was described; it was sold through Dodd, Mead, & Co. (see 'Pickering MS') to (2) E. Dwight Church, who sold it with his library in 1911 to (3) The HUNTINGTON LIBRARY.

COPY K: BINDING: (1) Stitched through ten holes into a dark Brown paper folder; (2) Between 1901 and 1937 pl. 1 was separated from the rest of the plates, which were stitched into the folder through two additional holes (missing from pl. 1); (3) The plates were reunited by 1939, when the last stitching had disappeared—the plates are now all loose.

HISTORY: (1) In the nineteenth century, pl. 1 was separated from the rest;[1] (**Ai**) Pl. 1 was sold anonymously (with property evidently once in the D'Israeli Collection—see *Europe* [A], p. 156) at Hodgson's, 14 Jan. 1904, lot 229,[2] for £20. 5s. to Maggs; (**Aii**) Sold posthumously for Sir Frederick Pollock at Sotheby's, 15 June 1937, lot 347,[2] for £29 to Gabriel Wells; (**Bi**) Pl. 2–18 were bought 'at Christie's (£30)' by Tregaskis, who offered them for sale 'some years ago' (according to Keynes [1921]); (**Bii**) Sold with the Library of the late Michael Tomkinson at Sotheby's, 3 July 1922, lot 1,153 for £90 to Dobell; (**Biii**) Acquired by W. E. Moss, lent to the Burlington

---

[1] Pl. 2–18 and the dark Brown paper wrapper have the same twelve stitch holes in groups of three, while pl. 1 has only ten stitch holes. This congruity suggests that pl. 1–18 were originally stitched to the cover through ten holes, and that after pl. 1 was separated pl. 2–18 were stitched to the cover again through two holes.

[2] The 1904 catalogue says that the work was 'presented by Blake to Sir Benjamin West', and Keynes & Wolf (on the basis of evidence unknown to me) amplify this by saying it was sold in 1904 'with a note that it came from Benjamin West's copy'. However, the 15 June 1937 catalogue says accurately that the references in the Keynes *Bibliography* (1921) and in the Moss sale catalogue (22 March 1937) 'to an inscription by Blake to West [*with pl. 1*], is due to a misunderstanding. There is no such inscription.' There appears to be no evidence from before 1904 associating West with this copy.

Fine Arts Club exhibition (1927), no. 80, and sold at Sotheby's, 2 March 1937, lot 169 (with Hayley's letter to Lady Portarlington),[1] for £620 to Gabriel Wells; (2) The reunited plates (plus the Hayley letter) were acquired by C. B. Tinker, lent to the Philadelphia exhibition (1939), no. 64, described in his Library Catalogue (1959), no. 272, and bequeathed at his death in March 1963 to (3) YALE. Reproduced in D. V. Erdman & J. E. Grant, ed., *Blake's Visionary Forms Dramatic* (1971), plus pl. a–c.

COPY L: BINDING: (1) Sewn and uncut in 1879; (2) Bound by Roger 'De Coverly' probably in the 1920s in three-quarter Green morocco over Green boards.

HISTORY: (1) Probably this is the copy offered in Ellis & White Catalogue 43 (?1879), lot 106 (sewn, uncut), for £21; (2) Bought in that year (according to the signature on the fly-leaf) by 'J. Frederick Hall. 1879'; it was rebound, probably in the 1920s, and sold with the Library of Arnold Hall at Sotheby's, 30 June 1927, lot 267 (as a 'facsimile reprint', in its present binding) for £4 to Hollings; (3) It was 'bought from Hollings by Rimell who offered it for sale, together with *Thel*, copy M, and *Visions of the Daughters of Albion*, copy K, in 1927, for £1600' (according to Keynes & Wolf); (4) Acquired by Owen D. Young, lent to the Fogg exhibition (1930), and given with his collection by Young and Dr. A. A. Berg in Memory of Henry W. Berg on 5 May 1941 to (5) The Henry W. and Albert A. Berg Collection of English and American Literature of the NEW YORK PUBLIC LIBRARY.

COPY M: BINDING: (1) Originally stabbed through two holes, 12·4 cm from the top and 11·7 cm apart, and remained in this state until 1905; (2) Bound for W. A. White by the Club Bindery in 1908 in Brown morocco (according to Keynes [1921]); (3) Disbound for the Blake Trust facsimile (1963), and the plates are now loose.

HISTORY: (1) Acquired by Richard Monkton Milnes (according to Gilchrist, [1863], i. 111–12), and probably reproduced by Ellis & Yeats (1893); (2) Sold by his son, the Earl of Crewe, at Sotheby's, 30 March 1903, lot 3 (unbound) for £295 to Quaritch; (3) W. A. White lent it (anonymously and still unbound) to the Grolier Club exhibition (1905), no. 17, evidently had it bound in 1908, and lent it to the Fogg exhibition (1924); (4) Acquired by his daughter, Mrs. William Emerson, who lent it to the Fogg exhibition (1930), and sold it posthumously at Sotheby's, 19 May 1958, lot 5, for £8,500 to Quaritch; (5) Acquired by Mr. *Paul Mellon*.

COPY N: BINDING: Bound in front of *Europe* (I) in early Victorian(?) Maroon embossed flowered cloth (now faded) with a Maroon leather spine in an Oxford hollow binding, the spine lettered sideways in Gold 'BLAKE.— AMERICA.—EUROPE', the edges trimmed.

HISTORY: (1) Inscribed in pencil, apparently by the first known owner Sir George Grey (1799–1882): 'I purchased this book at the sale of the effects of a deceased artist, (I now forget his name), who had obtained it direct from Blake' (the posthumous character of the printing of *America* suggests

---

[1] Sold with Blake's letter of 11 Dec. 1805 at Sotheby's, 28 July 1899, lot 262; for the Hayley text, see *Blake Records* (1969), 119–20.

that it had been obtained after Blake's death, perhaps from his widow); Grey gave it in 1882, with *Europe* (I) with which it was bound at a date later than the original stabbing, to (2) The AUCKLAND PUBLIC LIBRARY.

COPY O: BINDING: Bound, probably for John Linnell about 1824, in White vellum after *Europe* (K) to match his *Marriage* (H), *Songs* (R), and *Jerusalem* (C); in the binding is a fragment of p. 37 of Hayley's *Designs to a Series of Ballads*, for which Blake engraved designs in August 1802; each *America* plate is outlined in Red, as in *Europe* (K); each plate was disbound and mounted by 1970.

HISTORY: (1) Bought by John Linnell with *Europe* (K) ('not finished') for £1 on 8 Aug. 1821 (*Blake Records* [1969], 585), probably coloured later, bound with *Europe* (K) to match his *Marriage* (H), *Songs* (R), *Jerusalem* (C), lent by the Linnell Trustees to the exhibitions of the Tate Gallery (1913), no. 96, Manchester (1914), no. 145, Nottingham (1914), no. 122, the National Gallery of Scotland (1914), Case A, no. 3, and sold by the Trustees at Christie's, 15 March 1918, lot 172 (with *Europe* [K]), for £787. 10s. to Carfax for (2) T. H. Riches (husband of Linnell's grand-daughter), who lent them to the Burlington Fine Arts Club exhibition (1927), no. 81, and for whom a book-plate was inserted bequeathing it in 1935 to (3) The FITZWILLIAM MUSEUM, which received it in 1950; both were reproduced in colour microfilm by Micro Methods Ltd.

COPY P: BINDING: Bound, probably about 1833 for Samuel Boddington, in front of *Europe* (M) in heavily tooled Red morocco, g.e., similar to Boddington's *Jerusalem* (H).

HISTORY: (1) Acquired (perhaps from Tatham about 1833—see *For the Sexes* [D], p. 202) by Samuel Boddington, for whom it was apparently bound with *Europe* (M), and who put his book-plate on the original front marbled endpaper; (2) Acquired by Charles Fairfax Murray, described in his library catalogue (1899), Vol. II, p. 16, no. 142, and for whom a book-plate was inserted presenting the volume in July 1912 to (3) The FITZWILLIAM MUSEUM.

COPY Q: BINDING: (1) Bound by 1913 in Grey calf with *Europe* (L); (2) *America* was separated after 1913 and 'BOUND BY RIVIERE & SON' (with three water-colour copies of the designs on pl. 2, 15) in Blue levant morocco, g.e., by 1918.

HISTORY: (1) Perhaps copy Q and *Europe* (L) were the copies of *America* and *Europe* which, according to Samuel Palmer,[1] belonged to the late Sir Robert Peel (1788–1850); (2) Copy Q was sold by R. A. Potts at Sotheby's, 20 Feb. 1913, lot 59 (bound in Grey calf with *Europe* [L], not said to be coloured) for £66 to Sabin; (3) 'The volume was then broken up, [*cut down*], colouring added for Walter T. Spencer,[2] each work bound separately by Riviere, and sold [in the same year *by Spencer*] as original colouring to Herschel V. Jones' (according to Keynes & Wolf[2]); Jones added his book-plate and

---

[1] Palmer's letter to Gilchrist of about April 1861 (in the Yale University Library and quoted in *Anne Gilchrist: Her Life and Writings*, ed. H. H. Gilchrist [1887], 58) says also that a fine posthumous portrait of Blake by George Richmond was inserted; I have not traced the portrait.

[2] In 1921 Keynes wrote that 'the agent to whom Mr. Sabin sold the volume [*i.e. Spencer*]

sold *America* at Anderson Galleries, 2 Dec. 1918, lot 183 (bound by Riviere and coloured) for $3,600 to Rosenbach; (4) Acquired by A. E. Newton, who added his book-plate, lent it to the exhibition at the Fogg (1924) and in Philadelphia (1939), no. 65 (described as posthumously coloured), and sold it posthumously at Parke-Bernet, 16 April 1941, lot 127, for $5,500 to Wells; (5) Sold posthumously for Fred W. Allsopp at Parke-Bernet, 3 Dec. 1946, lot 21, for $6,000 to Paul H. Anderson, agent; (6) Acquired by Grace Lansing Lambert, who added her book-plate and gave it in Jan. 1960 to (7) PRINCETON.

COPY R:[1] BINDING: Bound by 1880 in Green morocco, g.e.

HISTORY: (1) Sold by George Smith at Christie's, 1 April 1880, lot 164, for £31. 10s. to (2) Quaritch, who lent it to Muir for his facsimile (1887) (according to Muir's title-page to *Europe* [1887]), and offered it in his catalogue (1887), lot 10,251, for £36; (3) *UNTRACED*. (If the printing colour and binding are correct, this cannot be identified with any other known copy.)

COPY a: BINDING: (1) The leaves with pl. (a, b), (c, 15ᵃ) were inlaid to 23·5 × 31·2 cm, and all the plates were bound about 1853 with many leaves of Blakeana including the 'Order' of the *Songs*; (2) They were separated after 1924 and bound by Macdonald (according to the 1927 catalogue) for George C. Smith, Jr., in Blue morocco.

HISTORY: For its History see the 'Order' of the *Songs* (p. 337).

COPPERPLATE OF Pl. a

HISTORY: (1) Sold anonymously (evidently from the Butts family) with 'William Blake's Working Cabinet', with copperplates engraved by Blake and Thomas Butts found in a secret drawer, at Sotheby's, 22 March 1910, lot 446, for £30. 10s. to Tregaskis; (2) W. E. Moss lent the copperplate separately to the exhibitions at Manchester (1914), no. 161, and the Burlington Fine Arts Club (1927), no. 91, and sold it at Sotheby's, 2 March 1937, lot 171, for £50 to Rosenbach for (3) Mr. LESSING J. ROSENWALD.

Pl. d: BINDING: See the Large Book of Designs (A) (p. 269).

HISTORY: For its History as part of the Large Book of Designs (A), see the Small Book of Designs (A) (p. 356).

Pl. d: BINDING: (1) Perhaps once bound as part of the Large Book of Designs (B); (2) Later bound 'somewhat irregularly in a cloth case' with *America* (A), 'The Accusers' (H) (see p. 77), *Song of Los* (B), *Visions* (F) pl. 1, *Europe* (A) pl. 1–2, 4–6, and 'Joseph of Arimathea Preaching' (F), but (3) Disbound in 1904, and now loose, mounted.

HISTORY: (1) Perhaps once part of A Large Book of Designs (B); (2) Probably acquired by the Earl of Beaconsfield (see *Europe* [A], p. 156); (3) For a time it was 'bound up somewhat irregularly in a cloth case' with

is unwilling to divulge its present whereabouts'; as a consequence, in 1921 Keynes listed the coloured and uncoloured states of each work as separate copies, both states of course untraced. Keynes gives the size of the earlier state as 22·5 × 33·5, that of the later as 22·5 × 26·5 cm (the true size is 22·0 × 24·0 cm). I do not know the evidence for these sizes; the 1913 sale catalogue does not give dimensions.

  [1] This corresponds, except in binding and printing colour, to Copy C.

America (A), *Song of Los* (B), *Visions* (F) pl. 1, *Europe* (A) pl. 1–2, 4–6, 'The Accusers' (H), and 'Joseph of Arimathea' (F), but disbound when sold anonymously at Hodgson's, 14 Jan. 1904, lot 223, for £42 to Osmaston;[1] (4) Sold by F. P. Osmaston's widow at Sotheby's, 14 Nov. 1928, lot 692, for £170 to G. Wells; (5) Sold by Mr. and Mrs. Anton G. Hardy at Parke-Bernet, 14 Jan. 1942, lot 20, for $575 to Rosenbach for (6) Mr. LESSING J. ROSENWALD; it was reproduced in Keynes & Wolf, p. 90.

Pl. 1: BINDING: Loose, mounted.
    HISTORY: (1) Lent by Greville Macdonald to the exhibitions in Nottingham (1914), no. 71, and the National Gallery of Scotland (1914), no. 73, and sold by him to (2) Francis Edwards, who offered it (?1931), lot 10, for £10; (3) *UNTRACED.*

Pl. 1: BINDING: Mounted and framed.
    HISTORY: (1) Perhaps once sold for the '10/6' on the verso; (2) Acquired by The ROSENBACH FOUNDATION.

Pl. 1: BINDING: Mounted, with pencil notes on the verso, e.g. '4/77'.
    HISTORY: (1) Sold after many years of ownership by a private collector to (2) The dealer Martin Breslauer, who sold it promptly in 1965 to (3) Mr. *Raymond Lister*.

Pl. 2, 5, 15: BINDING: Loose, mounted.
    HISTORY: (1) Acquired, probably from Frederick Tatham about 1834 (like the 'Nelson' drawing and *Europe* pl. 6–7, 12) by (2) John Defett Francis, who stamped his JDF monogram on them and gave them in 1878 to (3) The town of Swansea, where they were housed about 1966 in The GLYNN VIVIAN GALLERY.

Pl. 3: BINDING: Bound in three-quarter Red morocco by Hammond before 1887 among 30,000 extra-illustrations in 60 volumes with the John 'Kitto Bible' (?*Kitto's Pictorial Bible*, 1850), vol. IV, p. 572.
    HISTORY: (1) Apparently acquired by James, or more probably by the printseller John, Gibbs of London (whose initials occur on some leaves of the work below), who inserted it in the 'Kitto Bible' (?1850); (2) Acquired by Theodore Irwin, whose son (3) Theodore Irwin, Jr., sold it in 1919 to (4) The HUNTINGTON LIBRARY.

Pl. 3, 6, 10: BINDING: Loose; pl. 6 had been inserted in a copy of Mrs. Bray's *Life of Thomas Stothard* (1851) until it was extracted in 1941.
    HISTORY: Pl. 3 (1) Sold by the auctioneer Hodgson about 1924 to (2) *Geoffrey Keynes*. Pl. 6: (1) Acquired by *Geoffrey Keynes* in an extra-illustrated copy of Mrs. Bray's *Stothard* (1851), from which he removed it in 1941. Pl. 10: (1) Sold by W. E. Moss at Sotheby's, 2 March 1937, lot 170, to (2) *Geoffrey Keynes*. All three plates[2] are listed in Keynes's *Bibliotheca Bibliographici* (1964), no. 513.

---

[1] The 1928 catalogue says Osmaston acquired it from Quaritch in 1904.
[2] The two untraced and unidentified *America* plates exhibited in 1892 could be two of Keynes's pl. 3, 6, 10.

Pl. 4: BINDING and HISTORY: See *Thel* (a).

Pl. 15 and two other plates, BINDING: Loose.

HISTORY: (1) Pl. 15 was lent by Mrs. Gilchrist to the Boston Museum exhibition (1880), no. 1 ('Drowned Bodies washed up by the Sea'); (2) Pl. 15 and two others were lent by her son Herbert H. Gilchrist to the Philadelphia exhibition (1892), no. 187, 149–50; (3) *UNTRACED*.[1]

7

'*America*: A Prophecy.' *Poet-Lore*, v (1893), 363–71.

Transcribed from 'the facsimile', parts of which they clearly could not read.

8

A. *America. N.Y., 1947. Albion Facsimile No. 2. B. *n.d.

An uncoloured facsimile, with a 3 pp. Foreword by Ruthven Todd. B omits the imprint and Foreword.

9

*America a Prophecy [M]. London, 1963. The William Blake Trust.

Geoffrey Keynes, 'Description and Bibliographical Statement', is 5 pp.

A9

'America a Prophecy.' *Stony Brook*, 3/4 (1969), cover (recto and verso), 1–16.

A reduced facsimile in Black on Yellow paper of copy C or D, with no related text at all.

B9

*America: A Prophecy [E]. Introduction by G. E. Bentley, Jr. Normal, Illinois, 1974. Materials for the Study of William Blake: The American Blake Foundation, Volume I.

A monotone facsimile with Roger R. Easson, 'Editorial Comments' (pp. 1–2), G. E. Bentley, Jr., 'A Bibliographical Introduction' (pp. 3–13), and Roger R. Easson, 'A Check-List of Secondary Materials in English' (pp. 14–21). In addition to the plates of copy E, the limited edition repro-duces (a) pl. a–c, pl. d (LC), the copperplate of pl. a (LC), (N) pl. 4, (B) pl. 13, 'The Chaining of Orc' sketch (BMPR), and a possible title-page design (BMPR).

10. 'Ancient of Days' (?1794)

For Descriptions, etc., see *Europe*, p. 148.

COPY A: BINDING: Mounted and framed.

HISTORY: (1) Evidently once the property of Thomas Butts (according to the 1904 catalogue, below); (2) Acquired by W. B. Scott, lent by him to the Boston Museum of Fine Arts exhibition (1876), no. 268; perhaps this is the

---

[1] The two untraced and unidentified *America* plates exhibited in 1892 could be two of Keynes's pl. 3, 6, 10.

copy sold posthumously for Scott at Sotheby's, 14 July 1892, lot 177, for
£5. 15s.; (3) This may be the Butts copy which passed from Scott to 'Ross'
(according to the 1904 catalogue) and thence to (4) Sydney Morse, who lent
it to the Carfax exhibition (1904), no. 23, and sold it at Christie's, 26 July
1929, lot 20, for £135[1] to Colnaghi;[1] (5) Acquired by A. S. W. Rosenbach,
who bequeathed it to (6) The ROSENBACH FOUNDATION.

COPY B. BINDING: Loose.
    HISTORY: (1) This (or E) may be the copy sold posthumously for John
Giles (Samuel Palmer's cousin) at Christie's, 2 Feb. 1881, lot 184 (with
Europe [a]); (2) Perhaps this is the copy lent by Stopford Brooke to the Carfax
exhibition (1906), no. 80; (3) Sold posthumously for A. E., Newton at Parke-
Bernet, 16 April 1941, lot 130 (printed in Black[2]) for $125; (4) Sold anony-
mously at Christie's, 10 Feb. 1958, lot 11 (printed in Brown) for £231 to
Agnew for (5) Mr. *George Goyder.*

COPY C: BINDING: Loose, mounted.
    HISTORY: (1) Acquired by W. B. Scott, lent to the Burlington Fine Arts
Club exhibition (1876), no. 307, probably the copy sold by him at Sotheby's
21 April 1885, lot 178, for £10 to Thibeaudeau; (2) Acquired by Mrs.
Graham Smith[1] (see *Marriage* pl. 3–4, p. 301) and presumably inherited by
her nephew (3) Anthony Asquith, who sold it at Hodgson's in 1942 (according to Keynes below—see *Europe* pl. 2, p. 162) to (4) *Geoffrey Keynes,* who
reproduced it in his *Separate Plates* (1956), lent it to the exhibitions of the
British Museum (1957), no. 58, and (anonymously) the Whitworth Art
Gallery (1969), no. 11, and the National Library of Scotland (1969), no. 71,
and described it in his catalogue (1964), no. 557.

COPY D: BINDING: (1) Bound about 1853 with many leaves of Blakeana
including the 'Order' of the *Songs* (see p. 337); (2) Separated after 1924.
    HISTORY: For its History see the 'Order' of the *Songs.*

COPY E: BINDING: Mounted and framed.
    HISTORY: (1) W. A. White may have acquired the print, lent it anony-
mously, along with most of the rest of the exhibits, to the Grolier Club
exhibition (1905), no. 24, and sold it posthumously with much of the rest of
his collection through Rosenbach in 1929 to (2) Mr. LESSING J. ROSENWALD,
who had it by 1930.

COPY F: BINDING: Mounted and framed.
    HISTORY: (1) Coloured by Blake on his deathbed in Aug. 1827, signed
'Blake 1827', and sold for £3. 13s. 6d. to Frederick Tatham (*Blake Records*
[1969] 471); (2) This was 'No doubt . . . [*the one*] in the late Mr Geo Blamire's
sale at Christie's, 9 [*i.e.* 7] Nov. 1863',[3] lot 120 (described as 2 'Drawings *in
colours*') for £5. 7s. 6d. to Holsted; (3) Acquired by J. E. Taylor, who lent it
to the Burlington Fine Arts Club exhibition (1876), no. 267, and presented it

[1] G. Keynes, *Engravings by William Blake: The Separate Plates* (1956), 25.
[2] I presume this is a mistake.
[3] W. M. Rossetti's note appears in the margin of his copy (now in Harvard) of Gilchrist's
Life (1863), i. 360.

before 1913 to the WHITWORTH INSTITUTE, Manchester, reproduced in the Tate exhibition catalogue (1947), and frequently elsewhere.

'BALLADS MANUSCRIPT'; see 'PICKERING [BALLADS] MANUSCRIPT'.

11. 'Blake's Chaucer: An Original Engraving' (1810)

BIBLIOGRAPHICAL INTRODUCTION

Copy	Collection	Correction	Contemporary Owners
A	BMPR	—	
B	*Keynes*	—	Thomas Butts
C	HARVARD	—	

TITLE: 𝕭𝖑𝖆𝖐𝖊'𝖘 𝕮𝖍𝖆𝖚𝖈𝖊𝖗: / An Original Engraving by him from his Fresco Paint- / ing of Sir Jeffery Chaucer and his Nine and Twenty / Pilgrims setting forth from Southwark on their Journey / to Canterbury. / . . . G. Smeeton, Printer, 17, St. Martin's Lane, London

COLLATION. 4°: [A1–2]; one sheet, four pages.

CONTENTS. 'Blake's Chaucer: An Original Engraving' ([A1]ʳ–[A2]ʳ); [A2]ᵛ blank.

SHEET-SIZE: 25·3 × 20·1 cm.

WATERMARK: H WILLMOTT / 1810 (B, C).

PAGE NUMBERING: Pages 2–3 are correctly numbered in round brackets in the middle of the top margin.

RUNNING TITLE: None.

CARTCHWORDS: Correct, except for 'ing's' (p. 1), which corresponds, not to the top line of p. 2 ('Cook,'), but to l. 6 of p. 2 ('[morn-]ing's draught').

ORNAMENTS: None.

PUBLICATION: Blake probably sent copies of this leaflet to his friends such as Thomas Butts in 1810,[1] as he had the flyers advertising his exhibition and *Descriptive Catalogue* (1809).

ERRATA: (1) ¶3 'Squire and' should be 'Squire's'; (2) ¶4 'Tapster' should be 'Tapiser'; (3) ¶7, 'ef'; (4) ¶8, 'horrizon'; (5) ¶9, 'end' should be 'and'; (6) ¶9, 'Leneaments'.

COPY A: BINDING: Loose, with the remains of a wafer.
    HISTORY: (1) Sold by H. H. Gilchrist with other works for £150 on 12 June 1894 to (2) The BRITISH MUSEUM PRINT ROOM.

---

[1] The watermark of 1810 gives an initial terminus, and the publication of the engraving on 8 Oct. 1810 gives a probable final terminus.

COPY B: BINDING: Loose.

HISTORY: (**1**) Acquired by Thomas Butts, presumably; (**2**) Sold for his great-grandson Anthony Bacon Drury Butts at Sotheby's, 19 Dec. 1932, lot 128, for £10. 10*s*. to Quaritch; (**3**) Acquired by *Geoffrey Keynes* and described in his catalogue (1964), no. 579.

COPY C: BINDING: Loose.

HISTORY: (**1**) Sold for $125 by G. Simons to (**2**) C. R. Richmond, who gave it on 9 May 1948 to (**3**) HARVARD.

12. 'Blake's Chaucer: The Canterbury Pilgrims' (1809)

BIBLIOGRAPHICAL INTRODUCTION

Copy	Collection	Correction	Contemporary Owner
A	BMPR	—	

TITLE: BLAKE's CHAUCER, / *THE CANTERBURY PILGRIMS.* / — / THE FRESCO PICTURE, / Representing CHAUCER's Characters, painted by / WILLIAM BLAKE, / *As it is now submitted to the Public,* / ... *May 15th*, 1809. / = / Printed by Watts & Bridgewater, South-molton-Street.

COLLATION: Broadsheet: [A1], 1 sheet.

CONTENTS: 'Blake's Chaucer: The Canterbury Pilgrims' ([A1]^r); [A1]^v blank.

SHEET-SIZE: 18·7 × 22·8 cm.

WATERMARK: 1807 (as in the *Descriptive Catalogue* [1809]).

PUBLICATION: Blake probably sent copies of this prospectus to his friends in May 1809, as he did those advertising his exhibition and *Descriptive Catalogue* (1809).

ERRATA: 'dissemminated' (¶2).

COPY A: BINDING: Loose.

HISTORY: (**1**) Sold with other works by H. H. Gilchrist for £150 on 12 June 1894 to (**2**) The BRITISH MUSEUM PRINT ROOM.

13. 'Blake's Memorandum' (?August 1803)

BIBLIOGRAPHICAL INTRODUCTION

TITLE: 'Blake's Memorandum in Refutation of the Information and Complaint of John Scholfield, a private Soldier, &c.'

COLLECTION: *UNTRACED*. A transcript, apparently by a contemporary from Blake's original, is in Trinity College, Hartford, Connecticut.

WATERMARK: '1802', with a Britannia-type crowned shield.

DATE: ?Late August 1803.

Blake's 'Refutation' was clearly prepared after the Deposition of 16 Aug. and before Blake appeared at the Quarter Sessions on 4 Oct. 1803 to answer the charge of sedition.[1] Probably Blake collected his thoughts on the evidence shortly after the Depositions were made, in late Aug. 1803, and communicated them to his lawyer (?R. Daly), who had them transcribed for his own use.

DESCRIPTION: On a folded sheet are two documents apparently collected for the use of Blake's lawyer at his trial for sedition. The manuscript consists of: 1^r 'The Information and Complaint of John Scolfield';[1] 1^v–2^v 'Blake's Memorandum'.

BINDING: The contemporary copy of 'Blake's Memorandum' is on the same sheet as the '/Copy/' (in the same hand) of John Scolfield's official 'Information and Complaint' (see *Blake Records* [1969], 124 n. 1).

HISTORY: The original of 'Blake's Memorandum' is not known to have survived; the contemporary transcript was (1) Sold with Hayley's MSS at Sotheby's, 20 May 1878, lot 34, for 12s. to Quaritch; (2) Sold posthumously for H. Buxton Forman at Anderson Galleries, 26 April 1920, lot 64, for $17; (3) Acquired by Allan R. Brown and given by him in 1941 to (4) TRINITY COLLEGE, Hartford, Connecticut.

14. *The Book of Ahania* (1795)

BIBLIOGRAPHICAL INTRODUCTION

TABLE

Copy	Plates	Leaves	Water-marks	Blake numbers	Binding-order	Leaf-size in cm	Printing colour
‡A LC	1–6^1	6	—	—	‡1–6**[2]	23·2 × 28·8	*Black*
‡Ba *Keynes*	1^1	1	—	—	Loose	23·3 × 29·6	*Colour-printed*
‡Bb YALE	2^a, 2^b, 4	3	—	—[3]	Loose[3]	10·6 × 14·5*	Grey & Brown (2^a) *Colour-printed* (2^b) Black (4)
Bc MORGAN	5	1	—	—	Loose	16·5 × 21·6	Black

‡	Coloured by Blake or his wife.
‡	Pl. 1 faces pl. 2.
**	The identifiable offsets confirm the present order.
*	The edges are trimmed and gilt.
Black	Italicized printing colours indicate colour printing.

[1] Pl. 1 (Ba) belongs with copy A, and pl. 1 (A) should properly be called pl. 1 (Ba), for their Histories are quite separate.

[2] The leaves of copy A are loose, but the offsets suggest the order.

[3] The ink numbers (13–14, 45) on pl. 2^a, 2^b, 4 in copy Bb derive from the time when these leaves were bound with the 'Order' of the *Songs*. They are now bound as pl. 2^a, 2^b, 4.

[1] *Blake Records* (1969), 122–37.

TITLE: *THE | BOOK of | AHANIA | LAMBETH | Printed by W Blake 1795*

DATE: 1795, as on the title-page.

PUBLICATION: *Ahania* seems to be a *Second Book of Urizen*. It is etched in intaglio (not in the relief-etching of most other works in Illuminated Printing), the text is two columns of italic writing, very like *The Book of Los* (1795).

The complete copy (A) must have been colour printed in 1795, and probably the odd copies of pl. 1, 2 (2 copies), 4–5 were pulled at the same time. The version of the Urizen myth in *Ahania* clearly did not hold Blake's interest in this form, for he did not list the book with his other works for sale in his letters of 9 June 1818 and 12 April 1827.

One of pl. 1–5 may have been etched on the verso of *Europe* (1794) pl. 3, and the versos of the others may have served to carry *The Book of Los* (1795), as follows:

	Ahania		*Book of Los*		*Europe*	
pl. 1:	9·8×13·6			pl. 3	13·4×9·6	
pl. 2:	9·8×13·6	pl. 3:	9·8×13·7			
pl. 3:	9·8×13·6	pl. 4:	9·9×13·7			
pl. 4:	9·9×13·5	pl. 2:	9·8×13·5			
pl. 5:	9·8×13·6	pl. 5:	9·9×13·6			
pl. 6:	10·0×13·7	pl. 1:	9·9×13·7			

Thus Blake's only two coloured works in ordinary etching may have been etched on opposite sides of the same six copperplates. Perhaps the paucity of copies of *Ahania* and *The Book of Los* is due to the fact that the six copperplates on which they were etched were lost or damaged.

COLOURING: The work was sparingly coloured in printing. There are no designs or colouring on pl. 3–5.

CATCHWORDS: Pl. 4 ('Of'), pl. 5 ('But') correct.[1]

ORDER: Pl. 1–6. The offsets, chapter numbers, and stanza numbers combine to make the plate-sequence quite clear.

VARIANTS: None.

ERRATA: None.

Pl. 1. DESIGN: A nude woman kneels between the legs of a man seated with his head on his knees and looks up at him. (A pencil sketch for this design is in the BMPR, reproduced in the 1973 facsimile.)

COLOURING: Their SKIN is pale Purple (A), her HAIR is Grey (A) or Brown (Ba), and his Grey (A) or White (Ba). The BACKGROUND is Blue (A, Ba) and Black (A) or Red (Ba), and the GROUND is mottled (Ba).

Pl. 2. DESIGN: Below the title, a floating woman in a long dress seems to be holding apart impending clouds with her outstretched hands. (A similar design is in *Urizen* [1794] pl. 13.)

---

[1] Both pl. 4 and pl. 6 begin with 'But', but the order of chapters makes the correct sequence clear.

COLOURING: Her DRESS is faint Purple (A) or uncoloured (Bb, pl. 2ᵇ) and her HAIR is Brown (Bb, pl. 2ᵇ). The top is Grey (A) or Black and Purple (Bb, pl. 2ᵇ), the right BACKGROUND is Orange (Bb, pl. 2ᵇ), by the woman is Blue (A), and the bottom Green (Bb, pl. 2ᵇ).

Pl. 3. INCIPIT: 'AHANIA / Chap: 1ˢᵗ . . .'.

Pl. 4. INCIPIT: 'Chap: II: . . .'.

Pl. 5. INCIPIT: 'Of iron, from the dismal shade . . .'.

Pl. 6. INCIPIT: 'But I wander . . .'. DESIGN: At the bottom of column two lies a huge naked bearded man among rocks with a younger man face down before him.

COLOURING: His HAIR is orangish-Brown (A), and there is a Red mark on his SHOULDER (A). To the left is Black (A).

COPY A: BINDING: (1) pl. 1 was separated from pl. 2–6, probably between 1893 and 1903; (2) Another pl. 1 is now separately mounted with copy A; pl. 2–6 were stitched into an apparently nineteenth-century paper cover— there are twenty-five stitch-marks 1·1 cm apart *around* the margins.

HISTORY: (1) Pl. 1 (the frontispiece) was separated from the others in the nineteenth century;¹ (**Ai**) Pl. 2–6 were sold by the Earl of Crewe at Sotheby's, 30 March 1903, lot 7 ('unbound'), for £103 to Quaritch; (**Aii**) They were acquired by 'W A White 20 April 1903' from the 'Earl of Crew Sale / Quaritch' (according to notes on the cover); White lent them anonymously to the exhibitions of the Grolier Club (1905), no. 29, (1919) no. 146, and the Fogg (1924) and sold them posthumously through Rosenbach on 1 May 1929 to Mr. Rosenwald; (**Bi**) A different pl. 1 was sold anonymously at Sotheby's, 11 May 1895, lot 20, for £2. 6s. to R. Ward; (**Bii**) It may be this copy of pl. 1 which was sold by Paul Carton² at Sotheby's, 11 Dec. 1935, lot 622, for £34 to Ulysses; (2) All six plates were acquired by Mr. LESSING J. ROSENWALD by 1939, who allowed pl. 2–6 to be reproduced in the Blake Trust facsimile (1973). N.B. This provenance indicates that the copy of pl. 1 now with pl. 2–6 is not the one originally associated with them.

---

¹ In 1861 Gilchrist (*Life of William Blake*, ed. R. Todd [1945], 112) did not know of the frontispiece, for he says *Ahania* 'is quite unadorned, except by two vignettes, one on the title, the other on the concluding page'. Swinburne (*William Blake* [1925], 252, 254), writing in 1866, is ambiguous, for though he says *Ahania* consists of 'six leaves', he knows of only 'two illustrations', and though one of these he calls 'the frontispiece' the design he describes is that for the title-page. In 1892 Ellis wrote that 'Lord Houghton [*later Lord Crewe*] sends me the only known copy of the book of Ahania' (I. Fletcher, 'The Ellis–Yeats–Blake Manuscript Cluster', *To Geoffrey Keynes* [1972], 111), which he had presumably inherited from his father R. M. Milnes (1809–85) and which was reproduced with all 6 plates in Ellis & Yeats (1893). Crewe's copy of pl. 1 (now called copy Ba) has been separated from the rest of the plates and another one substituted for it.

It was probably copy Bb (not copy A as in Keynes [1921] and Keynes & Wolf) which was sold at Sotheby's in 1855.

² Keynes & Wolf suggest, on the basis of evidence unknown to me, that Carton's copy 'may be the same one which was obtained from a friend of Blake by Judge Bewley'.

COPY Ba: BINDING: (1) Pl. 1 was separated from copy A,[1] probably between 1893 and 1903; (2) It is now loose.

HISTORY: (1) Sold with the Earl of Crewe's Blakes at Sotheby's, 30 March 1903, lot 18, with *Europe* pl. 1 (Keynes) and another *Europe* plate,[2] *For the Sexes* (L) pl. 3, *No Natural Religion* pl. a1, plus two photographs and the frontispiece to Burger's *Leonora* (1796) for £10 to Tregaskis; (2) Sold for E. J. Shaw at Sotheby's, 29 July 1925, lot 162, with *Songs* (G) pl. 30–1 for £55 to Keynes; (3) *Keynes* lent it to the exhibitions of the Burlington Fine Arts Club (1927), no. 85, the British Museum (1957), no. 29 1, and the National Library of Scotland (1969), no. 56, described it in his catalogue (1964), no. 521, and allowed it to be reproduced in the Blake Trust facsimile (1973).

COPY Bb: BINDING: (1) Inlaid to *c.* 23×30 cm and bound about 1853 with many leaves of Blakeana including the 'Order' of the *Songs* (see p. 337); (2) Separated after 1924, 'BOUND BY JAMES MACDONALD CO / NEW YORK CITY', evidently for G. C. Smith, Jr., in Blue levant morocco, g.e.

HISTORY: For the History, see the 'Order' of the *Songs*.

COPY Bc: BINDING: (1) Bound in contemporary rough calf with other leaves of Blakeana, including *Thel* (a) (see pp. 130–2); (2) After 1906 it was separated and mounted separately.

HISTORY: For the History, see *Thel* (a).

15

*The Book of Ahania. London, [1892].
Apparently a William Griggs facsimile.

A15

*The Book of Ahania. London, 1973. The William Blake Trust.

Geoffrey Keynes, 'Commentary and Bibliographical History', is on 5 unnumbered pages. The facsimile consists of pl. 1 (copy Ba) plus pl. 2–6 (copy A). It is not really an eclectic facsimile, however, for pl. 1 (Ba), 2–6 (A) were apparently bound together in Blake's time, and the leaves were not separated, with the Atlantic between, until much later. Copy A (pl. 1–6), as presently constituted and identified, is rather the eclectic work.

---

[1] Keynes & Wolf say that 'the stitch-holes at the right-hand border match those of copy A'.

[2] This unidentified *Europe* plate 'in drab' did not reappear in the E. J. Shaw sale at Sotheby's, 29 July 1925, with the other plates above, and I have not traced it elsewhere.

16. *The Book of Los* (1795)

BIBLIOGRAPHICAL INTRODUCTION

TABLE

Copy	Plates	Leaves	Water-marks	Blake numbers	Binding-order	Leaf-size in cm	Printing colour
♯A BMPR	1–5	5	—	—	‡1–5**	24·8 × 29·4	*Black*
B MORGAN	4	1	—	—	Loose	15·8 × 20·2	Black

    ♯   Coloured by Blake or his wife.
    ‡   Pl. 1 faces pl. 2.
    **   The identifiable offsets confirm the present order.
    Black Italicized printing colours indicate colour printing.

TITLE: *THE | BOOK of | LOS | LAMBETH | Printed by W Blake 1795*

DATE: 1795, as on the title-page.

PUBLICATION: The only draft of *The Book of Los* is a sketch for Eno on pl. 1 (in the University of Texas).

The work is clearly another form of *Urizen* (1794). The italic text was etched in 1795 in two parallel columns in intaglio, rather than in the relief-form found in most other works in Illuminated Printing. The only copy must have been colour printed in that year, and probably the extra copy of pl. 4 was pulled at the same time. Blake evidently took little interest in it,[1] for he seems to have printed only one copy, and he did not mention it in his letters of 9 June 1818 and 12 April 1827 offering his other works for sale.

COLOURING: The work was lightly colour printed in shades which have probably faded, especially the greyish-Pink flesh in pl. 1, the Brown people in pl. 2–3, 5, and the rusty sun in pl. 5. There is no design or colouring on pl. 4.

CATCHWORDS: Pl. 1 ('Dark[*ness*]'), pl. 2 ('An') correct.

ORDER: Pl. 1–5, as in the unique copy.

VARIANTS: None.

ERRATA: None.

Pl. 1. DESIGN: A woman with very long hair, a long dress, and bare feet sits on the ground with her head on her knees and her mouth open as if in distress. (A drawing for the design in the University of Texas differs chiefly in showing both hands and feet spread beside her face.)

COLOURING: Her HAIR and DRESS are Grey. The top and bottom BACKGROUND is mottled a very dark Green and Orange; the edges to right and left are Blue, as if representing sky.

---

[1] It may have been etched on the versos of the *Ahania* plates (see p. 113), and perhaps the copperplates were then lost, for *Ahania* (1795) too exists only in a unique copy.

Pl. 2. DESIGN: Between the title and the imprint is a back view of a naked man apparently squeezed within the earth. (The effect is quite different from *For Children* (1793) pl. 5, *Urizen* [1794] pl. 9–10 where the earth-men seem to be struggling against their prisons.)

COLOURING: The man's HAIR is Orange, and the ROCKS are Brown.

Pl. 3. INCIPIT: 'LOS Chap. I . . .'. DESIGN: Flourishes form an oval round 'LOS' at the top of the plate. In the 'O' sits a tiny bearded man with an open book. Spreading symmetrically downward from the 'O' is a net enmeshing a naked boy at the bottom left and a nude girl at the bottom right.

On a flourish over 'Chap' is seated a clothed figure reading a book.

COLOURING: The PEOPLE are touched with Brown and the rest of the design with Olive.

Pl. 4. INCIPIT: 'Darkness round Los . . .'.

Pl. 5. INCIPIT: 'An immense Fibrous Form . . .'. DESIGN: Below 'The End of the / Book of LOS' in the second column is a globe, over which, in the air, is a naked man kneeling with his legs spread and his arms thrown out.

COLOURING: The SUN is rust-Brown, its BACKGROUND is Green and, at the bottom left, Brown, and the MAN is Brown.

COPY A: BINDING: (1) Originally stabbed through three holes, 9·6 cm from the top, 5·1, 6·3 cm apart; (2) Bound after July 1866 at the British Museum in half Brown morocco with crowns on the spine; (3) The leaves were remounted in heavy paper 'windows' and bound in Red morocco in 1969.

HISTORY: (1) Sold by G. E. Mason of 6 Barnards Lane, Beddgelert, North Wales, on 14 June 1866 for 10s. to the BRITISH MUSEUM, where it was bound, reproduced by Ellis & Yeats (1893), and 'Transferred to the Department of Prints and Drawings, [23] June 1953 / C. B. Oldman' (according to the note on the second fly-leaf), where it was bound again in 1969.

COPY B: BINDING: (1) Bound in contemporary rough calf with other leaves of Blakeana, including *Thel* (a); (2) After 1906 it was separated and mounted.

HISTORY: For its History, see *Thel* (a) (p. 131).

17

'The Book of Los: By William Blake: 1795.' *Century Guild Hobby Horse*, v (1890), 82–9.

First printing of the poem in conventional typography, with an introduction by F. York Powell (pp. 82–4).

18. *The Book of Thel* (1789)

BIBLIOGRAPHICAL INTRODUCTION

See Table on pp. 120–1

TITLE: THE / *BOOK* / *of* / THEL / *The Author & Printer Willm. Blake. 1789.*
DATE: 1789, the date on the title-page, seems reliable.[1]
PUBLICATION: The sixteen surviving copies of *Thel* were probably coloured and sold over a period of about thirty-eight years, as follows:

Date:	1789	1790	1790–5	1796	1796–1803	*c.* 1806	1815–27
Copies:	K, R	a, C	A–B, D–E	BMPR	G–J, L	F	M–O

Copies K and R are in State I (see VARIANTS, below) and therefore must be earliest, *c.* 1789. Copies a and C are in the transitional form of State II and must be next. Copies A and E belonged to Blake's early friends Cumberland and Stothard, and copies B and D are very like them; all were probably made early. The BMPR colour prints are from the Large and Small Books of Designs of 1796. Copy L belonged to Butts, to whom Blake began selling his works in the mid 1790s, and copies G–J, printed like copy L in Green, were probably made about the same time. Copy F, also in Green, may have been printed early, but the fact that the text is coloured suggests at least that it was coloured later than the others. Copies M–O, printed in reddish-Brown, seem to have been made later, for N and O are watermarked 1815 and have coloured texts.

It was described in the Prospectus of 10 Oct. 1793 as 'The Book of Thel, a Poem in Illuminated Printing. Quarto, with 6 designs [*on pl. 2–4, 6–8*], price 3 *s*'. This very low price must be for uncoloured copies, though none has survived in this state. In his letter to Dawson Turner of 9 June 1818 Blake lists it as '6 do [Prints] Quarto [£]2. 2. o', and to George Cumberland on 12 April 1827 he offered it for £3. 3*s*. Copies were acquired by George Cumberland (A), Thomas Stothard (E), Isaac D'Israeli (F), Francis Douce (I), T. F. Dibdin (J), J. J. Garth Wilkinson (K), Thomas Butts (L), and James Vine (O, produced and bound with *Milton* [D]).

COLOURING: All complete copies are coloured, most of them lightly and delicately,[2] the earlier ones with few colours at a time. Copies G, K use a great deal of pale Orange, copy I is darker than other copies, and copy J

---

[1] It has been inconclusively suggested on the basis of symbolism (*Prophetic Writings of William Blake*, ed. D. J. Sloss & J. P. R. Wallis [1926], ii. 267–8) and the alteration in form of the letter *g* (Erdman, p. 713) that pl. 1 and 8 were etched later than pl. 2–7, 'no earlier than 1791' according to Erdman.

[2] Copy F is not very successfully coloured, especially in pl. 7–8, and copy L, which is bold and flat in colouring with solid washes, seems uncharacteristic, particularly in pl. 3–4, 6–7. Keynes & Wolf do not comment on the peculiarities of copies F and L, but they do suggest that copies D and M may have been coloured by Mrs. Blake because of an 'almost exact similarity of the colouring', which I do not see.

is brightly coloured. In copies F, H, N, O many features are clarified in ink. Copy N, which has an ink-framing-line about 0·8 cm from the plate-mark of each plate, is lovely and bold in colouring. Gold is used in copy O, along with a great deal of greyish-Blue, though most colours are pale. Copy a is uncoloured and the BMPR pulls, made for the Large and Small Books of Designs, are colour printed and were mostly masked in printing. In copies F, N, O the text is partly coloured.

Thel, who is seen on pl. 2, 4, 6–7, is uniformly dressed in most copies: Yellow (A [yellowish-Green in pl. 2], F, K [orangish-], R [greenish-]), pale Pink (B), Green (C, G), pale Purple (D [pale Blue on pl. 2], M), Raspberry (E [in pl. 2 Pink, her hair Yellow], O), reddish-Brown (L [greyish-Brown on pl. 2, reddish-Purple on pl. 7]), and Grey (BMPR pulls). The irregular colouring of Thel's dress in copies I, J, N (her cheeks rouged throughout in N) is recorded in the notes. She is never shown with the 'white veil' of l. 92.

CATCHWORDS: Correct throughout: pl. 3 ('Why'), 5 ('III'), 6 ('But'), 7 ('IV'); none on pl. 1–2, 4, 8.

ORDER: Pl. 1–8.

Pl. 2–8 are in that order in all copies and are confirmed in this arrangement by Blake's etched numbers and the catchwords. The only ambiguity is with pl. 1, 'Thel's Motto', which is missing from copy E and is numbered and bound *after* the text in copies N and O. Evidently after 1815, when copies N and O were printed, Blake decided that 'Thel's Motto' should form a postscript rather than a prelude.

VARIANTS: There are at least two States of *Thel*,[1] found in pl. 3, l. 13, the fourth from last word. In copies K and R, the etched word reads 'gently':

And gentle sleep the sleep of dea*th* and gently hear the voice

In all other copies,[2] the etched word reads 'gentle':

And gentle sleep the sleep of dea*th* and gentle hear the voice

Careful examination makes it clear that the change was made on the copperplate—the 'gently' or 'gentle' is printed, not in manuscript—so copies K and R must have been printed before or after all the others.

The fact of a change will not in itself demonstrate whether 'gently' or 'gentle' was the first reading. However, in copy a (reproduced in *Thel* [1971], 6) and copy C, the terminal letter of the crucial 'gentle' on pl. 3 shows an etched 'e' written over a 'y', indicating that 'gently' was the first reading. The hypothesis that 'gently' is the earlier reading is supported by the fact that 'gentle' is found in the late copies N–O bearing watermarks of 1815. State 1, then, is identified by 'gently' and State 2 by 'gentle'.

Another change was effected on pl. 8, where ll. 121–2 were deleted in copies I and J. These erasures seem to have been made on the paper rather

---

[1] As Miss Nancy Bogen points out in her edition of *Thel* (1971), 3–9.
[2] My evidence for copy H derives from Miss Bogen's *Thel* (1971).

TABLE

Copy	Plates	Leaves	Watermark	Blake numbers[1]	Binding-order	Leaf-size in cm	Printing colour
#A Anon.	1–8	8	—	—	*1–8***[2]	18·2×26·5	golden-Brown
#B *Mellon*	1–8	8	—	—	1–8**	23·1×22·8*	Brown
#C MORGAN	1–8	8	—	—	1–8	22·0×28·3*	dull Brown
#D BMPR	1–8	8	—	—	1–8**	21·2×28·8*	golden-Brown
#E YALE	2–8	7	—	—	2–8	24·0×30·0	golden-Brown
#F LC	1–8	8	I TAYLOR (5); 1794 (7)	—	*1–8***[2]	26·9×37·1	golden-Brown
#G FITZWILLIAM	1–8	8	—	—	1–8	23·6×30·0*	greenish-Blue[3]
#H LC	1–8	8	—	—	1–8**	23·5×30·7	Green
#I BODLEY	1–8	8	—	—	*1–8***	23·4×29·3	Green
#J HARVARD	1–8	8	—	—	*1–8***	23·2×29·6*[4]	Green
#K YALE	1–8	8	—	—	1–8**	23·0×29·5	Green
#L HUNTINGTON	1–8	8	—	—	1–8**	23·9×30·3*	Green
#M NYP	1–8	8	—	—	1–8**	23·6×30·0	reddish-Brown (dark Orange)

Copy	Plates		Watermark		Binding order	Measurements	Colour
#N CINCINNATI	1–8	8	RUSE & TURNERS/1815 (6, 8)	2, 6–8 (on 3, 7–8, 1)	2–8, 1	23·0 × 28·0*	reddish-Brown (Orange)
#O LC	1–8	8	RUSE & TURNERS/1815 (3, 8)	—[5]	2–8, 1	21·0 × 27·8*[6]	reddish-Brown (near golden-Brown)
P,[7] Q[7]							
#R *Mellon* a	1–8	8	—	—	1–8	24·0 × 30·4	Brown
MORGAN	2–5, 7	5	J Whatman (2)	—	Loose	17·0 × 24·1 (2) 10·3 × 25·0 (3) 23·8 × 30·0 (4) 24·1 × 30·2 (5) 14·8 × 19·4 (7)	Black
#BMPR	2, 4, 6–7	4	*invisible*	—		19·0 × 26·0	*Colour-printed*
SAN FRANCISCO PUBLIC LIBRARY	2, 6	2			Loose	22·5 × 29·2 (2) 12·2 × 17·1 (6)	Black

\# Coloured by Blake or by his wife (not counting Grey washes).
** The identifiable offsets confirm this order.
* The edges are trimmed and gilt; in other copies, the edges are uneven.
1–8 Italicized binding-order numbers were so bound before 1835.

1 There are etched numbers (1–6) at the top right corners of pl. 3–8, though the colouring has obscured the number 1 in all copies but B; the 2 in F; the 3 in D, F; the 4 in F–G, L, N; the 5 in N; and the 6 in F, N.
2 The plates in copies A and F are loose, but the order is given by the offsets plus the printed numbers.
3 In copy G, pl. 1–3 are more Green than Blue.
4 In copy J, only the top edge is trimmed and gilt.
5 Copy O is numbered in ink over the same thing in pencil (like

Milton [D] with which it is bound): 1–8 on pl. 2–8, 1. Since in general pencil numbers seem to lack authority, it is reasonable to assume that these numbers are not by Blake even though confirmed in ink.
6 The edges of copy O are marbled (according to Keynes & Wolf; when I saw them, the leaves were so mounted as to make the edges invisible).
7 Copies P and Q were described as 8 plates on 8 leaves, coloured and sewn (Q uncut), in the Sotheby catalogues of 2 July 1895 (lot 502) and 24 Feb. 1897 (lot 806). They may well be the same as copies G or H.

than on the copperplate;[1] the paper is demonstrably roughened by erasure, and flying figures and scrolls (in I) or birds (in J) have been drawn over the erasures. Since these changes were made after the plates were printed, they do not constitute a State in the ordinary bibliographical sense and will tell us nothing clearly about when the copies showing the change were printed. The erasures were probably made to suppress the explicit erotic references:

> Why a tender curb upon the youthful burning boy!
> Why a little curtain of flesh on the bed of our desire?

The excisions in copies I and J may have been made at any time to please prudish patrons, perhaps Francis Douce and T. F. Dibdin who owned them; other copies may have been printed later with these two lines still standing.

The only significant colouring variants are the water added in some copies to pl. 6–7, creating islands, the frequent clouds added in later copies, and the trees added regularly in copy O.

ERRATA: In l. 29, 'o'erfired' may be an error for 'o'ertired'.

Pl. 1. INCIPIT: 'Thel's Motto . . .'.
  COLOURING: None (A, G–M); the title is touched with Red (B, C), Blue (C), and Green (D, R); the whole page is Blue (N), or the corners are touched with Grey and Blue (O).
  VARIANTS: The words are surrounded by a vine (F).

Pl. 2. DESIGN: A willow overarches the title and the design beneath it. At the left, Thel with her shepherdess crook looks at a tiny nude man who is emerging from a blossom and reaching towards a tiny clothed woman with raised arms by another blossom. Above them, between 'BOOK' and 'THEL', are two flying birds and a flying man. On the italicized letters in '*BOOK of THEL*' are tiny figures.
  COLOURING: THEL'S DRESS is rose-Pink (I), Green (J), uncoloured (N). The SMALL WOMAN'S DRESS is Pink (A, B [pale], E, K), Blue (C, R [skirt only]), Green (D [pale], F, H, and I [pale], L [yellowish-]), Yellow (G, J, BMPR pull), and uncoloured (M–O). The SKY is also touched with pale Orange (G, J [Gold]), Peach (K, L), Pink (G, J [Raspberry], N, O), Yellow (J, L), Grey (N), Purple (R), Black and Magenta (BMPR pull). The BLOSSOMS are Red (A, F, J, K, N [dark,] O, R), orangish-Brown (B), Yellow (C, G), pale Pink (D), Raspberry (G), dark Blue (E), dark Purple outlined in Red (I), reddish-Brown (L, BMPR pull), dull Green (M [two]), Brown (M [one plant]). The TITLE is Yellow (B, H [bright], N), Pink (C), Blue (D), Green (M), and Gold (O). The flying BIRDS are, from left to right, Blue and Yellow (C), Red and Red-and-Green (F), Blue and Red (K), and greyish-Blue (O).

---

[1] Despite the roughened paper, Miss Bogen (ed. *Thel* [1971], 5) believes that the changes found in copies I and J were made on the copperplates and simply confirmed on the paper. She therefore concludes that copies I and J constitute State III. I read the evidence differently, and other facts, such as watermarks and colouring of the text, make it difficult for me to believe that I–J are the last copies printed.

The MAN in the 'B' is Red (C). All the upper people are greyish-Blue save the angel on the 'L' who is Pink (O). The LEAVES of the flowering plant are Yellow (J).

VARIANTS: Thel's right foot is Green (H), perhaps accidentally. In the BMPR pull, the irrelevant title and imprint have disappeared, covered by a cloud, and the branches of the trees to the right are gone.

Pl. 3. INCIPIT: 'Thel / I / The daughters of Mne Seraphim...'. DESIGN: Five flying figures surrounding the title 'THEL' seem scarcely related to each other. Below the 'T', a naked man reclining on a plant looks up towards a woman in a long dress who is holding before her face a flying child. Over the 'T' a naked man is pointing towards an eagle, while below and after the 'L' we see the back of a naked man with a round shield on his left arm and a sword in his right hand.

COLOURING: The TITLE is Green (C [dark], R). The WOMAN'S DRESS is Red (C), Pink (A, D, H), uncoloured (E), Green (F [light], I [dull], L and N [yellowish-], M [pale], R), pale Orange (G), Blue (J), Brown (K), and Grey (O). The SKY is also touched with Purple (A–C, H, K, R), Yellow (B, G, I–L, N, O, R), Red (C, L), Pink (D, G, I, J [Raspberry], M–O, R), Orange (H [bright], K [pale]), and Brown (N), often vivid. The SHIELD is Brown (C) and Yellow (J), the men and child are Brown (J), the BIRD is Gold (K), pale Green (M), and Yellow (N).

VARIANTS: *State I*: l. 13 '. . . and gently hear the voice' (copies K, R).

State II: l. 13 'and gentle hear the voice' (copies A–J, L–O).

In copy C, the men at the left seem to be wearing pink tights; their heads and hands are uncoloured. In copy F, there are Grey and Pink clouds to the right (as there are in M), willows in the margins, and grass at the bottom. In copy O, there is Brown ground at the bottom, and a tree growing up the left margin produces a branch on which the first man lies.

Pl. 4. INCIPIT: 'Why should the mistress . . .'. DESIGN: Under the branches of a birch-tree which stands at the right, Thel regards a small lilly woman in a very long dress who emerges from the grass and bows towards her.

COLOURING: THEL'S DRESS is Brown (I), Yellow (J), and Pink (N). The LILLY WOMAN is uncoloured (A–G, K–M, O, R), White (H–J), and Grey (N, BMPR pull). The SKY is also touched with Pink (C [Raspberry], N, O), pale Orange (G, H [bright], L), Purple (H, K, R), Yellow (I, J, L–O), Green (K), Red (L, BMPR pull). The BLOSSOMS are Red (C) and Blue (D [pale], R), and the TREE a ghostly Blue (F).

VARIANTS: Clouds are regularly added in later copies. The tree is extended up the right margin in O.

Pl. 5. INCIPIT: 'II. / O little Cloud . . .'. DESIGN: At the top left and bottom right corners of the page small branches reach across the text.

COLOURING: Copies A, M are uncoloured; besides the frequent Blue, there are streaks of Yellow (B, J, N, O, R), Pink (O, J [Raspberry], N, O), Peach (K), Purple (K, R), and Grey (C [bluish-], N).

VARIANTS: Green grass at the top and bottom of copy F obscures the numbers.

Pl. 6. INCIPIT: 'III. / Then Thel astonish'd . . .'. DESIGN: Above the text, Thel stands with outstretched arms looking down left at a baby in the grass, while above her a naked man trailing a long robe flies away from her. The trunk of a birch-tree is visible to her right.

COLOURING: THEL'S DRESS is dark Pink (I), Green (J), and Grey (N). The cloud MAN'S ROBE is uncoloured (A, F, I, K, O), Yellow (C [brownish-], L), Blue (D, G, R), pale Green (E, F), Raspberry (M), and Grey (N). The SKY is also touched with Pink (A, D, J [Raspberry], K, N, O), bluish-Purple (B, C, R), Brown (C [pale], F), Peach (E), pale Green (F), Grey (I), Yellow (F, I, L [mustard-], M–O, R), Black (J), and Orange (BMPR pull). The TREE is pale Green (F) and the bottom of the design pale Yellow (B, N). The hair of all the people is brownish-Orange (L).

VARIANTS: Clouds are regularly water-coloured in (e.g. in H [Yellow], I, N [dark Brown]). A branch is added at waist-level and water to the left, brownish-Green ground is added below the text in F, the tree is obscured in I, and in O Thel is seen in full profile (as she is in the BMPR pull) looking down, the tree continues up to the top right margin, and roots at the bottom right cover the printed catchword.

Pl. 7. INCIPIT: 'But he that loves the lowly . . .'. DESIGN: Below the text (but above the catchword) Thel sits with her head bowed and her arms crossed on her knees, while before her a nude adolescent(?) child plays with a naked baby. Behind them are three very large plants, the two at the right bearing blossoms.

COLOURING: THEL'S DRESS is greyish-Purple (I), Raspberry (J), and yellowish-Green (N). The FLOWERS are Blue (A, D [the right one], F, K, O [dull], R), Pink (C, D [the left one], G, M), Purple (F [pale], L [greyish-], N), Red (H, I [brownish-], J [Raspberry], N), and yellowish-Brown (BMPR pull). The SKY is at least partly Yellow (A, B, F, H, J, K [pale Orange], L, N [strong], O), Pink (F, O, BMPR pull), Purple (H, I, R), Brown (L), Orange (L), Peach (L). The bottom is bluish- or greyish-Black (B, F), and Yellow and Pink (O). The text is Grey in N. The hair is all brownish-Grey (E), and in L the child's hair is Yellow.

VARIANTS: A cloud is added in H. Water surrounding the grass seems to make it an island in a swamp in copies I, N, O, BMPR pull, and grass is visible on our side of the water in N. Thel's face is clearly visible in N and O, and mountains are visible in the left background in O and the BMPR pull.

Pl. 8. INCIPIT: 'IV. / The eternal gates . . .'. DESIGN: At the foot of the page, after the last line of the text and almost engulfing 'The End', the design represents a bridled, open-mouthed serpent with a forked tongue and looping tail carrying three naked children left across the grass. (The design is almost exactly repeated, reversed, in *America* [1793] pl. 13.) The first child, a girl, holds the bridle, while the second grasps the hand of the smallest one. At the top left corner of the text is a branch.

COLOURING: The SERPENT is uncoloured (A, E, K), Green (B, D [the head Blue], J [the head Pink], R), Yellow and Brown (C, N), spotted with Black, Green, and Yellow (F), Yellow and Green scales (H), mottled Red and Green (I), Brown and Green (L), mottled Red and Brown (O); his head is Pink (G) and Green (M). The SKY is greyish-Purple (C, R), brownish-Green (F), Raspberry (J), Yellow (J, K [pale Orange], O), Pink (O). The GIRL is clothed in purplish-Pink (H). The leaf by 'The End' is Blue (H) and 'The End' is Green (B). In D the GRASS is Blue, and in N Green and Purple. The TEXT is Grey, Purple, Yellow, and Blue in N.

VARIANTS: Scroll-work and flying figures (like those in *Jerusalem*) in I and Pink water-colour in J half-heartedly cover the ineffective erasure of ll. 121–2. A tree is added in front of the serpent in O.

COPY A: BINDING: (1) Bound, probably for William Beckford shortly after 1835, in half calf labelled on the spine 'Blake's Work' (this binding is now with *Urizen* [F]) in front of *Urizen* (F)[1] and *Marriage* (A); (2) All three works were disbound probably for the 1891 Boston exhibition—the leaves are now loose.

HISTORY: (1) Sold with *Job* and '[*For Children: The*] Gates of Paradise' (C) among George Cumberland's Collection at Christie's, 6 May 1835, lot 61, for £3. 13s. 6d. to W. Bohn (a note with the detached cover [see *Urizen* (F), p. 181] says 'Cumberland sale / H. G. [?Bohn]'); (2) Numbered by William Beckford ('N.° 4029', see *Urizen* [F]) and sold posthumously with his library at Sotheby's, 29 Nov. 1883, lot 764 (bound with *Urizen* [F] and *Marriage* [A]) for £121 to Quaritch; (3) Quaritch inserted his Beckford sale book-plate and offered it in his Rough List No. 67 (Jan. 1884), lot 70, for £150; (4) Acquired by E. W. Hooper, who lent them to the Boston exhibition (1891), no. 273 (disbound); *Thel* went before 1921 to his daughter (5) Mrs. John Briggs Potter, who lent it to the exhibitions of the Fogg Museum (1924, 1930) and Philadelphia (1939), no. 22, and gave it to her daughter (6) Mrs. John Butler Swann, who deposited it on 1 July 1941 in Harvard, recovered it in 1971, and sold it to (7) H. P. Kraus, who was apparently the anonymous vendor who sold it at Parke-Bernet Galleries on 19 Oct. 1971, lot 343, for $21,000 through Warren Howell to (8) An *Anonymous* Collector.

COPY B: BINDING: (1) It was unbound in 1903; (2) Bound in '1904' by Douglas Cockerell (whose monogram is on the cover) in Green morocco, g.e.

HISTORY: (1) Probably acquired by R. M. Milnes and reproduced by Ellis & Yeats (1893); it was sold by Milnes's son the Earl of Crewe at Sotheby's, 30 March 1903, lot 2 ('unbound')[2] for £77 to Edwards; (2) Bound in 1904, acquired by Algernon Methuen, lent by him to the exhibition of the National Gallery (1913), no. 89, and by Lady Methuen to that of the Burlington Fine Arts Club (1927), no. 73, and sold for Algernon Methuen at Sotheby's,

---

[1] There is an offset of *Urizen* pl. 1 on the verso of *Thel* pl. 8.

[2] Most of the Blake works in the Crewe sale were, like *Thel* (B), unbound—*Visions* (M), *America* (M), *Europe* (C), *Urizen* (G), *Ahania* (A), *Song of Los* (E), *The Ghost of Abel* (A), *On Homer* (A)—suggesting that they were in original wrappers (like *Innocence* [E]) and were perhaps acquired from a contemporary of Blake's. The other works in the sale were either bound for Milnes (*No Natural Religion* [B], *Marriage* [F], *Jerusalem* [I]), or had apparently been previously bound (*Songs* [V]).

19 Feb. 1936, lot 501, for £420 to Quaritch for (3) Philip Hofer (see *Visions* [M], p. 476), who lent it to the Philadelphia exhibition (1939), no. 23; (4) Acquired by Mr. *Paul Mellon*.

COPY C: BINDING: 'BOUND BY RIVIERE' in Red crushed levant morocco, g.e.

HISTORY: (1) Apparently sold from an unknown '106 Cat June 30 1877' (according to the note on the first fly-leaf); (2) Acquired by Thomas Gaisford, who added his book-plate and sold it at Sotheby's, 23 April 1890, lot 185, for £29 to Quaritch, for whom it was described as 'Collated & Perfect / Ap! 24th 1890 / J. T'; (3) Acquired by 'W. A. White / 20 March 1891' (according to his note on the first fly-leaf), who lent it to the exhibition of the Grolier Club (1905), no. 10 (anonymously), perhaps to that of (1919), no. 51, and the Fogg (1924); after his death it was sold (according to Keynes & Wolf) to (4) John W. Frothingham, whose daughter [Elizabeth W. Frothingham] gave it [in 1940] (according to the undated note with it) to W. A. White's daughter (5) Mrs. William Emerson, who sold it posthumously at Sotheby's, 19 May 1958, lot 1, for £1,900 to Fleming; (6) Acquired by Mrs. Landon K. Thorne, who lent it to the Princeton exhibition (1969), no. 26, in whose catalogue (1971) it was described (no. 3), and who gave it in February 1972 to (7) The PIERPONT MORGAN LIBRARY.

COPY D: BINDING: (1) Bound, probably after Feb. 1856 in the British Museum, in half Green morocco, g.e.; (2) The leaves were remounted in heavy paper 'windows' and bound in Red morocco in 1969.

HISTORY: (1) This may be the copy sold by 'Sotheby, [?Dec.] 1854, 3*l* 2*s*';[1] it could alternatively be copies E, G, H, J, or M; (2) Sold by Messrs. Evans with *Songs* (T), *America* (H), *Song of Los* (A), and the Large (A) and Small Books of Designs (A) on 9 Feb. 1856 to (3) The BRITISH MUSEUM PRINT ROOM, where it was probably bound and used for the Pearson (1876) and Muir (1884) facsimiles.

COPY E: BINDING: (1) Originally stabbed with two fly-leaves through four holes 5·6, 6·5, and 6·4 cm apart; it was still 'sewed' in 1918, but (2) Now the plates are loose.

HISTORY: (1) This was 'Stothard's Copy'[2] (according to the note on the first fly-leaf); (2) Another erased pencil note on the fly-leaf reads: 'Bot[?] of [?] Hamilton[?] 1853' (see *Innocence* [A], p. 404); perhaps the buyer was Alexander Gilchrist, whose widow lent a copy to the Boston exhibition (1880), no. 43; (3) Sold anonymously (by Sir Robert Comyn, according to Keynes [1921]) at Sotheby's, 17 March 1893, lot 1811, for £14. 10*s*. to Robson; (4) Acquired by T. J. Wise and resold by him in 1899 (according to Keynes & Wolf); (5) Acquired by H. V. Jones, who added his book-plate, and sold it at Anderson Galleries, 2 Dec. 1918, lot 182, for $79 to Rosenbach; (6) Acquired before 1921 by A. E. Newton, who added his book-plate, lent it to the

---

[1] According to W. T. Lowndes, *The Bibliographer's Manual of English Literature* (1857), i. 215—see also *Marriage* (I), *Songs* (P), and *Jerusalem* (D), pp. 300, 419, 259.

[2] The 'marks of a painter's oily fingers' which Gilchrist ([1863], i. 78) reported are scarcely visible, but the copy is very battered.

exhibition in the Fogg (1924) and Philadelphia (1939), no. 26, and sold it posthumously at Parke-Bernet, 16 April 1941, lot 128, for $1,500, to Stonehill; (7) Acquired by Chauncey Brewster Tinker, who added his book-plate, for whom it was described in his catalogue (1959), no. 271, and who bequeathed it at his death in March 1963 to (8) YALE.

COPY F: BINDING: (1–2) Twice stabbed through three pairs of holes about 7 cm apart, perhaps to the old half Red morocco boards still with the plates, but (3) Now loose. (At one time the plates were mounted with paper labels at the margins.)

    HISTORY: (1) Probably acquired by Isaac D'Israeli (see *Europe* [A], p. 156); (2) Sold posthumously with the Library of his son the Earl of Beaconsfield at Sotheby's, 20 March 1882, lot 59, for £20 to Ellis & White; (3) Offered in Ellis & White Catalogue 50 (?Nov. 1882), lot 80, for £42; (4) Acquired by B. B. Macgeorge, described in his library catalogues (1892, 1906), lent to the exhibitions in the National Gallery (1913), no. 88, Manchester (1914), no. 157, Nottingham (1914), no. 123, the National Gallery of Scotland (1914), Case B, no. 3, and sold with his Library at Sotheby's, 1 July 1924, lot 110, for £290 to Quaritch; (5) Offered in Quaritch Catalogue 388 (Oct. 1924), lot 323, for £375; (6) Acquired by George C. Smith, Jr., listed in his anonymous catalogue (1927), no. 3, lent to the Fogg exhibition (1930), and sold with his Collection at Parke-Bernet, 2 Nov. 1938, lot 14, for $2,200 to Rosenbach for (7) Mr. LESSING J. ROSENWALD.

COPY G: BINDING: (1) Evidently only sewn in 1895; (2) Perhaps in that year it was bound for Ellis & Elvey by 'Lloyd & Wallis' in Green morocco 'super extra', but not yet trimmed; (3) Thereafter the edges were trimmed and gilt.

    HISTORY: (1) Perhaps this is the copy (P in Keynes & Wolf) sold anonymously at Sotheby's, 2 July 1895, lot 502 (8 coloured quarto leaves, sewn), for £14 to Ellis and (2) Offered in Ellis & Elvey Catalogues 81 and 82 (both ?1895), lot 50 in both (8 coloured plates, rough edges, Olive morocco super extra), for £31. 10s.; (3) Acquired by Charles Fairfax Murray (who had the edges gilt if nos. 1–2 above are accurate), who inserted his bookplate, had it described in his library catalogue (1899), and, according to another book-plate, gave it in July 1912 to (4) The FITZWILLIAM MUSEUM; reproduced in colour microfilm by Micro Methods Ltd.

COPY H: BINDING: (1) Evidently only sewn in 1897; (2) Bound (by Riviere, according to the 1905 catalogue) in Blue morocco by 1905.

    HISTORY: (1) Perhaps this is the copy (Q in Keynes & Wolf) sold anonymously at Sotheby's, 24 Feb. 1897, lot 806 (8 coloured leaves, uncut and sewn), for £18. 5s. to Gerrard; (2) Bound by Riviere and sold by 'a Gentleman' (F. P. Osmaston—see *Marriage* [F], p. 299) at Sotheby's, 3 June 1905, lot 772, for £67 to Dobell; (3) 'Mr Dobell believes that he sold it to another bookseller. It was bought from Tregaskis in 1906' (according to Keynes [1921]) by (4) Greville Matheson MacDonald, who added his book-plate, lent it to the exhibitions in Manchester (1914), no. 150, Nottingham (1914), no. 115, the National Gallery of Scotland (1914), Case A, no. 10, and sold it (according to Keynes [1921]) in March 1920 to Francis Edwards; (5) Sold anonymously at Anderson's, 21 May 1923, lot 10B (not lot 108 as in Keynes & Wolf), for $1,025 to Drake; (6) Acquired by Major W. Van R. Whitall, who added his book-plate and sold it at American Art Association, 14 Feb. 1927, lot 111, for $5,000 to Rosenbach for (7) Mr. LESSING J. ROSENWALD.

COPY I: BINDING: Bound by 1834 in half Brown calf over marbled boards with 'The Book of Thel' gilt sideways on the spine.

  HISTORY: (1) Acquired by Francis Douce, who added his book-plate and bequeathed it in 1834 to (2) The BODLEIAN LIBRARY, which listed it in the Douce Catalogue (1840), 32.

COPY J: BINDING: (1) Originally stabbed through three holes, 9·3 cm from the top and 6·0, 6·0 cm apart;[1] (2) It was interleaved with tissue paper watermarked J WHATMAN / 1811 and bound (by [John] Hering according to the 1880 and 1896 catalogues), probably for T. F. Dibdin (1776–1847) not long after 1816 (the third fly-leaf is watermarked 'S S / 1816') with *Visions* (G) in old straight grain Brown[2] morocco, t.e.g., the spine gilt with 'Book / of / Thel / By / Blake / 1789'.

  HISTORY: (1) Evidently acquired by Thomas Dibdin (1776–1847), who wrote 'very curious and extra rare T D' on the first fly-leaf; it was probably Dibdin who had it bound with *Visions* (G) after 1816; (2) Sold by George Smith at Christie's, 1 April 1880, lot 165, for £85 to Sotheran; (3) Offered by Sotheran at £105;[3] (4) Acquired by Quaritch, lent in 1887 to Muir for his facsimile (1920), and offered (1887), lot 13,845, for £85, and in his Catalogue 157 (March 1896), lot 36, for £85 again; (5) Bought 'about 1900 from Quaritch' (according to Keynes [1921]) by Amy Lowell, who added her book-plate, and bequeathed it in 1925 to (6) HARVARD.

COPY K: BINDING: (1) Originally stabbed through three holes, 7·5 and 8·1 cm apart; (2) Bound about 1885 in half Maroon morocco.

  HISTORY: (1) *Thel* (K) was evidently among 'the Designs, etc., of Blake's' which, according to his letter of 17 July 1839, Garth Wilkinson 'received . . . from Mr Clarke' (C. J. Wilkinson, *James John Garth Wilkinson* [1911], 30) and inherited from Wilkinson by his daughter (2) Mrs. M. J. Mathews, for whom it was sold posthumously at Christie's, 9 April 1945, lot 28, for £540 to Quaritch; (3) Offered for £700 by Quaritch in Catalogue 633 (Nov. 1945),

---

  [1] *Visions* (G) now has no stab holes, but it may have been stabbed with *Thel* (J), for *Visions* pl. 1 has left an offset on the verso of *Thel* pl. 8, though not on the tissue paper which is now between them.

  [2] The 1880 catalogue describes it as Blue morocco extra, g.e.; the 1896 catalogue calls it Olive morocco extra, g.e.; Keynes (1921) and Keynes & Wolf call it 'olive morocco', but the colour is now Brown. Dibdin had an interview with Blake about 1816 (*Blake Records* [1969], 242–3).

  [3] The 1880 catalogue describes it as bound 'by HERING' in blue morocco extra, g.e.; the 1896 catalogue says it is bound by Hering in Olive morocco extra, g.e.; Keynes & Wolf call it 'olive morocco', but the colour is now simply Brown.

  The 1887, 1896, and Keynes & Wolf catalogues agree erroneously that it was sold at Christie's in 1881; the two former specify, however, that it was bought then for £85 by a dealer [Sotheran] who later offered it for £105, so there can be no doubt that all three catalogues are describing the same work. The second fly-leaf is inscribed '£85'.

lot 13, Catalogue 638 (?May 1946), lot 648, One Hundredth Anniversary Catalogue (1947), lot 30, Catalogue 679 (1949), lot 122, Catalogue 678 (1951), lot 35; (3) Acquired by Mr. Paul Mellon and given by him in April 1951 to (4) YALE.

COPY L: BINDING: (1) Originally stabbed through three holes, about 5·2 cm from the top, and 10·6, 9·7 cm apart; (2) 'BOUND BY F. BEDFORD', probably for Frederick Locker, in Green levant morocco, g.e.

HISTORY: (1) Sold anonymously with the Collection of Thomas Butts (see *Songs* [E], p. 414) at Sotheby's, 26 March 1852, lot 51, for £2. 15*s*. to F. T. P.; (2) Acquired by 'F. T. Palgrave 1852', who wrote his name and the date on pl. 1; (3) Acquired by Frederick Locker, who was 'indebted to Mr Francis Palgrave for this volume' (according to his catalogue [1886]), and who added his book-plate, probably had it rebound by Bedford (see *Songs* [E]); and lent it to the Burlington Fine Arts Club exhibition (1876), no. 316; (4) Sold by Dodd, Mead and Co. in 1905 (see 'Pickering MS', p. 341) to E. D. Church; (5) Sold by Rosenbach (according to the receipt now with the volume) to the HUNTINGTON LIBRARY.

COPY M: BINDING: (1) Originally stabbed through three holes, 6·5 cm from the top, 8·6 and 7·6 cm apart; (2) Bound by Roger 'DE COVERLY', probably in the 1920s, in half Green morocco.

HISTORY: (1) Evidently once owned by 'Euphrasia Fanny (Haworth [?or Hanrott])', who wrote the first two names in ink and the last in pencil on pl. 1; (2) Apparently acquired by 'J Frederick Hall. 1873', who wrote his name and the date on the first fly-leaf; it was rebound, probably in the 1920s, and sold with the Arnold Hall Library at Sotheby's, 30 June 1927, lot 234 (as a 'facsimile reprint', in its present binding), for £4. 10*s*. to Rimell; (3) Offered by Rimell with *Visions* (K) and *America* (L) in 1927 for £1,600 (according to Keynes & Wolf); (4) Acquired by Owen D. Young, who lent it to the Fogg exhibition (1930) and gave it with Dr. A. A. Berg on 5 May 1941 to (5) The Berg Collection of the NEW YORK PUBLIC LIBRARY (see *America* [L], p. 104), where it was reproduced (1971).

COPY N: BINDING: (1) Bound with *Marriage* (G) and *Visions* (P);[1] (2 Rebound alone for Robson & Kerslake in 1890 in Red straight grain morocco, g.e.; each plate is outlined in Red ink about 0·8 cm from the platemark, as in *Marriage* (G) and *Visions* (P).

HISTORY: (1) Bound with *Marriage* (G) and *Visions* (P) and sold anonymously at Sotheby's, 17 Feb. 1890, lot 301, for £121 to Robson; (2) Robson & Kerslake had *Thel* rebound by Riviere, put their ticket on the back endpaper, and offered it (£32) and *Marriage* (£63) in a letter of 25 March 1890 (now with *Thel*) to (3) Alexander Mackay, who bought both, and whose widow sold *Thel* posthumously at Christie's, 26 April 1921, lot 1, for £205 to Shoebridge; (4) Acquired by Mr. John J. Emery, who signed the first endpaper, lent it to the Philadelphia exhibition (1939), no. 28, and gave it in 1969 to (5) The CINCINNATI ART MUSEUM.

[1] The three works were probably produced together, for they are printed in the same colour ink on paper with the same watermark and each has the plates outlined in ink.

COPY O: BINDING: (1) Originally stabbed through six holes about 4·6 cm from the top and 4·1, 3·9, 4·5, 4·5, 4·5 cm apart with *Milton* (D); (2) Stitched by 1838 with *Milton* (D) through twelve holes in old half russia, the edges marbled probably for James Vine, whose *Jerusalem* (J) and *Songs* (V) are in similar bindings; (3–4) Evidently disbound and rebound about 1930, again disbound about 1963 and rebound as before about 1967.

HISTORY: (1) Bound with *Milton* (D) and '*exquisitely finished in colours by Blake himself* . . . expressly for his principal patron Mr. Vine of the Isle of Wight' (d. 1837) for whom it was sold posthumously at Christie's, 24 April 1838, lot 297, '*h.b.*' (half bound), for £5. 12s. 6d. to H. Bohn;[1] (2) Offered by Henry G. Bohn (1841), lot 178 (no price) and (1847), £10. 10s.; (3) For a time it was 'in the library of the late B. G. Windus' (according to the 1923 catalogue below), from whom it was apparently inherited by (4) The Revd. G. P. de Putron (the grandson of B. G. Windus, according to Keynes & Wolf), after whose death it was sold at Sotheby's, 11 Dec. 1923, lot 252, for £3,400 to Pickering; (5) Acquired by Frank Bemis, who added his book-plate dated 1925, lent it (evidently disbound) to the Fogg Museum (1930, *Milton* only) and, anonymously, to the Philalelphia exhibition (1939), nos. 29 and 112; it was sold after his death through Rosenbach on 18 Sept. 1939 to (6) Mr. LESSING J. ROSENWALD, who had it disbound about 1963 for the Blake Trust facsimiles of *Thel* (1965) and *Milton* (1967), and rebound as before about 1967.

COPY P: HISTORY: Perhaps to be identified with copy G.

COPY Q: HISTORY: Perhaps to be identified with copy H.

COPY R: BINDING: (1) Originally stabbed through five holes in contemporary heavy Grey paper wrappers (which accompany the plates); (2) The plates were separated, evidently after 1953, and are now loose.

HISTORY: (1) Sold by H. A. Mair at Puttick & Simpson's, 19 Nov. 1900, lot 339, for £46 to Quaritch; (2) Probably acquired then by Marsden J. Perry (see *Visions* [H], p. 475), sold posthumously with his Library at American Art Association–Anderson Galleries, 11 March 1936, lot 37, for $2,000 to Drake; (3) 'Sold by Drake to a private collector, and in 1952 repurchased by them' (according to Keynes & Wolf); (4) Acquired by Hannah D. Rabinowitz, who put her book-plate on the slipcase, and sold it through Stonehill (according to Mr. R. J. Barry, Jr., of that firm) to (5) Mr. *Paul Mellon*, who lent it to the exhibitions at Cornell (1965, no. 4) and Winnipeg (1965).

COPY a: BINDING: (1) Bound in contemporary rough calf with other leaves of Blakeana (see the History); (2) After 1906 the plates were separated and are now loose.

HISTORY: (1) Bound in contemporary rough calf[2] with:

---

[1] According to the 1847 Bohn catalogue below (not in that of 1841). Blake went with John Linnell 'To Mr Vine's' on 8 April 1822 (*Blake Records* [1969], 275). Vine is not known to have owned other Blake works, besides *Job* (O), *Thel* (O), *Milton* (D), *Songs* (V), and *Jerusalem* (J).

[2] The 1905 and 1906 descriptions specify that it was in a binding 'contemporary with Blake'; the 1902 description says the plates are 'inserted in a scrap book'.

(1–2) *Thel* (a) pl. 2–3
(3) *Urizen* (I) pl. 4
(4) *For the Sexes* (J) pl. 7
(5–7) *Songs* (n) pl. 47, 44, 37
(8–10) *Europe* (b) pl. [11, 17], [9, 17], [16–17]
(11) *Songs* (n) pl. b
(12) *Europe* (b) pl. [2, *Jerusalem* pl. 74]
(13) *America* pl. 4
(14–15) *Europe* (b) pl. [4–5], [4, 9]
(16) *Jerusalem* pl. 28
(17) *Europe* (b) pl. 15
(18) *Jerusalem* pl. 56
(19) *Book of Los* (B) pl. 4
(20) *Ahania* (Bc) pl. 5
(21) *No Natural Religion* pl. a2
(22) *On Homer* (F)
(23) *Thel* (a) pl. 7
(24) 4 Virgil plates
(25–6) *Thel* (a) pl. 4–5
(27) *Jerusalem* pl. 45
(28) *Songs* (n) pl. 31
(29–36) *For the Sexes* (J) pl. 10, 18, 9, 16, 8, 2, 21, 20
(37–8) *Songs* (n) pl. 50, 13
(39) Pl. IV for Flaxman's article on sculpture for Rees's *Cyclopaedia* (1816), with Hesiod pl. 25 (1816) on the verso
(40) *For the Sexes* (J) pl. 19
(41) *Songs* (n) pl. 30
(42) Drawing of a soldier seated before a tomb [Morgan pressmark: III.45.E.1]
(43) Several sketches, perhaps for Dante [Morgan pressmark: III.45.D]
(44) Sketch of a female by a grave, called 'Beauty' [Morgan pressmark: III.45.E]
(45) *Urizen* (I) pl. 10
(46) Frontispiece to Lavater's *Aphorisms* (1788)
(47) Pl. 3 for Hayley's *Triumphs of Temper* (1803)
(48) Proof before letters representing a man leaning against a tree and playing a harp to an eagerly listening woman (?not by Blake)
(49) *Songs* (n) pl. 2
(50) Pl. 2 for Flaxman's *Iliad* (1805)
(51) Pl. [36, 12] for Flaxman's *Hesiod* (1817)
(52) Pl. 10 for Flaxman's *Odyssey* (1805)
(53) Proof of 'The Lion' for Hayley's *Ballads* (1802),

this volume[1] was sold with the Library of Robert Arthington at Sotheby's,

---

[1] The 1866 description says there are 'upwards of 60 engraved pages'; 1887 says there are 56 proofs, sketches, etc.; 1902 says there are '52 subjects'; in 1905 and 1906 there are said to be '61 examples'—the variation may be due to whether one counts a leaf printed on both sides as one example or two.

The order is based on a combination of the sometimes vague descriptions of (1) the 1902 catalogue, (2) a letter of William Muir, 19 May 1902, to 'Dear Sirs' (now with the collection), followed carefully by (3) the 1905 catalogue, and (4) the 1906 catalogue. The plates were given letters by subject (e.g. the *Europe* plates and the Hesiod plates are called 'F') and numbered following the Muir order.

17 May 1866, lot 24, for £11 to Pickering; (2) Sold anonymously at Christie's, 1 June 1887, lot 258, for £34 to White; (3) Sold with the Library of Henry White at Sotheby's, 21 April 1902, lot 270, for £87 to Roberts; (4) Sold anonymously at Sotheby's, 6 Dec. 1905, lot 921, for £80; (5) Sold anonymously at Sotheby's, 15 Dec. 1906, lot 482, for £155 to Abbey for (6) The PIERPONT MORGAN LIBRARY, where each leaf was mounted separately; *Jerusalem* pl. 28 is reproduced in D. V. Erdman, 'The Suppressed and Altered Passages in Blake's *Jerusalem*', *Studies in Bibliography*, xvii (1964), 10.

Pl. 2, 4, 6–7: BINDING: See the Small Book of Designs (A) (p. 356).
  HISTORY: For their History see the Small Book of Designs (A).

Pl. 2, 6: HISTORY: For their History see the 'Order' of the Songs, p. 337.

19

*_The Book of Thel_. [?Illustrated by] W. R. Kean. Printed as Manuscript [*sic*. Lambeth, 1917.]
  An eccentric reprint for the William Blake Society.

20

*_The Book of Thel_. London, 1920.
  The following note is inside the wrappers of the copy of Mr. Robert Essick: 'This Book is copied from a very richly coloured Original [*copy J?*] which was lent to me by Mr Bernard Quaritch of 15 Piccadilly in 1887ᴸ.ᴶ I now issue this edition of fifty copies through Messrs Quaritch of Grafton Streetᴸ,ᴶ Londonᴸ,ᴶ August 1920ᴸ.ᴶ Wm Muir'. (The previous Muir facsimile [1884] was from copy D; see p. 488.)

21

*_The Book of Thel_. London, 1924.
  A colour facsimile published by Frederick Hollyer.

22

A*_The Book of Thel_ [D]. London, 1928. B London & N.Y., 1928.
  A colour facsimile by Gollancz.

23

*_The Book of Thel_. N.Y., 1928 (vDVE).
  A facsimile.

24

*_The Book of Thel_. [San Francisco], 1930.
  Text printed for the Book Club of California with one 'Decoration by Julian A. Links'.

25

The Book of Thel. Pawlet [Vermont, 1949].
A typographical reprint by the Banyan Press.

26

*The Book of Thel [O]. London, 1965. The William Blake Trust.
Geoffrey Keynes, 'Description and Bibliographical Statement', is on 5
unnumbered pages.

27

*The Book of Thel: A [colour] Facsimile [of copy M] and a Critical Text.
Ed. Nancy Bogen. Providence [R.I.] & N.Y., 1971.
David V. Erdman, 'Foreword', is pp. xi–xii. To the 'Text' (pp. 34–49)
and its notes (pp. 65–73), Professor Bogen adds particularly an 'Introduction' (pp. 2–31) which stresses 'The Three States of *Thel*', 'Blake's Punctuation', and 'A New Interpretation'. The bibliographical details are novel and
important.

28

**Thel no Sho: [The Book of Thel]*. Tr. Bunsho Jugaku. Kyoto, 1933.
Translations into Japanese face facsimiles of the plates, which were
coloured by hand by the translator and his wife.

29

**Kniha Thel.* [Tr. O. F. Bäbler, illustrations by Jan Konupek.] Suaty
Kopeček [Czechoslovakia], 1935.

30

§*Thels Bog.* Ditg. Overs. af Kai Friis Møller. 1945.

31. 'A Descriptive Catalogue' advertisement (1809)

BIBLIOGRAPHICAL INTRODUCTION

TABLE

Copy	Collection	Correction	Contemporary Owner
A	Glasgow University Library[1]	—	Thomas Butts

[1] The only known copy of this flyer is bound with *Descriptive Catalogue* (O), and reproduced by Keynes, *Blake Studies* (1949). The printers of 'A Descriptive Catalogue', '[*Ann*] Watts & [*Edward*] Bridgewater, [*31*] Southmolton-street', were at this address about 1807–10 (W. B. Todd, *A Directory of Printers . . . 1800–1840* [1972]), not far from Blake, who was at 17 South Molton Street about 1803–21.

TITLE: A DESCRIPTIVE CATALOGUE / OF / *BLAKE's EXHIBITION*, / At No. 28, Corner of / BROAD-STREET, / GOLDEN-SQUARE. / . . . / Printed by Watts & Bridgewater, Southmolton-street.

COLLATION: Broadsheet, text [Al]ʳ, verso blank; 1 sheet, 2 pages.

CONTENTS: Text on [Al]ʳ.

LEAF-SIZE: 13·8 × 16·5 cm.

WATERMARK: None.

PUBLICATION: Blake probably sent copies of his advertisement for the *Descriptive Catalogue* (1809) to his friends, such as Thomas Butts, in the spring of 1809, as he had the flyer for the exhibition itself (p. 164).

COPY A: BINDING: Evidently mounted for Thomas Butts after 1820 (the watermark date on the mount) and bound with *Descriptive Catalogue* (O)— see p. 140.

　　HISTORY: For its History see *Descriptive Catalogue* (O).

32. *A Descriptive Catalogue* (1809)

BIBLIOGRAPHICAL INTRODUCTION

TABLE

Copy	Collection	MS change on page	Contemporary owner
A	BM	—	
B	BMPR	— 64	
C	*Keynes*	Title-page, 64	
D	HUNTINGTON	Title-page, 64	
E	VICTORIA & ALBERT	—	{ Samuel Boddington / Thomas Boddington
F	YALE	Title-page, 64	William Beckford
G	FITZWILLIAM	Title-page, 64	
H	BODLEY	Title-page, 64	Francis Douce
I	HARVARD	—	Robert Balmanno
J	*Mellon*	Title-page, 64	
K	LC	— 45	John Linnell
L	LC	Title-page, 64	
M	*Rosenbach*	—	
N	MORGAN	—	
O	GLASGOW UNIVERSITY LIBRARY	Title-page, 64	Thomas Butts
P	MORGAN	—	Frederick Tatham
Qⁱ			
R²			
S	*Taylor*³		Henry Crabb Robinson / Charles Lamb⁴

¹ Copy Q is probably the same as copy P.
² Copy R may be the same as copy D.
³ Information about copy S comes from Keynes, *Blake Studies* (1949).
⁴ Copies owned by George Cumberland, H. C. Robinson (three copies), and Robert Southey (*Blake Records*, 219, 226, 578) have not been traced.

TITLE: A / DESCRIPTIVE CATALOGUE / OF / PICTURES, / *Poetical and Historical Inventions*, / PAINTED BY / WILLIAM BLAKE, / IN / WATER COLOURS, / BEING THE ANCIENT METHOD OF / *FRESCO PAINTING RESTORED*: / AND / DRAWINGS, / *FOR PUBLIC INSPECTION*, / AND FOR / 𝔖𝔞𝔩𝔢 𝔟𝔶 𝔓𝔯𝔦𝔳𝔞𝔱𝔢 𝔠𝔬𝔫𝔱𝔯𝔞𝔠𝔱, / = / *LONDON*: / Printed D. N. SHURY, 7,[1] Berwick-Street, Soho, / for *J. BLAKE*, 28, Broad-Street, Golden-Square. / - / 1809.

COLLATION: 12mo in half-sheet imposition: [A]² (= G3–4) B–G⁶ (−G3–4), signed on the first three leaves of each quire (but G3 is unsigned); 36 leaves, 72 pages.

Note: In a 12mo in sixes, the first leaf of each gathering is conjugate with the sixth, the second with the fifth, and the third with the fourth, the third and fourth being cut free to insert between \$1–2 and \$5–6. In Signature G, the 'Index' was printed as G6, for it is conjugate with G1 in copy N.[2] However, the Index was, at least occasionally, a separate leaf, for the advertisement for 'A Descriptive Catalogue' (p. 133) offers '*an Index to the Catalogue gratis*' to those paying the price of admission but not buying a catalogue.

CONTENTS: Title-page ([A1]ʳ), 'Conditions of Sale' ([A1]ᵛ), 'Preface' ([A2]ʳ⁻ᵛ), 'Descriptive Catalogue, &c. &c.': 'Number I' (B1ʳ), 'Number II' (B1ᵛ–B4ʳ), 'Number III' (B4ʳ–D5ᵛ), 'Number IV' (D6ʳ–E1ᵛ), 'Number V' (E2ʳ–F2ʳ), 'Number VI' (F2ʳ), 'Number VII' (F2ᵛ), 'Number VIII' (F2ᵛ–F3ʳ), 'Number IX' (F3ᵛ–F6ʳ), 'Number X' (F6ʳ), 'Number[s] XI', 'XII', 'XIII' (F6ᵛ), 'Number XIV' (F6ᵛ–G1ʳ), 'Number XV' (G1ʳ–G2ᵛ, G5ʳ), 'Number XVI' (G5ʳ⁻ᵛ), 'Index' (G6ʳ⁻ᵛ); no blank pages.

LEAF-SIZE: about 11·5 × 19·0 cm. uncut (copies C, E, G), probably Medium paper.

WATERMARK: '1807 AP' edgemark, visible only in \$1, \$3 (in about half the gatherings, as we would expect in a 12mo in half-sheet imposition).

PAGE NUMBERING: Pages correctly numbered: iv ([A2]ᵛ) at the top left corner of the page; 2–66 (B1ᵛ–G5ᵛ) at the top middle of the page.

RUNNING TITLE: None except for the correct second page of the 'INDEX'.

CATCHWORDS: None.

PRESS FIGURES: None.

PUBLICATION: Probably very few copies of the *Descriptive Catalogue* were printed, perhaps fifty or a hundred. Only sixteen have been traced, and there are records of a few more copies. They were issued in unlabelled greyish-Blue wrappers (still preserved with copies C, G, K) to the 'Fit audience . . . tho' few' who paid 2*s*. 6*d*. to see Blake's exhibition in 1809–10.

---

[1] The address of Daniel Nathan Shury from 1801 to 1822 was apparently 17 (not 7) Berwick Street, Soho (according to W. B. Todd, *A Directory of Printers and Others in Allied Trades [in] London and Vicinity 1800–1840* [1972], 174).

[2] I am deeply grateful to Mr. Paul Needham of the Pierpont Morgan Library for help with this description. Keynes (1921) gives '[A]⁴, B–F⁶, G⁴', with blanks at [A]¹ and G4 and the 'Index' after the 'Preface' rather than as the last leaf.

CORRECTIONS: By an oversight, the crucial fact that the exhibition could be seen 'At N 28 Corner of Broad Street Golden Square' was left off the title-page. Blake corrected this error and another on p. 64 in Black ink, probably in most of the copies that were distributed at the exhibition (copies B¹–D, F–H, J, L, O). The copies without these corrections (A, E, I, K, M, N, P) probably were not disposed of until years later. Some confirmation of this conjecture may be seen in the facts that copy I was apparently not bound before 1818, copy P, also uncorrected, was evidently a gift to 'Frederick Tatham / from the Author, June 12, 1824', and copy K was sold to Linnell by Blake's widow in 1831.[2]

DISTRIBUTION DATES: This suggests that copies left Blake's hands:

In 1809–10:	B, C, D, F, G, H, J, L, O
After 1810:	A, E, M, N
After 1818:	I
In 1824:	P
In 1831:	K

ERRATA:[3] (1) Title-page, 'At N 28 Corner of Broad Street Golden Square' omitted; (2) ¶ 4, the question mark belongs at the end of the sentence, and the extra 'he' should be removed; (3) ¶ 5, sentences one and two evidently should be one sentence; (4) ¶ 5, in the last sentence 'W' should be lower case; (5) ¶ 7, sentences one and two should be one sentence; (6) ¶ 9, 'villany'; (7) ¶ 9 'falshood'; (8) ¶ 10, 'Hercules, Farnese' should have no comma; (9) ¶ 12, 'changing yellow' was perhaps meant to be 'changing to yellow'; (10) ¶ 14, there is an extra set of quotation marks in line 2 of the first quotation (this convention of extra quotation marks is used elsewhere in the volume only in ¶ 21); (11) ¶ 14, the semicolon after 'cavalcade' should evidently be a comma; (12) ¶ 21, the second set of quotation marks is redundant (see ¶ 14 above); (13) ¶ 24, the second full stop should evidently be a comma; (14) ¶ 26, the 'b' dropped out of 'but'; (15) ¶ 31, the first word, 'For', serves no purpose; (16) ¶ 34, the full stop after 'dispute' should evidently be a question mark; (17) ¶ 34, the closing double quotation mark is misprinted as an apostrophe and a single quotation mark; (18) ¶ 41, a Black quad shows in the left margin; (19) ¶ 48, the last sentence should evidently be two sentences, divided after 'temper'; (20) ¶ 50, 'Ruben's' should be 'Rubens''; (21) ¶ 54, the closing quotation marks are omitted; (22) ¶ 57, 'The' in 'The Reeve' should not be capitalized; (23) ¶ 59, the last full stop should be a question mark; (24) ¶ 64, 65, 67, quotation marks are omitted at the beginnings and ends of the quotations; (25) ¶ 68, the hyphen in 'statues' at the end of page 36

---

[1] B lacks the title-page alteration.

[2] *Blake Records* (1969), 596. Thomas Boddington, who bought *For the Sexes* (D) in 1833, may have acquired his copy of *Descriptive Catalogue* (E) at the same time.

[3] This Errata List omits minor eccentricities of punctuation and capitalization (which presumably reflect Blake's text), defects of type (e.g. ¶ 21, the initial quotation marks are defective; ¶ 34, the first 'i' of 'sublimity' is broken; ¶ 59, the 'f' in the last 'of' is in the wrong fount; ¶ 68, the hyphen in 'sta- / tues' appears to be broken), and the fact that pp. 44 and 47 have more lines than pp. 45–6. Keynes (ed., *The Complete Writings of William Blake* [1957], 913) says the book 'was on the whole carefully printed', but the above lapses on the part of compositor and proof-reader might justify another conclusion.

appears to be broken; (**26**) ¶ 68, 'God's' should apparently be 'gods'; (**27**) ¶ 68, the last exclamation mark probably should be a question mark; (**28**) ¶ 72, '*sat*' should be '*set*'; (**29**) ¶ 73, 'histori ans'; (**30**) ¶ 74, 'thin g'; (**31**) ¶ 77, 'The antiquities . . . is' should be 'The antiquities . . . are'; (**32**) ¶ 77, the semicolon after 'Voltaire' should be a comma; (**33**) ¶ 77, 'opinions' should be 'opinion'; (**34**) ¶ 78, there should be a mark of punctuation after 'remains of antiquity'; (**35**) ¶ 78, 'Painting and Sculpture as it exists . . . is Inspiration . . . it is perfect' should be 'Painting and Sculpture as they exist . . . are Inspiration . . . they are perfect'; (**36**) ¶ 80, 'The face and limbs that deviates or alters . . . is' should be 'The face and limbs that deviate or alter . . . are'; (**37**) ¶ 85, there is a Black quad between 'among' and 'the'; (**38**) ¶ 87, there should be a question mark after 'go naked'; (**39**) ¶ 110, 'idea of want' should be 'want of idea'; (**40**) ¶ 110, after 'intentions' there should be a question mark, not a full stop; (**41**) ¶ 110, 'line' is spelt 'lne'.

COPY A: BINDING: (**1**) Originally stabbed through three holes; (**2**) Bound after March 1864 at the British Museum in dark Brown leather with a crown on the front cover; rebound at the 'B.M. 1969' in three-quarter Red morocco.

HISTORY: (**1**) Perhaps this is the copy acquired by George Cumberland (see *Blake Records* [1969], 219); (**2**) Acquired 29 March 1864 by the BRITISH MUSEUM, where it was bound.

COPY B: BINDING: Bound after 1856 in the British Museum.

HISTORY: (**1**) This may be one of the four copies bought by Crabb Robinson on 23 April 1810 (*Blake Records* [1969], 578); (**2**) It was 'Presented by William Smith Esqre / 1856'[1] (according to the inscription on the title-page) to (**3**) The BRITISH MUSEUM PRINT ROOM, where it was bound.

COPY C: BINDING: Stitched in the original paper covers.

HISTORY: (**1**) Perhaps this is the copy offered by Messrs. Low Bros. of Birmingham (Feb. 1915) for 7*s.* 6*d.* (according to Keynes, *Blake Studies* [1971], who is the authority for what follows); (**2**) Sold by Maggs Bros. in 1916 to (**3**) William Bateson, who gave it in 1922 to (**4**) *Geoffrey Keynes*, who described it in his catalogue (1964), no. 578.

COPY D: BINDING: 'BOUND BY F. BEDFORD' in Brown levant morocco, g.e.

HISTORY: (**1**) This may be the copy (Keynes copy R) sold with the Robert Arthington Library at Sotheby's, 17 May 1866, lot 21, for £1. 9*s.* to James (it could alternatively be copies C, G, I, J, M, N, P); (**2**) Sold with the T. G. Arthur Library at Sotheby's, 15 July 1914, lot 45, for £24. 10*s.* to G. D. Smith; (**3**) G. D. Smith sold it for $350 to (**4**) The HUNTINGTON LIBRARY.

COPY E: BINDING: Bound in Red blind stamped morocco.

HISTORY: (**1**) Acquired (perhaps from Tatham about 1833—see *For the Sexes* [D], p. 202) by Samuel Boddington, who added his book-plate and gave it to (**2**) Thomas Boddington (Samuel's book-plate is inscribed 'T. Boddington

---

[1] I find no record of it in the BMPR acquisitions records.

from S B'), who added his book-plate, and with whose Library it was sold posthumously at Sotheby's, 4 Nov. 1895, lot 96, for £5. 5*s*. to W. Browne; (3) Acquired by William Cowan, who added his book-plate and sold it at Sotheby's, 4 Dec. 1912, lot 849, for £4 to Quaritch, from whom it went on 13 Dec. 1912 to (4) The VICTORIA & ALBERT MUSEUM.

COPY F: BINDING: (1) Originally stabbed through three holes; (2) Bound after 1825 (three of the fly-leaves are watermarked 'WEATHERBY / 1825') in Green morocco, with 'Blake's Catalogue' on the spine.

HISTORY: (1) Bound after 1825 (the watermark date on the endpapers), perhaps for the owner (? A. J. Oliver) whose erased and virtually illegible signature appears on the title-page; (2) Sold with the Beckford Library at Sotheby's, 2 July 1882, lot 957, for £9 to Quaritch; (3) Quaritch added his Beckford sale book-plate, offered it in his Rough List 58 (30 July 1882), lot 205, for £10, and in his Catalogue 157 (March 1896), lot 70, for £10. 10*s*. and 'Traded [*it*] to America';[1] (4) Acquired by W. A. White, who lent it to the exhibitions of the Grolier Club (1905), no. 36 (anonymously), and the Fogg (1924); (5) Bought by G. D. Smith (an undated note from him accompanies the book), who 'sold it to'[1] (6) Felix Isman, who sold it in 1932[1] to (7) A. S. W. Rosenbach, who in turn sold it in 1932 to (8) C. B. Tinker (a note of 1932 from Rosenbach to Tinker accompanies the book), who added his book-plate, in whose catalogue (1959), no. 284, it was described, and who bequeathed it at his death in March 1963 to (9) YALE.

COPY G: Bound by [John] 'LEIGHTON' *c*. 1830 in Blue morocco, g.e., over the original Blue paper cover.

HISTORY: (1) Perhaps this is the copy Southey bought when he saw Blake's exhibition;[2] (2) Acquired by C. F. Murray, who signed the wrapper, added his book-plate, listed it in his catalogue (1899), and gave it on 11 July 1912 to (3) The FITZWILLIAM MUSEUM.

COPY H: BINDING: Bound by 1834 in half Green leather over marbled boards, the spine gilt with 'Blake's Catalogue'.

HISTORY: (1) Acquired by Francis Douce, who added his book-plate and bequeathed it in 1834 to (2) The BODLEIAN LIBRARY, which described it in the Douce Catalogue (1840), 32.

COPY I: BINDING: Bound for the first time, probably for Robert Balmanno after 1818 (the watermark date on a fly-leaf), with Chaucer, *Prologue* (1812) (which like the *Descriptive Catalogue* has no other extra stab holes), and *Innocence* (U) in half Green morocco, labelled 'Tracts / by / Blake / London /1789 / 1809/ 1812', t.e.g.; (2) The *Descriptive Catalogue* is still stitched as a unit, but it has pulled free from the common binding.

HISTORY: For the History see *Innocence* (U) with which it was bound (p. 411).

---

[1] G. Keynes, *Blake Studies* (1971).
[2] *Blake Records* (1969), 226. On 8 May 1830 Southey wrote: 'I have nothing of Blake's but his designs for Blair's *Grave*' (p. 398), but in 1847 he described the *Descriptive Catalogue* (p. 226), so he must have kept his copy.

COPY J: BINDING: (1) In original boards before 1892; (2) 'BOUND BY RIVIERE' in Red morocco, g.e. by 1892 for B. B. Macgeorge.

HISTORY: (1) This may be one of the four copies bought by Crabb Robinson on 23 April 1810 (*Blake Records* [1969], 578); Robinson may have given it to (2) William Wordsworth;[1] (3) Acquired 'in original boards' (according to the 1892 catalogue below) by B. B. Macgeorge, who had it rebound by Riviere, described in his library catalogues (1892, 1906), and sold it at Sotheby's, 1 July 1924, lot 124, for £9. 10s. to Dobell; (4) Offered in Maggs Bros. Catalogue 456 (1924), lot 54, for £21; (5) Acquired by Willis Vickery, who added his book-plate, described it in his book (1927), and sold it at American Art Association–Anderson Galleries, 1 March 1933, lot 17, for $200; (6) Acquired by A. E. Newton, who added his book-plate, and sold it posthumously at Parke-Bernet, 17 April 1941, lot 149, for $275, to Gannon; (7) Acquired by *Mary Mellon*, who added her book-plate.

COPY K: BINDING: Bound, probably for John Linnell before 1846, in front of *A Catalogue of the Orleans' Italian Pictures* . . . for sale . . . the 26th of December, 1798, and following days, at Mr. Bryan's Gallery; *A Catalogue of the Orleans' Italian Pictures* . . . for sale . . . the 26th of December, 1798, and following days, At the Lyceum In the Strand; and Blake's *Poetical Sketches* (T), in simple Brown matted boards.

HISTORY: For its History see *Poetical Sketches* (T) with which it is bound (p. 353).

COPY L: BINDING: 'Bound by Zaehnsdorf' in Green morocco over the original Blue paper covers which are labelled in old ink: 'Blake's Catalogue'.

HISTORY: (1) Perhaps this is one of the four copies bought by Crabb Robinson on 23 April 1810 (*Blake Records* [1969], 578); (2) Sold anonymously at Sotheby's, 4 July 1895,[2] lot 1129, for £3. 3s. to Quaritch, who sold it promptly to (3) W. A. White (the fly-leaf is inscribed 'Sotheby 1 / 4 July / B.Q. £3. 3. 0+10% $17 / very cheap, B.Q. asked £10', 'W. A. White / 15 July '95'); White lent it anonymously to the Grolier Club exhibition (1905), no. 35, and perhaps to that of (1919), no. 18, and sold it posthumously through Rosenbach on 1 May 1929 to (4) Mr. LESSING J. ROSENWALD.

COPY M: BINDING: The pages were cut down to about 7·7 × 13·8 cm, inlaid to 10·7 × 17·6 cm, and 'BOUND BY F. BEDFORD' in Brown levant morocco, g.e.

HISTORY: (1) Perhaps this is the copy lent by George A. Smith to the Burlington Fine Arts Club exhibition (1876), no. 319; (2) Sold by 'a Lady' at Sotheby's, 2 May 1911, lot 323, for £10. 5s. to Tregaskis; (3) Acquired by W. E. Moss, who added his book-plate, lent it to the exhibition at Manchester (1914), no. 168, and sold it at Sotheby's, 2 March 1937, lot 196, for £50 to Rosenbach; (4) A. S. W. Rosenbach bequeathed it to (5) the ROSENBACH FOUNDATION.

---

[1] In a letter of 10 Aug. 1848 (now in Dove Cottage), Robinson suggested that Edward Quillinan should 'Enquire of M^{rs} W: whether she has not a copy of his *Catalogue*'.

[2] Not on 14 July 1895 (a Sunday), as in Keynes, *Blake Studies* (1949; 1971).

COPY N: BINDING: Bound in Buff boards; the front cover loose.

HISTORY: (1) This may be the copy of 'Blake's Catalogue' which was a 'present' from Flaxman's sister-in-law Maria Denman on 1 Oct. 1842 to (2) Crabb Robinson (according to his diary in Dr. Williams's Library); (3) Sold by E. J. E. Tunmer at Sotheby's, 15 June 1937, lot 346, for £37 to Robinson; (4) Offered by Messrs. Robinson in March 1938, for £60;[1] (5) Sold by 'Two N.Y. Private Collectors' (O. T. Bradley)[1] at Parke-Bernet, 6 Nov. 1944, lot 78; (6) Sold by a New York Collector at Parke-Bernet, 4 Nov. 1946, lot 46, for $225; (7) Sold for a Deceased N.Y. Collector at Parke-Bernet, 29 Jan. 1952, lot 51, for $140; (8) Acquired from the firm of Robinson by Dr. B. E. Juel-Jensen on 8 March 1953 and sold by him to Blackwells in 1959; (9) Acquired by Mrs. Landon K. Thorne, in whose catalogue (1971) it was described (no. 12), and who gave it in February 1972 to (10) The PIERPONT MORGAN LIBRARY.

COPY O: BINDING: Bound by 'J[*ohn*] LEIGHTON. BREWER STREET', evidently for Thomas Butts between 1820 (the watermark date in the bound-in mount) and 1830 (when Leighton died) in half Red morocco over patterned and stamped Red cloth with 'BLAKE'S CATALOGUE', 'LONDON / 1809' on the spine, t.e.g., with the 'Descriptive Catalogue' advertisement folded and mounted on a sheet (watermarked '1820') which is hinged to a stub.

HISTORY: (1) Probably owned by Thomas Butts, who evidently had it bound after 1820 with the advertisement to the catalogue and for whom it was sold posthumously at Foster & Son, 29 June 1853, lot 93 ('PROCESSION OF CANTERBURY PILGRIMS; *with explanations by the artist*'), for £10. 10s. to Stirling; (2) Sir 'William Stirling[-Maxwell]' added his book-plate, and from him it passed to his son (3) Sir John Maxwell Stirling Maxwell, who bequeathed it at his death in 1956 to (4) GLASGOW UNIVERSITY.

COPY P: BINDING: John Mitford (1781–1859) evidently made the notes in ink on pp. 9–10 and the fly-leaf after the text, in pencil on pp. 44, 46, 56, and had the book bound in Brown sprinkled calf (in the process the comments on pp. 9 and 46 were trimmed).

HISTORY: (1) Acquired by 'Frederick Tatham / from the Author. / June 12. 1824' (according to the title-page inscription); (2) Acquired by John Mitford (1781–1859), who signed the front cover and who probably made the marginal comments[2] on a fly-leaf and pp. 9–10, 44, 46, 56 (e.g. beside Blake's comment on p. 56 that 'Mr. B has . . . the courage to suffer poverty and disgrace, till he ultimately conquers' is: 'This He did, & is gone to receive his reward'); Mitford probably had it bound; (3) The inscription 'Burton[?] Opened 5 Ap [*18*]67' on the front cover may indicate another owner; (4) Sold for Sir Thomas Phillips at Sotheby's, 25 May 1946, lot 27, for £85 to Quaritch (with Quaritch's collation marks on the back cover); (5) Sold by Arthur Randle at Sotheby's, 11 Oct. 1948, lot 34, for £95 to

---

[1] According to G. Keynes, *Blakes Studies* (1971).

[2] An undated clipping from the catalogue of an unknown dealer (inserted by J. H. Anderdon in the extra-illustrated Royal Academy catalogues which he gave to the Royal Academy) offers a 'Presentation copy from the Author and MS. Memorandum by Mr. M. [*?Mitford*], &c., &c.' The description fits copy P; Keynes calls it copy Q.

Rosenbach, who in turn sold it to (6) Mrs. Landon K. Thorne, in whose catalogue (1971) it was described (no. 13), and who gave it in February 1972 to (7) The PIERPONT MORGAN LIBRARY.

COPY Q: HISTORY: This is probably copy P.

COPY R: HISTORY: This may be copy D.

COPY S: BINDING: Bound by Charles Lamb with his *Confessions of a Drunkard*, Southey's *Wat Tyler*, and the *Poems* of Rochester and Lady Winchelsea (see History).

HISTORY: (1) Henry Crabb Robinson bought four copies on 23 April 1810, one of which he gave to (2) Charles Lamb (*Blake Records* [1969], 537, 578), who had it bound with his *Confessions of a Drunkard*, Southey's *Wat Tyler* [?1817], the *Poems* [?1713 or ?1714] of Anne Finch, Countess of Winchelsea, Lord Rochester's *Poems*, and seven other works (according to the 1848 catalogues) and bequeathed it (1834) with the rest of his library to his friend (3) Edward Moxon,[1] who, after the death of Lamb's sister Mary (1847), destroyed all but about sixty volumes (according to the 1848 catalogues) and sold the rest for £10 to the New York store of (4) Bartlett & Welford, which sold them piecemeal in Feb. 1848;[2] the 54th lot, described as 'Tracts Miscellaneous, 1 thick volume, 12mo . . .', including *Descriptive Catalogue* (S) went for $4.50; (5) The volume of miscellaneous Tracts was sold anonymously (?by James T. Annan) through Cooley, Keese, & Hill of New York, 21 Oct. 1848, lot 376, for $4.25 to Campbell; (6) *UNTRACED* (see Addenda).

33. *Europe* (1794)

BIBLIOGRAPHICAL INTRODUCTION

See Table on pp. 142–3

TITLE: *EUROPE* / *a* / PROPHECY / *LAMBETH* / *Printed by Will: Blake 1794*

DATE: 1794, as on the title-page.

The work was not listed in the Prospectus of 10 Oct. 1793, but the earliest copies were colour printed about 1795, thus confirming the title-page date.

The only real problem in dating arises with pl. 3, of which only two copies are known (in copies H and K). The idiosyncratic nature of the formation of the letter 'g' in pl. 3, with a leftward serif used elsewhere only about 1791–1802, would suggest a date of etching contemporaneous with the other plates; on the other hand, the fact that Blake omitted pl. 3 in his description of *Europe* in 1818 but included it in the copy (K) which he sold to Linnell in

---

[1] According to Crabb Robinson's diary for 27 April 1848 (Dr. Williams's Library).

[2] The Bartlett & Welford list was printed in Anon., 'Charles Lamb's Library in New York,' *Literary World*, iii (5 Feb. 1848), 10–11, and offprinted for the commercial use of the firm.

TABLE

Copy	Plates	Leaves	Watermarks	Blake numbers	Binding-order	Leaf-size in cm	Printing colour
‡A *Mellon*	1–2, 4–18	17	1794 / J WHATMAN (4, 6, 8, 10–11, 16)	1–15[1]	‡1–2, 4–9, 11–14, 10, 15–18	22·0×30·5* (1–2, 4–6)[2] 26·4×37·3* (7–18)	olive Brown
‡B *Cunliff*	1–2, 4–18	17	I TAYLOR (8, 14)	1–15[1]	‡1–2, 4–9, 11–14, 10, 15–18**[3]	26·7×37·3*[4] *irregular*	*Brown* (1, 9–10), *Blue* (2, 7, 11, 13, 15–17), *Green* (4–6, 8, 12, 14, 18)
‡C HARVARD	1–2, 4–18	17	I TAYLOR (4, 10, 18) 1794 / J WHATMAN (9, 17)	1–15[1]	‡1–2, 4–9, 11–14, 10, 15–18**[5]	26·6×37·1[5]	*Green* (1–2, 4, 6, 8–10, 12–13, 16, 18), *Blue* (5, 7, 11, 14–15, 17)
‡D BMPR	1–2, 4–18	10[6]	I TAYLOR [[4–5] 14–15]	1–15[7]	‡1–2, 4–18**	25·7×36·0	*bluish-Green* (1–2, 4–7, 10–18), *Brown* (8–9)
‡E LC	1–2, 4–18	10[6]	I TAYLOR ([12–13])	3–17[8]	‡1–2, 4–18**	25·9×37·0	*bluish-Green* (2, 4–8, 11–18), *Brown* (1, 9–10)
‡F BERG	1–2, 4–18	10[6]	I TAYLOR ([14–15])	1–15[7]	‡*1–2, 4–18**	27·4×37·8	orangish-Brown (1, 8) *Green* (2, 4–7, 11–18) dark Brown (9–10)
‡G *Thorne*	1–2, 4–18	10[6]	I TAYLOR ([10–11] [14–15])	1–15[7]	‡1–2, 4–18	24·4×35·9* (1)[4] 25·0×35·9* (2, 4–18)[4]	*Brown* (1, 9–10) *Green* (2, 5–8, 11–18) *Green* (4)
H HARVARD	1–18	18	E & P (6, 9, 16, 17)	—	3, 2, 11, 4–9, 11–14, 10, 15–18**[3]	24·8×30·8	brownish-Black (1–2, 4–18) light Brown (3)
I AUCKLAND	1–2, 4–18	17	R & T (6–7, 10–12, 14–18) RUSE & TURNERS 1812 (1–2, 4–5, 8–9, 13)	1–17[9]	‡1–2, 4, 10, 9, 5–8, 11–18**	23·6×32·4*	Black
[*There is no J*]							
‡K FITZWILLIAM	1–18	18	J WHATMAN / 1818 (1, 4, 9), J WHATMAN / 1819 (6, 13), J WHATMAN / 1820 (7)	1–18	1–5, 10, 9, 6–8, 11–18	24·0×30·3	orangish-Red
L HUNTINGTON	1–2, 4–18	17	T STAINS (1–2, 4–7, 9–11, 13–18) T STAINS / 1813 (12)	1–17[9]	1–2, 4–5, 10, 9, 6–8, 11–18**	22·1×29·5*	Black
M FITZWILLIAM	1–2, 4–18	17	J WHATMAN / 18g[2?] (6–7)	—	1–2, 4–18**	22·8×28·0*	*reddish-Brown*

Copy	Plates		Watermark		Binding	Dimensions	Colours
a BMPR	1–2, 4–7, 9–11, 17, 18	8[10]	—		Loose	26·2 × 33·0 (1) 26·7 × 33·1 (2[4–5] 9–10 [11, 17]) 26·0 × 33·5 [[6–7]] 23·4 × 33·3 (18)	dark Green (2, 4–7, 11, 17–18) dark bluish-Green (1, 9–10)
b MORGAN	2, 4[a–b], 5, 9[a–b], 11, 15–16, 17[a–c]	7[11]	J WHATMAN / 1832 (15)	—	Loose	17·8 × 23·7 (2) 18·7 × 25·6 ([4[a], 9[a]]) 26·9 × 38·0 ([4[b], 5]) 19·3 × 25·6 ([9[b], 17[a]] [16, 17[c]]) 27·2 × 37·5 ([11, 17[b]]) 20·3 × 26·6 (1)	Black (2, 4[b], 9[a], 11, 17[b]) greenish-Black (4[b], 5, 9[b], 16, 17[a, c]) reddish-Brown (15)
c[12] *Baskin* LC NEWBERRY *UNTRACED*[13] NEW YORK *Ryskamp*	1–2, 4[a–c], 5[a–b], 6–7, 9[a–c], 10, 11[a, c], #11[b], 12–14, #15[a], 15[b], #16, 17[a, c], #17[b], 18[a–b]	19[14]	I T[AYLOR] [15[a]]	—[15]	Loose[16]	17·6 × 24·3 (1) 23·7 × 31·2 (2 [4[c], 9[b]] [5[b], 10] [6–7] [11[a], 12] [13–14] 15[a] [16, 17[b]]) 18·5 × 25·3 (4[a], 5[a])[17] 17·1 × 23·9 ([4[b], 9[b]])[17] 18·0 × 24·8 (9[a])[17] 17·6 × 23·7 ([11[b], 17[a]])[17] 19·3 × 25·6 25·6 ([11[c], 17[c]]) 17·4 × 31·4 (15[b]) 23·0 × 31·0 (18[a]) 23·5 × 29·2 (18[b])	Blue (1, 13–14[18]) Brown (2) reddish-Brown (4[a], 5[a], 9[a], 18[b]) Grey or Black (4[b–c], 5[b], 6–7, 9[b–c], 10, 15[b], 18[a]) dark Green or greyish-Green (11[a–c], 12, 16, 17[a–c]) *Brown* (15[a])
Mellon #*Preston*	1 1[a–b], 2[a–b]	1[19] 4[21]	— —		Loose Loose	16·3 × 23·0[20] 16·1 × 12·8 (1[a])[22] 16·1 × 16·6 (1[b])[22] 9·8 × 17·6 (2[a])[22] 15·6 × 15·6 (2[b])[22]	Brown Black (1[a]) Brown (1[a], 2[b]) reddish-Brown (2[a])
Keynes	1–2, #4, 5, #6–7, 10, #12	6[23]	—		Loose	18·4 × 25·1 (1) 19·3 × 25·7 (2) 17·0 × 14·3 (4)[22] 27·3 × 37·5 ([5, 10]) 16·5 × 13·0 ([6–7])[22] 16·6 × 23·0 (12)	bluish-Black (1) Black (2) Brown (4) Blue (5–7, 10) *Green* (12)
#*Crawford* TRINITY COLLEGE	2 #2, 18	1[24] 2	— —		Loose Loose	16·6 × 25·1[20] 17·3 × 23·5 (2)[22] 21·2 × 20·0 (18)[22]	dark greyish-Blue Brown (2) reddish-Brown (18)
#TATE VIVIAN GALLERY	6–7 6–7, 12	1[25] 3	— —		Loose Loose	16·6 × 9·2[22] 21·1 × 29·3(6) 20·3 × 27·4 (7, 12)	bluish-Grey reddish-Brown
#BMPR	10	1	*invisible*		Loose	26·8 × 34·3	greyish-Brown
#NATIONAL GALLERY OF VICTORIA	11	1	—		Loose	16·1 × 23·5	*greenish-Blue*
BUFFALO	18	1	*invisible*		Loose	16·5 × 16·7[26]	bluish-Grey

Coloured by Blake or his wife.
1–18 Italicized binding-orders indicate contemporary bindings.
Notes to Table on p. 144.

‡   Pl. 1 faces pl. 2.

**   The identifiable offsets confirm the present order.
*   The leaves are trimmed and gilt.
Brown Italicized printing colours indicate colour printing.

1821 suggests a late date of printing. Probably he etched pl. 3 early but omitted it from most copies. Even in copy H it seems to be printed in a different shade of ink, and therefore it may have been added to copy H at a later date.

PUBLICATION: There is a good deal of evidence about the growth of *Europe*. Sketches for what appear to be *Europe* designs are on *Notebook* pp. 8, 25, 74–5, 77, 96–8,[1] and there are seventy-six proofs of *Europe*, eighteen in

[1] Lines of text interrupted by the design on pl. 6, 15–6 suggest that on these plates some of the design preceded the text, while in pl. 4, 7–8, 15, 17–18 parts of the design seem to accommodate the text.

Notes to Table on pp. 142–3.

[1] In copies A–C, Blake's numbers are on pl. 4–9, 11–14, 10, 15–18.

[2] In copy A, pl. 1–2, 4–6 were separated from the rest of the work, cut down, inlaid to size, and then reunited with pl. 7–18.

[3] Copies B and H are disbound, but the numbers, offsets, and Keynes & Wolf agree confidently on the above orders.

[4] In copies B and G, the leaves are trimmed but not gilt.

[5] The plates of copy C are loose, but the leaf-numbers plus the offsets (12–13–14, 17–18) give the order; additional offsets (12–14–15) indicate that the leaves were once arranged in a different order.

[6] In copies D–G, pl. [4–5] [6–7] [8–9] [10–11] [12–13] [14–15] [16–17] are printed back-to-back.

[7] In copies D, F, G, Blake's numbers are on pl. 4–18.

[8] In copy E, there are odd numbers (3, 5, 7 . . . 17) on the rectos of pl. 4–18.

[9] If, as seems possible, copies I and L were printed posthumously, their ink numbers have little authority.

[10] In copy a, pl. [4–5] [6–7] [11, 17] are printed back-to-back.

[11] In copy b, the following plates are printed back-to-back: [2, *Jerusalem* 74] [4ᵃ, 9ᵃ] [4ᵇ, 5] [9ᵇ, 17ᵃ] [11, 17ᵇ] [16, 17ᶜ].

[12] In copy c, the plates are distributed as follows: pl. 1, 4ᵃ, 5ᵃ (*Baskin*); pl. 2, 5ᵇ, 9ᵃ, 10, 11ᵃ, 12, 18ᵃ⁻ᵇ (LC); pl. 4ᵇ, 9ᵇ, 11ᵇ, 16, 17ᵃ⁻ᵇ (NEWBERRY); pl. 4ᵃ, 9ᵃ, 13–14, 15ᵇ (*UNTRACED*); pl. 6–7, 15ᵃ (NEW YORK UNIVERSITY); pl. 11ᶜ, 17ᶜ (*Ryskamp*).

[13] The untraced plates of copy c were, like the rest of copy c, dispersed at the George C. Smith, Jr., sale at Parke-Bernet Galleries, 2 Nov. 1938, lots 30 (pl. [4ᶜ, 9ᶜ]) and 32 (pl. [13–14] 15ᵇ), from the catalogue of which the above information is taken.

[14] In copy c, the following plates are printed back-to-back: [2, *Jerusalem* 8] [4ᵇ, 9ᵇ] [4ᶜ, 9ᶜ] [5ᵇ, 10] [6–7] [11ᵃ, 12] [11ᵇ, 17ᵃ] [11ᶜ, 17ᶜ] [13–14] [16, 17ᵇ].

[15] The numbers in copy c (20, 33–5, 37, 39–43, 50–1 on pl. 2, 4ᵇ, 4ᵃ, 6, 15ᵃ, 11ᵇ, 5ᵃ, 16, 10, 12, 18ᵃ⁻ᵇ) derive from the time when the plates were bound with other pages with the 'Order' of the *Songs*.

[16] Pl. 18ᵃ⁻ᵇ of copy c are now bound between *Jerusalem* pl. 9 and *Jerusalem* pl. 19–20, 38ᵃ⁻ᵇ, 48, 50, 58, 78, but they were previously bound differently with the 'Order' of the *Songs*.

[17] Pl. 4ᵃ, [4ᵇ, 9ᵇ] 5ᵃ, 9ᵃ, [11ᵇ, 17ᵃ] in copy c are inlaid to size (23·8 × 31·1 cm).

[18] In the 1938 Weyhe catalogue, lot 123 describes the printing colour of pl. 14 as Green.

[19] In the Mellon proof, [*Europe* 1, *Jerusalem* 30] are printed back-to-back.

[20] The dimensions given for the Mellon and Crawford proofs are those visible within the frame.

[21] In the Preston proofs, the following plates are printed back-to-back: [1ᵃ, *Jerusalem* 41] [1ᵇ, *Jerusalem* 25] [2ᵃ, *Jerusalem* 32] [2ᵇ, *Jerusalem* 47].

[22] The Preston, Keynes (pl. 4, [6–7]), Trinity College, and Tate proofs are cut down beyond the plate-marks.

[23] In the Keynes proofs, pl. [2, *Jerusalem* 1] [5, 10] [6–7] are printed back-to-back.

[24] In the Crawford proof, pl. [2, *Jerusalem* 24] are printed back-to-back.

[25] The Tate proofs of pl. [6–7] are printed back-to-back.

[26] The Buffalo pull of pl. 18 is cut down to the design.

early states. Twenty-five leaves with proofs on both sides bear plates which were not printed back-to-back in the published form, including nine copies of pl. 1–2 with pulls from *Jerusalem* (1804–?20) on the back. Most of the proofs were printed about 1794 in shades of dark Green or dark Blue or colour printed about 1795, but nine seem to have been printed posthumously in reddish-Brown. The proofs reveal at least three states of some plates, but the copperplates do not seem to have been altered after the work was published.

Pl. 1–2, 4–18 exhibit the plate-maker's mark of JONES AND / PONTIFEX N⁰ 47 / SHOE LANE LONDON,[1] indicating that these are the versos of plates probably bearing earlier engravings on their rectos. The coincidence of dimensions suggests that most of the *Europe* plates were etched on the backs of the *America* plates:

America		Europe		
pl. 1	16·9 × 23·4	pl. 1	16·9 × 23·4	
pl. 2	16·7 × 23·5	pl. 6	16·7 × 23·6	
pl. 3	16·3 × 23·1	pl. 7	16·4 × 23·1	
pl. 4	16·6 × 23·8			
pl. 5	16·7 × 23·7	pl. 11	16·7 × 23·6	
pl. 6	16·4 × 23·2	pl. 17	16·5 × 23·3	
pl. 7	16·6 × 23·3	pl. 12	16·6 × 23·4	
pl. 8	16·7 × 23·4	pl. 13	16·7 × 23·4	
pl. 9	16·8 × 23·5	pl. 14	16·9 × 23·4	
pl. 10	16·7 × 23·5	pl. 18	16·6 × 23·4	
pl. 11	16·9 × 23·4	pl. 16	16·9 × 23·3	
pl. 12	16·9 × 23·5	pl. 10	17·0 × 23·4	
pl. 13	17·2 × 23·7	pl. 4	17·1 × 23·6	
pl. 14	17·3 × 23·5	pl. 15	17·3 × 23·4	
pl. 15	17·4 × 23·6	pl. 5	17·3 × 23·6	
pl. 16	17·2 × 23·6	pl. 8	17·2 × 23·6	
pl. 17	17·0 × 23·7	pl. 9	17·1 × 23·7	
pl. 18	17·1 × 23·8	pl. 2	17·3 × 23·9	
		pl. 3	13·4 × 9·6	*Ahania* pl. 1 9·8 × 13·6

In addition, the verso of *Europe* pl. 3 may have been used for an *Ahania* plate.

In its published form, *Europe* consists of seventeen, or in two copies of eighteen, plates. The early copies (D–G) were mostly colour printed about 1794–5 on ten leaves of large paper. The first copy may be F, which is like the others in watermark, number and size of leaves, and binding-order but is not in the experimental, colour printed form. Copies B–C, which are colour printed, differ in number of leaves, size, and binding-order, and may be marginally later, while copy H, which is uncoloured, on smaller paper, and has the extra pl. 3, may have been printed (like *America* [A] and *Visions* [G]) about 1800; it is apparently the only copy which Blake printed but did not colour. Copy A is much like H except that it lacks pl. 3, but the fact that

---

[1] First reported by M. J. Tolley, 'The Auckland Blakes', *Biblionews and Australian Notes & Queries*, 2S, ii (1967), 6–16.

its text is coloured as well as its designs suggests that it was not finished until after 1805.[1] Copy K is also much like copy H, except that it was printed in orangish-Red on paper watermarked 1818–20 with *America* (O), arranged in a new order, sold 'not finished'[2] to Linnell in 1821, and evidently coloured later.

This may complete the list of copies printed by Blake. The three remaining copies may all be posthumous. One (M), on seventeen small leaves watermarked 1832, is printed in reddish-Brown and bound in the order of the earliest copies. The last two (I, L) are printed on small leaves of paper watermarked 1812 and 1813 of a kind which was evidently used elsewhere for Blake's works only in the copies of *America* with which *Europe* (I, L) are bound and which also seem to be posthumous. They are arranged in the order found elsewhere only in the late copy K, which suggests that the printer (?Tatham) had access to Linnell's copy K.

This evidence seems to give a pattern as follows:

Copy	Approximate date	Watermark	Leaves	Leaf-sizes	Binding-orders			Printing colours
					1–18	1–9, 11–14, 10, 15–18	1–5, 10, 9, 6–8, 11–18	
‡F	1794	I TAYLOR	10	27×38	xxx			Brown, Green
‡D–E, G	1795	I TAYLOR	10	*c.* 26×36	xxx			*Brown, Green*
‡B–C	1796	I TAYLOR J WHATMAN	17	27×37		xxx		*Brown, Green, Blue*
H	?1800	E & P	18	25×31		xxx		brownish-Black
‡A	?1805	1794 / J WHATMAN	17	22×30		xxx		olive-Brown
‡K	1821	J WHATMAN / 1818–20	18	24×30			xxx	orangish-Red
I, L	?1833	RUSE & TURNERS 1812 T STAINS / 1813	17	*c.* 23×30			xxx	Black
M	1833	J WHATMAN / 1832	17	23×28	xxx			reddish-Brown

‡ means coloured by Blake.

Often copies of *Europe* (A–C, I–M)[3] were bound with *America* (1793) and sometimes (A, C, G) with *Visions* (1793) and *The Song of Los* (1795); one copy (D) was bound contemporaneously with the Large Book of Designs and another (B) with *Jerusalem* (1804–?20).

Blake offered *Europe* at £5. 5*s*. for 17 plates (pl. 1–2, 4–18) in his letter to Dawson Turner of 9 June 1818, and in his letter to George Cumberland of 12 April 1827 he gave the price as £6. 6*s*. Contemporary owners of *Europe* included ?Isaac D'Israeli (copy A), P. A. Hanrott (B), George Cumberland (C, sold to Thomas Butts in 1835), Ozias Humphry (D, lent to Cumberland, Crabb Robinson, and Richard Thomson), Linnell (K, bought with *America* [O] on 8 Aug. 1821 for £1 and coloured later), and Samuel Boddington (M, perhaps bought about 1833).

COLOURING: Almost all the copies of *Europe* which Blake produced are

[1] Copy G, which was evidently colour printed about 1795, may have been touched up with water-colour ten years later, for its text is also lightly coloured.
[2] *Blake Records* (1969), 585.
[3] *Europe* (K) was clearly produced with *America* (O), and *Europe* (M) with *America* (P).

coloured. Copies B–E and G were boldly and sombrely colour printed about
1795–6 and later touched with water-colour. It is clear that the colouring
was occasionally completed some time after printing, for copy H was never
coloured like the others, the style of colouring (about 1805) of copy A seems
to be rather later than its printing, and copy K was sold, 'not finished', in
1821, apparently before the colouring was added or completed. There are
only Grey washes on copies H (pl. 1–2, 4, 6–12, 14–16, 18) and I (pl. 1–2, 4,
6–9, 11–18). In copy L, the colouring was added about 1913, probably
imitating copy D, and is therefore not reported below.

Most of the colour on pl. 1, 5, 7–11, and 14 comes from the printing colour,
and, probably for this reason, the full-page designs (pl. 1, 9–10) were sometimes printed in a colour different from the rest of the plates (copies B, E–G, a).

The colouring of copies D, F, G seems very similar. The text is coloured in
copies A (greyish-Blue), G (Buff), and K (bluish-Grey) but is not recorded in
the notes on colouring below. The plates in copy K are outlined in Red, and
the colouring is glorious.

CATCHWORDS: Pl. 8 ('Arise'), correct, has the only catchword; it was
evidently necessary to show which plate (11) followed the two full-page
designs (pl. 9–10).

ORDER: Pl. 1–18.

There are essentially three variant orders for *Europe*[1] apparently based on
Blake's authority: First (*c.* 1794–5), pl. 1–2, 4–18 in five copies (D–G, M);
Second (*c.* 1796–1805), pl. 1–2, 4–9, 11–14, 10, 15–18 in four copies (A–C,
H[2]); Third (*c.* 1821), pl. 1–5, 10, 9, 6–8, 11–18 in three copies (I, K–L[3]). It
seems possible that Blake did not revert to an earlier order after he had
taken up another, though the evidence about this is not clear. The order
followed below is the first order.

In all three arrangements, only the full-page designs (pl. 1, 9–10) vary
significantly in order, except that once pl. 3 precedes, and once it follows,
the title-page. That is, the text is not affected by these differing plate-orders.

SIGNIFICANT VARIANTS:[4] Pl. 1, 4–5, 9–10, 17–18 exist in one or two
variant proof states,[5] but only pl. 17–18 have proof-changes in the text. Three
proofs of pl. 2 were adapted in sketches, and eleven proofs were cut down
beyond the plate-mark.

An almost identical version of pl. 1 was issued separately as 'The Ancient
of Days'.

A number of minor variants were created in the colouring. For example,
the angels in pl. 8 were given halos in one copy, sometimes the flesh in
pl. 9–10 was coloured Yellow or Green, and there are striking differences in
the treatment of nudity in pl. 18.

[1] The Keynes & Wolf orders for copies A, C, K are inaccurate.
[2] In copy H, the order of the first plates is: 3, 2, 1.
[3] Copies I and L (perhaps posthumous) lack pl. 3, and I has pl. 10, 9 after pl. 4.
[4] The minor variants inevitable in colour printing in copies B–E, G, such as the obscuring
of cross-hatching, are ignored here.
[5] My observations of these variants often differ significantly from those of Keynes & Wolf.

George Cumberland[1] wrote titles and verses, many of them probably from Edward Bysshe's *Art of English Poetry* (1702 ff.), on pl. 1, 2 verso, 4–12, 14–16, 18 of copy D. Cumberland may have had advice from Blake about these passages, which are often very illuminating.

ERRATA: 'lureing' (pl. 17, l. 226); 'flo[a]ting' (pl. 17, l. 229).

Pl. 1. DESIGN: The whole page is a design of a naked, kneeling, bearded man with long white hair flying to the left, who leans out from a bright sphere and with light emitted from his fingers forms a compass to divide the deep. A fragment of cloth shows by his left foot. Clouds surround and impinge on the sun but are broken by the god's arm.

A sketch for the design in the *Notebook* p. 96 is entitled: 'Who shall bind the Infinite' (see pl. 5, l. 29); a sketch of the side view of the figure (*c.* 1788), with the inscription from Proverbs below, is reproduced in *Blake's Pencil Drawings*, Second Series, ed. G. Keynes (1956) pl. 34, and is etched in *No Natural Religion* (?1788) pl. b10. A design similar to the *Europe* frontispiece, known as 'The Ancient of Days', differs fractionally from it in plate-size (16·8 × 23·2 *v.* 16·9 × 23·4 for *Europe* pl. 1), the shorter beard of the god, and the greater extension of the sun's rays at the bottom. J. T. Smith (1828) said that Blake saw the figure of the god in a vision 'at the top of his staircase' and that he especially enjoyed colouring it, finishing copy F on his deathbed (*Blake Records* [1969], 470, 471, 527–8). It is coloured like the frontispiece to *Europe*, and is known in seven copies:

Copy	Watermark	Leaf-size in cm	Printing colour
‡A ROSENBACH	—	22·7 × 30·8	Brown
‡B *Goyder*	*invisible*		Black
‡C *Keynes*	*invisible*	16·7 × 23·8	Orange and Brown (double-printed)
D *UNTRACED*		23·5 × 31·1	Black
‡E LC			Brown
‡F WHITWORTH			Yellow

(Information about copy D comes from the Parke-Bernet catalogue of G. C. Smith, Jr., 2 Nov. 1938, lot 28. It is just possible that copies B and D are identical.) Copy C is inscribed: 'When He set a compass upon the face of the depth / Proverbs [*8: 27.*]'

COLOURING: The SUN is Yellow (A [strong Orange], C [Ochre], D, E [golden], F, K, Preston pull [pl. 1ᵇ], 'Ancient of Days' [C]), Pink (B, 'Ancient of Days' [C]), Red (B, D [strawberry], G, 'Ancient of Days' [B]), Black (B). The CLOUDS are the printing colour or Black (A–G), Grey (D, 'Ancient of Days' [B]), Brown (C, G [dark]), Red (C [bright], K [raspberry]), Orange (E, Preston pull [pl. 1ᵃ]), Pink (Preston pull [pl. 1ᵇ]), and Purple ('Ancient of

---

[1] The inscriptions in copy D are unsigned, but the handwriting is that of Cumberland's letters of 1796 in the British Museum Department of Manuscripts.

Days' [A]), and its MARGINS are Red (A [dark], B, F [pinkish-]), or Brown (G). The CLOTH by the man's foot is sometimes Pink (B), Purple (G), or Blue (K).

VARIANTS: In the proofs, the clouds by the god's right knee are not hatched (a), there is no division between clouds at the top middle (a), the shafts of light do not extend far from his fingers (Mellon pull), and the top cloud impinges on the sun at the left (Keynes pull). All these features were altered in the published state.

A leaf has been added in water-colour in copy A.

In the Preston proofs, the top is cut off at the man's forehead (pl. 1ᵇ) or ankle (pl. 1ᵃ) to focus on the *Jerusalem* (1804–?20) plates on the verso.

Pl. 2. TITLE-PAGE. DESIGN: A huge, open-mouthed serpent coils between 'a' and the imprint. (Blake's Design I [1797] for Gray's 'Descent of Odin' is strikingly similar—see I. Tayler, *Blake's Illustrations to the Poems of Gray* [1971] for a reproduction.)

COLOURING: The SNAKE is mottled Brown (A–G, K, Preston proofs) with Blue (A, C–F, Preston pull [2ᵇ]), Black (A, E, Trinity College pull), Yellow (A, D [Ochre], K, Preston proof [pl. 2ᵃ], Crawford pull), Green (A, C, E–F, Preston proofs, Trinity College proof), Red (B–C and Trinity College pull [pinkish-], E–F), Purple (D), and Orange (Crawford pull); its TONGUE is often Red (B–C, E, G, Preston pull [pl. 2ᵇ]). The BACKGROUND is Grey (A–B), Pink (B, E), Peach (E), Green (F [pale], K), yellowish-Brown (F–G), Blue (K), or pale Purple (Trinity College pull).

VARIANTS: The proofs in copies b–c, Preston, Keynes, and Crawford have plates from *Jerusalem* (1804–?20) on the versos. In copy b and the Preston copy (pl. 2ᵃ) and Crawford proofs, the printed design was much altered with pencil. In all three, 'PROPHECY' was erased or (in the Crawford copy) obscured under squiggles, and 'EUROPE' is cut off in the Preston copy and covered by squiggles in Crawford's; in addition, the design is cut off in the Preston proofs, above the serpent's head and through the bottom coil (2ᵇ) or above the second line of the imprint (2ᵃ). In copy b, the snake's head is erased from the paper and a tail substituted for it. A flying figure descends from the first 'E' of 'EUROPE', and others are hinted at in pencil by the 'U' and 'R'. At the bottom is a man with a book and quill. In the Preston copy (pl. 2ᵃ), an alternate serpent head is drawn firmly to the right in water-colour; a nude woman lies on a coil, and another lies under the coils; where the word 'PROPHECY' was in the engraving, in this version a person is seated on a coil; and three others are in front. All the figures are in pencil. In the Crawford copy is added in ink a naked man facing us with his hands on the coils.

A hill rises to the right behind the lower coils in some copies (B, C [Grey], E [Pink], F [Blue], G [Purple]).

There are rays of the rising sun in F.

In copy G, the imprint has been retraced in Brown paint, so that it seems to read: 'Painted [*for* Printed] . . .'.

Pl. 3. INCIPIT: 'Five windows light . . .'. DESIGN: The only trace of decoration is a little foliage at the foot.

Pl. 4. INCIPIT: 'PRELUDIUM / The nameless shadowy female . . .'. DESIGN: Above the text, a clothed traveller with a staff and a large pack strapped to his back walks down a wooded road, while in a Black cave near by among rocks crouches a naked man with a dagger. (A sketch perhaps for the assassin appears in *Notebook* p. 97. A bearded assassin clad in an animal skin is shown in the same peculiar position, except that he has the dagger in his left hand, in a drawing of 1799 called 'Malevolence' [reproduced in *Blake Records* (1969), at p. 60].)

In the open places in the text are insects, birds, and foliage; in the bottom right corner a naked man falls headlong, apparently dragged down by a heavy Black metal weight, and below the text are the head and shoulders of a tormented, bat-winged man trailing what appear to me to be strips of cloth and to Keynes & Wolf 'the coils of a serpent'. (Sketches of this tormented figure appear in *Notebook* pp. 74, 75.)

COLOURING: The TRAVELLER is dressed in Blue (A, D, F, K, Keynes pull), Green (B–C, E), or Buff (G); his PACK is Black (B, D [greyish-]), Tan (C), Gold (F), or pale Blue (G), and its STRAPS are Yellow (A, F [golden]), or Black (B–C); his HAIR is Yellow in E, and his HAT Black in C. The ASSASSIN, ordinarily nude-Pink, is a vivid reddish-Purple in the Keynes pull, and his HAIR is Grey in E.

At the bottom, the WINGS of the tormented figure are Black (A–B, F–G [greyish-]), or deep Red (K), and the CLOTH is Blue (D, F [greenish-]) or Purple (D). The FALLING MAN is sometimes Blue (D) or Grey (F–G).

VARIANTS: The proofs reveal at least two preliminary stages of the etched design:

State 1: There are no White lines in the ruts in the road, on the traveller's pack, right shoulder, belly, crotch, or leg (copy b [pl. 4ᵃ⁻ᵇ]);

State 2: There are more White lines on each (copy a);

State 3: The published State adds yet more white lines.

The assassin has a tonsure in C.

Cuffs have been added to the traveller's ankles in copy E to make it clear that he is trousered and not naked, and in F the trousers end at the knee.

Pl. 5. INCIPIT: 'Unwilling I look up . . .'. DESIGN: The text on this and on pl. 6–8, 11, 14 is on clouds. Below the clouds, a naked bald man floating in air throttles two others, while in the top right margin another naked man, holding his head, flees away. (A sketch for the bottom figures, reversed, is pasted on to *Notebook* p. 8, and a sketch perhaps of the man at the top right is on p. 98.)

COLOURING: The figures are usually nude-Pink, but sometimes the STRANGLER is Blue (A) or greenish-yellowish-Gray (K), the VICTIM on the left is Green (D, F [bright], G), and the one on the right is Green (A–C), Blue (D, F [bright], G) or bluish-Grey (K). The SKY is Black (A, B [velvet bluish], C–D, E [brownish-], F–G, K), sometimes with some Green (A) or dark

Brown (C). The CLOUDS are occasionally dark Brown (B) or pale Raspberry (K) and Yellow (K).

VARIANTS: In *State 1* of the proofs, the clouds have not been extended by White line hatching, and the strangler's left foot is clear (b);

State 2 is the published form.

The bottom clouds have been coloured out in copy C, and they are extended below the men by the colouring in D.

The feet of all the lower men have been made clear in copy K.

Pl. 6. INCIPIT: 'A / PROPHECY / The deep of winter came . . .'. DESIGN: Beside the first letter ('A') sprout two tiny figures as palm-trees; below it a clothed figure seated on clouds bends over its knees; to its left a naked man flies to the right with a protesting woman in a long, trailing dress; and to its right a winged, naked, flying man kisses a winged, nude, flying woman. 'PROPHECY' sprouts in vegetation and seven tiny figures, and above the 'Y' float two more.

'Between the title and the text floats a large woman with heavy wings and a trailing skirt, clasping her neck. Under her head, by ll. 1–4, a small, naked man crouches in a flaming Yellow sphere.

Round the text are ten birds and seven tiny figures.

COLOURING: The large woman's DRESS is Yellow (A, G [pale], K [greenish-]), Green (B), Red (C [dark raspberry], F [pinkish-]), and Blue (D [pale], E [pale Purple]); her WINGS are Yellow (A–B), Brown (B–C, G), Red (C, E, K [pinkish-], Tate pull), Blue (B–C, D [Purple], E–G, K, Tate pull), Black (E), and Green (F, Tate pull), and her HAIR is sometimes Black (B, E). The SUN is Yellow or Pink (A), Red (A, E, G), Brown (B, C [orangish-]), or Orange (D, F). The small woman's DRESS is Olive (D), pale Purple (E), or Blue (F). The SKY in some places is Black (B, D [greyish-], G, K), Green (B), or pale Purple (D). The small people's WINGS are Blue (D, F), brownish-Black (E), or Brown (G), and some CLOUDS are Pink (D [pale], K) or yellowish-Green (K).

VARIANT: The bottom half of the plate, including part of the angel, is cut off in the Tate copy.

Pl. 7. INCIPIT: 'The shrill winds wake . . .'. DESIGN: By the text are insects, birds, and foliage, and by ll. 21–4 a larger nude (?female) figure tumbles headlong down the right margin.

Just below the text are three small, nude, sprawling women, and to the right a small, running, naked man kisses a running woman in a long dress. Below them, the main design shows a large nude woman on a cloud leaning over to draw a cloth over or from a naked man on the grass asleep face down on his arms; his head gives off flames.

COLOURING: The MANTLE is Blue (A [dark], C, D [vivid], G [purplish-]), Purple (B, F [bluish-]), reddish-Brown (E), or bluish-Grey (K). The large MAN is Green in F. The persons' HAIR is Brown (A [golden], B and G [orangish-], C–E). The bottom CLOUD is occasionally Yellow (A, C [golden], K), or Raspberry (K). The small woman's DRESS is Yellow (A) or Green (G), and the SKY is sometimes reddish-Brown (B) or Grey (D). The GROUND is sometimes iridescent dark Blue, Orange, and Green (B), brownish-Red with greenish-Yellow (C), or Brown (G).

VARIANTS: *State 1*: The prone man has a halo (copy a) which was removed in *State 2*.

The Tate copy is cut down and includes only ll. 16–31.

Pl. 8. INCIPIT: 'Now comes the night . . .'. DESIGN: Above the text, most of the page is occupied by a large, dark, naked, scaly, crowned man with a sword, standing between two angelic women with heavy wings and with crossed arms or piously clasped hands.

COLOURING: The DEVIL is uniformly Black (A–D, E and K [brownish-], F [greyish-], G [scales greyish-Blue]). The left angel's DRESS is Yellow (A–B, G), Brown (C [greyish-], E [yellowish-], F [golden]), or Pink (D, K [bluish-]), and her WINGS are Yellow (A, G) or mottled Blue (B–G) with Brown (B–D, G), and Red (E, G). The right angel's DRESS is Yellow (A–B, G), Blue (C), Pink (D, K [bluish-]), Brown (E [yellowish-], F [golden]), and her WINGS are mottled Blue (A–G) with Green (A), Brown (B–D, G), or Red (E, G); their HAIR is Brown in G. The BACKGROUND is Black (B, D–F), Brown (C [dark], E, G), Orange (K), or Yellow (K).

VARIANTS: The text is printed in Green and retraced without alteration in Blue in copy B.

The wings are extended downward in copies D and G, and the angels have been given Orange halos in copy K.

Pl. 9. DESIGN: The whole page is a design of two barefooted women in long dresses (the one on the right with a necklace) before a large fireplace in which a smoking coal fire heats a large cauldron, evidently prepared for the dead child stretched on a cloth in the foreground. The long-haired woman on the left seated on the floor bends over her raised knees, which she clasps with her arms, while the woman on the right in an elegant low chair looks up at the cauldron. (A sketch perhaps for this design appears in *Notebook* p. 77; the left woman appears in a design related to *Tiriel* [?1789], see ll. 257–61 note; and a virtually identical one for the baby is on *America* [1793] pl. 11.)

COLOURING: The left woman's DRESS is Blue (A, G), Red (B [dull Pink], C [raspberry], F [pinkish-], K [pale raspberry]), or pale Green (D, E [yellowish-]). The right woman's DRESS is Yellow (A, D, F), Red (B [dark], E [bold Pink], G [pinkish-]), rich reddish-Brown (C), or Grey (K), and her NECKLACE is Red (A, B [dark], C, D [pale], E–F), or Blue (G). The BABY, ordinarily nude-Pink, is sometimes greyish-Green (A), greyish-Pink (B), or Grey (K), and the CLOTH he lies on is pale Green (D) or Blue (F, G [greyish-]). The WALL is the printing colour or Yellow (A), Brown (C [dark], E, K [light]), or Grey (D, G). The women's HAIR is Brown (A [orangish-], B [orangish on the left, dark on the right], C, E, F [the left woman]), or Black (D, F [the right woman]). The CHAIR is sometimes Green (B [dull], C), Blue (F), or pale Red (K).

VARIANTS: The proofs reveal three stages of the etched design:

State 1 shows heavy Black shadows on the baby's ribs and above his face, in the cloth by the left woman's foot, and in the smoke (copy b [pl. 9ᵇ]);

State 2 has some White lines in the cloth on the child's side and above his face (copy a);

State 3, the published state, shows more White lines in all these areas.

The right woman's foot is sometimes strangely Yellow (B–C, D [orangish-]).

The left woman seems to have a kind of chair in copy K.

Pl. 10. DESIGN: The whole page is a design of a man in a long, dark coat and souwester-like hat carrying a large bell who walks past a brick wall with a door marked 'LORD / [H]AVE MERC[Y] / ON US' over a cross. In the bottom left corner a man in a singlet supports an apparently dying woman in a long dress, while to the right another with raised arms falls toward the ground. (A sketch for the three bottom figures appears on *Notebook* p. 25. The bellman and the two figures at the bottom are adapted from a design for 'Plague' [*c.* 1779] in the possession of Mr. Donald Davidson [reproduced in *Blake Newsletter*, vii (1973), 4 and cover]; the inscription 'Lord have / M^{er} on us' there appears on a massive church.)

COLOURING: The BELLMAN is Black (B, D–E, G, BMPR pull), or Blue (K), and his HAIR is White (B), Grey (D), or yellowish-Brown (E). The other MAN is Purple (A), Blue (B–C, F–G), Brown (D, E [reddish-]), or Green (K), and his HAIR is Red (B), Grey (D), yellowish-Brown (E), Blond (F), or Black (BMPR pull). The left woman's DRESS is Yellow (A), Red (B), Blue (C, E [pale Purple], F [purplish-]), Raspberry (D [pale], K), or purplish-Grey (G), and her HAIR is Orange (B, F [pale]), Grey (D), yellowish-Brown (E), or Black (BMPR pull). The right-hand woman's DRESS is Red (A [pale Pink], C [pale raspberry], G [pinkish-]), pale yellowish-Brown (B), pale Green (D), Blue (E–F), or bluish-Grey (K), and her HAIR is Brown (B and D [dark], E [yellowish-], F), or Black (BMPR pull). The WALL is the printing colour, or pale Orange (A), Grey (B, D, F), Black (C), or Brown (E, K).

VARIANTS: The proofs reveal at least one preliminary stage of the etching:

State 1: There are no White lines in the coat or hat of the bellman, on the chest or back of the lower man, on the back of the right woman's leg, or through the horizontal lines of the left woman's dress, and few in the women's hair (copy a); in copy c, the left woman's hair is indicated by scratching on the paper;

State 2, the published State, shows more White lines in all these areas.

The bellman and the two women have pale Green skin in B, and all the faces are tinged with Green in C.

The door is obscured in C and raised in K, and the cross is invisible in K.

The left woman's eyes are rolled upward, and a heavy shadow falls from the top left in copy D.

Pl. 11. INCIPIT: 'Arise O Rintrah . . .'. DESIGN: Below the text, most of the page is filled by a White-bearded man in a long robe who looks leftward with outstretched arms, while his legs are clasped by a woman in a long dress kneeling on the grass. (In some copies [e.g. B], the colouring makes it clear that the man is protecting the woman from enveloping darkness.) Behind them are clouds and, to the left, Black sky. (For related designs see *Tiriel* [?1789] ll. 257–61 note.)

COLOURING: The man's ROBE is Blue (A, B [dark velvet], D and F [purplish-], E [pale], G and National Gallery of Victoria pull [dark]), Buff (C), Grey (K), or uncoloured (c). The woman's DRESS is Yellow (A, D, F, Victoria pull), Brown (B [greyish-], E [golden]), Raspberry (C, K), pale Green (G), and lavender Pink (c), and her HAIR is Brown (B, G, K, Victoria pull), or Black (F, c). Some CLOUDS are Blue (A [greyish-], C, Victoria pull), Red (A, B [vivid velvet], K [raspberry], Victoria pull), dark bluish-Black (B, C [Red at the edges], E), or Grey (D, F [dark], G, K), or Yellow (K, c).

Pl. 12. INCIPIT: 'Enitharmon slept . . .'. DESIGN: Stalks of grain make a huge 'S' round the figures at the top and the text at the bottom. Within the top of the 'S', a nude, flying woman on the left and a naked man blow large, strange, curving horns from which spray dark particles.

COLOURING: The BACKGROUND is Yellow (A, K [pale], Keynes pull), Brown (B [greenish-], C, E, G), Green (D–G, Keynes pull [yellowish-]), or Grey (F). The woman's HAIR is Blond (A–B, K), or Black (D), and the man's Orange (A), Red (B), Black (D), or Yellow (K). The woman's HORN is Red (B, Keynes pull), dark Green (E), or Brown (G), and the man's is Brown (B [dark], E [reddish-], G), Red (C), or dark Blue (Keynes pull). The LEAVES and SPRAY are Black in B.

VARIANT: The man's right hand is Green in copy D.

Pl. 13. INCIPIT: 'In thoughts perturb'd . . .'. DESIGN: A large, open-mouthed serpent whose head emits flames writhes up the left margin in seven coils. (Blake's *Night Thoughts* drawing for Night V, p. 8 [?1796] shows in the left margin a similar crested serpent rising on seven coils and looking down at a kneeling, worshipping figure.)

COLOURING: The SNAKE is Black (A), or mottled Brown (B, D–G, K) with Green (B–C, E), Red (B–C, E), Blue (B, C [dark], E), and Yellow (E), and its TONGUE is Red (B).

Pl. 14: INCIPIT: 'Albions Angel rose . . .'. DESIGN: Above the text, most of the page is dominated by a fat man with huge, open, dark bat wings, an ornate robe, long, pointed ears, and a pope's triple-tiara, who is seated on a Gothic throne above a cloud with a book open on his knees. (In some copies [e.g. B], it appears as if his robe is faced with four embroidered human figures.) Before him bend a clothed angelic man (on the left) and woman with wings who cross wands headed with fleurs-de-lis over the text.

COLOURING: The pope's ROBE is Purple (A), pinkish-Peach (B), or Red (C–G, K), and his WINGS are Black (A [greenish-], E–F [greyish-]), or Brown (B); the FACINGS of his robe (A), his TIARA (A–C, E–G, K), and his THRONE (A, K) are Gold. The left angel's ROBE is yellowish-Green (A), Blue (B and F [pale], C, D [pale Lavender], G), yellowish-Brown (E), or bluish-Grey (K), and his WINGS are Blue (A, B [pale], E, G), Pink (C), Buff (D), Purple (E), Brown (E, G), and Green (E). The right angel's ROBE is yellowish-Green (A), pale Yellow (B), Blue (C, D [pale Lavender], F [pale], G), yellowish-Brown (E), or bluish-Grey (K), and her WINGS are Blue (A, B [pale], C, E, G), Brown (D [buff], E, G), Purple (E), and Green (E). The colouring of the BACKGROUND is Black throughout, and once the CLOUD is Yellow (K).

VARIANTS: In copy B, the pope's mouth is shut.

The top of the throne is obscured in copy C.

In copy G, the pope smiles weakly, and his bat-ears are not flesh-coloured, and therefore seem to be part of the throne-design, and his robe-facings are gone.

The pope's eyes are raised in copy K, and serpent-coils from the feet of the angels almost meet beneath the text.

Pl. 15. INCIPIT: 'And the clouds & fires . . .'. DESIGN: In the right margin and between ll. 114 and 115 are many insects near a huge, Black Spider's web, in which is wrapped, in the bottom right corner, a small, reclining, naked person with hands clasped as if in despair. At the bottom left are plants with large leaves.

COLOURING: The PERSON, ordinarily nude-Pink, is sometimes Grey (A [dark], F). The bottom SPIDERS are spotted with Red in B, the bottom BACK-GROUND is sometimes Yellow (B–C), and some PLANTS are dark Blue in B.

Pl. 16. INCIPIT: 'The red limb'd Angel . . .'. DESIGN: There is a spider in his web between ll. 137 and 138.

The bottom half of the page is filled by the design of a naked man seated on a low stone and chained by the ankles who raises his hands (?in horror) as he looks to the right towards a dark, scaled, naked man with keys who is ascending shadowed dungeon steps.

COLOURING: The PRISONER, ordinarily nude-Pink, is sometimes greyish-Pink (B), or orangish-Pink (C), and his HAIR is Brown (C, E [light], c). The JAILER is Green (A [strong], C–D and c [greyish-], E [yellowish-], F–G), greenish-Grey (K), or dark greenish-Blue (B), and his HAIR is Black (E). The WALLS are the printing colour or Brown (C–D [buff], F, c [peach]), or Black (B, E–F, G [brownish-]).

Pl. 17. INCIPIT: 'Ethinthus queen of waters . . .'. DESIGN: In the right margin and in open spaces in the text, particularly after ll. 153, 156, and 167, are luxuriant flames, insects, birds, and vegetation, and in the bottom margin are three serpents.

COLOURING: The design is touched with Brown and Green in all coloured copies, plus Black (B, D), Blue (B, E), and Red (C, E).

VARIANTS: The proofs reveal two preliminary states of the copperplate, plus two manuscript alterations:

State 1: In copies a, b (pl. 17ᵃ⁻ᵇ) and c (pl. 17ᵃ⁻ᶜ), l. 174 reads 'She ceas'd, and all went forth to sport beneath the solemn moon' and l. 177 reads 'Till morning ope'd the eastern gate, and the angel trumpet blew:'. In copy c (pl. 17ᵃ), ll. 174–9 were half-heartedly erased from the paper, and in copy c (pl. 17ᵇ) l. 174 above was altered in blue ink to read: 'She ceas'd. All were forth in sport beneath the solemn moon.'

State 2: In copy b (pl. 17ᶜ), l. 177 is in this early state, but l. 174 was altered to the final state.

State 3: The published State also eliminates the last five words from l. 177, perhaps because Newton had already 'siez'd the Trump, & blow'd the enormous blast' in l. 134.

Pl. 18. INCIPIT: 'Shot from the heights . . .'. DESIGN: In the margin, between ll. 186 and 187 and between ll. 192 and 193 are flourishing tendrils, insects, and birds.

Below the text, most of the page is taken up by a design of a naked man fleeing up steps to the left; he carries over his shoulder a limp woman in a long dress and holds a little girl by the arm, as flames surge across the page from the right. At the top of the steps there appears to be a broken classical column. (A similar design, reversed, appears in *Job* [1826] pl. 3.)

COLOURING: The woman's DRESS is Blue (A [strong], F–G), Grey (Buffalo), Yellow (B), brownish-Orange (C), Purple (D [pale], E [reddish-]), or White (C [the blouse], K), and her HAIR is Brown (B [dark], D–E, K), or Black (F). The child's DRESS is Green (A, E [pale]), Brown (B), orangish-Gold (C), Grey (D), pale Purple (F), purplish-Pink (G), uncoloured (K), or pale Grey (Buffalo pull), and her HAIR is Yellow (B, C [golden-]), Brown (D–E, K), or Black (F). The man's HAIR is Brown (B–D, K), or Black (E–F).

VARIANTS: There are two early states in the proofs:

State 1: In copy a, there are no White lines on the shoulder of the woman, on the right ankle of the man, or on the child's fingers; there is a squiggle (later removed) below 'Call'd' in l. 259, and l. 249 reads: 'Shot from the heights of Enitharmon, before the trumpet blew:'.

State 2: In copy c (pl. 18ᵃ), the text is unchanged but the design has been altered with White lines as in the published State.

State 3: In the published State, the last four words of l. 249 were removed from the copper, perhaps because the trumpet had already sounded in l. 203.

In copy D, there are lines on the man's left hip as if to represent cloth, but the cloth is not coloured; in copy F, a piece of loose cloth covers his genitals; in copy G, the penis is enormously long, extending to the upper edge of his right thigh.

In copy K, the child's face is turned towards the man.

The Trinity College and Buffalo proofs show the design only; they are cut off just above 'FINIS'.

COPY A: BINDING: (1) Originally stabbed through three holes, 8·9 and 7·0 cm apart; (2) Later mounted on hinges and bound in boards (according to Keynes [1921]); (3) Before 1856 pl. 1–2, 4–6 were separated, for a time they were bound 'somewhat irregularly in a cloth case' with *America* (A) and pl. d, 'The Accusers' (H), *Song of Los* (B), *Visions* (F) pl. 1, and 'Joseph of Arimathea Preaching' (F), but (4) Separated by 1904; at some point they were trimmed to about 22·0 × 30·5 and later inlaid to the size of the other plates with which they were reunited by 1906; (5) pl. 7–18 were 'BOUND BY RIVIERE & SON' in Brown levant morocco, Jansen style, g.e.; (6) When pl. 1–2, 4–6 were added to this volume the leaves in which they were inlaid were gilt rather more brightly than the rest.

HISTORY: (1) Probably bought before 1835 by Isaac D'Israeli[1] (1766–

---

[1] In 1835 Isaac D'Israeli referred to 'the ONE HUNDRED AND SIXTY designs I possess of Blake's' (T. F. Dibdin, *Reminiscences of a Literary Life* [1836], 788—see *Blake Records* [1969],

1848); (2) Pl. 1–2, 4–6 were separated from the others by 1856;[1] (**Ai**) Pl. 7–18 were sold by D'Israeli's son the Earl of Beaconsfield at Sotheby's, 20 March 1882, lot 57, for £8. 5s. to Bain; (**Aii**) They were listed in the library catalogue of B. B. Macgeorge (1892), who lent pl. 7, 9–18 to Muir for his facsimile (1887); (**Bi**) For a time pl. 1–2, 4–6 were bound 'somewhat irregularly' with *America* (A) and pl. d, 'The Accusers' (H), *Song of Los* (B), *Visions* (F) pl. 1, and 'Joseph of Arimathea Preaching' (F) before they were sold anonymously at Hodgson's, 14 Jan. 1904, lot 225, for £80 to Hopkins; (3) The reunited plates were all listed in the catalogue of B. B. Macgeorge (1906) and sold posthumously for him at Sotheby's, 1 July 1924, lot 116, for £500 to G. Wells; (4) Acquired by George C. Smith, Jr., listed in his anonymous catalogue (1927), lot 11, lent to the Fogg exhibition (1930), and sold posthumously at Parke-Bernet, 2 Nov. 1938, lot 26, for $13,000 to Sessler; (5) Acquired by Moncure Biddle, who added his book-plate, lent it to the Philadelphia exhibition (1939), no. 69, and sold it 'through Gannon' (according to Keynes & Wolf) to (6) Mr. *Paul Mellon*.

COPY B: BINDING: (1) Originally stabbed through three holes, 3·4 cm

243), and in 1862 his son the Earl of Beaconsfield sent W. M. Rossetti 'a list of his . . . "170 Drawings &c By W. Blake" . . . [*from* Urizen, Los, &c &c]' (*Letters of William Michael Rossetti*, ed. C. Gohdes & P. F. Baum [1934], 5). Beaconsfield's 1882 sale included:

Title	Number of Plates
Songs (A)	50
Europe (A)	12 (missing pl. 1–2, 4–6)
Visions (F)	10 (missing pl. 1)
Thel (F)	8
Urizen (B)	28
Marriage (D)	27
	——
	135 in all

The plates missing from	*Europe* (A)	5
and	*Visions* (F)	1
were once bound up with	*America* (A)	18
	America pl. d (LC)	1
	Song of Los (B)	8
	'The Accusers' (H)	1
	'Joseph of Arimathea Preaching' (F)	1
		——
and sold anonymously in 1904		35
		——
		170

These 170 plates were probably all in the collection when Beaconsfield described his '170' designs in 1862. The 10 plates added between 1835 (160 plates) and 1862 (170 plates) probably consisted of *Song of Los* (B) and two of the three loose plates.

This History suggests that the works sold anonymously in 1904 had belonged to D'Israeli (*America* [A] and one separate plate) or his son (*Song of Los* [B] and two separate plates). The *Europe* and *Visions* plates mislaid in 1856 (see also *Visions* [F], p. 473) and again in 1882 were still in the collection and known to its owner in 1862.

[1] Keynes (1921) and Keynes & Wolf say that 'Beaconsfield's library marks, dated 1856', show that the 5 plates were then missing (for similar marks see *Visions* [F] and *Urizen* [B], pp. 473, 180); however, neither Mr. Mellon's librarian Mr. Willis Van Devanter nor I can find these marks.

from the top and 9·0, 9·2 cm apart; (2) Bound about 1821 (the watermark date on three fly-leaves) with *America* (G), *Jerusalem* (B) in a Red Roxburgh binding over a black spine, the spine gilt with 'AMERICA. / — / EUROPE / — / JERUSALEM / — / BY / BLAKE'; (3) Disbound in June 1966.

HISTORY: The History is as in *America* (G), p. 102.

COPY C: BINDING: (1) Originally stabbed (perhaps with *America* [B]) through three holes, 6·5 cm and 7·7 cm apart; (2) Bound before 1835 with *America* (F), *Visions* (B), *Song of Los* (D); (3) *Europe* was extracted from the volume in 1852, and its leaves are now mounted.

HISTORY: (1) *Europe* (C) may once have been sewn with *America* (B) and then separated; (2) It was apparently copy C which was 'bound together' with *Visions* (B), *Song of Los* (D), and *America* (F) and sold with Blair's *Grave* in the library of George Cumberland at Christie's, 6 May 1835, lot 60, for £3. 18s. to Butts; (3) The same composite volume was sold anonymously with the Butts collection (see *Songs* [F], p. 414) at Sotheby's, 26 March 1852, lot 54, for £11 to 'M' (? R. M. Milnes);[1] (4) *Europe* was sold as the Property of Milnes's son the Earl of Crewe at Sotheby's, 30 March 1903, lot 5 (unbound), for £203 to Quaritch; (5) It was bought from the 'Earl of Crewe, Quaritch / £203. 5%+ex[*change*] / $1047' by 'W A White / 20 April, 1903' (according to notes on the loose blank leaf bearing an offset); White lent it anonymously to the Grolier Club exhibition (1905), no. 21, perhaps to that of (1919), no. 12, and to the Fogg exhibition (1924), and gave it (according to Keynes & Wolf) to his son-in-law (6) F. M. Weld, Jr.;[2] it was bought from the Weld Estate (according to Keynes & Wolf) by (7) Harold T. White, whose widow gave it (in accordance with his will) in Dec. 1963 to (8) HARVARD.

COPY D: BINDING: (1) Ozias Humphry probably had it bound with the Large Book of Designs (A); (2) Separated, mounted on linen stubs, and bound in the British Museum in half Green morocco with *Visions* (A); (3) The leaves of *Europe* and *Visions* were remounted in heavy paper 'windows' and bound, together, in Red morocco, in 1969.

---

[1] The auctioneer's copy in the British Museum gives as the buyer 'M' (not 'F. T. Palgrave, £11', as in Keynes [1921] and Keynes & Wolf—see *America* [F], p. 102), who is probably the same as 'R M M' (Richard Monckton Milnes), the buyer of lots 52, 55, 57, 59, 158–9, 167 in the same sale.

F. T. Palgrave and Milnes 'together attended Mr. Butts' sale of Blake's books, and each encouraged the other to become the possessor of many of his original drawings and engravings' (G. F. Palgrave, *Francis Turner Palgrave* [1899], 26). At the sale Palgrave bought *Thel* (L), but he already evidently owned *Europe* (D), while he lacked *America*, *Visions*, and *Song of Los*. Milnes owned, probably by this date (see *Thel* [B], p. 125), copies of *America* (M), *Visions* (M), and *Song of Los* (A), and consequently he needed only *Europe* from the Butts volume. Therefore, *Europe* (C) was extracted from the composite volume (its plates have been loose since its first positive identification in 1903) and retained by Milnes, while Palgrave got the rest of the volume.

This hypothetical provenance for *Europe* (C) is supported by W. A. White's note in the volume saying that 'Monckton Milnes bought it and others' from 'Butts'; they were 'bound up together in one volume which was broken up at [*i.e. before*] the Crewe sale'.

[2] A memorandum with the volume from F. M. W. inquires on 23 Dec. 1929 of 'MR. WHITE' which copy of *Europe* is the one he has.

HISTORY: (1) Probably acquired from Blake by Ozias Humphry,[1] apparently lent by him to George Cumberland (who wrote extensive quotations[2] from Bysshe's *Art of English Poetry* on pl. 1–2, 4, 6–18), and bequeathed to Humphry's natural son (2) William Upcott, who lent it to H. C. Robinson (who quoted it in 1811) and to Richard Thomson[3] (who described it in about 1827 as bound with the Large Book of Designs [A], see p. 269—*Blake Records* [1969], 447, 470–3), and for whom it was sold posthumously by Evans, 15 June 1846, lot 277 (with *America* [H] and with the Large [A] and Small Books of Designs [A] 'Inserted'), for £7. 2s. 6d. to Evans; (3) Evidently acquired by F. T. Palgrave;[4] (4) Acquired on 25 June 1859 by the BRITISH MUSEUM PRINT ROOM, bound with *Visions* (A), and probably used for Pearson's facsimile (1876); pl. 2, 5–6, 8 were used for the 1887 Muir facsimile.

COPY E: BINDING: 'BOUND BY F. BEDFORD' in Brown levant morocco.

HISTORY: (1) Acquired by 'Thos Gaisford', who added his book-plate and sold it at Sotheby's, 23 April 1890, lot 190, for £59 to Robson (at the back is the ticket of 'Robson & Kerslake Booksellers, 23, Coventry Street, Haymarket, London'); (2) Sold for the late widow of Alexander Mackay at Christie's, 26 April 1921, lot 2, for £600 to Shoebridge; (3) 'Bought in 1922' (according to Keynes & Wolf) by A. E. Newton, who added his bookplate, lent it to the Philadelphia exhibition (1939), no. 70, and sold it posthumously at Parke-Bernet, 16 April 1941, lot 129, for $8,000 to Rosenbach for (4) Mr. LESSING J. ROSENWALD.

COPY F: BINDING: Sewn through three holes, 9·6 and 8·0 cm apart, in the original heavy Buff wrappers, now rather battered.

HISTORY: (1) Perhaps this is the copy sold by Robert Arthington at Sotheby's, 17 May 1866, lot 23 (17 pages, coloured), for £6. 10s. to Pickering; (2) Acquired by a collector who stamped pl. 1 verso, pl. 2, and pl. 18 with his sign: a monogram D W J in a circle under a three-pronged crown; (3) Sold anonymously at American Art Association, 1 Feb. 1928, lot 8, for $11,300 to W. M. Hill; (4) Acquired by Owen D. Young, who lent it to the Fogg exhibition (1930), and gave it jointly with Dr. A. A. Berg on 5 May 1941 to (5) The Berg Collection of the NEW YORK PUBLIC LIBRARY (see *America* [L], p. 104).

COPY G: BINDING: (1) Originally stabbed through eight holes, 2·7 cm from the top, 4·2, 3·7, 2·6, 5·8, 5·7, 5·9, 3·8 cm apart; (2) Later bound in old (? contemporary) half Red morocco in front of *Song of Los* (C) (with which

---

[1] Probably not by Butts, for Butts seems to have owned copy C (q.v.), rather than copy D as in Keynes & Wolf.

[2] The quotations are unsigned, but the handwriting is the same as that in Cumberland's letters of 1796 in the British Museum. Cumberland's quotations are analogous to the titles added to the plates of the Small Book of Designs (B).

[3] Thomson describes pl. 12 ('two angels pouring out the black spotted plague upon England') as 'page 9'; pl. 12 was numbered '9' by Blake in copy D, but '10' in copy C. Therefore it must have been copy D which Thomson was describing for J. T. Smith's life of Blake (1828).

[4] D. G. Rossetti told Anne Gilchrist in 1863 that 'the [*British*] Museum copy of *Europe* [D] . . . belonged formerly' to 'a Mr. Palgrave' (*Letters of Dante Gabriel Rossetti*, ed. J. R. Wahl [1965], ii. 483).

the binding is now) and *Visions* (H), the edges trimmed but not gilt; (3) *Europe* was removed (still independently stitched) by 1905, and pl. 1 is now loose.

HISTORY: For its History see *Visions* (H), with which it was bound, p. 474.

COPY H: BINDING: (1) Bound in half calf in 1882, but (2) Disbound, trimmed, and each leaf mounted, probably by E. W. Hooper for the Boston exhibition (1891).

HISTORY: (1) Sold by H. G. Bohn in May 1835¹ to (2) William Beckford, and sold with the Beckford Library at Sotheby's, 4 July 1882, lot 955, for £12. 5s. to Ellis & White; (3) Offered in Ellis & White Catalogue 50 (?Nov. 1882), lot 83,² for £45; (4) Perhaps this is the uncut copy, 'not paged', sold anonymously at Sotheby's, 18 Dec. 1886, lot 1559, for £4. 15s. to J. Pearson; (5) Acquired evidently through Little, Brown, by Edwin William Hooper, who lent it to the Boston exhibition (1891), no. 6, and from whom it passed before 1921 to his daughter (6) Mrs. John Briggs Potter, who lent it to the exhibitions in the Fogg (1924, 1930) and Philadelphia (1939), no. 71, and gave it with her sisters in memory of her father on 1 July 1941 to (7) HARVARD.

COPY I: BINDING: Bound after *America* (N)—see p. 104.

HISTORY: The History is the same as that of *America* (N), with which it is bound.

COPY K: BINDING: Bound with *America* (O)—see p. 105.

HISTORY: The History is the same as that of *America* (O), with which it is bound.

COPY L: BINDING: (1) Bound in Grey calf with *America* (Q); (2) *Europe* was separated after 1913, the plates were trimmed erratically (the plates are at heights different from those of the facing offsets), and 'BOUND BY RIVIERE & SON' in Red levant morocco, g.e., by 1918.

HISTORY: (1) Sold by R. A. Potts at Sotheby's, 20 Feb. 1913, lot 59 (bound in Grey calf with *America* [Q], not said to be coloured), for £66 to Sabin; (2) The volume was broken up, 'colouring was added soon afterwards for Walter T. Spencer, who [*concealed his steps—see* AMERICA (*Q*), *p. 105— and*] sold it in the same year to Herschel V. Jones' (according to Keynes & Wolf); Jones added his book-plate and sold *Europe* at Anderson Galleries, 2 Dec. 1918, lot 184 (bound by Riviere and coloured), for $4,600 to G. D. Smith for (3) The HUNTINGTON LIBRARY.

COPY M: BINDING: Bound, probably about 1833 for Samuel Boddington, after *America* (P) in heavily tooled Red morocco with marbled endpapers, g.e., in a way similar to Boddington's *Jerusalem* (H).

¹ An inserted leaf says: 'notes [*probably by Beckford*] from the former binding:—May 1835 / H G Bohn / — / N° 955 of the . . . [*1882 sale*] / sold to Ellis & White for £12. 5. 0'; Keynes (1921) and Keynes & Wolf say it contained 'the inscription "May 1835 H. G. Bohn N. 732".'
It is evidently just coincidence that *For Children* (C) was sold by Cumberland in May 1835 to Bohn, who presented it in that month to Beckford.

² Described as having 17 leaves (it now has 18 leaves) bound in half calf (now disbound), 'printed in a single dark tint' (pl. 3 is in a conspicuously lighter shade than the other 17 plates); evidently pl. 3 (present among the 18 plates in the Beckford sale) was omitted from the Ellis & White description.

HISTORY: The History is as in *America* (P), with which it is bound; see p. 105.

COPY a: BINDING: (1) First stabbed through 5 holes, 2·0 cm from the top, 10·2, 6·6, 6·8, and 6·8 cm apart (pl. 1 missing the top hole, the stabs in the *right* sides of pl. 1 *and pl. 9*); on the verso of pl. 18 is a faint pencil sketch of a horse, with perhaps a small man standing in front of it; (2) now separately mounted, pl. 1–2, 9–10 pasted down.

HISTORY: (1) This is evidently the copy with 8 engraved leaves sold posthumously for Samuel Palmer's cousin John Giles at Christie's on 2 Feb. 1881, lot 184 (*'with a duplicate of the frontispiece, coloured'*—?'Ancient of Days' [B], ?making 9 leaves in all); (2) Perhaps pl. 11 [and 17] from copy a were lent by H. H. Gilchrist to the Pennsylvania Academy of the Fine Arts exhibition (1892), no. 151; (3) Copy a was sold by Major Alexander Sykes at Sotheby's, 29 July 1936, lot 1006 (in a portfolio), for £26 to Rimell; sold by James Rimell & Sons for £250 on 16 Nov. 1936 to (4) The BRITISH MUSEUM PRINT ROOM.

COPY b: BINDING: (1) Bound in contemporary rough calf with other leaves of Blakeana, including *Thel* (a); (2) After 1906 the plates of *Europe* were each separately mounted.

HISTORY: The History is as in *Thel* (a); see p. 131.

COPY c: BINDING: (1) Bound about 1853 with many leaves of Blakeana including the 'Order' of the *Songs*; (2) The *Europe* plates were separated after 1924; (3a) Pl. 18^{a-b} were bound with *Jerusalem* plates, probably by Macdonald for G. C. Smith, Jr.; (3b) All the other plates are now loose, pl. 4^a, 5^a mounted, pl. 1, 11^c, 17^c mounted and framed.

HISTORY: see the 'Order' of the *Songs*.

Pl. 1: BINDING: Loose.

HISTORY: For its History see *For the Sexes*, pl. 3, p. 204; *Keynes* lent it to the exhibitions of the British Museum (1957), no. 58, and (anonymously) the Whitworth Art Gallery (1969), no. 10, and the National Library of Scotland (1969), no. 70, and described it in his catalogue (1964).

Pl. 1: BINDING: Mounted and framed.

HISTORY: (1) This may be one of the two uncoloured copies[1] lent by A. Macmillan to the Burlington Fine Arts Club exhibition (1876), no. 269; (2) Perhaps W. A. White lent it (with *Jerusalem* pl. 30 printed on the verso) anonymously with the rest of his collection to the Grolier Club exhibition (1905), no. 23, and sold it posthumously with the rest of his Blake collection in 1929 to (3) A. S. W. Rosenbach, who lent it to the Philadelphia exhibition (1939), no. 72, and sold it in Nov. 1952 to (4) Mr. Rabinowitz, whose widow (as Mrs. Lester Albert Le Wars) sold it through Mr. Robert Barry, Jr., of Stonehill's in 1970 to (5) Mr. *Paul Mellon*.

Pl. 1^{a-b}, 2^{a-b}: BINDING: Loose.

HISTORY: For the History see *Jerusalem*, pl. 25, 32, 41, 47, with which they are printed, p. 262.

[1] For the other, see the 'Order' of the *Songs*, p. 337.

Pl. 2: BINDING: Loose.

HISTORY: (1) Acquired (with *Jerusalem* pl. 1 printed on the verso) by William Bell Scott, who added his monogram, and probably sold it at Sotheby's, 21 April 1885, lot 165 (*Jerusalem* pl. 1?), for 11s. to Fawcett: (2) Perhaps (like *Marriage* pl. 3–4, lot 167, in this sale sold to Fawcett) it was acquired by Mrs. Graham Smith and then by her nephew (3) Anthony Asquith, who sold it posthumously at Hodgson's in 1942[1] to (4) *Geoffrey Keynes*, who lent it to the exhibitions in the British Museum (1957), no. 293, and (anonymously) the Whitworth Art Gallery (1969), no. 17, and the National Library of Scotland (1969), no. 64, described it in his catalogue (1964), no. 523, and reproduced the *Jerusalem* frontispiece with the facsimile of *Jerusalem* (C) (1952).

Pl. 2: Loose, mounted.

HISTORY: (1) Sold posthumously for Stopford Brooke at Sotheby's, 9 April 1919, lot 447, for £12. 10s. to Edwards; (2) Acquired from Frederick Keppel & Co. of New York (according to letters of 6 Nov., 29 Dec. 1920 with the plate) by Allan R. Brown, who gave it on 31 Jan. 1940 to (3) TRINITY COLLEGE, Hartford, Connecticut.

Pl. 2: Mounted, framed.

HISTORY: (1) Sold posthumously with the Linnell Collection at Christie's, 15 March 1918, lot 176 (with *Jerusalem* pl. 24 on the verso); (2) Acquired by Lady Cameron, who allowed it to be reproduced in Keynes's *Bibliography* (1921) and lent it to the Burlington Fine Arts Club exhibition (1927), no. 82; (3) Acquired by the *Earl of Crawford and Balcarres*, who loaned it to the exhibitions in Tokyo (Oct. 1929) and the National Library of Scotland (1969), no. 44.

Pl. 4: BINDING: Loose.

HISTORY: (1) Given by George Richmond on 19 March 1890 to his son (2) John Richmond, whose wife sold it in 1927 to (3) *Geoffrey Keynes*, whose catalogue (1964), no. 520, is the authority for these facts.

Pl. 5, 10: BINDING: Loose.

HISTORY: (1) Acquired by the Earl of Crewe;[2] (2) Acquired by J. Tregaskis;[2] (3) Acquired by W. Graham Robertson in 1904,[2] lent to the Bournemouth exhibition (1949), no. 45, described in his catalogue (1952), no. 135, and sold posthumously at Christie's, 22 July 1949, lot 86, for £10. 10s. to Gain, for (4) *Geoffrey Keynes*, who described it in his catalogue (1964), no. 520, and lent it anonymously to the exhibitions of the Whitworth Art Gallery (1969), no. 14, and the National Library of Scotland (1969), no. 44.

Pl. 6–7: BINDING: Loose.

HISTORY: (1) Acquired from Mrs. John Richmond in 1922 by (2) The TATE GALLERY.

---

[1] G. Keynes, *Bibliotheca Bibliographici* (1964), no. 523. The only Asquith sales I can trace at Hodgson's (14–15 Jan., 29 April 1943) include no Blakes.

[2] *The Blake Collection of W. Graham Robertson*, ed. K. Preston (1952), no. 135.

Pl. 6–7: BINDING: Loose.

HISTORY: (**1**) Lent anonymously to the Grolier Club exhibition (1905), no. 25, perhaps by W. A. White who lent most of the rest of the works shown there; (**2**) Sold posthumously for Col. Gould Weston at Christie's, 15 July 1957, lot 28, for £26. 5.; (**3**) 'Given by John Fleming . . . [*in*] 1956 [*sic*]' to (**4**) *Geoffrey Keynes*, according to his catalogue (1964), no. 520.

Pl. 6–7, 12: BINDING: Loose.

HISTORY: (**1**) Acquired, probably from Frederick Tatham about 1834 (like the 'Nelson' drawing), by (**2**) John Defett Francis, who added his mark to each plate and 'J Defett Francis 1834' on the verso of pl. 6, and gave them in 1876 to (**3**) The town of Swansea, where they were housed about 1966 in the GLYNN VIVIAN GALLERY.

Pl. 10: BINDING: (**1**) Perhaps once bound with other Blakeana in an extra-illustrated Gilchrist (1863); (**2**) Now pasted on a loose mount.

HISTORY: (**1**) Perhaps this is the copy offered by Francis Harvey (?1864) for 10*s*.; (**2**) It may have been bound with 144 other Blake prints and drawings in the extra-illustrated 1863 Gilchrist (see *For the Sexes* pl. 15, p. 205) offered by John Pearson, Catalogue 58 (?1884), lot 363, for £52. 10*s*.; (**3**) Pl. 10 was sold separately by the Revd. J[?] Iden. Hart on 2 Oct. 1936 to (**4**) The BRITISH MUSEUM PRINT ROOM.

Pl. 11: BINDING: Loose, mounted; framed with three lines.

HISTORY: (**1**) Perhaps this is the 'design' Linnell bought for £1. 1*s*. in Aug. 1821 (*Blake Records* [1969], 585); it was lent to the Burlington Fine Arts Club exhibition (1876), no. 26, and sold posthumously with the Linnell Collection at Christie's, 15 March 1918, lot 178, to (**2**) The Felton Bequest for (**3**) The NATIONAL GALLERY OF VICTORIA, Melbourne, Australia, which received it on 13 March 1920.

Pl. 11, 17: BINDING: Loose.

HISTORY: See the 'Order' of the *Songs*, p. 337.

Pl. 12: BINDING: Loose.

HISTORY: (**1**) Lent by Dr. Greville MacDonald to the exhibitions in Nottingham (1914), no. 62, the National Gallery of Scotland (1914), no. 45, and sold by him to (**2**) Francis Edwards, who in turn sold it in 1928 to (**3**) *Geoffrey Keynes*, who lent it to the exhibitions of the British Museum (1957), no. 28 1, (anonymously) to the Whitworth Art Gallery (1969), no. 15, and the National Gallery of Scotland (1969), no. 44, and described it in his catalogue (1964), no. 520, which is the authority for these sales.

Pl. 18: BINDING: Loose, mounted.

HISTORY: (**1**) Probably acquired by 'Mrs Gilchrist', whose name is on the classical drawing miscalled 'Discuss Thrower' once fastened to the back of the *Europe* plate; Mrs. Gilchrist lent it to the exhibitions of the Burlington Fine Arts Club (1876), no. 74, and the Boston Museum (1880), no. 130, and (**2**) Her son H. H. Gilchrist lent it to the Pennsylvania Academy of the Fine Arts exhibition (1892), no. 160; (**3**) Sold by Emma W. Bucknell through American Art Association, 2 April 1928, lot 56, for $1,100; (**4**) Acquired by

Thomas B. Lockwood, who gave it by 1935 to what is now (5) The STATE UNIVERSITY OF NEW YORK AT BUFFALO, where it was described in *A Selection of Books and Manuscripts in the Lockwood Memorial Library of the University of Buffalo* (1935).

34

**Europe, a Prophecy. London, 1969. The William Blake Trust.

Geoffrey Keynes, 'Description and Bibliographical Statement', is on 6 unnumbered pages. The colour facsimile reproduces copy B (pl. 2, 6, 13–15, 17–18), copy G (pl. 1, 4–5, 7–12, 16), and copy K (pl. 9).

35. 'The Everlasting Gospel'

For a Description etc. of 'The Everlasting Gospel' see the *Notebook* (p. 321), where it is largely written; the History etc. here are for the loose leaves.

BINDING: A loose sheet, folded, with four stab holes along the centre crease, 1·5, 4·0, 2·3 cm apart.

HISTORY: (1) Seen by Swinburne (*William Blake* [1868], 175–6)[1] and acquired by E. J. Shaw, who sold it at Sotheby's, 29 July 1925, lot 166 [for £98 to Sawyer]; (2) Acquired by A. S. W. Rosenbach, who lent it to the Philadelphia exhibition (1939), no. 12, and gave it to (3) The ROSENBACH FOUNDATION.

36. 'Exhibition of Paintings in Fresco' (1809)

BIBLIOGRAPHICAL INTRODUCTION

TABLE

Copy	Collection	Corrections	Contemporary Owner
A	HUNTINGTON	[A1]$^{r-v}$	Ozias Humphry
B[2]	BODLEY	[A1]$^{r-v}$	

TITLE: EXHIBITION / OF / 𝔓𝔞𝔦𝔫𝔱𝔦𝔫𝔤𝔰 𝔦𝔫 𝔉𝔯𝔢𝔰𝔠𝔬, / Poetical and Historical Inventions, / By. Wм. BLAKE / – / . . . / . . . for Public Inspection and for Sale by Private / Contract, at / *No.* 28, *Corner of BROAD STREET, Golden-Square.* / — / '*Fit audience find tho' few*' MILTON. / — / Admittance 2s. 6d. each Person, a discriptive Catalogue included. / Watts & Co. Printers, Southmolton St.

COLLATION: Folio: [A1–2], 1 sheet, 4 pages.

CONTENTS: 'Exhibition of Paintings in Fresco . . . Watts & Co. Printers, Southmolton St.' ([A1]^r), 'The Invention of a Portable Fresco' ([A1]^v); [A2]$^{r-v}$ blank. Copy B lacks [A2].

[1] For the possibility that it had been with the *Notebook*, see pp. 321 ff.
[2] Copy B is reproduced in Keynes (1921).

LEAF-SIZE: 18·0 × 23·8 cm.

WATERMARKS: N HENDON[?] / 1802 (copy A).

PAGE NUMBERING: None.

RUNNING TITLES: None.

CATCHWORDS: None.

PRESS FIGURES: None.

PUBLICATION: This flyer was apparently sent out by Blake in May 1809 (the date he added at the end) to his friends, for the only surviving copies were folded to make envelopes and sealed with wafers, and copy A was addressed to Ozias Humphry and sent with a letter by Blake.

ERRATA: (1) ¶5 'discriptive'; (2) ¶10 'Gentleman' should be plural; (3) ¶11 'excluded'.

COPY A: BINDING: Loose, folded to make the envelope for Blake's letter of May 1809, with a wax seal.

   HISTORY: (1) Folded as an envelope for Blake's letter of May 1809 to Ozias Humphry; (2) Acquired by Alexander C. Weston, who lent it to the Burlington Fine Arts Club exhibition (1876), no. 320; (3) Sold by a Philadelphia Collector (Col. Henry D. Hughes—see Visions [L], p. 476) at American Art Association, 16 April 1923, lot 128 ('addressed in Blake's autograph on the back of the second leaf'—i.e. with the 1809 letter); (4) Acquired by 19 April 1926[1] by the HUNTINGTON LIBRARY.

COPY B: BINDING: (1) Evidently originally folded to make an envelope (there is a wafer but no address); (2) Now in a modern binding.

   HISTORY: (1) Evidently once folded to form an envelope and sealed with a wafer; (2) Acquired on 6 Dec. 1893 by the BODLEIAN LIBRARY, and reproduced in Keynes (1921).

37. 'A Fairy leapt' (?1793)

BIBLIOGRAPHICAL INTRODUCTION

COLLECTION: Library of Congress.

WATERMARK: None.

LEAF-SIZE: 14·1 × 18·9 cm.

DATE: About 1793.
   The date is somewhat uncertainly derived from the style of the poem, the form of the handwriting, and the hypothetical date of the drawing on the verso.

DESCRIPTION: The text, on one side of a single leaf, is in pencil and is quite

---

[1] Its 'Source [is] unknown', according to the Huntington accession record, and the date above is that of cataloguing.

difficult to read; the words 'Disguser', 'paltry', 'poisnous', 'hides', and 'Storm' are particularly doubtful.

On the verso is the drawing known as 'The Infant Hercules Throttling Serpents'.

BINDING: Loose; on the verso is Blake's sketch called 'The Infant Hercules Throttling Serpents' (*c.* 1793), reproduced in *Blake's Pencil Drawings*: Second Series, ed. G. Keynes (1956), no. 5.

HISTORY: (1) Offered and reproduced in James Rimell & Son Catalogue 288 (?1932), lot 64 (according to T. O. M[abbott], 'The Text of Blake's "A Faery Stepd upon my Knee"', *N&Q.*, clxiv [1933], 388–9);[1] (2) Sold by the Stonehill firm in 1937 to (3) Mr. LESSING J. ROSENWALD.

38. *The First Book of Urizen* (1794)

BIBLIOGRAPHICAL INTRODUCTION

See Table on pp. 168–9.

TITLE: THE / FIRST *BOOK* / *of* / *U R I Z E N* / *LAMBETH. Printed by Will Blake 1794*

DATE: 1794, as on the title-page.

PUBLICATION: In some respects, *Urizen* is Blake's most ambitiously designed work up to this time. Every plate is illustrated, and there are an unusual number of full-page designs, on pl. 9, 12, 14, 16–17, 21–2, 24, 26–7. Many of the designs illustrate the text more literally than was often Blake's custom (see pl. 1, 3–5, 7–8, *11–12*, 15, *17*, *19–21*, *23–8*), particularly with simple designs of naked men. In addition, there are tiny birds and foliage on text-plates 3–8, 10–11, 13, 15, 18–20, 23, 25, and 28. The logical, consecutive nature of the narrative is emphasized by chapter- and section-numbers and by running heads. The book was also printed with great care on one side of the leaves only, all copies being coloured and significant variants being made in each.

Copperplates: There is some evidence in the coincidence of plate-sizes that *Urizen* was etched on the versos of the plates for the *Marriage* (?1790–3):

		Urizen			*Marriage*
pl.	1	*10·3* × 14·9	pl. 26		*10·3* × 14·8
pl.	2	10·3 × 16·8			
pl.	3	10·0 × 14·8	pl. 14		10·1 × 14·9
pl.	*4*	*10·2* × *15·0*	*pl.*	*10*	*10·2* × *15·0*
pl.	5	10·5 × *14·9*	pl. 13		10·6 × *14·9*
pl.	6	11·7 × 14·2			
pl.	7	10·5 × *14·9*	pl.	8	10·4 × *14·9*

---

[1] It was quoted by Swinburne (*William Blake* [1868] 143–4 n.).

Urizen		Marriage			
pl. 8	10·1 × 15·0	pl. 9	10·1 × 15·1		
pl. 9	10·4 × 14·8	pl. 25	10·4 × 14·8		
pl. 10	9·9 × 14·7	pl. 24	9·8 × 14·8		
pl. 11	10·9 × 15·2	pl. 21	10·8 × 15·3		
pl. 12	10·2 × 15·4			Urizen pl. 22	10·1 × 15·6
pl. 13	10·2 × 16·5	pl. 17	10·1 × 16·5		
pl. 14	10·4 × 14·5	pl. 20	10·4 × 14·5		
pl. 15	10·9 × 14·8	pl. 22	10·8 × 14·9		
pl. 16	10·5 × 15·2	pl. 27	10·4 × 15·2		
pl. 17	9·1 × 14·8			Urizen pl. 26	9·2 × 14·9
pl. 18	10·9 × 15·0				
pl. 19	10·4 × 15·8				
pl. 20	10·1 × 15·2	pl. 6	10·1 × 15·1		
pl. 21	10·2 × 16·6	pl. 16	10·2 × 16·6		
pl. 22	10·1 × 15·6			Urizen pl. 12	10·2 × 15·4
pl. 23	10·2 × 15·0	pl. 15	10·2 × 14·9		
pl. 24	10·4 × 15·0	pl. 7	10·3 × 15·0		
pl. 25	10·3 × 16·3	pl. 18	10·3 × 16·4		
pl. 26	9·2 × 14·9			Urizen pl. 17	9·1 × 14·8
pl. 27	10·4 × 15·5	pl. 12	10·4 × 15·4		
pl. 28	10·3 × 15·1	pl. 2	10·3 × 15·1		

Pl. 14 and 27 are made from the bottom left and top left of Blake's unfinished engraving of 'The Approach of Doom' (?1788),[1] and pl. 5, 16–17, 20 also seem to be etched over other designs. The dimensions suggest that pl. 5 and 16 are from the right-hand side of 'The Approach of Doom', though the remaining lines of the original engraving are too faint to allow for confident identification. If *Urizen* pl. 5, 14, 16, 20, 27 are on the versos of *Marriage* pl. 6, 12–13, 20, 27, presumably these *Marriage* plates were themselves etched on the versos of previously engraved plates, though they do not show the plate-maker's-marks.

Plates Missing: *pl. 4 (D–G), 7–8 (C), 9 (E), 16 (C–F), 24 (E)*: The omission from some copies of pl. 9 (E), 16 (C–F), and 24 (E) does not seem very significant, because all are full-page designs, and pl. 9 and 16 are not very closely related to the text. Most copies in which pl. 16 is lacking are also missing pl. 4 (D–F). Pl. 9, 24 uniquely missing from copy E are further indications of the eccentricity of that copy.

Pl. 7–8, containing an inessential conclusion to Chapter III and a redundant chapter IV [a], are missing from copy C. This suggests that copy C is the earliest one printed and that pl. 7–8 were etched after the others. (They also differ from all other plates with text at the top of the page in having no running heads.)

However, it seems unaccountable that copies D–G should lack pl. 4, which bears the end of Chapter II and the beginning of Chapter III. The omission of the beginning of Chapter III is never rectified by corrections to the text in the copies lacking this plate, and its absence must have been very

---

[1] G. Keynes, *Engravings by William Blake*: The Separate Plates (1956), 13–14. Its dimensions are 21 × 29·7 cm.

TABLE

Copy	Plates	Leaves	Watermarks	Blake numbers	Binding-order	Leaf-size in cm	Printing colour
#A Mellon	1–28	28	I TAYLOR (15)[1]	—[2]	1–2, 22, 24, 3–4, 12, 5–7, 17, 8, 10–11, 14, 13, 18, 21, 19, 15–16, 20, 9, 23, 26, 25, 28, 27**[3]	18·0 × 25·4	orangish-Brown
#B MORGAN	1–28	28	1794 / J WHATMAN (18, 26) 1794 I TAYLOR (12–13, 24–5)	1–28	1–4, 14, 5–7, 10, 12, 8, 11, 22, 13, 9, 15–16, 18, 17, 19, 24, 20–1, 23, 25–8**[4]	27·1 × 37·4	Brown (1, 3–7, 9–17, 19, 21–2, 24–8) Green (2, 8, 18, 20, 23)
#C Mellon	1–6, 9–15, 17–28, 2[b]	26	—	—	1, 2[b], 2–4, 12, 5, 6, 9–11, 13, 22, 15, 14, 18, 17, 19, 21, 20, 23, 27, 24–6, 28**	24·3 × 30·3* (1–28) 17·3 × 28·3 (2[b])	orangish-Brown (1–2, 9, 12, 14, 17–28) Green (3–6, 10–11, 13, 15) pale Brown (2[b])
#D BMPR	1–3, 5–15, 17–28	26	J WHATMAN (2, 5) 1794 / J WHATMAN (20)	1–26	1–3, 5–15, 17–28**	18·0 × 26·0*	Brown
#E UNTRACED[5]	1–3, 5–8, 10–15, 17–23, 25–7	24	J WHATMAN (1 leaf)		1, 3, 5, 12, 2, 6, 14, 7, 10, 8, 11, 22, 13, 15, 18, 17, 19, 25,[5] 20–1, 23, 26–8	23·5 × 29·5	Green
#F HARVARD	1–3, 5–15, 17–28	26	—	—	1–3, 5, 12, 6–7, 14, 10, 8–9, 11, 13, 22, 15, 18, 17, 19–21, 23–8**[6]	18·3 × 26·5	Brown (1, 15) Green (2–3, 5–14, 17–28)
#G LC	1–3, 5–28	27	RUSE & TURNERS / 1815 (6, 14, 16, 18, 20–2)	1–27	1–3, 9, 5, 12, 6, 14, 7–8, 22, 10–11, 16, 13, 15, 17–21, 23, 27, 24–6, 28	23·0 × 28·9*	Orange
#H Rosenbloom	1, 4, 25	3	—	—[7]	Loose[7]	13·9 × 18·2 (1) 12·3 × 18·2 (4) 11·7 × 18·2 (25)	Orange (1) greyish-Brown (4) Green (25)
#I MORGAN	4, 10	2	—	—	Loose	14·8 × 20·4 (4) 17·4 × 21·7 (10)	Green
#ROSENBACH	1	1	invisible	—	Loose	10·0 × 14·0	Colour-printed
#BMPR	1–3, 5, 7–8, 10–12, 14, 17, 19, 21, 23–4, 27	16	1794 / J WHATMAN (17)[8]	—	Loose	c. 19·0 × 26·0 (2–3, 5, 7–8, 10–11, 17, 23–4, 27) 11·5 × 16·5 (12) 24·5 × 34·6 (14, 21) 16·1 × 26·1 (19)	Colour-printed

Copy	Pl.	Leaves	Watermark/No.	Binding	Leaf-size (cm)	Printing colour
#Keynes	1, 3, 25		—	Loose	18·2×26·0 (1) 15·0×9·9 (3) 18·4×25·7 (25)	*orangish-Brown* (1, 3) *Brown* (25)
#TATE	2	1	—	Loose	18·7×20·8 (2)	*Colour-printed*
#UNTRACED⁹	3	1	—	Loose	12·4×9·4	*Colour-printed*
#TEXAS	5	1	—	Loose	11·4×8·3	*Brown*
#YALE	5, 10	2	invisible	Loose	19·0×16·0	*Colour-printed*
#UNTRACED	9	1	invisible	Loose	12·6×17·0	Black
#Newton	9	1	13[10]	Loose	15·6×20·7	*Colour-printed*
#MORGAN	12	1	—	Loose	10·2×15·1	Black
#NATIONAL GALLERY OF VICTORIA	21	1	J WHATMAN	Loose	10·3×16·6	*Colour-printed*
#Holland	22	1	1794[11]	Loose	18·5×26·2[11]	*Colour-printed*

*   Coloured by Blake or his wife.
**   The identifiable offsets confirm the present order.
†   The leaves are trimmed and gilt.
Brown   Italicized printing colours indicate colour printing.

1 In copy A, pl. 4 and 8 are on paper conspicuously heavier than that of the others.

2 In copy A, there are numbers in Red ink (the colour with which the plates are touched up) on pl. 2–28, all of which but 1, 3, 6, and 24 on pl. 2, 4, 5, 27 have been erased. However, the 2(?), 5(?), 15, and 22 on pl. 3, 6, 22, and 24 are still legible, while the first numeral ('1') may still be read on pl. 12, 14, 16. This gives an order of:

[1] 2 3[?] 4 × 6[?] 5 × × × × × × × × 22 × × × × × × × 24 × 27 × × × which does not coincide with that of the binding, the offsets, or any other known copy.

3 The clear offsets in copy A give a quite different order:

1–2, 22, 24, 3–4, 12, 6, 17, 10–11, 8, 14, 13, 18, 21, 19, 15–16, 20, 9, 23, 26, 25, 28, 5, 7, 27

which does not correspond to that of the binding or to any other known copy.

4 The leaves of copy B are now loose, but the order is given by the numbers and offsets.

5 Details about the untraced copy E come from Keynes & Wolf and Keynes (1921). Both agree in saying that it 'Lacks pls. 4, 9, 16, 24', while describing it with two copies of pl. 12 and with no mention of pl. 25. It seems likely that the second pl. 12 given in the 'Arrangement' should be pl. 25.

6 The leaves of copy F are now loose, but the offsets, pencil numbers (9–34, for when the work was bound after *Thel* [A]), and Keynes & Wolf agree on the above order.

7 The numbers (31, 46, 47) on the leaves into which the leaves of copy H are inlaid indicate their order when they were bound with other leaves including the 'Order' of the *Songs*. Their present binding-order (1, 25, 4) is modern and irrelevant.

8 In the BMPR leaves, the watermarks are mostly invisible because the leaves are pasted down.

9 I saw the now-untraced pl. 3 at the Sotheby sale of 16 Dec. 1970 (lot 14). The plate was masked in printing so that only the design shows, 9·8×6·1 cm. The print seems genuine to me, but scholars whose judgement I respect have privately expressed doubts about its authenticity.

10 The number '13' may refer to a time when this plate was bound with other colour prints without text.

11 Mr. Holland's pl. 22 is now framed, so this information has been taken from Keynes & Wolf.

puzzling to anyone concerned with the narrative continuity of the poem. Further, the only copy (A) in which the text seems to have been altered to bridge the missing plate in fact has pl. 4. Moreover, the designs on pl. 1, 3–5, and 12 seem to derive from the text on pl. 4, and these designs must have seemed yet more enigmatic without pl. 4. Why Blake included it in copies A–C and offered it in 1818 but omitted it in copies D–G seems a mystery.

Printing: The absence in copy C of pl. 7–8, bearing a second and probably later version of Chapter IV, suggests that it was the first copy printed in 1794 (the date on the title-page). It was probably followed soon after by copies D–F, which have pl. 7–8 but lack pl. 16 (like copy C) and pl. 4. Copies A¹ and B, containing all the plates, may have been printed in 1795, after Blake had decided on and completed all the plates he wanted in the book. Probably at the same time the plates for the Large and Small Books of Designs and the other loose prints were colour printed, including all the full-page designs except pl. 26 but omitting many text-plates. Copy G, water-marked 1815, was printed some years later, and it too lacks pl. 4. The absence of pl. 4 was not permanent, however, for Blake described *Urizen* as consisting of '28 Prints Quarto' in his letter of 9 June 1818. No late copy answering this description is known, but clearly Blake was prepared to print pl. 4 as late as 1818. In this year the price was £5. 5s., but in his letter of 12 April 1827 he gave it as £6. 6s.

The printing order therefore appears to be as follows:

Copy	Approximate date	Watermark date	Plates missing	Colouring	Text coloured
C	1794	—	7–8, 16	*Colour-printed*	No
D–F	1794	1794	4, 16 [plus 9, 24 in E]	*Colour-printed*	No
A–B	1795	1794	—	*Colour-printed*	No
Separate prints	1796	1794	6, 13, 15–16, 18, 20, 26, 28	*Colour-printed*	
G	?1815	1815	4	Water-coloured	Yes

Ownership: Among Blake's contemporaries, copies of *Urizen* were owned by ?the first Baron Dimsdale (A), Isaac D'Israeli (B), William Beckford (F), Frederick Tatham (pl. 1, 'given me by his Widow' [1827–31]), John Giles (pl. 2, later acquired by George Richmond), E. Danniels (pl. 3), and Ozias Humphry (pl. 1–3, 5, 7–8, 10–11, 14, 17, 19, 21, 23–4, 27 in the Large [A] and Small [A] Books of Designs, inherited by his son William Upcott, who showed them to Richard Thomson to describe for J. T. Smith [1828]). Allan Cunningham (1830) described copy G, but did not say who owned it.[2]

Title: One problem with *The First Book of Urizen* is that there is no *Second Book of Urizen*. Perhaps Blake originally intended *The Book of Ahania* (1795) to fill this role, or perhaps *Vala* (?1796–?1807), which was at one point organized in 'Books', was to comprehend *Urizen*. At any rate, the 'First' in

---

[1] In copy A, pl. 3 and 5 were emended as if to accommodate the absence of pl. 4, and pl. 4 and 8 are on different paper, implying that they were later additions.
[2] *Blake Records*, 486.

the title, without a sequel, seems anomalous, and Blake removed the word on some (but not all) plates of copies A and G (the last copy). His final intention, at least, was to call it simply *The Book of Urizen*.

He may, however, have had other reasons for calling it *The First Book of Urizen*. Blake's Urizen is, like Moses' Jehovah, the creator of his world, and *Urizen* begins with the fall and the creation of the world and ends with the creation of religion and the exodus, as does Genesis, the first book of Moses. The parallels in action are conspicuous, and the parallel in titles may have been intended to emphasize those of the actions. Perhaps *Urizen* is the first book of 'The Bible of Hell' with which Blake threatened the world in the *Marriage* (?1790–3) pl. 24.

COLOURING: All seven copies of *Urizen*, and all the separate pulls, are coloured, and all but the last copy (G) are heavily colour printed and touched up with water-colours. Taking into account the deliberately tacky, mottled effect of colour printing, the colouring is very simple on the whole, with Pink flesh, Yellow and Red flames, Brown rocks, and so on, and some plates (e.g. pl. 3) have few or no significant variants in colouring. Ordinarily the whole area of the design was coloured, so that the original etched lines are very difficult to make out. One explanation for this very heavy colouring may be that as many as seven plates were etched on top of other designs, and the etched lines of *Urizen* may have revealed an awkward amount of the earlier designs.

In copy A, the colouring is heavy, with much rusty-Brown. B is mostly water-coloured and is very fine. In copy G, there are Orange framing-lines round the plates, much Gold is used, and the text is coloured; the effect is magnificent.

CATCHWORDS: None.

RUNNING HEADS: Correct (in the form 'I Urizen. C. viii.', pl. 23) on plates with text at the top of the page (pl. 4, 6, 11, 13, 15, 18, 20, 23, 28); missing on similar pl. 7–8 and on text-plates with designs at the top (pl. 2–3, 5, 10, 19, 25).

ORDER: Pl. 1–4, 12, 5–11, 13–28, with authoritative variants.

The problem of arranging the plates is confusing, for each of the seven copies is bound quite differently from the others, and three of these orders are justified by Blake's foliation. However, if we separate the plates bearing text from those consisting only of designs, the patterns become clearer.

Text: The order of the text is given in part by chapter- and section-numbers and by running heads as pl. 3–7, 10–11, 13, 18–20, 23, 25, 28; the positions of only pl. 8 and 15 are not clear from this evidence. Narrative continuity demonstrates that pl. 8 cannot follow pl. 10 (as it does in copies B, E–F), for it interrupts the seven ages in which Los binds Urizen; its only plausible position is between pl. 7 and pl. 10. Pl. 15 is not so clearly related to the other plates, and its place after pl. 19 in copy A is not impossible. Assuming that the title-page and 'PRELUDIUM' should be the first two plates, the order of the text then should be pl. 1–8, 10–11, 13, 15, 18–20 [*or*

18–19, 15 20], 23, 25, 28, and this is the order found in copies A (with the variant position for pl. 15),[1] C, D, and G. Copies B[1] and F are similar except that pl. 8 comes after pl. 10; copy E has pl. 2 and 25 in nonsensical places, but is otherwise like copies B and F.

Full-page Designs: The full-page designs on pl. 9, 14, 16, and 22 are not very closely related to the text, and, with the exception of pl. 16 (of which only three copies are known), they appear almost at random through the book, in five or six locations in the seven known copies.

Pl. 12 seems to show how Urizen 'arose on the waters' as described on pl. 4, and it is bound after pl. 4 (A, C) or 5 (E–G) in five copies. Pl. 17 depicts the 'globe of life blood' described on the last line of pl. 15 and the first of pl. 18; it could follow either pl. 15 (as it does in D, G) or pl. 18 (as it does in B–C, E–F), but it surely should not follow pl. 7 as it does in A. Pl. 21, showing Orc with Enitharmon and Los, must come after Orc's birth is described (pl. 19) and depicted (pl. 20); it follows pl. 20 plausibly in copies B, D–G, pl. 19 possibly in copy C, and pl. 18 eccentrically in copy A. Pl. 24, representing the birth of Urizen's sons, must follow pl. 23 (as it does in D, F) where this is described, or perhaps pl. 27 (as in C, G), but it is very puzzling after pl. 19 (B) or 22 (A). Pl. 26 represents 'The Dog at the wintry door' of pl. 25 and normally follows pl. 25 (B–D, F–G); after pl. 23 (A, E) it seems enigmatic. Pl. 27, which evidently shows Urizen involuntarily creating the web of religion as described on pl. 25, follows plausibly on pl. 26 (as in B, D–F) or pl. 28 (as in A), but seems strange after pl. 23 (as in C, G).

Whole Work: Thus if we accept the order for the text above, and place the full page designs as close as possible to the text they illustrate, as they are found in most copies, we create the following order: 1–4, 12, 5–8, 10–11, 13, 15–21 [*or 13, 18, 17, 19, 21, 15–16, 20*], 23–28 [*or 23, 25–26, 28, 27, 24*].

Conclusion: Despite the extraordinary inconsistency of the orders in which copies are numbered and bound, the proper arrangement of the text is fairly plain. Discounting two obvious errors in copy E, all copies agree except for one legitimate variant position for pl. 15 (found in copy A) and one eccentric variant position for pl. 8 (found in copies B, E–F). Similarly the full-page designs on pl. 12, 17, 21, 24, 26–7 are related with varying degrees of clarity to pl. 4, 15 or 18, 20, 23, and 25, and they are bound following these plates more often than not. Pl. 9, 14, 22, also bearing full-page designs, float disconcertingly from place to place, never resting in the same position in more than two copies, and no single authoritative order can be established for them. Of the three numbered copies, B seems to dislocate pl. 8, 12, and 24, and D and G to put pl. 12[2] or 27 in uncommon positions.[3] The most authoritative order (pl. 1–4, 12, 5–11, 13–28), is, therefore, eclectic, corresponding most closely to the numbered copy D, but chiefly based upon

---

[1] Keynes & Wolf are wrong about the orders of copies A–B.

[2] The dislocation of pl. 12 in copy D is explicable by the fact that copy D lacks pl. 4, which contains the textual passage on which pl. 12 seems to be based.

[3] This evidence suggests that copy A, with pl. 9, 14–15, 17, 21–2, 24, 27 bound in unique positions, is bound erroneously. The order suggested by its offsets seems to be even more mistaken. That of the erased foliation may have been consistent with the order suggested above for the fixed plates.

narrative consistency, foliation, binding, and the relationship of design to text.

SIGNIFICANT VARIANTS:[1] Except for the attempt to delete 'First' from the title, all the significant variants appear in only one copy, and no two copies are alike.

The 'FIRST' of the title was taken out irregularly from pl. 1 (G, Rosenbach pull), 2 (A, C [q.v.], G), 28 (A, G), and the 'I' in the running head, 'I Urizen . . .', was removed on pl. 4, 6, 11, 13, 18, 20, 28 (but left on pl. 15, 23) of copy A; the whole running head was removed from copy D pl. 12; and the 'I' is lacking on pl. 13, 15, 18, 20, 28, though present on pl. 6, 11, 23, of G.

One or more plates are missing from most copies—pl. 4 from D–G, 7–8 from C, 9 from E, 16 from E–F, 24 from E.

The text is sometimes retraced without change in copies A–B, D.

Pl. 3: 'Like' was altered to 'In his' in copy G.
Pl. 4, 5, 25: ll. 93–5, 109, 464 were removed in copy A, and l. 74 in copy C.
Pl. 6: Two of the falling figures are omitted in copy D.
Pl. 11: The skeleton has no chains in copy G.
Pl. 15: A boy and an eagle have been added in copy G.
Pl. 16: The man is bearded in copy A.
Pl. 24: Two of the men are omitted in copy D.
Pl. 25: l. 364 is erased in copy A.
Pl. 26: The door is obscured in copies A, D, F.

Blake masked the plates with text (pl. 1–3, 5, 7–8, 10–11, 19, 23) plus pl. 24 when he printed the designs for the Large and Small Books of Designs (BMPR, Keynes, Tate, Yale, Texas). Additionally, the plates for the Small Book of Designs (B) (pl. 1–3, 5, 9–10, 12, 21–2) have several framing-lines round the designs and inscriptions.

ERRATA: Pl. 7 has an extra 'his'; pl. 20, 'Op[*p*]pressd'.

Pl. 1. DESIGN: Over the title droops a thin, leafless tree. Between the title and the imprint a man in a long Grey robe and with a White beard which covers his feet sits on the ground with his knees raised and, with a quill in either hand, copies in mottled books or on stones to his left and right from a book under his feet. Behind him are what appear to be two Grey tombstones with curved tops. His eyes are downcast or shut, and his left foot shows through his beard. (An analogous design appears on *All Religions are One* [?1788] pl. 2.)

VARIANTS: 'FIRST' is erased from the paper and covered by a branch in copy G and the Rosenbach pull; the latter has the imprint cut off. The title is masked but the imprint is clear in the BMPR and Keynes pulls; in the latter the date is altered to '1796' and an inscription reads: '"Which is the Way" / "The Right or the Left"'.

---

[1] Minor variants caused by colour printing, such as the rock-shapes on pl. 9–10, 18, 21 or the folds of cloth on pl. 27, are ignored here.

Pl. 2. DESIGN: Between 'PRELUDIUM TO' and 'THE FIRST BOOK OF *URIZEN*', a floating woman on the right in a long, swirling dress reaches to the left towards a small, floating, naked child. Below them the text is engulfed in flame-like foliage. (A pencil sketch is in the Keynes [Fitzwilliam] collection.)

COLOURING: The woman's DRESS is Pink (A, B [pale Raspberry], C [2ᵇ], BMPR and Tate pulls), Purple (C [pale in 2ᵃ], F [greyish-]), Uncoloured (D), or bold Green (G), and her HAIR is Orange (C [2ᵃ]), Brown (F), or Yellow (BMPR pull). The BACKGROUND is Green (A–B [dull], C [2ᵃ⁻ᵇ]), Orange (B, F–G), Blue (G, BMPR and Tate pulls), and Pink (BMPR and Tate pulls).

VARIANTS: The 'FIRST' in 'FIRST BOOK OF *URIZEN*' is painted over in A and G; the plant comes up the right side and covers 'PRELUDIUM TO THE FIRST BOOK OF' in copy C (pl. 2ᵇ); and 'PRELUDIUM TO' is gone in the Tate copy.

An Orange cloud has been added at the top left in copy C (pl. 2ᵃ).

The woman's hair is in a bun, and she has shoes on, in copy G.

The Tate copy is inscribed, probably not by Blake, 'Teach these Souls to Fly'.

Pl. 3. INCIPIT: 'Chap: I . . .'. DESIGN: Above the text, a naked man looking away from the viewer runs leftwards with giant strides and outspread arms through enveloping flames. (A similar figure, reversed, in the Rosenwald Collection is reproduced in *Blake's Pencil Drawings*, ed. G. Keynes [1956], pl. 11.)

VARIANTS: In l. 11, 'Like' is mended to 'In his' in copy G.

In l. 44, '3' is absorbed into the design in copy G, probably because it lacks pl. 4. l. 44 is deleted in copy A.

'Chap: II' is erased in copy B (according to Erdman, p. 726).

The Keynes copy is inscribed: 'O flames of furious desire'.

Pl. 4. INCIPIT: 'Muster around the bleak desarts . . .'. DESIGN: Below the text, a naked man sits on the ground and holds his head. The design is covered by Black vertical lines evidently representing pelting rain. (The same figure, reversed and with a chain, appears in *No Natural Religion* [?1788], pl. b8.)

COLOURING: The BACKGROUND, ordinarily Green, is dark Brown in I.

VARIANTS: l. 74 is erased from the paper in copy C (according to Erdman, p. 726) and l. 93 from copy A.

Pl. 5. INCIPIT: 'In living creations appear'd . . .'. DESIGN: Above the text is an old man with a long White beard whose head emits rays of light. He holds open an enormous book, the pages of which are mottled and non-representational.

COLOURING: The man's ROBE, usually uncoloured or White, is sometimes Blue (B) or Grey (D), and the BOOK is mottled Yellow (A, D, G, Yale pull), Grey (A, C), Black (B–C, F–G), Red (B, D, Yale pull), Blue (B, D, BMPR pull [dark], Texas and Yale pulls), Brown (C, F), Green (Yale pull), and

Orange (Yale pull). The BACKGROUND is Black, plus Blue (F, BMPR pull [dark], Yale pull), and Yellow (G).

VARIANTS: ll. 95–6 were touched up in Red ink and then deleted in Blue ink in copy A.

l. 109 was erased from the paper and covered by a Green vine in copy A.

ll. 113, 114, 122 have 'he' altered to 'He' in copy A.

There are flames over Urizen in the BMPR pull.

The Yale pull is inscribed at the bottom: 'The Book of my Remembrance'.

Pl. 6. INCIPIT: 'As the stars are apart from the earth . . .'. DESIGN: Below the text, most of the page is occupied by three naked men wrapped in snakes who fall headlong through vertical flames. The central, largest, man has his arms outspread, while those on either side clutch their heads. Beside the central figure there seem to be the heads of an ?eagle (A–B) on the left and a lion (A–B, G).

COLOURING: The MIDDLE MAN is Green and the right one Blue in copy B. The SNAKES are usually Black or Brown, but sometimes the right and left ones are also Green (C) or Red (F) and the middle one Blue (C) or Red (F). The FLAMES are sometimes Grey (A), Black (D, G), or yellowish-Green (G).

VARIANTS: The figures on the right and left were painted over in copy D. After l. 142, there appears to be an erasure of two lines from the copperplate, sometimes covered by swirls (A, C, F–G).

Pl. 7. INCIPIT: '12: Los howld in a dismal stupor . . .'. DESIGN: Below the text, most of the page is taken up by a large naked man on his knees amidst flames with his arms wrapped round his throat, his mouth open, and his eyes staring, as if in torment.

COLOURING: The MAN is once greenish-Red (F), and the FLAMES are occasionally Black (A, D) and Purple (A).

Pl. 8. INCIPIT: '1: Los smitten with astonishment . . .'. DESIGN: Below the text, most of the page is absorbed by a skeleton seated in a foetal position, with its hands on its head.

COLOURING: The SKELETON, ordinarily Yellow and Brown, is sometimes partly Black (D, F) or yellowish-Green (G), and the BACKGROUND is Blue (A–B [strong, dark], D), Black (D, F, G, and BMPR pull [bluish-]), and Green (F).

VARIANT: The skeleton is surrounded by an Orange nimbus in copy G.

Pl. 9. DESIGN: The whole page is a design of a naked man with a long beard, kneeling with one knee raised and both hands on the ground, who seems to struggle to lift the enormous mass of rocks which presses him down. (There are similar scenes on pl. 10 and on *For Children* [1793] pl. 5, and *The Book of Los* [1795] pl. 2.)

COLOURING: The background ROCKS are mottled Grey (A, F–G) and Black (A, C–D, F, untraced and Newton pulls), Brown (B, D, F, Newton pull), Orange (B–C, F–G, Newton pull), Green (C, D and the untraced pull [dark], F, G [light], Newton pull), Gold (G), and Blue (G).

VARIANTS: There are Yellow rays from the man's head in copy B.

The Newton copy is inscribed: '"Eternally I labour on"'.

Pl. 10. INCIPIT: 'Chap: IV/1 Ages on ages roll'd over him . . .'. DESIGN: Above the text, a naked man with his back to us, in the position of a weight-lifter, seems to struggle with great rocks which press in upon him from all sides. (For similar scenes see pl. 9, *For Children* [1793] pl. 5, and *The Book of Los* [1795] pl. 2.)

COLOURING: The ROCKS, ordinarily Brown, are sometimes partly Black (A, D, F, I), Grey (B [brownish-], C [dark], G, Yale pull), Green (D [dark], G [light], Yale pull), Gold (G), Yellow (G), and Orange (Yale pull).

VARIANTS: The Yale copy is inscribed: '"Does the Soul labour thus"/"In the Caverns of the Grave"'.

Pl. 11. INCIPIT: '7. From the caverns of his jointed Spine . . .'. DESIGN: Half the page below the text is filled with a design of a partly fleshed skeleton fastened with Black balls and chains among flames; he is sitting on the ground with his knees drawn up and his head raised. On our right is a naked man with a great hammer seated in a contorted position with both hands on the ground. (A sketch for this plate is described in G. Keynes, *Bibliotheca Bibliographici* [1964], no. 491.)

COLOURING: The SKELETON, ordinarily Brown and White, is sometimes Green (B, G [yellowish-]), or Grey (C, BMPR pull).

VARIANTS: The skeleton has no chains in copy G.

Pl. 12. DESIGN: The whole page is a design of a naked man with a floating White beard who seems to be rising with raised knees and outstretched arms through deep water. (A man in a similar position is sketched from before and behind in *Vala* [?1796–?1807] p. 66.)

COLOURING: The WATER is Black (A [greenish-], G [bluish-], BMPR and Morgan pulls), dark Blue (B), or Green (C [dark], D, F, Morgan pull).

VARIANTS: The Morgan copy is inscribed in old Brown ink on the verso: 'I labour upwards into / futurity / Blake'.

Pl. 13. INCIPIT: 'Two nostrils bent down to the deep . . .'. DESIGN: In the middle of the page, after l. 251 in the first column and l. 265 in the second, a floating, long-haired, dark Grey woman with her back to us seems to be holding apart very dark clouds with outstretched arms. (A similar scene is in *Ahania* [1795] pl. 2.)

After l. 256 are two butterflies.

COLOURING: The background CLOUDS and SKY are Black (A [brownish-], C–D, F–G), Blue (B–D, F), and Brown (B).

VARIANTS: The running head is gone in copy D.

There are stars under the woman in copy G.

Pl. 14. DESIGN: The whole page is a design of a muscular, naked man with his back to us who seems to have floated to rest on his hands, head downwards, on rocks or clouds; his elbows and knees are bent.

COLOURING: The BACKGROUND is Black, with some Grey (A–C, BMPR pull), Brown (A, F), Green (C, F), greenish-Blue (D), Orange (G), and White (G). The man's HAIR is Yellow in the BMPR pull.

Pl. 15. INCIPIT: 'Thus the Eternal Prophet was divided . . .'. DESIGN: Most of the page, at the bottom, is taken up with the design of three men staring down from the dark sky at a gently curving mass which may be the earth, with streaks in the sky above it. The men on the left and right have long White beards and Grey robes; the one in the centre, who has dark hair and is beardless, leans down with his left hand on the earth, apparently to separate one part from another.

COLOURING: The ROBE of the man on the right, usually Grey, is sometimes yellowish-Brown (B) or Blue (G). The STREAKS in the sky are Red (A, C [raspberry], D [pinkish], F), Orange (B, G), Green (B), and Yellow (G). The SKY is sometimes very dark Green (A), Black (A), or Grey (F), and the EARTH is Black (A–D, F), or greyish-Green (G).

VARIANTS: The men's eyes are not visible in B; the old men's eyes are closed in C, F–G; and the right-hand man seems to have a cowl in F.

In G, there is a new head of a boy at the top left, with the outline of an eagle's head above it. (Keynes & Wolf imply erroneously that several copies have this variant.)

Pl. 16. DESIGN: The whole page is a design of a naked man crouched in flames with his hands behind his head.

VARIANTS: The man has a long White beard in copy A, and there are tears on his cheeks in B.

Pl. 17. DESIGN: The whole page is a design of a (?female) figure with long hair and a Red skirt (but no top) who holds her ears as she bends towards us over a flaming sphere; the background is Black.

COLOURING: Enitharmon's HAIR is Brown (A, D [dark]), Yellow (B), or Black (BMPR pull).

VARIANTS: There are clear Orange and Red veins on the globe which mount to Enitharmon's back in B and G, and in G she has lines at her wrist as of a garment. She has a bloody Red woven belt in C, and in D and G she has bloody veins on her legs.

Pl. 18. INCIPIT: '8. The globe of life blood trembled . . .'. DESIGN: Most of the page, below the text, is taken up by a design of a large, naked man (Los) with spread legs and outstretched arms holding a great Black hammer as he walks through rocky flames.

COLOURING: The ROCKS behind the flames are sometimes Green (B, C [dark], F), Black (C–D, F), or Grey (G), and Los's HAIR is Brown (A), or Yellow (F).

Pl. 19. INCIPIT: 'They call'd her Pity, and fled . . .'. DESIGN: Above the text, a nude woman with long hair bends away as if in distress from a naked man kneeling before her with his head in his hands.

COLOURING: The woman's HAIR is Brown (A [light], F, BMPR pull) or Orange (C), and the Man's Blond (A), Black (C, F), or Brown (BMPR pull). The BACKGROUND is Brown (A, D, F, G [greyish-]), Black (A, C–D, F, G and BMPR pull [bluish-]), dark reddish-Purple (B), or dark Grey (A, C, BMPR pull).

VARIANTS: A curious, uncoloured object, like a splash or like scratched-out vertical writing, appears to the left of the woman in copy A and is flame-coloured in G.

The man seems to be clothed (including his hands) in bloody Red in B.

A cloud goes from the man's knees to the woman's head in the BMPR pull.

Pl. 20. INCIPIT: 'Stretch'd for a work of eternity . . .'. DESIGN: Below the text, a small naked boy with spread arms and legs who emits flames falls through darkness towards the bottom right corner. (The design is very closely echoed from *America* [1793] pl. d.)

COLOURING: Orc's HAIR is Gold (F) and the BACKGROUND Black (A–B, D, F), or Brown (C, F).

VARIANTS: The genitals of the child (whose sex is obscure in some copies) are inked in in copy B.

Pl. 21. DESIGN: The whole page is a design of a nude woman (Enitharmon) with her arms by her side holding a cloth and looking down at a half-grown boy (Orc) who is embracing her, while to the right a bearded man (Los) leaning on a great hammer looks down at them. The man's chest is girdled by a large Red chain which falls between his legs. (Enitharmon and Orc are sketched on *Notebook* p. 74, and an analogous scene is in *Vala* [?1796–?1807] p. 60.)

COLOURING: Enitharmon's HAIR is Blond (A, D, F, BMPR and National Gallery of Victoria pulls), Orc's Brown (A and F and BMPR pull [pale], Victoria pull) or Yellow (D), and Los's Brown (A, D, F, BMPR and Victoria pulls). Los is usually coloured more darkly than the others (e.g. copy B and Victoria pull), and his HAMMER, which is usually Black, is White in G. The BACKGROUND is mottled Green (A [greyish], B–C, BMPR and Victoria pulls), Brown (A, C, F, Victoria pull), Black (A–B, D, G [bluish-]), Orange (B [bright], F), dark Red (D), Green (F), and Yellow (G [greenish-], Victoria pull).

VARIANTS: Enitharmon has her right hand in the small of Orc's back in A.

There is a vivid sun setting at the middle left in copies B–C, G, and the BMPR and Victoria pulls.

Los looks downward in C, F, and the BMPR pull, not at Enitharmon.

Pl. 22. DESIGN: The whole page is a design of a naked man with a long White beard whose head gives off light; he is seated on the ground with his knees up, and his eyes closed, and his wrists are fastened with Black manacles, apparently to his ankles.

COLOURING: The man's KNEES are touched with pale Green in C, and all his SKIN is sometimes Green (D [bluish-], F [greyish-]). His BEARD is dark Brown in the Holland copy. The BACKGROUND is Grey (A [dark], C), Brown (A–B [dark], F, Holland pull [pinkish-]), Orange (C), Yellow (F), and Black (F, Holland pull).

VARIANTS: There are tears in his eyes in G.

The Holland copy is inscribed: '"Frozen doors to mock" / "The World, while they within torments uplock"'.

Pl. 23. INCIPIT: 'Of life on his forsaken mountains . . .'. DESIGN: Below the text, half the page is filled by a man with a long White beard and wearing a long Grey robe; he walks to the right with huge strides, carrying in his right hand a heavy Red globe which emits rays. His left arm is raised, and beneath it appears a dim Brown lion. (The design is copied on *Vala* [?1796–?1807] p. 74.)

COLOURING: The BACKGROUND is Black, with Brown (C, G), and Purple (G), and twice the SKY is Lavender (C–D).

Pl. 24. DESIGN: The whole page is a design of four naked men apparently emerging from their elements. In the bottom left corner is the head of a man in a Black sea; to the right a man with a stubble beard climbs from the Green earth; across the middle of the page floats a man with his hands raised to shoulder level and a Red swirl coming from his chest; and above him are the head and spread arms of a man in flames.

COLOURING: The SEA-MAN is sometimes Purple (B), and Grey (F), and his HAIR is Blue (D, BMPR pull), or Black (F). The FIRE-MAN is Grey in B, and his HAIR is Yellow in F. The SKY is Grey (A [greenish-], F–G), Brown (B), Blue (C [dark], F, BMPR pull [greenish-]), heavy Yellow (D), Orange (G, BMPR pull), and Red (BMPR pull).

VARIANTS: There seems to be a Blue snake at the bottom in C.

Fuzon and Grodna are omitted, and there is an Ochre sun on a clear horizon, and Blue and Brown clouds at the top, in D.

The cloud-man has an Orange halo, and there is a sunset at the middle left in copy G.

The BMPR pull shows only the bottom half of the design, and in it only the sea-man.

Pl. 25. INCIPIT: 'The Ox in the slaughter house moans...'. DESIGN: Above the text is a confused design which appears to represent three nude women in the Green sea wrapped in the coils of a great winged worm.

COLOURING: The WORM is Brown (A, F, H [reddish-], Keynes pull), White (A), Green (A–C, F–H), Red (B–C, F, G [raspberry]), Black (C–D, Keynes pull), greyish-Blue (D, F, Keynes pull), Orange (F–G, Keynes pull), or Blue (F), and the SKY is sometimes Orange (B, Keynes pull), bright Red (C), or Black (F).

VARIANTS: The middle face is obscured in A.

l. 465 is erased on the paper and covered with a Red line in A. (It is present in all other copies, though Keynes & Wolf say self-contradictorily that l. 365 'is found only in copies B and E' [p. 71] or 'in only ... B, C and F' [p. 72].)

Pl. 26. DESIGN: The whole page is a design of a boy in a long dress standing with clasped hands to the right of a dog lying on the ground before a door and raising his head as if howling. (A sketch, perhaps for this plate, is in *Notebook* p. 15.)

COLOURING: The boy's GOWN, ordinarily uncoloured or White, is Green in G. The DOG is Black (A), White (A, F), Grey (B–C), or Brown (D, F–G), and the WALL behind them is Brown (A [rusty], B–C), Black (C), Yellow (G), and Pink (G).

VARIANTS: A Black shadow covers half the page, from top right to bottom left in A, F, from top left to bottom right in B, G, and there is light as if from a window at the top left in C.

The boy's mouth is open in A.

The door is obscured in copies A, D, F.

Pl. 27. DESIGN: The whole page is a design of a White-haired man in a long, pale robe who flees from us with his hands raised by his head as if in panic.

COLOURING: Urizen's ROBE, which is usually uncoloured or Grey, is dull yellowish-Green in B, and his HAIR is pale Yellow (D). The BACKGROUND is Black, with Grey (A [brownish-], C, F), Green (G), and Red (G).

VARIANTS. There is an orangish-Red light above the man's head in G.

Pl. 28. INCIPIT: 'They lived a period of years . . .'. DESIGN: Below the text, half the page is absorbed by the design of a man with a very long White beard and a long robe sitting with outstretched arms, wrapped in a net of very thick rope. (A similar design appears in 'The Human Abstract', *Songs* [1794] pl. 47.)

COLOURING: Urizen's ROBE is uncoloured or White (A, F–G), Brown (B, C [buff]), Grey (D, F), the ROPE, usually Black, is Orange and Yellow in G, and the BACKGROUND is Black (A–C, F), dark Blue (D), Brown (A [rusty], D), and greyish-Pink (G).

VARIANTS: Conclusion: 'FIRST' is erased from the paper in A, and painted over in G.

In two copies there are rays from his head, Orange in B, Red in D.

COPY A: BINDING: (1) 'Formerly in boards, probably original';[1] (2) 'In recent times'[1] bound for 'W H S' (W. H. Smith & Co.)[1] by Douglas Cockerell[1] in Red straight-grain morocco.

HISTORY: (1) Perhaps acquired by the 1st Baron Dimsdale (1712–1800); (2) Inherited by Major T. E. Dimsdale, who lent it to the Burlington Fine Arts Club exhibition (1929), no. 83, and to the National Book League exhibition (1947), no. 195,[2] and sold it at Sotheby's, 28 Feb. 1956, lot 531, for £6,800 to Howard Samuel; (3) Acquired by Mr. *Paul Mellon*.

COPY B: BINDING: (1) Originally stabbed through three holes, 11·4 cm from the top and 7·7, 6·7 cm apart; (2) In 1953 the leaves were 'now' mounted on stubs bound in old (?late-nineteenth-century) half Red morocco over greyish-Brown boards (very like *Visions* [F]), but (3) By 1965 all the leaves were loose.

HISTORY: (1) Probably acquired by Isaac D'Israeli (see *Europe* [A], p. 157); (2) Sold by his son the Earl of Beaconsfield[3] at Sotheby's, 20 March 1882, lot 60, for £59 to Ellis & White; (3) Offered by Ellis & White in their Catalogue 50 (?Nov. 1882), lot 82, for £75; (4) Acquired by B. B. Macgeorge,

---

[1] According to Keynes & Wolf; the evidence therefore is unknown to me. Keynes (1921) says Cockerell bound it 'Recently'.

[2] John Hayward, *English Poetry*: An Illustrated Catalogue (1950).

[3] A note at the bottom of pl. 1 ('133—Oct 15th 1856') is evidently the Beaconsfield Library Mark—see *Visions* (F), *Europe* (A), pp. 473, 157.

listed in his catalogues (1892, 1906), lent to the exhibitions in the National Gallery (1913), no. 99, Manchester (1914), no. 159, Nottingham (1914), no. 121, the National Gallery of Scotland (1914), Case B, no. 5, and sold posthumously at Sotheby's, 1 July 1924, lot 117, for £580 to G. Wells; (5) Acquired by A. E. Newton, who added his book-plate and a note, lent it to the Philadelphia exhibition (1939), no. 75, and sold it posthumously at Parke-Bernet, 16 April 1941, lot 131, for $8,250 to Rosenbach; (6) Acquired by Mrs. Landon K. Thorne, in whose catalogue (1971) it was described (no. 9), and who gave it in Feb. 1972 to (7) The PIERPONT MORGAN LIBRARY.

COPY C: BINDING: 'BOUND BY F. BEDFORD' in Brown morocco, g.e.; pl. 2b is inlaid and has two black framing-lines.

   HISTORY: (1) Offered in John Pearson's Catalogue (1854) for £55 (according to Keynes [1921]—perhaps Pearson wrote 'Cat No 42' on the endpaper); (2) Acquired by Thomas Gaisford, who added his book-plate and sold it at Sotheby's, 23 April 1890, lot 191, for £66 to Nugent; (3) Acquired for the Britwell Court Library, whose Librarian, Mr. Colman, added the pressmarks '8.F.' and '87.F.6' on the endpaper (as the next owner told me); (4) Inherited by Major S. V. Christie-Miller, who sold it posthumously at Sotheby's, 29 March 1971, lot 35, for £24,000 to Wynne Jeudwine for (5) A group headed by John Baskett, who sold it in the spring of 1972 to (6) Mr. *Paul Mellon*.

COPY D: BINDING: (1) Originally stabbed through three holes, 6·8 cm from the top, 5·3, 6·0 cm apart; (2) The plates were mounted on linen stubs and bound after June 1859 for the British Museum in half Green morocco, g.e.; (3) The leaves were remounted in heavy paper 'windows' and bound in Red morocco in 1969.

   HISTORY: (1) Acquired by Francis Palgrave, who sold it on 25 June 1859 to (2) The BRITISH MUSEUM PRINT ROOM, where it was bound and used for Pearson's facsimile (1876), and probably (with pl. 1, 16, 24 from copy G) for that of Ellis & Yeats (1893).

COPY E: BINDING: Bound 'by Clarke and Bedford' (who were partners 1841–50) in Brown morocco (according to Keynes [1921]).

   HISTORY: (1) Acquired from Sir Charles Dilke (according to the 1886 catalogue below) by (2) Frederick Locker, who added his book-plate (according to Keynes [1921]), lent it to the Burlington Fine Arts Club exhibition (1876), no. 313, and had it listed in his catalogue (1886); (3) Acquired through Dodd, Mead & Co (see the 'Pickering MS', p. 341) by E. D. Church (according to Keynes [1921]); (4) Acquired before 1921 by Mrs. Harry Payne Whitney, after whose death in 1942 it presumably went to her heirs (see *Visions* [N], p. 476); (5) *UNTRACED*.

COPY F: BINDING: (1) Bound, probably for William Beckford shortly after 1835, in half calf labelled on the spine 'Blake's Work' in between *Thel* (A) and *Marriage* (A); (2) It was disbound probably for the 1891 Boston exhibition, and the former binding is now with the loose leaves.

   HISTORY: (1) Acquired by William Beckford, who numbered it ('N° 4029') on the now detached binding; it was sold with his Library at Sotheby's,

29 Nov. 1883, lot 764 (bound with *Thel* [A][1] and *Marriage* [A]), for £121 to Quaritch; (2) Quaritch inserted his Beckford sale book-plate and offered it in his Rough List 67 (Jan. 1884), lot 80, for £150; (3) Acquired by E. W. Hooper who disbound the volume, lent *Urizen* to the Boston exhibition (1891), no. 7, and passed it before 1921 to his daughter (4) Mrs. Ward Thoron, who lent it to the Fogg exhibition (1924) and presented it in 1962 to (5) HARVARD.

COPY G: BINDING: (1) Originally stabbed through three holes, 4·0 and 4·0 cm apart; (2) The leaves were unbound in 1903 and 1905, but (3) They were mounted on stubs and bound by 'THE CLUB BINDERY, 1908' for W. A. White in Brown morocco, g.e.; each plate is framed with 1 orange line.

HISTORY: (1) Described by Cunningham (1830),[2] sold anonymously at Sotheby's, 20 Jan. 1852, lot 186, for £8. 15s. to Milnes; pl. 1, 16, 24 probably reproduced by Ellis & Yeats (1893) along with copy A, and sold by Milnes's son the Earl of Crewe at Sotheby's, 30 March 1903, lot 6 (unbound), for £307 to Quaritch; (2) Acquired by 'W A White / Apl 20—1903' from 'B Q £307 / 5% profit . . . $1610' (according to notes on the second and last fly-leaves), who lent it (unbound) to the exhibition of the Grolier Club (1905), no. 27, perhaps to that of 1919, no. 13 (anonymously), to that of the Fogg (1924), had it bound in 1908, and sold it posthumously on 1 May 1929 through Rosenbach to (3) Mr. LESSING J. ROSENWALD.

COPY H: BINDING: (1) Inlaid and bound about 1853 with many leaves of Blakeana including the 'Order' of the *Songs*; (2) Separated after 1924 and bound in Blue levant morocco, presumably by Macdonald for G. C. Smith, Jr.

HISTORY: For the History, see the 'Order' of the *Songs*, p. 337.

COPY I: BINDING: (1) Bound in contemporary rough calf with other leaves of Blakeana, including *Thel* (a); (2) After 1906 the *Urizen* plates were separated and mounted.

HISTORY: For the History, see *Thel* (a), p. 131.

Pl. 1: BINDING: Pasted on cardboard which in turn is mounted and framed.

HISTORY: (1) Probably acquired by W. A. White, lent anonymously with the rest of his collection to the Grolier Club exhibition (1905), no. 28, and sold posthumously in 1929 with the rest of his collection to (2) A. S. W. Rosenbach, who lent it to the Philadelphia exhibition (1939), no. 77, and gave it to (3) The ROSENBACH FOUNDATION.

Pl. 1: BINDING:

HISTORY: (1) Perhaps it was part of the Small Book of Designs (B), see p. 356); (2) 'This Coloured Print by Wm Blake was given me by his Widow [*Catherine, according to the note on the verso by* (3)] Frederick Tatham Sculptor'; (4) Acquired by Lord Killanin, lent by him to the Carfax Exhibition (1906), no. 79a, and sold at Sotheby's, 28 July 1947, lot 166, for £65 to (5) *Geoffrey Keynes*, who reproduced it in Keynes & Wolf, p. 85, and lent it to the exhibi-

---

[1] The note on a fly-leaf with the detached cover ('Cumberland sale / H. G. [?*Bohn*]') presumably applies only to *Thel* (A)—see p. 125; the history of the *Marriage* and *Urizen* before the Beckford sale is not known.

[2] *Blake Records* (1969), 486.

tions of the British Museum (1957), no. 27 1a, and (anonymously) the Whitworth Art Gallery (1969), no. 8a, and the National Library of Scotland
(1969), no. 51, and described it in his catalogue (1964), no. 522.

Pl. 1–3, 5, 7–8, 10–11, 17, 19, 23–4, 27: See The Small Book of Designs (A).

Pl. 2: BINDING: (1) Once stabbed through three holes 3·8 and 4·3 cm apart
with *Marriage* pl. 11, *Urizen* pl. 5, 10; (2) Now mounted, framed, with four
framing-lines round the design, inscribed, not by Blake, 'Teach these Souls
to Fly'.

HISTORY: (1) Perhaps once part of The Small Book of Designs (B);
(2) Acquired by Samuel Palmer's cousin John Giles, who sold it posthumously
at Christie's, 4 Feb. 1881, lot 440, to (3) Dr. Richard Sisley,[1] from whom it
was acquired by his daughter (4) Mrs. John Richmond,[1] who sold it in
1922[1] to (5) The TATE GALLERY.

Pl. 3: BINDING: Loose, mounted in a window. On the verso is an undefined
sketch and writing.

HISTORY: (1) Sold anonymously at Sotheby's, 17 Dec. 1970, lot 14, for
£80; (2) *UNTRACED.*

Pl. 3: BINDING: Framed in four lines, inscribed 'O flames of furious desire',
loose.

HISTORY: (1) According to a note on the verso presumed to be by C. L.
Trumpington, it was sold 'by either Mrs. Blake or a relation of hers' to
(2) 'E. Danniels, 53 Mortimer Street',[2] perhaps related to the E. T. Daniell
who bought a copy of *Job* in Sept. 1827 (*Blake Records* [1969], 353); (3)
Acquired successively by 'Ogden, Oxford',[2] (4) by Mr. C. Layle Trumpington, (5) by 'Mrs. Pollitt, 1897',[2] and (6) in 1904 by W. Graham Robertson,
in whose catalogue it was described[2] and who sold it posthumously at
Christie's, 22 July 1949, lot 87 (for £78. 15s. to Eames);[2] (7) Acquired by
Geoffrey Keynes, who described it in his catalogue (1964), no. 522.

Pl. 5: BINDING: Framed and mounted.

HISTORY: (1) Sold posthumously for Frederic Manning at Sotheby's,
3 July 1935, lot 563; (2) Acquired for $265 about 1951 (according to a note
by Mrs. Hanley of *c.* 1966) by T. E. Hanley, who sold it with his library in
the autumn of 1964 to (3) The UNIVERSITY OF TEXAS.

Pl. 5, 10: BINDING: (1) Stabbed through three holes 3·8 and 4·3 cm apart
with *Marriage* pl. 11, *Urizen* pl. 2, with three framing-lines round the designs,
pl. 5 inscribed 'The Book of my Remembrance', pl. 10 inscribed ' "Does the
Soul labour thus", / "In the Caverns of the Grave" '; (2) Now mounted and
framed.

HISTORY: (1) Perhaps once part of The Small Book of Designs (B); (2)
Acquired by the Revd. Stopford Brooke, who sold them posthumously at
Sotheby's, 9 April 1919, lots 448, 450, for £26 and £29 to Tregaskis; (3)
Offered in James Tregaskis Caxton Head Catalogue 815 (23 June 1919),
lots 1 (£65) and 2 (£70); (4) Acquired by Templeton Crocker, lent to the

---

[1] According to M. Butlin, *William Blake* [Tate catalogue] (1971), 33.
[2] *The Blake Collection of W. Graham Robertson*, ed. K. Preston (1952), no. 136*.

Philadelphia exhibition (1939), no. 78, and sold to (5) Channcey Brewster Tinker, described in his catalogue (1959), no. 261–2, and bequeathed at his death in 1963 to (6) YALE.

Pl. 9: BINDING: Framed and mounted, one black framing-line round the design.

HISTORY: (1) Acquired in the nineteenth century by James Leathart, from whom it passed to his grand-daughter (2) Mrs. Margaret C. Mele, who sold it at Christie's, 14 March 1967, lot *85, for £700 to Agnew; (3) *UN-TRACED*.

Pl. q: BINDING: Mounted and framed, with three ink lines framing the design, inscribed 'Eternally I labour on'.

HISTORY: (1) Perhaps once part of the Small Book of Designs (B); (2) Sold posthumously by the Revd. Stopford Brooke at Sotheby's, 9 April 1919, lot 451, for £38 to the dealer Tregaskis, who apparently sold it to the U.S. dealer (3) Gabriel Wells, who in turn sold it to (4) A. E. Newton, who wrote in a notebook with it: 'I bought it from Gabriel Wells when we were in London together in the summer of 1921, and I paid a pretty stiff price for it, too'; Newton lent it to the Philadelphia exhibition (1939), no. 80, and sold it at Parke-Bernet, 16 April 1941, lot 133, for $150 to the dealer Sessler, apparently for Newton's daughter (5) *Miss Caroline Newton*, who placed it on deposit in Princeton.

Pl. 12: BINDING: Mounted and framed, inscribed on the verso 'I labour upwards into / futurity / Blake'.

HISTORY: (1) Perhaps once part of The Small Book of Designs (B); (2) This is probably the *Urizen* plate ('Man sinking in Water') sold for W. B. Scott at Sotheby's, 21 April 1885, lot 177, for £6. 6s. to Fawcett; (3) Acquired by the Revd. Stopford Brooke, who sold it posthumously at Sotheby's, 9 April 1919, lot 449 for £32 to Tregaskis; (4) Acquired by Herschel V. Jones, who gave it to his daughter (5) Miss Tessie Jones, who bequeathed it in 1968 to (6) the PIERPONT MORGAN LIBRARY.

Pl. 14, 21: See The Large Book for Designs (A).

Pl. 21: BINDING: Mounted, with three framing-lines round the design.

HISTORY: (1) Perhaps once part of The Large Book of Designs (B); (2) Acquired by John Linnell, listed in Gilchrist (1863), ii. 202, and sold posthumously at Christie's, 15 March 1918, lot 177, for £90 to Martin; (3) Presented by The Felton Bequest to (4) The NATIONAL GALLERY OF VICTORIA, Melbourne, Australia.

Pl. 22: BINDING: Mounted and framed, with one framing-line round the design, inscribed below: '"Frozen doors to mock" / "The World: while they within torments uplock."'

HISTORY: (1) Perhaps once part of The Large Book of Designs (B); (2) Sold for H. B. Forman at Anderson Galleries, 15 March 1920, lot 66, for $1,060 to Rosenbach; (3) Acquired by A. E. Newton, who lent it to the Philadelphia exhibition (1939), no. 82, and sold it at Parke-Bernet, 14 April 1941, lot 132, for $300 to 'private', i.e. (4) Mr. *Joseph Holland*.

Plate 25: BINDING: Loose.

HISTORY: (1) Perhaps this was included among the 30 drawings and specimen plates for *Urizen, Visions, Jerusalem* '&c' sold anonymously at Sotheby's, 24 Feb. 1897, lot 809; (2) Acquired by Richard Johnson, who stamped his initials on the verso and sold it posthumously at Sotheby's, 28 May 1934, lot 173 (with 6 Mora plates); (3) Acquired by *Geoffrey Keynes*, who listed in his library catalogue (1964), no. 519.

39

**The Book of Urizen* [A]. Reproduced in [colour] Facsimile With a Note by Dorothy Plowman. London, Toronto & N.Y., 1929.
   'A Note on William Blake's Book of Urizen' is on pp. 11–25.

40

**The Book of Urizen* [G]. London, 1958. The William Blake Trust.
   It includes a 2-page 'Bibliographical Statement' by Geoffrey Keynes and another unpaginated, untitled, and unsigned statement. The facsimile is reproduced in no. 41.

41

**The Book of Urizen* [G]. Introduction by Clark Emery. Coral Gables (Florida), 1966. University of Miami Critical Studies No. 6. B. Second Printing, 1969.
   A black-and-white copy of the Blake Trust facsimile (1958), no. 40. The introduction is divided into 'The Background' (pp. 1–20), dealing largely with Gnosticism, and 'The Poem' (pp. 21–54).

42

A*Urizen no Sho [*The Book of Urizen*]. Tr. Bunsho Jugaku. Kyoto, 1932.
   The translation into Japanese is illustrated by reproductions of some but not all the plates.

43. *For Children: The Gates of Paradise* (1793)

BIBLIOGRAPHICAL INTRODUCTION

See Table on p. 186

TITLE: *For Children | The | Gates | of | Paradise | — | 1793 | Published by W Blake N⁰ 13 | Hercules Buildings Lambeth | and | J. Johnson S! Pauls' Church Yard*

TABLE

Copy	Plates	Leaves	Water-marks	Blake numbers[1]	Binding-order	Plate-size in cm	Printing colour
A LC	1–18	18	MAFRINS[2] (13, 15)	—	‡*1–18*	9·6 × 13·9*	Black
B BMPR	1–18	18	—	—	‡1–18**	10·3 × 13·5* *irregular*	Black
C *Anonymous*	1–18	18	—	—	*1–18*	10·5 × 12·9	Black
D LC	1–18, *For the Sexes* 2, 19–20	21	—	—	‡*1–2, For the Sexes* 2, *19–20, For Children* 0 *18*	10·2 × 12·7*	Black
E *Mellon*	1–18	18	—	1–18[3]	‡*1–18*	11·5 × 13·5	Black

‡   Pl. 1 faces pl. 2.
1–18 Italicized binding-orders indicate copies still in bindings of before 1835.
**   The identifiable offsets confirm the present order.
*   The edges are trimmed and gilt.

[1] There are etched numbers (2–16) on pl. 4–18.
[2] The almost illegible and perhaps fragmentary watermark in copy A has not been confidently identified or dated. The 'FRIN' is especially dubious. G. Keynes (ed., *The Gates of Paradise* [1968], i. 47) suggests that it may be 'MARAIS', part of 'PAPETRIE DU MARAIS', which has been 'found in a book dated 1797'. 'MARTIN' also seems a possibility. Pl. 2 in copy A is on clearly different paper.
[3] The numbers on copy E are on pl. 1, 3–18 and the fly-leaf following pl. 18.

DATE: 17 May 1793.

All the plates except pl. 2 and 15 bear this date in the imprint, in some form of:

Publishd by W Blake 17 May 1793

on pl. 1, 4–5, 7–8, 10–12, 18 (except that 'Publishd' is reduced to 'Pub^d' on pl. 7, 11, and 'Lambeth' is added to pl. 10), or

Publishd 17 May 1793 by W Blake Lambeth

on pl. 3, 6, 9, 13–14, 16–17 (except that pl. 3 omits 'Lambeth'). On pl. 2 there was no necessity for this imprint, and on pl. 15 there was no room for it. All the evidence suggests that the work was designed, engraved, and all copies printed at about this date.

PUBLICATION: *For Children* is an emblem book. Blake filled his *Notebook* with emblem sketches, and he went through them several times numbering them on odd pages from p. 15 to p. 101.[1] The sketches on pp. 15, 17, 19, 34, 40, 45, 52, ?58–9, 61, 63, 68–9, 71, 75, 91, 93–5, and ?98 were chosen as emblems to use as *For Children* pl. 1, 3–18, those for pl. 10, 13, 16–17 with captions as in the printed version, those for pl. 1, 3–9, 15, 17–18 with variant legends. These designs were reproduced in simple line engravings, first in a proof

[1] Except for pp. 21, 33, 53, 77, 99, and plus pp. 18, 22, 24, 34, 58, 60, 72, 94, 98. All the odd pages without numbers except for p. 77 have sketches used in *For Children* on adjacent pages.

state without the imprints (copy A) and next with the imprints of '17 May 1793' and some minor alterations in engraving.

Presumably copy A was simply a proof copy, never really published. All the rest were printed on small leaves, about 11 × 14 cm, probably shortly after the date of the imprint, as follows:

Copy	Approximate date	State
A	early spring 1793	State 1 (proof)
B–E[1]	late spring 1793	State 2 (as published)

Very few copies were printed, for only five have survived, and only one (E) is known to have gone into the hands of a child. There is no evidence beyond that on the title-page that Joseph Johnson ever sold the book; in particular, he never advertised it in his journal, *The Analytical Review*.

Blake listed it in his Prospectus of 10 Oct. 1793 as 'The Gates of Paradise, a small book of Engravings. Price 3s.', but he did not mention it in his list of works for sale in his letters of 9 June 1818 or 12 April 1827. Among Blake's contemporaries, copies were owned by Mrs. Bliss (copy A, acquired by P. A. Hanrott and sold to William Beckford in 1833), George Cumberland (copy C, acquired by Beckford in 1835), Frederick Tatham (copy D)[1] and John Henry Fuseli (copy E, who gave it to his five-year-old friend Harriet Jane Moore on 22 Nov. 1806).

The significance of the emblems was made rather clearer when Blake revised and expanded the series in *For the Sexes: The Gates of Paradise* (?1818)—see pp. 193–200.

COLOURING: None.

CATCHWORDS: None.

ORDER: Pl. 1–18 in all copies, confirmed by the etched numbers.

VARIANTS: The five known copies are in two States:

State 1: There are no imprints, the numbers are in slightly different places, and there are small differences in the engraved lines in the first State (A).

State 2: The second State is the one as published (copies B–E—but see pl. 4 of copy E).

For further variants, see *For the Sexes* (?1818), pp. 193–200.

ERRATA: None observed.

Pl. 1. INCIPIT: 'What is Man!' DESIGN: At the bottom is a chrysalis on a leaf with the head of a sleeping baby, while over it is a caterpillar on a leaf. (A sketch with an inscription for this plate, labelled 'Frontispiece', is on *Notebook* p. 68.)

VARIANTS: *State 1*: There is no imprint, the word 'Frontispiece' is missing, there is no shading above the chrysalis, no line beneath its chin, and less shading on its face and upper body (copy A).

State 2: The published State is found in copies B–E.

---

[1] Copy D is clearly a sport, with pl. 2, 19–20 from *For the Sexes* (?1818) added to it twenty-five or more years later.

Pl. 2. DESIGN: Between 'For Children' and 'The Gates', a small figure in a long robe flies to the right.

VARIANTS: *State 1*: In copy A, there are only two lines in the gown by the feet of the figure (later there are four), the rule is 1·5 cm below 'Paradise' (not 0·8 cm as in the published State), and there is nothing below the rule. Between the rule and 'Paradise' are words which seem to be erased both from the copperplate and from the paper. They begin with the letter 'P' and end with 'ey', with space between for something like

P[*ublishd by J. Dodsl*]ey

State 2. The published State is found in copies B–E.

Pl. 3. INCIPIT: 'I found him beneath a Tree'. DESIGN: Beneath a willow bending over the page from the left, a woman in a long dress which leaves her right knee exposed holds a baby in the folds of her skirt while she plucks another, mandrake-like, from the ground. (A reversed sketch for this design on *Notebook* p. 63 is inscribed: 'I found him beneath a tree in the Garden'.)

VARIANTS: *State 1*: There is no imprint or number or shading on the left ankle, and fewer lines in the woman's hair (copy A).

State 2: The published State is found in copies B–E.

In copy C is sketched in pencil a nude human leg protruding from the design, echoing that of the engraved woman. It may be by George Cumberland, and the sketches on the versos of pl. 6 and 17 may be his too.

Pl. 4. INCIPIT: 'Water'. DESIGN: Beneath the branch of a leafless tree on the right, a naked man on an island or peninsula sits with his hands on his knees while rain pelts round him. (A sketch for this plate is on *Notebook* p. 95, with an inscription from *Hamlet*.)

VARIANTS: *State 1*: There is no imprint, and the engraved '2' is in a slightly different place in the bottom left corner (copy A).

State 2: The published State is found in copies B–E, except that copy E strangely has an engraved number in the bottom right corner.

Pl. 5. INCIPIT: 'Earth'. DESIGN: A naked man with his arms over his head seems to try to climb through enveloping rock. (The design is sketched on *Notebook* p. 5, and, reversed, on p. 93, with a caption from *Hamlet*. For similar designs, see *Urizen* [1794] pl. 9–10, and *The Book of Los* [1795] pl. 2.)

VARIANTS: *State 1*: There is no imprint, and the number is in a slightly different place (copy A).

State 2: The published State is found in copies B–E.

Pl. 6. INCIPIT: 'Air'. DESIGN: On a cloud sits a naked man with his chin on his right knee and his hands on his forehead. In the sky are fourteen stars. (Two sketches for this plate are on *Notebook* p. 94, with an inscription from Ezekiel, and another on p. 98 may be for it as well.)

VARIANTS: *State 1*: There is no imprint, the number is in a slightly different place, and there is no vertical hatching on the cloud to the left of the man (copy A).

State 2: The published State is found in copies B–E.

Pl. 7. INCIPIT: 'Fire'. DESIGN: Amid soaring flames a naked man stands defiantly with outspread arms bearing a spear and a shield. (On *Notebook* p. 91 is a reversed sketch for this splendid design, with a caption from *Paradise Lost.*)

VARIANTS: *State 1*: There is no imprint, and the number is written differently in copy A.

State 2: The published State is found in copies B–E.

Pl. 8. INCIPIT: 'At length for hatching ripe he breaks the shell'. DESIGN: A winged child emerges from an egg in a cloudy sky. (A sketch for this plate, with the quotation ascribed to Dryden, [*Fables Ancient and Modern* (1700)], appears on *Notebook* p. 69.)

VARIANTS: *State 1*: There is no imprint, the number is in a different place, there is no hatching on the cherub's left arm, and more shading round the top of his left leg in copy A.

State 2: The published State is found in copies B–E.

Pl. 9. INCIPIT: 'Alas!' DESIGN: A boy in knee-breeches tries to knock down a tiny, naked, flying child with his hat, while another such child lies sprawled on the ground in front of him. In the background are a hedge and a cloudy sky. (A sketch with an inscription for this plate is on *Notebook* p. 19.)

VARIANTS: *State 1*: There is no imprint, the number is in a slightly different place, and there is a heavy line from the boy's chin to his ear (later removed) in copy A.

State 2: The published State is found in copies B–E.

Copy B is inscribed: 'Noi jiam' verme, / nati a formar l'angelical forfall' from Dante.

Pl. 10. INCIPIT: 'My Son! my Son!' DESIGN: At the left, a naked boy with a huge spear in his left hand threatens an old man with a long beard. The latter is seated on a huge stone chair, resting his cheek on his left hand and his right hand on a sword. From the right arches a tree, and in the background are hills and a cloudy sky.

(A reversed sketch for this design appears on *Notebook* p. 34, and another reversed sketch [BMPR, reproduced in *Blake Newsletter*, V (1972), 234] shows the boy with a cape and a quiver shaking a spear at the old man who is in armour but swordless; behind the old man is a broken classical column.)

VARIANTS: *State 1*: There is no imprint, the number is in a slightly different place, the old man's right leg is shaded only on the calf, there is no shading on the old man's feet, right thigh, right wrist, or above his left ankle, and there are several lines on his right shoulder, like a bandage (later removed), in copy A.

State 2: The published State is found in copies B–E.

Pl. 11. INCIPIT: 'I want! I want!' DESIGN: A tiny man mounts a ladder propped against a quarter moon, while two others watch him. In the background are seven stars in a dark, cloudless sky. (A reversed sketch for this design is on *Notebook* p. 40.)

VARIANTS: *State 1*: There is no imprint, the number is in a slightly different place, and the rungs on the ladder mount only to the second star on the right (not to the third star as in State 2) in copy A.

State 2: The published State is found in copies B–E.

Pl. 12. INCIPIT: 'Help! Help!' DESIGN: A naked man in the sea raises his hand with outspread fingers towards a dark sky. (A sketch perhaps for this plate appears on *Notebook* p. 58.)

VARIANTS: *State 1*: There is no imprint, and the number is in a slightly different place, in copy A.

State 2: The published State is found in copies B–E.

Pl. 13. INCIPIT: 'Aged Ignorance'. DESIGN: Beneath the branch of a tree stretching from the left sits an old man with a long beard, closed eyes, a long robe, and spectacles; he is cutting with huge scissors the wings of a naked boy running to the right towards a speckled rising sun. (*Notebook* p. 52 bears a sketch for this design.)

VARIANTS: *State 1*: There is no imprint or number in copy A.

State 2: The number and imprint are supplied in copies B–E.

Pl. 14. INCIPIT: 'Does thy God O Priest take such vengeance as this?' DESIGN: A bearded man (Ugolino) crouches between two boys of about ten (his grandsons) who seem to be clutching him, while two young men (his sons) lean against the left and right margins with their hands on the ground. All are naked, and the background is an undifferentiated Black. (A tentative sketch for this design is in the V & A [no. 8763 B, reproduced in *Pencil Drawings* [1927], pl. 9], a very similar one is in the *Notebook* [p. 59, the left figure on p. 75], a closely related design is in the *Marriage* [?1790–3] pl. 16, related designs are entitled 'How I pity' (?1793), and 'Is all joy forbidden' (?1793), a quite different version is in the background of Blake's portrait of Dante for Hayley's library [*c*. 1801] [reproduced in Wm. Wells, *William Blake's 'Heads of the Poets'* (1969) pl. 32], and a very similar drawing for Dante [1824–7], with two angels added overhead [reproduced in A. S. Roe, *Blake's Illustrations to the Divine Comedy* (1953), pl. 68], was copied in a tempera [1827] owned by Sir Geoffrey Keynes [reproduced in the Arts Council exhibition catalogue, *The Tempera Paintings of William Blake* (1949), pl. xi].)

VARIANTS: *State 1*: There is no imprint, the number is in a slightly different place, and there is much less hatching on the old man's left leg, on the left leg of the boy on his left, on the right leg of the boy on his right, and on the right leg of the man at the bottom left, in copy A.

State 2: The published State is found in copies B–E.

Pl. 15. INCIPIT: 'Fear & hope are — Vision'. DESIGN: A man, a woman, and two children kneel on either side of a low bed on which seems to be a corpse and stare upwards at the figure of a man with a long gown and long beard who stands, as it were, on the foot of the bed and raises his left arm. The background is an undifferentiated Black. (The reversed sketch for this plate on *Notebook* p. 61 is entitled 'What we hope to See'.)

VARIANTS: *State 1*: The number is in a slightly different place, the background behind the spirit is not hatched horizontally, and '&' reads 'or' in copy A.

State 2: The published State is found in copies B–E.

Pl. 16. INCIPIT: 'The Traveller hasteth in the Evening'. DESIGN: A man in a large Black hat and a swallow-tailed coat and carrying a staff in his right hand walks with long strides before a hedge towards the right. (A sketch for the design appears in *Notebook* p. 15, and a similar figure appears in *All Religions are One* [?1788] pl. 7.)

VARIANTS: *State 1*: There is no imprint, and the number is in a slightly different place in copy A.

State 2: The published State is found in copies B–E.

Pl. 17. INCIPIT: 'Death's Door'. DESIGN: An old man with a long beard, a long swirling robe, and a crutch under his left arm seems to be hurried by the wind through an open stone doorway. (A sketch perhaps for this design appears on *Notebook* p. 17, and another is on p. 71. An almost identical figure appears on *America* [1793] pl. 14 and again in the design [1805] called 'Death's Door' for Blair's *Grave* [1808].)

VARIANTS: *State 1*: There is no imprint, and the number is in a slightly different place in copy A.

State 2: The published State is found in copies B–E.

Pl. 18. INCIPIT: 'I have said to the Worm . . .'. DESIGN: Beneath the branches or roots of a dark tree crouches a person clothed apparently in a cowl and shroud. In the figure's right hand is a vertical rod, and round its feet wraps a worm, while on the ground to the right are the profiles of two or more men the same colour as the earth. (The design is sketched on p. 45 of the *Notebook*, and a quite similar drawing is in the Pierpont Morgan Library [16·2 × 20·8 cm, reproduced in *The Gates of Paradise*, ed. G. Keynes (1968), i. 39]; the latter omits the worm and shows the figure as clearly feminine.)

VARIANTS: *State 1*: There is no imprint, and the number is in a slightly different place, in copy A.

State 2: The published State is found in copies B–E.

COPY A: BINDING: (1) Originally stabbed through three holes, 3·2 cm from the top, and 3·9 and 3·8 cm apart; (2) Bound about 1805 (the date on the fourth fly-leaf) identically with *Songs* (P) (see p. 419), probably for Mrs. Bliss, in Red straight-grain morocco, g.e., the spine gilt with 'BLAKE'S / GATES / OF / PARADISE'.

HISTORY: (1) Bound about 1805, probably for Mrs. Bliss, with whose elaborately bound Bibliotheca Splendissima it was sold by Saunders & Hodgson, 26 April 1826, lot 10 (in its present binding), for 8s., perhaps to (2) P. A. Hanrott, with whose Library it was sold by Evans, 20 July 1833, lot 894, for £1. 16s. to Thorpe (evidently for Clarke, whose name is written after the price in the BM copy of the catalogue); (3) Acquired by William Beckford, who wrote on the fly-leaf 'Hanrott July 1833', numbered it ('no 3764'), and sold it posthumously with *The Beckford Library* at Sotheby's, 4 July 1882, lot 953, for £16 to Bain; (4) Acquired by B. B. Macgeorge, described in his Library catalogues (1892, 1906), lent to the exhibitions in the National Gallery (1913), no. 94, Manchester (1914), no. 156, Nottingham (1914), no. 117, the National Gallery of Scotland (1914), Case A, no. 8, and sold posthumously at Sotheby's, 1 July 1924, lot 112, for £175 to Maggs; (5) Offered in Maggs Catalogue 456 (1924) for £275; (6) Acquired by W. E. Moss, who lent it to the Burlington Fine Arts Club exhibition (1927), no. 8, had six copies printed of photographic reproductions (?1942) and sold it for £460 to Rosenbach for (7) Mr. LESSING J. ROSENWALD.

COPY B: BINDING: (1) Stitch marks suggest that it was bound before 1862, (2) When it was acquired by the British Museum, pasted on to larger leaves (15·8×21·1 cm), which were mounted on stubs and bound in half Green morocco, g.e.; (3) The leaves were mounted in heavy paper 'windows' and rebound in Red morocco in 1969.

HISTORY: (1) Sold by Colnaghi & Co. on 12 July 1862 to (2) The BRITISH MUSEUM PRINT ROOM, where the leaves were mounted and bound.

COPY C: BINDING: Bound, perhaps about 1835 for William Beckford, in Brown half calf with 'BLAKE'S WORK' on the spine; the rather crude sketches on pl. 3 and the versos of pl. 6 and 17 may be by George Cumberland.

HISTORY: (1) Acquired by George Cumberland, who probably made the sketches (on pl. 3 and the versos of pl. 6, 17) and the note (on the penultimate fly-leaf: 'Mrs Blake now lives at N 17 Charlton St Fitzroy Square at a Bakers. 1830'—see *Blake Records* [1969], 568), and sold it with *Job* and *Thel* (A) at Christie's, 6 May 1835, lot 61, for £3. 13s. 6d. to W. Bohn; (2) Acquired by William Beckford, who perhaps had it bound, wrote 'a present from H. G. Bohn / 19th May 1835 / No 3783' on the first fly-leaf, and for whom it was sold at Sotheby's, 4 July 1882, lot 954, for £12. 12s.; (3) Acquired by Thomas Brooke, who added his book-plate; sold by Lady Brooke at Sotheby's, 24 Nov. 1913, lot 62, for £91 to Spencer; (4) Acquired by H. V. Jones, who added his book-plate and sold it at Anderson Galleries, 2 Dec. 1918, lot 185, for $610 to Rosenbach; (5) Acquired by A. E. Newton, who added his book-plate, lent it to the exhibitions at the Fogg (1924) and in Philadelphia (1939), no. 32, and sold it posthumously at Parke-Bernet, 16 April 1941, lot 134, for $3,000 to Sessler; (6) Acquired by Mary S. Collins, who added her book-plate; (7) From her it passed into an *Anonymous* collection.

COPY D: BINDING: 'BOUND BY F. BEDFORD' by 1886, probably for Frederick Locker, in Green morocco, g.e., with *For the Sexes* pl. 1, 19, 20; the little drawings on the latter may be by Frederick Tatham.

HISTORY: (1) 'It came from Mr Tatham'[1] (according to a manuscript note on the fly-leaf by Frederick Locker), 'who my Father knew', and who apparently sold it to (2) Locker's father; (3) Acquired by Frederick Locker, who added his book-plate, lent it (or *For the Sexes* [E]) to the Burlington Fine Arts Club exhibition (1876), no. 311, probably had it bound by Bedford (see *Songs* [E], p. 414), described in his *Rowfant Library* (1886), and sold posthumously through Dodd, Mead & Co. (see the 'Pickering MS', p. 341) to (4) 'W. A. White / 27 Apl 1905', who wrote his name and the date on the

---

[1] See also *For the Sexes* (L), p. 203.

fly-leaf, perhaps lent it anonymously to the Grolier Club exhibition (1919), no. 8, and to that in the Fogg (1924), and probably sold it after his death through Rosenbach on 1 May 1929 to (5) Mr. LESSING J. ROSENWALD; it was reproduced in the Blake Trust facsimile (1968).

COPY E: BINDING: Bound in contemporary marbled boards without a label.

HISTORY: (1) Given by John Henry Fuseli (according to the inscription on the front fly-leaf) (2) 'To Harriet Jane Moore [*then 5 years old, the daughter of James Carrick Moore (1762–1860) and grand-daughter of John Moore (1729–1802), family physician to Fuseli's patrons the Lockes of Norbury Park*] / from her friend Henry Fuseli / Nov. 22*nd* 1806'; (3) Acquired by her sister Julia Moore (1803–1904) (according to the 1949 catalogue below, the authority for the rest of the History); (4) Acquired by a cousin on Julia's death; (5) Acquired by Mrs. M. C. Heath, who sold it at Sotheby's, 4 April 1949, lot 75D, for £320 to King; (6) Acquired by Mr. *Paul Mellon*.

44

*The Gates of Paradise. For Children [A]. The Plates before Imprint Enlarged Two Diameters. N.p., n.d. [1942?]

There is a preface of 3 pp. by William E. Moss. In the Bodley copy Moss added a manuscript note saying 6 copies were made.

45. *For the Sexes: The Gates of Paradise* (?1818)

BIBLIOGRAPHICAL INTRODUCTION

See Table on pp. 194–5

TITLE: *For the Sexes | The | Gates | of | Paradise |*
                  Mutual Forgiveness of each Vice
                  Such are the Gates of Paradise
                  Against the Accusers chief desire
                  Who walkd among the Stones of Fire
                  Jehovahs Finger Wrote the Law
                  Then Wept! then rose in Zeal & Awe
                  And the Dead Corpse from Sinais heat
                  Buried beneath his Mercy Seat
                  O Christians Christians tell me Why
                  You rear it on your Altars high

DATE: ?1818.

The first revisions of *The Gates of Paradise* seem to have been made about 1818. One indication of date is the watermark of 1818 in the second State of *For the Sexes* (B). Another is the similarity of the poetry added in *For the Sexes*

TABLE

Copies	Plates	Leaves	Watermarks	Blake numbers[1]	Binding-order	Leaf-size in cm	Printing colour
A *UNTRACED*[2]	1–21	21	*no dated watermark*	—	—	11·2 × 15·8	
B BMPR	1–21	21	J WHATMAN/1818 (2, 10, 13)	—	‡1–2, 19–20, 3–18, 21**	10·6 × 15·2 to 11·4 × 17·0	Black
C BM	1–21	21	J WHATMAN/18[25] (1, 9–10, 18)	17–19[3]	2, 1, 3–21**	14·0 × 22·5*	Black
D MORGAN	1–21	21	J WHATMAN/1825 (3, 8, 16–17)	17–19[3]	1–21**	14·3 × 22·8	Black
E ROSENBACH	1–21	21	—	—	‡1–2, 19–21, 3–18**	19·2 × 25·8*	Black
F HUNTINGTON	1–18, 21	19	J WHATMAN/1826 (1, 5, 7, 11–13, 16)	—	1–18, 21[4]	24·0 × 34·4 *irregular*	Black
G *Mellon*	1–18, 20–1	20	J WHATMAN/1826 (3, 6–9, 12, 14, 17)	—	‡2, 1, 3–18, 21 20**	23·9 × 34·0*[5]	Black
H *Newton*	1–3, 9–15, 20–1	12	J WHATMAN/1826 (13, 15, 20–1)	—	‡2, 1, 3, 9–15, 20–1[6]	23·0 × 33·2	Black
I YALE	1–18, 20–1	20	J WHATMAN/1826 (2, 4, 6, 12–13, 18)	—	‡2, 1, 3–18, 21, 20	24·2 × 34·3 (1–18) 19·1 × 19·7 (20–1)	Black
J MORGAN	2, 7–10, 16, 18–21	10	—	—	Loose	27·0 × 37·2 (1) 26·5 × 36·7 (7) 18·3 × 20·3 (8) 9·5 × 11·5 (9) 9·8 × 13·0 (10) 25·5 × 34·5 (16) 8·7 × 11·5 (18) 26·2 × 37·4 (19) 26·6 × 39·2 (20) 26·2 × 35·4 (21)	Black

Copy	Present order of plates	(no.)	Offsets	Binding order	Size (cm)	Ink
K LC	1–3, 8–9, 11, 13–16, 18–21	14	—	Loose	26·5 × 37·5	Black Black
L *Keynes* LC	2–8, 10–14, 16–18, 21	16	—	2–8, 10–14, 16–18, 21[7]	22·5 × 31·0[8]	Black Black
	2, 19–20, *For Children* (D) 1–18	21	—	*For Children* 1–2, *For the Sexes* 1, 19–20, *For Children* 1–18	10·2 × 12·7	
Keynes	6–7	2	—	Loose	7·3 × 8·9	Black
HUNTINGTON	12	1	—		8·5 × 10·8	Black
TRINITY COLLEGE	14	1	—	Loose[9]	24·8 × 32·9	Black
BMPR	15	1	*invisible*	Loose	10·7 × 12·1	Black

++   Pl. 1 faces pl. 2.   *1–21* Italicized binding-order numbers indicate copies still in bindings of before 1835.

**   The identifiable offsets confirm the present order.   * The edges are trimmed and gilt.

1 Since pl. 3–18 have etched numbers (1–16), only pl. 19–21 needed supplementary numbers.

2 The information about copy A, which has not been traced, is taken from *The Poetical Works of William Blake*, ed. J. Sampson (1905), 368, 373, 375.

3 In copies C and D, Blake's extra ink numbers 17–19 are on pl. 19–21.

4 The leaves of copy F are now loose, but the offsets plus the pencil numbers (1–19) give the above order.

5 Only the top edges of copy G are gilt.

6 The leaves of copy H are loose, but the stab-marks and etched numbers give the order above.

7 The leaves of copy L were loose when Keynes acquired them. Pl. 3 in copy L has a quite distinct history and was not associated with copy L until Keynes acquired it.

8 Pl. 8, 10–12, 14, 16–18 in copy L are trimmed to about 0·3 cm from the plate-marks and inlaid to size.

9 The Trinity College pl. 14 was bound after 1871 (the watermark date on the fly-leaf) with *The Ghost of Abel* (D) and *On Homer* (D). Since pl. 14 in *For the Sexes* and *For Children* is identical, the chief indication that this pl. 14 is from *For the Sexes* is the very large size. It could have come from the very miscellaneous copy J.

to that in 'The Everlasting Gospel' (?1818) (p. 323). Compare, for example:

'The Everlasting Gospel'	For the Sexes
Mutual forgiveness of each Vice	Mutual forgiveness of each Vice⌊,⌋
. . . oped the Gates of Paradise	Such are the Gates of Paradise
[*part b, ll. 26–7*]	[*pl. 2, ll. 1–2*]
Reasoning upon its own dark Fiction	Two horn'd Reasoning Cloven Fiction
In doubt which is Self Contradiction	In Doubt which is Self contradiction
[*part k, ll. 98–9*]	[*pl. 19, ll. 13–14*]
Cease finger of Cod to write	Jehovah's Finger Wrote the Law
[*part f, l. 23*]	[*pl. 2, l. 5*]

Similarly, the 'Laocoon' (?1820) with its serpents named 'Evil' and 'Good' 'propagating Generation & Death' (p. 268) seems akin to the designs of *For the Sexes*.

This fragmentary evidence is not very satisfactory, but it does seem to point to a date of about 1818 for the composition of pl. 2, 19–20 and the engraving of the revised *Gates of Paradise*, a time when Blake was turning once again to his works in Illuminated Printing.[1]

PUBLICATION: *For Children* (1793) clearly had a very small circulation, for only five copies have survived, and one of these was given away in 1806 and another came into the hands of Frederick Tatham, who acquired all Blake's effects from his widow. Blake may at one time have considered making a companion work, to be called 'For Children: The Gates of Hell', but this evidently got no further than a draft title-page (see p. 215).

It was probably not until about 1818 that he began writing new verses (pl. 2, 19–21) for *The Gates of Paradise* and improving his engravings, but the few copies which survive suggest that he never completed the work to his own satisfaction and that most of the duplicate copies of the final State were printed and sold posthumously.

Blake's extensive revisions of *For the Sexes* may have occupied part of his time for the rest of his life. The dates of 1825 and 1826 in all but the first water-marked copy suggest that it was not until several years after 1818 that he was sufficiently satisfied with the work to pull prints. Indeed, since only one complete copy exists in the final State of the plates, it seems likely that Blake never was entirely satisfied with the work. Probably he printed copies primarily as working proofs, and the fragmentary copies were pulled post-humously by his widow (1827–31) or by Tatham.

Three facts in particular point to the conclusion that most copies were printed posthumously. In the first place, copies F–L are fragmentary, all but two lacking pl. 19, which is the first half of 'The Keys'. An explanation of this omission may be that pl. 19 was engraved on the verso of pl. 20 and was thus easy to overlook. The effect, however, was to make nonsense of the

---

[1] See his letter of 9 June 1818. A yet later date for the composition of pl. 2, 19–21 and the first engraved revisions seems quite possible.

crucial Key to the work, and it is difficult to believe that Blake would have been responsible for such an oversight.

In the second place, the first five copies (A–E) are printed on paper of the size Blake called Octavo, about 14×20 cm (though copy E is 19×26 cm). However, except for some isolated prints, all other copies are much larger, about 24×34 cm or larger, and the watermark is 1826. This distinction in size is conspicuous and seems significant when we observe that it obtains only in incomplete copies using 1826 paper.

In the third place, a significant number of copies can be traced to Tatham,[1] who received Blake's works from his widow. He gave copy F away on 23 October 1831 as a memorial of Catherine Blake's funeral, he sold copy E to Locker, and he evidently also sold pl. 2, 19–20 to Locker with *For Children* (D). Thomas Boddington, who dated his copy (D) '1833', must have got it from Tatham, and his brother Samuel Boddington presumably acquired his copy (C) from Tatham at the same time that he bought his other posthumous copies of works by Blake.[2] Since copies A–B, K belonged to John Linnell, who might well have bought them from Catherine (she lived with him in 1827–8) or Tatham, it is clear that all complete copies were possibly (A–B, K) or almost certainly (C–F) sold posthumously.[3]

The dates of *For the Sexes* may then have been as follows:

Copy	Watermark date	Approximate dates of: Printing	Sale
A–B	1818 *or* n.d.	1818	?1827
C–E	1825 *or* n.d.	1825	1833 ff.
F–L	1826 *or* n.d.	1827–8	1831 ff.

Among Blake's contemporaries, copies were owned by John Linnell (A, B, K), Samuel Boddington (C), Thomas Boddington (D, dated '1833'), Frederick Tatham (F, given to Mr. Bird on 23 Oct. 1831), and ?Joseph Dinham (H).

COLOURING: None.

CATCHWORDS: None.

ORDER: Pl. 1–21, with authoritative variants.

The surviving copies are bound in five different orders:

Order	Copies
1–21	D, F*
2, 1, 3–21	C
‡2, 1, 3–18, 21, 20	G*, ?H*, I*
1–2, 19–20, 3–18, 21	B
‡1–2, 19–21, 3–18	E

* indicates a copy missing one or more plates.

---

[1] He quotes *For the Sexes* in his 'Life of Blake' of about 1832 (*Blake Records* [1969], 527).

[2] His copies of *America* (P), *Europe* (M), *Jerusalem* (H), *Songs* (c) are watermarked 1831 and 1832, and his *Descriptive Catalogue* (E) is without Blake's authenticating corrections.

[3] This may lend some weight to the hypothesis advanced by E. Wolf 2nd in the Philadelphia Catalogue (*William Blake* [1939], 63) that the last alterations in the copperplates of *For the Sexes* were made by Tatham, though Keynes (ed., *The Gates of Paradise* [1968], i. 50) and I think this unlikely.

Pl. 3–18 do not vary in order and are confirmed by the etched numbers.

The frontispiece (pl. 1) seems indifferently to precede (B, D–F) or to follow (C, G–I) the title-page (pl. 2), and the stab-marks and early bindings give authority to each arrangement.

Pl. 19–20 ('The Keys') twice follow pl. 3–18 (C–D, both numbered by Blake), twice plausibly follow the title-page (B, E), and in two defective and perhaps posthumous copies (G, I) follow pl. 21. Blake's numbers (19–21 on pl. 17–19 in C–D) seem to give decisive weight to the order pl. 3–20, with pl. 2, 19–20, 3–18 a plausible variant.

Pl. 21 ('To the Accuser') is sometimes the last plate (B–D, F), sometimes follows pl. 20 (C–E), and sometimes succeeds pl. 18 (B, C, I). Blake's numbers in copies C–D seem to give authority to the order pl. 3–21.

Each order seems plausible, but pl. 1–21, which is justified both by Blake's numbers and by contemporary binding, seems the most satisfactory.

VARIANTS:[1] Four States of pl. 2 have been observed in *For the Sexes*, two for pl. 1, 3–9, 13, 15, 19, and one for pl. 10–12, 14, 16–18, 20–1. (The preliminary State of pl. 1–18 is taken to be that in the published State of *For Children* [1793], and in the first State below are noted variants from *For Children*.) In each plate, the hatching is darker and more subtle in *For the Sexes* than in *For Children*, and the lines are more firmly engraved. In pl. 1–2, 4–7, 9, 13, the captions are expanded. In *For Children*, the genitals of all the naked figures are invisible, but a hint of them was added in *For the Sexes* pl. 13.

ERRATA: None observed.

Pl. 1. VARIANTS: *State 1*: The caption is expanded (B–D).

State 2: In the final State there is added double shading above and to the left of the baby's face and heavier lines to the right of the caterpillar (E–L).

Pl. 2. VARIANTS: *State 1*: Below 'For' in the first line of the *For Children* plate is added another flying figure, and on each side of 'The' below it are three more. Between 'of' and 'Paradise' is a rising sun with a floating angel with arms folded over breast on each side. 'Children', the rule, and the imprint have been removed, and in their places have been put 'the Sexes' and the verses. (Lines to keep the writing level are visible in C.) l. 5 reads 'fingers', and ll. 7–8 read 'And in the midst of Sinais heat / Hid it beneath His Mercy Seat' (A–B).

State 2: l. 5 was altered as at present to read 'Finger Wrote' (B).

State 3: ll. 7–8 were altered as at present to read 'And the Dead Corpse from Sinais heat Buried beneath his Mercy Seat' (C–D).

State 4: The sun's rays were added in the final State (E–L).

Pl. 3. VARIANTS: *State 1*: A shadow has been added across the foreground of the *For Children* plate, and the contours of field and hill are clearer (B–D).

---

[1] Useful information about variants is to be found in J. Sampson, ed., *Poetical Works of William Blake* (1905), G. Keynes (1921), L. Binyon, *The Engraved Designs of William Blake* (1926), and [E. Mongan & E. Wolf 2nd] *William Blake* (Philadelphia exhibition catalogue, 1939), but the standard authority is G. Keynes, ed., *The Gates of Paradise* (1968), i, which yet does not describe graphic variants of *For the Sexes* in detail.

State 2: In the final State, the clear sky above the woman's left elbow is hatched, the ground to the right of her skirt is hatched diagonally, and her skirt covers more of her left leg (E–L).

Pl. 4. VARIANTS: *State 1*: There is a new line separating the earth and water, not found in the *For Children* plate, most of the tree trunk is rubbed down and reworked, roots were added, and the caption was expanded (B–D).

State 2: In the final State, there is added a heavy shadow on the tree, shading on the man's right calf, extra shading above his left hand, more lines by his mouth and eye and forehead and on his left biceps (E–L).

Pl. 5. VARIANTS: *State 1*: The Black recess over the man's right arm in *For Children* has been removed so that the rock presses on his arm, the shadows on the rocks round the figure are lightened, and the caption has been expanded (B–D).

State 2: In the final State, the lower lip curls to the right, there is more hatching on the man's left hand and arm, and dashes have been added on either side of 'Earth'.

Pl. 6. VARIANTS: *State 1*: The man's left shoulder has been added to the *For Children* plate, his right shoulder is made more muscular to match the left, and the caption has been expanded (B–D).

State 2: In the final State, the clear patch in the cloud to the left of the man's right shoulder has been cross-hatched, hatching has been added to his chin, there are more lines on his left knee and many more on his arms, and dashes have been added before and after 'Air' (E–L).

Pl. 7. VARIANTS: *State 1*: The *For Children* plate has been much reworked. The man's eyes are closed, scales have been added to his belly and in the flames at the left, right, and top margins, the shading is lighter behind his head, there are suggestions of ram-like horns in his hair, and the caption has been extended (B–D).

State 2: In the final State, there are vertical lines on the man's right leg, more shading on his left leg, scales on his upper thighs, the scales rise higher on his belly, the shield-strap over his arms is stronger, there is more hatching on his cheeks, and his chest is darker (E–L).

Pl. 8. VARIANTS: *State 1*: The egg in the *For Children* plate has been outlined, the sky and the shadow on the shell have been lightened, the pale margin of the top cloud has been extended, another fragment of shell has been added, the cracks in the shell are shorter, a strong shadow has been added under the shell, there is less stipple on the cherub's face, he has less hair, and his wing-shapes are altered (B–D).

State 2: In the final State there is more shading on the cherub's right leg (E–L).

Pl. 9. VARIANTS: *State 1*: Much of the shading in the *For Children* plate has been lightened, there are fewer lines on the boy's belly, the lower limits of his breeches are obscured so that he might almost be naked, his features are altered, and the caption is expanded (B–D).

State 2: In the final State, there are more than five lines of shading inside the boy's hat, his forearm and collar and the flying child's right leg are shaded, there is more hatching on the boy's legs and much more on the legs and arms and across the back of the fallen child, and the tree trunk has more lines (E–L).

Pl. 10. VARIANTS: The cloud shapes of *For Children* are altered, the back of the throne and the grass in the centre are lightened, the shadow of the old man's legs is removed, and vertical lines are added to the old man.

Pl. 11. VARIANTS: There is a trifle less striation in the sky than in *For Children*, and the shadow below the figures at right is somewhat longer.

Pl. 12. VARIANTS: The top and left sky is considerably darker than in *For Children*, a mass apparently representing land was added to the right, the sea was lightened, there is less shading on the man's arms and fingers, and his face is clearer and lighter.

Pl. 13. VARIANTS: *State 1*: Compared to the *For Children* plate, folds and shading have been added to the old man's robe, the bush behind him is darker, the boy has been given faint genitals, and the caption has been extended (B–D).

State 2: In the final State, there is a dark line just above the sun, the lines on the boy's legs are darker, the lines on the man's biceps are completed, there are lines on the boy's right calf and on the man's right wrist, and more lines on the man's lap, shoulder, and beard (E–L).

Pl. 14. VARIANTS: The floor and wall of the *For Children* plate have been lightened, the shapes of the cut stones in the walls are clearer, and shading has been added to the figures, especially to the one on the right.

Pl. 15. VARIANTS: *State 1*: The background of the *For Children* plate, especially the vertical lines, has been darkened, extensive shading has been added to all the figures, particularly the children's faces, the children's mouths are open and the left-hand child is seen almost full face rather than in profile, the woman's mouth is less open, the hands of the corpse are obscured, and a halo has been added to the spirit (B–D).

State 2: In the final State, there are lines on the arm of the man at the bottom left, more lines on his leg, hip, and back, horizontal lines on the side of the couch, more lines on the spirit's right arm, on the corpse, and on the faces of the children, and there are lines on the spirit's left arm (E–L).

Pl. 16. VARIANTS: The contrasts of the *For Children* plate have been darkened, the lines for the man's eyebrow and neck are heavier, and the sky is darker.

Pl. 17. VARIANTS: The outline of the door is clearer than in *For Children*, folds were added to the bottom of the old man's robe, lines were added to his beard, the shadow of his foot was made narrower, and the shadow of his crutch was made distinct.

Pl. 18. VARIANTS: Everything in the *For Children* plate is clarified, especially the roots of the tree and the faces in the earth. There are fewer shadows on the person's face, which seems more feminine, and the effect is lighter.

Pl. 19. INCIPIT: 'The Keys . . .'. DESIGN: On each side of 'The' in the title are tiny flying figures, and on the first 'T' is an embracing couple.

VARIANTS: *State 1*: In A–B, the sky and Satan are light, and in l. 15 the pronoun reads 'I'. In B, 'Doubt Self Jealous' in l. 9 is written over an erasure of printing which may read 'In Doubt . . . y'.

State 2: The sky and Satan were darkened, in l. 9 the MS change was confirmed on the copperplate, and in l. 15 the pronoun was altered to 'We' in copies C–L.

Pl. 20. INCIPIT: 'He meets his Saviour in the Grave . . .'. DESIGN: Before or after ll. 28, 32–3, 36, 38, 40–2 are tiny human figures. In l. 35, the apostrophe in 'Time's' is a bird.

Pl. 21. INCIPIT: 'To The Accuser . . .'. DESIGN: Between 'The God of This World' and l. 1 creeps a serpent with ten numbered coils.

Below the text is a naked sleeping man with a staff in his right hand. Over him floats a Black man with arms outspread and wings bearing two circles (sun and moon) and ten stars. (The winged figure is very similar to one in 'The Flight of Moloch' for Milton's 'Nativity Ode' [the undated Huntington copy is reproduced in the Huntington catalogue (1957), the Whitworth copy dated '1809' is reproduced in D. Figgis, *The Paintings of William Blake* (1925), pl. 37], except that the legs are in a different position and the stars and circles are omitted.)

COPY A: BINDING: Unknown.

HISTORY: (1) Acquired by John Linnell, from whom (according to J. Sampson, ed., *Poetical Works of William Blake* [1905], 368) it passed to (2) John Linnell, Jr.; (3) Probably this is the copy sold anonymously at Puttick & Simpson's, 1 Aug. 1906, lot 142 (21 plates, pl. 19 with an alteration by Blake [as in A], in wrappers);[1] (4) *UNTRACED*.

COPY B: BINDING: Mounted on linen stubs and 'BOUND BY ZAEHNSDORF 1906' in Brown morocco.

HISTORY: (1) Acquired by John Linnell, from whom (according to Sampson, as above) it passed to (2) James T. Linnell, who evidently sold it to (3) The dealer Francis Edwards,[2] who apparently had it bound and sold it in 1906 to (4) Miss A. G. E. Carthew, who added her book-plate (dated 1906), inscribed the fly-leaf,[2] lent it to Hollyer for the 1925 facsimile and to the Burlington Fine Arts Club exhibition (1927), no. 87, and bequeathed it on 13 July 1940 to (5) The BRITISH MUSEUM PRINT ROOM.

COPY C: BINDING: Bound between 1908 and 1921 for T. J. Wise in

---

[1] T. J. Wise, who saw it at the 1 Aug. 1906 sale, 'states that it was a tattered copy in grey paper wrappers' (according to Keynes, ed., *Gates of Paradise* [1968], i. 49). Keynes (ibid.) states erroneously that this copy was sold at Sotheby's, 27 June 1906, lot 142, for £22. 1s. The source of the error may be *Book Prices Current* for 1906, which lists lot 142 in the Sotheby sale twice, once (correctly) as Dryden's *Hind and the Panther* and once (erroneously) as the *Gates of Paradise*.

[2] The last fly-leaf is inscribed: 'This book was bought by me from Mr Edwards of High Street Marylebone in 1906. He got it from the Linnells. A G E Carthew 1906'.

Green leather, g.e., with the Wise owl on the front cover and a harp on the back.

HISTORY: (1) Acquired by Samuel Boddington, who added his book-plate; (2) Perhaps this is the copy of the *Gates* with 21 plates sold posthumously for John Giles (Samuel Palmer's cousin) at Christie's, 2 Feb. 1881, lot 185; (3) Sold by R. A. Potts in 1908 (according to Keynes, *Bibliography* [1921]) to (4) T. J. Wise, who had it bound with the Wise owl, added his book-plate in the back, and gave it with the Ashley Library in 1938 to (5) The BRITISH MUSEUM.

COPY D: BINDING: (1) Originally stabbed through three holes, 6·9 cm from the top, 3·6 and 3·6 cm apart; (2) Bound in old (?contemporary) half Brown calf over marbled boards, with 'THE GATES OF PARADISE BY BLAKE 1793' gilt sideways on the spine.

HISTORY: (1) Acquired, probably from Tatham (who owned most of Blake's works in 1833), by 'Thomas Boddington / 1833', who wrote his name and the date on the front endpaper and added his initialled book-plate; it was sold posthumously with his Library at Sotheby's, 4 Nov. 1895, lot 94, for £21 to Quaritch; (2) It was 'bo't through Quaritch at his Sale at Sotheby's 4 Nov '95' by 'W A White 18 Novʳ '95' (according to manuscript notes, the first below Boddington's signature, the second on the fly-leaf), who had it reproduced in a privately printed facsimile (?1897) and probably by Max Plowman in his edition of Blake's *Poems & Prophecies* (1927 ff.), lent it to the exhibitions of the Grolier Club (1905), no. 13 (anonymously), perhaps to that of 1919, no. 9, and to that in the Fogg (1924) and probably sold it posthumously with much of the rest of his collection in 1929 to Rosenbach; (3) Lent by A. S. W. Rosenbach to the Philadelphia exhibition (1939), no. 106; (4) Acquired by Mrs. Landon K. Thorne, in whose catalogue (1971) it was described (no. 11) and who gave it in 1973 to (5) The PIERPONT MORGAN LIBRARY.

COPY E: BINDING: 'BOUND BY F. BEDFORD' by 1886, perhaps for Frederick Locker, in Brown levant morocco, g.e.

HISTORY: (1) Acquired, perhaps from Tatham (see *For Children* [D], p. 192) by Frederick Locker, who added his book-plate, perhaps had it bound by Bedford (see *Songs* [E], p. 414), described in his catalogue (1886), and sold through Dodd, Mead & Co. (see the 'Pickering MS', p. 341) to (2) 'W. A. White', who put his name on the second fly-leaf, and probably sold it posthumously in 1929 to (3) A. S. W. Rosenbach, who lent it to the Philadelphia exhibition (1939), no. 107, and bequeathed it to (4) The ROSENBACH FOUNDATION.

COPY F: BINDING: Stabbed after 1827 (the watermark date on the cover) through three holes, 12·8 cm from the top and 4·4, 3·5 cm apart, into a Green paper folder; the string was still through pl. 15 in May 1965, but the other plates were loose.

HISTORY: (1) Given by 'Frederick Tatham / [from *del*] / to Mʳ Bird / on his attendance at the Funeral / Oct 23ʳᵈ 1831 — / being the day on which the / widow of the author was / Buried in Bunhill Fields / Church Yard' (according to the inscription on the Green paper folder); (2) Sold with the T. G. Arthur Library at Sotheby's, 15 July 1914, lot 260, for £72 to G. D. Smith for (3) The HUNTINGTON LIBRARY; it was reproduced in the 1968 facsimile.

COPY G: BINDING: Bound in Brown half morocco, t.e.g.

HISTORY: (1) Perhaps this is the copy of the *Gates* sold posthumously for George Blamire at Christie's, 6 Nov. 1863, lot 21, for £5. 5*s*. to Quaritch; (2) Acquired by the Earl of 'Southesk / 1864', who wrote his name and the date on a fly-leaf, added his book-plate and other notes on the fly-leaf, and transcribed from pl. 19 (here missing) couplets below the platemarks; (3) Sold at Sotheby's, 19 Oct. 1954, lot 279, for £370 to Stonehill; (4) Acquired by Mr. *Paul Mellon*.

COPY H: BINDING: (1) Originally stabbed through three holes, 12·5 cm from the top and 4·5, 4·5 cm apart; (2) In 1876 nine of the plates were exhibited 'in three frames'; (3) All the plates are now loose.

HISTORY: (1) Acquired by William Bell Scott, who added his monogram, lent nine plates to the Burlington Fine Arts Club exhibition (1876), nos. 285–7, and sold it at Sotheby's, 21 April 1885, lot 166, for £10. 2*s*. 6*d*. to Bain; (2) Sold by Miss Boothby Heathcote at Sotheby's, 29 July 1925, lot 168, for £31 to Parsons; (3) Acquired by George C. Smith, Jr.,[1] described in his anonymous catalogue (1927), lot 17, sold posthumously at Parke-Bernet, 2 Nov. 1938, lot 52, for $750 to Rosenbach; (4) Acquired by Mrs. Landon K. Thorne, who lent it to the Philadelphia exhibition (1939), no. 110, and from whom it passed through John Fleming about 1960 to (5) *Miss Caroline Newton*, who lent it to the Princeton exhibitions (1967) and (1969), no. 37.

COPY I: BINDING: (1) Originally stabbed through three holes, 4·8 and 4·8 cm apart in a wrapper; (2) By 1929 the wrappers and pl. 19 had disappeared, and pl. 2 has now pulled loose.

HISTORY: (1) Perhaps it was 'given by Blake to Joseph Dinham, sculptor' (as was 'Believed' according to the 1929 catalogue below); (2) Sold by the grandson of Joseph Dinham at Sotheby's, 27 March 1929, lot 417 (missing the wrappers and pl. 19) for £215 to G. Wells; (3) Acquired by C. B. Tinker, lent to the Philadelphia exhibition (1939), no. 109, described in his catalogue (1959), no. 280, and bequeathed at Tinker's death in March 1963 to (4) YALE.

COPY J: BINDING: (1) Bound in contemporary rough calf with other leaves of Blakeana, including *Thel* (a); (2) After 1906 the plates of *For the Sexes* were each separately mounted.

HISTORY: The History is as in *Thel* (a), p. 131.

COPY K: BINDING: Loose.

HISTORY: (1) Evidently originally John Linnell's; (2) Sold by his grandson Herbert Linnell through Lionel Robinson, according to the description (still with the collection) in July 1937 to (3) Mr. LESSING J. ROSENWALD.

COPY L: BINDING: (1) Pl. 8, 10–12, 14, 16–18 trimmed and inlaid to size, all plates (but the extra pl. 3) bound about 1853 with many leaves of Blakeana including the 'Order' of the *Songs*; separated by 1886; (2) Bound after 1953

---

[1] The Fogg Museum exhibition catalogue (1930) ascribes it in error to Rosenwald.

for Geoffrey Keynes by Gray of Cambridge in Red niger morocco with separate pl. 3.

HISTORY: For the History, see the 'Order' of the *Songs*, p. 337.

Pl. 1. 19–20: BINDING: They are bound with *For Children* (D).

HISTORY: For the History, see *For Children* (D), p. 192.

Pl. 3: BINDING: (1) The plate was apparently loose from 1903 until it was (2) Bound after 1953 with *For the Sexes* (L).

HISTORY: (1) Inscribed on the verso 'From the Earl of Crewe' and sold with his Blake collection at Sotheby's, 30 March 1903, lot 18 (with *Europe* pl. 1 and another *Europe* plate, *Ahania* pl. 1, *No Natural Religion* pl. a1, the frontispiece to Burger's *Leonora* [1796], and two photographs) for £10 to Tregaskis; (2) Sold by E. J. Shaw at Sotheby's, 29 July 1925, lot 157 (with *Europe* pl. 1 and four other engravings) for £31 to *Keynes*; (3) Keynes bound and described *For the Sexes* pl. 3 in his catalogue (1964), no. 582, as if it belonged to copy L, the history of which is quite distinct.

Pl. 6–7: BINDING: (1) Bound, with *America* pl. 6 and *Songs* pl. b, 51, in an extra-illustrated copy of Mrs. Bray's *Life of Thomas Stothard* (1851); (2) Disbound and mounted after 1941.

HISTORY: For the History, see the 'Order' of the *Songs*, p. 337.

Pl. 12: BINDING: Mounted and bound before 1887 by Hammond in three-quarter Red morocco at Vol. V, p. 715 of a copy of the Bible, ed. John Kitto (?1850), extra-illustrated and expanded to sixty volumes.

HISTORY: The History is as in *America* pl. 3 (Huntington), p. 107.

Pl. 14: BINDING: Bound between 1871 (the fly-leaves seem to be watermarked J WHATMAN 1871) and 1884 (when they were first offered for sale together) in half Red morocco over Red boards with *On Homer* (D), *The Ghost of Abel* (D), and Blake's portrait of Joseph Wright of Derby.

HISTORY: (1) Perhaps this is the copy lent by A. A. Weston to the Burlington Fine Arts Club exhibition (1876), no. 8; (2) Offered by John Pearson in Catalogue 58 (?1884), lot 100, with *On Homer* (D), *The Ghost of Abel* (D), and Blake's portrait of Joseph Wright of Derby,[1] for £12. 12s.; (3) Acquired by B. B. Macgeorge, described in his library catalogues (1892, 1906—described under *The Ghost of Abel*), and sold posthumously at Sotheby's, 1 July 1924, lot 126, for £50 to Quaritch; (4) Offered by Quaritch in Catalogue 388 (Oct. 1924), lot 325, for £75; (5) Bought from Quaritch (the receipt with the collection is dated 10 Dec. 1924) by Allan R. Brown, who lent them to the Philadelphia exhibition (1939), no. 126, and gave them (with his memorial book-plate) in 1940 to (6) TRINITY COLLEGE, Hartford, Connecticut.

Pl. 15: BINDING: (1) Perhaps bound with 144 other leaves of Blakeana with an extra-illustrated Gilchrist (1863) in 1884, but (2) Now separated and mounted with 'The Accusers' (B).

---

[1] With a note: 'During the last twenty years we have been endeavouring to discover and unearth every scrap of Blake's work, yet we have never seen nor heard of any copies of the above occurring for sale.'

HISTORY: (1) Perhaps bound with 144 other prints and drawings[1] in the extra-illustrated 1863 Gilchrist (2 vols. quarto, 1 vol. octavo, in uniform half Brown morocco, g.e.) offered by John Pearson, Catalogue 58 (?1884), lot 363, for £52. 10*s*.; (2) Pl. 15 was acquired by H. H. Gilchrist, lent to the Pennsylvania Academy exhibition (1892), no. 138 (8), sold, with other works, by H. H. Gilchrist on 12 June 1894 for £150 to (3) The BRITISH MUSEUM PRINT ROOM.

46

*For the Sexes: The Gates of Paradise [?D]. N.Y., [?1897].
    A facsimile privately printed for W. A. White.

47

*For the Sexes: The Gates of Paradise [B]. London, 1925.
    A facsimile by Frederick Hollyer.

48

*The Gates of Paradise: For Children, For the Sexes. Introductory volume by Geoffrey Keynes with Blake's preliminary sketches. [3 vols.] London, 1968. The William Blake Trust.

Vol. I is the Introductory volume, with a 'Publisher's Note' by A. D. F[awcus], 'Introduction' (pp. 1–5), 'Commentary' (pp. 7–22), list and reproduction of drawings for the *Gates* (pp. 23–46), and an important 'Census' (pp. 47–51) of *For Children* and *For the Sexes* by Sir Geoffrey Keynes.

Vol. II is a facsimile of *For Children* (D) and Vol. III reproduces *For the Sexes* (F).

The Four Zoas, see *Vala.*

49. *The French Revolution* (1791)

BIBLIOGRAPHICAL INTRODUCTION

TABLE

Copy	Collection	Corrections	Contemporary Owner
A	HUNTINGTON	—	John Linnell

TITLE: THE / FRENCH REVOLUTION. / A POEM, / IN SEVEN BOOKS. / BOOK THE FIRST / LONDON: / PRINTED FOR J. JOHNSON, Nº 72, ST PAUL'S CHURCH-YARD. / MDCCXCI [1791]. / [PRICE ONE SHILLING.]

[1] Described as including 'original illustrations from "The Gates of Paradise," "Jerusalem," "Europe," "Triumphs of Temper," Hayley's "Ballads," 4to Edition, "Blair's Grave," "Elements of Morality," &c., many in proof states, also 70 fine portraits and plates mentioned in the work'; the volume 'has been illustrated [*?by Pearson*] purely as a labour of love, and has occupied 10 years in getting together the unique contents'. H. H. Gilchrist, who may have acquired the volume, lent plates from all the works described to the Pennsylvania Academy exhibition (1892).

COLLATION: 4°: [A1–2], B1–C[4]; B1–2, C1–2 signed; 10 leaves, 20 pages.

CONTENTS: Title-page ([A1]ʳ), 'Advertisement' ([A2]ʳ), 'Book the First' (B1ʳ–C4ᵛ); [A1]ᵛ, [A2]ᵛ blank. No fly-leaves or half-title.

LEAF-SIZE: 22·2 × 29·6 cm.

WATERMARK: None.

PAGE NUMBERING: Pages 2–16 are correctly numbered in the middle of the top margin within square brackets.

RUNNING TITLES: None.

CATCHWORDS: Correct throughout.

PRESS FIGURES: B1ᵛ '1'; C1ᵛ '2'.

ORNAMENTS: None.

PUBLICATION: Not published. There are a number of reasons[1] for believing that *The French Revolution* never got beyond the stage of proof: (1) Only one copy has been traced; (2) The register is defective, suggesting that the formes were never quite ready to be printed; (3) The impression of the type is extraordinarily heavy, occasionally nearly piercing the thin paper; (4) Thumb marks, presumably of the printer, may be seen on some pages; (5) The inking is uneven, and the ends of the lines are often somewhat blurred; (6) The last words, 'END OF THE FIRST BOOK', are not properly centred; (7) A number of simple misprints, such as 'Eeternally' (l. 46), 'were away' for 'wear away' (l. 76), the '8' upside-down on p. 8, have not been corrected; (8) None of the other 'seven books' promised on the title-page is known.

Perhaps the book was suppressed by author or publisher because of fear of public prosecution or because events in France took a turn not envisaged in the poem.

CORRECTIONS: None.

ERRATA:[2] (1) l. 40, 'spiders' should be 'spiders''; (2) l. 46, 'Eeternally'; (3) l. 74, 'bonds' perhaps should be 'bands'; (4) l. 76, 'were away' should be 'wear away'; (5) l. 83, 'antientest' should be 'ancientest'; (6) l. 92 'is' should be 'are'; (7) ll. 114, 125, 'Neckar' should be 'Necker'; (8) l. 147, 'Is' should be 'Are'; (9) l. 159, 'When' should be lower case; (10) ll. 162–4, the punctuation seems wrong; (11) l. 176, the punctuation seems wrong; (12) l. 203, the comma and semicolon should be reversed; (13) l. 207, though 'vallies' is a Blakean spelling, yet 'valleys' is spelled conventionally in ll. 220, 224; (14) l. 208, 'is' should be 'are'; (15) l. 219, the full stop should be an exclamation mark or a question mark; (16) ll. 273–4 seem to be mispunctuated; (17) l. 283, 'war-living' should probably be 'was, living' or 'war—living'.

BINDING: Sewn through three holes into greyish-Blue paper wrappers.

HISTORY: (1) Signed at the top 'John Linnell. Red Hill 1860' (though

---

[1] These points are largely summarized from the notes of Horace Hart in *The Poetical Works of William Blake*, ed. J. Sampson (1925), xxxii, li.

[2] The regularity of the capitalization, of the spelling, and (on the whole) of the punctuation, suggests that these aspects of Blake's manuscript were considerably revised in the printing-house.

presumably acquired long before), and sold posthumously at Christie's, 15 March 1918, lot 191, for £131. 5*s*. to G. D. Smith for (2) The HUNTINGTON LIBRARY.

50. 'Genesis. The Seven Days of the Created World.'

The manuscript so entitled in Blake's hand (now in Princeton) is 'a close translation [probably by Hayley] of the opening lines of Tasso's *Le Sette Giornate del Mondo Creato*' (as Povey has shown, no. 2438); Blake was merely the scribe.

BINDING: Bound as a small notebook with heavy Blue paper covers; two leaves have been cut out.

HISTORY: (1) Transcribed by Blake for William Hayley, presumably between 1800 and 1803 when he was Hayley's neighbour in Felpham; (2) Sold for Joseph Mayer at Sotheby's, 19 July 1887, lot 188, for £2. 7*s*. to Pearson; (3) Acquired by H. B. Forman, who added his book-plate, and sold it posthumously through Anderson Galleries, 15 March 1920, lot 68, for $1,350; (4) Offered in Rosenbach Catalogue 20 (Oct. 1920), lot 8, for $2,500; (5) Acquired by P. H. Bonner, who added his book-plate and lent it to the Fogg exhibition (1930), and with whose Library it was offered by Dutton's (1931), lot 21, for $8,500; sold by Bonner at American Art Association–Anderson Galleries, 15 Feb. 1934, lot 17, for $10·50 [*sic*]; (6) Lent by Dr. Gabriel Wells to the Philadelphia exhibition (1939), no. 97; (7) Acquired by Grace Lansing Lambert, who added her book-plate and gave it in Jan. 1960 to (8) PRINCETON.

A 50

Genesis: Verses from a manuscript of William Blake. Cummington [Massachusetts], 1952.

This elegantly produced little book gives no indication that Blake was merely the scribe and not the composer of the lines in the manuscript. This is a transcript, not a facsimile.

51. *The Ghost of Abel* (1822)

BIBLIOGRAPHICAL INTRODUCTION

TABLE

Copy	Plates	Leaves	Watermarks	Blake numbers	Binding-order	Leaf size in cm	Printing colour
A LC	1–2	2	J WHATMAN / 1821 (1)	—	Loose	23·2 × 28·8	Black
B *Keynes*	1–2	2	—	—	Loose	24·5 × 34·2	Black
C HUNTINGTON	1–2	2	—	—	Loose	24·2 × 34·5	Black
D TRINITY COLLEGE	1–2	2	J WHATMAN / 1820 (2)	—	1–2[1]	23·5 × 33·0	Black

[1] Copy D is bound before *On Homer* (D) and *For the Sexes* pl. 14.

TITLE: THE GHOST of ABEL / *A Revelation In the Visions of Jehovah* / *Seen by William Blake* / . . . / *1822 W Blakes Original Stereotype was 1788*

DATE: 1822, as given in the colophon.

PUBLICATION: Blake evidently wrote *The Ghost of Abel* at least in part in response to the iconoclasm of Lord Byron, to whom the work seems to be dedicated and whose *Cain, A Mystery* was published in 1821. It is etched in relief, probably on both sides of a single copperplate.

Only a few copies were printed, evidently in the year of etching if one is to judge from the watermarks of 1820 and 1821. Blake probably gave a few copies to friends such as Butts (A) and Linnell (B, C), often in conjunction with *On Homer* (?1820) (copies A, B, D), but he did not bother to list it with his other works offered for sale in his letter to George Cumberland of 12 April 1827.

COLOURING: None.

CATCHWORDS: None.

ORDER: Pl. 1–2. The context makes the order quite clear.

VARIANTS: None.

ERRATUM: 'Transgres[*s*]or', l. 35.

Pl. 1. INCIPIT: 'THE GHOST of ABEL . . .'. DESIGN: The text is scattered with tiny figures, tendrils, birds, and scenes. To the left of 'THE GHOST of ABEL' are two clothed figures, on the letters of 'ABEL' are four more, and to the right are an additional five.

To the left of 'Seen by William Blake' is a bounding stag chased to the right by a lion, and to its right are two naked figures apparently fleeing to the left from flames.

Two tiny figures are on the long tail of the S in 'Scene'.

After 'Adam!' in l. 1 lies a naked man, while another flees to the right. To the left is a star which seems to approach the corpse.

To the left of 'Is this Death?' in l. 2 is a horizontal figure in a long robe.

Before 'Adam!' in l. 2 are three robed figures flying to the left, and to the right are fruit and a leaf, towards which writhes a serpent.

To the left of ll. 3–6 a naked couple stands beneath a tree bent with fruit.

After l. 9 is a robed figure.

To the left of ll. 11–13, a figure reclines between two trees, and another hovers above it.

To the left of ll. 18–22 stand two naked figures beneath a drooping, leafless tree.

Pl. 2. INCIPIT: 'Alive & not Dead . . .'. DESIGN: To the left of ll. 25–6 a bent figure, apparently carrying a large book, walks to the right.

To the left of ll. 29–33 a nude figure running to the right seems to strike in passing a seated (?female) figure.

Below the first 'Abel' of l. 36 is a floating robed figure.

To the left of ll. 38–42 a nude female hovers over a naked reclining male. After 'My Will' in l. 43 are nine tiny walking and flying figures.

To the left of ll. 43–5 two naked figures stand on either side of the massive trunk of a fruit tree, wrapped round which seem to be serpent coils.

Below l. 50 but above the colophon is a horizontal figure in a fur skirt leaning on the ground, while above it to the right hovers the head and arms of a man who points to the words 'The Voice of Abels Blood'.

COPY A: BINDING: (1) Stitched with *On Homer* (A) and 'The Man Sweeping the Interpreter's Parlour' between 1852 and 1912, but (2) Now loose.

HISTORY: (1) Probably this is the copy sold anonymously with the Collection of Thomas Butts (see *Songs* [E], p. 414) at Sotheby's, 26 March 1852, lot 55 (presumably bound as in 1912), for £2 to R. M. M.; (2) Sold by R. M. Milnes's son the Earl of Crewe at Sotheby's, 30 March 1903, lot 8 (4 leaves, including *The Ghost* [2 leaves], 'The Man Sweeping the Interpreter's Parlour' [1 leaf], plus *On Homer* [A] [1 leaf]) for £43 to Quaritch; (3) Acquired by William A. White, who lent them ('sewn' together)[1] to the exhibitions of the Grolier Club (1905), no. 37a, b, c, (1919), no. 19a, b, c, and the Fogg (1924) and sold them posthumously through Rosenbach on 1 May 1929 to (4) Mr. LESSING J. ROSENWALD.

COPY B: BINDING: Loose.

HISTORY: The History is as in *On Homer* (B) (see p. 336); it is reproduced in *The Prophetic Writings of William Blake*, ed. D. J. Sloss & J. P. R. Wallis (1926), i. 644.

COPY C: BINDING: Loose.

HISTORY: (1) Perhaps this is the copy lent by H. H. Gilchrist to the Pennsylvania Academy of the Fine Arts exhibition (1892), no. 146; (2) Lent by the Linnell Trustees to the exhibitions in Manchester (1914), no. 93, Nottingham (1914), no. 70, the National Gallery of Scotland (1914), no. 50, and sold at Christie's, 15 March 1918, lot 200, for £29. 8s. to Edwards; (3) Sold by 'a Prominent Pennsylvania Collector' (Col. Henry D. Hughes, according to Keynes & Wolf) at American Art Association, 22 April 1924, lot 70, for $400 to James F. Drake for (4) The HUNTINGTON LIBRARY.

COPY D: BINDING: Bound with *For the Sexes* pl. 14.

HISTORY: The History is as in *For the Sexes* pl. 14, p. 204.

52

El Fantasma de Abel. With a Prefatory Note by P. Berger. La Plata, Argentina, 1943.

An unillustrated anonymous translation.

---

[1] According to A. G. B. Russell, *The Engravings of William Blake* (1912), the three works were then still bound together, though they are now loose.

53. 'I asked a thief' (1796)

BIBLIOGRAPHICAL INTRODUCTION

COLLECTION: Princeton.

WATERMARK: Chain lines 3·3 cm apart, slightly crooked.

LEAF-SIZE: 13·5 × 12·3 cm.

DATE: Dated '1796' by Blake.

DESCRIPTION: The poem is written in Brown ink on one side of the leaf. The first line is smudged, and the paper has three folding creases. The poem is copied with no verbal changes from the draft on p. 114 of the *Notebook*.

BINDING: Loose.

HISTORY: (1) Acquired by Oliver R. Barrett, and inherited by his son (2) Roger W. Barrett, who sold it at Parke-Bernet, 30 Oct. 1950, lot 93, for $1,350 to Grace Lansing Lambert; (3) Mrs. Lambert gave it in 1959 to (4) PRINCETON.

(54–73.) INSCRIPTIONS ON DESIGNS

BIBLIOGRAPHICAL INTRODUCTION

See Table opposite

The inscriptions are written on the designs themselves. Each inscription is only a few words, except for those on the 'Fall of Man', 'Epitome of Hervey', Gray, Milton, Dante, and Genesis.

For titles and descriptions of other pictures, see the *Notebook* (?1793–?1818) (p. 321), 'The Accusers' (1793) (p. 76), *America* (1793) pl. 2–3 (pp. 92 ff.), The Small Book of Designs (?1795),[1] The Large Book of Designs (?1795),[2] 'Albion Rose' (?1796) (p. 78), *Vala* (?1796–?1807) p. 100, l. 4 (p. 459 n.), *Jerusalem* (1804–?20) pl. 97 (p. 257), 'To the Queen' (1807) (p. 451), *Descriptive Catalogue* (1809) ¶ 6, 8 (pp. 134 ff.), 'Joseph of Arimathea' (?1809) (p. 266), 'Mirth' (?1820) (p. 321), and 'Laocoon' (?1820) (p. 269).

This section yet omits most of the simple titles Blake wrote on his pictures. Some of these are:

'Death of Earl Goodwin' (Royal Academy, 1780)
'A breach in a city, the morning after a battle' (Royal Academy, 1784)
'War unchained by an angel, Fire, Pestilence, and Famine following' (Royal Academy, 1784)
'Joseph making himself known to his brethren' (Royal Academy, 1785)

---

[1] i.e. *Marriage* (?1790–3) pl. 11, 14 (p. 294), *Visions* (1793) pl. 2, 10 (p. 468 n.), *Urizen* (1794), pl. 1–2, 5, 9–10, 12 (p. 173).
[2] *Urizen* pl. 22 (p. 172).

TABLE

Title	Date	Collection	Watermark	Leaf-size in cm
'Father & Mother'	?1793	LC		
'The Bible of Hell'	?1793	UNTRACED[1]		
'Is all joy'	?1793	BMPR	*invisible*	27·5 × 23·3
'How I pity'	?1793	BMPR	*invisible*	10·7 × 13·2
'Visions of Eternity'	?1793	BMPR	—	20·3 × 27·2
'For Children The Gates of Hell'	?1793	*Keynes*		12·0 × 13·5
'Behold your King'	?1795	BMPR	*invisible*	14·1 × 19·2
Gray Designs	1797	*Mellon*	1794 / J WHATMAN (51–2, 57–8, 61–2, 67–8, 71–2, 77–8, 81–2, 89–90, 105–8, 119–20, 127–30, 133–4, 141–2, 153–4)	32·1 × 41·3
Blair's *Grave* title-page	1806	HUNTINGTON		20·3 × 24·1
'The Fall of Man'	1807	V & A		38·2 × 49·2
'Epitome of Hervey'	after 1808	TATE		29·0 × 43·0
L'Allegro	?1816	MORGAN	M & J LAY / 1816 (1–2, 6)	
Il Penseroso	?1816	MORGAN	M & J LAY / 1816 (3–4, 6)	
'Return Alpheus'	?1816	BMPR	*invisible*	16·4 × 19·5
'All Genius varies'	?1819	*Vanderhoef*		
List of Apostles	?1823	FITZWILLIAM	1802	c. 14·5 × 22·5
Dante Designs no. 3–4, 7, 14–17, 36, 51, 56, 86, 90, 99, 101	1824–7	Birmingham (3) TATE (4, 14) FOGG (7, 17) Melbourne (15–16, 36, 51, 56, 90, 99) ASHMOLEAN (86) BMPR (101)	W ELGAR / 1796 (15–16, 51, 56, 90, 99) Crest (36)	c. 37·0 × 52·8
'Illuminated Genesis MS'	1827	HUNTINGTON	J WHATMAN 1821 (1) J WHATMAN 1826 (2, 7)	27·3 × 36·8

[1] The only reference to these words is in Ellis & Yeats, *The Works of William Blake* (1893), i. 46.

'Joseph ordering Simeon to be bound' (Royal Academy, 1785)
'Joseph's brethren bowing before him' (Royal Academy, 1785)
'The Bard, from Gray' (Royal Academy, 1785)
'Edward & Elinor' (engraving, 1793)
'Job / What is Man That thou shouldest Try him Every Moment? Job vii C 17 & 18' (engraving, 1793)
'Ezekiel / I take away from thee the Desire of thine Eyes, Ezekiel xxiv C 16' (engraving, 1794)
'Newton' (?1795)[1]
'Nebuchadnezzar' (?1795)[1]
'Elohim Creating Adam' (?1795)[1]
'God speaking[?] to Adam' (?1795)[1]
'Lamech and his two Wives' (?1795)[1]
'The House of Death Milton' (?1795)[1]
'The last supper[:] "Verily I say unto you, that one of you shall betray me." Matt. chap. 26. ver. 21' (Royal Academy, 1799)

[1] M. Butlin, *William Blake* (1971), colour-prints in the Tate.

'The loaves and fishes' (Royal Academy, 1800)

Hebrew for 'And Enoch walked with God, and he was not: for God took him', Genesis v. 24 (engraving, *c.* 1807)

'Jacob's Dream: Vide Genesis, chap. xxviii. ver. 12' (Royal Academy, 1808)

'Christ in the sepulchre, guarded by angels' (Royal Academy, 1808)

'Adam and Eve' (?1809)[1]

'Canute Dark Hair & Eyes' (? 1819)[2]

'The Egyptian Taskmaster who was killed and Buried by Moses' (?1819)[3]

'Saul King of Israel somewhat influenced by the Evil Spirit' (?1819)[4]

'Corinna the Rival of Pindar', 'Corinna the Grecian Poetess' (?1819)[2, 4]

'The Three Tabernacles / The Lamb of God'[3]

'The Church Yard'[3]

'Death'[3]

'Mirth'[3, 1]

'Hope'[3]

'Pilgrim's Progress', 'Christian returning home', 'Apollyon' (?1824)[5]

'Here Lieth, Thomas Day aged 100' (*Night Thoughts* drawing [?1797] for Night IX, p. 6, British Museum Print Room)

54. 'All Genius varies Thus . . .' (?1819)

DATE: ?1819, when Blake's interest in the Visionary Heads was raised by Varley and his interest in phrenology was re-aroused by Spurzheim. The drawing survives with a collection of Visionary Heads and may therefore be associated with them in time.

DESCRIPTION: Blake's words are inscribed at the bottom of a drawing of Nine Grotesque Heads.

BINDING: Loose.

HISTORY: (1) Sold with the Linnell Collection at Christie's, 15 March 1918, lot 166 (with five Visionary Heads); (2) Offered in Maggs Catalogue 366 (May 1918), no. 156 (with thirteen Visionary Heads), for £210; (3) It was in the possession of Mrs. George Madison Millard in 1924, (4) And in that of Horace Gedney Young in 1925; lent to the Little Museum of La Miniatura exhibition (1936), no. 9, and bequeathed by his widow to (5) Mr. *F. Bailey Vanderhoef, Jr.*

---

[1] *Blake's Pencil Drawings*, ed. G. Keynes (1956).

[2] C. H. Collins Baker, *Catalogue of William Blake's Drawings and Paintings in the Huntington Library*, rev. R. R. Wark (1957).

[3] *The Blake Collection of W. Graham Robertson*, ed. K. Preston (1952).

[4] *Pencil Drawings by William Blake*, ed. G. Keynes (1927).

[5] These titles appear on designs no. 1, 11, 20 for Bunyan's *The Pilgrim's Progress* (watermarked J WHATMAN / 1824) in the Frick Collection, New York. The wicket gate in no. 10 is marked 'KNOCK AND IT SHALL BE OPENED'. Most of the drawings in the series bear other inscriptions, which I believe to be by Tatham; 'Apollyon' (above) may be in Tatham's hand as well.

55. 'Angels to be . . .' (see *America* pl. 2)

The inscription is on a drawing perhaps for a title-page for *America*; see p. 93.

BINDING: Loose, mounted.

HISTORY: (1) Given by John Defett Frances on 12 Dec. 1874 to (2) The BRITISH MUSEUM PRINT ROOM.

56. 'Behold your King' (?1795)

DATE: ?1795. Perhaps it is related to the Bible series for Butts of 1795 ff.

DESCRIPTION: A figure (?Pilate) in a conical hat at the left of a rough sketch points to another figure (?Christ) at the top right.

BINDING: Pasted into an album in the British Museum Print Room (press-mark: 198 b 2) after 1874.

HISTORY: (1) Given by John Defett Francis on 12 December 1874 to (2) The BRITISH MUSEUM PRINT ROOM.

57. 'The Bible of Hell' (?1793)

DATE: ?1793; see p. 480.

DESCRIPTION: The words are written 'in title-page form' on the back of 'A drawing', according to E. J. Ellis & W. B. Yeats (*The Works of William Blake* [1893], i. 46).

BINDING: ?Loose.

HISTORY: The only known reference to this inscription is in *The Works of William Blake*, ed. E. J. Ellis & W. B. Yeats (1893), i. 46: 'A drawing also exists with the words, "The Bible of Hell, in Nocturnal Visions collected. Vol. I, Lambeth," written on the back in title-page form.'

58. Blair's *Grave* (1806) title-page

DATE: 1806.

DESCRIPTION: At the sides of a tomb are two women, one, on the left, with bat wings and one with heavy, moth wings, while from the top of it rises a thinly draped woman with clasped hands. The tomb is inscribed: 'A Series of Designs / Illustrative of / The Grave, / a Poem / by Robert Blair. / Invented & Drawn by William Blake / 1806'.[1]

---

[1] The design is reproduced in C. H. Collins Baker, *Catalogue of William Blake's Drawings and Paintings in the Huntington Library*, rev. R. R. Wark (1957), pl. xxx. A different title-page design was published, with the etched title: THE / GRAVE, / A Poem. / *Illustrated by twelve Etchings* / EXECUTED / *BY* / LOUIS SCHIAVONETTI, / *From the Original* / Inventions / *OF* / WILLIAM BLAKE. / 1808.

BINDING: Loose.

HISTORY: (1) Acquired by B. B. Macgeorge, described in his catalogues (1892), p. 10, (1906), p. 15, and sold for him at Sotheby's, 7 July 1924, lot 123; (2) Lent by Mrs. Louise Ward Watkins to the exhibitions of the Little Museum of La Miniatura (1936), no. 2, and of Philadelphia (1939), no. 121; (3) Given by Mr. Keith Spalding in 1946 to (3) The HUNTINGTON LIBRARY.

59. Dante Designs (1824–7)

DATE: 1824–7.

Blake was at work on his 102 designs and his seven engravings for Dante's *Divine Comedy* from 1824 to 1827.[1]

DESCRIPTION: Blake's identifications and comments appear chiefly in pencil on parts of the designs which might otherwise have been obscure.

Most of the Dante designs have as well an ink inscription by Blake at the bottom saying something like 'HELL Canto 4' (as on No. 7), the same thing (often erased) in pencil, frequently at the bottom right; something similar in pencil on a corner of the verso; and perhaps the same thing in pencil erased in the middle of the verso.

All the Dante designs are reproduced in *Illustrations to the Divine Comedy of Dante by William Blake* (1922) and in A. S. Roe, *Blake's Illustrations to the Divine Comedy* (1953); the latter is the source of the uniform numeration.

BINDING: Loose.

HISTORY: All the Dante drawings, commissioned by John Linnell, were sold posthumously with the Linnell Collection at Christie's, 15 March 1918, lot 192, to the National Art Collections Fund, which reproduced them (1922) and distributed them around the world:

No. 3 to BIRMINGHAM ART GALLERY

No. 4, 14 to The TATE GALLERY

No. 7, 17 to The FOGG MUSEUM

No. 15–16, 36, 51, 56, 90, 99 to The NATIONAL GALLERY OF VICTORIA, Melbourne, Australia

No. 86 to The ASHMOLEAN MUSEUM, Oxford

No. 101 to The BRITISH MUSEUM PRINT ROOM.

All the Dante designs were again reproduced by Albert Roe, *Blake's Illustrations to the Divine Comedy* (1953).

60. 'Epitome of Hervey's *Meditations among the Tombs*' (after 1808)

DATE: After 1808, like the drawing.[2]

DESCRIPTION: Blake's water-colour called 'Epitome of Hervey's *Meditations*

---

[1] *Blake Records* (1969), 290 ff.
[2] M. Butlin, *William Blake*: a complete catalogue of the works in the Tate Gallery (1971), 45–6.

among the Tombs' has many inscriptions identifying the figures as they rise toward or fall from heaven.

BINDING: Mounted, framed.

HISTORY: (1) Thomas Butts sold it posthumously at Foster & Sons, 29 June 1853, lot 135, for £2. 10s. to Money; (2) Acquired by George Thomas Saul, who lent it to the Burlington Fine Arts Club exhibition (1876), no. 69, and presented it in 1878 to (3) The National Gallery, which transferred it in 1909 to (4) The TATE GALLERY.

61. 'The Fall of Man' (1807)

DATE: '1807 W Blake inv' is inscribed on the drawing and presumably applies to the words on the back of the drawing as well.

DESCRIPTION: On the cardboard back of his water-colour-and-ink drawing of 'The Fall of Man' Blake has written his description in his Copperplate hand in pencil.

BINDING: Mounted, framed.

HISTORY: (1) Sold with the Collection of Thomas Butts at Foster's, 29 June 1853, lot 89, for £6. 6s. to Stirling; (2) Acquired from Sir William Stirling Maxwell by Captain Archibald Stirling, who lent it to the Carfax exhibition (1906), no. 36; (3) Acquired by Lt.-Col. William Stirling, who lent it to the exhibition at the Tate (1947), no. 27, and sold it in 1953 to (4) The VICTORIA & ALBERT MUSEUM.

62. 'Father & Mother . . .' (?1793)

DATE: ?1793, Mr. Martin Butlin's estimate for the date of the drawing.

DESCRIPTION: The faint sketch of a woman with butterfly wings is numbered '11 [9 *del* 10 *del* 13 *del*]'. The intention of the drawing and its relation to the words on the page are not clear. On the verso is a sketch for *Milton* pl. 45.

BINDING: Loose, mounted.

HISTORY: (1) Acquired by W. A. White, who lent it to the Fogg exhibition (1924) and sold it posthumously with other Blakes through Rosenbach in 1929 to (2) Mr. LESSING J. ROSENWALD.

63. 'For Children The Gates of Hell' (?1793)

DATE: ?1793, like *For Children: The Gates of Paradise* (1793).[1]

DESCRIPTION: The text is the title on a sketched title-page. Nothing more is known of the work.

[1] G. Keynes (*The Gates of Paradise* [1968], i. 3) suggests that the date is 'perhaps about 1818', when Blake was revising *For Children* as *For the Sexes*.

BINDING: Loose.

HISTORY: (1) Acquired by Frederick Tatham,[1] presumably from Mrs. Blake at her death in 1831; (2) Acquired by Quaritch;[1] (3) Acquired by W. Graham Robertson in 1886,[1] described in his Collection (1952),[1] and sold posthumously at Christie's, 22 July 1949, lot 63 (with designs for *Thel* pl. 5 and three other drawings), for £18. 18s. to Agnew; (4) Bought from Maggs Bros. in 1949 by *Geoffrey Keynes*, according to his catalogue (1964), no. 481 reproduced in *The Gates of Paradise* (1969), i. 40.

64. Poems and Descriptions of Designs for Gray's *Poems* (1797)

DATE: 1797.

In a letter of *c.* 1–4 Nov. 1797,[2] Nancy Flaxman said that 'Flaxman has employ'd him [*Blake*] to Illuminate the works of Grey for my library'. Cumberland reported that Blake asked only ten guineas for the designs,[3] which is the price of friendship, not of commerce.

DESCRIPTION: The leaves of the title-page and pp. 43–158 of POEMS / BY / MR. GRAY / [*in pencil*: DRAWINGS / by / WILLIAM BLAKE] / — / A NEW EDITION. / — / LONDON: / PRINTED FOR J. MURRAY, (No. 31.) FLEET- / STREET. / MDCCLXXXX [*1790*] (watermarked with chain lines and about 8·6 × 14·7 cm) are inset into 58 much larger leaves of 1794 / J WHATMAN paper. On each of the larger leaves is a drawing by Blake in illustration of Gray's poems, and on the verso of the last leaf of each poem is a manuscript list by Blake of the lines illustrated by, or the titles of, the drawings for the succeeding poem. Occasional mistakes indicate that: (1) The centres of the WHATMAN sheets were cut out; (2) The leaves of POEMS BY MR. GRAY were inset, with the recto of the text leaves always over-lapping at the outer margin and the verso always partly obscured by the larger sheet; (3) A Red border was carefully drawn on the larger sheet just outside the incision and occasionally showing on the inner sheet; (4) Often while this Red border was still wet, the surrounding designs were drawn in pencil and water-coloured;[4] (?5) The design titles and the poems were written;[5] (?6) The pages were numbered in ink at the top outer corners; (7) The work was bound in contemporary three-quarter calf over marbled boards[6] and has been repeatedly rebacked since then[7] without being trimmed

---

[1] *The Blake Collection of W. Graham Robertson*, ed. K. Preston (1952), no. 91.

[2] BM Add. MSS 39790, ff. 3–4. For the date, see M. K. Woodworth, 'Blake's Illustrations for Gray's Poems', *N&Q*, ccxv (1970), 312–13.   [3] *Blake Records* (1969), 187.

[4] Occasionally the pencil or water-colour overlaps the wide border or the inset page (e.g. pp. 67, 71, 75, 126, 134, 148, 150, 153, 155) or the water-colour has made the Red border run (e.g. p. 131).

[5] The pencil Xs by the lines illustrated may or may not have been made by Blake. Similar symbols, some of them probably not by Blake, are used in the drawings for Young's *Night Thoughts*.

[6] The designs are coloured so close to the inner margins that they could not have been bound when Blake was colouring them. Further, the water-colours when wet have occasionally blurred on to pages not now facing each other.

[7] The two fly-leaves in front and the one in the back all have different watermarks.

or gilt; (8) A drawing lettered 'William Blake / Drawn by John Flaxman' was pasted to the fly-leaf facing the title-page, *over* an offset of the Red border from the title-page, probably long after the volume was bound. There are clear Brown fingerprints on the title-page, pp. 58, 158, and occasionally elsewhere on the designs.

BINDING: (1) The title-page and pp. 43–158 of POEMS / BY / MR. GRAY / LONDON: / PRINTED FOR J. MURRAY, (No. 31.) FLEET- / STREET. / MDCCLXXXX [*1790*] were inset into windowed leaves of paper water-marked 1794 / J WHATMAN; (2) Blake made his designs on the larger sheets, which were then (3) Bound in old (?contemporary) three-quarter calf over marbled boards with 'GRAY' on the spine; the spine has been rebacked, in 1966 the title-page was loose and pp. 143–4 almost loose; (4) The leaves were disbound in 1967 for the Blake Trust facsimile.

HISTORY: (1) They were inlaid, bound with Gray's *Poems* (1790), and apparently given to Nancy Flaxman in 1797; (2) Sold posthumously with Flaxman's collection at Christie's, 1 July 1828, lot 85 (with 'Blake's Portrait by Mr Flaxman'), to Clarke; (3) Probably acquired by William Beckford, and inherited from him by his son-in-law (4) The Duke of Hamilton; (5) Sold by the Duke of Hamilton in 1966 to (6) Mr. *Paul Mellon.*

65. 'How I pity' (?1793)

DATE: ?1793.

DESCRIPTION: At the centre of concentric circles, like a web, in a pencil design similar to *For Children* (1793) pl. 14, an old man crouches before two smaller, prone, childish figures, who seem to be wrapped in webs.

BINDING: Pasted down on a leaf in a bound volume of drawings (pressmark: 198 b 2).

HISTORY: (1) Given by John Defett Francis on 12 Dec. 1874 to (2) The BRITISH MUSEUM PRINT ROOM.

66. 'Illuminated Genesis Manuscript' (1827)

DATE: 1827, the date given by Gilchrist,[1] is confirmed by the very tentative nature of the latter part of the transcription and designs.

DESCRIPTION: The eleven leaves of Blake's illuminated transcription of Genesis consist of one tentative and one fairly finished sketch of a title-page plus nine leaves of illuminated text. The text is in pencil confirmed in Green ink at first (through II. 5, except for the title of Chapter II). The ruled portion of leaf 11 is mostly blank.

In transcribing Genesis, Blake frequently altered punctuation and capitalization, changed 'and' to '&', and omitted the 'e' in the past tense; he often shortened 'unto' to 'to' (II. 19, 24; III. 6, 17 ['to the voice'], IV. 5, 7)

---

[1] A. Gilchrist, *Life of William Blake* (1863), i. 246; (1942), 259.

and reversed 'shalt' and 'thou' (III. 16, 19 [twice]; IV. 12). The most significant addition is 'Adamah' written over (II. 7, 19), or in parentheses after, 'the ground' (II. 9; III. 19; IV. 10, 11, 12).

BINDING: Loose.

HISTORY: (1) Made by Blake for John Linnell in 1827 (*Blake Records* [1969], 322 n. 2), and sold posthumously at Christie's, 15 March 1918, lot 192; (2) Acquired by the HUNTINGTON LIBRARY.

67. 'Is all joy forbidden' (?1793)

DATE: ?1793. Embracing figures at the top left are similar to those at the bottom of the title-page of the *Marriage* (?1790–3).

DESCRIPTION: The pencil drawing (related to *For Children* [1793] pl. 14 and reproduced in *Pencil Drawings* [1927], pl. 7) represents an old man brooding over a book, as one weeping child stands at the left and two more lie at the right.

BINDING: Pasted down on a leaf in a bound volume of drawings entitled Period IV, Vol. 12 (Case 121*).

HISTORY: (1) Given by John Defett Francis on 12 Dec. 1874 to (2) The BRITISH MUSEUM PRINT ROOM.

68. List of Apostles (?1823)

DATE: ?1823.

   The date could be almost any time from 1802, when the *Ballads* (1802) leaves came into Blake's hands, until his death in 1827. They were probably used after 1805, when publication of the 1802 *Ballads* was officially abandoned, and before 1824, when the *Job* pencil sketches which they accompany must have been completed and, when Blake had made his engravings, given to Linnell. The '1823' below Blake's initials may date the apostles as well.

DESCRIPTION: Pages iii–iv, 37–8[1] of the 1802 *Ballads* were used as a wrapper for Blake's *Job* sketches 'Done for me John Linnell' (according to the inscription on the innermost wrapper) probably about 1824. They bear fifty versions of the initials WB, including Blake's usual monogram:

There is also an A D like Dürer's, a sketch of a head for *Job*; two rough sketches of the dog on *Job* pl. 3, 22, and the list of disciples.

   The list could be for subjects of a series of paintings—or it could have served a great many other purposes.

   [1] The two leaves were folded and are now divided along the creases into four leaves; p. 38, the dirtiest page, was probably the outside wrapper.

BINDING: (1) Once stitched as the cover of 30 leaves of *Job* sketches; (2) Disbound.

HISTORY: (1) The leaf with the List of Apostles (pp. 37–8 of Hayley's *Designs to A Series of Ballads* [1802]) was used as a wrapper for the 'Drawings & studies' 'Done for me John Linnell'; after Linnell's death (1882), they were sold by the Linnell Trustees at Christie's, 15 March 1918, lot 150, for £504 to Messrs. Carfax for (2) T. H. Riches, who bequeathed them in 1935 to (3) The FITZWILLIAM MUSEUM, which received them in 1950.

69. Milton, Descriptions of *L'Allegro* and *Il Penseroso* Designs (?1816)

DATE: *c.* 1816.

The *L'Allegro* and *Il Penseroso* designs were probably made about 1816 and their descriptions are presumably from the same date. At the same time Blake engraved 'Mirth' from *L'Allegro* and called on Thomas Frognall Dibdin to discuss 'Milton's minor poems'.[1]

DESCRIPTION: Blake wrote descriptions of his six *L'Allegro* and six *Il Penseroso* drawings, one each on twelve sheets of paper, and numbered them 1–12. The titles are on one side (now pasted down on larger leaves and only legible against strong light), and the descriptions on the other. Each description leaf seems to have a horizontal crease near the top, as if it had been folded.

BINDING: According to typescript notes made in the Morgan Library, 'the drawings and the accompanying notes in Blake's hand were mounted in a folio volume bound in russian leather, the binding apparently dating from the mid-nineteenth century. Both drawings and notes were pasted down flat on the leaves of the folio and were left so when the drawings and texts were placed on individual mats.' The descriptions are now pasted on larger sheets, so that the backs with the titles are invisible.

HISTORY: (1) The twelve *L'Allegro* and *Il Penseroso* designs 'with the artist's descriptions' were sold posthumously with the Collection of Thomas Butts at Foster & Son's, 29 June 1853, lot 99, for £7. 7s. to Milnes; (2) Sold by R. M. Milnes's son the Earl of Crewe at Sotheby's, 20 March 1903, lot 16, for £1,960, to A. Jackson; (3) Acquired by Marsden J. Perry, who put his stamp on a blank leaf, lent them anonymously to the Grolier Club exhibition (1905), no. 88, and sold them in 1907 to (4) W. A. White, who evidently lent them anonymously to the Grolier Club exhibition (1919), no. 43; (5) Acquired by Alfred T. White, at whose death in 1921 they were inherited by his daughter (6) Mrs. Adrian Van Sinderen, whose husband sold them on 21 Nov. 1949 for $25,000 to (7) The PIERPONT MORGAN LIBRARY.

[1] *Blake Records* (1969), 242.

70. 'Nelson' Drawing (1805)

DATE: 1805, like the painting.

DESCRIPTION: The inscription is on the verso of the drawing.

BINDING: Loose, mounted.

HISTORY: (A) (1) Acquired in 1834 by John Defett Francis (the verso is inscribed 'JDF 1834'), and given by him on 12 Dec. 1874 to (2) The BRITISH MUSEUM PRINT ROOM.

(B) (1) Offered by Francis Harvey (?1864) with 15 other designs for £3. 3s.; (2) UNTRACED.

71. 'Pitt' Painting (1805)

DATE: 1805.

DESCRIPTION: 'The Spiritual Form of Pitt . . .' is inscribed with a title-description.

BINDING: Mounted, framed.

HISTORY: (1) Acquired by Samuel Palmer; (2) Offered by his son A. H. Palmer at Christie's, 20 March 1882, lot 108 (bought in), and sold in 1882 to (3) The National Gallery, which transferred it in 1931 to (4) The TATE GALLERY, the catalogue of which is the authority for this history.

72. 'Return Alpheus'[1] (?1816)

DATE: ?1816, like *L'Allegro* and *Il Penseroso*?

DESCRIPTION: A very rough sketch may represent a river god lifting his head from the waves while the personified valleys scatter flowers.

BINDING: Pasted on to a leaf in a bound volume of drawings (pressmark: 198 b 2).

HISTORY: (1) Given by John Defett Francis on 12 Dec. 1874 to (2) The BRITISH MUSEUM PRINT ROOM.

73. 'Visions of Eternity' (?1793)

DATE: ?1793, like *Visions* (1793).

DESCRIPTION: On the verso is a rough sketch of a standing man with out-spread arms; on the recto is a sketch of a title-page, with branches and flying figures.

[1] *Lycidas*, ll. 132–5:

> Return *Alpheus*, the dread voice is past,
> That shrunk thy streams; Return *Sicilian* Muse,
> And call the Vales, and bid them hither cast
> Their Bels, and Flourets of a thousand hues.

BINDING: Pasted on to a leaf in a bound volume of drawings (pressmark: 198 b 2).

HISTORY: (1) Given by John Defett Francis on 12 Dec. 1874 to (2) The BRITISH MUSEUM PRINT ROOM.

74. *An Island in the Moon* (?1784)

BIBLIOGRAPHICAL INTRODUCTION

COLLECTION: Fitzwilliam Museum.

WATERMARKS: A design 7·1×11·3 cm on pp. 3–16, O–P represents a fleur-de-lis above a rectangular shield in a triple border, divided into four compartments. In the bottom left compartment are sheep, and in the bottom right one a harp.

The *countermark* (2·8×3·9 cm) on pp. 1–2, A–N consists of 'G R' under a small crown.[1]

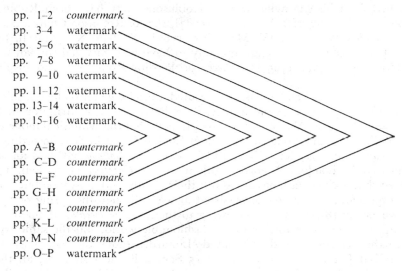

pp. 1–2	*countermark*
pp. 3–4	watermark
pp. 5–6	watermark
pp. 7–8	watermark
pp. 9–10	watermark
pp. 11–12	watermark
pp. 13–14	watermark
pp. 15–16	watermark
pp. A–B	*countermark*
pp. C–D	*countermark*
pp. E–F	*countermark*
pp. G–H	*countermark*
pp. I–J	*countermark*
pp. K–L	*countermark*
pp. M–N	*countermark*
pp. O–P	watermark

SIZE: 18·3×30·8 cm.

DATE: ?Autumn 1784. The date of the *Island in the Moon* is a vexed and difficult question. A number of internal references point to the autumn of 1784.

'Holy Thursday' was first celebrated in St. Paul's Cathedral (as it is in the poem in Chap. 11) on Ascension Day, 2 May 1782,[2] and the poem must

---

[1] The marks are similar to but distinct from figures 19 and 25 in Thomas Balston, *James Whatman, Father and Son* (1957). Miss Phyllis M. Giles, Librarian of the Fitzwilliam Museum, has provided me with a great deal of information about the watermarks in the *Island*.

[2] *European Magazine*, i (June 1782), 388: 'This day one of the noblest spectacles in the world

therefore have been composed after 2 May 1782. The impulse to 'Hang Italian songs' in favour of 'English Genius forever' and the references to the commercial success of 'Doctor Clash And Signior Falalasole' (Chaps. 9, 11) may have arisen from the Handel Festival of May 1784.[1] The allusion to a new method of printing (p. A) may be connected with George Cumberland's experiments on the subject between Jan. and Oct. 1784.[2] Jacko in Chap. 8 may have been inspired by the monkey of that name which was brought to Astley's circus in 1784.[1] The reference to 'Vauxhall & Ranelagh' (¶ 27) suggests the warm months when those gardens were open; the fact that Suction plans to 'knock them all up' in the May Royal Academy exhibition 'next year' implies that the setting, and perhaps the time of writing, are between June and Dec.;[3] and the 'swallows . . . on their passage' (¶ 3) seem to point to autumn.

The most precise contemporary references come from the fashionable Miss Gittipin's envy of 'Miss Filligreework . . . & her maids & Stormonts & Balloon hats & a pair of Gloves every day & the sorrows of Werter & Robinsons & the Queen of Frances Puss[4] colour' (Chap. 8).[5] These fashions were of a butterfly longevity, as Miss Gittipin clearly knew, and as Blake may have learned from his engraving work.[6] 'Robinsons' may have been Robinson Gowns (*Lady's Magazine*, XIV [April 1783], 187) or Robinson Chapeaux and Hats (*Lady's Magazine*, XIV [May, Dec. 1783], 268, 650; XV [March, June 1784], 154, 303), but they are unlikely to have long survived the fall from fashion on 18 Jan. 1785 (*Gazetteer*) of Perdita Robinson, who inspired them.

The first manned balloon ascents created a brief rage for balloon fashions. The first '*chapeaux au ballon*' appeared in Paris, and a contributor to the *European Magazine*, IV (Dec. 1783), 406, hoped 'that this whimsical mode will not be introduced among the people of England', but in fact, according to the *Lady's Magazine*, XIV (Dec. 1783), 650, 'The *Balloon* hat' had already appeared in London. A correspondent of the *Gazetteer* of 19 Feb. 1784 hoped that 'balloon fashions are about their zenith, and must soon burst and be forgotten!', but the mode persisted at least through the spring of 1784. However, by 18 Sept. 1784, according to the *Morning Herald*, 'Balloon' was losing its influence as a name in the fashionable world, and the same styles were thenceforth to be denominated 'Lunardis' (after the balloonist who electrified London by his ascent on 15 Sept.). By next summer, all these fashions had dispersed, according to the *Gazetteer* of 26 July 1785: 'The balloon hat has had its day;—the Werter, Lunardi [*also*] . . .'.

was exhibited in St. Paul's cathedral. Upwards of 6000 charity children were arranged under the dome . . .'.

[1] See D. V. Erdman, *Blake: Prophet Against Empire* (1969).

[2] See his articles in *New Review*, vi (Oct. 1784), 318–19, and *European Magazine*, vi (Nov. 1784), 345.

[3] Blake himself exhibited at the Royal Academy in 1780, 1784, 1785, and 1799.

[4] The first use of the word 'puce' recorded in the *Oxford English Dictionary* is in 1787.

[5] As Palmer Brown has shown in unpublished studies made about 1951.

[6] For example, his plate for *The Lady's Pocket Book* of Nov. 1782 shows '*A Lady in the full Dress, & another in the most fashionable Undress now worn*'.

The ephemeral nature of these fashions means that Miss Gittipin's allusions and Blake's satire would have been virtually meaningless after 1785. The period when these fashionable Robinsons, Werters, and Balloon Hats were flourishing, in 1784, is almost certainly the period as well when Blake was writing his *Island in the Moon*.

DESCRIPTION: The manuscript consists of sixteen unnumbered leaves, thirty-two pages. Apparent gaps in the text and in the watermark–countermark pattern suggest that two or more leaves are missing between the eighth and ninth leaves. I have therefore numbered the pages 1–16 and A–P. The text of the *Island* is on pp. 1–16, A; pp. B–O are blank; while p. P (the verso of the sixteenth leaf) is a jumble of sketches, including six horses' heads, a lion lying down with a lamb (drawn twice), the head of a man, in the middle 'Numeration', and scattered round it six 'N's, an 'm', 'nu', 't' twice, 'B', 'Bla' written backwards, and 'William Blake' three times. Before these sixteen leaves are three others (one with proofs from Blake's woodcuts for Thornton's Virgil [1821] and one with A. H. Palmer's statement of the provenance of the proofs), and at the end are two more, all the extra leaves watermarked 'VAN GEL[DER?]'.

Page 16 ends with a song by Sipsop as the last of a series of burlesques of Italian opera. Page A begins abruptly with 'thus Illuminating the Manuscript' and ends abruptly half-way down the page. There is no context for p. A, and the immediately preceding pages may have been removed because they reveal too directly or too inaccurately Blake's secret method of Illuminated Printing. If the manuscript was originally a bound gathering of leaves issued as a notebook, it may have consisted of eight or ten sheets, or a multiple thereof. Pages O–P are sewn in separately and may once have been in a different position, though their watermark corresponds neatly to the countermark on pp. 1–2. There are the same number of leaves with watermarks (pp. 3–16, O–P) and with countermarks (pp. 1–2, A–N), so that no conclusion can be drawn from an imbalance there. If anything was removed, it probably consisted of at least one sheet, two leaves bearing watermark and countermark. Thus it seems likely that at least four pages are missing between p. 16 and p. A of the *Island in the Moon*.

Inks: There are three shades of ink used in the manuscript, suggesting seven periods of work on it: (1) *Brown*, p. 1 to p. 8 middle; (2) *Grey*, p. 8 (from 'are always talking . . .') through p. 9; (3) *Brown*, p. 10 ('Chap 9') to p. 12 ('. . . its a shame'); (4) *Grey*, p. 12 (including the deletion of the last two-and-a-half Brown lines) to p. 14 (the first line after 'Holy Thursday', '. . . & Mrs Sistagatist'); (5) *Brown*, p. 14 (including the deletion and replacement of the last three words) to p. 16 ('in such a serious humour'); (6) *Black*, the rest of p. 16; (7) *Brown*, p. A. *Deletions and Corrections* are in the same ink as the original except for the following changes in *Grey* ink: p. 3 '[Ass *del*] Arse' is deleted and 'Ass' restored; pp. 5, 8, the deletions ('what is this gim' and 'O what a scene . . . disguise'); p. 15, 'turd' deleted and 'tansy' substituted.

Title: The conventional title, *An Island in the Moon*, is an adaptation of the first words of the work.

All Blake's lines begin at the left margin, and it is therefore sometimes difficult to know where he intended a new paragraph to begin.

BINDING: Bound in Red morocco, lettered on the front 'Original Manuscript / William Blake / Island in the Moon'.

HISTORY: (1) Acquired before 1893¹ by Charles Fairfax Murray, who gave it in 1905 to (2) The FITZWILLIAM MUSEUM.

75. *Jerusalem* (1804–?20)

BIBLIOGRAPHICAL INTRODUCTION

See Table on pp. 226–7

TITLE: *Jerusalem / The / Emanation of / The Giant / Albion / 1804/ Printed by W Blake S^{th} Molton S^{t}*

DATE: 1804–?20.

The composition, etching, and printing of *Jerusalem* evidently went on over a long period of time, probably from 1804 to 1820. There are some internal references to this long gestation period, as well as a few outward and visible signs.

In his letters of 1803, Blake refers to a very long poem, which may have fragmented into *Milton* (1804–?8) and *Jerusalem*. Both must have been begun by 1804, the date they bear on their title-pages, but no known surviving copy can have been printed that early. Blake described the genesis of *Jerusalem* on pl. 38, ll. 40–2:

> I heard in Lambeths shades [*where he lived 1790–1800*];²
> In Felpham [*1800–3*] I heard and saw the Visions of Albion⌊.⌋
> I write in South Molton Street [*1803–21*] what I both see and hear⌊.⌋

Confirmation of this post-1803 dating may be seen in the use throughout of the orthodox 'g' with the rightward serif, which is characteristic of his datable works from 1803 on.³ The references to Privates Scolfield and Cock, to Lieutenant Hulton, and to Justices of the Peace Brereton, Peachey, and

---

¹ *The Works of William Blake*, ed. E. J. Ellis & W. B. Yeats (1893), i. 186–7. In 1863 Mrs. Gilchrist told W. M. Rossetti about 'a long thing which I really believe even Mr Swinburne will pronounce pure rubbish'; later Rossetti heard that she had destroyed it (*Rossetti Papers* [1903], 42). The work referred to could be the *Island* if Mrs. Gilchrist did not destroy her copy, or if what she had was a transcript. 'Leave, Oh leave me to my sorrow', 'Phoebe drest like Beauty's Queen', and 'This city and this country' were first printed in *The Light Blue* (1867), no. 2155.

² 'Lambeths Vale Where Jerusalems foundations began' (*Milton* pl. 4, l. 16) may refer to the poem as well as to the woman-place Jerusalem.

³ This suggestion was first made in D. V. Erdman's important article, 'The Suppressed and Altered Passages in Blake's *Jerusalem*', *Studies in Bibliography*, xvii (1964), 1–54, and was refined in Erdman's 'Dating Blake's Script: the "g" hypothesis', his 'postscript' to this note, and in GEB's 'Blake's Sinister "g", from 1789–93 to ?1803' in *Blake Newsletter*, iii (1969), 8–13, 42, 43–5.

Quantock throughout the poem allude to his trials in October 1803 and January 1804. Perhaps the early references in the preface (pl. 3) to 'love and friendship' were deleted about 1804.

However, the early version of the poem, like that of *Vala* (?1796–?1807), was clearly much modified in succeeding years, for there are many indications of alterations in *Jerusalem*. The title-page (pl. 2) seems to have described once a work different from the four chapters we now have, perhaps as 'In XXVIII Chapters'. There are etched variants on pl. 1, 20, 28, 37, 45, and 53, and early scratched numbers differing from the present ones on pl. 3, 19–20, 37–8, 45, and 50 were later deleted and others in the present order substituted. Pl. 14 once concluded with 'End of the 1st Chap:', suggesting that there may have been four chapters (as at present) of fourteen or fifteen plates each. This corresponds fairly well with the news in George Cumberland's notebook in the summer of 1807 that 'Blake has eng⁰ 60 Plates of a new Prophecy!'[1]

We may be able to account for many of the plates added to *Jerusalem* after 1807. The catchwords on pl. 11, 19, 53, 66, and 70 do not match those on any other plates well, and these and other catchwords suggest that pl. 8 (an insertion), 10 (an insertion), 11, 19, 53, 66, and 70 were once in different positions. Similarly, pl. 16 seems to be out of place, and has a striking number of errata, suggesting haste and lateness. Pl. 35 seems to interrupt the sequence of pl. 34 and 36 and may be an insertion. Pl. 42–3 seem to interrupt pl. 41 and 44 (which are alike in script and different from pl. 42–3) and may also be insertions. Pl. 46 is introduced by a line added to pl. 45 and is therefore presumably contemporaneous with the additional line on pl. 45. Pl. 55–6, 60, 65–6 seem, partly from the awkwardness with which they fit into their present places, to be later additions. Pl. 59 does not comfortably follow pl. 58, and pl. 67, l. 1 does not seem to follow persuasively any other plate. The number of errata on pl. 82 is striking, suggesting hasty tardiness, and pl. 34, 56, 61 are written in a similar, and unusual, large script. Of these apparently late plates, pl. 10, 16, 34, 43, 55–6, 60–1, 77, and 82 have little or no decoration, suggesting that absence of decoration and lateness are associated with each other.

In addition, the conditions of the copperplates themselves[2] sometimes indicate that they were late. Pl. 33, 56, 63, 71–2, 92–3, and 100, which have disfiguring copperplate-maker's-marks, were presumably utilized only when other, more perfect, materials were exhausted. Something else seems to have been originally engraved under the present etchings on pl. 47, ?64, 94–6, and

---

[1] *Blake Records* (1969), 187. Since *Jerusalem* is Blake's only known work with as many as sixty plates, Cumberland must be referring to *Jerusalem*. Blake was evidently not ready at this time to print it, for on 19 Dec. 1808 he wrote to Cumberland that he had 'now so long been turned out of the old channel' of 'my former pursuits of printing' 'that it is impossible for me to return to it'.

[2] Forty-two of the 52 (or more) copperplates needed for *Jerusalem* could have been formed from the centres of Blake's engravings for Young's *Night thoughts* (1797) left blank (except for p. 65) for the typeset text.

Night Thoughts centres: 15·4 to 17·5 cm wide by 20·7 to 25·0 cm high.
Jerusalem plates: 13·8 to 17·1 cm wide by 20·1 to 22·7 cm high.

TABLE

Copy	Plates	Leaves	Watermarks	Blake numbers[1]	Binding-order	Leaf-size in cm	Printing colour
A BMPR	1–100	100	J WHATMAN / 1818 (2–3, 5, 9, 21–2, 25, 27, 30, 36, 43, 46–7, 53, 62, 66, 72, 78, 88) J WHATMAN / 1819 (76) J WHATMAN / 1820 (58, 69, 74, 82, 89)	1–100[2]	1–28, 33–41, 43–6, 42, 29–32, 47–100**	26·5 × 32·7*	Black
#B *Cunliffe*	1–25	25	J WHATMAN / 1818 (6–10, 16)	1–25	‡1–25**[3]	26·7 × 37·2 *irregular*	brownish-Red
C *Harvey*	1–100	100	J WHATMAN / 1818 (22, 25, 33, ?40, 42, 47, 49, 59) J WHATMAN / 1819 (19) J WHATMAN / 1820 (11, 16, 24, 51, 60, 66, 68, 72–3, 84, 88, 91, 93)	1–100	1–28, 33–41, 43–6, 42, 29–32, 47–100**	25·0 × 32·0	Black
D HARVARD	1–100	100	J WHATMAN / 1820 (4, 7–8, 22–4, 30, 37–9, 41, 44, 60–1, 68, 72, 83–4, 90, 99–100)	1–100	1–100[3]	26·6 × 33·3*	Black
#E *Mellon*	1–100	100	J WHATMAN / 1820 (4–5, 7, 10, 17, 22, 31, 40–1, 43, 45–6, 50–1, 53–4, 56, 61–2, 75, 78, 81, 88, 90, 97)	1–100	1–100	27·0 × 34·5*	Orange
F MORGAN	1–100, 28ᵇ, 45ᵇ, 56ᵇ	103[4]	J WHATMAN / 1824 (20, 23, 27, 38, 65) J WHATMAN / 1826 (5, 8–9, 21, 34, 40, 44, 50, 54, 59, 71, 74–5, 79, 81, 86, 95, 99) EDMEADS & PINE / 1802 (28ᵇ, 45ᵇ, 56ᵇ)	‡1–100[5]	1–27, 28ᵇ, 28–44, 45ᵇ, 45–55, 56ᵇ, 56–100**	27·0 × 37·1* (1–39, 41–100)[6] 26·1 × 36·1 (40)[7] 17·4 × 23·7 (28ᵇ) 21·3 × 27·8 (45ᵇ) 20·6 × 29·2 (56ᵇ)	Black
G *UNTRACED*[8]							
H FITZWILLIAM	1–100	100	J WHATMAN / 1831 (7–8, 12, 14, 39, 44–5, 47–8, 51, 53, 65, 68, 82, 86, 92, 100)	—	1–100**	23·1 × 28·5*	reddish-Brown
I LC	1–100	100	J WHATMAN / 1832 (4, 24, 34, 60, 66) J WHATMAN / 1831 (4–5, 8, 10, 12, 25, 57, 67, 69, 75, 96–7) J WHATMAN / 1832 (9, 28, 56)	—	1–100**	23·5 × 28·8*	reddish-Brown
J *Rosenbloom*	1–15, 17–100, 20ᵇ	100	J WHATMAN / 1831 (1, 7, 26, 33–4, 39, 41, 43, 45, 57, 62–3, 65, 69, 91–2, 94)	—	‡1–9, 11, 10, 12–15, 20ᵇ, 17–98, 100, 99[9]	24·3 × 30·4 *irregular*	reddish-Brown

Copy	Plates coloured	Watermark	No.		Binding	Leaf-size (cm)	Colour
METROPOLITAN MUSEUM, N.Y.	1	J WHATMAN / 1831	1	—	Loose	17·8×24·1	orangish-Brown
Keynes	1, #37, #51, 100[10]	—	4	—	Loose	19·3×25·7 (1) 16·8×23·1 (37)	Orange & Black (1) Black (37) bluish-Green (51) reddish-Brown (100)
Malone	4, 18–19, 28, 35, 37	—	3[11a]	—	Loose[11]	16·0×6·7 ([4, 37], [28, 35]) 16·1×4·4 ([18–19])	Blue
BMPR	5, 53	—	1[12]	—	Loose	28·4×35·1	Blue
Mrs. Greenberg	6	unknown	1	—	Loose	14·4×16·2[13]	greenish-Blue
LC	8, #9, 19–20, 38[a-b], 48, 50, 58, 78	EDMEADS & [PINE] (9) J WHATMAN / 1818 (58)	10[14]	—[15]	Loose	23·7×31·2 (8) 16·9×22·9 (9, 48) 23·6×31·1 (19–20, 38[a-b], 50, 78) 23·7×28·6 (58)	orangish-Brown & Black (8) Black (9, 20, 38[a], 48, 50, 58, 78) greenish-Blue (19, 38[b])
VICTORIA & ALBERT	9, 11	—	1[16]	—	Loose	28·9×35·3	Green
Crawford	24	—	1[17]	—	Loose	19·6×26·2[18]	orangish-Brown
Preston	25, 32, 41, 47	—	4[19]	—	Loose	16·1×16·6 (25)[13] 9·8×17·6 (32)[13] 16·1×12·8 (41)[13] 15·6×15·6 (47)[13]	Brown (25, 32, 47) orangish-Brown (41)
Harvey	28	—	1	—	Loose	15·5×10·3[13]	reddish-Brown
Mellon	28, 30, 35	—	2[20]	—	Loose	15·4×10·4 ([28, 35])[13,18] 15·8×21·6 (30)[18]	Blue (28, 35) Brown & Black (30)
VIVIAN GALLERY *UNTRACED*[21]	35, 50–1, 99	*invisible* WHATMAN / 1832 (51)	1 3	—	Loose Loose	16·4×9·3[13] 16·8×23·2 (50) 17·4×23·8 (51) 16·2×23·2 (99)	reddish-Brown Black (50) reddish-Brown (51, 99)
NATIONAL GALLERY OF VICTORIA	51	—	1	—	Loose	27·7×33·8	Red
MORGAN	74	—	1[22]	—	Loose	17·8×23·7	Orange

#++   Copies so marked were coloured by Blake.
      Pl. 1 faces pl. 2.
**   The identifiable offsets confirm the present binding-order.

*   The edges are trimmed and gilt.
1–100   The binding seems to date from before 1835.
Black   The plates were printed in more than one colour.

Notes to Table on p. 228.

99, indicating that Blake was casting about for copperplates when he etched them, presumably when his clean surfaces had all been used. The unusual plate-sizes of pl. *47, *56, *64, *71, 77–8, 89, *92, *95–*6, and *99 strikingly echo the above eccentricities, the plates with asterisks sharing some of the other peculiarities above suggesting late use.

There are, then, indications that some thirty-seven plates were etched later than their immediate neighbours: Chapter I: pl. 8, 10–11, 16, 19; Chapter II: pl. 33–5, 42–3, 46–7; Chapter III: pl. 53, 55–6, 59–61, 63–7, 70–2; Chapter IV: pl. 77–8, 82, 89, 92–6, 99–100. Most of them are in Chapters III and IV.

Some passages refer to 1808–9. The phrase on pl. 43, l. 36, 'A pretence of Art to destroy Art', also appears in the marginalia (?1808) to Reynolds' *Works* (1798), p. 2. The references throughout to Hand, who evidently represents the three Hunt brothers, must date from 1808 or later, when they attacked Blake in their *Examiner*; in particular, the passage on pl. 93 referring

Notes to Table on pp. 226–7

¹ For Blake's printed numbers, see the *Numbers* below.

² In copy A, numbers 56–7, 59–66 are over erasures, and pl. 26 is bound upside-down.

³ The leaves of copies B and D are loose, but the numbers and offsets clearly give the orders above. Pl. 1 (B) has three stab holes in the right margin and many stitching holes in the left indicating that it was stabbed with the frontispiece facing the title-page but reversed when bound about 1821.

⁴ The extra pl. 28ᵇ, 45ᵇ, 56ᵇ with copy F were previously among the proofs with *Thel* (a) and were only bound with *Jerusalem* (F) when *Thel* (a) was broken up in this century.

⁵ Copy F is numbered 1–100 on pl. 1–28, 33–41, 43–6, 42, 29–32, 47–100. (Keynes & Wolf report the numbering inaccurately.) Some numbers are in a very wavering hand, and numbers 29, ?34, and 36 are over erasures, the '36' on pl. 32 perhaps over '40'. The presence of ink numbers in the bottom left corners shows that pl. 51, 100 have been bound upside-down.

⁶ In copy F, only the top edge is gilt.

⁷ Pl. 40 in copy F is inscribed in pencil, on authority unknown to me, 'from another copy'. It did not come with *Thel* (a), like the other extra plates in copy F.

⁸ Information about copy G comes from Keynes & Wolf. It may well be a ghost.

⁹ Pl. 51 is bound upside-down in copy J.

¹⁰ Keynes pl. [1, *Europe* pl. 2] are printed back-to-back. Details concerning pl. 51 are taken from G. Keynes, *Bibliotheca Bibliographici* (1964).

¹¹ Mrs. Malone's pl. [4, 37] [18–19] [28, 35] are printed back-to-back. They are now all mounted on a single sheet.

¹² BMPR pl. [5, 53] are printed back-to-back.

¹³ The Greenberg, Preston, Harvey, Mellon (pl. 28, 35), and Vivian Gallery pulls are cut down to the designs (Mr. Mellon's pl. 35 is cut off after l. 9).

¹⁴ LC pl. [8, *Europe* pl. 2] are printed back-to-back.

¹⁵ The numbers (20–1, 23–6, 28, 44, 49) on LC pl. 8, 78, 9, 48, 19–20, 50, 38ᵇ, 58 refer to their order when bound with other plates including the 'Order' to the *Songs*.

¹⁶ V & A pl. [9, 11] are printed back-to-back.

¹⁷ Lord Crawford's pl. [24, *Europe* pl. 2] are printed back-to-back.

¹⁸ The measurements for Lord Crawford's and Mr. Mellon's pulls are those of the exposed surface in the frame.

¹⁹ Preston pl. [25, *Europe* pl. 1ᵇ] [32, *Europe* pl. 2ᵃ] [41, *Europe* pl. 1ᵃ] [47, *Europe* pl. 2ᵇ] are printed back-to-back.

²⁰ The Mellon pl. [28, 35] [30, *Europe* pl. 1] are printed back-to-back.

²¹ When the volume of proofs including the 'Order' of the *Songs* was broken up, these plates were sold at Parke-Bernet Galleries, 2 Nov. 1938, lot 41.

²² Morgan pl. [74, *Europe* pl. 2] are printed back-to-back.

to the Hunts as Anytus, Melitus, and Lycon (as he did in his 'Public Address' [*c*. 1810–11]) seems to quote their cruel review (17 Sept. 1809) of his *Descriptive Catalogue* (1809). Blake himself apparently described *Jerusalem* as unfinished in his *Descriptive Catalogue* (1809), ¶ 75:

The Strong man represents the human sublime. The Beautiful man represents the human pathetic, which was in the wars of Eden divided into male and female. The Ugly man represents the human reason. They were originally one man, who was fourfold; he was self-divided, and his real humanity slain on the stems of generation, and the form of the fourth was like the Son of God. How he became divided is a subject of great sublimity and pathos. The Artist has written it under inspiration, and will, if God please, publish it; it is voluminous, and contains the ancient history of Britain, and the world of Satan and Adam.

Other passages refer to 1811–15. Crabb Robinson noted in his journal for 24 July 1811 that recently 'Southey had been with Blake . . . he showed S. a perfectly mad poem called Jerusalem—Oxford Street is in Jerusalem.'[1] (Apparently *Jerusalem* was not then complete, for nineteen years later Southey wrote that Blake's 'designs for his own compositions in verse were not ready for sale when I saw him, nor did I ever hear that they were so'.)[2] Some plates, however, must have been finished about this time, for in 1812 Blake lent 'Detached Specimens' of *Jerusalem* to the exhibition of the Water Colour Society.[3] He was probably at work on the poem when George Cumberland Jr. reported to his father on 21 April 1815 that Blake's 'time is now intirely taken up with Etching & Engraving'.[4]

Blake pulled a good number of proofs, particularly in Chapter I (pl. 1, 4–5, 8–9, 11, 18–20, 24–5) and Chapter II (pl. 28, 30, 32, 35, 37–8, 41, 45, 47–8, 50), as well as in III (pl. 51, 53, 56, 58, 74) and IV (78, 99–100). Some of them (pl. 1, 8, 24–5, 30, 32, 41, 47, 74) are on the versos of left-over *Europe* proofs, and a few are on paper watermarked '1802', though the proofs were probably pulled some time later than this.

No surviving copy, however, can have been printed before 1818, according to the watermarks, and indeed every complete copy contains watermarks as late as 1820.

It seems likely, therefore, that the poem records experiences of Blake between 1790 and 1820, that it was written after 1803, that it was etched from 1804 on, sixty plates being completed by 1807,[5] and the last forty over the next twelve or thirteen years, but that it was not printed, except for proofs, before 1818–19, and that no complete copy was ready before 1820.

PUBLICATION: Chapter I in copies A and B may have been printed as early as 1818, the date of the watermark. Chapter II in copy A could have been printed in 1819, according to its watermark, and that in copy C certainly

---

[1] *Blake Records*, 229. Oxford Street is only in *Jerusalem* pl. 38, l. 57.

[2] *Blake Records*, 398.

[3] *Blake Records*, 230–1. The most likely possibilities are Mrs. Malone's pl. 4, 18–19, 28, 35, 37, or Mr. Preston's pl. 25, 32, 41, 47.

[4] *Blake Records*, 235–6. *Jerusalem* does not appear in Blake's list of his works ready for sale in his letter of 9 June 1818.

[5] It is of course likely that some of the sixty plates completed in 1807 were later altered or abandoned in favour of others.

was, for Linnell bought it for 14*s.* on 30 Dec. 1819.[1] Copies D and E
have leaves watermarked 1820 in each chapter, and in copy F each chapter
has leaves watermarked 1826. In every copy, at least some plates in Chapters
III and IV are watermarked at least as late as 1820, and the work was
probably ready for sale at this time, for it stimulated an extravagant piece of
puffing by T. G. Wainewright in a letter to *The London Magazine* for Sept.
1820:

my learned friend Dr. Tobias Ruddicombe, M.D. is, at my earnest entreaty, casting
a tremendous piece of ordnance,—*an eighty-eight pounder!* which he proposeth to fire
off in your next. It is an account of an ancient, newly discovered, illuminated manuscript, which has to name 'Jerusalem the Emanation of the Giant Albion! ! ! ' It
contains a good deal anent one '*Los*,' who, it appears, is now, and hath been from the
creation, the *sole* and fourfold dominator of the celebrated city of *Golgonooza*! The
doctor assures me that the redemption of mankind hangs on the universal diffusion
of the doctrines broached in this M.S.[2]

Blake may have produced few if any more than the half-dozen contemporary copies which survive,[3] and even these few he found difficult to
sell. On 12 April 1827, a few weeks before his death, he wrote to George
Cumberland:

The Last Work I produced is a Poem Entitled Jerusalem the Emanation of the
Giant Albion, but find that to Print it will Cost my Time the amount of Twenty
Guineas⌊.⌋[4] One I have Finishd [?*i.e. coloured.*] It contains 100 Plates but it is not
likely that I shall get a Customer for it⌊.⌋

According to Cunningham, he 'wrought incessantly' on it, 'tinting and
adorning it', but the lack of sale 'sank to the old man's heart'.[5] This coloured
copy (E) was still in his hands at his death, and his widow was no more
successful in selling it, for she still had it when she died in 1831. Her executor
Frederick Tatham evidently felt that he must write a biography of Blake
to be bound with the coloured copy, to make it more saleable.

Among Blake's contemporaries, copies were acquired by William Young
Ottley (copy ?A),[6] P. A. Hanrott (copy B, bound with *America* [G] and
Europe [B]), John Linnell (C), Frederick Tatham (E), Samuel Boddington
(H),[7] and Thomas Butts (I).

Considering the narrowness of its circulation, the poem was noticed
surprisingly widely just after Blake's death. J. T. Smith quoted pl. 3, 52,
77 in 1828; an anonymous writer in *The London University Magazine* apparently alluded to it in March 1830; in the same year Allan Cunningham

---

[1] Linnell may have bought Chapter III for £1 on 10 Dec. 1820, and he did buy the
'Balance' on 4 Feb. 1821 for 15*s.* (*Blake Records*, 581, 585). If we are to believe the watermarks,
Chapters I, III (including pl. 51), and IV of copy C could not have been printed before
1820.

[2] *Blake Records*, 265–6.

[3] Some plates of copies A, C, D, and I are poorly printed, with disfiguring smudges and
splatter.

[4] Cunningham (1830) gave the price as twenty-five guineas (*Blake Records*, 490).

[5] *Blake Records*, 501.

[6] Copy A was bought for £5. 5*s.* on 11 Aug. 1827, the day before Blake died (*Blake Records*,
594, 341, 347).

[7] Boddington may have acquired copy H when he got his *For the Sexes* (D) in 1833.

called it 'exclusively wild' and found that 'The crowning defect is obscurity', but he held 'many of the figures' in copy E to be 'worthy of Michael Angelo'; and Tatham quoted 'thrilling lines' from pl. 27 and 52 in his manuscript memoir of about 1832.[1] Tatham obviously valued the work highly, or at least thought it saleable, for when the copperplates passed into his hands in 1831 on the death of Mrs. Blake, he printed at least three copies (H–J) in reddish-Brown on paper watermarked 1831 and 1832.

DESIGNS: *Jerusalem* is generously decorated with large designs, many of them of very remarkable beauty, distributed in the following pattern:

	Plates
FULL-PAGE DESIGNS:	1–2, 26, 51, 76, 100
DESIGNS AT TOP OR BOTTOM (*italicized* when occupying more than a quarter of the page):	*4*, 6, *8–9*, *11*, *14–15*, 19, *21–2*, 24, *25*, *28*, *30*, 31, *32*, *35*, *36*, *37*, *39*, *41*, *44–5*, *46–7*, *50*, *53–4*, 57, 62, 64, 67, 69, 74, *75*, *78*, *84–5*, *87*, 91, *93–5*, 97, 98, *99*
INTERLINEAR DESIGNS (*italicized* when over a quarter of the page):	3, 18, 20, 23, 33, *58–9*, 63, *70*, *71–3*, *81*, *92*
SMALL DESIGNS IN RIGHT MARGIN (usually figures; *italics* indicate minimal designs):	5, 7, *12–13*, 29, 38, 40, 42, *43*, *48*, 49, *60*, 65–6, *79*, 80, *82–3*, 89, 96 (large)
NOTHING OR VIRTUALLY NO DESIGN (*italics* indicate the first plate of a chapter):	*10*, *16–17*, *27*, *34*, *52*, *55–6*, *61*, *68*, *77*, 86, 88, 90

Of these designs, those on pl. 1–2, 11, 26, 35, 37, 51, 53, and 76 are in White line; that is, they are engraved in the ordinary manner, but with Blake's method of intaglio printing, in which the ink prints from the surfaces rather than from the hollows, the engraved lines appear White or blank rather than dark, ink-coloured.

COLOURING: In most contemporary copies of *Jerusalem* (A, C, D, F, LC pl. 38ᵃ), the only colouring is a Grey wash, normally added to darken the background. Only copies B and E and some proofs are coloured. Since copy B has only twenty-five plates, all colouring reported below in the notes to the plates for pl. 26–100 is for copy E, except for the coloured proofs.

In copy A, a few words and designs are outlined in ink.

Copy B is lightly but firmly coloured. The text has colouring between the lines (which is not recorded in the plate-notes below). The dominant colours are greyish-Blue and Yellow. Some words and designs are clarified in pencil (pl. 5, 7–10), in Red ink (pl. 8), or in Black ink (pl. 9–11, 15, 19–22, 25). Parts of the design on pl. 11 seem to be printed also in Black.

In copy C at the bottom of pl. 16 there seems to be some accidental Green colouring, and the plates are often dirty (e.g. pl. 29–30, 48). In copy D, there is a Black framing-line around each plate, and pl. 21, 46, 69, 85 are touched up in ink.

In copy E, all the plates are framed by a single Red line, and pl. 1–2 have simple border designs like those in *Songs* (W). The text is usually coloured

[1] *Blake Records*, 458, 463; 383; 489, 490, 501; 520, 532.

greyish-Blue, and the designs are often magnificently coloured. Some text (e.g. on pl. 80) is touched in Black ink.

In copy F, some Chinese White has been used, and there are a few ink additions, e.g. on pl. 21, 25, 32, 73, 82, 87, 99.

Mrs. Malone's pl. 4, 18–19, 28, 35 have Blue wash over all, Sir Geoffrey Keynes's pl. 37 has greyish-Pink wash over the text, and the Victoria pl. 51 has three framing-lines.

CATCHWORDS:

Plate	Catchword	Matching incipit on plate
5	His	6; also 17, 19, 31, 38
7	[Con *del*][1]	9
8	Con[2]	9
9	To[3]	11; also 65, 77
11	[One (?) *del*][1]	14, *implausible*
12	And[4]	13; also 15, 25, 30, 37 (an added line), 57, 59, 70–2, 75
13	One[5]	14
18	[His *del*]	19; also 6, 17, 31, 38
19	[Jeru- *del*][6]	4, 23, 27, 28, 53, 78, *all implausible*
30	His	31; also 6, 17, 19, 38
37	His[4]	38; also 6, 17, 19, 31
38	By	39; also 67
40	Bath[7]	41; also 45, 46
43	With	44
47	These	48
48	The[8]	49; also 5, 50, 60, 74, 90
49	The	50; also 5, 49, 60, 74, 90
53	The[9]	5, 49, 50, 60, 74, 90, *all implausible*
53	In[10]	54; also 10 ('Into'), 58, 66
65	In	66; also 10 ('Into'), 54, 58
66	And[11]	13, 15, 25, 30, 37 (an added line), 57, 59, 70–2, 75, *none persuasive*
70	His[12]	6, 17, 19, 31, 38, *all implausible*
79	En-	80; also 93

Conclusions: The catchwords, mostly in Chapters I and II, link pl. 5–6, 8–9–11, 12–13–14, 18–19, 30–31, 37–38–39, 40–41, 43–44, 47–48–49–50, 53–54, 65–66, 79–80. They tell us nothing about the crucial plates in Chapter II (pl. 28–29, 32–33, 41–42–43, 46–47).

[1] I cannot read the '[Con *del*]' (pl. 7) or '[One (?) *del*]' (pl. 11) reported by D. V. Erdman, 'The Suppressed and Altered Passages in Blake's *Jerusalem*', *Studies in Bibliography*, xvii (1964), 44.

[2] Obscured in B.   [3] Covered in B and E.   [4] Obscured in E.

[5] Obscured in E and F.   [6] Invisible in most copies.

[7] Deleted in C. The scansion suggests that 'Bath' may be the last word of the text, crowded below l. 61, rather than a catchword.

[8] Covered with a wash in D.

[9] Visible only in the BMPR proof; altered ineffectively to 'In' in all other copies.

[10] Erdman (see note 1 above) reads this as '[The *del*]'.

[11] The 'And' is little more than a blur in the bottom right corner.

[12] Erased in A; correctly altered with a pen to 'And' in C.

Pl. 8 may be an insertion between pl. 7 and pl. 9, and pl. 10 is an insertion between pl. 9 and pl. 11. Pl. 11, 19, 53, 66, 70 were linked by catchwords with plates which apparently do not survive. Pl. 18 must have been temporarily followed by another plate to justify the deletion of its correct catchword.

PRINTED NUMBERS:[1] Two series of numbers were scratched on some of the plates of *Jerusalem*. The earlier set here was later deleted:

Number	Plate	Copy
2	3	A (fairly clear)
illeg	19	H–I
16	20	LC pull (clear)
37 8	37	H
6	38	A, LC pl. 38^b (clear; not in C, D, LC pl. 38^a; altered to '38' in E)
39	45	J (almost illegible)
49 or 1900	50	H or J

These variant numbers are in Chapter I (3, 19–20) and Chapter II (37–8, 45–6, 50).

The early numbers on pl. 3, 46, 50 suggest that one numbering system ignored pl. 1 or perhaps pl. 10. The '16' on pl. 20 implies that four of the plates now numbered 1–19 were then omitted (probably pl. 1, 10, 16–17), and the '39' apparently on pl. 45 suggests that two more were then omitted between pl. 20 and pl. 45.

In the second numeration, correct printed numbers were put in the top right corners of pl. 2–7, 11, 16–100,[2] except that pl. 18, 22–3, 32, 45, 47, 50–4, 57, 59, 72, 78, 82, 92 have no numbers. All but nos. 46, 56, 65, 68, 74–5, and 96 are in White line, which is very thin and faint. The numbers are most easily visible in the posthumous copies, particularly J. No printed numbers are visible in B.

Since the printed numbers on pl. 29–46 contradict the numbers Blake added with a pen in copies A, C, F, it is important to know whether the numbers were scratched on the copperplates before copies A, C, and F were printed. This, however, is exceedingly difficult to determine. In each of copies A, C, F, there is heavy printing and Grey wash which might have obscured these faint White lines. It is therefore almost impossible to be sure that the absence of a printed number on the paper means that there was no number scratched on the copper plate from which it was printed. In copies A–B, none of the second series of numbers is clear; in copy C, only the number on pl. 40 seems to be present, though deleted in pencil; and in copy F can be seen the numbers on pl. 3, 16, ?17, 28 (not 28^b), 38, ?49, 56, 68, 85, 90, 96. This may suggest that the numbers were scratched on the copperplates after most of the proofs and copy A (perhaps plus copy C)

---

[1] I cannot read the '25' or '23' (pl. 9, LC pull), '16' (pl. 19), '1⁰' (pl. 28, A, C), '31' (pl. 35, A), '36' (pl. 37, A), '45' (pl. 46, F), nor the correct numbers on pl. 1, 8–10, 12–15, 18, 22–3, 32, 47, 50–4, 59, 72, 78, 92 reported by D. V. Erdman, 'The Suppressed and Altered Passages in Blake's *Jerusalem*', *SB*, xvii (1964), 49–50.

[2] The numbers on pl. 48–9, 83, 90 (only the '9' is clear), and 94 are somewhat doubtful.

were printed. The printed numbers in copy F, contradicted by its numbers added with a pen, suggest that Blake first indicated the new arrangement on the copperplates but carelessly copied the former order when he numbered them with a pen. In the other copies (B, D–E), the printed numbers and the pen numbers are congruent.

INK NUMBERS: So far as Blake's ink numbering is concerned, the order of Chapters I, III–IV is constant. The only variant occurs in Chapter II, where pl. 42, 29–32 are placed after pl. 46 in copies A, C, and F.[1]

ORDER: There is only one variant in the order of the plates of *Jerusalem*.[2] Chapters I, III, and IV do not vary in order, but in Chapter II pl. 29 46 were arranged in two different ways. In copies D and E they were numbered 29–46, but in copies A, C, and F pl. 42 and 29–32 were placed in Blake's numbering after pl. 46.

Of these two orders, that of copies A and C is apparently the earliest, for Chapter II in copy C was printed in 1819 and Chapters I and II of copy A may have been, whereas copies D and E can be no earlier than their watermark dates of 1820. Further, the etched design on pl. 20 is different in A and C from that in D–F. It is plausible to suppose that the numbering of copies A and C preceded that of D and E, as their printing did.[3] The two arrangements, then, are as follows:

	Plates	Contemporary copies
FIRST ORDER:	pl. 1–28, 33–41, 43–6, 42, 29–32, 47–100	A, C, F
SECOND ORDER:	pl. 1–100	D, E

Blake's numbering in copy F, which is watermarked 1826, reverts to the First Order. Further, faint numbers were scratched on most of the copperplates, evidently after copies A–C were printed and are visible in copies D–J. Thus the pen numbers in copy F contradict the printed numbers.

In the First Order, the narrative transition at every junction later dislocated (pl. 41–43, 46–42–29, 32–47) is plausible, except in the case of pl. 33, which fits awkwardly after pl. 28. In the Second Order, the transitions between pl. 28 and pl. 29 and between pl. 32 and pl. 33 are good, but those between pl. 41 and pl. 42 and between pl. 46 and pl. 47 are distinctly awkward.

Each order entails its own beauties and difficulties. The Second Order has been followed below, because it is, in a sense, the later of the two, and because it is the one followed in the copy (E) on which Blake expended the greatest pains, perhaps working on its colouring in the last months of his life.

---

[1] Copy F was bound by Bedford in the late nineteenth century to match the order of copies D and E and the posthumous copies H and I. The eccentric order of posthumous copy J is clearly without Blake's authority. Copy B, which has only pl. 1–25, is irrelevant here. Pl. 56–7, 59–66 in copy A are presently numbered over erasures.

[2] The extra plates in copies F and J and the plate missing from J clearly lack Blake's authority.

[3] No light is thrown on the order of Chapter II by the catchwords.

PLATE-SIZES: Most of the plates fall approximately (within 0·2 or 0·3 cm) within three sizes:

Size	Plates
16·3 × 22·4 cm:	pl. 1–9, 11–14, 18–20, 23–9, 31–2, 35, 37–43, 45–6, 48, 50–3, 65–6, 70, 74–6, 79–80, 82–3; *50 plates in all*
15·1 × 21·2 cm:	pl. 15, 17, 21–2, 30, 34, 36, 44, 49, 54–5, 57–8, 60, 62, 67–9, 81, 84–8, 90–1, 93–4, 97–8; *30 plates in all*
14·8 × 22·4 cm:	pl. 10, 16, 33, 59, 63, 72–3, 100, plus 61; *9 plates in all*
exceptions:	pl. (47, 78), (71, 77), (89, 92), (95, 56), (96, 64), 99; *11 plates in all*

Almost all the plates of *Jerusalem* seem to have been etched on the versos of other *Jerusalem* plates. In the list below, perfect matches are *in italics*, and an asterisk (*) indicates the presence of a copperplate-maker's-mark.

Plate	Matches	Plate
pl. 1 (16·2 × 22·3)	=	*pl. 27 (16·2 × 22·3)*
pl. 2 (16·2 × 22·5)	=	pl. 40 (16·3 × 22·5)
pl. 3 (16·4 × 22·5)	=	*pl. 6 (16·4 × 22·5)*
pl. 4 (16·3 × 22·5)	=	*pl. 5 (16·3 × 22·5)*
pl. 7 (16·3 × 22·4)	=	*pl. 76 (16·3 × 22·4)*
pl. 8 (16·2 × 22·2)	=	pl. 70 (16·1 × 22·2)
pl. 9 (16·4 × 22·5)	=	*pl. 11 (16·4 × 22·5)*
pl. 10 (15·0 × 22·5)	=	**pl. 72 (15·0 × 22·5)*
pl. 12 (16·4 × 22·5)	=	*pl. 14 (16·4 × 22·5)*
pl. 13 (16·3 × 22·3)	=	*pl. 31 (16·3 × 22·3)*
pl. 15 (15·1 × 21·3)	=	*pl. 44 (15·1 × 21·3)*
pl. 16 (14·7 × 22·3)	=	*pl. 100 (14·8 × 22·4)
pl. 17 (15·0 × 21·3)	=	pl. 69 (15·0 × 21·2)
pl. 18 (16·4 × 22·5)	=	*pl. 26 (16·4 × 22·5)*
pl. 19 (16·3 × 22·5)	=	*pl. 28 (16·3 × 22·5)*
pl. 20 (16·3 × 22·6)	=	*pl. 23 (16·3 × 22·6)*
pl. 21 (15·2 × 21·4)	=	*pl. 49 (15·2 × 21·4)*
pl. 22 (15·2 × 21·3)	=	*pl. 30 (15·2 × 21·3)*
pl. 24 (16·5 × 22·6)	=	pl. 35 (16·5 × 22·5)
pl. 25 (16·3 × 22·2)	=	*pl. 83 (16·3 × 22·2)*
pl. 29 (16·2 × 22·3)	=	*pl. 43 (16·2 × 22·3)*
pl. 32 (16·3 × 22·3)	=	pl. 53 (16·4 × 22·3)
pl. 34 (15·0 × 21·2)	=	*pl. 36 (15·0 × 21·2)*
pl. 37 (16·3 × 22·6)	=	*pl. 45 (16·3 × 22·6)*
pl. 38 (16·2 × 22·5)	=	pl. 51 (16·1 × 22·5)
pl. 39 (16·0 × 22·4)	=	pl. 82 (16·1 × 22·2)
pl. 41 (16·2 × 22·4)	=	pl. 48 (16·4 × 22·4)
pl. 42 (16·3 × 22·5)	=	*pl. 46 (16·3 × 22·5)*
pl. 47 (16·1 × 21·1)		

Plate	Matches	Plate

pl. 50 (16·3× 22·6) = *pl. 52 (16·3× 22·6)*

pl. 54 (14·9× 21·1) = *pl. 55 (14·9× 21·1)*

pl. 57 (14·9× 21·0) = *pl. 62 (14·9× 21·0)*
pl. 58 (14·9× 21·1) = *pl. 60 (14·9× 21·1)*
pl. 59 (14·6× 22·4) = pl. 61 (14·4× 22·5)

*pl. 63 (14·9× 22·5)

pl. 65 (16·2× 22·3) = *pl. 66 (16·2× 22·3)*

pl. 67 (15·1× 21·3) = *pl. 91 (15·1× 21·3)*
pl. 68 (14·9× 21·1) = *pl. 81 (14·9× 21·1)*

pl. 73 (14·8× 22·5) =*pl. 33 (14·8× 22·5)*
pl. 74 (16·5× 22·6) = pl. 75 (16·4× 22·7)

pl. 77 (17·0× 22·1) = *pl. 71 (17·1× 22·1)
pl. 78 (16·1× 21·0)
pl. 79 (16·1× 22·0) = pl. 80 (16·1× 22·1)

pl. 84 (15·0× 21·1) = pl. 85 (14·9× 21·1)

pl. 86 (15·1× 20·9) = *pl. 87 (15·1× 20·9)*

pl. 88 (15·0× 20·9) = pl. 94 (15·2× 21·2)
pl. 89 (14·5× 20·2) = *pl. 92 (14·6× 20·3)
pl. 90 (15·1× 21·1) = *pl. 93 (15·1× 21·1)*

pl. 95 (14·0× 20·1) = *pl. 56 (13·8× 20·1)
pl. 96 (14·4× 20·3) = *pl. 64 (14·5× 20·4)
pl. 97 (14·9× 21·0) = *pl. 98 (14·9× 21·0)*

pl. 99 (15·4× 22·7)

The plates of *Jerusalem* combine in thirty perfect marriages, eleven half-perfect marriages, and seven approximate marriages, leaving four bachelors. The *copperplate-maker's-mark* on pl. 33, 72, 100 is:

WHITTON[1] & HARRIS
N? 31 SHOE LANE
LONDON

Part of that on pl. 71 is:

OW & SON
[SH]OE LANE
LONDON

The plate-maker's-mark on pl. 56, 63, 92, 93 might be either of the above. The mark on pl. 64 has not been identified. Pl. 5 (copy A) and 57 (copy H) also seem to show plate-maker's marks.

---

[1] The undated trade-card of 'Benjamin Whitton / Copper and Brass Plate- / Maker / At the Crown in Shoe Lane, / opposite the White Swan near S! Andrew's Church, / HOLBORN, /London' is reproduced in A. Heal, *London Tradesmen's Cards of the XVIII Century* (1968), pl. xxi.

VARIANTS: In each case but pl. 4, 20, the etched variants are between isolated proofs and completed copies:

Etched Variants (ignoring numbers)

pl. 1: The words are clear in the Keynes proof; deleted in others
pl. 4: The third star was added after copy B was printed
pl. 20: The design in the LC proof, A, and C is different from D–F, H–J
pl. 28: The design in the Morgan proof is different from others
pl. 37: l. 10 'pale' in the Keynes proof was altered to 'blue' in others
pl. 45: l. 40, omitted in the Morgan proof, is present in others
pl. 53: The catchword in the BMPR proof is gone in others

Significant Variants Made by Hand (ignoring catchwords covered by wash)

pl. 37: 'blue' was altered to 'pale' in A
pl. 51: The names were added in the Keynes pull
pl. 56: 'earth-worm' was extended to 'earth-worms' in F
pl. 69: l. 1, 'conjoined' was altered to 'combined' in E
pl. 84: A sun was added to the design in E
pl. 97: Shorts were added to the naked man in E
p. 98: l. 45, 'the Coven[an]t of Jehovah' was altered to 'thy Covenant Jehovah' in E.

ERRATA:[1]

'laying' for 'lying' (pl. 1, l. 7)
'incohererent' (pl. 5, l. 3)
'ou[t]side' (pl. 8, l. 25)
'Fals[e]hood' (pl. 12, l. 13)
'cartaact[s]' (pl. 13, l. 41)
'heaves' for 'heave' (pl. 16, l. 9)
'Glou[ce]ster' (pl. 16, l. 45)
'Cornwal[l]' (pl. 16, l. 46)
'Harford' for 'Hertfordshire' (pl. 16, l. 47)
'Nott[in]gham[shire]' (pl. 16, l. 48)
'Hunt[in]g[do]n[shire]' (pl. 16, l. 48)
'Camb[ridgshire]' (pl. 16, l. 48)
'Heref[ordshire]' (pl. 16, l. 49)
an extra 'the' (pl. 16, l. 51)
'Hadd[i]n[g]t[on]' (pl. 16, l. 53)
'Kincard[ine]' (pl. 16, l. 53)
'Edinbur[g]h' (pl. 16, l. 54)

'Roxbro' for 'Roxburgh' (pl. 16, l. 54)
'Berwi[c]k' (pl. 16, l. 54)
'Ab[e]rdeen' (pl. 16, l. 54)
'Cla[c]kman[n]an' (pl. 16, l. 55)
'Invernes[s]' (pl. 16, l. 55)
'Ca[i]t[h]nes[s]' (pl. 16, l. 55)
'Linlithgo[w]' (pl. 16, l. 55)
'Renfru' for 'Renfrew' (pl. 16, l. 56)
'Sutherlan[d]' (pl. 16, l. 56)
'Glasgo[w]' (pl. 16, l. 57)
'Dumbart[o]n' (pl. 16, l. 57)
'Kir[c]ku[d]bri[g]ht' (pl. 16, l. 58)
'Lanerk' for 'Lanark' (pl. 16, l. 58)
'Kinros[s]' (pl. 16, l. 58)
'Murra' for 'Moray' (pl. 16, l. 58)
'Kromarty' for 'Cromarty' (pl. 16, l. 58)

1 This list omits variants of proper names which do not seem to have a standard orthography: Brereton (pl. 5, 19, 36), Brertun (pl. 32, 71); Coban (pl. 5, 7, 9, 18–19, 36, 71), Koban (pl. 8, 32, 58); Guantok (pl. 19), Gwantock (pl. 36), Gwantok (pl. 32), Gwantoke (pl. 71), Kwantok (pl. 5); Hutton (pl. 5, 19, 36), Hutn (pl. 7), Huttn (pl. 32, 71); Kock (pl. 32), Kox (pl. 5, 7–8, 19, 36, 43, 71); Peachey (pl. 5, 19, 71), Peachy (pl. 32, 36); Schofield (pl. 7), Scofeld (pl. 19, 43), Scofield (pl. 5, 7, 11, 43, 60), Skofeld (pl. 8, 15, 32, 36, 67, 71, 90), Skofield (pl. 17, 22, 51, 58, 68); Slade (pl. 36, 71), Slaid (pl. 32), Slayd (pl. 5, 19).

'wooe' for 'woo' (pl. 17, l. 10)

'suspition' (pl. 18, l. 24, pl. 19, l. 26)

'nouris[*h*]d' (pl. 22, l. 6)

'was' for 'were' (pl. 27, ¶ 6)

'acros[*s*]' (pl. 27, l. 43)

'Op[*p*]pressors' (pl. 30, l. 27)

'involve[*s*]' (pl. 33, l. 47)

'have thou elevate' ?for 'hast thou elevated' (pl. 34, l. 10)

'fals[*e*]hoods' (pl. 40, l. 19)

'trajic' (pl. 41, l. 29)

an extra 'of' (pl. 43, l. 37)

'suspition' (pl. 45, l. 8)

'conjoinining' (pl. 45, l. 37)

'Uncircuncision' (pl. 49, l. 44)

'Fals[*e*]hood' (pl. 55, l. 65)

'Ca[*i*]thnes[*s*]' (pl. 58, l. 46)

'enterance' (pl. 59, l. 1)

'Forgive[*ne*]ss' (pl. 61, l. 12)

'Familys' for 'Families' (pl. 63, l. 32)

'frownining' (pl. 64, l. 31)

'Daug[*h*]ters' (pl. 65, l. 21)

an extra 'him' (pl. 65, l. 62)

'disagre[*em*]ents' (pl. 70, l. 8)

'plea[*sa*]ntness' (pl. 73, l. 49)

'St[*r*]eet' (pl. 74, l. 55)

'Natwre' (pl. 77, l. 20)

'encompas[*s*]ing' (pl. 77, l. 29)

'Ephra[*i*]m' (pl. 79, l. 30)

'instr[*u*]ments' (pl. 79, l. 48)

'Fals[*e*]hood' (pl. 82, ll. 17, 19, 20)

'Defo[*r*]mity' (pl. 82, l. 69)

'siste[*r*]s' (pl. 82, l. 72)

'soften[*in*]g' (pl. 82, l. 77)

'Furna[*c*]es' (pl. 82, ll. 78, 79)

'rejoi[*c*]e' (pl. 83, l. 18)

'Fals[*e*]hood' (pl. 84, l. 31)

'Bends' for 'Bend' (pl. 86, l. 10)

'Arou[*n*]d' (pl. 86, l. 36)

'sendinding' for 'sending' (pl. 88, l. 30)

'Hermaph[*r*]oditic' (pl. 89, l. 4)

'Presbuterion' (pl. 89, l. 6)

'Cai[*a*]phas' (pl. 93 design)

'Worship[*p*]ing' (pl. 93, l. 23)

'Chastitity' (pl. 94, l. 23)

'incompreh[*en*]sible' (pl. 98, l. 11)

'Coven[*an*]t' (pl. 98, l. 45)

Pl. 1. FRONTISPIECE, INCIPIT: 'there is a Void . . .'. DESIGN: A traveller wearing a short, belted coat and a flat-brimmed hat and carrying in his right hand a round object which gives off rays steps with his right foot through an open arched doorway in a stone wall. (His attitude is similar to that of the female 'Soul exploring the recesses of the Grave' with a candle in her right hand for Blair's *Grave* [1808]; and 'Death's Door' for the same work and for *For Children* [1793] and pl. 97 below are also related to it.)

Beside and on the archway, Blake engraved eleven lines which can be read confidently from the Keynes proof, where they are outlined in Black. Later they were deleted on the copperplate with lines for the brick-work and further obscured in the printing and colouring processes, though they can also be made out from posthumous copies, particularly copies H and I.

COLOURING: The man's COAT is greyish-Red (B) or bluish-Grey (E), his HAT Black (B); the BALL of fire is Yellow (B) and Red (B, E) of course; the WALL is reddish-Grey (B), or shades of Brown (E), and the DOORWAY is Black (B).

VARIANTS: *State 1*: The words appear clearly, though three were erased from the paper (Keynes pull).

State 2: The words were deleted on the copper (all other copies).

The traveller's fingers extend through the central cone of light in B, not just through its rays as elsewhere.

Some rays from the globe are Black in D; they extend throughout the page in E.

Pl. 2. TITLE-PAGE: DESIGN: Above the title floats a clothed woman with rounded moth wings; to the left of 'Jerusalem' flies a woman with narrow butterfly wings; to the left of 'Albion' sits a clothed woman with large, demonic wings resting her head on her left hand; below her but above the imprint a large woman with arms extended over her head lies asleep as her body vegetates into a wing-like leaf decorated with stars, two dark circles, and two crescent moons; in the bottom right corner stands an even larger figure with somewhat similar wings (decorated with stars and a crescent moon) holding its head in its hands; and between the words are tiny moths, birds, and three flying humans.

Below 'Albion' is a deletion *'before etching'* which I find illegible except for 'V' but which Erdman (p. 731) reads with certainty as 'In XXVIII Chapters'. The imprint is in White line.

COLOURING: The BACKGROUND is Blue (B, E), Orange (E), and Green (E); the WINGS at top are Yellow with Red (B) or Blue (E); the vegetating woman's WING-PETALS are Yellow with Red (B) or Red veins (B, E); the woman at the middle left is Yellow (E); the bottom WINGS are Blue (E), and the other WINGS are Green (E).

VARIANT: The projections to the left of the leaf-woman's head are different in B, like the pincers of a huge earwig, as Keynes notes in the facsimile of B (1974).

Pl. 3. INCIPIT: 'To the Public . . .'. DESIGN: To the left of and below ll. 5–10 is a person with enveloping, flame-like wings—perhaps she is turning into a leaf—while to the right of the poem are leaf-like flourishes. Many words are deleted from the copperplate.

Pl. 4. INCIPIT: 'Jerusalem / Chap: 1 . . .'. DESIGNS: Below 'Jerusalem' a figure in a long robe and a cowl sits with arms extended towards naked youths sitting on each side. To the right of the right-hand figure there seem to be flames. From beside the one at the left four nude women float to the left and to the top of the page. The topmost woman points above the title to three stars and a crescent moon, in which is written:

Movos o Iεσоυς

that is, 'Jesus only' (cf. Mark 9: 8; Luke 9: 36; John 8: 9).

To the right of the text are a series of curious intersecting lines like a web.

COLOURING: The woman's ROBE is yellowish-Brown (B) or dark Blue (E), and the SKY is Black (B, E) and dark Blue (E).

VARIANT: The cloud by the moon is coloured out in E.

Pl. 5. INCIPIT: *State 1*: The etched star above the 's' of 'Jerusalem' is not present in B.

State 2: The star was added in other copies. DESIGN: INCIPIT: 'The banks of the Thames . . .'. In the right margin are five small women, the top and bottom ones nude with clasped hands looking upwards, the second from the top nude with outspread arms, the third one perhaps clothed, kneeling with clasped hands, and the fourth kneeling in a long dress with head bowed down in a Magdalen-like position.

COLOURING: The flame-like BACKGROUND is Grey in B. The two women in the middle have DRESSES of Yellow and Brown in the BMPR pull.

Pl. 6. INCIPIT: 'His Spectre driv'n . . .'. DESIGN: Between ll. 2 and 3, and between ll. 7 and 8 are flames curling from below the text where a naked man leans on his hammer on his forge and looks upward at a bat-winged figure with its hands to its ears who seems to be whispering to him. To the right may be seen a huge bellows and an even larger chain, while to the left is a flaming hearth with large tongs standing before it.

COLOURING: Los and the spectre are a similar greyish-Pink in B, but in E Los is Brown and the spectre dark Blue; the FORGE is Grey (B), the BELLOWS greyish-Red (B), and the HEARTH reddish-Grey (B).

VARIANT: In B, the tongs are not visible; the man's right forefinger is extended, his left hand goes round the handle of the hammer (not over the top), the bellows at right have only one pleat, and the chain above the bellows is invisible.

Pl. 7. INCIPIT: 'Was living: panting . . .'. DESIGN: To the right of the text are large swirls, in which stand three figures, representing, from top to bottom, a ?clothed woman pointing upward, a naked man standing with his left arm raised, and a nude figure with its back to us plunging head downward.

Pl. 8. INCIPIT: 'Rose up against me . . .'. DESIGN: Below the text, a naked woman with a harness round her breasts and genitals walks to the left pulling a moon-like circle through the sky.

COLOURING: The SKY is Black (B, E); the CLOUD and centre of the MOON are Grey in B; the centre of the MOON is dark Brown in E and its lighted part Yellow.

VARIANTS: In B, in the right margin above l. 19 a tree is added by hand, with a winged figure below it who seems to be gesturing towards an angry swan below him.

The catchword is obscured in B.

In copy E, three stars were added beside and above the woman.

Pl. 9. INCIPIT: 'Condens'd his Emanations . . .'. DESIGNS: Between ll. 11 and 12 are a herd of sheep, with a tiger lying on its paws at the left, a bounding dog next to him, a kneeling person beside a shape which may be a sleeping lion, and a shepherd leaning against a tree at the right playing a flute.

Between ll. 22 and 23 at the left sits a man with bowed head and extended legs, while a woman in a long dress crawls away from him apparently to take a round object from an enormous serpent.

Below the text is a large design of two clothed figures at the left tearing their hair, another kneeling with head down as if in grief beside the foreshortened body of a prostrate, naked man, while to the right is another clothed seated figure. In the background are two enormous stars and, perhaps, lightning.

COLOURING: In the top scene, the SHEPHERD is clothed in Pink (B) or pale Lavender (E). In the middle scene, the PERSON on the left is pale Blue

(V&A pull), and the WOMAN has a Pink dress (V&A). In the bottom scene, the kneeling WOMAN in the middle has a Grey dress (B, V&A) or a Blue one (E); the two figures at the left are uncoloured (B), Brown and Blue (E), Purple and Grey (V&A), or Blue (LC pull); the right WOMAN is Brown (E); the CORPSE is greyish-Pink (B); the bottom SKY is Yellow (E, V&A) or greyish-Pink (V&A); the GROUND is Yellow (B); and the STARS are Brown (E, LC), and Yellow (V & A).

VARIANT: The catchword is invisible in B and E.

Pl. 10. INCIPIT: 'Into the Furnaces . . .'.

Pl. 11. INCIPIT: 'To labours mighty. . .'. DESIGNS: Above the text, a naked human with the wings, neck, and head of a swan sits in water with its head on the water, apparently blowing bubbles. In the background, the shore with roughly engraved trees is visible, and behind the figure is a fish.

In the right margin of the text are four fish.

Below the text floats a naked woman with heavy pearl necklaces, bracelets, and ear-rings, who seems to have spiny flames protruding from all parts of her body.

COLOURING: The FIGURES are uncoloured (B), the BACKGROUNDS are Black (B [?colour-printed], E), Grey and Orange (E).

Pl. 12. INCIPIT: 'Why wilt thou give to her . . .'. DESIGN: In the right margin are three small figures. The top one is a woman in a swirling gown holding on an elegant hat with both hands. Below her, a naked man plunges downwards with compasses to span what seems to be a terrestrial globe with regular intersections (similar to the one on pl. 54), while in the bottom a clothed woman reaches up to the globe.

COLOURING: The DRESSES are Pink (B, E), the GLOBE greyish-Blue (B).

VARIANT: In E, the globe is completed on the left, and the catchword is obscured.

Pl. 13. INCIPIT: 'And that toward Eden . . .'. DESIGN: At the top of the right margin is a large insect; below it are two leaves; below them is a large ?bat above a small, kneeling, clothed figure with raised arms.

COLOURING: The WOMAN is dark Green (E), the INSECT Grey (B), and the BAT Grey (B) or dark Blue (E).

VARIANTS: The catchword is obscured in E–F.

Pl. 14. INCIPIT: 'One hair nor particle of dust . . .'. DESIGNS: To the right of the text are five circles of various sizes (one lumpy like the earth and one with a belt around it), a crescent moon, and two stars.

Below the text, a large naked man in a position like that of a funeral effigy lies on his left elbow looking upward at a small woman floating above him with regular swirling wings or draperies. (She is sketched nude on pp. 31–2 of Hayley's *Designs to a Series of Ballads* [1802] in the BMPR; both figures are seen in the sketch in the V&A, reproduced in *Pencil Drawings* [1927] pl. 37.) Around her are six large stars and a crescent moon, and over her is a rainbow. Perhaps the man is Los viewing Enitharmon, 'his vegetated mortal Wife' (l. 13) or Jerusalem 'Like a pale cloud' (l. 34). Below and to the left of the last line is a deletion which seems to read: 'End of the / 1st Chap:'.

COLOURING: The woman's ROBE is Yellow, Pink, and greyish-Blue (B) or all Blue (E); the RAINBOW from top to bottom is Red (B, E [pinkish-]), Yellow (B), Green (B), Blue (B, E), Pink (B), Green (E), Gold (E), Yellow (E), and Orange (E); the PLANETS at the top are pale Yellow (B); the BACKGROUND is Grey and Brown (E); and the FIGURES are Blue (E).

VARIANTS: In B, curving lines over the man's head are completed to make a circle (with faint continents on it) complementing the moon at the left.

Pl. 15. INCIPIT: 'And Hand & Hyle . . .'. DESIGN: Below the text, a large, naked, bearded man with outstretched arms seems to run or float to the right over a much smaller naked man almost lying on the ground with his right arm in the air, who is turning into roots and branches. There seem to be veins in the soil, especially in E.

COLOURING: The BACKGROUND is Yellow and Pink in B.

Pl. 16. INCIPIT: 'Hampstead Highgate Finchley . . .'. DESIGN: The only design is a tiny figure standing at the end of ll. 18–21.

Pl. 17. INCIPIT: 'His Spectre divides . . .'. DESIGN: The design consists only in small leaves and flourishes in the right margin.

Pl. 18. INCIPIT: 'From every-one of the Four Regions . . .'. DESIGNS: Between ll. 10 and 11 a naked winged man with lilies in his hair floats to the left, and a nude, winged woman perhaps with roses in her hair floats to the right. Over their extended right arms are crescent moons with masts and sails, and from their arms a naked boy (at the right) floats to kiss a floating nude girl.

To the right of ll. 14–20, 26–32, 34–5 are three naked figures falling head-long.

COLOURING: The WINGS are touched with Yellow (B) or pale Blue (E), the woman's roses are pale Red (B), the SKY is Grey (B), Red, Yellow, and Black (E), and the MOONS are Yellow (E).

Pl. 19. INCIPIT: 'His Children exil'd from his breast . . .'. DESIGN: Below the text lies a large, naked man, contorted as if in agony; beneath his shoulder, his left hip, and on his right hip lie three other tiny naked figures, two more tiny clothed figures kneel as if in mourning by his head, and two more stand in mourning at his feet. To the right is a heavy sunset, and up the right margin and across the top of the page rise nine naked men and women, the four at the top with overlapping wrists.

COLOURING: The CLOTHES are greyish-Blue (B), the SUN is Red (B) or Yellow (E), and the SKY is partly Pink (B) or Orange (E).

VARIANT: The prostrate figure below the giant's hip is invisible, apparently coloured out, in B.

Pl. 20, INCIPIT: 'But when they saw Albion . . .'. DESIGNS: Above the text, two small figures float together head-to-head.

Between ll. 11 and 12 are four stars and three moons.

Between ll. 13 and 14 two tiny clothed figures seem to pull to the left a flaming roller pushed by other figures, and to the right a woman in a long dress seems to crawl after them amid stars. (A related woman, reversed, appears in *Vala* [?1796–1807], p. 82.)

Between ll. 20 and 21 are flames.

Between ll. 26 and 27 four tiny clothed figures pull to the left a flaming star which is followed by a floating woman.

In the bottom right corner are two large stars.

COLOURING: The CLOTHES are Blue (B [greyish-], E [middle figure only]).

VARIANT: The points of the flame in the top right corner in A, C, LC pull (B indeterminate) are extended and differentiated from those in D–F, H–J, for no obvious purpose.

Pl. 21. INCIPIT: 'O Vala! O Jerusalem! . . .'. DESIGN: Below the text, three small nude women at the left cower away from another naked figure flourishing three studded lashes in each hand.

COLOURING: The BACKGROUND is Yellow (B, E) at the right, Blue at the left (E).

Pl. 22. INCIPIT: 'Albion thy fear has made me tremble . . .'. DESIGNS: Above the text floats a naked woman near what may be an angel.

Below the text is a symmetrical design of three huge cog-wheels; over the central one two angelic figures stretch towards each other, and over those at the right and left similar figures stretch towards the margins where they are presumably to be met by other angels.

COLOURING: The COGS are dark Grey (B) or Black (E), the ANGELS Pink, including their wings (E), and the SKY at bottom Yellow (B, E).

Pl. 23. INCIPIT: 'Jerusalem! Jerusalem! . . .'. DESIGNS: Between ll. 13 and 14 lies a nude, heavy, winged woman apparently turning into vegetation, with a flower at each side. From her hair extend long, curious scrolls at each side, and up the right margin are two winged insects with human bodies.

Between ll. 28 and 29 are four small naked men imprisoned in the earth beneath tree roots.

Below the text are seven more similar tiny naked men entrapped among rocks and tree roots.

COLOURING: The top woman's WINGS are Grey, Yellow, and Pink (B), and her ribbon or scroll is Pink (B); the FLOWERS are Yellow (B); the bottom FIGURES are Blue (E), and the bottom BACKGROUND is yellowish-Grey (B).

Pl. 24. INCIPIT: 'What have I said? . . .'. DESIGNS: Above the text, a large moon is raised apparently on heavy waves. Resting on the moon are a person's head and outstretched arms or wings.

Between ll. 11 and 12 four clothed women crawl to the right, and down the right margin are clouds and a kneeling woman with her arms crossed over her head. To the left of the crawling woman there appear to be three open-mouthed heads; cf. pl. 50.

COLOURING: The MOON is Yellow (B, E), or Grey (Crawford pull); the top BACKGROUND is Grey (B), dark Blue (E), or Black (Crawford pull); the WAVES are Black (Crawford pull); and the right MARGIN is Grey and Pink (B).

Pl. 25. INCIPIT: 'And there was heard . . .'. DESIGN: Below the text, two-thirds of the page is taken up by the design of a naked man kneeling with his hands behind his back and his head on the right knee of a seated nude woman whose forehead is on her left hand as she looks down at him. On his right thigh are a star and a round, flaming face; on his right shoulder is a star; on his left thigh are seven stars and a crescent moon; on his belly are three stars; and from his belly extends a bloody cord held in the fists of a nude woman seated to the right. Over the scene broods a nude woman from whose outstretched hands depend bloody lines. (An analogous scene of a man on the ground between a man[?] at the right and a nude woman at the left, both with knives in their hands, is in the BMPR, and a similar victim appears in 'The Blasphemer' [*c.* 1800], illustrating Leviticus 24: 23 and reproduced in M. Butlin's Tate catalogue: *William Blake* [1971], 45.)

COLOURING: The MAN is Grey (B), his SUN, STARS, and MOON Yellow (B); the women's HAIR from left to right is Yellow (two) and orangish-Brown (E); the VEINS and lines running from the women's fingers are Red (B, E); the BACKGROUND is Yellow (B, E), Brown, and Black (E); and the GRASS at the bottom is Green (E), of course.

VARIANTS: In E, tears have been added to the face of the woman at the right, and there seem to be eyes in the moon on the man's thigh.

A cloth over the right leg of the woman at the right has been added with a fine pen in F.

Pl. 26. DESIGN: The whole page is a splendid White-line design, sideways, of a naked man in flames walking to the left with outstretched hands with spikes in the palms and looking backward at a woman in a long dress standing with her hands raised at waist level. (The scene is sketched in pencil in the BMPR, reproduced in *Pencil Drawings* [1927], pl. 38.) They are labelled 'HAND [*and*] JERUSALEM' at the bottom of the design. Sideways to the figures is written a poem, the first two lines to the left of Hand, the third between Hand and Jerusalem, and the fourth behind Jerusalem:

<blockquote>
SUCH VISIONS HAVE / APPEARD TO ME
AS I MY ORDERD RACE HAVE RUN ⌊:⌋
JERU / SALEM / IS NAMED / LIBERTY
AMONG THE SONS / OF ALBION⌊.⌋   [*4*]
</blockquote>

COLOURING: The BACKGROUND is Black in E.

Pl. 27. INCIPIT: 'To the Jews . . .'. DESIGN: The only decoration is a long-stemmed flowering plant between the two columns of the poem.

Pl. 28. INCIPIT: 'Jerusalem. / Chap. 2 . . .'. DESIGNS: Above the text is a huge, floating, six-petalled lotus on which a naked couple embraces, each with the left arm behind the partner's head and the right arm behind the partner's back. (A similar lotus is on *Vala* p. 24.)

In the right margin are four indeterminate, sea-shell-like creatures, including a starfish.

COLOURING: The SKY is partly Orange (E, Mellon pull); the PETALS are uncoloured (E) or Green (Mellon pull); the BACKGROUND is Yellow and

Brown (E) or Blue (Mellon pull); and the HAIR is Brown (E, Mellon pull [orangish-]).

VARIANTS: *State 1*: In the Morgan proof, a coil like hair or a worm appears below the buttock of the right-hand person; the right person's left leg is fairly clearly doubled over to the left of the left person; the division in the right person's buttocks to the right is fairly clear; the left person's left leg and the right person's right leg are invisible; and the right person's back is lumpishly muscular. The couple seem to be copulating.

(*N.B.* The Keynes & Wolf description of this plate is misleading.)

State 2: In all other copies, the worm, the left leg, the buttock-line, and heavy muscles of the right-hand person are removed, and a right leg is added to the right. The two persons seem to be sitting with their legs in opposite directions, the left person's to the left and the right one's to the right.

In copy E, a star was added above the left leaf, the hand on the left person's hip is invisible, and the right person's buttocks are clear.

Pl. 29. INCIPIT: 'Then the Divine Vision . . .'. DESIGN: By ll. 13–32 in the right margin, a nude woman stands with upraised arms, apparently in flames, and to the right of ll. 44–52 and 56–62 there seem to be two naked falling figures.

Pl. 30. INCIPIT: 'And the Two that escaped . . .'. DESIGNS: Above the text, a naked man at the right kneels and extends his upturned hands towards a nude, running woman, who apparently has butterfly wings, while behind her is another figure with bat wings on his arms and legs.

Below the text is a tendril with seven leaves.

COLOURING: The WINGS are Red and the BACKGROUND Yellow.

VARIANT: The wings of the central figure are extended behind the head of the man at the right in copy E.

Pl. 31. INCIPIT: 'His western heaven . . .'. DESIGN: Below the text to the right lies a nude woman enveloped in a web by another nude woman lying on her stomach with her left arm extended between her legs holding thread and her right hand above her head holding a spindle.

Pl. 32. INCIPIT: 'Leaning against the pillars . . .'. DESIGN: Below the text, two-thirds of the page is taken up by a lovely design of a woman in a long robe holding a mantle over her head as she looks at a nude woman with a nude girl on each side of her. To the right, a nude girl floats toward the sky, toward which she points; below her in the background is a Gothic church with waves in front of it; and to the left is a baroque dome surmounted by a cross. (The design is sketched on *Notebook* pp. 16, 76, 80; cf. pl. 81 for the figures and pl. 57, 84 for the buildings.)

COLOURING: The ROBE and MANTLE are light Blue (E, Preston pull), and the HAIR light Yellow (Preston pull); the SKY is partly dark Grey at the right (Preston pull) and the CLOUD yellowish-Green (E).

VARIANTS: In E, the domed building at the left is put in anew, the dome is raised, there is a turret on top of it, and its cross touches the mantle.

Pl. 33. INCIPIT: 'Turning his back to the Divine Vision . . .'. DESIGN: Between ll. 16 and 17 a ?naked, bearded man bends over a plough pulled by two oxen with bearded, human heads. In the background are low hills.

COLOURING: The MAN and BEASTS are Grey, the EARTH Brown.

Pl. 34. INCIPIT: 'Elevate into the Region of Brotherhood . . .'. DESIGN: After ll. 29–31 is a flying, nude woman.

Pl. 35. INCIPIT: 'Then the Divine hand . . .'. DESIGNS: About a third of the page, above the text, is taken up by a large, clothed figure with outstretched hands floating in flames. His hands and feet show stigmata.

To the right of the text are flames, and in another third of the page below the text is a design of a large naked man stretched out on the ground with his eyes shut as from his ribs emerges a naked person in flames looking upward. (A similar scene is on *All Religions are One* [?1788] pl. 5.)

COLOURING: The top MAN and top BACKGROUND are Grey; the bottom BACKGROUND is dark Green (E).

VARIANT: The stigmata are invisible on the man's hands in E.

Pl. 36. INCIPIT: 'Reuben returnd to his place . . .'. DESIGN: Above the text, a small naked man on the left kneels and swings a huge hammer with an enormous stroke towards a light-giving sphere resting on an anvil in the centre, while to the right another man runs away.

COLOURING: The left MAN is uncoloured, and the SUN is Orange.

Pl. 37. INCIPIT: 'And One stood forth . . .'. DESIGNS: Above the text, a third of the page is taken up by a naked man collapsed backwards in the arms of a kneeling clothed man with a nimbus. To the left there appears to be a palm-tree, to the right is the trunk of a huge oak-tree, and beneath the naked man's right foot is a circle with long, tapering wings. The scene evidently represents pl. 23, ll. 24–6: 'beneath the Palm tree & the Oak of weeping . . . Albion sunk Down in sick pale languor' into the arms of Jesus (see pl. 24, ll. 59–60, pl. 48, ll. 1–2).

To the right of the text are stars, while beneath it another third of the page is taken up by a huge, pterodactyl-like creature with outspread wings brooding over a rigidly outstretched woman who seems to be vegetating (cf. pl. 2). To the left is a blazing sun, and to the right is a crescent moon. (Analogous scenes are on *Visions* pl. 6 and *America* pl. 15 [pp. 470, 97]. Perhaps it represents a 'Spectre rising . . . insane, and most deform'd' (ll. 2, 4).

COLOURING: The bottom GLOBES are Yellow; the top GLOBE and its WINGS reddish; the FIGURES are yellowish-Brown, the SPECTRE reddish, and the SKY dark Blue.

VARIANTS: *State 1*: In l. 10, in place of 'blue' the Keynes proof reads 'pale'.

State 2: The copper was mended to make the word read 'blue' in all other copies, but in A 'blue' was restored in ink to 'pale'.

The catchword is covered in E.

NOTE: l. 1: The first six words are engraved (not etched) in intaglio, and the last four words are incised in White line (not raised in stereotype).

Pl. 38. INCIPIT: 'His face and bosom . . .'. DESIGN: In the left margin are intertwined lines like a vine or a heavy chain, and in the right margin are swirling lines which may include (by ll. 27–33) a kneeling woman and (by ll. 43–54) a falling woman turning into vegetation.

COLOURING: The FIGURES are pale Yellow.

VARIANT: ll. 40–3 in LC pl. 38ª are underlined in Red ink, there is a Red line above them, and two brackets in Red ink at each side, for reasons obscure to me.

Pl. 39. INCIPIT: 'By Satans Watch-fiends . . .'. DESIGNS: Above the text, a naked, bald, bearded man with bat wings sits a bounding horse (?with bat wings) as he aims a triple bow backwards towards the left. (A reversed sketch [*c.* 1800–5] for this plate on unwatermarked paper is in the Rosenwald Collection [reproduced in *Pencil Drawings*, ed. G. Keynes [1956], no. 28], and Sir Geoffrey Keynes has another possibly related sketch, according to Mr. Martin Butlin.)

Below the text is a large semicircle with spiky rays showing over the ?sea.

COLOURING: The MAN and HORSE are orangish-Pink; the SUN is Yellow; the BACKGROUND is dark Blue; and the SEA is dark Green.

Pl. 40. INCIPIT: 'Los shudderd at beholding Albion . . .'. DESIGN: In the top left margin are tendrils, and in the right margin are flourishing tendrils and leaves with (by ll. 16–26) a small naked man walking with outstretched arms (similar in position to Hand on pl. 26, though reversed) and raised head, and (by ll. 46–60) a nude woman reaching upward, apparently for grapes on a vine.

Pl. 41. INCIPIT: 'Bath who is Legions . . .'. DESIGN: Below the text, half the page is taken up with a design of a naked man seated with his head resting on a scroll on his knees.

The scroll unrolls to the left, and on it may be read in mirror-writing:

> Each Man is in / his Spectre's power
> Untill the arrival / of that hour,
> When his Humanity / awake
> And cast his Spectre / into the Lake⌊.⌋   [*4*]

Seated on the scroll at the bottom left is a small man with a pen in his right hand who seems to be reading it. (A sketch for this design on unwatermarked paper is in the Rosenwald Collection.)

NOTE: The poem was drafted on *Notebook* p. 12.

COLOURING: The bottom left MAN is uncoloured (E, Preston pull); the SCROLL is Yellow (E); the BACKGROUND is dark Blue (E); and the CLOUD behind the man is orangish-Blue (E).

Pl. 42. INCIPIT: 'Thus Albion sat . . .'. DESIGN: In the right margin is a column of seven naked figures supporting one another, the bottom one lying down, the next one kneeling with his hands behind his head, the next three standing on one another's shoulders, and the top two being women reaching for a huge bunch of grapes.

COLOURING: The GRAPES are Purple.

Pl. 43. INCIPIT: 'They saw their Wheels . . .'. DESIGN: In the right margin are swirling lines, perhaps representing clouds, and, by ll. 56–69, a clothed, kneeling figure with its hands clasped above its head.

Pl. 44. INCIPIT: 'With one accord . . .'. DESIGNS: Above the text are two angelic figures at the right, the left-hand one pointing to a light-giving, winged house on a moon-shaped boat riding on the waves.

Below the text is a long, open-mouthed snake (like those on pl. 72, 98) which turns into tendrils with berries at the right.

COLOURING: The ARK is pale Brown; the ark WINGS and ANGELS pale Blue; the SKY at left Black; and the SEA Grey.

VARIANT: In copy E, the ark is more boat-shaped and less moon-shaped, and the waves in front of it are suppressed.

Pl. 45. INCIPIT: 'Bath, healing City! . . .'. DESIGNS: Above the text at the right, a nude, long-haired figure floating over the sea on a cloud apparently holds a net which seems to be attached to a prone, naked man at the left with his head in his hands and his left leg in the air, who turns into bare, spiky branches.

In the right margin are a plant, three fishes, and an open-mouthed snake or eel, and between ll. 2 and 3 is a large fish into whose open mouth three smaller ones are swimming.

COLOURING: The FIGURES are pale Purple; the CLOUD is pale Yellow; and the top SKY is Black.

VARIANTS: *State 1*: l. 40 does not appear in the Morgan proof.
State 2: l. 40 is added in White line in copies A–J.

Pl. 46. INCIPIT: 'Bath, mild Physician . . .'. DESIGN: Below the text, almost half the page is devoted to a magnificent design of a bearded old man in a long robe and a woman with long hair seated at the right in a flaming chariot whose wheels and yoke are huge serpents and whose two bearded, man-headed oxen are ridden by tiny figures in the rough shapes of humans but with wings on arms, shoulders, and thighs, and with chicken heads (similar figures are on pl. 78 and *Vala* [?1796–?1807] p. 40). The oxen have single, curving horns, wreathed at the base, ending in hands; the near horn reaches back for a pen proffered by its gnome, while the far one stretches forward. (A similar colour print [1795] called 'God Judging Adam' [copies owned by the Tate Gallery, reproduced in the 1957 catalogue; by the Metropolitan Museum of New York; and by Mrs. William Tonner, both reproduced in the *Burlington Magazine*, C (1958), 40] shows God in a sphere of fire drawn to the left by ruddy horses resting his left hand on a book and stretching his right arm towards a naked man with bowed head.)

COLOURING: The RIDERS are yellowish-Orange; the OXEN are pale purplish-Blue; the WREATHS are Green; and the SERPENTS mottled Green and Black.

VARIANT: The woman may have a veil in E.

Pl. 47. INCIPIT: '& From Camberwell to Highgate . . .' at the top of the page is deleted. DESIGN: Between ll. 10 and 11, about two-thirds of the page is taken up by a design of a naked man on the right with his right foot on a rock, his hands to his head, and his torso twisted sharply from us. To the left are two nude women, the one on the left standing with her arms crossed over her head, and the one in the centre falling headlong with her left hand reaching upward.

COLOURING: The MAN is greyish (Preston pull); the left woman's HAIR is Blond and the right one's Brown (Preston pull); the ROCK is Yellow (E), and the BACKGROUND dark Blue (E) or Grey to Black (Preston pull).

Pl. 48. INCIPIT: 'These were his last words . . .'. DESIGN: In the right margin, by ll. 2–8, is a tiny, clothed, bending figure, and below are flying birds, bats, moths, and other insects.

VARIANT: The catchword is coloured over in D.

Pl. 49. INCIPIT: 'The secret coverts of Albion . . .'. DESIGN: In the right margin are long tendrils bearing a few leaves or fruit, and, after ll. 42–60, a naked man standing with his hands behind his head, looking upward.

Pl. 50. INCIPIT: 'The Atlantic Mountains . . .'. DESIGN: Below the text, a naked man sits on a rocky islet resting two of his three crowned heads on his hands. From his chest a naked, two-headed young man emanates to the left, while from the young man's chest in turn emanates another naked man to the right, who similarly engenders a fourth naked man. In the background are a circle like the earth and perhaps lightning to the left, and a moon, another earth-like circle, and a setting sun on the right.

COLOURING: The HAIR and CROWNS are Yellow, the ROCKS Brown with Green on top.

Pl. 51. DESIGN: The whole page is a sideways design of three figures in flames; the one at the left, in a long robe, is seated with her crowned head in her left hand and holding a sceptre headed with a fleur-de-lis in her right hand; the naked one in the centre squats with his head between his knees and his arms round his ankles; and the naked, bald man at the right walks to the right bearing chains from his wrists and ankles. (A sketch for it in the possession of Mr. David J. Black shows the same scene, reversed, with the addition on the left [corresponding to the right of pl. 51] of an extraordinary naked[?] man with flying hair crawling towards us—see the reproduction in *Blake Newsletter*, vii [1973], 6. The right-hand figure is similar to the one on the right of the colour print [1795] which Blake called 'The House of Death Milton [*PARADISE LOST, XI.* 477–93]' [copies in the Fitzwilliam Museum, the British Museum, and the Tate Gallery (reproduced in the 1971 Tate catalogue)], the chief differences being that the figure is reversed and has a dagger in his left hand rather than chains.) In the bottom left corner is Blake's monogram.

COLOURING: The FLAMES are dark Red, apparently emanating from the man at the right (E); the FLESH is dark reddish-Brown (E); the person's ROBE is Grey with Green (E) or Blue (National Gallery of Victoria pull); the central CLOUD is dark Blue (Victoria pull).

VARIANTS: The monogram does not appear in C and is apparently covered by wash in D–E.

In the Keynes copy, the figures are labelled from left to right 'Vala Hyle   Skofeld'.

Pl. 52. INCIPIT: 'To the Deists . . .'. DESIGN: The poem is written in two columns on either side of flourishing tendrils, with the seventh stanza beneath the others.

The poem was drafted in much more extensive form in the *Notebook*, p. 12, and many of the omitted stanzas, with a few duplicated ones, appear in 'The Grey Monk' in 'The Pickering [Ballads] Manuscript' (p. 342).

Pl. 53. INCIPIT: 'Jerusalem / Chap 3'. DESIGNS: Above the text, about half the page is taken up with a fine White-line design of a clothed woman seated on a curving throne on a huge floating sunflower-blossom with her chin on her hands and resting her elbows on her knees. She seems to have three crowns, one above another, and behind her is a canopy decorated with six stars on each side, on the left a crescent moon, and on the right a circle with regular intersections like a terrestrial globe (like that on pl. 12).

After ll. 4–10 there is a seated, clothed woman against whom a child is leaning, and after ll. 13–25 a naked figure plunges head downward to a nude woman reaching up to it.

COLOURING: The woman's DRESS is dark Blue (E) or Magenta (BMPR pull), her immediate BACKGROUND Red (E, BMPR [edges]), Blue (E, BMPR), and Yellow (E); the SUNFLOWER is Yellow (E) or Green (BMPR); the WATER is bluish-Black (E); and the BACKGROUND is Black (BMPR).

VARIANTS: *State 1*: The catchword 'The' is clear (BMPR pull).

State 2: The catchword is gone in all other copies.

ll. 8, 24 appear to be squeezed into stanza breaks.

Pl. 54. INCIPIT: 'In Great Eternity . . .'. DESIGNS: After ll. 1–8 and between ll. 8 and 9 are many birds, and between ll. 14 and 15 is a lumpy circle (like that on pl. 72) labelled in the centre: 'This World', at the top: 'Reason', at the right: 'Wrath', at the bottom: 'Desire', and at the left: 'Pity'. It is flanked by ten soaring, naked men, women, and children.

To the right of the remaining lines and below the text are many winged insects, and at the bottom are four male heads (cf. pl. 92), apparently all extending from the same neck, looking upward past five large stars.

COLOURING: The WORLD is Yellow.

Pl. 55. INCIPIT: 'When those who disregard . . .'.

Pl. 56. INCIPIT: 'Then Los heaved . . .'. DESIGN: The only decoration is a few lines in the right margin which seem to coalesce after ll. 12–13 and ll. 24–6 into cobwebs.

VARIANT: l. 37: 'earth-worm' is extended with a pen to 'earth-worms' in copy F (by Blake).

Pl. 57. INCIPIT: 'And the voices of Bath . . .'. DESIGNS: Above the text, two large, nude women with lines extending from their hands bend towards the right and look leftward. Over them is an arch, and around them are eleven large stars. They are walking or kneeling on part of a semicircle holding buildings including a dome like St. Paul's, labelled at each side 'York London'.

Below the text, a large, nude woman floats on her right side amid lines which seem to emanate from her body. (Her right leg, which is bent upward at the knee, seems to have been first represented as more nearly parallel to the left one.) Around her are three large stars, and above her in a segment of the circle interrupted above is a building with three pointed towers labelled 'Jerusalem'.

COLOURING: The ARCH is Orange and the EARTH Green.

VARIANT: The titles of the cities in the designs are coloured over and difficult to read in copy E.

Pl. 58. INCIPIT: 'In beauty the Daughters of Albion . . .'. DESIGNS: Between ll. 12 and 13 is a bat-winged vagina, with hair above.

Between ll. 43 and 44 is a prone skeleton amid flames which seem to lick up the right margin.

COLOURING: The VAGINA is Pink with some Blue; the HAIR above it is Brown; and the SKELETON is greyish-Green.

Pl. 59. INCIPIT: 'And formed into Four precious stones . . .'. DESIGN: Between ll. 21 and 22 are three clothed women beside two spinning wheels, the one at the left seated and the two at the right kneeling.

COLOURING: The women's DRESSES are, from left to right, Blue, pale Lavender, and pale Orange, and the BACKGROUND is Yellow.

Pl. 60. INCIPIT: 'The clouds of Albions Druid Temples . . .'. DESIGN: The only decoration apart from swirling lines is a nude woman kneeling with upraised, clasped hands after ll. 15–22.

Pl. 61. INCIPIT: 'Behold: in the Visions of Elohim Jehovah . . .'. DESIGN: The only decorations are flying birds in the right margin, between ll. 2 and 3, between ll. 13 and 14, between ll. 27 and 28, and between ll. 46 and 47.

VARIANT. l. 51: 'Garments' was written 'Garents', and an 'm' over a caret was faintly etched to correct it, and touched up in A and D.

Pl. 62. INCIPIT: 'Repose on me . . .'. DESIGN: Above the text is the tormented head of a giant apparently enwrapped in serpent coils and surrounded by peacock feathers with eyes in them: fingers show at the Black margin just above the text as if he is supporting himself by them.

Below the text are two huge, flaming feet, apparently of the same giant, and between them stands a tiny naked man with arms outspread. (Cf. *Vala* [?1796–?1807] p. 16, where is sketched a small figure looking at two enormous feet, and p. 31, ll. 9–10: 'I see not Luvah as of old⌊;⌋ I only see his feet Like pillars of fire travelling thro darkness & non entity'.)

COLOURING: The peacock FEATHERS are Green at the top left to Blue at the right, and the GROUND is Green.

VARIANT: The giant's tongue is clear in E.

Pl. 63. INCIPIT: 'Jehovah stood among the Druids . . .'. DESIGNS: Between ll. 23 and 24 on a cloud lies a nude, tormented woman wrapped in the coils of a huge worm. Above her calves is a crescent moon which gives off Black rays.

Between ll. 25 and 26, between ll. 31 and 32, between ll. 35 and 36, and between ll. 41 and 42 are many flying birds.

COLOURING: The MOON is Red and its RAYS Pink; the CLOUD is Blue with a Pink edge, and the SKY is Yellow.

Pl. 64. INCIPIT: 'Of the Mundane Shell . . .'. DESIGNS: Above the text, a clothed figure whose head gives off dark light sits on the ground with its head resting on what seems to be a low, Regency chair, while to the right two nude women holding a scroll or thread float toward the right in a cloud of light.

Below the text, a prone, bearded man with a long robe marks his place in a large open book with his right forefinger and looks upward to the left, as if at the irradiated dreamer above.

COLOURING: The top person's ROBE is pale Blue, his NIMBUS Yellow to Orange; the bearded man's ROBE is Orange; the CLOUD to the right is pale Green; and the GRASS at the bottom is, of course, Green.

Pl. 65. INCIPIT: 'To decide Two Worlds . . .'. DESIGN: The only decoration is a large chain (broken by ll. 6–8 and ll. 13–16) which dangles down the right margin.

Pl. 66. INCIPIT: 'In awful pomp & gold . . .' DESIGN: After ll. 21–39 is a small woman sitting on the back of a kneeling figure, and what appear to be flames lick up the entire margin.

Pl. 67. INCIPIT: 'By those who drink their blood . . .'. DESIGN: Below the text, a naked young man with a belt is stretched across the page on grass by chains fastened to gyves on his wrists and ankles. Above the chains are five flying birds.

COLOURING: The BACKGROUND is Purple.

Pl. 68. INCIPIT: 'O Skofield why art thou cruel? . . .'. DESIGN: The only decorations are a few flourishes and seven flying birds in the right margin.

Pl. 69. INCIPIT: 'Then all the Males . . .'. DESIGN: Below the text, a naked man is seated on the grass with arms outspread in a despairing attitude, and what appear to be gyves are on his wrists and ankles. On either side of him are nude women flourishing knives, the one at the left with a vague, dripping object somewhat like a scalp in her left hand, and the one at the right with what appears to be a cup in her left hand. Over the man is a crescent moon, over the right-hand woman are four large stars, and below her left arm are several large, dolmen-like rocks.

VARIANT: l. 1: 'conjoined' seems to have been altered in the copper from 'combined' and was restored to 'combined' in copy E.

Pl. 70. INCIPIT: 'And this the form of mighty Hand . . .'. DESIGN: On a hill between ll. 16 and 17 stands a giant cromlech framing clouds, a crescent moon, and three tiny figures on a road. Above it are tiny birds, and in the background are low hills.

COLOURING: The DOLMEN is pale Brown, and the MOON is a whole circle (not just a crescent) of Yellow.

VARIANT: The catchword was erased from copy A.

Pl. 71. INCIPIT: 'And above Albions Land . . .'. DESIGNS: In the right margin are flourishing tendrils with a few leaves.

Between ll. 49 and 50 a swan with outspread wings and lowered head looks to the right at a nude woman lying on her left elbow.

COLOURING: The SWAN is pinkish-Orange and the WOMAN Grey.

Pl. 72. INCIPIT: 'And the thirty-two Counties . . .'. DESIGNS: In the right margin are a few vague flames, emanating from between ll. 31 and 32, where there is a large, irregularly shaped circle (like the one labelled 'This World' on pl. 54) with vague objects on it, one in the centre rather like the continent of Africa. Coiling round it are the words 'Continually Buildin*g*, Continually decaying because of Love & Jealousy'. On each side amid the flames stand clothed, winged figures with their hands to their faces.

Below the text is an open-mouthed serpent, beneath which is written in mirror-writing: 'Women the comforters of Men become the Tormentors & Punishers'.

COLOURING: The WORLD is Yellow.

Pl. 73. INCIPIT: 'Such are Cathedron's golden Halls . . .'. DESIGN: Between ll. 21 and 22, a naked man squatting on his heels swings a hammer towards the sun which rests on oblong stones.

COLOURING: The SUN is Orange and the FORGE Black.

VARIANT: The sun's rays extend downward into the text in E.

Pl. 74. INCIPIT: 'The Four Zoa's clouded rage . . .'. DESIGNS: After ll. 3–14 and ll. 26–33 are soaring, nude women.

Below the text lies a naked man from whose head, hands, and genitals extend lines (coloured bloody Red in E), as if he were vegetating.

COLOURING: The SKY is a heavy Orange and the vegetating LINES a bloody Red.

Pl. 75. INCIPIT: 'And Rahab Babylon the Great . . .'. DESIGNS: Between ll. 9 and 10 is a series of eleven intersecting circles containing standing figures with spread wings, every alternate figure with wings raised so as not to interfere with its neighbours.

Below the text are a naked man (at the left) and a nude woman, both crowned, who seem to turn at the hips into serpents; they embrace large serpents with seven heads. The serpent embraced by the woman is marked with intersecting circles like those between ll. 9 and 10. Above her is a crescent moon.

COLOURING: The SERPENT-halves of the bottom figures are mottled Green, Pink, and Blue, and the bottom BACKGROUND is pale greenish-Yellow.

Pl. 76. DESIGN: The whole page is a splendid White-line design of a naked man with outspread arms and spread legs looking upward at the figure of Christ nailed to the forked branches of a huge tree. Christ has a large, vivid nimbus, to the left is a ?rising sun, and between and to the right of the worshipper's legs is written 'Albion Jesus'. The second word is faint and sometimes (e.g. F) invisible. (Erdman [p. 733] reports that '"Albion" is deleted in copies D E; "Jesus" in copies C D E F', but the obscurity appears to me to be the result of ineffective printing rather than deletion. 'Jesus' is certainly faintly visible in C.)

(A sketch for this design, *c.* 1780, reproduced in *Pencil Drawings* [1927] pl. 2, is in the V&A, with a sketch for 'Albion Rose' on the verso, and approximately the same design, reversed, but without the cross, Christ and his worshipper both standing, was used in Blake's ninetieth Dante design, *c.* 1824–7. A similar design is in the Bunyan series [?1824], no. xiv, reproduced in *Pilgrim's Progress* [1941]. In 'The Archangel Michael Foretelling the Crucifixion' for *Paradise Lost*, XII. 411–19 is a similar Christ, reversed, on a cross, with Adam standing naked with clasped hands to the right; there are three copies, one of 1807 [reproduced in C. Baker, *Catalogue of William Blake's Drawings and Paintings in the Huntington Library*, rev. R. R. Wark (1957), pl. xii], one of 1808 [in the Boston Museum, reproduced in M. R. Pointon, *Milton & English Art* (1970), 156], and one of 1822 [reproduced in the Fitzwilliam catalogue by D. Bindman, *William Blake* (1970), pl. 36].)

COLOURING: The BACKGROUND is Black.

VARIANT: Fruit has been added to the tree in water-colour in E, F.

Pl. 77. INCIPIT: 'To the Christians . . .'. DESIGN: To the right of the first poem, in front of regular vertical lines, a tiny clothed figure rolls up a ball which leads beneath the poem and above 'Devils are' at the left. (*Night Thoughts* design 362 represents a boy in a forest rolling up a ball of string.)

NOTE: The draft of this poem is on *Notebook* p. 46.

VARIANT: The bottom left and bottom right corners are covered by heavy inking in contemporary copies (A, C–F).

Pl. 78. INCIPIT: 'Jerusalem, C 4 . . .'. DESIGNS: Above the text, a naked, rooster-headed man sits on a rock beside the sea with his beak on his left hand and looks at a huge ?rising sun below the title.

In the right margin are large tendrils, and between ll. 20 and 21 are two tiny flying birds.

COLOURING: The BEAK is Yellow, the COMB Red, the SUN a heavy yellowish-Brown, the RAYS from the sun Red, and the SKY Black.

Pl. 79. INCIPIT: 'My tents are fall'n . . .'. DESIGN: In the right margin are leaves, two flying birds, and a bunch of grapes.

COLOURING: The BIRDS are Green, the GRAPES reddish.

Pl. 80. INCIPIT: 'Encompassd by the frozen Net . . .'. DESIGN: In the right margin are three nude women with worms coiled round them.

COLOURING: The WORMS are Pink.

Pl. 81. INCIPIT: 'I have mockd those . . .'. DESIGN: Between ll. 14 and 15, about two-thirds of the page is taken up by a design of a nude woman with her hair in a bun; her left hand is 'Upon her back behind her loins' (as

Gwendolen's is in pl. 82, l. 21) and her right hand points to mirror-writing on a cloud to the left which reads:

> In Heaven the only Art of Living
> Is Forgetting & Forgiving
> Especially to the Female
> But if you on Earth Forgive
> You shall not Find where to Live⌊.⌋   [5]

(The last two lines are written in a solid Black part of the margin and may be an afterthought.) Gwendolen is facing another nude woman with her hand on her breasts and her left hand on her vagina, while behind her ten nude women float up from her feet. (Gwendolen and Cambel are sketched, reversed, on *Vala* [?1796–?1807] p. 33.)

COLOURING: The BACKGROUND is Blue, the CLOUD White.

VARIANT: In copy E, the central woman has her fingers and thumb extended and not, as in other copies, on her vagina.

Pl. 82. INCIPIT: 'I have heard Jerusalems groans . . .'. DESIGN: The only design is a long worm in the right margin, and perhaps a trace of flame.

Pl. 83. INCIPIT: 'Corruptibility appears upon thy limbs . . .'. DESIGN: In the right margin are clouds on which are a small naked figure and a tiny figure.

Pl. 84. INCIPIT: 'Highgates heights & Hampstead . . .'. DESIGN: Below the text, a small boy leads a bearded old man leaning on crutches to the left past a brick wall (at the right), a domed church (London), and a Gothic church (Jerusalem). (The foreground is echoed, reversed, from 'London' in *Experience* [1794] pl. 46.)

COLOURING: The CLOTHES are greyish-Blue, and the HAIR of both the old man and the boy White.

VARIANTS: There is no White ground under the figures in C.

A Gold sun with Red rays ?rises above the church in the left margin in E.

Pl. 85. INCIPIT: 'Became a Space & an Allegory . . .'. DESIGNS: Between ll. 21 and 22 is a branch with leaves.

Below the text at the right kneels a nude woman holding in her hands tendrils with leaves and grapes, which she draws from the right margin and, apparently, from the side of the naked man kneeling to the left. In the background are clouds, a crescent moon, two stars—one trailing rays—and a series of concentric circles giving off eight rays, perhaps the sun.

COLOURING: The HAIR is White, the GRAPES Green, the SUN Yellow, the SKY round it Peach and below it Magenta, and the CLOUD Pink.

VARIANT: There is no White ground at the bottom in C.

Pl. 86. INCIPIT: 'I see thy Form . . .'.

Pl. 87. INCIPIT: 'Repelling weeping Enion . . .'. DESIGN: Above the text, half the page is a design divided into sections by quarters of four contiguous circles. A woman (Enion) in a long dress runs stooping from the lower left one after two naked children (Los and Enitharmon) in the lower right and upper right sections. (The scene is sketched, reversed and slightly altered, in *Vala* [?1796–?1807] p. 9.) In the upper left section is a naked, bearded man with spread arms and legs, and in the lower left, behind the woman, is a head.

COLOURING: The woman's DRESS is pale Yellow, the two FIGURES behind her are Grey, and the BACKGROUND is Grey and Brown.

Pl. 88. INCIPIT: 'Los answerd sighing . . .'. DESIGN: The only decoration, besides vague wavy lines, represent flying birds between ll. 1 and 2 and in the right margin.

Pl. 89. INCIPIT: 'Tho divided by the Cross . . .'. DESIGN: In the right margin are a plant at the bottom, birds, and a small figure reaching up to take a huge ?crown from a clothed figure plunging downward from the top corner.

COLOURING: The top person's DRESS is yellowish-Green, and the person below is Lavender.

Pl. 90. INCIPIT: 'The Feminine separates . . .'. DESIGN: The only decoration is tendrils in the right margin.

Pl. 91. INCIPIT: 'It is easier to forgive an Enemy . . .'. DESIGN: In the right margin are swirls, perhaps representing leaves, and below the text lies a small naked man from whom lines extend to two circles on either side, that on the right like a ball of rope, and that on the left with a six-pointed Star of David over it.

COLOURING: The STAR is yellowish-Green.

Pl. 92. INCIPIT: 'What do I see! . . .'. DESIGN: Between ll. 10 and 11, half the page is taken up with the design of a large woman in a clinging dress inscribed at the right 'Jerusalem' who sits on the ground from which the heads of four men emerge (cf. pl. 54), that in front of her representing a bearded, old man. In the background are two or more tiny cromlechs.

NOTE: Erdman (p. 733) observed that the text of ll. 1–26 underlies the design on pl. 95; l. 27, which does not appear there, is in effect an addition.

COLOURING: The woman's DRESS is very pale Yellow, and the SKY behind her Pink.

Pl. 93. INCIPIT: 'Enitharmon heard . . .'. DESIGNS: Above the text, three naked men, with their left knees on the ground and right knees raised, point with their right index fingers to the right. Their names are on their backs, their thoughts on Lycon's right thigh, and the opinion of Caiaphas on the left thigh of Melitus, as follows: 'Anytus⌊,⌋ / Melitus / & Lycon / thought Socrates / a Very Pernicious / man⌊.⌋ / So Cai[a]phas / thought Jesus'.

Below the text is a nude woman who seems to be lying slightly below ground-level amid flames which lick up the right margin.

VARIANTS: In C, the top left is solid Black over the men, with no lines.

In copy E, the colouring has almost obscured the lettering on the figures at the top.

Pl. 94. INCIPIT: 'Albion cold lays on his Rock . . .'. DESIGNS: Above the text, two or more naked men lie with their heads back on the ground, with lines extending from them to the left margin.

Below the text, a clothed figure lies prostrate as if in despair over the stiff body of a bearded old man stretched across the page. (The design was first etched in the middle of pl. 95, and similar designs are on *America* [1793] pl. 2 and *Milton* [1804–?8] pl. 38.) In the background is a low hill surmounted by a cromlech, behind which are the rays of a ?rising sun.

COLOURING: The bottom FIGURES and STONES are Grey, the EARTH is dark greenish-Brown, the SUN is Gold, and its RAYS Red.

VARIANTS: In copy C, there are no stones, and there is solid Black over the figures' feet as high as the text.

In copy E, what looks like a dolmen in uncoloured copies has its opening coloured stone-Grey, as if it were solid stone, rather than the Blue of the sky or the Pink of the sunrise.

Pl. 95. INCIPIT: 'Her voice pierc'd Albions clay cold ear . . .'. DESIGN: Above the text, half the page is taken up by a man squatting in flames as he rests his left hand on a rock and raises his right to the top right corner. (At the bottom right show the feet of the corpse on pl. 94, and his head may be dimly seen at the left [clearly in copy E]; the design on pl. 94 was first etched on this plate and then deleted ineffectively.)

COLOURING: The FLAMES, scarcely coloured, are a creamy-Blue. The lines between the man's legs, which in uncoloured copies might be taken for flames, are flesh-Pink in the only coloured copy (E).

VARIANT: A worm was added at the bottom of the text in E.

Pl. 96. INCIPIT: 'As the Sun & Moon lead forward . . .'. DESIGN: ll. 1–25 are curtailed, because of the design at the right, two-thirds of the height of the page, representing a bearded man in a long robe embracing a nude woman.

COLOURING: The COUPLE are Orange and Pink, the BACKGROUND pale Grey.

Pl. 97. INCIPIT: 'Awake! Awake Jerusalem . . .'. DESIGN: Below the text, about two-thirds of the page is taken up by a splendid design of a naked man carrying a large circle (related to that on pl. 1) in his left hand as he takes an enormous stride across the grass toward the left and raises his right arm over his head. The circle gives off huge rays of light which almost obscure two stars and a crescent moon.

(A very similar sketch for Young's *Night Thoughts* [c. 1796], Night I, p. 6 [BMPR] substitutes a staff for the globe and adds a coffin at the right and, overhead, kites flown by two boys at the left. A reversed sketch of c. 1818 for this *Jerusalem* design [BMPR; 20·9 × 24·1 cm; watermark invisible; reproduced in *Pencil Drawings* (1927), pl. 39] shows a man in trousers striding through a mountain pass with a staff in his right hand; it is labelled across the sky 'Journey of Life'.)

COLOURING: His HAIR is Brown, the GLOBE Pink at the centre and Yellow at the edges, and the SKY is vividly Yellow and Black.

VARIANTS: The light to the left and below the globe is gone in C.

The man is given long, transparent shorts in copy E (cf. *Milton* [1804–?8], pl. 29, 33).

Pl. 98. INCIPIT: 'Then each an Arrow flaming . . .'. DESIGNS: Above the text are the coils of a large, open mouthed serpent (cf. pl. 44, 72).

Between ll. 15 and 16 are flying birds, in the right margin are branches and birds, and between ll. 55 and 56 are many birds and, from left to right, a snail, a toad, a butterfly, a caterpillar, a spider, a moth, and a large worm.

COLOURING: The SERPENT is Grey, the WORM reddish-Brown.

VARIANT: l. 45: 'the Coven[an]t of Jehovah' was altered in ink to 'Thy Covenant Jehovah' in copy F.

Pl. 99. INCIPIT: 'All Human Forms identified . . .'. DESIGN: Below the text, nine tenths of the page is taken up by a design of a bearded old man, in a long robe and with an enormous halo, pressing to him the loins of a nude woman with open arms. In the background are enveloping flames.

COLOURING: The whole page is very dark; the nude WOMAN is reddish-Brown, the man's ROBE is Grey, his HALO dark Blue, the flames at the top Grey, and the rest Orange and Red.

VARIANT: The bottom left corner is Black in C.

Pl. 100. DESIGN: The entire page is a dark sideways design of a naked man holding a great hammer in his right hand and fire-tongs in his left. On the left, a naked figure seems to carry the sun on its shoulder away from us, and on the right a nude woman with upraised arms holds in her left hand something like a spindle and in her right lines from which depend a crescent moon. In the sky are stars, and below them are a series of cromlechs in a circle in the centre extending in symmetrical looped wings on each side.

COLOURING: The STONES are orangish-Grey, the SUN and MOON Yellow, and the SKY Black.

VARIANTS: In copy E, Yellow rays extend across the plate from the sun, and a bloody thread extends from the woman's spindle to her right hand and drips from there on to the moon. Two extra stars have been added above her left arm, one extra within the crescent of four stars to her left, and two more above her.

COPY A: BINDING: (1) Mounted on stubs and bound when received at the British Museum in 1847 in dark Green half morocco over marbled boards, g.e.; (2) the leaves were remounted in heavy paper 'windows' and bound in Red morocco in 1969.

HISTORY: (1) On 11 Aug. 1827 (the day before Blake died), 'Mr [*William Young*] Ottley [*gave Linnell £5. 5s.*] for Mrs Blake for a copy of Jerusalem' (*Blake Records* [1969], 594, 341, 347), perhaps this copy; Young's copy ('*one hundred engravings from wood*') was sold at Sotheby's, 21 July 1837, lot 306, for £3. 18s. to Bohn; (2) This may have been the copy purchased from W. Evans on 18 March 1847 by the BRITISH MUSEUM PRINT ROOM, which put it into a BM binding; reproduced in colour microfilm by Micro Methods Ltd.

COPY B: BINDING: (1) Originally stabbed through three holes, 14·2 cm from the top, 4·2, 4·3 cm apart; (2) Later bound about 1821 (the date on three fly-leaves) in a Roxburghe binding with *America* (G) and *Europe* (B) (which have quite different patterns of stab holes), the spine gilt with 'AMERICA / — / EUROPE / — / JERUSALEM / — / BY / BLAKE'; (3) Disbound in June 1966.

HISTORY: The History is as in *America* (G), p. 102.

COPY C: BINDING: Bound, probably about 1824 for John Linnell, in White vellum to match Linnell's *America* (O), *Marriage* (H), *Europe* (K), and *Songs* (R), the spine gilt with 'JERUSALEM'; the spine was mended in 1931 at the British Museum and given White morocco hinges.

HISTORY: (1) Bought by John Linnell (Chapter 2[1] on 30 Dec. 1819 for 14s., the 'Balance' on 4 Feb. 1821 for 15s.—see *Blake Records* [1969], 581, 585), who had it bound, and sold posthumously at Christie's, 15 March 1918, lot 194, for £89 to Edwards; (2) Acquired before 1921 by Frank Rinder, whose wife lent it to the exhibitions of the Burlington Fine Arts Club (1927), no. 88, and the British Council (Tate, 1947, no. 41), it was inherited by their daughter (3) *Mrs. Ramsey Harvey*; one Blake Trust facsimile (1952, 1955) was made from this volume.

COPY D: BINDING: (1) Originally stabbed through three holes, 10·5 cm from the top, 4·1 and 5·0 cm apart; (2) Evidently later bound, for the edges are gilt; (3) Disbound evidently for E. W. Hooper before the Boston exhibition (1891), and now each plate is loose and mounted; there is one Black framing-line round each plate.

HISTORY: (1) This may be the copy sold at 'Sotheby, Dec. 1854, 4*l* 16s' (according to W. T. Lowndes, *The Bibliographer's Manual of English Literature* [1857], i. 216)—it could alternatively be copies F, H, or J; (2) It was evidently bought at auction by the dealer John Pearson for £100,[2] used for his facsimile (of 1877, according to a note by Hooper in copy D) and sold by Pearson (according to the note) to (3) Edwin William Hooper, who lent it to the Boston exhibition (1891), no. 8a; (4) It was lent anonymously to the Philadelphia exhibition (1939), no. 113 (unbound), and given in his memory by his daughters Mrs. John Briggs Potter, Mrs. Ward Thoron, Mrs. Bancel Lafarge, Mrs. Greeley Stevenson Curtis, and Mrs. Roger Sherman Warner (according to the book-plate) on 1 July 1941 to (5) HARVARD.

COPY E: BINDING: (1) Mounted on stubs and bound by 1863 with Tatham's 'Life of Blake' (?1832) on paper watermarked 'J WHATMAN / TURKEY MILL / 183[2?]' and portraits of Blake and of his wife in dark Green morocco, g.e.; all plates have one Red framing-line, and pl. 1–2 have decorated borders; (2) Disbound in 1948 to allow the facsimile to be made, and rebound, as before, by Gray & Son of Cambridge (according to Keynes in *William Blake*, ed. A. H. Rosenfeld [1969], 415–16).

HISTORY: (1) Acquired by Frederick Tatham, probably at the death of Catherine Blake in 1831; Tatham evidently wrote his 'Life of Blake' (?1832)

---

[1] Chapter 2, evidently the first one printed, is the only one in which all the leaves are watermarked before 1820.

[2] Pearson's Catalogue 58 (?1884) contains an advertisement for his facsimile of *Jerusalem* (1877) made from this copy, the original of which he says 'cost at an auction £100'; no such auction is known, and the price seems enormous—compare the nineteenth-century sales of copies A, D, E, G, I.

to recommend the sale of *Jerusalem* (E) (*Blake Records* [1969], 507), and this Life plus the drawings of William and Catherine have been bound with the volume since the first clear record of it in 1887; (2) Sold posthumously for George Blamire at Christie's, 6 Nov. 1863, lot 213, for £50. 8s. to Daniels; (3) Sold anonymously at Christie's, 1 June 1887, lot 255, for £166 to Quaritch; (4) It 'was bought by me [*Archibald Stirling*] from Quaritch about 1893' (according to a note of 12 Feb. 1922 signed A. S. on the second fly-leaf), and lent to the Burlington Fine Arts Club exhibition (1927), no. 89; (5) Acquired by his son William Stirling, who apparently allowed it to be used for the Blake Trust facsimile (1951), and sold it in 1952 through Scribner's (according to Keynes & Wolf) to (6) Mr. *Paul Mellon*, who lent it to the Washington exhibition (1957).

COPY F: BINDING: 'BOUND BY F. BEDFORD' in Red straight grain morocco, t.e.g., pl. 51, 100 bound wrong side out, in the order of the 1877 facsimile (1–100), not of the numbers; (2) After 1906 the extra pl. 28, 45, 56 were mounted on larger leaves and tipped in.

HISTORY: (1) Acquired by the dealer James Toovey, who added his 'BURNHAM ABBEY BUCKS' book-plate and sold it[1] in 1899 to (2) The PIERPONT MORGAN LIBRARY.

N.B. The extra pl. 28, 45, 56, which Keynes & Wolf describe with copy F, came later with *Thel* (a), and had no prior connection with copy F.

COPY G: BINDING: Perhaps bound in Olive morocco extra, g.e.

HISTORY: (1) Perhaps this is the copy in Olive morocco extra,[2] g.e., sold with the Library of the late Francis Bedford at Sotheby's, 21 March 1884, lot 120, for £5. 12s. 6d. to Quaritch; (2) Acquired before 1921 by Felix Isman, who evidently reported to Keynes & Wolf on 2 March 1939 that it was 'somewhere in storage'; twenty-five years later his widow 'has no recollection of having seen a copy of *Jerusalem* in their library', and 'it was not in the library when he died [*in 1943*]';[3] (3) *UNTRACED*—perhaps a ghost.

COPY H: BINDING: Bound, probably in 1833 for Samuel Boddington, in Yellow morocco heavily tooled and gilt, g.e., in a way similar to Boddington's *Europe* (M), the spine with a Red label gilt sideways with 'JERUSALEM. W. BLAKE. 1804'; the plates are still stitched together, but they have pulled free of the binding.

HISTORY: (1) Acquired (perhaps about 1833 from Tatham—see *For the Sexes* [D], p. 202) by Samuel Boddington, who may have had it bound about 1833 and added his book-plate;[4] (2) Acquired by Charles Fairfax Murray,

---

[1] According to Keynes & Wolf, it was sold by 'his son, Charles J. Toovey, in 1899', but it is listed (with 100 plates) in the *Catalogue of a Collection of Books* formed by James Toovey principally from the library of the Earl of Gosford the property of J. Pierpont Morgan (1901). Toovey may have taken pl. 40 'from another copy' (as it is marked) and added it to copy F.

[2] Keynes & Wolf suggest that this is copy H, but since H is in contemporary Yellow morocco, and all other traceable copies have similar irreconcilable features, copy G seems most likely, if it is not a ghost.

[3] D. V. Erdman, 'The Suppressed and Altered Passages in Blake's *Jerusalem*', *Studies in Bibliography*, xvii (1964), 42.

[4] Not 'Sold at Sotheby's, November 1895' (as in Keynes & Wolf), or at Thomas Boddington's sale (4–7 Nov.) or at any other time, so far as I can discover.

who had it described in his library catalogue (1899), added his book-plate, and gave it in July 1912 to (3) The FITZWILLIAM MUSEUM.

COPY I: BINDING: Bound after March 1852 for R. M. Milnes (by Leighton,[1] according to Keynes [1921]) in Red morocco with the Milnes Golden wheatsheaf on the cover, g.e.

HISTORY: (1) Sold anonymously with the Collection of Thomas Butts (see *Songs* [E], p. 414) at Sotheby's, 26 March 1852, lot 57, for £10. 15s. to R. M. M.; (2) Bound with the wheatsheaf design of R. M. Milnes on the cover, and sold by his son the Earl of Crewe at Sotheby's, 30 March 1903, lot 15, for £83 to Quaritch for (3) 'W. A. White 20 Apl 1903', 'Earl of Crew Sale B Quaritch' (according to the notes on the fly-leaf), who lent it to the exhibitions of the Grolier Club (1905), no. 32 (anonymously), and (1919), no. 16 (anonymously) and to that in the Fogg (1924); sold after his death through Rosenbach on 1 May 1929 to (4) Mr. LESSING J. ROSENWALD.

COPY J: BINDING: Bound probably for James Vine (whose *Thel* [O], *Milton* [D], and *Songs* [V] are in similar bindings) in contemporary Brown half russia over Brown marbled boards, g.e., with the spine lettered sideways like the leather label on the front cover, 'BLAKE's / JERUSALEM'; on pl. 13–15, 17–22, 24, 27–8 are marginal comments in pencil, e.g. 'East [*is*] the Holy or Internal' (pl. 14).

HISTORY: (1) Acquired by James Vine, who may have made the extensive marginal notes, and for whom it was sold posthumously at Christie's, 24 April 1838, lot 298, '*h.b.*' (half bound) for £2. 17s. to H. Bohn; (2) Offered with other Blakes from the Vine sale by Henry G. Bohn (1841), lot 176 (half bound) for £5. 5s.; (3) Offered by C. J. Sawyer (June 1928) (according to Keynes & Wolf); (4) Acquired by Cortlandt Bishop, who added his book-plate, and sold it at American Art Association, 5 April 1938, lot 280, for $2,700 to Sessler; (5) Acquired by Mr. *Charles J. Rosenbloom*, who added his book-plate.

Pl. 1: BINDING: Loose, mounted.

HISTORY: (1) Acquired by Mr. Dick, with whose collection it went about 1917 to (2) The METROPOLITAN MUSEUM, New York.

Pl. 1: BINDING: Loose.

HISTORY: The History is as in *Europe* pl. 2, printed on its verso; see p. 162.

Pl. 3: BINDING: Loose.

HISTORY: (1) Lent by H. H. Gilchrist to the Pennsylvania Academy of the Fine Arts exhibition (1891), no. 152; (2) *UNTRACED.*

Pl. 4, 18–19, 28, 35, 37: BINDING: Mounted on one sheet in windows, showing, on the recto, pl. 4 at the top, pl. 19 in the middle, pl. 28 at the bottom.

HISTORY: (1) Perhaps these were the three or four plates including 'Jerusalem, chap. 2' (pl. 28) lent by A. Macmillan to the Burlington Fine Arts Club exhibition (1876), no. 270; (2) These are probably the copies sold posthumously for H. Buxton Forman at Anderson Galleries, 15 March 1920,

---

[1] John Leighton flourished as a binder 1813–30; either Milnes added only his crest to a Leighton binding, or John Leighton did not bind it; or it was bound by a different Leighton.

lot 67 (six coloured *Jerusalem* plates on three leaves, including a title [?pl. 4, 28]), for $610 to G. D. Smith; (3) Acquired by Arthur F. Egner, and inherited by his daughter (4) *Mary E. Malone*.

Pl. 5, 53: BINDING: (1) Once stabbed with pl. 9, 11 (below) through five holes, 10·6 cm from the top, 5·8, 2·1, 3·1, 2·1 cm apart, perhaps with 144 other leaves of Blakeana in an extra-illustrated Gilchrist (1863); (2) Loose and mounted since 1906.

HISTORY: (1) Perhaps bound with 144 other Blake prints and drawings in the extra-illustrated 1863 Gilchrist (see *For the Sexes* pl. 15, p. 205) offered by John Pearson, Catalogue 58 (?1884), lot 363, for £52. 10s.; (2) Pl. 5, 53 were lent by H. P. Horne to the Carfax exhibition (1904), no. 26, and sold by Carfax & Co. on 19 July 1906 for £60 to (3) The BRITISH MUSEUM PRINT ROOM.

Pl. 6: BINDING: Loose, mounted.

HISTORY: (1) Acquired by 'Mr. Evans, Strand' (according to A. Gilchrist, *Life of William Blake* [1863], ii. 207, no. 49), who may have sold it to (2) Horace Elisha Scudder, who lent it to the Boston exhibitions (1880), no. 5, (1891), no. 8b, and from whom it passed (according to Mr. Balch below) to his granddaughter (3) Mrs. Ingersolle Bowditch (*née* Sylvia Scudder), who gave it to her great-niece's husband (4) Mr. Franklin Balch, who sold it in 1966 to (5) Mr. Richard Cole, from whom it passed to his widow (6) Deborah, who is now (1971) *Mrs. Jack Greenberg*.

Pl. 8: BINDING: See *Europe* (c), p. 161.

HISTORY: For its History with *Europe* (c), see the 'Order' of the *Songs*, p. 340.

Pl. 9, 11: BINDING: (1) Once stabbed with pl. 5, 53 (above) through five holes, 11·0 cm from the top, 5·7, 2·2, 3·1, and 2·1 cm apart, perhaps with the Gilchrist (1863); (2) Loose and mounted since 1899.

HISTORY: (1) Once stabbed with pl. 5, 53 above, perhaps with the Gilchrist; (2) Offered for sale in an unidentified catalogue for £7. 7s. (a clipping from it accompanied the plates, and pl. 11 is marked '7 gns'); (3) Bought in 1899 by the VICTORIA & ALBERT MUSEUM.

Pl. 9, 19–20, 38ᵃ⁻ᵇ, 48, 50, 78: BINDING: (1) Pl. 9, 48 were inlaid to size, and all the plates were bound about 1853 with many leaves of Blakeana including the 'Order' of the *Songs*; (2) Separated after 1924, and bound, probably by Macdonald by 1927 for G. C. Smith, Jr., in Blue morocco with *Europe* pl. 18ᵃ⁻ᵇ.

HISTORY: For the History, see the 'Order' of the *Songs*, p. 341.

Pl. 24: BINDING: See *Europe* pl. 2, p. 162.

HISTORY: For the History, see *Europe* pl. 2 with which it is printed.

Pl. 25, 32, 41, 47: BINDING: See *Europe* pl. 1ᵃ⁻ᵇ, 2ᵃ⁻ᵇ, p. 161.

HISTORY: (1) These are probably the 'Detached Specimens of an original illuminated Poem, entitled "*Jerusalem . . .*"' listed in the *Catalogue of the Fifth Annual Exhibition by the Associated Painters in Water Colours* (1812), no. 324;[1] (2) If

---

[1] Pl. 4, 18–19, 28, 35, 37 (Mrs. Malone), pl. 5, 53 (BMPR), pl. 9, 11 (Victoria & Albert), pl. 24 (Crawford), pl. 28, 30, 35 (Mellon), pl. 51 (Keynes, Melbourne) might have been in-

so, they were probably disposed of abruptly, for 'the landlord siezed the contents of the gallery in distraint of rent';[1] they seem to have passed in 1827[2] from Blake[2] to his widow[2] and on her death in 1831 to (3) Frederick Tatham,[1] who may have sold them anonymously at Sotheby's, 29 April 1862, lot 191 (five 'subjects from his published works, *highly finished in colours*'), for 8s. to (4) Col. Weston, from whom they were inherited by (5) Miss Nora Hunter,[2] who gave them in 1957 to (6) Kerrison Preston, who described them in his catalogue (1960), no. 13, lent them to the National Library of Scotland exhibition (1969), no. 65, allowed them to be reproduced in the facsimile of *Jerusalem* (B) (1974), and for whom they were sold posthumously at Sotheby's, 21 March 1974, lots 18–21, to (7a) W. R. Cummings (pl. 25, £7,000; pl. 32, £12,000; pl. 41, £13,000) for The NATIONAL GALLERY OF ART, Canberra, Australia, and to (7b) *H. Moss* (pl. 47, £11,000).

Pl. 28: BINDING: Loose, mounted.

HISTORY: (1) Perhaps it was among the thirty leaves of Blakeana (see *Urizen* pl. 9, p. 185) sold anonymously at Sotheby's, 24 Feb. 1897, lot 809, to Quaritch; (2) Sold posthumously with the Collection of Stopford Brooke at Sotheby's, 27 July 1917, lot 795; (3) Acquired by Frank Rinder, and inherited by his daughter (4) *Mrs. Ramsey Harvey*.

Pl. 28, 35: BINDING: Mounted, framed.

HISTORY: (1) Perhaps this is the untitled coloured *Jerusalem* plate lent by H. E. Scudder to the Boston exhibition (1880), no. 85; (2) Probably acquired by W. A. White, lent anonymously with the rest of his collection to the Grolier Club exhibition (1905), no. 33, and sold posthumously in 1929 with other Blakes to (3) A. S. W. Rosenbach,[3] who sold the leaf in Nov. 1952 to (4) Mr. Rabinowitz, whose widow, as Mrs. Lester Albert LeWars, sold it through Mr. Robert Barry, Jr., of Stonehill's in 1970 to (5) Mr. *Paul Mellon*.

Pl. 28, 45, 56: BINDING: Tipped into *Jerusalem* (F).

HISTORY: The History is as in *Thel* (a), p. 131.

N.B. These plates were tipped into *Jerusalem* (F) after they were acquired for the Morgan Library (after 1906); they had nothing previously to do with that copy, despite the impression given by Keynes & Wolf.

Pl. 30: BINDING: See *Europe* pl. 1, p. 161.

HISTORY: The History is as in *Europe* pl. 1 (Mellon), on the verso of which it is printed.

Pl. 35: BINDING: Loose.

HISTORY: (1) Acquired, probably from Frederick Tatham about 1834

---

cluded among those exhibited in 1812; uncoloured plates, or plates from completed copies, seem less likely.

[1] J. L. Roger, *History of the Old Water Colour Society* (1891), i. 271.

[2] Geoffrey Keynes, ed., *Jerusalem* (B) (1974) gives little evidence for these conclusions; in particular, he does not give the lot number or the price of the 1862 sale or state the relationship of Miss Hunter to Col. Weston.

[3] This is the leaf mistakenly described as consisting of *Jerusalem* pl. 28–9 'now in the possession of the Rosenbach Company' by Keynes & Wolf (1953, p. 111).

(like the 'Nelson' drawing and *Europe* pl. 6), by (2) John Defett Francis, who gave it in 1876 to (3) The town of Swansea, where it was housed about 1966 in the GLYNN VIVIAN GALLERY.

Pl. 37, 100: BINDING: Loose.
HISTORY: For the History, see *Marriage* pl. 3–4 (Keynes), p. 301.

Pl. 50–1, 99: BINDING: Loose.
HISTORY: For the History, see the 'Order' of the *Songs*, p. 341.

Pl. 51: BINDING: Mounted, framed.
HISTORY: (1) Acquired by Francis Harvey;[1] (2) Perhaps this is the coloured copy lent to the Burlington Fine Arts Club exhibition (1876), no. 108, and sold by George Smith at Christie's, 16 July 1880, lot 100, for 12s. to Baker; (3) Acquired by E. Parsons;[1] (4) Acquired by W. Graham Robertson on 14 Jan. 1911,[1] reproduced in D. Figgis, *The Paintings of William Blake* (1925), pl. 93, lent to the exhibitions of the Tate (1947), no. 84, and the Bournemouth Arts Club (1949), no. 44, described in his catalogues (1920), (1952), no. 137, and sold posthumously at Christie's, 22 July 1949, lot 88, for £46. 4s. to Dunn for (5) *Geoffrey Keynes*, who lent it to the British Museum exhibition (1957), no. 30 1, and described it in his catalogue (1964), no. 523.

Pl. 51: BINDING: Loose, mounted.
HISTORY: (1) Probably this is the unidentified design, of exactly the size of *Jerusalem* pl. 51, lent by Linnell and his trustees to the exhibitions of the Burlington Fine Arts Club (1876), no. 27, the National Gallery (1913), no. 101, Manchester (1914), no. 77, Nottingham (1914), no. 63, the National Gallery of Scotland (1914), no. 46, and sold at Christie's, 15 March 1918, lot 158 (described as a water-colour) for £73. 10s. to Martin; (2) Acquired by the Felton Bequest for (3) The NATIONAL GALLERY OF VICTORIA, Melbourne, Australia, which received it on 13 March 1920.

Pl. 74: BINDING: See *Europe* pl. 2, p. 162.
HISTORY: The History is as in *Thel* (a), p. 131.

76

*Jerusalem: The Emanation of the Giant Albion [D], 1804. [London, 1877.]
A facsimile. The publisher, who is not given, was evidently Andrew Chatto, whose ledgers (now with the firm of Chatto & Windus, transcribed by my friend Morton Paley, who generously brought them to my attention) record an order on 17 Nov. 1877 for printing 100 sets of 'Blake reproductions' and binding them on 26 Jan. 1878 by Sotheran at a total cost of £139. 10s.

77

Jerusalem. Ed. E. R. D. Maclagen and A. G. B. Russell. London, 1904. The Prophetic Books of William Blake. Cf. no. 119. 'Introduction' is pp. ix–xvii.

---

[1] *The Blake Collection of W. Graham Robertson*, ed. K. Preston (1952), no. 137.

78

*Jerusalem [E]. A [colour] Facsimile of the Illuminated Book. [Five fascicles.] London [1951]. The William Blake Trust.
'Preludium' (pp. v–vi) by Joseph Wicksteed; 'Bibliographical Statement' (pp. vii–ix) by Geoffrey Keynes.

79

A. **Jerusalem* [C]. Foreword by Geoffrey Keynes. London, 1952. B. N.Y., 1955. C. London, 1955. The William Blake Trust.
Includes a transcript of the poem and the 'Foreword' (1 p.).

80

Kiralis, Karl. 'Critical Edition (in Two Volumes) of William Blake's *Jerusalem*, The Emanation of the Giant Albion (1804–1820).' Brown Ph.D., 1954. Cf. *DA*, xiv (1954), 2347–8 (vMKN).

81

A. *Blake, William. *Jerusalem*: A Simplified Version. Ed. William R. Hughes. London, 1964. B. N.Y., 1964.

82

Gerusalemme, L'Emanazione del Gigante Albione. Milano, 1943. Breviari Mistici No. 13 (vMKN).
The author of the 'Introduzioni' (pp. 5–33) and the Italian prose translation is not identified.

A 82

*Jerusalem The Emanation of the Giant Albion [B]. London, 1974. The William Blake Trust.
Geoffrey Keynes, 'Commentary and Bibliographical History' (on 9 unnumbered pages), deals largely with variants, including those of the proofs of pl. 25, 32, 41, 47, here also reproduced.

83. 'Joseph of Arimathea' (1773, ?1785, ?1809)

BIBLIOGRAPHICAL INTRODUCTION

TABLE

Copy	State	Watermark	Size in cm	Printing colour
A *Keynes*	1	—	*c.* 15·2 × 26·2	pale Brown
B BMPR	2	—	24·6 ×(*o.* 34·4	*Colour-printed*
C BMPR	2	—		
D *Keynes*	2	—		
E *Keynes*	2	J WHATMAN/1825		*Colour-printed*
F LC	2	—	24·0 × 32·0	
G *UNTRACED*[1]	2	—		
H TRINITY COLLEGE	2			

[1] Information about the untraced copy G derives from the Christie catalogue of 22 July 1949, lot 83.

DATE: *State 1*: 1773; MS on copy A, ?1785, *State 2*: ?1809.

State 1: The date of 1773 for the original engraving is given in State 2. The date of the MS inscription could be any time after Blake's apprenticeship ended in 1779; perhaps he inscribed it when he kept a print shop in 1785.

State 2: The character of the inscription is much later than the original engraving, for 'the Rock of Albion' does not appear before *Vala* (?1796–?1807) p. 24, l. 8 (a late addition) and *Milton* (1804–?8) pl. 25, l. 23. The engraving was thoroughly reworked and has grown from a promising work to a powerful one. Perhaps both re-engraving and inscription may be associated with Blake's re-examination of his ideas about art visible in the Reynolds Marginalia (?1808), the *Descriptive Catalogue* (1809), and the projected 'Work on Art' (?1809) and dated very tentatively ?1809.

PUBLICATION: No contemporary buyers or critics are known. Blake clearly valued the design, for he kept the copperplate by him from 1773, when he first copied it from Michelangelo, until at least 1825, the date of the watermark in copy E. State 1 has no printed words but was inscribed by Blake in MS; State 2 is largely re-engraved.

DESIGN: A muscular old man with crossed arms wearing a long hooded shirt (not a 'sheepskin') strides to the right across barren cliffs beside the sea. The title is on a rock above him, and the rest of the inscription appears below his feet. It attributes the design to a 'drawing by Salviati' (i.e. Giuseppe Porta, 1538–85) which has not been identified, but a very similar print attributed to Beautrizet is reproduced in G. Keynes, *Engravings by William Blake*: The Separate Plates (1956), pl. 3. The design is taken from Michelangelo's fresco of the crucifixion of St. Peter in the Capella Paolina in the Vatican.

COPY A: BINDING: Loose.
HISTORY: (1) Sold by Frederick Izant at Sotheby's, 14 Dec. 1939, lot 5, for £2. 1s. to (2) *Geoffrey Keynes*, who described it in his catalogue (1964).

COPY B: BINDING: See the Large Book of Designs (A), p. 269.
HISTORY: (1) Acquired 11 June 1864 by the BRITISH MUSEUM PRINT ROOM.

COPY C: BINDING: Loose, pasted down.
HISTORY: (1) Acquired 11 June 1864 by the BRITISH MUSEUM PRINT ROOM.

COPY D: BINDING: Loose.
HISTORY: (1) Probably this is the copy offered by Quaritch (1887), lot 13,844, for £4; (2) Sold by Robson & Co. about 1916 (according to Keynes, *Separate Plates* [1956]) to (3) W. E. Moss, who sold it at Sotheby's, 2 March 1937, lot 138, for £9. 10s. to Edwards; (4) Acquired by *Geoffrey Keynes*, who reproduced it in his *Separate Plates* (1956), lent it to the British Museum exhibition (1957), and described it in his catalogue (1964), no. 551.

COPY E: BINDING: Loose.
HISTORY: (1) Perhaps acquired by George Richmond; (2) Sold by his daughter-in-law Mrs. John Richmond in 1927 to (3) *Geoffrey Keynes*, who lent it to the British Museum exhibition (1957), and gave the history in his catalogue (1964), no. 551.

COPY F: BINDING: (1) Perhaps it was once bound with the Large Book of Designs (B) (p. 269); (2) For a time it was 'bound up somewhat irregularly in a cloth case' with *America* (A) and pl. d, *Song of Los* (B), *Visions* (F) pl. 1, *Europe* (A) pl. 1–2, 4–6, and 'The Accusers' (H) (see p. 77); (3) Disbound by 1904 and now loose and mounted.
HISTORY: (1) Perhaps it was once part of the Large Book of Designs (B); (2) It was probably owned by the Earl of Beaconsfield (see *Europe* [A], p. 156); (3) For a time it was 'bound up somewhat irregularly in a cloth case' with *America* (A) and pl. d, *Song of Los* (B), *Visions* (F) pl. 1, *Europe* (A) pl. 1–2, 4–6, and 'The Accusers' (H), before it was disbound and sold separately at an anonymous Hodgson sale, 14 Jan. 1904, lot 228 (called 'John the Baptist'); (4) Acquired by W. A. White, lent to the exhibitions of the Grolier Club (1905,) no. 40, perhaps to that of (1919), no. 23, and the Fogg (1924), and sold posthumously on 1 May 1929 through Rosenbach to (5) Mr. LESSING J. ROSENWALD.

COPY G: BINDING: Loose.
HISTORY: (1) Perhaps this is the copy lent by Mrs. Gilchrist to the Burlington Fine Arts Club exhibition (1876), no. 281, and (2) Lent by her son H. H. Gilchrist to the Pennsylvania Academy exhibition (1892), no. 154; H. H. Gilchrist is probably the descendant of Alexander Gilchrist who sold it at Sotheby's, 24 June 1903, lot 34 (with 'Democritus' for Lavater's *Physiognomy*); (3) Acquired by W. Graham Robertson, lent to the Bournemouth exhibition (1949), no. 51, described in his Collection (1952), no. 129, and sold posthumously at Christie's, 22 July 1949, lot 83, for £18. 18s. to Agnew; (4) *UNTRACED.*

COPY H: BINDING: Loose.

HISTORY: (1) This may be the copy apparently sold by Frederick Tatham (like the 'Pickering [Ballads] MS') to (2) Francis Harvey, who offered it in a catalogue (c. 1864) for £1. 4s., from which it was apparently bought, with a number of other items such as the 'Pickering MS', by (3) The Revd. Samuel Prince, for whom it was sold posthumously at Sotheby's, 11 Dec. 1865, lot 280, for £1. 2s. to ?Timmins ?Francis; (4) Perhaps this is the copy lent by H. E. Scudder to the Boston exhibitions (1880), no. 13, (1891), no. 119; (5) Given by Allan R. Brown in 1940 to (6) TRINITY COLLEGE, Hartford, Connecticut.

84. 'Laocoon' (?1820)

BIBLIOGRAPHICAL INTRODUCTION

TABLE

Copy	Plates	Leaves	Watermark	Blake numbers	Binding-order	Leaf-size in cm	Printing colour
A[1] Keynes	1	1	—[2]	—	Loose	27·6 × 38·2	Black
B Rosenbloom	1	1	invisible	—	Loose	27·7 × 22·9 irregular	Black

[1] Copy A is reproduced in G. Keynes, *Engravings by William Blake*: The Separate Plates (1956) and elsewhere.

[2] Keynes (ibid.) says, on the basis of evidence unknown to me, that copy A is on 'Whatman paper without watermark'.

DATE: ?1820.

The earliest likely date is 1815, when Blake was commissioned to make a commercial engraving (dated 1 Oct. 1815) of Laocoon to illustrate Flaxman's article on sculpture for Rees's *Cyclopaedia* (1802–20). Parallels to 'The Everlasting Gospel' (?1818) and *On Homer* (?1820), particularly in ¶ 3 and 15, suggest a date of ?1820.

PUBLICATION: In 1815 Blake went to the Royal Academy to make a drawing from the cast[1] preparatory to his engraving of 'Laocoon' for Rees's *Cyclopaedia* (1802–20). Within the next few years he evidently saw the relevance of the statue to his own beliefs and made another engraving of the subject, 'Drawn & Engraved by William Blake', which he filled with aphorisms and observations, sideways, round the figures, and in almost every empty space. Since the words are written higgledy-piggledy, it is difficult to establish the order in which they should be printed.

Probably very few copies were pulled and given to friends. One (A) was acquired by John Linnell.

COLOURING: None.

VARIANTS: None.

[1] *Blake Records* (1969), 238.

ERRATA: None.

DESIGN: The design represents a naked man and two naked boys enmeshed in the coils of two serpents.

It is based on the cast (in the Royal Academy) of the original in the Vatican representing the Trojan priest and his two sons being punished by two great sea serpents for offending Apollo (or Athena) during the Trojan wars. In 1815 Blake made a sketch (reproduced in *Blake's Pencil Drawings*: Second Series, ed. G. Keynes [1956], no. 30) and an engraving of the subject for Rees's *Cyclopaedia* (1802–20). He also made a drawing of Laocoon in his priestly robes called 'Jehovah with his Sons Satan and Adam' (reproduced in the work above, no. 31, from the sketch in the possession of Sir Geoffrey Keynes).

The original sketch and the engraving for Rees are faithful copies of the cast, showing it without the hands, arms, and serpent heads. In his annotated engraving, Blake has restored the missing parts.

COPY A: BINDING: Loose.

HISTORY: The History is as in *On Homer* (B), see p. 336; it is reproduced in Keynes (1921).

COPY B: BINDING: Loose, pasted to a mount.

HISTORY: (1) Sold by Emma W. Bucknell at American Art Association, 2 April 1928, lot 76, for $610; (2) Acquired by Paul Hyde Bonner, lent to the Fogg exhibition (1930), and offered with his Library by Dutton's (1931), lot 31, for $1,750; (3) Sold posthumously by George C. Smith, Jr., at Parke-Bernet, 2 Nov. 1938, lot 57, for $475 to Sessler for (4) Mr. *Charles J. Rosenbloom*.

85. Large Book of Designs

The origin and constitution of The Large Book of Designs are given under The Small Book of Designs.

COPY A: BINDING: (1) By 1827 'Albion Rose' (C), *Urizen* pl. 14, 21, 'The Accusers' (G), *Visions* pl. 1, 7, 'Joseph of Arimathea Preaching' (B?), and *America* pl. d were bound at the end of *Europe* (D); (2) They were disbound, probably by 1846, and pasted on mounts in the British Museum after Feb. 1856.

HISTORY: For its History, see the Small Book of Designs (A), p. 356.

COPY B: BINDING and HISTORY: On the analogy of Large Book of Designs (A), 'Accusers' (H), 'Albion Rose' (D), *America* pl. d, *Urizen* pl. 21–2, 'Joseph of Arimathea' (F), and *Visions* pl. 1, 7 may once have formed part of a Large Book of Designs (B), though they vary in size and have little in common except colour printing. They have long been widely scattered.

86. Letters (1791–1827)

BIBLIOGRAPHICAL INTRODUCTION

Many of Blake's letters bear no postmark, presumably because they were either delivered by messenger or enclosed in another sheet (bearing the address) which has since disappeared. Since an ordinary letter consisted of a single sheet folded so as to form its own envelope, the opening of the letter entailed tearing it, and consequently one or more of the postmarks may be hard to read or even torn off entirely. Naturally, for letters for which the manuscripts have not been traced, there is no information as to postmark or watermark in the Table below.

TABLE

Symbols

(Ph)	Transcribed from a Photograph, Photostat, or Microfilm; all other manuscripts are transcribed from originals.
(Gilchrist)	Transcribed from Alexander Gilchrist,[1] *Life of William Blake* (1880), i. 143, 163–4, 194–5, 205–6, 209–13, 215–16, 218–20, 222–3 because the manuscripts have not been traced.
(Sotheby)	Transcribed from the Sotheby catalogue of Hayley Correspondence, 20 May 1878, lots 4, 21, 22, 25, 32 because the manuscripts have not been traced.
*	A *wafer* sealed the letter
+	A *wax seal* is on the letter. The only clear seal (19 Oct. 1801) represents an owl on a perch. That of 27 Jan. 1804 seems to represent a classical head.
1791 Oct. 18	Dates in italics indicate the letter is written *to* Blake.

For notes to the Table see pp. 273–4

Date	Postmark	Watermark	Collection
1791 Oct. 18	C OCT / 7 / . . .¹	CURTEIS & SON	HUNTINGTON
[*1791 Oct.?*]			*UNTRACED*²
[*1794 Oct.*]			*UNTRACED*³
[*1794 Nov.*]			*UNTRACED*³
1795 Dec. 6	*C DE / 10 / 95	[ ]TH	BM
[*1796 Jan.*]			*UNTRACED*³
[*1796 Feb.*]			*UNTRACED*³
[*1796 May*]			*UNTRACED*³
1796 Dec. 23	—	*chain lines*	BM
1799 Aug. 16	—	*design*	BM
[*1799 Aug.*]			*UNTRACED*⁴

¹ A comparison of the Gilchrist transcripts with the manuscripts of the traceable letters which he quotes reveals that he consistently normalized capitalization, spelling ('conceived' for 'Concievd'), punctuation, grammar ('you were' for 'you was', 7 April 1804), and paragraphing, and expanded contractions ('&' to 'and', 'tho' to 'though'). Occasionally such changes significantly affect meaning. Additionally, the Gilchrist transcripts were often startlingly casual. For example, in the letter of 14 Jan. 1804, ten words were omitted in the first sentence, plus five in the last; 'Mʳˢ Lambert' became 'Mr. Lambert', and 'wicked' changed twice into 'wretched'. Presumably he made similar changes in the letters for which the original manuscripts have not been traced.

Date	Postmark	Watermark	Collection
1799 Aug. 23	*BRIDGE·S^T / WEST-MINSTER B·AU· / 28 / ·99[5]	chain lines	BM
1799 Aug. 26	*BRIDGE S^T / ... AU / ... / 99	chain lines	BM
1800 Feb. 18			(Gilchrist)
1800 April 1	†BRIDGE / WEST-MINSTER A / 1 / 1800	design	Lady Radcliffe
1800 April 17	CHICHESTER		G. Keynes[6]
1800 May 6	†C·MA· / 6 / 800	design	HARVARD
1800 July 2	*C JY / 2 / 800	design	LC
1800 Sept. 12	2 o'Clock / 12·SP / 1800 A·N O[?] Unpaid	design	MORGAN
1800 Sept. 14	—	1798	MORGAN
1800 Sept. 16	*BRIDGE / WEST-MINSTER A·S·E· / 16 / 800	179[ ]	HUNTINGTON
1800 Sept. 21	*CHICHESTER	design	YALE
1800 Sept. 22	†CHICHESTER SEP 23 / 1800	design	WESTMINSTER PUBLIC LIBRARY
[*1800 Sept.*]	—	1798	WESTMINSTER PUBLIC LIBRARY[7]
1800 Oct. 2	—	1798	WESTMINSTER PUBLIC LIBRARY
1800 Nov. 26			(Gilchrist)
[*1800 Autumn?*]			UNTRACED[8]
1801 May 10	*—	design	WESTMINSTER PUBLIC LIBRARY
1801 July 31	AJY / 31 / 801	—	FOLGER (Ph)
1801 Sept. 11	*—	F HAYES / 1798	WESTMINSTER PUBLIC LIBRARY
1801 Oct. 7	† ... [1]801	design	FITZWILLIAM
1801 Oct. 19	†CHICHESTER / 63[?] F / OCT 21 / 1801	BUTTANSHAW / 18[00?]	MORGAN
[*1801 Autumn*]			UNTRACED[9]
1802 Jan. 10	*CHICHESTER	A BLACKWELL / 1798	WESTMINSTER PUBLIC LIBRARY
[*1802?*]			UNTRACED[10]
1802 Nov. 22	—	F HAYES / 1798	WESTMINSTER PUBLIC LIBRARY
1802 Nov. 22	—	design	WESTMINSTER PUBLIC LIBRARY
[*1802 Nov.*]			UNTRACED[11]
[*1803 Jan.?*]			UNTRACED[12]
1803 Jan. 30	—	chain lines	LC
[*1803 April*]			UNTRACED[13]
1803 April 25	†—	A BLACKWELL / 1798	WESTMINSTER PUBLIC LIBRARY
1803 July 6	—	A BLACKWELL / 1798	WESTMINSTER PUBLIC LIBRARY
1803 Aug. 16	†—	F HAYES / 1798	WESTMINSTER PUBLIC LIBRARY
1803 Sept. 19			(Sotheby)
1803 Oct. 7	—	A B[LACKWELL?]	Mrs. D. F. Hyde
1803 Oct. 26			(Gilchrist)
1803 Dec. 13	†—	A BLA[CKWELL] / 1798	MAINE HISTORICAL SOCIETY (Ph)
1804 Jan. 14	*JA / 16[?] / ...	A BLACKWELL / 1798	HARVARD
1804 Jan. 27	†B·JA· / 27 / 804	A BLACKWELL / 1798	HARVARD

Date	Postmark	Watermark	Collection
[*1804 Feb.*]			*UNTRACED*[14]
1804 Feb. 23	*—	*design*	BM
1804 March 12	*B·M·R / 12 / 804	*design*	*Malone*
[*1804 March*]			*UNTRACED*[15]
1804 March 16	—	*design*	MORGAN
[1804 March 19?]			*UNTRACED*[16]
1804 March 21	—	*design*	PENNSYLVANIA HISTORICAL SOCIETY (Ph)
1804 March 31	†C MR / 31 / 804	*design*	TRINITY COLLEGE (Hartford, Conn.)
1804 April 2			(Gilchrist)
1804 April 2			*UNTRACED*[16]
1804 April 7	*A AP / 7 / 804	*design*	HARVARD
1804 April 27	*C·AP / 27 / 804	*design*	MORGAN
1804 May 4			(Gilchrist)
1804 May 28			(Gilchrist)
1804 June 22	†B·JU· / 22 / 04	*design*	MORGAN
1804 July 16	*—	*design*	*F. W. Hilles* (Ph)
1804 Aug. 7			(Sotheby)
1804 Aug. 9			(Sotheby)
1804 Sept. 28	—	*design*	LC
[*1804 Oct.*]			*UNTRACED*[17]
1804 Oct. 23			(Gilchrist)
[*1804 Nov.*]			*UNTRACED*[18]
1804 Dec. 4	†B[?]·D·E· / 4 / 80[ ]	W D[AC]IE & CO. 1804	LC (Ph)
1804 Dec. 18			(Gilchrist)
1804 Dec. 28	C·D·E· / 29 / 804	—	PENNSYLVANIA HISTORICAL SOCIETY (Ph)
1805 Jan. 19	—	*design*	HAVERFORD COLLEGE (Ph)
1805 Jan. 22			(Gilchrist)
1805 March 22	†A·MR· / 25 / 805	W DA[CI]E / 1803	HARVARD
1805 May 17			(Sotheby)
1805 June 4			(Gilchrist)
1805 Nov. 27	—	*design*	HARVARD
1805 Dec. 11	†[ ] DE / 11 / 805	*design*	*G. Keynes*
[1806 June?]			*UNTRACED*[19]
1807 May			*UNTRACED*[20]
1807 Oct. 14	*TWO PENNY / POST / . . . . . . OC / 1807	180[2?]	BOSTON PUBLIC LIBRARY (Ph)
1808 Jan. 18 [A]	—	IVY MILL / 1806	*R. W. Barrett*
1808 Jan. 18 [B]	—	IVY MILL / 1806	Lord *Egremont* (Ph)
1808 Feb. [C]	—	IVY MILL / 1806	Lord *Cunliffe*
1808 Dec. 18	*[*2 indecipherable round stamps*]	1806	BM
1808 Dec. 19	—	—	BM
[1809 May?]	†—	*design*	TRINITY COLLEGE (Hartford, Conn.) (Ph)
[*1810 July?*]			*UNTRACED*[21]
[1810 Aug.?]			*UNTRACED*[22]
[*1810 Aug?*]			*UNTRACED*[23]
1815 July 29			*UNTRACED*[24]
1815 Sept. 8	—	—	WEDGWOOD MUSEUM (Ph)

Date	Postmark	Watermark	Collection
1818 June 9	R J[U?] / 9 / 1818	*design*	ROSENBACH FOUNDATION[25]
1819 Oct. 11	—	—	UNIVERSITY OF TEXAS (Ph)
1823 March 25	—	*design*	YALE
[1824 Aug. 4?]	—		LC
[1825 March?]	*—	1818	HUNTINGTON
[1825 June 7?]	*—	*chain lines*	HUNTINGTON
1825 Oct. 11	*TP STRAND CO 8·MORN·8/12·OC / 1825 10[?]·F·NO[ON?] . . . / OC·12 / 1825	*probably none*[26]	HUNTINGTON
1825 Nov. 10	*TP / STRAND CO 8·MORN·8 / 11·NO / 1825	*design*	HUNTINGTON
1826 Jan. 31	*T·P / STRAND CO 4[?]·EVEN / 31 JA / 18[ ]	RUSE & TURNERS / 1810	HUNTINGTON
[1826 Feb. 5?]	—	*chain lines*[27]	HUNTINGTON
1826 March 31	—	*chain lines*[27]	MORGAN
[1826 April?]	—	—	YALE
1826 May 19	*T·P / STRAND CO 10·F[?]·NOON·10 / [ ]Y / 1826	*chain lines*[27]	HUNTINGTON
1826 July 2	*T·P / STRAND CO 12 NOON· / 2·JY / 1826	*chain lines*[27]	ST. JOHN'S SEMINARY
1826 July 5	—	*chain lines*[27]	HUNTINGTON
1826 July 14	—	SMITH & ALLNUTT / 1815	MORGAN
1826 July 16	*T·P / STRAND CO 10[?]·NOON·10 / 17·JY / 1826	RUSE & TURNERS / 1810	HUNTINGTON
1826 July 29	*T·P / STRAND CO 2·A·NOON·2 / 29·JY / 1826	*chain lines*[27]	HUNTINGTON
1826 Aug. 1	*T·P / STRAND CO 10·F·NOON·10 / 2·AU / 1826	*chain lines*[27]	HUNTINGTON
1826 Nov. 4	WORCESTER / NO 3 D2 / 117 D / PAID / 4 NO 4 / 1826	R BARNARD / 1825	*Miss J. L. Ivimy*[28]
1826 Dec. 29	*—	—	TEXAS
[*1827 Jan.*]			*UNTRACED*[29]
1827 Jan. 27	*—	*chain lines*[27]	HUNTINGTON
[1827 Feb.?]	—	—	HUNTINGTON
[1827 Feb.?]	*—	*chain lines*	LC
1827 March 5			*UNTRACED*[30]
1827 March 15	*—	*chain lines*[27]	FITZWILLIAM
1827 March 18	*—	*chain lines*[27]	BERG COLLECTION (NYP)
1827 April 12	*—	RUSE & TURNERS / 1810	FITZWILLIAM
1827 April 25	*—	*chain lines*[27]	HUNTINGTON
1827 July 3	*—	*chain lines*[27]	HUNTINGTON
1827 Nov. 25			*Miss J. L. Ivimy*

[1] The only really clear part of the postmark is the '7', which seems to contradict the written date of 'Oct 18'.

[2] The draft of Blake's letter to Reveley is on the verso of Reveley's letter to Blake; the fair copy sent has not been traced.

3 In his Journal, Captain John Gabriel Stedman included 'Blake' in a list of letters he wrote in October 1794; 'I wrote to . . . Blake' in November 1794; in 'January and February [*1796*] I write . . . to Blake—3 times—dº [*i.e. in London*]'; and under '*Correspondence*' for May 1796 he noted '12 letters to Blake' (*Blake Records* [1969], 48, 50, 51), but none of these letters has been traced.

4 Dr. Trusler's untraced letter to Blake is known only from the references in Blake's letter of 26 Aug. 1799.

5 The clear postmark date of 28 Aug. (which contradicts the clear written date of 23 Aug.) must be a mistake.

6 Quoted from *The Letters of William Blake*, ed. G. Keynes (1956).

7 Butts's letter to Blake is known only from his rough draft.

8 The last known location is the Sotheby catalogue of H. V. Morten, 5 May 1890, lot 22. Keynes (*Letters* [1968], 49–50) prints this letter from an anonymous Sotheby catalogue of 3 Dec. 1888, lot 13, which I cannot trace.

9 Butts's letter is referred to in Blake's of 10 Jan. 1802.

10 [O. Crawfurd] 'William Blake: Artist, Poet, and Mystic', *New Quarterly Magazine*, ii (1874), 475.

11 Blake's untraced letter to his brother James was enclosed in his letter of 22 Nov. 1802.

12 Blake's letter from his brother is mentioned in the letter of 30 Jan. 1803.

13 James Blake's 'pressing letter' is mentioned in William's of 25 April 1803.

14 Prince Hoare's letter is mentioned in Blake's of 23 Feb. 1804.

15 On 16 March Blake refers to Hayley's letter to him.

16 On 2 April 1802 Blake said he sent letters to his solicitor, Mr. R. Dally, 'a fortnight ago' and 'by this post'.

17 Blake's letter of 23 Oct. 1804 mentions Hayley's letter to him.

18 Blake's letter of 4 Dec. 1804 mentions Hayley's letter to him.

19 *Monthly Magazine*, xxi (1 July 1806), 520–1.

20 Anon., 'The Life and Works of Thomas Stothard, R.A.', *Gentleman's Magazine*, N.S., xxxvii (1852), 149–50.

21 C. H. B. Ker wrote to George Cumberland, probably in August 1810, that he had 'some time before written to him [*Blake*]' (BM Add. MSS. 36516, f. 56—*Blake Records* [1969], 227).

22 Blake's reply to Ker is summarized in the letter above.

23 In another letter to Cumberland, postmarked 27 Aug. 1810, C. H. B. Ker mentioned that 'I wrote' to Blake (BM Add. MSS. 36502, f. 273—*Blake Records* [1969], 228). In this letter Ker refers to a series of exchanges with Blake which may have been verbal or may represent further lost letters.

24 My transcript derives from a photostat of the office copy on flimsy paper watermarked 'watts & co. soho / staffordshire' in the Wedgwood Museum. The original has not been traced.

25 A beautiful manuscript copy on unwatermarked paper was made by Dawson Turner, bound in a volume with an index (identifying it as a 'copy') dated 1837, and given in 1890 to Trinity College, Cambridge.

26 The letter is mounted on linen, and the watermark is therefore obscured.

27 The chain lines in Blake's otherwise unwatermarked letters of 1826–7 are the same distance apart as those in his letters bearing the watermark ruse & turners / 1810. All the letters of 1826–7 (except that of 14 July 1826) may therefore be on the same paper.

28 The postmark is on the letter to Linnell (also with the Ivimy MSS) in which the letter to Blake was enclosed.

29 Blake mentions Linnell's letter in his of 27 Jan. 1827.

30 Cumberland wrote on 5 March 1827 that he 'Sent . . . [*a*] Lett[*er*] . . . to *Blake*' (*Blake Records* [1969], 340), which has not been traced.

HISTORIES

I omit here the Histories of letters known only through contemporary references. These may be traced through the Table of Letters (pp. 270–4).

1791 oct. (1) The letters of 31 Jan. 1826; 7 June 1825; 25 April 1827; Oct.

1791,[1] March, 11 Oct., 10 Nov. 1825, 5 Feb., 19 May, 5, 16, 29 July, 1 Aug. 1826, 27 Jan., Feb. ['I calld this Morning . . .'], 3 July 1827 were sold with the Linnell Collection at Christie's, 15 March 1918, lots 208 (£30. 10s.); 209 (£25. 4s.); 213 (£26. 5s.), 214[1] (£84) to G. D. Smith for (2) Henry E. Huntington, who gave them to the HUNTINGTON LIBRARY.

1795 DEC. 6. (1) The letters of 6 Dec. 1795, 23 Dec. 1796,[2] 16, 23, 26 Aug. 1799, 18, 19 Dec. 1808 were given with the Cumberland Correspondence by George Cumberland in 1849[3] to (2) The BRITISH MUSEUM.

1796 DEC. 23, 1799 AUG. 16, 23, 26. As in 6 Dec. 1795.

1800 FEB. 18. Known only from A. Gilchrist, *Life of William Blake* (1880), i. 143—see the note to 26 Nov. 1800—p. 277, below.

1800 APRIL 1. (1) Sold with the Hayley Correspondence at Sotheby's, 20 May 1878, lot 2, for £1. 5s. to Naylor; (2) Sold by Henry Goldsmith at Anderson's, 10 Jan. 1908, lot 20 (reproduced), for $50; (3) Sold at Sotheby's, 5 July 1909, lot 106, for £3. 18s. to Quaritch;[4] (4) 'Offered for sale in several catalogues of . . . James Tregaskis about 1910' (with a facsimile);[5] (5) Sold anonymously at Sotheby's, 2 June 1919, lot 113, for £18 to Campbell; (6) Sold by a Lady at Sotheby's, 2 June 1932, lot 492, for £22 to Tufnell; (7) Sold by Professor Charles Singer at Sotheby's, 31 July 1934, lot 428, for £18. 10s. to Maggs for (8) Lady Charnwood (according to the Maggs Bros. records); after Lady Charnwood's death it was placed by (9) Her daughter Lady Radcliffe on deposit in the BRITISH MUSEUM.

1800 APRIL 17. (1) Offered by Tregaskis, June 1928, for £85;[6] (2) Sold at Sotheby's, 17 Feb. 1932, for £3. 10s. to King;[6] (3) Offered by Raphael King in a catalogue, lot 25, for £5. 5s. (4) Acquired by Sir *Geoffrey Keynes*.

1800 MAY 6. (1) The letters of 6 May 1800, 14, 27 Jan., 7 April 1804, 22 March 1805 were sold with the Hayley Correspondence at Sotheby's, 20 May 1878, lots 1 (£3. 3s.), 9 (£2. 15s.), 10 (£5), 15 (£2. 19s.), 6 (£3. 5s.) to Naylor; (2) They were acquired by Frederick Locker Lampson, put into an album, described in his *Rowfant Library* (1886), and sold to Dodd Mead & Co. about 1905 (see the 'Pickering [Ballads] MS', p. 341); (3) Acquired by Paul M.

---

[1] Lot 214 in the Linnell sale is described as eight single-leaf quarto letters to Linnell (1825–7) plus two letters (one in pencil) to Mrs. Linnell [11 Oct. 1825, 5 Feb. 1826], plus '2 short Autograph Notes' [Feb. 1826, Feb. 1827], making a total of '11' (i.e. 12) letters. Two letters (Oct. 1791 [Blake's letter from Willey Reveley and his reply] and 3 July 1827 [in octavo]) are apparently not covered by this description but seem to have passed to Huntington from the Linnell Collection and may have come (as Keynes, *Bibliography* [1921], ed., *Letters* [1956, 1968] asserts without discussion) with lot 214.

[2] The letter of 23 Dec. 1796 is reproduced in A. G. B. Russell, ed., *Letters* (1906), 56, and E. Gosse, *English Literature*: An Illustrated Record (1903), iii. 19.

[3] *Catalogue of Additions to the Manuscripts in the British Museum in the Years MDCCCC–MDCCCCV* (London, 1907), 122.

[4] Keynes, ed., *Letters* (1968); the only Sotheby sale of this date which I can trace consists entirely of coins.

[5] Keynes (1921), Keynes, ed., *Letters* (1956, 1968).

[6] Keynes, ed., *Letters* (1968).

[7] I have seen only an undated clipping from this catalogue in the W. E. Moss collection in Bodley.

Warburg, from whom it passed to his daughter (4) Mrs. Samuel P. Grimson, who with her husband gave the album on 12 Jan. 1960 to (5) HARVARD.

1800 JULY 2. (1) Sold by T. G. Arthur at Sotheby's, 11 April 1893, lot 187, for £5 to Pearson; (2) Sold posthumously for Charles Fairfax Murray at Sotheby's, 5 Feb. 1920, lot 18, to Morton; (3) Offered in Maggs Bros. Catalogues 394 (Summer 1920, lot 1,037), 433 (1922, lot 2,980) for £78 and again in no. 449 (April 1924, with a facsimile of the last two pages); (4) Offered on 7 Jan. 1925 to Alan R. Brown for $390 by Gannon;[1] (5) Sold at American Art Association–Anderson Galleries, 25 May 1938, lot 73;[2] (6) Acquired by Mr. LESSING J. ROSENWALD.

1800 SEPT. 12. (1) Sold at the Flaxman-Denman sale at Christie's, 26 Feb. 1883, lot 287;[3] (2) Sold by B. B. Macgeorge at Sotheby's, 1 July 1924, lot 134, for £55 to Sawyer; (3) Offered on 7 May 1925 to A. R. Brown for $525 by Weyhe;[4] (4) Acquired by Miss Tessie Jones, and bequeathed by her in 1968 to (5) The PIERPONT MORGAN LIBRARY.

1800 SEPT. 14. (1) Sold at the Flaxman-Denman sale at Christie's, 26 Feb. 1883, lot 290; (2) Acquired by 1921 by the PIERPONT MORGAN LIBRARY.

1800 SEPT. 16. (1) Sold with the Hayley Correspondence at Sotheby's, 20 May 1878, lot 3, for £2. 17s. to Webster; (2) Sold by Louis J. Haber at Anderson's, 9 Dec. 1909, lot 47, for $55 to G. H. Richmond; (3) Acquired by Henry E. Huntington and given to the HUNTINGTON LIBRARY.

1800 SEPT. 21. (1) Given by John Flaxman to (2) John Thomas Smith for publication in *Nollekens and his Times* (1828) (*Blake Records* [1969], 461); (3) Sold posthumously for Charles Fairfax Murray at Sotheby's, 5 Feb. 1920, lot 19, to Morton; (4) Offered in Maggs Bros. Catalogues 394 (Summer 1920, lot 1,036, £85), 425 (Summer 1922, lot 964, £85), 464 (1925, lot 868, 'SOLD'); (5) Acquired by Chauncey Brewster Tinker, who lent it to the Philadelphia exhibition (1939), no. 282, and bequeathed it at his death in March 1963 to (6) YALE.

1800 SEPT. 22. (1) The letters of 22 Sept., end of Sept., 2 Oct. 1800, 10 May, 11 Sept. 1801, 10 Jan., 22 Nov. (both parts) 1802, 25 April, 6 July, 16 Aug. 1803 were sold 'about 1906'[4] by Captain Frederick Butts (the grandson of the recipient) to (2) W. Graham Robertson, who allowed them to be reproduced (1926) and bequeathed them in 1948 to (3) Mr. Kerrison Preston, who gave them in 1967 to (4) The WESTMINSTER PUBLIC LIBRARY.

1800 END OF SEPT., OCT. 2. As in 22 Sept. 1800.

1800 NOV. 26. (1) The letters of 26 Nov. 1800, 26 Oct. 1803, 4, 28 May, 9 Aug., 23 Oct., 18 Dec. 1804, 22 Jan., 17 May, 4 June 1805 were sold with the Hayley Correspondence at Sotheby's, 20 May 1878, lots 33 (£3. 14s.),

---

[1] In a letter now in Trinity College, Hartford, Conn.
[2] Keynes, ed., *Letters* (1968).
[3] This may be the 'letter from William Blake to Flaxman', the property of the mendacious R. C. Jackson, described in the unreliable Goddard & Smith catalogue of his property, 23–5 July 1923, lot 298.
[4] Keynes, ed., *Letters* (1968).

32 (£3), 17 (£4), 18 (£5. 10s.), 32 (£3), 23 (£6. 14s.), 27 (£5. 10s.), 30 (£4. 8s.), 25 (£5. 5s.), 31 (£3. 15s.), to Quaritch and were (2) Offered in Quaritch's *General Catalogue* (1880), lot 12,803 (only the first and last ones dated) for £52. 10s.; (3) *UNTRACED*.[1]

1800 AUTUMN? (1) Perhaps this is Blake's 'Short Note to Flaxman' sold with the Flaxman collection by the Denman family at Christie's, 26 Feb. 1883, lot 289 (with Blake's letter of 18 March 1827 and the receipt of 1799); (2) Sold anonymously at Sotheby's, 3 Dec. 1888, lot 13;[2] (3) Sold by H. V. Morten at Sotheby's, 5 May 1890, lot 22, for £2. 2s. to Ellis; (4) *UNTRACED*.

1801 MAY 10, SEPT. 11. As in 22 Sept. 1800.

1801 OCT. 7. (1) Sold at Sotheby's, 8 Nov. 1927, lot 289 (with seventeen letters from Flaxman to Hayley), for £23 to Maggs; (2) Offered by Maggs Bros. in Catalogue 544 (Summer 1930), lot 855, for £12. 10s., and in 1932, lot 168 (including both parts); (3) Acquired by A. N. L. Munby, who reproduced it with an article in the *Connoisseur*, CXVIII (1946), 26, and sold it on 2 June 1949 to (4) The FITZWILLIAM MUSEUM.

1801 OCT. 19. (1) Sold with the Flaxman-Denman Collection at Christie's, 26 Feb. 1883, lot 288; (2) Sold posthumously for William Harris Arnold at Anderson Galleries on 10 Nov. 1924, lot 53; (3) Acquired in 1926 from Rosenbach by Mrs. Alice Bemis Taylor;[3] at the time of her death in June 1942 she gave it (according to Mrs. Thompson) to her niece (4) Mrs. Charles G. Thompson, who gave it in 1972 to (5) The PIERPONT MORGAN LIBRARY.

1802 JAN. 10, NOV. 22 (both parts). As in 22 Sept. 1800.

1803 JAN. 30 (1) Sold at Hodgson's, 21 March 1917, lot 168, for £31 to Dobell;[4] (2) 'Afterwards acquired by Messrs. Maggs',[4] who sold it[4] to (3) W. E. Moss, who in turn sold it at Sotheby's, 2 March 1937, lot 281 (where it is reproduced), for £150 to Rosenbach for (4) Mr. LESSING J. ROSENWALD.

1803 APRIL 25, JULY 6, AUG. 16. As in 22 Sept. 1800.

1803 SEPT. 19. (1) Sold with the Hayley Correspondence at Sotheby's, 20 May 1878, lot 4, for £2. 2s. to Naylor; (2) *UNTRACED*.

1803 OCT. 7. (1) Sold with the Hayley Correspondence at Sotheby's, 20 May 1878, lot 5, for £4. 4s. to Webster; (2) Acquired by R. B. Adam, in whose catalogues (1921, 1929) it is partly quoted, and from whom it passed to (3) *Mrs. Donald Hyde*.

1803 OCT. 26. As in 26 Nov. 1800.

---

[1] The firm now has no record of the purchaser of these letters. In the 1880 catalogue eleven letters are offered, but though Quaritch is known to have bought eleven Blake letters at the 1878 sale, the letter of 23 Feb. 1804 bought then was promptly sold to the British Museum. The unidentified letter in the 1880 catalogue may have been that of 18 Feb. 1800, only known from the Gilchrist transcript (1880).

[2] Keynes, ed., *Letters* (1968). It does not appear in the only Sotheby sale of this date which I can trace (R. S. Turner, 23 Nov. 1888 and thirteen following days).

[3] According to the records of Mrs. Taylor's Collection in the Taylor Museum, Colorado Springs, Colorado, Blake's letter was never the property of the Taylor Museum, despite the statement in the Keynes edition of Blake's *Letters* (1956).

[4] Keynes, ed., *Letters* (1968).

1803 DEC. 13. (1) Offered by John Pearson in Catalogue 6 (?1858), lot 34, for £5. 5s.; (2) Sold with the Hayley Correspondence at Sotheby's, 20 May 1878, lot 8, for £2. 7s. to Naylor; (3) Acquired by Dr. John S. H. Fogg, who bequeathed it at his death in 1893 to (4) The MAINE HISTORICAL SOCIETY.

1804 JAN. 14, 27. As in 6 May 1800.

1804 FEB. 23. (1) Sold with the Hayley Correspondence at Sotheby's, 20 May 1878, lot 11, for £4. 4s. to Quaritch; (2) 'Purch^d of B. Quaritch 15 June 1878' (according to the note on the address page) by the BRITISH MUSEUM.

1804 MARCH 12. (1) Sold with the Hayley Correspondence at Sotheby's, 20 May 1878, lot 7, for £2. 15s. to Waller; (2) Sold posthumously for Joseph Mayer at Sotheby's, 19 July 1887, lot 189 (with letters of 31 March, 27 April, 28 Sept. 1804), for £10. 5s. to Robson; (3) Sold posthumously for H. Buxton Forman at Anderson Galleries, 15 March 1920, lot 69, for $125; (4) Acquired by Arthur F. Egner by 1925;[1] (5) Inherited by his daughter *Mrs. John Malone.*

1804 MARCH 16. (1) Sold with the Hayley Correspondence at Sotheby's, 20 May 1878, lot 12, for £3. 3s. to Naylor; (2) Sold by F. Naylor in the Sotheby sale of 27 July–1 Aug. 1885, lot 1,030 (with the Linnell letter of April 1826) for £4. 16s. to Pearson; (3) Acquired by Mr. Shepherd (successor of John Pearson) of 46 Pall Mall, who gave William Muir 'the use' of it for reproduction in his edition of *Milton* (1886); (4) Sold posthumously for Charles Fairfax Murray at Sotheby's, 5 Feb. 1920, lot 20, to Morton; (5) Offered in Maggs Bros. Catalogues 394 (Summer 1920, lot 1,038), 433 (1922, lot 2,981 [the last page reproduced]) for £52; (6) Bought on 8 Feb. 1944 from James F. Drake for $292 by the PIERPONT MORGAN LIBRARY.

1804 MARCH 21. (1) Sold with the Hayley Correspondence at Sotheby's, 20 May 1878, lot 13, for £3. 5s. to Naylor; (2) Sold by F. Naylor at Sotheby's, 27 July 1885, lot 97, for £3. 7s. to Waller; (3) Acquired by Simon Gratz, who gave it with his collection on 4 Oct. 1907 to (4) The PENNSYLVANIA HISTORICAL SOCIETY.

1804 MARCH 31. (1) Sold with the Hayley Correspondence at Sotheby's, 20 May 1878, lot 14 (with the letter of 2 April 1804), for £4 to Waller; (2) Sold posthumously for Joseph Mayer at Sotheby's, 19 July 1887, lot 189 (with letters of 12 March, 27 April, 28 Sept. 1804), for £10. 5s. to Robson; (3) Acquired by H. Buxton Forman, lent to A. G. B. Russell to print in his edition of Blake's *Letters* (1906), and sold posthumously at Anderson Galleries, 15 March 1920, lot 70, for $120; (4) Acquired by Alan R. Brown and given by him in 1940 to (5) TRINITY COLLEGE, Hartford, Connecticut.

1804 APRIL 2. (1) Sold with the Hayley Correspondence at Sotheby's, 20 May 1878, lot 14 (with the letter of 31 March 1804), for £4 to Waller; (2) *UNTRACED.*

1804 APRIL 7. As in 6 May 1800.

---

[1] Keynes, ed., *Letters* (1968).

1804 APRIL 27. (1) Sold with the Hayley Correspondence at Sotheby's, 20 May 1878, lot 16, for £2. 10s. to Waller; (2) Sold posthumously for Joseph Mayer at Sotheby's, 19 July 1887, lot 189 (with letters of 12, 31 March, 28 Sept. 1804), for £10. 5s. to Robson;(3) Sold posthumously for H. Buxton Forman at Anderson Galleries, 15 March 1920, lot 71, for $170; (4) Acquired by Mrs. Landon K. Thorne, in whose catalogue (1971) it was described (no. 17), and who gave it in 1973 to (5) The PIERPONT MORGAN LIBRARY.

1804 MAY 4, 28. As in 26 Nov. 1800.

1804 JUNE 22. (1) Sold with the Hayley Correspondence at Sotheby's, 20 May 1878, lot 19, for £4. 4s. to Weston; (2) Acquired by 1921 by the PIERPONT MORGAN LIBRARY.

1804 JULY 16. (1) Sold with the Hayley Correspondence at Sotheby's, 20 May 1878, lot 21, for £3. 1s. to Naylor; (2) Sold by F. Naylor at Sotheby's, 27 July 1885, lot 98, for £3. 9s. to Bennett; (3) Sold posthumously for John Lawrence Toole at Sotheby's, 8 Nov. 1906, lot 119 (as by 'W. Black', bound with other letters in Green morocco); (4) Acquired by Toole's relative B. L. Simpson and sold by him anonymously at Sotheby's, 2 May 1966, lot 237, to Goodspeed; (5) Offered in Goodspeed's *Flying Quill* (Sept. 1966) for $2,000 and bought from them by (6) Professor *F. W. Hilles.*

1804 AUG. 7. (1) Sold with the Hayley Correspondence at Sotheby's, 20 May 1878, lot 22, for £3. 10s. to Naylor; (2) Sold by F. Naylor at the Sotheby sale of 27 July–1 Aug. 1885, lot 1,031 (with slightly different excerpts), for £3. 18s. to Molini; (3) *UNTRACED.*

1804 AUG. 9. As in 26 Nov. 1800.

1804 SEPT. 28. (1) Sold with the Hayley Correspondence at Sotheby's, 20 May 1878, lot 24, for £2. 13s. to Waller; (2) Sold posthumously for Joseph Mayer at Sotheby's, 19 July 1887, lot 189 (with letters of 12, 31 March, 27 April 1804), for £10. 5s. to Robson; (3) Sold posthumously for H. Buxton Forman at Anderson Galleries, 15 March 1920, lot 72, for $140; (4) Acquired by George C. Smith, Jr., described in his anonymous catalogue (1927), no. 53, and sold posthumously for him at Parke-Bernet, 2 Nov. 1938, lot 6 (p. 1 reproduced), for $325 to Rosenbach, who sold it to (5) Mr. LESSING J. ROSENWALD.

1804 OCT. 23. As in 26 Nov. 1800.

1804 DEC. 4. (1) Sold with the Hayley Correspondence at Sotheby's, 20 May 1878, lot 26, for £4 to Naylor; (2) Sold by F. Naylor at Sotheby's, 27 July 1885, lot 99, for £3. 12s. to Molini; (3) Sold at Anderson Galleries, 16 April 1914, lot 55, for $275 to Mrs. Breckinridge Long; (4) Given by 1964 to the LIBRARY OF CONGRESS.

1804 DEC. 18. As in 26 Nov. 1800.

1804 DEC. 28. (1) Sold with the Hayley Correspondence at Sotheby's, 20 May 1878, lot 28, for £7. 10s. to Naylor; (2) Sold by F. Naylor at Sotheby's, 27 July 1885, lot 100, for £3. 5s. to Barker, who put his name and the date (J. E. Barker, 1886) in the top left corner of the address leaf; (3) Lent by

Ferdinand J. Dreer to the Boston Museum of Fine Arts exhibition (1891), no. 147, and given formally on 1 March 1890 to (4) The HISTORICAL SOCIETY OF PENNSYLVANIA.

1805 JAN. 19. (1) Sold with the Hayley Correspondence at Sotheby's, 20 May 1878, lot 29, for £3. 16s. to Naylor; (2) Sold by F. Naylor at Sotheby's, 27 July 1885, lot 101, for £3. 5s. to Thibaudau; (3) Acquired by Charles Roberts and given by his widow in 1902 to (4) HAVERFORD COLLEGE.

1805 JAN. 22. As in 26 Nov. 1800.

1805 MARCH 22. As in 6 May 1800.

1805 MAY 17, JUNE 4. As in 26 Nov. 1800.

1805 NOV. 27. (1) Sold by Robert Hoe at Anderson Galleries, 25 April 1911, lot 397, for $180; (2) Acquired by Amy Lowell and bequeathed by her in 1925 to (3) HARVARD.

1805 DEC. 11. (1) Lent by Mr. Daniel to E. J. Ellis & W. B. Yeats for *The Works of William Blake* (1893), i. 172; (2) Sold anonymously at Sotheby's, 28 July 1899, lot 262 (with Hayley's letter to Lady Portarlington about Blake), for £5. 5s. to Thomas; (3) Sold anonymously at Hodgson's, 22 June 1922, lot 272, for £20. 10s. to Edwards; (4) Acquired from Sessler for $3,000 with *Songs* (j, see p. 428) on 13 July 1925 by A. E. Newton, who gave them both by 1939 to his daughter (5) Miss Caroline Newton, who gave the letter, according to an inscription on the case by the recipient, in Dec. 1956 to (6) Sir *Geoffrey Keynes*.

1806 JUNE. (1) Sent by Blake to the Editor (Sir Richard Phillips) of the *Monthly Magazine*, who published it; (2) *UNTRACED*.

1807 MAY. (1) Acquired after 1830 by Allan Cunningham and thence by his son (2) Peter, who lent it for publication in the *Gentleman's Magazine* (1852) (*Blake Records* [1969], 184–7); (3) *UNTRACED*.

1807 OCT. 14. (1) Acquired by Mellen Chamberlain, who gave it with his Collection in 1893 to (2) The BOSTON PUBLIC LIBRARY.

1808 JAN. 18 (A) (1) Evidently acquired by William Upcott (the natural son of the recipient) and lent by him to J. T. Smith for publication in his *Nollekens and his Times* (1828) (*Blake Records* [1969], 473–4); (2) Sold by Major C. H. Simpson at Sotheby's, 15 March 1916, lot 33, for £51 to G. D. Smith; (3) Acquired by Oliver R. Barrett and inherited by his son (4) Mr. *Robert W. Barrett*.

1808 JAN. 18 (B). (1) Presumably sent with the picture to Lord Egremont at Petworth House, where it was discovered in 1952 by the present (2) *Lord Egremont*.

1808 FEB. (C). (1) Sent (according to the note on the last page) by Ozias Humphry to (2) The Earl of Buchan; it was sold with Buchan's MSS by R. H. Evans, 14 June 1836, lot 312 (with four letters of other men), for £1. 2s. to Thorp; (3) Offered by Thomas Thorp 'in 1837 for 15s.';[1] (4) Sold

---

[1] Keynes, ed., *Letters* (1968). It is not in the ten Thorp catalogues of 1837 which I have seen.

anonymously[1] at Puttick & Simpson's, 19 Dec. 1862, lot 28, for £1. 11s. to Anderdon; (5) Lent by J. H. Anderdon to Gilchrist for his *Life of William Blake, 'Pictor Ignotus'* (1863), I. 212, and evidently sold at auction in 1879;[1] (6) Apparently acquired by the dealer 'Waller. 5/5 1880', who signed the bottom right corner of the last page; (7) Acquired by Henry Cunliffe,[2] on whose death it went to his great-nephew, (8) Lord Cunliffe,[2] from whom it was inherited by his son (9) The present *Lord Cunliffe*.

1808 DEC. 18, 19. As in 6 Dec. 1795.

1809 MAY. (1) Presumably the letter and the 'Exhibition of Paintings' (A) which served as its cover were both owned by Alexander C. Weston when he lent the latter to the Burlington Fine Arts Club exhibition (1876), no. 320; (2) The letter was sold by C. J. Toovey at Sotheby's, 25 April 1912, lot 10, for £14 to Maggs; (3) Offered for £35 in Maggs Bros. Catalogues 293 (July–August 1912 [with a facsimile], lot 2890), 329 (1914, lot 2126); (4) The letter and 'Exhibition' leaf were sold by a Philadelphia Collector [Col. Henry D. Hughes] at American Art Association, 16 April 1923, lot 128, for $125; (5ai) For the History of the cover leaf, see the 'Exhibition of Paintings' (A)— p. 165; (5bi) The message leaf was acquired by Alan R. Brown and given by him in 1940 to (ii) TRINITY COLLEGE, Hartford, Connecticut.

1815 JULY 29. (1) *UNTRACED*. A contemporary copy is in the Wedgwood Museum, Barlaston, Stoke-on-Trent.

1815 SEPT. 8. (1) In the Wedgwood firm since receipt; now in the WEDGWOOD MUSEUM, Barlaston, Stoke-on-Trent.

1818 JUNE 9. (1) Sold posthumously with the Dawson Turner MSS at Puttick & Simpson's, 6–10 June 1859, lot 676 (with six volumes of MSS), for £24; (2) 'Later offered by S. J. Davey for £6. 6. 0';[3] (3) Acquired by W. A. White, lent by him to the exhibitions of the Grolier Club (1905), no. 137 (anonymously), and the Fogg (1924), and sold at his death in 1929 with his collection to (4) A. S. W. Rosenbach, who lent it to the Philadelphia Exhibition (1939), no. 283, and bequeathed it to (5) The ROSENBACH FOUNDATION.

1819 OCT. 11. (1) 'In the possession of Goodspeed . . . in 1925';[3] (2) Sold posthumously for George C. Smith, Jr., at Parke-Bernet, 2 Nov. 1938, lot 7, for $45 to Sessler; (3) Sold by Moncure Biddle at Parke-Bernet, 29 April 1952, lot 117, for $100 to Schwartz; (4) Acquired by Dr. E. Hanley and sold by him in 1965 to (5) The UNIVERSITY OF TEXAS.

1823 MARCH 25. (1) Sold for The Linnell Trustees at Christie's, 2 Dec. 1938, lot 62 (with account books and receipts for *Job*), for £78. 15s. to W. H. Robinson; (2) Presented by Otis T. Bradley in 1942[3] to (3) YALE.

1824 AUG. 4? (1) Acquired by Mr. LESSING J. ROSENWALD.

---

[1] The 1862 vendor may have been William Smith (1808–76), for a note on the folder for the manuscript says: 'Smith, the celebrated picture dealer in Newport St., obtained this letter from William Upcott [*the son of O. Humphry*] . . . . From Smith it passed into the hands of Mr. Anderdon . . . at whose sale in [*?30–31 May*] 1879 at Sotheby's it was purchased.'

[2] Keynes, ed., *Letters* (1968).

[3] Keynes, ed., *Letters* (1968).

1825 MARCH?, JUNE 7?, OCT. 11, NOV. 10; 1826 JAN. 31, FEB. 5. As in Oct. 1791

1826 MARCH 31. (1) John Linnell made a copy (now with the Ivimy MSS) and gave the original on 10 Feb. 1830 (*Blake Records* [1969], 378) to (2) Abraham Cooper; (3) Offered in John Pearson Catalogue 6 (?1858), lot 33, for £3. 3s.; (4) Sold posthumously for Emma W. Bucknell at American Art Association, 2 April 1928, lot 73, for $390 to Gabriel Wells; (5) Sold by David M. Newbold at Henkel's, 9 Oct. 1928, lot 399, for $350 to Wells (6) 'Offered with the estate of Gabriel Wells for $350.00 by Boesen, N.Y. March 1948';[1] (7) Acquired by Mrs. Landon K. Thorne, in whose catalogue (1971) it was described (no. 18), and who gave it in 1973 to (8) The PIERPONT MORGAN LIBRARY.

1826 APRIL? (1) Sold by F. Naylor at the Sotheby Sale of 27 July–1 Aug 1885, lot 1,030 (with the letter of 16 March 1804), for £4. 16s. to Pearson (2) Sold anonymously at Sotheby's, 31 July 1893, lot 1,100 (with *Innocence* [Q] and 4 drawings), for £49. 10s. to Heath; (3) They were all 'Sold by Quaritch in 1900'[2] to Marsden J. Perry, who in turn sold them to (4) W. A. White, who lent the letter to the exhibitions of the Grolier Club (1905) no. 138 (anonymously), and the Fogg (1924), and gave them all to his brother[2] (5) Alfred T. White, who bequeathed them to his daughter (6) Mrs. Alfred van Sinderen, whose husband sold the letter in July 1965 to (7) YALE.

1826 MAY 19. As in Oct. 1791.

1826 JULY 2. (1) Sold with the Linnell Collection at Christie's, 15 March 1918, lot 210, for £30. 9s. to Dobell; (2) Offered in Albert J. Scheuer Catalogue 3 (1927), lot 860 (with a facsimile), for $300; (3) Bought from Dawson's Book Shop (Los Angeles) by (4) Mrs. Edward L. Doheny, who gave it on 14 Oct. 1940 to (5) ST. JOHN'S SEMINARY, Camarillo, California.

1826 JULY 5. As in Oct. 1791.

1826 JULY 14. (1) Found among Linnell's papers by Linnell's great-grandson Bryan Palmer (Samuel Palmer's grandson) in 1959 and sold on 15 Feb 1960 for $400 to (2) The PIERPONT MORGAN LIBRARY.

1826 JULY 16, 29, AUG. 1. As in Oct. 1791.

1826 DEC. 29. (1) Kept in an album begun about 1826 by Mrs. Aders; (2) Sold by 'a Lady' [the Hon. Audrey Pauncefote] at Sotheby's, 16 Dec 1958, lot 483, for £24 to J. Schwartz— the album, sold as lot 482, is now in Harvard; (3) Acquired by Dr. E. Hanley and sold by him in 1965 to (4) The UNIVERSITY OF TEXAS.

1827 JAN. 27. As in Oct. 1791.

1827 FEB. ['I thank you ...'] (1) Sold with the Linnell Collection at Christie's, 15 March 1918, lot 211, for £30. 9s. to Swayne; (2) Sold anonymously at American Art Association–Anderson Galleries, 25 May 1938, lot 74; (3) Acquired by Mr. LESSING J. ROSENWALD.

1827 FEB. ['I calld this Morning. . . .'] As in Oct. 1791.

[1] Keynes, ed., *Letters* (1968).   [2] Keynes & Wolf.
[3] Keynes, ed., *Letters* (1968).

1827 MARCH 15. (**1**) Sold with the Linnell Collection at Christie's, 15 March 1918, lot 212, for £31. 10s. to Carfax for (**2**) T. H. Riches, who bequeathed it at his death in 1935 to (**3**) The FITZWILLIAM MUSEUM.

1827 MARCH 18. (**1**) Sold with the Flaxman-Denman Collection at Christie's, 26 Feb. 1883, lot 289 (with the receipt of 1799 and a 'Short Note to Flaxman' [perhaps the letter of ?1800]); (**2**) Sold posthumously for Charles Turner at Henckel's, 8 Nov. 1912, lot 554, for $30 to Manning; (**3**) Owned by W. T. Spencer from 1913[1] 'until about 1930';[2] (**4**) Acquired by the BERG COLLECTION of the NEW YORK PUBLIC LIBRARY.

1827 APRIL 12. (**1**) Sold by T. G. Arthur at Sotheby's, 11 April 1893, lot 188 (with Cumberland's card), for £5. 5s. to Pearson; (**2**) Sold posthumously for Charles Fairfax Murray at Sotheby's, 5 Feb. 1920, lot 21, to Morton; (**3**) Offered in Maggs Bros. Catalogue 597 (Summer 1934), lot 287 (with a facsimile of the last page), for £150 and sold by them on 17 Oct. 1935 to (**4**) The FITZWILLIAM MUSEUM.

1827 APRIL 25, JULY 3. As in Oct. 1791.

87

'Letters of William Blake to George Cumberland.' Ed. Richard Garnett. *Hampstead Annual*, 1903, pp. 54–69.

Introduction by Garnett and text of four letters from Blake to Cumberland, and two to the Revd. John Trusler; in addition, several letters referring to Blake, from the Cumberland papers in the British Museum.

88

A. *The Letters of William Blake*, together with a Life by Frederick Tatham. Ed. Archibald G. B. Russell. London, 1906.   § B. N.Y., 1906.

'Introduction' (pp. xvii–xlvii); Frederick Tatham, 'The Life of William Blake' (pp. 1–49) is reproduced in facsimile in Wittreich (1970) and transcribed anew in *Blake Records* (1969).

89

'Ein unveröffentlicher Brief von William Blake.' Ed. Stefan Zweig and Archibald G. B. Russell. *Deutsche Almanach auf das Jahr 1907*. Leipzig, 1907, pp. 75–7.

The letter is to Trusler, 23 Aug. 1799.

90

A. *Letters from William Blake to Thomas Butts 1800–1803*. Printed in Facsimile with an Introductory Note by Geoffrey Keynes. Oxford, 1926.   B. §* Folcroft, Pennsylvania, 1969.

---

[1] Keynes (1921).   [2] Keynes, ed., *Letters* (1968).

The introduction is pp. vi–ix. Blake's letters and the debtor–creditor account are in facsimile, while the letter *from* Butts is a transcript.

91

A Letter of William Blake [of 7 Oct. 1803 in facsimile and letterpress]. With Christmas Good Wishes from [R. B. Adams] and [R. B. Adams, Jr.] Christmas, 1929.

92

Keynes, Geoffrey. 'Blake and Hayley: A New Letter.' *TLS*, 31 July 1930, p. 624.

Text of a letter, 7 Oct. 1803.

93

A. *The Letters of William Blake*. Ed. Geoffrey Keynes. London, 1956. *B. § N.Y., 1956. C. London, 1968. D. *Blake no Tegami* [*The Letters of Blake*]. Tr. Narumi Umetsu. Tokyo, 1970.

A–C. Comprehends fairly full notes, some related documents such as receipts, and provenances.

D. Includes a chronological history of Blake's life.

94

A Letter from William Blake. Northampton, 1964.

Text of letter of 10 Jan. 1802; 6 representations of Blake by Leonard Baskin.

95

Frederick W. Hilles. 'A "New" Blake Letter [*16 July 1804*].' *Yale Review*, LVII (1967), 85–9.

Acquired by Hilles.

96

'William Blake'. Tr. Pierre Leyris. *L'Ephémère*, No. 12 (1969), 466–519, 552–3.

Excerpts in French from Blake, Linnell, Palmer, T. S. Eliot (pp. 466–9), 11 'Lettres' (470–519), and 19 reproductions.

97. Excerpt from Malkin's *Father's Memoirs of his Child* (1806)

BIBLIOGRAPHICAL INTRODUCTION

TITLE: A / FATHER'S MEMOIRS / OF / HIS CHILD. / BY / *BENJ. HEATH MALKIN, ESQ.* / M.A. F.A.S. / = / Great loss to all that ever him did see; / Great loss to all, but greatest loss to me. / *ASTROPHEL.* / = / LONDON: / PRINTED FOR LONGMAN, HURST, REES, AND ORME, / PATERNOSTER ROW; / *BY T. BENSLEY, BOLT COURT, FLEET STREET.* / 1806.

PUBLICATION: Bensley printed 1,000 copies of Malkin's *Memoirs* for the author in Jan. 1806[1] with four plates probably engraved by R. H. Cromek (only the first is so signed), the frontispiece after Blake's design of Malkin's son, the other three after the son himself. Between 7 Feb. 1806 and 1810, Malkin took 52 copies of the book himself;[2] in Aug. 1811 450 copies were pulped;[3] and by June 1815 445 copies had been sold, leaving 53 on hand.[3] The book was scantly noticed in the public press,[4] and clearly it sold very slowly—about 45 copies a year for ten years.

CONTEXT: In the introductory letter to Thomas Johnes, M.P. (pp. xvii–xli), dated 4 Jan. 1806, Malkin gives an account of Blake, including the reprinting of some of his poems.[5]

98. *The Marriage of Heaven and Hell* (?1790–3)

BIBLIOGRAPHICAL INTRODUCTION

See Table on pp. 286–7

TITLE: *THE* / *MARRIAGE* / *of* / *HEAVEN* / *and* / *HELL*

DATE: Composed ?1790–3; etched ?1790–3; published 1793.

Internal evidence indicates dates of composition from 1790 to 1793. On pl. 3 is a reference to the 'thirty-three years since . . . [*the*] advent' of the Last Judgement which, according to Swedenborg, had occurred in 1757, and, to clarify the implication of the passage, '1790' is written by it in copy F. Similarly, the spread of revolutionary ideas to Spain, Rome, and the rest of the world, described on pl. 25–7, seems to allude to 1792–3. Pl. 25–7 may have been conceived after the rest of the work was completed, but they are clearly integral to *The Marriage*, for they are included with all copies (A–I) containing more than four of the twenty-seven plates.

---

[1] Longman Impression Book No. 3, f. 14, with the firm of Longman Green & Co., London.
[2] Longman Commission and Divide Ledger, ff. 187, 302, Commission Ledger I, f. 30.
[3] Longman Commission Ledger I, f. 30.   [4] *Blake Records* (1969), 181, 182.
[5] *Blake Records*, 421–31.

TABLE

Copy	Plates	Leaves	Watermarks	Blake numbers	Binding-order	Leaf-size in cm	Printing colour
#A HARVARD	1–27	15¹	E & P ([19–20])	—	Loose²	18·4×26·8	golden-Brown
B BODLEY	1–27, 'Our End'³	16¹	—	—	1–27**	15·0×23·5	reddish-Brown (1, 3, 6, 8, 12, 14–15, 18–19, 22–3, 26–7) light Brown (2, 4–5, 7, 25) brownish-Black (10–11) greenish-Black (13, 16–17, 20–1, 24, 'Our End')
#C MORGAN	1–27	15¹	J WHATMAN (1, [11–12])	—	1–27	17·9×20·9	bluish-Green
#D LC	1–27	27	I TAYLOR (10) 1794/I TAYLOR (4, 13, 17, 27)	1–27	1–27**	26·8×38·0 *irregular*	Green⁴
#E *Keynes*	1–27	27	—⁵	—	1–27⁶	19·7×26·6	*golden- to dark Brown*
#F MORGAN	1–27	27	E & P (2, 9, 13, 16, 19, 24–5)	—	1–27**	19·3×26·0*	*dark Brown*
#G HARVARD	1–27	27	RUSE & TURNERS/1815 (1–2, 6, 15, 18, 24–5)	1–27	1–11, 15, 14, 12–13, 16–27	23·1×28·2*	reddish-Brown
#H FITZWILLIAM	1–27	15¹	—	1–27	1–27	13·2×20·4	reddish-Brown (1–9, 12, 14–15, 18–19, 22–3, 25–7) Green (10–11, 13, 16–17, 20–1, 24)
#I FITZWILLIAM	1–27	27	J WHATMAN/1825 (2, 8, 14, 16–17, 21, 26–7)	1–27	1–27	23·8×29·7	Red

Copy	Plates	Leaves	Binding order		State	Dimensions	Colour
K *FITZWILLIAM*	21-4	2[1]	—	—	21-4	14·5×23·7	Black
L *Harvey*	25-7	2[1]	C BALL ([25-6], 27)	—	25-7	17·4×21·3	Black
M *UNTRACED*[8]	25-7	2[1]	—			*Octavo*	Black
Keynes	3-4	1	—		Loose	15·0×23·8	Brown (3) Black (4)
UNTRACED[9]	5-6	1	*invisible*		Loose	11·7×15·9	*Sepia*
Newton[10]	11	1	*invisible*		Loose	17·9×12·9	*Colour print*
BMPR[10]	11, 14, 16, 20	4			Loose	18·9×26·0	*Colour print*
LC	14	1	—	9[10]	Loose	18·8×12·1	*Colour print*

‡‡ Water-coloured by Blake or his wife.

1-27 An italicized binding-order indicates that the binding appears to date from before 1835.

* The leaves are trimmed and gilt.

** The identifiable offsets confirm this order.

dark-Brown An italicized printing colour shows that the work is colour printed.

---

[1] Plates (3-4) (5-6) (7-8) (9-10) (11-12) (13-14) (15-16) (17-18) (19-20) (21-2) (23-4) (25-6) are printed back-to-back in copies A-C, H, K-M.

[2] The rectos of the leaves of copy A were numbered 35-48 in the normal order (1-27), evidently some time between about 1835, when it was bound after *Thel* (A) and *Urizen* (F), and 1891, by which time the works were separated.

[3] Copy B includes the separate print 'Our End is come' (dated 5 June 1793) as a frontispiece. Since this extra leaf appears to be conjugate with the succeeding leaf, pl. 1 (the other even-numbered leaves are certainly or probably conjugate with the succeeding odd-numbered leaves, making eight sheets), since it is printed in the same colour as other plates, and since it is stabbed in the same pattern as the other leaves, Blake clearly intended it to form part of *Marriage*.

[4] In copy D, the designs on pl. 2, 10-11, 14-16, 20-4 are printed in Brown.

[5] I could not find the 'E & P' watermark on three leaves of copy E reported by the Grolier Club catalogue (1905) and Keynes & Wolf.

[6] From about 1813 to 1957 copy E was (according to Keynes & Wolf) bound in the order 1-3, 5-10, 4, 11, 14, 12-13, 16-27, 15. This order is clearly confirmed by the offsets (1-2, 5-6-7-8-9, 10-?4, 11-14, 12-13-16 through 27-15), except that pl. 21 is offset on pl. 3 and pl. 16 is also offset on pl. 15. Keynes (the present owner) has had it rebound in the conventional order (1-27).

[7] The two leaves of copy L are conjunct, as in copy B.

[8] Information about the untraced copy M derives from the catalogue of the Linnell sale at Christie's, 15 March 1918, lot 198. (Keynes & Wolf copy N—27 numbered and coloured leaves—is only known from the catalogue of the Thomas Gaisford sale at Sotheby's, 23 April 1890, lot 193; the Sotheby master copy of this catalogue [in the BM] describes it in MS as a 'reprint'. Copy N is, therefore, a ghost.)

[9] Pl. 5-6 have not been traced since they were removed from the volume containing the MS 'Order' of the *Songs* and sold at Parke-Bernet, 2 Nov. 1938, lot 36.

[10] The loose plates in the collections of Miss Newton, BMPR, LC were evidently parts of the Small Books of Designs, with which some were numbered.

The genesis of *The Marriage* may perhaps be seen in Blake's comments (?1789) on Swedenborg's *Divine Love and Divine Wisdom* (1788). His ambivalent attitude toward the New Jerusalem Church and the rapid progress of political developments after 1790 may have protracted the etching of the work from 1790 to 1793. The change in the formation of the letter 'g'[1] from conventional (g, with the serif on the right) on pl. 2–3, 5–6, 11–13, 21–4 to idiosyncratic (ᵷ, with the serif on the left) on pl. 4, 7–10, 14–20, 25–7 may indicate differences in date of etching, the conventional 'g' appearing on the plates etched earlier.[2]

The date of publication is almost certainly 1793. For one thing, the earliest copies (K–M, A–C) are printed on paper without dated watermark, implying a date before 1794. In the second place, the plate called 'Our End is come', integrally printed with copy B, is dated 5 June 1793. And in the third place, *The Marriage* is advertised in the Prospectus of 10 Oct. 1793. There can thus be little doubt that the work was first printed in 1793.

PUBLICATION: The only known drafts for *The Marriage* are the sketches for *Nebuchadnezzar* (pl. 24) on *Notebook* pp. 44, 48.[3]

The nine complete copies of *The Marriage* (A–I) and the three fragments (K–M) which have survived were probably printed, coloured, and sold at two widely separate periods:

Approximate date	1793	1794	1795	1821	1825–7
Copies	K–M, A–C	D	E–F	H	G, I

The fragmentary copies K–M are apparently early proofs, for K lacks the design on pl. 24, L shows part of a line later removed from the copperplate of pl. 25, and M lacks the last eight lines (the 'Chorus') on pl. 27. These proofs, like copies A–C, were printed on both sides of rather small leaves without dated watermark. Copies K–M, A–C must have been printed about 1793, and copy B was listed in the Prospectus of 10 Oct. 1793 as 'The Marriage of Heaven and Hell, in Illuminated Printing. Quarto, with 14 designs, price 7s. 6d.'[4] Copy D, watermarked 1794, was printed on very large leaves, probably in the year the paper was made, and copies E, F, and pl. 11 (2 copies), 14 (2), 16, 20 (for the Small Book of Designs), also printed on only one side of the leaves, were probably colour printed in the next year.

After the printing of copies K–M, A–F, there seems to have been a long hiatus. *The Marriage* was omitted from lists of works for sale in Blake's letters

---

[1] As observed by Erdman, *Poetry and Prose of William Blake* (1967), p. 723.

[2] The style of lettering (vertical or roman on pl. 2, 7 [all but the top two lines], 8–10, slanted or italic on the rest) is probably not indicative of date.

[3] For suggestions that pl. 6, 12–13, 20, 27 were etched on the versos of plates bearing previous engravings, including 'The Approach of Doom' (?1788), and that versos of pl. 2, 5–10, 12–18, 20–2, 24–7 were used for *Urizen* (1794), see p. 167.

[4] This account of '14 designs' seems to refer to the fourteen designs on pl. 1–5, 10–11, 14–16, 20–1, 24, plus 'Our End is come' printed integrally as the frontispiece to copy B. (Keynes & Wolf suggest somewhat implausibly that the fourteenth design is to be found in the second design 'on pl. 4' [evidently meaning pl. 3].) The price must be that for an uncoloured copy, and copy B is the only complete copy without extensive colouring.

of 9 June 1818 and 12 April 1827. Copy H may have been printed about 1793,[1] but it was coloured for Linnell in 1821. Copy I (watermarked 1825) is probably the copy ordered by T. G. Wainewright in Feb. 1827, and copy G (watermarked 1815), which is the same in size and colouring, may have been made at the same time.

Contemporary owners of copies of *The Marriage* included William Beckford (copy A),[2] (?George) Dyer (B, which passed to Francis Douce in 1821), probably Isaac D'Israeli (D), Thomas Butts (F), John Linnell (H—bought 30 April 1821 for £2. 2s.—and copies L, M), T. G. Wainewright (?I), Henry Crabb Robinson (K, probably acquired accidentally on 10 Dec. 1825), Ozias Humphry (pl. 11, 14, 16, 20 in the Small Book of Designs [A], which passed to his son William Upcott after 1809), and John Varley (pl. 14).

COLOURING: The colouring of *The Marriage* is more intricate and variable than that for most of Blake's works. Copies B, K–M are uncoloured, except for touches of Blue on pl. 1–4 of B. Copies A and C are very lightly coloured, and the text is not coloured. Copies C and D are clear and lovely and are quite similar in colouring. All these were presumably coloured by about 1794.

Copies E[3] and F and pl. 11 (2 copies), 14 (2), 16, 20[4] were colour printed about 1795, copy F particularly splendidly, and the designs (especially the smaller ones) were water-coloured. In all these colour-printed plates, mottled effects are common, and in F the flesh is usually a greyish-Pink and the flames dark Red. There are ink margins round the plates in copies E, G–I.

Copy H was coloured about 1821 in a very curious fashion. The printed text was written over by hand with the most extraordinary care, repeating the same letters (e.g. 'Improvent' on pl. 10) and anarchic punctuation, in Black, Red, Yellow, Green, Blue, Lavender, Brown, and Pink. Sometimes two colours are used in a single line, but more often several consecutive lines are done in the same colour, so that a block of Red may be followed by a block of Green.

Copies G and I were coloured very similarly, perhaps about 1827, and in copy I the flames are often coloured Blue. In all the later copies, the text (including almost the whole page in pl. 6–9, 12–13, 17–19, 22–3, 25–7) is horizontally streaked with colour, particularly Blue (copies A–I), Pink (A, C–E, G–H), Grey (A, D, F), Yellow (C–D, F–G, I), Purple (C, E), Green (D–E, G), Brown, Orange, Red, and Black (D). The colouring of the text is not recorded in the notes below.

RUNNING HEAD: 'Proverbs of Hell' (pl. 8–10) is correct.

CATCHWORDS: There are no catchwords on pl. 1–4, 7, 10–11, 13–15, 20, 24–7; on the other plates they are given correctly ('-ah' on pl. 5; 'ro' pl. 6;

---

[1] Copy H is like copies A–C in being printed in Green and reddish-Brown on both sides of small unwatermarked leaves.

[2] Copy A does not seem to have belonged to George Cumberland, *pace* Keynes & Wolf.

[3] Copy E was cleaned at the British Museum in 1913.

[4] When pl. 11, 14, 16, 20 were printed for the Small Book of Designs, the texts were masked, so that only the designs show.

'The' pl. 8–9;[1] 'would' pl. 12; 'to' pl. 16; 'root' pl. 17; 'us' pl. 18; 'num[*ber*]' pl. 19; 'one' pl. 21; 'great[*est*]' pl. 22; '-pulse' pl. 23).

ORDER: Pl. 1–27.

The conventional order is clearly pl. 1–27; copies B–C, H were bound thus in contemporary bindings, and D, H–I were so numbered by Blake.

Copies	Order
A–D, F, H–M	1–27
E	1–3, 5–10, 4, 11, 14, 12–13, 16–27, 15[2]
G	1–11, 15, 14, 12–13, 16–27[2]

The order of copy E may have no authority, but that of copy G clearly does, for it was numbered by Blake. G is a late copy, watermarked 1815, but it must precede copy I, which is watermarked 1825 and is in conventional order. The order of copy G is clearly therefore only a temporary alteration. There are at least two authoritative orders for the plates in *The Marriage*, but most copies, including the earliest and latest, are in the order 1–27.

SIGNIFICANT VARIANTS:

Pl. 3: '1790' is added above the text (F).

Pl. 5: Another ball has been added to the design (I).

Pl. 10: The scene is altered to an island (C, H, I).

Pl. 11: The scene is altered in some copies to a cave (G, I); in others the sea is not distinguishable from the island (D, Newton pull). Once it is inscribed '"Death & Hell" / "Teem with Life"' (Newton pull).

Pl. 14: Inscribed '"A Flaming Sword" / "Revolving every way"' (LC pull).

Pl. 20: ¶73 is obscured in every coloured copy (A, C–I, BMPR).

Pl. 21: Dawn seems to rise behind the man in a few copies (D, G, H), and in D two Brown pyramids have been added.

Pl. 24: The design does not show (K).

Pl. 25, l. 6: Five more words are printed in copy L.

Pl. 27: The eight-line 'Chorus' is missing in M.

The changes on pl. 24–5, 27 were made very early on the copperplate; all the others were made in the process of colouring.

ERRATA:

Pl. 7, Proverb 13: 'whol[*e*]som[*e*]'.

Pl. 10, Proverb 66: 'improv[*em*]ent'.

Pl. 20: 'with[*h*]eld'.

None of the errata was ever corrected by Blake.

Pl. 1. TITLE-PAGE. DESIGN: Above 'HEAVEN' are leafless trees, among which are two figures walking at the left, one kneeling over the second 'E'

---

[1] There is no ambiguity about the identical catchwords on pl. 8–9, because pl. 10 clearly concludes the 'Proverbs of Hell' with 'Enough! or Too much' and therefore pl. 10 must follow pl. 9.

[2] The plates out of order are 4 ('The voice of the Devil'), 14 ('The ancient tradition . . .'), 15 ('I was in a Printing house in Hell . . .'). Of course, in copies printed with conjugate leaves, such as B and L, little variation in order was possible. The catchwords and contents firmly link in the present order all but pl. 3–4, 11, 14–15.

near cattle; above them are flying birds. Below 'HELL' a nude woman coming horizontally from the left embraces a naked man coming from the right. (These two are sketched in 'Is all joy forbidden' [?1793].) From the bottom left come gigantic flames which reach across most of the page below 'HEAVEN' towards clouds billowing from the bottom right. Between 'HELL' and 'HEAVEN' are four other embracing naked couples and nine or more single naked figures.

COLOURING: The large LOVERS are Pink darkening to Purple in A. The FLAMES, ordinarily Red, are occasionally Pink (A), dark orangish-Brown (F), or Yellow (G). The SKY is sometimes touched with Pink (C, G, I) or Green (G), and the CLOUDS in a few copies are Brown (A, E), or Blue, Red, and Yellow (G).

Pl. 2. INCIPIT: 'The Argument. / Rintrah roars . . .'. DESIGN: In a tree in the right margin, a woman in a long swirling dress supports herself by her left hand while she leans down to put something in the hand of another clothed woman standing at the foot of the tree. (The outlines of the lower girl's dress are somewhat ambiguous, and in most copies she appears to be nude. A similar scene is in *Songs* [1789] pl. 7 ['The Ecchoing Green'].) At the foot of the page is a curious plant with long wandering tendrils and two or three far smaller nude women lying on the ground leaning on their elbows. (The woman in the middle has an outline beside her head which may represent either another woman or a first draft of her own head. This extra line does not seem to be functional and is neither coloured like a person nor removed in coloured copies.) Between ll. 16 and 17, and between ll. 20 and 21 are five flying birds.

COLOURING: The TOP GIRL's dress is flesh Pink (A), Green (C, D), pale Brown (F), Blue (G [pinkish], H), or Raspberry; the LOWER GIRL's dress is flesh Pink (A, C, E, F [reddish-], G [Raspberry]), Yellow (D), Green (H), or Blue (I). The reclining FIGURES at the foot are pinkish-Blue in G, the SKY is occasionally Pink (D [brownish-], E), and the bottom BIRD is Blue (A) or Red (C).

VARIANTS: The lower girl's dress does not reach as high as her breasts in F. In D, a Brown cloud has been added at right.

Pl. 3. INCIPIT: 'As a new heaven is begun . . .'. DESIGN: Above the text, a nude (?female) figure with long hair and outspread arms seems to fly horizontally feet-foremost through flames toward the left.

Below the text, a nude woman prostrate on clouds reaches towards the left corner as she gives birth to a baby whose head and upraised arms may be clearly seen. To the right, two small naked figures run to the right.

On this and succeeding pages, there are tiny figures, birds, animals, and flourishes in most openings in the text.

COLOURING: The TOP PERSON's HAIR is blond (C) or Brown (E). The FLAMES are occasionally Brown (D [reddish-], E [orangish-]), Orange (G), orangish-Yellow (D, G), and Pink (G), and the CLOUDS at bottom are sometimes Grey (E, H), dark Red and Brown (F), or yellowish-Green (G).

VARIANTS: The bottom woman is on a cloud in A.

The last two letters of 'XXXIV' are obscure in C.

The hands of the man at the right are obscured in D.

Above the figure over 'new' in l. 1 is '1790' in dark Blue ink in F.

Pl. 4. INCIPIT: 'The voice of the / Devil / All Bibles . . .'. DESIGN: To the left of 'The voice of the / Devil' are two figures in long robes blowing trumpets, and to the right is a third. Below the text to the right is a naked man trying to fly from flames though chained by the left ankle. (The chain, which is not on the etched plate [B], has been added in the colouring [e.g. in I].) To the left, another naked man runs across the sea carrying a naked child. Behind him is the sun near the horizon. (The design, which Blake called 'The Good and Evil Angels', is repeated in a similar water-colour in the Cecil Higgins Art Gallery, Bedford [reproduced in J. Beer, *Blake's Humanism* (1968), pl. 30], and, reversed, in the two large colour prints dated 1795 in the Tate Gallery [reproduced in M. Butlin, *William Blake* (Tate catalogue) (1971), 40] and in the collection of Mr. and Mrs. John Hay Whitney [reproduced in (E. Mongan & E. Wolf 2nd) *William Blake* (Philadelphia exhibition) (1939), p. 136]. In the water-colour and in both colour prints, the angel in flames is chained and the sun is on the horizon; in the Tate print, the angel in flames is blind.)

COLOURING: The ADULTS are reddish-Pink and the CHILD Grey (D). The FLAMES are sometimes Pink (A), pale Orange (C), Yellow (D, G), or Black (D); the SKY is occasionally Pink (A, G), Green (D), Purple (D), Red (E), orangish-Brown (F), Yellow (G), or Grey (H); the SEA is dark Grey (A, C, I), Black (D, E [bluish-], H), greyish-Blue (F), greenish-Brown (G). The SUN is sometimes Red (D–E, G–H) or orangish-Brown (F).

VARIANTS: The chained figure looks downward in I.

Pl. 5. INCIPIT: 'Those who restrain desire . . .'. DESIGN: Above the text are flames reaching upward towards a sword, an upside-down man with spread arms and legs, a curious, curved object—half a (?chariot-)wheel with spokes and, at the top, a swirling cloth—a small circular object (?the sun), and a horse head-downward, all of which seem to be falling.

Above the bottom paragraph is a serpent.

COLOURING: The HORSE is dapple-Grey (C), orangish-Brown (D), Grey and dark Brown (F), or Grey with Pink (G). The CLOTH is Blue (C, D), dark Red (F), or greyish-Pink (G), and the WHEEL is uncoloured except in D, where it is Blue. The FLAMES are Yellow in D, and the SKY is occasionally Purple (A), Pink (A), Yellow (C, G, I), Grey (D, H), Red, Black, and Brown (E), dark orangish-Brown (F) or reddish-Black (G). The SUN is Red (C, D [orangish]), or Yellow (I), and the SERPENT is Grey with Red spots in F.

VARIANTS: The robe and wheel are the same colour, as if they were the same object in D.

The bottom of the page is Green, as if it were earth, in G.

In I, there is a Red ball to the left of the man, a Grey cloud to the left and a Raspberry one to the right.

Pl. 6. INCIPIT: '[Messi-]ah fell. & formed . . .'. DESIGN: Below the words 'A Memorable Fancy' are flames, into which a tiny figure at the right falls head-foremost with arms outspread. To the left of the title is a figure in a long robe.

Below the text there appear to be non-functional lines including the letters 'WOH . . .' in mirror-writing, which Blake made no effort to obscure in coloured copies and which seem indeed to be emphasized by the colouring in some copies (e.g. C, D, G).

Like pl. 6, pl. 7–9, 12–13, 17–19, 22–3, 25–7 have only small interlinear designs.

Pl. 7. INCIPIT: '[cor-]roding fires he wrote . . .'. DESIGN: To the left of 'Proverbs of Hell', a tiny woman stoops beneath a leafless tree, while to its right is a woman with a child on either side of her, all with upraised arms.

After Proverb 6 is grass and a figure running to the right, while in the bottom right corner is a figure in a flowing robe blowing a trumpet.

COLOURING: The bottom FIGURE is occasionally Yellow (D, G).

Pl. 8. INCIPIT: 'Proverbs of Hell / Prisons are built . . .'. DESIGN: To the left of 'Proverbs of Hell' and Proverbs 21, 30, 34, 37 and after Proverbs 21–6, 39 are leaves and grapes. After Proverbs 28–9 are four flying birds; after Proverb 30 are a flying bird, a lion, two crawling humans, and three sheep; after Proverbs 32–3 is a figure standing before a leafless tree; after Proverbs 34–6 is a little bay beside a cliff from which one tree grows, with two sailing boats and a dory in the water, and eight birds in the air; and after Proverb 37 are a serpent and a bounding stag.

COLOURING: The CLIFF is Green (A, G), Grey (C), or Brown (D), and the SEA is Blue (A, C, D [greenish-], G), or Grey (F).

Pl. 9. INCIPIT: 'Proverbs of Hell / The fox provides . . .'. DESIGN: To the left and right of 'Proverbs of Hell' are naked figures, and in the bottom right corner is a clothed flying couple.

Pl. 10. INCIPIT: 'Proverbs of Hell. The head Sublime . . .'. DESIGN: Below the text, a man with bat wings kneels on grass between two clothed scribes and points to part of a long unrolled scroll. Behind him there appears to be a table covered with a pillow or cloth.

At the ends of Proverbs 63–4, 66–7 are many tiny floating and dancing figures.

COLOURING: The LEFT MAN is Gold (A), Blue (C, D [dark], H), bright Red (E), Brown (F [dark], I [purplish-]), or Grey (G); the MIDDLE MAN, who is ordinarily nude-Pink (A, C, D and E [greyish-], G–H), is sometimes a striking Grey (F) or Blue (I), with Red WINGS (E); the RIGHT MAN is bluish-Purple (A), Yellow (C–D), Buff (E), Black (F), Raspberry (G), Blue (H), or Brown (I). The SKY is occasionally Grey (H), Yellow to Orange (D), oddly mottled Red, Brown, and Blue (F), or Red (H).

VARIANTS: The figures seem to be on an Island, though the sea is not shown (C) or is coloured Black (H, I).

In the bottom margin and licking up the sides are Grey, Red, and Blue flames (G).

The Central figure is seen in full profile in copy I.

Pl. 11. INCIPIT: 'The ancient Poets . . .'. DESIGN: Above the text, a woman in a long dress on an island lies beside a naked baby beneath a huge plant. Behind her is a tree stump bearing the face of a bearded man in its base (which is accentuated in copy D), and to the left a naked crowned figure with long hair like a sunrise stands in the sea with outspread arms.

Below the text are a naked figure perhaps swimming to the left and the bearded head and outspread naked arms of an old man.

At the end of paragraph 28 are four tiny figures kneeling with clasped hands and bowed heads before a much larger standing figure with a sword.

COLOURING: The MOTHER'S DRESS is light Green (A), Raspberry (C), or Pink (I), and once (I) her BABY has on a Blue dress. The MAN in the sea has on a Green blouse (C), and his HAIR AND CROWN are Gold (C, BMPR pull). All the PERSONS are pinkish-Blue in G. The SKY is sometimes shaded with Grey (A), Buff (A), Purple (D), yellowish-Green (D), Red and Green (E), vivid Red and dark Blue streaks (F, I), Orange and Red (Newton pull), Pink (G [bluish-], BMPR pull), Yellow (I), and dark greenish-Blue (Newton pull). The ISLAND, which is ordinarily Green, is occasionally dark Brown (F) or Yellow (H), and sometimes the SEA is Yellow to Green (D), dark greenish-Blue (Newton pull), or Green as if it were foliage (BMPR pull). The BOTTOM is Brown (A [dark], D), Grey (C), Black (D–E, G), or dark Blue (F).

VARIANTS: The sky is indistinguishable from the sea (E, F, BMPR pull).

A cave-mouth is drawn in Brown (G, I [streaked with Raspberry]), giving the impression that the viewer is looking out from the cave on to the ocean.

An inscription in Black ink (?by Blake) in the Newton pull reads: '"Death & Hell" / "Teem with Life"'. In the same copy, the stump is extended upward, and the island is not distinguishable from the water (also in D). The stump is a green sheaf in the BMPR pull.

Pl. 12. INCIPIT: 'A Memorable Fancy. / The Prophets Isaiah and Ezekiel . . .'. DESIGN: The only designs on the page are naked figures flanking 'A Memorable Fancy' and at the ends of paragraphs 33 and 34, and flourishes.

Pl. 13. INCIPIT: 'would at last be proved . . .'. DESIGN: Two tiny figures floating above the text and a third recumbent below it are the only significant designs on the page, other than flourishes.

Pl. 14. INCIPIT: 'The ancient tradition . . .'. DESIGN: Above the text lies a naked man stretched out rigidly as if in death. He is engulfed in flames, over which hovers a naked figure with outstretched arms.

After ¶ 42 are leaves, and at the end of ¶ 44 is a galloping horse.

COLOURING: The CORPSE is touched with Blue (A, I [pale]), Grey (C [bluish-], D–E, G), dark greyish-Brown (F), or greenish-Pink (H). The GOD is the same dark greyish-Brown as the corpse in F; his HAIR is Brown (D) or brownish-Black (BMPR pull). The FLAMES are sometimes Orange (C), blackish-Red (D), Yellow (G, H), Black (G, LC pull), Green (H), or Blue (LC pull), and the SKY is sometimes buff (A), Yellow (D, E [brownish-], I, LC pull), Pink (G), yellowish-Grey (BMPR pull), or Black (LC pull).

VARIANTS: The LC pull is inscribed (?by Blake) in Black ink: '"A Flaming Sword" / "Revolving every way"'.

Pl. 15. INCIPIT: 'A Memorable Fancy / I was in a Printing house . . .'. DESIGN: On each side of 'A Memorable Fancy' are floating figures with outspread arms.

Below the text is an eagle with outspread wings and raised head grasping a long, open-mouthed serpent. Above the eagle is another, very small bird.

Before ¶ 47 is a tiny human figure, and after ¶ 48 are two more.

COLOURING: The BIRD is Brown, sometimes touched with Pink (C), Red and Black (G), or Gold (H). The SNAKE is Green and Black (A), or Brown (D [dark], E [with Red], G [with Red and Black], H [with Gold]). The SKY is occasionally greenish-Blue (E) or orangish-Brown (F).

VARIANTS: In some copies clouds are added in water-colour.

Pl. 16. INCIPIT: 'The Giants who formed . . .'. DESIGN: Above the text are five clothed figures, a bearded old man between two pairs of boys, sitting on the grass with their heads bowed over their knees. (For similar designs, see *For Children* [1793] pl. 14.)

After ¶ 54 is a floating figure, and after ¶ 56 are two more.

COLOURING: The CLOTHES of the figures from left to right are: (1) Pink (A, I [Raspberry]), Grey (C), Blue (D), Green (E [very dark], G–H), Brown (F), Black (BMPR pull); (2) Yellow (A [greenish-], G, BMPR pull), Green (C, F [dark], H), Purple (D), dark Red (E), Blue (I); (3) Purple (A [bluish-], C [pale], I), Brown (D), Grey (E–F, H, BMPR pull), Raspberry (G); (4) Green (A, H), Red (C), Purple (D), Buff (E), Black (F), Blue (G, BMPR pull), Orange (I); (5) Grey (A, C), Yellow (D), Green (E, H, I), dark Red (F), Violet (G), Brown (BMPR pull). The WALL behind them is Grey (A, C [touched with Green]), Black (A, BMPR pull), Brown (D, E and F [very dark], G).

VARIANTS: The left man has no shirt in H and is almost invisible in the murk in the BMPR pull.

The father appears to be blind in the BMPR pull.

Pl. 17. INCIPIT: 'to reconcile them seeks to destroy existence . . .'. DESIGN: After ¶ 59 are a man, a standing horse, and a leaping horse. To the left of 'A Memorable Fancy' is a man standing under a drooping tree; over it is a soaring bird, and after it are five more flying birds.

Pl. 18. INCIPIT: 'root of an oak . . .'. DESIGN: A few flourishes form the only designs.

Pl. 19. INCIPIT: 'us with all the fury . . .'. DESIGN: The only significant designs are birds at the ends of ¶ 67–9, a pair of tiny floating figures one above the other at the end of ¶ 67, a tiny running figure before ¶ 69, and two figures soaring towards one another and touching hands at the end of ¶ 69.

VARIANTS: The top of the page seems to have been rather carelessly extended about 0·6 cm in copy I.

Pl. 20. INCIPIT: 'number of monkeys . . .'. DESIGN: Below the text (but above 'Opposition is True Friendship') is a huge, open-mouthed serpent coiling through the sea.

At the end of ¶ 70 are three tiny figures, perhaps representing monkeys.

COLOURING: The SERPENT, whose colour is largely determined by the colour of the printing-ink, is water-coloured greenish-Blue (A), Yellow (C), Red (D), Black streaked with livid Red (E), mottled Red and Blue (F), greenish-Brown (G), Red, Gold, and Black (H), dotted with Red, Blue, Brown (I), mottled Black and Red (BMPR pull); its EYE is rimmed with Red (A), and its TONGUE is Red (F, BMPR pull). The SEA is Black (A, C–D, H–I, BMPR pull), dark Blue (E, F), greenish-Brown (G), and the SKY is sometimes dark reddish-Brown (F), Yellow (G, I), Brown (E, G), Orange (G, I), Black (E, G–H, BMPR pull), or Red (H, BMPR pull [brick]).

VARIANTS: ¶ 73 is obscured by the colouring (partly because it is in White line) but barely visible in all coloured copies (A, C–I, BMPR pull).

By the end of ¶ 72 is 'N.B.' in pencil (C).

A Pink cloud appears over the Serpent (A, C), and a Black cloud is at the left with sunbeams from it to the serpent's head (G); other clouds are added in I.

Pl. 21. INCIPIT: 'I have always found that Angels . . .'. DESIGN: Above the text, a naked man with splayed legs sits on a little hill and looks upward. (A very similar figure appears in *America* [1793] pl. 8, the top of the design [1805] called 'Death's Door' for Blair's *Grave* [1808], and the Unnamed Print described and reproduced in G. Keynes, *Engravings by William Blake*: The Separate Plates [1956], pl. 23–4 and no. XIV.) Under his left knee is a skull.

On foliage just above the text are four tiny figures, the one at the right apparently reading a book.

COLOURING: The MAN's skin is occasionally bluish-Pink (A, I). The GROUND is mottled Blue (E, F), Red (E, F), Black (E), and Brown (F), and the SKY is sometimes a vivid purplish-Blue (A), Yellow (C, G), Pink (C, G), Brown (E [dark], F [reddish]), Black (E, F), Orange (G), Grey (G), pale Purple (H).

VARIANTS: There are clouds arching over the page (A, I [Green, Pink, and Yellow]).

A Yellow and Red dawn rises behind the man (D).

In D there are two Brown pyramids added in water-colour, one behind the man and one to the left.

In ¶ 75, the initial letter of 'already' is capitalized by hand in D.

Rays of light emanate from the man (G, H [gold]), and in G there is a semicircle of light around him.

Pl. 22. INCIPIT: 'one on earth that ever broke a net . . .'. DESIGN: At the end of ¶ 80 are three flying birds; to the left of 'A Memorable Fancy' is a reclining figure, and to its right is a running man with a bow who appears to have shot another figure with upraised arms.

Pl. 23. INCIPIT: 'greatest men best . . . .'. DESIGN: The only significant designs are three tiny naked figures floating beneath the text.

COLOURING: The FIGURES are Green and Red in D.

Pl. 24. INCIPIT: '[im-]pulse, not from rules . . .'. DESIGN: Between ¶ 89 and 90 is a crowned, open-mouthed, naked old man crawling to the left before what appear to be huge tree trunks. (The design, reversed and without the crown, is sketched on *Notebook* pp. 44, 48, and *Night Thoughts* drawing for Night VII, p. 27 [BMPR] and repeated in the three colour prints of 1795 which Blake called 'Nebuchadnezzar' [reproduced in M. Butlin, *William Blake* (Tate catalogue) (1971) 36, G. Keynes, *William Blake's Illustrations to the Bible* (1957) pl. 84c (Minneapolis Institute of Fine Arts copy), and D. V. Erdman, *Blake Prophet Against Empire* (1954) pl. VIIb (Boston Museum of Fine Arts copy)].)

At the end of ¶ 86 are a tiny bowed figure and another running; between ¶ 87 and ¶ 88 are five or more tiny seated figures; and after ¶ 88 is a running figure.

COLOURING: NEBUCHADNEZZAR'S SKIN is sometimes Red (D), dark reddish-Brown (E, F), or brownish-Pink (H), his HAIR AND BEARD, which are ordinarily White (e.g. in A), are occasionally Yellow (C–D), and his CROWN is Yellow (C, H and I [gold]). The TREE TRUNKS are Grey (A, E, I [bluish-]), Green (C, E [mottled], G [pale], H [greyish-]), or an odd Blue and reddish-Brown (F). In D the SMALL FIGURES are Yellow and Pink (D).

VARIANTS: The plate was masked in printing, so that nothing shows of the design in K.

Pl. 25. INCIPIT: 'A Song of Liberty . . .'. DESIGN: Except for leaves, the only representational designs are birds after ll. 4 and 9 and a floating woman in a long dress after l. 7.

COLOURING: The BIRDS are dark Red in F.

VARIANTS: l. 6 reads: 'And weep and bow thy reverend locks' in L, which seems to be an early proof copy. When the words were removed from the copperplate, no design was added to replace them.

l. 6: The defective exclamation mark appears as a full stop in D.

Pl. 26. INCIPIT: 'hurl'd the new born wonder . . .'. DESIGN: After l. 10 is a bounding stag; after l. 11 is a figure falling headlong; after l. 12 are two or more seated figures; and after l. 17 are five standing figures.

VARIANTS: l. 16: The defective terminal 'a' makes the name appear to read 'Urthonu' (B, D).

Pl. 27. INCIPIT: 'he promulgates his ten commands . . .'. DESIGN: After l. 18 are two figures, one kneeling and one running; after l. 19 are two leaping horses, one ridden by a man; on either side of 'Chorus' are leaping horses; and after 'Chorus' are six flying birds.

COLOURING: The HORSES are Grey (C) or Brown (E, F [dark]).

VARIANTS: Copy M lacks 'the 8-line Chorus at the end', according to the Christie sale catalogue of 15 March 1918, lot 198, which is the only record of this copy.

COPY A: BINDING: (1) Bound, probably for William Beckford shortly after 1835, in half calf labelled on the spine 'Blake's Works' (this binding is now with *Urizen* [F]) after *Thel* (A) and *Urizen* (F); (2) The volume was disbound probably for the 1891 Boston Exhibition, and the *Marriage* leaves were inserted individually into large pieces of fine cardboard split at the right side to allow entry, with a flap opening to show the plates.

HISTORY: (1) Numbered by William Beckford ('Nº 4029'— see *Urizen* [F], p. 181) and sold with his Library at Sotheby's, 29 Nov. 1883, lot 764 (bound with *Thel* [A][1] and *Urizen* [F]), for £121 to Quaritch; (2) Quaritch inserted his Beckford sale book-plate (see *Urizen* [F]), lent it for the Muir facsimile (1885), and offered it (Jan. 1884), lot 80, for £150;[2] (3) Acquired by E. W. Hooper, who had it disbound before he lent it to the Boston Exhibition (1891), no. 3; the *Marriage* was acquired before 1921 by his daughter (4) Mrs. Bancel Lafarge, who lent it to the Philadelphia exhibition (1939), no. 34, and bequeathed it on 7 May 1948 to (5) HARVARD.

COPY B: BINDING: (1) Originally stabbed through three holes, 7·7 cm from the top and 3·2, 4·0 cm apart, including 'The Accusers' (B) (which is printed integrally with the work); (2) Bound by 1834 in half Red morocco over marble boards, the spine gilt with 'MARRIAGE OF HEAVEN & HELL'. There may be indecipherable pencil notes on the versos of 'The Accusers' and pl. 27 which are very dirty; the last page may read: 'These extraordinary fig[*ures?*] / to rapt old'.

HISTORY: (1) Apparently advertised in Blake's Prospectus (10 Oct. 1793) and acquired by (?George) Dyer; (2) 'Blake's mar. of heaven & hell [*was acquired from*] Dyer' in April 1821 by (3) Francis Douce (according to Douce's acquisition list—Bodley, MS Douce e. 67, f. 40ᵛ), who added his book-plate and bequeathed it in 1834 to (4) The BODLEIAN LIBRARY, which described it in the catalogue of his gift (1840).

COPY C: BINDING: Bound in contemporary tree calf, gilt, rebacked, the spine lettered 'Marriage / of / Heaven / & Hell'.

HISTORY: (1) Sold by Mons. L. F. le Beaumonte, of Geneva, at Sotheby's, 18 May 1892, lot 1,192, for £50 to Bain; (2) Acquired by Robert Hoe, who added his book-plate, had it described in his catalogue (1895), lent it anonymously to the Grolier Club exhibition (1905), no. 12, and sold it posthumously at Anderson Galleries, 25 April 1911, lot 391, for $3,500 to (3) The PIERPONT MORGAN LIBRARY, where pl. 1–24 were reproduced in J. K. Singer, *The Unholy Bible* (1970).

COPY D: BINDING: (1) Originally stabbed through six holes, 1·2, 4·2, 3·8, 2·9, and 5·2 cm apart (the second hole disappears in some leaves); (2) Bound in boards, with a leather back, uncut, interleaved, from 1884 to 1924, but (3) Mounted on hinges and bound in Red morocco (by Macdonald, according to the 1927 catalogue) for G. C. Smith, Jr., by 1927, with two water-colours which were separated after 1938.

HISTORY: (1) Probably acquired by Isaac D'Israeli (see *Europe* [A], p. 156); (2) Sold posthumously by his son the Earl of Beaconsfield at Sotheby's, 20 March 1882, lot 61, for £50 to Bain; (3) Acquired by B. B. Macgeorge, listed in his Library catalogues (1892, 1906), and sold with his

---

[1] The note on a fly-leaf with the detached cover (see *Urizen* [F], p. 181)—'Cumberland sale / H. G. [?Bohn]'—presumably applies only to *Thel* (A); the history of the *Marriage* and *Urizen* before the Beckford sale is not known.

[2] It seems to be referred to in Anon., 'The Blake Drawings in the Quaritch Collection', *Critic*, xvi (1 March 1890), 110.

Library at Sotheby's, 1 July 1924, lot 115, for £660 to Maggs; (4) Acquired by G. C. Smith, Jr., listed in his anonymous catalogue (1927), lot 4 (with water-colours of pl. 1–2 [by Hotten] attributed to Blake[1]), lent to the Fogg Exhibition (1930), and sold posthumously at Parke-Bernet, 2 Nov. 1938, lot 35 (still with the water-colours), for $8,800 to Rosenbach for (5) Mr. LESSING J. ROSENWALD, who allowed the Blake Trust to make a facsimile of it (1960).

COPY E: BINDING: (1) Bound in half Maroon morocco (according to Keynes & Wolf), perhaps not long after 1813 (the date, according to a MS note by Keynes, on an endpaper—I could not find this watermark); (2) In 1957 Keynes had it 'Bound by Gray of Cambridge', with the leaves rearranged, in native dyed Red niger morocco.

   HISTORY: (1) Offered by Quaritch Catalogue 157 (March 1896), lot 37, for £60; (2) Acquired from 'Quaritch' for '£60–0–0' by 'W A White / 30 Apl. 96' (according to the note on the front fly-leaf), apparently then in the half [Maroon] roan and unique plate-order in which Keynes (1921) describes it; the darkened pigments were restored at the British Museum in 1912 (according to Keynes [1921]; a note on the last fly-leaf says: '£290 Aug 29 1913 / Dr[?] Littlejohn / £14 for cleaning'); White lent it to the exhibitions of the Grolier Club (1905), no. 11 (anonymously), perhaps to that of (1919), no. 6, and to that in the Fogg (1924); after his death in 1927 it was acquired by his daughter (3) Mrs. William Emerson, who lent it to the Fogg (1930) and Philadelphia (1939, no. 35) exhibitions, and (according to a note below White's signature) gave it to (4) 'Geoffrey Keynes / from Frances White Emerson / 5 Dec 1956'; *Keynes* had it interleaved and 'the leaves rearranged in the correct order' and rebound in 1957, and described it in his catalogue (1964), no. 510.

COPY F: BINDING: Bound after March 1852 for R. M. Milnes in Orange morocco with the Milnes wheatsheaf on the front panel, g.e.

   HISTORY: (1) Sold anonymously with the Thomas Butts collection (see *Songs* [E], p. 414) at Sotheby's, 26 March 1852, for £5. 5s. to R. M. M.; (2) Stamped on the cover with the wheatsheaf of R. M. Milnes, who allowed Camden Hotten to reproduce it [1868]; (3) Sold by his son the Earl of Crewe at Sotheby's, 30 March 1903, lot 12, for £260 to Osmaston; (4) F. P. Osmaston added his book-plate, offered it (according to Keynes & Wolf) anonymously at Sotheby's, 3 June 1905, lot 770, but apparently withdrew it (Stephens, £150); it was sold by Osmaston at Christie's, 5 April 1917, lot 1,987, for £350 to Stevens & Brown; (5) Acquired before 1921 by A. E. Newton, who added his book-plate, lent it to the exhibitions of the Fogg (1924) and in Philadelphia (1939), no. 36, and sold it posthumously at Parke-Bernet, 16 April 1941, lot 135, for $6,300 to Rosenbach; (6) Acquired by Mrs. Landon K. Thorne, who lent it to the Princeton exhibition (1969), no. 38, in whose catalogue (1971) it was described (no. 4), and who gave it in 1973 to (7) The PIERPONT MORGAN LIBRARY.

   [1] These water-colours came from J. C. Hotten, were offered in J. W. Bouton's *Original Drawings in Watercolor and India Ink by the Celebrated William Blake* (N.Y., 1875) (according to the 1923 catalogue below) and were sold by Charles Eliot Norton at American Art Association, 2 May 1923, lot 15.

COPY G: BINDING: (1) Bound in calf with *Thel* (N) and *Visions* (P) until Feb. 1890; (2) Rebound, evidently by March 1890, in Blue straight grain morocco, g.e.; there are ink frames around each plate.

HISTORY: (1) Bound in calf with *Thel* (N) and *Visions* (P) and sold anonymously at Sotheby's, 17 Feb. 1890, lot 301, for £121 to Robson; (2) Robson & Kerslake had the *Marriage* rebound, put their ticket in back, and offered it (for £63) and *Thel* (for £32) in a letter of 25 March 1890 (now with *Thel*) to (3) Alexander Mackay, who bought both, and whose widow sold the *Marriage* posthumously at Christie's, 26 April 1921, lot 3, for £460 to Shoebridge; (4) 'Acquired in 1922 from Gabriel Wells' (according to Keynes & Wolf) by Amy Lowell[1] and bequeathed by her in 1925 to (5) HARVARD.

COPY H: BINDING: Bound, probably about 1824 for John Linnell, in White vellum tooled to match his *American* (O), *Europe* (K), *Songs* (R), *Jerusalem* (C), the spine gilt sideways with 'THE MARRIAGE OF HEAVEN AND HELL'; each plate is surrounded by a Red framing-line.

HISTORY: (1) Bought by John Linnell on 30 April 1821 for £2. 2s., according to the receipt (*Blake Records* [1969], 581), bound in White vellum to match his copies of *America* (O), *Europe* (K), *Songs* (R), and *Jerusalem* (C), lent by his Trustees to the exhibitions at the Tate Gallery (1913), no. 90, Manchester (1914), no. 146, Nottingham (1914), no. 116, the National Gallery of Scotland (1914), Case A, no. 6, and sold posthumously at Christie's, 15 March 1918, lot 195, for £756 to Carfax for (2) T. H. Riches, who lent it to the Burlington Fine Arts Club exhibition (1927), no. 27, and for whom a book-plate was inserted saying it was bequeathed in 1935 to (3) The FITZWILLIAM MUSEUM, which received it in 1950.

COPY I: BINDING: The leaves are mounted on stubs and bound in hal leather; each plate is framed in a Red line.

HISTORY: (1) This is probably the copy ordered by T. G. Wainewright by Feb. 1827 (*Blake Records* [1969], 339)—in watermark, foliation, colouring, and framing-lines it is very like *Songs* (X) which Blake made for Wainewright; (2) It may be the copy sold at 'Sotheby, Dec. 1854. 4l. 16s.' (W. T. Lowndes, *The Bibliographer's Manual of English Literature* [1857], i. 216—this could alternatively be copies C, E, or N); (3) Acquired by 'Richard Edward Kerrick/August 31st 1856' (according to the inscription on the second fly-leaf), who bequeathed it at his death on 13 May 1872 to (4) The FITZWILLIAM MUSEUM; reproduced in colour microfilm by Micro Methods Ltd.

COPY K: BINDING: (1) Probably loose between 1825 and 1900; (2) 'BOUND BY RIVIERE & SON' in Blue morocco for C. F. Murray between 1900 and 1912.

HISTORY: (1) It was probably already loose in the cover of *Songs* (Z) (p. 424), when that work was acquired on 10 Dec. 1825 by H. C. Robinson, who gave it to (2) E. W. Field, who allowed it to be transcribed in a review of Gilchrist by W. F. Rae, 'The Life and Works of William Blake', *Fine Arts Quarterly*, iii (1865), 65–6, and gave it to (3) Sir Frederick Burton, who

---

[1] This may be the copy of the *Marriage* lent to the Fogg exhibition (1924) and identified as Huntington's; Huntington is not known to have owned a copy of the *Marriage*.

gave it on his deathbed to (4) Charles Fairfax Murray, who had the *Marriage* bound, added his book-plate, wrote on the first fly-leaf: 'This fragment of Blakes Marriage of Heaven & Hell came to me with the Songs of Innocence, bequeathed to me by Sir Fred^k Burton, I found it loose in the cover', and gave it in July 1912 (according to another book-plate) to (5) The FITZWILLIAM MUSEUM.

COPY L: BINDING: Loose.
N.B. The three plates are printed on one sheet.

HISTORY: (1) Sold posthumously with the John Linnell Collection at Christie's, 15 March 1918, lot 197, for £11. 11s. to Tregaskis;[1] (2) Acquired by Frank Rinder, and inherited from him by his daughter (3) *Mrs. Ramsey Harvey.*

COPY M: BINDING: Probably loose; untraced.

HISTORY: (1) Sold posthumously with the Collection of John Linnell at Christie's, 15 March 1918, lot 198, for £8. 18s. 6d. to Tregaskis; (2) *UN-TRACED.*

COPY N: HISTORY: The copy of the *Marriage* (N) with 27 numbered leaves, coloured by Blake, uncut, described as if an original in the Sotheby catalogue of the Library of Thomas Gaisford, 23 April 1890, lot 193 (sold for £2. 10s. to Quaritch) is described in MS in the Sotheby master copy in the British Museum as a 'reprint'. Copy N, therefore, is a ghost.[2]

Pl. 3–4: BINDING: Loose.

HISTORY: (1) W. B. Scott acquired the *Marriage* pl. 3–4 and *Jerusalem* pl. 37, 100, added his monogram to each, lent perhaps *Jerusalem* pl. 100 ('Study of the Human Figure') and pl. 37 ('touched by hand') to the Burlington Fine Arts Club Exhibition (1876), no. 288, 302, and sold them at Sotheby's, 21 April 1885, lot 167 (the *Jerusalem* plates described as two plates from *Jerusalem* and *America*) for £1. 5s. to Fawcett; (2) The *Marriage* (and presumably the *Jerusalem*) plates were acquired by Mrs. Graham Smith (see Keynes, below); (3) Anthony Asquith sold all four at Hodgson's in 1942 (see *Europe* pl. 2 and Keynes, below), where they were bought by (4) *Geoffrey Keynes*, who reproduced pl. 37 in Keynes & Wolf, p. 106, lent them to exhibitions of the British Museum (1957), no. 29 4, 30 4, the Whitworth Art Gallery (1969), no. 19 (*Jerusalem* pl. 100, anonymously), and the National Library of Scotland (1969), no. 66 (ditto), and described them in his catalogue (1964), no. 511, 523.

Pl. 5–6: BINDING: (1) Inlaid and bound about 1853 with other leaves of Blakeana including the 'Order' of the *Songs*; (2) Disbound after 1924, and now loose.

HISTORY: The History is given under the 'Order' of the *Songs*, p. 337.

---

[1] A note with the volume by Mrs. Rinder states (evidently erroneously) that it had been in the Edward Dowden sale of 1916.

[2] Keynes (1921) identifies as copy N the untraced copy 'acquired . . . many years ago' by Oswald Crawfurd which later passed to his widow (according to A. G. B. Russell). I have no more information about this Crawfurd copy.

Pl. 11: BINDING: See Small Book of Designs (B), p. 356.

HISTORY: (1) Originally perhaps part of the Small Book of Designs (B); (2) Acquired by Alexander Gilchrist's son H. H. Gilchrist, who lent it to the Pennsylvania Academy Exhibition (1892), no. 159; (3) 'Bought by Carl Edelheim from H. Gilchrist in 1893' (according to A. E. Newton's note on the back of the frame); Edelheim gave it (according to Keynes & Wolf) to his son-in-law (4) A. E. Newton, who lent it to the Philadelphia exhibition (1939), no. 81, and from him it passed to his daughter (5) *Miss Caroline Newton*, who lent it to the Princeton exhibitions of 1967 and 1969 (no. 52).

Pl. 11, 14, 16, 20: BINDING and HISTORY: See the Small Book of Designs (A), p. 356.

Pl. 14: BINDING: See the Small Book of Designs (B), p. 356.

HISTORY: (1) Perhaps originally part of the Small Book of Designs (B); (2) Acquired by John Varley (according to Keynes & Wolf); (3) Sold by Sydney Morse at Christie's, 26 July 1929, lot 19 (described as 'The Soul hovering over the Body'), for £78. 15s. to Colnaghi; (4) Acquired by Mr. LESSING J. ROSENWALD.

99

*The Marriage of Heaven and Hell [F]. London, [1868].
     Camden Hotten colour facsimile.

100

'William Blake's Marriage of Heaven and Hell.' *Century Guild Hobby Horse*, II (1887), 135–57.
     The first printing in conventional typography, with an Introductory Note [by H. P. Horne] (pp. 135–6).

101

The Marriage of Heaven and Hell. London, 1906. The Venetian Series.

102

The Marriage of Heaven and Hell. Boston, 1906 (vMKN).

103

The Marriage of Heaven and Hell and a Song of Liberty. With an Introduction by Francis Griffin Stokes. London, 1911.
     'Introduction', pp. 7–43.

104

The Marriage of Heaven and Hell [I]. Reproduced in [colour] Facsimile, With a Note by Max Plowman. London, Toronto & N.Y., 1927.

'A Note on William Blake's "Marriage of Heaven and Hell"', pp. 7–21, is reprinted as pp. 92–101 of Max Plowman's *The Right to Live* [ed. Dorothy L. Plowman], London, 1942. The facsimile is reproduced in no. 108.

105

§*The Marriage of Heaven and Hell.* Bristol, 1928.

106

The Marriage of Heaven and Hell. Maastricht, Holland, 1928.
A typographical reprint by the Halcyon Press.

107

The Marriage of Heaven and Hell [D]. London, 1960. The William Blake Trust.
'Descriptive and Bibliographical Statement' by Geoffrey Keynes (4 pp.).

108

A. *the marriage of heaven and hell* [I]. Introduction by Clark Emery. Coral Gables (Florida), 1963. University of Miami Critical Studies No. 1.   B. Second Printing, 1968.   C. Third Printing, 1970.

A black-and-white copy of Max Plowman's colour facsimile (1927) of copy I. The paraphrastic 'Introduction' is on pp. 1–104.

109

The Marriage of Heaven and Hell, drawings by Clark Stewart. Knoxville, Tennesee, 1972.

The 13 designs of naked women are unrelated to Blake's.

110

§*Le Mariage du Ciel et de l'Enfer.* Tr. Charles Grolleau. [Ed. Lucien Chamuel.] Paris, 1900.

111

A. 'Le Mariage du Ciel et de l'Enfer.' Tr. André Gide. *La Nouvelle Revue Française*, XIX (1922), 129–47.   B. *Le Mariage du Ciel et de l'Enfer.* Tr. André Gide.

Charlot, 1922.   C. Paris, 1923.   D. 1942. Collection Romantique. E. Paris, 1965. Collection Romantique No. 2.

The introductory and explanatory matter in A is almost invisible; in B & E the 'Introduction' covers pp. 7–8, and in C pp. 9–11.

112

Le Mariage du Ciel et de l'Enfer. Tr. Daniel-Rops [Jules Charles Henri Petiot]. Paris, 1946.

The Introduction is pp. 15–25; 'William Blake: Poésie et Prophétie' (pp. 71–92) is reprinted from no. 1458; 'Un Apocalypse pour notre temps' (pp. 95–111) is reprinted from no. 1460. There are 9 plates 'gravés sur bois en deux tons par Jean Vital Prost' which are scarcely related to Blake's. The French translation is translated into Italian in no. 116.

113

La boda del Cielo y del Infierno. (Primeros libros proféticos.) Versión castellana con introducción y notas por Edmundo Gonzalez-Blanco. Madrid, 1928.
    Introduction (pp. 5–82).

114

Snoubení Nebe a Pekla. Tr. Otto F. Babler. Olomouc [Czeckoslovakia], 1931.

115

El matrimonio del Cielo y del Infierno. Tr. Xavier Villaurrutio. With a Prefatory Note taken from G. K. Chesterton. [Mexico,] 1942 (vMKN).

116

La sposalizio del cielo e dell'inferno. [French tr. by Daniel Rops (i.e. J. C. H. Petiot), Italian tr. by Emma Manacorda Lantermo.] Firenze, 1951.
    Facing translations, Introduction, and 'Due studi su William Blake di Daniel Rops'.

117

Le Mariage du Ciel & de l'Enfer. Tr. Stephane Lamy, frontispice de Claude Weisbuch, pointes-sèches de Yves Charnay. Fontenay-aux-Roses, 1965.
    The 'Avant-propos' are 5 pp.; the 11 plates are not Blake-like.

118. *Milton* (1804–?8)

BIBLIOGRAPHICAL INTRODUCTION

See Table on p. 305

TABLE

Copy	Plates	Leaves	Watermarks	Blake numbers	Binding-order	Leaf-size in cm	Printing colour
#A BMPR	1-45	45	J WHATMAN/1808 (1, 3, 8, 18)	1-45[1]	1-45**	17·6×23·7*	Black
#B HUNTINGTON	1-45	45	J WHATMAN/1808 (3, 6, 8, 10, 24, 29, 31, 36, 40)	1-45	1-45**	16·8×23·3	Black
#C NYP	1, 3-45, a-e	49	J WHATMAN/1808 (4, 7, 26, 41, c, e)	1-2, 1, 3-8, 8*, 9-32, 32, 33-46[2]	1, b, 3, a, 4-8, c, 9-16, d, 17-20, 22-3, 25-6, 24, 27-32, e, 33-42, 21, 43-5	14·8×23·0*	Black
#D LC	1, 3-45, a-f	50	RUSE & TURNERS/ 1815 (4, 7, 10, 14-15, 25, 32, 40, 43, e-f)	1-50[3]	1, 3, b, a, f, 4-8, c, 9-16, d, 17-20, 22-3, 25-6, 24, 27-31, e, 32-42, 21, 43-5**	22·0×27·8*[4]	Red, plus *Red & Black* on 1, 3, 8, 13, 15, 21, 29, 32-3, 38, 41, 44, a, c
Harvey	38	1	—	—	Loose	15·7×23·4	Black

indicates coloured copies.
1-45   indicates copies in contemporary bindings.
**   indicates that the present binding-order is confirmed by the identifiable offsets.
*   indicates that the edges are trimmed and gilt.
Black   Italicized printing colours indicate colour printing.

[1] In copy A, numbers 16-17 are over erased numbers; that under 16 is perhaps '15'.
[2] In copy C, the numbers on pl. a-b, 3-5, 17-21, 24-8, 32, 43-5 are over erasures.
[3] Since the ink numbers in copy D are over the same thing in pencil, they may have no more authority than pencil numbers, which are ordinarily posthumous.
[4] The edges of copy D are marbled.

TITLE: *MIL | TON a Poem | in 12 Books | The Author | & Printer W Blake | 1804 | To Justify the Ways of God to Men*

'*TON . . . Books*' is written sideways from top to bottom in the right margin; '*The Author . . . 1804*' is written sideways from bottom to top in the left margin.

DATE: 1804–?8

In the autumn of 1801, as he was walking through the Sussex countryside,[1] Blake beheld in astonishment and terror the sun approach him and Los step from it. He described the experience in a poem which he sent to Thomas Butts 'above a twelvemonth' later on 22 Nov. 1802, and he incorporated it as the central event of *Milton* (see especially pl. 20–1, 40). He may have connected this experience with Milton partly because of his portrait of Milton for Hayley's library, his designs for *Comus* (1801), and his proposed (but unrealized) engravings for Cowper's translations of Milton's *Latin and Italian Poems* eventually published in 1808.[2]

Blake came to think that the purpose of his life in Felpham in 1800–3 was to write *Milton*: 'Los . . . set me down in Felphams Vale . . . that in three years I might write all these Visions To display Natures cruel holiness: the deceits of Natural Religion' (pl. 36, ll. 21, 23–5). *Milton* seems to be the poem referred to in his letter of 25 April 1803:

none can know the Spiritual Acts of my three years Slumber on the banks of the Ocean[3] unless he has seen them in the spirit or unless he should read My long Poem descriptive of those Acts for I have in these three years composed an immense number of verses on One Grand Theme Similar to Homers Iliad or Miltons Paradise Lost⌊.⌋ the Persons & Machinery intirely new to the Inhabitants of Earth (some of the Persons Excepted)⌊.⌋ I have written this Poem from immediate Dictation twelve or sometimes twenty or thirty lines at a time without Premeditation & even against my Will. *T*he Time it has taken in writing was thus renderd Non Existen*t*, & an immense Poem Exists which seems to be the Labour of a long Life all producd without Labour or Study. I mention this to shew you what I think the Grand Reason of my being brought down here⌊.⌋

It must be the same poem which he refers to in his letter of 25 July 1803:

I hope that all our three years trouble [*will*] . . . speak to future generations by a Sublime Allegory which is now perfectly completed into a Grand Poem⌊.⌋ I may praise it since I dare not pretend to be any other than the Secretary⌊;⌋ the Authors are in

[1] Blake was walking to Lavant to meet his sister, presumably as she came on the stage from London to Felpham. According to his letter of 11 Sept. 1801, she had just then returned to London; perhaps she had come not long before. If so, the experience described in the poems may have occurred about early Sept. 1801.

[2] Letters of 26 Nov. 1800, 19 Oct. 1801, 30 Jan. 1803. Blake had later experiences with Milton as well, for on 17 Dec. 1825 he told Crabb Robinson: 'I saw Milton [lately] in Imagination And he told me . . . he wished me to shew [in a poem or picture] the falsehood of his doctrine that the pleasures of *sex* arose from the fall— The fall could not produce pleasure. . . . I declined⌊.⌋ I said I had my own duties to perform'. Three weeks later he told Robinson that 'he had been command^d . . . to write abo^t Milton And that he was applauded for refusing⌊;⌋ he struggled with the Angels and was victor' (*Blake Records* [1969], 316–17, 544, 320).

[3] 'My three years slumber on the banks of the Ocean' appears in *Jerusalem* (1804–?20), pl. 3, ¶ 1.

Eternity⌊.⌋ I consider it as the Grandest Poem that this World Contains. . . . This Poem shall by Divine Assistance be progressively Printed & Ornamented with Prints & given to the Public. But of this work I take care to say little to Mʳ H. since he is as much averse to my poetry as he is to a Chapter in the Bible⌊.⌋ He knows that I have writ it for I have shewn it to him & he has read Part by his own desire & has looked with sufficient contempt to inhance my opinion of it.

These letters cannot refer exclusively to *Jerusalem* (1804–?20), which is not markedly autobiographical, nor can the 'immense Poem' refer just to the much shorter *Milton*. Perhaps Blake had in draft a poem which comprehended the actions that were later divided between *Milton* and *Jerusalem*. Moreover, the poem 'perfectly completed' cannot be *Milton* as we now have it, for parts of it were clearly written after 1803. Perhaps the clearly autobiographical portions of *Milton* dealing with the quarrel of Blake–Palamabron, Catherine Blake–Elynittria, and Hayley–Satan on pl. 3–11, his visions of Ololon (who only appears in *Milton*), of Los and Milton on pl. 12–22, 29–45, and the songs of Beulah on pl. 24, 31–2, 34, f were drafted but not yet 'Ornamented with Prints' or etched by the summer of 1803.

The title-page is dated 1804, and presumably it and some of the other plates were etched then. Blake refers on pl. a to 'South Molton Street', where he lived from late 1803 until 1821. His reference on pl. 17 to 'Scofield' is connected with Private John Scolfield's accusation (15 Aug. 1803) that Blake had '*damned the King*', which led to Blake's indictment (4 Oct. 1803), trial, and acquittal (11 Jan. 1804) on the charge of sedition.[1] The passages concerning South Molton Street and Scolfield must have been composed after the summer of 1803.

There were yet years of revision and addition before the poem could be 'given to the Public'. The condemnation in the 'Preface' (pl. 2) of the low prices given by 'fash[i]onable Fools' for works of genius and the 'expensive advertizing boasts that they make of such works' evidently stems from Blake's experiences with R. H. Cromek, who bought Blake's designs for Blair's *Grave* in the autumn of 1805. Cromek immediately began advertising them vigorously, with a crescendo of notices when the work was published in the summer of 1808. The 'Preface' allusions to Cromek must have been written after 1805. It seems likely that the passages describing 'the Persons & Machinery' of eternity on pl. 5, 11, 14, 16–17, 24, 26–8, 30, 32, 34–5, 37, b–c, e–f, and Los's struggles in heaven (pl. 22–8) were also drafted later than the more personal passages.

The villain named 'Hand', who appears on pl. 17 and 22, is evidently to be identified with Leigh Hunt and his two brothers, who attacked Blake in their *Examiner* on 7, 28 Aug. 1808, and 17 Sept. 1809 as a 'visionary' (in the first) and an 'unfortunate lunatic' (in the last).[2] Hand is only slightly defined in *Milton*, but in *Jerusalem* (1804–?20) his 'Three Brains in contradictory council' (pl. 70, l. 5) and his three pointing hands (pl. 93) are clearly associated with the three Hunts, whose contributions to the *Examiner* were often signed with the symbol of a pointing hand. The appearance of Hand in *Milton*, then, probably dates from after August 1808. Probably the 'Preface'

---

[1] *Blake Records* (1969), 125, 131, 140.   [2] *Blake Records*, 195, 198–9, 216.

(pl. 2) was written at the same time, for in it Blake defends himself against the 'ignorant Hirelings' of the press, as he does in the *Descriptive Catalogue* (1809) ¶ 48 and, in different terms, in the 'Public Address' (?1810–11).

Since pl. 12–22 are similar to each other in form, with regular catchwords, small figures in the right margin, and 60–62 lines per page when there is no large design, the references to Hand on pl. 17 and 22 suggest that they were all etched after August 1808. Pl. 43, which condemns those pretenders to the arts who 'mock [*inspiration*] with aspersion of Madness' (l. 8) probably also comes after August 1808.

Since pl. 2, containing references evidently to 1808, is present in the earliest copies of *Milton* (A B), the poem cannot have been finished before then. The watermark of 1808 demonstrates that the work was printed after that time in its first published state. If, as seems likely, the work was finished with a rush, with at least pl. 2, 17, 22, and 43 being etched in or after 1808, the extra pl. a–e may have been completed, etched, printed, and added to copy C at the end of 1808 as well. Pl. f, which appears only in copy D watermarked 1815, may have been etched almost any time in the ten years before then. I should guess that it was etched about 1808, just after copy C was completed.

The dates of *Milton* may therefore be as follows:

Approximate date	Of composition of passages on plates	Of etching of plates
1803	1, 3–22, 24, 29–45, f	
1804–6	5, 11, 14, 16–17, 22–8, 30, 32, 34–5, 37, a–c, e–f	1, 3–11, 24–41
1808	2, 17, 22, 43	2, 12–23, 42–5, a–f

PUBLICATION: *Milton* was written and etched over a period of six or more years (1803–8). It is organized in 'Books' like *Thel* (1789), *Urizen* (1794), *Ahania* (1795), *The Book of Los* (1795), and parts of *Vala* (?1796–?1807), and at one point it consisted of 'an immense number of verses'. This bulk is indicated on the title-page, where it is described as 'a Poem in 12 Books'. However, the work does not correspond to this description, and on 28 March 1826 T. G. Wainewright wrote anxiously: 'The title says in 12 books. My copy has but 3! yet "*Finis*" is on the last page! How many should there be?'[1] Either Wainewright was careless in describing his copy, or his was different from any that survives today, for all known copies have only two books, and in copies A and C Blake obscured the first numeral of '12' to make it correspond with the work as published. It seems likely that the long delay in completing the poem may have been partly caused by the labour of reducing the 'immense number of verses' to the present two books of *Milton*.

By the time he came to etch it, Blake's resources were even more limited than previously, and some of the copper he chose had already been used for other purposes. Pl. c seems to be etched over another design, and pl. 26

---

[1] *Blake Records* (1969), 327.

shows (under the bottom cliff) the plate-maker's-mark stamped on the versos of copperplates.

The work was a bulky one, with few of the designs which apparently attracted most of his customers, and he evidently printed very few copies. Three of those that survive (A–C) were apparently printed about 1808,[1] as the watermark date suggests, and then pl. 21 and 24 were rearranged, pl. 2 was removed, and pl. a–e were added to copy C, perhaps also at the end of 1808. Finally, in or after 1815, a fourth copy was printed with yet another new plate (f), bringing the total number of plates in copy D to fifty. It must be this last copy which was offered in Blake's letter of 9 June 1818 as '50 do [Prints] Quarto [£]10. 10. 0', for no other copy has that number of plates. He did not mention *Milton* in his list of writings in the letter of 12 April 1827. Among Blake's contemporaries, copies were acquired by Thomas Butts (?A), T. G. Wainewright (?B, bought shortly before March 1826), William Beckford (C), and James Vine[2] (copy D, bound with *Thel* [O]).

Milton attracted little attention, and only two other possible contemporary references to it are known. The anonymous author of an article in *Urania* (1825) reported that Blake 'has, as he affirms, . . . now by him a long poem nearly finished, which was recited to him by the spirit of Milton', and Allan Cunningham wrote in 1830 that 'Milton, in a moment of confidence, entrusted him with a whole poem of his, which the world had never seen'.[3] However, Blake said that *Milton* was inspired by the 'Daughters of Beulah' (pl. 3) and that 'the Authors are in Eternity'. If these references of 1825 and 1830 are indeed to *Milton*, they must be somewhat garbled.

COLOURING: Pl. 1, 8, 13, 15, 21, 29, 33, 38, 41, and 45 are full-page plates, and there are smaller designs on pl. 3–4, 12, 14, 16, 24, 26, 30, 32, 36, 42–4, a, and c. In these designs the genitals of the males are regularly invisible or obscured (pl. 8, 12–14, 16, 21, 29, 33, 38). There are no designs of significant size on pl. 2, 5–7, 9–11, 17–20, 22–3, 25, 27–8, 31, 34–5, 37, 39–40, b, d–f; of these, pl. 2, 34–5, 37, 39 have no designs at all, pl. 17–20, 22–3, 25, 28, and b have small nudes in the margin, and the rest have only tiny figures, insects, foliage, or incidental flourishes at the right. Pl. 1, 13, 38, 41 are engraved in White line, and therefore the effect is dark, the chief colour being that of the printing-ink.

In all copies of *Milton*, the designs are coloured, and the text is streaked with colour, chiefly greyish-Blue, Pink, and Yellow. In copies A–C, the colouring is sombre, and the larger figures are greyish-Pink. In copy B the dominating colour is greyish-Blue, some Gold is used, and the colouring is stronger in Book II. In copy C, there is a Black framing-line about 0·8 cm from the plate-mark, there is some Gold, and the text is occasionally clarified in pencil (pl. 11) or in ink (pl. 25, 39). In copy D, the full-page designs plus

[1] Between printing copies A and B, he altered the copperplate of pl. 3 and erased a line on pl. 24.
[2] On 8 April 1822 Blake went with John Linnell 'To Mr Vine's' (*Blake Records* [1969], 275), perhaps to deliver *Milton* (D) and *Thel* (O), which were said to have been '*exquisitely finished in colours* . . . expressly for his principal patron Mr. Vine of the Isle of Wight' (H. G. Bohn's 1847 catalogue).
[3] *Blake Records*, 297, 488.

pl. 3, 32, 44, a, c, and e are printed in Red and Black, and the colouring is lighter and stronger than in the other copies. Some letters and details of features are touched in ink, and the effect is splendid.

CATCHWORDS: The catchwords are all correct: pl. 9 ('For'), 10 ('Sick'), 14 ('To'), 16 and 18 ('And'), 20 ('Can'), 24 ('Loud', erased or covered in C–D), 25 ('These', erased in C), 27 ('For'), 30 ('Into'), 31 ('And'). The only ambiguities are caused by the 'For' on pl. 9 and 27, corresponding to the incipits on pl. 10 and 28; by the 'To' on pl. 14, corresponding to the incipits on pl. 15, 43, 45; and by the 'And' on pl. 16 and 18, corresponding to the incipits on pl. 7, 17, 19, 32, 34, 39, d–e. However, in each case the continuity of the narrative removes any uncertainty as to which incipit matches which catchword.

ORDER: Pl. 1–3, b, a, f, 4–8, c, 9–16, d, 17–31, e, 32–45, with authoritative variants.

Pl. 1–20, 22–3, 25–45 are invariably in that order in relation to each other. Copies A–B agree in arranging the plates 1–45, and pl. 2 (the 'Preface') invariably follows pl. 1 when it is present (A–B). In copies C–D, pl. 2 was omitted, pl. a–e (plus pl. f in D) were added, and pl. 21 and 24 were moved to new positions. The change in order came about while copy C was being put together, perhaps at the end of 1808 shortly after the first two copies had been finished.

Copy C was first numbered without pl. a–e, probably in the order of copies A–B.[1] Then pl. 2 was removed, pl. a–b, d were added, pl. 21 and 24 were put in their new positions, and the numbers on pl. 3–5, 17–21, 24–8, 43–5 were altered to accommodate the new order: pl. 1, 3, b,[2] a, 4–16, d, 17–20, 22–3, 25–6, 24, 27–42, 21, 43–5. Pl. 24 follows pl. 26 without greatly disrupting the text, after Blake erased its catchword in copies C–D. The full-page design on pl. 21 clearly derives from a passage on pl. 20 which it first followed in copies A–C; its significance after pl. 42 seems obscure. Pl. b begins with the same words as pl. 5—'By Enitharmons Looms'—but it was evidently intended to follow pl. 3,[2] and pl. a is effective after pl. b.[2] However, pl. 4 fits very ill after either pl. a or pl. b, because it begins with a sentence fragment. Pl. d appropriately begins with 'And' to match the catchword on pl. 16.

Finally pl. c and e were added to copy C, with extra numbers (8*, 32*). Pl. c fits between pl. 7 and pl. 9 well enough, but pl. e is very awkward after pl. 32.

Copy D, which was made not before 1815, is bound like copy C except for three plates: pl. b is correctly bound after, rather than before, pl. 3; pl. f is

---

[1] The confused numbering at the beginning of copy C suggests that pl. 2 may have been included in the first foliation.

[2] In copy C, pl. b is numbered '2' to follow the '1' on pl. 3. However, the binder evidently became confused because there is also a '1' on pl. 1, so he erroneously made the initial order: pl. 1, b, 3, a, 4–8 . . . This is clearly an impossibility, for it makes the poem begin with a sentence fragment. The sense of the text demonstrates that pl. a must follow pl. b (as it does in copy D) and not pl. 3 (as it does in the erroneously bound copy C). Copy D, and all other evidence in copy C except the binding, demonstrate that pl. b should follow pl. 3, and that pl. a should follow pl. b.

persuasively added after pl. a; and the awkward pl. e somewhat more satisfactorily precedes pl. 32 rather than following it.

Taking copies A–B as standard, the authoritative variants in order, then,
are these: pl. 2 was removed and pl. a–e were added (plus pl. f in D), pl. 21
was awkwardly moved to follow pl. 42, and pl. 24 was not inappropriately
placed after pl. 26. Pl. e proved to be rather unsatisfactory after either
pl. 31 or pl. 32, and the opening sentence on pl. 4 was never altered to
accommodate its interruption by pl. b, a.

The order suggested above, then, is a composite one, combining pl. 2 with
pl. a–f, though they are never found in the same copy, and inserting the
extra plates into the earlier order.

VARIANTS:

Pl. 1: '12' was altered to '2' in copies A and C.
Pl. 2 was omitted in copies C–D.
Pl. 3: 'That' in copy A was altered to 'What' in copies B–D.
Pl. 4: the last two words were deleted in copies C–D.
Pl. 5: l. 1 was erased in copies C–D.
Pl. 9 (C) and 10 (B) have a rainbow over the text.
Pl. 22: l. 30, 'Pitying' was altered to 'Saying' in copy D.
Pl. 23: 'raving' was altered to 'roaring[?]' in copy B.
Pl. 24: l. 60 was erased from copies B–D, and the catchword from copies C–D.
Pl. 25: the catchword was erased in copy C.
Pl. 29, 33: shorts have been added to the naked men in copies B–D, though
  not in pl. 14, where the same figure and action appear.

ERRATA: 'fash[i]onable' (pl. 2), 'mou[n]tains' (pl. 7), 'Forgivenes[s]' (p. 15),
'Transgres[s]ors' (pl. 20), 'thun[d]ers' and 'arou[n]d' (pl. 23), 'laceratin[g]'
(pl. 24), 'from' omitted (pl. 25), 'pos[s]essors' (pl. 27), 'danc[e]', blocked by
the plate margin (pl. 31), 'enterance' (pl. 35), 'Rahah' for 'Rahab' (pl. 37),
'Femi[ni]ne', an extra 'ann be' (pl. 42), 'tim[e]', blocked by the plate margin,
'Fem[in]ine' (pl. 43), 'Individiality' (pl. a), 'Enitharman' (pl. c), 'Halle[l]ujah'
(pl. e), 'crue[l]ties' (pl. f).

Pl. 1. TITLE-PAGE. DESIGN: A dark naked man walks from us with his
right arm outstretched. To the left of his head are the letters '*MIL*'; vertically
to the right of his extended hand is '*TON a Poem* / *in 12 Books*'; vertically
to the left of him, the other way up, is '*The Author* / *& Printer W Blake* / *1804*';
and beneath his feet is the motto, '*To Justify the Ways of God to Men*'.

COLOURING: The BACKGROUND is Black (A–B, D), dark Blue (B), and
Grey (C), and the GROUND at the left is Yellow (A) or flame Orange to Red (D).

VARIANTS: The '1' in '12' is virtually obscured by a swirl in copies A and
C, though it is clear in B and D.

Pl. 2. INCIPIT: '*PREFACE . . .*'.

Pl. 3. INCIPIT: '*MILTON* / *Book the First . . .*'. DESIGN: In the top right
corner a huge Red star throws vivid light upon the title on which six figures

are resting amidst foliage. Below and beside 'Book the First' are a naked, floating man (on the left) and a woman with their arms above their heads.

COLOURING: The star's RAYS are Pink (A, D) and Yellow (B–D), and the BACKGROUND is Pink (A), Black (B, D), or Brown (C).

VARIANTS: l. 21: 'That' in A was mended in the copper to 'What' in B–D.

Pl. b. INCIPIT: 'By Enitharmons Looms when Albion . . .'. DESIGN: At the side of ll. 3–8, 10–21 are three small nude female figures.

Pl. a. INCIPIT: 'Beneath the Plow of Rintrah . . .'. DESIGN: Between ll. 14 and 15 are a cromlech and several other cromlech-like stones, with tiny people at their feet at the left.

Below the text, a third of the page is taken up with a complicated design of a clothed woman at the bottom left kneeling with her hands to her head; beside her stands a clothed woman with a long staff (?a distaff), similar in position to a nude (?female) figure with its back to us also with a distaff and holding an object like a plumb bob over distant cromlechs in the background. In the centre is a large, elliptical rock with a kneeling figure on it, and in the background is a cliff with larger cromlechs on it.

COLOURING: The women's DRESSES are Grey (C [left and right]) and Pink (D), and the SKY is partly Pink (C–D), Yellow (C–D), and Black (C–D).

Pl. f. INCIPIT: 'Palamabron with the fiery Harrow . . .'. DESIGN: In the bottom left corner is a small nude woman in flames. ll. 41–4 are indented round the design in the bottom left corner, and each line is written on two or three levels.

Pl. 4. INCIPIT: 'From Golgonooza the spiritual . . .'. DESIGN: Between ll. 26 and 27, about a third of the page is taken up with a gigantic Grey cromlech beneath a cloudy sky with a crescent moon. At the base of the cromlech are a tiny horse and rider and trees.

VARIANTS: l. 35: The last two words, '& Woven', are erased from the paper (C) or perhaps from the copperplate (D).

The scene is coloured as if it were daylight in copy B.

Pl. 5. INCIPIT: 'By Enitharmons Looms . . .'. DESIGN: After ll. 21–2, 27–8, 31–3 are three tiny human figures.

VARIANTS: l. 1 is erased from the paper in copies C–D, and replaced by tendrils in D.

ll. 4–5: The last half of l. 4 and the first half of l. 5 are erased, apparently from the paper, in all copies.

Pl. 6. INCIPIT: 'Mean while wept Satan . . .'. DESIGN: After ll. 10–11, 14–15, 20–2 and below the text are four tiny human figures.

Pl. 7. INCIPIT: 'And all Eden descended . . .'. DESIGN: After ll. 7–10 is a tiny human flourishing large leaves, after ll. 28–9 is a tiny floating figure, and after ll. 34–42 there seem to be two tiny figures climbing a tree.

Pl. 8. DESIGN: The whole plate is a design of a naked man and woman (?Los and Enitharmon) at the left, who look right towards a naked man (?Orc) on a small pedestal in flames. The background is Black.

COLOURING: The BACKGROUND behind the couple at the left is orangish-Pink (B) or greyish-Blue (D). The FLAMES are sometimes pale yellowish-Green (A), Grey (A, C), Yellow (B–D), and greyish-Blue (B).

VARIANTS: Light comes from the top right in copy C.

In copy D, the man at the left has a short beard, and the pedestal has been extended to the right margin.

Pl. c. INCIPIT: 'then Los & Enitharmon knew . . .'. DESIGN: Below the text, a third of the page is taken up by the design of an old woman in a long dress rushing with outspread arms in front of an arched doorway.

COLOURING: The BACKGROUND is Black (D), pale Yellow (D), and pale Blue (D).

Pl. 9. INCIPIT: 'He set his face against Jerusalem . . .'. DESIGN: After ll. 14–15, 18–20, 33–6 are three tiny figures, the one at the bottom in a large hat apparently playing a flute. In openings in the text are flourishing tendrils and birds.

COLOURING: The two top FIGURES are yellowish-Green in copy D.

VARIANTS: In copy C is a rainbow over the text from the top left to the middle right. From top to bottom it is coloured Orange, Green, greyish-Blue, and Raspberry.

Pl. 10. INCIPIT: 'For her light is terrible to me . . .'. DESIGN: To the right of ll. 6–7, 11–15, 24–5, 31–3, 42 are six tiny figures.

VARIANTS: In copy B there is a rainbow (presumably of Elynittria, ll. 14–15) from the middle right to the bottom. It is coloured (from top to bottom) Red, Yellow, Blue, and Purple.

Pl. 11. INCIPIT: 'Sick couch bears the dark shades . . .'. DESIGN: After ll. 8–10, 16–19, 32–5, 47–8 are four tiny human figures, the top one seated in a chair.

Pl. 12. INCIPIT: 'According to the inspiration . . .'. DESIGN: Between ll. 3 and 4 a small naked man lies sprawled at the left and another runs away to the right. In the background are branches and what appears to be a stone wall (?an altar).

COLOURING: The SKY is sometimes Yellow (B) or Raspberry (C).

Pl. 13. DESIGN: The plate is a splendid full-page design of a naked man with a nimbus standing with raised arms holding White garments. Behind him is a ?rising Yellow sun. The scene evidently represents Milton as 'He took off the robe of the promise, & ungirded himself from the oath of God' (pl. 12, l. 13).

COLOURING: The BACKGROUND is Black (A [very dark purplish-], C–D) or dark Brown (B). MILTON is dark greyish-Red (B), his HAIR is golden-Brown (D), and his NIMBUS is dark reddish-Black (A), White (C), or Red (D). The sun's RAYS are Yellow (B–C), Orange (C), and Red (D).

VARIANTS: In copy D, the rays from the nimbus extend almost to the margins, and Milton's hair extends to the tops of his shoulders.

Pl. 14. INCIPIT: 'As when a man dreams . . .'. DESIGN: After ll. 7–10,

19–22, 33–6 are four tiny human figures, the one at the top being a kneeling woman who holds a small child on her knees.

Between ll. 46 and 47 is depicted on the left a small falling man (?Blake) exactly in the position of the one on pl. 29, with a star entering his left foot; in the centre is a stone wall like that on pl. 12; and on the right is a clothed woman (?Catherine Blake) with her hands to her head.

COLOURING: In copy C, the two figures at the bottom of the right margin are dressed in yellowish-Green and Raspberry.

VARIANTS: The face of the falling man is turned slightly towards us in copy D.

Pl. 15. DESIGN: The whole plate is a design of a naked man standing with his back to us with his hands on the throat or shoulders of an old man with a long White beard and a Grey robe whose hands are on stone tablets on the left and right which seem to read:

$$\text{שסטה} \ / \ \text{יזמ—} \quad \text{—ואסש} \ / \ \text{ה:וס} \ / \ \text{חח}$$

The naked man is stepping across what seems to be a stream, on which is written: 'To annihilate the Self-hood of Deceit & false Forgivenes[s]'. The scene perhaps represents the strife of Milton and Urizen (pl. 17, ll. 25–6). On a curving Black hill in the background is a man with two women on each side of him. They are playing instruments, from left to right a straight horn, a tambourine, a harp, a curved horn, and a tambourine again. Behind them is brilliant light as of a rising sun.

COLOURING: From left to right, the musicians' CLOTHES are: (1) Blue (A [pale], D), Pink (B), Green (C); (2) Green (A), Grey (B–C), Blue (D); (3) Blue (A), naked-Pink (B–D); (4) Pink (A), Grey (B), Blue (C–D); (5) Grey (A), Pink (B, D [yellowish-]), light Orange (C). The SKY is Yellow (A [strong], B [orangish-]), Green (A), and Red (B), and once the HILL in the background is partly mottled Green (B).

VARIANTS: In copy C there are Gold flames under the young man's feet, and the stone tablets are illegible.

In copy D, the left-hand tambourine player looks at us, and the harper has a clear halo.

Pl. 16. INCIPIT: 'In those three females . . .'. DESIGN: Above the text, three women on an elegant Regency couch at the right look away from three writhing women at the left.

Below the text, a naked man at the left looks warily at a tree with a human torso and legs which stretches bare Brown branches horizontally towards him above a bearded face in the ground.

COLOURING: The three women on the right are wearing DRESSES of bluish-Grey (A–B), Blue (C), and pale Red (D); from left to right, those on the left are in (1) Pink blouse, Green skirt (A), Pink (B), Green (C), Blue (D); (2) Grey (A), uncoloured (B), Blue (C–D); (3) Pink (A–C), Blue (D). The SKY is partly Orange (A, C), Purple (A), Pink (A), Brown (A), orangish-Red (B), Yellow (C), and Green (D).

VARIANTS: In copy D the women on the right are looking towards curious

Red and Yellow objects which might be torch-bearers; there is nothing of the kind in A.

Pl. d. INCIPIT: 'And Tharmas Demon of the Waters . . .'. DESIGN: After ll. 9–14 there appears to be a tiny figure.

Pl. 17. INCIPIT: 'And he also darkend . . .'. DESIGN: At the right of ll. 1–4, 6–9, 11–15, 17–23, 32–7, 40–4, 55–60 are eight small figures.

Pl. 18. INCIPIT: 'Two yet but one . . .'. DESIGN: After ll. 19–33, 35–42, 53–9 are small, naked human figures, and after ll. 6–12 is a bunch of grapes.
    COLOURING: The GRAPES are Green in copy D.

Pl. 19. INCIPIT: 'And down descended . . .'. DESIGN: After ll. 7–15, 24–31, 35–42, 45–53, 56–9 are five small naked figures.

Pl. 20. INCIPIT: 'Tho driven away . . .'. DESIGN: After ll. 1–24, 28–34, 36–47, 52–7 are five small naked figures, the two at the top plummeting downwards.
    COLOURING: The top (A) and bottom right figures (A, D) are Blue.

Pl. 21. DESIGN: The whole page is a design of a naked man stepping from a flaming Yellow circle, while before him on grass kneels another naked man wearing a sandal on his right foot, who looks over his shoulder at the sun-god.
    COLOURING: The FLAMES in the sun are sometimes pale Grey (B) or Blue (C).
    VARIANTS: Both men have been given transparent shorts in copy C and a kind of flesh-Pink girdle in D.

Pl. 22: INCIPIT: 'Can you have greater Miracles . . .'. DESIGN: To the right of ll. 11–20, 24–8, 33–6, 40–4 are four small figures.
    COLOURING: The second and fourth figures (counting from top to bottom) are dressed in Pink and greyish-Blue in copy B; all the figures are bluish-Grey in copy D.
    VARIANTS: l. 30: the first word seems to be altered to 'Saying' in copy D.

Pl. 23. INCIPIT: 'Of Palamabrons Harrow . . .'. DESIGN: To the right of ll. 1–16, 20–8, 30–43, 51–63, 67–74 are five small, naked figures.
    VARIANT: l. 66, 'roaring' in copy B is altered from 'raving' in copies A, C–D.

Pl. 24. INCIPIT: 'But the Wine-press of Los . . .'. DESIGN: Between ll. 24 and 25 are a 'Centipede', a 'ground Spider', a 'Beetle', an 'Earth-worm', a 'Grasshopper', a 'Toad', and a dragon-headed, short 'Serpent' (of ll. 11–22), and above them in the right margin are birds and a moth.
    VARIANT: l. 60 was erased, apparently from the paper, in copies B–D, and the catchword was erased from copies C–D, because pl. 25 (which it matches) does not follow pl. 24 in these copies.

Pl. 25. INCIPIT: 'Loud shout the Sons of Luvah . . .'. DESIGN: After ll. 27–35, 59–63 are two tiny human figures.
    VARIANT: The catchword is erased in copy C, though it is followed by pl. 26 which matches the catchword.

Pl. 26. INCIPIT: 'These are the Sons of Los . . .'. DESIGN: Between ll. 15 and

16, and between ll. 43 and 44 are strange, uncoloured or Grey rocky shapes, perhaps representing cliff-sided islands, with one town at the left of the upper island and another at the right of the lower one.

COLOURING: The bottom island is Green on top in copy D.

Pl. 27. INCIPIT: 'Some Sons of Los . . .'. DESIGN: In the right margin are many birds of different sizes, including a dragon-like one at the top right, and between ll. 43 and 44 is a long, curling, leafless tendril.

Pl. 28. INCIPIT: 'For in this Period . . .'. DESIGN: To the right of ll. 1–20, 23–8, 31–9 are four small naked figures.

Pl. 29. DESIGN: The whole page is a design of a naked man labelled 'WILLIAM' falling backwards with outstretched arms on to grass and three stone steps, as a large star falls in flames on his left foot. (He is a reversed version of the design labelled 'ROBERT' on pl. 33, evidently representing William Blake and his beloved brother Robert. A figure almost exactly like the one here is on pl. 14.)

COLOURING: The star's RAYS are pale Yellow (B, C [golden]) and Pink (B), and its flames are once Blue (C). The BACKGROUND is Black (A–B, D) or Brown (C), and behind the man in A it is Yellow.

VARIANTS: The man has been given shorts which are transparent Pink (B), Yellow (C), or Green (D).

Pl. 30. INCIPIT: 'Milton / Book the Second . . .'. DESIGN: To the left and right of 'Book the Second', two small naked figures fall headlong, while two small women in long dresses beneath the titles run towards them. To the left of and above the title is lightning, and to the right a small nude woman floats upwards. Above the heavy clouds surrounding the title is written in mirror-writing: 'How wide the Gulf & Unpassable between Simplicity and Insipidity', while between 'Milton' and 'Book the Second' in mirror-writing is: 'Contraries are Positives⌐;⌐ A Negative is not a Contrary'.

COLOURING: The women's DRESSES are greyish-Blue (D [left]) and Green (D), and the SKY is partly Yellow (A, C–D), Raspberry (C–D), and Black (D).

VARIANTS: Copy A is surrounded by a border of linked floating, naked Brown figures.

Pl. 31. INCIPIT: 'Into this pleasant Shadow . . .'. DESIGN: In the right margin are several shapes which may represent a flower, among other things.

Pl. e. INCIPIT: 'And Milton oft sat up . . .'. DESIGN: In the right margin and partly filling the spaces between stanzas are tendrils and leaves.

Pl. 32. INCIPIT: 'And the Divine Voice was heard . . .'. DESIGN: Below the text are four intersecting flaming circles marked with the cardinal points and the names of the Zoas: 'N   Urthona / E   Luvah / S   Urizen / W   Tharmas'. In the centre is a flaming egg, the northern and southern portions of which are labelled 'Adam / Satan' while from the south-east comes a line passing through 'Satan' to 'Adam', identified as 'Miltons Track'.

COLOURING: The CIRCLES are Grey (A, C [bluish on right, pinkish on bottom]), Brown (B [top one yellowish, right one greyish, bottom one reddish, last one greenish], D [reddish, top one greyer]), and yellowish-Orange (C [top one]). The EGG is bluish-Grey (A, C), uncoloured (B), or dark Blue (D), the outer FLAMES are Yellow, with some Magenta (B), Raspberry (C), bluish-Grey (C), and greyish-Blue (D), and the BACKGROUND is once reddish-Purple (A).

Pl. 33. DESIGN: The whole page is a design carefully echoing that on pl. 29, representing a naked man labelled 'ROBERT' falling with outspread arms backwarks on three stone steps, as a flaming star falls on his right foot.

   COLOURING: The MAN is Grey (A), the background SKY is Black (A, B–D [bluish-]) and dark Raspberry at top right (C), the STAR is uncoloured (A–B) or Yellow (C), and its FLAMES are sometimes bluish-Grey (A), pale Blue (B), and Yellow (C).

   VARIANTS: Robert Blake has been given decorous Pink (B), transparent Yellow (C), or pale Green (D) shorts, as William was on pl. 29. A fragmentary fourth (top) step has been added in copy D.

Pl. 34. INCIPIT: 'And all the Songs of Beulah . . .'. DESIGN: There is a small, worm-like object after l. 7.

Pl. 35. INCIPIT: 'Are here frozen . . .'.
   VARIANTS: In copy B, the bottom right is Orange and Yellow as if with rising flames.

Pl. 36. INCIPIT: 'When on the highest lift . . .'. DESIGN: Below the text is a design of a White-walled thatched house labelled 'Blakes Cottage / at Felpham'. Below walks a small man in the garden looking up at a figure in the sky (over the pump) in swirling draperies. To the right are trees with very few leaves, and over the house are seven birds.

   COLOURING: BLAKE is dressed in pale Grey (A) or pale Blue (B–D), OLOLON is uncoloured (A–B), Pink and Gold (C), or pale Blue (D), once the DOOR FRAME is Pink (B), and the SKY is partly Pink (A–B, D), Orange (B–C), and Yellow (B–C).

   VARIANT: There is a sunrise over the house in copy C.

Pl. 37. INCIPIT: 'The Virgin answerd . . .'.

Pl. 38. DESIGN: The whole plate is a very dark design of a naked man asleep on a rock beside a nude woman, who lies with her arm across his chest. In the near and far background is the Black sea, and over them stretches an eagle with outspread wings and open beak in a Black sky. (A similar eagle is on *America* [1793] pl. 15, and another is in the engraving to illustrate Hayley's *Ballad* [1802] of 'The Eagle'; a sketch for the *Milton* design is in the BMPR, reproduced in *Blake Newsletter*, v [1972], 226.)

   COLOURING: The ROCKS are a curious Green (A), yellowish-Black (B–C), pinkish-Black (C), or yellowish-Brown (D).

   VARIANTS: There is no water at the bottom in copy B.
   In copy D, the man's left thumb on the woman's left leg has been extended to place it on her vagina.

Pl. 39. INCIPIT: 'And the Forty-eight Starry Regions . . .'.
   VARIANT: In copy B, Yellow rays descend from the right.

Pl. 40. INCIPIT: 'Till all things become One . . .'. DESIGN: After ll. 25–8, 41–3 are two tiny human figures.

Pl. 41. DESIGN: The whole plate is a very dark design of a naked man whose head gives off light supporting a kneeling, drooping, White-haired figure in a long robe. The naked man seems to be standing in a river or small lake. (A very similar sketch for this design is in the V&A, reproduced in *Pencil Drawings* [1927], pl. 33.)

 COLOURING: The figure's ROBE is Grey (A, D), or pale greyish-Blue (B–C), the saviour's NIMBUS is Yellow (B) or Red (C–D), and his HAIR is Brown (A) or Yellow (C). The SKY is Black (A) or dark greyish Blue (C D), and the ROCKS behind the figures are orangish-Yellow (A), Black (B [yellowish-], D) and luminous Grey (C).

 VARIANTS: In copy B, the saviour's eyes seem to look down, not to the right.

 The kneeling figure's hands are bluish-Grey like the robe, in copy C.

 The rays from the saviour's head extend to his waist and to the margins in copy D.

Pl. 42. INCIPIT: 'Before Ololon Milton stood . . .'. DESIGN: Below the text, a naked man at the right kneels with his hands extended before him towards a dense Brown wood in which are visible a serpent tail, an open-mouthed dog, and a dragon-head.

 COLOURING: The SERPENT is once Magenta (A), and the DOG is Red (B), Yellow (B), Brown (C, D [reddish-]), and Orange (C).

Pl. 43. INCIPIT: 'To bathe in the waters of Life . . .'. DESIGN: Above the text, six nude women holding hands float through an intricate pattern in front of flames.

 VARIANT: In copy B, the arms of the two women at the right are confused.

Pl. 44. INCIPIT: 'Becomes a Womb . . .'. DESIGN: After ll. 1–3, 11–14, 24–7 are what appear to be three tiny figures.

 Below the text, a nude horizontal woman hovers over grain (shaped like tightly pressed humans) with outstretched arms from which rain seems to descend.

 COLOURING: The GROUND is once Yellow (D) and the SKY purplish-Grey (A).

Pl. 45. INCIPIT: 'To go forth to the Great Harvest . . .'. DESIGN: Most of the page, below the text, is taken up with a design of a nude woman with flourishing hair and trailing a veil; she stands with arms raised over a young man at either side; they look at her as their lower bodies turn into giant ears of grain. (A sketch for this plate is in the Rosenwald Collection, on the verso of a page with an inscription—see p. 215.)

 COLOURING: The VEIL is Green (A, B [pale], C), Gold (C), and Blue (D), the woman's LEGS are Green (A, B [pale]), and her HAIR is Brown (B, D [yellowish-]). The PLANTS are pale Pink (A, C [streaked with Gold], D [top]), brownish- or pinkish-Orange (B), and yellowish-Green (D [bottom]), the SKY is sometimes Orange (A), greyish-Blue (B), Pink (D), Red (D), and Yellow (D), and behind the woman is Orange and Gold in copy C.

VARIANT: The woman has no eyeballs in copy B.

COPY A: BINDING: (**1**) Originally stabbed through three holes, 7·0 cm from the top, 3·5, 4·2 cm apart; (**2**) Mounted on stubs and bound in old half Green morocco, g.e.; (**3**) The leaves were mounted in heavy paper 'windows' and rebound in Red morocco in 1969.

HISTORY: (**1**) This (or copy B) may be the copy sold anonymously with the Collection of Thomas Butts (see *Songs* [E]) at Sotheby's, 26 March 1852, lot 53, for £9 to Toovey, perhaps for (**2**) Francis Palgrave (who bought *Thel* [L] at the same sale), and who sold copy A on 25 June 1859 to (**3**) The BRITISH MUSEUM PRINT ROOM, where it was reproduced by Muir (1886), and probably (with pl. a, c–e from copy C) by Ellis & Yeats (1893); reproduced in colour microfilm by Micro Methods Ltd.

COPY B: BINDING: (**1**) Originally stabbed through three holes about 6·2 cm from the top and 4·6, 4·6 cm apart; (**2**) Now bound in contemporary Brown calf, blind tooled and gilt, with 'MILTON / ——— / BLAKE / — / 1804' gilt on the spine.

HISTORY: (**1**) Perhaps this is the copy which T. G. Wainewright said on 28 March 1826 he had 'lately purchased';[1] (**2**) Acquired by Robert Hoe, who added his book-plate and signature on the first fly-leaf, had it described in his catalogue (1895), lent it anonymously to the Grolier Club exhibition (1905), no. 34, and sold it posthumously through the Anderson Auction Co., 25 April 1911, lot 393, for $9,000 to (**3**) The HUNTINGTON LIBRARY.

COPY C: BINDING: (**1**) Originally stabbed through five holes, later bound, g.e.; (**2**) The leaves were cut out of this binding (the original stubs, about 0·6 cm wide and still sewn together, are with the book), mounted on stubs, and 'Bound by J. Mackenzie' by *c.* 1850 in Blue morocco, also of course g.e.; there is a Black framing-line about 0·8 cm from each plate.

HISTORY: (**1**) Numbered by William Beckford on the second fly-leaf ('N° 1856'), probably bound for him, and sold posthumously for him at Sotheby's, 4 July 1882, lot 952, for £230 to Quaritch; (**2**) Quaritch inserted his Beckford sale book-plate, and offered it (30 July 1882), lot 203, for 'o o o'; (**3**) Bought from this Quaritch catalogue for £270 by Robert Lenox Kennedy, who offered it to the New York Public Library (according to documents now with the book); (**4**) After his death (1887), it was purchased with his Library by the Lenox Library of the NEW YORK PUBLIC LIBRARY; pl. a, c–e were reproduced (probably with copy A) by Ellis & Yeats (1893).

COPY D: BINDING: (**1**) Originally stabbed through six holes, 4·1, 3·9, 4·4, 4·5, 4·5 cm apart, with *Thel* (O); (**2**) Later stitched with *Thel* (O) through 12 holes in old half russia, the edges marbled; (**3**) Evidently

---

[1] *Blake Records* (1969), 327. 'The Title says in *12* books [*as is clear in copies B and D*]! My copy has but *3*!' All known copies have two books. If Wainewright's copy has been traced, it should be copy B, for copy D was '*finished*' for Mr. Vine.

disbound and rebound about 1930, disbound again about 1963, rebound about 1966.

HISTORY: The History of copy D (which appears in Blake's list of works in his letter of 9 June 1818) is as in *Thel* (O), with which it was bound; see p. 130.

Pl. 38: BINDING: Loose, mounted.

HISTORY: (1) Perhaps this is the design from *Milton* sold by W. B. Scott at Sotheby's, 21 April 1885, lot 185, for £1. 1s. to Pincott; (2) Acquired from A. H. Palmer for 15s. (according to notes with the volume) by (3) Edward Dowden, who sold it (auctioneer not mentioned), 20 Jan. 1916, lot 264, for £3. 5s. (according to the note), to (4) Frank Rinder, who lent it to the Burlington Fine Arts exhibition (1927), no. 71; (5) Acquired by his daughter *Mrs. Ramsey Harvey.*

119

Milton. Ed. E. R. D. Maclagen & A. G. B. Russell. London, 1907. The Prophetic Books of William Blake.

This is the second and last volume in this projected series (see no. 77); the 'Introduction' is pp. v–xvi.

120

*Milton [D], a Poem. London, 1967. The William Blake Trust.

Geoffrey Keynes, 'Description and Bibliographical Statement', is on 13 unnumbered pages.

121. 'Mirth' (?1820)

BIBLIOGRAPHICAL INTRODUCTION

TABLE

Copy	State	Watermark
A BMPR	1	—
B *Keynes*	2	

DATE: ?1816, ?1820.

State 1 was etched in stipple without an inscription, probably about the time of the *L'Allegro* designs (see p. 219), *c.* 1816. Perhaps Blake intended to engrave the whole series.

State 2 is thoroughly reworked and could be almost any time thereafter; 1820 is only a guess.

PUBLICATION: Perhaps only the unique known proof of each unfinished State was pulled. No contemporary reference to the print is known.

DESIGN: A girl in a diaphanous gown dances toward the viewer, accompanied by some twenty-five floating figures, two of whom are identified as 'SPORT that wrinkled CARE derides' and 'LAUGHTER holding both his sides' (*L'Allegro* ll. 31–2). Blake's comment appears below the design.

COPY A: BINDING: Loose, mounted.

HISTORY: (1) Lent by the Linnell Trustees to the exhibitions in the National Gallery (1913), no. 76, Manchester (1914), no. 85, Nottingham (1914), no. 69, the National Gallery of Scotland (1914), no. 49, and sold at Christie's, 15 March 1918, lot 190 (with other works), for £54. 12s. to [A.] Martin for (2) The BRITISH MUSEUM PRINT ROOM, and reproduced by Keynes, *Separate Plates* (1956), p. 35.

COPY B: BINDING: Loose, mounted.

HISTORY: (1) Reproduced by A. G. B. Russell, *Engravings of William Blake* (1912); (2) Bought from Robson & Co. in June 1916 by (3) W. E. Moss, who sold it at Sotheby's, 2 March 1937, lot 200, for £70 to (4) *Keynes*, who reproduced it in his *Separate Plates* (1956), lent it to the British Museum exhibition (1957), and described it in his Catalogue (1964), no. 561.

122. *Notebook* (?1793–?1818)

BIBLIOGRAPHICAL INTRODUCTION

COLLECTION: BRITISH MUSEUM Department of Manuscripts.

WATERMARKS: Pages 1–116 have chain lines 2·65 cm apart, plus a circular watermark with a radius of about 1·5 cm perhaps representing a fleur-de-lis. The top, partly triangular, section of the watermark is visible on twenty-eight leaves, while the bottom, more curvilinear part is on thirty leaves. Arranging the pages as they were when Blake wrote on them,[1] the pattern of gatherings seems to be as follows ('Top' and 'Bottom' referring to the portion of the watermark visible):

Gatherings:	2 leaves	6 leaves		12 leaves		12 leaves
Top: pp.	9–10		1–4, 15–16		25–36	49–60
Bottom: pp.	5–6	13–14, 11–12, 7–8		17–24 [*4 pages missing*]	37–48	
Gatherings:	12 leaves	12 leaves		4 leaves		
Top: pp.	73–84		97–108	[*8 pages missing*]		
Bottom: pp.	61–72	85–96		109–16		

[1] See the ORDER below. The side facing the mould when the paper was made is indented with the lines of the mould, and the verso facing the felt is smooth. When a sheet or group of sheets is folded once, all the mould-sides will uniformly face either towards or away from the fold, thus: pp. 1–2 (mould–felt) FOLD pp. 3–4 (felt–mould). In every leaf of the *Notebook*, the felt- and mould-marks confirm the watermark pattern above and indicate that (whatever the sequence of leaves) the present rectos were all rectos when Blake first used the *Notebook*. (This line of argument was privately conveyed by Mr. Howard Nixon to Mr. Erdman and thence to me.)

The eight pages missing at the end could not well have been after p. 116 when Blake was using the book, for p. 116 is dirty from use as an outside cover; nor could they have been between p. 108 and p. 109, for these pages are linked by transferred blobs of Blake's ink. It seems likely, therefore, that the eight pages missing at the end were removed before William Blake began using the *Notebook*. By analogy, it seems likely that the four pages missing from pp. 17–24 and the unknown number probably missing from pp. 1–16 were also removed before the poet used the book.

Pages 117–20 have neither chain lines nor watermark.

The fragment of a leaf pasted on p. 8 has part of a circular watermark very much larger than that on pp. 1–116.

LEAF-SIZE: 15·7×19·5 cm, irregular. A fragment 7·4×11·3 cm was cut from the top outer corner of pp. 71–2, probably by 1847.[1]

DATES:

(1) *By 1787*: Sketches *by Robert Blake* (d. 1787) on pp. 5, 7–9, 11, 13.

(2) *About 1793*: Poems (pp. 4, ?78, 98–101, 103, 105–109, 111, 113–15, including *Songs of Experience* [1794] on pp. 101, 103, 105–109, 111, 113–115); prose (pp. 10 [June 1793], ?92, 116); vignettes (pp. 2, 8, 15–37, 39–61, 63, 65, 67–75, 77–79, 81, 83–89, 91–102, 106–108, 110–112, including *For Children* [1793] on pp. 15, 17, 19, 34, 40, 45, 52, ?58, 59, 61, 63, 68–69, 71, 75, 91, 93–95, ?98, *Marriage* [?1790–3] on pp. 44, 48, 'Job' [1793] on p. 20, *Visions* [1793] on pp. 28, 30, 32, ?50, 74, 78, 81, 92, *America* [1793] on pp. ?29, ?49, ?75, ?77, *Songs of Experience* [1794], on pp. 43, 54, 57, 65, 74, *Europe* [1794] on pp. 8, 25, 74–75, ?77, 96, ?97, ?98, *Urizen* [1794] on p. ?15, 74, *Song of Los* [1795] on pp. ?13, ?60, 'Elohim Creating Adam' [?1795] on p. 54, 'Satan Exulting over Eve' [?1795] on p. 112).

(3) *1801–3*: Poems (pp. 2–3, ?5, 6–7, 12, 14, 46 [for *Jerusalem* (1804–?20)], 56, 93) and sketches (pp. 2–4, 6, 12, 16, 19, 21, 38, 40, 47, 54, 66–67, 69–70, 73–76, 80–82, 90, 92, including Hayley's *Designs to A Series of Ballads* [1802], on pp. 6, 73, 92, portrait-like sketches on pp. 2–4, 12, 19, 21, 40, 47, 54, 66–67, 69–70, 74, 82, *Vala* [?1796–?1807] on p. ?90, *Jerusalem* [1804–?20] on pp. 16, 76, 80).

(4) *1807*: Prose (pp. 10 [20 Jan.], 64, 88–89 [Aug.]); poems (p. 54, 96–97); and a sketch for *Paradise Lost* [?1807] (p. 104).

(5) *1809*: Poem (p. 40).

(6) *1810*: 'Vision of the Last Judgment' ('For the Year 1810') (pp. 68–72,

---

[1] The probable date is established by the fact that the words cut out are missing from the early transcripts by D. G. Rossetti, one in manuscript made shortly after he acquired the book in 1847 on paper watermarked 1844 and bound with the *Notebook*, another printed in Gilchrist's *Life of William Blake*, 'Pictor Ignotus' (1863), ii. 161 ff.

On 27 Nov. 1864 W. M. Rossetti wrote to Horace Scudder: 'if I can find a convenient little bit to snip out [*of the NOTEBOOK*], I shall have great pleasure in sending it to you, just as a specimen of writing' (MS in Harvard). S. F. Damon (*A Blake Dictionary* [1965], 437) supposes that the bit snipped off may have been from pp. 71–2 of the *Notebook*, but the chronology above invalidates the suggestion.

76–87, 90–95); miscellaneous prose (pp. 67 [23 May], 72); and a poem (p. 87).

(7) *1810–11*: 'Public Address' (pp. 1, 17–21, 23–25, 38–39, 44, 46–47, 51–53, 55–67, 71, 76, 78, 86); poems associated with the 'Public Address' (pp. 21, 23–43, 47, ?50, 52, 60–63, 65, 70, 73, 79, 89); a translation (p. 64); a transcript (p. 59 [4 Aug. 1811]); and 'Blake's Chaucer' (pp. 117–119).

(8) *1812*: Poems (pp. 6, 22).

(9) ?*1818*: 'The Everlasting Gospel' (pp. 21, 33, 48–54, 98, 100–101, 120).

DESCRIPTION

Title: The volume now generally known as the *Notebook* was for many years called 'The Rossetti Manuscript', from its best-known owner, D. G. Rossetti, who owned it between 1847 and 1882.

Contents: The *Notebook* is made up of fifty-eight leaves[1] (pp. 1–116) with the same watermark, plus two leaves (one sheet, pp. 117–20) consisting of the inner margin of pp. 45–6 of William Hayley's *Designs to A Series of Ballads* (9 Sept. 1802).[2] These sixty leaves are mounted on stubs, interleaved, and bound with thirty-three leaves of Dante Gabriel Rossetti's transcript of the *Notebook* in half morocco over marbled boards, with an older leather spine lettered 'BLAKE / M.S.'. When the leaves were disbound, they were not trimmed, for the writing goes quite to the three outer margins, and sewing holes are still visible in the inner margin, sometimes overlapping with the designs and some writing (e.g. p. 10).

Pages 1 and 116 are very dirty, suggesting that the leaves may once have been without a cover and that pp. 117–120 (which are separately hinged and much cleaner) were not added to the others until they were bound. The writing throughout the *Notebook*, especially that in pencil, appears to have faded noticeably since the facsimile of 1935 was made. The outer margins of all the leaves are rather dirty, and a few chips have broken off the outer edges.

On p. 8 has been pasted a roughly L-shaped fragment (9·6 × 7·3 cm at the largest dimensions) with a sketch for *Europe* (1794) pl. 5, and, on the verso, lines for a much larger sketch.

The *Notebook* was paginated 1–120 in the upper outer corners in the present order by W. A. White,[3] who owned it from 1887 to 1927.

Order: In the original order of the *Notebook*, the designs apparently by Robert Blake (pp. 5, 7–9, 11, 13) were evidently at the front, in the following

---

[1] For evidence that there may have been at least twelve pages more at one time, see the *Watermark* description above.

[2] The paper can be identified from the fragments of printing on pp. 118 and 120. Blake designed, engraved, and printed the plates for the book, and was given the printed sheets to sell for his own benefit. In later years he used the unsold sheets for scrap paper, for example in 'The Ballads MS'.

[3] *The Poetical Works of William Blake*, ed. J. Sampson (1905), 138.

order: pp. 5–6?, 9–10,[1] 13–14,[1] 11–12?, 7–8,[2] 1–2,[2] 3–4,[3] 15–20,[3] 21–116.[4] Later, perhaps when pp. 117–20 were added to the others, the leaves were rearranged and rebound in their present order: pp. 1–120. The alteration is now of considerable venerability, for pl. 1 is much dirtier than the other pages, the tiger on p. 6 has offset on p. 7, the design on p. 9 has offset on p. 8, and some words on p. 10 have offset on p. 11. The pages were presumably in this new order in 1847 when D. G. Rossetti bought the *Notebook* and inscribed the fly-leaf. The pages of the *Notebook* are here referred to in the order of the present binding.

COMPOSITION: The first user of the book was evidently Robert Blake, who started making designs at the front. After his death in 1787, William Blake made sketches in it from front to back in about 1792 and 1793. Then he turned the book round and wrote lyrics in it, starting at the back, in approximately 1793 and 1794. Some years later he picked it up again, and began making memoranda and drafting poems and prose starting at the front, in about the years 1801–3, 1807, 1809–11, and 1818.

DESIGNS

* Means there is no writing on the page except inscriptions for the designs (pp. 8–9, 11, 13, 15–16, 45, 102, 104, 110, 112).

  Undecipherable designs are on pp. 15 (bottom), 16 (bottom), 25 (bottom), 32 (bottom), 50 (top), 53, 59 (bottom), 64 (erased), 66 (middle), 79 (numbered '[8 *del*] 12'), 89 (numbered '21[?]'), 99 (erased), 107 (in the centre, small), 114 (sideways).

  No designs appear on pp. 1, 10, 14, 62, 74–75, 103, 105, 109, 113, 115–120.

  All sketches, numbers, and inscriptions are *in pencil* unless otherwise specified.

p. 2   A woman is apparently turning into a tree; a more finished version is on p. 36, and a third version is in the British Museum. *Upside-down* at the bottom is a face.

p. 3   A naked man(?) bending to the right is at the top of the page. Below is the head of a man in a fez-like hat facing left.

p. 4   At the top are two unfinished profiles. In the middle, partly obliterated by the sketch, is: 'Ideas / of / Good & Evil'. Below are

----

[1] A stain in the top margin 4·2 cm from the outside appears on pp. 10 and 13, indicating that pp. 9–10, 13–14 were sequential.

[2] A chip is missing in the top inner margin on pp. 7–8, 1–2, indicating that these pages were once sequential.

[3] A large ink or *aqua fortis* blob at the top outer corner appears in steadily diminishing size on pp. 1–2, 3–4, 15–16, 17–18, 19–20, indicating clearly that these pages were once sequential: 1–4, 15–20. Further, there is a clear offset of writing from p. 4 to p. 15, and a probable offset from p. 2 to p. 3. In addition, transferred blobs of ink indicate the relationship of pp. 14–11, 24–25, 48–49, 54–55, 59–61, 78–89, 80–81, 90–91, 96–97, 98–99, 106–107, 108–109, 110–111, 112–113.

[4] Erdman (*Poetry and Prose of William Blake* [1967], pp. 768, 774–5, 781) suggests this order; some of the evidence given here was pointed out privately by Erdman. I have not observed evidence which demonstrates the position of p. 6–p. 9, and p. 12–p. 17 in this sequence. Page 116 is smudged as if it had been the outside page for some time.

a man(?) lying in bed and a woman(?) sitting on the edge of the bed taking off long stockings.[1]

p. 5   *Sideways* at the bottom is a tall figure with its arms raised, with other erased figures above it, perhaps *by Robert Blake*.[2]

p. 6   Most of the page is taken up by a pencil sketch confirmed in ink of a tiger (quite finished) and a fleeing man (somewhat rough) for Blake's second plate (not reversed) for Hayley's *Designs to A Series of Ballads* (1 July 1802). Below these is a finished head of the tiger approximately in the attitude of the 1802 tiger.[3]

p. 7   *Sideways* in the middle are three large, rather stiff robed figures which may be *by Robert Blake*.[4]

*p. 8   Three faint, tall figures facing a smaller one drawn *sideways* may be *by Robert Blake*. Pasted on to the bottom of the page was an irregularly shaped scrap of paper with the three struggling figures etched in *Europe* (1794), pl. 5. (On the verso of the scrap are lines of a larger sketch; the scrap was listed and mounted separately after 1966.)

*p. 9   The page is entirely filled *sideways* with an ink-and-Grey-wash drawing of a poorly proportioned knight, apparently with a drawn sword, rushing from a Gothic cloister after a woman into a wood; it may be *by Robert Blake*.[4]

*p. 11 Drawn *sideways* is a crowned figure in a long robe with arms outstretched towards another figure which turns away. Behind them are groups of other, smaller figures. At the bottom are two children by a recumbent figure. All are probably *by Robert Blake*.[4]

p. 12   In the middle is a pudgy boy, perhaps Henry VIII aged about 8. Below, to the right, is a different face.

*p. 13 The page is taken up with a full-page ink-and-Grey-wash sketch of a crowned king and queen on a flower, with angelic figures hovering over them, probably *by Robert Blake*.[4] This design was copied on the cover of the 1880 Gilchrist; a similar design was used in *Song of Los* (1795) pl. 5.

*p. 15 In the centre is the design for *For Children* (1793), pl. 16, numbered '39' and entitled: 'The traveller hasteth in the Evening'. Above this is a rough, winged man carrying a tiny man in his mouth,[5] which is repeated twice more below the first sketch, and on pp. 16–17. In the top left corner is the back of a man standing with his legs apart and urinating. (An offset of this design appears on p. 14.) In the bottom left corner is a dog looking up at a man, perhaps related to *Urizen* (1794) pl. 26. Other lines seem indecipherable. At the bottom is

[1] The sketch may be related to the couplet at the bottom of the page:
When a Man has Married a Wife he finds out whether
Her knees & elbows are only glued together[.]
[2] Suggested by Keynes (ed., *The Note-Book* [1935], 149).
[3] Its attitude is not that of the beast in 'The Tyger' (*Songs* [1794] pl. 42).
[4] Suggested by Keynes (ed., *The Note-Book* [1935], 149, 150).
[5] Cf. p. 22, ll. 5–6: 'Not only in his Mouth his own Soul lay But my Soul also'.

some offset ink writing, not in Blake's hand, which may read: 'sweet of them'.

*p. 16   At the top centre are two sketches of the flying man with a tiny human figure in his mouth attempted on pp. 15, 17. At the bottom left side is the back of a nude man. To his right is a woman with outspread arms sheltering three(?) children, similar to the design on pp. 76 and 80 for *Jerusalem* (1804–?20) pl. 32. Other lines are indecipherable.

p. 17   At the top are two sketches of the mouth of the giant with a man in his mouth, more fully given on pp. 15–16. In the centre, a man walks forward, perhaps through a door, and meets a skeleton.[1] The design is numbered '40' and entitled 'Are glad when they can / find the grave'.[2]

p. 18   A man on horseback followed by another figure (a woman?) carrying something is numbered '34'.

p. 19   In the top left corner is a man's left profile, like the bearded profile on p. 21. In the centre is a sketch for *For Children* (1793), pl. 9, numbered '[6 *del*] 8' and inscribed:

> Ah luckless babe born under cruel star
> And in dead parents baleful ashes bred⌊,⌋
> Full little weenest thou what sorrows are
> Left thee for portion of thy livelihed⌊.⌋
>
> Spenser [*FAERIE QUEENE, II. ii. 2. 1–4*]

p. 20   Four(?) figures sitting round a fifth who is looking at the sky are reminiscent of the engraving of 'Job' ('18 August 1793').

p. 21   At the top left is a fine bearded profile, very like the beardless profile on p. 19. In the top middle are three studies of lips, as on p. 33. In the centre is a man looking up at a woman springing from a flower (not unlike *Songs* [1794] pl. 39), and below it are lines from Shakespeare's Sonnet XV:

> Every thing that grows
> Holds in perfection but a little [*moment.*]

p. 22   Two figures stand on either side of a seated one, before whom kneels a fourth, while a fifth turns away; the very faint sketch is numbered '17'.

p. 23   A cage hanging from a tree holds a crouching person; the design is numbered '30[?]'.

p. 24   Two figures in a wood are threatened by a bearded man; the scene, numbered '18', may perhaps be Adam and Eve driven from Paradise.

p. 25   In the centre, numbered '[32 *del*] 23', are five despairing figures; the three at the left were used for *Europe* (1794) pl. 10, the third from the left reversed.

---

[1] A related design was used in *For Children* (1793) pl. 17, *America* (1793) pl. 14, Blair's *Grave* (1808), and *Jerusalem* (1804–?20) pl. 1; it is repeated on p. 71.
[2] Job 3: 22.

p. 26   A large, complicated sketch seems to represent naked soldiers with shields, standards, and swords, landing from a boat; they may be connected with the proposed engraving (*Notebook*, p. 116) of 'The Landing of Julius Caesar'.[1]

p. 27   Two(?) smudged figures looking down on a prostrate man are numbered '[33(?) *del*] 24' and inscribed with a quotation from Milton's Sonnet XVII, to Sir Henry Vane:

> [*Whether to settle peace, or to unfold*]
> The drift of hollow states, hard to / be spelld⌊.⌋

p. 28   In the centre is a large sketch for *Visions* (1793) pl. 3, reversed.

p. 29   A slight figure hovering in the air over a prostrate person, numbered '[32(?) *del*] 19', may be related to *America* (1793) pl. 2.

p. 30   Four faint figures dancing in the air (for *Visions* [1793] pl. 2, reversed) are inscribed:

> A fairy vision of some gay
> Creatures of the element who
> In the colours of the rainbow live
> Milton[2]

p. 31   A figure apparently standing on a cloud and going through a door to be received by three waiting people is numbered '35'.

p. 32   In the centre is a large clear sketch for *Visions* (1793) pl. 6, reversed.

p. 33   At the top are two pairs of lips, as on p. 21. In the centre is an indistinct figure lying on a bed, with another holding a child(?) kneeling beside the bed.

p. 34   The rough sketch for *For Children* (1793) pl. 10 is numbered '16' and inscribed, as on the print: 'My son My son'.

p. 35   A woman standing on a cloud and leading two children with each hand is numbered '[2 *del*] 13'.

p. 36   A woman reaching upwards and turning into a tree (like the design on p. 2) is inscribed: 'As Daphne was root bound / Milton'.[3]

p. 37   A group of five(?) people gathered round a figure on a bed is numbered '[10 *del* 25(?)*del*] 26'.

p. 38   In the centre is a rough sketch of muscular shoulders. In the middle of the right margin is a pointing index finger darkened in ink (perhaps related to Hand—see *Milton* [1804–?8] pl. 17).

p. 39   Three figures looking down at a fourth lying in bed (not like the sketch on p. 37) is somewhat like Blake's second plate for Mary

---

[1] Suggested by M. Wilson, *Life of William Blake* (1948).

[2] *Comus*, ll. 298–300: 'I took it for a faëry vision / Of some gay creatures of the element / That in the colours of a Rainbow live . . .'.

[3] *Comus*, ll. 659–62: 'Nay Lady sit; if I but wave this wand, / Your nervs are all chain'd up in Alabaster, / And you a statue; or as *Daphne* was / Root-bound, that fled *Apollo*.'

Wollstonecraft's *Original Stories* (1791);[1] it is numbered '[26 *del* 26 *del* 14 *del*] 25'.

p. 40   In the centre is a faint sketch used in *For Children* (1793) pl. 11, reversed. In the bottom right is a smudged and scribbled-over miniature portrait; a similar head is on p. 47.

p. 41   In front of a Gothic door a man and a woman are kissing, respectively, a girl and a boy; the drawing is numbered '[32 *del* 14 *del* 27 *del*]'.

p. 42   An old man leaning on a stick reaches for a butterfly.

p. 43   A vague sketch for *Songs* (1794) pl. 29, reversed, is numbered '[15 *del*] 28'.

p. 44   In the centre is a clear sketch for the *Marriage* (?1790–3) pl. 24, reversed, as on p. 48.

*p. 45   Below the rough sketch for *For Children* (1793), pl. 18, numbered '[13 *del* 7(?) *del*] 1', is the title: 'I have said to corruption thou art / my father, to the worm thou art / my mother & my Sister⌊.⌋ / Job' (17: 14).[2]

p. 46   A man sitting on the edge of a bed and looking apprehensively upward is entitled: 'Murder'.

p. 47   Two figures with outstretched arms are springing upwards, and between their arms are two other figures also rising up; the sketch is numbered '2[?]29[?]'. Below them, in the bottom margin and somewhat overlapping them, is a clear face with an elaborate head-dress, not unlike that on p. 40.

p. 48   In the centre is a faint sketch for the *Marriage* (?1790–3) pl. 24, reversed, as on p. 44.

p. 49   A rough figure standing with his hands to his head beside another prostrate on the ground (similar to the standing man in *America* [1793], pl. 3, or to 'Cain Standing over the Body of Abel') is numbered '[4(?) *del* 21(?) *del* 23 *del*] 15'.

p. 50   In the centre is a naked man falling, apparently after having stabbed himself; a very similar design is on p. 75, and the general attitude is like that of the bottom figure in *Visions* (1793) pl. 2.

p. 51   In the centre, numbered '[40 *del*] 42', are five rough figures dancing in a circle at the foot of a tree. At the top of the tree there seems to be seated a larger figure blowing a curling horn; this musician is repeated on a larger scale at the bottom left corner.

p. 52   The clear sketch for *For Children* (1793) pl. 13 is labelled, like the etched plate: 'Aged Ignorance'.

p. 54   At the top is a fine, fairly finished head. In the middle is the design etched in *Songs* (1794) pl. 46, reversed. At the bottom is a fine sketch for the colour print which Blake called 'Elohim creating Adam' (?1795).

[1] Suggested by Keynes (ed., *The Note-Book* [1935], 154).
[2] The etched title is: 'I have said to the Worm Thou art my mother & my sister'.

p. 55   A very faint child kneeling before a seated figure is numbered '5[?]'.

p. 56   A figure running over the edge of a cliff is held by the ankle by another person (of whom only the head and restraining arm are visible).

p. 57   A sketch for *Songs* (1794) pl. 30, reversed, is numbered '[8(?) *del*] 34'.

p. 58   A faint sketch, perhaps that used in *For Children* (1793) pl. 12, is numbered '[45 *del*] 33'; another sketch may be for pl. 11 of the same work; a third is undecipherable.

p. 59   The design used in *For Children* (1793) pl. 14 is numbered '[44 *del* 29 *del*] 30'.

p. 60   A man kissing, from behind, the neck of a woman running away from him, numbered '[29 *del*]', is similar to that in *The Song of Los* (1795) pl. 4.

p. 61   The sketch (numbered '[26 *altered to* 29 *del*] 31') used in *For Children* (1793) pl. 15, reversed, is inscribed: 'What we hope to See'.[1]

p. 63   The pencil, ink, and wash design used in *For Children* (1793) pl. 3, reversed, is numbered '[10 *del*] 15' and entitled: 'I found him beneath a tree in the Garden'.[2] Beneath is a second sketch of the mandrake.

p. 65   The pencil, ink, and wash sketch (numbered '[45(?) *del*] 46') for *Songs* (1794) pl. 41, reversed, does not show the wings of the etched version.

p. 66   At the top is a profile face like that on p. 67, evidently representing Blake himself.

p. 67   At the top is a clear profile like that on p. 66. In the centre are two rough figures standing before a door, numbered '[48(?) *del*] 47'.

p. 68   The sketch labelled above 'Frontispiece', for *For Children* (1793) pl. 1, seems to be very faintly inscribed: 'What is Man that thou shouldest / Magnify him & that thou shouldest set / Thine heart upon him[?] / Job' (7: 17).[3]

p. 69   The sketch used in *For Children* (1793) pl. 8 is numbered '[5 *del*]' and labelled: 'At length for hatching ripe he breaks / the Shell / Dryden'.[4] Above this is a rough head.

p. 70   At the top left is a face in ink; a related sketch is on p. 74. Below are two adults surrounded by three children.

---

[1] The etched plate is called 'Fear & Hope are—Vision'.
[2] The etched plate omits the last three words.
[3] Only the first three words are inscribed under the etching itself.
[4] Translation of Chaucer's Knight's Tale, Book III (Dryden, *Fables Ancient and Modern* [1700], 87, reprinted in E. Bysshe, *The Art of English Poetry* [1710]):

> So Man, at first a Drop, dilates with Heat,
> Then form'd, the little Heart begins to beat;
> Secret he feeds, unknowing in the Cell;
> At length, for Hatching ripe, he breaks the Shell,
> And struggles into Breath, and cries for Aid;
> Then, helpless, in his Mothers Lap is laid.

p. 71   The design, numbered '35', is labelled, as it is in *For Children* (1793) pl. 17 (p. 17) 'Deaths Door'.

p. 72   In the centre is a figure with upraised arms numbered '48'.

p. 73   At the top and left are three sketches of the eagle bearing a child used as pl. 7 of Hayley's *Designs to A Series of Ballads* (1 July 1802). In the centre a woman holding a baby in her arms is numbered '[18(?) *del*] 36' and inscribed: 'Yet can I not persuade / me thou art dead / Milton' ('Death of a Fair Infant', l. 29).

p. 74   There are approximately five horizontal rows of sketches. In the top middle is a left profile. The first figure in the second row (repeated as the second figure in the third line) is the bowed figure in *Visions* (1793) pl. 7, 10. The second figure in the second row is the woman etched reversed in *Songs* (1794) pl. 33. The third sketch is a finished head related to that on p. 70. The fourth is a standing figure clasping another person, used in *Urizen* (1794) pl. 21. The first figure in the third row is flying with outstretched arms and a robe whirling upward; it is perhaps related to the flaming god in *Visions* (1793) pl. 2. The third sketch in this row is a left profile portrait. In the fourth row the first and second figures kneel or sit with bowed heads, like the central woman in *Visions* (1793) pl. 10. The third figure in the row is for *Songs* (1794) pl. 28. The first figure in the fifth row, tormented, with his arms clutched round his shoulders, is apparently that used for the bat-winged figure at the bottom of *Europe* (1794) pl. 4; it seems to be repeated on p. 75. The second figure in this row, quite similar, seems to be the model for the flaming god at the bottom of *Visions* (1793) pl. 2.

p. 75   Three rows of sketches fill the page. At the top left is a bowed figure related to that for *Europe* (1794) pl. 4 on p. 74. To the right is a seated figure with head bowed, like the left person in *For Children* (1793) pl. 14. In the top right corner two tormented figures falling, related to *America* (1793) pl. 7, are inscribed: 'A vision of fear'. To the left of the next row is a man falling backward, very like the figure on p. 50. In the centre, two embracing figures on their knees with a child between them is inscribed to the right: 'A vision of hope'. Below, in the bottom row at the left, there are faint lines apparently representing a bearded figure. In the middle of the bottom row is a sketch for *For Children* (1793), pl. 5 (p. 93), numbered '[16 *del*] 38'.

p. 76   Three faint adults with children on either side (like the designs on p. 80 and *Jerusalem* [1804–?20] pl. 32) fill most of the page.

p. 77   In the centre is a flying child, with an illegible deleted number. At the bottom, partly razored out after the writing was added to the verso, is a prostrate child related to those etched reversed in *America* (1793) pl. 11 and *Europe* (1794) pl. 9.

p. 78   A large sketch for *Visions* (1793) pl. 11, reversed, fills most of the page.

p. 80   The clear design of a woman sheltering a group of children is like those on p. 76 and *Jerusalem* (1804–?20) pl. 32.

p. 81   The figure, numbered '[14 *del*] 32', was used, reversed, for the top right one, in *Visions* (1793) pl. 2.

p. 82   At the bottom, *upside-down*, is a head, perhaps of Catherine Blake,[1] perhaps of a man.

p. 83   A clear seated woman with a rigid child on her knees is numbered '37' and inscribed:

> Sweet rose⌊,⌋ fair flower⌊,⌋ untimely pluckd⌊,⌋ soon faded⌊,⌋
> Pluckd in the bud & faded in thine Spring⌊.⌋[2]

p. 84   Two figures near a corpse walk beneath a crescent moon.

p. 85   A man, manacled(?) and seated before a rock(?), is numbered '[20 *del* 2 *del*] 2' and inscribed:

> Whose changeless brow
> Neer smiles nor frowns
> Donne[3]

p. 86   Three faint women extend *sideways* from margin to margin.

p. 87   A faint standing figure beside one reclining is numbered '6'.

p. 88   A large faint *sideways* sketch represents a standing figure holding his hand over another person engulfed in serpent coils.

p. 90   A *sideways* sketch of a reclining man looking upward is rather like that on *Vala* (?1795–?1807), p. 48.

p. 91   The design, reversed in *For Children* (1793) pl. 7, is numbered '[4 *del*] 6' and inscribed: '[Forthwith upright *del*] he rears from off the pool / His mighty stature / Milton' (*Paradise Lost*, I. 221–2).

p. 92   At the top is a sketch for the doorway (like that on p. 6) etched for pl. 2 of Hayley's *Designs to A Series of Ballads* (1 June 1802). Below is the design reversed in *Visions* (1793) pl. 7.

p. 93   The design, reversed in *For Children* (1793) pl. 5 (p. 75), is numbered '3' and '2' and inscribed: 'Rest Rest perturbed Spirit / Shakespeare' (*Hamlet*, I. v. 183).[4]

p. 94   Two sketches for the figure in *For Children* (1793) pl. 6 (p. 98) show his elbows in different positions; the central one in ink-and-wash is numbered '5' and inscribed: 'Thou hast set thy heart as / the heart of God / Ezekiel'.[5]

---

[1] Suggested by Keynes (ed., *The Note-Book* [1935], 159).

[2] 'The Passionate Pilgrim', ll. 131–2 (accurate except for 'the spring'); '*fade* is always spelt *vaded*' in Jacobean printings (*The Plays and Poems of William Shakspeare*, ed. E. Malone [1790], x. 326).

[3] 'The Progresse of the Soule', ll. 35–6: 'Great Destiny . . . whose changelesse brow Ne'r smiles nor frownes . . .'. Blake made a large drawing of the subject, called 'Fate' (*The Note-Book*, ed. G. Keynes [1935], 160).

[4] The words are those Hamlet speaks to his father.

[5] Ezekiel 28: 6–7: 'thus saith the Lord God; because thou hast set thine heart as the heart of God . . . thou shalt die . . .'.

p. 95   The design used in *For Children* (1793) pl. 4 is numbered '[*number del and illeg*] 4' and inscribed:

> O that the Everlasting had not fixd
> His canon gainst self-slaughter
> Shakespeare [*Hamlet, I. ii. 131–2; the first word should be 'Or'.*]

p. 96   The rough *sideways* sketch for *Europe* (1794) pl. 1 is inscribed at the right side from *Europe* pl. 5. 'Who shall bind / the Infinite [?]'

p. 97   The crouching man with a knife, numbered '[20(?) *del* 32 *del*] 33', is related to the ones in *Europe* (1794) pl. 4 and in the picture called 'Malevolence'[1] which Blake described in his letter of 16 Aug. 1796.

p. 98   The *sideways* figure with his hands clasped over his head and numbered '5' at the top left may be related to the one in *For Children* (1793) pl. 6 (p. 94), or to the one in the top right corner of *Europe* (1794) pl. 5.

p. 100   The half-reclining figure gazing beneath his hand fills the whole page *sideways*.

p. 101   The faint man pushing a woman from him is numbered '[26 *del*] 50' and inscribed: 'Begone & trouble me no / more'.

*p. 102 The stiff nude man and woman, with lines as if of trees beside them, almost fill the page *sideways*.

*p. 104 Christ, with arms outspread, flies to kiss God, who sits with bowed head, while over him broods the Holy Ghost, with wings spread. Similar large designs are on pp. 106 and 108 and were repeated in Blake's *Paradise Lost* illustration (1807?).

p. 106   A large, very rough, *sideways* design may be for the Trinity, as on pp. 104, 108.

p. 108   The large, almost undecipherable *sideways* sketch may be for the Trinity, as on pp. 104, 106.

*pp. *110–111   These pages were used *sideways* for a single sketch representing a robed figure on the right inclining toward a seated figure, with, below them on p. 111, another naked figure falling. The subject may be God, Christ, and Satan.

*p. 112 The *sideways* sketch of Satan for the colour print of 'Satan Exulting over Eve' (?1795) entirely fills the page.

DESIGN NUMBERS: The decipherable numbers attached to the drawings are both so incomplete and so redundant as to make it very difficult to draw any reliable conclusions from them. In the list opposite, numbers in brackets are deleted.

The facts that pl. 3–9 of *For Children* are numbered approximately accurately (though pl. 12, 14–18 are inaccurate) and that several numbers are duplicated suggest that more than one series of numbers may be included here.

---

[1] Reproduced in *Blake Records* [1969], pl. x.

Design number	Found on page number									
1				45						
2			[35]	?47				85 [85]	93	
3									93	
4				[?49]					[91] 95	
5					?55	[69]			94 98	
6	[19]							87	91	
7				[?45]						
8	19				[?57]		[79]			
9										
10			[37]			[63]				
11										
12							79			
13			35	[45]						
14			[39]	[41]				[81]		
15				[43]	49	63				
16			34				[75]			
17		22								
18		24					[?73]			
19		29								
20								[85]	[?97]	
21				[?49]				?89		
22										
23		25		[49]						
24		27								
25			[?37] 39							
26			37 [39]			[61]				[101]
27				[41]						
28				43						
29				?47	[59,	60, 61]				
30		?23			59					
31						61				
32		[25, ?29]		[41]				81	[97]	
33		[?27]			58				97	
34	18				57					
35			31				71			
36							73			
37								83		
38							75			
39	15									
40	17				[51]					
41										
42					51					
43										
44					[59]					
45					[58]	[?65]				
46						65				
47						67				
48					[?67]	72				
49										
50										101

BINDING: (1) Once bound in leather with 'BLAKE / M.S.' on the spine; (2) Between April 1847, when D. G. Rossetti acquired the MS, and 1882, when he sold it, the *Notebook* leaves were mounted on stubs and bound in a mistaken order with thirty-three leaves of the Rossettis' transcript of the

Notebook (on paper watermarked R. TURNER / 1844) in half leather and marbled boards with the previous spine; (3) Rebound in half morocco and interleaved about 1934 (according to *The Note-Book of William Blake*, ed. G. Keynes [1935], xii); the corner of pp. 71–2 was probably missing in 1847, and pp. 117–20 were apparently tipped in at a later date. The volume is now rather fragile.

HISTORY: (1) Blake evidently left the *Notebook* at his death in 1827 to (2) Catherine Blake, from whom it passed to (3) Samuel Palmer's brother William; (4) The fly-leaf is inscribed:

I purchased this original M.S. of [*William*] Palmer, an attendant in the Antique Gallery at the British Museum, on the 30ᵗʰ April, 1847. Palmer Knew Blake personally, and it was from the artist's wife that he had the present M.S. which he sold me for 10 . . . . D. G. C. R[*ossetti*].

Rossetti made a manuscript transcript of thirty-three leaves on paper watermarked 1844 still bound with the *Notebook*, allowed William Allingham to make a transcript (now in the Turnbull Library, Wellington, New Zealand), about 1854, and arranged the transcript published in Gilchrist (1863); (5) Sold posthumously with Rossetti's household effects by T. G. Wharton, Martin & Co., on 7 July 1882, lot 483, for £110; (6) Offered by Ellis & White (?1883) with D. G. Rossetti's annotated Gilchrist (1863), lot 67, for £250; sold by F. S. Ellis at Sotheby's, 18 Nov. 1885, lot 608 (again with the Gilchrist), for £85, to Ellis & Scrutton;[1] (7) The MS was 'traded' to Dodd, Mead & Co. in 1884[1] and sold by (8) 'Dodd Mead & Co' to 'W A White / Brooklyn / 26 Janry '87 / $825' (according to White's notes on the fly-leaf); White paginated the *Notebook* [and Rossetti's transcript] (*The Poetical Works of William Blake*, ed. J. Sampson [1905], 38) and lent it anonymously to the Grolier Club exhibitions (1905), no. 139, (1919), no. 57; from White (d. 1927) it passed to his daughter (9) Mrs. Frances White Emerson, who had it rebound and allowed a facsimile to be made of it (1935), lent it to the Philadelphia exhibition (1939), no. 10, and gave it in 1957 to (10) The BRITISH MUSEUM DEPARTMENT OF MANUSCRIPTS.

123

*A. *The Note-Book of William Blake* Called the Rossetti Manuscript. Ed. Geoffrey Keynes. London, 1935. *B. N.Y., 1970 [i.e. 1971].

The 'Introduction' (pp. v–xiii) was revised in Keynes's *Blake Studies* (1949, 1971). The 1935 work is both a photographic facsimile and a transcript; the inaccuracies in the transcript are partly due to the fact that Keynes could not revise the proofs. The 1970 version is evidently merely a facsimile of the facsimile.

---

[1] *The Note-Book of William Blake*, ed. G. Keynes (1935), xi.

A 123

*The Notebook of William Blake: A Photographic and Typographic Facsimile. Ed. David V. Erdman with the assistance of Donald K. Moore. Oxford, 1973.

An edition of major importance.

124. *On Homers Poetry [&] On Virgil* (?1821)

BIBLIOGRAPHICAL INTRODUCTION

TABLE

Copy	Plates	Leaves	Water-marks	Blake numbers	Binding-order	Leaf-size in cm.	Printing colour
A LC	1	1	—	—	Loose	23·3 × 28·9	Black
B *Keynes*	1	1	—	—	Loose	24·5 × 34·3	Black
C *UNTRACED*[1]	1	1	1821[1]				Black
D TRINITY COLLEGE	1	1	—	—	Loose[2]	22·0 × 32·9	Black
E NEW YORK UNIVERSITY	1	1	—	—	Loose	21·6 × 31·0	Black
F MORGAN	1	1	—	—	Loose	24·4 × 34·2	Black

[1] According to both Keynes (1921) and Keynes & Wolf, copy C was 'Similar to copy B. Also in the Linnell collection, but not included in the sale.' I do not know the source of this information. Copy C may be the one with a 'water-mark . . . dated 1821' reproduced [by MUIR] for H. P. Horne, 'Blake's Sibylline Leaf on Homer and Virgil', *Century Guild Hobby Horse*, ii (1887), 115–16.

[2] Copy D was bound after 1871 (the date of the watermark in the fly-leaf) with *Ghost* (D) and *For the Sexes* pl. 14.

TITLE: *On Homers Poetry | . . . | On Virgil*

DATE: ?1821.

The general character of the ideas expressed in *On Homer* is late, but there are few clear indications of date. The citation of the same passage from Virgil referred to in 'Laocoon' (?1820), the similarity of format to *The Ghost of Abel* (1822), and the watermark of 1821 tentatively suggest a date of about 1821.

PUBLICATION: The text is etched over another work, as can be seen from the fragments at the bottom of the design (especially in copies E–F). Blake probably printed a few copies about 1821 and gave them to friends such as Thomas Butts (?A) and John Linnell (B–C).

COLOURING: None.

VARIANTS: None.

ERRATA: None observed.

Pl. 1. DESIGN: To the left of 'On Virgil' are four figures standing beside a tree and a man playing a harp. To the right are descending flames or roots, and at the bottom strange figures divide the text from flames.

COPY A: BINDING: (1) Stitched with *The Ghost of Abel* (A) and 'The Man Sweeping the Interpreter's Parlour' between 1852 and 1912; (2) Now loose.

HISTORY: For the History, see *The Ghost of Abel* (A), p. 209.

COPY B: BINDING: Loose.

HISTORY: (1) This may be the copy apparently sold by Frederick Tatham (like the 'Pickering [Ballads] MS') to (2) Francis Harvey, in whose catalogue (c. 1864) it was offered with *The Ghost of Abel* (?B), *No Natural Religion* (evidently pl. a2), and 'The Man Sweeping the Interpreter's Parlour' for £6. 6s. and acquired, with a number of other items such as 'The Pickering MS', by (3) The Revd. Samuel Prince, for whom it was sold posthumously at Sotheby's, 11 Dec. 1865, lot 270 (only *The Ghost of Abel* is listed), for £3. 18s. to Toovey; (4) Evidently acquired by John Linnell (who later owned copies of *The Ghost of Abel*, *On Homer*, and *No Natural Religion* pl. a2); (5) 'Laocoon' (B), *On Homer*, and *The Ghost of Abel* (B) were reproduced (numbered 1–4) by Ellis & Yeats (1893), *The Ghost of Abel* was lent to the National Gallery exhibition (1913), no. 103, and all three were sold with the Linnell Collection at Christie's, 15 March 1918, lot 199, for £37. 16s. to Quaritch; (6) All three works were acquired before 1921 by *Geoffrey Keynes*, *The Ghost of Abel* was lent to the exhibitions of the Burlington Fine Arts Club (1927), no. 90, and (anonymously) the Whitworth Art Gallery (1969), no. 20, and the National Library of Scotland (1969), no. 68, and all three were described in his catalogue (1964), no. 524–5.

COPY C: BINDING: Loose?

HISTORY: (1) Perhaps this is the copy which was lent by H. H. Gilchrist for reproduction in the *Century Guild Hobby Horse*, II (1887), 115–16, and to the Pennsylvania Academy of the Fine Arts exhibition (1892), no. 145, and which was later (2) 'In the Linnell Collection';[1] (3) *UNTRACED*.

COPY D: BINDING: Bound with *For the Sexes* pl. 14; see p. 204.

HISTORY: For the History, see *For the Sexes* pl. 14.

COPY E: BINDING: (1) Bound about 1853 with many leaves of Blakeana including the 'Order' of the *Songs*; (2) Separated after 1924, and now loose.

HISTORY: For the History, see the 'Order' of the *Songs*, p. 337.

COPY F: BINDING: (1) Bound in contemporary rough calf with other leaves of Blakeana including *Thel* (a); (2) After 1906 it was separated and mounted by itself.

HISTORY: For the History, see *Thel* (a), p. 131.

---

[1] Keynes (1921) and Keynes & Wolf give no evidence for this statement, and I know of none to support it.

125. 'The Order in which the Songs of Innocence and Experience ought to be paged' (? after 1818)

BIBLIOGRAPHICAL INTRODUCTION

COLLECTION: LIBRARY OF CONGRESS.[1]

WATERMARK: None.

LEAF-SIZE: 19·6 × 27·1 cm.

DATE: ? after 1818.

The only copy of the *Songs* arranged in the order given in 'The Order' (copy V) is on paper watermarked '1818'. Therefore 'The Order' was probably produced after 1818.

DESCRIPTION: The manuscript consists of a sheet of paper, folded to make four pages, with stitching marks in the inner margin and the number '102' at the top of p. 1 added when the sheet was part of a volume of Blakeana formed about 1853. A note on the first page describes its provenance, the text is on pp. 2–3, and p. 4 is blank and somewhat dirty. The text is in Black ink.

There are two series of checks in the margins by most numbers. The left-hand series includes all the numbers but 1 and 44, corresponding to no known copy of the *Songs*. The right-hand series includes all but nos. 17–18, 23, 28–34, 46–9, 51–4 (with Xs before nos. 1, 5–6), corresponding to copy F of *Innocence*, except that F has no. 23.

BINDING: (1) Bound about 1853 in half Red morocco, t.e.g., in a volume with other works (see below); (2) The 'Order' was separated after 1924, mounted probably by James Macdonald for G. C. Smith, Jr., by 1938, and bound with *Songs* pl. 11, 30–32, 37, 40, 44, 47, 50, in half Blue morocco.

HISTORY: (1) 'About 1853'[2] George A. Smith collected, numbered, and bound a volume of Blakeana consisting of the MS of Cunningham's Life of Blake and:[3]

(1) *Songs* pl. 42
(2–6) *Songs* pl. 11, 37, 30, 31, 40 (verso pl. 50) (LC)[4]
(7) Two portraits on one sheet
(8) *On Homer* (E)
(9) *Songs* pl. 51
(10–12) *Songs* pl. 32, 44, 47 (LC)[4]
(*13–*14) *Ahania* (Bb) pl. 2ᵃ⁻ᵇ

---

[1] A lithographic facsimile was published with the Muir facsimile of the *Marriage* (1885).

[2] G. Keynes, *Separate Plates* (1956), 6. (In his *Bibliography* [1921], 319, Keynes cites 'a prefatory note signed "G. A. S. 1855"'; I have not traced this note.) The *Marriage*, *Urizen*, and *Experience* plates here may be comprehended in Butts's 10s. 6d. payment for 'Urizen, Heaven &c & Songs of Experience' in 1805 (*Blake Records* [1969], 573).

[3] This list is compiled from the catalogues (chiefly that of Maggs Bros.) and from the numbers (identified by asterisks) on many plates.

[4] *Songs* pl. 30–32, 37, 44, 47 may have been part of the fall-out of the plates printed in Grey from copy a.

(*15–*17) *America* (a) pl. a (verso pl. b), 15^b, c (verso pl. 15^a)

(18) *America* (a) pl. 11–12

(*19) *America* (a) pl. 4

(*20) *Europe* (c) pl. 2 (verso *Jerusalem* pl. 8)

(*21) *Jerusalem* pl. 78 (LC)

(22) [?*Europe* (c) pl. 13–14]

(*23–*6) *Jerusalem* pl. 9, 48, 19, 20 (LC)

(27) [?*Europe* (c) pl. 11^c, 17^c]

(*28) *Jerusalem* pl. 50 (LC)

(29) *Jerusalem* pl. 99

(30) *Thel* pl. 2

(*31) *Urizen* (H) pl. 1

(32) [?*Jerusalem* pl. 38^a (LC)]

(*33–*5) *Europe* (c) pl. 4^b (verso pl. 9^b), 4^a, 6 (verso pl. 7)

(36) *Europe* (c) pl. 4^c (verso pl. 9^c)

(*37) *Europe* (c) pl. 15^a (NYU)

(38) *Europe* (c) pl. 15^b (*UNTRACED*)

(*39–*43) *Europe* (c) pl. 11^b (verso pl. 17^a), 5^a, 16 (verso pl. 17^b), 10 (verso pl. 5^b), 12 (verso pl. 11^a)

(*44) *Jerusalem* pl. 38^b (LC)

(*45) *Ahania* (Bb) pl. 4

(*46–7) *Urizen* (H), pl. 4, 25

(48) *Thel* pl. 6

(*49) *Jerusalem* pl. 58 (LC)

(*50–*1) *Europe* (c) pl. 18$^{a–b}$

(52–3) 'Little Tom the Sailor' pl. 1–2 (i.e. the leaf cut in two)

(54) *Marriage* pl. 5–6

(*55) *For the Sexes* (L) pl. 2

(*56–*7) *No Natural Religion* (L^2) pl. a3–4^1

(58–9) [?*All Religions are One* pl. 1, *No Natural Religion* pl. a1]^1

(*60) *No Natural Religion* (L^2) pl. a8^1

(61–3) [?*No Natural Religion* (L^1) pl. b1, 3–4]^1

(*64) *All Religions are One* pl. 1

(65–71) [?*No Natural Religion* (L) pl. b6–12]^1

(72) [?*Songs* pl. b]

(73) [?'The Man Sweeping the Interpreter's Parlour']

(*74–*87) *For the Sexes* (L) pl. 10–11, 16, 13, 18, 17, 8, 12, 14, 6, 5, 7, 4, ?21

(88–9) [?*For the Sexes* pl. 6–7]

(90) [?*America* pl. 6]

(*91) 'Albion Rose' (B)

---

^{1} In his copy of *No Natural Religion* (C), Frederick Locker noted that when this '4° vol of Miscellaneous pieces by Blake was sold at Christies 1 Apl 1880 . . . it contained some pieces' (*All Religions are One* pl. 1 [two copies], *No Natural Religion* [L^1] pl. b2, 6–11, which he described) not contained in his copy. He did not mention *No Natural Religion* (L) pl. a2–4, 8, b3–4, 12, which his copy already contained, but the numbers on pl. a3–4, 8 indicate that they must then have been present.

(92) *Jerusalem* pl. 51
(93) *Europe* (c) pl. 1¹
(*94) 'The Accusers' (F)
(*95) *Europe* (c) pl. 9ᵃ
(*96) *America* (a) pl. 1
(*97) Hayley's *Ballads* (1802) pl. 14, with the 'Riddle MS' on the verso²
(98) 'The Chaining of Orc' (LC)
(99) Sketch of Thomas Hayley
(100) [?'The Ancient of Days' (D)]
(101) [?*Jerusalem* pl. 50 (*UNTRACED*)]
(*102–3) The 'Order' of the *Songs*

this volume was sold by Smith at Christie's, 1 April 1880, lot 168, for £66 to Quaritch; (2) Quaritch evidently sold it to William Muir, who extracted some plates, wrote 'Wm Muir / Edmonton / 1886' on the fly-leaf of *No Natural Religion* (L¹), reproduced *Songs* pl. b and the 'Order' of the *Songs* ('which have lately come into my possession') as an 'Appendix' to his facsimile of the *Marriage* (a copy of which [now in the Newberry] he sent to the Editor of the *Athenaeum* with a note on 28 Dec. 1885), reproduced *No Natural Religion* (L), and *On Homer* [E] in his facsimiles of these works (1886), and *Europe* (?c) pl. 1, 4 in his facsimile of *Europe* (1887).

(A1) *Songs* pl. b, 51, *America* pl. 6, *For the Sexes* pl. 6–7 were evidently extracted,³ later bound in an extra-illustrated copy of Mrs. Bray's *Life of Thomas Stothard* (1851) which was bought in 1941 by (A2) *Geoffrey Keynes*, who extracted the plates, reproduced *Songs* pl. b in Keynes & Wolf (p. 54), lent *America* pl. 6 to the British Museum exhibition (1957), no. 26 2, and *Songs* pl. b (anonymously) to the exhibitions at the Whitworth Art Gallery (1969), no. 5, and the National Library of Scotland (1969), no. 41, and described all four plates in his catalogue (1964), no. 513, 515, 517 (*Songs* pl. 51 with *Songs* [1]), 582.

(B1) *For the Sexes* (L) pl. 2, 4–8, 10–14, 16–18 were extracted from the 'Order' volume and sold anonymously at Sotheby's, 21 July 1953, lot 484 (loose, with pl. 1, 3, 9, 15 of Muir's facsimile), for £64, to (B2) *Sir Geoffrey Keynes*, who described them (with pl. 21 and his extra pl. 3 added to and bound with them) in his catalogue (1964), no. 582.

(C1) *No Natural Religion* (L²), *All Religions are One* pl. 1, and *For the Sexes* (L) pl. 21 were extracted from the 'Order' volumes and sold anonymously (for Sir Hickman Bacon, according to Keynes, below) at Sotheby's, 21 July 1953, lot 470 (with pl. a2–5, 7, 9 of the Muir facsimile of *No Natural Religion* watermarked J WHATMAN 1811, all the *No Natural Religion* plates described

---

¹ This may be one of the two uncoloured copies lent by A. Macmillan to the Burlington Fine Arts Club exhibition (1876), no. 269; for the other, see *Europe* pl. 1, p. 161.
² The 'T J G W' at the corners of the print suggest that it may once have belonged to Blake's friend Thomas Griffiths Wainewright.
³ *Songs* pl. b and the 'Order' to the *Songs* came to Muir at the same time and may have come from the same source. The subsequent history of *Songs* pl. 51, *America* pl. 6, and *For the Sexes* pl. 6–7 associate them with *Songs* pl. b. If *America* pl. 6 was once in the volume with the 'Order' of the *Songs*, it should be associated with copy a.

as the Muir facsimile), for £42 to Abbott for (**C2**) *Keynes*, who lent *No Natural Religion* anonymously to the National Library of Scotland exhibition (1969), no. 21, described them in his catalogue (1964), no. 506–7, and lent *No Natural Religion* pl. b10 for reproduction in the 1971 facsimile.

(**D1**) *No Natural Religion* (L¹) was sold anonymously at Sotheby's, 21 July 1953, lot 469 (described as a Muir facsimile), for £205 to Schwartz; (**D2**) Jacob Schwartz sold it in December 1953 to (**D3**) Mrs. Landon K. Thorne, who gave it to (**D4**) The PIERPONT MORGAN LIBRARY, which lent it for reproduction in the 1971 facsimile, and in *The Illuminated Blake*, ed. D. V. Erdman (1974).

(**E1**) The second copy of *All Religions are One* pl. 1 is *UNTRACED*.

(3) The depleted volume, still including the 'Order' of the *Songs*, was offered by Quaritch (1887), lot 10,252, for £80; (4) It was described in B. B. Macgeorge's Library catalogue (1906), p. 17, and sold posthumously at Sotheby's, 1 July 1924, lot 133, for £345 to Parsons; (5) Offered in Maggs Catalogue 456 (1924), lot 53, for £630; (6) Acquired by George C. Smith, Jr., broken up, separately bound by Macdonald, listed in Smith's anonymous catalogue (1927), no. 6 (the 'Order' and seven proofs of the *Songs*), 10 (*America* [a]), 12 (18 *Europe* plates), 13 (*Urizen* [H]), 14 (*Ahania* [Bb]), 15 (11 *Jerusalem* proofs), 16 (*On Homer* [E]), 36 ('Albion Rose' [B]), lent to the Fogg exhibition (1930) (the 'Order' and seven *Songs* plates, *America* [a], *Urizen* [H], *Ahania* [Bb], *Jerusalem* pl. 9, 19, 20, 38, 48, 50, 58, 78, *Europe* pl. 18ᵃ⁻ᵇ, *On Homer* [E], 'The Accusers' [F], and 'Albion Rose' [B]), and sold posthumously at Parke-Bernet, 2 Nov. 1938.

(**A1**) Lot 15 (*Thel* pl. 2, 6) for $45 to Stonehill, who sold them in 1938 to (**A2**) Dr. John W. Robertson, who bequeathed them to his son-in-law (**A3**) Edwin Grabhorn, who gave them to his brother (**A4**) Robert Grabhorn (whose partner Mr. Andrew Hoyem is the source of the post-Stonehill information), who offered them anonymously at Sotheby's, 11 Dec. 1973, lots 26–7, withdrew them, and gave them in 1974 to (**A5**) The SAN FRANCISCO PUBLIC LIBRARY.

(**B1**) Lot 18 (the 'Order' plus *Songs* pl. 11, 30–2, 37, 40, 44, 47, 50) for $550 to Stonehill for (**B2**) Mr. LESSING J. ROSENWALD.

(**C1**) Lot 19 (*Songs* pl. 42, 51) for $160 to Rosenbach; (**C2**) *UNTRACED*.

(**D1**) Lot 23 (*America* [a]) for $500 to (**D2**) Mr. LESSING J. ROSENWALD— pl. c was reproduced in Keynes & Wolf, p. 42 and pl. a–c in *The Illuminated Blake* (1974).

(**E1**) Lot 27 (*Europe* [c] pl. 2, *Jerusalem* pl. 8) for $150; (**E2**) Acquired by 1939 by Mr. LESSING J. ROSENWALD.

(**F1**) Lot 28 ('Ancient of Days' [D]) for $300 [to private buyer]; (**F2**) *UNTRACED*.

(**G1**) Lot 29 (*Europe* [c] pl. 1, 4ᵃ, 5ᵃ) for $245 (to Sessler, according to Miss Mabel Zahn of Sessler's, who is also the authority for **G2** and **G4** below); (**G2**) Sold by Sessler's to (**G3**) Moncure Biddle (a note on the verso of pl. 1 says it is from the Smith and Biddle collections) and bought again at his sale by (**G4**) Sessler's; (**G5**) Acquired by Mr. *Leonard Baskin*.

(**H1**) Lot 30 (*Europe* [c] pl. 4ᶜ, 6–7, 9ᶜ, 15ᵃ) for $140 to Gannon; (**H2a**) pl. [6–7], 15ᵃ were bought from the collection of a deceased New York dealer by Professor Joel Egerer about 1964, from whom they passed to (**H2b**) NEW YORK UNIVERSITY; (**H3**) Pl. [4ᶜ, 9ᶜ] are *UNTRACED*.

(**I1**) Lot 31 (*Europe* [c] pl. 5ᵇ, 9ᵃ, 10, 11ᵃ, 12) for $280; (**I2**) Acquired by 1939 by Mr. LESSING J. ROSENWALD.

(**J1**) Lot 32 (*Europe* [c] pl. 11ᶜ, 13–14, 15ᵇ, 17ᶜ) for $160 to Weyhe; (**J2**) Offered by Weyhe (Dec. 1938), lot 123 (pl. 15ᵇ) sold, lot 124 (pl. 13–14) for $150, lot 125 (pl. 11ᶜ, 17ᶜ) for $125; (**J3a**) Pl. 11ᶜ, 17ᶜ were bought from Allen of New York about 1964 by Mr. *Charles Ryskamp*, who lent them to the Princeton exhibition (1969), no. 43; (**J3b**) Pl. 13–14, 15ᵇ are *UNTRACED*.

(**K1**) Lot 33 (*Europe* [c] pl. 4ᵇ, 9ᵇ, 11ᵇ, 16, 17ᵃ⁻ᵇ) for $90 to Gannon; (**K2**) Bought from a dealer in the spring of 1943 by the NEWBERRY LIBRARY.

(**L1**) Lot 34 (*Urizen* [H]) for $250; (**L2**) Acquired by Mr. *Charles J. Rosenbloom*.

(**M1**) Lot 36 (*Marriage* pl. 5–6) for $40; (**M2**) *UNTRACED*.

(**N1**) Lot 37 (*Ahania* [Bb])¹ for $140 [to Gannon]; (**N2**) Acquired by C. B. Tinker, who added his book-plate, listed in his catalogue (1959), no. 274, and bequeathed at Tinker's death in March 1963 to (**N3**) YALE.

(**O1**) Lot 39 (*On Homer* [E]) for $260 [to Gannon]; (**O2**) Bought from the collection of a deceased New York dealer about 1964 by Professor Joel Egerer, from whom it passed to (**O3**) NEW YORK UNIVERSITY.

(**P1**) Lot 40 (*Jerusalem* pl. 9, 19–20, 38ᵃ⁻ᵇ, 48, 50, 58, 78, *Europe* pl. 18ᵃ⁻ᵇ) for $500 to (**P2**) Mr. LESSING J. ROSENWALD.

(**Q1**) Lot 41 (*Jerusalem* pl. 50–1, 99) for $300; (**Q2**) Offered by Weyhe (Dec. 1938), lot 120 (pl. 51) for $200, lot 121 (pl. 50) sold, lot 122 (pl. 99) for $250; (**Q3**) *UNTRACED*.

(**R1**) Lot 42 ('The Accusers' [F], 'The Chaining of Orc', 'Albion Rose' [B], and 'The Man Sweeping the Interpreter's Parlour') for $450 to Rosenbach for (**R2**) Mr. LESSING J. ROSENWALD.

(**S1**) Lot 50 (the 'Riddle MS') was sold for $70; (**S2**) Acquired in 1968 by G. E. Bentley, Jr., and reproduced in 'A New Blake Document: The "Riddle" Manuscript', *Library*, 5S, XXIV (1969), 339.

126. 'Pickering [Ballads] Manuscript' (?after 1807)

BIBLIOGRAPHICAL INTRODUCTION

COLLECTION: PIERPONT MORGAN LIBRARY.

WATERMARK: None. The paper is that used in Hayley's *Designs to A Series of Ballads* (1802).²

---

¹ These are probably the '3 designs' of *Ahania* sold at 'Sotheby, 1855, 1*l*. 13*s*.' (W. T. Lowndes, *The Bibliographer's Manual of English Literature* [1857], i. 216). Keynes & Wolf suggest that the work sold in 1855 is *Ahania* (A), but that copy has six plates.

² At the bottom left of p. 16 appear fragments of an erased printed word which is evidently the catchword 'With' on p. 20 of Hayley's *Designs to A Series of Ballads* for which Blake made engravings published on 1 July 1802. Blake's Ballads Manuscript paper was obtained by taking the abandoned *Ballads* (1802) sheets and cutting off the sections bearing Hayley's text and the '1802' watermark, leaving the wide inner margins for Blake's own poems.

LEAF-SIZE: 12·5 × 18·4 cm.

DATE: ?after 1807.

The earliest possible date, as shown by the use of leaves from Hayley's *Ballad* of 1 July 1802, is June or July 1802. Three of the poems ('Mary', 'The Grey monk', and 'The Golden Net') seem to be copied from drafts of 1803. Other leaves from unsold copies of the *Ballads* (1802) were apparently used between 1807 and 1824.[1]

This evidence suggests that the Ballads Manuscript poems were transcribed in their present form after 1805, when publication of the separate quarto *Ballads* (1802) was abandoned (see Blake's letter of 22 Jan. 1805), and probably after 1807. The dates of original composition may well be 1800–4 for the Ballads Manuscript poems.

DESCRIPTION: The manuscript consists of 22 pages (11 leaves) numbered 1–22 in the top outer corners of the pages in the Black ink in which the text is written. The text is fairly copied in ink which is uniformly Black except for some corrections. There are faint offsets from the writing on many pages.

The poems are 'The Smile' (p. 1), 'The Golden Net' (pp. 1–2) drafted on *Notebook* p. 14, 'The Mental Traveller' (pp. 3–7), 'The Land of Dreams' (pp. 7–8), 'Mary' (pp. 8–10), 'The Crystal Cabinet' (pp. 10–11), 'The Grey Monk' (pp. 12–13) drafted on *Notebook* p. 12 and revised on *Jerusalem* (1804–?20) pl. 52, 'Auguries of Innocence' (pp. 13–18), 'Long John Brown & Little Mary Bell' (p. 19), and 'William Bond' (pp. 20–2).

TITLE: The manuscript has long been called 'The Pickering Manuscript', after B. M. Pickering, who owned it for a few years, but 'The Ballads Manuscript' seems a more useful title, since it describes both the poems themselves and the paper on which they are written.

BINDING: (1) Once stitched through three holes, 3·9 cm from the top and 4·5, 4·6 cm apart, probably in a dark Olive-tinted cover; (2) About 1866 it was 'BOUND BY F. BEDFORD / FOR B. M. PICKERING' in Red morocco, g.e.

HISTORY: (1) Acquired from Catherine Blake, at her death in 1831, by (2) Frederick Tatham,[2] who offered it 'to several gentlemen for 25 guineas' (according to the Harvey catalogue below) and then sold it to (3) Francis Harvey, who 'lent [*it*] to Mr Gilchrist, who has reprinted a portion of it',[3] and then offered it in his catalogue (*c.* 1864) for £15. 15*s.*; (4) Acquired by the Revd. Samuel Prince, for whom it was sold posthumously at Sotheby's, 11 Dec. 1865, lot 83, for £7. 5*s.* to Pickering;[4] (5) 'BOUND BY F. BEDFORD FOR

---

[1] See 'The Date of Blake's Pickering Manuscript', *Studies in Bibliography*, xix (1966), 232–43.

[2] A letter from Tatham printed in the Harvey catalogue says: 'The MS you purchased of me was part of the possessions into which I came by legacy from Mrs. Blake'.

[3] D. G. Rossetti wrote to Alexander Gilchrist, 27 Aug. 1861, 'I have been reading [*and copying*] the Blake MS' (*Letters of Dante Gabriel Rossetti*, ed. J. R. Wahl [1965], ii. 418).

[4] W. M. Rossetti was evidently mistaken when he wrote to Anne Gilchrist, 2 March 1880 (letter in the collection of Mrs. L. K. Thorne), of 'a little M.S. book belonging to Lord Houghton at that time [*c. 1863*] but now to Mʳ Pickering'. W. M. Rossetti said in a letter to John Sampson that it was 'then, to the best of his recollection, stitched into a darkish olive-tinted cover' (*Poetical Works of William Blake*, ed. J. Sampson [1905], 265).

B. M. PICKERING' and printed by Pickering in 1866;[1] (6) Acquired by William Mitchell, who added his book-plate; (7) Acquired by Frederick Locker, who added his book-plate, lent it to the Burlington Fine Arts Club exhibition (1876), no. 315, described it in his catalogue (1886), and sold it through Dodd, Mead & Co.[2] to (8) 'W. A White 27 Apl 1905' (according to the note on the second fly-leaf), who lent it to the exhibitions of the Grolier Club (1919), no. 58 (anonymously) and the Fogg (1924) and allowed pp. 13–14 to be reproduced in G. Keynes, *Bibliography of William Blake* (1921); it was sold, probably after White's death (1927) with many of his other Blakes in 1929, to (9) Rosenbach; lent by A. S. W. Rosenbach to the Philadelphia exhibition (1939), no. 105; (10) Acquired by Mrs. Landon K. Thorne, in whose catalogue (1971) it was described (no. 16), and who gave it in 1971 to (11) The PIERPONT MORGAN LIBRARY, which reproduced it (1972).

127

*The Pickering Manuscript. Introduction by Charles Ryskamp. N.Y., 1972.
   The first facsimile of the manuscript (22 pages), with a factual 'Introduction' of four pages.

128. *Poetical Sketches* (1783)

BIBLIOGRAPHICAL INTRODUCTION

See Table on p. 344

TITLE: POETICAL / SKETCHES. / — / By W. B. / — / LONDON: / Printed in the Year M DCC LXXXIII [1783].

COLLATION: 4° (half sheet imposition): [A1–2], B–K4 (*J omitted*); signed on first two leaves of each quire except in quire A; 38 leaves, 76 pp. K4 present in copies B, C, E, G, H, I, R.

CONTENTS: Title-page ([A1]ʳ), 'Advertisement' ([A2]ʳ), 'Miscellaneous Poems': 'To Spring' (B1ʳ⁻ᵛ), 'To Summer' (B1ᵛ), 'To Autumn' (B2ʳ), 'To Winter' (B2ᵛ), 'To the Evening Star' (B3ʳ), 'To Morning' (B3ᵛ), 'Fair Elenor' (B4ʳ–C1ᵛ), 'Song [How sweet I roam'd]' (C1ᵛ), 'Song [My silks and fine array]' (C2ʳ), 'Song [Love and harmony combine]' (C2ᵛ), 'Song [I love the jocund dance]' (C3ʳ), 'Song [Memory, hither come]' (C3ᵛ), 'Mad Song' (C4ʳ), 'Song [Fresh from the dewy hill]' (C4ᵛ), 'Song [When early morn walks forth]' (D1ʳ), 'To the Muses' (D1ᵛ), 'Gwin, King of Norway' (D2ʳ–D4ʳ), 'An Imitation of Spencer' (D4ᵛ–E1ᵛ), 'Blind-Man's Buff' (E1ᵛ–E2ᵛ); 'King Edward the Third' (E3ʳ–H4ʳ), 'Prologue, intended for a dramatic piece of King Edward the Fourth' (H4ᵛ), 'Prologue to King John' (I1ʳ–I1ᵛ), 'A War Song to Englishmen' (I1ᵛ–I2ʳ), 'The Couch of Death' (I2ᵛ–I3ᵛ), 'Contemplation' (I4ʳ⁻ᵛ), 'Samson' (I4ᵛ–K3ᵛ); [A1]ᵛ, [A2]ᵛ K4ʳ⁻ᵛ blank.

---

[1] *Songs of Innocence and Experience, with Other Poems* [ed. R. H. Shepherd] [1866].
[2] *Poetical Works of William Blake*, ed. J. Sampson (1905), 265, says Dodd, Mead & Co. bought the Locker Collection 'in June [*sic*] 1905'.

TABLE

Copy	Collection	Corrections on page	Contemporary owner
A	BM	—	
B	BM	4, 9, 15^{a-b}	?Thomas Butts
C	HUNTINGTON	4, 7, 12, 15^{b}	Charles Tulk
D	CINCINNATI ART MUSEUM	9, 15^{b}	George Cumberland
E	*Martin*	4, 7, 9, 15^{a-b}	John Flaxman, William Long
F	TURNBULL LIBRARY	4, 9, 15^{a-b}, 24^{b}[1]	Nancy Flaxman, Isaac Reed, Richard Heber
G	WELLESLEY	—	Samuel Palmer
H	PFORZHEIMER	—	?Samuel Palmer
I	PRINCETON	—	
[*There is no J*]			
K	TORONTO	—	
L	TRINITY COLLEGE, Cambridge	—	
M	*UNTRACED*	—[2]	
N	YALE	—	?Samuel Palmer
O	TEXAS	4, 9, 15^{a-b}	
P	*UNTRACED*	—[3]	
Q	WESTMINSTER PUBLIC LIBRARY	4, 5, 7, 9, 12, 15^{a-b}, 24^{b}, 25, 28	
R	ROSENBACH	—	Samuel Palmer
S	HUNTINGTON	4, 7, 9, 15^{a-b}, 29	John Flaxman, William Hayley, ?Thomas Kemble, Duke of Devonshire
T	LC	4, 15^{b}, 24^{a-b}, 44, 46, 64^{a}	John Linnell
U	LIVERPOOL PUBLIC LIBRARY	—	?Samuel Palmer
V	TEXAS CHRISTIAN	4, 7, 12, 15^{b}, 24^{a}, 44, 46, 64^{a-b}	
W	UNIVERSITY COLLEGE (LONDON)	2, 4, 9, 15^{a-b}, 20, 24[4]	
X	MORGAN	—	

[1] Copy F has corrections and comments in three different hands: (1) Blake's Black ink corrections on pp. 4, 7, 9, 15^{a-b}, 24^{b} of a kind Blake made elsewhere; (2) corrections on pp. 7, 13, 17, 24 of a unique kind in Brown ink and (I think) in another hand; (3) pencil corrections and comments on pp. 2, 7, 11–17, 24–25, 30, 45–46, 52, 55, 60, 62–64, certainly not by Blake. (The inserted 'Songs by Shepherds' are in a fourth hand; see p. 363, below.) The ink changes are reproduced in D. F. McKenzie, 'Blake's *Poetical Sketches* (1783)', *Turnbull Library Record*, i, no. 3 (March 1968), 8.

[2] The Anderson Galleries catalogue of H. B. Forman's Library (15 March 1920, lot 35) says that there are 'two corrections in Blake's own hand at pp. 12 and 15, and possibly two others, according to a note in Mr. Forman's hand', but Keynes (*Blake Studies* [1949], 37) asserts that the 'corrections in the text [*were*] copied by him [*Forman*] from copy B'. I do not know Keynes's authority, but the statements are difficult to reconcile, since copy B has corrections only on pp. 4 and 15, while the 1920 catalogue claims four corrections for copy M, including two on pp. 12 and 15.

[3] Keynes (*Blake Studies* [1949]) implies that there are no corrections.

[4] The hand which made the corrections does not look like Blake's.

LEAF-SIZE: 13·9 × 22·3 cm (R).

WATERMARK: Chain lines 2·8 cm apart. Paper defective, perhaps an odd lot.

PAGE NUMBERING: Pages numbered correctly 2–70 (B1v–K3v) at the outside corners of pages with running heads; in square brackets in the middle of the top margin when the first line of the page is the title of the piece that follows (except that pp. 15–16 are in round brackets).

RUNNING TITLES: Correct, except for p. 26, 'BLIND-MAN'S BUFF.', which should be 'AN IMITATION OF SPENCER.', and p. 56, 'A WAR SONG TO ENGLISHMEN.', which should be 'PROLOGUE TO KING JOHN.'

CATCHWORDS: Correct, except for p. 43, '*Prince*' which should be '*Prince.*' and p. 55, 'PROLOGUE' which should be 'PROLOGUE,'.

PRESS FIGURES: None.

ORNAMENT: p. 10.

FACSIMILE PAGES:[1] H1–K4 (in copies K, L, U), I1–K4 (in copy P), [A2] (in copy Q).

The facsimile pages were printed on paper watermarked 'MICHALLET',[2] sometime before 1887, when they were described in a Pearson catalogue, and probably before the death in 1883 of Francis Bedford, who bound copies K and U.

PUBLICATION: According to J. T. Smith (1828), John Flaxman and A. S. Mathew paid for the printing of Blake's *Poetical Sketches* and gave the copies 'to Blake to sell to friends, or publish, as he might think proper'.[3] He did not show much interest in the thirty-eight leaves stitched into bluish-Grey wrappers. A few copies he evidently gave away himself: George Cumberland probably received his copy (D) about 1783; Thomas Butts is likely to have acquired a copy (B) soon after he became Blake's patron about 1795; and Charles Tulk was presumably given his copy (C) after 1810 when, at the age of twenty-four, he began working with John Flaxman in the interest of Swedenborg. Other copies were given away by the Flaxmans in Blake's interest; Flaxman gave one copy (S) to William Hayley on 26 April 1784,[4] and another (E) to William Long, almost certainly at the same time,[4] while Nancy Flaxman gave copy F away on 15 May 1784, perhaps to Isaac Reed.

CORRECTIONS: In all these copies which were given away by or for Blake, the author made neat corrections in ink in a kind of printing hand.

---

[1] The clearest indication of the facsimile is in the last words on p. 59, where the penultimate 'Prepare' is under the 'w' of 'welcome' in genuine copies and under the 'c' in the facsimile.

[2] Oddly enough, the 1890 Griggs facsimile of the *Poetical Sketches*, which is typographically quite distinct from the inserted facsimile leaves, is also printed on paper watermarked 'MICHALLET', and a fly-leaf in copy X is on the same paper.

[3] *Blake Records* (1969), 456. Keynes (*Blake Studies* [1949], 26) calculated that they probably paid about £6 to have fifty copies printed.

[4] *Blake Records*, 27–8. Crabb Robinson owned two copies (?A, ?O).

Apparently he corrected copies unsystematically, as he happened to notice errors afresh. In all copies which he improved, Blake corrected the misspelling on page 15, and in all but one he made the same deletion on page 4, but the other changes seem almost random.[1]

Incidence of MS changes in POETICAL SKETCHES

Copy	Pages																		Totals
	2	4	5	7	9	12	15^a	15^b	20	24^a	24^b	25	28	29	44	46	64^a	64^b	
B		*			*		*	*											4
C		*		*			*	*											4
D			*					*											2
E		*		*	*		*	*											5
F		*			*		*	*				*							5
O		*			*		*	*											4
Q		*		*	*	*	*	*		*	*		*	*					10
S		*		*	*	*		*			*								6
T		*						*		*	*				*	*	*		7
V		*			*	*	*	*							*	*	*	*	9
W	*	*		*	*			*	*										6
11	1	10	1	5	8	3	7	11	1	2	3	1	1	1	2	2	2	1	

UNCORRECTED COPIES: At his death Blake left a number of copies as they had come to him from the printer, unstitched, uncut, and uncorrected. Five copies (G–I, ?N, R) seem to have come into Samuel Palmer's hands in this pristine state.[2] Copies K, L, P, U probably survived in the original sheets until the last three or four quires were accidentally damaged, for in each copy these last quires were supplied in facsimile. All these copies (G, H, I, K, L, P, R, U) are uncorrected, and with them may be associated copies A, M, N, and X which also lack changes by Blake. Copies A, G, H, I, K, L, M, N, P, R, U, X were probably all in Blake's possession at his death and are, therefore, in a sense, 'posthumous' copies.

Dates at which POETICAL SKETCHES left Blake's hands

Date	Copies
1783–4	D, E, F, S
c. 1795	B
c. 1810	C
1783–1827	O, Q, V, W
Posthumous	A, G, H, I, K, L, M– P, R, T (1831), U, X

[1] Blake evidently made corrections in some copies well before they were disposed of, for copy T, which Linnell bought from his widow in 1831 (*Blake Records*, 596), has extensive corrections.

[2] According to a note in copy G by 'John Linnell jun.', 'I found in Mr S. Palmer's store room at Furze Hill House [*where Palmer lived from 1862 until his death in 1881*], *3* copies of this book *in sheets*, (one [*?copy U*] not quite perfect)— S. P. told me to take one [*copy G*] for my self...'. A. H. Palmer sold 'two [*?more*] copies of Blake's "Poetical Sketches"' which he had found 'among my father's papers and books' to the dealer Pearson (according to his note with copy N), perhaps copies H and R. Palmer also probably gave copy I to Gilchrist.

ERRATA:[1] (1) p. 4, l. 11, there is an extra 'in'; (2) p. 7, l. 6, 'cheeks' should be singular; (3) p. 12, l. 16, 'her' should be 'his'; (4) p. 14, ll. 6, 8 are not indented like ll. 14, 16; (5) p. 15, l. 4, 'unfold' should be 'infold'; (6) p. 15, l. 7, 'beds' should be 'birds'; (7) p. 18, l. 6, 'greeen'; (8) p. 18, l. 9, 'chrystal'; (9) p. 22, ll. 78, 80, 'doth' should be 'do'; (10) p. 24, 'Spencer' is mis-spelled; (11) p. 24, l. 8, 'yields' should be 'yieldst'; (12) p. 24, l. 14, 'others' should be singular; (13) p. 24, l. 15, 'cares' probably should be 'ears'; (14) p. 26, l. 1, 'Snow' should be lower case; (15) p. 27, ll. 30, 40, the closing quotation marks are omitted; (16) p. 28, l. 64, there is an extra full stop; (17) p. 28, l. 66, the semicolon should probably be a comma; (18) p. 29, the Dramatis Personae omits the 'Minstrel' and 'Warriors'; (19) p. 29, in the scene heading '*Nobles before it*' should evidently omit the last two words; (20) p. 32, l. 20, 'phlsophic'; (21) p. 35, 'Cressey' for 'Cressy'; (22) p. 36, l. 10, 'ere' for 'e'er'; (23) p. 43, '*Exeunt*' should be '*Exit*'; (24) p. 44, l. 235, 'her' should be 'his'; (25) p. 46, l. 291, 'them' should be 'him'; (26) p. 50, the direction '—*to him*' is misplaced; (27) p. 56, l. 1, 'For' should be lower case; (28) pp. 63–4, the first speech should have quotation marks all down the left margin, like the second speech; (29) p. 64, 'in the house when I grew up; he was my school-fellow' should be repunctuated; (30) p. 65, 'ly' is mis-spelled; (31) p. 67, 'withs' for 'withes'; (32) p. 67, 'falshood'.

COPY A: BINDING: Bound after June 1890 in the British Museum in Brown morocco, with a crown.

    HISTORY: (1) Perhaps this is the copy given by Crabb Robinson in May 1848 to (2) J. J. G. Wilkinson;[2] (3) Copy A was sold by Quaritch for £42 on 19 June 1890 to (4) The BRITISH MUSEUM, where it was bound.

COPY B: BINDING: Stabbed through three holes into the original greyish-Blue wrappers.

    HISTORY: (1) Sold posthumously with part of the Library of Captain Butts[3] at Sotheby's, 2 May 1906, lot 801 (a clipping from the catalogue is still with the volume), for £60 to Wise; (2) T. J. Wise gave it with the Ashley Library in 1937 to (3) The BRITISH MUSEUM.

COPY C: BINDING: (1) In 1906 it was in the original light Blue cloth boards with a Red leather label on the spine; (2) It was bound, apparently for Robert Hoe, at 'THE CLUB BINDERY 1908' in Citron levant morocco, g.e.

    HISTORY: (1) It came 'To Charles Tulke Esq[re], / from William Blake' (according to the inscription on the title-page); (2) Sold by Edward Duperner at Sotheby's, 20 June 1906, lot 937 (in 'original light blue cloth boards' and

---

[1] This Errata List omits defects of type such as p. 27, l. 49, p. 42, l. 182; the defective 'T', p. 31, l. 7; the defective 'g', p. 45, l. 253; the defective 't' in 'tir'd'. The conventionality of the spelling, punctuation, and capitalization, compared with Blake's usual later practice, suggests that someone corrected the printer's copy fairly carefully.

[2] Wilkinson thanked Crabb Robinson on 24 May 1848 for 'your kind gift of Blake's Poetical Sketches' (letter in Dr. Williams's Library).

[3] Nothing is said of its having belonged to the Captain's grandfather Thomas Butts. The collection obviously represents in part the acquisitions of subsequent generations, for some of the books in it were published as late as 1905.

a Red leather label on the spine), for £109 to B. F. Stevens; (3) Acquired by Robert Hoe, who evidently had it bound in 1908, added his book-plate, and sold it posthumously at Anderson's, 25 April 1911, lot 389, for $725 to (4) The HUNTINGTON LIBRARY.

COPY D: BINDING: (1) Originally stabbed through three holes, 3·2 and 2·9 cm apart; (2) Now bound in contemporary Brown half calf over marbled boards, with 'POETICAL / SKETCHES' blind stamped on it.

HISTORY: (1) Acquired by George Cumberland, who wrote his name on the title-page, pasted in his Message Card and 'The Man Sweeping the Interpreter's Parlour', and made notes on pp. 2 ('To Spring' is '*fine*') and 63 ('Contemplation' is 'Beautiful—G. C.'); (2) It was sent 'From George Cumberland [*Jr*] / to [(3)] John Linnell 1866 / See letter / &c' (according to the note on the first fly-leaf); it was sold posthumously with the Linnell Collection at Sotheby's, 3 June 1918, lot 3, for £60 to Pickering; (4) Acquired before 1921 by Beverly Chew, who added his book-plate on the back cover, and sold it posthumously at Anderson's, 8 Dec. 1924, lot 28, for $900 to Rosenbach; (5) Acquired by John J. Emery, who put his name on the front endpaper, lent it to the Philadelphia exhibition (1939), no. 1, and gave it in 1971 to (6) The CINCINNATI ART MUSEUM.

COPY E: (1) Bound in half calf with contemporary plays in 1919; (2) Bound by 1924, apparently for Col. Henry D. Hughes, by Macdonald (according to the 1924 catalogue) in dark Green morocco, g.e.

HISTORY: (1) Presented 'To M^r [*William*] Long / from J Flaxman' (according to the inscription on the title-page), probably about April 1784 (see *Blake Records* [1969], 27–8); (2) Offered in a catalogue of Thomas Thorpe of Guildford (Dec. 1919),[1] bound in half calf with contemporary plays, for £60; (3) *Poetical Sketches* was separately bound by Macdonald and sold by 'a Prominent Pennsylvania Collector' (Col. Henry D. Hughes, according to Keynes, *Blake Studies* [1949]) at American Art Association, 22 April 1924, lot 58, for $525; (4) Acquired by George C. Smith, Jr., described in his anonymous catalogue (1927), no. 1, lent to the Fogg exhibition (1930), and sold posthumously at Parke-Bernet, 2 Nov. 1938, lot 9, for $350 to Gabriel Wells; (5) Sold by E. W. Keese at Sotheby's, 14 March 1961, lot 503, for £1,300 to Hollings; (6) Acquired by Mr. *Henry Bradley Martin*.

COPY F: BINDING: (1) Stabbed by 1784, evidently with sheet C misfolded and thus bound (pp. 11–12, 9–10, 15–16, 13–14);[2] (2) Four unstabbed leaves with Blake's poems were bound, perhaps for Isaac Reed by 1807, with the correctly folded trimmed leaves in Red crushed morocco with 'BLAKE' on the spine.

---

[1] I have only seen a clipping with *Poetical Sketches* (G), without indication of seller or date, saying the copy there offered has a presentation inscription from Flaxman on the title-page; Keynes (*Blake Studies* [1949]) says he was offered copy E bound 'with several dramatic works' by Thorpe in Dec. 1919 for £60 (for a similarly bound copy, see copy S). I have combined the descriptions of Keynes and the clipping.

[2] The misfolding is indicated by erased ink notes on pp. 8 ('page 9 overleaf'), 10 ('page 11 two leaves back'), and 12 ('page 13 two leaves forward'), apparently in the same hand as the '1784' inscription on the title-page.

HISTORY: (1) It was a '[present *del*] from Mrs Flaxman May 15, 1784' (according to the note on the title-page), perhaps to the Flaxmans friend (2) Isaac Reed, who may have added the leaves with 'Songs by Shepherds', and with whose library it was sold by King & Lochee, 5 Dec. 1807, lot 6,577 (the second fly-leaf has 'Reeds Sale 1807 ˢ6 ᵈ6'), for 6s. 6d. to Heber; (3) This was the copy in Richard 'Heber's Sale [*by Evans, 8 Dec.*] 1834', lot 99 (according to the inscription in a contemporary hand), where it sold for 2s., probably to (4) J. H. Anderdon, who added his dated book-plate ('J H A / 1834'); (5) It may have been acquired by B. M. Pickering, with the second edition of whose *Songs of Innocence and of Experience*, ed. R. H. Shepherd (1868), two of the shepherd's 'Songs' were published; (6) Sold by a deceased Gentleman at Sotheby's, 1 June 1907, lot 419, for £27 to Gundy; (7) Sold anonymously at Sotheby's, 22 March 1910, lot 448, for £52 to Francis Edwards, who sold it to (8) Alexander Turnbull; after Turnbull's death in 1918 it was given to (9) The TURNBULL LIBRARY, Wellington, New Zealand.

COPY G: BINDING: Bound in the late 19th century for John Linnell, Jr., in half morocco over marbled boards, the edges dappled.

HISTORY: (1) Samuel Palmer gave it to (2) John Linnell, Jr.,[1] who had it bound, and sold it posthumously at Hodgson's, 29 May 1906, lot 517, for £16. 5s. to Dobell;[2] (3) Offered in Maggs Bros. Catalogue 71, p. 13, for £32. 10s.; apparently bought for '£28. 0 [*from*] Maggs 117' (according to the note on the penultimate fly-leaf) by (4) George Herbert Palmer, who added his book-plate, described it in his catalogue (1923), lent it to the Fogg exhibition (1924), and gave it in 1924 to (5) WELLESLEY COLLEGE.

COPY H: BINDING: 'BOUND BY F. BEDFORD' in the manner of Roger Payne in Green levant morocco, t.e.g.

HISTORY: (1) Perhaps it was inherited from Samuel Palmer by his son (2) A. H. Palmer (see copy N), who may have sold it for £20 to John Pearson; (3) Sold with the Pearson Library at Sotheby's, 7 Nov. 1916, lot 40, for £51 to Dobell;[3] (4) Sold with the Library of Herschel V. Jones at Anderson Galleries, 2 Dec. 1918, lot 181, for $445 to G. D. Smith; (5) Acquired by 1936 for the PFORZHEIMER LIBRARY.

COPY I: BINDING: (1) Apparently bound by Bedford in Brown morocco, t.e.g., at least from 1884 to 1896; repairs were made to the corners of the title-page, and the 'Advertisement' page before 1914; (2) Bound by 'LORTIC FRÈRES' in Red levant morocco, t.e.g., by 1914.

---

[1] The verso of the first fly-leaf was inscribed, evidently after Samuel Palmer's death in 1881: '*John Linnel jun.* I found in Mˢ S. Palmer's store room at Furze Hill House [*where Palmer lived 1862–81*], *3* copies [*?G, R, U*] of this book *in sheets*, (one [*?U*] not quite perfect)— S. P. told me to take one for my self—I had this copy half bound in morocco—this [*G*] is the copy—it should have been left untrimmed at the edges [*it is 12·6×20·9 cm*]— A. H. Palmer sold one of his copies [*?R*] for £20 (I believe he told me).' The complete copy left in sheets is evidently R.

[2] Not to Maggs, as in Keynes, *Blake Studies* (1949).

[3] A clipping in copy G from an unidentified catalogue, perhaps Dobell's, offers copy H for £70.

HISTORY: (1) This may be the uncut copy which (according to the 1888 catalogue) belonged to Alexander Gilchrist[1] and which was (2) Sold anonymously at Sotheby's, 19 March 1888, lot 183, for £16 to Pearson; a note on the first fly-leaf of copy I says 'A46 / Td. / Pearson'; (3) Probably this is the copy bound by Bedford, t.e.g., sold anonymously at Sotheby's, 20 June 1896, lot 588, for £40 to Conway; (4) Copy I was acquired by Thomas G. Arthur, who added his book-plate, apparently had it bound by Lortic Frères, and sold it with his library at Sotheby's, 15 July 1914, lot 46, for £56 to (5) G. D. Smith; sold by Smith (according to Keynes, *Blake Studies* [1949]) on 8 Nov. 1918 for $400 to (6) A. E. Newton, who added his book-plate, lent it to the exhibitions at the Fogg (1924) and in Philadelphia (1939), no. 2, and sold it posthumously at Parke-Bernet, 16 April 1941, lot 124, for $225, to Papantonio of Seven Gables Bookshop; (7) Mr. Papantonio bought it for stock and believes he sold it to Sessler's (according to his letter to me of 1967); (8) Acquired by A. E. Newton's daughter Caroline Newton, who added her book-plate, lent it to the Princeton exhibition (1967), and gave it in the spring of 1971 to (9) PRINCETON UNIVERSITY.

COPY K: BINDING: (1) Bound by Bedford in calf; (2) The binding apparently became rough, and it was later 'BOUND BY SANGORSKI & SUTCLIFFE, LONDON', in Red morocco, g.e., apparently before 1951.

HISTORY: (1) Sold with the Library of R. A. Potts at Sotheby's, 20 Feb. 1913, lot 71, for £8. 5s. to Dobell; (2) Offered as the property of the late P. M. Pittar at Sotheby's, 25 July 1918, lot 1,045 (bound by Bedford) [£10, Protheroe], apparently bought in, and sold as Pittar's property at Sotheby's, 17 Dec. 1919, lot 27 (bound by Bedford), for £8 to G. D. Smith; (3) Sold posthumously by G. D. Smith at Anderson's, 28 April 1921, lot 28 (with the book-plate of R. A. Potts), for $10; (4) 'In 1936 said to be in the possession of Mr. Francis J. Underhill',[2] who may be the anonymous owner who sold it at Sotheby's, 11 April 1938, lot 285 (bound by Bedford), for £10 to King; (5) Offered in Raphael King's Catalogue 34 (Jan. 1940) for £65,[2] apparently rebound, and sold in 1951 by King to (6) George R. Day (according to a letter of 5 Dec. 1951 from King to Day shown me by Day's son);[3] (7) Sold (according to Day's son) posthumously to Philip Duschnes, who in turn sold it in 1966 to (8) The UNIVERSITY OF TORONTO.

COPY L: BINDING: (1) Evidently bound with Wordsworth's *Letter to a*

---

[1] Gilchrist (d. 1861) wrote that the rarity of *Poetical Sketches* forced him 'to abandon the idea of myself owning the book. I have had to use a copy borrowed from one of Blake's surviving friends' (*Life of William Blake*, 'Pictor Ignorus' [1863], i. 23). The surviving friend was probably Samuel Palmer, who seems to have allowed Gilchrist to keep the borrowed copy.

[2] According to Keynes, *Blake Studies* (1949).

[3] In this letter King says: 'There is little to tell of its provenance, as it was found in a nineteenth century calf binding in rough condition. It is certainly not one of the "known" copies.' However, the identification of the King–Day copy with the Potts–Pittar copy seems virtually certain. For one thing, the Potts–Pittar and King–Day copies each have pp. 49–70 in facsimile. For another, King owned the Potts–Pittar copy and sold the King–Day copy, but is not known to have owned any other copy of the *Poetical Sketches*. Evidently King was merely uninformed about the previous history of this copy.

friend of Robert Burns (1816), [T. H. E. A.], *Remarks on Professor* [G. P. G] *Rossetti's* '[*Disquizione sullo*] *Spirito Antipapale*' [1832], 'and others', until at least 1897; (2) Rebound by 1911 in Red straight grained morocco, g.e.

HISTORY: (1) Perhaps this is the copy bound in half calf with works by Wordsworth 'and others' and sold anonymously at Sotheby's, 7 Feb. 1897, lot 498, for £33 to Dobell; (2) Copy L was sold by 'a Lady' at Sotheby's, 2 May 1911, lot 321, for £49 to Quaritch; (3) Sold by H. T. Butler at Hodgson's, 14 June 1934, lot 439, for £92 to Robinson; (4) Acquired by Lord Rothschild, who lent it to the National Book League exhibition (1947), no. 193,[1] and gave it in 1969 to (5) TRINITY COLLEGE, Cambridge.

COPY M: BINDING: Bound by Roger de Coverly in the 20th century in Blue levant morocco, g.e.

HISTORY: (1) Acquired by H. Buxton Forman before 10 June 1883 (the date of the sonnet he wrote on the fly-leaf), bound for him, and sold posthumously at Anderson Galleries, 15 March 1920, lot 35, for $410; (2) *UNTRACED*.

COPY N: BINDING: 'BOUND BY F. BEDFORD' in Green morocco, t.e.g.

HISTORY: (1) Acquired by Thomas Gaisford, who added his book-plate, and sold it at Sotheby's, 23 April 1890,[2] lot 184, for £48 to Quaritch; (2) Acquired by B. B. Macgeorge, listed in his catalogues (1892, 1906), lent to the exhibitions in the National Gallery (1913), no. 86, Manchester (1914), no. 166, Nottingham (1914), no. 113, the National Gallery of Scotland (1914), Case B, No. 2, and sold posthumously at Sotheby's, 1 July 1924, lot 109, for £118 to Quaritch; (3) Offered by Quaritch (Oct. 1924), lot 322, for £135; (4) Acquired by Willis Vickery, who added his book-plate, described it in his book (1927), and sold it posthumously at American Art Association–Anderson Galleries, 1 March 1933, lot 15, for $975 to Beyer; (5) Acquired by C. B. Tinker, who added his book-plate, described in his catalogue (1959), no. 265, and bequeathed at his death in March 1963 to (6) YALE.

COPY O: BINDING: Bound by Thomas 'FAZAKERLEY LIVERPOOL' in Red morocco, the edges trimmed, especially at the bottom, sometimes affecting the catchwords; the top 2·6 cm of the title-page was cut off (presumably removing an owner's name) and repaired.

HISTORY: (1) Perhaps this is Crabb Robinson's 'second copy' of 'Blakes Poet[1] Sketches' (cf. copy A) which was 'bound in a Vol. of tracts' (according to Robinson's Diary of 24 May 1848 in Dr. Williams's Library); copy O was rebound in the 19th century and (2) Sold by W. E. Moss at Sotheby's, 2 March 1937, lot 141, for £80 to Sawyer; (3) Acquired for The Miriam Lutcher Stark Collection of the UNIVERSITY OF TEXAS, where it appeared in the catalogue of 1940.

---

[1] John Hayward, *English Poetry*: An Illustrated Catalogue (1950).

[2] With copy N is a note of 5 May 1890 from A. H. Palmer to the dealer Pearson saying: 'The two copies of Blake's "Poetical Sketches" you have just purchased [*?from Palmer*], are, to the best of my belief, all that existed [*?after my father's death*] among my father's papers or books.' It seems likely that Palmer's note refers to copies H and R, and not to copy N, which had already been sold twice by May 1890.

COPY P: BINDING: Bound by Riviere in Green morocco, gilt, untrimmed (according to Keynes, *Blake Studies* [1949]).

HISTORY: (1) Acquired from Quaritch about 1900 by (2) General Archibald Stirling of Keir (according to Keynes, *Blake Studies* [1949]), from whom it passed to (3) Lt.-Col. William Stirling, who sold it; (4) *UNTRACED.*

COPY Q: BINDING: 'Bound by Zaehnsdorf' with the 'Advertisement' leaf in facsimile in Green levant morocco, g.e.

HISTORY: (1) Sold anonymously[1] at Sotheby's, 21 March 1898, lot 108 (the advertisement leaf in 'excellent facsimile'), for £6. 17s. 6d. to C. Brown; (2) Sold anonymously at Hodgson's, 20 Nov. 1901, lot 596, for £12. 10s. to Quaritch; (3) Sold from Quaritch Catalogue 234 (Oct. 1904), lot 175, for £16 (according to the Quaritch files) to (4) W. Graham Robertson, who gave it in 1940 to (5) Kerrison Preston, who described it in his Catalogue (1960), no. 1, and gave it in 1966 to (6) WESTMINSTER PUBLIC LIBRARY, London.

COPY R: BINDING: Unbound, unstabbed, untrimmed, uncut, unfolded— in every respect (except a little dirt) as the sheets were delivered from the press.

HISTORY: (1) 'Formerly in the possession of Samuel Palmer' (according to the Grolier Club catalogue below); (2) Perhaps sold by Palmer's son A. H. Palmer for £20 to (3) The dealer Pearson (see copy N); (4) Acquired by W. A. White, who lent it to the exhibition of the Grolier Club (1905) (anonymously), perhaps to that of (1919), no. 1, to that in the Fogg (1924), and probably sold after his death (1927) with other Blakes in 1929 to (5) A. S. W. Rosenbach, who lent it to the Philadelphia exhibition (1939), no. 3, and gave it to (6) The ROSENBACH FOUNDATION.

COPY S: BINDING: Bound about 1825 (the fly-leaves are watermarked G & R TURNER / 1825) for the Duke of Devonshire (whose monogram, WS in a D, is at the foot of the spine) in front of (b) R. Steele, *The School of Action*, Steele, *The Gentleman*, and Addison's fragment of a Tragedy [1809], (c) Robert Jephson, *Two Strings to your Bow* (1791), (d) Anon., songs to a pantomime, *Mago and Dago*; or, Harlequin the Hero (1794), (e) John Peter Roberdeau, *Fugitive Verse and Prose* (1803), and a manuscript table of contents, in polished calf, gilt, with 'PLAYS / VOL. 30' on the spine, all the contents trimmed to size.

HISTORY: (1) It was sent on 26 April 1784 (see *Blake Records* [1969], 27–8) as a gift 'For[?] William Ha[y]le[y] / From J Flax[man]' (according to the trimmed inscription on the title-page); (2) Acquired by the Duke of Devonshire, who had it bound about 1825 with his crest and a manuscript table of contents with four plays and a volume of poetry evidently bought from

---

[1] Not described in the 1898 catalogue as part of the Maurice Johnson Library, as in Keynes, *Blake Studies* (1949). Copy Q may have been transcribed by William Allingham (in a Notebook now in the Turnbull Library, Wellington, New Zealand), incorporating the changes found in copy Q and adding the one on p. 17. No original copy now known incorporates *all* these corrections.

Thomas Kemble about 1825;[1] (3) Sold in 1914[2] by the 6th Duke of Devonshire with the Kemble–Devonshire Plays and the Chatsworth Caxtons through Sotheby's (according to T. S. Wragg, the present librarian at Chatsworth) to (4) The HUNTINGTON LIBRARY.

COPY T: BINDING: Bound with *Descriptive Catalogue* (K); see p. 139.

HISTORY: (1) On 25 Aug. 1831 Linnell paid 2s. 6d. each 'to Mrs Blake for a [*DESCRIPTIVE*] Catalogue [*K*]' and 'Poems' (evidently *Poetical Sketches* [T]) (*Blake Records* [1969], 596), which he bound with two other works, signed 'John Linnell / 38 Porchester Terrace / Bayswater / — / 1846' (on the front cover), and gave (2) 'To James T L / 1866' (as the above note continues); (3) It was sold by James's son Herbert Linnell through Lionel Robinson in July 1937 (according to Robinson's description with the volume) to (4) Mr. LESSING J. ROSENWALD.

COPY U: BINDING: Bound in Brown calf, g.e., by Francis Bedford (according to the 1885 catalogue); the 'Spine [*was*] repaired June 1962' (according to the note inside the cover).

HISTORY: (1) This may have been Samuel Palmer's copy (see copy G); (2) It was sold by his son A. H. Palmer to (3) Pearson, who described it as bound in 'calf super extra, gilt leaves by F. Bedford', with the 'last three sheets beautifully facsimiled', and offered it in his Catalogue 60 (?1885), lot 132, for £7. 10s. (this could alternatively be copy K); (4) Acquired and dated by H. F. Hornby ('H. 10. 10. 87'), and given posthumously in 1899 with his Library and memorial book-plate to (5) LIVERPOOL PUBLIC LIBRARIES, where it was listed in his catalogue (1906).

COPY V: BINDING: Stabbed through three holes into the original bluish Grey wrappers.

HISTORY: (1) Acquired by Frederick Locker,[3] who added his bookplate, described in his *Rowfant Library* (1886), and sold posthumously through Dodd, Mead & Co. (see the 'Pickering MS'); (2) Sold posthumously with the Library of Dr. James B. Clements at Parke-Bernet, 8 Jan. 1945, lot 70, for $2,000; (3) Acquired by William Luther Lewis, with whose collection it was sold (after his death in 1952) to (4) The Amon G. Carter Foundation, which on 27 May 1955 loaned, and then on 6 Aug. 1958 gave it to (5) TEXAS CHRISTIAN UNIVERSITY.

COPY W: BINDING: Bound in '1904', by Douglas Cockerell (according to a University College Librarian), for University College, London, in Green morocco.

---

[1] It was not sold at Sotheby's, 16–20 July 1886, as suggested by M. R. Lowery, 'A Census of Copies of William Blake's *Poetical Sketches*, 1783', *Library*, 4th Ser. xvii (1936), 354–60.

[2] It was an '*en bloc* purchase 1914', according to the Huntington accession card.

[3] Perhaps this is the copy with the second correction of 'Mad Song' ('birds' from 'beds'), but not the first ('infold' from 'unfold') which Southey quoted in *The Doctor*, vi (1847), 126. The only other such copies belonged at this time to Tulk (C), Cumberland (D), and Linnell (V).

HISTORY: (1) Acquired before 1852[1] by UNIVERSITY COLLEGE, London, where it was rebound in 1904.

COPY X: BINDING: 'BOUND BY BEDFORD' in olive Brown morocco, the top edge gilt, in a style similar to many other Britwell Court books.

HISTORY: (1) Acquired for the Britwell Court Library, where it was apparently bound and where shelf-marks ('8. D', '87. E. 3') were added on the blank binder's leaf; (2) Inherited by Major S. V. Christie-Miller, for whom it was sold posthumously at Sotheby's on 29 March 1971, lot 34, for £3,800 to Fleming for (3) The PIERPONT MORGAN LIBRARY.

129

Poetical Sketches. Now First Reprinted from the Original Edition of 1783. Ed. Richard Herne Shepherd. London, 1868.
    'Preface' (pp. vii–xiv).

130

Poetical Sketches. By W. B. London: Printed in the Year M DCC LXXXIII. [London, 1890.]
    A very persuasive facsimile by William Griggs.

131

Poetical Sketches. Decorations Designed and Cut on the Wood by Charles Ricketts. London, 1899.

132

A. *Poetical Sketches* [A]. London, 1926. The Noel Douglas Replicas. B. N.Y., 1927. The Noel Douglas Replicas. C. N.Y., 1927. The English Replicas.
    A is published by Noel Douglas, B & C by Paysen & Clarke. A slip inserted in some copies of C says: 'This Book is now published in the United States by Columbia University Press for the Facsimile Text Society'.

133

Poetical Sketches. [Ed. Eric Partridge.] With an Essay on Blake's Metric by Jack Lindsay. London, 1927.
    Eric Partridge, 'Introduction. A Note on Blake's Lyrical Poetry, with especial reference to the Poetical Sketches' (pp. ix–xxiv) is reprinted in part from no. 354; Jack Lindsay, 'The Metric of William Blake', is pp. 1–20.

PROSPECTUS; see *To the Public*.

    [1] It appears in a manuscript catalogue of 1852, but not in the previous one used until about 1849.

134. *Receipts signed by Blake*

Separate receipts signed by Blake are given in *Blake Records* (1969), 571–84.

	Payer	Date	Sum £ s. d.	Location of MS
1	John Flaxman	14 Dec. 1799	9 0 8	HAVERFORD
2	Thomas Butts	8 July–20 Aug. 1803	14 14 0	unprinted; Sotheby, 24 June 1903
3	,, ,,	22 Jan. 1805	12 12 0	WESTMINSTER PUBLIC
4	,, ,,	5 July 1805	5 7 0	*Joseph Holland*
5	,, ,,	7 Sept. 1805	4 4 0	WESTMINSTER PUBLIC
6	,, ,,	3 March 1806 (for 12 May 1805 to 3 March 1806)	66 0 0	,, ,,
7	,, ,,	30 June 1806	21 10 0	,, ,,
8	,, ,,	9 Sept. 1806	6 6 0	*Ruthven Todd*
9	,, ,,	15 Oct. 1806	5 5 0	WESTMINSTER PUBLIC
10	,, ,,	29 Jan. 1807	21 0 0	printed in A. Briggs, *Connoisseur* (1907)
11	,, ,,	3 March 1807	28 6 0	WESTMINSTER PUBLIC
12	,, ,,	2 June 1807	12 1 6	,, ,,
13	,, ,,	13 July 1807	15 15 0	,, ,,
14	,, ,,	6 Oct. 1807	10 10 0	,, ,,
15	,, ,,	14 Jan. 1808	26 5 0	,, ,,
16	,, ,,	29 Feb. 1808	10 0 0	,, ,,
17	,, ,,	29 July 1808	10 0 0	,, ,,
18	,, ,,	3 Nov. 1808	5 5 0	,, ,,
19	,, ,,	7 Dec. 1808	5 5 0	,, ,,
20	,, ,,	7 April 1809	21 0 0	,, ,,
21	,, ,,	29 June 1809	10 10 0	Sotheby, 19 Dec. 1932
22	,, ,,	10 July 1809	10 10 0	WESTMINSTER PUBLIC
23	,, ,,	10 Aug. 1809	10 10 0	,, ,,
24	,, ,,	4 Oct. 1809	10 10 0	,, ,,
25	,, ,,	25 Nov. 1809	20 0 0	,, ,,
26	,, ,,	16 Jan. 1810	21 0 0	,, ,,
27	,, ,,	3 March 1810	10 10 0	,, ,,
28	,, ,,	14 April 1810	21 0 0	,, ,,
29	,, ,,	30 June 1810	5 5 0	,, ,,
30	,, ,,	14 July 1810	15 15 0	,, ,,
31	,, ,,	20 Sept. 1810	10 10 0	,, ,,
32	,, ,,	18 Dec. 1810	10 10 0	,, ,,
33	John Linnell	12 Aug. 1818	2 0 0	YALE
34	,, ,,	11 Sept. 1818	5 0 0	*Keynes*
35	,, ,,	19 Sept. 1818	7 0 0	YALE
36	,, ,,	9 Nov. 1818	5 0 0	,,
37	,, ,,	31 Dec. 1818	3 15 0	,,
38	,, ,,	27 Aug. 1819	1 19 6	,,
39	,, ,,	30 Dec. 1819	14 0	,,
40	,, ,,	30 April 1821	2 2 0	,,
41	,, ,,	1 March 1822	3 0 0	,,
42	Accounts between Blake & Linnell	March 1823 to Nov. 1825		,,
43	John Linnell	14 July 1826	150 0 0	,,
44	Mrs Aders via John Linnell	29 July 1826	2 5 0	,,
45	John Linnell (receipt signed for Mrs. Blake by Tatham)	18 May 1829	1 11 6	,,

135. 'The Riddle Manuscript' (?1802)

BIBLIOGRAPHICAL INTRODUCTION

COLLECTION: *G. E. Bentley, Jr.*

LEAF-SIZE: 10·6 × 15·5 cm.

WATERMARK: None.

DATE: ? Summer 1802. See below.

DESCRIPTION: On the verso of the 'Riddle MS' is a proof before letters of Blake's 14th engraving, dated 9 Sept. 1802 in the published state, for Hayley's *Designs to A Series of Ballads*. The leaf was trimmed to conform to the proof, and this trimming has removed the beginnings of the lines and perhaps some lines at the top (the letters at the top and left are legible only with some hesitation) of the text written the other way up on the recto. Since the MS fairly clearly preceded the print, Sept. 1802 is the latest likely date. Since Blake is unlikely to have taken much pains to preserve such a trifle, Sept. 1800, when he moved to Felpham, is the earliest likely date. Summer 1802 seems a good guess.

The page may be a list of riddles playing with words—'Love lie Girl' may equal 'Lovely Girl', 'Love Errs' equals 'Lovers', 'Isinglass' equals 'Eyes in Glass', 'an Ell ['*L*'] taken from London is Undone [*ondon*]'.

BINDING: Loose, mounted in a window of a larger sheet.

HISTORY: The History is as in the 'Order' of the *Songs*, p. 337.

136. Small Book of Designs

COPY A: BINDING: (1) *Thel* pl. 2, 4, 6–7, *Urizen* pl. 1–3, 5, 7–8, 10–11, 17, 19, 23–4, 27, *Marriage* pl. 11, 14, 16, 20, *Visions* pl. 3, 10 were stabbed through three holes, 7·2 and 8·8 cm apart in a small quarto volume, perhaps bound in half morocco, (2) Which was apparently disbound by 1846, and pasted on mounts after 1856 in the British Museum.

HISTORY: (1) About 1796[1] Blake 'Printed for Mr [*Ozias*] Humphry . . . a selection from the different Books of Such as could be Printed without the Writing' (as he told Dawson Turner on 9 June 1818), which Richard Thomson described as 'seven [*i.e. 8*] separate engravings upon folio pages, without letterpress'[2] (the Large Book of Designs [A]) 'At the end'[2] of *Europe* [D] and 'a small quarto volume of twenty-three [*colour-printed*] engravings of various sizes and shapes' (the Small Book [A]); (2) Both Large and Small Books were acquired by Humphry's natural son William Upcott, who showed them to Richard Thomson to describe for J. T. Smith's life of Blake, apparently disbound them after 1827, and sold them posthumously (as 'original draw-

---

[1] The date on *Urizen* pl. 1 (Keynes) in copy B altered to '1796' suggests that the Large and Small Books were made at that time.

[2] *Blake Records* (1969), 471–2.

ings' 'Inserted' with *Europe* [D] and *America* [H]) through Evans, 15 June 1846, lot 277, for £7. 2s. 6d. to Evans; (3) Sold by Messrs. Evans with *Songs* (T), *Thel* (D), *America* (H), and *Song of Los* (A) on 9 Feb. 1856 to (4) The BRITISH MUSEUM PRINT ROOM, where they were mounted and given accession numbers[1] in the following order:

Large Book (A)

> (1) 'Albion Rose' (C)
> (2) *Urizen* pl. 21
> (3) 'The Accusers' (G)
> (4–5) *Visions* pl. 7, 1
> (6) 'Joseph of Arimathea Preaching' (B?)
> (7) *Urizen* pl. 14
> (8) *America* pl. d

Small Book (A)

> (1) *Urizen* pl. 1
> (2) *Marriage* pl. 11
> (3) *Urizen* pl. 17
> (4–6) *Marriage* pl. 16, 14, 20
> (7–9) *Urizen* pl. 23, 24, 3
> (10) *Thel* pl. 2
> (11–15) *Urizen* pl. 27, 2, 8, 19, 10
> (16) *Thel* pl. 6
> (17) *Visions* pl. 3
> (18–19) *Urizen* pl. 7, 11
> (20) *Visions* pl. 10
> (21) *Urizen* pl. 5
> (22–3) *Thel* pl. 7, 4

COPY B: BINDING: (1) *Marriage* pl. 11, *Urizen* pl. 2, 5, 10 were once stabbed together through three holes, 3·8 and 4·3 cm apart; (2) They may have also been associated with *Marriage* pl. 14, *Urizen* pl. 1, 3, 9, 12, 22, *Visions* pl. 10 in a volume similar to the Small Book of Designs (A); all these plates have three or four framing-lines and (save *Visions* pl. 10) inscriptions.

[1] These accession numbers seem to be determined by matching plates of the same size on a mount and not by the original order (the 1846 catalogue description implies that they were even then loose). The certain offset (*Marriage* pl. 20 followed by *Urizen* pl. 17) and the conjectural ones (*Marriage* pl. 11—*Urizen* pl. 7—*Marriage* pl. 20; *Urizen* pl. 10—*Marriage* pl. 14—*Urizen* pl. 24; *Thel* pl. 2—*Urizen* pl. 2; *Urizen* pl. 19—*Visions* pl. 13) have no relation to the accession-number order.

Keynes (1921) says that Small Book (A) was 'bound in half-morocco', and seems confident that the accession-number order (except for nos. 17 and 20) was the binding-order. The BMPR 'Register of Purchases and Presentations' says nothing of binding, nor does it distinguish between Large and Small Books of Designs. However, the Large Book is listed before the Small one and is distinguishable from it by uniform differences in leaf size (24·5 × 34·5 cm versus 19·0 × 26·0 cm) and stab holes (the Large Book has none, the Small Book has three, 7·2 and 8·8 cm apart).

The volume (if it existed) must have been broken up by 1831; (3) Now the plates are loose, and most of them are mounted and framed.

HISTORY: Stab marks, framing-lines, colour printing, and inscriptions indicate that *Marriage* pl. 11, *Urizen* pl. 2, 5, and 10 were once bound together. Perhaps they formed a volume, similar to the Small Book of Designs (A), with *Marriage* pl. 14 (numbered '9'), *Urizen* pl. 1, 3, 9 (numbered '13'), 12, 22, *Visions* pl. 10 (numbered '22'), which are like the former except that they lack the stab holes (perhaps they were trimmed off) and that *Visions* pl. 10 has no inscription. If they were once all gathered together, the facts that *Urizen* pl. 2 belonged to Samuel Palmer's cousin John Giles and that *Urizen* pl. 3 was given by Catherine Blake to Tatham suggest that the volume was broken up early.

For their subsequent Histories, see the individual plates.

137. *The Song of Los* (1795)

BIBLIOGRAPHICAL INTRODUCTION

TABLE

Copy	Plates	Leaves	Water-marks	Blake numbers	Binding-order	Leaf-size in cm.	Printing colour
‡A BMPR	1–8	8	—	—	‡1–8**	24·5 × 34·5*	*Brown* (1, 3–8) *Grey* (2)
‡B LC	1–8	8	—	2–4, 6–8, 10–11[1]	Loose	24·0 × 32·0	*greyish-Black*
‡C MORGAN	1–8	8	—	—	*1, 8, 2–4, 6–7, 5*[2]	24·8 × 35·9	*olive-Brown* (1, 3–8) *olive-Green* (2)
‡D BMPR	1–8	8	—	—	‡1–8**	25·6 × 37·0	*Brown* (1, 3–8) *greyish-Green* (2)
‡E HUNTINGTON	1–8	8	—	—	‡1–3, 8, 4, 6, 5, 7**	26·0 × 36·4[3]	*Grey*

‡ Coloured by Blake or his wife.
‡ Pl. 1 faces pl. 2.
1–8 Italicized binding-orders indicate contemporary Bindings.
** The identifiable offsets confirm the present order.
* The leaves are trimmed and gilt.
Brown Italicized printing colours indicate colour printing.

[1] The ink numbers on pl. 1–2, 4–8 of copy B plus those on (3) 'The Accusers' (H), (5) 'Joseph of Arimathea' (F), and (9) *America* pl. d (LC) indicate that the order of these works, before they were sold at Hodgson's, 14 Jan. 1904, lots 224, 227–8, 223, was: *Song of Los* pl. 1 (‡2), 'The Accusers' (‡3), *Song of Los* pl. 2 (‡4), 'Joseph of Arimathea' (‡5), *Song of Los* pl. 4–6 (‡6–8), *America* pl. d (‡9), *Song of Los* pl. 7–8 (‡10–11). The first plate of this oddly combined work may have been *Song of Los* pl. 3 (not accounted for above) or *Visions* (F) pl. 1 or *America* (K) pl. 1, the last two of which were lots 226 and 229 in the same sale.
[2] The clear offset-order is: [1] 2–3–4–6–8 [?5] [?7] in copy C.
[3] In copy E, only the top edge is gilt.

TITLE: *THE | SONG of | LOS | Lambeth printed by W Blake 1795*

DATE: 1795, as on the title-page.

PUBLICATION: *The Song of Los* is a companion to *America* (1793) and *Europe*

(1794) in size (about 17×23 cm¹) and in subject, divided as it is between 'AFRICA' and 'ASIA', and it was sometimes bound with them—copy B with *America* (A), *Europe* (A) and *Visions* (1793) (F); copy C with *Europe* (G) and *Visions* (H); copy D with *America* (F), *Europe* (C), and *Visions* (B). Blake sometimes extra-illustrated the text with other plates: 'The Accusers', 'Joseph of Arimathea', and *America* pl. d in copy B and 'Albion Rose' in copy E.

The first five lines of text, the prelude, are etched in italic, the rest in roman characters.

All five surviving copies were probably colour printed in 1795, and thereafter Blake seems to have lost interest in the work, for he did not list it with other books for sale in his letters of 9 June 1818 or 12 April 1827. The only contemporary owner known is George Cumberland, whose copy (D) was sold to Butts in 1835.

COLOURING: All copies are sombrely colour printed, with mottled effects common, greyish-Pink flesh, and occasional touches of water-colour. Copies A and C are particularly similar, and copy E is the clearest and most handsome one.

CATCHWORD: None.

ORDER: Pl. 1–8. The plates bearing text (pl. 3–4, 6–7) and the frontispiece and title-page (pl. 1–2) are always in the same order with respect to each other. It is only the plates with full-page designs (pl. 5, 8) which move disconcertingly in copies C and E. Since all known copies seem to have been printed about the same time, and since all have some claim to Blake's authority, the only safe conclusion is that Blake most often used the order 1–8 but that he experimented freely with the position of pl. 5 and 8.

SIGNIFICANT VARIANTS: The colour printing makes many minor variants, such as the number of birds in pl. 2.

Pl. 5 in copy D is inscribed: 'King and Queen of the Fairies'.

ERRATA: None.

Pl. 1. FRONTISPIECE. DESIGN: A barefooted man in a long skirt kneels on a Green lawn over a Grey altar, over which hovers a huge, mottled sphere emitting four large rays.

COLOURING: The man's SKIRT is Grey (A, B, D), pale Pink (C) or White (E), and his HAIR is pale Grey (D) or White (E). The SUN is mottled Yellow (A, C, D, E) with Blue (A) and Black (A, C–E), or yellowish-Brown with flecks of Green, Black, and dark Orange (B), and its RAYS are Black and yellowish-Brown (A) or greyish-Gold (D). The SKY is Grey-Brown-Black (C) or Grey (D, E [dark]), and the GROUND is mottled Green (C, D), Brown (C, D), Blue (D), and Grey (D).

Pl. 2. TITLE-PAGE. DESIGN: Above the imprint lies a bearded man in a long robe leaning on his left elbow with his hand on a skull. (He is sketched

¹ The plates that are chiefly or entirely design (pl. 1–2, 5, 8) average 17·4×23·6 cm, while those with text are much narrower: 13·6×22·4 cm.

in a few strokes in a sheet belonging to Mr. David Bindman—see *Visions* [1793] pl. 2.) He is looking upward to the title, by which are a varying number of birds. Behind him in the distance are hills and the sea stretching across the horizon.

COLOURING: The MAN'S ROBE is Grey (A, C, D, E [pale]), and his EYES Blue (B). The HILL is Green (A, C–E) or Brown (C), the WAVES Grey (A, E), Black (C–D) and Green (C), the BACKGROUND Blue (A [dark], E), Black (B), or Orange (E), FLAMES at the bottom left Orange (A) and Red (A, D), and the BIRDS Red (A–C) and Green (B). The SKULL is a faint Green in E.

Pl. 3. INCIPIT: 'AFRICA / I will sing you . . .'. DESIGN: At the top of the page are insects, lush vegetation, and a huge, open-mouthed serpent writhing through 'AFRICA'.

Between ll. 5 and 6 lies a naked child with a sheep.

The margins are dark Green.

COLOURING: The SNAKE is Brown (A, D, E), Black (A, B [greenish-]), Red (C), Blue (C), Green (C, D–E), and dark Orange (D), and its TONGUE Red (A–C, E). The BUTTERFLIES at the top are touched with Red (C, E), Yellow, Black, and Blue (E), and the boy's HAIR is Brown (A) or Yellow (E).

Pl. 4. INCIPIT: 'These were the Churches . . .'. DESIGN: After ll. 38–42 is a naked man with huge, narrow, bat wings.

Below the text a naked man runs across grass to the right with a woman in a flowing skirt; his left arm is round her waist and her left arm is round his head. To the left are two birds with heavy wings. (A similar design, reversed, is in Blake's *Notebook* p. 60.)

COLOURING: The bat WINGS are dark Blue (A, D), Green (B), or dark Brown (E). The woman's SKIRT is Yellow (A [dull], B [mottled], D [strong]), yellowish-Brown (C) or pale Grey (E), and the couple's HAIR is Brown (A) or Yellow (D, E). The middle background is a solid (A) or streaked (B, E) Red, as if of flame, and the SKY is deep Blue (B, E), very dark Brown (C), or Ochre (D).

VARIANTS: There seems to be a fragment of another printed design above and to the left of the platemark in copy B.

There is a leaf by the last line in B and C.

In the bottom right are Blue mountains in D.

Pl. 5. DESIGN: The whole page is taken up by a design of a woman in a long dress who lies asleep in a huge, dark Green lily with cream-coloured petals, while a crowned man with a mantle and sceptre sits in another beside her. Above them, stars twinkle in a dark bluish-Black sky. (A similar design perhaps by Robert Blake, is in the *Notebook*, p. 13, and an almost identical [though reversed] design, probably preliminary, now in an anonymous private collection, is reproduced in L. H. Dudley, 'Blake Exhibition', *Fogg Art Museum Notes*, II [1930], 285–304. This separate design is on paper watermarked only with a fleur-de-lis and measuring 16·3×21·2 cm, compared with 17·5×23·2 for pl. 5.)

COLOURING: The woman's DRESS is Yellow (A [pale], B, E), the king's ROBE Red (A and E [dark], B–C, D [rusty]), his MANTLE Red (A [bright], C, E),

Grey (B), or Purple (D), and their HAIR orangish-Brown (A), Gold (B), Orange (C–D), or Yellow and Auburn (E).

VARIANTS: The leaves and stars differ somewhat in each copy.

In C, the king looks upward.

At the bottom of copy D is an old pencil inscription: 'King and Queen of the Fairies'. The queen's foot and the king's leg are obscured in this copy.

Pl. 6. INCIPIT: 'ASIA / the Kings of Asia . . .'. DESIGN: In the letters of 'ASIA' are four or more tiny figures, and between them and the text is the mouth of a cave, in which squats a naked man holding a limp woman in a long dress. The background is mottled Green and Brown.

To the right of ll. 15–24 crouches a naked man with his left knee raised, his right one horizontal, and his head on his arms.

COLOURING: The woman's DRESS is Yellow (A [clear], D [dark]) or very pale Pink (C) and her SKIN Grey (B). The CAVE is bright Yellow and Brown (E), the SKY Yellow (A), Raspberry (A), Black (B), orangish-Rose (B), Red (C, D [pale]), and dark Blue (E). The CLOUDS are Black (D) or Pink (E).

VARIANTS: There seems to be Blue sea to the right of 'ASIA' in B.

Pl. 7. INCIPIT: 'To cut off the bread . . .'. DESIGN: To the right of ll. 32–40 a naked man with bent knees and elbows falls headlong through a dark sky. Round the text is dark Green and Brown foliage.

COLOURING: The top right is a rusty Orange (A) or dark Blue (C, D, E).

Pl. 8. DESIGN: The whole page is taken up with a design of a naked man leaning on a huge Black hammer kneeling on a cloud with his legs apart and looking downward at a large Red globe which gives off Red rays beneath him and behind the clouds in a bluish-Black sky.

COLOURING: The man's HAIR is Brown (B [golden-], D and E [orangish-]), or Auburn (C), the CLOUDS are Brown (A, B, D [dark], E [reddish-]), Orange (A, D, E), Red (B, C), Green (B), Blue (B), and the SUN is Black (A, C), Red (C, D [bloody], E [dark]).

VARIANTS: There are no rays from the top of the sun in B.

The man's eyes are more nearly closed in C and D.

COPY A: BINDING: (1) Originally stabbed through three holes, 7·2 cm from the top, 8·5 and 10·0 cm apart; (2) Bound after Feb. 1856 at the British Museum in half dark Green morocco, g.e.

HISTORY: (1) Sold by Messrs. Evans with *Songs* (T), *Thel* (D), *America* (H), and the Large (A) and Small Books of Designs (A) on 9 Feb. 1856 to (2) The BRITISH MUSEUM PRINT ROOM, where it was bound; reproduced by Muir (1890), probably this or copy D is the one (pl. 2–7) reproduced in Ellis & Yeats (1893); reproduced in colour microfilm by Micro Methods Ltd.

COPY B: BINDING: (1) Once bound 'somewhat irregularly' with *America* (A) and pl. d, 'The Accusers' (H) (q.v.), *Visions* (F) pl. 1, *Europe* (A) pl. 1–2, 4–6, and 'Joseph of Arimathea Preaching' (F), but (2) Disbound in 1904, and now loose.

HISTORY: (1) Probably bought by the Earl of Beaconsfield between 1856

and 1862 (see *Europe* [A]); (2) For a time it was 'bound up somewhat irregu-
larly in a cloth case with' *America* (A) and pl. d, *Visions* (F) pl. 1, *Europe* (A)
pl. 1–2, 4–6, 'The Accusers' (H)—see p. 77, and 'Joseph of Arimathea
Preaching' (F), but it was disbound when it was sold anonymously at
Hodgson's, 14 Jan. 1904, lot 224, for £144 to Quaritch; (3) Acquired by
William A. White, who lent it anonymously to the exhibitions of the Grolier
Club (1905), no. 30, perhaps to that of (1919), no. 15, and to the Fogg (1924);
it was sold after his death (1927) through Rosenbach on 1 May 1929 to
(4) Mr. LESSING J. ROSENWALD.

COPY C: BINDING: (1) Originally stabbed through three holes, 8·6 cm
fom the top, 9·6 and 10·3 cm apart; (2) Later bound with *Visions* (H) (which
has quite different stab holes) and *Europe* (G) in old (?contemporary) half Red
morocco (repaired later still) without lettering; (3) The volume was disbound
by 1905, the *Song of Los* leaves remaining stitched together but quite detached
from the binding which still accompanies them.

HISTORY: For its History, see *Visions* (H), with which it was bound.

COPY D: BINDING: (1) Bound with *Visions* (B), *America* (F), *Europe* (C),
until 1852, when *Europe* was extracted; (2) The other works were rebound
together after July 1859 by the British Museum in Yellow morocco, stamped
and gilt with the Royal Arms, g.e.; (3) The leaves of the three works were
mounted in heavy paper 'windows' and bound together in Red morocco in
1969.

HISTORY: The History is as in *America* (F); see p. 102. Probably this or
copy A is the one reproduced in Ellis & Yeats (1893), and pl. 4–5, 7–8 were
reproduced in *The Illuminated Blake*, ed. D. V. Erdman (1974).

COPY E: BINDING: (1) Originally stabbed through three holes, 10·4 and
10·4 cm apart,[1] with 'Albion Rose' (D); (2) Later 'BOUND BY RIVIERE & SON'
in Red levant morocco, t.e.g., with 'Albion Rose' (D); (3) In 1953 'Albion
Rose' was removed from the binding.

HISTORY: (1) Sold by the Earl of Crewe at Sotheby's, 30 March 1903,
lot 9,[2] for £174 to Sabin, apparently for (2) Frederic Robert Halsey,[3] who
had it bound with 'Albion Rose' (D)[4] and sold it with his Library in 1915 to
(3) The HUNTINGTON LIBRARY, which removed 'Albion Rose' from the binding in 1953.

[1] The top stab hole is 7·0 cm from the top in the *Song of Los* and 7·4 cm from the top of
'Albion Rose', corresponding to the differences in size (36·4 cm high in the former, 36·7 in
the latter); evidently when the top edge of the *Song of Los* was trimmed and gilt 'Albion Rose'
was not touched.

[2] It is described as eight unbound leaves, '4 of which are full-page figures without text'.
Since five of the eight plates of *Song of Los* have text (though the title-page very little), this
implies that the cataloguer miscounted either the number of leaves without text or the total
number of leaves; if the latter, 'Albion Rose' (D), earlier and later bound with *Song of Los* (E),
may have been sold with it in 1903.

[3] Not 'Robert T. V. Halsey', as in Keynes & Wolf.

[4] The last fly-leaf has a note, evidently by Halsey: '1903 / £cnt. / binding £ce.x.x'.
'Albion Rose' may have been part of a Large Book of Designs (B).

138. 'Songs by Shepherds' (?1787)

BIBLIOGRAPHICAL INTRODUCTION

COLLECTION: The original MS is not known. A contemporary transcript is on two fly-leaves of *Poetical Sketches* (F) in the Alexander Turnbull Library, Wellington, New Zealand (reproduced in D. F. McKenzie, 'Blake's *Poetical Sketches* [1783]', *Turnbull Library Record*, I, No. 3 [March 1968], at pp. 8–9).

WATERMARK: Chain lines 2·8 cm apart, like those in *Poetical Sketches*, but the paper is slightly heavier and darker.

LEAF-SIZE: 13 × 20·5 cm, as in *Poetical Sketches* (F).

DATE OF COMPOSITION: *c.* 1787.

One of the MS poems was etched in a modified form for *Songs of Innocence* (1789), which were evidently composed 1784–9. 1787 is little more than a guess within this period.

DATE OF TRANSCRIPTION: *c.* 1787.

The printed leaves of *Poetical Sketches* (F), stabbed in incorrect order through three holes, were a 'present from Mrs Flaxman May 15, 1784' (according to an inscription on the title-page), perhaps to the Flaxmans' friend Isaac Reed. Later, the mistaken order of the sheets was pointed out in an unknown hand[1] which also transcribed Blake's poems on two unstabbed leaves. It seems likely, therefore, that the poems were transcribed before the sheets were put into their present binding. Since a contemporary hand has written 'Reeds Sale 1807' at the top of f. 2ʳ (bearing a Blake poem), it seems clear that this binding took place before 1807. The poems must, then, have been transcribed and bound between 1784 and 1807; once again, 1787 is little more than a guess.

MANUSCRIPT: Two fly-leaves have been added at the beginning and two more at the end of *Poetical Sketches* (F). The 'Songs by Mʳ Blake' are on the verso of the first leaf (which is pasted to the marbled endpaper) and on recto and verso of the second leaf. There are four distinct hands affecting Blake's text in the volume: (1) Blake's neat ink corrections to the printed text; (2) Other corrections in a different hand and ink; (3) The pencil corrections to the text; and (4) The manuscript poems. The last three hands have not been identified.

For the BINDING and HISTORY, see *Poetical Sketches* (F).

---

[1] Comparison with MSS of Isaac Reed dated 1762, 1773, 1776, 1781, 1790, 1800 (in the Folger Shakespeare Library) makes it clear that the hand is not that of Reed. Nor is it that of Blake or John Flaxman. I do not agree with McKenzie (see above) that the poems are in the hand of the presentation inscription.

139. *Songs of Innocence and of Experience* (1789, 1794)

BIBLIOGRAPHICAL INTRODUCTION

HEADNOTES: In order to avoid the tedious repetition of *Innocence* and *Experience* when identifying individual copies, the letters representing copies of the combined *Songs* are italicized. Thus, in the context of the *Songs*, 'copies A, D, *C, W*' means '*Innocence* copies A, D, *Songs* copies C, W'.

In Keynes & Wolf, *Innocence* plates are given one order when they appear in the separate *Songs of Innocence* and a quite different order when they are in the combined *Songs*. To avoid this duplication, I refer to the *Innocence* plates uniformly in the order used in the *Songs*.[1]

N.B. Because *Songs of Experience* are inextricably involved with *Songs of Innocence*, both series are described here.

See Table on pp. 365–72

---

[1] For conversion purposes, it may be useful to have a list of the relationships between the Keynes & Wolf *Innocence* order and their *Songs* order for the same plates:

Keynes & Wolf *Innocence* ORDER

Innocence pl.	1	2	3	4	5–7	8	9	10–11	12	13	14	15	16–17	18–19	20–1	22	23	24
Songs pl.	2	3	4	26	34–6	8	11	6–7	18	12	25	5	20–1	16–17	13–14	24	19	27

Innocence pl.	25–6	27	28	29–30	31
Songs pl.	22–3	53	15	9–10	54

Keynes & Wolf *Songs* ORDER

Songs pl.	2	3	4	5	6–7	8	9–10	11	12	13–14	15	16–17	18	19	20–1	22–3	24	25
Innocence pl.	1	2	3	15	10–11	8	29–30	9	13	20–1	28	18–19	12	23	16–17	25–6	22	14

Songs pl.	26	27	34–6	53	54
Innocence pl.	4	24	5–7	27	31

TABLE

Songs of Innocence (1789)

Innocence copy	Plates missing or added[1]	Leaves[2]	Watermarks	Blake numbers	Leaf-size in cm.	Printing colour
#A McKell	—	17	—	—	13·2×18·7[3]	Brown
#B LC	—	17[4]	—	—	12·7×17·7*	Brown
#C WELLESLEY	—	17	J WHATMAN ([8, 11])	—	13·5×18·2*[5]	golden-Brown
#D MORGAN	—	17	—	—	12·6×16·1*	orangish-Brown
#E NYP	—	17	J WHATMAN (3) E & P ([19, 24])	—	13·6×19·1	golden-Brown
#F HARVARD	—6–7, 19, 24	15	E & P ([15, 9] [26, 34])	—[6]	13·3×18·2*	golden-Brown
#G Mellon	—	17	J WHATMAN ([8, 11])	—	13·6×19·0	orangish-Brown
#H UNTRACED[7]	—	17	—	—	13·0×19·0	Brown
#I HUNTINGTON	—	17[8]	E & P ([23, 53])[9]	—	12·6×18·1	Green plus Blue (2–3)
#J Anonymous	—13–15, 19–21, 34–6, 53	12[10]	E & P ([10, 54] [23, 11] [24, 12])	—	12·0×16·2	Green
#K PFORZHEIMER	—34–6	16[11]	—	—	11·6×17·3*	Brown
#L BODLEY	—26, 34–6	15	—	—	13·3×18·9	reddish-Brown
#M Anonymous	—26, 34–6	15	E & P ([6–7] [8, 11])	—	12·0×18·4*	Brown

Songs of Innocence (1789)

Innocence copy	Plates missing or added¹	Leaves²	Watermarks	Blake numbers	Leaf-size in cm.	Printing colour
#N DOHENY	−34–6, 54	27	—	1–27	13·0×19·8*	Brown
#O TEXAS	−6–7, 34–6	26	BUTTANSHAW/180[ ] (10, 17, 26)	1–4, 7–28	13·7×19·4*¹² plus 13·0×19·4* (20)	Brown¹³
#P YALE	−10, 17, 34–6	26	J WHATMAN/1[ ]¹⁴ (2, 12) EDMEADS & PINE 1802 (8, 21)	—	12·3×17·7*	pale Orange
#Q at SYRACUSE	−34–6	28	J WHATMAN/1804 (4, 8) EDMEADS & PINE 1802 (23, 27)	1–28	12·5×17·6*¹⁵	orangish-Brown plus dark Brown (17)
#R Keynes	−3–18, 21, 34–6, 53–4	9	—	1, 18–19, 22–5, 27–8	14·5×20·9¹⁵	Brown plus Blue (19–20, 24)
#S CINCINNATI	−34–6	28	J WHATMAN/1808 (9, 25)	2–28¹⁶	13·7×19·1 to 15·2×20·7	Black plus Green (2) Brown (3–4, 12, 26–7)
#T Taylor	−15, 53	29	J WHATMAN/1[ ]4[?] (2–3, 11, 24, 26, 54)	—	13·1×18·2	Black
#U HARVARD	+9ᵇ	32	J WHATMAN (54)	—	11·8×18·9*⁵	Black
#V¹⁷ UNTRACED	−3	30				
#W¹⁷ UNTRACED	−9–10, 13–14, 34–6, 53	22	J WHATMAN (on one plate)		11·5×20·2	Brown
#X Lister	−2–12, 15, 20–3, 26, 34, 53	6¹⁸	E & P ([13–14])	—	13·5×18·7 irregular	Green
#Y¹⁷ UNTRACED	−2–3, 19–27, 34–6, 53–4	15	BUTTANSHAW (6, 15–16)	3–17	13·5×20·0 to 15·0×21·2	pale Brown

Songs of Innocence and of Experience (1794)

Songs copy	Plates missing or added[1]	Leaves[2]	Watermarks	Blake numbers	Leaf-size in cm.	Printing colour
A BMPR	−1, 50−2	50	I TAYLOR (6, 36, 39, 53)[19]	1–26 (*SI*), 1–20 (*SE*)[20]	27·1 × 38·0	Brown plus Green (28–34, 37–49, 53–4)
B BMPR	−52, +a	30	—	—	13·5 × 19·0 *irregular*	Brown[21]
C LC	−52, +a	30	E & P ([23, 53]) I TAYLOR ([46, 42]) J WHATMAN ([32, a])	—	12·3 × 18·0*	*Brown*[22] plus *Green* (47)
D *Houghton*	−52, +a	30	E & P (3, [8, 11] [19, 24])	—	12·3 × 17·5*	Brown[23]
E HUNTINGTON	+15[b] [24]	32[25]	J WHATMAN ([50, 37] [33, 43])	1–54[16]	11·4 × 17·6*	Brown[26] plus Green (13–14, 20–1, 34–6, 50, 15[b]) Black (32)
F *Mellon*	−1, 39, 44–5, 48, 52	34[27]	E & P ([16–17])	1–34[28]	11·8 × 18·4*[12]	*Green*[29] plus *Brown* (29, 41, 49, 54) *Black* (30, 37) *Blue* (42)
G[30] *Keynes*	−1–29, 33–6, 39, 44–5, 48, 52–4	15	—	—	11·5 × 18·2 plus 12·5 × 19·3 (37) 10·2 × 18·2 (42) 10·7 × 18·2 (43)	Green plus *Brown* (37, 43) *Blue* (30)
Lister	(40)	1	—	—	11·3 × 18·0 (40)	Orange (40)
H *Crawford*	−1–27, 34–6, 39, 44–5, 48, 52–4	17	J WHATMAN (29–30)	—	12·5 × 19·0	*Brown* plus *Green* (30–1, 33, 41–3, 46) *Blue* (38)

Songs of Innocence and of Experience (1794)

Songs copy	Plates missing or added[1]	Leaves[2]	Watermarks	Blake numbers	Leaf-size in cm.	Printing colour
#I HARVARD	—	54	—	1–54	13·0 × 18·6 plus	dark Brown
#J Blunt	–28	53	—	—	13·0 × 17·2 (27) various[31]	Brown[32]
#K[33] MORGAN	–1–27, 39, 53–4	24	—	30–52[33]	13·6 × 18·2 plus, 13·6 × 17·7 (28), 13·6 × 18·7 (35), 12·7 × 18·1 (40), 13·2 × 17·7 (48), 12·7 × 17·8 (30–3, 37, 41, 44–7, 50–2)[34] irregular	dark Brown
#L Mellon	—	54	—	1–54	12·5 × 18·2*	dark Brown
M[35] YALE	—	54	—	2–54[16]	12·0 × 18·9*	dark Brown
#N HUNTINGTON	–1–28, 54	25	—	30–54	13·4 × 19·6*	Black
#O HARVARD	+1ᵇ, 54ᵇ	56	—	1–29 (SI), 1–27 (SE)	13·3 × 18·3 (SI) irregular, 13·7 × 20·0 (SE) irregular	Brown[36]
#P Anonymous	—	54	BUTTANSHAW/1802 (18, 24, 41)	1, 1–28 (SI), 2–26(SE)[37]	9·6 × 13·8*	Brown
Q Dennis	—	54	BUTTANSHAW/1802 (31, 38, 42, 50) [J Wh]ATMAN/[1]804 (4)	1–28 (SI), 1–26 (SE)	12·4 × 18·3	Brown[38]
#R FITZWILLIAM	—	54	I TAYLOR (12, 17, 26, 41) J WHATMAN/1808 (42)	1–53[39]	21·3 × 30·0	Grey

Copy			Watermark		Dimensions	Colour
#S CINCINNATI	—	54	J WHATMAN/1808 (2, 8, 21, 26–7)	1–25 $(SE)^{16}$ / 1–28 (SI)	$12·8×18·1*^{12}$	Brown (1, 28–52) Black (2–27, 53–4)
#T$^{1-2}$ BMPR	—	52^{40}	RUSE & [TU]RNERS/ [181]5 (4, 13, 18, 21, 25, 27, 36, 45, 54)	$1–54^{41}$	$11·7×18·5*$	Orange plus Brown (6–7, 19, 24, 28, 33, 38, 41, 43, 51) Green (32, 40, 42, 47, 49–50)
#T$^{1-2}$ NATIONAL GALLERY OF CANADA	29–31, 38, 41, 43, 46–7, 49–51	11	RUSE & TURNERS/1815 (41, 50, 51)	38, 41, 43, 47, 49–51^{41}	c. $14·7×23·6$ plus $12·0×18·6$ (29) $12·6×19·4$ (30, 31, 46)	Orange plus Green (29–31, 46)
#U PRINCETON	1–54	54	RUSE & TURNERS/1815 (4, 11–12, 18, 21, 26, 29, 31, 38, 41, 44, 47–48)	1–54	$13·9×22·2*$	Orange
#V MORGAN	1–54	54	J WHATMAN/1818 (5, 9, 12, 18, 25, 28, 31, 34–5, 43–4, 52–3)	1–54	$27·2×33·0*^{42}$	Orange
#W KING'S COLLEGE	1–54	54	J WHATMAN/1818 (15) J WHATMAN/1825 (11, 17, 20, 22, 27, 30–1, 33, 35, 42–4, 49, 54)	1, 3–54^{16}	$22·2×28·3*$	reddish-Brown
#X *Anonymous*	1–54	54	J WHATMAN/1825 (2–3, 5, 10, 12, 22–3, 25, 30, 39, 49–50, 53)	1–54	$20·0×26·4*$	Orange
#Y METROPOLITAN MUSEUM	1–54	54	J WHATMAN/1825 (12, 15, 20, 23–4, 26, 41, 43, 46–8, 50)	1–54	$14·1×15·7$	reddish-Brown
#Z LC	1–54	54	J WHATMAN/182[5?] (2, 7–8, 13–14, 21, 24–5, 30–1, 33–5, 47–8, 52)	1–54	$13·0×21·6*$	Orange
#AA FITZWILLIAM	1–54	54	J WHATMAN/18[ ] (7, 12, 17, 37)^{43}	1–54	$10·7×15·5$ to $13·0×18·3$	Orange

Songs of Innocence and of Experience (1794)

Songs copy	Plates	Leaves[2]	Watermarks	Blake numbers	Leaf-size in cm.	Printing colour
BB[44] UNTRACED	1–54, b?	55				
a BM	1–14, 16–54, b	54	J WHATMAN/1831 (6, 8, 10, 13–14, 16, 19, 28–9, 32–3, b) J WHATMAN/1832 (48)	—	19·4 × 24·4 plus 19·2 × 27·5 (30–2, 37, 44–5, 47–8, 50–2, 54, b)	Grey plus Brown (30–2, 37, 44–5, 47, 50–1, b)
b HARVARD	1–54	54	J WHATMAN/1831 (3, 11, 16, 23, 29, 32, 40, 43, 45, 47–8, 51)	—	14·6 × 18·2*[42]	reddish-Brown
c Drysdale	1–51, 53, 54, b	54	J WHATMAN/1831 (9, 11, 16–17, 25, 27, 29, 33, 37, 45, 47)	—	15·3 × 17·9*	reddish-Brown
d[7] UNTRACED	1–14, 16–29, 33–6, 38–43, 46, 49, 52–3	42	J WHATMAN/1831	—	11·0 × 18·0*	Brown
e[45] MORGAN	1–29, 34–6, 38–40, 42–3, 48–9, 54	40	J WH[AT]MAN/[ ]1[?] (1, 3, 12–13, 15, 17, 20, 24, 35, 39, 43, 48)	—	13·2 × 12·8*	orangish-Brown[46]
f[7] UNTRACED	1–54	54	J WHATMAN/1831	—	16·5 × 18·5*	reddish-Brown
g[1] PRINCETON	3–10, 12–14, 16–27	23	J WHATMAN/1831 (8, 13–14, 16–17, 22, 24)[47]	—	20·1 × 24·2 plus 19·0 × 24·2 (19)	Grey
g[2] LC	28–9, 31, 33–6, 38–9, 41–4, 46, 49, 52–4	18	J WHATMAN/1831 (33, 39, 42, 44)[48]	—	19·6 × 24·5	Grey plus Orange (44)
h[49] UNTRACED	1–54, 1[b], plus 2 pl. ?	57	J WHATMAN/1832	—		Black (1[a]+33 others) Brown (1[b]+ 22 others)

Copy	Plates	Count	Watermark		Dimensions	Colour
i Cunliffe	1–14, 16–28, 30, 33–6, 38–43, 46, 48–9, 52–4	44	J WHATMAN/1831 (6, 8, 10–11, 14, 16–17, 19–20, 22, 24, 27–9, 33, 39, 42)47	—	22·3×24·5 plus 16·6×24·5 (48)	Grey
j35 Newton	1–54	54	various31	—51		Red
k Keynes	30, 43, 45, 48, 52	5	J WHATMAN/1831 (30, 45)	—	16·2×20·4	reddish-Brown
l Keynes	29, 33, 38–9, 41–3, 46, 49, 51–2	11	—	—	19·0×27·2 plus 8·1×13·2 (51)	Grey
m Keynes	3, 10–11, 19, 22, 54	6	[J W]HATMAN/1831 (10)	—	20·0×24·5	Grey
n MORGAN	2, 13, 30–1, 37, 44, 47, 50, b	9	J WHA[TMAN]/183[ ] (13)52	—	19·6×24·2 (2) / 17·0×19·5 (13) / 18·6×27·7 (30, 47) / 19·2×25·7 (31) / 19·2×24·9 (37) / 13·1×18·3 (44) / 17·2×21·3 (50) / 17·8×23·1 (b)	Grey plus reddish-brown (13)
o Bentley	39	1	[J WHA]TMAN/[18]31 (39)	—	18·6×28·0	orangish-Brown
o53 UNTRACED	31, 38 plus 14 others	16	1832	—		yellowish-Brown (including 31) Red (38) Black
TATE	3a–b, 22, 48a–b	5	J WHATMAN/1831 (22, 48a)	—	20·0×24·5 plus 20·0×20·4 (3b)	Black
#HARVARD	6–7	1	—	—	10·5×18·3	Green
Fuel-Jensen	#7, 10, 33	3	—	—	various31	Brown
	44	1	—	—	13·7×21·0 (44)	Black (44)

Songs of Innocence and of Experience (1794)

Songs copy	Plates	Leaves	Watermarks	Blake numbers	Leaf-size in cm.	Printing colour
Keynes	#9–10, b	2⁵⁴	—	—	13·7 × 18·9 ([9–10]) / 15·9 × 21·2 (b)	Green (9–10) / Grey (b)
LC	11, 30–2, 37, 40, 44, 47, 50	8⁵⁵	J W[HATMAN] (44)	—	7·8 × 11·6 (11) / 9·0 × 13·9 (30 44) / 8·1 × 12·4 (31–2, 37) / 18·2 × c. 19·0 ([40, 50]) / 7·2 × 11·9 (47)	Grey plus Orange (11, 40, 50)
Bentley	22, 28, 30, 40, 44–6, 48ᵃ⁻ᵇ	9	J WH[ATMAN]/1[ ] (45–6, 48ᵇ)	—	20·1 × 24·3 (22) / 15·5 × 20·2 (28) / 12·1 × 18·2 (30) / 16·3 × 20·3 (40, 44–6) / 19·6 × 21·4 (48ᵇ) / 16·0 × 19·8 (48ᵃ)	Brown plus Grey (22, 30, 48ᵇ)
*UNTRACED*⁵⁶	#24–5, 31, 37, #40, 47	6	— (40)	—	11·4 × 17·8 (24) / 11·3 × 18·0 (40)	Blue (24) / Buff (40)
#*Blunt*	28	1	—	29	12·3 × 16·2	Black
HARVARD	29–30, 37	3	J WH[ATMAN]/TURKE[Y MILL]/ 18[ ] (29)	—	11·2 × 18·5	Black
#*UNTRACED*⁵⁷	38	1				Green
#*UNTRACED*⁵⁸	42, 51	2		24 (on 51)	11·3 × 12·1 (42) / 22·9 × 31·3 (51)	Green (42) / Brown (51)
#*UNTRACED*⁵⁹	42	1				Brown
Holland	a	1	*invisible*	—		Brown

\# The plates are water-coloured by Blake or his wife.
* The edges have been trimmed and gilt.
Brown   Italicized printing colours indicate that the plates were colour printed.

Notes to Table on pp. 365–72

¹ For *Innocence*, the normal plates are 2–27, 34–6, 53–4; for the combined *Songs* they are 1–54.

² In copies with fewer leaves than plates (*Innocence* [A–M], *Songs* [B–F]), the following plates are printed back-to-back: (5, 25) (6–7) (8, 11) (9, 15) (10, 54) (12, 18), (13–14) (16–17) (19, 24) (20–21) (22, 27) (23, 53) (26, 34) (35–36) (30–31) (32, a) (33, 43) (37, 50) (38, 41) (39, 44) (40, 49) (42, 46) (45, 47) (48, 51), with some noted exceptions.

³ The edges of copy A are gilt but not trimmed.

⁴ In copy B, pl. (22–23) (27, 53) are printed back-to-back.

⁵ In copies C and U, only the top edges are gilt.

⁶ Copy F is numbered I–XXVII (perhaps by the binder) in the centre of the page above the platemark in the order of binding.

⁷ *Innocence* (H) and *Songs* (d, f) have not been traced, and details about them are taken from Keynes & Wolf.

⁸ In copy I, pl. (5, 9) (8, 24) (11, 34) (12, 22) (15, 26) (18–19) (25, 27) are printed back-to-back.

⁹ The watermark in copy I is not J WHATMAN on two leaves, as in Keynes & Wolf.

¹⁰ In copy J, pl. (5, 9) (8, 22) (11, 23) (12, 24) (18, 26) (25, 27) are printed back-to-back.

¹¹ In copy K, pl. (22, 26) are printed back-to-back, and the verso of pl. 27 is blank.

¹² The leaves of *Innocence* (O) and *Songs* (F, S) are trimmed but not gilt.

¹³ Not 'brown and green', as in Keynes & Wolf.

¹⁴ Not J WHATMAN / 1804, as in Keynes & Wolf.

¹⁵ Pl. 21 of copy Q and pl. 20, 23 of copy R are trimmed more than the others.

¹⁶ There are no numbers on *Innocence* (S) pl. 2, *Songs* (E) pl. 32, *Songs* (M) pl. 3, *Songs* (S) pl. 1, and *Songs* (W) pl. 2.

¹⁷ Since copies V–W, Y have not been traced, their descriptions are taken from the Sotheby catalogues of 12 March 1891, lot 350 (V); 28 June 1940, lot 260 (W), and 30 April 1941, lot 641 (W); and 12 March 1962, lot 151 (Y).

¹⁸ Pl. (13–14) (16–17) (18, 25) (19, 54) (24, 27) (35–36) are printed back-to-back in X.

¹⁹ Not 'I TAYLOR 1794, on one leaf', as in Keynes & Wolf.

²⁰ The ink numbers in copy A omit the frontispieces and title-pages in *Innocence* and *Experience*. There are pencil numbers giving an order (29, 28, 30–3, 35–6, 34, 37, 39, 38, 40–9, 53, 3, 4–27, 54) which corresponds to that in no other copy of the *Songs* and which, from the misplacing of the first leaf of 'The Little Girl Lost' (pl. 34), is manifestly erroneous.

²¹ In copy B, plates 1, 28–33, 37–51, a are printed in orangish-Brown with some details (normally vegetation) printed in *Black*; the rest (2–27, 34–6, 53–4) are printed in a flat Brown.

²² In copy C, the printing colour is flat Brown on pl. 1–29, 34–6, 53–4; orangish-Brown on pl. 30–3, 37–46, 48–51, a. Pl. 1, 28, 30, 32–3, 37–51 seem to be colour printed.

²³ Copy D is printed in golden-Brown on pl. 1, 12–14, 18, 20, 26, 28–51, and in dark Brown on the rest (pl. 2–11, 15–17, 19, 21–5, 27, 53–4, a).

²⁴ The two pl. 15s in copy E are a printing fault, not a binding error, for they are on the rectos of pl. 9 and 34.

²⁵ In copy E, pl. (15, 34) are printed back-to-back, and the versos of pl. 26, 32, 52 are blank.

²⁶ In copy E, the printing colour is golden-Brown on pl. 1, 3–7, 16–17, 25, 28–31, 33, 38–49; Brown on pl. 2, 8–12, 15, 18–19, 22–4, 26–7, 37, 52–4; pale Red on pl. 51.

²⁷ In copy F, pl. (5, 9) (8, 24) (10, 27) (11, 25) (12, 22) (15, 26) (18–19) (34–5) (36, 54) are printed back-to-back, while the *Experience* plates are printed on one side of the leaf only.

²⁸ The leaves of copy F are foliated on rectos (except for pl. 18 which is numbered on the verso) in ink in *Experience*, in pencil in *Innocence*.

²⁹ In copy F, only pl. 31–3, 38, 40, 43, 46–7, 50 are colour printed in Green; *Innocence* is not colour printed.

³⁰ Pl. 33, 41, 46, 49 in copy G have not been traced since they were offered in Quaritch's *General Catalogue* (1877), lot 9741, and their colours, sizes, etc., are not known.

³¹ In copies J, j, and Dr. Juel-Jensen's plates (7, 10, 33), the leaves were cut down to about 0·5 cm from the platemark. If pl. 28 of copy J went to copy T, the original size of the leaves of copy J must have been 11·7 × 18·5 cm.

³² In copy J, pl. 1–2, 5–7, 12, 15–16, 21, 29–30, 32–4, 36, 38–40, 43, 45–6, 48–9, 53 are printed in a Brown (almost Black) darker than the other plates.

³³ In copy K, the figures include pl. 30–3, 37, 41, 44–7, 50–2 from what Keynes & Wolf call copy e, which were once part of copy K. The K plates are uncoloured, the e plates in K coloured. This combined K, e was evidently stabbed and numbered before 1817 with *Innocence* from *Songs* (O). The last plate (52) is not numbered.

³⁴ The leaves from copy e (pl. 30–3, 37, 41, 44–7, 50–2) are gilt on the top and outsides, but not at the bottom as the rest of the leaves in copy e are.

³⁵ The colouring of copies M and j does not appear to be Blake's.

³⁶ Both *Innocence* and *Experience* in copy O are printed in the same dark Brown, not 'dark red-brown' in *Innocence* and 'dark brown' in *Experience*, as in Keynes & Wolf.

³⁷ Not '1–28 and 1–25' as in Keynes & Wolf. Apparently Blake accidentally numbered the frontispiece of *Innocence* (pl. 2) as if it were to go with *Experience*.

³⁸ In copy Q, *Innocence* is printed in a uniform orangish Brown, *Experience* in a uniform dark Brown.

³⁹ The first plate (pl. 1) is not numbered in copy R, and there are duplicate numbers (1–25) in *Experience*.

⁴⁰ In copy T, pl. (6–7) (19, 24) are printed back-to-back. Copy T was originally two copies of the *Songs*, one (T¹) early, colour-printed, and unnumbered, which was merged with a late, numbered copy (T²) printed in Red. Some of the plates discarded from this combined T are in the National Gallery of Canada; the other (hypothetical) discarded plates are *UNTRACED* and are not tabulated here.

⁴¹ In copy T² (BMPR), Blake's numbers in Red appear only on the plates printed in Orange (1–5, 8–18, 20–3, 25–7, 29–31, 34–7, 44–6, 48, 52–4) and fairly clearly would have been 1–54 if completed with pl. 38, 41, 43, 47, 49–51 (National Gallery of Canada) and other (now *UNTRACED*) plates.

⁴² The leaves in copies V and b are trimmed and marbled.

⁴³ The watermarks in copy AA are extremely difficult to see because the leaves are pasted down.

⁴⁴ Details about copy BB, which has not been traced, are taken from the Sotheby catalogue of 13 Jan. 1830, lot 41.

⁴⁵ Pl. 30–3, 37, 41, 44–7, 50–2 from what Keynes & Wolf call copy e are described under copy K. The remaining plates of copy e were coloured posthumously.

⁴⁶ In copy e, pl. 4, 7–9, 11–13, 17–18, 23–5, 29, 35 are nearer to golden-Brown, and pl. 10, 26 are nearer to reddish-Brown.

⁴⁷ Pl. 19 in copy g¹ and pl. 48 in copy i are on thinner paper than the other leaves.

⁴⁸ Pl. 31 in copy g² is on a smaller leaf of paper different from that of the rest of the leaves.

⁴⁹ All information about copy h comes from the Anderson Gallery catalogue of 15 March 1920, lot 53.

⁵⁰ In copy j, the crucial watermark was mostly cut off when the leaves were heavily trimmed, and in none is it clear. The critical plates are 13–14, 22, 40 in which ATMAN / 31 can be read tentatively or (pl. 40) confidently.

⁵¹ In copy j, the plates in each of the two volumes are numbered 1–27 (in the same Red ink in which the border lines are drawn and the text is printed) in a hand which seems to me unlike Blake's. *Experience* is in 'VOL. 1' and *Innocence* in 'VOL. 2'.

⁵² In copy n, pl. 2 is on heavier paper than the other leaves.

⁵³ This description of copy o combines information from Keynes & Wolf and from the Weyhe catalogue (1938); the reference in the latter to 'Night' and 'Nurse's Song' could be to pl. 20 or 21, 24 or 38.

⁵⁴ Pl. (9–10) are printed back-to-back.

⁵⁵ Pl. (40, 50) are printed back-to-back.

⁵⁶ Pl. 24–5, 31, 37, 40, 47 are known only from the catalogues of the Burlington Fine Arts Club (1876), no. 289; Boston Museum (1880), no. 14; Pennsylvania Academy of the Fine Arts (1892), no. 126–7, 142–4, 148; Sotheby, 15 July 1912, lot 213; Sotheby, 6 May 1936, lot 719; and Colnaghi (1972), no. 111; pl. 40 now belongs to Mr. *Lister*.

⁵⁷ The only record of this pl. 38 comes from the Manchester catalogue (1914), no. 83.

⁵⁸ Details of pl. 42, 51 are taken from the catalogue of the Parke-Bernet Galleries, 2 Nov. 1938, lot 19.

⁵⁹ The untraced pl. 42 is known only from the Ellis & Elvey catalogues 81–2 (?1895), lot 51 in each.

IDENTIFICATION OF PLATES

Pl. 1   Combined title-page of the *Songs of Innocence and of Experience*
Pl. 2   Frontispiece to *Innocence*; a shepherd looking at a child on a cloud
Pl. 3   *Innocence* title-page
Pl. 4   'Introduction' to *Innocence* (begins 'Piping down the valleys wild')
Pl. 5   'The Shepherd'
Pl. 6–7   'The Ecchoing Green' (pl. 7 begins: 'They laugh at our play')
Pl. 8   'The Lamb'
Pl. 9–10   'The Little Black Boy' (pl. 10 begins: 'For when our souls . . .')
Pl. 11   'The Blossom'
Pl. 12   'The Chimney Sweeper' for *Innocence* (begins: 'When my mother died . . .')
Pl. 13   'The Little Boy lost'
Pl. 14   'The Little Boy found'
Pl. 15   'Laughing Song'
Pl. 16–17   'A Cradle Song' (pl. 17 begins: 'Wept for me . . .')
Pl. 18   'The Divine Image'
Pl. 19   'Holy Thursday' for *Innocence* (begins: 'Twas on a Holy Thursday . . .')
Pl. 20–21   'Night' (pl. 21 begins: 'When wolves and tygers . . .')
Pl. 22–23   'Spring' (pl. 23 begins: 'Little Girl Sweet and small')
Pl. 24   'Nurses Song' for *Innocence* (begins: 'When the voices of children are heard on the green And laughing is heard on the hill')
Pl. 25   'Infant Joy'
Pl. 26   'A Dream'
Pl. 27   'On Anothers Sorrow'
Pl. 28   Frontispiece to *Experience*: a shepherd with a winged child on his head
Pl. 29   *Experience* title-page
Pl. 30   'Introduction' to *Experience* (begins: 'Hear the Voice of the Bard!')
Pl. 31   'Earth's Answer'
Pl. 32   'The Clod & the Pebble'
Pl. 33   'Holy Thursday' for *Experience* (begins: 'Is this a holy thing to see')
Pl. 34–6   'The Little Girl Lost' (pl. 34–5) and 'The Little Girl Found' (pl. 35–6) (pl. 35 begins: 'Leopards, tygers play' and pl. 36 begins: 'Famish'd weeping weak')
Pl. 37   'The Chimney Sweeper' for *Experience* (begins: 'A little black thing among the snow')
Pl. 38   'Nurses Song' for *Experience* (begins: 'When the voices of children are heard on the green And whisprings in the dale')
Pl. 39   'The Sick Rose'
Pl. 40   'The Fly'

Pl. 41   'The Angel'
Pl. 42   'The Tyger'
Pl. 43   'My Pretty Rose Tree', 'Ah! Sun-Flower', 'The Lilly'
Pl. 44   'The Garden of Love'
Pl. 45   'The Little Vagabond'
Pl. 46   'London'
Pl. 47   'The Human Abstract'
Pl. 48   'Infant Sorrow'
Pl. 49   'A Poison Tree'
Pl. 50   'A Little Boy Lost'
Pl. 51   'A Little Girl Lost'
Pl. 52   'To Tirzah'
Pl. 53   'The School Boy'
Pl. 54   'The Voice of the Ancient Bard'
Pl. a   Design of five winged cherubs carrying a naked man
Pl. b   'A Divine Image'

ORDER OF THE PLATES IN *Songs of Innocence*

Innocence copy	Order of the plates
A	‡2–4 (5, 25) (16–17) (15, 9) (10, 54) (6–7) (24, 19) (27, 22) (23, 53), (26, 34) (35–6) (11, 8) (13–14) (20–1) (12, 18)**
B	‡2–4 (5, 25) (27, 53) (19, 24) (15, 9) (10, 54) (6–7) (12, 18) (26, 34) (35–6) (13–14) (16–17) (22–3) (11, 8) (20–1)**
C	‡2–4 (16–17) (13–14) (18, 12) (27, 22) (23, 53) (8, 11) (26, 34) (35–6) (15, 9) (10, 54) (19, 24) (6–7) (20–1) (25, 5)**
D	‡2–4 (6–7) (15, 9) (10, 54) (11, 8) (26, 34) (35–6) (24, 19) (25, 5) (20–1) (13–14) (18, 12) (16–17) (27, 22) (23, 53)**
‡E¹	‡2–4 (18, 12) (6–7) (11, 8) (15, 9) (10, 54) (5, 25) (27, 22) (23, 53) (24, 19) **(14, 13)** (26, 34) (35–6) (20–1) (16–17)**
F	2–4 (5, 25) (8, 11) (15, 9) (10, 54) (13–14) (18, 12) (16–17) (20–1) (27, 22) (23, 53) (26, 34) (35–6)
‡G²	‡2–4 (26, 34) (35–6) (8, 11) (6–7) (18, 12) (25, 5) (20–1) (16–17) (13–14) (24, 19) (27, 22) (23, 53) (15, 9) (10, 54)
H	2–4 (5, 25) (15, 9) (10, 54) (6–7) (16–17) (20–1) (24, 19) (11, 8) (27, 22) (23, 53) (13–14) (26, 34) (35–6) (12, 18)
I	‡2–4 (5, 9) (10, 54) (16–17) (11, 34) (35–6) (8, 24) (25, 27) (13–14) (12, 22) (23, 53) (15, 26) (19, 18) (6–7) (20–1)**
J	2–4 (5, 9) (10, 54) (18, 26) (6–7) (27, 25) (8, 22) (23, 11) (24, 12) (16–17)
‡K	‡2–4 (6–7) (15, 9) (10, 54) (11, 8) (26, 22) (23, 53) (25, 5) (16–17) (24, 19) (12, 18) (13–14) (20–1) 27
‡L	2–4 (5, 25) (24, 19) (27, 22) (23, 53) (15, 9) (10, 54) (6–7) (16–17) (13–14) (8, 11) (18, 12) (20–1)
M	‡2–4 (25, 5) (15, 9) (10, 54) (27, 22) (23, 53) (16–17) (19, 24) (6–7) (8, 11) (18, 12) **(21, 20)** (13–14)**

¹ The order of copy E is that of the pencil numbers; the plates are now loose.
² The order for the loose plates of copy G is that of Keynes (1921), who evidently saw it before the stitching came out.

N   2, **4**, 3, 5–8, 19, 24, 16–17, 15, 9–10, 26, 12–14, 27, 11, 20–1, 53, 22–3, 25, 18**

O   2–5, 25, 9–10, 27, 22–3, 15, 53–4, 12, 8, 19, 18, 20–1, 26, 16–17, 11, 24, 13–14

P¹   ‡2–4, 25, 6–7, 22–3, 18–19, 53, 13–14, 27, 26, 15, 11, 20–1, 8, 5, 54, 12, 24, **9, 16**

Q   ‡2–4, 6–7, 11, 22–3, 25, 54, 5, 9–10, 27, 16–19, 8, 12, 26, 53, 15, 24, 13–14, 20–1

R²   2   19–20   22–5   26–7

S³   ‡2–21, 53, 22–5, 54, 26–7

T⁴   3, **2**, 4–5, 25, 27, 19, 24, 9–10, 54, 6–7, 12, 18, 26, 34–6, 13–14, 16–17, 22–3, 11, 8, 20–1

U⁵   3, **2**, 4, 6–7, 9ᵇ, 9–12, 15, 8, 53, 24, 13–14, 20–1, 19, 26, 16–17, 25, 54, 22–3, 5, 27, 18, 34–6**

V   *unknown*

W   *loose*

X   (35–6) (18, 25) (16–17) (13–14) (24, 27) (19, 54)⁶

Y   4–18

Songs copy	*Order of the plates* INNOCENCE

A   3, ‡**2**, 4, 22–3, 6–7, 9–10, **13**, 20–1, 11, 24, 27, 54, 15, 18, 12, 19, 53, **14**, 8, 5, 16–17, 26, 25

‡B   ‡1–4 (6–7) (15, 9) (10, 54) (5, 25) (24, 19) (11, 8) (27, 22) (23, 53) (16–17) (12, 18) (20–1) (13–14)**

C   ‡2, 1, 3–4 (25, 5) (16–17) (8, 11) (24, 19) (6–7) (27, 22) (23, 53) (18, 12) (15, 9) (10, 54) (20–1) (13–14)**

D   ‡2, 1, 3–4 (15, 9) (10, 54) (27, 22) (23, 53) (6–7) (16–17) (20–1) (5, 25) (24, 19) (8, 11) (18, 12) (13–14)**

E   1–4 (5, 25) (11, 8) (15, 9) (10, 54) (18, 12) (16–17) (6–7) (27, 22) (23, 53) (24, 19) (13–14) (20–1) 26**

F   ‡2–4 (5, 9) (10, 27) (6–7) (12, 22) (23, 53) (15, 26) (13–14) (8, 24) (34–5) (36, 54) (18–19) (16–17) (25, 11) (20–1)**

¹ Despite the contemporary binding of copy P, its authority is much diminished by the fact that the last halves of 'The Little Black Boy' (pl. 10) and 'A Cradle Song' (pl. 17) are missing; someone, presumably Blake, has scratched out the catchwords on pl. 9 and 16, to suggest that no following plates were needed.

² Part of copy R was evidently lost in a fire; the above order is that of Blake's foliation and the 1952 binding. The missing leaf of 'Night' (pl. 21) presumably would have been numbered '20' and come in after pl. 20.

³ Pl. 2 in copy S has stitch holes in the *left* margin, suggesting that it was not originally bound to face pl. 3. In the light of the page numbering, probably by Blake, it is likely that that 1920 Quaritch catalogue 'full collation' (pl. 3–4, 16–17, 13–14, 18, 12, 27, 22–23, 53, 8, 11, 26, 15, 9–10, 54, 19, 24, 6–7, 20–21, 25, 5) was not meant to suggest that the plates were bound in this erroneous order.

⁴ In copy T, pl. 18, 27 have unidentifiable offsets that do not come from the facing plates. Keynes & Wolf say erroneously that the order is 1–5.

⁵ The order of the loose leaves of copy U derives from the pencil numbers confirmed by the offsets. In the facsimile of copy U (1883), the order of the plates is: 3, 2, 4, 6–7, 9–11, 24, 15, 12, 25, 8, 13–14, 20–1, 53, 27, 16–19, 22–3, 54, 26, 5, 34–6, which corresponds to that of no other known order of *Innocence* and probably lacks authority.

⁶ The leaves were loose in 1964.

Songs copy	*Order of the plates* INNOCENCE
G–H	*Experience* only
I	2, 1, 3–5, 11, 9–10, 22–3, 19, 6–7, 25, 8, 24, 15, 12, 18, 26–7, 53–4, 16–17, 20–1, 13–14**
J¹	1–5, 22–3, 19, 15, 24, 18, 8–10, 25, 6–7, 16–17, 53, 20–1, 27, 26, 13–14, 11–12, 54
K	*Experience* only
L	1, ‡2–4, 6–7, 12, 9–10, 19, 22–4, 5, 26, 16–17, 20–1, 11, 13–14, 25, 8, 54, 15, 18, 27**
M	3, 1–2, 4, 8, 6–7, 15, 20–1, 19, 18, 13–14, 27, 9 10, 26, 11, 54, 5, 22 5, 16–17, 12**
N	*Experience* only
O	1–5, 12, 19, 6–7, 11, 15–17, 25, 27, 24, 54, 22–3, 18, 53, 8, 26, 13–14, 9–10, 20–1**
P	‡2, 1, 3–7, 25, 9–10, 27, 22–3, 15, 53–4, 12, 8, 19, 18, 20–1, 26, 16–17, 11, 24, 13–14
Q	‡2–4, 6–7, 5, 11, 22–3, 12, 54, 53, 25, 15, 26, 8–10, 16–17, 19, 24, 27, 13–14, 20–1
R	1–21, 53, 22–5, 54, 26–7**
S	2–21, 53, 22–5, 54, 26–7**
T¹,²	1–5 (6–7) 8–18 (19, 24) 20–3, 25–7
U	1–27**
V²	1–4, 6–8, 5, 25, 9–10, 15, 22–3, 16–17, 24, 19, 11–12, 18, 20–1 26–7, 13–14**
W–Y	1–27
Z	1–27**
AA	1–27**
BB	*unknown*
♯a	1–14, 16–27
♯b	1–27
♯c	1–4, 6–7, 25, 11–12, 9–10, 19, 15, 8, 5, 20–1, 16–17, 22–3, 27, 24, 34–6, 53, 26, 54, 13–14, 18
♯d	*unknown*
♯e	*loose*
♯f	*unknown*
♯g¹	3–4, 6–8, 5, 25, 9–10, 22–3, 16–17, 24, 19, 12, 18, 20–1, 26–7, 13–14
♯h	*unknown*
♯i³	1–14, 16–25, **48**, 26–7
♯j	1–27
♯k–l	*Experience* only

¹ The validity of this order for copy J is confirmed by the 1839 reprint of the *Songs*, which gives the poems in the above order. In his letter of 12 Feb. 1818 describing copy J (*Blake Records* [1969], 251–3), Coleridge implies the present order, except that he accidentally omits 'The Human Abstract' (pl. 47) and seems to count pl. 28, which is missing now.

² The order in copy V is the same as that in the 'Order' of the *Songs* (?1818)—see p. 337— which was probably made for copy V.

³ The plates of copy i are loose, but pencil numbers 2–12, 14–26, together with the presumed positions of pl. 1 and 13, which are not numbered, give the above order, which does not correspond to that in any other copy known.

♯m–o   *loose*
pl. 4–18   4–18

♯   Means that the order of the plates is dubious, normally not supported by contemporary binding or by Blake's numbering or by consistent offsets.
Bold-face Letters indicate contemporary bindings.
Bold-face Numbers are conspicuously irregular.
**   The identifiable offsets confirm the binding-order.
‡   The frontispiece faces the title-page.

ORDER OF THE PLATES IN *Songs of Experience*

Songs copy	*Order of the plates*
A	29, ‡**28**, 30–1, 40, 32, 41, 37, 42, 48, 45, 38, 47, 34–6, 44, 49, 46, 39, 33, 43
♯B	‡28–9 (30–1) (48, 51) (42, 46) (45, 47) (**26**, 34) (35–6) (44, 39), (37, 50) (40, 49) (41, 38) (33, 43) (32, a)**
C	‡28–9 (30–1) (48, 51) (38, 41) (39, 44) (45, 47) (**26**, 34) (35–6) (50, 37) (40, 49) (46, 42) (43, 33) (32, a)**
D	‡28–9 (30–1) (40, 49) (46, 42) (39, 44) (**26**, 34) (35–6), (48, 51) (47, 45) (50, 37) (41, 38) (33, 43) (32, a)**
E	28–9 (30–1) (**15ᵇ**, 34) (35–6) (50, 37) (42, 46) (44, 39) (38, 41) (45, 47) (40, 49) (48, 51) (33, 43) 52, 32**
F	‡28–32, 38, 33, 46, 41, 49, 42, 50–1, 37, 47, 43, 40**
G	*loose*
Hᴵ	‡28–32, 42, 38, 43, 49, 33, 41, 37, 50, 40, 46, 51, 47**
I	28–33, 48, 41, 39–40, 50–1, 43, 37, 45, 49, 44, 46–7, 38, 42, 34–6, 52**
J	29–31, 48, 32, 44, 40, 42, 50, 33, 43, 41, 38, 34–6, 47, 37, 52, 49, 51, 46, 39, 45**
K²	28–32, 38, 48, 42, 33, 41, 46, 40, 47, 45, 50–1, 44, 34–7, 49, 43, 52**
L	‡28–31, 34–6, 42, 40, 33, 48, 32, 37, 52, 45, 47, 44, 50, 41, 39, 38, 49, 46, 51, 43, 53**
M	28–32, 49, 42, 41, 39, 52, 44, 50–1, 37, 47, 34–6, 38, 48, 45, 40, 46, 53, 43, 33*
N	29–32, 37, 49, 48, 42, 40, 39, 47, 51, 34–6, 44, 41, 43, 50, 52, 46, 45, 33, 38, 53**
O	1ᵇ, 28–32, 38, 34–6, 42, 48, 37, 44, 39, 46, 43, 49–50, 40, 47, 45, 51, 41, 33, 54ᵇ, 52**
P	‡28–31, 48, 42, 40, 32, 34–6, 49, 39, 33, 47, 38, 51, 50, 52, 43, 46, 45, 37, 41, 44
Q	28, **1**, 29–31, 48, 42, 37, 34–6, 38, 32, 40, 50, 47, 52, 39, 44, 46, 51, 41, 49, 45, 33, 43**
R	28–49, 52, 51, 50**
S	**1**, 28–32, 38, 42, 37, 49, 45, 33, 43, 47, 50, 41, 48, 34–6, 46, 44, 39–40, 51–2**

¹ The order for the loose plates of copy H is that reported for it in the Sotheby catalogue of 20 Dec. 1948, lot 98 (when it was still 'loosely sewn in old paper wrappers') and confirmed by the offsets. This does not correspond to the order in which the plates are described in J. T. Smith's 1828 life of Blake (*Blake Records* [1969], 468–70)—28–32, 49, 40, 33, 37, 46, 42, 50, 47, 41, 43, 38, 51; Smith's order was probably not intended as that of the binding.
² This order for copy K combines numbers and very clear offsets from copies K and e of the *Songs*.

T¹   ‡28–48, 50–1, 49, 52–4
U   28–54**
V²   28–31, 38, 40, 42, 34–6, 32, 45, 33, 49, 4¹, 39, 52, 54, 43–4, 50, 48, 53, 46,
         5¹, 37, 47**
W   28–54
X   28–54**
Y   28–54
Z   28–54
AA   28–54
BB   *unknown*

‡a   28–9, 33–6, 38–43, 46, 49, 52–3, 48, 54, 30–1, 47, 37, 32, b, 5¹, 50, 44–5
‡b   28–54
‡c   29, 28, 30, 44, 48, 39, 37, 45, 33, 47, 42, 40, b, 31, 43, 49, 46, 38, 5¹, 32,
         50, 41
‡d   *unknown*
‡e²   *loose*
‡f   *unknown*
‡g²   ‡28–9, 31, 38, 42, 34–6, 33, 49, 4¹, 39, 52, 54, 43–4, 53, 46
‡h   *unknown*
‡i³   28, 33, 30, 34–6, 38–43, 46, 49, 52–4
‡j   28–54
‡k   *loose*
‡l³   29, 33, 38–9, 41–3, 46, 49, 52, 51
‡m–o   *loose*

‡   Means that the order of the plates is dubious, normally not supported by contemporary
     binding or by Blake's numbering or by consistent offsets.
Bold-face Letters indicate contemporary bindings (probably before 1835).
Bold-face Numbers are conspicuously irregular.
**   The identifiable offsets confirm the binding-order.
‡   The frontispiece faces the title-page.

TITLES: [General title-page:] SONGS / Of / *INNOCENCE* / and Of /
        EXPERIENCE / Shewing the Two Contrary States / of the Human SOUL
        [*Innocence* sub-title:] SONGS / of / *INNOCENCE* / *1789* / The
        Author & Printer W Blake
        [*Experience* sub-title:] SONGS / *of* / EXPERIENCE / *1794* / The
        Author & Printer W Blake

DATES: Written: 1784–?1797.
  First Published: 1789 (pl. 2–27, 34–6, 53–4)
                   1794 (pl. 1, 28–33, 37–51, a)
                   ?1797 (pl. 52).
  Not published by Blake: (pl. b).

  Three poems later etched in *Innocence* (pl. 13, 19, 24) were used in the
Island in the Moon of *c.* 1784, and one more (pl. 15) appeared as 'Song 2ᵈ by
a Young Shepherd' (*c.* 1787). The rest of the *Innocence* poems were presum-

  ¹ The numbers on pl. 38, 41, 43, 47, 49–51 (T², National Gallery of Canada) indicate that
they were once placed in sequence in copy T.
  ² Copy V is arranged as in the MS 'Order' of the *Songs* (?1818) (see p. 337).
  ³ The leaves of copies i and l are loose, but pencil numbers give the orders above, which
correspond to that of no other copy known.

ably drafted about 1787–9, and the book with pl. 2–27, 34–6, 53–4 was first published in 1789, the date on the title-page of *Innocence*.

In his *Notebook*, Blake made drafts for most of the poems (pl. 31–3, 37–50)[1] and some of the designs (pl. 28–30, 33, 41, 46) of *Experience*, some of them (pl. 30, 33, 37–8, 41–2, 47–8, b) carefully contrasting with specific *Innocence* poems. He evidently felt that he was ready to issue the separate *Songs of Experience* by 10 Oct. 1793, when he advertised them in his Prospectus, but no surviving copy corresponds to the '25 designs' he specified there, and it seems likely that they were not in fact published until 1794, the date on their title-page. Perhaps *Experience* (pl. 28–51) was issued for a time separate from *Innocence* (pl. 2–27, 53–4) before they were issued together with a combined title-page (pl. 1).

Pl. b ('A Divine Image') may have been etched about 1794, but no surviving copy was printed by Blake. Pl. 52 ('To Tirzah') is not found in the earliest copies of *Experience* (*A–D, F–H*), is later in symbolism, and was probably written and published somewhat later, perhaps in 1797

PUBLICATION: The *Songs of Innocence* were advertised and evidently sold separately from 1789 to at least 1818.

Songs of Experience were advertised separately in the Prospectus of 10 Oct. 1793 and Blake's letter of 9 June 1818, and the first copies were probably intended for separate sale. In seventeen copies of the *Songs* (*A–I, K, N–T*), *Experience* was produced separately from *Innocence*, as is demonstrated by the distinctly different sets of printing colours (*A–C, ?D, ?E, F, Q, S–T*), numbers (*A, F, O–S*), and stab holes (*A, E, I, K, O, Q, T*) in *Innocence* and *Experience*, and the survival of some copies of *Experience* (*G–H, K, N*) without accompanying copies of *Innocence*.[2] In particular, *Experience* (*B–C, F–H, O, T¹*) were printed about 1795 and then added to copies of *Innocence* printed either somewhat earlier (*B–C, F*) or twenty years later (*O, T²*). It was apparently only in the last nine years of his life that Blake uniformly produced *Innocence* and *Experience* together.

Copperplates: There is clear evidence that some plates of the *Songs* were etched on the versos of others. For one thing, the sixteen electrotype copies of the *Songs* plates for Gilchrist's life of Blake (1863) were made from only ten pieces of copper,[3] indicating that at least six plates were etched on the versos of others. Secondly, copperplate-maker's-marks are visible on nine plates of the *Songs*,[4] all of them in *Experience*. And

---

[1] Except for 'Ah! Sun-Flower' on pl. 43; this is also one of the handful of *Experience* poems etched in roman letters. Note that there is a design but no text in the *Notebook* for pl. 30. The *Innocence* plates appear to be both etched and engraved but the *Experience* plates only etched.

[2] Copies *K* and *N*, however, were once numbered consecutively with copies of *Innocence*.

[3] A. Gilchrist *Life of William Blake*, '*Pictor Ignotus*' (1863), ii. 267. The electrotypes were of pl. 3, 6, 8, 16, 18, 24, 27, 29, 33–34, 36, 43, 46–48, 53.

[4] Part of the plate-maker's-mark

JONES Nº. 4[7?]
SHOE LANE LONDON

may be seen on posthumous pulls of pl. 1 (copy *c*), pl. 28 (*a, c, g, i*, Bentley pull), pl. 29

thirdly, the plates may be arranged in pairs of strikingly similar dimensions, as follows:

DIMENSIONS IN CENTIMETRES OF

Innocence plates	*Experience* plates		*Innocence* plates	*Experience* plates	*Experience* plate
(*2*) 7·0×11·0 =	(**28**) 7·0×11·0	(*18*) 7·0×11·2 =	(**1**) 7·0×11·2		
(*3*) 7·4×12·0 =	(**51**) 7·3×12·0	(*20*) 6·9×11·1 =	(**41**) 6·8×11·1		
(*5*) 6·9×11·1 =	(**38**) 6·9×11·1	(*21*) 6·8×11·0 =	(**50**) 6·8×11·0		
(*6*) 7·0×11·0 =	(**43**) 7·0×11·0	(*25*) 6·8×11·1 =	(**39**) 6·8×11·1		
(*9*) 6·9×11·1 =	(**37**) 6·9×11·1	(*27*) 7·1×11·2 =	(**33**) 7·3×11·3		
(*10*) 6·7×11·1 —	(**44**) 6·0×11·1		(**29**) 7·2×12·4 =	(*30*) 7·2×12·4
(*12*) 7·3×11·2 =	(**32**) 7·3×11·3	(*34*) 6·6×11·2 =	(**47**) 6·6×11·2		
(*13*) 7·2×11·8 =	(**40**) 7·3×11·8	(*35*) 6·8×11·1 =	(**49**) 6·8×11·1		
(*14*) 7·2×11·7 =	(**31**) 7·2×11·7	(*36*) 6·9×11·1 =	(**46**) 6·9×11·1		
(*15*) 6·7×11·1 =	(**45**) 6·6×11·1	(*53*) 6·9×11·1 =	(**48**) 7·0×11·1		
(*16*) 7·2×11·3 =	(**52**) 7·2×11·4	(*54*) 6·3×11·0 =	(**42**) 6·3×11·0		

28 Bold-face Numbers represent a copperplate-maker's-mark.
2 Italic numbers identify dimensions which match perfectly.

Apparently, then, at least six, and perhaps as many as twenty-two *Experience* plates were etched on the versos of other *Songs* plates.

Metamorphoses in Plates: The sequence in which copies of *Innocence* and the *Songs* were printed may have been something like this:

1789–1800

Copies	A–G, I–J, X	B–C	G–H, T¹	F²	A, O (SE)	M, D	K–L
Watermark Date		1795¹	1795¹	1795¹			
Plates Back-to-Back	—	—		—		—	—
Pl. 34–6 not in *Innocence*		—					
Plates Numbered				—	—		
Text Coloured							—²
Pl. 53–4 not in *Innocence*							
Purchase Date					1795 (O)		

1800–1806

Copies	P	J	Q	E	N, K–N, O (SI)	O, P	Q
Watermark Date	1802		1804			1802	1804
Plates Back-to-Back			—				
Pl. 34–6 not in *Innocence*	—	—	—	—		—	—
Plates Numbered		—	—	—		—	—
Text Coloured		—	—	—		—	
Pl. 53–4 not in *Innocence*							
Purchase Date	1805			1806²	1814 (O)		

1814–1827

Copies	R, I	T U	S, R–S	T²–U	V	W, Y–AA	X
Watermark Date		...4	1808	1815	1818	1825	1825
Plates Back-to-Back							
Pl. 34–6 not in *Innocence*	—	—	—	—	—	—	—
Plates Numbered	—		—	—	—	—	—
Text Coloured	—	—	—	—	—	—	—
Pl. 53–4 not in *Innocence*	—		—	—	—	—	—
Purchase Date			1819 (R)	by 1822 (U)		1825 (Z–AA)	1827

(*b–c, e, k*, Harvard pull), pl. 32 (*b–c*), pl. 33 (*a*), pl. 37 (*b–c*, Harvard pull), pl. 46 (*a*, electrotype), pl. 47 (*a*, electrotype), and pl. 49 (*c*).

¹ '*1795*' means that the *Experience* plates were colour printed (in 1795).
² *Songs* (*E–F*) and perhaps *Innocence* (*K–L*) seem to have been printed early but coloured late.

The *Songs of Innocence* and *Songs of Innocence and of Experience* repeatedly altered over the years in the distribution and characteristics of the plates. The earliest copies of *Innocence* (A–G, I–J, X), *c.* 1789–93, consisted of pl. 2–27, 34–6, 53–4, printed on both sides of the leaf. At first, *Experience* apparently consisted of pl. 1, 28–33, 37–51,[1] but very shortly thereafter pl. 34–6 were added to the new work (in copies A–E,[2] K–AA). The earliest copies of the *Songs* printed all together (B–D) include pl. a, without text, but thereafter this plate was omitted. Later pl. 52 ('To Tirzah') was added to *Experience* (E, I–AA), perhaps to replace pl. a. From about 1795[3] Blake began printing the plates on one side of the leaf only (N–U, A, G–AA). From at least 1806,[4] he began numbering his copies (N–O, Q–S, A, E–F, I, K–AA) and colouring the text as well as the designs (K–L, N–O, R–T, E, I–P, R–W, Y–AA). By 1818[5] he moved pl. 53 to *Experience* (T, L–N, T–AA); by 1819[6] he began putting framing-lines or scroll work round the designs (O, R–AA) and settled on a fairly stable order of pl. 1–54 for the plates (S, R–U, W–AA); and by 1822[7] he moved pl. 54 to *Experience* as well (O, T–AA).

Letter Face: Almost all *Innocence* (pl. 3–27, 34–6, 53) is etched in miniscule upright roman letters, while only six poems from *Experience* (pl. 42, 43 ['Ah! Sun-Flower' only], 46, 49, 50 [ll. 1–4 only], b) are in roman. All the rest is in Blake's usual slanting italic, including most of *Experience* (pl. 30–3, 37–45, 47–8, 50–2) and one poem from *Innocence* (pl. 54, 'The Voice of the Ancient Bard').[8]

Sale: In the Prospectus of 10 Oct. 1793, *Innocence* and *Experience* are described as being 'in Illuminated Printing. Octavo, with 25 designs [*each*], price 5*s.* [*each*]'. In the letter of 9 June 1818, they are listed as, respectively, 28 Prints (?pl. 1–27, 54) and 26 Prints (?pl. 28–53), octavo, for £3. 3*s.* each. In his letter of 12 April 1827, Blake gives the price for the combined *Songs* as £10. 10*s.*

Blake's lyrical *Songs* appealed to his contemporaries far more than did his narrative poetry. Wordsworth and his circle casually admired individual poems which were occasionally reprinted in biographical notices and elsewhere.[9] In 1807 Wordsworth copied pl. 15, 19, and 42 into a commonplace

---

[1] The only colour printed plates in the *Songs* (pl. 1, 28–33, 37–51) appear in *Experience* (B–C, F–H, T[1]). Since pl. 34–6, 52–4 were not colour printed, it seems likely that the colour printing took place before pl. 34–6 were added to *Experience*.

[2] In copies B–E, pl. 34–6 seem to have been printed with *Innocence* but bound with *Experience*. This would explain why pl. 15 and 26 are in the wrong section in these copies.

[3] Colour printing is thought to have been done in 1795. Some colour-printed copies (B–C, F) are printed on both sides of the leaf and some (G–H, T[1]) on only one side.

[4] Copy E was sold in 1806.

[5] The letter of 9 June 1818 describes *Innocence* as having 28 Prints (?pl. 1–27, 54) and *Experience* as having 26 (?pl. 28–53).   [6] Copy R was sold in 1819.

[7] Copy U belonged to James Boswell [Jr], who died in 1822.

[8] These varieties of letter face were remarked first in *The Poetical Works of William Blake*, ed. J. Sampson (1905), 69.

[9] Poems were reprinted as follows: Pl. 4 (1811, 1830), pl. 8 (*1830), pl. 12 (*1824, *1830), pl. 15 (*1806, *1830), pl. 16–17 (1830), pl. 18 (1806, 1830), pl. 19 (1806, 1811, *1818, *1830), pl. 30 (1830), pl. 42 (*1806, *1811, *1830), pl. 44 (*1811, 1830), pl. 49 (1830)—*Blake Records* (1969), 254, 284, 381, 382, 384–5, 425–8, 430–1, 443–6, 479, 483–4, 504–5. Asterisks (*) represent unauthoritative substantive variants.

book, and later said that he thought the *Songs* delightful though showing an interesting madness.[1] Crabb Robinson transcribed parts of *Songs* (*D*) in 1810 for an article he published in *Vaterländisches Museum* next year, and he read some of the *Songs* to Hazlitt, who was struck by 'The Chimney Sweeper'.[2] In 1818 C. A. Tulk lent *Songs* (*J*) to Coleridge, who returned them with an elaborate list of 'Dyspathies ... and Sympathies', indicating that he especially liked pl. 9–10, 18, 20–1, and 34–6.[3] Charles Lamb thought 'The Tyger' 'glorious' when he heard it recited,[4] and he sent a copy of pl. 12 to be published by James Montgomery in *The Chimney Sweeper's Friend* (1824), where it was admired by Bernard Barton.[5]

Most of those who saw the *Songs*, however, probably agreed with Richard Thomson, who wrote in 1828 that the poems were 'of no great degree of elegance or excellence'.[6] Blake's contemporaries were evidently more interested in the tinted designs than they were in the poems. Perhaps for this reason, Blake coloured copies more and more elaborately and heavily, even colouring over the texts, until in a number of copies some poems are virtually illegible.

Among Blake's contemporaries, copies of *Innocence* were owned by ?Dr. William Long (A), R. H. Clarke (B), Samuel and Henry Rogers (C), John and Nancy Flaxman (D), C. Newman (E), Edward Fitzgerald (H), John Linnell (I), Sir Charles W. Dilke (1810–69) (K), the first Marquis of Bute (M), Arthur Champernowne (O), B. H. Malkin and Thomas Johnes (P, gift of 1805), the first Baron Dimsdale (R), T. F. Dibdin (?S, acquired by 1816), and Robert Balmanno (U); copies of the *Songs* were owned by Isaac D'Israeli (*A*), Judge Charles Warren (*B*), Elizabeth Iremonger (by 1810) and Miss C. L. Shipley (*D*), Thomas Butts (*E*, bought for £6. 6s. on 9 Sept. 1806), George Cumberland (*F*), Ozias Humphry and William Upcott (*H*), Thomas or H. W. Phillips (*I*), Charles Augustus Tulk (*J*), John and Nancy Flaxman and Maria Denman (*O*, *Experience* perhaps bought in 1795 for 10s. and *Innocence* bought in July 1814 for £1), Mrs. Bliss and P. A. Hanrott (*P*), the Revd. Mr. Joseph Thomas (1765–1811) (?*Q*, bought for £10. 10s.), John Linnell (*R*, bought for £1. 19s. 6d. on 27 Aug. 1819; *X*, *AA*); James Boswell (d. 1822, son of Johnson's biographer), Thomas Edwards and William Beckford (*U*), Sir Thomas Lawrence (?*V*, bought for £12. 12s.?), Sir Francis Chantrey (?*V*, bought for £21?), Bishop John Jebb (*W*, bought March 1830 for £10.10s.), Thomas Griffiths Wainewright and James Weale (*X*, ordered Feb. 1827, bought for £10. 10s.), Edward Calvert (*Y*), H. C. Robinson (*Z*, bought for £5. 5s., delivered 10 Dec. 1825), Mrs. Charles Aders (*AA*, bought for £5. 5s., delivered 10 Dec. 1825), Robert Balmanno (*BB*), Hannah Boddington (*b*), Samuel Boddington (*c*), William Odell Elwell (*d*), and ?Frederick Tatham (*i*).

COLOURING: The designs in the *Songs* are more often literally illustrations

---

[1] *Blake Records*, 430 n. 1; 231; 536.   [2] *Blake Records*, 224; 432–55; 229.
[3] *Blake Records*, 251–3.
[4] *Blake Records*, 285. On the other hand, William Beckford thought it 'trash' such as might be found 'on the walls of Bedlam'—ibid. 431 n. 1.
[5] *Blake Records*, 284.   [6] *Blake Records*, 470.

than is true in Blake's other works in Illuminated Printing. In the reports of colouring below, I give the colours only of figures of substantial size or importance. The most extensive consequent omissions are on pl. 6–7, 15, 19, 53–4.

Blake normally tinted the plates of his *Songs*, and only a few are left un-coloured (U, W, *M*, *O* [*Innocence*], Q^1). Sometimes he clearly did not complete the colouring he had begun, for some plates of *K* were coloured and others were not, while in Dr. Juel-Jensen's plates the colouring is unfinished even on individual plates; for example, on pl. 7, the kite-boy's left trouser-leg is coloured (Green) and the right one is uncoloured.

The colours are bold in A; pale and delicate in C–D, I–J, M–Q, X, *A–D*, *F* (*Innocence*), *L*, *V*; plain and simple in B, E–H, S; heavy in K, *S* (in which some plates, e.g. pl. 2, are stippled), Blunt pl. 28; bright in R, *I–J*, *O* (*Experience*), *R*, *Y*; colour-printed in B–C, F–H, T^1 (sometimes [*F–G*] the colours have altered badly, especially in flesh which has turned Grey); careful in *E*; elaborate but light in *P*; rich in *R*; and elaborate, extensive, and splendid in *U*, *W–X*. *Innocence* (T) seems to have been printed in a runny ink and boldly but carelessly coloured, perhaps by Mrs. Blake; the details are often poor—for example, on pl. 9 the features of the boy are like a pumpkin. *Songs* (*R*) is not very successfully coloured, and in it *Innocence* is better and perhaps earlier than *Experience*. T^2 is dull.

In the colouring of individual details, such as clothes, there are a number of colouring-groups: I–J, *A*; K–L; N–Q (sombre); *B–E*; F, *F*; *I–L*, *N–P*; *U–V*; *W–X*; *Z–AA*. It must be recognized, however, that the definition of these subject-groups is highly subjective.

Some colouring details may be roughly dated:

	Early		*Late*
pl. 10	Left child Caucasian	pl. 10	Left child Negro (F, L–O, Q, S, *E, I–J, L, P, R–Y*)
pl. 18	Plant predominantly Green (A–E, G, K, M, T, *B, D*)	pl. 18	Plant Yellow (I–J, N, P–Q, X, *A, C, E–F, I–J, L, T–U, X–AA*)
pl. 34	Boy naked (A–G, I, T, *A–E, I, Z–AA*)	pl. 34	Boy clothed (F, *J, L, N–P, R–Y*)
pl. 36	Tree trunk Green (A–F, I, T, X, *B–C, E, X*)	pl. 41	Woman crowned (D, *J, L, O, R, T²–AA*)

In general, late copies were more extensively coloured. The designs were often extended for a few millimetres at the sides, and particularly at the bottom with a stream,[2] and on some plates a halo was added.[3] In late

---

[1] There is some Grey and pale Brown wash in *Experience* (*Q*).

[2] Pl. 4 (N, T, *J, V, X, Z–AA*), pl. 7 (T, *U, X, Z–AA*), pl. 8 (T, *S–V, X–AA*), pl. 12 (*AA*), pl. 18 (T), pl. 20 (T, *T, V, Z*), pl. 21 (T, *T, X, Z–AA*), pl. 23 (N–P, *E, J, S–V, X–AA*), pl. 24 (*U*), pl. 32 (*V, AA*), pl. 35 (*U*), pl. 47 (*N, T²–V, X, Z–AA*), pl. 49 (*V*). N.B. Streams were frequently added in T, *T–V, X, Z–AA*, but only twice in *Y*.

[3] Pl. 10 (K, O–P, *D, P, S, V, Y, AA*), pl. 11 (*X, Z*), pl. 12 (*W–X, Z*), pl. 14 (*M, AA*), pl. 18 (*Q, S–T, S, V, X–Y*), pl. 21 (K–Q, *T, J, Q, U–Y, AA*), pl. 25 (*T, Z*), pl. 28 (*Z*), pl. 30 (*W, Y–AA*), pl. 31 (*Y*), pl. 41 (*K, Z*), pl. 44 (*U–V, X*).

copies, the text is often coloured (K–L, N–O, R–T, *E*, *I–L*, *N–P*, *R–S*, *T²–W*, *Y–AA*),[1] the text is sometimes illegible (B, I, Q, T, *D*, *H*, *L*, *N*, *R*, *U–Y*, *AA*), and Blake clarified details by hand (I–Q, S, *B–E*, *J*, *L*, *P–R*, *T²–X*, *Z*). Occasionally Gold was used (*R*, *N*, *S*, *U*, *W–Z*, *e*), and framing-lines were made round the plates (J,[2] O, *R–AA*, *j*).[3]

Posthumous Colouring: A number of copies were printed posthumously (*a–o*; *a*, *i* poorly printed), and some were coloured posthumously: *M* is crudely coloured in a style not significantly like that of any other copy; *c* has touches of greyish-Green on a few plates; *e* is coloured crudely and very heavily, unlike any other copy; *i* pl. 29 is coloured; *j* was heavily coloured in a unique but very Blake-like way.

CATCHWORDS: Catchwords were needed only for poems which bridge two plates. They are given correctly as 'They' (pl. 6), 'For' (pl. 9), 'Wept' (pl. 16), 'When' (pl. 20), 'Little' (pl. 22), 'Leopards' (pl. 34), and 'Famish'd' (pl. 35), all in *Innocence*.

ORDER: The plates of *Innocence* and the combined *Songs* were arranged in thirty-four distinct ways. Among *Innocence* (A, C–N, P–Q, U) and *Songs* (*A–O*, *Q*), no two copies are arranged alike, and, in the rest, there are essentially three orders, two of which obtain in only two copies each. In chronological sequence, they are as follows:

(1) *Innocence* (B, T):[4] 2–5, 25, 27, 53, 19, 24, 15, 9–10, 54, 6–7, 12, 18, 26, 34–6,
   c. 1790?   13–14, 16–17, 22–3, 11, 8, 20–1

(2) *Innocence* (O),[5] *Songs* (P): 2–7, 25, 9–10, 27, 22–3, 15, 53–4, 12, 8, 19, 18, 20–1,
   after 1802   26, 16–17, 11, 24, 13–14

(3) *Innocence* (S),[6] *Songs* (*R–AA*):[6] 1–54
   by 1819

Within this bewildering variety there is, however, a little regularity at the beginning and end of *Innocence* and at the beginning of *Experience*. *Innocence* normally begins with pl. ‡2–4 in separate copies of *Innocence* or with pl. 1–4 when bound with the combined *Songs*.[7] Further, *Innocence* is more likely than not to end with either pl. 20–1 (B, I, L, Q, T, *F*, *O*, *Q*) or pl. 13–14 (*M*, *O*, *B–D*, *I*, *P*, *V*).[8]

Experience begins regularly with pl. 28–31,[9] or even with pl. 28–32 (*F*, *H–I*, *K*, *M–O*, *R–U*, *W–AA*), but there seems to be no common ending until all the plates were bound in uniform order in *T–U*, *W–AA*.

---

[1] Details of the colour of the text are not recorded below.

[2] Only the first four plates in *Innocence* (J) have framing-lines.

[3] Instead of the ordinary Red framing-lines, there are borders of scrolls (*W*) or foliage (*Y*) in two copies, the former evidently added by Mrs. Blake.

[4] T lacks pl. 15 and 53 and has pl. 2 after pl. 3.   [5] *Innocence* (O) lacks pl. 6–7.

[6] *Innocence* (S) of course lacks pl. 1, 28–52; *Innocence* (S) and *Songs* (*R–S*) have pl. 53, 54 after pl. 21, 25; *R* ends: pl. 52, 51, 50; *S* has a unique *Experience* order; and *T* has pl. (19, 24) from *T*¹ after pl. 18 and pl. 49 after pl. 51.

[7] Except for pl. 2, 4, 3 in N; pl. 3, 2, 4 in T–U, *A*; pl. 3, 1–2 in *M*; or pl. 2, 1, 3–4 in C–D, I, P. *F*, *Q*, *S* lack pl. 1 in *Innocence*.

[8] It must be remembered also that in copies printed back-to-back, the varieties of order are necessarily more limited than with other copies.

[9] *A* begins with pl. 29, 28, 30–1; *Q* has pl. 28, 1, 29–31.

Blake's final intention, confirmed in the 'Order' of the *Songs* (see p. 337), was clearly to arrange the plates in the order 1–54. It must be realized, how-ever, that in this late order plates 34–6, 53–4 are in *Experience*, while they were in *Innocence* in the earliest copies.

Plates Printed Back-to-Back: The plates printed back-to-back on the same leaf are relatively constant, with 90 per cent consistency among 552 pulls. In twelve copies (A, C–H, L–M, *B–D*), the plates exactly fit the standard pattern with the same plates always printed back-to-back. In three (B, K, *E*) the exceptions are minor, but in four others (I, J, X, *F*) they are numerous. There seems to be no significant pattern within these exceptions.

Recto and Verso: Some leaves are regularly bound with the same plate as recto:[1] (6–7) (15, 9) (10, 54) (*18, 12*) (*13–14*) (16–17) (*24, 19*) (*20 21*) (27, 22) (23, 53), (26, 34) (30–31) (32, a) (*33, 43*) (35–36), (40, 49) (*45, 47*) (48, 51) (*50, 37*). Others are bound with one plate as recto or verso almost indif-ferently: (5, 25), (11, 8) (38, 41), (39, 44) (42, 46).

There are simple explanations of why some plates appear regularly as rectos. Five leaves bear two halves of a poem or two intimately connected poems,[2] and six leaves bear poems which are completed on adjacent leaves.[3] Pl. a, without text, on the verso of pl. 32 was used as a concluding plate in the only three copies of the *Songs* in which it appears. Naturally, in these cases the contents determine which poem is on the recto and which on the verso, and the only exceptions (*E* pl. [14, 13], *M* pl. [21, 20]) are clearly mistakes.

There is no such easy explanation for why pl. (40, 49) (48, 51) should invariably be bound with the same plates as rectos or why pl. (18, 12) (24, 19) (33, 43) (50, 37) (45, 47) should normally be so bound.

Pl. 1–3, 28–9, bearing frontispieces and title-pages, and pl. 4, with the 'Introduction' to *Innocence*, always appear on leaves with blank versos. It is notable that pl. 52 never appears on a leaf bearing another plate, pre-sumably because it was added to the *Songs* only after Blake stopped printing plates back-to-back.

SIGNIFICANT VARIANTS: *N.B.* Because the *Songs* represent over 45 per cent of the total of surviving Illuminated Prints, it has not been feasible to report variants of them in as great detail as with his other works, and more judgement has had to be exercised as to whether a variant is 'significant' or not.

Pl. 9, 16: The catchwords were deleted in P because pl. 10, 17 are missing.
Pl. 10: The left child is Caucasian in early copies, Negro in late ones.
Pl. 17, ll. 31–2: 'are . . . smiles . . . beguiles' was altered to 'like . . . smile . . . beguile' in *J*.

---

[1] Leaves occasionally reversed are printed *in italics*.
[2] Pl. 6–7 with 'The Ecchoing Green'; pl. 13–14 with 'The Little Boy lost' and 'The Little Boy found'; pl. 16–17 with 'Cradle Song'; pl. 20–21 with 'Night'; pl. 30–31 with the 'Intro-duction' to *Experience* and 'Earth's Answer'; and pl. 35–36 with 'The Little Girl Found'.
[3] Pl. (15, 9) (10, 54) with 'The Little Black Boy'; pl. (27, 22) (23, 53) with 'Spring'; and pl. (26, 34) (35–6) with 'The Little Girl Lost'.

Pl. 21, l. 48: 'As I' was altered to 'And' in Q.

Pl. 32, l. 5: 'sung' was mended to 'sang' in Z.

Pl. 34–6 were issued with *Innocence* in early copies but with *Experience* after about 1794.

Pl. 42, l. 12: '& what' was altered to 'Formed thy' in P and 'forged thy' in Malkin (1806).

Pl. 52 is not in the earliest copies of the *Songs* (*A–D, F–H*).

Pl. 53–4 were ordinarily issued with *Innocence*, but in very late copies they were moved to *Experience*.

Pl. a is found only with early copies of the *Songs* (*B–D*).

Pl. b is found only in posthumous pulls.

See also the Colouring variants.

ERRATA: 'is' for 'are' (pl. 9, l. 16); 'moves' for 'move' (pl. 20, l. 11); 'head . . . bed' for 'heads . . . beds' (pl. 20, ll. 23–4); 'fo[r]lorn' (pl. 26, l. 5); 'controll' (pl. 30, l. 8).

Pl. 1. COMBINED TITLE-PAGE. DESIGN: Below the sub-title lies a nude woman with her head twisted to face the viewer, and above her a naked man with leaves around his loins cowers away from flames surging from the right. To the right of the first 'Of' above flies a bird, and on the first 'S' of 'SONGS' are two tiny figures.

COLOURS: The FLAMES are sometimes strangely Blue (O^b, *W*), Green (*W*), or strong Purple (Z).

VARIANT: In some copies (*B–D, e*), the colouring makes the woman face down.

Pl. 2. *INNOCENCE*, FRONTISPIECE. DESIGN: A shepherd in tights holding a pipe in his hands leads his grazing flock through a forest and glances upward at a naked boy on a cloud among the trees.

COLOURING: The SHEPHERD'S TIGHTS are shades of Green (A, D, *C*, *U*, *AA*), Yellow (B, I, *E*), Blue (C, J, L, O–P, *B, D, R–T, V–W, Y*), Pink (E, G, M, Q, *F, I, J, L, P, X*), Brown (F, S, *A*), Red (K, N, *Z*), and Orange (R, T, *Z*), and the CLOUD is sometimes Pink (A, F, M, *A, F, L, S, V, AA*), Blue like a patch of sky (B–C, G, N, P–Q, T, *B, E, L, U, Z–AA*), Yellow (K, R, W, *Y*), Purple (*C–D*), or Red (*Y*). The TREE is once Blue (I).

VARIANTS: The shepherd has acquired a belt in *E*, and the head of a sheep has been added between the shepherd and the tree to our right in *T*.

Pl. 3. *INNOCENCE*, TITLE-PAGE. DESIGN: Between 'Innocence' and 'The Author . . .', in the bottom left, a woman in a kind of mob cap and a long dress sitting in a chair shows a book to a small boy and girl at her knees (similar figures appear on pl. 4 and on *All Religions are One* [?1788] pl. 8). To the right is a broken ?apple-tree (with '1789' to the right), on the 'I' leans a tiny man with a wide hat playing a pipe (a similar figure appears on *America* [1793] pl. 18), on 'ONG' are ?three other tiny figures, and from the letters of 'SONGS' luxuriate plant-like flourishes.

COLOURING: The WOMAN'S DRESS is shades of Blue (A–B, K, M, Q, *S*, *Y, U*), Purple (C, I, L, *A, F, R, T, V–X, Z*), Brown (D, G, N–O, S, *E*), Yellow

(E, *C*, *J*, *L*), Pink (F, P, T), Green (J, *AA*), Grey (*B*, *D*), and Orange (*I*, *P*);
the LEFT CHILD is in Blue (G, N, P–Q, *C*, *I*, *J*, *L*, *W–X*), Green (J, T, *U*, *Z–AA*),
Grey (K, *T*), Brown (M, *E*), Yellow (*D*), and Red (*T*); the RIGHT CHILD is in
Blue (C, F, I, P, *I–J*, *L*, *V–W*, *Z*), Pink (G, K, N–O, *P*, *U*), Purple (I–J),
Brown (M, *C*, *E*, *X*), Green (Q), Orange (T), Yellow (*B*, *F*, *T*, *AA*), or Red
(*T*); and the SKY is partly Yellow (A, J, O, Q, S–T, *L*, *V–W*, *AA*), Pink
(D, K–M, O, *E*, *P*, *S*, *U*, *X*, *AA*), Purple (J, Q, *W*), Red (L, *L*, *V*, *T*), Green
(*E*), Orange (*J*, *Z–AA*), Magenta (*AA*), and Brown (*X*).

Variant: In copy M is an old inscription beneath the imprint: 'who was
deranged in his Intellects'.

NOTE: For the 'Motto to the Songs of Innocence & of Experience', see
Notebook p. 101.

Pl. 4. 'Introduction'. DESIGN: On each side of the text are inter-twining
vines forming sets of four tiny vignettes. Those on the left represent, from
top to bottom, (1) a seated adult showing a book to a child (as in pl. 3);
(2) a walking naked figure (in the position of 'Albion rose' [?1796]); (3)
a standing man looking down at ?sheep (like pl. 5 reversed); and (4) ?a
woman looking down at a cradle (like pl. 17 reversed). The vignettes on the
right represent (1) a standing man; (2) a man reading; (3) a walking person;
and (4) ?a seated couple.

COLOURING: The designs are so small that they are never coloured
distinctly.
NOTE: Title: The MS of the 'Introduction', supposed (probably erroneously)
to be by Blake, was offered in Quaritch's *General Catalogue* (1880), lot 12,804
(with other works from the Collection of a friend of Blake), for £10, but it is
UNTRACED.

Pl. 5. 'The Shepherd'. DESIGN: Up the right margin grows a tree, and below
the text stands an adolescent shepherd, with tights and a crook, looking
over a densely packed grazing flock (a similar scene appears on pl. 4,
reversed). In the background are forested hills, to the left is a large, exotic,
soaring bird, and in the centre are three or more small birds.

COLOURING: The SHEPHERD'S CLOTHES are Green (A, G, *D*, *R*), Blue
(B, E, I, K–L, N, P–Q, S–T, *B*, *F*, *I–J*, *L*, *P*, *T–T*), Yellow (C, D, J, *A*, *AA*),
Brown (D, *E*), Grey (F, *S*), Orange (M), Pink shirt (O), or Red (*Z*); and the
SKY, normally partly Yellow (A, D–E, J–Q, S, *B*, *L*, *R–S*, *W*, *T*) and Pink
(B, F, J–K, M, O–Q, S, *E–F*, *I–J*, *L*, *R*, *U–V*), is sometimes Purple (E, *D*,
T–U, *T*, *Z*), Red (L), Brown (*A*), Green (*P*), Magenta (*P*), or Orange (*S*).

VARIANTS: The background hills have been made into sky in *A*, *L*, and
there is a sunrise in copies S, X, *Z–AA*.

Pl. 6. 'The Ecchoing Green' (pl. 1). DESIGN: Above the text is a large tree
with a circular bench round it, on which sit two men with flat hats (the one
at the left with a child at his knees) and two women, each with two children
at her knees. To the left of the tree are two boys hitting a ball, while at the
right walk three more boys.

Beside the text are flourishing tendrils with ?grapes and a flying, fork-tailed bird, to the left of the first stanza is a boy with a cricket-bat, and to the right another runs after a hoop.

COLOURING: The LEFT WOMAN'S DRESS is Yellow (A, E, P, *B*, *T*, *V*, *Y*), Green (C, G, I–J, T, *A*, *E–F*), Pink (D, K–N, Q, S, *I*, *P*, *R–S*, *U*, *AA*), Blue (*B*, *J*, *L*), Red (*X*, Harvard pull), or Brown (*Z*); and the RIGHT WOMAN'S Magenta (A), Purple (B, J, T, *C–D*, *T–U*, *W*, *Z–AA*), Blue (C, I, K–M, Q, S, *F*, *I*, *P*, *R–S*, *X*), Yellow (D, N), Red (E), Pink (G, I, P, *J*, *L*, *V*, *Y*), Brown (*A*), Grey (*B*), or Red (*E*). In most coloured copies (A, C, G, I–J, L–N, P–Q, S–T, *A–E*, *I–J*, *L*, *P*, *R–AA*, Harvard pull), the trousers of some boys, particularly those at the bottom, are coloured differently from their shirts (which are usually uncoloured).

VARIANTS: Occasionally the boy at the far right is painted out with Green (e.g. E), and the catchword is painted over (e.g. P).

Pl. 7. 'The Ecchoing Green' (pl. 2, INCIPIT: 'They laugh at our play . . .'). DESIGN: A large vine growing from the bottom right corner borders the bottom and sides of the text, which is at the top. To the left of the text a boy stretches upward towards an enormous bunch of grapes, while a second boy lying on the branch beneath the text holds down another bunch of grapes to a girl in a flat hat below (the last two figures are echoed in *Marriage* [?1790–3] pl. 2). This girl is the last of a procession across the bottom of the page consisting of (from left to right) a girl, a boy with a large kite, a boy with a cricket-bat, a man in a large hat pointing left with his right hand, a small child, a woman carrying a baby, a boy in a hat, and the grape-receiver.

COLOURING: The MAN is dressed in Brown (A–D, K, T, *A*, *C–D*, *V*, *X*, *Z–AA*, Harvard pull), Blue (E, L, *E*, *I*, *T*), Grey (*G*, J, M, P–Q, *L*, *P*, *U*, *Y*), Green (N, S, *J*, *R–S*, *W*, *Y*), or Yellow (*B*), and the SKY is partly Yellow (A–B, D, G, L, N, P, S, *A–B*, *D*, *R*, *T*, *V*), Purple (B, E, J, T, V, *A*, *X*), Pink (D–E, N, S, *E*, *P*), Orange (L, P, S, *R–S*), Brown (*A*), and Red (*C*).

VARIANTS: The top left boy has a belt in N, the children at the bottom right are carrying grapes in *W–X*, and in l. 17 the first 'Such' is not visible in *J*.

Pl. 8. 'The Lamb'. DESIGN: Sparsely leaved trees on each side arch over the text, beneath which are a thatched barn at the right with two doves on the crest, a large flock of sheep, and a small naked boy holding his hands out to a lamb.

COLOURING: The THATCHED ROOF, normally of course shades of Yellow or pale Brown, is occasionally Green (C, G, I), and the SKY above it is often vivid with Purple (A–C, E, J, M, T, *C–D*, *F*, *L*, *V–AA*), Orange (A, *L*, *S*), Pink (F, I, O, Q, *I–J*, *P*, *U–W*), Green (I, N, *E*, *S*), Yellow (J, L–M, *P*, *X*), and Red (L, N).

Pl. 9. 'The Little Black Boy' (pl. 1). DESIGN: Above the text is a large tree, beneath which sits a dark woman in a skirt bending over a dark child who points up with his left hand. On the horizon at the right is the rising sun.

COLOURING: The MOTHER and CHILD are uniformly dark shades of Brown or Grey; the SKIRT, often uncoloured, is sometimes Blue (C, G, *Z*), Pink (E),

Yellow (F, *F*), Brown (N–O, S, *A, J, L, P*), or Grey (*E, R, T, V*); and the sky, normally sunrise Yellow (A–B, E, G, I–J, L, O–P, T, *A–E, L, P, V–X, AA*) or Pink (C–D, F, I–J, N, S, *F, I–J, R–U, X–Y*), is sometimes Black (D), Red (K, P, *W, Z*), Brown (K), Orange (L, *C, L*), Purple (P, *A*), or Magenta (*AA*).

VARIANT: The catchword is scratched from the paper in P, because pl. 10 (to which it refers) is missing in this copy.

Pl. 10. 'The Little Black Boy' (pl. 2, INCIPIT: 'For when our souls . . .').
DESIGN: Beneath a tree arching under the text from the right sits a bearded, Christ-like shepherd with a crook; he is looking down at a naked child with clasped hands by his knees. Behind is another naked child and a flock of grazing sheep, and at the foot there seems to be a stream.

COLOURING: The LITTLE ENGLISH BOY at Christ's knee is uniformly Caucasian-Pink or once (*E*) Caucasian-Blue; the LEFT CHILD is generally Caucasian-Pink in early copies, evidently representing them 'When I from black and he from white cloud free' (l. 23), but he is Negro-Grey or Negro-Brown in most late copies (F, L–O, Q, S, *E, I–J, L, P, R–Y*). CHRIST'S ROBE, usually uncoloured or White, is occasionally coloured palely in Yellow (A, T, *R*), Grey (*J*), Green (*U*), Blue (*Y, AA*), Purple (*Z*), or Red (Juel-Jensen pull), and the sky is often partly Yellow (B–C, I–K, M–N, *E, L, R, V, X–Y*), Purple (C, E, I, *F, L*), Pink (D–E, G, J–K, N, Q, S, *J, X*), Red (L–M, *R–S, Y*), Orange (L, T, *L*), or Green (*L*).

VARIANTS: In early copies, the left-hand child is coloured as a Caucasian, and in later copies as a Negro (as above). Christ has been given a halo in some late copies (K, O–P, *D, P, S, V, Y, AA*). ll. 27–8 are underlined in Grey wash in K.

Pl. 11. 'The Blossom'. DESIGN: From the bottom right corner springs a huge, flame-like plant, on whose flourishing branches above the text play six naked winged children (two of them kissing) and a larger, clothed, winged figure bending over a baby.

COLOURING: The FLAME-PLANT, normally Green (A–C, E, J, L, T, *C–D, J, T–U*) or Yellow (D, F, K, S, *E, R, U, Z–AA*), is often strangely Purple (G, J, N, *J*), Pink (I, O–P, *F, S–V, X, AA*), Blue (L, P, *I, T–U, X–Y*), Orange (L), Magenta (M), Grey (Q, *B, J, P*), Brown (*A*), or Red (*L, W, Y–Z*). The LARGE ANGEL is clothed in Blue (B, Q, T, *X*), Pink (C, E–F, K, S, *I, R, U–V*), Green (G, I, L, N, *A, E, P, Y–AA*), Orange (M), or Yellow (*B, L, T, W*), and the sky is often partly Yellow (G, J, L, N–O, Q, *B, I–J, L, P, T–V, Y*), Purple (*I*), Orange (L, M, *I, V*), or Pink (*E*).

VARIANTS: The sun is visible at the top left in copy *T*, sunrise colours are seen in N and *U*, and the larger angel has a halo in *X, Z*.

Pl. 12. 'The Chimney Sweeper'. DESIGN: Beside and between the stanzas of text are flourishes as of branches, and below the text is a very small design of an adult in a long robe at the bottom right helping a child to rise from the Black earth, while to the left are ?nine naked boys running and fighting joyously.

COLOURING: The design is so small that it is rarely coloured distinctly.
VARIANT: The angel has a halo in *W–X, Z*.

392 I. WRITINGS Songs of Innocence and of Experience, no. 139

Pl. 13. 'The Little Boy lost.' DESIGN: Above the text is a large tree, beneath which a boy in a long dress walks left with outstretched arms towards a triangular gleam.

On each side of both stanzas floats an angel, and another pair (making six in all) floats beneath the text.

COLOURING: The BACKGROUND is uniformly dark, ordinarily Grey (A, E–F, L, O, Q, S–T, X, *A–F, I–J, L, R–S, V, X, Z*) or Brown (B–C, E–G, K, M, *Y, AA*), but sometimes Blue (D, S, *P, AA*), Green (I, N, *X*), Orange (K), or Pink (K), and the LITTLE BOY'S DRESS, usually uncoloured or White, is sometimes Pink (B, G, I, T, *T*), Yellow (C), Blue (P), or Grey (Q, *E, S, V, Y–AA*). The GLEAM, normally uncoloured, is Red to Blue in N, S–T, *B, D–F, R–V, AA*, and the ANGELS are coloured, most frequently Pink, in A, C–G, I, M, Q, S, X, *B, E, I, L, R–S, V, Y–AA*.

VARIANTS: The background trees are formed almost entirely by the colouring and are therefore various in shape; the gleam is often greatly expanded; and the boy is given a hat in coloured copies.

NOTE: The poem is sung in the *Island in the Moon* (?1784) p. 14.

Pl. 14. 'The Little Boy found'. DESIGN: Above the text, a Christ-like figure with a halo walks through a forest of huge trees leading by the wrist a small boy with a hat or halo.

To the right of the text floats a figure with outstretched arms.

COLOURING: The BACKGROUND is dark, usually Grey (A, E, Q, S–T, X, *C, F, J, L, R, V*), or Brown (B–D, F–G, K–L, *B, T, Y*), but it is sometimes Green (N–O, S, *S, X*), Blue (O, *X*), or Yellow (*X*). CHRIST'S CLOTHES are usually uncoloured or White but are occasionally pale Yellow (F), Grey (O, *E, T, V, Y*), Blue (*P, AA*), or Purple (*T*), and the BOY'S CLOTHES are somewhat more frequently palely coloured Pink (B, G, I, T, *T*), Yellow (C, F), Grey (E, O, *E, V, Y, AA*), Blue (*P, S, AA*), or Green (*Z*). Christ's HALO, often scarcely visible in early copies, in late copies is Brown (K), Pink (N, *V*) Gold (O–Q, *U, AA*), Red (*J, L, S, W–Y*), and Orange (*Z*).

VARIANTS: The background trees, being formed almost entirely by the colouring, differ in each copy. The bottom angel has a halo in *AA*.

Pl. 15. 'Laughing Song'. DESIGN: Above the text is a long table with, on the viewer's side, a woman (at the left) and a man with wineglasses seated on low-backed chairs at the ends and, in the centre, a standing man holding aloft his hat and glass. Across the table are five seated women, the ones at the ends with hats, and in the background is a forest.

Beneath the text are birds and a flourishing vine.

COLOURING: Of the persons on the viewer's side of the table, the SEATED WOMAN at the left is dressed in Green (A, C, E–G, *B, F*), Purple (B, *W, Z*), Blue (F, *E^a, L, P, S*), Yellow (K–L, Q, *A, C–D, Y*), Magenta (M, *R*), Red (N), Brown (O), Pink (P, *E^b, J, T, V, X*), Grey (S, *U*), or Orange (*AA*); the STANDING MAN'S TIGHTS are Magenta (A), Pink (B, L, *L, S, U*), Blue (C, F, N–Q, *E^a, I–J, R, X–Y*), Red (D–E, G, I, K, *A–D, Z*), Green (D, *V, AA*), Orange (M, S, *E^b, AA*), Yellow (*B, D, F, P*), Grey (*T*), and Purple (*W*); and the SEATED MAN at the right has tights of Blue (A, D, F–G, K–M, P, *B–E^a, V*),

Yellow (B, E^a, R), Red (C, E, N, S, *J*, *Y*), Green (I, *A*, *F*, *AA*), Brown (O, *X*), Pink (Q, *P*), Orange (E^b, *L*, *S*, *W*), and Grey (*T*).

VARIANTS: The seated man at the right faces the standing man rather than the table in *T*, *X*, and the hair of the woman seated to the left is altered in L–M, E^a, B.

NOTE: An earlier version, called 'Song 2d by a Young Shepherd', was copied about 1787 in *Poetical Sketches* (F)—see p. 363.

Pl. 16. 'A Cradle Song' (pl. 1). DESIGN: The only decorations are flourishing branches and leaves round the text and between stanzas; at the end of l. 4 there appears to be a tiny woman lying on a leaf with a seated one bowed above her; on 'A' leans a piper; in 'C' and 'D' are figures; to the left of ll. 5–8 is a standing figure; by ll. 9–10 is a flying one; by ll. 11–12 is a sitting one; and by ll. 21–3 is a standing one.

COLOURING: The details are so minute that they are rarely coloured very individually.

VARIANT: The catchword is scratched out on the paper in P, because pl. 17 (to which it refers) is missing in this copy.

Pl. 17. 'A Cradle Song' (pl. 2, INCIPIT: 'Wept for me...'). DESIGN: Beneath the text, a woman in a long dress and sitting in a wicker chair bends over a baby in a large hooded wicker cradle; in the background is a curtain-screen. The scene is similar to one on pl. 4.

To the left of ll. 26–8 stands a person, to the left of l. 29 there appears to be a cherub, and by the text are plant-like flourishes.

COLOURING: The WOMAN'S DRESS is Blue (A, E–F, K–L, Q, *D–E*, *S*, *W*), Red (B, D, *Y*) Pink (G, I, N–O, S–T, *I–J*, *L*, *P*, *S*, *U–V*, *X*), Purple (J, *C*, *F*, *R*, *Z–AA*), Yellow (M, X, *A*), or Green (*B*, *T*), and the CURTAIN is Green (A–B, F, T, *C–D*, *F*, *W–X*), Blue (C, G, M–O, Q, S, X, *A*, *E*, *J*, *L*, *P*, *V*, *Y–Z*), Brown (D, L, *R*, *AA*), Purple (E, *I–K*, *T*), Black (T, *I*), Grey (*B*), or Yellow (*R*). The rush FLOOR is often iridescent with Green, Blue, Brown, and Yellow, but sometimes including Purple, Orange, Red, Grey, and Pink.

VARIANT: ll. 31–2: The terminal 's' in 'smiles' and 'beguiles' and the word 'are' were deleted and 'like' was substituted for 'are' in a hand like Blake's in *J*.

Pl. 18. 'The Divine Image'. DESIGN: A huge flame-plant makes a backward 'S' from the bottom right corner, under the text, back between the third and fourth stanzas, up the right margin, and across above the title. At its extremity in the top left corner are a tiny walking woman and a floating man; before them are two more figures kneeling with clasped hands; and at the base of the plant is a standing, Christ-like figure raising from the plant with a gesture of his right hand a naked man, while a nude woman lies beneath the plant. (The fallen man and his Saviour are repeated, reversed, in *No Natural Religion* [?1788] pl. b1, and in Young's *Night Thoughts* [1797] p. 90.)

COLOURING: The FLAME-PLANT, normally Green (A–E, G, K, M, T, *B*, *D*, *U–V*) or Yellow (I–J, N, P–Q, X, *A*, *C*, *E–F*, *I–J*, *L*, *T–U*, *X–AA*), is sometimes oddly Brown (J, O, T), Orange (L, *S*, *U*), Pink (*S*, *U*), Red

(P, W–Z), Purple (R), or Blue (W–X). The figures are so small that they are rarely coloured with much individuality.

VARIANTS: The CHRIST-LIKE FIGURE at the bottom has a halo in copies Q, S–T, S, V, X–Y, and a stream has been added at the bottom in T.

Pl. 19. 'Holy Thursday'. DESIGN: Above the title, nine pairs of tiny boys walk to the right behind two adults, one bearing a mace, while below the text seven pairs of girls walk to the left behind a man.

Above and below each line of text is luxuriant foliage.

COLOURING: The children are uncoloured in early copies (C, E, G, A–D, F, M, O, Q), but in later copies they are not only 'in red ⌊*rarely*⌋ & blue & green' (l. 2) but also in Yellow, Purple, Brown, Orange, Grey, and Pink.

VARIANT: l. 6: When the text was clarified in Q, the second 'a' of 'radiance' was altered, presumably accidentally, to an 'e', making it 'radience'.

NOTE: The poem was sung in the *Island in the Moon* (?1784) p. 14.

Pl. 20. 'Night' (pl. 1). DESIGN: Up the right margin grows a tree with three tiny winged persons and two birds on it, and at the base, apparently in a cave, lies a lion. In the left margin are ?four more tiny winged figures and the moon.

COLOURING: There is rarely more colouring than Green for foliage and shades of Blue or Grey for the sky.

VARIANTS: In coloured copies stars are often added, in F a moth was added in the left margin, and in copies J and T the catchword was covered by the colouring.

Pl. 21. 'Night' (pl. 2, INCIPIT: 'When wolves and tygers . . .'). DESIGN: To the right of the text are leafy branches, and below the text are five figures, three abreast on the left talking toward two others, one of whom points toward the three.

COLOURING: In late copies were added stars (e.g. T–U, W–Z) and haloes for all the figures (K–Q, T, J, Q, U–Y, AA). In copy B, it is not night. In copy Q, l. 48 is clarified in ink and altered to read 'And guard'.

Pl. 22. 'SPRING' (pl. 1). DESIGN: Above the text, a woman with ?coiled hair and a long gown sits beneath a spreading tree and holds on her knees a naked baby who is reaching towards a nearby flock of sheep.

Beneath the text is flourishing foliage with, to the right, two winged figures on it, one seated playing a pipe and one reclining. The first is apparently 'Sound[*ing*] the Flute' as in l. 1.

COLOURING: The MOTHER'S DRESS is Magenta (A, Y), Blue (B, O, T, I, L), Yellow (C, G, I–J, L–M, R–S, A, D, R), Green (D, F, U), Brown (E, K, B), Pink (F, N, P–Q, C, J, P, S, V, X), Purple (J [skirt], E, W, Z–AA), or Lavender (T), and the SKY, usually partly sunrise Yellow (A–B, D, G, J, N–O, Q–R, T, A–D, J, L, S–T, V–X, AA), or Pink (B–C, E, J, N–Q, T, A–B, D–E, I, P, R–S, X–Y), is sometimes Brown (K), Red (L, S, L, U–V), Magenta (M), Purple (P, U), (R, J, S, Z). The SHEEP are once Pink and Gold (Z).

VARIANTS: The woman's hair is represented differently in E, G, J, Q, T, *S*, *V*, *Z*; sheep were added in O, P, *T*; and there are vines (*R*) or wheat tendrils (S) beside the top design twice.

Pl. 23. 'Spring' (pl. 2, INCIPIT: 'Little Girl . . .'). DESIGN: Beneath the text, a naked baby between two sheep fondles a lamb.

To the right of the text are large ornamental flourishes bearing two winged figures, the top one standing and the bottom one sitting with bowed head.

COLOURING: The SKY, normally partly Yellow (A–B, J, N, R, *E, L, T*) and Pink (A, I, Q–R, T, *F, I, L*), is sometimes Purple (B–C, F, J, *A*), Orange (*R, T*), or Magenta (*P*).

VARIANT: There is a rainbow over the text in *AA*.

Pl. 24. 'Nurse's Song'. DESIGN: By the title and to the right of the text are luxuriant branches; a tiny figure climbs the 'N'; two more are on the 'S'; two others lie on the descender of the 'g'; another sits on a flourish above 'e's'; after l. 2 is a tiny figure; and to the right of ll. 7–13 is a weeping willow bending over a pool.

Below the text, a tree at the left arches over a seated woman reading a book and seven children running in a circle with joined hands. In the background are low hills meeting in a valley.

COLOURING: In early copies, all the tiny figures are uncoloured; in later ones the NURSE at the bottom is dressed in Purple (B–C, E, I–J, T, X, *C, R, V, X, Z–AA*), Brown (D, G, O–P, S, *W*), Pink (K, Q), Orange (L [skirt],*P*), Blue (M–N, *A, D, F, I–J, S, U, T*), Grey (R, *B, T*), or Yellow (*E, L*), and the SKY, especially in the valley, is often partly sunset-Yellow (A–B, D, G, J–M, Q–R, X, *A, D, I, S, V, X, Z*), Pink (C, I, N, R, X, *E, L, X*), Brown (D), Orange (J, O, Q, T, *B, S*), or Red (M, *D*).

NOTE: A variant of the poem was sung as 'my mothers song' in the *Island in the Moon* (?1784) p. 14.

Pl. 25. 'Infant Joy'. DESIGN: From the bottom right corner grow two enormous blossoms: one closed in the right margin, and one open above the text and containing a child with moth wings standing before a seated woman in a long dress with a baby in her lap.

COLOURING: The BLOSSOMS, ordinarily conventional shades of Red (B–F, I, K–Q, S–T, *A–C, J, L, P, R–S, U–W, T–AA*), Yellow (J), or Ochre (*T*), are sometimes strangely Blue (A, G, X, *D–F, I, X*). The MOTHER'S DRESS is Green (A–D, F–G), Blue (E, J–L, N, *J, L, S–T, V–W, T*), Yellow (I, P–Q, S, *A, E–F, P, R, Z*), Purple (M, *D*), Pink (O, X, *I, AA*), Brown (T), or Red (*X*); the ANGEL'S DRESS is Pink (A, G), Blue (B, F, T), Green (C, E, *D, AA*), Yellow (D, K–L, N, *B, V, Z*), Brown (S, *T*), or Grey (*X*); its WINGS are sometimes Yellow, Blue, Brown, or Pink (I, L, P, S, *B–C,P, X*); and the SKY is often partly Brown (K, N), Pink (N, R, *E, V, X*), Yellow (O, R, *E, J, L, S–V, X–T*), Orange (R, *I, S*), Green (R), or Purple (T, *U*).

VARIANTS: The angel has a halo in *T, Z*, and a Green plant was added at the top right in *X*.

Pl. 26. 'A Dream'. DESIGN: Round the text is luxuriant foliage, and in the bottom right corner a tree-trunk outlines a tiny man in a broad-brimmed hat carrying a tall staff to which a lantern is fastened at the top. On the first two letters of the title are reclining figures, and beneath the 'e' of 'Dream' there seems to be a floating figure.

COLOURING: The details are too small to admit of much individual colouring.

VARIANTS: Stars were added in some late copies (e.g. T, *T–U*, $\mathcal{Z}$); in l. 14 'near' did not print in copy P; and the watchman has lost his right arm and lantern in T.

Pl. 27. 'On Anothers Sorrow'. DESIGN: In the bottom left margin a tiny figure playing a pipe leans against a thin tree which twines up round another tree in which a second tiny figure is climbing; at the top are two other figures reaching upwards. In the right margin is a bird and a thin tree twined with a luxuriantly bearing grape-vine.

COLOURING: The tiny details are rarely coloured with much individuality.

VARIANT: In l. 31, the last word, 'tear' (which extends into the right margin), was defectively etched; it scarcely printed in I, E, P, T, was covered by a leaf in L, and had to be darkened in O.

Pl. 28. *EXPERIENCE*, FRONTISPIECE. DESIGN: The whole page is a design of a shepherd in knee-length tights who holds the hands of a winged child sitting on his head. (They are sketched on *Notebook* p. 74.) Round the shepherd graze sheep; a large tree forms the right and top margins, another is to the left; and a hill mounts steeply to the right.

COLOURING: The SHEPHERD'S CLOTHES are Blue (*A, D* [shirt], *E, L, S*), Yellow (*C, AA*), Green (*D* [pants], *F, H, T, $\mathcal{Z}$*), Orange (*F*), Purple (*I, R, U, W*), Pink (*O–P, X*), Red (*U, V*, Blunt pull), and Magenta (*Y*); and the SKY is usually partly Orange (*A, E–F, I, L, P, R–S, V, X–Y*, Blunt pull), Pink (*B–C, H*), Yellow (*C, E, H–I, O–P, R–W, Y*), Brown (*C, $\mathcal{Z}$*), Purple (*D*), Red (*E–F, U, W*), or Green (*F*). The SHEEP are once Orange (*F*) and the TREE once pale Blue (*Y*).

VARIANTS: There is a sun in *A, E, O, S, W*; the child has a halo in $\mathcal{Z}$; and in *S* the top left corner is a heavy Brown, as if it were a branch or a cave mouth, and something like a small branch descends above the cherub's right hand.

Pl. 29. *EXPERIENCE*, TITLE-PAGE. DESIGN: Below 'EXPERIENCE', an adolescent boy and girl bend in mourning on either side of an aged couple stretched rigidly on a kind of couch; behind them are rigidly rectilinear shapes like a stone tomb, with '1794' on the right. (The design is sketched, reversed, on *Notebook* p. 43.)

To the left of 'of' floats a woman in a long dress, and, to the right, in mirrored position, is a naked man. On the first 'S' of 'SONGS' is a tiny figure in a long robe, and round 'SONGS' are flowers, including lilies and a thistle, and flourishes.

COLOURING: The BOY mourning at the left is dressed in Blue (*A–B, E, I–J, L, N–O, R–S, T²–U, W–$\mathcal{Z}$*), Green (*C, V*), Purple (*D, AA*), Yellow (*F*), Magenta (*H*), Pink (*I, N, P*), or Red (*T¹*); and, at the right, the GIRL'S DRESS is Yellow (*A, E*), Green (*B, D, H, T¹, U, Z*), Pink (*C, I-J, L, N-P, S, W-T*), Red (*F*), Blue (*R*), Purple (*T², AA*), or Lavender (*V*). The CORPSES are uniformly uncoloured or a dead-Grey. The COUCH is sometimes Grey (*A, T¹*), Blue (*I, S, T*), or Purple (*N-O, R, W*); and the WALL behind is Yellow (*A-C*), Grey (*E, H-I, N, S-T¹, X*), Brown (*R*), Blue (*T*), or Green (*Z*).

VARIANTS: The date is coloured over in *A-B, D*, and the hair of the mourning girl is long (not in a bun) in *H*.

Pl. 30. 'Introduction'. DESIGN: The text is on a cloud in a starry sky, below which a nude woman leans on a pillow on a couch with swirling drapery which in turn is on a cloud. (The design is sketched, reversed, on *Notebook* p. 57.)

COLOURING. The SKY surrounding the clouds is uniformly Black or dark Blue, and the COUCH is sometimes Yellow (*E, L, N, R-S, W, T, AA*), Pink (*F*), Blue (*I, O-P, V, X*), Red (*K*), or outlined in Green (*H*).

VARIANT: The woman has been given a halo in *W, T-AA*.

Pl. 31. 'Earth's Answer'. DESIGN: Below the text, an open-mouthed snake moves to the right; between and beside the stanzas is flourishing foliage; and to the right of ll. 9–11 is a great bunch of grapes.

COLOURING: The SNAKE is sometimes Blue (*F-H*), Red (*F*), Gold (*N*), or Purple (*U*).

VARIANTS: In *F*, the snake's tail rises further up the right margin; it has a circle of Brown, Purple, and White round its head in *T*; the grapes are gone in *Z*; and Mrs. Blake added rams' heads in the corners in *W*.

NOTE: 'Earths Answer' was drafted on *Notebook* p. 111.

Pl. 32. 'The Clod & the Pebble'. DESIGN: Above the text, four sheep and two oxen drink from a stream beneath a tree at the right, while beneath the text is a lily pond with a duck, two frogs, and a worm. To the right of the text is a flourishing plant.

COLOURING: The SKY is often partly Yellow (*A, E, I, K-L, N-O, U-V, X, AA*), Pink (*C, E, L, O, S*), Green (*C, K, U*), Orange (*I-J, L, S-T, V, X*), or Red (*K, N, U*).

VARIANTS: There is a sunset in copy *A*, and in copy *Z* when the text was clarified in Red ink 'sung' in l. 5 was mended to 'sang'.

NOTE: The poem was drafted without title on *Notebook* p. 115.

Pl. 33. 'Holy Thursday'. DESIGN: Above the title, a woman looks down as if in horror at a naked dead child (very like that in *America* [1793] pl. 11) lying rigidly on the ground. Over her arches a tree from the right, and in the distance are a lake and precipitous hills. (The woman is sketched, reversed, on *Notebook* p. 74.)

To the right of ll. 5–9, a child with his head in his arms stands before a kneeling woman who is being clasped by a naked child, while among foliage in the bottom right corner lies the foreshortened body of a naked male (similar in position to the figure on pl. 49).

COLOURING: The TOP MOTHER'S DRESS, uncoloured in early copies, is sometimes Red (*K*), Grey (*O, S, T*), Yellow (*R*), Blue (*V-W, AA*), or Purple

(Z); the MIDDLE MOTHER'S DRESS is Grey (B), Purple (D, W, Z, Juel-Jensen pull), Pink (E, $\mathcal{J}$, N, S–T, V, X–Y), Magenta (H), Red (K), Blue (L, P, R, AA), or Brown (O); the STANDING BOY beside her is in Blue (A, D, H, $\mathcal{J}$, N, T, V, X–Y), Grey (O–P, S), naked Pink (R), or Orange (Z); and the SKY is often partly Orange (A, F, I, L), Yellow (A, K–L, N, R), Red (E–F, K, R), Green (F, K), or Pink (H, N–O, V). The TOP BABY, ordinarily uncoloured or Grey, is twice pale Blue (V, Y).

VARIANT: Briars were drawn around the design in copy Y.

NOTE: 'Holy Thursday' was drafted on *Notebook* p. 103

Pl. 34. 'The Little Girl Lost' (pl. 1). DESIGN: In the right margin, a naked adolescent boy clasps and kisses a clothed girl who steps from him pointing toward the drooping willow above them and the exotic, fork-tailed bird above it. Up the left margin rises a sinuous vine, with a branch between l. 8 and l. 9 bearing a fork-tongued serpent.

COLOURING: The GIRL'S DRESS is Blue (A–B, F, I), Green (C–E, G, I, D, V, Y), Purple (T, R, W), Yellow (A, Z–AA), Grey (B,F), Orange (E), or Pink ($\mathcal{J}$, L, N–P, S–T, X), or Red (U). The BOY is naked-Pink in early copies (A–G, I, T, A–E, I, Z–AA), but later is dressed in Rose trousers (F), Blue ($\mathcal{J}$, O–P, R–Y), or Grey (L, N). The SKY is often partly Pink (A, F–G, F, $\mathcal{J}$, L, N, T, X), Green (B, E, T, X, AA), Purple—particularly behind the lovers (E–F, I, A, C–E, T–W, Y), Red (E–F, B–C, E, R), Brown (A, N), Yellow (B–C, F, I, N–O, V–W, AA), Orange (F, R, AA), or Ochre (O, S).

NOTE: Early copies of pl. 34–6 (A–I, T–U, X, F) are bound with *Innocence*, late ones with *Experience*.

Pl. 35. 'The Little Girl Lost' (pl. 2) and 'Found' (INCIPIT: 'Leopards, tygers play . . .'). DESIGN: Below the end of 'The Little Girl Lost' is a dense forest in which lies a girl (Lyca) leaning on her right hand.

To the right of 'The Little Girl Found' stands a tiger beneath a leafless little tree, while to the left are flourishes of a plant.

COLOURING: The GIRL'S DRESS is Green (A, E–F, F), Pink (B, G, I, T, E, I, L, N–O, S–T, V, X, AA), Brown (C), Yellow (X, B, R), Blue (U), Red (W), Magenta (Y), or Orange (Z), and the TIGER is often oddly Pink (E, D, P, X), Green (I,B, U), Red (C,E, U, Y), Blue (C, U, V–W, Y), and Purple (W).

VARIANTS: There is an extra tree in A, U, and the trees are sometimes Blue (C, I).

Pl. 36. 'The Little Girl Found' (pl. 2, INCIPIT: 'Famish'd weeping . . .'). DESIGN: To the right of the text are two enormous twining trees; beneath the text is a lioness (at the left) ridden by a naked child, whose left hand is held by a larger nude girl, while to the right a third naked child leans on a couching lion. Beside the lioness a nude woman stretches beautifully, and up the left margin is twining foliage.

COLOURING: The TREE TRUNK, which one might expect to be Brown or Black, is often Green (A–F, I, T, X, B–C,E, X) or Yellow (U), and the LIONS are occasionally iridescent (L) or spotted Red and Blue (W).

Pl. 37. 'The Chimney Sweeper'. DESIGN: Beneath the text, a Black boy bearing a Black bag on his shoulder stands at a street corner in Black snow.

He is clearly the 'little black thing among the snow Crying weep weep' (ll. 1–2). To the right of the text are foliage-like swirls.

COLOURING: The SNOW is occasionally Blue (*D*) or Gold (*X*).

VARIANT: The design is surrounded as if in a snow-cloud in *Y*.

NOTE: 'Chimney sweeper' is drafted on *Notebook* pp. 106, 103.

Pl. 38. 'Nurses Song'. DESIGN: Below the text, a woman standing in a doorway combs the hair of a standing boy; at his feet sits another child reading. On either side of them are very large plants bearing grapes, while by the title, in the right margin, and between ll. 2 and 5 are other plants.

COLOURING: The NURSE'S DRESS is Yellow (*A–B, G*), Green (*C, V*), Blue (*D, P, AA*), Ochre (*E*), Red (*H, T*¹), Pink (*I–J, L, R S, U, W–Y*), Brown (*N–O*), and Purple (*T*², *Z*); the STANDING BOY is in Blue (*A–B, C–D* plus *L, X* [shirt], *F, G–J, O, R* [pants], *S–T*¹⁻²), Yellow shirt (*D, P, R*), Brown (*L* plus *N, X* [pants], *W*), Green (*N* [shirt], *U, Y–AA*), or Pink (*P* [shirt], *V*); and the SITTING CHILD is in Blue (*A, C, G, P, S, X*), Grey (*B, N*), Purple (*D*, T², *W, Y*), Green (*E, T*¹, *U–V*), Red (*H*), Orange (*I–J*), Pink (*O, AA*), or Yellow (*R, Z*). The DOORWAY is sometimes Blue (*S, U, Z*) like the sky.

NOTE: The poem was drafted without title on *Notebook* p. 109.

Pl. 39. 'The Sick Rose'. DESIGN: From the bottom left corner grows a huge, thorny rose-bush on the branches of which, above the text, are a caterpillar and two tiny crouching women, while below the text is a large folded blossom from which emerges a tiny woman, with outspread arms, wrapped round by a worm.

COLOURING: The ROSES are fairly conventionally Red (*A, E, R, Z*), brownish-Grey (*B*), Pink (*C, I–J, L, N–P, S–X, AA*), or pinkish-Purple (*D*).

VARIANT: In *S*, there is a very thin extension of the worm to the left.

NOTE: 'The sick rose' was drafted on *Notebook* p. 107.

Pl. 40. 'The Fly'. DESIGN: Beneath the text, a woman in a mob cap bends to hold the two hands of a child who is apparently learning to walk; behind her a girl is about to hit a shuttlecock with a racquet. In the right margin are a leafless tree and one flying bird.

COLOURING: The GIRL'S DRESS is Yellow (*A, D, F, U*), Green (*C, T, V*), Pink (*E, J, M–O, R, AA*), or Brown (*P, S, W, Z*); the WOMAN'S DRESS is Purple (*A, D, U–W*), Grey (*B–C, N*), Yellow (*E, G*), Blue (*F, O, R, X*), Magenta (*H, Y*), Brown (*I, S, T, Z* [skirt]), Orange (*J*), Pink (*L, Z* [blouse]), or Green (*P, AA*); and the BABY'S DRESS, usually uncoloured or White, is occasionally Yellow (*B*), Green (*F, V, Z*), Grey (*J*), Buff (*W*), or Pink (*AA*). In most copies a CLOUD has been added behind the nurse, which is Yellow (*A–D, G, R, T, W–X*), Green (*F*), Blue (*F, T*), Ochre (*H*), Pink (*I*), Orange (*N, R*), or Brown (*T, Y*).

NOTE: The poem was drafted without title on *Notebook* p. 101.

Pl. 41. 'The Angel'. DESIGN: Beneath a tree arching from the left above the text, a woman in a belted dress lies with her head on her left hand and her right hand round the face of a standing winged child whose hands are on her arm. (The design is sketched, reversed, on *Notebook* p. 65, showing the angel without wings.) There is foliage in the right margin and by the title.

COLOURING: The WOMAN'S DRESS is Pink (*A, E, H, L, T²–U*), Green (*B–C*), Yellow (*D*), Red (*F*), Blue (*I, N–O, R, X–Y*), Brown (*T¹, V*), Purple (*W*), Grey (*Z*), or Orange (*AA*); the ANGEL'S SKIN is sometimes pale Blue (*P*), bluish-Grey (*S*), or pinkish-Purple (*W*), and his WINGS are often iridescent with Purple (*A, X*), Red (*B, D, H, P, T¹*), Blue (*B–C, H, P, W–X*), Brown (*C*), Pink (*C, K, N–O*), Yellow (*E, O, W*), and Grey (*N*), The SKY is partly Yellow (*A, C, I, N, T²*), Pink (*C, H–J, N–P, T², V, Z*), Orange (*F, R, S, X, AA*), or Red (*X*).

VARIANTS: The woman's hair is variously arranged, sometimes in a scarf (*M, T², a*), sometimes hanging long (*B–C, E, H, K, N, P*), but in later copies she was regularly given a crown which is often Gold (*D, J, L, O, R, T²–AA*). In *K* and *Z*, the angel has been given a halo.

NOTE: 'The Angel' was drafted on *Notebook* p. 103 and ll. 15–16 on pp. 111, 113.

Pl. 42. 'The Tyger'. DESIGN: In the right margin is a huge tree, and below the text stands a tiger looking left. By the title is a flying bird.

COLOURING: The TIGER is seldom coloured realistically and is sometimes (e.g. *N*) almost iridescent, with Yellow (*A, C, G, N, P, T, W–X*), Brown (*A, C, F–H, K, O, R, T, AA*), Blue (*A, C, E–H, K, N, O, T, Y*), Pink (*B, D–E, O, X*), Green (*B, E–F, O, Z*), Black (*D, L, N, T, V*), Red (*F, H–I, K, V–W, Y*), and Orange (*L, N, R–S*), and the SKY is sometimes partly Pink (*I, L, O, X*), Yellow (*I, L, V, X*), and Orange (*I*). The TREE is Blue in *V* and *Y*.

VARIANT: In copy *P*, '& what' was erased and 'Formed thy' carefully substituted in ink in l. 12 (see the reproduction in Keynes & Wolf); it was altered to 'forged thy' in Malkin (1806) (*Blake Records* [1969], 431).

NOTE: 'The Tyger' was drafted on *Notebook* pp. 108–9.

Pl. 43. 'My Pretty Rose Tree', 'Ah! Sun-Flower', 'The Lilly'. DESIGNS: To the right of 'My Pretty Rose Tree' is a branching tree, and under it is a woman lying on her left elbow with a bowed figure before her (a similar figure appears on *No Natural Religion* [?1788] pl. a9 and, reversed, on *All Religions are One* [?1788] pl. 3). Between them are ten flying birds, and below them by the title are three more.

To the left of 'Ah! Sun-Flower' is a tiny figure with long flying hair and a flowing robe, looking upward with clasped hands (perhaps the personified sunflower), and by all three poems are flourishes.

COLOURING: The KNEELING PERSON is Blue (*A–B, G, I–J, L, O, R, T²–U, W–X, Z–AA*), Grey (*C, N, S*), Green (*D, H, V*), Pink (*E*), Gold (*F*) or Orange (*P*), and the RECLINING WOMAN is Brown (*A*), Grey (*B, P, T²*), Pink (*C, I–J, L, N–O, R–T¹, U–X, AA*), Purple (*D, Z*), Green (*E*), Red (*F*), or Ochre (*H*).

VARIANT: 'The Lilly' l. 4: the last word ('bright') is below the line in the position of a catchword and is covered, presumably accidentally, by a Green flourish in copy *S*.

NOTE: 'My Pretty Rose Tree' was drafted on *Notebook* p. 115 and 'The Lilly' on p. 109 (without title).

Pl. 44. 'The Garden of Love'. DESIGN: Above the text kneel a boy and a girl, each with clasped hands, and a tonsured monk who holds an open book and gestures toward an open grave. (A large, early sketch [reversed] in McGill represents a curly-haired boy holding a handkerchief to his nose, a long-haired girl, a man not identified as a cleric, a shovel, and a *lighted* lantern; the background is indistinguishable.) In front of them is a tombstone, beside them is a window with diamond-shaped panes, and behind them is a tree. To the right of the text are two curling worms, and in the bottom margin are thorny branches.

COLOURING: The PERSONS are dressed in shades of Grey (*A, E, I–J, L, N–P, R–T, V–Z̧*), Pink (*C*), or Blue (*U, AA*), except that the MONK is some-times also in Grey (*B, D*), Brown (*C, AA*), or Black (*K*); and the BACKGROUND is Black and Brown (*B*), Grey (*D, O–P, U*), Green (*I, K–L, N, S, Z̧*), or Yellow (*U, AA*).

VARIANTS: The monk is quite bald in *A* and *V*; the window is invisible in *D–E*; there is a Black hat in *K*; and the monk's head gives off light in *U–V, X*.

NOTE: The poem was drafted without title on *Notebook* p. 115.

Pl. 45. 'The Little Vagabond'. DESIGN: Above the text, in a dense, dark forest, a bearded old man whose head gives off rays kneels with his left arm over a naked boy kneeling facing him.

Below the text is a fire, with a kneeling man in tights and a standing child to the left and a woman with two naked, clinging children to the right.

COLOURING: The OLD MAN'S ROBE is Purple (*A, J, O, R–S, X*), Gold (*I*), Red (*L, N, V*), Grey (*P, W*), Blue (*T, AA*), and the NAKED BOY before him is sometimes dressed in Grey (*A, L, N, P*), Blue (*I*), or Brown (*R*).

VARIANT: Both figures at the top are naked in *C*, and the naked boy is dressed in *A, I, L, N, P, R*.

NOTE: 'The little Vagabond' was drafted on *Notebook* p. 105.

Pl. 46. 'London'. DESIGN: Above the text, a small boy leads a blind, bearded old man on crutches past a stone wall with a door in it. (The design is sketched, reversed, on *Notebook* p. 54, and repeated, also reversed, on *Jerusalem* [1804–?20] pl. 84, where it is described as 'London blind & age-bent begging thro the Streets of Babylon', a similar man, reversed, is on *For Children* [1793] pl. 17, *America* [1793] pl. 14, 'Death's Door' in Blair's *Grave* [1808], *Job* [1826] pl. 6.)

To the right of ll. 5–12 a small boy warms his hands before a large fire.

COLOURING: The OLD MAN is in Grey (*A, E, J–K, N, P, R–S, W*), Blue (*F, K, L, O, T²–V, X–AA*), or Green (*I*); the BOY leading him is Blue (*A, T²–U*), Green (*D, F, J, V, X–AA*), Grey (*E, K, N, P, T¹*), or Pink (*W*); and the BOY by the fire is Green (*A–B, D–F, P, Z̧–AA*), Blue (*C, H, T²*), Pink (*J, U–V, Y*), or Grey (*T¹*). The WALL is Grey (*A, H–I, N, P*), Brown (*B–C, E, K–L, R–V, X–AA*), Black (*C–D*), pale Green (*D*), Yellow (*S–T¹*), and Pink (*S*).

VARIANT: In copy *K*, the doorway is the Blue of the sky.

NOTE: 'London' was drafted on *Notebook* p. 109.

Pl. 47. 'The Human Abstract'. DESIGN: In the right margin is a tree, and beneath the text crouches a bearded old man lifting a heavy rope above himself. (A similar design appears on *Urizen* [1794] pl. 28.)

COLOURING: The MAN'S CLOTHES are normally Grey (*A, E, H, J, L, N–O, S, T*², *Z–AA*) or Blue (*I, P, V–Y*), but are once brownish-Gold (*U*). The SKY is occasionally Pink (*E, V*), Ochre (*H*), Yellow (*O, W*), or Orange (*O*).

VARIANT: In *K*, a setting sun at the left sends garish Red light over the whole page.

NOTE: 'The human Image' was drafted on *Notebook* p. 107.

Pl. 48. 'Infant Sorrow'. DESIGN: In the right margin and below the text is a curtain behind a naked child on a bed; over the child a woman in a mob cap is bending with outstretched arms.

COLOURING: The WOMAN'S DRESS is Yellow (*A, I, R*), Blue (*B, U–V, Y, AA*), Brown (*C, E–F*), Pink (*D, J, O–P, W–Y*), Red (*L, S, Z*), Purple (*N*), or Green (*T*); and the CURTAINS are Blue (*A–B, D, I–J, L, N–P, S, W–X*), Ochre (*B, E*), Yellow (*C, J*), Green (*C, Z–AA*), Pink (*E, T–V*), Brown (*F*), Purple (*R*), Orange (*AA*). The rush FLOOR is often iridescent with Green, Red, Black, Yellow, Grey, Pink, Orange, and Brown, and twice (*J, W*) the woman's HAIR is Pink.

VARIANT: The woman's cap has disappeared in *J, R, W–X*.

NOTE: 'Infant sorrow' was drafted as a much longer poem on *Notebook* p. 113.

Pl. 49. 'A Poison Tree'. DESIGN: In the right margin is a leafless tree, and below the text lies a foreshortened naked man with outspread arms (similar in position to the figure on pl. 33).

COLOURING: The CORPSE, ordinarily uncoloured or shades of Grey (*A, F, N–O, R–T*¹⁻², *V–Z*) or Brown (*L*), is twice Pink (*D, P*), and once Blue (*U*). The SKY is sometimes heavy with Brown (*A–B, Z*), Purple (*C, R*), Yellow (*E*), Pink (*E, I–J, O, V, X*), Orange (*F*), or Black (*F, V*).

NOTE: The poem was drafted as 'Christian forbearance' on *Notebook* p. 114.

Pl. 50. 'A Little Boy Lost'. DESIGN: In the right margin are large plants, while beneath the text, in the left corner, is a fire before which two people crouch, with ?two smaller people behind them, ?one standing.

COLOURING: The PERSONS are most often Grey.

NOTE: The poem was drafted without title on *Notebook* p. 106.

Pl. 51. 'A Little Girl Lost'. DESIGN: In the right margin is a large tree with a few tendrils and leaves, while ?twenty-five birds fly to the left and right of ll. 1–4, between ll. 29 and 30, and between the branches of the tree. A squirrel is in the main fork of the tree.

COLOURING: Except for the birds, all copies are conventionally coloured.

VARIANT: A branch divides the page after l. 19 in copy *K*.

Pl. 52. 'To Tirzah'. DESIGN: Beneath the fruit of a tree branching from the right below the text, two standing women at the left endeavour to raise a limp, naked body, while to the right a pitcher is offered by a bearded old man on whose robe is etched vertically: 'It is Raised / a Spiritual Body' from 1 Corinthians 15: 44: 'It is sown a natural body; it is raised a spiritual body'.

COLOURING: The LEFT WOMAN'S DRESS is Pink (*E, I, K–L, N–O, R, T–U, W–X, Z*), Blue (*J, V*), Brown (*P, AA*), Grey (*S*), or Red (*Y*); the RIGHT WOMAN'S DRESS is Blue (*E, I, L, O, R, U, W–Y*), Pink (*J–K, S–T, V*), Green (*N*), Brown (*P, Z*), or Yellow (*AA*); the CORPSE, ordinarily shades of Grey (*I–J, N–O, R–S, U, W–Z*), is sometimes pale Blue (*E, K*), Brown (*L*), or Pink (*T, AA*); and the OLD MAN'S ROBE is Brown (*E, N, AA*), Blue (*I–K, V*), Grey (*L, O–P, R–U, X*), or Yellow (*W, Y*). The PITCHER is sometimes shades of Yellow (*I, K–L, O, S, U–V, Z*) and once Blue (*Y*).

NOTE: Pl. 52 is not found in the earliest copies of the *Songs* (*A–D, F–H*).

Pl. 53. 'The School Boy'. DESIGN: Below the text crouch and sit three boys playing marbles; in the left margin are twining vines with a person, a ?worm, and, at the top, a large bird; and in the right margin are larger twining vines, up which three boys are climbing, perhaps for a very large bunch of grapes, and at the top is perched a fourth boy, who is reading.

COLOURING: The BOTTOM LEFT BOYS are most frequently Blue, Green, and Yellow; the BOTTOM RIGHT BOY Pink and Blue; and the TWO LOWER CLIMBERS Pink, often naked.

NOTE: In early copies, pl. 53 was bound with *Innocence*, in late copies (*L–N, T–AA*) with *Experience*.

Pl. 54. 'The Voice of the Ancient Bard'. DESIGN: Below the text, a White-bearded harper (echoed in *Job* [1826] pl. 21) is flanked by two embracing ?children on the left, and by two children, a man, and three women standing on the right before a kneeling figure. Beside the text are tendrils.

COLOURING: The HARPER'S ROBE is Blue (F, Q, *I, O, T, Z–AA*), Grey (*I, K, M, O, X, E, P, S, V*), Yellow (*L, W*), Brown (*S, C, X*), or Purple (*R*); the THREE ADULTS on the right are dressed, from left to right, in (1) Red (A, C, F), Green (B, E, I, L–M, T, *A, C, O*), Blue (D, G, J–K, Q, *D–F, J, U–V, Y*), Brown (E, S, T), Pink (O, U, W), Purple (P, X, *B*), Orange (*I, L, P*), Yellow (*R–S, X*), Grey (*Z–AA*); (2) Brown (A, F, *A*), Yellow (B, *B, W*), Purple (C, M, *L*), Pink (E, I–L, *E, J, O, T, V, X–Y, AA*), Green (G, S, *F, Z*), Blue (O–Q, *C, I, P, R–S, U*), Orange (T, X); (3) Purple (B, I–J, L, T, *R*), Brown (C), Pink (D, G, O, S, *Z*), Green (E, K, P–Q, *C–D, F, L, T, Y, AA*), Blue (F, M, *A–B, E, I–J, O, W–X*), Yellow (X, *I, P*), Orange (*S*), Grey (*V*); and the KNEELING PERSON is in Green (A–G, T, X, *B, J, T, V*), Yellow (I–J, L, O, Q, *A, D–F*), Blue (K, P, U, *Y*), Grey (M, *AA*), Orange (S, *R*), Pink (*I, L, P, S, X*), Purple (*W*), or Brown (*Z*). The SKY is partly Purple (A, C–E, G, I–J, M, P, X, *A, F, T, V–W*), Yellow (C, I–J, M, P, *A–C, E, J, L, O, V–W, Y*), Pink (D, G, J, L, *D, F, O*), Green (K), or Orange (*J, L, W*).

VARIANTS: The third person from the right is seen in profile in copy T, and the fragment of a tree on the right is extended in copy *W*, perhaps by Mrs. Blake.

NOTE: Pl. 54 was bound with *Innocence* in early copies, with *Experience* in late copies (*O, T–AA*).

Pl. a. DESIGN: The whole page is a design of a naked man supported in the air by five naked cherubs.

COLOURING: The BACKGROUND is Yellow in *B–D*.

NOTE: The plate was only issued with a few early copies of the *Songs* (*B–D*).

Pl. b. 'A Divine Image'. DESIGN: Beneath the text, a naked kneeling man with a huge hammer is about to strike a flaming head (the sun) on an anvil at the right. (Very similar designs are on *Jerusalem* [1804–?20] pl. 36, 73.) Before l. 1 stands a figure with outstretched arms, and between stanzas is a ?vine with ?six figures by it.

NOTE: Pl. b is only known in posthumous copies and of course is not coloured.

Songs of Innocence

COPY A: BINDING: (1) Originally stabbed through three holes, about 2·2 cm from the top and 6·8, 7·6 cm apart; (2) It was later stitched into an account-book cover,[1] but the stitching had come loose by 1900 when (3) It was bound for Robert Hoe at the 'CLUB BINDERY 1900 LEON MAILLARD FINISHER', in Citron morocco inlaid with Red levant morocco borders, the edges gilt but not trimmed.

HISTORY: (1) 'Stitched into an account book cover by Blake' and 'given by Blake to his Doctor' (according to the 1897 catalogue below);[2] (2) It was apparently purchased from 'Ellis[?] / [*Catalogue*] 350[?] / From the Library of / Sir Thomas W. Hamilton [? *or* Wetherton]' (according to the erased inscription on the verso of pl. 1—for a similar name see *Thel* [E], p. 126); (3) Sold anonymously at Sotheby's, 24 Feb. 1897, lot 752, for £42 to B. F. Stevens; (4) Acquired by Robert Hoe, who added his book-plate on the first fly-leaf (which is offset on to the *third* fly-leaf), inscribed it,[2] had it bound in 1900, lent it anonymously to the Grolier Club exhibition (1905), no. 3, and sold it posthumously at Anderson's, 8 Jan. 1912, lot 452, for $665 to Graham; (5) Christine Alexander Graham added her book-plate on the first fly-leaf and sold it (as by A Maryland Lady) at Parke-Bernet, 23 Nov. 1943, lot 48, for $3,300 to G. Wells; (6) Acquired by David McC. McKell (a note in his hand says it came from the above sale), and inherited by his son (7) Dr. *David McC. McKell, Jr.*

COPY B: BINDING: (1) Bound after 1825 (the front fly-leaf is watermarked BEILK / & / KNOT / 1825), perhaps for R. H. Clarke, in Brown blind-stamped russia with 'SONGS / OF / INNOCENCE' on the front panel, g.e.; the spine was cracked by 1906 and later rebacked; (2) The volume was disbound in 1954 for the Blake Trust facsimile and later rebound in the same binding by Peter Francke.

---

[1] See its History. On the basis of evidence unknown to me, J. Sampson (ed., *Poetical Works of William Blake* [1905], 72) says it was 'Originally in worn-out red leather binding'. Perhaps the account-book cover was red leather.

[2] The 1897 description is echoed in Hoe's note on the second fly-leaf: 'This is the copy colored by Blake & given by him to his physician. It has been preserved loose between leather covers until I bound it [*in 1900*]. R. H.' The identity of Blake's physician is not known; Messrs. Birch and Long are possibilities.

HISTORY: (1) Acquired by 'R H Clarke' (the son of Hayley's friend J. S. Clarke [1765?–1834]), who signed the first fly-leaf in ink and pencil; (2) Sold anonymously at Sotheby's, 26 May 1906, lot 267 (the plates unnumbered, the binding 'cracked'), for £83 to Robson; (3) Acquired by W. E. Moss, who added his book-plate, lent it to the Manchester exhibition (1914), no. 148, and sold it at Sotheby's, 2 March 1937, lot 143, for £750 to Rosenbach for (4) Mr. LESSING J. ROSENWALD, who wrote a note saying that it was disbound (and subsequently rebound) by Peter Francke when it was sent to Paris for the Blake Trust facsimile (1954), and who allowed it to be reproduced again in 1971.

COPY C: BINDING: 'BOUND BY F. BEDFORD' before 1875 in Green levant morocco inset with Brown morocco, t.e.g.

HISTORY: (1) It was 'executed' for Samuel Rogers[1] (1763–1855), who added his book-plate on a fly-leaf; (2) Acquired by 'Henry Rogers' (who predeceased Samuel), who added his book-plate on the verso of the fly-leaf bearing his brother's book-plate; (3) Sold anonymously in its present binding by a relative and representative of the family[1] at Sotheby's, 8 June 1875, lot 20, for £27. 10s. to Bain (apparently for Pearson[1]); (4) Offered by Quaritch (Feb. 1915), lot 4,511, for £220, and sold from the catalogue (the penultimate fly-leaf is inscribed '$900.00 Quaritch') on 15 April 1915 (according to a letter from the purchaser now with the book) to (5) George Herbert Palmer, who lent it to the Fogg Exhibition (1924), described it in his catalogue (1923), and added his book-plate, together with another presenting it (in 1924) to (6) WELLESLEY COLLEGE.

COPY D: BINDING: (1) Originally stabbed through three holes, 2·7 cm from the top, 4·9, 6·4 cm apart; (2) Probably later bound after 1801 (the date on one fly-leaf); (3) 'BOUND BY F. BEDFORD' in Citron levant morocco inlaid with Red and Green morocco, g.e.

HISTORY: (1) 'Coloured by Blake for Flaxman' (according to the 1876 catalogue below—see *Songs* [O], p. 419) and acquired by Flaxman's wife, who signed the third fly-leaf ('A Flaxman') probably not long after 1801 (the watermark date in the fly-leaf), sold among the John Flaxman Collection at Christie's, 26 April 1876,[2] lot 4, for £30 to Pearson, who evidently inscribed the second fly-leaf 'bought at Flaxmans Sale at Christies . . .' and had it bound; (2) Offered by John Pearson on 6 March 1883 (in a letter now with *Songs* [O]), lent for the Muir facsimile (1884), and disposed of at his sale at Sotheby's, 7 Nov. 1916, lot 41, for £205 to Sawyer; (3) Offered in an American Catalogue for $2,000 (according to a catalogue clipping now with *Innocence* [C]); (4) Acquired by Herschel V. Jones, and bequeathed to his daughter (5) Miss Tessie Jones, who bequeathed it in 1968 to (6) The PIERPONT MORGAN LIBRARY.

COPY E: BINDING: (1) Originally stabbed through three holes, 4·6 cm

---

[1] According to R. H. Shepherd ('Blake's Songs of Innocence' *Academy*, viii [June 1875], 636), who was shown the book by John Pearson in June 1875.

[2] Not 'June 1875', as in Keynes & Wolf.

from the top, 4·3, 3·5 cm apart, into Buff paper covers (still with the plates);
(2) It was later laid between the leaves of a volume of Scott's *Geography*
which bore a leather label: 'C. Newman Born July 21st 1804'; the plates
were still stitched in 1899, but (3) By 1926 they had become separated, and
the string has now disappeared.

HISTORY: (1) Apparently acquired by 'C. Newman Born July 21st 1804',
for whom it was put (with a leather label bearing this information)[1] 'between
the pages of another book [*Scott's* GEOGRAPHY[1]]' (according to the 1926
catalogue below); (2) Acquired 'at Leicester in or about the year 1899' by
Charles R. Robson, then stitched in the order of the pencil numbers (according to the 1926 catalogue), and sold by him at Sotheby's, 15 Dec. 1926, lot 612
(then unstitched), for £450 to 'Spencer v[ia] Q[uaritch]' (according to the
marked Quaritch file); (3) Acquired by Owen D. Young, who lent it to the
Fogg exhibition (1930), and gave it with Dr. A. A. Berg on 5 May 1941 to
(4) The Berg Collection of the NEW YORK PUBLIC LIBRARY (see *America* [L],
p. 104).

COPY F: BINDING: (1) Originally stabbed through three holes, 5·7 and
5·9 cm apart; (2) Interleaved and bound in contemporary Brown[2] morocco
elaborately gilt, the edges goffered and gilt, by C. Lewis (according to the
1892 catalogue), the spine gilt with 'Songs of / Innocence / W. Blake. / [*and
sideways at the bottom:*] 1789'.

HISTORY: (1) Probably pl. (6–7) (19, 24) went to *Songs* (T) before 1836,
by when *Innocence* (F) was bound; (2) Sold by Edwin Henry Lawrence at
Sotheby's, 9 May 1892, lot 60 (?twenty-one plates, bound by C. Lewis
[1786–1836] in Olive morocco, edges gilt and goffered), for £52 to Pearson;
(3) Returned from the Lawrence sale, sold with all faults at Sotheby's,
26 April 1893,[3] lot 1,086, for £18 to Pearson; (4) 'Acquired by Thomas J.
Wise . . . [*and*] resold by him in 1899 [*to Quaritch*]' (according to Keynes &
Wolf); (5) Acquired by Amy Lowell, who added her book-plate dated in
manuscript 1899,[4] and bequeathed by her in 1925 to (6) HARVARD.

COPY G: BINDING: (1) In 1921 (Keynes) it was still stitched through
bluish-Grey paper wrappers and a Buff spine, but (2) The plates were 'now
loose' in 1953 (Keynes & Wolf) (the cover is still with the plates).

HISTORY: (1) Perhaps this is the copy sold anonymously by Puttick &
Simpson, 4 March 1872, lot 1,121; (2) It was sold anonymously at Sotheby's,
2 July 1895, lot 501,[5] for £20 to Quaritch; (3) Bought by W. A. White,
and given by him to his daughter (4) 'Frances W. Moffat / 10 August 1895 /
with love' (according to the inscription on the recto of pl. 1; an accompanying
letter of 9 Aug. 1895 is also with the volume); Mrs. Emerson (W. A. White's
daughter) lent it to the exhibitions of the Grolier Club (1905), no. 2, perhaps

---

[1] This information comes from Keynes & Wolf; the label and Scott's *Geography* are not
now with the volume and are not mentioned in the 1926 catalogue.

[2] Not 'olive', as in the 1892 catalogue and Keynes & Wolf.

[3] It was not part of the J. B. Ditchfield Library, as in J. Sampson, ed., *Poetical Works of
William Blake* (1905), 70, and in Keynes & Wolf.

[4] Keynes & Wolf say she bought it 'some time after 1900'.

[5] Then stitched and said to be lacking a (non-existent) second plate to 'Infant Joy'.

the other of (1919), no. 2 (anonymously), and to that of the Fogg (1924), and in Philadelphia (1939), no. 13, and sold it posthumously at Sotheby's, 19 May 1958, lot 2, for £3,800 to A. Stonehill; (5) Acquired by Mr. *Paul Mellon*.

COPY H: BINDING: The leaves were mounted on paper guards and bound by J. Smith [*c*. 1840] in Green morocco (according to Keynes [1921]).

HISTORY: (1) Bought in 1833[1] by Edward FitzGerald, who signed the fly-leaf with the date 1834;[2] (2) Acquired by Thomas Gaisford, who added his book-plate inside the cover,[2] and sold it at Sotheby's, 23 April 1890, lot 186, for £41 to Quaritch; (3) Acquired by General Archibald Stirling of Keir,[2] and subsequently by his son (4) Lt.-Col. William Stirling, who sold it; (5) *UNTRACED*.

COPY I: BINDING: (1) Originally stabbed through three holes, 3·9 cm from the top, 4·8, 4·9 cm apart; (2) Bound after 1796 (the date on the third and fourth fly-leaves) in contemporary mottled calf, with a gilt emblem in the middle of the panel, and the spine gilt sideways with 'BLAKE'S / SONGS'; both covers are now detached.

HISTORY: (1) 'This Copy was coloured by W. Blake himself' according to the note (written by John Linnell, according to the 1911 catalogue below); (2) Acquired by Robert Hoe, who wrote on the second fly-leaf: 'I paid £4. 4. 0 for this book. R. H.', added his book-plate, had it described in his catalogue (1895), lent it anonymously to the Grolier Club exhibition (1905), no. 4,[3] and sold it posthumously at Anderson's, 25 April 1911, lot 390, for $700 to G. D. Smith for (3) The HUNTINGTON LIBRARY.

COPY J: BINDING: Bound in old (?contemporary) half leather (later rebacked) over marbled boards, gilt, lettered 'SONGS' sideways on the spine; kept in an extraordinary 19th-century embroidered cover (by Mrs. Reginald Frampton, according to the 1925 catalogue) with 'SONGS OF / INNOCENCE / WILLIAM / BLAKE' stitched on it; the first four plates are outlined in Red.

HISTORY: (1) Sold anonymously[4] at Sotheby's, 20 Nov. 1899, lot 116, for £13. 15*s*. to Quaritch; (2) Acquired before 1921 by E. J. Shaw, who sold it at Sotheby's, 29 July 1925, lot 159, for £150 to Spencer; (3) Sold at American Art Association, 14 April 1926, lot 75, for $1,200 to W. Clarkson; (4) Given by Dr. J. W. Robertson to his son Edwin Grabhorn (according to Mr. Warren Howell); (5) Offered in John Howell's Catalogue 34 (1963), lot 98, for $7,500; (6) Acquired by an *Anonymous* collector.

COPY K: BINDING: 'Bound by C. MURTON'[5] *c*. 1838 in Black straight grain morocco, g.e.; an illegible name on the verso of pl. 2 is erased and partly cut off.

[1] On 25 Oct. 1833, FitzGerald wrote to W. B. Donne: 'I have lately bought a little pamphlet which is very difficult to be got, called The Songs of Innocence . . .' (*Letters & Literary Memoirs of Edward FitzGerald*, ed. W. A. Wright [1902], i. 26).

[2] According to Keynes & Wolf.

[3] It was erroneously said to have been 'given by Blake to his physician', referring to Hoe's copy A in the same sale.

[4] Not, as Keynes & Wolf say, as part of 'the collection of H. A. Mair'; the H. A. Mair sale was at *Puttick & Simpson's*, 19 Nov. 1900.

[5] Not 'Murdon', as in Keynes & Wolf.

HISTORY: (1) Acquired by Sir Charles W. Dilke (1810–69), who signed the second fly-leaf, and added his book-plate ('Catalogue No. 293'); (2) Evidently lent by his son (Sir C. W. Dilke [1843–1911]) to the Burlington Fine Arts Club exhibition (1876), no. 312,[1] and offered posthumously at Christie's, 9 May 1911, lot 55 (£250, Tennent), but withdrawn (according to Keynes & Wolf); (3) Apparently acquired by the dealer G. D. Smith in 1918 (the second and last fly-leaves are inscribed 'C[?] & P [*for* Collated & Perfect] Hinds 5 / 2 / 18' and 'G. D. S. 12 / 1918'); (4) Acquired before 1921 by Carl H. Pforzheimer, who added his book-plate, lent it to the Philadelphia exhibition (1939), no. 17, and bequeathed it to the institutionalized (5) CARL H. PFORZHEIMER LIBRARY.

COPY L: BINDING: (1) Originally stabbed through three holes, 5·0 cm from the top, 4·0, 3·6 cm apart, but (2) Unbound by 1902; (3) The plates were mounted on stubs and 'Bound by Zaehnsdorf' in Brown morocco.

HISTORY: (1) Sold anonymously at Sotheby's, 22 July 1902, lot 396 (then 'unbound'), for £19. 10s. to E. Parsons; (2) Acquired before 1921, perhaps for the '15/—/—' on the verso of pl. 2, by Miss Carthew, who added her book-plate, and who may have had it bound; it was 'Bequeathed by Miss A. G. E Carthew July 1940' (according to a manuscript note in it) to (3) The BODLEIAN LIBRARY.

COPY M: BINDING: The plates were mounted on stubs and bound, perhaps not long after 1804 for the Marquis of Bute, in bluish-Purple velvet with Magenta silk doublures, the edges goffered and gilt, with eight fly-leaves at the front and fifteen[2] at the back (the 3rd, 12th, and 22nd water-marked E & P / 1804); the volume is preserved in an early 19th-century Brown calf case.

HISTORY: (1) It may have been acquired by the first Marquis of Bute, whose sister, the Countess of Portarlington, was solicited by Hayley for patronage for Blake in 1803 (*Blake Records* [1969], 120); (2) Sold by the fourth Marquis of Bute at Sotheby's, 28 June 1948, lot 262, for £1,250 to Sawyer; (3) Acquired by an *Anonymous* collector, who lent it anonymously to the National Library of Scotland exhibition (1969), no. 27.

COPY N: BINDING: 'BOUND BY F. BEDFORD' in Green levant morocco, g.e., in a style very similar to, and with some of the same tools used in, *Songs* (E).

HISTORY: (1) Apparently acquired by 'B. M. Pickering', whose stamp is on the first fly-leaf; (2) It 'recently came to light in Cornwall'[3] and was sold by 'A Collector' at Sotheby's, 3 April 1933, lot 157, for £410 to Quaritch; (3) Offered in Quaritch Catalogues 486 (1934), lot 69, and 491 (1934), lot 354, both for £600; (4) Acquired by Mrs. George Millard, who sold it on

---

[1] No. 312 is described, apparently in error, as *Songs of Innocence and of Experience*.

[2] Not 14, as in Keynes & Wolf.

[3] From the place of its discovery, the 1933 catalogue (followed by the Quaritch catalogues and Keynes & Wolf) surmises that it may have been owned by Blake's Cornish patron John Hawkins, but the 'B. M. Pickering' stamp suggests that it was owned in London in the 19th century and that the place of its discovery was unrelated to the original ownership. *Innocence* (N) strikingly complements the *Experience* in *Songs* (O).

1 Feb. 1935 (according to the inscription on the last fly-leaf: 'Millard / 2–1–35') to (5) Estelle Doheny, who lent it to the exhibitions of the Little Museum of La Miniatura (1936), no. 14, and in Philadelphia (1939), no. 20, and gave it on 14 Oct. 1940 to (6) The Edward Laurence Doheny Memorial Library of ST. JOHN'S SEMINARY, Camarillo, California.

COPY O: BINDING: Bound in contemporary half Black roan over Green marbled boards gilt but without lettering, greyish-Green endpapers, the leaves trimmed but not gilt; the plates framed in ink; pl. 12, 23 have large pencil scribbles over them.

  HISTORY: (1) Acquired by Arthur Champernowne (1767–1819); (2) Sold by his great-grandson A. M. Champernowne at Sotheby's, 6 May 1936, lot 718, for £180 to Schwartz; (3) Acquired in 1937 from Schwartz (according to letters with the volume) by (4) T. E. Hanley, who lent it to the Philadelphia exhibition (1939), no. 21, and sold it in 1965 to (5) The UNIVERSITY OF TEXAS.

COPY P: BINDING: (1) Originally stabbed through three holes, 8·3, 8·3 cm apart; (2) Bound about 1805 in contemporary gilt Black straight grain morocco with Brown velvet set into the panels into which are set in turn diamond-shaped pieces of leather (one on each board) bearing the crest of Thomas Johnes (two battle-axes saltireways sable), the spine lettered 'Blake's / Songs / 1789', g.e.

  HISTORY: (1) It was '[*words illeg*]' the gift of / Mʳ Malkin 1805—' (according to the inscription on the verso of pl. 21), evidently to (2) Thomas Johnes of Hafod, whose crest is on the cover, and to whom Malkin dedicated his *Memoirs of his Child* (1806) with its account of Blake; (3) Acquired by Lawrence W. Hodson, who added his book-plate, and sold it at Sotheby's, 3 Dec. 1906, lot 64, for £107 to Tregaskis; (4) Acquired by Dr. Greville MacDonald, lent to the exhibitions in Manchester (1914), no. 149, Nottingham (1914), no. 114, and the National Gallery of Scotland (1914), Case B, no. 1, and sold in 1920 (?March—see *Thel* [H], p. 127) to (5) Francis Edwards (according to Keynes [1921]); (6) Bought 'from Gabriel Wells in April 1922 for $1400'[1] by Frank Brewer Bemis, who added his book-plate, and lent it to the Fogg exhibition (1930) and (anonymously) to the Philadelphia exhibition (1939), no. 18; (7) Bought through Rosenbach in 1940 by Chauncey Brewster Tinker, who added his book-plate, in whose catalogue (1959), no. 268, it was described, and who bequeathed it at his death in March 1963 to (8) YALE.

COPY Q: BINDING: (1) Originally stabbed through three holes, 3·1 cm from the top, 4·8 and 4·4 cm apart; (2) Bound about 1828 in heavily blindstamped Green calf, the spine gilt with 'SONGS / OF / INNOCENCE / BY / WM BLAKE', g.e., interleaved, with marbled endpapers and nineteen fly-leaves in front and sixteen in back (the 21st, 25th, 29th, and 31st watermarked, J WHATMAN / TURKEY MILL / 1828), and two drawings (probably not by Blake); in 1964 the drawings were removed.

  HISTORY: (1) Sold as the Property of a Lady at Sotheby's, 31 July 1893,

[1] According to Keynes & Wolf.

lot 1,100 (with two designs said erroneously to be by Blake, Blake's letter of ?April 1826, and Schiavonetti's sketch for his engraving of Phillips's portrait of Blake), for £49. 10s. to Heath; (2) *Innocence* was 'Purchased in 1900 from Quaritch' (who said it was 'Linnell's copy')[1] by Marsden J. Perry, who put his stamp ('M J P') on the first fly-leaf, and sold it[1] to (3) W. A. White, who lent it to the exhibitions of the Grolier Club (1905), no. 5–6[2] (anonymously), and the Fogg (1924), and gave it to his brother (4) Alfred T. White,[3] who bequeathed it to his daughter (5) Mrs. Adrian Van Sinderen, who lent it to the Philadelphia exhibition (1939), no. 19, and deposited it (with the two drawings) in (6) SYRACUSE UNIVERSITY LIBRARY, for which it is destined.

COPY R: BINDING: (1) Originally stabbed through three holes, 2·6 and 3·5 cm apart (trimmed off pl. 25); (2) A binding was probably damaged in a bonfire in the 1890s from which the plates were rescued; (3) In 1952 they were detached and hinged into a volume bound in Green straight grain morocco; (4) After 1952 each plate was mounted separately.

HISTORY: (1) Acquired by the first Baron Dimsdale (1712–1800) (according to a family tradition reported in the 1952 catalogue below); the leaves were 'rescued by their owner from a bonfire' (according to Keynes & Wolf) 'in the 1890's' (according to Keynes [1964]); (2) Sold by Major T. E. Dimsdale at Sotheby's, 24 Nov. 1952, lot 99 ('detached and hinged into a 4to volume, green straight-grained morocco—gilt', some leaves stained by fire), for £240 to Armstrong; (3) Acquired by Sir *Geoffrey Keynes*, who had the plates bound and matted, lent them to the exhibitions in the British Museum (1957), no. 32 2–4, 6–7, 33 2–6 and (anonymously) the National Library of Scotland (1969), no. 28, the Whitworth Art Gallery (1969), no. 3, and described them in his catalogue (1964), no. 508.

COPY S: BINDING: (1a) Pl. 3–27 were originally stabbed through three holes, 6·2 cm from the top, 2·8 and 2·8 cm apart; (1b) Pl. 2 was originally separately stabbed through three holes, 5·6 cm from the top and 3·9 and 4·2 cm apart; (2) The plates were hinged on to larger leaves and 'BOUND BY RIVIERE & SON' in crushed Brown levant morocco, the larger leaves g.e., pl. 2 being added between 1920 and 1922.

HISTORY: (1) This (or copies G, J, L, N, O, Q, T) may be the one 'Mr. Masquerier...induced me [*T. F. Dibdin*] to purchase' by 1816;[4] (2) Acquired by Quaritch (the last fly-leaf has a pencil note 'June '20') and offered, without pl. 2, in his Catalogue 361 (Dec. 1920) for £350, and again with pl. 2,[5] in Catalogue 368 (March 1922), lot 108,[6] at £400; (3) Sold with Mrs. Phoebe A. D. Boyle's Library at Anderson's, 19 Nov. 1923; lot 46, for $1,100 to

---

[1] J. Sampson, ed., *Poetical Works of William Blake* (1905), 73.
[2] Nos. 5 and 6 in the 1905 catalogue clearly describe the same copy.
[3] According to Keynes & Wolf.
[4] T. F. Dibdin, *Reminiscences of a Literary Life* (1836)—see *Blake Records* (1969), 243.
[5] The copy of pl. 2 supplied may have been the one from the Collection of a friend of Blake offered by Quaritch (1880), lot 12,804 (with four drawings and the MS of *Songs* pl. 4) for £10.
[6] Described in the unique page-order of copy C, which Quaritch had offered in Feb. 1915; the order given for copy S in the catalogues of 1920 and 1922 is probably therefore insignificant.

G. D. Smith; (4) Acquired by G. C. Smith, Jr., described in his anonymous catalogue (1927), no. 2, lent to the Fogg exhibition (1930), and sold posthumously at Parke-Bernet, 2 Nov. 1928, lot 16, for $2,300 to Gannon; (5) Sold about 1941 by Scribner's to Albert Rouillier Galleries of Chicago (according to Mr. Harold E. Graves, Manager of Scribner's Rare Book Department); (6) It was part of the 'Bequest of Herbert Greer French, 1942' (according to a slip pasted in) to (7) The CINCINNATI ART MUSEUM.

COPY T: BINDING: Bound (by J. Smith, according to the 1890 catalogue) in old (?contemporary) russia, blind tooled and gilt, the spine gilt with 'SONGS / OF / INNOCENCE / — / BLAKE / 1789'; the hinges have been mended.

HISTORY: (1) Sold anonymously at Hodgson's, 21 April 1910, lot 246, for £47 to Edwards; (2) Offered by Maggs Bros. (1911), item 35, for £110; (3) It was 'Bought May—1911 F. B.' (according to the inscription on the first fly-leaf), evidently someone close to (4) Miss Catherine Bullard, who owned the book in 1921 and lent it to the Fogg Exhibition (1924); (5) Acquired about 1953 from Goodspeed's of Boston by Mr. *Robert H. Taylor* of Princeton, who lent it to the Princeton exhibitions of 22 Oct–19 Dec. 1954 ('Illustrated Books from the 15th Century to the 20th', no catalogue published), of Nov. 1964–Jan. 1965 (*Landmarks of English Literature*), and of 1969 (no. 25).

COPY U: BINDING: (1) Originally stabbed through three holes; (2) Sewn through seven about 1818 (the watermark date on the front fly-leaf), probably for Robert Balmanno, with *Descriptive Catalogue* (I) and Chaucer's *Prologue* (1812) into a half Green morocco binding over marbled boards, labelled 'Tracts / by Blake / London / 1789 / 1809 / 1812', t.e.g.; (3–4) The *Innocence* plates were disbound, probably when they were exhibited in Boston in 1891.

HISTORY: (1) Acquired by Robert Balmanno, who probably had it bound about 1818 with *Descriptive Catalogue* (I) and Chaucer's *Prologue* (1812), and 'who died in Brooklyn N.Y. about 1865' (according to the note by E. W. Hooper on the *Descriptive Catalogue* fly-leaf); (2) It may have been acquired by 'H. D. Chapin / 60 Beacon St / Boston / High 3–4 / 40 inches' (according to the enigmatic note on pl. 14); (3) Acquired by E. W. Hooper, who put his initials on the *Descriptive Catalogue*, lent *Innocence* to the Boston exhibition (1880), no. 137, and *Innocence* and *Descriptive Catalogue* to the Boston Exhibition (1891), no. 1a, 146[1] and allowed *Innocence* to be used for the Boston facsimile (1883); at his death it passed to his daughter (4) Mrs. Greely S. Curtis, Jr., who owned it in 1921; (5) Given by Mrs. Curtis's sister Mrs. Ward Thoron in memory of their father on 15 Nov. 1950 to (6) HARVARD.

COPY V: BINDING: Half bound (?in leather).

HISTORY: (1) Sold by W. H. Crawford at Sotheby's, 13 March 1891, lot 350, for £8 to Tregaskis; (2) *UNTRACED*.

COPY W: BINDING: Loose in a morocco binding.

---

[1] Hooper also lent to the 1891 Boston exhibition (no. 1d) a 'Modern Impression' of 'The Little Black Boy' (pl. 9 or 10) printed in black, which I take to be a late 19th-century facsimile rather than one of Tatham's pulls.

HISTORY: (1) Sold by a Nobleman at Hodgson's, 28 June 1940, lot 260, for £25 to 'Private'; (2) Sold at Sotheby's, 30 April 1941, lot 641, for £50 to B. F. Stevens; (3) *UNTRACED*.

COPY X: BINDING: (1) Originally stabbed through three holes, 5·3 cm from the top, 3·8 and 3·9 cm apart; (2) They were loose and very soiled when sold in 1964, but (3) They were cleaned (according to the owner) and 'BOUND BY GRAY OF CAMBRIDGE' in Cream leather for Raymond Lister in 1965.

HISTORY: (1) Sold anonymously at Sotheby's, 9 Nov. 1964, lot 112 (loose, soiled), for £220 to Alan G. Thomas, who sold them to (2) Mr. *Raymond Lister*, who had them cleaned and bound, and added a family book-plate.

COPY Y: BINDING: Loose.

HISTORY: (1) Sold by 'a gentleman' at Sotheby's, 12 March 1962, lot 151, for £1,000 to Fairbrother (i.e. the dealer Nicolas Rauch of Geneva);[1] (2) *UNTRACED*.

Songs of Innocence and of Experience

COPY A: BINDING: (1a) *Innocence* was originally stabbed through four large holes (which have been repeatedly used), 11·0 cm from the top (four small holes together), 4·5 (2), 2·0 (3), and 6·0 cm apart (2); (1b) *Experience* was separately stabbed through three holes, 10·5 cm from the top and 7·3, 8·1 cm apart; (2) The leaves were pasted on cardboard[2] and bound in two enormous volumes in heavy White vellum; the top edges of the cardboard are gilt, but Blake's leaves are not.

HISTORY: (1) Probably acquired by Isaac D'Israeli (see *Europe* [A], p. 156); (2) Sold by his son the Earl of Beaconsfield at Sotheby's, 20 March 1882, lot 56,[3] for £85 to Dowdeswell; (3) Acquired by Bernard Buchanan Macgeorge, listed in his library catalogues (1892, 1906), and sold with his collection at Sotheby's, 1 July 1924, lot 111, for £760 to Martin; (4) 'Presented by Mrs B. B. Macgeorge as a Memorial of The Macgeorge Library ... 1927 7 26' to (5) The BRITISH MUSEUM PRINT ROOM (according to the printed title-page of Vol. I).

COPY B: BINDING: (1) Originally stabbed through three holes, 4·1 cm from the top and 5·5, 6·5 cm apart; (2) the leaves were pasted to heavy sheets[4] and bound in modern ugly heavy Blue morocco; in May 1964 the plates were hinged on to the same sheets so that the versos could be seen.

[1] M. Rauch's sale records were not preserved after his death by his successor, André Cottet.

[2] Keynes (1921) and Keynes & Wolf say erroneously that the leaves are inserted in slide mounts.

[3] *Innocence* and *Experience* are said to have 29 and 21 plates respectively, though they now have 28 and 22.

[4] Keynes & Wolf say 'The leaves, which show the original stitch-holes, have not been bound since Blake's covers were removed. Now mounted on stiff leaves and bound'; apparently they do not count the present cover as a binding of the leaves. However, there are *both* stitch and stab holes in the plates, and they were almost certainly sewn into a binding between Blake's stabbing and the present binding. The plates were evidently disbound by 1876, when they were exhibited as four separate lots.

HISTORY: (1) 'Originally in the possession of Judge Charles Warren, who obtained it directly from Blake or his wife '(according to Keynes & Wolf, who are evidently reporting a family tradition); (2) Given to Warren's daughter, Lady Stafford Carey, who gave it to her daughter (according to Keynes & Wolf) (3) 'b / Emily J. Carey / Candie / Guernsey' (according to the inscription on the verso of pl. 2), who lent it to the Burlington Fine Arts Club exhibitions (1876), nos. 273–4, 277–8, and '*Anonymously*' (1927), no. 75; it was the '. . . GIFT OF MISS E. J. CAREY 1932' (according to the lettering on the spine) to (4) The BRITISH MUSEUM PRINT ROOM; reproduced in colour micro-film by Micro Methods Ltd.

COPY C: BINDING: Bound in contemporary gilt Citron morocco, with a label reading 'SONGS / OF / INNOCENCE' (*Experience* omitted) on the spine and small diamond-shaped panels with blind-stamped stars in the middle on the boards, g.e.

HISTORY: (1) Sold as the Property of a Clergyman at Sotheby's, 16 March 1909, lot 172, for £166 to Dobell; (2) Offered in Tregaskis' Golden Head Catalogue 699 (26 April 1909), lot 76 (according to A. G. B. Russell, *The Engravings of William Blake* [1912], no. 16), 'for 245 guineas' (according to Keynes [1921]); (3) Acquired by W. E. Moss, who added his book-plate, lent it to the exhibition in Manchester (1914), no. 147, allowed pl. a to be reproduced in Keynes (1921), and sold it at Sotheby's, 2 March 1937, lot 144, for £1,400 to Rosenbach for (4) Mr. LESSING J. ROSENWALD.

COPY D: BINDING: Bound after 1796 (The watermark date on the fourth and fifth fly-leaves) in contemporary blind tooled and gilt straight grain Citron morocco with 'SONGS / OF / INNOCENCE / &c' gilt on the spine, heavy Blue endpapers and three fly-leaves at each end, g.e.

HISTORY: (1) This is probably the copy quoted in 1811 by Crabb Robinson (*Blake Records* [1969], 433 n. 1) and sold for Elizabeth Iremonger by King & Lochee, 26 April 1813, lot 165 ('*elegantly bound*'), perhaps to (2) Miss Iremonger's friend 'C L Shipley',[1] whose signature appears on the first fly-leaf; (3) The next owner was evidently 'Fanny F S Milner' (d. 1876), who also wrote her name on the first fly-leaf; (4) 'This copy is from the collection of [*Miss Milner's nephew*] Major [*G. M. L.*] Egerton[,] Town[s]hend House[,] York[,] Sale early in 1916 before March 11' (according to a note with the volume); (5) Acquired by Quaritch[2] presumably at this sale (the last fly-leaf bears the note probably for Quaritch: 'no Tirzah [*pl.* 52] other-wise C[*ollated*] A[*nd*] P[*erfect*] E H Denis[?] 13/3/16 cxts/—'); (6) Acquired before 1921 by A. E. Newton, who added his book-plate, lent it to the exhibitions at the Fogg (1924) and in Philadelphia (1939), no. 41, and sold it posthumously at Parke-Bernet, 16 April 1941, lot 136, for $6,100 to Rosenbach; (7) Acquired by Mr. *A. A. Houghton*, who added his initialled book-plate.

---

[1] For Miss Iremonger's friendship with Miss Shipley, see *Blake Records* (1969), 222. 'A Dream' is only found in *Experience* (as transcribed in Robinson's Commonplace Book, in Dr. Williams's Library) in copies *B–D*.

[2] Quaritch had it in March 1916, according to Keynes (1921).

COPY E: BINDING: (**1a–b**) *Innocence* was originally stabbed through three holes, about 5·0 cm from the top and 3·5, 3·4 cm apart,[1] while no stab holes are visible in the *Experience* plates;[2] (**2**) Trimmed and bound, apparently after 1806 for Thomas Butts, 'in an old weekly washingbook', with a parody of the 'Introduction' to *Innocence*; (**3**) Frederick Locker had it again 'BOUND BY F. BEDFORD' in Green crushed morocco, g.e. (according to the 1886 catalogue), with the addition of pl. 32, and Gilchrist's letter of 25 Oct. 1861.

HISTORY: (**1**) This is evidently the copy of 'Songs of Innocence &c' for which Thomas Butts paid £6. 6s. on 9 Sept. 1806 (*Blake Records* [1969], 575); it was sold with a parody of the 'Introduction' to *Innocence*,[3] and 'with the printed Poem [*evidently the 1839 edition in conventional typography*] . . . 3 vols.' anonymously among the Collection of Thomas Butts[4] at Sotheby's, 26 March 1852, lot 50, for £12. 12s. to Arthington; (**2**) Sold with the collection of Robert Arthington at Sotheby's, 17 May 1866, lot 17 (still in three volumes, with a letter [of 25 Oct. 1861] from Gilchrist), for £13. 15s. to Pickering; (**3**) Pickering had the first fly-leaf stamped 'B. M. Pickering'; (**4**) Acquired by Frederick Locker, who added his book-plate, put his name on pl. 1, 28, and the first fly-leaf, wrote on the unnumbered pl. 32; 'I inserted this— ?Colouring more modern', 'rescued it' from the washing book (according to his catalogue [1886]) by having it rebound by Bedford,[5] and lent it to the Burlington Fine Arts Club exhibition (1876), no. 309; it was sold through Dodd, Mead & Co. (see the 'Pickering MS', p. 341) to (**5**) E. Dwight Church (according to Keynes & Wolf); (**6**) Acquired by Beverly Chew, who added his book-plate, and sold it *en bloc* with the rest of his collection in Dec. 1912 to (**6**) The HUNTINGTON LIBRARY.

COPY F: BINDING: Bound in old (?contemporary) half Brown calf with 'BLAKES WORK' gilt sideways on the spine.

HISTORY: (**1**) 'G Cumberland' wrote his name on the verso of pl. 28, but did not sell the work with his Collection in 1835; (**2**) Sold posthumously for Henry Burgess at Sotheby's, 17 April 1929, lot 583, for £1,900 to Spencer; (**3**) Sold by Scribners to Edison Dick (according to Mr. Graves of Scribners), and (**4**) Bought back by Scribners in 1947; sold through Gannon in 1947 for $13,200 (according to Keynes & Wolf) to (**5**) Mr. *Paul Mellon*.

---

[1] It was apparently stabbed again irregularly through the same holes, for all but pl. (15, 9), (10, 54), (18, 12), (24, 19) have another hole 3·0 cm below the bottom one listed above, and these same plates (except pl. 1) also have another hole 3·1 cm above the top one.

[2] There are three stabs in pl. (48, 51), 3·7 cm from the top and 3·2, 3·9 cm apart which seem quite unrelated to any others in the book.

[3] For the text of the parody and a discussion of its authorship, see 'A Piper Passes', *N & Q* ccix [1964], 418–19.

[4] None of the Blake books in the sale has any indication in it that Butts owned it, but several of the pictures sold then are known to have been sold by Blake to Butts, e.g. the 'Wise and Foolish Virgins' (lot 165 in the 1852 sale) described as on the stocks for Butts in the letter of 6 July 1803, and 'Paul Preaching' (lot 161) paid for by Butts in the account of 3 March 1806 (*Blake Records* [1969], 571). Gilchrist (1863) identifies the sale as that of 'Mr. Butts' son'.

[5] Apparently almost all Locker's Blake books were bound for him, as *Songs* [E] was, by Bedford in ornate Green morocco (*No Natural Religion* [C], *Thel* [L], *America* [I], *For Children* [D], and the unsigned case for *Poetical Sketches* [V]) or Brown morocco (*For the Sexes* [E]).

COPY G: BINDING: (**1a–d**) Divers sets of stab holes (three holes 4·2 and 4·6 cm apart in pl. 31–2, 38, 42; two more in pl. 38; three holes 5·7 and 6·8 cm apart in pl. 37; none in pl. 30, 43, 47, 50, 51) indicate that these plates were originally stabbed separately; (**2**) Perhaps bound with *Songs* (N), *The World Turned Upside Down*, and several other works in half Red morocco, uncut, in 1859 and 1860; (**3**) Separately bound in half calf in 1877; (**4**) After that date the plates were probably scattered loose; pl. 38 was framed and glazed in 1937.

HISTORY: (**1**) Offered by Quaritch in Catalogue 147 (15 May 1859) (bound with *The World Turned Upside Down* [and *Songs* (N)][1] in half Red morocco, uncut), for £10. 10s., in Catalogue 156 (24 Feb. 1860) (40 plates [*Songs* (G), 15 plates, plus *Songs* (N),[1] 25 plates], bound with several other works, including *The World Turned Upside Down*), for £8. 10s., and in (1877), lot 9,741 (15 plates [pl. 30–2, 38, 37, 42, 33, 50, 46, 40, 49, 41, 43, 47, 51] in half calf), for £25; (**2**) These fifteen plates were probably separated; they may include: (**Ai**) Eight unbound 'Colour Plates' sold with the Library of Julian Marshall at Sotheby's, 11 July 1904, lot 36, for £13 to Quaritch; these too may have been later separated and disposed of; (**Bia**) Pl. 37 was given by Francis Edwards in Jan. 1925 to (**Bib**) *Geoffrey Keynes*; (**Biia**) Pl. 30–1 (with *Ahania* pl. 1) were sold by E. J. Shaw at Sotheby's, 29 July 1925, lot 162, to (**Biib**) *Geoffrey Keynes*; (**Biiia**) Pl. 50–1 were lent by J. A. Fuller Maitland to exhibitions in Manchester (1914), no. 81, and Nottingham (1914), no. 124; (**Biiib**) Acquired by *Geoffrey Keynes*; (**Biva**) Pl. 38 was lent by Miss A. M. Butterworth to the exhibition in Manchester (1914), no. 38, and sold at Sotheby's, 6 May 1936, lot 719; (**Bivb**) Sold anonymously at Sotheby's, 21 Dec. 1937, lot 333, for £12. 12s. to Armstrong; (**Bivc**) Acquired by *Geoffrey Keynes*; (**Bva**) Pl. 42–3, formerly the property of Kenneth Grahame, (**Bvb**) Were sold by W. G. O. Thomas at Sotheby's, 28 July 1947, lot 117, for £75 to (**Bvc**) *Geoffrey Keynes*; (**Bvia**) The pl. 32 and 49 (coloured) sold by J. W. Ford at Sotheby's, 12 May 1902, lot 75, for £5. 17s. 6d. to Tregaskis may have dwindled to the (**Bvib**) Pl. 32 probably sold by Greville Macdonald to (**Bvic**) Francis Edwards, who offered it [?1931], no. 12, for £30, and evidently sold it (with *Visions* pl. 10) to (**Bvid**) *Geoffrey Keynes*, who said that this and pl. 47[2] were acquired 'at various dates from various sources' (Keynes & Wolf, echoed by Keynes [1964] below); pl. 30–2, 37–8, 42–3, 47, 50–1 were lent by Keynes to the British Museum exhibition (1957), no. 34 2–4, 6–7; 35 2–3, 5–7, and described in his catalogue (1964), no. 514; (**Bviia**) Pl. 40 was sold anonymously to (**Bviib**) Colnaghi's, which put it in an exhibition catalogued as *Original Printmaking in Britain 1600–1900* (2 Nov.–1 Dec. 1972), no. 101 and sold it in 1972 for £1,200 to (**Bviic**), *Mr. Raymond Lister*; (**Ci**) Pl. 33, 41, 46, 49 (listed in the 1877 Quaritch catalogue) are *UNTRACED*.

COPY H: BINDING: (**1**) Originally stabbed through three holes, 5·1 cm

---

[1] It seems likely that the miscellaneous work containing 40 plates from Blake's *Songs* offered by Quaritch in 1859 and 1860 is the same as the two copies of *Songs of Experience* (G and N, q.v.) containing 15 and 25 plates offered by Quaritch in 1877.

[2] Perhaps this is the copy of pl. 47 sold for 'the George D. Smith Book Company Inc In Liquidation' at Anderson Galleries, 21 May 1928, lot 179A.

from the top, 3·7 and 6·0 cm apart, into ancient, dirty, ragged greyish-Buff wrappers; (2) In 1953 they were still stitched through three stubs, but in May 1964 the cord had entirely disappeared.

HISTORY: (1) Probably acquired by Ozias Humphry (1742–1810) and inherited by his natural son (2) William Upcott, who lent it to Richard Thomson to describe for J. T. Smith's life of Blake (*Blake Records* [1969], 468–70), and with whose Library it was sold posthumously by Messrs. Evans, 15 June 1846, lot 65, for £1. 14*s*. to Evans; (3) Evidently acquired by 'R. Sykes' (perhaps a relative of the famous bibliophile Sir Mark Masterman Sykes ⌈1771–1823⌉), who wrote his name on the verso of pl. 28; (4) Sold with Robert Arthington's Library at Sotheby's, 17 May 1866, lot 18, for £1. 1*s*. to Pickering; (5) Sold for C. H. Jephcot at Sotheby's, 20 Dec. 1948, lot 98 ('loosely sewn'), for £340 to Lord Crawford, i.e. (6) The Earl of *Crawford and Balcarres*, who lent it anonymously to the National Library of Scotland exhibition (1969), no. 39.

COPY I: BINDING: (1) Originally stabbed through three holes, 4·5 cm from the top, 3·4, 3·4 cm apart;[1] (2) Bound about 1830 in Brown cloth with 'Blake's Songs' on the spine.

HISTORY: (1) '*It* was given by Blake' (according to the 1902 catalogue below) to 'H. W. Phillips' (who signed the second fly-leaf) or perhaps to his father;[2] (2) Acquired 'from Phillips' daughter' (according to the 1902 catalogue) by (3) 'The present [*1902*] owner', perhaps 'Gerald Massey' (whose name appears on the second fly-leaf); Massey may have been the anonymous vendor at Sotheby's, 3 June 1902, lot 140, for £216 to Quaritch; (4) Sold by Quaritch after 1905 (according to Keynes [1921]) to (5) George C. Thomas of Philadelphia; (6) Exhibited by Rosenbach (Dec. 1911), no. 74, and sold by him to (7) The Library of Harry Elkins Widener, in whose *Catalogue* (1918) it is described, and given with the Widener Collection in 1915 to (8) HARVARD where pl. 1–2, 4–11, 13–15, 17, 19–23, 25–6, 28–33, 37–42, 44–5, 47–52 were reproduced in *The Illuminated Blake*, ed. D. V. Erdman (1974).

COPY J: BINDING: The leaves[3] were trimmed to within 0·5 cm of the etching, skilfully inlaid into larger sheets (13·1 × 19·7 cm), carefully indented at the join of the inner and outer leaves (perhaps, as Keynes & Wolf suggest, 'by putting each print, damped, in press with blank plate') to look like plate-marks, and 'BOUND BY RIVIERE' (before 1880, say Keynes & Wolf, using

---

[1] Trimming, evidently, has removed one (pl. 1, 15, 40), two (pl. 2, 34), or three of the stab holes (pl. 3, 54); most of the plates from an early *Innocence* (pl. 4–7, 9–12, 16–23, 26–7, 35–6, 53) have as well extra stab holes, ordinarily (pl. 4–7, 9–10, 12, 16–23, 26, 53) very closely approximating the above set, suggesting that perhaps *Innocence* was stabbed first, and later *Experience* was added stabbed through approximately the same holes, making pairs of holes in most of *Innocence*.

[2] Since Henry Wyndham Phillips (1820–68) was only seven when Blake died, it is improbable that he had it directly from Blake. Perhaps Blake gave it to H. W. Phillips's father Thomas, who painted Blake's portrait in 1807.

[3] If pl. 28 from copy J went to copy T, the original size of the leaves must have been 11·7 × 18·5 cm or larger.

evidence unknown to me) in Brown morocco, g.e.; pl. 28 was loosely inserted by 1927.

HISTORY: (1) Lent by Blake's friend Charles Augustus Tulk to S. T. Coleridge, who described it in a letter of 12 Feb. 1818 (*Blake Records* [1969], 251–3), and also to Garth Wilkinson, whose edition of the *Songs* (1839) follows the plate-order of copy J;[1] (2) 'Bought in 1870 by James Bain, the bookseller, from a member of Tulk's family then resident in Australia';[2] (3) 'For a time in the possession of Dew-Smith of Cambridge';[2] (4) 'Rebought by Bain about 1900, and soon after sold to [5] Lord Rothschild';[2] (6) 'after his death in the possession of Lady Rothschild, who [*lent it to the Burlington Fine Arts Club Exhibition* [*1927*], *no. 76, and*] in 1933 gave it to her grandson, [7] The present Lord Rothschild. Given by Lord Rothschild in 1949 to'[2] (8) Sir *Anthony Blunt* who lent it to the Ferens Art Gallery exhibition (1959), no. 13.

COPY K: BINDING: (1) Originally stabbed through three holes, 2·6 and 2·8 cm apart, and numbered (1–52) in old Brown ink with the *Innocence* plates of *Songs* (O) and the plates coloured by Blake from copy e (pl. 30–3, 37, 41, 44–7, 50–2),[3] the whole work consisting of pl. 1–38, 40–54; (2) By 1899 the uncoloured plates of *Experience* (copy K) were separated and are now loose; see copies O and e for the subsequent binding of the other plates.

HISTORY: (1) Originally the uncoloured plates of K were stabbed with pl. 30–3, 37, 41, 44–7, 50–2 (all water-coloured) of copy e and the *Innocence* plates of *Songs* (O); the plates of K were apparently loose when (2) Acquired by the dealer James Toovey, who sold them in 1899 to (3) The PIERPONT MORGAN LIBRARY.[4]

COPY L: BINDING: (1) Originally stabbed through three holes, 3·3 and 4·0 cm apart; (2) Later bound (probably by C. Lewis [by 1836], according to the 1938 catalogue) in gilt Green straight grain morocco, the spine lettered 'Songs / of / Innocence / & / Experience', with Pink endpapers and interleaved with tissue paper, g.e.

HISTORY: (1) Perhaps the '1799 / J S' (on the recto of pl. 2) is an acquisition or early library mark; (2) Acquired by 'Henry Little' (according to the deleted signature on the verso of the first fly-leaf); (3) Sold by Alfred G. Gray at Sotheby's, 15 Dec. 1926, lot 613, for £1, 350 to 'Spencer v[*ia*] Q[*uaritch*]' (according to the marked Quaritch file); (4) Acquired by Cortlandt F. Bishop, who added his book-plate, and sold it at American Art Association, 5 April 1938, lot 279, for $5,400 to Sessler; (5) Acquired by Moncure Biddle, who added his book-plate, lent it to the Philadelphia exhibition (1939),

---

[1] Perhaps pl. 28 went to copy T, before 1856.

[2] According to Keynes & Wolf. Keynes (1921), from which the early history here is repeated, adds that Lord Rothschild left it 'in Mr. Bain's hands for nearly twenty years'. Lord Rothschild lent it to the National Book League Exhibition (1947), no. 194 (John Hayward, *English Poetry*: An Illustrated Catalogue [1950]).

[3] The congruence among the plates of copies K, O, and e is exactly confirmed by the ink numbers, offsets, printing colours (dark Brown), quality of water-colouring, paper, and approximate leaf-size.

[4] It is listed in the *Catalogue of a Collection of Books* formed by James Toovey principally from the library of the Earl of Gosford the property of J. Pierpont Morgan (1901).

no. 49, and sold it through Gannon (according to Keynes & Wolf) to **(6)** Mr. *Paul Mellon.*

COPY M: BINDING: The plates are mounted on stubs, and 'BOUND BY SANGORSKI & SUTCLIFFE, LONDON, ENGLAND'[1] in Red levant morocco, g.e.

HISTORY: **(1)** Evidently crudely painted posthumously (the offsets show the colouring); sold by Sir William Tite at Sotheby's, 19 May 1874, lot 292 (coloured, blind-tooled morocco extra), for £61 to Pearson; **(2)** Acquired by Thomas Gaisford, who added his book-plate, and sold it at Sotheby's, 23 April 1890, lot 187, for £87 to Robson; **(3)** Sold posthumously for Mrs. Alexander MacKay at Christie's, 26 April 1921, lot 4, for £170 to Shoebridge; **(4)** Acquired by Chauncey Brewster Tinker,[2] who added his book-plate, in whose catalogue (1959), no. 273, it was described, and who bequeathed it at his death in March 1963 to **(5)** YALE.

COPY N: BINDING: **(1)** Perhaps bound with *Songs* (G), *The World Turned Upside Down*, and several other works in half Red morocco, uncut, in 1859 and 1860, but separated by 1877; **(2)** Now bound in Maroon morocco, g.e., with two fly-leaves watermarked V[*ictoria*] R[*egina*].

HISTORY: **(1)** Copy N seems to have been separated from a numbered copy of *Innocence* printed in Black consisting of pl. 1–28, 54 (note that it lacks these plates and that it is numbered 30–54), pl. 28 numbered '29';[3] the reduced copy N was offered in Quaritch catalogues of 15 May 1859, 24 Feb. 1860 (with copy G, q.v.), 1877 (lot 9,741, £48), and 1880 (lot 3,407, £42); **(2)** Sold for Howell Wills at Sotheby's, 11 July 1894, lot 92, for £40 to Quaritch; **(3)** Acquired by Robert Hoe, who added his book-plate, had it described in his catalogue (1895), lent it anonymously to the Grolier Club exhibitions (1905), no. 9, (1919), no. 4, and sold it posthumously at Anderson's, 25 April 1911, lot 392, for $700 to G. D. Smith for **(4)** The HUNTINGTON LIBRARY.

COPY O: BINDING: **(1a)** The *Experience* plates (including pl. 1[b]) were stabbed, perhaps in May 1797,[4] through three holes, about 5·4 and 6·9 cm apart, through bluish-Grey wrappers (one of which still adheres to pl. 1[b]); **(2)** The plates are now loose, perhaps disbound for the 1891 Boston exhibition; **(1b)** The *Innocence* plates (plus pl. 1[a]) were evidently stabbed through three holes, 2·6 and 2·8 cm apart, numbered in old Brown ink at the top right corner (1–29 for *Innocence*, 30–52 for *Experience*) with *Songs* (K) (pl. 28–9, 34–6, 38, 40, 42–3, 48–9) and the numbered plates of copy e (pl. 30–3, 37, 41, 44–7, 50–2), all printed in dark Brown, unwatermarked, and about the

---

[1] Not 'Bound . . . by Riviere', as in Keynes & Wolf.

[2] Letters with the volume suggest that the dealer Gabriel Wells had it from 1937 to 1939 trying to establish the authenticity of the colouring, and that he sold it to Tinker in the autumn of 1939.

[3] Professor Blunt's copy of pl. 28 answers this description.

[4] *Experience* may be the work referred to as 'Blakes Book' or 'Blakes Engravings' for which Flaxman paid 10s. 6d. and 4s. in early 1795 and Oct. 1795, and 'Blake's Book, binding, 3[s.]' paid for in the week ending 13 May 1797. Its colouring could be comprehended by one or more of the payments to 'Blake' of 24 July 1796 (£5. 5s.), Oct. 1797 (£2. 2s.), 28 May (£2), 9 July (£2) 1814 (*Blake Records* [1969], 569, 570, 578).

same leaf-size (*c.* 13·0 × 18·3 cm); (**2b**) *Innocence* was separated by April 1817, and its leaves are now loose, perhaps disbound for the 1891 Boston exhibition; for the subsequent binding of the other leaves, see copies K and e.

HISTORY: (**1Ai**) The coloured *Experience* (which strikingly complements *Innocence* [N]) was probably bought by John Flaxman in 1795 (see BINDING) and given to his wife, who wrote 'A Flaxman' in pencil on pl. 28; (**Bi**) The uncoloured plates of *Innocence* were evidently stabbed and numbered with uncoloured *Songs* (K, e) and the numbered and coloured plates of copy e (pl. 30–3, 37, 41, 44–7, 50–2); (**Bii**) *Innocence* was probably separated from *Songs* K and e, bought as 'Blake's Song's' for £1 by Flaxman in the week ending 30 July 1814 (*Blake Records* [1969], 578), and given to his wife, who wrote 'Mrs Flaxman / April 1817' on pl. 2; the *Experience* plates have separate histories under copies K and e; (**2**) The combined plates of copy O were inherited by Mrs. Flaxman's sister, Maria Denman, lent by her to Ruskin (whose letter of thanks is still with it), and sold with the *Remaining Works of John Flaxman* at Christie's, 26 April 1876, lots 5 and 6 (each described as *Songs of Innocence and of Experience*, lot 6 adding 'coloured'), both of which were 'ret[urne]ᵈ';[1] they were sold again at Christie's, with the *Remaining Works of . . . John Flaxman*, 26 Feb. 1883, lots 244 (*Innocence*) and 245 (*Experience* and Ruskin's letter); (**3**) Acquired by E. W. Hooper, who lent them to the 1891 Boston exhibition (nos. 1b, 5a) and bequeathed them before 1921 to his daughter (**4**) Mrs. Roger S. Warner, who lent them to the exhibitions in the Fogg (1924 and 1930, *Experience* only in each) and in Philadelphia (1939), no. 47, and gave them with her sisters in memory of their father on 1 July 1941 to (**5**) HARVARD.

COPY P: BINDING: Bound, probably for Mrs. Bliss about 1805, to match *For Children* (A)[2] in two volumes in Red straight grain morocco, with gilt fillets round the sides, the panels blind stamped with stars in the corners, marbled endpapers, the spines gilt with 'BLAKE'S / SONGS / VOL. / I [II]', g.e.

HISTORY: (**1**) Evidently used for facsimiles (belonging now to Paul Mellon and Anon.) about 1825,[3] and sold with the Bibliotheca Splendissima of Mrs. Bliss by Saunders and Hodgson, 26 April 1826, lot 11 (in its present binding), for £1, perhaps to (**2**) P. A. Hanrott, with whose library it was sold by Evans, 30 July 1833, lot 893, for £2. 1*s.* to Thorpe; (**3**) Evidently this is the copy of the *Songs* in '2 vols, 8vo' sold at 'Sotheby, 1855, mor. 12*l.* 5*s.*' (W. T. Lowndes, *The Bibliographer's Manual of English Literature* [1857], i. 215); (**4**) Sold by Charles E. Willis at Sotheby's, 31 July 1931, lot 624, for £1,600 to Quaritch —it bears the Quaritch collation marks; (**5**) Acquired by Mrs. William Emerson, who lent it to the Philadelphia exhibition (1939), no. 48, and sold

---

[1] The misdescription, and the consequent dissatisfaction of the purchaser, may be explained by the fact that a title-page (pl. 1) for *Innocence and Experience* exists with both *Innocence* and *Experience*. Since *Experience* is coloured and *Innocence* is not, lots 5 and 6 must represent *Innocence* and *Experience* respectively.

[2] A rubbing of the *For Children* (A) binding now with the *Songs* shows that the two are virtually identical. *For Children* (A) may have been bound about 1805.

[3] 'Two Contemporary Facsimiles of *Songs of Innocence and of Experience*', *Publications of the Bibliographical Society of America*, lxiv (1970), 450–63.

it posthumously at Sotheby's, 19 May 1958, lot 3, for £3,600 to Quaritch, who soon sold it to (6) Mr. George Goyder, who sold it about Jan. 1971 to Quaritch, who sold it for £12,000 to Warren Howell who sold it to (7) An *Anonymous* collector.

COPY Q: BINDING: (1a) The *Innocence* plates were originally stabbed through three holes, about 4·4 cm from the top and 4·0, 3·7 cm apart; (1b) The *Experience* plates were originally separately stabbed through three holes, 3·4 and 4·0 cm apart; (2) They were later bound in two volumes in matching gilt Green half calf over marbled boards (the spines bearing different ornaments), *both spines* gilt with 'SONGS / OF / INNOCENCE'.

HISTORY: (1) This is probably the set which the Revd. Joseph Thomas (1765–1811) bought on Flaxman's recommendation from Blake for £10. 10s.;[1] from Thomas it is likely to have passed, in 1811, like the second folio Shakespeare which Blake helped to illustrate, to (2) Mrs. Thomas,[2] thence many years later to her daughter[2] (3) Mrs. John Woodford Chase, and thence to Mrs. Chase's son[2] (4) Drummond Percy Chase (1820–1902); D. P. Chase gave it in about 1863[3] to (5) 'Alex. Macmillan', who signed the fly-leaf of each volume, and from whom it was inherited by his daughter, (6) Mrs. Lewis Dyer;[3] (7) It was acquired by Weyhe of New York (according to Keynes & Wolf), and was given (before 1953) to his daughter (8) *Mrs. Seth Dennis*.

COPY R: BINDING: (1a–b) *Innocence* was stabbed separately and *Experience* numbered separately before they were (2) Bound together, probably for John Linnell about 1824 (the watermark date on the second fly-leaf), in tooled White vellum to match his copies of *America* (O), *Europe* (K), *Marriage* (H), and *Jerusalem* (C), the spine gilt with 'SONGS / OF / INNOCENCE / BLAKE'; the designs are framed in three or four sepia lines.

HISTORY: (1) *Innocence* was apparently produced before *Experience*, both were bought by Linnell for £1. 19s. 6d. on 27 Aug. 1819 (according to the receipt Blake gave Linnell—*Blake Records* [1969], 581, 585), who had them bound after 1824; (2) The volume was 'Given to William Linnell / by John Linnell sen Apl 28 1863' (according to the note on the second fly-leaf); it was probably while the book was in the Linnell family that a rather childish hand wrote in it: 'The gentle Reader is earnestly requested not to touch these drawings with finger or thumb, not even ever so lightly'; it was bequeathed in 1906 to William Linnell's daughter (3) Mrs. T. H. Riches (d. 1950); a book-plate states that it was bequeathed by T. H. Riches in 1935 to (4) The FITZWILLIAM MUSEUM, which received it in 1950.

---

[1] According to A. Gilchrist, *Life of William Blake, 'Pictor Ignotus'* (1863), i. 124. Gilchrist says that 'For such a sum Blake could hardly do enough, finishing the plates like miniatures.' Copy Q is almost uncoloured, but its history seems quite clear. Perhaps Gilchrist's price and description do not apply to the Thomas copy.

[2] According to a note by D. P. Chase in the 1632 Shakespeare folio in the British Museum Print Room.

[3] According to Keynes (1921). Keynes told L. Parris ('William Blake's Mr. Thomas', *TLS*, 5 Dec. 1968, p. 1390) that these details were given to him by Mrs. Dyer. D. P. Chase said he sold the 1632 Shakespeare to Macmillan in 1880.

COPY S: BINDING: (1) Perhaps originally stabbed through heavy greyish-Brown wrappers (such as the leaf now separating *Innocence* from *Experience*); (2) Bound about 1822 (one flyleaf is watermarked '1 /1822') in Brown calf, the panels gilt with one framing-line, the spine blind stamped and gilt with 'SONGS / OF / INNOCENCE / BLAKE. / 1794=5'; the trimming of the edges may have removed the stab holes (if they existed).

HISTORY: (1) Perhaps bought by Sir Francis Chantry;[1] (2) This is probably the copy (54 coloured leaves, bound in gilt calf, octavo) sold anonymously at Sotheby's, 15 Aug. 1890, lot 3,173, for £48 to Maggs; (3) Acquired before 1905 by Mrs. John R. Wade of Brooklyn (J. Sampson, ed., *Poetical Works of William Blake* [1905], 74); (4) Acquired before 1921 by Beverly Chew, who added his book-plate and sold it at Anderson Galleries, 18 Dec. 1924, lot 29, for $5,500 to Rosenbach; (5) Acquired by Mr. John J. Emery, who signed the front cover, lent it to the Philadelphia exhibition (1939), no. 42, and gave it in 1969 to (6) The CINCINNATI ART MUSEUM.

COPY T: BINDING: Bound in modern Brown morocco, g.e.; there is a Red framing-line round the designs on pl. 1–5, 8–18, 20–3, 25–7, 29–31, 34–7, 39, 44–6, 48, 52–4.

HISTORY: (1) Evidently the plates now in copy T were originally parts of two separate copies, called here T[1] and T[2]. T[1] probably consisted of *Experience* pl. 28–33, 37–51 (or perhaps only of the surviving pl. 29–33, 38, 40–3, 46–7, 49–51) which were colour printed about 1795 on untrimmed, unwatermarked leaves about 12·6×19·4 cm and stitched through three stab holes. T[2] must have been a complete copy of the *Songs* (pl. 1–54) printed much later in Orange on untrimmed paper about 14·7×23·6 cm watermarked RUSE & TURNER / 1815, with Red framing-lines round the plates, numbered 1–54 in Red in the top right corners, and sewn through three different stab holes. (2ai) Copy T[2] is evidently the coloured copy sold anonymously at Sotheby's, 20 Jan. 1852, lot 45, for £4. 14s. to Evans; it was then evidently incomplete, for the printed description of 'Fifty-four designs' (presumably deriving from the '54' on the last plate) was altered by hand in the BM copy to 'Fifty-two'. Other plates (?damaged ones) were evidently removed, and pl. 1–5, 8–18, 20–3, 25–7, 29–31, 34–7, 39, 44–6, 48, 52–4 of T[2] were merged with pl. 32–3, 38, 40–3, 47, 49–51 from T[1], with pl. (6–7), (19, 24) (?from *Innocence* [F]), and with pl. 28 (?from *Songs* [J]), all were trimmed to 11·7×18·5 cm, bound as copy T, and sold by Messrs. Evans on 9 Feb. 1856 with *Thel* (D), *America* (H), *Song of Los* (A), and the Large (A) and Small Book of Designs (A) to (2aii) The BRITISH MUSEUM PRINT ROOM. (2bi) Pl. 29–31, 46 from T[1] and pl. 38, 41, 43, 47, 49–51 from T[2] were sold by E. Parsons & Son of London to (2bii) The NATIONAL GALLERY OF CANADA. (2ci) Pl. 28, 37, 39, 44–5, 48 from T[1] and pl. 6–7, 19, 24, 28, 32–3, 40, 42 from T[2] are *UNTRACED*.

COPY U: BINDING: Bound before 1824 by Charles Lewis according to

[1] According to Gilchrist ([1863], i. 124–5, 357–8), 'In the last years of his life, Sir Thomas Lawrence, Sir Francis Chantrey, and others, paid as much as twelve and twenty guineas [*for* highly finished *copies of the* SONGS, Blake] . . . printing off only one side of the leaf, and expanding the book by help of margin into a handsome quarto.' No copy has evidence of ownership by Lawrence or Chantry, and *most* copies of *Songs* are printed on one side only.

the 1824 and 1828 catalogues, in gilt Green crushed levant morocco, the spine gilt with 'Blake's Songs of / Innocence', g.e.; a single line frames each plate.

HISTORY: (1) Evidently this is the copy of James Boswell (1778–1822, the son of Johnson's biographer) (according to the 1828 catalogue), which was probably the one (2) Offered by Rivington & Cochran (1824), lot 11,795 (54 coloured plates '*bound by Charles Lewis*' [1786–1836] in '*green morocco, extra, g.l.*'), for £8. 8s.; (3) Sold with the property of the bookseller Thomas Edwards by Stewart, Wheatley, & Adlard, 15 May 1828, lot 940 ('SONGS OF INNOCENCE[1] . . . *from the Collection of the late James Boswell*' '*bound by Lewis in venetian morocco extra, gilt leaves*'), for £2. 19s. to Clarke the first fly-leaf is inscribed in pencil '940' and 'Edwards May 1828'; (4) Numbered by William Beckford on the first fly-leaf ('No 3851'), and sold with his Library at Sotheby's, 4 July 1882, lot 951, for £146 to Quaritch; (5) Quaritch added his Beckford sale book-plate, and offered it in Rough List 58 (30 July 1882), lot 202, and *General Catalogue* (1887), lot 10,250, each for £170; it was used for the facsimiles of Muir (1885) and Quaritch (1893), and bought 'of B. Q. / £170' (according to the note at the bottom right corner of the last fly-leaf) by (6) 'W A White / 23 Oct. 1895' (according to the pencil note on the first fly-leaf), who lent it anonymously to the Grolier Club exhibition (1905), no. 7, and gave it to his daughter (7) Mrs. Hugh D. Marshall (according to a letter to me from White's grandson Mr. Alexander M. White); Mrs. Marshall lent it to the Philadelphia exhibition (1939), no. 43, and sold it to her brother (8) Harold T. White (according to Mr. A. M. White); (9) It was 'Given to Emily de F. White [*Mrs. H. T. White*] Xmas 1947 by H T W' (according to an inserted note); (10) Given by Miss Caroline Newton on 21 March 1967 to PRINCETON.

COPY V: BINDING: (1) Originally stabbed through three holes, 10·9 cm from the top, 5·3, 5·3 cm apart; (2) Bound, probably for James Vine (whose *Thel* [O], *Milton* [D], and *Jerusalem* [J] are in similar bindings) in half Brown russia over Blue marbled boards, the edges marbled; there are four lines framing each plate, with a pale water-colour wash between the second and third lines on all but pl. 44, 51, as follows: Blue (pl. 1, 9, 14, 16, 21, 29, 31, 37, 46, 50, 52), Green (pl. 2, 17, 32), Pink (pl. 3, 5, 8, 10, 22, 27, 33, 36, 38, 40, 47), yellowish-Green (pl. 4, 6–7, 11, 18–19, 23–5, 28, 35, 49, 53–4), Yellow—only marginally distinguishable from the yellowish-Green—(pl. 12, 15, 34, 39, 42), Grey (pl. 13, 20, 26, 43, 45, 48), Purple (pl. 30), and Brown (pl. 41).

HISTORY: (1) Probably this is the copy sold posthumously for James Vine[2] at Christie's, 24 April 1838, lot 299, 'h.b.' (half bound) for £7. 15s. to

[1] The misdescription as 'SONGS OF INNOCENCE' for this copy of *Songs of Innocence and o Experience* may be due to the fact that the spine says 'SONGS OF INNOCENCE' and no more. The inscription ('Edwards May 1828') on *Songs* (U) indicates that it was the copy sold in May 1828; the 54 plates in the 1824 description indicate that it too was the combined *Songs*; therefore Keynes & Wolf are probably wrong in suggesting that Boswell's copy was *Innocence* (F).

[2] Keynes & Wolf, echoing Keynes (1921), say, on evidence unknown to me, that copy V was 'Originally in the possession of Thomas Butts. Then acquired by Richard Monckton Milnes, Lord Houghton, and from him passed to his son the Earl of Crewe.'

Bohn;[1] (2) Offered with 54 coloured plates 'hf. bd.' by Henry G. Bohn (1841), lot 177 (no price); (3) Probably acquired by R. M. Milnes and sold by his son the Earl of Crewe at Sotheby's, 30 March 1903, lot 1, for £300 to Quaritch; (4) Acquired by Algernon Methuen, lent by Lady Methuen to the exhibitions of the National Gallery (1913), no. 87, and the Burlington Fine Arts Club (1927), no. 77, and sold for Algernon Methuen at Sotheby's, 19 Feb. 1936, lot 499, for £1,050 to Rosenbach; (5) Acquired by Mrs. Landon K. Thorne, who lent it to the Philadelphia exhibition (1939), no. 46, in whose catalogue (1971) it was described (no. 7), and who gave it in February 1972 to (6) The PIERPONT MORGAN LIBRARY.

COPY W: BINDING: (1) Originally stabbed through three holes, 9·2 cm from the top, 4·2 and 4·7 cm apart; (2) Bound (by Bedford, say Keynes & Wolf using evidence unknown to me) in Red morocco, g.e.; round the borders of the plates are rather ineffective scrolls, leaves, and decorations not related to the text, usually in Green, sometimes in Blue, Orange, or Grey, which 'Mrs Blake . . . added . . . after Blake's death'.[2]

HISTORY: (1) Described by Catherine Blake as being 'especially precious from having been "Blake's own"';[3] (2) Bought for £10. 10s. from Catherine Blake by Haviland Burke for John Jebb, Bishop of Limerick, on 2 March 1830 (*Blake Records* [1969], 379); on Jebb's death in 1833 (3) 'This book came into the possession of [*his curate*] the Rev. Charles Forster' (according to a note by L. M. Forster pasted in);[4] 'it was left by the Rev. Charles Forster to his eldest daughter [4] Laura Mary Forster[4] signed by her June 27, 1903' (as the above note continues); she added her book-plate and gave it on 'New Year's Day, 1904' (as the note concludes) to her nephew (5) E. M. Forster; it was willed by Forster (according to a note of 8 Sept. 1939 with the book) and then given by him for his birthday (according to an accompanying letter of 7 July 1959 to A. N. L. Munby, the Librarian) to (6) KING'S COLLEGE, Cambridge.

COPY X: BINDING: (1) 'Originally bound in boards covered with light green calico'; (2) By 1905 the sheets were 'mounted in a book of white drawing paper, 12 × 15 inches' and 'Half-bound in morocco' (J. Sampson, ed., *Poetical Works of William Blake* [1905], 75); (3) 'BOUND BY RIVIERE & SON' by 1918 in elaborate Red crushed levant morocco, g.e.; a Red line frames each plate.

HISTORY: (1) Ordered by T. G. Wainewright by Feb. 1827 (*Blake Records* [1969], 339) and apparently described by Blake on 12 April 1827 as the copy he was 'now Printing . . . for a Friend at Ten Guineas' which would require at least 'Six Months'; 'It was executed by the highly gifted artist

---

[1] Bohns' copy could alternatively be J or S.

[2] George Richmond told this to Mrs. L. M. Forster, who repeated it to her nephew E. M. Forster on 14 May 1923 in a letter (now with the book).

[3] Gilchrist (1863), i. 365. 'Mr Blake's Nursery Rhyme' (which Keynes [1921] and Keynes & Wolf report to be 'laid in loose') cannot now be traced by either the late Mr. Forster (according to his letter to me) or by Mr. A. N. L. Munby, the book's present custodian.

[4] Keynes & Wolf say it was 'Given by Bishop Jebb to the Misses Thornton, daughters of Henry Thornton, M.P. The youngest, Laura, married the Rev. C. Forster.'

expressly for his friend, Mʳ Wain[e]wright, to whom, I am told, he was at the time under considerable pecuniary obligations . . . J. W. May 1835' (according to a note pasted in); (2) It came 'From the Library of James Weale Esqʳ 1840' (according to a pencilled note below the former one); (3) This was evidently the copy for which John Linnell paid on 13 Dec. 1842 'to Mʳ White for a Copy of Blakes Songs Colᵈ 10—' (according to Linnell's 'Cash Book' no '3' for 1837–48 with the Ivimy MSS); (4) It was 'Given to John Linnell, Junʳ by John Linnell senʳ—April 28, 1863' (according to a note on the third fly-leaf); the first fly-leaf is inscribed 'John Linnell junʳ / 1863', and the second fly-leaf has a note, presumably by a Linnell: 'These Drawings should not be touched with the finger'; it was bound for the Linnells and sold with their Blake Collection at Christie's, 15 March 1918, lot 201, for £735 to Dighton; (5) It is described as 'My Copy / B L D' (on the verso of the second fly-leaf under a cutting from the 1918 catalogue); (6) It was sold by 'a Lady' at Sotheby's, 9 June 1921, lot 3, for £510 to Sabin; (7) Acquired by George C. Smith, Jr., described in his anonymous catalogue (1927), no. 5, lent to the Fogg exhibition (1930), and sold posthumously at Parke-Bernet, 2 Nov. 1938, lot 17, for $9,000 to Sessler; (8) Acquired by Mary S. Collins (Mrs. Philip Collins), who added her book-plate, and lent it to the Philadelphia exhibition (1939), no. 44; she left it in 1947 (according to Keynes & Wolf) to her daughter-in-law (9) Dorothea Collins (Mrs. Alan Collins); from Mrs. Alan Collins it passed into an (10) *Anonymous collection.*

COPY Y: BINDING: (1) Once stitched; (2) Now loose, mounted on huge mats (35×59 cm), mostly two plates per mat; there are non-representational leaf borders round all the plates, up to 1·0 cm wide, often elaborate and fine, sometimes very modest, mostly in Green, sometimes in Orange, Red, or Black.

HISTORY: (1) Acquired from Blake by Edward Calvert (according to the 1893 and 1901 catalogues below); (2) Bought, evidently from 'the Calvert family', by (3) Ellis & Elvey, who offered it in their Catalogue 75 (?1893), lot 34, for £150; sold with the F. S. Ellis Library at Sotheby's, 4 Nov. 1901, lot 5 for £700 (4) to A. Jackson; (5) Acquired by 1905 by Marsdon J. Perry (according to J. Sampson, ed., *Poetical Works of William Blake* [1905], 76), who lent it anonymously to the Grolier Club exhibition (1905), no. 8, and 'sold it about 1906'[1] to (6) W. A. White who evidently lent it anonymously to the Grolier Club exhibition (1919), no. 3, and sold it 'through Dodd'[1] in Oct. 1917 to (7) The METROPOLITAN MUSEUM OF ART of New York.

COPY Z: BINDING: Bound about 1826 (the fourth and eighth fly-leaves are watermarked J WHATMAN / 1826) for Crabb Robinson in dark Purple straight grain levant morocco, gilt and blind stamped, the front panel gilt with 'BLAKE'S / SONGS / OF / INNOCENCE / AND / EXPERIENCE', the spine with 'SONGS / OF / INNOCENCE / AND / EXPERIENCE / BY / BLAKE', with Green marbled endpapers, eight fly-leaves at the front, six at the rear, g.e.; unbound by Peter Francke in 1953 and rebound by him in 1956 in the same covers— —perhaps it was at this time that the plates were mounted on hinges (Keynes

[1] According to Keynes & Wolf.

& Wolf do not mention hinges); there is one Red water-colour framing-line round each plate; *Marriage* (K) was loose in the cover until 1912.

HISTORY: (1) 'This copy I received from Blake himself[1]—And coloured by his own hand which I present with great pleasure to Edwin W. Field—/ H. C. Robinson / March 11ᵗʰ 1863. / 30 Russell Square / London' (according to the note on the sixth fly-leaf); Robinson inserted his book-plate, and wrote on it in pencil; 'ætat 88 / to / [2] Edwin W Field / 11 Mar 1863'; (3) 'Given to F. W. Burton / by Mʳˢ Edwin Field / in memory of her husband / Oct 6 1871' (according to the note on the second fly-leaf); (4) 'Directed by my uncle Sir Frederic Burton (when dying) to be given to Chaˢ Fairfax Murray Esq / 20.6.1900 / H B Burton' (according to the note on the second fly-leaf); sold posthumously for Murray at Sotheby's, 7 July 1919, lot 8, for £600 to Sabin; (5) Acquired by Willis Vickery, who added his book-plate, described it in his book (1927), and sold it posthumously at American Art Association–Anderson Galleries, 1 March 1933, lot 16, for $6,000 to Rosenbach; (6) Acquired by Frank Lewis Bemis, who added his book-plate, lent it anonymously to the Philadelphia exhibition (1939), no. 45, and sold it posthumously on 4 Nov. 1938 through Rosenbach to (7) Mr. LESSING J. ROSENWALD, who wrote on the last fly-leaf: 'In ca. 1953 this volume was sent to Peter Francke to be unbound in order to have a facsimile made by the Trianon Press (for the Blake Trust). Upon completion the book was rebound by Peter Francke in 1956. Lessing Rosenwald / 2/8/56'; another facsimile was made in 1967.

COPY AA: BINDING: Pasted on large sheets (21·5 × 27·6 cm) and bound in Red cloth; there is a Red framing-line round each plate.

HISTORY: (1) Delivered to Mrs. Charles Aders on 10 Dec. 1825, who paid £5. 5s. for it on 29 July 1826, according to Blake's receipt,[2] and sold it for £6. 6s. after Aug. 1835 to (2) John Linnell;[2] (3) 'Given to James Thoˢ Linnell / by John Linnell senʳ April 28 / 1863' (according to the note on the second fly-leaf), and sold for J. T. Linnell's Trustees at Christie's, 15 March 1918, lot 215, for £735 to Carfax for (4) T. H. Riches, who lent it to the Burlington Fine Arts Club Exhibition (1927), no. 78, and for whom a book-plate was inserted bequeathing it in 1935 to (5) the FITZWILLIAM MUSEUM, which received it in 1950; reproduced in colour microfilm by Micro Methods Ltd.

COPY BB: BINDING: Bound in elegant Brown calf.

HISTORY: (1) The copy with '55 *Plates, brown calf, elegant*' sold anonymously (by Robert Balmanno, according to the BMPR catalogue) at Sotheby's, 13 Jan. 1830, lot 41, for £1 to Glynn is the only copy known with fifty-five plates, and none of the copies now in contemporary Brown calf can be identified with it; (2) *UNTRACED*.

N.B. All the following copies were printed after 1830.

COPY a: BINDING: (1) Once sewn (the stitching marks show at the left of

---

[1] It was apparently delivered on 10 Dec. 1825 and paid for (£5. 5s.) on 15 April 1826 (*Blake Records* [1969], 323, 591). Until 1912 *Marriage* (K) accompanied it.
[2] *Blake Records* (1969), 319–20, 583, & n. 1.

the plates); (2) The plates were mounted on stubs and bound after Jan. 1864 in the British Museum in Brown morocco with the King's Arms.

HISTORY: (1) Sold by [B. M.] Pickering on 7 Jan. 1864 for £9. 9s. to (2) The BRITISH MUSEUM where it was bound[1] with the royal arms and used for Pearson's facsimile (1876).

COPY b: BINDING: Bound after 1831 (the watermark date on the leaves) in Green gilt seal-grain morocco, with 'Songs of Innocence. & Experience. W. Blake' on the spine, and the initials ('h B') of Hannah Boddington on the boards, marbled edges.

HISTORY: (1) Acquired by Hannah Boddington and with her 'h B' on the boards; (2) Acquired by the Comtesse de Montebello (Hannah Boddington's sister, according to Keynes & Wolf), who added her book-plate numbered '2134'; (3) Sold by 'a Gentleman' at Sotheby's, 30 June 1906, lot 861, for £2. 12s. to Maggs; (4) Offered in Maggs Catalogue 255 (1910), lot 513, for £15. 15s.; (5) Acquired before 1921 by W. E. Moss, and sold at Sotheby's, 2 March 1937, lot 145, for £50 to Quaritch; (6) Acquired by Philip Hofer, who added his book-plate, lent it to the Philadelphia exhibition (1939), no. 51, and gave it on 1 July 1941 to (7) HARVARD; reproduced in facsimile (1947, 1973).

COPY c: BINDING: Bound in heavy Red morocco with an owl on the front cover and a harp or lyre on the back,[2] g.e.

HISTORY: (1) Acquired by Samuel Boddington, who added his book-plate; (2) Perhaps acquired and bound by T. J. Wise (like *For the Sexes* [C]); (3) Acquired by Stopford Brooke, and inherited (according to the present owner) by his granddaughter (4) *Mrs. William Drysdale*.

COPY d: BINDING: Pl. 30–2, 37, 44–5, 47, 50–1, 54, b, were apparently transferred to copy a before the work was bound in russia with the first type-set edition of the *Songs* (1839) (according to the 1914 catalogue).

HISTORY: (1) The 'title-page' (? pl. 1) is inscribed 'Wm Odell Elwell [Elwill *according to the 1937 catalogue*] 1840' (according to Keynes [1921]);[3] (2) Sold anonymously at Sotheby's, 16 March 1909, lot 145 (bound in russia), for £6. 6s. to Tregaskis; (3) Offered by 'Tregaskis in one of his catalogues shortly afterwards (36 g)' (according to Keynes [1921]); (4) Offered in Maggs Catalogue 325 (1914), lot 254 (bound in morocco), for £12. 12s.; (5) Acquired before 1921 by W. E. Moss and sold at Sotheby's, 2 March 1937, lot 146, for £32 to Maggs; (6) Acquired by the dealer Stonehill in 1937; (7) *UNTRACED*.[4]

[1] Pl. 30–2, 37, 44–5, 47, 50–1, 54, b, printed in Brown (rather than Grey), and differing in size from the others (19·2 × 27·5 cm rather than 19·4 × 24·4 cm), may have been taken from copy d (which is printed in brown and is missing all these plates plus pl. 15, 48), or copy e (missing these Brown plates plus pl. 33, 41, 46, 53). Pl. 30–2, 37, 44, 47 printed in Grey (LC) may be the Grey plates missing from copy a. The fragmentary copy o, also owned by Pickering, may also have contributed leaves to copy a.

[2] The binding style appears to me to be of perhaps the 1830s, but the ornaments seem to be those of T. J. Wise.

[3] If the missing plates (except pl. 15, 48) went to copy a, the rest of copy d must have been cut down from the 19·2 × 27·5 cm of the added plates of copy a to the present 11·0 × 18·0 cm of copy d.

[4] The Stonehill firm now has no record of who bought it. Keynes & Wolf say it is 'now in

COPY e: BINDING: (1) Pl. 30–3, 37, 41, 44–7, 50–2 (coloured by Blake) were originally stabbed through three holes, 2·6, 2·8 cm apart, with the uncoloured *Songs* (K) and the *Innocence* plates of *Songs* (O); (2) The *Songs* (O) plates were separated by 1817; the plates of copy e above were sewn with the other plates of copy e in Yellow morocco (according to the 1901 catalogue), g.e. (the plates formerly stabbed with copies K and O not gilt at the bottom) and coloured after 1862; (3) All the plates of copy e were disbound after 1899 and are now loose and mounted.

HISTORY: (1) Originally pl. 30–3, 37, 41, 44–7, 50–2 (coloured) were stabbed with copy K (uncoloured) and copy O (*Innocence* only, uncoloured); copy O was separated by 1817 and K probably later; (Ai) The forty un-numbered and apparently posthumous leaves of copy e were probably the ones sold as the property of 'An Amateur' (? Tatham) at Sotheby's, 29 April 1862, lot 196 (not said to be coloured), for £1. 6s. to Toovey; these plates were probably coloured for Toovey (the colouring does not show in the offsets) and stitched with the (Bi) Thirteen genuinely coloured plates acquired elsewhere; (2) The composite work was sold by James Toovey in 1899 to (3) The PIERPONT MORGAN LIBRARY,[1] where the plates were disbound.

COPY f: BINDING: Bound by Leighton in 1869 in straight grain Black morocco, in borders inlaid with Red, g.e. (according to Keynes [1921]).

HISTORY: (1) An early owner 'dated the book 1836' (according to a note on the fly-leaf);[2] (2) Acquired by Frederick Collins Wilson, who added his book-plate,[2] (3) Sold anonymously at Sotheby's, 18 Dec. 1919, lot 447, for £39 to Sabin; (4) *UNTRACED*. This may have been sophisticated into copy j.

COPY g¹: BINDING: The plates were mounted on linen stubs and 'BOUND BY RIVIERE & SON FOR H. BUXTON FORMAN' by 1920 in Maroon morocco.

HISTORY: (1) Acquired by H. Buxton Forman, who had it bound, added his book-plate, and sold it at Anderson Galleries, 15 March 1920, lot 51, for $60 to Rosenbach; (2) Acquired by A. E. Newton, who added his book-plate, and sold it posthumously at Parke-Bernet, 16 April 1941, lot 159, for $70 to Sessler; (3) Sold by Sessler to Knoedler (according to Keynes & Wolf); (4) Acquired by Grace Lansing Lambert, who added her book-plate, and gave it in Jan. 1960 to (5) PRINCETON.

COPY g²: BINDING: The plates were mounted on linen stubs and 'BOUND BY RIVIERE & SON FOR H. BUXTON FORMAN' by 1920 in Maroon crushed levant morocco, Jansen style.

HISTORY: (1) Acquired by H. Buxton Forman, who had it bound, added his book-plate, and sold it posthumously at Anderson Galleries, 15 March 1920, lot 52, for $65 to Rosenbach; (2) Acquired by R. B. Adam, who added his book-plate, and sold it at Anderson Galleries, 15 Feb. 1926, lot 36, for $50 to Rosenbach; (3) A. S. W. Rosenbach gave it in the autumn of 1938 to (4) Mr. LESSING J. ROSENWALD.

the Yale University Library', but Miss Marjorie G. Wynne (Research Librarian, Yale University Library) wrote to me that it 'is not at Yale and never has been'.

[1] It is described in the *Catalogue of a Collection of Books* formed by James Toovey principally from the library of the Earl of Gosford the property of J. Pierpont Morgan (1901).

[2] According to Keynes (1921).

COPY h: BINDING: The plates were mounted on linen stubs and bound by Riviere & Son for H. Buxton Forman by 1920 in Maroon morocco, Jansen style (according to the 1920 catalogue).

HISTORY: (1) Sold posthumously by H. Buxton Forman at Anderson Galleries, 15 March 1920, lot 53, for $90 to Rosenbach; (2) *UNTRACED*.

COPY i: BINDING: Loose, never sewn.

HISTORY: (1Ai) All but pl. 48 were evidently sold anonymously (? by Tatham) at Sotheby's, 29 April 1862, lot 195 ('43' plates) for £4. 6s. to Toovey; (Bi) The paper, size, printing colour, and numbers (revised after pl. 48) all suggest that pl. 48 was acquired separately; (2) All the plates were acquired by Henry Cunliffe, and bequeathed by him to his great-nephew[1] (3) Lord Cunliffe, on whose death in 1963 they passed to his son (4) The present *Lord Cunliffe*.

COPY j: BINDING: The plates were printed posthumously (the watermark is J W[H]ATMAN / [18]31), trimmed down to within 0·5 to 0·8 cm of the etching, inlaid, a Red line was drawn round the inlaid leaves (leaving ink on both the outer and inner leaves), numbered in the same Red ink, and sewn into two volumes of contemporary straight grain Green morocco, gilt and blind stamped, with 'W. BLAKE / — / SONGS OF INNOCENCE / AND / EXPERIENCE / VOL. 1 [2.]' on the spines (*Experience* in Vol. I, *Innocence* in Vol. II), with greyish-Brown endpapers, interleaved and with twenty-four fly-leaves in Vol. I, thirty in Vol. II of the same paper as the leaves in which the plates are inlaid, g.e.

N.B. The binding itself seems to Keynes & Wolf and to me to be contemporary, and the endpapers and adjacent fly-leaves look to be of the same date. However, the gilding appears to Keynes & Wolf to be more recent than the binding—it looks about mid 19th-century to me—and the fly-leaves, interleaves, and the paper in which the plates are inlaid all seem mid 19th-century. Additionally, the colouring, though often plausible, does not seem to be by Blake, particularly in pl. 22, 35, 40, 46, 48. It seems likely, therefore, that the plates were cut down to obscure the watermark, inlaid, bordered, numbered, and coloured before 1925 (perhaps in the late 19th century——see copy e), and sewn into two bindings which were already fifty to one hundred years old.

HISTORY: (1) This may be copy f (last traced in 1919) sophisticated; it is 'From the collection of Julian Marshall' (according to the note on the second fly-leaf of Vol. II); (2) Bought from Sabin in July 1925 for £550 ($2,640) by (3) Sessler's and sold (with Blake's letter of 11 Dec. 1805) on 13 July 1925 for $3,000 (according to a letter of 5 Jan. 1965 from Miss Mabel Zahn of Sessler's, now with the volumes) to (4) A. E. Newton (d. 1941), who added his bookplate, and wrote a note on the fly-leaf of Vol. I saying that he gave it 'Many years ago' to his daughter (5) *Miss Caroline Newton*, who in turn added her book-plate, and lent it to the exhibitions in Philadelphia (1939), no. 50, and Princeton (1967), (1969), no. 47.

---

[1] According to Keynes & Wolf.

COPY k: BINDING: The plates were mounted in a frame in 1937, but after that date they were dismounted, and are now loose.

HISTORY: (1) Copies k and m were probably the plates lent 'In frames' by Mme Bodichon to the Burlington Fine Arts Club exhibition (1876), nos. 275–6;[1] and (2) Copy k was sold 'in one frame' for the late Mrs. J. M. Morse at Christie's, 19 March 1937, lot 45 (with *Songs* [m], framed), for £26. 5s. to (3) *Keynes*, who dismounted and described them in his catalogue (1964), no. 516, 518.

COPY l: BINDING: (1) Once sewn (there are stitch holes in the left margins), but (2) Now loose.

HISTORY: (1) Sold in Jan. 1925 by Francis Edwards[2] to (2) *Geoffrey Keynes*, who described it in his catalogue (1964), no. 517 (with *Songs* pl. 51), and lent it anonymously to the exhibitions at the Whitworth Art Gallery (1969), no. 6, and the National Library of Scotland (1969), no. 40.

COPY m: BINDING: Mounted in a frame in 1937, but now loose.
    HISTORY: The History is as in copy k.

COPY n: BINDING: (1) Bound in contemporary rough calf with other leaves of Blakeana including *Thel* (a), but (2) Now loose and mounted.
    HISTORY: The History is as in *Thel* (a), p. 131.

COPY o: BINDING: Loose.
    HISTORY: (1) Bought from B. M. Pickering in 1869[3] (according to Keynes & Wolf) by (2) Charles Eliot Norton; (3) Acquired by Paul Hyde Bonner and offered with his Library by Dutton's (1931), no. 34, for $350; (4) Acquired and broken up, apparently by Weyhe, in whose catalogue (Dec. 1938) were offered pl. 20 (? and 21) (lot 128, $75), pl. 38 (lot 126, $50), pl. 39 (lot 127, $50); pl. 39 (marked 'Chas E. Norton Coll.') was acquired from Weyhe in 1963 for $75 by (5 **Ai**) *G. E. Bentley, Jr.*; (**Bi**) The rest of the plates are *UNTRACED*, unless some are to be found in copy k.

ELECTROTYPES: HISTORY: (1) Blake's copperplates evidently came through Mrs. Blake's hands to Frederick Tatham, from whom most of them were stolen. A few survived for a time, for, according to D. G. Rossetti, 'the original plates [*3, 6, 8, 16, 18, 24, 27, 29, 33–4, 36, 43, 46–8, 53*] of the *Songs* . . . were recovered by Mr. Gilchrist [*who died in 1861*], being the only remnant of the series still in existence on copper'.[4] Electrotypes were made of these and were printed for Macmillan in Gilchrist's *Life of William Blake* (1863, 1880), Vol. ii. The copperplates from which these electrotypes were made then disappeared. The electrotypes seem to be identical in form with Blake's plates except for pl. 29 (the title-page to *Experience*), which lacks some details, such as the '1794' and the flourish on the 'T' in the imprint, and adds others, particularly the shading on the couch-tomb. I cannot account for these variants.[5] The electrotypes were preserved by Macmillan's printer,

---

[1] Keynes & Wolf call this copy CC.   [2] According to Keynes & Wolf.
[3] Copy o may have contributed some leaves to copy a, which was also owned by Pickering.
[4] Gilchrist (1863), ii. 267.
[5] John Sampson (ed., *Poetical Works of William Blake* [1905], 105) says that 'the titlepage would appear to have been engraved twice by Blake. In Gilchrist's reprint the date is

Richard Clay & Co., until about 1961, when (according to letters to GEB from the Macmillan firm) they were destroyed by Clay & Co. on instructions from Macmillan; before their destruction, however, electrotypes of the Macmillan electrotypes were made for (**2 Ai**) Keynes, from which sets of prints were pulled for Keynes & Ruthven Todd (1941), and which Keynes gave in 1955 to (**Aii**) The VICTORIA & ALBERT MUSEUM, (**Bi**) Pl. 33 was acquired by the BRITISH MUSEUM PRINT ROOM; (**Ci**) A set was acquired by the FITZ-WILLIAM MUSEUM, from which in turn an electrotype set was made in 1964 for (**Di**) *G. E. Bentley, Jr.*

Pl. a: BINDING: Loose.

HISTORY: (**1**) This may be the 'Typical Figure of Immortality' lent by Mrs. Gilchrist to the Burlington Fine Arts Club exhibition (1876), no. 293; (**2**) Perhaps this is the copy acquired before 1911[1] by Stopford Brooke, and sold posthumously at Sotheby's, 27 July 1917, lot 792; (**3**) Offered in Tregaskis Catalogue 810 (20 Jan. 1919) for £23 (according to Keynes [1921], 115 n); (**4**) Acquired by R. B. Adam, who gave it (according to the 1941 catalogue below) to (**5**) A. E. Newton, who lent it to the Philadelphia exhibition (1939), no. 52, and sold it posthumously at Parke-Bernet, 16 April 1941, lot 137, for $400; (**6**) Acquired by Mr. *Joseph Holland*.

Pl. b: BINDING: Bound as in *America* pl. 6; see p. 339.

HISTORY: For its History, see the 'Order' of the *Songs*, p. 337.

Pl. 3^{a-b}, 22, 48^{a-b}: BINDING: Loose.

HISTORY: (**1**) Given by Mrs. John Richmond in 1922 to (**2**) The TATE GALLERY.

Pl. 6–7: BINDING: Loose, mounted.

HISTORY: (**1**) Perhaps this is the unidentified and apparently coloured *Innocence* leaf lent by Mrs. Gilchrist to the Burlington Fine Arts Club exhibition (1876), no. 289; (**2**) Acquired by E. W. Hooper, who lent it to the Boston exhibitions (1880), no. 44, (1891), no. 1c, and given in his memory by (**3**) His daughters on 1 July 1941 to (**4**) HARVARD.

Pl. 7, 10, 33: BINDING: Trimmed to about 0·2 cm of the etching, loose, mounted.

HISTORY: (**1**) Perhaps owned by 'C Dew', whose name is on the verso in modern Blue ink;[2] (**2**) Sold by Henry Martin at Sotheby's, 31 July 1961, lot 485, for £17 to Parker, who sold them to (**3**) Dr. *B. E. Juel-Jensen*.

Pl. 9–10: BINDING: (**1**) Originally stabbed through three holes, 1·0 and 1·9 cm apart; (**2**) Later bound in an extra-illustrated Gilchrist (1863), but (**3**) Disbound after 1941, now loose.

---

omitted . . . In some [*original*] copies the date has evidently been inserted by hand.' I have not observed hand-inserted dates on copies the Blakes printed and know no evidence suggesting that Blake engraved pl. 28 twice except for the duplicate plate with the electrotypes, which I cannot explain. Perhaps the electrotype of pl. 29 is a facsimile (not an electrotype) made in the middle of the nineteenth century.

[1] A. G. B. Russell, *The Engravings of William Blake* (1912), no. 16.

[2] Dr. Juel-Jensen understands that they were acquired by a soldier who offered them to Mr. Goyder. They may be the three coloured plates sold with *Songs* (h) in 1920.

HISTORY: (**1**) Bound in an extra-illustrated copy of Gilchrist (1863) which was acquired by (**2**) *Geoffrey Keynes*, who removed the leaves, and described those of the *Songs* in his catalogue (1964), no. 509.

Pl. 11, 30–2, 37, 40, 44, 47, 50; BINDING: (**1**) Pl. 30–2, 37, 44, 47 may once have formed part of copy a; (**2**) Mounted and bound about 1853 with other leaves of Blakeana including the 'Order' of the *Songs*; (**2**) The volume was broken up and the *Songs* plates were bound with the 'Order' after 1924, probably by Macdonald for G. C. Smith, Jr., in Blue morocco.

HISTORY: For their History, see the 'Order' of the *Songs* with which they were bound, p. 337.

Pl. 22, 28, 30, 40, 44–6, 48ᵃ⁻ᵇ: BINDING: Loose.

HISTORY: (**1**) Sold anonymously at Sotheby's, 9 Nov. 1964, lot 113, for £32 to Blackwell's, who in turn sold them in 1965 to (**2**) *G. E. Bentley, Jr.*

Pl. 24–5, 31, 37, 40, 47: HISTORY: (**1**) Mrs. Gilchrist lent one unidentified *Innocence* plate to the exhibition of the Burlington Fine Arts Club (1876), no. 289, and pl. 25 to that of the Boston Museum (1880), no. 14; (**2**) Her son H. H. Gilchrist lent pl. 24–5, 31, 37, 40, 47 to the Pennsylvania Academy of the Fine Arts exhibition (1892), no. 126–7, 142–4, 148; (**3ai**) Gilchrist's may be the coloured copy of pl. 24 sold by the late William Harcourt Hooper at Sotheby's, 15 July 1912, lot 213, for £7. 5s. to Maggs; (**3aii**) All the plates are now *UNTRACED*.

Pl. 28: BINDING: Mounted, framed.

HISTORY: (**1**) Acquired by Sir *Anthony Blunt* with *Songs* (J), with which it was associated some time between 1818 (when Coleridge omits it from his description of this copy—see *Blake Records* [1969], 251-3) and 1921[1] (when Keynes described it with copy J in his *Bibliography*).

Pl. 29–31, 38, 41, 43, 46–7, 49–51: BINDING: (**1a**) The colour-printed leaves (pl. 29–31, 46) were originally stabbed through three holes, about 2·7 cm from the top and 5·6, 6·7 from each other; (**1b**) The other leaves (pl. 38, 41, 43, 47, 49–51) were originally stabbed through three different holes, about 6·7 cm from the top and 4·1, 3·7 cm apart—probably with copy T; (**2**) Before 1856, these eleven plates were removed from copy T and are now separately mounted.

Pl. 29–30, 37: BINDING: Loose, since 1891.

HISTORY: (**1**) 'Taken in 1838: From the original plates / in the possession of Mr. Tatham' (according to a note in an unknown hand on the verso of pl. 29); (**2**) Acquired by E. W. Hooper, who lent them to the Boston exhibition (1891), no. 5b; (**3**) Given by Mrs. Ward Thoron with *Innocence* (U) on 15 Nov. 1950 to (**4**) HARVARD.

Pl. 42: BINDING: Loose.

HISTORY: (**1**) Offered in Ellis & Elvey Catalogues 81 and 82 (both ? 1895), lot 51 in both (one leaf, coloured), for £1. 10s.; (**2**) *UNTRACED*.

[1] It may have been part of *Songs* (N) and separated before 1859.

Pl. 42, 51; BINDING: Loose.
HISTORY: For their History, see the 'Order' of the *Songs*, p. 337.

Pl. 44: BINDING: For a time tipped into a copy of Gilchrist, but now loose.
HISTORY: (1) Tipped into a copy of Gilchrist's *Life* which was acquired 'many years' before 1967 (according to the present owner) by (2) Dr. *B. E. Juel-Jensen*, who removed it from the Gilchrist.

Pl. 51: BINDING: Mounted on a larger sheet (16·6 × 21·5 cm) and bound as in *America* pl. 6; see p. 339.
HISTORY: For the History, see the 'Order' of the *Songs*, p. 337.

140

The Songs of Experience. With designs by Celia Levetus. London, [1902].
Pre-Raphaelite designs for children.

141

Songs of Experience. London [1911]. Langham Booklets.

142

Songs of Experience. London [1912]. Arden Books.

143

*Songs of Experience [? *A*]. London, 1927. B. N.Y., (? 1927).
A colour facsimile by Ernest Benn, evidently of copy *A* (as in no. 160), though the plate-order is that of copy V.

144

*Blake Centenary 1927. The Songs of Experience [A, T]. Facsimiled by Joseph Patrick Trumble, Sophia Elizabeth Muir and William Muir, from the Beaconsfield Original [A] in the British Museum (22 plates) with, as an appendix, (four plates) from the other British Museum copy [T]. Also one plate [b] for which no colouring is known (The Divine Image), which seems to belong to the Songs though not included in them by Blake. London, 1927 (vDVE).

A 144

Songs of Experience. Yellow Springs [Ohio], 1928 (v Dr. Walter Kahoe).

145

Songs of Experience [b]. N.Y., [1947?].

The black-and-white facsimile and transcript is accompanied by a 19-page essay by Joseph H. Wicksteed called 'Songs of the Heart's Experience'. This little volume is a companion to no. 164 and was reprinted (without Wicksteed's essay) in no. 186.

146

Munyo no Uta [*Songs of Experience*]. Tr. Bunsho Jugaku. Kyoto, 1935.

Translations into Japanese face facsimiles of the poems, most of which were coloured by hand by the translator and his wife after several facsimiles.

147

Songs of Innocence. Reproduced by photography from a perfect black and white copy [U] of the original issue of 1789, Containing all the Poems afterwards called Songs of Innocence, and three more which were afterwards issued among the Songs of Experience. Boston, 1883.

148

Blake, His Songs of Innocence. Oxford, 1893.

149

Songs of Innocence. With Illustrations by Geraldine Morris. London & N.Y., 1902. Flowers of Parnassus—XII.

150

Songs of Innocence: Lyrics from the Works of William Blake. Portland, Mains, 1904. The Old World Series, No. 35 (vMKN).

151

Songs of Innocence. London & N.Y., [1905]. The Broadway Booklets.

152

Songs of Innocence. Illustrated by Olive Allen. London & Edinburgh [1906].

153

Songs of Innocence. With a Preface by Thomas Seccombe and Twelve Coloured Illustrations by Honor C. Appleton. London [1911].

'Preface' (pp. vii–xvii); the illustrations are distressing.

154

Songs of Innocence. London [1911]. Langham Booklets.

155

Songs of Innocence. London, 1911.

156

Songs of Innocence. Decorated by Charles Robinson & Mary H. Robinson. London & N.Y., [1912].
    The decorations are lamentable.

157

Songs of Innocence. London [1912]. Arden Books.

158

Songs of Innocence [I]. London, 1923.
    A colour facsimile by Frederick Hollyer.

159

Songs of Innocence. San Francisco, 1924.
    There is no text besides the poems in this privately printed Grabhorn edition.

160

A. *Songs of Innocence* [A]. London, 1926. B. N.Y., 1926.
    A colour facsimile by Earnest Benn; see no. 143.

161

Songs of Innocence. Illustrated by Jacynth Parsons. With a Prefatory Letter by W. B. Yeats. London & Boston, 1927.
    'Prefatory Letter' (pp. vii–viii); the illustrations are dreadful.

162

Blake Centenary 1927. The Songs of Innocence [A]. Facsimiled [in colour] by Joseph Patrick Trumble, Sophia Elizabeth Muir and William Muir, from the Beaconsfield Original in the British Museum (28 plates). London, 1927 (vDVE).

A 162

Songs of Innocence. Yellow Springs, [Ohio], 1928 (v R. E. Thompson).

163

Songs of Innocence. [Written out by Helen Hinkley and decorated by James Guthrie.] Flansham [England], 1939.

164

**Songs of Innocence* [b]. N.Y., [1947?]
    The black-and-white facsimile and transcript is accompanied by a 4-page introduction by Ruthven Todd. This little volume is a companion to no. 145 and was reprinted (with Todd's essay) in no. 186.

165

**Songs of Innocence* [B]. London, 1954. The William Blake Trust.
    Geoffrey Keynes, 'Bibliographical Statement', is 2 pp.

166

A. *Songs of Innocence*. With Decorations by Harold Jones. London, 1958.
B. N.Y., 1961.
    The designs, intended for children, are unBlakelike and lamentable.

167

Songs of Innocence. Illustrations by Ellen Raskin. Garden City, N.Y., 1966.
    E. R., 'Note' (p. 7) says the designs 'make no attempt to follow Blake's style or subject'.

168

**Songs of Innocence*. N.Y., 1971.
    The 'Publisher's Note' (2 pp.) explains that this is a colour facsimile of copy B. Most of the words are also given in conventional typography.

169

*Muzen no Uta [*Songs of Innocence*]. Tr. Bunsho Jugaku. Kyoto, 1932.
    Translations into Japanese face facsimiles of the poems, which were coloured by hand by the translator and his wife.

170

Chansons d'Innocence, Tr. Pierre Messiaen. Paris, 1934.

171

A. *Songs of Innocence and of Experience*. Shewing the Two Contrary States of the Human Soul. [Ed. James John Garth Wilkinson.] London, 1839. B. London, 1839. C. London, 1925.

Wilkinson's 'Preface' is pp. iii–xxi in A and B, pp. iii–xxiii in C, dated 9 July 1839 in all three. The poems from the *Songs* are in the order of copy J and are supplemented with the 'Dedication of the Poem of The Grave.' B. The second issue omits 'The Little Vagabond'.

172

[*Songs of Innocence and of Experience*. London, 1843?]

In the BM copy is the following note:

This copy of Blake's *Songs of Innocence and Experience* was printed by Mr Charles Augustus Tulk [*d. 1849*], a Friend of Blake's, and a dear friend of my Wifes and mine;—and spaced as in the Original, in order that any who chose, might copy in the paintings with which the original is adorned. Twelve copies only were printed.

J. J. Garth Wilkinson

April 9, 1886

The sheets are watermarked 1843.

173

**Facsimile of the Original Outlines before Colouring of The Songs of Innocence and of Experience* [U]. With an Introduction By Edwin J. Ellis. London, 1893.

The 'Introduction' is pp. v–xxi.

174

A. §**Songs of Innocence; and Songs of Experience*. Boston, 1901. B. § London, 1901.

175

Songs of Innocence and of Experience: Showing the two Contrary States of the Human Soul. [Ed. Ralph Fletcher Seymour.] Chicago, 1906 (vDVE).

176

**Songs of Innocence and Songs of Experience*. London & Guildford, 1911.

177

**Songs of Innocence* [*and of Experience*]. London, 1911.

The plates are not by Blake.

178

Songs of Innocence and of Experience. Liverpool, 1923.
  51 copies were coloured, the rest (100) are plain.

179

A. *Songs of Innocence and of Experience.* Ed. George H. Cowling. London, 1925.
Methuen's English Classics. *B. London, 1926. C. § 1951. D. § 1953. . . .
*F. London, 1958. *G. London, 1960.
  'Introduction', pp. xi–xx, 'Notes' ('a little friendly chat'), pp. 45–70.

180

Songs of Innocence and of Experience. Ed. Arthur D. Innes. London, Glasgow,
& Bombay, 1926.
  'Introduction' is pp. 7–14.

181

Songs of Innocence and Experience. New Rochelle [N.Y.], 1935 (vMKN).
  The 5 plates are adapted from Blake.

182

§*Songs of Innocence and of Experience.* London, 1936.

183

Songs of Innocence and Experience. Mount Vernon [N.Y., 1937] (vDVE).

184

A. *Songs of Innocence and Experience.* London, 1938. B. 1941.

185

Songs of Innocence and of Experience. Sixteen designs printed from electrotypes
of the original plates for Ruthven Todd and Geoffrey Keynes. London, 1941.
  One Bodley copy has a note by Keynes saying 20 copies were made.

A 185

Songs of Innocence and Experience. London, 1941. Zodiac Books.

186

A. *Songs of Innocence & of Experience* [b]. London & N.Y., 1947. Albion
Facsimiles No. 1. B. §*[Folcroft, Pa.], 1969.

This black-and-white facsimile seems to consist of the same plates used in the separate 1947 *Innocence* (no. 164) and *Experience* (no. 145). Ruthven Todd's 4-page introduction is also reprinted in the 1947 *Innocence*.

187

*Songs of Innocence and of Experience [Z]. London, 1955. The William Blake Trust.

Geoffrey Keynes, 'Bibliographical Statement', is 3 pp.

188

A. **Songs of Innocence and of Experience*. Ed. Andrew M. Wilkinson. London, 1958. B. §1962. C. §1962. D. 1965. E. §1969. F. 1970.

'Introduction' (pp. vii–xx).

189

Songs of Innocence and Experience. Mount Vernon, [N.Y., 1958].

190

A. **Songs of Innocence and Of Experience* [Z]. London, 1967. B. N.Y., 1967.

A facsimile 'printed in 6- and 8-colour offset', with facing transcript and following explication. The 'Publisher's Note' by Arnold Fawcus is pp. vii–viii, the 'Introduction' by Geoffrey Keynes pp. ix–xvii.

191

Songs of Innocence and of Experience: Shewing the Two Contrary States of the Human Soul. Supplementary Material by Ruth E. Everett. N.Y., 1971.

'The Life of William Blake' (pp. 7–18), 'The Significance of Blake' (pp. 19–22), 'Structure and Special Qualities of the *Songs of Innocence and of Experience*' (pp. 22–3), 'Editions' (pp. 24–5), notes on each poem (e.g. '*wight*: creature', p. 66), 'Famous Quotations from *Songs of Innocence and of Experience*' (pp. 136–43), 'Questions for Study' (pp. 144–6), 'Locations of Major Collections of Blake's Paintings and Illustrations' (p. 147, including, oddly, 'Newberry Library, Chicago'), 'Additional Reading' (pp. 148–55), 'Audio-Visual Materials' (pp. 156–60). Apparently a school text in which accuracy is not a prime consideration.

A 191

§*Songs of Innocence and of Experience*: Facsimile of sixteen original plates etched by William Blake. London, 1971. Academy Editions.

B 191

Songs of Innocence & of Experience [b]. [Norwood, Pa.], 1973.
A slightly enlarged black-and-white facsimile.

192

A. *Chants d'Innocence et d'Experience*. Tr. M. L. & Philippe Soupault. Paris,
1927. B. Paris, 1947. 'Poésie et Théâtre.'

193

§*Les Chants de l'Innocence et de l'Expérience*. Tr. Pierre-Louis Matthey. Lausanne,
1947.

194

Söngvar Sakleysisins og Ljoð Lifsreynslunnar [*Songs of Innocence and of Experience*].
Tveir Ljóðaflokkar eftir William Blake. Tr. þorador Gudmunsson. Reykjavik
[Iceland], 1959.

195

§ *Unschuld und Erfahrung*: Die beiden Kontrasten der Menschenseele. Tr.
Kaathe Wolf-Gumpold. Vienna, 1966.

196. 'then she bore Pale desire' (?1783) and 'Woe cried the muse' (?1783)

BIBLIOGRAPHICAL INTRODUCTION

COLLECTION: The Berg Collection of the NEW YORK PUBLIC LIBRARY.

WATERMARK: Vertical chain lines 2·7 cm apart, as in *Poetical Sketches* (1783).

LEAF-SIZE: 12·0 × 19·0 cm.

DATE: *c.* 1783.

There is general agreement that the works were written in the 1770s or
1780s and that they are the earliest of Blake's manuscripts which have
survived. The handwriting is early, the mythology unformed, the metrical
style uncertain, the subject-matter conventionally sentimental (reminiscent
of 'Fair Elenor' in *Poetical Sketches* [1783]). One indication of date may be the
reference to the death of the Roman Empire, 'A sacrifice done by a Priestly
hand' (p. 2), apparently echoing similar assertions in Gibbon's *Decline and
Fall of the Roman Empire* (Vols. I–III, 1776, 1781). The 'Envy that Inspires
my Song' (p. 3) may be associated with the envy expressed by Quid-Blake
in the *Island in the Moon* (? 1784)—'they envy me my abilities' (p. A) and with
Flaxman's envious 'blasting my character as an Artist to Macklin my
Employer' ('Public Address' in the *Notebook* p. 53) in 1782–3,[1] perhaps

[1] Blake's plates for Macklin are dated 10 and 21 Aug. 1782, 30 March and 1 Oct. 1783.

corresponding to the time in 'Woe cried the muse' when 'Grief perch't upon my brow'. The date 1783 for 'then she bore Pale desire' and 'Woe cried the muse' is, however, admittedly very tentative.

DESCRIPTION: The manuscript consists of four leaves mounted on larger leaves. The last leaf is pasted down so that the verso (p. 8) is invisible. There are horizontal creases in the pages. The first words on p. 1 suggest that a preceding section is missing.

Order: Though the four leaves are now detached and separate, it can be seen[1] that leaves 2 and 3 were originally conjugate, because the missing *e* of 'Shame in a mist' on 2ᵛ (p. 4) is to be found on 3ʳ (p. 5), and the *l* of 'Smouldring' on 2ᵛ is also visible on 3ʳ. This leaves no difficulty in establishing the order of leaves 1–3ʳ (pp. 1–5), for 'then she bore Pale desire', followed by 3ᵛ (p. 6) with 'Woe cried the muse'. Various symbols link the isolated fragments on 4ʳ (p. 7) to pp. 4, 5, 6. A flourish 4·5 cm from the bottom of 3ʳ (p. 5) separates 'then she bore Pale desire' from 'Woe cried the muse' on 3ᵛ (p. 6), while a stroke 2·4 cm from the bottom of p. 6 in turn separates 'Woe cried the muse' from the additions on p. 7.

Writing and Ink: The pages are written to the very margin in Blake's usual hand. The ink is Brown up to p. 3; after 'Solid Ground' on that page the ink becomes Grey; at the top of p. 5, beginning with the word 'Hate', the same Brown ink as on the first three pages recurs. All of p. 6 ('Woe cried the muse') is written in Black ink with a sharp pen. On p. 7, the first insertion ('She brings humility . . . to know—&ᶜ &ᶜ') is in dark Brown ink; the second ('Conceit . . . around the World') is in pencil; the third ('then Shame bore . . . with Pride', the first word converted in ink to 'And') in pencil; and the fourth ('Swift as the . . . Infant Bud' for p. 6) in the same Black ink and sharp pen as p. 6. A correction on p. 1 ('observ[d and *del*]ing inly') and an insertion on p. 4 ('in the darkning Storm') are in Black ink. On p. 6 'Shadowy' and on p. 7 'humility, her Daughter' are deleted in pencil, and the 'awful' replacing 'Shadowy' is written in pencil.

Lineation: The actual lineation of Blake's prose text may be seen in Erdman's transcript.[1] W. M. Rossetti, the first editor of the work,[2] persuaded himself that the metrical prose was intended as verse, and he put slash marks onto Blake's manuscript (together with two notes on the last page) to direct his printer how to set up the text as iambic pentameter.

BINDING: The four leaves bearing 'then she bore Pale desire' and 'Woe cried the muse' are mounted on larger leaves, and the last leaf is pasted down.

HISTORY: (1) The MS with 'then she bore Pale desire' and 'Woe cried the Muse' was acquired from John Defett Francis about 1876 by (2) W. M. Rossetti (according to 'The Passions: An Unpublished Poem by William Blake', ed. W. M. Rossetti, *Monthly Review*, XII [1903], 123–9), from whom

---

[1] D. V. Erdman, 'A Blake Manuscript in the Berg Collection: "then She bore Pale desire" and "Woe cried the Muse"', *BNYPL*, lxii (1958), 191–201.

[2] 'The Passions: An Unpublished Poem by William Blake', ed. W. M. Rossetti, *Monthly Review*, xii (1903), 123–9.

it passed to his daughter (3) Mrs. Rossetti-Angeli, who lent it to J. Sampson (ed., *Poetical Works of William Blake* [1905], xxx), and sold it at Sotheby's, 27 March 1929, lot 529, for £440 to Spencer; (4) Acquired by Owen D. Young, who gave it jointly with Dr. A. A. Berg on 5 May 1941 to (5) The Berg Collection of the NEW YORK PUBLIC LIBRARY (see *America* [L], p. 104) which permitted it to be reproduced in no. 198.

197

'*The Passions*, an Unpublished Poem by William Blake.' Ed. William M. Rossetti. *Monthly Review*, xii (Aug. 1903), 123–9.
  The first printed text of 'then she bore Pale desire'.

198

*'A Blake Manuscript in the Berg Collection: "then She bore Pale desire" and "Woe cried the Muse".' Ed. David V. Erdman. *BNYPL*, LXII (1958), 191–201. For a 'Postscript', see no. 1172.

199

A. *then She bore Pale desire* . . . from a manuscript fragment by william blake illustrated by jeff nuttall. Brighton [1969]. B. § N.Y., 1970 [i.e. 1971].
  A hand-printed work with apparently non-representational designs.

200. *There is No Natural Religion* (?1788)

For the Bibliographical Introduction to *There is No Natural Religion*, see *All Religions are One*, p. 79.

Pl. a1. INCIPIT: 'The Author & . . .'. DESIGN: Two naked youths at the right stand before a clothed elderly couple seated at the left. Trees arch over the scene from the sides, in the middle distance is a field, and in the far distance are Green hills or trees. The mirror-imprint at the foot is often difficult to read.
  COLOURING: The old COUPLE is uniformly uncoloured, the FIELD is Brown (A and G¹ [pale], C), Orange (B, M [yellowish-]), or Yellow (D–F, I–J), and the SKY is Pink (C, E–G¹, H–K, M).

Pl. a2. INCIPIT: 'THERE / is NO / . . .'. DESIGN: An arched Gothic window with six (?) figures represented in the margins surrounds the title of the book.
  COLOURING: None.

Pl. a3: INCIPIT: 'The Argument . . .'. DESIGN: Beneath the text, a woman seems to sit with a standing child to the right and a prone figure to the left. In either margin are leafless(?) trees.
  COLOURING: The WOMAN is dressed in Blue (A), Yellow (E–F), yellowish-Green (G¹), yellowish-Brown (H–K), or pale Orange (M), and the right child once is Red (G¹).

Pl. a4. INCIPIT: 'I Man cannot naturally . . .'. DESIGN: Beneath the text, a tree arches from the right over a naked, White-bearded old man who is leaning on a staff and looking down at a Black-and-White dog which is gazing up at him. In the background are Green trees.

Pl. a5. INCIPIT: 'II Man by his reasoning power . . .'. DESIGN: Beneath a leafless tree which arches over the text from the left, a kneeling woman holds by the waist a kneeling small child who is reaching for a bird or butterfly. (Blake engraved a similar design for Young's *Night Thoughts* [1797] p. 12.)
    VARIANT: 'W. Blake: S' is added in copy D.

Pl. a6. INCIPIT: 'III From a perception . . .'. DESIGN: In the right margin and above the text spirals a vine, while below the text sits a man with a short beard and a winged boy with his right arm raised.

Pl. a7. INCIPIT: 'IV None could have . . .'. DESIGN: By the number is a flying, fork-tailed bird, while below the text a seated man in a low, flat hat plays a pipe to distant sheep.

Pl. a8. INCIPIT: 'V Mans desires . . .'. DESIGN: From the left leafless branches arch over the text, while below the text a naked boy walks with open arms towards a swan floating at the left. He apparently 'desire[s] what he has . . . perciev'd'.

Pl. a9. INCIPIT: 'VI The desires & perceptions . . .'. DESIGN: From the right arches a thin tree with a few leaves, while below the text a bearded man leans on his left elbow. Over him arches what appears to be Black grass. (A very similar figure appears, reversed, in *All Religions are One* [?1788] pl. 3 and *Songs* [1794] pl. 43.)

Pl. b1. DESIGN: The whole page is a design of a bearded, Christ-like figure at the left raising with a gesture of his left hand a naked figure from the ground. (The figures are repeated in Blake's plate for Young's *Night Thoughts* p. 90 and, reversed, in *Songs* [1789] pl. 18.) In the background are Gothic arches.

Pl. b3. INCIPIT: 'I Mans perceptions are not bounded . . .'. DESIGN: Below the text lies a man with a long beard.
    VARIANT: 'I' is altered, presumably not by Blake, to 'IV' to make it fit copy H.

Pl. b4. INCIPIT: 'II Reason or the ratio . . .'. DESIGN: Below the text is stretched a horizontal person on a Black couch.

Pl. b5 does not survive. In his facsimile (1886), William Muir suggested plausibly: 'The perceptions of the poetic or prophetic character are not bounded as the perceptions of the senses are.'

Pl. b6. INCIPIT: 'IV The bounded is loathed . . .'. DESIGN: At the top and bottom of the page are vines and flourishes.

Pl. b7. INCIPIT: 'V If the many become . . .'. DESIGN: By the number are leafy branches, and at the bottom, on each side of the isolated 'Man', floats a tiny figure in a long robe.

Pl. b8. INCIPIT: 'VI If any could desire . . .'. DESIGN: Below the text is a naked man (? on a cloud) with a chain from his right ankle; he seems to be tearing his hair with both hands and to illustrate the words 'despair must be his eternal lot'. (The same figure, reversed and unchained, appears in *Urizen* [1794] pl. 4.)

Pl. b9. INCIPIT: 'VII The desire of Man . . .'. DESIGN: By the number are leafy branches, and below the text floats a naked man with outspread arms.

Pl. b10. INCIPIT: 'Application . . .'. DESIGN: Below the text and between what may be huge tree trunks kneels a bearded man drawing a circle on the ground with a compass. (Mr. Michael Phillips points out [*No Natural Religion* (1971)] that the figure is adapted from one, associated with Newton, in the frontispiece to Vol. II of James Hervey's *Meditations among the Tombs* [1748]. A Blake sketch [*c.* 1788] for the design in the Mellon Collection, with a non-Blakean inscription from Proverbs 8: 27, is reproduced in *Drawings of William Blake*, ed. G. Keynes [1970], pl. 6. A similar design, reversed, is in the great colour print of 'Newton' [1795], another, seen from the other side, is in *Night Thoughts* design [?1796] no. 509, and another, seen from the front, is in *Europe* [1794] pl. 1) He may represent the words: 'He who sees the Ratio only sees himself only.'

Pl. b11. INCIPIT: 'Conclusion . . .'. DESIGN: The decorations consist of flourishes in the margins and from some letters.

Pl. b12. INCIPIT: 'Therefore God becomes . . .'. DESIGN: Below the text, a naked man with rays from his head lies on a couch-like wave.

COLOURING: The WAVE is ordinarily Black, but once (M) it is a pale clear Yellow, and the SKY is once orangish-Brown (M).

COPY A: BINDING: (1) Apparently loose in 1862; (2) Mounted on larger sheets (18·0 × 23·9 cm), which in turn are mounted on stubs and bound in Green morocco, the larger leaves g.e.; (3) The leaves were mounted in heavy paper 'windows' and rebound in Red morocco in 1969.

HISTORY: (1) Perhaps copy A (eleven plates) was among the fifty 'Plates for a very small work' sold anonymously (?by Tatham) with copies B (eleven plates) and G (twenty-eight plates) at Sotheby's, 29 April 1862, lot 197, for 16s. to Milnes; (2) 'Presented by Francis Palgrave, Esqre' (according to the gilt panel) on 12 Jan. 1878 to (3) The BRITISH MUSEUM PRINT ROOM, and reproduced in the Muir facsimile (1886) and in Ellis & Yeats (1893).

COPY B: BINDING: (1) Apparently loose in 1862, but (2) Bound thereafter for R. M. Milnes in Brown russia with the Milnes wheatsheaves on the front cover, t.e.g. (not g.e., as in Keynes & Wolf).

HISTORY: (1) Presumably copy B (eleven plates) was among the '50) 'Plates for a very small work, *some duplicates*' sold anonymously (?by Tatham' at Sotheby's, 29 April 1862, lot 197 (with copy A [eleven plates] and copy G [twenty-eight plates]), for 16s. to Milnes; (2) R. M. Milnes had copy B bound with his wheatsheaf on the front cover; (3) Sold by Milnes's son the Earl of Crewe at Sotheby's, 30 March 1903, lot 10, for £53 to Quaritch; (4) It was acquired from the 'Crewe Sale' by 'W A White 20 April 1903' (according to notes on the fly-leaf), who lent it anonymously to the Grolier Club exhibitions (1905), no. 38, (1919), no. 20, and to that in the Fogg (1924); (5) It was obtained by his daughter 'F. W. Emerson / Mch. 11. 1929. From W. A. W's heirs / $1600' (according to other notes on the fly-leaf), and 'offered by Rosenbach / at that date / £200'; Mrs. Emerson lent it to the Fogg (1930) and Philadelphia exhibitions (1939), no. 4, and sold it in 1941 through Gannon for '$2100' (according to the fly-leaf) to (6) Mr. *Paul Mellon*.

COPY C: BINDING: (1) Pl. a2 was apparently once sewn (there are stitching holes in the left margin); (2) Later it was inlaid to size with the other leaves and 'BOUND BY F. BEDFORD' for Frederick Locker in Green levant morocco, g.e.

HISTORY: (1) Acquired by B. M. Pickering, who had the fly-leaf stamped with his name; (2) Acquired by Frederick Locker, who added his book-plate, lent it to the Burlington Fine Arts Club exhibition (1876), no. 310, with notes on the second fly-leaf (identifying the *No Natural Religion* plates in the volume containing the 'Order' of the *Songs* and remarking that he added pl. a2, 3, 5¹ to copy C on 26 July 1878), and had it bound by Bedford (see *Songs* [E], p. 414), and described in his catalogue (1886), and sold through Dodd, Mead & Co. (see the 'Pickering MS', p. 341) to (3) White, who wrote on the third fly-leaf: 'W A White / 27 Apl 1905', lent it to the Fogg exhibition (1924), and sold it posthumously on 1 May 1929 through Rosenbach to (4) Mr. LESSING J. ROSENWALD, who lent pl. a2, 4, 8–9 for reproduction in the 1971 facsimile.

COPY D: BINDING: (1) Once sewn through stitching holes in the left margins (except of a1, where they are in the right margin), perhaps 'in boards' as in Keynes & Wolf; (2) Now loose and mounted.

HISTORY: (1) Acquired by E. W. Hooper, lent to the Boston exhibition (1891), no. 9, and inherited by his daughter (2) Mrs. Greely Curtis,² who lent it to the Philadelphia exhibition (1939), no. 6; it was given by Hooper's daughters in his memory on 1 July 1941 to (3) HARVARD.

COPY E: BINDING: Sewn in embossed coloured paper wrappers (like wallpaper).³

HISTORY: (1) Copy E was part of 'A pile of leaves of *There is No Natural Religion* . . . bought many years ago in a shop in Edinburgh' (according to Keynes [1921]) by (2) R. A. Potts and Stopford Brooke, and sold posthumously by Brooke at Sotheby's, 27 July 1917, lot 791 ('loose in original embossed and coloured paper wrappers'), for £38 to Tregaskis; (3) Bought from Tregaskis 16 March 1918 (according to the bill still with the work) by (4) Frank Rinder, from whom it was inherited by his daughter (5) *Mrs. Ramsey Harvey*.

COPY F: BINDING: (1) All but pl. a7 were sewn through three stab holes 4·0 and 3·6 cm apart through dark Brown paper wrappers; (2) After 1923 (1941) the plates became loose.

---

¹ Not 'the title-page and last two leaves [*pl. a1, 8–9*]', as in Keynes & Wolf.

² In his *Bibliography* (1921), Keynes said the work was then in the family of Mrs. R. S. Warner, evidently meaning her sister Mrs. Curtis.

³ Mrs. Harvey, the owner, says they have been thus sewn during her lifetime, but the 1917 catalogue, Keynes (1921), and Keynes & Wolf say they were loose.

HISTORY: (**1Ai**) Pl. a1, 3–4, 8–9, b3–4, 12 were a part of 'A pile of leaves of *There is No Natural Religion*' 'in a shop in Edinburgh' bought by (**Aii**) Stopford Brooke and R. A. Potts 'many years ago' (according to Keynes [1921]); they were sold with the R. A. Potts Library at Sotheby's, 20 Feb. 1913, lot 65 (eleven leaves), for £13 to Tregaskis; (**Bi**) Pl. a7 is inscribed in an unknown hand 'drawing by Wᵐ Blake given me by Mʳ Tatham'; (**2**) All nine plates were sold anonymously at American Art Association, 21 May 1923, lot 10A (pl. a7 with the inscription described as 'an extra plate . . . inserted', i.e. not stitched with the rest); (**3**) Sold by 'a prominent Pennsylvania Collector' (Col. Henry D. Hughes)[1] at American Art Association, 22 April 1924, lot 59, for $600 to (**4**) A. E. Newton, who lent copy F to the Philadelphia exhibition (1939), no. 7, and sold posthumously at Parke-Bernet, 16 April 1941, lot 153, for $1,500 to Rosenbach for (**5**) Mr. LESSING J. ROSENWALD, who lent pl. a1, 3 for reproduction in the 1971 facsimile.

COPY G: BINDING: Loose, mounted.

HISTORY: (**1**) Copy G (twenty-eight plates) was perhaps among the '50' 'very small' plates (not further identified), sold anonymously (?by Tatham) with copy A (eleven plates) and copy B (eleven plates) at Sotheby's, 29 April 1862, lot 197, for 16s. to Milnes; (**2**) The plates were 'Later in the possession of his son the Earl of Crewe';[1] (**3**) Sold through Scribner's 3 July 1952 to Mrs. Landon K. Thorne; in 1952 Mrs. Thorne gave all but pl. a5–a6 (G²) to (**4ai**) The PIERPONT MORGAN LIBRARY, which retained copy G¹ (pl. a5–7 of which it lent for reproduction in the 1971 facsimile), and in 1953 gave (**4aii**) Pl. a3ᵈ, a4ᵈ (copy G³) to HARVARD; (**4bi**) Pl. a5–a6 (G²) were for a time retained by Mrs. Thorne, described (no. 1) in her catalogue (1971), and were then given in 1973 to (**4bii**) The PIERPONT MORGAN LIBRARY.

COPY H: BINDING: 'BOUND BY RIVIERE & SON' in Brown morocco, inlaid.

HISTORY: (**1**) Perhaps this was the imperfect copy which Mr. Burt lent to William Muir for his facsimile (1886); (**2**) Acquired before 1921 by T. J. Wise, who added his book-plate, lent it to the Burlington Fine Arts Club Exhibition (1927), no. 72, and gave it in 1938 with the Ashley Library to (**3**) The BRITISH MUSEUM.

COPY I: BINDING: Loose.

HISTORY: (**1**) The plates of copy I were apparently among the 'pile of leaves of *There is No Natural Religion*' bought 'in a shop in Edinburgh' 'many years ago' by (**2**) Stopford Brooke and R. A. Potts (according to Keynes [1921], see copies E and F), for (**3**) They 'were presented to Mr. Forman by R. A. Potts, and the presentation letter accompanies the plates' (according to the Forman catalogue); H. Buxton Forman sold them posthumously at Anderson Galleries, 15 March 1920, lot 48, for $625 to Rosenbach; (**4**) Offered in Rosenbach Catalogue 20 (Oct. 1920), lot 9, for $1,800; (**5**) Acquired by George C. Smith, Jr. (but not described in his anonymous catalogue [1927]), lent to the Fogg exhibition (1930), and sold posthumously at Parke-Bernet, 2 Nov. 1938, lot 13, for $1,000 to Rosenbach; (**6**) Acquired by Mrs. Landon K. Thorne, who lent copy I to the Philadelphia exhibition

---

[1] According to Keynes & Wolf.

(1939), no. 8, in whose catalogue (1971) it was described (no. 2), and who gave it in 1973 to (7) The PIERPONT MORGAN LIBRARY.

COPY J: BINDING: Inlaid to size (g.e.) and bound (II, 3, 6, 36, 94, 112, 162, 168, 184) by 1870 (according to Keynes & Wolf, using evidence unknown to me) in an extra-illustrated set of Gilchrist (1863) in Red morocco, with scores of other leaves of engravings, drawings, MS, etc., extraordinarily like copy K.

HISTORY: (1) Bound by 1870 in an extra-illustrated Gilchrist (1863) in a style virtually identical with copy K and sold by Weyhe 'about 1930' (according to Keynes & Wolf) to (2) Allan R. Brown, who inserted his book-plate, lent it to the Philadelphia exhibition (1939), no. 9, and gave it in 1941 to (3) TRINITY COLLEGE, Hartford, Connecticut.

COPY K: BINDING: Inlaid to size (g.e.) and bound (II, 2, 6, 36, 94, 112, 162, 168, 184) in an extra-illustrated set of Gilchrist (1863) in Red morocco inlaid with green morocco, with scores of other leaves of engravings, extraordinarily like copy J.

HISTORY: (1) Bound in an extra-illustrated Gilchrist (1863) in a style virtually identical with copy J and sold posthumously by George C. Smith, Jr., at Parke-Bernet, 2 Nov. 1938, lot 65, for $600 to Sessler; (2) Acquired by Mr. *Charles J. Rosenbloom*, who added his book-plate.

COPY L: BINDING: (1) Mounted on larger leaves and bound about 1853 with many other leaves of Blakeana including the 'Order' of the *Songs* in half Red morocco, t.e.g.; (2a) Copy L was separated after 1880, L¹ was stitched by 1886 by William Muir into a Brown paper wrapper with four framing-lines round each plate; (2b) The plates of L² are now loose.

HISTORY L ¹⁻². For the History, see the 'Order' of the *Songs*, p. 337.

COPY M: BINDING: (1) In 1876 the plates were in 'Three frames'; (2) Now all the plates are mounted on one large sheet.

HISTORY: (1) Acquired with *All Religions Are One* pl. 1 by Mrs. Tulk, and lent by her to the Burlington Fine Arts Club exhibition (1876), nos. 304–6; (2) Bequeathed by John A. Tulk in 1956 to (3) The VICTORIA & ALBERT MUSEUM.

Pl. a2: BINDING: (1) Bound in contemporary rough calf with *Thel* (a), but (2) Disbound after 1906 and now loose, mounted.

HISTORY: The History is as in *Thel* (a), p. 131.

Pl. a2: BINDING: Loose.

HISTORY: (1) Perhaps this is the copy (evidently of pl. a2) offered in Francis Harvey's catalogue (*c.* 1864) with *On Homer* (? B), *The Ghost of Abel* (? B), and 'The Man Sweeping the Interpreter's Parlour' for £6. 6s.; (2) It may as well be the copy sold by the Earl of Crewe at Sotheby's, 30 March 1903, lot 18 (with *Europe* [K] pl. 1 and another *Europe* plate, *Ahania* [Bb] pl. 1, *For the Sexes* pl. 3, the frontispiece to Burger's *Leonora* [1796], and two photographs), for £10 to Tregaskis; (3) Sold with the John Linnell Collection at Christie's, 15 March 1918, lot 203, with *All Religions Are One* pl. 2–10, for £84 to G. D. Smith for (4) The HUNTINGTON LIBRARY.

Pl. a8: BINDING: Pasted on a mount.

HISTORY: (1) 'Presented by Miss [*C. J.*] Sketchley' (according to the note on it) on 19 Oct. 1949 'in accordance with the wishes of the late Miss R. E. D. Sketchley' (according to BMPR acquisitions records) to (2) The BRITISH MUSEUM PRINT ROOM.

201

**There is No Natural Religion* [*D*]. [Cambridge, Mass.], 1948.
Philip Hofer's 'Foreword' to this tiny colour facsimile is 2 pp.

202

**There is No Natural Religion*. London, 1971. The William Blake Trust.
The work is in two volumes, Series a in a small volume, Series b in a large one. Geoffrey Keynes, 'Description and Bibliographical Statement', is on 10 unnumbered pages in the larger volume. The facsimile is eclectic, reproducing parts of Copy F (pl. a1, a3), Copy C (pl. a2, a4, a8–a9), Copy G (pl. a5–a7), and Copy L (pl. b1–b4, b6–b12). In his essay, Keynes alters the identification and order of the plates as follows:

1971 designation: a1—a2—a3—a9; b1, b3–b10—b11—b12
1953 Keynes & Wolf, designation: a2, a1, a3–a9; b2, b3–b10, a10, b11

203. *Tiriel* (?1789)

BIBLIOGRAPHICAL INTRODUCTION

COLLECTION: British Museum.[1]
WATERMARK: Britannia type, with the countermark 'G R'.[1]
SIZE OF TEXT: 15·7×21·0 cm.
SIZE OF DRAWINGS: *c.* 18·0×27·0 cm.
DATE: ? 1789.
Some indications of an early date, preceding Blake's confident adoption of his technique of Illuminated Printing about 1789, are as follows: (1) The characters of the handwriting and the drawing are early; (2) The poem is incomplete, with some lines left unfinished; (3) The characters and events of the poem were scarcely used in Blake's later myth; (4) The work was never etched for publication; (5) The designs are physically separate from the text and quite different in shape and character from the illuminations for his etched works; (6) ll. 360, 370 are repeated in *Thel* (1789) and the *Marriage* (?1790–3). The time of composition might, however, range from 1785 to 1793.

[1] The manuscript, watermark and traceable designs are reproduced in the 1967 edition of *Tiriel*, from which some descriptions are repeated here.

DESCRIPTION: The manuscript consists of eight leaves enclosed within light bluish-Grey wrappers inscribed, perhaps by Blake: 'Tiriel / MS by M.̣ Blake'. The rectos are correctly foliated in pencil 2–9 at the top right corners of pp. 1, 3, 5, 7, 9, 11, 13, 15, and there are section numbers (1–8) on pp. 1, 3, 5, 7, 10, 11, 13, 14. Most pages on which a section ends (pp. 2, 6, 9, 12, 13, 15) are only partly filled with writing.

Ink and Writing: The same greyish-Black ink is used throughout the poem, with very minor changes. The hand is clear but not copperplate, and there are numerous changes in the text, including some thirty-nine deleted lines, but there are few enough minor alterations to make one wonder whether this was intended as a fair copy.

DRAWINGS: Twelve separate finished drawings for *Tiriel* are known,[1] but only nine of them have been traced, as follows:

Drawing	Collection	Lines illustrated	Subject
1	*Mellon*	19–20	Tiriel Supporting Myratana[2]
2	FITZWILLIAM	59–60?	Har and Heva Bathing
3	*UNTRACED*[3]	75–84?	Har Addressing Mnetha
4	BMPR	84–6	Har Blessing Tiriel
5	*UNTRACED*[3]	123?	Har and Heva Playing Harps
6	*Essick*	149–52	Tiriel Leaving Har and Heva
7	VICTORIA & ALBERT	215–33	Tiriel Carried by Ijim
8	*Keynes*	257–61	Tiriel Denouncing his Four Sons and Five Daughters
9	*UNTRACED*[3]	271–7	Tiriel's Sons Awed by their Father's Curse
10	*Kain*	321–7	Har Walking with Hela
11	*Keynes*	347–8	Har and Heva Asleep
12	*Hanley*	393	Tiriel Dead before Hela

There can be no doubt that the twelve designs form a sequence, for the characterization is quite consistent.[4] In Drawings 1, 4, 6–8, 10, 12, Tiriel is shown as a 'blind' old man, 'bald' except for a fringe of white hair at the ear-line (ll. 28, 29), with a White beard, and a long-sleeved, unbelted, loose-fitting gown that reaches to his ankles. Har in Drawings 2, 4, 6, 11 is an old

[1] Southgate & Barrett sale, 8 June 1854, lot 643, 'Twelve elaborate Subjects'; Sotheby sale, 1 May 1863, lots 377–88; A. Gilchrist, *Life of William Blake* (1863), ii. 253, (1880), ii. 273—1863 somewhat different from 1880 in details.

[2] A sheet bearing pencil sketches for this design in the Tate Gallery is reproduced in M. Butlin, *William Blake* (1971), 29.

[3] Nos. 3, 5, and 9 are last known from the references by W. M. Rossetti in Gilchrist.

[4] There are as well some remarkable inconsistencies. Tiriel's hair and beard are described as 'grey' in the text (ll. 14, 196) but are conspicuously White in the designs. Har says Tiriel's beard is 'shriveld' (l. 88), but the designs show it full and cut straight across the bottom. There are frequent references in the text to the countless wrinkles of Tiriel's face (ll. 14, 88, 93, 115, 135, 315, 334) but such wrinkles are not conspicuous in the designs. Har says Tiriel has 'no teeth' (l. 89), but the designs do not show him with the fallen cheeks of toothless age. Tiriel is not 'outstretchd at Har & Hevas feet' (l. 393) in Drawing 12 but at Hela's feet.

More puzzling is the inconsistent representation of Heva and Mnetha, who are 'aged' women in the text (ll. 58, 63) and in Drawings 4–6 but are beautiful young women with clear foreheads, smooth necks, and firm breasts in Nos. 2 and 11.

man of about the same apparent age as Tiriel, with a smooth, trouble-free face, and 'very long' silvery hair and beard (l. 114). In Drawings 1, 7–8, one of the sons addressed by Tiriel, evidently Heuxos, has a fair curling beard and wears a knee-length dark gown, a pale mantle, and a strange, spiked crown. In Drawings 7–8, 10–12, Hela has 'dark hair' (l. 321) and a clinging, belted gown which leaves her knee and right breast bare. Since this characterization is consistent in all nine drawings which have been traced, we may be confident that the designs belong together.

Further, it is clear that Drawings 1, 4, 6–8, 10, 12 are closely related to the text of *Tiriel*, sometimes illustrating it quite literally. A few designs are difficult to relate to Blake's poem, but since the characters in them are demonstrably the same as those in the closely related drawings, we must conclude that Blake meant them all to illuminate *Tiriel*.[1]

CATCHWORD: None.

ORDER: Pp. 1–15.

The order of the pages is given clearly by Blake's ink section numbers and by the narrative continuity of the poem. The order and position of the Drawings is much more problematical.

ERRATA: 'was' for 'were' (l. 154); 'the[*e*]' (ll. 170, 297, 310); '&' for 'as' (l. 239); 'here' for 'hear' (l. 255).

BINDING: (A1) Stabbed through two sets of three holes each, very close to one another, about 5·0 cm from the top and 5·0, 5·0 cm apart, into light bluish-Grey wrappers, the front one inscribed, perhaps by Blake: 'Tiriel /MS by M⸢r⸣ Blake'; (2) These were bound after 1908 at the British Museum in Blue morocco.

HISTORY: (A1) The 'MS. was, until recently [*1874*], the property of Mrs. [*Alexander*] Gilchrist' (*Poetical Works of William Blake*, ed. W. M. Rossetti [1874], cxxiii); (2) It was published by W. M. Rossetti (above), lost for a time, discovered in a box in the office of Rossetti's publisher, George Bell & Son (E. J. Ellis, *The Real Blake* [1906], 158–9), and sold at Sotheby's, 29 July 1903, lot 458, for £28 to Quaritch; (3) It was 'Purchased of B. Quaritch, 13 Feb. 1909' (according to the inscription on the MS) by (4) The BRITISH MUSEUM; the MS and the traceable drawings were reproduced in 1967.

(B1) The twelve drawings may have been acquired from Catherine Blake at her death in 1831 by (2) Frederick Tatham, who may have sold them, along with 'many' other Blake drawings,[2] to (3) The dealer Joseph Hogarth; Hogarth sold them with sixty-six other Blake drawings at Southgate & Barrett's, 8 June 1854, lot 643, for £3; (4) Acquired by Elhanan Bicknell,

---

[1] In the British Museum Print Room are two drawings of about the time of *Tiriel* which have sometimes been associated with the poem. One represents a Black-bearded man embracing a dark-haired woman (in a position like that in *Tiriel* Drawing 2, reversed), as they kneel on a rug and bolster before a figured curtain. The second represents the same couple kneeling as they warm their hands before a fire in the forest. In details of appearance and situation, they bear no other close resemblance to the characters or actions of *Tiriel*.

[2] W. Partington, 'Some Marginalia', *TLS*, 28 Jan. 1939, p. 64, quoting Hogarth's notes about Blake and Tatham.

and sold posthumously for him at Christie's, 1 May 1863, lots 377–88;
(5) The twelve designs were separated and came to rest as above.

204

*Tiriel: Facsimile and Transcript of the Manuscript, Reproduction of
the Drawings and a Commentary on the Poem by G. E. Bentley, Jr.
Oxford, 1967.
    The 'Introduction' (pp. 1–57) is on the history, description, and signifi-
cance of drawings and manuscript.

205

Tiriel. [Tr. Otto F. Babler.] Olomouc [Czechoslovakia], 1927.
    This consists of the text of *Tiriel*, printed in purple, and nothing more.

206. *To the Public*: Prospectus (10 October 1793)

BIBLIOGRAPHICAL INTRODUCTION

TABLE

Copy	Plates	Leaves	Water-marks	Blake numbers	Binding-order	Leaf-size in cm.	Printing colour
A UNTRACED[1]	? 2[2]	1				c. 19·0 × 27·9	Blue

DATE: 10 October 1793, as given in the heading.

PUBLICATION: The Prospectus was probably composed, 'engraved',[1]
printed, and distributed rapidly in the autumn of 1793. No copy is known
today, and the only information about it derives from Gilchrist.[1]

COLOURING: Probably none.

CATCHWORD: Probably none.

ORDER: Pl. 1–2, if there were two plates.

VARIANT: None.

ERRATUM: None observed.

BINDING: Loose presumably.

HISTORY: (1) Transcribed for Gilchrist (*Life of William Blake* [1863], ii.
263–4) through the kindness 'of Mr. Frost'; (2) *UNTRACED*.

---

    [1] A Gilchrist, *Life of William Blake*, '*Pictor Ignotus*' (1863), ii. 263.
    [2] I should guess that there were two plates, printed on recto and verso of one leaf, the
second plate beginning with ¶5.

207. 'To the Queen' (April 1807) from Blair's *Grave* (1808)

BIBLIOGRAPHICAL INTRODUCTION

PRINTED TITLE: THE / GRAVE, / A POEM. / BY / ROBERT BLAIR. / —/ ILLUSTRATED BY / Twelve Etchings / EXECUTED FROM / ORIGINAL DESIGNS. / — / LONDON: / *PRINTED BY T. BENSLEY, BOLT COURT,* / FOR THE PROPRIETOR, R. H. CROMEK, N° 64, NEWMAN STREET; / AND SOLD BY / CADELL AND DAVIES, J. JOHNSON, T. PAYNE, J. WHITE, LONGMAN, HURST, REES, AND / ORME, W. MILLER, J. MURRAY, AND CONSTABLE AND CO. EDINBURGH. /1808.

ENGRAVED TITLE: THE / GRAVE, / A Poem. / Illustrated by twelve Etchings / Executed by / Louis Schiavonetti, / From the Original / Inventions / OF / WILLIAM BLAKE. / 1808.

COMPOSITION: The publication of Blake's designs for Blair's *Grave* was evidently first undertaken by R. H. Cromek in Sept. 1805 (see Blake's letter of 27 Nov. 1805), and the first proofs are dated Feb. and June 1806. According to a letter from Cromek to James Montgomery, between the 17th and the 20th of April 1807:

Blake's Drawings for 'The Grave' . . . [*were*] presented to the Queen & Princess at Windsor— I received a Letter . . . stating Her Majesty's wish that M! Blake would dedicate the Work to Her— This circumstance has so much pleased Blake that he has already produced a *Design* for the Dedication & a poetic Address to the queen marked with his usual Characteristics— Sublimity, Simplicity, Elegance and Pathos, his wildness *of course*.[1]

Cromek goes on to 'transcribe the Lines' in a form which differs from the published version only in accidentals and in the insertion above Blake's name of the words 'Your Majesty's devoted Subject and Servant'.[2]

PUBLICATION: 688 copies of the quarto edition were published in Aug. 1808 for 578 subscribers, ordinary copies at £2. 12s. 6d., proof copies at

---

[1] Cromek's letter (written 17 April 1807, with the above postscript on the 20th) is in the Sheffield Public Library.

[2] A similar contemporary MS copy, called 'dedication to the Grave', is among the poetry collections of Nancy Flaxman (BM Add. MSS 39788, f. 89, not in Blake's hand). Except for accidentals, it differs from the printed version only in l. 7 inserted in pencil in the right margin, 'Region' for 'regions' in l. 15, and the termination of the quotation marks at the end of l. 18.

L. Binyon (*Catalogue of Drawings by British Artists . . . in the British Museum* [1898], i.128) reports that the first six lines ('"The Door of Death . . . golden Keys," &c.') were 'just decipherable' in pencil on Blake's sketch for the dedication to *The Grave*, but seventy years later I can only make out the first two words. Blake's water-colour (23·6 × 30·0 cm) represents a body at the foot of the page, from which the soul, bearing two keys, floats up toward a golden double-door with two locks (see the reproduction in *Blake Records* [1969], 184).

£5. 5s. A folio edition was published in the same year. The whole work was republished twice in '1813'[1] without significant change in the text of Blake's poem.[2] 'To the Queen' did not accompany the reduced editions of the work published in 1847 and 1858 or the reissue of the plates with a poem by Jose Joaquin de Mora in 1826.

The only known published contemporary comment on the poem complained that:

> The dedication of this edition of the Grave to the Queen, written by Mr. Blake, is one of the most abortive attempts to form a wreath of poetical flowers that we have ever seen. Should he again essay to climb the Parnassian heights, his friends would do well to restrain his wanderings by the strait waistcoat. Whatever licence we may allow him as a painter, to tolerate him as a poet would be insufferable.[3]

BINDING: Loose?

HISTORY: (1) The MS of Blake's 'Autograph Dedication of his Visions to the Queen' was offered by Thomas Thorpe (1833), lot 140, for 4s.; (2) This MS is *UNTRACED*, but a copy was made by R. H. Cromek in his letter to James Montgomery of 17–20 April 1807 (in the Sheffield Public Library), another copy (not by Blake) is in the collection of poetry made for Nancy Flaxman (d. 1820), with no significant variants (BM Add. MSS. 39788, f. 89), and the original was, of course, printed in Blair's *Grave* (1808).

208. 'Upcott's Autograph Album' (16 January 1826)

BIBLIOGRAPHICAL INTRODUCTION

COLLECTION: Berg Collection of the NEW YORK PUBLIC LIBRARY.[4]

WATERMARK: None on Blake's page.

LEAF-SIZE: 21·0 × 27·0 cm.

DATE: 16 Jan. 1826 is the date of Blake's autograph. The signatures with which it is bound are dated from 1820 to 1828; the portraits which illustrate the signatures (including Phillips's portrait of Blake engraved for Cunningham's *Lives* [1830]) have dates running into the 1830s; the index[5] is dated

---

[1] The 1813 title-page is expanded with the information: TO WHICH IS ADDED / A LIFE OF THE AUTHOR. / = / LONDON: / *PRINTED BY T. BENSLEY, BOLT COURT,* / FOR THE PROPRIETOR, R. ACKERMANN, 101, STRAND; / AND SOLD BY / CADELL AND DAVIES, J. JOHNSON, T. PAYNE, J. WHITE, LONGMAN, HURST, REES, AND / ORME, W. MILLER, J. MURRAY, AND CONSTABLE AND CO. EDINBURGH. / 1813. Two editions bear the same title page, one of 1813 and one of ?1874.

[2] The poem appears on an unsigned leaf in all four editions.

[3] Anon., review of *The Grave* in *Antijacobin Review and Magazine*, xxxi (1808), 234; see *Blake Records* (1969), 208.

[4] The MS is reproduced in D. V. Erdman, 'Reliques of the Contemporaries of William Upcott, "Emperor of Autographs"', *BNYPL*, lxiv (1960), 581–7. William Upcott (1779–1845) was the natural son of Ozias Humphry and was, like his father, a friend and patron of Blake.

[5] In the index appears: 'Blake (William) artist & author of designs for Blair's Grave &c.— [*Page*] 19'.

27 Sept. 1833; and the title-pages are dated 1833. It is clear that Blake's signature was secured on 26 Jan. 1826, and that the materials were arranged in volumes, indexed, and bound in 1833.

DESCRIPTION: Blake's autograph appears below that of B. R. Haydon on a leaf inserted in Volume II of a two-volume collection of autographs. The hand-lettered title-page of Volume II reads: 'RELIQUES / OF MY / CONTEMPORARIES. / — / WILLIAM UPCOTT. / — / WITH POR-TRAITS. / AUTHORS, ARTISTS, FOREIGNERS & MISCEL-LANEOUS. / My Life steals on:— / ROGERS. / 1833'; the title to the first volume is the same in substance except for a motto from Crabbe.

BINDING: 'BOUND BY HERING' in 1833 in dark Green morocco in Vol. II of William Upcott's Reliques of My Contemporaries, 1833, p. 19.

HISTORY: (1) Made and bound in 1833 for William Upcott; (2) Acquired by Owen D. Young, who gave it jointly with Dr. A. A. Berg on 5 May 1941 to (3) The Berg Collection of the NEW YORK PUBLIC LIBRARY (see *America* [L], p. 104).

209. *Vala* or *The Four Zoas* (?1796–1807)

BIBLIOGRAPHICAL INTRODUCTION

TITLE: The Four Zoas / [VALA *del*] / [or *del*] / The torments of Love & Jealousy in / The Death and / Judgement / of Albion the / [Eternal *del*] Ancient Man / [A DREAM / of Nine Nights *del*] / by William Blake 1797

COLLECTION: BRITISH MUSEUM Department of Manuscripts (Add. MSS 39764).

WATERMARKS: 1794 J WHATMAN[1] on (1–2) (9–10) (23–4) (25–6) (31–2) (39–40) (41–2) (51–2) (67–8) (77–8) (79–80) (81–2) (137–8)
   [LE]PARD[2] (97–8) (109–10) (119–20)
   . . . R (perhaps I TAYLOR) on (141–2)

LEAF-SIZES:
   31·3 × 39·7 cm (1–2)

   [1] Pages 1–18, 23–86, 91–96, 99–108, 111–18, 121–140 seem to be the same 1794 J WHAT-MAN paper, of which pp. 43–86, 91–140 were used for *Night Thoughts* proofs. On 24 June 1796 Fuseli reported that Richard Edwards, who had commissioned the *Night Thoughts* proofs, had supplied Blake with 'ab. 900 pages' of 'large half sheet[s] of paper' (*Blake Records* [1969], 52), clearly this 1794 J WHATMAN paper.
   [2] Paper watermarked 'LE[P]ARD 1803' was used in proofs of Flaxman's then unpub-lished designs for the *Divina Comedia* (1793), probably in preparation for the 1807 Longman edition (G. E. Bentley, Jr., *The Early Engravings of Flaxman's Classical Designs* [1964], 49).

31·3 × *c*. 41·3 cm (3–4) (21–2)[1]

c. 32·8 × *c*. 41·4 cm (5–6)[2] (9–10) (25–6) (111–12) (127–8)[3]

c. 31·9 × *c*. 40·9 cm (7–8) (13–14) (15–16) (29–30) (31–2) (37–8) (85–6)[4] (121–2)

c. 32·4 × *c*. 41·2 cm (11–12)[5] (17–18) (23–4) (27–8) (47–8)[2] (73–4) (77–8) (81–2) (117–18) (133–4)[3]

33·3 × 25·4 cm (19–20)[1]

c. 32·8 × *c*. 40·5 cm (33–4) (93–4) (123–4)[3] (125–6)[3] (135–6)[3]

c. 32·8 × *c*. 42·2 cm (35–6) (39–40) (41–2) (43–4)

c. 33·0 × *c*. 39·5 cm (45–6)[2] (97–8) (109–10) (119 20)

c. 32·4 × *c*. 40·8 cm (49–50) (51–2) (53–4) (61–2)

c. 32·3 × *c*. 39·4 cm (55–6) (67–8) (113–14) (129–30)[3] (137–8)

32·4 × *c*. 42·0 cm (57–8) (71–2)

32·9 × 41·0 cm (59–60)

c. 32·3 × *c*. 40·4 cm (63–4) (65–6) (69–70) (83–4), (89–90)[6] (91–2) (95–6)[3] (131–2)[3]

33·2 × 42·2 cm (75–6)

32·2 × 32·5 cm (79–80)

31·4 × 40·5 cm (87–8)[6]

32·9 × 37·0 cm (99–100)

33·5 × 36·4 cm (101–2)[7]

32·6 × *c*. 39·9 cm (103–4)[3] (105–6)[3]

33·3 × 37·1 cm (107–8)

30·6 × 41·6 cm (115–16)

31·8 × 37·3 cm (139–40)

9·7 × 16·6 cm (141–2)

16·2 × 10·4 cm (143–4) irregular

14·4 × 23·3 cm (145–6)

DATES:

(1) ?1796–7 *Vala* probably drafted in a notebook.

(2) 1797 Copperplate fair copy (pp. 1–18, 23–42) plus perhaps drafts of Nights IV–IX.

(3) ?1797–1802 revised.

[1] Pages 19–22 are two halves of a large, vague sketch. The paper has chain lines. The bottom of pp. 19–20 was evidently cut off.

[2] Pages 5–6 have a curious wavy crease, made after the writing, as if from a heavy weight. Pages 45–6 were creased horizontally and pp. 47–8 vertically *after* the *Night Thoughts* engravings were printed but *before* the sketches were completed.

[3] Made of two halves of overlapping leaves, with widths of 21·3 cm (95–6) (127–8) (131–2), 20·8 cm (95–6) (123–4) (133–4), 20·6 cm (both in 103–4) (133–4), 19·7 cm (105–6), 21·0 cm (105–6) (135–6), 21·1 cm (123–4), 20·2 cm (125–6) (129–30), 21·6 cm (125–6) (127–8) (135–6), 20·3 cm (129–30), 20·5 cm (131–2). The leaves were joined before the *Night Thoughts* engravings were printed on them.

[4] Pages 85–6 have a small patch at the side, 5·4 × 3·0 cm.

[5] Pages 11–12 seem to have been trimmed at the top, for several letters go off p. 12 *and return*.

[6] Pages 87–90 are two halves of Blake's engraving called 'Edward & Elinor', from which *c*. 8 cm were removed when they were separated.

[7] The top of the engraving is missing in pp. 101–2.

(4) ?1802 fair copy (pp. 43–84, 112) plus perhaps drafts of Nights VIIb–IX

(5) ?1803–7, revised, pp. 19–22, 85 ff. transcribed, pp. 99–118 recopied again, title changed to *The Four Zoas*.

(1) It is likely that *Vala* was drafted on separate pages, perhaps in a note-book like pp. 141–4 (though no such pages are known to survive), for the earliest surviving draft is clearly a fair copy, the original of which must have been written elsewhere. This lost draft was probably composed between 1795,[1] when *Ahania* and *The Book of Los* were etched, and 1797, when the fair copy was dated.

(2) The fair copy was first transcribed in the Copperplate Writing on large blank sheets and dated '1797'[2] on the title-page. This date presumably applies to the pages originally in the Copperplate Hand (pp. 1–14, 17–18, 23–30) plus pp. 15–16[3] in the Modified Copperplate Hand, which were all stitched together. Probably in the same year, pp. 31–42 were transcribed in the Modified Copperplate Hand and stitched with pp. 1–18, 23–30 through a distinct set of stab holes. (Probably the rest of the poem was also transcribed from the hypothetical notebook on to other leaves later discarded and now lost.)

The other pages of *Vala* are quite distinct from pp. 1–18, 23–42 in hand-writing, in being written on sheets previously used for proofs (chiefly for *Night Thoughts*[4]) or sketches, and in stab holes. Pages 1–18, 23–42 in the Copperplate Hands were heavily revised, with about eight deleted lines and twelve added lines to a page, compared to pp. 19–22, 43–139, which have only about one deleted line and three and a half added ones to a page. This suggests that pp. 1–18, 23–42 were first transcribed in their present form earlier than the rest.[5]

(3) The whole poem was probably revised extensively between 1797 and about 1802. In the process, some pages, such as pp. 4–8, became difficult to read. Blake partially transcribed at least pp. 7–8 in a little notebook, of which only pp. 144, 143 survive.

(4) Blake transcribed p. 48, and probably the rest of the poem, after June 1802.

The evidence for the date of p. 48 is relatively simple, for underneath ll. 11–29 is a mirror-image of the type from [William Hayley] *Designs to A Series of Ballads* (1 June 1802) p. 9. The image was transferred when Blake

---

[1] It may be related to 'The Bible of Hell: which the world shall have whether they will or no' announced in the *Marriage* (?1790–3) pl. 24, ¶89, and to 'The Bible of Hell, In Nocturnal Visions collected' (?1793) for which he made a separate title-page.

[2] It is unlikely that Blake would have used the WHATMAN paper supplied him for his *Night Thoughts* work (see *WATERMARKS* above) for his fair copy of *Vala* before June 1797, when the *Night Thoughts* was published (*Blake Records* [1969], 59).

[3] Pages 15–16 differ from pp. 1–14, 17–18 in handwriting, in stab holes, and in their omission from the earliest page- and line-numeration.

[4] Like *Night Thoughts*, *Vala* is organized in nine Nights.

[5] An alternative hypothesis is that Blake first (?c. 1796) copied out the whole poem in the Usual Hand and then in 1797 recopied as far as mid Night III on proof sheets in the Copper-plate Hands, discarding originals as they were copied. However, this hypothesis cannot, it seems to me, satisfactorily account for such diverse factors as symbolism, stab holes, correc-tions, and handwriting.

used his *Night Thoughts* proof sheet as a backing in printing his engraving on p. 9 of Hayley's *Ballad*.[1] *Vala* p. 48 must, then, have been written after 1 June 1802.

Page 48 is similar in character to pp. 43–7, 49–86, 91–140 in being written on *Night Thoughts* proofs in the Usual Hand, and all these pages differ from pp. 1–18, 23–42 in these respects and in stabholes and symbolism. Probably, therefore, pp. 43–140[2] were all transcribed after June 1802.

Pages 43–84, 111–12 were once stabbed together (p. 112 evidently as an illustration for Night IV), separate from the other leaves, from which they also differ in symbolism. Probably they are all that survive of the 1802 transcript.

(5) Pages 19–22, 85 ff.,[3] and revisions of the whole were probably made from 1803 to about 1807. The evidence for these dates is of several kinds.

On *Vala* p. 3 Blake wrote two passages in Greek. He learned Greek from Hayley in 1801–3,[4] and by 30 Jan. 1803 he felt that he could 'read Greek as fluently as an Oxford scholar'. The Greek is therefore likely to have been added after 1802.

Further, the Greek passages are from the New Testament and deal with the nature of Christ and the mission of his disciples. Such enthusiastic Christian references are scarcely visible in the earliest surviving drafts of Nights I–VIIa or in Blake's letters much before 1803. However, after 1803 Blake's letters and poetry take on an explicitly Christian character. On 23 Oct. 1804 he wrote:

Suddenly, on the day after visiting the Truchsessian Gallery of pictures, I was again enlightened with the light I enjoyed in my youth, and which has for exactly twenty years been closed from me as by a door and by window-shutters.

This renewed revelation probably accounts for the Hebrew and Christian symbolism found in the additions to pp. 1–18, 23–84 (Nights I–VIIa). However, such symbolism is found in the earliest surviving lines of Nights VIIb–IX, suggesting that they were transcribed in their present form after Nights I–VIIa had been revised. This distinction in symbolism in Nights VIIb–IX is confirmed by the fact that I–VIIa were stabbed, whereas VIIb–IX were not. The present drafts of VIIb–IX seem, then, to be later than 1803.[5]

The growing explicitness of the Christian and Hebrew symbolism suggest that the surviving drafts were written in this order: VIIa, VIIb, IX, VIII.[6]

---

[1] At the bottom of *Vala* p. 48 is an indentation the size ($11 \cdot 5 \times 8 \cdot 0$ cm) of Blake's engraving of an elephant for *Ballads* (1802) p. 9.

[2] Pages 87–90 seem from other evidence to be even later than the immediately preceding pages. Since pp. 85–6 with the first 'End of the Seventh Night' were not stabbed, they presumably replace pages ending Night VIIa which were stabbed and then discarded.

[3] With the exception of pp. 19–20, 111–12, none of these pages was ever stabbed with pp. 1–18, 23–42 or with pp. 43–84.

[4] *Blake Records*, 86, 89.

[5] Most of Nights VIIb–IX (pp. 95–110, 115–16, 121–36, 139–40) are made of leaves which are odd sizes (pp. 99–102, 107–8, 115–16, 139–40), patched together (pp. 95–6, 103–6, 123–36), or creased (pp. 97–8, 109–10, 121–2). Pp. 111–14, 117–18 are even later additions to Nights VIII–IX.

[6] For detailed evidence for these conclusions, see *Vala* (1963), 162–5.

The present Night VIII must replace a discarded draft[1] of the time of VIIb or IX (that is, of perhaps 1803–5).[2]

Pages 19–21 are an insertion into Night I which incorporates references to 'the Council of God', which is found elsewhere only as additions to pp. 55–6; this plus their Hebrew, Christian, and Druid symbolism suggest that they were the last complete pages added to the poem.

One of the last changes was the substitution in the title of *The Four Zoas* for *Vala*; its lateness is demonstrated by the facts that each chapter is still headed 'Vala' rather than 'The Four Zoas' and that the word 'Zoa' never appears in the text of the poem at all.[3] The date must be about 1807, for the word 'Zoa' is found in *Milton* (1804–?8) and *Jerusalem* (1804–?20), zoas are clearly depicted in Blake's drawings for *Paradise Lost* (1807–8), and they are described in his letter of 18 Jan. 1808 and in his *Descriptive Catalogue* (1809) ¶ 75, where *Vala* is apparently referred to.

DESCRIPTION: The manuscript consists of seventy-three leaves (146 pages), of which pp. 66, 76, 89, 112, 114, 140, and 146 have no writing and pp. 2, 88 have only prose perhaps not integral to *Vala*. The writing is in Black ink except for a few Brown ink lines and seventy-three lines in pencil, including all of pp. 2, 20, 142.

The text is written on five different kinds of paper which represent roughly chronological divisions of the work. (1) Pages 1–18, 23–42 are on blank 1794 J WHATMAN paper, meticulously written in the Copperplate Hands, with light strokes to keep the writing level,[4] careful punctuation, catch-words,[5] and sketches on all but p. 34.

(2) Pages 43–86, 91–140 are written in the Usual Hand mostly on the same paper, on which Blake had previously pulled proofs of his engravings for Young's *Night Thoughts* (1797). These engravings were designed to leave a space in the centre for Young's text; in this blank centre of the proofs and on the versos Blake wrote Nights IV–IX of *Vala*. The proof is regularly on the recto, except for pp. 113–14, 139–40, where the proofs on the versos are title-pages which scarcely left room for writing. In general, the *Night Thoughts* engravings seem to have had little effect upon the text and designs of *Vala*.

(3) Pages 87–90 were originally one leaf bearing Blake's engraving of 'Edward & Elinor' (18 Aug. 1793), which was cut in two; the engraving is on pp. 87–8.

(4) Pages 19–22 are written on a leaf which originally contained a large, vague sketch, which was cut in two.

[1] Page 145 seems to be notes for the revision of this earlier draft.

[2] Over 120 lines in the earliest surviving forms of I–VIIb and IX were moved from *Vala* to *Jerusalem* (1804–?20), but the traffic seems to have gone from *Jerusalem* to *Vala* in lines from the earliest surviving form of Night VIII (see especially p. 105, ll. 31–54) and in additions to other Nights.

[3] The addition of 'Albion' on the title-page is also late, for 'Albion' is found only in added passages and is not found after p. 56.

[4] Pages 2–9 have no strokes, probably because p. 2 was not meant for text and pp. 3–9 were obscured by repeated erasures.

[5] There are catchwords on pp. 3–6, 8–10, 12–13, 15–17, 26, 28–9, 32, 37–8, 40, 42.

Proofs of Young's Night Thoughts (*1797*) *used in* Vala

Vala Page	Night Thoughts Page	Vala Page	Night Thoughts Page	Vala Page	Night Thoughts Page
43	63	75	75	111	*73
45	*90	77	12[1]	114	*65[2]
47	49[1]	79	55	115	73
49	12[1]	81	*8[1]	117	*41[3]
51	33[1]	83	*54[3]	119	*86
53	*7[1]	85	*93[2]	121	*40[4]
55	87	91	*15[1]	123	*16[1]
57	*70[1]	93	*57	125	31[1]
59	73	95	*35[1]	127	25[1]
61	86	97	*90	129	*37
63	23[1]	99	*24[1]	131	*40[4]
65	*80[2]	101	*13[1]	133	*8[1]
67	*72[2]	103	*27[1]	135	*26[1]
69	92	105	*19[1]	137	*88[2]
71	*7[1]	107	4[1]	140	Title-page[1]
73	43	109	*95		

* indicates a proof state; for the differences between proof and published states, see *Vala* (1963), 209.

N.B. Pulls of all the *Night Thoughts* plates were used except for pl. 1, 10, 17, 46. Pages 7–8, 12, 40, 86, 90 were used twice and p. 73 thrice. No *Night Thoughts* proof in *Vala* is dated after 27 June 1796.

[1] The published imprint is 27 June 1796. *Vala* pp. 53, 57, 71, 81, 91, 105, 123, 133 are proofs before date.

[2] The published imprint date of 1 June 1797 was not yet engraved in *Vala* pp. 65, 67, 85, 114, 117, 137.

[3] The published imprint date of 22 March 1797 is missing in both proofs in *Vala* (pp. 83, 117).

[4] The published imprint date of 4 Jan. 1797 is missing in both proofs in *Vala* (pp. 121, 131).

(5) Pages 141–6 are scraps of paper with related texts not integral to the present form of *Vala*; pp. 141–2 are probably drafts of the poem but they are not used in the surviving text; pp. 143–4 are revisions of pp. 7–8; and p. 145 is a revision for Night VIII.

There is some confusion about the headings to five Nights. Night I (p. 3) is headed 'Night the First', Night II (p. 23) is also 'Night the [First *del*] First', and p. 8 has an inserted 'Night the Second' though pp. 18–19 each still have 'End of The First Night'. Night III (p. 37) is headed 'Night the [Fourth (?) *del*] Third'. The present order of Nights I–III is clear, but Blake's original intentions are matters for speculation.

Blake left two Nights headed 'Night the Seventh', one (pp. 77–90) called here Night VIIa and the other (pp. 91–9) called here Night VIIb. They seem to form a continuous narrative, but the evidence of stab holes and symbolism suggests that Night VIIa was transcribed distinctly before Night VIIb.

Most of *Vala* is clearly fair copy, but the text is sometimes overwhelmed with corrections, inversions, deletions, and additions, and a number of passages are obviously incomplete, with crucial words deleted, for example, or with directions to add otherwise unknown passages. As it stands, the poem is clearly unfinished, and its transcription is especially complex. Through most of its revisions Blake called it *Vala*, but eventually he changed the title to *The Four Zoas*.

There is no known reference to *Vala* by Blake's contemporaries, and the first printed mention of it is in the catalogue in Gilchrist's *Life* (1863). The text was first transcribed and partly reproduced in Blake's *Works*, ed. E. J. Ellis & W. B. Yeats (1893); independent transcripts of a more satisfactory kind were made in *The Writings*, ed. G. Keynes (1925 . . . 1972), *The Prophetic Writings*, ed. D. J. Sloss & J. P. R. Wallis (1926), in *Vala*, ed. H. M. Margoliouth (1956), with the complete facsimile (1963), and in *Poetry and Prose*, ed. D. V. Erdman (1967).

HANDWRITING: Blake used three discrete styles of handwriting in *Vala*, probably at discrete times.[1] In general, the more careless the handwriting, the later it was used.

(1) The Copperplate Hand is large, elaborate, beautiful, and clear, apparently a fair copy with about 16 lines to a page on pp. 1–14, 17–18, 23–30. It is rarely used to replace a later hand.[2] (2) The Modified Copperplate Hand is hastier, exhibits fewer punctilios of punctuation, and also has about 16 lines to a page on pp. 15–16, 31–42 and revisions to pp. 4–5, 14, 18. It is rarely substituted for the Usual Hand. (3) The Usual Hand which Blake used for his correspondence is hastily written; individual words are often hard to decipher, there is very little punctuation, and stanza breaks are sometimes hard to identify. About seven-eighths of the poem is in this hand, including all of pp. 19–22, 43–145 and revisions and additions to early pages, with about 30–37 lines to a page. There is a reduced and hurried form of the Usual Hand on pp. 85 (l. 32)–90, 113, 142.

DRAWINGS: Eighty-four pages have *Vala* sketches, most of which seem to have been made after the text was transcribed. The majority of the drawings were begun in pencil;[3] some were confirmed in ink[4] or crayon;[5] and a few were continued in water-colour wash.[6]

Nights III–VIIa (pp. 37–90) originally ended after nine pages of text, and the tenth page (pp. 46, 56, 66, 76, 86) was left blank for a design. In Nights

---

[1] A table of the handwriting on each page may be found in *Vala* (1963), 210–13.

[2] The Modified Copperplate Hand turns into the most beautiful Copperplate Hand at p. 42, l. 10.

[3] The sketches on pp. 1–2, 10–12, 16, 19, 21–2, 30, 39–41, 48, 89, 96, 139, 144 are in pencil only. The *Vala* sketches are reproduced in the facsimile (1963) and described in the OET edition of his *Writings* (in press).

[4] The sketches on pp. 3–5, 50, 116, 128 are in ink as well as pencil.

[5] Pages 6–9, 13–14, 17–18, 20, 23–4, 26–9, 31–2, 35–6, 38, 42, and all the rest to p. 138 (save pp. 48, 70, 84, 88, 90, 96, 114) are in Black crayon as well as pencil; on pp. 14, 60, 62, 68, 86, 98, 100, 102, 104, 106, 108, 110, 118, 122, 130, 134, 136 the background is shaded in crayon; pp. 25, 31, 37 are in crayon only.

[6] There are water-colour washes on pp. 3 (Brown, Blue, Grey, Black), 4 (Grey, Brown, Black), 5 (Blue, Grey, Pink, Brown, Black), 7 (Black, Grey), 15 (Brown), 31 (Grey, Brown), and 128 (Blue, pinkish-Purple, Brown). Some lines are deleted in Grey wash (e.g. pp. 6, 8) even though Grey wash is not used in the designs on these pages.

III, V–VIIa Blake completed the designs in the spaces he had left for them, but on p. 55 in Night IV he made a note to himself to 'Bring in here the Globe of Blood as in the B of Urizen'; he erased 'The End of the Fourth Book' and added thirty-two more lines which filled the space he had left for a design on p. 56. Apparently he then made a design on a separate leaf (now p. 112) illustrating the passage to be borrowed on p. 55 from *Urizen*, and stabbed pp. 111–12 with pp. 43–84. (Later, when he needed paper for additions to Night VIII, he used the recto of this drawing. Therefore p. 111 belongs in Night VIII and p. 112 apparently with Night IV.)

The text on pp. 16, 19, 22, 54, 58 is written *over* large, vague sketches which precede and are presumably not related to the poem. The large drawings on pp. 16, 58 (q.v.) are for *Night Thoughts* (1797) p. 65 and probably not for *Vala* at all.[1] Pp. 20, 126, 132 have childish scrawls *over* the text[2] which presumably do not illustrate *Vala*.

PAGE-NUMBERS: Blake wrote ink numbers (1–9, 11–14) on pp. 3–11, 13–14, 17–18. All the rest of the numbers are in pencil; most were demonstrably added after 1893, and all probably lack Blake's authority.[3]

LINE-NUMBERS: Blake numbered the lines of Nights I–II early in pencil by hundreds and then later, after many revisions, in ink by fifties. The rest of the Nights were generally numbered early in ink in fifties (including the last line) and later in pencil in fives or tens. Since both pencil and ink line-numbers include some added lines but omit others added still later, it seems fairly clear that Blake added the line-numbers during the course of his revisions.[4]

The ink line-numbers link pp. 3–18, 23–32, 33–6, 37–46, 47–54, 55–6,[5] 57–66, 67–76, 77–84, 91–8, 99–110, 117–39. Pages 19–22, 87–90, 111–16 have no line-numbers.

STAB HOLES: Pages 1–20, 23–42 seem to have been stitched four times through seven stab holes; the First is *c.* 9·1 cm from the top, the Second 0·24 cm lower, the Third *c.* 1·1 cm lower, the Fourth *c.* 7·5 cm lower, the Fifth 0·8 cm lower, the Sixth *c.* 7·2 cm lower, and the Seventh *c.* 5·1 cm lower. (1) Firstly pp. 1–18, 23–30 were stitched through the Second, Fifth, and Seventh holes. (2) Secondly, pp. 31–42 were added to these pages (pp. 16–15 now reversed) through the First, Fourth, and Sixth holes.[6] (3) Thirdly, to put pp. 15–16 right,[7] pp. 1–18, 23–42 were stitched through the

---

[1] The *Night Thoughts* engravings found in *Vala* do not seem to have exerted an appreciable effect upon the text or designs.

[2] Perhaps these scrawls are by John Linnell's children. The erasures of erotic drawings might have been made by Blake, by Linnell, or by Linnell's children.

[3] For fuller details of the pencil page-numbers, see *Vala* (1963), 197, 207.

[4] For detailed arguments about which lines are counted and which omitted in the line-numeration, see *Vala* (1963), 202–6.

[5] The line-number joining p. 55 with p. 54 is wrong by only one, and the sense joins the two pages perfectly.

[6] The first hole does not appear in pp. 15–16.

[7] The catchword demonstrates that the order should be 15–16.

First, Fifth, and Seventh holes. (4) Fourthly, pp. 19–20 were stitched with pp. 1–14, 17–42 through the First and Third holes.[1]

Pages 43–84, 111–12 were separately stabbed through three holes about 15 cm from the top and 4·15, 4·8 cm apart. The two sections (pp. 1–20, 23–42, and pp. 43–84, 111–12) were never stitched together.

N.B. Pages 21–2, 85–110, 113–40 were never stabbed at all.

CATCHWORDS: The catchwords are 'In' (pp. 3, 40), '[Enion *del*] So' (p. 4), '[Where[2] *del*] Reard' (p. 5), '[And(?) *del*] [Till(?) *del*]' (p. 6), '[Why *del*]' (p. 8), '[But(?) *del*]' (p. 9), 'I' (p. 10), 'They' (pp. 12, 15), 'Stretch' (p. 13), 'Enion' (p. 16), 'Why' (p. 17), 'And' (p. 26), 'That' (p. 28), 'Spread' (p. 29), 'The' (p. 32), 'Infolded' (p. 37), 'Raise' (p. 38), '[Leaping (?) *del*]' (p. 42, after l. 20). All the catchwords match the following pages in the present order except for replaced catchwords and pp. 6, 8, 42. Pages 9, 43 begin with additions in a hand different from the catchwords, and the lines to which the catchwords refer are evidently lost. Apparently the page beginning with words to match the catchword on p. 6 is also lost.

The catchwords associate pp. 3–4, 5–6, 9–14, 15–18, 25–30, 31–4, 37–42.

ORDER: Pages 1–18, 21–2, 19(–20), 23–104, 113–16, 105–12, 117–39.

In 1889, when Ellis & Yeats began to transcribe *Vala*, 'it was un-paged and unsorted'.[3] How had Blake arranged it?

Pages 3–18, 23–36, 37–46, 47–56, 57–66, 67–76, 77–84, 91–8, 99–110, 117–39 are linked by Blake's *page-numbers* (pp. 3–11, 13–14, 17–18), by his *line-numbers* (pp. 3–18, 23–32, 33–6, 37–46, 47–56, 57–66, 67–76, 77–84, 91–8, 99–110, 117–39), and by his *catchwords* (pp. 3–4, 5–6, 9–14, 15–18, 25–30, 31–4, 37–42). If we further link the title-page (p. 1) and 'The End' of one Night with the beginning of the next, the pattern becomes pp. 1–18, 23–84, 91–110, 117–39.

Pages 19–22, 85–90, 111–16, which are missing from this sequence, can be fitted in without great difficulty. Since 'messengers from Beulah' arrive on p. 21 (l. 6) and finish their message on p. 19 (l. 6), p. 19 seems to follow pp. 21–2. Page 19 concludes with 'End of The First Night', so pp. 21–2, 19 presumably come after the 'End of The First Night' on p. 18.[4] Page 20 does not fit well with p. 19 or with any other passage; it seems to be an additional fragment never integrated with the rest of the poem.

Page 84 is strongly linked to p. 85 by narrative continuity. Pages 87–90 are written on two halves of a large leaf in the hand in which the last additions were made to p. 86 and continue its narrative. The text on pp. 85–7, 90 is essentially a single addition to Night VIIa.

---

[1] In pp. 1–2, 33–4, 37–8, the Third stab hole missed the paper. This accounts for all the stab holes in these pages, but other explanations might suffice. For details of the stab-holes in each leaf, see *Vala* (1963), 214–15. There are from one to thirteen holes in the top margin of pp. 47–50, 53–4, 57–8, 91–6, 99–108, 117–18, 121–2, 125–6, 129–30, 133–40, which do not seem to have been used for stitching.

[2] ? Or 'When'.

[3] *The Poetical Works of William Blake*, ed. E. J. Ellis & W. B. Yeats (1893), ii. 300. The page-numbers of *Vala* refer to the order of pages as bound in the British Museum.

[4] However, D. J. Sloss & J. P. R. Wallis (ed., *The Prophetic Works of William Blake*) rather awkwardly add pp. 21–2, 19–20 to the apparent end of Night I on p. 9.

Page 112 bears a design which apparently illustrates a passage to be added on p. 55. The text on the recto (p. 111) seems intended as a replacement for p. 110, ll. 29–37 which were deleted. Probably yet later p. 110, ll. 38–41 were added to replace p. 111; if so, p. 111 was abandoned and, like pp. 20, 141–5, is not integral to *Vala*.

According to inserted directions, the top passage on p. 113 was to be entered on p. 104, and the bottom passage on p. 113 plus its continuation on p. 115[1] was to be entered on p. 106. The direction on p. 106 to 'turn back three leaves' to p. 113 and the one on p. 116 to 'turn over leaf' to p. 106 clearly indicate that the order here was pp. 103–4, 113–16, 105–6. The overall order then should be pp. 1–18, 21–2, 19(–20), 23–104, 113–16, 105–12, 117–39.[2]

Pages 141–6 were small leaves apparently never bound by Blake with pp. 1–140. The order of the text indicates that p. 144 should precede p. 143 and that they are presently bound backwards.

Errata:[3]
  'has[t]' (p. 4, l. 12)
  'des[c]ending' (p. 5, l. 1)
  'Speterous' for 'Spectrous' (p. 9, l. 8)
  'warr' (p. 12, l. 18)
  'Luvah[*s*]' (p. 13, l. 9)
  'let' ?for 'led' (p. 19, l. 3)
  'As[c]ending' (p. 30, l. 34)
  'hum[m]ing' (p. 34, l. 73)
  'su[l]phuireous' (p. 44, l. 7)
  'gnasshing' (p. 44, l. 16)
  'strugg[l]ing' (p. 50, l. 21)
  'ribbs' (p. 54, l. 13)
  '& &' (p. 58, l. 9)
  'firma[m]ent' (p. 58, l. 25)
  'wire' for 'were' (p. 70, l. 31)
  'stre[t]chd' (p. 73, l. 34)
  'his' for 'him' (p. 75, l. 11)
  'excentric' (p. 75, l. 38)
  'be' for 'you' or 'ye' (p. 80, l. 3)
  'Urizen[*s*]' (p. 90, l. 59)
  'crumb[l]ing' (p. 91, l. 7)
  'trapppings' (p. 91, l. 29)
  'in' for 'on' (p. 94, l. 33)
  'Mo[u]rning' (p. 95, l. 3)
  'B[r]other' (p. 95, l. 6)

---

[1] Page 113 ends with Los saying 'Hear me repeat my Generations' and p. 115 begins with a list of 'the Sons of Los & Enitharmon'.

[2] At a late stage, Blake turned Night VIIb inside out, so that the order there should be p. 95 (l. 15)–98, 91–5 (l. 14).

[3] Ignoring oddities in overly or insufficiently deleted passages.

'to' apparently omitted (p. 95, l. 32)
'the[e]' (p. 98, l. 28)
'writ[h]ing' (p. 101, l. 12)
'deci[e]t' (p. 101, l. 26)
'fal[l]ing' (p. 102, l. 29)
?'come' omitted (p. 103, l. 17)
'num[m]ing'[1] (p. 103, l. 30)
'Jerusa[le]m' (p. 104, l. 1)
'divin[e]' (p. 104, l. 53)
'Fo[r]lorn' (p. 104, l. 65)
'rec[iev]ing' (p. 105, l. 57)
'dec[i]etful' (p. 106, l. 34)
'forn' for 'form' (p. 106, l. 47)
'Eyes' for 'Eye' (p. 107, l. 9)
'whereever' (p. 110, l. 26)
'thou[sa]nd' (p. 113, l. 27)
'wherefor[e]' (p. 115, l. 13)
'des[c]ended' (p. 115, l. 26)
'infinitie' for 'infinite' or 'infinity' (p. 122, l. 24)
'ou[t]braving' (p. 123, l. 3)
'hipocrisy' (p. 123, l. 31)
'ornaminted' (p. 124, l. 11)
'horse[s]' (p. 124, l. 15)
'ha[n]d' (p. 124, l. 26)
'vall[e]y' (p. 128, l. 19; p. 129, l. 12)
'mour[n]d' (p. 129, l. 18)
'fa[i]nt' (p. 129, l. 30)
'l[i]ght' (p. 129, l. 36)
'roon' for 'room' (p. 135, l. 8)
'wodd' for 'wood' (p. 137, l. 25)
'beholds' for 'beheld' (p. 138, l. 25)

BINDING: (1) Pages 1–18, 23–30 were stabbed together;[2] (2) Pp. 31–42 were added to pp. 1–18, 23–30;[2] (3a) Pp. 19–20 were separately added to pp. 1–18, 23–42;[2] (3b) Pp. 43–84 were stabbed separately;[2] (3c) The other leaves were not stabbed, but the last leaves seem to have been in a fixed order: pp. 91–104, 113–16, 105–12, 117–40;[2] (4) All the leaves were loose from 1889[2] until 1918, when (5) They were bound in the British Museum; (6) Rebound '25 Aug 1960' (according to the stamp) in half Black morocco over Blue boards, with every leaf mounted; interleaved.

HISTORY: (1) Given by William Blake to John Linnell,[3] whose family

---

[1] 'numming' is Blake's ordinary spelling for 'numbing'.
[2] See the Description above.
[3] John Linnell, Jr., wrote on 7 Jan. 1893: 'my father *often told me as well as others* that Mr. Blake gave him the MS. The exact date of the gift he said nothing about' (E. J. Ellis, *The Real Blake* [1907], 411; cf. A. T. Story, *The Life of William Blake* [1892], i. 170, and *The Poetical Works of William Blake*, ed. J. Sampson [1905], 339).

allowed Gilchrist (d. 1861), and Swinburne to see it,[1] W. M. Rossetti to catalogue it (1863), and E. J. Ellis & W. B. Yeats to transcribe it (1889) and partly reproduce it (1893) and sold it at Christie's, 15 March 1918, lot 206 (seventy loose leaves 'besides several fragments'), for £420 to Pearson; (2) Presented anonymously on 11 May 1918 to the BRITISH MUSEUM DEPART-MENT OF MANUSCRIPTS, where the loose leaves were bound, and it was published in facsimile (1963).

210

*William Blake's Vala: Blake's Numbered Text. Ed. H. M. Margoliouth. Oxford, 1956.
   'Introduction' (pp. xi–xxvii), 'Notes' (pp. 97–181). An attempt to disentangle Blake's first draft from later ones.

211

'William Blake's Four Zoas.' 2 vols. Ed. G. E. Bentley, Jr. Oxford D.Phil., 1956.

212

*Vala or The Four Zoas. A Facsimile of the Manuscript, a Transcript of the Poem and a Study of its Growth and Significance. Ed. G. E. Bentley, Jr. Oxford, 1963.
   The study of the poem's 'Growth and Significance' is pp. 155–217.

213. *Visions of the Daughters of Albion* (1793)

BIBLIOGRAPHICAL INTRODUCTION

See Table on pp. 466–7

TITLE: *VISIONS | of | the Daughters of | Albion | The Eye sees more than the Heart knows. | Printed by Will.ᵐ Blake: 1793.*

DATE: 1793.
   There seems to be no reason to doubt the date on the title-page.

PUBLICATION: Blake made sketches in his *Notebook* for pl. 2 (the top right figure, reversed, on p. 81, the grotesque head on p. 74), pl. 3 (reversed, on p. 28), pl. 6 (reversed, on p. 32), pl. 7 (the bowed figure on p. 74, the whole scene, reversed, on p. 92), pl. 10 (the bowed figures on p. 74), pl. 11 (reversed, on p. 78).

---

[1] E. J. Ellis, *The Real Blake* (1907), 172.

The sixteen copies of *Visions* which have survived were probably printed and coloured over a period of about thirty-two years:

Date	1793–5	1795	1796–1800	1821–5
Copies	A–E,[1] a[2]	F, BMPR, Tate, Keynes[3]	G,[4] H,[5] F+, I–L, M[6]	N–P

The earliest copies, of about 1793–5, are printed in shades of Brown on both sides of the leaf, and the colour prints (F plus the fragments) must be from 1795. These were followed by a series of *c*. 1796–1800 printed in Green on large paper in which the cloud shapes round the sun in pl. 1, at the top left of pl. 2, to the right and below the flying figure in pl. 11 were obscured in the process of printing or colouring.[7] Finally a number of copies were printed about 1821 on one side only of small paper watermarked RUSE & TURNERS / 1815 in reddish-Brown ink, heavily coloured in text and design, and numbered by Blake.

In the Prospectus of 10 Oct. 1793, Blake offered the *Visions* as a 'Folio, with 8 designs [*pl. 1–3, 6–7, 9–11*], price 7*s*. 6*d*.'; in his letter of 9 June 1818 he described it as '8' folio prints selling for £3. 3*s*., and in that of 12 April 1827 he advertised them for £5. 5*s*. Copies were acquired by George Cumberland (B), D'Israeli (F), Dibdin (G, ?in 1816), and H. C. Robinson (O, after 10 Dec. 1825).

For the link between an unknown work called 'Outhoun' and the *Visions* (1793), see p. 482.

COLOURING: The ordinary colours, in addition to the usual pattern, are: sun Red to Yellow, sea bluish-Black to dark Green (especially in copies printed in Green), clouds uncoloured or Buff or Grey or Blue. The text is coloured in copies G (pl. 7), M, O, P, and Gold is used in N and O. The figures are outlined in ink in copy L, and O and P have Red framing-lines round

---

[1] Copies A, E are on undated small paper, B–D on large paper, all printed on both sides.

[2] In copy a, the leaves are cut down to the designs.

[3] Copy F and the loose pulls are colour printed on one side only of the leaves.

[4] Copy G was printed with the early clouds on 11 small leaves, probably about 1796, coloured over the text, numbered, and sold about 1816.

[5] Copy H (like A–G) shows the clouds on pl. 1–2, 11, while in copies F+, I–M they are obscured; all are on large undated paper.

[6] The coloured text and numbers in copy M suggest that it was finished after 1805.

[7] Keynes & Wolf imply that the changes were made permanently on the etched copper-plate; the lines [visible in A–H, a] were 'removed and in subsequent impressions . . . [*do*] not appear'; copies I–M (and presumably N–P) are 'all of the second issue'. (In the descriptions of the individual copies they say nothing of the states of copies F+, L, N, O, P, but their general remarks apply to all copies after H.) However, it is clear that the obscuring of the cloud outlines did not take place on the etched copperplate, for these outlines are visible in exactly the same form in late copies O and P (watermarked 1815) as in early copies A–H, a. The differences must be due to temporary changes in style of printing and colouring. The cloud outlines are probably obscured under layers of paint (especially in copies J and K) or wiped off in the printing process (M) as the margins were uniformly wiped off. The cloud-outlines are a little different in pl. 1 (I, L, M), 2 (L), 11 (I, L, P) and gone in the rest of copies I–M.

TABLE

Copy	Plates	Leaves	Watermarks	Blake numbers[1]	Binding-order	Leaf-size in cm.	Printing colour
‡A BMPR	I–II	6[2]	—	—	2–II, I	21·2×30·1[3]	golden-Brown
‡B BMPR	I–II	6[2]	J Whatman ([2–3] [6–7])	—	‡I–II	25·3×36·2	Brown
‡C Cunliffe	I–II	6[2]	J Whatman ([8–9])	—	‡I–II	25·7×36·0*[4]	Brown
‡D Harvard	I–II	6[2]	J Whatman ([10–11])	—	‡I–II[5]	27·2×38·1	golden-Brown
‡E Huntington	I–II	6[2]	J Whatman ([2–3])	—	‡I–II	21·1×24·3*	orangish-Brown
‡F Morgan	I–II, 1^b, 2^b, 3^b	13[6]	1794 / J Whatman (7, 10)	—	‡Loose**[7]	27·0×38·2[8] plus 20·4×29·0 (1)	*reddish-Brown* (1–11) dark Green (1^b, 2^b, 3^b)
‡G Harvard	I–II	11	1794 / J Whatman (10)	I–II	2, I, 3–II**	23·2×29·5*[9]	brownish-Black
‡H Rosenbach	I–II	6[2]	J Whatman ([2–3])	—	‡Loose[10]	24·4×35·9	Green
‡I Mellon	I–II	6[2]	—	—	‡I–II	24·7×34·6*	Green
‡J LC	I–II	6[2]	E & P ([4–5], [10–11])	—	‡I–II	26·1×38·0	Green
‡K NYP	I–II	6[2]	E & P (1, [6–7] [8–9])	—	‡I–II	27·0×37·5	Green
‡L Princeton	I–II	6[2]	—	—	‡I–II**	25·5×36·3	Green

Copy	Plates	Leaves	Watermark	Blake's nos.	Order	Size (cm)	Printing colour
‡M Hofer	1-11	6[2]	E & P ([6-7])!	—	‡1-11	26·1 × 36·4*[9]	Green
‡N UNTRACED[11]	1-11	11	RUSE & TURNERS/ 1815 (on 2 leaves)	1-11	1-11	22·5 × 28·5*	brownish-Red
‡O BMPR	1-11	11	RUSE & TURNERS/ 1815 (1)	1-11	1-11	22·0 × 28·0	reddish-Brown
‡P FITZWILLIAM	1-11	11	RUSE & TURNERS/ 1815 (5, 9, 11)	1-11	1-11	23·0 × 28·2*	reddish-Brown
‡Q UNTRACED	1-11	11		1-11			
a LC	1-3, 7, 9-10	6	—	—	1-3, 7, 9-10	11·2 × 6·8 (1) 12·7 × 15·1 (2) 9·9 × 8·7 (3) 11·5 × 7·0 (7, 9) 11·2 × 4·7 (10)	Black
BMPR[12]	1, 3, 7, 10	4	*invisible*	—		24·5 × 34·5 (1, 7) 19·0 × 26·0 (3) 17·8 × 26·0 (10)	*Colour-printed*
TATE	1, 7	2	—	—	Loose	26·7 × 34·5 (1) 24·5 × 28·4 (7)	*Colour-printed*
Keynes	6, 10	2	—	—	Loose	6·5 × 11·5 (6) 18·4 × 27·0 (10)	*Colour-printed*

‡ Water-coloured by Blake or his wife.
++ The frontispiece (pl. 1) faces the title-page (pl. 2).
** The identifiable offsets confirm this order.
1-11 An italicized binding-order indicates that the binding appears to date from before 1835.
* The leaves are trimmed and gilt.
reddish-Brown An italicized printing colour is colour-printed.

Notes to Table on p. 468.

the plate-marks. The early copies, A–E, H–L, are lightly and simply coloured, and C is particularly clear and lovely. The later colouring in G, M–P is more extensive and heavy; in O it is especially happy. The colouring of copies A, C, F, J, L seems to be fairly idiosyncratic, while there is a good deal in common in the colour-patterns of copies B, D, E, K, O, P.

Keynes & Wolf suggest that Mrs. Blake may have been responsible for the comparatively uninteresting colouring of copies D, H, J, K, L, M; of these, copies D, H, M seem to me credible as Blake's work, and for the others the evidence for Mrs. Blake's hand is at least extremely tentative.

CATCHWORD. None.

ORDER: Pl. 1–11.

The order of the plates with text (2–11) is uniform in all copies and is confirmed by Blake's numbers, the offsets, and the narrative order, though there are no catchwords. The only uncertainty arises with the frontispiece (pl. 1), which is bound facing pl. 2 or numbered by Blake at the beginning of all but two copies. In copy A, pl. 1 was bound about 1847 after pl. 11, and there is no evidence to indicate that this was Blake's intention. In copy G, it was bound about 1816 to *follow* pl. 2, but this as well may not represent Blake's intention. In all other copies, Blake clearly meant pl. 1 to serve as the frontispiece; in copies A and G, in which pl. 1 appears elsewhere, there is some doubt as to whether Blake was responsible for its position.

VARIANTS: For colouring variants, see the note to Publication above on p. 465.

ERRATUM: None observed.

Pl. 1. FRONTISPIECE. DESIGN: At the left, a crouching, naked, bearded man with heavy chains on his ankles and hair standing on end is staring

---

Notes to Table on pp. 466–7.

1 There are etched numbers (2–3, 5–7) at the top right corners of pl. 5–6, 8–10 though the colouring has obscured the number 5 in copies D–F, O, the 6 in F, the 7 in B–D, F, H–J, O, and all the numbers in copies G, P, a.

2 Pl. [2–3], [4–5], [6–7], [8–9], [10–11] are printed back-to-back in copies A–E, H–M.

3 The leaves of copy A are inlaid to 25·5 × 36·2 cm.

4 The edges in copy C are trimmed but not gilt.

5 In copy D, pl. 1 is loose, but the stab-marks in the right side indicate that it faced pl. 2 when stabbed.

6 In copy F, pl. [2b–3b] are printed back-to-back and pl. 1b, 2b are marked 'Inserted'.

7 In copy F, stab marks in the right side of pl. 1b indicate that it faced 2b when stabbed. The extra plates in this copy are identified as 'F+'.

8 In copy F, the width ranges from 26·5 to 27·9 cm.

9 In copies G and M, only the top edges are gilt.

10 The facts that in copy H pl. 1 is numbered in pencil on the verso, whereas the other odd-numbered plates are numbered on rectos, and that the pin-holes and stains in pl. 1–2 exactly match each other indicate that pl. 1 faced pl. 2. The pencil numbers give the order as 1–10.

11 The information about copy N, which has not been traced, comes from the catalogues of 29 Jan. 1878 (Sotheby), 1886 (Rowfant Library), and Keynes & Wolf.

12 Pl. 1, 3, 7, 10 in the BMPR evidently once formed parts of the Large and Small Books of Designs.

wide-eyed to the left. His arms behind his back are evidently chained to those of a nude kneeling woman whose back is to him and whose head is bowed. Above her on the rocks crouches another naked man with his right arm wrapped round his head. Beyond them is the sea over which a low sun appears in a break in the heavy clouds. Overarching all are rocks from which dangle leaves, suggesting that the viewer is seeing the scene from inside a cave. The bottom margin is very dark.

COLOURING: The PEOPLE, ordinarily nude-Pink, are in copy F from left to right strongly contrasted reddish-Grey, Pink, and dark Grey; their hair is Brown (two) and Yellow (G), Yellow (J), or Brown (K). The CLOUDS are Purple (B–E, F+, H–L, O, P), Blue edged with Red (G), pale Orange (M), to Black (BMPR pull). The SUN, ordinarily Red (B, G, H, K, P, Tate pull), Orange (J, L), or Yellow, is sometimes yellowish-Green (D), whitish-Pink (F), or Gold-and-Pink (O). The SKY is sometimes Yellow (B–D, G, O, P) to Orange (F+, H, K, M) to Red (F, L). The ROCKS, ordinarily Brown, are sometimes Green (K–M).

VARIANTS: The cracks in the rocks often differ—in D, for example, at the bottom right the cracks are diagonal rather than vertical. In the BMPR pull, there is no colouring distinction between the sky and the cave.

Copy B is inscribed in pencil (?by George Cumberland): 'Rocks on the Coast'.

Pl. 2. TITLE-PAGE. DESIGN: At the bottom, between the title and the motto, a nude woman with raised arms runs across a Black sea between the crests of two rightward-moving waves and looks upward at a bearded figure whose clasped arms and heavy extended wings are in flames. (A similar bearded figure is in Blake's two sketches [BMPR] and his engraving after Fuseli of Anubis for Darwin's *Botanic Garden* [1791], at 127.) Across the title, from the bottom left to the top right, extends a rainbow in which five dim clothed and naked figures (who usually take its colours) are sporting. (The figures in the rainbow are sketched, reversed, on *Notebook* p. 30, with a quotation from *Comus*.) At its top a naked man seated on a cloud (which is very dark to the right) reaches with both hands toward the word 'of'. Under the 'V' of 'VISIONS' two naked figures resting on the same cloud reach over and look down at a third lying on a lower cloud (below 'the'), who looks up at them. Between the 'g' and 'b' is a crouching figure. (Sketches related to figures on this page are on *Notebook* pp. 50, 74, 81; six sketches in red chalk are in the BMPR: 1885-5-9-1618; Mr. David Bindman has a sketch [*c.* 1793] with figures related to the flaming man and to the man on the cloud, reproduced in D. Bindman, 'An Unpublished Blake Drawing of the Lambeth Period', *Blake Newsletter*, iv [1970], 38, inscribed 'The Dead [*two words illeg. like* bad doers]'.)

COLOURING: The CLOUDS are usually Grey but are sometimes pale Purple (A, D, M), Lavender (F+), Orange (F, J), Pink (M), or Yellow (D). The RAINBOW is coloured from top to bottom with Yellow (Orange in A, Red in C, Pink in D), Green and Blue; these colours are preceded by Pink

(B), Red (D), Orange (F+, F, H, I–M), or Blue and Red (G), and succeeded by Pink (A, E, F+, F, H, I–L, O), Purple (B, C, M) Red (D), or Grey (P). The top right MAN is Green (F).

Pl. 3. INCIPIT: 'The Argument . . .'. DESIGN: Below the text, a nude kneeling woman holding her breasts kisses a tiny flying figure (repeated at the top of *America* pl. 2) who seems to spring from a flower (?marygold) in the grass in the bottom right corner. Etched rays from the bottom right corner are carefully coloured to represent a sunrise (the sun is visible in G). (A reversed sketch for the design is on *Notebook* p. 28.)

COLOURING: The SKY is Raspberry (A), Yellow (B–E, F+, G–I, K, O, P, BMPR pull), Pink (C, M, P, BMPR pull), Orange (F, G, M, O, BMPR pull), Red (F, BMPR pull), pale Green (F+, I), Purple (I, L), Mustard (J), Grey (P), or Brown (BMPR pull), particularly in the bottom right, The FLOWER is Orange (H), and the HAIR orangish-Brown (L).

VARIANTS: In F+, M, the colours are not related to the rays.

Copy B is inscribed 'Birth of a Daisy'. In a, there seem to be three obscured words to the right of Albion.

Pl. 4. INCIPIT: 'Visions / Enslav'd the Daughters . . .'. DESIGN: A nude woman seated on the 'V' of 'Visions' blows a wreathed trumpet, while another woman reclines on a cloud (which looks like a horse, especially in later copies) above the first 'i'. A naked, flying archer over the 'n' shoots an enormous arrow at the second 'i', while another archer over the second 's' is reaching over his left shoulder, apparently for an arrow. Below the 'ns', a figure in a trailing robe flies leftward.

Below the text, a nude woman (on the left) and man sprawl in exhaustion on rocks.

COLOURING: The top SKY is Blue plus Purple (A, C–E, H, M), Yellow (C, E, F), Orange (F, H, L), Red (H), and Pink (K, L). The bottom ROCKS are Brown in B. The ROBED FIGURE is usually uncoloured but is sometimes Purple (B, K), Green (C), or Yellow (G). The second PERSON from the top left is Blue (E) or Yellow (D). The first, third, and fifth PEOPLE from the top right are Blue (F). The bottom WOMAN is Green (G).

Pl. 5. INCIPIT: 'Now thou maist marry Bromions harlot . . .'. DESIGN: The central design is a small (*c.* 1·0 cm high) vignette between ll. 39 and 40 representing the trunk of an almost horizontal tree bending to the right, against which a pick is leaning, and a prone naked man (uniformly *coloured* greyish-Brown to Black) raising himself from the ground at the left. In the top of the left margin is a nude woman falling headlong.

COLOURING: The SKY, ordinarily Blue or uncoloured, is sometimes pale Purple (A, J), Brown (B, C), Yellow (D, M, O), Raspberry (G, K), or Pink (I, O). The TREE, usually Brown or Green, is once Blue (L).

Pl. 6. INCIPIT: 'And none but Bromion . . .'. DESIGN: Below the text, an eagle with outspread wings attacks the midriff of a nude woman spread in abandon on a cloud. (A reversed sketch appears on *Notebook* p. 32, and related scenes appear in *America* [1793] pl. 15 and *Jerusalem* [1804–?20] pl. 37.)

COLOURING: The conventional tinting is varied with shades of Pink and Yellow (B, E, G, K, M, P) or Purple (H, J, L) in the CLOUD and a purplish-Black (G) or yellowish-Brown (L) SKY.

VARIANTS: In copy C, the cloud extends behind the eagle's wing and tail at left. The clouds are not joined under the eagle's wing (F). In copy I, the bird seems to be blind.

Pl. 7. INCIPIT: 'Wave shadows of discontent . . .'. DESIGN: Above the text, by a large rock at the left, a robed seated figure bows his head over his hands, which are resting on his knees. Over him from the left impends a wave containing a nude woman clasping her hands, from whose left foot dangles a chain. (The whole design is sketched in *Notebook* p. 92 and the man alone on p. 74.) Over a dark sea at the right a low sun (of differing sizes) is added in the colouring.

COLOURING: The MAN'S ROBE is Blue (A, B, G, J, O), Green (C), Purple (D, I), Pink (E), Black (E), reddish-Brown (H), pale Brown (K, Tate pull), Yellow (L), Green (M), or Grey (BMPR pull). The WOMAN, usually nude-Pink, is sometimes yellowish-Green (G) or Green (I). The SKY is bright with Purple (A–C, E, K–M), Pink (B, P), Yellow (D, G, M, O, P), Red or Orange (E–G, I, K, M, O, P, BMPR and Tate pulls) or Mustard (J). The SUN, usually Yellow or Orange, is Red (A, G) or pale Green (D).

VARIANTS: There is no sun in copies B, C, H, and the Tate pull. In B, C, E, L, there are Grey or Purple clouds from the wave to the right margin. Ordinarily the sun is a semicircle, but in E, F, I, M only one quarter of the sun is visible, and in O, P one eighth is visible, while in L we see the whole sun. In F, a thin, leafless Brown tree is added in ink in the bottom right margin.

Copy B is inscribed 'Solitary Coast'.

Pl. 8 INCIPIT: 'But when the morn arose . . .'. DESIGN: There are two designs, a small (*c.* 2·0 cm high) vignette between l. 143 and 144, representing a prone woman in a very long skirt, and a tendril with leaves which extends across the page after l. 113.

COLOURING: The SKIRT is pale Green (A, C, J, L), pale Purple (B, D, E), Blue (F, G, M), yellowish-Brown (H), Raspberry (I, K, O), or Pink (P). The BLOUSE, normally skin-coloured as if she had no blouse on, is pale Green (B, K) or Purple (H).

Pl. 9. INCIPIT: 'And a palace of eternity . . .'. DESIGN: Below the text, a naked man reclining on a cloud at the left flourishes a studded whip at a nude woman who strides away from him with her face in her hand.

COLOURING: The PEOPLE are normally nude-Pink, but the MAN is Grey in O and both are greyish-Pink in P. The CLOUD, ordinarily uncoloured or Grey, is sometimes Black (D), Purple (H, J), Pink (M, O, P), Yellow or Orange (O, P). The SKY is blue or streaked with pale Purple (A, C, L), Yellow to Orange (B, D, H, J, K), or Pink (B, C, M).

VARIANTS: In C, Pink rays from a whole Yellow sun at the bottom right suffuses the page with Pink light. In L, a Purple cloud covers the woman's vagina. In M, P, all the clouds are different; in P the bottom right cloud continues up the margin.

Pl. 10. INCIPIT: 'In happy copulation . . .'. DESIGN: At the top of the plate, a confusing mass of huddled figures seems to represent primarily three large seated figures: one in the centre seen from the side with head between legs, another to the right seen from the front with head on knees (sketched on *Notebook* p. 74), and between them the head of a woman with flying hair looking upward. To the left of the central figure crouches another facing the opposite direction. Above the back of this last figure are some lines which may represent further small crouched figures.

COLOURING: The CENTRAL PERSON is pale Green (A, I), Purple (B, M), uncoloured (C), Raspberry (E, J, O, P), Blue (F), Yellow or Gold (D, G, L, BMPR pull), Buff (H, Keynes pull), Green (I), or yellowish-Green (J). The FIGURE to the RIGHT is Raspberry (A, D, G, I, L), Green (B, F, K), Yellow (C, E, H, M, O), Blue (J), Purple (P), or Red (BMPR and Keynes pulls). The WOMAN LOOKING UPWARD is uncoloured or Grey (A, C, E, H, I, L, M), Blue (B, O, P), Yellow (D, BMPR pull), Purple (K), Red (F), Green (G), or Raspberry (J). The SMALL CROUCHING FIGURE at the LEFT is uncoloured (A, I), Purple (B, H, K, BMPR pull), Pink (C), Green (D, E, G, M, O, P), Orange (F), or Yellow (J). The SKY, ordinarily dark, ominous, and lurid, has shades of Grey (A–D, F, K, M), Purple (E, I), Pink (F), Black (G), Red (I, BMPR, Keynes pulls), Brown (J, L), Orange (J, P), Green (L, P), and Yellow (O).

VARIANTS: Copy B is inscribed 'Evening clouds'.

Pl. 11. INCIPIT: 'Where the cold miser . . .'. DESIGN: Below the text, three people crouching on a rock to the right at the edge of a dark sea clutch one another and (the two on the right) look upward at a naked figure on a cloud with flying hair and outstretched arms enwrapped in flames (an echo of the title-page figure, though beardless and wingless). (A reversed sketch appears on *Notebook* p. 78.)

COLOURING: The PEOPLE from left to right are: (1) pale Green (A, H, P), Blue (B, F), Brown (C, K [pale]), Grey (D), Raspberry (E, I, L), Yellow (G, J, O), or Pink (M); (2) pale Raspberry (A, D, G, J, K, O), uncoloured (B), Magenta (C), Yellow (E, L), Purple (H), Green (I), Blue (F, M, P); (3) Blue or greyish-Blue (A, G, I, J, O), Raspberry (B, K, M, P), pale Brown to Orange (C, F, H), greyish-Green (D), Purple (E, I, L). The SKY is sometimes Grey (A, F), Pink (F), Orange (G), or Purple (I). The CLOUD is Black and Gold (G), pale Brown (C, H), Yellow and Grey (J), Green, Pink, and greyish-Brown (L), Purple and yellowish-Brown (M), or greyish-Pink (P). The SEA is Brown (D).

VARIANT: In I the waves are different.

Copy B is inscribed 'anxiety'.

COPY A: BINDING: (1) The leaves were mounted on stubs and bound at the British Museum after March 1847 with *Europe* (D) in half Green morocco; (2) The leaves of both works were mounted in heavy paper 'windows' and rebound in Red morocco in 1969.

HISTORY: (1) Purchased, perhaps for the '1/11/6' on the verso of pl. 1, from W. Evans on 18 March 1847 by (2) The BRITISH MUSEUM PRINT ROOM, where it was bound with *Europe* (D), and reproduced by Muir (1884) and by Ellis & Yeats (1893).

COPY B: BINDING: (1) Bound with *America* (F), *Song of Los* (D), *Europe* (C) until 1852, (2) When *Europe* was abstracted; the other three works were rebound together at the British Museum after July 1859 in Yellow morocco, stamped and gilt with the Royal Arms, g.e.; (3) The leaves of the three works were remounted in heavy paper 'windows' and bound in Red morocco in 1969.

HISTORY: The History is as in *America* (F), see p. 102. *Visions* (B) was used for the Pearson facsimile (1876).

COPY C: BINDING: (1) Originally stabbed (perhaps with *America* [C]) through three holes, 9·0 cm from the top, 7·5, 7·3 cm apart; (2) Bound about 1850 in three-quarter Maroon morocco over Brown marbled boards, the edges trimmed but not gilt.

HISTORY: (1) It may have been sewn with *America* (C) when it was acquired by 'H I Reveley' (who signed the free endpaper), perhaps a relative of Willey Reveley with whom Blake corresponded in 1791; (2) This (or copies D, E, I, L, N, P, or Q) may be the copy sold with the Robert Arthington Library at Sotheby's, 17 May 1866, lot 22, for £6 to Pickering; (3) Notes on the fly-leaves of prices ('7.7.0', '8/0/0', 'Toovey 8/8/-') suggest that it went through several hands before it was bought 'from C. J. Toovey'[1] by Cunliffe, who added his book-plate ('Henry Cunliffe') and bequeathed it[1] to his great-nephew (4) Lord Cunliffe, who in turn (according to the present owner) bequeathed it in 1963 to his son (5) The present *Lord Cunliffe*.

COPY D: BINDING: (1) Originally stabbed through three holes, 8·2 and 8·2 cm apart; (2) Later (by 1895) stitched in wrappers.

HISTORY: (1) Sold anonymously at Sotheby's, 2 July 1895, lot 503, for £19 to Quaritch; (2) It was bought by 'W A White / 15 July 95 / Sotheby's 1/4 July thro B.Q./£19.+10% $103' (according to a MS note); White lent it to the Grolier Club exhibition (1905) no. 14 (anonymously), and perhaps to that of (1919), no. 10, and the one in the Fogg (1924); it was acquired from White's estate for $9,000 (according to a note of 9 Jan. 1928 with the volume) by his daughter (3) Frances White Emerson, who lent it to the Fogg exhibition (1930), and sold it 'in May 1935' (according to Keynes & Wolf) to (4) Roger Amory, who gave it on 12 Dec. 1944 to (5) HARVARD.

COPY E: BINDING: Bound in modern (19th-century) Red levant morocco, g.e.

HISTORY: (1) Acquired by Ralph Brocklebank, who added his book-plate, and sold it at Christie's, 10 July 1922, lot 69, for £185 to F. Sabin; (2) Offered in Maggs Catalogue 428 (1922), lot 184, for £315; (3) Sold by Thomas J. Gannon in Jan. 1923 to (4) The HUNTINGTON LIBRARY.

COPY F: BINDING: (1a) Pl. 2–11 (and probably pl. 1) were stabbed through three holes, 9·9 cm from the top and 9·4, 7·2 cm apart; (1b) Later

[1] According to Keynes & Wolf.

they were bound in half Red levant morocco over Grey boards (very like *Urizen* [B]); (1c) Pl. 1 was separated from the other plates by 1856 and bound somewhat irregularly for a time in a cloth case with *America* (A) and pl. d, *Song of Los* (B), *Europe* (A) pl. 1–2, 4–6, 'The Accusers' (H), and 'Joseph of Arimathea Preaching' (F); (1d) But it was disbound by 1904, trimmed (removing any stab holes), inlaid to size (by Riviere, according to the 1906 catalogue) by 1906; (1e) Pl. 1^b–3^b were originally stabbed through three holes, 10·3 cm from the top and 7·6, 8·0 cm apart; (2) Pl. [2^b–3^b] were added to copy F by 1882 and pl. 1^b by 1892—these removals and additions necessitated repeated stabbing approximately through the stab holes in the original plates; (3) All the plates are now loose.

HISTORY: (1) It probably belonged to Isaac D'Israeli (see *Europe* [A], p. 156); pl. 1 was separated from the other plates by 1856;[1] (2 Ai) Pl. 2–11 were sold posthumously by D'Israeli's son the Earl of Beaconsfield at Sotheby's, 20 March 1882, lot 58, for £4 to Ellis & White; (Aii) Pl. 2–11 plus 2^b and 3^b were offered in Ellis & White Catalogue 50 (?Nov. 1882), lot 81, for £63; (Aiii) Pl. 2–11, 1^b, 3^b were listed in the *Catalogue of the Library of Bernard Buchanan Macgeorge* (1892); (Bi) Pl. 1 was for a time 'bound up somewhat irregularly in a cloth case' with *America* (A) and pl. d, *The Song of Los* (B), *Europe* (A) pl. 1–2, 4–6, 'The Accusers' (H), and 'Joseph of Arimathea Preaching' (F), before it was disbound and sold anonymously at Hodgson's, 14 Jan. 1904, lot 226, for £29 to Hopkins; (3) Pl. 1–11, 1^b, 2^b, 3^b (the work as presently constituted) were listed in the catalogue of B. B. Macgeorge's Library (1906), lent to the exhibitions in the National Gallery (1913), no. 91, Manchester (1914), no. 152, Nottingham (1914), no. 119, the National Gallery of Scotland (1914), Case A, no. 5, and sold at Sotheby's, 1 July 1924, lot 113, for £385 to Quaritch; (4) Offered for £525 in Quaritch Catalogues 388 (Oct. 1924, lot 324), 401 (May 1926, lot 217), and 405 (Dec. 1926, lot 242); (5) Acquired by Paul Hyde Bonner, who added his book-plate, lent it to the Fogg exhibition (1930), offered it through Dutton (1931), lot 24, for $10,000, and sold it at American Art Association–Anderson Galleries, 15 Feb. 1934, lot 11, for $5,200 to Rosenbach; (6) Acquired by Mrs. Landon K. Thorne, who lent it to the exhibitions in Philadelphia (1939), no. 54, and Princeton (1969), no. 39, in whose catalogue (1971) it was described (no. 5), and who gave it in 1972 to (7) The PIERPONT MORGAN LIBRARY.

COPY G: BINDING: Bound as in *Thel* (J); see p. 128.

HISTORY: The History is the same as in *Thel* (J), with which it was probably bound not long after 1816.

COPY H: BINDING: (1) Originally stabbed through four holes, 6·2 cm from the top, 5·8, 6·0, 9·0 cm apart; (2) Later trimmed (all but removing these stab holes) and bound with *Song of Los* (C) (which has quite different stab holes) and *Europe* (G) in old (?contemporary) half Red morocco (repaired later still) without lettering (the binding is now with *Song of Los* [C]); (3) The volume was disbound by 1905, and the *Visions* plates are now loose.

[1] A note on pl. 11 verso ('10—Oct—15—1856') suggests that there were only ten plates in 1856, and that pl. 1 was then missing.

HISTORY: (1) Sold by H. A. Mair at Puttick & Simpson's, 19 Nov. 1900, lot 338 (bound with *Europe* [G], *Song of Los* [C], and three water-colour drawings), for £225 to Quaritch; (2) The composite volume became the property 'of M J Perry who got it from Quaritch's cat in 1899 [*i.e. after Nov. 1900*]' (according to the note by W. A. White on the fly-leaf of *Europe*); (3) It was acquired by 'W A White / March 2d, 1908' (according to this note), who broke up the volume, lent it anonymously to the Grolier Club exhibition (1905), no. 15, 22, 31, and gave the parts to his daughter (4) 'Frances / July 22, 1917' (according to the same note); Frances White Emerson lent them to the Fogg exhibitions (1924, 1930), and sold them posthumously at Sotheby's, 19 May 1958, lot 4, for £23,000 to Fleming; (5 Ai) *Visions* was acquired by The ROSENBACH FOUNDATION; (Bi) *Europe* (G) and *Song of Los* (C) were sold by Fleming to Mrs. Landon K. Thorne, who allowed a facsimile to be made of *Europe* by the Blake Trust (1969), lent it to the exhibitions of the Whitworth Art Gallery (1969), no. 13, and the National Library of Scotland (1969), no. 45; *Europe* and *Song of Los* were described in her catalogue (1971, no. 8, 10), and *Song of Los* was given in February 1972 to (Bii) The PIERPONT MORGAN LIBRARY.

COPY I: BINDING: Bound in 19th-century half dark Green morocco, g.e.

HISTORY: (1) This may be the coloured copy with six leaves in half morocco, g.e., sold with the collection of Sir William Tite at Sotheby's, 19 May 1874, lot 293, for £30 to Pearson; (2) Acquired by Thomas Gaisford, who added his book-plate and sold it at Sotheby's, 23 April 1890, lot 188, for £26 to Ellis; (3) Offered in Ellis & Elvey Catalogues 69 (?1890), lot 88, for £42, and 79 (?1894), lot 41, for £35; (4) Sold anonymously at Hodgson's, 14 April 1904, lot 514, for £39 to Quaritch—a note on the last fly-leaf says 'Perfect / pp B Quaritch / F S. Ferguson / 15. iv. 1904'; (5) Offered by Quaritch (1904), lot 1,601, for £90, and bought by (6) 'W A White July 18 1904' (according to the note on the first fly-leaf), who lent it to the exhibitions of the Grolier Club (1905), no. 16 (anonymously) and the Fogg (1924); (7) It was acquired by his niece, Mrs. Adrian Van Sinderen, who lent it to the Philadelphia exhibition (1939), no. 55; (8) Acquired by Mr. *Paul Mellon.*

COPY J: BINDING: Bound in Black levant morocco (by Riviere, according to the 1905 catalogue).

HISTORY: (1) Sold anonymously (by F. P. Osmaston—see *Marriage* [F], p. 299) at Sotheby's, 3 June 1905, lot 771, for £105 to Leighton; (2) Acquired (in 1906) by G. M. Macdonald, who added his book-plate, lent it to the exhibitions in Manchester (1914), no. 151, Nottingham (1914), no. 120, National Gallery of Scotland (1914), Case A, no. 7, and sold it (in March 1920, according to Keynes & Wolf) to Francis Edwards; (3) Acquired by George C. Smith, Jr., described in his anonymous catalogue (1927), no. 7, lent to the Fogg exhibition (1930), and sold posthumously at Parke-Bernet, 2 Nov. 1938, lot 20, for $3,700 to Rosenbach for (4) Mr. LESSING J. ROSEN-WALD, who allowed pl. 2–11 to be reproduced in *The Illuminated Blake*, ed. D. V. Erdman (1974).

COPY K: BINDING: (1) Originally stabbed through three holes, 10·4 cm from the top, 7·9, 10·0 cm apart; (2) Bound by 'DE COVERLY', probably in the 1920s, in half Green morocco.

HISTORY: (1) Acquired by 'J Frederick Hall. 1878', who wrote his name and the date on the first and last fly-leaves; it was rebound probably in the 1920s, and sold with the Arnold Hall Library at Sotheby's, 30 June 1927, lot 268 (as a 'facsimile reprint') for £7. 15s. to Rimell; (2) Offered by Rimell with *Thel* (M) and *America* (L) in 1927 for £1,600;[1] (3) Acquired by Owen D. Young, who lent it to the Fogg exhibition (1930), and gave it with Dr. A. A. Berg on 5 May 1941 to (4) The Berg Collection of the NEW YORK PUBLIC LIBRARY (see *America* [L], p. 104).

COPY L: BINDING: The plates are mounted on linen stubs and bound in half Maroon morocco over buckram.

HISTORY: (1) Sold anonymously at Sotheby's, 28 July 1919, lot 222, for £195 to Maggs; (2) Sold by a 'Philadelphia Collector' (Col. Henry D. Hughes)[1] at American Art Association, 16 April 1923, lot 117, for $1,450 to James Williams; (3) Acquired by George C. Smith, Jr., described in his anonymous catalogue (1927), no. 8, lent to the Fogg exhibition (1930), and sold posthumously at Parke-Bernet, 2 Nov. 1938, lot 21, for $2,500 to Gannon; (4) Acquired by Mrs. Gerard B. Lambert, who added her book-plate and gave it in Jan. 1960 to (5) PRINCETON.

COPY M: BINDING: (1) Unbound in 1903; (2) Bound by Douglas Cockerell in 1904 (the back board is stamped '19 Ⓓ 04') in Green morocco, t.e.g. (plates only, not the fly-leaves).

HISTORY: (1) Sold by the Earl of Crewe at Sotheby's, 30 March 1903, lot 4 (unbound), for £122 to Edwards; (2) Bound in 1904, acquired by Algernon Methuen, lent to the National Gallery Exhibition (1913), no. 92, and sold at Sotheby's, 19 Feb. 1936, lot 503, for £540 to Quaritch; (3) 'Bot by P[*hilip*] H[*ofer*] (thru Quaritch) Sotheby's 1936 (Feb 19) fr £540+10% to Quar. ($5⁰⁰ £). Paid £420+10% for Book of Thel [*B*], same sale' (according to a note in the volume); *Hofer* added his book-plate and that of 'Frances Hofer', and lent it to the Philadelphia exhibition (1939), no. 58.

COPY N: BINDING: Bound by Riviere in Red morocco extra, g.e. (according to the 1878 catalogue).

HISTORY: (1) Perhaps this is the work called *Outhoon* offered by Catherine Blake to James Ferguson (Gilchrist, [1863], II. 262); (2) It is apparently the copy sold among the A. G. Dew-Smith Library at Sotheby's, 29 Jan. 1878, lot 196, for £30 to Quaritch; (3) Evidently it is the copy Frederick Locker lent to the Burlington Fine Arts Club exhibition (1876), no. 314, and described in his catalogue (1886), which was sold through Dodd, Mead & Co. in 1905 (see the 'Pickering MS', p. 341); (4) Acquired before 1921 by Mrs. Harry Payne Whitney, 'and presumably now the property of her heirs'[2] (according to Keynes & Wolf); (5) *UNTRACED*.

COPY O: BINDING: (1) Originally stabbed through two holes, 14·0 cm

---

[1] According to Keynes & Wolf.
[2] Inquiries among all the surviving heirs named in her will have been unsuccessful.

from the top, 4·8 cm apart (perhaps a higher stab hole was lost in the binding process); there is a Red framing-line round each plate; (2) It was unbound in 1916; (3) The plates were mounted on stubs and later 'Bound by
Zaehnsdorf, London, England' in Brown calf; (4) The leaves were mounted
in heavy paper windows and bound in Red morocco in 1969.

HISTORY: (1) Acquired by 'H. C. Robinson', who wrote his name on the
third fly-leaf, beneath which another hand has written: 'bought by him from
Blake for / he thinks 1 guinea & presented / by him to [2] Edwin W Field /
2 June 1865', who added his book-plate; (3) Presented by Miss Field to the
Red Cross and St. John Sale at Christie's, 26 April 1916, lot 2,009, and sold
for £210 to Miss Carthew; (4) Miss A. G. E. Carthew added her book-plate
and a note on the last fly-leaf saying she bought it in 1916 'Unbound', and
bequeathed it on 13 July 1940 to (5) The BRITISH MUSEUM PRINT ROOM.

COPY P: BINDING: (1) Bound in calf with *Thel* (N) and *Marriage* (G) until
Feb. 1890; (2) Rebound, evidently by March 1890, in Maroon straight
grained morocco, g.e.; there is a reddish-Brown framing-line round each
plate.

HISTORY: (1) Bound with *Thel* (N) and *Marriage* (G) and sold anonymously
at Sotheby's, 1 Feb. 1890, lot 301, for £121 to Robson; (2) Robson &
Kerslake had *Visions* rebound and sold it (for £60, according to Keynes
[1921]) to (3) Alexander Mackay, for whose widow it was sold at Christie's,
26 April 1921, lot 5, for £260 to Riches; (4) T. H. Riches lent it to the
Burlington Fine Arts Club Exhibition (1927), no. 79, and bequeathed it in
1935 (according to the book-plate) to (5) The FITZWILLIAM MUSEUM, which
received it in 1950; reproduced in colour microfilm by Micro Methods Ltd.

COPY Q: BINDING: Uncut and sewn (according to the 1897 catalogue).
HISTORY: (1) Sold anonymously at Sotheby's, 24 Feb. 1897, lot 807
(eleven coloured leaves, uncut and sewn) for £20. 5s. to Gerrard; (2) *UN-
TRACED*.

COPY a: BINDING: (1) The plates (perhaps then cut down) were in
A Manuscript Book (probably pasted in) written by members of the Chevalier
family in 1910; (2) By 1937 the cut-down plates were mounted and 'Bound
by Zaehnsdorf' for W. E. Moss in Red straight grain morocco, the mounts
g.e.

HISTORY: (1) Sold by [Ellen M. Chevalier Dobinson] the great-
granddaughter of Thomas Chevalier (1767–1824) [and of C. H. Tatham,
great-niece of George Richmond and of Frederick and of Arthur Tatham,
according to genealogical notes with the volume] at Sotheby's, 1 Dec. 1910,
lot 125 ('A Manuscript Book, written by members of the Chevalier family,
containing two prints[1] by Blake . . .') for £3. 3s. to Dobell; (2) Acquired
before 1921 by W. E. Moss, who removed *Visions* (a) from the MS book,

---

[1] There are six plates in copy a, but Keynes & Wolf say without qualification that *Visions*
(a) was included with lot 125. I have not traced this MS book, but according to Keynes &
Wolf 'It was there stated that the prints were done by Blake for the children of Thomas
Chevalier, surgeon . . . who was a friend of Blake and is said to have attended him.'

bound it, and sold it (with the MS book) at Sotheby's, 2 March 1937, lot 178, for £10 to Stonehill, from whom (3) *Visions* (a) was acquired by 1939 by Mr. LESSING J. ROSENWALD.

Pl. 1, 7: BINDING: See the Large Book of Designs (A).

HISTORY: For their History as part of the Large Book of Designs (A), see the Small Book of Designs (A).

Pl. 1, 7: BINDING: Mounted and framed; there are three framing-lines round each plate.

HISTORY: (1) Perhaps they were part of the Large Book of Designs (B); (2) Perhaps these are the two coloured 'stamped prints' of the *Visions* sold by George Smith at Christie's, 16 July 1880, lot 123, for 10s. to Colnaghi; (3) Pl. 1 was lent by the Linnell Trustees to the exhibitions in the National Gallery (1913), no. 93, Manchester (1914), no. 80, Nottingham (1914), no. 60, National Gallery of Scotland (1914), no. 47, and both plates were sold with the Linnell Collection at Christie's, 15 March 1918, lots 174–5, to Martin for the National Art Collections Fund, which gave it to (4) The TATE GALLERY, where they were reproduced (M. Butlin, *William Blake* [1971], 32–3).

Pl. 3, 10: BINDING and HISTORY: See the Small Book of Designs (A), p. 356.

Pl. 6: BINDING: In 1960 in a sketchbook of Samuel Prout, but now loose.

HISTORY: (1) Removed from a sketchbook of Samuel Prout and sold at Sotheby's, 26 Nov. 1960,[1] lot 11, according to the buyer, (2) Sir *Geoffrey Keynes*, who described it in his catalogue (1964), no. 512.

Pl. 10: BINDING: Loose; there are four framing-lines round the plate.

HISTORY: (1) It may have been part of the Small Book of Designs (B); (2) Perhaps this was the unidentified plate from the *Visions* lent by H. H. Gilchrist to the Pennsylvania Academy Exhibition (1892), no. 147; (3) Perhaps it was among the thirty leaves of Blakeana (see *Urizen* pl. 9, p. 184) sold anonymously at Sotheby's, 24 Feb. 1897, lot 809, to Quaritch; (4) Acquired by Dr. Greville Macdonald, by whom it was sold to (5) Francis Edwards, who offered it in a catalogue (?1931), no. 2, for £60, and sold it in 1936 to (6) *Geoffrey Keynes*, who listed it in his catalogue (1964), no. 522.

214

**Visions of the Daughters of Albion* [A]. Reproduced in Facsimile. With a Note by John Middleton Murry. London, Toronto, & N.Y., 1932.

'A Note on William Blake's Visions of the Daughters of Albion' is pp. 11–25.

215

Visions of the Daughters of Albion. Pawlet [Vt.], 1957.

---

[1] I cannot trace this Sunday sale.

216

Visions of the Daughters of Albion [C]. London, 1959. The William Blake Trust.

Bibliographical Statement by Geoffrey Keynes (4 pp.).

217

Cherry, Charles Lester. 'Critical Edition of William Blake's Visions of the Daughters of Albion.' *DA*, xxix (1969), 4452A. North Carolina Ph.D. (1968).

'Woe Cried the Muse'. For the Bibliographical Introduction, &c., see 'then she bore Pale desire', p. 439.

218. WORKS LOST

INTRODUCTION

In this section are descriptions of works alluded to in Blake's writings or elsewhere of which no significant text is known. Some may be titles of works never written, some may be alternative titles for known works, and others may have been written but lost.

Blake told Crabb Robinson: 'I have written more than Voltaire or Rousseau—Six or Seven Epic poems as long as Homer and 20 Tragedies as long as Macbeth.'[1] At his death he 'left volumes of verse, amounting, it is said, to nearly an hundred, prepared for the press'.[2] No manuscript works 'prepared for the press' survive, but the bulk of unpublished writings was apparently at one time formidable.

Many manuscripts seem to have been destroyed by Blake's friends. Blake himself told Crabb Robinson on 18 Feb. 1826:

'I have been tempted to burn my MSS but my wife wont let me⌊.⌋⌊ ⌋⌊'⌋She is right⌊,⌋'⌋ said I— ⌊'⌋You have written these, not from yourself but by a higher order⌊.⌋ The MSS. are theirs not your property— You cannot tell what purpose they may answer; unforeseen to you⌊.'⌋ He liked this And said he wo[d] not destroy them⌊.⌋'[1]

Even if Blake kept his word, poverty may have forced his widow to discard some of his works which no one else seemed to want.

At the death of Catherine Blake, almost all Blake's drawings, copperplates, books, and manuscripts evidently passed into the possession of their devoted friend Frederick Tatham. Tatham printed a few of the works in Illuminated Printing in the 1830s and sold them along with a good many of the drawings. Later Tatham became 'a zealous Irvingite' and was persuaded 'by some very influential members of the Sect . . . that Blake was inspired . . . by Satan

---

[1] *Blake Records* (1969), 322. No completed tragedy survives, and none of his epics is as long as Homer's.

[2] Cunningham, *Lives* (1830) (*Blake Records*, 506–7).

himself—and was to be cast out as an "unclean spirit"'.[1] Though Edward Calvert implored Tatham not to destroy Blake's works,[2] 'Tatham . . . enacted the holocaust of Blake manuscripts—not designs, I think, as I have heard from his own lips'.[1] The destruction was not complete, for about 1860 he said 'that he had destroyed some of Blake's manuscripts and kept others by him, which he had sold from time to time'.[3] The only manuscript he is known to have kept by him was the 'Pickering [Ballads] MS', which he sold about 1864.

Others also apparently destroyed Blake manuscripts of less importance. When D. G. Rossetti acquired the *Notebook* in 1847, 'there were many loose papers in the book. . . . Many of these loose sheets contained verses which were so bad that Rossetti threw them into his waste-basket, from which Swinburne rescued a few fragments not quite so worthless as the rest.'[4] Mrs. Gilchrist wrote to W. M. Rossetti about the Blake manuscripts 'your brother destroyed', but W. M. Rossetti did 'not distinctly recollect' such an action.[5] Mrs. Gilchrist herself had 'a long thing which I really believe even Mr Swinburne will pronounce pure rubbish'.[5] W. M. Rossetti described it as

a prose narrative of a domestic, and also fantastic, sort, clearly intended by its author to count as humouristic or funny, and somewhat in the Shandean vein. I read this performance, and heartily confirmed Mrs Gilchrist in the conviction of its being rubbish; yet I was startled to learn soon afterwards that, on receiving my letter, she had burned the MS. The thing was stupid, but it was Blake's, and a curiosity.[5]

It seems likely, therefore, that Blake's friends destroyed many manuscript works by Blake of which we have no knowledge. The fragments below[6] are all apparently quite minor, with the possible exception of the 'Work on Art'.

'Barry a Poem' (?1808)

On *Notebook* p. 60 (?1808), Blake wrote fourteen satirical lines 'to come in Barry a Poem', but no other reference to the work is known. Their subject and style are similar to other poems in the *Notebook* of about 1808.

'The Bible of Hell' (?1793)

In the *Marriage* (?1790–3) pl. 24, Blake wrote that he had 'The Bible of Hell: which the world shall have whether they will or no.' He evidently seriously intended to produce such a work, for he made a tentative draft title-page for it (see p. 213): 'The Bible of Hell, in Nocturnal Visions collected Vol. I.

---

[1] As Anne Gilchrist reported in a letter of 9 Nov. 1862 in *Anne Gilchrist: Her Life and Writings*, ed. H. H. Gilchrist (1887), 129–30.

[2] [S. Calvert] *A Memoir of Edward Calvert Artist* (1893), 59.

[3] A. Symons, *William Blake* (1907), 241, reporting a conversation between Dr. Garnett and Tatham.

[4] E. J. Ellis, *The Real Blake* (1907), 299, quoting an unnamed 'friend of D. G. Rossetti'. Perhaps one of the fragments was part of 'The Everlasting Gospel' which Swinburne printed in *William Blake* (1868), 175–6.

[5] *Rossetti Papers 1862 to 1870*, ed. W. M. Rossetti (1903), 41–2.

[6] They are given in alphabetical order because their dates are so uncertain.

Lambeth'. The date must be 1790–1800, when he was living in Hercules Buildings, Lambeth.

No other direct reference to the work has survived.[1] Perhaps it became *Vala* (?1796–?1807), which is subtitled 'a Dream of Nine Nights'. Alternatively, his promise, on one of the first plates (?1790) etched for the *Marriage*, to produce 'The Bible of Hell' may have been fulfilled in the 'Proverbs of Hell' on *Marriage* pl. 7–10, which were apparently etched rather later (?1793).

'The Book of Moonlight' (?1809)

In his *Notebook* (p. 46), Blake made a note to himself about lines to be inserted 'in the Book of Moonlight p 5', apparently a work in verse about art, but nothing remotely like such a poem has survived. Its concern for design and its reference to Titian suggest that it may have been composed about 1809 (cf. *Descriptive Catalogue* [1809]).[2]

Descriptions of the *Comus* Designs (?1801)

Among the property of Thomas Butts was 'Milton's Comus, 8 [*drawings*], with the artist's descriptions',[3] but there is no other evidence that Blake made Descriptions of the drawings. In his letter of 19 Oct. 1801 Blake spoke of sending his 'Designs for Comus' to the Revd. Joseph Thomas. If the Descriptions existed, they were probably written at this time.

'For Children ⌊:⌋ the Gates of Hell' (?1793)

Blake drafted a title-page for a work to be called 'For Children ⌊:⌋ the Gates of Hell' (see p. 215), but no more of the work is known. It is clearly analogical to *For Children: The Gates of Paradise* (1793) and perhaps related to 'The Bible of Hell' (?1793), above.

'The History of England' (?1793)

In his Prospectus of 10 Oct. 1793 Blake offered 'The History of England, a small book of Engravings. price 3s.' Evidently it was not to be printed in colours, for it is not described as 'in Illuminated Printing' as *Thel* (1789), *Visions* (1793), *America* (1793), and the *Songs* (1789–94) are. On the other hand, Blake may have intended to include some text, as he did in *For Children* (1793), which is also described in the Prospectus as 'a small book of Engravings. Price 3s.' The identity in price of the two works may suggest that the 'History of England' was to have about eighteen plates, like *For Children*. On p. 116 (?1793) of the *Notebook* Blake made a list of about twenty subjects (to which five were later added) dealing with the history of England, with a 'frontispiece' to represent 'The Ancient Britons according to Caesar'. Probably the subjects in this list were intended for the work advertised in the Prospectus, but none of the subjects is known to have been engraved.

---

[1] Unless it is related to 'For Children ⌊:⌋ the Gates of Hell' (?1793), below.
[2] It is unlikely to be related to Edward Lord Thurlow's *Moonlight A Poem* (1814).
[3] Sold at Foster's, 29 June 1853, lot 98.

Names of Gods (?1783)

W. M. Rossetti described a 'scrap of paper in the same [*Blake's*] handwriting, giving a few details about names of Gods in different mythologies. It is a mere memorandum. . . . The spelling is very bad, & must belong to B's youth.'[1] The piece sounds somewhat similar to 'then she bore Pale desire' (?1783), which deals with the origins of the passions and which W. M. Rossetti owned. No other reference is known to Blake's 'memorandum' 'about names of Gods in different mythologies'.

'Outhoun' (?1793)

Catherine Blake offered to James Ferguson, probably after Blake's death (1827–31), 'A work called Outhoun. 12 Plates, 6 inches more or less. Price £2 2s. 0d.'[2] This work sounds rather like *Visions of the Daughters of Albion* (1793), in which Oothoon is the chief character.

The details, however, do not fit the *Visions* very precisely. It has eleven plates (not '12'), the leaves are 11″ to 15″ high, the plate size is about 4¾″ × 6¾″ (though this could, I suppose, be '6 inches more or less'), and the price in Blake's letter of 12 April 1827 was £5. 5s. (not £2. 2s.). Probably 'Outhoun' is the *Visions* rather inaccurately described.

'Twelve Good Rules' (?1803)

From May 1803 to 1808 George Cumberland regularly made notes to himself in his pocket-book to discover 'who has Plate of the 12 good Rules [engraved] by Blake lost'.[3]

Perhaps the work is related to 'King Charles' "Twelve Good Rules"', which normally consisted of a decorative design, such as the king's execution, and the following uplifting maxims: (1) Urge no healths; (2) Profane no divine ordinances; (3) Touch no state matters; (4) Reveal no secrets; (5) Pick no quarrels; (6) Make no comparisons; (7) Maintain no ill opinions; (8) Keep no bad company; (9) Encourage no vice; (10) Make no long meals; (11) Repeat no grievances; (12) Lay no wagers. These 'Twelve Good Rules' of King Charles were very popular among country people. They are referred to by Goldsmith in *The Deserted Village* and by Crabbe in *The Parish Register* (ll. 51–2), and Thomas Bewick (1753–1828) said they were 'common to be seen when I was a boy in every cottage and farm house throughout the country'.[4]

If Blake had wanted to deal with a popular subject, particularly when he was living in the country, in Felpham (1800–3), he might have engraved 'King Charles' "Twelve Good Rules"' for sale among his rural neighbours. To save money and trouble, he may have engraved them on pewter by the process which he described in his *Notebook* and recommended to his friends.[5]

---

[1] *Letters of William Michael Rossetti*, ed. C. Gohdes & P. F. Baum (1934), 131, 132.
[2] A. Gilchrist, *Life of William Blake*, '*Pictor Ignotus*' (1863), ii. 262.
[3] *Blake Records* (1969), 118 & n. 4.
[4] *A Memoir of Thomas Bewick*, ed. A. Dobson (1887), 261.
[5] *Notebook* p. 10. On 12 April 1813 Blake 'recommended [*to George Cumberland*] Pewter to Scratch on with the Print' (*Blake Records* [1969], 232).

If so, they may be related to the 'Illustrations by W. Blake—pewter-types 13' which are recorded in a sale catalogue[1] but are untraced.

No other reference to Blake's 'Twelve Good Rules' is known.

'Version of Genesis' (date unknown)

Crabb Robinson reported that on 18 Feb. 1826 Blake 'shewed me his Version (for so it may be called) of Genesis—"as understood by a Christian Visionary" in which in a style resembl⁸ the Bible—The spirit is given⌐.⌐ He read a passage at random⌐.⌐ It was striking⌐.⌐'[2] Nothing like such a work has survived.[3] It probably gave the 'infernal or diabolical sense' of the Bible, a work which, he promised in the *Marriage* (?1790–3) pl. 24, that 'the world shall have if they behave well'. The date could be almost any time between 1793 and 1826.

'A Work on Art' (?1809)

Several references are known to Blake's unpublished 'Work on Art'. As early as 10 Jan. 1802 he had, as he wrote to Butts, 'recollected all my scatterd thoughts on Art', and perhaps from this date he began to cast about for ways of publishing them. When he returned to London in 1803 he evidently talked to his friends about this project. In the summer of 1807 George Cumberland wrote in his Diary that Blake 'Intends to publish his new method [*of engraving*] through means[?] of stopping lights', and next spring he wrote more specifically: 'Blakes new mode of Stopping lights to be published in Nicholson'. That autumn he wrote again: 'Blakes new Mode of Engraving to be Published by me at his desire',[4] and on 18 Dec. 1808 he wrote to Blake proposing this:

> You talked also of publishing your new method of engraving—send it to me and I will do my best to prepare it for the Press.—Perhaps when done you might with a few specimens of Plates make a little work for subscribers of it—as Du Crow [*Ducros*] did of his Aqua Tinta—selling about 6 Pages for a guinea to non Subscribers—but if you do not chuse this method, we might insert it in Nicholsons Journal [OF NATURAL PHILOSOPHY, CHEMISTRY, AND THE ARTS] or the Monthly Magazine—with reference to you for explanations⌐.⌐

On the 19th Blake replied declining Cumberland's offer: 'I have Myself begun to print an account of my various Inventions in Art for which I have procured a Publisher[5] & am determind to pursue the plan of publishing what I may get printed without disarranging my time'.

[1] Sale of Mrs. Steele's collection at Christie's, 7 Feb. 1893, lot 186.

[2] When he revised this passage in his 'Reminiscences', Robinson said Blake 'read a wild passage in a sort of Bible Style' from his '[Vision . . . *del*] Version of Genesis' (*Blake Records* [1969], 322, 547).

[3] The Illuminated Genesis Manuscript (1827) gives the Bible literally, and the 'Genesis' manuscript, a translation (probably by Hayley) of Tasso's *Sette Giornate del Mondo Creato*, is not by Blake (but was transcribed by him), is not 'striking', and is not 'in a style resembl⁸ the Bible'. Perhaps the 'Version of Genesis' is related to 'The Bible of Hell' above.

[4] *Blake Records* (1969), 187, 188, 211 n. 3.

[5] This phraseology suggests that Blake was printing the work at his own expense and planned to distribute it through a bookseller selling on commission. Blake may be referring here to the *Descriptive Catalogue* (1809).

The work is described further in the advertisement of his exhibition (15 May 1809):

Fresco Painting is properly Miniature, or Enamel Painting: every thing in Fresco is as high finished as Miniature or Enamel, although in works larger than Life. The Art has been lost: I have recovered it. How this was done, will be told, together with the whole Process, in a Work on Art, now in the Press.

And in the *Descriptive Catalogue* (1809), ¶ 9 are more details:

Whether Rubens or Vandyke, or both, were guilty of this villa[i]ny [*first bringing oil Painting into general opinion and practice*], is to be enquired in another work on Painting, and who first forged the silly story and known fals[e]hood, about John of Bruges inventing oil colours . . . .

Thus Blake twice says positively that the work is actually being printed. It seems at least possible that it was published, for in 1828 J. T. Smith wrote that Blake 'proposed an engraving from his fresco picture [*of the Canterbury Pilgrims*], which he publicly exhibited in his brother James's shop window, at the corner of Broad-street [*an address James Blake left in 1812*], accompanied with an address to the public, stating what he considered to be improper conduct'.[1] If it was printed, however, no copy has been traced. Perhaps the 'Public Address' (p. 323) was part of the text.

[1] *Blake Records* (1969), 465. Smith may be referring to the *Descriptive Catalogue* (1809), which does complain in passing of 'improper conduct' and mentions the Chaucer engraving, but it cannot accurately be described as a prospectus for the engraving. The advertisements for the engraving, on the other hand, do not contain accusations of 'improper conduct'.

Section B

COLLECTIONS AND SELECTIONS

219. **Ægteskabet mellem Himmel og Helvede og andre skrifter.* Tr. Niels Alkjær. København, 1952. Religion og Livsvisdom.
The introduction, 'William Blake', is pp. 5–12, 'Noter' pp. 92–4.

220. *Auguries of Innocence.* Printed for E. V. Lucas [London] 1905.

221. *Auguries of Innocence.* Written out by Lillian Frost. Flansham [England], 1914.

222. *Auguries of Innocence.* Birmingham, 1930.
A tiny school exercise, consisting of 8 poems only.

223. A. **Auguries of Innocence.* Wood Engravings by Leonard Baskin. Northampton [Mass.], 1959. B.* N.Y., 1968.
The illustrations are not intended to be Blake-like except for the portrait. B is a 'facsimile' of A.

224. §*Auguries of Innocence.* Bronxville (N.Y.), 1968.

225. A. *Auguries of Innocence.* Illustrated by Paul P. Piech. Bushey Heath (Hertfordshire), [1970]. Taurus Poem No. 13. B. §*N.Y., 1970 [i.e. 1971].
The illustrations are not related to Blake designs.

226. *Blake.* Selected poetry. Ed. Ruthven Todd. [N.Y., 1960.] The Laurel Poetry Series. B. §1963. C. §1964. D. §1966. E. §1967. F. §1969. G. §1970. H. §1971. I. §1973.
Introduction (pp. 11–21), Notes (pp. 157–9).

227. A. **Blake Jojoshisho Shishu [Selected Romantic Lyrics].* Tr. Bunsho Jugaku. Tokyo, 1931. . . . E. §5th Printing. 1935. . . . H. *8th Printing. 1937. 101 pp. . . . K. *11th Printing, Second Edition, Revised. 1940. 122 pp. L. *12th Printing. 1949. M. *13th Printing. 1957. 116 pp.
Revised in *Blake Shishu.*

228. A. § 'Blake no Kotoba [Proverbs].' Tr. Soetsu (Muneyoshi) Yanagi. *Shirakaba [The White Birch],* V (1914), 98–109. B. *Blake no Kotoba.* Tr. Soetsu (Muneyoshi) Yanagi. Tokyo, 1921. 103 pp.
In B, there are 37 plates.

229. A. **Blake Senshu [Selected Poems].* Tr. Makoto Sangu. Tokyo, 1919 (vHK). B. Tokyo, 1922. 270 pp.

230. A. §*Blake Shisen [Selected Poems].* Tr. Kochi Doi. Tokyo, 1946. B. *1948. 210 pp. C. Republished as *Blake's Shishu [Poems].* Tokyo, 1950. 210 pp. D. *1953. 177 pp.
The verso of the title-page of B says: Poetical Works of William Blake.

231. *Blake Shishu* [*Poems*]. Tr. Masatomo Watanabe. Tokyo, 1923. 200 pp.

232. *Blake Shishu.* Tr. Iwaichi Ozeki. Tokyo, 1926. 134 pp.

233. *Blake Shishu.* Tr. Masao Hataya. Tokyo, 1927.
A duplicate title-page in English calls it *Poems of Wm. Blake* (Memorial Volume). With an Introduction by Genjiro Yoshida.

234. *Blake Shishu.* Tr. Naosuke Irie. Tokyo, 1943. 228 pp.
Includes a translation of the preface to Yeats's Muse's Library Blake (no. 293).

235. A. *Blake Shishu.* Tr. Bunsho Jugaku. Tokyo, 1950. 225 pp. B. *1968. 168 pp.
Republication of the works in *Blake Jojoshisho*, with alterations and additions.

236. A. §*Blake's Poems.* Ed. Makoto Sangu. Tokyo, 1929. Kenkyusha Pocket English Series. 120 pp. B. Revised Edition. Tokyo, 1962.
In B, the Introduction is pp. i–xiv, the Notes pp. 67–117.

A236. §*Blake's Poems.* Ed. Aileen Ward. Cambridge [England], 1973. Limited Editions Club.

237. *The Book of Thel. Songs of Innocence. And Songs of Experience.* With Decorations by Charles Ricketts. London, 1897.
The 'Decorations' are terrible and unBlakelike.

238. A. 'The Chimney-Sweeper.' *The Chimney-Sweeper's Friend, and Climbing-Boy's Album.* Dedicated, by the most gracious permission, to His Majesty. Arranged by James Montgomery. With illustrative designs by Cruickshank. London: Printed for Longman, Hurst, Rees, Orme, Brown, and Green, Paternoster-Row. 1824. Pp. 343–4. (BM & GEB) B. Second edition, with alterations and additions. London: Published by Harvey and Darton, Grace-Church Street; and W. Alexander and Son, York. 1825[–1826]. Pp. 209–10. (Harvard).
A. Blake's poem, with only very minor alterations, was 'communicated by Mr. Charles Lamb, from a very rare and curious little work'. At the end of the book (pp. 402–13) is 'The Climbing-Boy's Soliloquies. No. II. The Dream', by Montgomery, which Lamb said in a letter of 15 May 1824 (see no. 2094) was 'awkwardly paraphras'd from B'. However, I can see no significant relationship between this poem and any of Blake's.
B. According to the advertisement, the second edition was issued in twelve sixpenny parts, with new matter and a new arrangement for which Montgomery was not responsible. The part with Blake's poem exactly as before is no. 5. The probable terminal date is established by a quotation in the last number (p. 455) from the *Sheffield Iris* for 14 April 1826.

239. A. *The Chimney Sweeper.* Bushey Heath [Herts.] [1969]. Taurus Poem 10 B. §*N.Y., 1970 [i.e. 1971].
Three folded leaves with a design by Peter Paul Piech.

240. *_A Choice of Blake's Verse_. Ed. Kathleen Raine. London, 1970.
The 'Introduction' is pp. 11–19; 'The text . . . is taken from . . . Keynes'.

241. _The Complete Poetry and Selected Prose of John Donne & The Complete Poetry of William Blake_. With an Introduction by Robert Silliman Hillyer. N.Y., 1941. A Modern Library Giant.
The 'Introduction' is pp. xv–lv. The text of Blake, pp. 493–1045, is taken from that of Keynes. There is no reason why Blake should have been bound up with Donne.

The Complete Writings of William Blake, ed. Geoffrey Keynes (1957 ff.); see _The Writings of William Blake_. ·

242. 'A Cradle Song.' _The Little Keepsake for 1844_. [Ed. Mrs. S. (Pamela Chandler) Colman.] Boston [?1843]. P. 94 (vDVE).
In a story about 'The Baby', sister Helen says to mamma:
'O dear, I am afraid she is going to cry; may I sing that little song to her that I learnt in William Blake's "_Songs of Innocence_," mamma?'
'Yes, Helen, you may, if it is not very long.'
'No, mamma, it is not, —and it is all about a little baby.'

243. _A Cradle Song. The Divine Image. A Dream. Night._ Printed and hand illuminated by Valenti Angelo. N.Y., 1949 (vDVE).

244. §_Les Dits de l'Enfer_. Paris, 1949.

245. _A Divine Image:_ Four poems by William Blake, Lino-cuts by Duine Campbell. Leicester, 1968.
Campbell's 'Introduction' (one page) says it is 'an experiment'. The plates are not related to Blake's.

246 A. §_The Divine Image._ Illustrated by Paul P. Piech. Bushey Heath, 1970. B. §*London, 1971.

247. *Donne: John Donne, _Uta to Sonet: Songs and Sonnets_ [tr. by various], Blake: William Blake, _Keiken no Uta: Songs of Experience, Tengoku to Jigoku to no Kekkon: The Marriage of Heaven and Hell_ [tr. Kochi Doi], [Tokyo, 1969].
The Blake works are translated into Japanese on pp. 122–228.

248. ['The Ecchoing Green' called] 'A Summer Evening on a Village Green.' Pp. 274–5 of _Pictorial Calendar of the Seasons_ exhibiting the Pleasures, Pursuits, and Characteristics of Country Life for Every Month in the Year and embodying the whole of Aiken's Calendar of Nature. Ed. Mary Howitt. London, 1854.

249. 'The Edition of the Works of Wm. Blake' by 'The Blake Press at Edmonton', England (1884–90). (This title comes from the description of the series in _The Song of Los._)
John Pearson & Co., who had published _Jerusalem_ (?1877), announced in a 'PROPOSAL FOR THE PUBLICATION OF THE PROPHETIC BOOKS, AND THE SONGS OF INNOCENCE AND OF EXPERIENCE'

(?1884) (copy in the collection of Mr. Raymond Lister) and in his catalogue 58 (?1884) the first of a series of 'William Blake's Works', 'For Subscribers only, limited to 50 Copies'; 'after this has been done *the materials will be destroyed*'. Pearson published *Innocence*, *Thel*, *Visions*, and *Experience*, but (according to a letter from William Muir to The Editor of *The Athenaeum*, 28 Dec. 1885, in the Newberry copy of the *Marriage*) 'When Mr. Pearson left business last March [*1885*] I arranged with his excellent successor Mr Shepherd that Mr Quaritch should be my agent'. Quaritch issued separate 4-page ads. for Muir's 'FACSIMILE OF THE WORKS OF WM. BLAKE' in May 1885, Nov. 1886 (copies in the Newberry *Thel* and *America*) and May 1887 (according to Keynes [1921]) and published the rest of the volumes In 1912, Thomas Wright (no. 3016) said that 'Mr. Muir has still a few copies . . . for sale' of the *Marriage*, *Gates*, 'Ancient of Days', *Europe*, *Milton*, *Experience*, *America*, *No Natural Religion*, and 'Little Tom', and Keynes said that everything but the *Songs* were 'recently coloured by Mr. Muir' and 'still to be obtained' as late as 1921.

'Volume I' consisted of separately issued facsimiles in quarto (all but h–i water-coloured) as follows:

(a) *Songs of Innocence* [D] produced by Wm Muir, Emily J. Druitt, J. D. Watts, Joseph B. Muir, Hannah T. Muir. London, 1884. (For another Muir facsimile [1927], see no. 162.)

(b) *The Book of Thel* [D]. London, 1884.

Muir's drawings for this facsimile are in the possession of Mr Raymond Lister. For another Muir facsimile (1920), see no. 20.

(c) *Visions of the Daughters of Albion* [A]. Edmonton, 1884.

(d) *Songs of Experience* [U]. Edmonton, 1885. (For another Muir facsimile [1927], see no. 144.)

(e) *The Marriage of Heaven and Hell* [A]. Edmonton, 1885.

In an 'Appendix' are facsimiles of the 'Order' of the *Songs* and 'A Divine Image' (*Songs* pl. b).

(f) *Milton* [A], A Poem in 2 Books. Facsimilied by Wm. Muir, J. D. Watts, H. T. Muir, and E. Druitt. Edmonton, 1886.

Muir's 'Preface to Milton' is 5 pages; a facsimile of Blake's letter of 16 March 1804 is included.

In a letter of 25 May 1886 (with *Milton* [C]), Quaritch says that Muir 'will reproduce the 5 additional leaves [*found in copy C but not in A*]—as a *supplement*'.

(g) *There is No Natural Religion*. Facsimilied by Wm. Muir, E. Druitt, H. T. Muir, and J. D. Watts. Edmonton, 1886.

The work includes *All Religions are One* pl. 1. In the Preface, Muir wrote that 'This edition is made up from the portion in the British Museum [A] and from some pages in my own possession [L]', but according to his title-page for *Europe* (1887), he worked 'from three imperfect copies, viz. my own, Mr Burt's copy [?H], and the British Museum copy'.

(h) *On Homer's Poetry* [&] *On Virgil* [?C]. Edmonton, 1886.

This separate leaf was also published with H. P. Horne's article (see no. 1885).

(i) 'Little Tom the Sailor.' Edmonton, 1886. See no. 470.

This single leaf was issued with *Milton* (Newberry), separately, and in *The Century Guild Hobby Horse*, I (1886), at p. 121.

'Volume II' consisted of separately issued facsimiles in folio:

(j) *America* [R], A Prophecy. Facsimilied by W. Muir, H. T. Muir, E. Druitt, & M. Hughes. Edmonton, January 1887.

Some copies (e.g. Newberry) were issued uncoloured, and 'About six' (e.g. BM, watermarked '1886') were coloured 'in recent years after copy B [*i.e. A*]' (according to Keynes [1921]).

(k¹) *Europe*, A Prophecy. Facsimilied [in colour] by W. Muir, S. E. Muir, H. T. Muir, and M. Hughes. Edmonton, September 1887.

According to Muir's 1887 title-page (Newberry), pl. 1 and 4 are 'from originals [*?of copy c*] in Mr Muir's possession', pl. 2, 5-6, 8 are from copy D, and pl. 7, 9-18 from Copy A.

(k²) *Europe*, A Prophecy. Facsimilied Anno 1931 from [copy D] . . . by Fredᵏ Hollyer, Sophia E. Muir & Wᵐ Muir.

At least one copy (University of Washington at Seattle) has the 1887 title-page altered thus in manuscript.

(l) *The First Book of Urizen* [B]. Facsimilied [in colour] by Wm. Muir, H. T. Muir, I. D. Watts, and A. F. Westcott, from the splendid original belonging to Mr. Macgeorge, of Glasgow. Edmonton, 1888.

According to Keynes (1921), 'Only about twenty-five copies were done; the plates . . . have since been lost.'

(m) *The Gates of Paradise*. Etched by Mary Th. A. Hughes [*or* Facsimilied by Mary Hughes and Wm. Muir]. Edmonton, 1888.

The plates are from *For the Sexes*, except for the title-page, which is from *For Children*. The prologue and 'The Keys' (*For the Sexes* pl. 1, 19-20) are reproduced in conventional typography.

(n) *The Song of Los* [A]. Facsimilied by W. C. Ward, E. Druitt, H. T. Muir, S. E. Muir, and Wm. Muir. Edmonton, November 1890.

The plates are coloured in an opaque medium which Muir explains in a letter of 12 Feb. 1891 to The Editor of *The Athenaeum* (with the Newberry *Song of Los*). According to Keynes (1921), 'Only about twenty-five copies . . . were made. Some additional copies have been executed [*i.e. coloured?*] recently.'

In the last work issued (*Song of Los*), Muir explained that he had not reproduced *The French Revolution* and *Ahania* because he could not 'Get originals to work from'; that *Jerusalem* is missing from the series because Pearson had already reproduced it (no. 76); and that *The Book of Los* was omitted because someone else [?Ellis & Yeats] was doing it.

250. *Eien-no-Fukuin [*The Everlasting Gospel*]. Tr. Bunsho Jugaku. Kyoto, 1938.

251. *Eight Songs of Innocence*. For Treble Voices, Unison and Two Part. Words by William Blake. Music by D. Wauchope Stewart. London, 1926. The Year Book Press Series of Unison and Part-Songs. No. 264.

252. A. *Eight Songs of William Blake*, N.Y., 1925. B. N.Y., 1926.

A was 'Printed by William Edwin Rudge for his Friends Christmas 1925', while B consisted of '200 copies for sale'.

253. §*England awake! Awake! Awake!* Kettering, Northamptonshire, 1968.

254. **Exoteric Writings of William Blake*. Ed. Bunsho Jugaku. Kyoto, 1933.

According to the 'Preface' (1 page), 'By "exoteric" the editor means "intelligible to plain readers"'.

255. *The Fly*. Illustrated by Paul P. Piech. Bushey Heath, Herts. [1968]. Taurus Poem No. 6.

256. §*The Four Seasons*. Seattle, 1949.

257. §*Gedichte*. Tr. Alexander von Bernus und Walter Schmiele. Heidelberg, 1958.

258. *Gedichte*. Tr. Georg von der Vring. Wiesbaden, 1958.

The 'Nachwort' is pp. 49–54.

259. *A Grain of Sand. Poems for Young Readers. Ed. Rosemary Manning. London, Sydney, Toronto, 1967.

'The Voice of William Blake' is pp. 9–20.

260. A. ['Holy Thursday' from *Innocence*.] [Jane & Ann Taylor.] *City Scenes, or A Peep into London*. For Children. London. Printed & Sold by Darton, Harvey & Darton, 55, Gracechurch Street, 1818. Price Half a Crown Half Bound. Pp. 67–8. (Essex County Library, Toronto Public.) B. *City Scenes, or A Peep into London*. London. Published by Harvey & Darton, Gracechurch Street, 1828. P. 68. (BM, Essex County Library, GEB) C. §1840. D. §1844. E. §n.d.

In Scene 70 of this guide for children is a description of the setting of 'Holy Thursday' from *Innocence*, with a crude print of 'Charity Children' and Blake's poem (somewhat damaged) attached. The poem and most of the description do not appear in the editions of 1809 and 1814.

261. *Ideas of Good and Evil*. Yellow Springs, [Ohio] 1927 (vE Wolf).

A261. **The Illuminated Blake*: All of William Blake's Illuminated Works with a Plate-by-Plate Commentary. Annotated by David V. Erdman. Garden City, N.Y., 1974.

The monotone reproductions consist of:

All Religions are One (A)

No Natural Religion (F) pl. a1, 3, (C) pl. a2, 4, 8–9, (G) pl. a5–7, (L) pl. b1–4, 6–12.

Thel (F) pl. 1, (I) pl. 2, 6, 8, (N) pl. 3–4, 7, (D) pl. 5

Songs (I) pl. 1–2, 4–11, 13–15, 17, 19–23, 25–6, 28–33, 35, 37–42, 44–5, 47–52, (U) pl. 1, 4, (Gilchrist [1863]) pl. 3, 16, 18, 24, 27, 34, 36, 43, 46, 53–4, (b) pl. 12

Marriage (C) pl. 1–2, 8, 21, (E) pl. 3–7, 9–10, 12–14, 17–19, 22–7, (I) pl. 11, 15–16, 20

Visions (I) pl. 1, (J) pl. 2–11, (C) pl. 4 with variant
America (N) pl. 1–2, 4–16, 18, (K) pl. 3, 17, (a) pl. a–d
Europe (I) pl. 1–2, 4–18, (H) pl. 3, (b) pl. 2, ('private collection' [i.e.,
    Lord Crawford]) pl. 2, (Preston [p. 398] or Westminster Public Library
    [p. 416] [i.e., Australian National Gallery]) pl. 2
Song of Los (A) pl. 1, (E) pl. 2–3, 6, (D) pl. 4–5, 7–8
Urizen (B) pl. 1–5, 7–18, 20–28, (A) pl. 6, (G) pl. 19
Ahania (A) pl. [?1], 2–6
Book of Los (A)
Milton (A) pl. 1–32, 34–45, (C) pl. 33, (D) pl. a–f
Jerusalem (E) pl. 1, 99–100, (D) pl. 2–98, (F) pl. 28 with variant
On Homer (D)
The Ghost of Abel (D)
'The Accusers' (B)
For Children (E)
For the Sexes (G)
The text consists of an 'Introduction' (pp. 10–21), about 300 words of
description and 'Commentary' accompanying each plate (pp. 23–399), and
an important 'index to the pictures' (pp. 400–15). This is a major work of
scholarship and an important piece of criticism.

262. A. *Infant Sorrow*. Leicester, 1970. B. §*London, 1971.
Illustrations by Duine Campbell to three poems.

263. **Introduction, The Will and the Way, Love's Secret*. London [?1925].
A broadside from The Poetry Bookshop headed 'The Rhyme Sheet
No. 3. Poems and decorations by William Blake.'

264. A. ['Introduction' to *Innocence*], 'The Tiger', 'The Blossom', 'The
Angel'. *Nightingale Valley*: A Collection, Including a Great Number of the
Choicest Lyrics and Short Poems in The English Language. Ed. Giraldus
[William Allingham]. London, 1860. Pp. 54–5, 95–6, 116–17, 235. B. *Choice
Lyrics and Short Poems; or, Nightingale Valley*. London, [1871]. Pp. 54, 95, 116,
235.
'Note J' in this anthology (pp. 273–6 in both editions), the longest of the
notes, is a brief biography and comment on Blake.

265. **Jerusalem e no Michi*: Blake Shibunsen [*The Way to Jerusalem*: Selected
Poems and Prose of Blake]. Tr. Bunsho Jugaku. Kyoto, 1947. 276 pp.

266. **Jerusalem, Selected Poems and Prose*. Ed. with Introduction, Notes, and
Commentary by Hazard Adams. N.Y., Chicago, San Francisco, Atlanta,
Dallas, Montreal, Toronto, London, Sydney, 1970.
The 'Introduction' is pp. v–xix, 'Notes and Commentaries', pp. 685–747.

267. **Kiyoi Kokoro no Uta*: Haha to Ko no Shishu [*Songs of Innocence*: A Collec-
tion of Poems for Mothers and Children]. Tr. Yoshijiro Ito. Tokyo, 1965.
The text consists of 19 *Songs of Innocence*, plus 'The Tyger'. 'Blake to
Sono Jidai [Blake and his Age]' (pp. 205–55) is divided into 'Blake no
Shogai [Blake's Life]' (pp. 205–24) and 'Blake no Jidai no Tokushoku

[Characteristics of Blake's Age]' (pp. 225–55). A commentary on the songs is on pp. 67–206.

268. 'The Lamb.' *New Jerusalem Magazine*, XVI (Sept. 1842), 40.

269. *The Lamb.* Oxford, 1889.
For Ruth Daniel; see no. 331.

270. *The Land of Dreams*; Twenty Poems Selected and Illustrated by Pamela Bianco. N.Y., 1928.
Introduction (pp. xiii–xvi).

271. 'Lavater's "Aphorisms (Ningen Kingenshu) on Man" Annotated by W. Blake.' Tr. Shuden Fujishima. *Eigo Kyoiku: The English Review*, XIV (1950), 665–9, 682.

272. §*Lettres et entretiens de William Blake.* Tr. Georges Le Breton & Eileen Souffrin. Paris, 1948. Éditions de la Revue *Fontaine*.

273. §'The Little Boy Lost' and 'The Little Boy Found'. *Child's Gem.* Ed. Mrs. S. Colman [Pamela (Chandler) Colman]. Boston, 1845. P. 69.

274. A. *London.* Illustrated by Paul Piech. Bushey Heath, Herts., [1968?] Taurus Poem No. 12. B. §*London, 1971.

275. A. **The Lyrical Poems of William Blake.* Text by John Sampson, with an Introduction by Walter Raleigh. Oxford, 1905. B. §1906. C. §1921. D. §1926. E. *1935.
The 'Introduction' (pp. vii–li in A and C) is reprinted as 'William Blake'. Pp. 251–88 of Raleigh's *Some Authors*: A Collection of Literary Essays 1896–1916. Oxford, 1923.

276. *Il Matrimonio del Cielo e dell'Inferno, Canti dell'Innocenza e Altri Poemi.* Prima Traduzione Italiana e Prefazione di Edmondo Dodsworth. Lanciano, n.d. [1923?]
Preface is pp. 5–28.

277. *A Memorable Fancy.* Lithographs by Rosemary Killen. [Northampton, Mass.], 1965.
One page from Blake's *Marriage*, illustrated.

278. 'Nurse's Song.' *Longmans' Series of Recitations.* Standard II. No. 7. London, N.Y., Bombay, n.d.

A278. §*Oeuvres.* Tr. Pierre Léyris. Vol. I. Paris, 1974.
A bilingual edition (English and French on facing pages) containing *An Island, Songs,* and parts of *Poetical Sketches.*

279. 'On Another's Sorrow.' *Harbinger*, III (31 Oct. 1846), 333 (vMKN).

280. A. 'On Another's Sorrow', 'Night', and 'The Little Black Boy'. *Poetry for Home and School.* [Ed. Mrs. Anna Cabot (Jackson) Lowell.] Boston, 1843. Pp. 68–9, 74–5, 85–6. B. *Gleanings from the Poets, for Home and School.* [Ed.

Mrs. A. C. (J.) Lowell.] Boston, 1855. Pp. 49, 52, 61 (vDVE). C. A New
Edition, Enlarged. Boston, 1862. Pp. 49–50, 52–3, 61–2.

281. §'The Piper ["Introduction" to *Innocence*].' *Folk Songs*. Ed. John
Williamson Piper. N.Y., 1861.

282. **Poemas y profecias*. Versión y Prólogo de Enrique Caracciolo Trejo.
Cordoba [Argentina], 1957.

A282. §*Poemas Profeticos y Prosas*. Version y prologo de Christobal Serra.
Barcelona, 1941.

283. A. *Poèmes choisis*. Tr. Madeleine L. Cazamian. Paris, [1943] (vMKN).
B. §Paris, 1950.
   In A, the Introduction is pp. 9–92. The poems, facing each other in
English and French, include *Songs*, *Thel*, *Urizen*, 'The Everlasting Gospel',
and extracts from *The Marriage* and *Milton*.

284. *Poèmes choisis*. Tr. Veva & Étienne Vauthier. Paris–Bruxelles, 1946.
   Étienne Vauthier, 'William Blake (1757–1827)' is pp. 7–10. There are
21 poems facing each other in French and English.

285. *Poems*. Ed. Monica Redlich. With an Introduction by E. de Selincourt.
London, Edinburgh, Paris, Melbourne, Toronto, & N.Y., [1937].
   'Introduction' (pp. 15–56) reprinted from no. 148.

286. *Poems*. Ed. Ruthven Todd. London, 1949. Crown Classics.
   'Introduction' (pp. 7–13).

287. A. **The Poems & Prophecies of William Blake*. Ed. Max Plowman. London,
Toronto, & N.Y. [1927]. Everyman's Library. B. §*London, Toronto, &
N.Y., 1934. C. **Poems and Prophecies*. [Ed. Max Plowman.] London & N.Y.,
1950. Everyman's Library 792. D. **Blake's Poems and Prophecies*. Ed. Max
Plowman. London & N.Y., 1954. E. **Blake's Poems and Prophecies*. Ed. Max
Plowman. Supplementary note, select bibliography, and revisions to the
notes by Geoffrey Keynes. London & N.Y., 1959. F. London, 1970.
   The 'Introduction' to A & B is pp. vi–xviii; to C & D (though quite
unchanged) pp. vii–xxvi; in E it is vii–xxvii, with a 'Supplementary Note'
by Keynes on pp. xxvii–xxviii ('The text of the writings remains exactly as
it was'), and 'Notes' on pp. 435–9. *For the Sexes* (copy C or D) is reproduced.

288. *Poems and Prose of William Blake*. Ed. Floyd Dell. Girard, Kansas, 1925.
Little Blue Book No. 677.
   The Introduction (pp. 6–8) is reprinted.

289. A. *Poems by William Blake*. Ed. Alice Meynell. London, 1911. Red
Letter Library. B. *Poems*. Introduction by Alice Meynell. London &
Glasgow, [1927].
   Introduction is pp. iii–xii in both A & B.

290. *Poems from William Blake's Songs of Innocence*. [8] Drawings by Maurice
Sendak. London, 1967.
   The plates are only barely related to Blake's.

291. *Poems of Blake.* Ed. Laurence Binyon. London, 1931.
'Introduction' (pp. ix–xl), 'Note on Blake's Metrical Experiments' (pp. 359–68).

292. A. *The Poems of William Blake* comprising Songs of Innocence and of Experience together with Poetical Sketches and Some Copyright Poems Not in Any Other Edition. [Ed. R. H. Shepherd.] London, 1874. B. London, 1887.
'Introduction' is pp. v–xiv in both A & B in this Pickering edition. The newly printed Copyright Poems are from the Ballads or Pickering MS.

293. A. *The Poems of William Blake.* Ed. W. B. Yeats. London, 1893. The Muses Library. B. N.Y., 1893. C. London & N.Y. [1905]. D. *Mr. William Butler Yeats Introduces the Poetical Works of William Blake.* London, 1910. Books that Marked Epochs. E. *Poems of William Blake.* N.Y., [1920]. Modern Library. F. London, 1969. The Muses Library.
The introductions are pp. xv–liii in A; pp. xi–lxix in C; pp. xi–xlix in D, E. The text originated in no. 369, and Yeats's introduction is incorporated into no. 234 in Japanese, and the 1905 version reproduced in facsimile in Wittreich (1970).

294. *The Poems of William Blake.* Ed. John Sampson. London, 1921.
'Preface' (pp. v–xxiii).

295. **Poems of William Blake.* Ed. Amelia H. Munson. N.Y., 1964.
'William Blake' (pp. 1–9).

296. A. **The Poems of William Blake.* Ed. W. H. Stevenson, Text by David V. Erdman. London, 1971. Longmans' Annotated English Poets. B. *London, 1972. A Longman Paperbook.
F. W. Bateson, 'Note by the General Editor', is on p. ix and Stevenson's 'Preface' on pp. xi–xiv. The text (pp. 1–864) is extracted from *The Poetry and Prose of William Blake,* ed. D. V. Erdman (1965), with 'spelling and punctuation . . . modernized' (p. xii) and with *Vala* Nights I–II, VII, and *Milton* rearranged. The edition is extremely valuable for Stevenson's voluminous annotations presenting 'essential details of fact and background' (p. xi), particularly Biblical echoes pointed out by Michael Tolley. Blake's prose is generally omitted except for *The Marriage.*

297. *Poems: Poèmes.* Tr. M. L. Cazamian. Paris, 1968. Bilingue Aubier Flammarion [11].
The 'Introduction' and 'Notes', both in French, are on pp. 7–87, 313–14; in the text, French translations face Blake's English poems.

298. A. *The Poems, with Specimens of the Prose Writings, of William Blake.* With a Prefatory Notice, Biographical and Critical, by Joseph Skipsey. London, 1885. The Canterbury Poets. B. London, Felling-on-Tyne, N.Y., & Melbourne, [1904?]. The Canterbury Poets.
'Introductory Sketch' (pp. 10–35 in A, 9–35 in B).

299. A. *The Poetical Works of William Blake*, Lyrical and Miscellaneous. Ed., with a Prefatory Memoir, by William Michael Rossetti. London, 1874. The Aldine Edition of the British Poets. B. *London, 1875. C. *Third Edition. London, 1880. D. *London, 1890. E. *London, 1911. F. *London, 1914. Bohn's Popular Library.

The 'Prefatory Memoir' is pp. ix–cxxxiii. The Miscellaneous poems include the first publication of *Tiriel*.

300. A. *The Poetical Works of William Blake*. A New and Verbatim Text from the Manuscript Engraved and Letterpress Originals with Variorum Readings and Bibliographical Notes and Prefaces. Ed. John Sampson. Oxford, 1905. B. Photographically reprinted in Oxford, 1947. C. §Kennebunkport, Maine, 1971.

The 'General Preface' of both editions is pp. v–xxxi. This is a work of pioneer scholarly importance, well-informed, meticulously accurate, well-balanced and intelligent—virtues that were never collectively applied to Blake's text before this time. It is particularly valuable on the *Songs*, *Gates of Paradise*, *Notebook*, and Pickering MS.

301. *The Poetical Works of William Blake*. Ed. Edwin J. Ellis. In Two Volumes. London, 1906. Cf. *The Works of William Blake* (1893), no. 369.

The introduction is in Vol. I, pp. xiii–xxxiv.

302. A. *The Poetical Works of William Blake*, Including the unpublished French Revolution together with the Minor Prophetic Books and Selections from The Four Zoas, Milton & Jerusalem. Ed. John Sampson. London, Edinburgh, Glasgow, N.Y., Toronto, Melbourne & Bombay, 1913. Oxford Edition. B. 1914. C. 1925. D. §1928. E. §1934. F. 1938. G. §1941. H. §1943. I. §1948. J. §1949. K. §1952. L. §1956. M. §1958. N. 1960. Oxford Standard Authors.

The 'Bibliographical Introduction' of A, B, C, F, and N is pp. xv–lii. There seems to be no alteration in the various printings. As the title indicates, Sampson did not think of the 'Prophetic Books' as 'Poetical'. The 'unpublished' on the last fourteen title-pages is of course grossly misleading.

Within its titular limitations, this is an important and useful edition. (The text is reprinted in no. 275.)

303. A. *Poetry and Prose of William Blake*. Complete in One Volume. Ed. Geoffrey Keynes. London & N.Y., 1927. B. §London & N.Y., 1927 C. §London & N.Y., 1932. D. §London & N.Y., 1939. E. London & N.Y., 1943. F. London & N.Y., 1948. G. London & N.Y., 1956. See no. 241, 370.

'The Editor's Preface' is 2 pp. and the 'Preface to the Fourth Edition' (1939) is 1 p. The work was reset, and the pages repaginated, in the editions of 1939 and after. *The Gates of Paradise* is reproduced in full.

A table of page correspondences for the fourth and later editions will be found in A. S. Roe, *Blake's Illustrations to the Divine Comedy* (1953).

304. A. *The Poetry and Prose of William Blake*. Ed. David V. Erdman. Commentary by Harold Bloom. Garden City (N.Y.), 1965. B. *1965 [i.e. Second Printing, 1966]. C. *Third Printing. D. *Fourth Printing 1970.

The 'Preface' is pp. xxiii–xxiv; Erdman's important 'Textual Notes' are pp. 709–806; Bloom's 'Commentary' (not covering 'the lyrics' [p. xxiv] or the last 260 pages) is pp. 807–89. The pagination for text is not changed for successive Printings. The Second Printing (so identified only on p. xxiv) has many corrections, and the Fourth Printing has more changes on 41 pages.

This edition, containing almost all Blake's writings (the omissions are chiefly letters), presents Blake's own punctuation and is editorially of the first importance. (Erdman's text of the poetry is reprinted, with some modifications, in *The Poems of William Blake*, ed. W. H. Stevenson [1971].)

305. *The Poetry of William Blake.* Containing: Several Songs of Innocence & Experience; and Other Poetical Works [N.Y.?] 1952.
The edition is noteworthy only for the typography.

306. A. **The Portable Blake.* Ed. Alfred Kazin. N.Y., 1946. Viking Portable Library. B. Reprinted as **The Indispensable Blake.* N.Y., 1950. C. Reprinted as *The Portable Blake.* N.Y., 1953. D. Reprinted as **The Essential Blake.* London, 1968. . . . U. §*The Portable Blake.* 21st Printing, 1974.
'Dr. Keynes . . . did the real work for this volume' (1946, p. xi) by providing Blake's text. Kazin's 'Introduction' (pp. 1–55 in A and D) is reprinted in no. 199, and at the end (pp. 675–94 in A and D) are selections from Crabb Robinson's 'Reminiscences'. All the plates for *Job* and 17 from *For Children* (?D) are reproduced.

307. *Premiers Livres prophétiques.* Tr. Pierre Berger. Paris, 1927. Philosophie: Collection dirigée par Pierre Morhange. See no. 313.
'Introduction Biographique: William Blake, Sa vie, ses œuvres et ses idées' (pp. 2–36).

308. *Primeros Libros Proféticos: Poemas.* Prólogo y traducción de Agustí Bartra. Mexico [City], 1961.
The 'Prólogo' is pp. 7–21, the 'Esquema Interpretativo de los Poemas' pp. 181–92.

309. A. **The Prophetic Writings of William Blake.* In Two Volumes. Ed. D. J. Sloss & J. P. R. Wallis, with a General Introduction, Glossarial Index of Symbols, Commentary, and Appendices. Oxford, 1926. B. **1957. C. **1964.
The 'General Introduction' is Vol. II, pp. 1–121, and the 'Index of Symbols' is Vol. II, pp. 124–263. The fresh transcriptions and bibliographical notes are of value, as is the 'Index of Symbols' if it is used for the evidence it collects rather than for the conclusions it comes to.

310. **Prose & prophecy*: Selections from the Prose and Prophetic Books of William Blake. Franklin, New Hampshire, 1964.
The anonymous Preface is on pp. xiii–xvi of this miniature volume.

311. *Proverbs of Hell.* Pasadena, 1929.
There are nine proverbs from the *Marriage of Heaven and Hell* 'Printed [on two leaves] by Gregg Anderson for private distribution and especially for Mr. Arthur M. Ellis'.

A311. *Proverbs of Hell.* Introduction Jack Schofield illustrations Duine Campbell. Leicester, 1972.
'Introduction' on 4 pp., text from the *Marriage*.

312. A. §*Pu-lai-k'o Shih-hsuan* [*A Selection of Poems by Blake*]. Tr. Yuan K'o-chia. Peking, 1957. B. Hong Kong, 1960.
In Chinese.

313. *Seconds Livres prophétiques.* Contenant Milton; Poèmes et Fragments divers; L'Évangile Éternel, tr. Pierre Berger. Paris, 1930. Philosophie: Collection dirigée par Pierre Morhange. See also 307.
'Introduction' (pp. 11–77).

314. A. *Select Poems of William Blake.* Ed. Makoto Sangu. Tokyo, 1925. Kenkyusha English Classics. B. *Second Edition.* 1935. C. *1948. Kenkyusha British & American Classics LXI. D. *1953. E. §1956. F. §1958. G. *1960. H. *1963.
The 'Introduction' (pp. i–xlvii in A) is in Japanese, the poems in English, the 'Notes' (pp. 151–335 in A–D, G–H) in Japanese and English.

315. A. *Selected Poems.* Ed. Stanley Gardner. London, 1962. The London English Literature Series. B. 1965.
'Introduction' (pp. 11–50), 'Notes' (pp. 136–87).

316. A. *Selected Poems by William Blake.* Ed. Basil de Selincourt. Oxford, 1927. The World's Classics. B. 1951. C. 1957. D. London, 1963. E. 1968.
'Introduction' (pp. v–xix in A and D).

317. *Selected Poems of William Blake.* Selected by J. C. Bloem. Amsterdam, 1945.
An unpretentious 62-page anthology in English.

318. A. *Selected Poems of William Blake.* Ed. F. W. Bateson. London, Melbourne, Toronto, 1957. B. §1961. C. §1963. D. §1964. E. 1965. F. 1966.
'Introduction' (pp. xi–xxx); the notes are original and illuminating.

319. *Selected Poetry and Prose of William Blake.* Ed. with an Introduction by Northrop Frye. N.Y., 1953. The Modern Library.
The excellent 'Introduction' is pp. xiii–xxviii, the 'Notes' pp. 459–65.

320. *Selected Writings.* Ed. Robert F. Gleckner. N.Y., 1967. Crofts Classics.
The 'Introduction' is pp. ix–xxii.

A320. [*Selections*]. Tr. S. I. Marshak. Preface by V. Zhirmunsky. Moscow, 1965.
182 pp., in Russian; V. Zhirmunsky, ['William Blake (1757–1827)]' is pp. 5–34.

321. 'Selections from Blake's Poems.' *The Harbinger*, VII (8 July 1848), 73.
Text of 'To the Evening Star', 'To Morning', 'Song [How sweet I roam'd]', 'Song [My silks and fine array]', 'Song [Love and harmony combine]' from *Poetical Sketches*.

322. *Selections from Songs of Innocence and Experience By William Blake.* Pen Written by Reynard Biemiller. N.Y., 1946.

323. *Selections from the Symbolic Poems of William Blake.* Ed. Frederick E. Pierce. New Haven & London, 1915.
'Introduction' (pp. vii–x).

324. *Selections from the Works of William Blake.* Ed. Mark Perugini. London, 1901. The Little Library.
'Introduction' (pp. ix–xli).

325. *Selections from the Writings of William Blake.* Ed. Laurence Housman. London, 1893.
'Introduction' (pp. ix–xxxi).

326. *Selections from William Blake.* London, Liverpool, Bournemouth, & Boston, [1923].

327. *Selections from William Blake.* Berkeley, California, 1964.

328. *Seven Poems from Blake's 'Songs of Innocence.'* Decorated in colours by G. Spencer Watson. Set to Music by Geoffrey Gwyther. London, [1949?].
The decorations are remarkably bad.

329. *Songs.* Los Angeles, 1935.
Five *Songs of Innocence* 'Printed by Janet and Ward Ritchie for Jonathan Baird Ritchie born July 17, 1935.'
For more *Songs* for another child, see no. 338.

330. *Songs and Poems.* With an Introduction by Michael Kingsdowne. London, [1920]. Stead's Poets, No. 75.
'William Blake: The Poet of Childhood' (pp. 3–8).

331. *Songs by William Blake.* Oxford, 1885.
This was evidently sent by 'Rachel and Ruth [Daniel] to their child friends these with Christmas greetings.' At the end is a list of 32 of 'Our Child Friends'. See no. 269.

332. *The Songs of Innocence.* With Designs by Celia Levetus. London, 1899.
Includes poems besides those in *Innocence*.

333. *Songs of Innocence.* [San Francisco, 1938.]
Five poems.

334. A. *Songs of Innocence and of Experience, and Other Works*: Songs of Innocence and of Experience; The Book of Thel; The Marriage of Heaven and Hell; Visions of the Daughters of Albion; The Everlasting Gospel; with a Selective Appendix of shorter poems from Blake's manuscripts. Ed. R. B. Kennedy. London & Glasgow, 1970. Collins Annotated Student Texts. B. §London, 1972.
'Preface' (pp. 10–12), 'Notes' (pp. 143–248), and ten 'Critical Extracts' (pp. 249–62); text selectively modernized from Erdman, no. 304.

335. A. *Songs of Innocence and Experience with Other Poems.* [Ed. R. H. Shepherd.] London, 1866. B. *Songs of Innocence and of Experience* Showing the Two Contrary States of the Human Soul [and other Miscellaneous Poems]. Ed. Richard Herne Shepherd. London, 1868.

The 'Preface' in A (pp. vii–xii) is expanded in B (pp. v–xii). The 'Other Poems' include those from the 'Pickering Manuscript' ('now in the possession of the Publisher' Pickering), 'The Grey Monk' and 'Long John Brown & Little Mary Bell' for the first time (the others were printed in Gilchrist [1863]); 'Mary' stanza 5 and 'Auguries of Innocence' ll. 113–14 were 'suppressed for sufficient reasons [*the use of the word* 'whore']', and asterisks substituted'. (A variant, pre-asterisk state is reported in no. 2867.)

B. In the second edition, 'Song by a Shepherd' and 'Song by an Old Shepherd' are printed silently from the MSS with *Poetical Sketches* (F).

336. *Songs of Innocence and Other Poems.* London [1911].

337. *Songs of Innocence And Other Poems.* London [1912].

338. *Songs (Second Series).* Los Angeles, 1941.
Four songs by Blake 'Printed by Janet and Ward Ritchie for Duncan Ward Ritchie born May 16, 1941'. See no. 329 for the first series.

339. *Taivaan ja Helvetin Avioliitto ja Muuta Proosaa.* [Tr. Tuomas Anhava.] Hämeenlinna [1959].
The introduction, 'William Blake', is pp. 5–29, the notes pp. 137–59.

340. 'The Tiger' and 'The Child and the Piper' [i.e. the 'Introduction' to *Innocence*]. *The Children's Garland*, from the best poets. Ed. Coventry Patmore. London & Cambridge, 1862. Pp. 158–9, 1–2.

341. 'The Tiger' and 'The Little Black Boy'. *The Estray*: A Collection of Poems. [Ed. Henry Wadsworth Longfellow.] Boston, 1847. Pp. 36–7, 103–4.

342. A. §'The Tiger', 'The Little Black Boy', 'My Silks', 'The Garden of Love' and 'On Another's Sorrow'. *The Household Book of Poetry*. Ed. Charles A. Dana. N.Y., 1857. B. 'The Tiger', 'Chimney Sweeper', 'The Little Black Boy', 'The Garden of Love', and 'On Another's Sorrow'. *The Household Book of Poetry*. Ed. Charles A. Dana. N.Y., 1858. Pp. 74, 162–3, 688, 785 (vDVE). C. N.Y. & London, 1859. Pp. 74, 162–3, 688, 785. . . . K. §Eleventh Edition, revised and enlarged. 1867. L. 'The Tiger', 'The Little Black Boy', 'Song [My Silks]', 'The Garden of Love' and 'On Another's Sorrow'. *The Household Book of Poetry*. Ed. Charles A. Dana. Eleventh Edition—Revised and Enlarged. N.Y. & London, 1868. Pp. 73, 159–60, 312–13, 706, & 807–8. M. N.Y. & London, 1869. Pp. 73, 159–60, 312–13, 706, & 807–8. 6. §1875. O. §1882. P. §N.Y. & London, 1903.

343. *Tigre.* Tr. E.T. [Emilie Terza.] n.p., [1906].

344. 'To Spring', 'To Summer', 'To Autumn', 'To Winter'. *Harbinger*, VII (24 June 1848), 57.
From *Poetical Sketches*.

A344. *Twelve Poems.* Ed. J. L. Carr. London, 1972. Florin Poet Series.

345. A. *Tyger Tyger.* Illustrated by Paul Piech. Bushey Heath, Herts. [1969]. Taurus Poem No. 5. B. §*London, 1971.

346. *Versek és Prófécidk.* [Ed. Kardos László.] Budapest, 1959.
'William Blake' (pp. 5–25) and the notes (pp. 317–34) are by Szenczi Miklós. Each poem seems to have a different translator.

347. *Visiones de las Hijas de Albion y el Viajero Mental.* Tr. Pablo Neruda. Buenos Aires, 1947.

348. *Visioni di William Blake.* Tr. Giuseppe Ungaretti. Verona, 1965.
The 'Discorsetto del Traduttore' is on pp. 11–15, 'Notizie Biografichie' pp. 451–68, 'Simboli e probabili fonti' pp. 469–535. English and Italian versions face one another.
The 37 plates include all those for Dante and *For the Sexes: The Gates of Paradise.*

349. *Werke.* [Ed. Gunther Klotz, tr. Walter Wilhelm.] Berlin, 1958.
'Einleitung' (pp. 7–56), 'Anmerkungen' (pp. 379–89); the English and German texts face each other.

350. *William Blake.* Edinburgh, 1884. The Jewel Poets.
The introductory essay, 'William Blake' (pp. 5–8), is by Henry J. Nicoll.

351. *William Blake.* [Ed. Edward Thompson.] London, [1925?] Augustan Books of Poetry.

352. *William Blake.* Tr. Jean Rousselot [assisté par Anne-Marie Rousselot]. Paris, 1964. Poètes d'aujourd'hui 118.
Introduction (pp. 5–77), 'Choix de Poèmes' (pp. 81–184).

353. *William Blake.* Ed. Vivian de Sola Pinto. London, 1965.
'Introduction' (pp. 1–58), 'Notes' (pp. 181–90); another popular selection.

354. *William Blake.* Ed. Leonard Clark. [London] 1969. Longman's Poetry Library.
Eleven poems on 13 pages.

355. *William Blake,* Ed. John Adlard. London, 1970. Studio Vista Pocket Poets.
'Introduction' (pp. 7–12).

356. *William Blake.* Ed. Francis Léaud. Paris, 1968. Collection U/U2. Série 'Étude anglo-américaine'.
'Présentation' (pp. 5–147), 'Anthologie' in English (pp. 150–247).

357. *William Blake 1757–1827.* Kettering [Northamptonshire] [1968].
Fifteen selections, mostly lyrics.

358. 'William Blake (1757–1827).' Pp. 33–101 of *The Romantics on Milton*: Formal Essays and Critical Asides. Ed. Joseph Anthony Wittreich. Cleveland & London, 1970.
Includes Keynes's text of *Milton.*

359. A. *William Blake: An Introduction.* With illustrations from Blake's paintings and engravings. Ed. Anne Malcolmson. London, 1967. B. N.Y., 1967.
'Blake, the Man' (pp. 9–32).

360. A. *William Blake*: A Selection of Poems and Letters. Ed. J. Bronowski. Harmondsworth [England], 1958. 'The Penguin Poets D42.' B. §1961. C. 1964. D. §1965. E. §1966. F. §1968. G. §1970. I. §1972. J. 1973.
Introduction (pp. 9–13).

361. *William Blake*: Ausgewählte Dichtungen Übertragen von Adolph Knoblauch. [2 vols.] Berlin, 1907.

362. *The William Blake Calendar*: A Quotation for Every Day in the Year. Selected by Thomas Wright. London, 1913.

363. *William Blake, die Ethick der Fruchtbarkeit.* Zusammengestellt aus seinen werken und aufzeichnungen ubersetzt und eingeleitet von Otto von Taube. Jena, 1907.
'Einleitung von der Person und den Werken William Blakes' (pp. i–li).

364. *William Blake: Dikter och Profetior.* I Urval av Folke Isaksson. [Tr. by Isaksson and others.] Stockholm, 1957 (vDVE).
Introduction (pp. 5–16).

365. *William Blake.* Poems ed. A. T. Quiller-Couch. Oxford, [1908]. Select English Classics.

366. *William Blake*: Selected Poems. Eds. G. D. H. & M. I. Cole. London, 1927.

367. *William Blake*: Selected Poems. With an Introduction by Denis Saurat. London, 1947.
'Introduction' (pp. 7–23); text (pp. 25–120) from the Keynes editions.

368. *Works by William Blake.* Songs of Innocence [copy a]. 1789. Songs of Experience [copy a]. 1794. Book of Thel [copy D?]. 1789. Vision[s] of the Daughters of Albion [copy B]. 1793. America: A Prophecy [copy F?]. 1793. Europe: A Prophecy [copy D?]. 1794. The First Book of Urizen [copy D]. 1794. The Song of Los [copy A or D]. 1794 [i.e. 1795]. Reproduced in Facsimile from the Original Editions. One Hundred Copies printed for Private Circulation. [London] 1876.
The publisher is not given.

369. A. *The Works of William Blake, Poetic, Symbolic, and Critical.* Ed. with Lithographs of the Illustrated 'Prophetic Books,' and a Memoir and Interpretation by Edwin John Ellis & William Butler Yeats. In Three Vols. London, 1893. B. *London, 1973.
The contents are:
Vol. I: Memoir (pp. 1–172); 'The Literary Period' (pp. 175–232); 'The Symbolic System' (pp. 235–420);
Vol. II: 'Interpretation and Paraphrased Commentary' (pp. 3–301); 'Blake the Artist' (pp. 305–403); 'Some References [to the Mythological Characters]' (pp. 405–35);

Vol. III: Blake's works, with 296 lithographs which include *All Religions are One* (A), 'Laocoon' (B), *On Homer* (B), *Ghost* (B), *Marriage* (?F), *Book of Los* (A), *Urizen* (D plus G), *Ahania* (A), *Thel* (B), *Visions* (A), *Song of Los* (A or D), *America* (?M), *Europe* (?F), *Milton* (C plus A or B), and *Jerusalem*, in all of which the quality is poor.

On 3 May 1900 Yeats wrote:

The writing of this book is mainly Ellis's. The thinking is as much mine as his. The biography is by him. He wrote and trebled in size a biography of mine. The greater part of the 'symbolic system' is my writing; the rest of the book was written by Ellis working over short accounts of the books by me, except in the case of the 'literary period', the account of the minor poems, and the account of Blake's art theories which are all his own except in so far as we discussed everything together.

[H. Adams, *Blake and Yeats* (1955), 47.]

The enthusiasm and comprehensiveness of this work are of considerable historical importance, but the reproductions are unreliable, the transcriptions inaccurate, the biography surprisingly fictional, and the criticism and interpretation thoroughly coloured by the editors' peculiar preconceptions. The edition is likely to prove useful only to adepts in both Blake and Yeats. Small fragments of the MS are in Reading University Library.

B is a photographic reprint.

370. A. **The Writings of William Blake*. In Three Volumes. Ed. Geoffrey Keynes. London, 1925. B. **The Complete Writings of William Blake* with All the Variant Readings. Ed. Geoffrey Keynes. London & N.Y., 1957. C. **The Complete Writings of William Blake* with Variant Readings. Ed. Geoffrey Keynes. London, N.Y., Toronto, 1966. §D. 1966. E. 1967. F. London, Oxford, N.Y., 1969. *G. §London, 1971. H. §London, 1972.

In A, the 'Editor's Preface' is in Vol. I, pp. xi–xviii. In B & C, 'The Editor's Preface' is pp. ix–xv, 'The Notes' pp. 883–927, and the plates include those of *For the Sexes: The Gates of Paradise*.

In C, the 'Preface to this Edition' (p. viii) says the page references are the same as in 1957, in order to make the work useful for the Concordance (no. 1579), from which corrections have been made on 124 pp. of text (though not including all known variants) and in some notes; a 'Supplement' of new material (pp. 928, 939–44) includes some of the matter which had come to light since 1957.

N.B. In A–H, Blake's works are intermingled in chronological order, though in B–H the letters are gathered together. B (Nonesuch) contains a significant number of minor additions to A, and is in turn slightly extended in C–H (Oxford). Until the publication of Erdman's edition (no. 304), there was no doubt concerning the fact that Keynes's editions of Blake above (A & B) were the best available.

PART II

REPRODUCTIONS OF DRAWINGS
AND PAINTINGS

Section A

ILLUSTRATIONS OF INDIVIDUAL AUTHORS

ORGANIZATION. Books whose *raison d'être* is their reproduction of Blake's paintings or drawings are organized alphabetically here under the name of the author illustrated (Dante, Milton, etc.). Collections which include more than one author (e.g. *Pencil Drawings*) are listed separately in Section B. Catalogues and exhibitions of Blake's art, and books for which he made engravings are given in Parts III and IV.

ALIGHIERI; see DANTE

BIBLE

371. *The Bible for My Grandchildren.* Ed. Ruth Hornblower Greenough. With Illustrations from designs by William Blake. Decorations by Rudolph Ruzicka. [2 vols.] [Boston], 1950.
   There are 31 plates.

372. *The Home Bible, Arranged for Family Reading.* Ed. Ruth Hornblower Greenough. With Illustrations from Designs by William Blake, and Decorations by Rudolph Ruzicka. N.Y., 1950.
   Thirty-one Blake plates.

373. **Blake Seisho Gashu* [*Blake's Bible Illustrations*]. Ed. Munemoto Yanagi. Tokyo, 1958. Thirty-two pp., 76 plates.

BIBLE: *Job.*

374. *Illustrations of the Book of Job by William Blake*: Being all the Water-Colour Designs Pencil Drawings and Engravings Reproduced in Facsimile. With an introduction by Laurence Binyon and Geoffrey Keynes. N.Y., 1935.
   'The History of the Designs' (pp. 3–15, revised and reprinted in Keynes's

8181515   R

Blake Studies [1949, 1971]), 'The Interpretation' (pp. 16–19), 'The Water-Colours, the Pencil Drawings, and the Engravings' (pp. 50–4), 'Reproductions of the Engravings' (pp. 55–7), and 'The Stage Version' (pp. 58–61, revised and reprinted in his *Blake Studies* [1949, 1971]) are by Keynes; 'The Place of the New Zealand Set' (pp. 47–9) is by Binyon; and 'The Variations in the Designs' (pp. 20–46) is by Binyon & Keynes. The 134 plates of this excellent Pierpont Morgan edition include Blake's pencil drawings and water-colours and proofs of his engravings. For the genesis of *Job*, it is of crucial importance.

375. *Illustrations of the Book of Job*. Reproduced in Facsimile from the original 'New Zealand' set made about 1823–4, in the possession of Philip Hofer. With a Note by Philip Hofer. London & N.Y., 1937.

'A Note on William Blake's Illustrations of The Book of Job' (pp. 5–9). A letter of 1844 from Linnell about *Job* is quoted (p. 8).

376. *Wright, Andrew. *Blake's Job*: A Commentary. Oxford, 1972.

Reproduction of the 22 engravings with about a page of conventional commentary for each (pp. 2–51), plus 'Appendix I: The Biblical Texts and Blake's Alterations' (pp. 53–64).

BUNYAN, John

377. *The Pilgrim's Progress*. Illustrated with 29 watercolour paintings by William Blake now printed for the first time. Ed. G. B. Harrison. With a new introduction by Geoffrey Keynes. N.Y., 1941. Limited Editions Club.

Keynes's 'Introduction' (pp. vii–xxxii) is revised and reprinted in his *Blake Studies* (1949, 1971).

378. *The Pilgrim's Progress* from This World to That Which Is to Come Delivered Under the Similitude of a Dream. Illustrated with Water-Colors by William Blake. N.Y., 1942.

John T. Winterich, 'How this Book Came to Be' (pp. xi–xix) only mentions Blake perfunctorily. The 12 plates are in colour.

379. *The Pilgrim's Progress*. Including an Introduction to the Book and a Note on the William Blake Designs by A. K. Adams together with an Essay on John Bunyan by Thomas Babington Macaulay. Sixteen pages of illustrations including reproductions of the frontispiece and eight designs for the First Part by William Blake. N.Y., 1968. Great Illustrated Classics.

A. K. Adams, 'Note on the Designs by William Blake' (pp. xxi–xxiii); 9 designs are by Blake, 7 by others.

DANTE ALIGHIERI

380. A. *Illustrations to the Divine Comedy of Dante by William Blake*. London, 1922. B. N.Y., 1968.

In each, the unsigned 'Introduction' is one page. A, printed for The National Art-Collections Fund, has 102 plates; B, a 'slightly enlarged version' in a portfolio, has 109 plates, the 102 drawings photographed from the 1922 edition, the 7 engravings added to them.

381. *The Divine Comedy of Dante Alighieri* translated into English Verse by Melville Best Anderson; with notes and elucidations by the translator, an introduction by Arthur Livingston, and thirty-two drawings by William Blake, now printed for the First Time. N.Y. [1944]. Heritage Book Club.

'A Note on This Edition', p. [iv], includes a comment on the drawings.

382. *Blake's Illustrations for Dante*: [20] Selections from the Originals in the National Gallery of Victoria, Melbourne, Australia and the Fogg Art Museum, Cambridge, Massachusetts. Cambridge, 1953. Fogg Picture Book No. 2.

Helen D. Willard, 'Introduction', is 4 pp.

383. *The Melbourne Dante Illustrations*. Ed. Ursula Hoff. Melbourne, 1961. Special Bulletin for the Centenary Year, 1961, The National Gallery of Victoria.

'William Blake's Illustrations to Dante's Divine Comedy' (pp. 1–4) is followed by reproductions of the 36 National Gallery Dante drawings.

GRAY, Thomas

384. A. *William Blake's Designs for Gray's Poems*, Reproduced Full-Size in Monochrome or Colour from the Unique Copy Belonging to His Grace the Duke of Hamilton. With an Introduction by H. J. C. Grierson. London, Edinburgh, Glasgow, Copenhagen, N.Y., Toronto, Melbourne, Cape Town, Bombay, Calcutta, Madras, Shanghai, 1922.

Grierson's essay, 'Blake's Illustrations to Gray's Poems' (pp. 5–18), is reprinted in B. 'Blake & Gray.' Pp. 200–55 of *The Background of English Literature*. London, 1925. There are 116 plates, 6 in colour.

385. **William Blake's Water-Colour Designs for the Poems of Gray*, Introduction and Commentary by Geoffrey Keynes, Kt. London, 1972. The William Blake Trust.

The work is issued either loose in a portfolio or bound in three volumes; the 1972 text at the end of Vol. III—'Introduction' (pp. 1–6) and 'Commentary' (pp. 9–28)—is mostly reprinted without acknowledgement from the 1971–2 exhibition catalogue.

MILTON, John. *L'Allegro.*

386. *L'Allegro*, with the Paintings by William Blake, together with a Note upon the Poems by W. B. Trent. N.Y., 1954.

'A Note upon the Poems' (pp. 7–16), 'Blake's Inscriptions on his Paintings' pp. 41–3.

MILTON. *Comus.*

387. *Illustrations of Milton's Comus*: Eight Drawings by William Blake. Reproduced by William Griggs. London, 1890.

The 8 colour plates are no. 112–19 (separately published) of Quaritch's *Facsimiles of Choice Examples selected from Illuminated Manuscripts, Unpublished Drawings and Illustrated Books of Early Date* (London, 1890).

388. *Comus: A Mask.* With Eight Illustrations by William Blake. Preface by Darrell Figgis. London, 1926.

'Preface' (pp. ix–xviii).

MILTON: *On the Morning of Christ's Nativity.*

389. *On the Morning of Christ's Nativity.* Milton's Hymn with [six] Illustrations by William Blake and a Note by Geoffrey Keynes. Cambridge [England], 1923.

'Note on the Illustrations' (pp. 31–2).

MILTON. *Paradise Lost.*

390. *Paradise Lost.* Illustrations [in colour] by William Blake. Liverpool, 1906.

'Preface' (pp. v–viii) is signed S. S., probably for Sidney Style, to whom several drawings belonged.

391. *Paradise Lost.* With the Illustrations by William Blake Printed in Color for the First Time and with Prefaces by Philip Hofer and John T. Winterich. N.Y., 1940. The Heritage Press.

Philip Hofer, 'How these Illustrations came to be' (pp. vii–xiv), accompanies the 9 Boston designs.

392. *Paradise Lost.* N.Y., 1947. An American Studio Book.

Colour facsimiles of Blake's designs, without Milton's text. Henry P. Rossiter, 'William Blake', is on 1 page.

MILTON. *Il Penseroso.*

393. *Il Penseroso,* with Paintings by William Blake, together with a Note upon the Paintings by Chauncey Brewster Tinker. N.Y., 1954.

'A Note upon the Paintings' (pp. 7–16) is reprinted from no. 2845; 'Blake's Inscriptions on his Paintings' is pp. 43–4.

MILTON. *Poems.*

394. *Poems in English* with Illustrations by William Blake. [2 vols.] London, 1926.

The 'Notes on Blake's Illustrations to Milton's Poems' (Vol. I, pp. 271–9) and 'Notes on Blake's Illustrations to Paradise Lost' (Vol. II, pp. 355–9) are by Geoffrey Keynes.

YOUNG, Edward.

395. *Illustrations to Young's Night Thoughts, Done in Water-Colour by William Blake.* Thirty pages, five reproduced in colour and twenty-five in monotone from the original water-colours. With an introductory essay by Geoffrey Keynes. Cambridge [Mass.] & London, 1927.

Keynes's 'Introductory Essay' (8 pp.) was revised and reprinted in his *Blake Studies* (1949, 1971). The 'Prefatory Note' by Chester W. Greenough is 2 pages.

N.B. The 537 water-colour designs in The British Museum Print Room are available in colour microfilm from the EP Group of Companies [formerly Micro Methods], Bradford Road, East Ardsley, Wakefield, Yorkshire.

Section B

COLLECTIONS AND SELECTIONS

396. *The Act of Creation, by William Blake.* Berwyn [Pa.], 1925.
The reproduction of the frontispiece of *Europe* has a 1-page introduction by
A. E. Newton.

397. **And the Third Day* . . . A Record of Hope and Fulfilment. Ed. Sir
Herbert Grierson. Pictures Chosen by John Rothenstein. London, 1948.
Eight pictures by Blake are among those reproduced.

398. A. *Blake.* Ed. G. Keynes. London, [1945]. The Faber Gallery. B. N.Y.,
1949. C. London, 1954.
'Introduction by Geoffrey Keynes' (pp. 2–5, 24), 10 colour plates.

399. **Blake.* London, 1965. The Masters 6.
Geoffrey Keynes, 'William Blake 1757–1827' (pp. 2–6), 38 plates.

400. *Blake and the Youthful Ancients* Being Portraits of William Blake and his
Followers Engraved on Wood by Leonard Baskin and with a Biographical
Notice by Bennett Schiff. Northampton [Mass.], 1956.
Bennett Schiff's untitled 3-page essay is about Blake's young friends and
his wonderful death. There are eighteen portraits, including 6 of Blake.

401. *The Blake–Varley Sketchbook of 1819* in the Collection of M. D. E. Clayton-
Stamm. Ed. Martin Butlin. [2 vols.] London, 1969.
In Vol. I is M. D. E. Clayton-Stamm, '"Gratias Tibi Ago"' (pp. xi–xiv),
Martin Butlin, 'Introduction' (pp. 1–18) and 'Commentary' (pp. 19–34).
Vol. II includes 36 Visionary Drawings by Blake.

402. *Blake's Pencil Drawings.* Second Series. Ed. Geoffrey Keynes. London,
1956. (For the first series, see *Pencil Drawings* [1927].)
'Blake's Pencil Drawings Second Series' (pp. vii–xi); there are 57 plates,
39 of which are reproduced (darker) in the 1970 *Drawings*.

403. A. §*The Book of Peace.* [Being a Collection of Prose & Verse Made by
Pamela Tenant with Illustrations from the Drawings of William Blake.]
London, 1900. B. §1900. C. 1901. D. 1905. E. §1910.
Of the 6 plates, three are by Blake.

404. A. Binyon, Laurence. *The Drawings and Engravings of William Blake.*
Ed. Geoffrey Holme. London, 1922. B. N.Y., 1967.
Binyon's Introduction is pp. 1–29, and there are 108 plates.

405. **Drawings of William Blake*: 92 Pencil Studies. Ed. Sir Geoffrey Keynes.
N.Y., 1970.
The 'Introduction' (pp. v–xi); most of the drawings are repeated, rather
darker, from the *Pencil Drawings* of 1927 (27) and 1956 (39).

406. A. *The Heads of the Poets.* (Eighteen in number—of which seventeen have not hitherto been published.) With an Introduction by Thomas Wright. Olney, Bucks., 1925. B. §Second Edition. 1925.

'William Blake's Heads of the Poets' is 6 pp. There is a 1-page report of 'The Thirteenth Annual Meeting of the Blake Society'.

407. *The Influence of Joy upon the Workman and his Work* by H. Bendelack Hewetson. Illustrated by Autotype Facsimiles of Drawings by William Blake, Miss Frederica Marsh, Edward Stanley [i.e. Stanley Inchbold], and the Author; and an Autotype Plate of Beverley Minster. London, 1880.

Two Blake plates from Blair.

408. *The Paintings of William Blake.* Ed. Darrell Figgis. London, 1925.

'William Blake in the Plan of his Days' (pp. 1–117); the 102 plates include sets for *Paradise Lost* and *Paradise Regained.* (Keynes, 'Blake Drawings', points out that two of the designs are not by Blake.)

409. *Pencil Drawings by William Blake.* Ed. Geoffrey Keynes. London, 1927. (For the Second Series, see *Blake's Pencil Drawings* [1956].)

'Blake's Pencil Drawings' (pp. vii–xvi); there are 82 plates (including the 22 *Job* sketches), 27 of which are reproduced in the 1970 *Drawings.*

410. *Twenty-Seven Drawings by William Blake* being Illustrations for Paradise Lost, Comus and The Bible. McPherson, Kansas, 1925.

There is a 1-page 'Foreword' by C[arl] J. S[malley], the publisher. The plates include the Boston series of *Paradise Lost* and *Comus.*

411. *William Blake.* Ed. Bertram Anthony. London & N.Y., 1948. The World's Masters—New Series.

'Introduction' (pp. 3–10), 'Notes to the Illustrations' (pp. 12–15); 50 small plates.

412. A. *William Blake* by Martin Butlin. London, 1966. The Tate Gallery Little Book Series. B. 1968. C. §1972.

'William Blake, 1757–1827' is 12 pp., followed by 32 plates from the Tate Gallery.

413. *William Blake: Etchings from his Works* by William Bell Scott. With Descriptive Text. London, 1878.

Scott's essay 'William Blake' is pp. 3–5, and 'Description of the [10] Etchings' pp. 6–8.

A413. *William Blake The Artist* by Ruthven Todd. London & N.Y., 1971. Studio Vista / Dutton Pictureback [sic].

118 plates interspersed with staccato chronological text 'about the manner in which William Blake lived as an artist' (p. 7).

414. *William Blake water-color drawings* [in the] Museum of Fine Arts, Boston. Prepared by Helen D. Willard, ed. Peter A. Wick. Boston, 1957.

H. D. W., 'Introduction' (pp. 5–10). The 37 Boston Museum Blakes, including 9 for *Paradise Lost* and 8 for *Comus,* are reproduced but only cursorily described.

PART III

COMMERCIAL BOOK ENGRAVINGS

Section A

ILLUSTRATIONS OF INDIVIDUAL AUTHORS

'Engravings' in this Part is taken to include line engravings, ordinary etchings, woodcuts—all the processes which Blake used to multiply designs to illustrate the works of other men.

All the plates in this Section (save those for *Job* and Dante) are to be reproduced in R. R. Easson & R. N. Essick, *William Blake: Book Illustrator*; Vol. I has already appeared (see 1972 in Part IV, Catalogues) with plates designed *and* engraved by Blake.

ORGANIZATION. Books for which Blake designed or engraved plates are listed alphabetically under the name of the author of the book or, in the case of periodicals, under the title of the magazine. Books with collected reproductions of his engravings are listed separately in Section B. *Catalogues* of his engravings will be found in Part IV, under Catalogues.

COPYRIGHT. In 1734 (8 Geo. II), Parliament passed 'An Act for the Encouragement of the Arts of Designing, Engraving, and Etching historical and other Prints, by vesting the Properties thereof in the Inventors and Engravers', according to which the designers, engravers, etc., 'shall have the sole Right and Liberty of Printing and Reprinting the same for the Term of Fourteen Years, to commence from the Day of the first Publishing thereof, which shall be truly engraved with the name of the Proprietor on each Plate and printed on every such Print or Prints'. As a consequence, the dates on engravings are of some importance as establishing copyright.

STATIONERS' HALL: A careful search has been made for the entry of each of the works for which Blake made engravings in the Stationers' (i.e. copyright) Register, in Stationers' Hall, London, but only seven were found. However, this conclusion must be treated cautiously, for the searcher must rely on a faulty index of publishers and an eccentric index of titles. For instance, Varley's *A Treatise on Zodiacal Physiognomy* might equally well be found under 'A' or 'Treatise'; in fact, it appeared in the *title* index under 'Varley'. No publisher consistently entered all his publications, and the general principle seems to have been the protection of a potentially popular work—children's books, voyages, etc. The publisher had to deposit nine copies of the work, and generally this was thought to be rather a high price to pay for somewhat dubious protection. It is also difficult to be sure at what stage of its production a book was entered at Stationers' Hall, but reason and utility suggest that the date of entry and the date of publication must have been almost synonymous. For instance, on 28 May 1804 Blake wrote to Hayley that Phillips desired

me to tell you that the *Life of Washington* was not put to press till the 3rd of this month (May), and on the 19th he had deliver'd a dozen copies at Stationer's Hall, and by the 16th five hundred were out. This is swift work if literally true, but I am not apt to believe literally what booksellers say.

PUBLISHERS. The original publishers of works containing Blake's engravings have been traced, but the only ones to survive are (1) Harrison & Sons Ltd., 44–47 St. Martin's Lane, London, W.C.2; (2) Longmans, Green & Co. Ltd., 48 Grosvenor Street, London; (3) Sir John Murray, 50 Albemarle Street, London, W.1. Of these, the first (successor to the Harrison company of 18 Paternoster Row) have no records of works with which Blake was connected; Longmans have voluminous records cited here under the relevant entries; and Sir John Murray's records cover (so far as Blake is concerned) only Cunningham's *Lives*, q.v. To the officers of each of these companies I am deeply grateful for patient assistance.

ATTRIBUTION. There are three kinds of 'signature' which make it difficult to attribute engravings to Blake.

(1) The first is a simple lack of signature, as in Salzmann's books. Here the grounds for attributing the work to Blake are generally stylistic and shaky.

(2) The second difficulty is in works signed with another name, generally Basire (as in Bryant and Gough), Blake's master. Occasionally there is biographical information pointing clearly to Blake's authorship (as in Gough), but often the grounds are merely stylistic or symbolic. No work signed by another has been attributed to Blake here without clear biographical evidence.

(3) The third difficulty is in the commonness of the name Blake. 'A Collection of Prosaic William Blakes' (no. 1165) records 23 London contemporaries of the poet who bore his names. The most troubling of these is the 'Blake W[illiam] S. Engraver & Printer, 16, Change alley' listed in W. *Holden's Triennial Directory* from 1799 to 1824, and his work has often been confused with the poet's. The only book for which he is known to have made engravings is THE / POETRY / OF VARIOUS / GLEES, SONGS, &c. / AS PERFORMED AT THE / Harmonists. [?Ed. George Fryer.] / [Ornament] / *LONDON:* / Printed at the Philanthropic Reform, London-Road, / *St. George's Fields,* / — / 1798, with a frontispiece (11·0 × 16·5 cm) of three singing cherubs on clouds below a wreathed lyre surmounted by a light-giving head. In some copies (e.g. BM, GEB), it is unsigned, but in others (as Keynes [1921] reports) it is signed '*Blake sc. Change Alley*'.

Therefore the precise details of the inscriptions on Blake's engravings are often of considerable importance. Plates have often been ascribed to Blake on insufficient evidence, and for many years it was common to identify the poet with the 'Change Alley Blake. In this Part, I have simply ignored books with engravings assigned to Blake on insufficient or misapplied evidence. Many of these omitted works will be found, listed but also rejected, in the catalogue of A. G. B. Russell (1912).

BLAKE'S COMMERCIAL COPPERPLATES: Though Blake designed or engraved over 800 plates which we can identify, few have survived. Linnell kept the plates which he commissioned or bought, those for *Job*, Dante, and Virgil. All the plates for Gough's *Sepulchral Monuments* were given to Bodley in anticipation of a second edition; Schiavonetti's etchings after Blake's *Grave* designs are in the Rosenwald Collection; Blake's plate after Hogarth for Gay's *Beggar's Opera* belongs to Mr. Philip Hofer; and the 'Canterbury Pilgrims' is in the Carnegie Institute of Pittsburgh. A few others were extant after Blake's death in 1827 but cannot be traced today; Cumberland's *Outlines* (1829) reprinted 4 Blake plates; his large engraving for *Romeo and Juliet* was reprinted in 1832; 3 plates for Flaxman's *Letter* (1799) appeared in the Flaxman sale of 1 July 1828; Grego printed 'Mrs Q' as late as 1906; his plates for Wedgwood were printed repeatedly through the first half of the nineteenth century; Flaxman's Hesiod and *Iliad* plates were printed in the 1880s; according to Keynes's *Separate Plates* (1956), Cumberland's calling card has been reprinted 'in recent times'; and some time after 1903 impressions were taken of 'Christ Trampling Urizen'.

The total numbers of copperplates from which posthumous impressions were taken (or, in the case of Gough and Flaxman, could have been taken) are as follows: *America* (19*), *Songs* (55*), *Europe* (17*), *Jerusalem* (100*), Cumberland (4*), Shakespeare (1*), Wedgwood (18*), Flaxman (43*), Dante (7), *Job* (22), Gough (8), Virgil (20), 'Mrs Q' (1), Blair (13), Separate Plates (4). (An asterisk after a number indicates that these plates disappeared between 1828 and 1920.) Of the 800 and more plates which Blake designed and engraved, at least 330 were in existence at his death, but of these only 76 can be traced today.

ALIGHIERI: see DANTE

ALLEN, Charles

415. A NEW AND IMPROVED / HISTORY OF ENGLAND, / FROM / THE INVASION OF JULIUS CÆSAR TO THE END OF THE / THIRTY-SEVENTH YEAR OF THE REIGN / OF KING GEORGE THE THIRD. / — / *By CHARLES ALLEN, A.M.* / AUTHOR OF THE ROMAN HISTORY, &c. / — / THE SECOND EDITION, / EMBELLISHED WITH FOUR COPPER PLATES, AND A CHRONOLO-/ GICAL CHART OF THE REVOLUTIONS IN GREAT BRITAIN. / — / Concluding with a short but comprehensive Historical View / of

Europe, from the abolition of the Monarchical form of / government in France; the military and naval operations, / with the conquests and revolutions in Italy to the / peace of Udina. The changes and revolutions in the / political state of the French Republic, and a more particular detail of the British History during that period. / — / LONDON: / PRINTED FOR J. JOHNSON, NO. 72, ST. PAUL'S / CHURCH-YARD. / — / 1797. (Yale)

There are 4 plates signed '*Blake: s. [sc.]*', '*London. Published Dec.* 1, 1797 by J. Johnson, S.* Paul's Church Yard.'*

 1. At '*P. 15*' is '*Alfred and the Neat-herd's Wife.*'
 2. At '*P. 78*' is '*King John Absolved by Pandulph.*'
 3. At '*P. 128*' is '*Wat Tyler and the Tax-Gatherer.*'
 4. At '*P. 224.*' is '*Queen Elizabeth and Essex.*'

Keynes (1921) has 'no doubt' that Fuseli designed the plates for both of Allen's histories, though none of them is so signed. There are no plates in the first edition of the *History of England* [1793].

416. A NEW AND IMPROVED / ROMAN HISTORY, / FROM THE / FOUNDATION OF THE CITY OF ROME, / TO ITS FINAL / DISSOLUTION AS THE SEAT OF EMPIRE, / IN THE / YEAR OF CHRIST 476, / Including a Period of about 1228 Years, / FROM ITS / *COMMENCEMENT UNDER ROMULUS.* / — / By CHARLES ALLEN, A. M. / AUTHOR OF THE HISTORY OF ENGLAND, &c. / — / THE SECOND EDITION. / EMBELLISHED WITH FOUR COPPER PLATES. / = / LONDON: / PRINTED FOR J. JOHNSON, NO. 72, ST. PAUL'S / CHURCH-YARD. / — / 1798. (GEB, Harvard, Huntington, LC, McGill, Princeton, Trinity College [Hartford, Conn.], West Sussex Record Office, Westminster Public, Yale)

There are 4 plates, signed '*Blake: s. [sc]*', '*London, Published Dec.* 1, 1797 by J. Johnson, S.* Paul's Church Yard.'*

 1. '*P. 2.*' '*Mars and Rhea Silvia.*' (Design size: 8·2 × 14·5 cm).
 2. '*P. 33.*' '*The Death of Lucretia.*' (8·4 × 15·1 cm).
 3. '*P. 174*', '*C. Marius at Minturnum.*' (8·4 × 14·7 cm).
 4. '*P. 292.*' '*The Death of Cleopatra.*' (8·1 × 14·7 cm).

There are no plates in the first edition of [1789] (BM). Keynes (1921) is confident that the unsigned plates in the 1798 edition were designed by Fuseli, and stylistic evidence strongly supports the speculation.

ARIOSTO, Lodovico

417. A. ORLANDO FURIOSO: / TRANSLATED FROM THE ITALIAN OF / LODOVICO ARIOSTO; / WITH NOTES: / By JOHN HOOLE. / — / IN FIVE VOLUMES. / VOL. I[–V]. / — / LONDON: / Printed for the AUTHOR: / Sold by C. BATHURST; T. PAYNE and SON; / J. DODSLEY; / J. ROBSON; T. CADELL; G. NICOL; J. MURRAY; / J. WALTER; T. and W. LOWNDES; J. SEWELL; / J. STOCKDALE; and J. PHILLIPS. / M.DCC.LXXXIII [1783]. (BM, Bryn Mawr, California [Berkeley], Case Western Reserve, Denver, Detroit Public, Folger, GEB, Harvard, Indiana, Iowa, Kansas State, LC, Lehigh, Library Company of Philadelphia,

Michigan, New Brunswick Theological Seminary, North Carolina, Pennsylvania, Stanford, Texas, Yale)

B. THE SECOND EDITION. / — / LONDON: / PRINTED FOR GEORGE NICOL, BOOKSELLER / TO HIS MAJESTY, STRAND. / M.DCC. LXXXV [1785]. (Amherst, BM, California [Berkeley], Catholic University, Colorado College, Cornell, Johns Hopkins, LC, National Library of Scotland, North Carolina, Texas, Westminster Public)

C. THE / ORLANDO / OF / *ARIOSTO*, / REDUCED TO XXIV BOOKS; / THE NARRATIVE CONNECTED, / AND THE / STORIES DISPOSED IN A REGULAR SERIES: / By JOHN HOOLE. / *TRANSLATOR OF THE ORIGINAL WORK / IN FORTY-SIX BOOKS.* / IN TWO VOLUMES. / VOL. I [II]. / LONDON: / PRINTED FOR J. DODSLEY, PALL-MALL. / M.DCC.XCI [1791]. (BM, Bryn Mawr, Cincinnati, Huntington, Johns Hopkins, Library Company of Philadelphia, New York, Texas, West Sussex Record Office, Yale)

D. ORLANDO FURIOSO: / TRANSLATED / FROM THE ITALIAN / OF / *LUDOVICO ARIOSTO*; / WITH / NOTES: / BY JOHN HOOLE. — / *IN FIVE VOLUMES.* / — / VOL. I[–V]. / — / [Vignette of Ariosto on Vol. I only] / *LONDON*: / PRINTED FOR OTRIDGE AND SON; R. FAULDER; J. CUTHELL; J. WALKER; / R. LEA; OGILVY AND SON; LACKINGTON, ALLEN, AND CO.; CADELL / AND DAVIES; T. N. LONGMAN; W. I. AND J. RICHARDION; / AND VERNOR AND HOOD. / — / 1799. (Boston Public, Free Library of Philadelphia, GEB, Harvard, Library Company of Philadelphia, Massachusetts Historical Society, McGill, Newberry, Peabody Institute, Princeton, Texas, Vassar, Virginia, Wisconsin, Yale)

There are 6 plates, one of which is unsigned. The only one by Blake is:

1. At '*Vol. 3. Page 164.*' It represents Orlando uprooting a pine and is signed '*Stothard del.*', '*Blake sc.*' (Plate-size: ?13·5 × 19·0 cm). (Stothard's drawing is in the Rosenwald Collection. A proof is in the Royal Academy.)

A. In the 1783 edition the plate, with the wrong placement direction as above, was used as the frontispiece to Vol. III. It may not have been published until 1784, for an advertisement dated 'January 24, 1784' is at the end of Vol. V (BM copy; the ad in the GEB copy is at the beginning of Vol. I and undated).

B. In the 1785 edition, the plate by Blake was correctly placed at Vol. III, p. 164.

C. In 1791, the plate was placed at Vol. I, p. 461, with a corresponding change in the page reference at the top of the plate.

D. In 1799, an inscription was added to the plates: '*Published by Vernor & Hood, Dec*. 1, 1798.', and Blake's plate was, as directed, at Vol. III, p. 164. In the GEB set, the publishing information varies curiously from volume to volume, perhaps because it was a remainder (a pasted-in label says it was '*Sold at reduced prices by Lackington, Allen & Cº*'). Vol. II is called 'A NEW EDITION' and the imprint reads 'J. NUNN; / J. WALKER . . . / CADELL

AND DAVIS; LONGMAN & REES; . . . RICHARDSON'; Vol. III also substitutes 'LONGMAN & REES' for 'T. N. LONGMAN' and corrects to 'RICHARDSON'; and Vol. IV–V have 'J. NUNN; J. WALKER; / . . . OGILVY & SON . . . CADELL AND DAVIES; / LONGMAN & REES . . . RICHARDSON'.

BELLAMY'S PICTURESQUE MAGAZINE

418. BELLAMY'S PICTURESQUE MAGAZINE, / AND LITERARY MUSEUM. / VOL. I. / FOR THE YEAR MDCCXCIII [1793]. / [Vignette] / LONDON. / Printed for T. BELLAMY, by Spilsbury & Son, / and Sold by T. Evans, N?. 46 Pater-noster Row. (Harvard, Pennsylvania)

1. The tenth plate, between pp. 48 and 49, represents the arrest of an aristocratic woman; it is entitled the 'F. REVOLUTION' and was '*Publish'd by T. Bellamy Aug. 1?. 1793*', '*C. R. Ryley del.*', '*Blake sc*' (plate-mark: 19·5 × 14·5 cm). It illustrates an unsympathetic 'Account of the Revolution in France, from its Commencement to the Death of Louis XVI. Accompanied with engravings from the designs of C. R. Ryley', extracted from a history by J. P. Rabaut, translated by James White (pp. 37–40, 50–1).

BIBLE

419. THE / Protestants Family Bible. / CONTAINING THE / Old and New Testaments. / WITH THE / *APOCRYPHA,* / ILLUSTRATED BY / EXPLANATORY NOTES. / WITH / *A Complete Concordance,* / AND / *GENERAL INDEX.* / By a Society of Protestant Divines. / I.H.S. / *LONDON*: / Printed for Harrison and C?. N?. 18, Paternoster-Row [1780–81]. (BM & GEB)

The 300 unnumbered gatherings of *The Protestant's Family Bible* were probably issued on Saturdays in 60 weekly numbers of 5 gatherings each (see the analogous *Novelist's Magazine*, no. 485–7, where the evidence is much clearer). Two of the plates are dated, the frontispiece on Saturday 2 Sept. 1780 and that for Acts VII. 59 forty weeks later on Saturday 9 June 1781.

All 58 plates (except the title-page above) are in elaborate frames, and 5 are signed '*Blake sculp.*', '*Publish'd as the Act Directs by Harrison & C?. N?. 18, Paternoster Row*'. All Blake's are after Raphael (and only he engraved after Raphael in this volume); nos. 1, 4–5 below are signed '*Raphael de Urbin Del?. [or del.]*', but no. 2–3 are erroneously labelled '*Rubens del.*' Blake's plates are:

1. 'GENESIS. / XVIII. 2.' '*Abraham & the Three Angels.*' (Plate-size 15·2 × 20·0 cm).
2. 'Gen: / XIX. 26.' '*Lot's Escape.*' (15·1 × 20·0 cm).
3. 'Gen, / XXXVII, 28.' '*Joseph sold to the / Ishmeelites.*' (15·2 × 19·8 cm).
4. 'Exodus. / XXXII. 19.' '*The Israelites Idolatry.*' (15·2 × 20·1 cm).
5. 'Joshua. / IV. 16.' '*Joshua passing over Jordan*' (15·2 × 20·0 cm).

420. THE / ROYAL UNIVERSAL / *FAMILY BIBLE; / OR, A COM-PLETE LIBRARY OF / DIVINE KNOWLEDGE: / CONTAINING THE

SACRED TEXT OF THE / *Old and New Testaments, / WITH THE / APOCRYPHA AT LARGE; / ILLUSTRATED WITH / *NOTES, CRITICAL, HISTORICAL, THEOLOGICAL AND PRACTICAL, / WHEREIN / The difficult Passages are explained, the seeming Contradictions reconciled, the Mis-translations corrected, / the deistical Objections refuted, and the Sacred Scriptures represented in their original Purity, / as the only Means of reconciling offending Man to his offended God. / WITH / *PRACTICAL REFLECTIONS ON EACH CHAPTER. / The whole calculated to promote the Interest of Virtue and Piety, and make Men wise unto / Salvation. / *TO WHICH IS ADDED / I. At the End of each Book a Connection between Civil and / Sacred History. / II. An Account of the great Men who flourished in the Hea- / then Nations in those Times, their Characters and Wri- / tings. / III. The State of Religion in the Heathen Nations, before / the Incarnation. / IV. Ancient and Modern Geography compared, shewing the / Difference in the Names of Places since the Christian Æra. / V. An Explanation of the Duty of all the Officers mentioned / in the Old and New Testaments. / VI. An Explanation of all the Scripture Terms, Names, and / Phrases. / VII. The History of the Old and New Testaments connected. / VIII. An Explanation of the Divine Offices used in the Jewish / Church, both before and after the Captivity. / IX. A Reconciliation of Sacred Chronology with the Records / of the Heathens. / X. A complete Concordance to the Old and New Testaments. / XI. A Critical and Historical Account of all the English Translations of the Bible. / XII. A complete Index to the Bible. / — / *By the Reverend JOHN HERRIES, A.M. and Others. / — / [2 mottos] / — / [2 vols.] VOL. I. / — / *LONDON: / PRINTED FOR FIELDING & WALKER, PATER-NOSTER-ROW, / *MDCCLXXX [1780, i.e. 1781]; VOL. II. / — / *LONDON: / PRINTED FOR J. FIELDING No. 23, PATER-NOSTER-ROW, / *MDCCLXXXI [1781, i.e. 1782]. (BM, GEB, Harvard, Toronto Public) [Lines preceded by an asterisk are printed in red.]

A prospectus in the John Johnson Collection of Ephemera in Bodley (b. 79) announced Herries's *Royal Universal Family Bible* as a new venture for 1 June 1782 but after the first run in numbers had been completed. It may fairly be presumed that the new issue was on approximately the same terms as the first. The work could be obtained in 'One Hundred Numbers' 'To be continued Weekly' 'at 6d each' with three sheets of letterpress and engravings 'ornamented with curious borders by Mr. *Clowes*' 'or elegantly bound in one Volume Calf, lettered, 2l. 18s. and 3l. 3s. bound in two Volumes'. The special attractiveness of the work was said to consist in the new type, the superfine paper, and 'ONE HUNDRED *of the most elegant* COPPER-PLATES *that were ever yet given in the* Sacred Scriptures', 'The Engraving of which has cost the Publisher upwards of Seven Hundred Pounds' (or about £7 each).

In the first issue, the work appeared in 100 fascicules over two years. Volume I began on 27 May 1780 and was completed with the fifty-second fascicule on 19 May 1781. Volume II began with the last signature-and-a-half of fascicule fifty-two on 19 May 1781 and continued through the hundredth fascicule in the late spring of 1782, each fascicule bearing the volume number and fascicule number as well as the signature (e.g. 'Vol. I.—No. 3. G'). Probably a plate was issued with each fascicule, for though the BM copy has only 93 plates and the GEB copy 99, one of the plates is numbered '100'. However, the plates were not issued with the fascicules with which they were to be bound, for the dates and numbers on the plates do not correspond with those of the fascicules. For instance, the plates bound eventually with the first four fascicules were issued originally with fascicules 1, 2, 79, and 82. Some of the plates are numbered, and almost all are dated, and a correlation of these numbers and dates indicates that the fascicules and plates were issued at very regular weekly intervals. (There are a few minor slips, such as two plates numbered '35' and no plate for no. 36, but not enough to cause difficulty in understanding the mode of issue.) The plates were regularly '*Published . . . by* Fielding & Walker' up to 31 March 1781 (the forty-first fascicule), but thereafter they were published by Fielding alone.

Clearly the title-pages themselves were issued with the first rather than the last fascicules of their respective volumes, for though they are unsigned they form part of the first and fifty-second fascicules. There is also a separate title-page in the middle of Volume II which reads:

THE / NEW TESTAMENT / OF OUR / LORD AND SAVIOUR / JESUS CHRIST; / WITH / NOTES, / CRITICAL, HISTORICAL, AND THEOLOGICAL, / AND / PRACTICAL REFLECTIONS / ON / EACH CHAPTER. / THE WHOLE CALCULATED TO PROMOTE THE INTEREST OF VIRTUE AND PIETY, / AND MAKE MEN WISE UNTO SALVATION. / — / BY THE REVEREND / JOHN HERRIES, A.M. / AND OTHERS. / — / LONDON: / PRINTED FOR J. FIELDING, No. 23, PATER-NOSTER-ROW. / MDCCLXXXI [1781].

It is a little difficult to be sure when the last fascicules were issued, for the weekly series runs steadily up to no. 97 on 30 March 1782, but no. 99 is 27 July 1782, and no. 100 is 27 April 1782. There were no page-numbers, and the signatures begin a new series in Volume II, though this second series is not broken by *The New Testament*.

Only 10 of the plates are signed by a designer and 47 are not signed by an engraver. Each plate has an elaborate dedication to a bishop or dean ('ornamented . . . by Mr. *Clowes*', as we know from the prospectus), and all are, or should be according to the 'Directions for the Binder', bound opposite the verse they illustrate. Blake's five plates are:

1. Vol. I, 'NUMBERS / Chap. 13 Ver. 23 [*i.e. 25, representing the children of Israel showing the fruits of the land to Moses and Aaron*]' (plate size: 28·0 × 18·5 cm), '*Blake sculp*', '*Published Sept! 16, 1780, by* Fielding & Walker, *Paternoster Row London*'. It was issued with fascicule seventeen and in the 'Directions for the Binder' it is described as no. '13 The Children of Israel stopping at the Brook of Eshcol'.

2. Vol. II, 'JONAH / Chap. 3. Ver. 4.' (plate-size: 28·0 × 18·5 cm). It is signed merely '*Blake Sc*', as are the next two, the '& Walker' has been

dropped, and the date is '*Octo*? *13 1781*'. It was issued with fascicule seventy-three and is described in the 'Directions' as no. '49 Jonah entering the City of Nineveh'.

3. Vol. II, 'JUDITH, / Chap. 13, Ver. 10' (plate-size: 28·2 × 17·7 cm) is dated '*Dec*? *22, 1781*', was issued with fascicule eighty-three, and is called in the 'Directions' no. '65 Judith giving the Head of Holofernes to her Maid'.

4. Vol. II, 'MATTHEW, / Chap. 3. Ver. 13' (plate-size: 28·3 × 18·0 cm) is dated '*Aug*? *18, 1781*', was issued with fascicule sixty-five, and is entitled in the 'Directions' no. '85 Christ baptized by John in the River Jordan'.

5. Vol. II, 'REVELATIONS [*sic*], / Chap. 1, Ver. 12 & 13 [*& 16*]' (plate-size: 27·1 × 17·2 cm) is signed '*Blake d & sc*' and dated '*Feb*? *23 1782*'. It was issued with fascicule 92 and is described in the 'Directions' as no. '91 The Vision of the seven golden Candlesticks'. (Blake's drawing for this engraving is in the BMPR.)

At the end of Volumn II (the last fascicule) is bound a 'List of Subscribers' containing 750 names.

Family Bibles were obviously extremely profitable in the late 18th century, and works with these words in the title were published in 1735–7, 1741, 1761, 1763–7, 1764–6, 1765–7, 1769–71, 1770–1, 1771, 1772–3, 1773, 1777, 1780, 1781–5, 1782, 1785?, 1790?, 1793, 1793–5, and 1800? inter alia. Of these a number, including those of 1735–7, 1741, and no. 419, were issued in parts (see R. M. Wiles, *Serial Publication in England before 1750* [1957]). A work by Thomas Sisson entitled *The Complete Family Bible; or, the Christian's Treasury*, published in 1785, reprints many of the Herries plates above, re-engraved on smaller plates and many of them reversed, but none of Blake's plates was re-engraved or reprinted.

BIBLE: *Job*

421. A. ‎ספר איוב‎ / = / ILLUSTRATIONS of / The / Book / of / JOB / Invented & Engraved / by William Blake / 1825 / [Seven angels] / London Published as the Act directs March 8: 1825 by William Blake N⁰ 3 Fountain Court Strand [1826]. (BM, Bodley, GEB, Huntington, LC [2], London, Morgan, National Gallery of South Australia, Newberry, Princeton [2], Syracuse, Texas)

B. 1874. (Toronto)

Copies of unrecorded date: Adelaide, Albright-Knox Gallery [Buffalo], Berg Collection [NYP], BMPR [3], Boston Museum, Boston Public, California [Berkeley], California [San Diego], Carnegie Institute [Pittsburgh], Chicago, Chicago Art Institute, Cincinnati Museum, City College [N.Y.], Cleveland Museum, Detroit Institute of Art, Detroit Public, Fitzwilliam, Glasgow, Harvard [3], Huntington, Liverpool Public [3], London, Los Angeles County Museum, McGill, Metropolitan Museum [N.Y.] [2], Minneapolis Institute, Montreal Museum, National Gallery of Canada, National Library of Australia, National Library of Scotland, National Library of Wales [2], NYP, Newberry, North Carolina, Northwestern, Ohio

State, Pforzheimer, Philadelphia Free Library, Philadelphia Museum, Prints Division [NYP], Rijks Museum [Amsterdam], St. John's Seminary [Camarillo, Calif.], Spencer Collection [NYP], Swarthmore, Tate Gallery, Texas Christian, Toronto Public, Trinity College, [Hartford, Conn.], V&A, Virginia, Wellesley, Whitworth Art Gallery, Wichita Art Gallery, Williams, Yale [3]

A. The story which Blake called 'Job's Captivity' fascinated him all his life. He alluded to it throughout his drawings and writings, made a large separate print of Job in 1793, and then a series of twenty-one designs (now in the Morgan) for his faithful patron, Thomas Butts, about 1810. Some ten years later his new friend John Linnell discovered that Blake was in want, and 'in hopes of obtaining a profit sufficient to supply his future wants . . . the publication of Job was begun at my suggestion and expense' (as Linnell wrote in 1830; see *Blake Records* [1969], 395). In the autumn of 1821 the Job designs were borrowed back from Butts, and for several days Blake and Linnell worked together as they 'Traced outlines from Mr Blakes designs from Job all day' (according to Linnell's Journal for 7 Sept. 1821; see *Blake Records* 274); this set is now largely in the Fogg. Blake coloured these tracings and then made a third set of 'reduced Drawings & studies for the Engravings of the Book of Job Done for me John Linnell' (as Linnell inscribed the set in the Fitzwilliam). A fourth set (known as the New Zealand set) was probably made by Linnell or one of his friends and is now in the collection of Mr. Paul Mellon. (For fuller details on watercolours, sketches, and working proofs, see Binyon & Keynes [1935], no. 374, or, preferably, Lindberg, *William Blake's Illustrations to the Book of Job* (1973), with its superb *catalogue raisonnée*.)

A contract drawn up on 25 March 1823 specified that for Blake's twenty engravings Linnell was to pay

one hundred Pounds for the set part before and the remainder when the Plates are finished, as Mr Blake may require it, besides which J. Linnell agrees to give W. Blake one hundred pounds more out of the Profits of the work as the receipts will admit of it. [*Blake Records*, 277.]

According to Linnell's *Job* accounts, he 'Paid [£150. 19. 3] to Mr Blake on account of Job', plus £4. 11s. 7d. for twenty 'copper Plates for Job' (*Blake Records*, 598–605).

These twenty copperplates bear on the versos the platemakers' marks; pl. 2–13, 15, 17–21 have:

I PONTIFEX & Co
22 LISLE STREET
SOHO, LONDON

and pl. 1 has:

G. HARRIS
N° 3
SHOE LANE
LONDON

Pl. 15 and 17, which exhibit no platemakers' marks, are on the versos of pl. II–III of Henri Louis Duhamel du Monceau, *A Practical Treatise of Husbandry* [tr. John Mills] (1762)—see the reproductions in no. 1163. The *plate-sizes* (measured on the versos) are:

pl. 1	16·5 × 21·3 cm.
pl. 2, 17	16·6 × *c.* 20·1 cm.
pl. 3–14, 16, 18–22	*c.* 17·1 × *c.* 21·9 cm.
pl. 15	16·6 × 10·8 cm.

There are two kinds of 'proofs' of *Job*: Blake's working proofs, and the first 215 published copies marked 'Proof'. There are working proofs in the BMPR, Fitzwilliam, *Keynes* (13), Rosenwald Collection (66), and Texas (11). Pl. 2 of the Texas set is inscribed (by J. E. Strange on the authority of Tatham, from whom he bought them): 'not a complete set as some Blake did not prove', and pl. 7 in the BMPR is inscribed: 'printed by Blake himself or by Mrs Blake at his own press'. The imprint was sometimes altered to '*by J. Linnell N° 6 Cirencester Place, Fitzroy Square*' (pl. 1–2, 17, 19, 21 in Texas, pl. 12, 17, 20–21 in BMPR).

According to Linnell's *Job* accounts, 150 'Proof' sets on India paper (watermarked J WHATMAN TURKEY MILL 1825) and 65 on French paper (watermarked J WHATMAN 1825) were printed by Lahee in March 1826. Then the word 'Proof' was removed from the plates (though it is still faintly visible on the copperplates and in some pulls), and 100 sets were printed on drawing paper. The total printing cost was £124. 12s. 1d. These sets were issued with a label:

ILLUSTRATIONS / OF THE / 𝕭𝖔𝖔𝖐 𝖔𝖋 𝕵𝖔𝖇, / IN TWENTY-ONE PLATES, INVENTED AND ENGRAVED BY / WILLIAM BLAKE, / *Author of Designs to* 'BLAIR'S GRAVE,' 'YOUNG'S NIGHT THOUGHTS,' &c. / = / 𝕷𝖔𝖓𝖉𝖔𝖓: / PUBLISHED BY THE AUTHOR, 3, FOUNTAIN COURT, STRAND, AND / MR. J. LINNELL, 6, CIRENCESTER PLACE, FITZROY SQUARE. / — / March 1826. *Prints* £[3. 3. 0. *in MS*] *Proofs* £[6. 6. 0.]

500 copies of the label were printed by Mr Tickman on 22 March 1826, according to the *Job* accounts (*Blake Records*, 590), where contemporary buyers are identified (pp. 586–601).

All the plates have '*W Blake inv & sculp*' and the same imprint as on the title-page, except that most have '*Willm*' instead of 'William', and pl. 2 is accidentally dated '1828'. Linnell wrote to Macmillan & Co, 11 Feb. 1864 (letter with the Ivimy MSS): 'the same [*date*] was engraved at the bottom of each plate by Blake himself . . . on all the plates except the first which follows the title and that plate has 1828—which was a mistake I have no doubt but of which I was not aware till now.'

All the plates have inscriptions above and below the design:

1. The first Job plate is the title-page.
2. '1'; 'Our Father which art in Heaven hallowed be thy Name'; 'Thus did Job continually'; 'There was a Man in the Land of Uz whose Name was Job, & that Man was perfect & upright & one that feared God &

eschewed Evil & there was born unto him Seven Sons & Three Daughters'; 'The Letter Killeth / The Spirit giveth Life / It is Spiritually Discerned'.

3. '2'; 'I beheld the Ancient of Days', 'The Angel of the Divine Providence', 'בלי יהוה'; 'I shall see God'; 'Thou art our Father'; 'We shall awake up in thy Likeness'; 'When the Almighty was yet with me, When my Children were about me'; 'There was a day when the Sons of God came to present themselves before the Lord & Satan came also among them to present himself before the Lord'.

4. '3'; 'The Fire of God is fallen from Heaven'; 'And the Lord said unto Satan Behold All that he hath is in thy Power'; 'Thy Sons & thy Daughters were eating & drinking Wine in their eldest Brothers house & behold there came a great wind from the Wilderness & smote upon the four faces of the house & it fell upon the young Men & they are Dead'.

5. '4'; 'And there came a Messenger unto Job & said The Oxen were plowing & the Sabeans came down & they have slain the Young Men with the Sword'; Satan 'Going to & fro in the Earth & walking up & down in it'; 'And I only am escaped alone to tell thee.'; 'While he was yet speaking there came also another & said The fire of God is fallen from heaven & hath burned up the flocks & the Young Men & consumed them & I only am escaped alone to tell thee'.

6. '5'; 'Did I not weep for him who was in trouble[?] Was not my Soul afflicted for the Poor'; 'Behold he is in thy hand: but save his Life'; 'Then went Satan forth from the presence of the Lord'; 'And it grieved him at his heart / Who maketh his Angels Spirits & his Ministers a Flaming Fire'.

7. '6'; 'Naked came I out of my mothers womb & Naked shall I return thither / The Lord gave & the Lord hath taken away. Blessed be the Name of the Lord'; 'And smote Job with sore Boils from the sole of his foot to the crown of his head'.

8. '7'; 'What! shall we recieve Good at the hand of God & shall we not also recieve Evil'; 'And when they lifted up their eyes afar off & knew him not they lifted up their voice & wep*t*, & rent every Man his mantle & sprinkled dust upon their heads towards heaven'; 'Ye have heard of the Patience of Job and have seen the end of the Lord'.

9. '8'; 'Lo let that night be solitary & let no joyful voice come therein'; 'Let the Day perish wherein I was Born'; 'And they sat down with him upon the ground seven days & seven nights & none spake a word unto him for they saw that his grief was very great'.

10. '9'; 'Shall mortal Man be more Just than God? Shall a Man be more Pure than his Maker? Behold he putteth no trust in his Saints & his Angels he chargeth with folly'; 'Then a Spirit passed before my face / the hair of my flesh stood up'.

11. '10'; 'But he knoweth the way that I take / when he hath tried me I shall come forth like gold / Have pity upon me! Have pity upon m*e*, O ye my friends / for the hand of God hath touched me / Though he

slay me yet will I trust in him'; 'The Just Upright Man is laughed to
scorn'; 'Man that is born of Woman is of few days & full of trouble / he
cometh up like a flower & is cut down[;] he fleeth also as a shadow / &
continueth not And dost thou open thine eyes upon such a one / &
bringest me into judgment with thee'.

12. '11'; 'My bones are pierced in me in the night season & my sinews take
no rest'; 'My skin is black upon me & my bones are burned with heat';
'The triumphing of the wicked is short, the joy of the hypocrite is but
for a moment'; 'Satan himself is transformed into an Angel of Light &
his Ministers into Ministers of Righteousness'; 'With Dreams upon my
bed thou scarest me & affrightest me with Visions'; 'Why do you persecute me as God & are not satisfied with my flesh? Oh that my words
were printed in a Book[,] that they were graven with an iron pen & lead
in the rock for ever For I know that my Redeemer liveth & that he shall
stand in the latter days upon the Earth & after my skin destroy thou This
body yet in my flesh shall I see God whom I shall see for Myself and mine
eyes shall behold & not Another tho consumed be my wrought Image';
'Who opposeth & exalteth himself above all that is called God or is
Worshipped'.

13. '12'; 'For God speaketh once yea twice & Man percieveth it not'; 'In
a Dream in a Vision of the Night in deep Slumberings upon the bed
Then he openeth the ears of Men & sealeth their instruction'; 'That he
may withdraw Man from his purpose & hide Pride from Man[.] If there
be with him an Interpreter[,] One among a Thousand / then he is
gracious unto him / & saith Deliver him from going down to the Pit /
I have found a Ransom'; 'For his eyes are upon the ways of Man & he
observeth all his goings'; 'I am Young & ye are very Old wherefore
I was afraid'; 'Lo all these things worketh God oftentimes with Man to
bring back his Soul from the pit to be enlightened with the light of the
living'; 'Look upon the heavens & behold the clouds which are higher
than Man'; 'If thou sinnest what dost thou against him or if thou be
righteous what givest thou unto him'.

14. '13'; 'Who is this that darkeneth counsel by words without knowledge';
'Then the Lord answered Job out of the Whirlwind'; 'Who maketh the
Clouds his Chariot & walked on the Wings of the Wind'; 'Hath the
Rain a Father & who hath begotten the drops of the Dew'.

15. '14'; 'Canst thou bind the sweet influences of Pleiades or loose the bands
of Orien'; 'Let there be / Light'; 'Let there Be A /Firmament'; 'Let the
Waters be gathered together into one place & the Dry Land appear';
'And God made two Great Lights / Sun / Moon'; 'Let the Waters bring
forth abundantly'; 'Let the Earth bring forth Cattle & Creeping thing
& Beast'; 'When the morning Stars sang together, & all the Sons of
God shouted for joy'.

16. '15'; 'Can any understand the spreadings of the Clouds / the noise of his
Tabernacle'; 'Also by watering he wearieth the thick cloud / He
scattereth the bright cloud also[,] it is turned about by his counsels'; 'Of
Behemoth he saith, He is the chief of the ways of God / Of Leviathan he

saith, He is King over all the Children of Pride'; 'Behold now Behemoth which I made with thee'.

17. '16'; 'Hell is naked before him & Destruction no covering'; 'Canst thou by searching find out God[?] Canst thou find out the Almighty to perfection'; 'The Accuser of our Brethren is Cast down / which accused them before our God day & night'; 'It is higher than Heaven⌊,⌋ what canst thou do[?] It is deeper than Hell⌊,⌋ What canst thou know[?] / The Prince of this World shall be cast out'; 'Thou hast fulfilled the Judgment of the Wicked'; 'Even the Devils are Subject to Us thro thy Name⌊.⌋ Jesus said unto them I saw Satan as lightning fall from Heaven'; 'God hath chosen the foolish things of the World to confound the wise And God hath chosen the weak things of the World to confound the things that are mighty'.

18. '17'; 'He bringeth down to the Grave & bringeth up'; 'we know that when he shall appear we shall be like him for we shall see him as He is'; 'When I behold the Heavens the work of his hands[,] the Moon & Stars which thou hast ordained, then I say What is Man that thou art mindful of him? & the Son of Man that thou visitest him'; 'I have heard thee with the hearing of the Ear but now my Eye seeth thee'; 'He that hath seen me hath seen my Father also / I & my Father are One'; 'If you had known me ye would have known my Father also and from henceforth ye know him & have seen him / Believe me that I am in the Father & the Father in me⌊.⌋ He that loveth me shall be loved of my Father for he dwelleth in you & shall be with you'; 'At that day, ye shall know that I am in my Father & you in me & I in you / If ye loved me ye would rejoice because I said I go unto the Father'; 'He that loveth me shall be loved of my father & I will love him & manifest myself unto him And my Father will love me & we will come unto him & make our abode with him / And the Father shall give you Another Comforter that he may abide with you for ever⌊,⌋ Even the Spiritual Truth which the World cannot recieve'.

19. '18'; 'Also the Lord accepted Job'; 'And my Servant Job shall pray for you'; 'And the Lord turned the captivity of Job when he prayed for his Friends'; 'I say unto you Love your Enemies⌊,⌋ bless them that curse you⌊,⌋ do good to them that hate you & pray for them that despitefully use you & persecute you / That you may be the children of your Father which is in heaven, for he maketh his sun to shine on the Evil & the Good & sendeth rain on the Just & the Unjust⌊.⌋ Be ye therefor perfect as your Father which is in heaven is perfect'.

20. '19'; 'The Lord maketh Poor & maketh Rich', 'He bringeth Low & Lifteth Up', 'who provideth for the Raven his Food When his young ones cry unto God'; 'Every one also gave him a piece of Money'; 'Who remembered us in our low estate For his Mercy endureth for ever'.

21. '20'; 'How precious are thy thoughts unto me O God / how great is the sum of them'; 'There were not found Women fair as the Daughters of Job in all the Land & their Father gave them Inheritance among

their Brethren'; 'If I ascend up into Heaven thou art there / If I make my bed in Hell behold Thou art there'.

22. '21'; 'Great & Marvellous are thy Works Lord God Almighty'; 'Just & True are thy Ways O thou King of Saints'; 'So the Lord blessed the latter end of Job more than the beginning'; 'After this Job lived an hundred & forty years & saw his Sons & his Sons Sons even four Generations⌊.⌋ So Job died being old & full of days'; 'In burnt Offerings for Sin thou hast had no Pleasure'.

Coloured Copies: At least two coloured sets are known:

A. A complete series (1) Acquired by Wm Courthope (1806–66), who added his College of Arms bookplate; (2) Acquired by Sir Frederick W. Burton (d. 16 March 1900), according to Keynes, *Blake Studies* (1971), 186 n.; (3) Offered by Tregaskis in his catalogue 493 (1901), according to Keynes, above; (4) It was sold by Sabin to Sessler, who apparently sold it to Col. H. D. Hughes (according to the 1938 catalogue), who sold it anonymously at American Art Association, 16 April 1923, lot 118; (5) Acquired by George C. Smith, who described it in his anonymous catalogue (1927), no. 18, and sold it at Parke-Bernet, 2 Nov. 1938, lot 58, for $3,125; (6) Acquired by Mary S. Collins, who added her bookplate, and at whose death it passed into (7) An *Anonymous* Collection.

B. Pl. 11, 16, 19, 21 are in the Fitzwilliam.

In 1830 Linnell said that 'The work has never yet been advertised', and he offered to make Colnaghi 'the seller with a liberal allowance' (MS in the Osborn Collection), but apparently they could not agree on terms. Later Linnell 'proposed [JOB] to be published' by Messrs Longman, Brown, Green, and Longmans, sometime between 1841 and 1856 (the only period during which the firm was so named), but the negotiations broke down over the question of whether Longman was 'to pay the expense of engraving the Designs . . . before a division of profits' (*Blake Records*, 376 n. 2). On 30 Dec. 1863 Linnell wrote to Macmillan & Co.

that only about 300 [*i.e. 315*] sets including the India proofs & French proofs have been printed, they were all taken from the plates when just finished & not any taken since. There are no plain [*i.e. drawing paper*] impressions left [*but there are some of the India at £10. 10s. and the French at £5. 5s.*]. . . . Mr Linnell does not intend printing any more at present.

(A transcript of this letter made by Herbert Palmer is with the Ivimy MSS.)

B. On 6 May 1892 John Linnell, Jr., wrote to Bernard Quaritch that after the 1826 printing:

Mr Linnell then put the plates away, & they were never again used after this time until the year 1874. At this time my father wishing to have some prints [*i.e. not proofs*] of the Job to offer for sale, (the original 100 copies having long since been exhausted) he had 100 copies printed from the plates upon India paper. . . . The above named impressions, taken at the two dates specified, are all that have been taken from the plates, of the Job. My father considered the plates at the last were as good as they ever were, for the work being cut with the graver, and not etched, it is durable— and is not worn by the printing as is the case with an etching.

At the time of the publication of the Job a certain number of copies of the 'proofs' were stuck into books of paper in boards,— These copies have become more or less spotted through damp. The unbound sets however in our possession have been kept well wrapped up since 1826—and are as good as when—finished.

(The pencil draft of this letter is with the Ivimy MSS.)

A receipt from Holdgate Bros., Steel & Copper-Plate Printers, 39, London St., Fitzroy Square, dated 23 March 1874, is made out to Mr. Linnell for 'paper and printing as estimated Illustrations "Book of Job" 100 ea[ch of] 22 plates 2200 a[t] 3£ [per hundred:] £66. 0. 0' (Ivimy MSS). The 1874 issue seems to have been printed on India paper over very heavy, unwatermarked paper. *Job* copies on India paper lacking the word 'Proof' are probably the 1874 issue.

No more pulls were taken between 1874 and 1919, when the copperplates went to the British Museum Print Room. The total number of sets printed, therefore, was 315 sets in 1826 and 100 in 1874. Sixty-eight sets were still in the family when the Linnells' Blakes were sold at Christie's, 15 March 1918, lots 183–9.

Copperplates: Blake's copperplates were given by Herbert Linnell on 28 May 1919 to the British Museum Print Room. All but pl. 14 have pounding marks on the versos.

In addition, in the John Johnson Collection (Bodley) are reduced copper-plates of pl. 6, 22, and in McGill are full-sized, unpublished copperplate facsimiles of pl. 3, 15, 17 (see no. 1163).

422. *William Blake's Illustrations of the Book of Job*. With Descriptive Letter-press, and A Sketch of the Artist's Life and Works by Charles Eliot Norton. Boston, 1875.

'William Blake' is pp. 11–31. The plates are full-size 'heliotypes'.

423. *Illustrations of the Book of Job*. London & N.Y., 1902.

Excellent full-size facsimiles, distinguishable most easily from genuine originals by a label to be found on some copies and by the watermark 'T H SAU . . . RS 1900'.

424. §*Illustrations of the Book of Job* Invented and Engraved by William Blake. A New Edition. London, 1903. The Illustrated Pocket Library of Plain and Coloured Books.

Keynes (1921) remarks that the reduced-size plates were also issued separately in a portfolio.

425. *Illustrations of the Book of Job* Invented and Engraved by William Blake. A New Edition. N.Y., 1903.

A very much reduced facsimile.

426. *William Blake*. Volume I. Illustrations of the Book of Job with a General Introduction by Laurence Binyon. London, 1906.

'Blake the Man' is pp. 3–15; 'Blake the Artist', pp. 19–31; 'Blake the Poet', pp. 35–49 (reprinted as 'Shijin to shiteno Blake', tr. Makoto Sangu on pp. 291–322 of his *Shigaku ni Noboru* [*Ascent of Poetic Mountain*], Tokyo, 1925);

and 'The Illustrations to Job', pp. 53–62. This series was never continued beyond these full-size reproductions of Blake's 22 engravings.

427. Coutts, Francis. *The Heresy of Job*: with the Inventions of William Blake. London & N.Y., 1907.

428. *Illustrations of the Book of Job*. Reproduced in reduced facsimile from impressions in the British Museum. London & Glasgow, 1912.

429. §*William Blake's Illustrations to the Book of Job*. Enlarged Facsimiles in Platinotype from the original edition by Frederic Evans. N.p., 1914.
  Twenty-five copies were privately printed, says Keynes (1921).

430. סבו איוב *Illustrations of The Book of Job* Invented & Engraved by William Blake 1825. London, 1923.
  A Frederick Hollyer facsimile.

431. *The Book of Job*: With the Twenty-Two Engravings of William Blake. London, 1927.

432. A. *Job*: Invented & Engraved by William Blake. Introductory Note by Kenneth Patchen. N.Y., 1947. B. *Illustrations of the Book of Job* Invented & Engraved by William Blake. The Doctrine of Job by S. Foster Damon. N.Y., 1950.

A. The gist of the 2-page essay, 'Blake', is: 'Hurrah! Hurrah! Hurrah! Hurrah for William Blake!' The 1947 edition was evidently issued in several forms: Some copies are bound, and others have the leaves loose in a portfolio; Reprinted on the versos of some copies, and separately bound and pasted into some others, is an essay by Damon entitled 'Blake's Doctrine of Job' slightly modified from his *William Blake: His Philosophy and Symbols*, pp. 225–6; Some copies have a pasted-in label saying the British distributor is Faber. The *Job* plates are reproduced photographically.

B. The Patchen essay is abandoned in the 1950 edition by the same publisher, the United Book Guild, and the Damon essay is printed a paragraph or more at a time opposite the plates they discuss.

433. A. *Blake's Job*: William Blake's Illustrations of the Book of Job with an Introduction and Commentary by S. Foster Damon. Providence (Rhode Island), 1966. B. Providence, 1967. C. N.Y., 1969. D. 1972.
  The 'Introduction' is pp. 3–7, the 'Commentary' is one page per engraving. (The text is distinct from Damon's 1950 'Doctrine of Job'.)

434. *King, Horace Mowbray. *Songs in the night*: A Study of the Book of Job with illustrations by William Blake. Gerrards Cross [Bucks.], 1968.
  Blake's 22 engravings are reproduced but not discussed.

BLAIR, Robert

435. A. THE / GRAVE, / A POEM. / BY / ROBERT BLAIR. / — / ILLUSTRATED BY / Twelve Etchings / EXECUTED FROM / ORIGINAL DESIGNS. / — / LONDON: / *PRINTED BY T. BENSLEY, BOLT COURT,* / FOR THE PROPRIETOR, R. H. CROMEK, No 64, NEWMAN

STREET; / AND SOLD BY / CADELL AND DAVIES, J. JOHNSON, T. PAYNE, J. WHITE, LONGMAN, HURST, REES, AND / ORME, W. MILLER, J. MURRAY, AND CONSTABLE AND CO. EDIN-BURGH. / 1808. ([*Printed as a folio*:] Berg Collection [NYP], Harvard, Huntington, Metropolitan Museum [N.Y.], Morgan, New York University)

B. ([*Printed as a quarto*:] Bodley, BM, BMPR, Berg Collection [NYP], Cornell, Emory, Fitzwilliam, GEB [2 copies], Harvard, Huntington [3 copies, 1 coloured], Sir John Soane Museum, London University, Metropolitan Museum [N.Y.], Morgan, National Library of Scotland, Newberry, Princeton [2], Signet Library [Edinburgh], Smith College, Syracuse, Texas Christian, Texas [2], Victoria & Albert [2], Westminster Public, Yale [2])

([*Copies of unrecorded format*:] Alberta, American Antiquarian Society, Buffalo and Erie Public, California [San Diego], Cincinnati, Colorado, Columbia, Durham, Illinois, Indiana, Iowa, LC, Lehigh, London University, McGill, Missouri, National Museum of Wales, North Carolina, Oregon, St. John's Seminary [Camarillo, Calif.], South Carolina, Stanford, Turnbull, Vancouver Public, Wellesley, Whitworth Art Gallery)

C. THE / GRAVE, / A POEM. / BY / ROBERT BLAIR. / — / ILLUS-TRATED BY / 𝔗𝔴𝔢𝔩𝔟𝔢 𝔈𝔱𝔠𝔥𝔦𝔫𝔤𝔰 / EXECUTED FROM / ORIGINAL DESIGNS. / — / TO WHICH IS ADDED / A LIFE OF THE AUTHOR. / = / LONDON: / *PRINTED BY T. BENSLEY, BOLT COURT*, / FOR THE PROPRIETOR, R. ACKERMANN, 101, STRAND; / AND SOLD BY / CADELL AND DAVIES, J. JOHNSON, T. PAYNE, J. WHITE, LONG-MAN, HURST, REES, AND / ORME, W. MILLER, J. MURRAY, AND CONSTABLE AND CO. EDINBURGH. / 1813. ([*Printed as a folio*:] Harvard, Princeton)

D. ([*Printed as a quarto*:] Art Institute [Chicago], Ashmolean, BM [3], BMPR, Buffalo, Edinburgh University, Fitzwilliam, Harvard [2], National Library of Scotland, Newberry, Princeton, Royal Academy, Smith College, Toronto, Toronto Public, Trinity College [Cambridge], Yale)

E. 1813 [i.e. London: John Camden Hutten, 1870; printed as a folio] (GEB, Huntington, Princeton, Westminster Public)

([*Copies of unrecorded format*:] Auckland Public, Boston Athenaeum, Boston Museum, Boston Public, Brooklyn Museum, Brigham Young, Bryn Mawr, California [Berkeley], Carleton, Cincinnati Public, Cleveland Public, Cornell, Florida, Free Library of Philadelphia, Kansas, Kent State, LC, McGill, Metropolitan [N.Y.] [2], Michigan, Minnesota, NYP, Ohio State, Pennsylvania, Syracuse, University College of South Wales, Victoria University, Washington, Waterloo University, West Sussex Record Office)

F. THE GRAVE, / A POEM, / BY / ROBERT BLAIR. / WITH ILLUS-TRATIONS, FROM DESIGNS / BY / WILLIAM BLAKE. / — / NEW YORK: / A. L. DICK, 66 FULTON STREET. / — / 1847. (S. F. Damon)

G. . . . NEW YORK: / STANFORD & DELISSER, / 508 BROADWAY. 1858. (GEB, Huntington, Toronto Art Gallery)

H. *The Grave*: A Poem. Illustrated by Twelve Etchings Executed by

L. Schiavonetti from the Original Inventions of William Blake. London, 1903. The Illustrated Pocket Library of Plain and Coloured Books.

I. *The Grave*. A Poem with Eleven Photogravures and One Half-Tone Reproduction after Designs by William Blake, A Photogravure Portrait after T. Phillips, R.A., and a Note on the Illustrations by Henry Fuseli. London & N.Y., 1906. The Photogravure Series.

J. *William Blake*. Twelve Designs for 'The Grave' by Robert Blair, Now First Separately Printed from the Original Plates in the Possession of an American Collector. N.Y., 1926.

K. *Blake's Grave*, A Prophet Book: Being William Blake's illustrations for Robert Blair's *The Grave*, arranged as Blake directed. With a Commentary by S. Foster Damon. Providence (Rhode Island), 1963.

L. *William Blake's Illustrations to The Grave*. Seattle, 1969. Double Elephant– San Vito Press Series, No. 3.

M. London, 1973.

On 18 Oct. 1805, John Flaxman reported that the entrepreneur R. H. Cromek had

employed Blake [*for £21*] to make a set of 40 drawings from Blair's poem of the Grave⌊,⌋ 20 of which he proposes [*to*] have engraved by the Designer . . . [*Among*] the most Striking are, The Gambols of Ghosts according with their affections previous to the final Judgment— A widow embracing the turf which covers her husbands grave   (*Blake Records* [1969], 166–7.)

Cromek issued a prospectus in 'Nov 1805' specifying that there were to be: FIFTEEN PRINTS FROM DESIGNS INVENTED AND TO BE ENGRAVED BY *WILLIAM BLAKE* . . . The Preface [CONTAINING AN EXPLANATION OF THE ARTIST'S VIEW IN THE DESIGNS] will be contributed by BENJAMIN HEATH MALKIN . . . . The work will be printed by T. BENSLEY, in Imperial Quarto. The Price to SUBSCRIBERS will be TWO GUINEAS . . . .   [*Princeton*]

Blake etched 'Death's Door' for the series himself, but (as Stothard told his son) 'Cromek found . . . [*it*] etched . . . so indifferently and so carelessly . . . that he employed Schrovenetti [i.e. *Schiavonetti*] to engrave them' (*Blake Records*, 172). Consequently, apparently without telling Blake of the change, Cromek issued another prospectus in 'Nov. 1805' in which he announced that there were to be 'TWELVE [*not 15*] VERY SPIRITED ENGRAVINGS BY *LOUIS SCHIAVONETTI* [*not by Blake*]' (BM: Add. MSS 33404, f. 144).

There were yet a number of other changes. (*a*) An early puff (in *Monthly Literary Recreations*, III [Sept. 1807], 239, echoed in *Literary Annual Register*, I [Oct. 1807], 437) was similar to later ones except in describing 'a fac simile of Blair's hand writing, from the Original Manuscript' and omitting reference to the frontispiece-portrait of Blake. Apparently the decision to introduce the 'fac simile' was made between November 1805 and September 1807. It was abandoned shortly thereafter. (*b*) Thomas Phillips painted a portrait of Blake (exhibited at the Royal Academy in the spring of 1807), which he 'presented to Mr. Cromek' (according to the *Antijacobin Review*, XXXI [Nov. 1808]) and which Schiavonetti etched for the frontispiece. (*c*) According to a letter from Cromek of 17 and 20 April 1807 (in Sheffield Public Library), between those dates the Queen gave Blake permission to dedicate the designs to her, and Blake instantly made a dedicatory poem and design, the first of which was printed with the book and the second of which was rejected with contumely by Cromek in a letter to Blake of May 1807. (*d*) There is no 'Preface' to this edition (as announced in the 1805 prospectus), and nothing is signed by Malkin, but the description 'Of the Designs' serves as a kind of preface, and as it does give 'the artist's view in the designs' (as Malkin's preface was said in the 1805 prospectus to do), it is probably by Malkin.

Two other prospectuses for the 1808 *Grave* are known, both probably from late 1808, both beginning: 'BLAKE's / ILLUSTRATIONS OF BLAIR. / — / Just published . . .'. One, giving the titles of the engravings, is bound with *Reliques of Robert Burns* (1808). The other, which omits the titles of the designs and differs in other small particulars, was issued as a separate flier (BM: Add. MSS 33397, f. 144, and bound with Bodley's copy of Carey's *Chaucer* [1808]). The latter concludes: 'A few Copies remain unsold, printed on large Elephant Quarto paper, with Proof Impressions of the Plates, on French Paper. *Price Four Guineas.*'

The book was evidently published in July and Aug. 1808 (the date depending on when Cromek delivered copies to subscribers). There were announcements in the *Artist* (1 Aug. 1807, p. 6), the *Literary Panorama* (Nov. 1807, column 304, 'to be printed . . . [*by*] Ballantyne'), *Monthly Magazine* (1 June 1808), *Athenaeum Magazine* (June 1808), *Monthly Literary Advertiser* (9 July 1808), and *Edinburgh Review* (Jan. 1809, p. 500), and reviews in the *Examiner* (7 Aug. 1808), *Antijacobin Review* (Nov. 1808), and *Monthly Magazine* (1 Dec. 1808), the first two reviews virulently hostile.

ORDER OF EDITIONS

A. The first issue of the first edition was evidently the 1808 folio, marked 'Proof Copy' on the plates.

B. In the second printing, the 1808 quarto, the same type was used, leaded rather less generously and with altered signatures. A scratch on pl. 1 in the 1808 quarto which does not appear in the 1808 folio seems to indicate that the quarto issue came second. In any case, since the type is the same in both, B is a different issue from A rather than a different edition.

C–D. The second edition was in 1813 with issues as in 1808 in large folio, using plates printed for the 1808 issues, and in quarto, with plates redated 1813, with paper watermarked 'EDMEADS & Cº 1811' (Newberry, Toronto, Toronto Public) and 'EDMEADS & PINE 1802' (Toronto Public), with the same type but with altered signatures.

E. The 'third edition' was the small folio facsimile (?forgery) on unwatermarked paper with the '1813' title-page set out as in C–D but with text completely reset line-for-line in 1870.[1] Much of the evidence about order of

---

[1] The [1870] folio has fewer lines to the page in the list of subscribers and in the description 'Of the Designs'. In the [1870] folio, 'ORIGINAL DESIGNS' on the title-page is

editions here derives from an article on 'The Printings of Blake's Designs to Blair's *Grave*' for *The Book Collector* (1975—generously shown me in typescript), in which R. N. Eassick & M. D. Paley demonstrate brilliantly and conclusively that the '1813' small folio was in fact set in type created in 1860, printed for John Camden Hotten in 1870, and regularly bound in late Victorian stamped cloth;[1] they also display minutely the changes in state of the plates.

Between the genuine 1813 edition (two issues) and the edition of [1870], the plates were re-used for Jose Joaquin de Mora, *Meditaciones Poeticas* (1826), for which the English inscriptions on the plates (except for the names of the designer and engraver) were replaced with Spanish. Afterwards the Spanish inscriptions were erased (traces of the Spanish are still faintly visible on the steel-faced copperplates now in the Rosenwald Collection), and the original words were carefully but not flawlessly imitated on the copper once more— e.g. ''Tis' (1808) on pl.7 was altered to 'Tis' [1870]. In this form, the plates are markedly fainter—for example, on the engraved title-page the flames at left show virtually no shading.

A & B. In most respects the folio and quarto printings are identical, printed from the same type, and what follows applies to both unless otherwise specified.

One of Blake's designs appears on the supplementary etched title-page, which is lettered:

THE / GRAVE, / A Poem. / *Illustrated by twelve Etchings* / EXECUTED / *BY* / LOUIS SCHIAVONETTI, / *From the Original* / Inventions / OF / WILLIAM BLAKE. / 1808.

A one-page dedicatory poem 'To the Queen' by 'William Blake' is on an unnumbered page without signature. (Blake's 'Autograph' MS was offered by Thomas Thorpe in 1833 [no. 545] but has not been traced further. It was copied within a day or two of composition by Cromek in a letter of 20 April 1807 [now in the Sheffield Public Library; see no. A1152]; another copy, in an unknown hand, is among the verses collected by Nancy Flaxman [BM. Add. MSS 39788, f. 89]. Blake transcribed at least the beginning of the poem on his unused design for the dedication in the BMPR.)

A six-page 'List of Subscribers' records 578 subscribers for 688 copies. An 'Advertisement' signed by R. H. Cromek and dated July 1808 (pp. xi–xii) contains a reference to Blake—though it is remarkable that the typeset title-page does not. An appreciation, signed by Henry Fuseli (pp. xiii–xiv), also mentions Blake; it is reprinted in Russell (1912), no. 603, and Knowles (1831), no. 2066. The unsigned description 'Of the Designs' (pp. 33–6) is probably by B. H. Malkin—see above. An advertisement for Stothard's Chaucer and a 'Prospectus' for it occupy pp. 37–40.

filled in (it is in outline in the 1813 quarto), and it uses short 's' for the long 'f' of the 1813 quarto. This is the 'third edition' in the sense that it is the third edition of Blair illustrated by Schiavonetti's plates.

[1] I cannot account for the fact that part of the blind-stamping on one 1813 quarto (Toronto) with the plates in a separate portfolio exactly matches that on one 1847 copy (Brown) and on one [1870] folio (GEB).

A 'Subscribers' Copy' was issued with the following label: 'BLAKE'S /
ILLUSTRATIONS / OF / BLAIR'S 𝔊𝔯𝔞𝔟𝔢, / ENGRAVED BY SCHIAVO-
NETTI. / — / 13 Plates. Price—2*l.* 12*s.* 6*d.*' (Huntington, Sir John Soane
Museum, Texas, Yale) Keynes (1921) reports another label as well: '*Blake's
Illustrations of Blair's Grave, Engraved by Schiavonetti. 13 Plates. —Price Four
Guineas.*' At the bottom of folio copies is: '*Proof copy R.H.C. Price 5 . . 5 . . o.*'
(Princeton). This was replaced by '*Subscribers' Copy.*', which is the only way
of distinguishing subscribers' copies. The 1808 quarto on laid paper is
watermarked 'J WHATMAN / 1808' (GEB, Newberry, Texas), and the folio
on wove paper 'J WHATMAN / 1801' (Berg Collection).

There is a frontispiece of 'William Blake', engraved by L. Schiavonetti
after the fine portrait by T. Phillips, which is now in the National Portrait
Gallery (London). (There are copies of this portrait, perhaps by Phillips, in
the Huntington [two, one watermarked '1810'], the Morgan, the Keynes
Collection, and the Barrett Collection, and a proof before letters is owned
by Keynes.)

All twelve plates in ordinary copies are inscribed: '*Drawn by W. Blake.*'
'*Etched* [no. 1–4, 6, 8–9, 11–12, or *Engraved*, no. 5, 7, 10] *by L. Schiavonetti*',
'*London, Published May 1ˢᵗ 1808, by Cadell & Davies, Strand.*', except for the
frontispiece and title-page, which are '. . . *by R. H. Cromek. N*.° *64 Newman
Street*'. The engravings are:

1. The engraved title-page, called, in the description 'OF THE DESIGNS',
   'THE SKELETON RE-ANIMATED' (plate-size: 27·8 × 36·6 cm).
   (The design is very like Young's *Night Thoughts* [1797], p. 19; a sketch
   once owned by F. J. Shields [A. G. B. Russell, *The Engravings of William
   Blake* (1912), 125] is untraced. A sketch for the trumpeter, reproduced
   in the Sotheby catalogue for 29 April 1971, lot 12, is in the collection of
   Mr. Paul Mellon, and Keynes owns a proof before title lettering.)

2. '*Christ Descending into the Grave. | Eternal King! whose potent Arm sustains |
   The Keys of Hell and Death.*' '*P. 1*' (plate-size 20·2 × 28·0 cm). (In the
   Huntington is a proof lettered: '*London, Published by R. H. Cromek. June
   1ˢᵗ 1806*', and a related sketch is in the BMPR.)

3. '*The meeting of a Family in Heaven.*' (Plate-size: 15·7 × 27·9 cm.) (Keynes
   owns a proof, a proof without letters is in the collection of Mr. Robert
   N. Essick, a sketch was in the Robertson catalogue [1952], no. 82, and
   a related sketch is in the BMPR.)

4. '*The Counsellor, King, Warrior, Mother & Child in the Tomb.*' '*P. 11*' (plate-
   size: 21·4 × 26·7 cm). (A proof without letters is in the collection of
   Mr. Robert N. Essick. The sketch for this design owned by the Earl of
   Crawford & Balcarres is evidently the one reproduced in Keynes [1921]
   at p. 220.)

5. '*Death of the Strong Wicked Man. | . . . . Heard you that groan? | It was
   his last.*' '*P. 12*' (plate-size: 24·1 × 28·1 cm). (A sketch in the V&A is
   reproduced in *Pencil Drawings* [1927].)

6. '*The Soul hovering over the Body reluctantly parting with Life. | . . . How
   wishfully she looks | On all she's leaving, now no longer hers!*' '*P. 16*' (plate-
   size: 21·4 × 26·7 cm). (A proof before letters is in the Princeton Art

Museum. The Tate sketch for it is reproduced in the Tate catalogue [1971], and another copy in the Rosenwald Collection is perhaps the one reproduced in J. Sheringham, *Drawings in Pen and Pencil* [1922].)

7. *'The descent of Man into the Vale of Death. | . . . .'Tis here all meet!' 'P. 21'* (plate-size: 17·0 × 27·9 cm). (A sketch is in the Rosenwald Collection, and one in the BMPR is related.)

8. *'The Day of Judgment.' 'P. 28'* (plate-size: 25·3 × 32·0 cm). (Keynes owns a proof.) (Schiavonetti delivered pl. 8 and asked £60 for it, according to his letter to Cromek of 21 July 1807, now in the possession of GEB.)

9. *'The Soul exploring the recesses of the Grave.'* (Plate-size: 15·9 × 28·6 cm.) (A rough sketch in the BMPR is reproduced in *Pencil Drawings* [1927].)

10. *'The Death of The Good Old Man. | . . . . Sure the last end | Of the good Man is peace! How calm His exit!' 'P. 30'* (plate-size: 24·0 × 27·7 cm). (A proof without letters except for signature is in the collection of Mr. Robert N. Essick.)

11. *'Death's Door | 'Tis but a Night, a long and moonless Night, | We make the Grave our Bed, and then are gone!' 'P. 32'* (plate-size: 17·5 × 29·7 cm). (A sketch for it, $12\frac{1}{2}'' \times 17\frac{1}{2}''$, shows the old man and two versions of the risen man; it belonged to F. J. Shields, is reproduced in I. Langridge, *William Blake* [1907], 184, and described in A. G. B. Russell, *The Engravings of William Blake* [1912], 129, but is presently untraced. Keynes has a Schiavonetti proof before the verses were added. A single proof of this design as etched by Blake himself is known, and Keynes comments [*Separate Plates* (1956), 41]: 'As far as is known this design of "Death's Door" is the only one of the series that Blake himself transferred to metal.' In the collection of Mr. Robert N. Essick is a proof (mentioned by Russell [1912]) inscribed *'London Published by R H Cromek Feby 1st 1806'*. A very curious related print consists of the bottom half of the design engraved twice on the same plate [reproduced in *Separate Plates*]. Sketches are in the Liverpool Public Library, BMPR, Rosenbloom Collection, and Widener [Harvard].)

12. *'The Reunion of the Soul & the Body.' 'P. 32'* (plate-size: 23·3 × 30·2 cm). (Keynes has a proof lettered as in the proof of pl. 2.)

A number of unused designs are known. One for the title-page in the Huntington lettered 'Invented & Drawn by William Blake 1806' is reproduced in the Huntington catalogue (1957). Another, owned by Mr. Gregory Bateson, is apparently the one reproduced in Keynes (1921). A third, inscribed '1806 W Blake inv' is in the BMPR. A fourth belongs to Mrs. Seth Dennis. The dedication design in the BMPR is reproduced in *Blake Records* (1969), at p. 184. The 'Widow Embracing the Turf which Covers her Husband's Grave' (mentioned in Flaxman's letter, above) is owned by Mr. Paul Mellon and reproduced in *Blake Records* (1969), at p. 166 (a sketch is in the BMPR: 1867-10-12-198). But the other drawing which Flaxman mentions, 'The Gambols of Ghosts', has not been traced.

A design belonging to Professor Robert Essick (reproduced in *Blake Studies*, IV, 2 [1972]) represents a naked, bearded figure with heavy wings ('Death') at the top of a flight of steps, from the bottom 'verge' of which a woman (the soul of the man 'quite unfurnish'd for that world to come') 'sinks to everlasting ruin' (*Grave* [1808], 16).

Blake's *Grave* designs were certainly the best-known ones he made, and they were frequently commented upon in accounts of Blake and sometimes copied. R. J. Lane copied 'Death's Door' about 1816 (BMPR). An anonymous engraver copied 'The Meeting of a Family in Heaven', reversed (plate-size: *c.* 9·9 × 17·0 cm), and entitled it *'Lord! here we are and the Children / which thou hast given us'* (McGill). Another copy of 'Deaths Door, Drawn by William Blake' with a quotation from the poem was 'Etched by P. D'Aiguille' at an unknown date (design size: 13·9 × 23·6 cm) (Morgan). Pl. 5 and 11 were copied by G. Hamilton in 1832–3, all the designs were adapted for Mora's *Meditaciones Poeticas* (1826), and 'Death's Door' was used as the design for Whitman's tomb.

The copperplates, now in the Rosenwald Collection, have been steel-faced, and on the versos is the plate-maker's-mark: 'Whitton & Harris / No. 31 Shoe Lane / London'. Mr. Rosenwald's curator Miss Mongan told me about 1962 that in recent times a few proofs had been pulled but that no more will be taken.

A 'Proof Copy' such as that in the Huntington differs in several ways from ordinary copies. Most plates (no. 2, 5–7, 10–12) have no quotation, and almost all (no. 2–6, 8–12) have 'Davies' mis-spelled 'Davis'. In addition, no. 6 is inscribed *'W: Blake del.'* and no. 7 is called *'The Valley of Death'* instead of *'The descent of Man into the Vale of Death.'* In both 1808 and 1813 the frontispiece was printed on India paper, though the rest of the plates are on ordinary paper.

The numbers on the plates refer to the pages of text on which the quotations appear (plates 2, 5–8, 10–12) or to the action which they summarize (plate 4). The unnumbered plates (1, 3, and 9) do not appear to derive from a specific incident or metaphor in the poem, as the others do, but to be Blake's own additions to the subject-range of the poem. (*N.B.* Often one or more of the page-numbers are missing, and the above list is a composite from several copies.)

The plates do not always appear at the same places in the text, nor are they invariably in the same order. In both folios and quartos recorded above, they are found opposite the text they illustrate and in the order given above. That is, they face pp. 1, 9, 10, 12 or 14, 16, 21, 28, 29, 30, 32, and 32 (i.e. the twelfth plate faces the verso of the eleventh). This is probably the normal order, for it is the one which obtains in the Harvard and Sir John Soane Museum quartos which bear the signatures of the original subscribers. (The quartos in the Morgan, Cornell, Signet, and Texas libraries also have evidence of which original subscribers they went to.)

However, in this arrangement the binder had to cut some of the leaves before he could insert the plates. It would have been far easier to gather the plates together all in one place (as in the BM copy), and, perhaps partly for this reason, a note at the head of the description 'Of the Designs' states:

By the arrangement here made, the regular progression of Man, from his first descent into the Vale of Death, to his last admission into Life eternal, is exhibited.

These Designs, detached from the Work they embellish, form of themselves a most interesting Poem.

In this description, the order of the plates is: 2, 7, 11, 5, 10, 6, 9, 4, 1, 12, 3, and 8. It seems probable that in 1808, as in 1813, the designs were occasionally issued 'detached from the Work they embellish' and bound separately, though I have no record of copies thus arranged.

On some large folio copies (Princeton, Harvard) is preserved a label:

THE / GRAVE, / 𝔄 𝔓𝔬𝔢𝔪, / BY ROBERT BLAIR: / ILLUSTRATED WITH / *THIRTEEN ENGRAVINGS*, / BY L. SCHIAVONETTI. / — / Published at R. ACKERMANN's, 101, Strand, London. / *Price £2. 12s. 6d.*

At the bottom of the engraved title-page of large-paper copies (Harvard, Princeton) is: 'Proof Copy R. H. C. Price 5..5..0', as in 1808. In these 'Proofs' the date-lines have not been altered—they read as in the ordinary 1808 copies—and the frontispiece is on India paper. These 1813 folios with 1808 imprints indicate that the 1813 large folios must have been printed before the 1813 quartos.

The [1870] folio copies have the plates in the midst of the poem, while the 1813 quartos and large folios have them gathered together at the end. In the small [1870] folio the order of the plates is normally different from 1808:

no.   2 p.   1
no.   5 p. 14
no.   6 p. 18
no.   7 p. 22
no.   4 p. 26
no.   9 p. 30
no. 12 p. 32
no. 10 p. 34
no.   3 p. 36
no. 11 p. 37
no.   8 p. 42

The waters seem to be muddied by the Ackermann list (1815) (Mellon Collection) which described:

Blair's Grave, illustrated . . . by W. Blake; with Biographical Accounts of Blair, Schiavonetti, and Cromek [*i.e. 1813.*] *First Edition, with proof Impressions of the Plates.* Atlas 4to. Boards . . . 3 13 6 N.B. *A few Copies only left of this Edition.* Ditto, (Second Edition) Elephant 4to. Boards . . . 2 12 6⌊.⌋

'First' and 'Second Edition' here presumably refer to the large 1813 quarto printings. Probably it is the same works which were offered in an undated prospectus (BM: 11902 bbb23, Vol. I, f. 246ʳ) for

A SECOND EDITION [*1813*] OF . . . BLAIR's GRAVE; Illustrated by . . . Mr. Blake . . . Printed on large Elephant Quarto, price 2l. 12s. 6d. extra boards.— A few copies on Quarto Atlas, price 3l. 13s. 6d. Boards⌊.⌋

Another anomaly is that, though Ackermann appears on the title-page, the *London Catalogue* for 1818 and 1831 gives Murray as the publisher.

In both 1813 and [1870] editions of the *Grave*, the same dedication, list of subscribers, 'Advertisement', and appreciation appear as in the

1808 printings, though the order varies. In addition, in 1813 there is a 'Biographical Sketch of Robert Blair' (pp. xv–xxix) in which Blake is mentioned; a 'Biographical Sketch of Lewis Schiavonetti' (pp. xxxii–xliv); and a 'Biographical Sketch of Robert Hartley Cromek' (pp. xlv–liv), which also refers to Blake (p. xlvii).

The plates, including the engraved title-page dated '1808', are unchanged in both quarto and folio 1813 printings in ordinary copies, except that each engraving is now inscribed: '*London, Published* [or *Pub^d*] *Mar*[*ch*] *1*[*st*] *1813, by R. Ackermann,* [*at*] [*101*] *Strand.*' On the last page of text of both quarto and folio 1813 editions is the colophon: 'T. Bensley, Printer, Bolt Court, Fleet Street.'

Probably the normal order of the text is the same in the 1813 quarto as in the 1813 folio, though in both the dedication and appreciation have no signatures and in both the order varies.

F–G. The works of 1847 and 1858 were different issues of the same work. The engraved title-page reads:

THE / GRAVE / A Poem / BY / BLAIR, / *With Illustrations from Designs* / BY / WM. BLAKE. / 1847.

They reprint Cromek's advertisement, Fuseli's appreciation, and the essay 'Of the Designs', and add a new biography of Blair and a biography of 'William Blake' (pp. v–vi) compiled chiefly from Cunningham (1830) (no. 143). The plates were reduced to about a quarter of their original size, and were re-engraved with the following inscription: 'Wm Blake del.', 'A. L. Dick sc.' This legend appears even upon Phillips's portrait of Blake. Plate 3, 'The meeting of a Family in Heaven', was omitted, presumably for prudish reasons; and the genitals of the naked gentlemen on plates 1 and 8 were decorously covered with filmy drapery.

H. The reduced reprint of 1903 follows the 1808 edition.

I. The much-reduced edition of 1906 follows that of 1813.

J. The 1926 edition, which omits the text of Blair, consists entirely of the plates except for an 'Introductory Note' by A. J. Smith about Cromek's acquisition of Blake's designs. The anonymous collector was George C. Smith Jr., whose anonymous 1927 catalogue lists the Blair copperplates.

K. Damon's essay on 'Blake's Grave' is on 10 unnumbered pages.

L–M. A note by the publishers states that the work is 'printed by offset photolithography from the original edition of 1804 [*?i.e. 1808*]', but without Blair's poem.

BONNYCASTLE, John

436. A. AN / INTRODUCTION / TO / MENSURATION, / AND / PRACTICAL GEOMETRY. / WITH NOTES, CONTAINING THE REASON OF EVERY / RULE, CONCISELY AND CLEARLY DEMON-STRATED. / By JOHN BONNYCASTLE, / Author of the SCHOLAR's GUIDE TO ARITHMETIC. / [Vignette] / LONDON: Printed for J. JOHNSON,

N° 72, / St. Paul's Church Yard. 1782. (Columbia, GEB, Harvard, Hull University, National Library of Scotland, Princeton)

B. . . . EVERY RULE, / CONCISELY AND CLEARLY DEMON-STRATED. / By JOHN BONNYCASTLE, / OF THE ROYAL MILITARY ACADEMY, WOOLWICH. / The SECOND EDITION corrected and improved. / [Vignette] / LONDON: Printed FOR J. JOHNSON, N° 72, / ST. PAUL'S CHURCH YARD. 1787. (Bodley, Cambridge, St. Andrews)

C. . . . The Third Edition corrected and improved. / [Vignette] / LONDON: Printed FOR J. JOHNSON, N° 72, / St. Paul's Church-Yard. 1791. (Academy of Natural Sciences [Philadelphia], Princeton, Queen's [Kingston, Ontario], Virginia)

D. . . . EVERY RULE / By JOHN BONNYCASTLE, / . . . / The Fourth Edition . . . / [Vignette] / LONDON: Printed for J. JOHNSON, N° 72, / . . . 1794. (Nottingham)

1. The only design is a vignette on the title-page of six naked boys playing with geometrical shapes. It is unsigned, but a proof of it in The British Museum Print Room is lettered 'Stothard del', 'Blake. Sc' (see the reproduction in Keynes's article, no. 2009). The proof is part of a collection of Stothard prints formed by Robert Balmanno (1780–1861), a friend of Stothard, executor of Fuseli, and patron of Blake (he owned *Innocence* [U], *Descriptive Catalogue* [I], *Job*, and perhaps *Songs* [BB]). A similar Balmanno 'collection after Stothard' (in an extra-illustrated set of Bray's life of Stothard [1851] in the Huntington Library [pressmark 152250]) came *en bloc*, according to Balmanno's inscription of 1819 on it, 'from Chas. Heath', an engraver, and the son of an engraver (1757–1834) who often engraved plates after Stothard for the same books Blake did and who must have known Blake. If the BMPR Stothard proofs also came through the Heaths, and if the inscriptions are by Charles or James Heath or by Balmanno, they have very considerable authority. Certainly the style of the plate is consonant with the work of Stothard and Blake at the time.

The plate-size was cut down at the bottom and left from 6·8 × 9·2 cm in 1782 to 6·1 × 8·4 cm in 1787 to 5·8 × 8·2 cm in 1791, and the ground shadows were made heavier and more uniform. The Third Edition plate of 1791 seems to have been worked over once more, and the Princeton copy is inscribed in pencil 'Stothard del', 'Blake sc'.

The same design was re-engraved for the Fifth Edition of 1798 (Bodley, GEB, Peabody Institute) and the frequent succeeding editions.

Boydell's Shakspeare

437. BOYDELL'S / Graphic Illustrations / of the / DRAMATIC WORKS, / of / 𝖲𝗁𝖺𝗄𝗌𝗉𝖾𝖺𝗋𝖾; / CONSISTING OF / 𝔄 / 𝔖𝔈ℜ𝔍𝔈𝔖 𝔒𝔣 𝔓ℜ𝔍𝔑𝔗𝔖 / *Forming an elegant and useful Companion to the / Various Editions of his Works,* Engraved from PICTURES, **purposely painted** / *By the very first* 𝔄𝔯𝔱𝔦𝔰𝔱𝔰, *and lately exhibited at /* THE SHAKSPEARE GALLERY. / = / 𝔏𝔬𝔫𝔡𝔬𝔫 /

Published by Mess.rs BOYDELL & CO. *Cheapside* [?1803]. *Tomkins Scrip.t Halliwell Sculp.t* (Boston Public, Brooklyn Public, Chicago, GEB, Folger, Keynes [defective], LC, Library Company of Philadelphia [defective], Princeton, Western Reserve Historical Society).

The 100 plates in this work (some dated 1803) include all those for *The Dramatic Works of Shakspeare*, no. 497 (q.v.), plus one additional portrait of Alderman Boydell. There is a descriptive index of drawings, which makes no mention of the engravers.

1. The ninety-fifth plate is Blake's variation of Opie's painting of the supposed death of Juliet (see no. 497).

Most copies are, of course, rebound, but one which is not (Toronto) bears *on the cover* a typeset (not engraved) title-page as follows:

BOYDELL'S / GRAPHIC ILLUSTRATIONS / OF / THE DRAMATIC WORKS / OF / SHAKSPEARE; / CONSISTING OF / A SERIES OF ONE HUNDRED PRINTS, / FORMING AN ELEGANT AND USEFUL COMPANION TO THE VARIOUS EDITIONS OF HIS WORKS. / ENGRAVED FROM PICTURES / PURPOSELY PAINTED BY THE VERY FIRST ARTISTS, AND LATELY EXHIBITED AT / THE SHAKSPEARE GALLERY. / LONDON: / = / PUBLISHED BY MESSRS. BOYDELL AND CO. CHEAPSIDE. / PRINTED BY W. BULMER AND CO. CLEVELAND-ROW, ST. JAMES'S. / 1813.

The plates are unwatermarked, but the very brief type-set text is watermarked 1812 / W BALSTON (Toronto), with a perplexing intermixture of J WHATMAN / 1801 in one copy (GEB). This is presumably the edition which was offered in a Boydell flyer of February 1813 (in the John Johnson Collection in Bodley) as either a single volume at £12. 12s. or 'published in Twelve Monthly Parts, price One Guinea each'. Indeed, it is distressing to observe that the evidence for the existence of an 1803 edition is all inferential while that for an 1813 edition is plain and direct.

The Blake plate is not included in *The Boydell Shakespeare Prints*, ed. A. E. Santaniello (N.Y. & London, 1968), a conflation of the *Graphic Illustrations* (above) and the *Collection of Prints, from Pictures Painted for the Purpose of Illustrating . . . Shakspeare* (1805), both much reduced in size.

BROWN, John

438. THE / ELEMENTS OF MEDICINE / OF / *JOHN BROWN, M.D.* / TRANSLATED FROM THE LATIN, / WITH COMMENTS AND ILLUSTRATIONS, / BY THE AUTHOR. / — / A NEW EDITION, REVISED AND CORRECTED. / WITH / A BIOGRAPHICAL PREFACE / BY THOMAS BEDDOES, M.D. / AND / A HEAD OF THE AUTHOR. / — / 'The coincidence of some parts of this work with correspon- / 'dent deduc- / 'tions in the BRUNONIAN ELEMENTA MEDICINAE—a work (with / 'some exceptions) of great genius—must be considered as a confirma- / 'tion of the truth of the theory, as they were probably arrived at by / 'different trains of reasoning.' / DR. DARWIN, ZOONOMIA, p. 75. / — / IN TWO VOLUMES. / — / VOLUME I [II]. / — / LONDON: / PRINTED FOR

J. JOHNSON, NO. 72, ST. PAUL'S / CHURCH-YARD. / — / MDCCXCV [1795]. (Bodley, Harvard, LC, National Library of Scotland, Princeton, U.S. National Library of Medicine, Virginia, Yale)

The only plate is the frontispiece to Volume I:

1. 'JOHN BROWN, M.D.', '*Donaldson Pinx!*', '*Blake Sculp!*', '*London, Published May 1, 1795, by J. Johnson, S! Paul's Church Yard.*' (Oval size: 10·9 × 13·2 cm.)

BRYANT, Jacob

439. A. A / NEW SYSTEM, / OR AN / ANALYSIS / OF / ANCIENT MYTHOLOGY: / Wherein an Attempt is made to divest TRADITION of FABLE; / and to reduce the TRUTH to its Original Purity. / In this WORK is given an HISTORY of the / BABYLONIANS, / CHALDEANS, / EGYPTIANS, / CANAANITES, / HELLADIANS, / IONIANS, / LELLEGES, / DORIANS, / PELASGI: / ALSO OF THE / SCYTHÆ, / INDO-SCYTHÆ, / ETHIOPIANS, / PHENICIANS. / The Whole contains an Account of the principal Events in the first Ages, from the / DELUGE to the DISPERSION: Also of the various Migrations, which ensued, and / the Settlements made afterwards in different Parts: Circumstances of great Conse- / quence, which were subsequent to the GENTILE HISTORY of MOSES. / — / VOL. I [II] [III]. / — / By JACOB BRYANT, / Formerly of KING's COLLEGE, CAMBRIDGE; and Secretary to his Grace the / late Duke of MARLBOROUGH, during his Command abroad; and Secretary / to him as Master General of his Majesty's Ordnance. / = [Vols. I–II:] LONDON: / Printed for T. PAYNE, MEWS-GATE; P. ELMSLY, in the / STRAND; B. WHITE, in FLEET-STREET; and / J. WALTER, CHARING-CROSS. M.DCC.LXXIV [1774]. [Vol. III:] M.DCC. LXXVI [1776]. (BM, Bodley, GEB.)

B. THE SECOND EDITION [of Vols. I–II:] / — / . . . M.DCC. LXXV [1775]. (Bath Public, Bodley, GEB)

A. Not counting maps and diagrams, there are 31 plates in the three volumes of the first edition, signed by Blake's master Basire (28), T. Chambers (2), and F. Bartolozzi (1); all but one are in Vols. I–II. It is highly likely that Blake had some hand in at least a few of Basire's engravings; on the somewhat tenuous evidence of Blake's later iconography, Ruthven Todd (*Tracks in the Snow* [1946], 38) puts the case for considering as Blake's that in Vol. III, p. 601.

(The Second Edition and Vol. III have minor variations of lineation on the title-page.)

B. The plates in the second edition are the same as those in the first, though in Vol. II they have been moved two pages forward.

The third volume does not have a 'Second Edition' on the title-page and was clearly issued in an extra-large printing to complete the sets of the first and second editions of Vols. I–II. It was intended to publish Vol. III in 1775, for an advertisement bound with some copies of [J. Bryant], *A Vindication of the Apamean Medal* (1775) announced that a second edition of Bryant's *Ancient*

Mythology Vols. I–II would appear next month and that the third volume was scheduled for December.

The six-volume 'Third Edition' (1807) was reduced in size from quarto to octavo, and as a consequence all the old plates had to be re-engraved (chiefly by J. LeKeux) to supplement ten new plates.

BÜRGER, Gottfried Augustus

440. LEONORA. / A TALE, / *TRANSLATED AND ALTERED FROM THE* / 𝕲𝕰𝕽𝕸𝕬𝕹 / OF / GOTTFRIED AUGUSTUS BÜRGER. / = / *BY J T STANLEY, ESQ. F.R.S.* &c. / = / 'Poetry hath Bubbles, as the water has: / 'And these are of them.'— / — / Does not th'idea of God include / The notion of beneficent and good; / Of one to mercy, not revenge inclin'd, / Able and willing to relieve mankind? / = / A NEW EDITION. / — / LONDON: / *PRINTED BY S. GOSNELL,* / FOR WILLIAM MILLER, OLD BOND STREET. / — / 1796. (BM, BMPR, Bodley, Fitzwilliam, Harvard, LC, National Library of Scotland, NYP, Princeton, Trinity College [Hartford, Connecticut], Westminster Public, Yale [3].)

All three plates are signed '*Blake in*[*v.*]:', '*Perry. sc*[:]'.

1. Beneath the frontispiece is written:

> *O! how I dreamt of things impossible,*
> *Of Death affecting Forms least like himself;*
> *I've seen, or dreamt I saw the Tyrant dress,*
> *Lay by his Horrors, and put on his Smiles;*
> *Treacherous he came an unexpected Guest,*
> *Nay, though invited by the loudest Calls*
> *Of blind Imprudence, unexpected still;*
> *And then, he dropt his Mask.*
> > *Alter'd from Young.*

(Design size: 16·6 × 20·1 cm. The engraving in fact illustrates Bürger pp. 10–11 and has no over-all similarity to any of Blake's other *Night Thoughts* drawings or engravings.) (A proof is in the possession of Mr. Robert N. Essick.)

2. On p. 1, at the top of the first page of the poem, is an untitled picture of a group of soldiers, wives, and children (plate size: ?18·9 × 12·8 cm).

3. On p. 16, at the bottom of the last page, is an untitled engraving of a soldier running to a woman on a couch (plate size: 15·2 × 9·7 cm). (Blake's sketch, in a somewhat different form, is in the collection of Sir Geoffrey Keynes.)

Bürger's poem was very popular, for there were three editions in 1796 in London alone; Blake's design was not, for *The British Critic*, VIII (Sept. 1796), 277, found the frontispiece 'distorted, absurd', the product of 'depraved fancy', and the *Analytical Review*, XXIV (Nov. 1796), 472, said it was 'perfectly ludicrous, instead of terrific' (*Blake Records* [1969], 54–5).

CATULLUS

441. THE / POEMS / OF / CAIUS VALERIUS / CATULLUS, / *IN ENGLISH VERSE*: / WITH THE LATIN TEXT REVISED, AND CLASSICAL

NOTES [by John Nott]. / PREFIXED ARE ENGRAVINGS OF / CATUL-
LUS, AND HIS FRIEND CORNELIUS NEPOS. / IN TWO VOLUMES
/ — / [four-line motto] / — / VOL. I [II]. / — / LONDON: / PRINTED FOR
J. JOHNSON, ST. PAUL'S CHURCH-YARD. / M DCC XCV [1795]. (Bodley,
Cincinnati, GEB, Harvard, Indiana, LC, Library Company of Philadelphia,
Newark Public, NYP, Ohio Wesleyan, Princeton, South Carolina, South-
ampton)

The only two plates are the frontispieces, which are signed '*Blake sculpsit.*',
'*Xaverius Della Rosa, Veronæ, delin.*', 'Apud effigiem antiquam curiæ senatûs
veronensi superpositam.', '*London Published March 10 1795 by J Johnson
St Pauls Church Y^d [or Yard]*'.

1. Vol. I: 'C: VAL: CATVLLVS.' (frame size: 10·0 × 16·8 cm)
2. Vol. II: 'CORNELL: NEPOS.' (frame size: 10·5 × 16·9 cm)

CHAUCER, Geoffrey

442. THE / POETICAL WORKS / OF / GEOFF. CHAUCER. / IN
FOURTEEN VOLUMES. / THE MISCELLANEOUS PIECES / From
Urry's Edition 1721, / THE CANTERBURY TALES / from *Tyrwhitt's*
Edition 1775. / = / [30 lines of verse] / = / VOL. XIII. / EDINBURGH: / AT
THE 𝔄𝔭𝔬𝔩𝔩𝔬 𝔓𝔯𝔢𝔰𝔰, BY THE MARTINS. / *Anno* 1782 [i.e. 1783]. (American
Antiquarian Society, Bodley, BM, Colorado, Harvard, LC, Minnesota,
Virginia)

The title-page of Vol. XIII is dated 1782, but at the end of the table of
contents is the date 22 March 1783 and Blake's frontispiece is dated May
1783, so the real date is clearly 1783. Chaucer is fourteen volumes of what
a label on each plate calls '*BELL'S EDITION* / The POETS of GREAT
BRITAIN / *COMPLETE* [in 109 volumes] *FROM* / CHAUCER to
CHURCHILL.' In the John Johnson Collection in Bodley is a set in
original marbled paper covers.
Stothard designed the frontispieces for all fifteen plates for Chaucer; that
for Vol. XIII is inscribed:

1. 'CHAUCER VOL. XIII. / Sampson yhad experience / That Women
were ful trew ifound / *In praise of Women* L 81, 82.' '*Stothard del*', '*Blake
sculp*' 'London Printed for John Bell British Library Strand May 24th.
1783.' (Framing-line: 6·7 × 10·6 cm)

In some sets of this work (e.g. BM, Bodley, GEB) Blake's plate was re-
engraved by Cooke and dated 16 Feb. 1787, though the title-pages were
unchanged.

The dated colophons (7 Sept. 1782 to 22 March 1783, regularly in volume-
order) and engraved imprints (1 Aug. 1782 to 29 May 1783, mostly in
volume-order) indicate that most of the set was published in 1783.
Blake's plate was withdrawn, and Cook's substituted for it, in later editions
of the Chaucer set in Bell's English Poets (§1784, §1786–7, §1799–1800, 1807).

443. THE / PROLOGUE AND CHARACTERS / OF / Chaucer's Pilgrims, /SELECTED FROM HIS / CANTERBURY TALES; / INTENDED TO ILLUSTRATE / A PARTICULAR DESIGN / OF / MR. WILLIAM BLAKE, / WHICH IS ENGRAVED BY HIMSELF. / And may be seen at Mr. COLNAGHI's, Cockspur Street; at / Mr. BLAKE's, No. 28, Broad Street, Golden Square; and at the / Publisher's, Mr. HARRIS, Bookseller, St. Paul's Church Yard. / — / *Price two shillings and sixpence.* / — / MDCCCXII [1812]. (BM, Harvard, Huntington, LC, Morgan, Trinity College [Hartford, Conn.], Yale)

There are only two plates:

1. The frontispiece (7·9 × 13·2 cm) is inscribed *'Publish'd Dec. 26. 1811. by Newberry St Pauls Ch: Yard'*, *'W Blake inv & sc'*, and, under the characters represented: *'Reeve. Chaucer. Oxford Scholar. Cook. Miller. Wife of Bath. Merchant.'*
2. At the bottom of p. 58 is a vignette (7·3 × 4·9 cm) of a cathedral and trees.

The preface, signed by 'THE EDITOR', contains a puff for Blake's 'Canterbury Pilgrims' engraving (pp. iii–iv) and states that 'The original reading is copied from the edition of Thomas Speight, printed Anno. 1687; and the Translation from Mr. Ogle's edition, 1741.' The anonymous editor may be Malkin, as Gilchrist (1863) plausibly suggests. The 'Mr. Blake' whose address is given on the title-page is the poet's brother James.

COMMINS, Thomas

444. AN ELEGY, / *set to Music by* / *Thos. Commins,* / *Organist of Penzance, Cornwall.* / LONDON. / *Printed & Sold by J: Fentum, N°. 78, corner Salisbury S^t. Strand* [1786]. (BMPR, Keynes)

Commins's *Elegy* consists of five pages of engraved music, with the above title at the top of the first page.

1. On the cover is an engraving of a man jumping from a boat to the open arms of a woman and child, illustrating the words:

> *The shatter'd bark from adverse winds*
> *Rest in this peaceful haven finds*
> *And when the storms of life are past*
> *Hope drops her anchor here at last.*

It is signed *'W. Blake del^t. & sculp^t.'* and *'Publish'd July 1, 1786 by J. Fentum N° 78 Corner of Salisbury Street'* (plate-mark: 20·0 × 27·8 cm). The BMPR copy is lightly coloured. (Keynes [1921] reports a sketch for the engraving in the hands of a bookseller named Robson in 1913.)

CUMBERLAND, George

445. = / AN ATTEMPT TO DESCRIBE / HAFOD, / AND THE NEIGHBOURING SCENES ABOUT THE / BRIDGE OVER THE FUNACK, COMMONLY CALL- / ED THE DEVIL'S BRIDGE, IN THE COUNTY OF / CARDIGAN. / AN ANCIENT SEAT BELONGING TO THOMAS / JOHNES, ESQ. MEMBER

FOR THE COUNTY OF / RADNOR. / = / BY GEORGE CUMBERLAND. / = /
[6 lines from] / *Dryden's Virgil.* / = / LONDON: / Printed by W. Wilson, St.
Peter's Hill, Doctors' Commons, / And sold by T. Egerton, Whitehall. / — /
M DCC XCVI [1796]. (Bodley, Toronto)

1. The only plate is a folding map bound after the text (18·3 × 36·1 cm)
inscribed with various place-names and entitled '*A Map of part of the Estate
of Thomas Johnes Esq: M P at Havod in the County of Cardigan: Jan.ᵧ 1796*'. It is
unsigned, but D. V. Erdman and Sir Geoffrey Keynes (no. 2037) attribute
it to Blake on the basis of the sinister formation of the 'g' throughout (for
discussion of this 'g', see no. 1217 40, 43–44).

However, since pl. 2–3, 5–11, 22 signed with some variant of 'Engraved
by G: C:' in Cumberland's *Thoughts on Outline* (1796) exhibit this eccentric,
sinister 'g', it seems likely that Cumberland too used this 'g'. (Otherwise, we
must assume that Blake lettered the plates signed 'Engraved by G: C:'.)
Without further evidence, therefore, we should assume that the plate in
Hafod was engraved by Cumberland, as we might otherwise expect, rather
than by Blake.

In a letter of 23 March 1796 (quoted in Keynes, above), Cumberland said
that he had 'only printed 50 [4° large Paper *copies*]—and 450 small [*octavo*]'
of *Hafod*.

446. A. OUTLINES FROM THE ANTIENTS / EXHIBITING THEIR PRIN-
CIPLES OF COM- / POSITION IN FIGURES AND BASSO-RELIEVOS
/ TAKEN CHIEFLY FROM INEDITED MONU- / MENTS OF GREEK
AND ROMAN SCULPTURE / WITH AN INTRODUCTORY ESSAY /
BY GEORGE CUMBERLAND, ESQ / — / LONDON / SEPTIMUS
PROWETT / — / MDCCCXXIX [1829] (BM, BMPR, Boston Public,
Bristol Public, Drexel Institute of Technology, GEB, LC, McGill, Penn-
sylvania, Princeton, Trinity College [Hartford, Conn.], Yale)

B. OUTLINES FROM THE ANTIENTS, / EXHIBITING THEIR
PRINCIPLES OF COMPOSITION IN / FIGURES AND BASSO-RE-
LIEVOS TAKEN CHIEFLY / FROM INEDITED MONUMENTS OF
GREEK / AND ROMAN SCULPTURE. / BY GEORGE CUMBERLAND,
ESQ. / EIGHTY-ONE PLATES. / [*vignette of urn*] / LONDON: / SEPTI-
MUS PROWETT. / — / MDCCCXXIX [1829]. (Robert Essick)

Among the 81 plates in A and B are reprinted pl. 19, 14, 15, and 23 (in
that order) from Cumberland's *Thoughts on Outline* of 1796. The only significant change is the addition of numbers to make the group fit in with the
present work, though a mistake was made in the order (80, 78–79, 81).

A. Cumberland's text consists of an 'Introduction' (pp. i–xxiv) and short
descriptions before each group of subjects (pp. 1–44), with an 'Appendix'
(p. [45]) on the plates from the earlier work, in which Blake is mentioned.

B. In the other version, the title-page was reset, the text omitted, and the
plates issued with a new table of contents, with '*IV. Plates, from Compositions*

by G. Cumberland, outlined by Blake.' Pl. 78 and 81 are given variant titles: 'Sufferings of Cupid and Psyche from Passion of Love' and 'The Bath, with Innocence Protected.'

The *Outlines* was in fact issued in four numbers, though this is not apparent from the rebound copies. The evidence comes from Cumberland's notebook, where under 27 April 1828 he noted that the work 'is to come out in 4 numbers 2 already out or ready' (BM Add. MSS 36521, f. 179); on 29 May 1829 his son (also named George) wrote that 'The 3ʳᵈ number of the outlines are finished & bound up' and on 21 July he sent the last number (BM Add. MSS 36512, ff. 196–7, 202).

Among the Cumberland MSS (GEB) are 30 leaves watermarked '1820' containing a draft 'Appendix' (with no reference to Blake) and 12 plates, including pl. 13–15, 19, 23 engraved by Blake, bearing a note: 'NB of these plates very few impressions were made', plus two tracings of 'the original outlines which I made when in Rome'. The sketches for the new engravings are in the BMPR in a collection labelled OUTLINES BY G. CUMBERLAND Senʳ FROM VARIOUS EMINENT WORKS OF ART ITALIAN GREEK &c (Accession no. 1866-2-10-586 irregularly to 674).

447. = / THOUGHTS ON OUTLINE, SCULPTURE, AND THE SYSTEM / THAT GUIDED THE ANCIENT ARTISTS IN COMPOSING THEIR / FIGURES AND GROUPES: / ACCOMPANIED WITH FREE RE- MARKS ON THE PRACTICE OF / THE MODERNS, AND LIBERAL HINTS CORDIALLY INTENDED / FOR THEIR ADVANTAGE. / TO WHICH ARE ANNEXED TWENTY-FOUR DESIGNS OF CLASSICAL SUBJECTS INVENTED ON THE PRINCIPLES RE- / COMMENDED IN THE ESSAY BY GEORGE CUMBERLAND. / = / AINSI IO SON PITTORE. / = / LONDON. PRINTED BY W. WILSON, ST. PETER'S-HILL, DOCTORS'-COMMONS: AND SOLD / BY MESSRS. ROBIN-SON, PATERNOSTER-ROW; AND T. EGERTON, WHITEHALL. MDCCXCVI [1796]. (Bodley, BM, BMPR, Bristol Public, California [Berkeley], Free Library of Philadelphia, GEB, Harvard, London University, Minnesota, National Library of Scotland, NYP, Ohio State, Peabody Institute, Pennsylvania, Princeton, Trinity College [Hartford, Conn.], V&A, Washington, Westminster Public, Yale)

The Plates: Of the 24 plates, 15 were engraved by Cumberland, 8 by Blake, and one (the frontispiece) is unsigned. All Blake's have the legend: 'From an original [*or* Original] Invention by G. Cumberland [*or* G: C:]. Engᵈ by W. Blake [*or* B]: Published [*or* Publish(')d] as the Act directs November [*or* Nov(ʳ)] 5: [17]94', except that on the last two the date is changed to 'January [*or* Janʸ] 1 1795', the date on Cumberland's engravings. Blake's 8 plates are:

1. Pl. '12', 'PSYCHE DISOBEYS' (15·9 × 12·0 cm).
2. Pl. '13', 'PSYCHE REPENTS' (16·2 × 12·3 cm).
3. Pl. '14', 'VENUS COUNCELS CUPID' (16·5 × 12·1 cm).
4. Pl. '15', 'THE CONJUGAL UNION OF CUPID' (17·2 × 12·8 cm).

5. Pl. '16', 'CUPID & PSYCHE' (23·9 × 17·4 cm).
6. Pl. '18', 'IRON AGE' (24·5 × 14·8 cm). Above the plate is:

Then cursed steel & more accursed gold
Gave mischief birth & made that mischief bold.
Ovid. Iron age

7. Pl. '19', 'ARISTOPHANES CLOUDS. SCENE. I.' plus identification of the characters in Greek (22·5 × 18·6 cm).
8. Pl. '23', 'ANACREON ODE LII' (20·9 × 15·0 cm).

Blake's plates, for which he was paid 'about Two guineas each and the coppers' (according to Cumberland's letter of 10 Jan. 1804 to Longman, now like the other Longman letters below, with the firm of Longmans, Green, & Co., Ltd.), are praised on pp. 47–8. Cumberland's designs are in the BMPR, as are proofs for pl. 2–24. Among the Cumberland MSS (GEB) is a Pink sheet with 'THOUGHTS ON OUTLINE, SCULPTURE &c. BY G. CUMBERLAND.' printed on it three times, one above another, evidently to be cut up and used as labels. (*N.B.* Plates signed by both Blake and Cumberland exhibit the eccentric 'g' with a leftward serif which, it has been argued—see Erdman and Bentley—was peculiar to Blake.)

Publication. Cumberland sent a copy to 'Mr Blake' in Aug. 1796 (*Blake Records* [1969], 55), for which Blake thanked him on 23 Dec. 1796. Cumberland himself entered the *Thoughts on Outline* at Stationers' Hall on 22 Nov. 1796. After he had sent out complimentary copies,

Finding an error of the Printer on the motto, I had a correct Motto printed, and [*copies were*] . . . corrected by pasting it over the other . . . it should be Anche io sono pittore

(as he wrote to Longman on 17 Feb. 1804). Consequently some copies (e.g. Harvard) were uncorrected, some (e.g. GEB) were corrected by hand ('AINCH' IO SON PITTORE'), and some (e.g. BM) have a corrected, printed label over the motto. Some copies were 'printed on very strong sized paper', and there were 'some [*with*] red printed Titles' (as Cumberland wrote to Longman in the letter of 17 Feb. 1804).

For unspecified reasons, Cumberland 'was obliged to withdraw' it from the bookseller, and 'Of the *Outline* not a single copy was ever sent to Mess Robinsons' (as he said in his letters to Longman of 10 Jan. and 17 Feb. 1804). The work was, therefore, sold privately in effect, and very slowly, and probably most copies were simply given away. In 1804 he arranged for Longman to sell the remainder, and between Jan. 1804 and June 1807 they took '99 copies, Boards' and '94 —— D°, Sheets' (according to their ledgers). They sold a few, gave away some for the author, and there were '89 returned to M͟r C. Oct 1 1811' (according to the Longman ledgers). On 11 Oct. 1813 Cumberland sent 74 copies to the bookseller White, who managed to sell only 7 copies by 21 April 1815, when he returned the rest to Cumberland (*Blake Records* [1969], 236 n. 4). Probably the rest were given away or scrapped.

As early as 5 Feb. 1804, Cumberland told Longman that 'I must be at liberty to apply [the Plates] to some other purposes', and a work by Cumberland called *Principles of the Composition of the Antients*, with 60 plates, was announced in *The Repository of Arts*, III (June 1810), 378. Publication was actively undertaken in 1824–5 (*Blake Records* [1969], 283–8, 300) and was finally achieved in 1829 under the title *Outlines from the Antients*, using again four of Blake's engravings.

Dante Alighieri

448. A. BLAKE'S ILLUSTRATIONS OF DANTE. / *Seven Plates, designed and engraved by* W. Blake, *Author of 'Illustrations of / the Book of Job,' &c. &c.* / Price £2. 2s. India Paper. / — / PLATE I. / . . . and like a corse fell to the ground. / Hell; Canto v. line 137. / PLATE II. / . . . . seiz'd on his arm, / And mangled bore away the sinewy part. / Hell; Canto xxii. line 70. / PLATE III. / . . . . . so turn'd / His talons on his comrade. / Hell; Canto xxii. line 135. / PLATE IV. / . . . lo! a serpent with six feet / Springs forth on one, / Hell; Canto xxv. line 45. / PLATE V. / He ey'd the serpent and the serpent him. / Hell; Canto xxv. line 82. / PLATE VI. / . . . Then two I mark'd, that sat Propp'd 'gainst each other, / Hell; Canto xxix. line 71. / PLATE VII. / 'Wherefore dost bruise me?' weeping he / exclaim'd. / Hell; Canto xxxii. line 79. / CARY'S DANTE. [London, 1838, paper watermarked '1822' or unwatermarked] (Fitzwilliam, Huntington [2 copies], LC, Princeton).

B. §[London, ?1892].

C. [1955] (Fitzwilliam, Huntington, National Gallery of Victoria [Melbourne, Australia]).

D. [1968] (BMPR, GEB).

Copies of unrecorded date: Albright-Knox Art Gallery (Buffalo, N.Y.), Berg Collection (NYP), Boston Museum, Boston Public, Chicago, Cincinnati Museum, Columbia, Cornell, Detroit Institute of Art, Harvard, London University, Metropolitan (N.Y.), Montreal Museum, Morgan, National Gallery of Canada, NYP (Prints Division), Philadelphia Museum, Rosenbach Foundation, St. John's Seminary (Camarillo, California), Tate Gallery, Texas Christian, Trinity College (Hartford, Conn.), Wellesley, Yale (3 copies, 2 in the Mellon Collection).

A. The label (above) pasted on the cover of the seven Dante engravings is undated, but it was probably printed in 1838. The unfinished engravings had been commissioned by John Linnell, and they became his property after Blake's death, at which time only a few engraver's proofs had been pulled. In his 'List of John Linnell Senior's Letters and Papers' (now with the Ivimy MSS), John Linnell, Jr., wrote that the seven Dante plates

have been printed at two dates, after a few proofs by Blake—J[ohn]. L[innell].sen in 1 S[eries]—(at Bayswater[)] had India proofs taken (all disposed of)[;] soon after J. L s death (J. L. jnr.)—had 50 copies (india on drawing paper) printed by Holdgate—

Elsewhere in the Ivimy MSS are two receipts from the printers Dixon & Ross, 26 Sept. 1838 for '25 each of 7 Plates Dante India 2.15.0' (called Artist's Proofs), and 2 Oct. 1838 for '95 Imp.rs of 7 Plts. Dante India. 1. 10 0'.

The daybook of Dixon & Ross, now known as Thomas Ross & Son (generously transcribed by Mr. Iain Bain) records work on

> Wednesday 26 September 1838
> Mr Linnell 25 of each of 7 plts Dante Ind[*ia*]
>   87¼ Sh[*ee*]ts. of th[*ic*]k. pl[*a*]t[*e*] Col[*ombier*] [*i.e. 2 pulls per sheet*]
>   25   ,,   of India [*7 pulls per sheet*]
> Saturday Septr 29th 1838
> Mr Linnell 95 Imp^ns of 7 plts Dante India [*i.e. 13⁴⁄₇ sets*]
>   47 Shts of Plt. Col. [*2 pulls per sheet*]
>   13⁴⁄₇ ,, of India [*7 pulls per sheet*]

Linnell's nephew James H. Chance sold at least some of the India-paper copies, for he wrote to Linnell on 30 Dec. 1856 (in a letter now with the Ivimy MSS):

I received the case quite safe with the 2[?] sets[?] of Dante & Two proofs of Emmaus[?] which are very beautiful (yesterday), and possibly I may be able to do something with them amongst my connexion. The Dante & Blake I have entirely on my own speculation being partial to them and if I can do any thing with them I shall be happy to enter into some agreements for 25 Copies ...

Confirmation that he carried out this speculation may be found in a note on the fly-leaf of one set (described in the Sotheby catalogue of 21 April 1943, lot 312):

A few copies may be had of Mr. Chance, 28 London Street, Fitzroy Square, W, Artists Proofs £3.13.6. Only 25 copies printed

B. In the draft of a letter to B. Quaritch of 6 May 1892 (in the Ivimy MSS), John Linnell [Jr.] wrote that

These [*Dante*] proofs (with the exception of two or three copies, one of which my brother sent you)—being disposed of, we are about to obtain a few more copies of proofs—similar to the former ones.

The second commercial printing of the Dante plates therefore consisted of 50 copies printed about 1892, of which 11 appeared in the 15 March 1918 Christie Linnell sale, lots 179–81.

C. Notes on the Huntington and Melbourne sets of Dante plates signed by Lessing J. Rosenwald say that they were printed for him in 1955. According to Keynes (*Blake Studies* [1971], 229), 20 sets were made in 1954.

D. Twenty-five more sets were made in 1968 (see Ruthven Todd, no. 2849), each plate on unwatermarked paper inscribed and dated by Lessing J. Rosenwald.

The copperplates were loaned by the Linnell Trustees to the BMPR, but in July 1937 they were sold (with other Blakes) through William H. Robinson Ltd. to Mr. Lessing J. Rosenwald. On the verso of each plate are a copperplate-maker's-mark: 'A Pontifex & Co / 22 Lisle Street / Soho, London' and corrections for the recto. (The records of the firm, now The

Farringdon Works & H. Pontifex & Sons, Ltd., 9–13 George Street, Man chester Square, London, do not go back as far as Blake's lifetime.)

Blake's plates have no lettering except for no. 1, on the design of which Blake wrote at the bottom right: 'The Whirlwind of Lovers from Dantes Inferno Canto V'.

Plate	Plate-size (cm.)	Location of drawing
1	27·9 × 35·4	Birmingham City Art Gallery
2	27·8 × 34·5	Fogg Art Museum
3	28·0 × 35·3	Birmingham City Art Gallery
4	27·8 × 35·3	National Gallery of Victoria, Melbourne, Australia
5	28·0 × 35·2	Tate Gallery
6	27·6 × 35·2	Tate Gallery
7	27·5 × 35·1	Birmingham City Art Gallery

There are proofs of each in the BMPR, one of no. 4 in the Fitzwilliam, and another of no. 1 in the Princeton Art Gallery. For the *drawings* to Dante, see Part II.

449. *The Inferno* from La Divina Commedia of Dante Alighieri as translated by the Reverend Henry Francis Cary and illustrated with seven engravings of William Blake. N.Y., 1931.

On one page, unsigned, is 'A Note on the Engravings of William Blake'.

[DARWIN, Erasmus]

450. A–B. THE / BOTANIC GARDEN; / = / *A Poem, in Two Parts.* / = / PART I. / CONTAINING / THE ECONOMY OF VEGETATION. / — / PART II. / THE LOVES OF THE PLANTS. / WITH / Philosophical Notes. / = / LONDON, / PRINTED FOR J. JOHNSON, ST. PAUL's CHURCH-YARD. / = / MDCCXCI [1791]. / Entered at Stationers Hall. (BM, GEB)

C. ... GARDEN. / *A POEM,* / IN TWO PARTS. / ... PHILOSOPHICAL NOTES. / = / THE THIRD EDITION. / = / LONDON: / ... PAUL'S ... / MDCCXCV [1795]. / *ENTERED AT STATIONERS' HALL.* (BM, GEB, LC, NYP, New York, Southampton, Westminster Public)

D. ... GARDEN, / A POEM. / ... THE FOURTH EDITION. / ... 1799. (BM, GEB, LC, NYP, Princeton, Swansea)

E. THE / POETICAL WORKS / OF / ERASMUS DARWIN, / M.D. F.R.S. / CONTAINING THE BOTANIC GARDEN, IN TWO PARTS; / AND THE TEMPLE OF NATURE. / WITH / PHILOSOPHICAL NOTES AND PLATES. / IN THREE VOLUMES. / VOL. I [II] [III]. / CONTAINING THE ECONOMY OF VEGETATION [CONTAINING THE LOVES OF THE PLANTS] [CONTAINING THE TEMPLE OF NATURE]. / LONDON: / PRINTED FOR J. JOHNSON, ST. PAUL'S CHURCH-YARD, / BY T. BENSLEY, BOLT COURT, FLEET STREET. /1806. (Toronto, Turnbull [Wellington, N.Z.])

The two Parts of *The Botanic Garden* were apparently issued quite separately up to the Fourth Edition of 1799. Part II, The Loves of the Plants, was published first in 1789; a second edition appeared in 1790; 'The Third Edition' in 1794; 'The Fourth Edition' in 1794; and a presumably piratical 'Fourth Edition' in 'Dudlin' in 1796. The separate title-pages of the first three editions of Part I read:

A. THE / BOTANIC GARDEN. / PART I. / CONTAINING / THE ECONOMY OF VEGETATION. / *A POEM.* / WITH / Philosophical Notes. / = / It Ver, et Venus; et Veneris prænuncius ante / Pennatus graditur Zephyrus vestigia propter; / Flora quibus mater, præ-spergens ante viai / Cuncta, coloribus egregiis et odoribus opplet. Lucret. / = / LONDON, / PRINTED FOR J. JOHNSON, ST. PAUL's CHURCH-YARD. / — / MDCCXCI [1791]. (BM, Bodley, GEB)

B. THE SECOND EDITION. / . . . MDCCXCI [1791]. (BM)

C. THE THIRD EDITION. / . . . MDCCXCV [1795]. (BM, GEB)

The first two editions of Part II and the first three editions of Part I were issued in several combinations with the 1791 general title-page. The third edition of Part I was usually bound with 'The Fourth Edition' (1794) of Part II. In Johnson's Fourth Edition of 1799, the separate Parts have only half-titles (lacking the imprint), and in other editions (1798, 1824, 1825), all three title-pages are congruent.

Johnson entered Part II of *The Botanic Garden* at Stationers' Hall on 6 March 1789, but it was not until 10 May 1792 that the first Part (along with the second again) was entered. It seems surprising that Part I should not have been published until six months after the date on the engravings, but such is the suggestion of the entry in the Stationers' Register.

There are 10 plates in the 1791 Economy of Vegetation, of which Blake seems to have engraved 5:

1. At p. 127 is 'Fertilization of Egypt.' 'H Fuseli. RA: inv', 'W Blake. sc.' 'London, Publish'd Dec.^t 1st 1791. by J. Johnson, St Pauls Church Yard.' No. 3–5 below have the same imprint. (Design size: 15·4 × 19·6 cm.) (Fuseli's sketch and Blake's adaptation, adding the bearded rain-god like that in *Visions* pl. 2, are in the BMPR. Keynes [1921] reports a caricature of Fuseli's design in Giorgione di Castel Chiuso [Peter Bayley], *Sketches from St. George's Fields* [1821], 95, but I find nothing like it in the first series [1820, LC] or the 'Second Series' [1821, Cornell].)

2. At p. 53 (of the notes) is: 'The Portland Vase'. (17·8 × 25·3 cm). There is no imprint, and, as with no. 3–5, the engraver is not identified. Blake's responsibility for the plate is indicated by Joseph Johnson's letter to Erasmus Darwin of 23 July 1791: 'Blake is certainly capable of making an exact copy of the vase' (*Blake Records* [1969], 43); see also no. 10, below.

3. At p. 54 is another view of the same scene: '*The first Compartment.*' (15·6 × 27·4 cm).

4. At p. 55 is: '*The second Compartment.*' (15·3 × 25·7 cm).

5. At p. 58 is: '*The Handles & Bottom of the Vase.*' (14·4 × 24·6 cm).

B. In 'The Second Edition' of 'The Economy of Vegetation' (1791), the same plates are in the same places without change, except that there is no date on no. 1 ('Fertilization of Egypt') and that the directions to the binder do not mention it.

C. 'The Third Edition' of 'The Economy of Vegetation' (1795) has the same plates as B, with the following addition:

6. At p. 168 is: '*Tornado.*' '*H Fuseli RA: inv:*' '*W Blake: sc:*', '*London, Published Aug! 1ˢᵗ 1795, by J. Johnson, S! Paul's Church Yard.*' (17·0 × 21·4 cm). (Proofs are in the BMPR and the collection of Professor Robert N. Essick.)

D. Johnson's 'Fourth Edition' (1799) was reduced from quarto to octavo size, and the plates were somewhat crudely re-engraved. 'Nightmare' was engraved by T. Holloway and dated 1 June 1791. The other plates, dated and inscribed like those in the 'Third Edition' (1 Dec. 1791), were evidently commissioned and executed at the same time as those for the first edition, and it is of course possible that Johnson's letter referred only to these octavo plates. Blake's responsibility is made explicit by the signature on pl. 10 below; his part in copying his plates for no. 7–9, 11 can be established only by analogy and by similarities of style.

7. At p. 145 is a design like no. 1 above (design size: 7·9 × 13·0 cm).
8. At p. 352 is a design like no. 2 above (7·7 × 10·9 cm).
9. At p. 355 is a design like no. 3 above (8·5 × 16·0 cm).
10. At p. 357 is a design like no. 4 above, signed '*Blake*' (8·5 × 15·6 cm).
11. At p. 362 is a design like no. 5 above (8·5 × 16·5 cm).

E. The collected edition of 1806 uses the reduced-size octavo plates of the 1799 edition, at Vol. I, pp. 145, 335, 338, 340, and 344.

Blake's plates were not included in other editions of New York (1798), London (1824, 1825), Dublin (1796), or in *O Jardim Botanico de Darwin* (Lisboa, 1803—Part I is 1804), and there are no plates at all in *Gli Amori delle Piante* (Milano, 1805), or *Les Amours des Plantes* (Paris, An VIII [1800]).

DONNE, John
A450. THE / POETICAL WORKS / OF / Dr. JOHN DONNE, / DEAN OF ST. PAUL'S, LONDON. / IN THREE VOLUMES. / WITH THE LIFE OF THE AUTHOR. / = / [10 line motto from] / BEN. JOHNSON. / = / VOL. I[–III]. / EDINBURGH: / AT THE Apollo Press, BY THE MARTINS. / Anno 1779.[1]

A proof engraving before letters on unwatermarked paper in the Balmanno Collection in the British Museum Print Room (1853 12 10 198) marked '*Stothard del.*', '*Blake. sc.*' (plate size: 10·3 × 14·5 cm) seems to be a rejected plate for Vol. II of Donne's Poetical Works in Bell's Edition of The Poets of Great Britain Complete from Chaucer to Churchill. It represents a winged figure flying away from the viewer, with cartouches at top and bottom very like those for Bell's Poets (see the reproduction in *Blake Newsletter*, VI [1972],

[1] There are normally three title-pages to each volume in Bell's English Poets, one in conventional typography like that above, another in conventional typography giving more information about the contents, and a third, engraved, with a large design.

237) and dimensions like other plates for the series. It was clearly intended for Bell's English Poets but abandoned.

It is not easy to say where the plate was intended to go, for none of the designs in the 109 volumes of the first four editions (1779–83, 1784, 1786–8, 1799–1800) or the 122 volumes of the fifth edition (1807) are significantly like the one Blake engraved. However, A. C. Coxhead, *Thomas Stothard* (1906), 84, says that Stothard made three designs for Donne, the second of which he describes as 'A figure flying in a cloud, back turned to the spectator'. This sounds remarkably like the Blake engraving, and, though Coxhead does not give the evidence for his statement, we may hesitantly accept its accuracy, *faute de mieux*.

The problem is that no such design appears in any set of Donne in Bell's English Poets known to me. The Stothard plates Coxhead ascribes to Vols. I and III are common enough, but the plate in Vol. II is designed by Edwards and engraved by Delattre (copies in Bodley, Chicago, Library Company of Philadelphia, Minnesota, NYP, Princeton, Texas, Virginia [2]). What happened to Blake's plate?

The title-page illustrations for Bell's English Poets were designed at first, in 1777–8 according to the engraved imprints, chiefly by Mortimer (38), who died in 1779, and Edwards (10); they were continued in 1779–83 largely by Stothard (41), Angelica Kauffman (8), and Rebecca (4). It seems likely that Edwards had made a series of designs for Donne's poems, at least one of which, for Vol. II, was engraved by Delattre in '1778'. When Stothard was brought into the undertaking in 1779, he was evidently asked to make designs for each of the three Donne volumes. All three were engraved, that for Vol. I by Delattre (24 Sept. 1779), that for Vol. II by Blake, then (autumn 1779) just out of his apprenticeship, and that for Vol. III by Grignion (17 Aug. 1779).[1] Then the duplication of Blake's plate with the one already engraved after Edwards for Vol. II was discovered, and Blake's was abandoned. Perhaps the only copy of Blake's engraving which survives is that in the BMPR.

The Donne volumes in Bell's English Poets belong in this bibliography, then, only because Blake apparently engraved a plate for them which was later rejected.[2]

EARLE, James

451. A. PRACTICAL OBSERVATIONS / ON THE / OPERATION FOR THE STONE. / — / By *JAMES EARLE, Esq.* / SURGEON EXTRA-ORDINARY TO HIS MAJESTY'S HOUSEHOLD, / AND / SENIOR SURGEON TO ST. BARTHOLOMEW'S HOSPITAL. / — / LONDON: / PRINTED FOR J. JOHNSON, ST. PAUL'S CHURCH-YARD. / — /

[1] According to the colophons, Vols. I–III were printed on 29 July, 5 and 12 Aug. 1779, but the dates on the plates, if accurate, indicate that they cannot have been published before the end of Sept. 1779.

[2] The Edwards plate for Donne Vol. II survived with a curious persistence. Not only did it displace Blake's (as it were), but, when the Donne volumes were omitted from the 1807 edition, it was given a new inscription and used to illustrate Edward Moore in Vol. CVI (1807).

1793. (BM, Cleveland Public, College of Physicians of Philadelphia, LC, McGill [Osler Collection], National Library of Medicine [Washington], N.Y. Academy of Medicine [N.Y.])

B. . . . STONE. / = / SECOND EDITION, / WITH AN APPENDIX, / CONTAINING / A DESCRIPTION OF AN INSTRUMENT CALCU-LATED TO / IMPROVE THAT OPERATION. / — / *By JAMES EARLE*, *Esq. F.R.S.* / SURGEON . . . / 1796. (McGill [Osler Collection], National Library of Medicine [Washington], St. Bartholomew's Hospital Medical School Library [London])

C. . . . OPERATION / FOR / *THE STONE.* / SECOND EDITION. / WITH / AN APPENDIX, / CONTAINING / A DESCRIPTION OF AN INSTRUMENT CALCULATED / TO IMPROVE THAT OPERATION. / = / BY SIR JAMES EARLE, F.R.S. / Surgeon Extraordinary to the King, and to his Majesty's Household; and / Senior Surgeon to St. Bartholomew's Hospital. / = / *LONDON*: / *Printed by W. Flint, Old Bailey;* / And sold by J. JOHNSON, St. Paul's Church-yard. / — / 1803 (College of Physicians of Philadelphia, Harvard, Kentucky, National Library of Medicine [Washington])

The first edition had two plates signed '*Blake*[:] *sc*[:]':

1. At '*P. 52*' is a plate of a curved surgical 'gorget' and of a 'staff' (p. 52) invented by Earle (10·8 × 17·7 cm).
2. At '*P. 74*' is a plate of four stones extracted from an 18-year-old boy (12 × 20 cm).

In the 1796 edition an appendix was added with a new, unsigned fold-out plate (29·5 × 16 cm) marked '*To face P. 8, Appendix.*' which Sir Geoffrey Keynes ('William Blake and Bart's', *Blake Newsletter*, VII [1973 (74)], 9) says 'was certainly executed by Blake', but the evidence of 'engraving technique' and 'lettering' seems far from conclusive to me.

Blake's plates were reprinted in the editions of 1796 and 1803 but not in Earle's *Practical Observations* printed in Dr. Percivall Pott's *Chirurgical Works* (1808, 1819).

The presence of Blake's plate was first reported by Professor Leslie F. Chard in an essay called 'Two "New" Blake Engravings', which he generously showed me in draft.

EMLYN, Henry

452. A. A / PROPOSITION / FOR / A NEW ORDER / IN / ARCHITEC-TURE, / WITH / RULES / FOR DRAWING the several PARTS. / = / By HENRY EMLYN, of WINDSOR. / = / LONDON; / PRINTED BY J. DIXWELL, ST. MARTIN'S LANE, CHARING CROSS, / M.DCC.LXXXI [1781] (LC, Sir John Soane Museum)

B. . . . WINDSOR. / = / THE SECOND EDITION, / WITH THE ADDITION OF ELEVEN PLATES AND THE EXPLANATION, / Shewing the INTERCOLLUMNIATIONS and ARCADES of the Composition, / And how it is adapted to assemble with the GRECIAN and ROMAN Orders; also, the / Manner of placing it over the DORIC, IONIC, COMPOSITE, and CORINTHIAN / Orders; with some concluding REMARKS. / = / LONDON; / PRINTED BY J. DIXWELL, ST. MARTIN'S LANE, CHARING CROSS; / M·DCC·LXXXIV [1784]. (BM, Cambridge University)

A. The New Order in Architecture is associated with the Order of St. George. 'PLATES II. and III.' represent '*The Pedestal of the lesser and greater Way*' (p. 9), the former with an elaborate coat of arms, the latter representing St. George slaying the dragon. In the first edition there were 10 plates, of which only one is identified as Blake's.

1. 'Pl: II.', signed '*Blake Sculp*' (design size, including the signature: 36 × 53 cm).

Paul Bremen (book catalogue 14 [April 1971], item 12) and Minnick & Gibson (*Blake Newsletter*, VI. 1 [1972], 12–17) conclude from stylistic evidence such as 'similar sweeping rhythms' that the anonymous pl. V is perhaps also by Blake, and Gibson & Minnick, perhaps observing that such evidence applies equally to other plates, suggest that all the anonymous plates in 1781 (pl. I, III, V–X, XVIII) are Blake's. The evidence does not seem persuasive to me.

B. In the Second Edition, the 11 new plates are anonymous (pl. XVIII) or signed by Sparrow (pl. XI–XVII, XIX–XXI). The first 10 plates seem unchanged.

The Third Edition of 1797 (BM) has a considerably expanded title-page and 'THIRTY-ONE COPPER-PLATES', somewhat reduced in size. The '*Blake*' plate, very carefully copied by an anonymous engraver, is now pl. IV and *c.* 27 × 44 cm.

(Gibson & Minnick believe that the 1781 plate Blake signed was 're-worked, rather than re-engraved entirely' in the 1797 edition, but they say nothing of the 1781 pl. I, III, V–X, XVIII in the 1797 edition. A minute examination of such features as the feathers at the bottom right and middle left persuades me that the 1797 pl. III is entirely distinct from the similar pl. II in 1781 and 1784.)

ENFIELD, William

453. A. THE / SPEAKER: / OR, / MISCELLANEOUS PIECES, / SELECTED / FROM THE BEST ENGLISH WRITERS, / AND DIS-POSED / UNDER PROPER HEADS, WITH A VIEW TO FACILITATE / THE IMPROVEMENT OF YOUTH / IN / READING AND SPEAKING. / TO WHICH IS PREFIXED / AN ESSAY ON / ELOCUTION. / BY WILLIAM ENFIELD, LL.D. / LECTURER ON THE BELLES LETTRES IN THE / ACADEMY AT WARRINGTON. / ——— Oculos, paulum tellure moratos, / Sustulit ad proceres; expectatoque resolvit / Ora sono; nec abest facundis *gratia* dictis. / OVID. / LONDON: / PRINTED FOR JOSEPH JOHNSON, ST. PAUL'S CHURCH-YARD. / MDCCLXXIV [1774, i.e. 1780]. (BM)

B. SELECTED FROM THE / BEST ENGLISH WRITERS, / AND

DISPOSED UNDER PROPER HEADS, / WITH A VIEW TO FACILI-
TATE THE / IMPROVEMENT OF YOUTH / . . . WARRINGTON. /
THE SIXTH EDITION, CORRECTED. / . . . gratia . . . MDCCLXXXI
[1781]. (GEB)

C. A NEW EDITION, CORRECTED. / . . . J. JOHNSON . . . /
MDCCLXXXV [1785]. (GEB[2])

D. A NEW EDITION, CORRECTED AND ENLARGED. / TO WHICH
ARE PREFIXED / TWO ESSAYS: / I. ON ELOCUTION. II. ON
READING WORKS OF TASTE. / . . . / *EMBELLISHED WITH FOUR
ELEGANT PLATES.* / . . . dictis. OVID. / . . . -YARD; / *By whom only the
genuine and complete Edition is published.* / — / MDCCXCV [1795]. (Liverpool)

E. M DCC XCVII [1797]. (Yale)

A. The earliest edition here is clearly a reissue of the 1774 sheets (which had
no plates) with the addition of 4 engravings signed '*Stothard del.*' and inscribed '*Publish'd as the Act directs, by J. Johnson, in S! Pauls Church Yard 1 Aug.
1780.*' One or more of the 4 plates were inserted, apparently in a rather
random fashion, in many of the succeeding issues. Stothard's designs appear
in some copies of editions of [1780], 1781, 1785, 1795, 1797, 1799, 1800,
1801, 1805, 1807, and 1820, but there are no plates at all in some copies of
editions of 1774, 1782, 1785, 1789, 1790, 1791, 1792, 1801, 1803, 1804, 1805,
1806, 1815, and 1822.

There is only 1 plate by Blake:

1. At p. 302 is 'Clarence's Dream.' '*Book VII. Chap. 22*'

> ——— *Then came wand'ring by*
> *A shadow like an Angel, with bright hair*
> *Dabbled in blood, and he shriek'd out aloud;*
> '*Clarence is come, false, fleeting, perjur'd Clarence,*
> *That stabb'd me in the field by Tewksbury;*
> *Sieze on him, furies, take him to your torments!*'
> *Shakespeare.*

'*Blake sc.*' (Plate-size: 11·7 × 17·6 cm.) (A sketch is in the BMPR, and
Keynes [1921] reports a copy in the W. E. Moss collection, which was
dispersed in 1937.)

B–E. In the editions of 1781 and 1785, Blake's plate, apparently unchanged,
is at p. 289; in those of 1795 and 1797 it is at p. 305; in 1795 it was touched
up, especially at the top left; in 1797 it was darkened throughout.

Blake's plate was crudely copied in a line engraving bearing Stothard's
name and the date 1 June 1799 which was inserted in some copies of the
1799 edition (e.g. Bodley, GEB); the same design was copied more skilfully
in a stipple engraving lacking the names of designer and engraver and dated
7 January 1800 which is found in other copies of the 1799 edition (BM); a
different line engraving (or perhaps the 1800 stipple plate heavily revised),
lacking the names of designer and engraver and dated 1 May 1801, was
inserted in some copies of the editions of 1801 (Princeton), 1805 (Bodley),
and 1807.

EULER, Leonard

454. ELEMENTS / OF / ALGEBRA, / *By LEONARD EULER.* / TRANS-
LATED FROM THE FRENCH [by Francis Horner], / WITH / THE
CRITICAL AND HISTORICAL NOTES / OF / *M. BERNOULLI.* / To
which are added / THE ADDITIONS OF M. DE LA GRANGE; / SOME
ORIGINAL NOTES BY THE TRANSLATOR; / MEMOIRS OF THE
LIFE OF EULER, WITH AN ESTIMATE OF / HIS CHARACTER; /
AND A PRAXIS TO THE WHOLE WORK, CONSISTING OF / ABOVE
TWO HUNDRED EXAMPLES. / IN TWO VOLUMES. / = / VOL. I
[II]. / = / LONDON: / PRINTED FOR J. JOHNSON, ST. PAUL'S
CHURCH-YARD. / — / 1797. (BM, Bowdoin, Bristol, California [Berkeley],
Christ's College [Cambridge], Cornell, John Crerar Library, LC, Literary
and Philosophical Society [Newcastle], Mittag-Leffler Library [Stockholm],
National Library of Scotland, Oregon, Princeton, Queen's College [Cam-
bridge], Royal Institution [London], St Andrews, Stanford, Yale)

The only plate is the frontispiece to Vol. I:

1. 'LEONARD EULER. / *From a Medallion, as large as life,* / *by Ruchotte, in the*
possession of / *John Wilmot Esq!.*', '*Blake Sculp.*' (Bust size: 6·8 × 11·0 cm.)
There is no plate in the 1822 edition.

FENNING, D., & COLLYER, J.

455. A. A NEW / SYSTEM / OF / GEOGRAPHY: / OR, / A General Description of the World. / CONTAINING / A CIRCUMSTANTIAL ACCOUNT
of all the COUNTRIES, / KINGDOMS, and STATES of / EUROPE, ASIA, AFRICA,
and AMERICA; / Their Situation, Climate, Mountains, Seas, Lakes,
Rivers, &c. / The RELIGION, MANNERS, CUSTOMS, MANUFACTURES, TRADE,
and BUILDINGS / of the INHABITANTS: / WITH / The BIRDS, BEASTS, FISHES,
REPTILES, INSECTS, the various VEGETABLES and MINERALS / found in
different REGIONS: / ALSO, / A Concise but Comprehensive HISTORY of each
COUNTRY from the earliest Times; / An INTRODUCTORY TREATISE on the
SCIENCE of GEOGRAPHY; / And, AN HISTORICAL ACCOUNT OF EACH OF THE
SIX VOYAGES ROUND THE WORLD, / PERFORMED BY BRITISH NAVIGA-
TORS, DURING THE LAST TWENTY YEARS. / EMBELLISHED
WITH / A New and Accurate Set of MAPS, by the best GEOGRAPHERS; /
And a great Variety of COPPER-PLATES, exhibiting various Subjects of
Natural History; / Views of the most remarkable Cities, Structures, or
Ruins; Representations of memorable / Historical Events, engraved from
masterly Designs; singular Customs, Ceremonies, and Dresses / prevailing
in the World, particularly among the SOUTH SEA ISLANDERS; and many other
/ curious and interesting Subjects. / — / By the late D. FENNING and
J. Collyer. / — / A NEW EDITION, REVISED, ENLARGED, and IMPROVED,
by / FREDERICK HERVEY, Esq; / Author of the NAVAL HISTORY of
GREAT BRITAIN, in Five Volumes Octavo. / The Account of NORTH AMERICA
Corrected and Improved, by / CAPTAIN CARVER, / Author of TRAVELS into
the interior Parts of that Country. / — / — *Mores hominum multorum vidit, et*
urbes, HOR. / — / VOL. I[–II]. / = / LONDON: / Printed for J. JOHNSON,

N⁰ 72, and G. and T. WILKIE, N⁰ 71, in / St. Paul Church-Yard. / M.DCC.LXXXV [1785]. [Vol. II¹ is M.DCC.LXXXVI (1786).] (BM)

B. . . . SCIENCE of GEOGRAPHY; / And, AN HISTORICAL ACCOUNT OF ALL THE VOYAGES OF DISCOVERY PERFORMED / BY BRITISH NAVIGATORS, DURING THE LAST TWENTY YEARS. / . . . [omits the late] / The Account of NORTH AMERICA Corrected and Improved, by / CAPTAIN CARVER, / Author of TRAVELS into the interior Parts of that Country. / A NEW EDITION, REVISED, ENLARGED, and IMPROVED, by / FREDERICK HERVEY, Esq; / Author of the NAVAL HISTORY of GREAT BRITAIN, in Five Volumes Octavo. / . . . M.DCC.LXXXVII [1787]. (Explorers Club, N.Y.)

A. The date of the earlier of these two issues should clearly be 1786, as the plates in Vol. I are dated as late as 31 Dec. 1785, and in Vol. II the dates run into 1786—and the title-page to Vol. II is dated 1786. All title-pages are printed in Red and Black.

Not counting 28 maps, there are 44 plates, 27 of them in Vol. I, all but 15 of which (11 in Vol. I) are signed by an engraver. Most of the plates (like the two by Blake) were 'Engraved for Herveys New System of Geography.'

1. The unsigned 'FRONTISPIECE VOL. I.' represents 'ASIA and AFRICA Characterised by a representation of their Various Inhabitants.' 'Published June 6ᵗʰ 1784; by G. Wilkie, Sᵗ Pauls Church Yard.' (Design size: 12·4 × 17·5 cm; outer frame: 18·1 × 25·4 cm.) For the evidence connecting this plate with Blake, see below.

2. At 'Vol. I. page 583.' are portraits of five Pacific Islanders, the first two of which, 'A MAN [and A WOMAN] of PRINCE WILLIAM'S SOUND.', are 'In Latitude 62° North.' In the centre is 'POULAHO KING of the FRIENDLY ISLANDS.' The last two, 'A MAN [and A WOMAN] of VAN DIEMEN'S LAND.' are 'In Latitude 43° South.' It is labelled 'N° 16.', 'Blake sc', and 'Publish'd April 16ᵗʰ 1785 by G. & T. Wilkie, Sᵗ Pauls Church Yard.' (Plate size: 17·4 × 20·4 cm.)

B. In the edition of 1787 there are 42 plates in the two volumes plus 39 maps. The only change in the Blake plates is in the dates, namely:
1. 'July 16ᵗʰ 1787'.
2. 'April 16ᵗʰ 1787'.

There is a certain amount of bibliographical confusion about the editions of the New System of Geography. This is compounded by the reference beside the proof of the first of these two plates in the Balmanno Collection of engravings after Stothard in the British Museum Print Room: 'The four quarters of the World. Frontispiece to a system of Geography. 1779', 'Stothard delᵗ', 'Blake sc'.² This is the only evidence known to me of the connection of either Stothard or Blake with the design, but the style is not alien to either man. The anonymous annotator got both title and date wrong, apparently, but he was followed by (or perhaps he followed?) Gilchrist, [1942] pp. 27–8, where Blake is said to have produced 'a well engraved frontispiece after Stothard . . . (The Four quarters of the World), to A System of Geography (1779)'.

¹ The title-page of Vol. II of A is like that of B except for the date.
² See the reproduction in Blake Newsletter, v (1972), 241.

No 1779 edition of Fenning and Collyer's book is known, and it is suspicious that Gilchrist did not mention the plate which Blake in fact signed. It is possible, perhaps, that 1779 refers to the date at which the drawing or the engraving was made. I accept the ascription of the frontispiece to Blake with some hesitation.

The first edition of Fenning and Collyer's *New System* was apparently the volumes of 1764–5 (copies in John Rylands Library, Harvard, LC), which naturally have no Blake plates. My only record of a second edition is in Watt (no. 533) who dates it 1771. The 'Third Edition' was dated 1770 (National Library of Scotland—see below) and 1771 (Princeton), and 'The Fourth Edition' was dated 1772–3 (William L. Clements Library of the University of Michigan) and 1773 (Bibliothèque Nationale, Paris), and they were originally issued without Blake's plates as well.

In the earlier editions the Frontispiece to Volume I represents 'The Goddess Vesta presenting to the Figure of Geography the Graphical Description of the World, & instructing Her in that Science', 'Hall Sculpsit.'

Frederick Hervey's name does not appear in any of the first four editions, but he was probably commissioned by Johnson (who sold the book from 1770 on) to bring up to date such a profitable title. Probably the first edition with which he was associated was that of 1785, for the preface to that work is dated December 1784, while the previous preface by Collyer had been dated September 1st 1770 (in the 1770 edition). The previous editions had made some claim to be 'enriched with the latest Discoveries' (1770), and clearly one of the first duties of an editor was to incorporate the latest geographical knowledge. This was accomplished by the addition of an 'Appendix to Volume the First' in which, as promised in the 1785 title-page, there was given 'a concise though comprehensive account of the six voyages round the world, which have been performed in the course of the last twenty years'. This is continuously paginated with the rest of the work (beginning at p. 521), and can be confidently dated about 1785, for the death of Captain King at 'the latter end of the year 1784' is mentioned (p. 615 n.).

Clearly this appendix was a valuable addendum for owners of earlier editions of the work, and it seems to have been sold separately, for it is found in the following: *A New System of Geography*: or, A General Description of the World. Containing A Particular and Circumstantial Account of all the Countries, Kingdoms, and States of Europe, Asia, Africa, and America. Their Situation, Climate, Mountains, Seas, Rivers, Lakes, &c. The Religion, Manners, Customs, Manufactures, Trade, and Buildings of the Inhabitants. With The Birds, Beasts, Reptiles, Insects, the various Vegetables, and Minerals, found in different Regions. Embellished with A New and Accurate Set of Maps, by the best Geographers; And Great Variety of Copper-Plates, containing Perspective Views of the Principal Cities, Structures, Ruins, &c. The Third Edition. [2 vols.] London: Printed for J. Payne, and sold by J. Johnson, No. 72, in St. Paul's Church-Yard 1770. We can be confident that the appendix was a later addition and that the 1770 text and title-page were not simply reissued or reprinted in 1785 because (*a*) the directions to the binder mention nothing after p. 480;

(b) the appendix is on paper different from the rest of the text; and (c) the third edition would not have been issued fourteen years after the appearance of the fourth edition. We may therefore be sure that when copies of the *New System* dated before 1785 appear, with the appendix and Blake's plate at Vol. I, p. 583 (as in the National Library of Scotland copy), the appendix and its plates are late additions and were not issued at the same time that the rest of the volumes appeared. (I am deeply grateful to Mr. W. B. Jay for assistance in describing the anomalous 1770 copy.)

FLAXMAN, John

456. A. COMPOSITIONS FROM THE / WORKS DAYS AND THEOGONY OF HESIOD. / [Design] / DESIGNED BY JOHN FLAX-MAN, R.A. P.S. / ENGRAVED BY WILLIAM BLAKE. / = / THERE, LET ME BOAST THAT VICTOR IN THE LAY / I BORE A TRIPOD EAR'D, MY PRIZE AWAY / Works—Elton's Hesiod. / *Published by Long-man, Hurst, Rees, Orme & Brown, London, Jan. 1, 1817.* (Bibliothèque Nationale [Paris], BM, BMPR, Bodley, Boston Museum, California [Los Angeles], Chicago, Chicago Art Institute, Clarke Library [Los Angeles], Columbia, Connecticut College for Women, Edinburgh, GEB [3], Harvard, Hunting-ton, Illinois, LC, Liverpool Public, London Library, McGill, Metropolitan [N.Y.] [3], Michigan, National Library of Ireland, NYP, Philadelphia Museum, Princeton [2], Queens, Royal Academy [2], Syracuse, Toronto, Trinity College [Cambridge] [2], Trinity College [Hartford, Conn.], V&A, Westminster Public, Western Ontario, Yale)

B. COMPOSITIONS FROM THE / WORKS AND DAYS, AND THEOGONY / OF / HESIOD / DESIGNED BY JOHN FLAXMAN, R.A., SCULPTOR. / ENGRAVED BY WILLIAM BLAKE. / [Bell emblem] / LONDON: / BELL AND DALDY, YORK STREET, / COVENT GARDEN. / 1870.

C. COMPOSITIONS / FROM THE / 'WORKS AND DAYS' AND 'THEOGONY' / OF / HESIOD. / DESIGNED BY JOHN FLAXMAN ... / ENGRAVED BY WILLIAM BLAKE. / LONDON / . . . 1881.

A. The Hesiod project may have originated in Rome in 1792, when Flaxman began his great series for *The Iliad* (engraved 1793), *The Odyssey* (engraved 1793), Dante (engraved 1793), Aeschylus (engraved 1795), and Bunyan (not engraved), for a leaf of Flaxman sketches signed 'J Flaxman 1792' (in the collection of Mr. Christopher Powney) has on the verso a list of sub-jects for designs including both Homer ('Telephus healed by Achilles 101') and Hesiod ('308 Hesiod Cupid delivered to the cow herd').

According to the contract with his publishers dated 24 Feb. 1816, 'Mr Flaxman agrees to furnish a series of Drawings to illustrate Hesiod and Messrs Longman & Co agrees to be at the expense of engraving the same.' The profits were to be divided equally between Flaxman and Longman & Co. (BM Add. MSS 39791, f. 21.)

Flaxman's 38 bound designs (including 2 title-pages) watermarked 1809 and 1813 were in Dec. 1970 in the possession of the dealer H. D. Lyon; a

further 24 in Grey wash were bound with other Flaxman designs in the
Metropolitan Museum; sketches for pl. 2, 4–5, 7, 9–10, 12–14, 16–26, 28,
30–1, 33–5 are in the British Museum Print Room; and others are noted
below.

Longmans preserve a record of the engraving costs in a volume of Miscellaneous Publication Expenses, ff. 269ʳ–268ᵛ (sic):

		Blake's Hesiod	[£	s	d]
		[Paid to Blake for each of the] Plates	5.	5.	0
1814		10–10–0——— 17/10			
Sep.	22	To Mʳ Blake for 2 plates & 2 Coppers	11	7	10
	24	,, Rylance [for] Reading MS—	—	10	6
Oct	7	,, Mʳ B for plates 10–10–— Coppers 17/6	11	7	6
	27	,, Mʳ B for Dᵒ — 10–10–— Copper 5/4	10	15	4
Nov.	15	,, Dᵒ ——— for 2 Dᵒ — 10–10–— copper 25/10	11	15	10
Decʳ	3	,, Dᵒ ——— 2 Dᵒ — 10–10–— & dᵒ 16/7½	11	6	7½
	30	,, Dᵒ ——— 2 Dᵒ — 10–10–— & 2 Coppʳ 16/6	11	6	6
[1815]					
Feb	10	,, Dᵒ ——— 3 Dᵒ ———————————	15	15	
		,, Dᵒ ——— for 4 Coppers ———————	1	14	4½
Mar	11	,, Dᵒ ——— for 2 plates ———————	10	17	6
June	15	,, dᵒ ——— for 1 Plate & Copper———	5	13	6
Dec.	7	,, Dᵒ ——— for 2 plates ———————	10	10	
		,, Dᵒ ——— Coppers———————		17	6
1816					
Jan'y	4	,, Dᵒ ——— for a plate ———————	5	13	6
Apr.	10	,, Dᵒ ——— for plates & Coppers ———	11	3	—
	18	,, Dᵒ ——— for 1 plate & Copper ———	5	11	6
May	17	,, Dᵒ ——— for 2 plates & Coppers ———	11	4	
June	21	,, Jeffreys Writing to 14 plates @ 7/. ———	4	18	—
		,, Cox & B[arnett]—proof 14 plates ———		7	—
	29	Mʳ Blake for 2 plates & Coppers ———	10	18	6
Augᵗ	26	,, do——— do ———	11	1	6
Oct.	18	—— dᵒ——— 2 pl & co ———	11	3	—
		[Carry] to opposite page	185	18	
1816		Blake's Hesiod			
		From opposite page	185	18	
		10–10–— 12/6			
Decʳ	10	To Mʳ B—— For 2 plates & 2 Coppers	11	2	6
		,, Jeffreys writing to 20 plates ———	7	—	
1817		altering writing of 6 plates	1	1	—
Jan	23	Mʳ B for 3 plates £15..15..0			
		3 Coppers ,, 18 ,,	16	13	,,
		,, Cox & B— proofs 6/. Dec 7— 3/. Dec 28		9	—
	28	,, Jeffreys altering 5 plates ———		5	—
Feb	10	,, do writing to pl. 1. 12. 37 ———	1	1	—
	21	,, do label ———		10	6
Jan	11	,, C & B 31 proofs 15/6——— feb 15 ——— 4 proofs	2/ 17	6	
			224	17	6

In the Bodleian Library are proofs before letters of the 37 plates, watermarked 1811 (pl. 7, 11), 1813 (pl. 21), 1815 (pl. 16), and 1816 (pl. 1, 17,
32, 36); some are called 'Blake's Hesiod' (pl. 2, 7, 11, 16, 22, 29, 37), and

some labelled 'Flaxman's Hesiod' or 'Flaxman' (pl. 18, 34–5). Many are dated in MS, and these dates correspond to the days on which Blake was paid for his engravings by Longman & Co., as follows: 15 Nov. (pl. 7), 13 Dec. (pl. 2), 30 Dec. 1814 (pl. 22, 26), 11 March (pl. 14, 37), 15 June 1815 (pl. 39), 5 Jan. (pl. 18), 10 April (pl. 34–5), 18 April (pl. 13), 17 May (pl. 15, 30), 29 June (pl. 16, 33), 27 Aug. (pl. 28, 32), and 18 Oct. 1816 (pl. 17, 31). Apparently it was at first hoped that the work could be published earlier, for pl. 2 is inscribed in MS: 'London, Published by Longman, Hurst, Rees, Orme & Brown Paternoster Row June 1816', but when June came eleven plates were not yet finished. The '14 plates' to which Jeffreys added writing on 21 June 1816 were probably the fourteen dated 1 Nov. 1816 (pl. 3–11, 22–3, 25–7). At that time Jeffreys had in hand, but did not add the writing to, pl. 2, 13–15, 18, 29–30, 34–5, 37, and two others. The Cox & Barnett proofs were clearly pulled in order to read the new writing added to the plates by Jeffreys. (Blake presumably pulled the Bodley proofs on his own press.)

The Longmans accounts summarize the publication expenses as follows (Impression Book No. 6, f. 70):

1817
Feb

Flaxmans Hesiod (200)			
Engraving 37 plates @ 5 guineas, Blake—	194	5	—
copper for do —— do	13	13	—
Writing to 37 plates @ 7/. Jeffreys	12	19	—
alterations —	1	6	—
Printing 200 sets @ 6/. Cox & B	22	4	—
proofs —	2	—	—
7½ reams plate medium 80/.	30	—	—
Rylance reading MS	—	10	6
Boarding 200 @ 2/9	26	8	—
Advertising	30	—	—
	333	5	6
Engraving label		10	6
Paper & print of 200 do		12	—
	334	8	—

None of the 37 stippled plates is signed, all have some variant of 'Elton's Hesiod—Works', a number, a quotation at the bottom right, and an imprint similar to the one on the title-page; pl. 3–11, 22–3, 25–7 are dated 1 Nov. 1816, and pl. 1–2, 12–21, 24, and 28–37 are dated 1 Jan. 1817.

1. The first page is the title-page (plate-size: 28·0 × 21·7 cm).
2. 'HESIOD ADMONISHING PERSES.' (35·3 × 25·3 cm.) (Mr. Christopher Powney has a drawing for it.)
3. 'PANDORA GIFTED.' (27·9 × 25·2 cm.) (Mr. Christopher Powney has two drawings for it.)
4. 'PANDORA ATTIRED.' (35·4 × 25·1 cm.)
5. 'PANDORA SHEWN TO THE GODS.' (35·4 × 25·1 cm.)

6. 'PANDORA BROUGHT TO EARTH.' (26·6 × 21·6 cm.)
7. 'PANDORA BROUGHT TO EPIMETHEUS.' (35·5 × 25·2 cm.) (Mr. Christopher Powney has two drawings for it.)
8. 'PANDORA, OPENING THE VASE.' (35·6 × 25·3 cm.) (A sketch is in the Fogg.)
9. 'GOLDEN AGE.' (27·9 × 20·2 cm.) (A proof is in the BMPR.)
10. 'GOOD DÆMONS.' (35·3 × 25·0 cm.)
11. 'SILVER AGE.' (27·9 × 20·2 cm.)
12. 'BRAZEN AGE.' (27·6 × 21·5 cm.) (A sketch is in the Huntington, and a proof before letters is in the Morgan.)
13. 'MODESTY AND JUSTICE RETURNING TO HEAVEN.' (22·6 × 27·9 cm.) (A proof before letters is in the BMPR.)
14. 'IRON AGE.' (38·0 × 25·8 cm.)
15. 'THE EVIL RACE.' 'THEY THRUST PALE JUSTICE FROM THEIR HAUGHTY GATES.' (28·0 × 22·6 cm.)
16. 'THE EVIL RACE.' 'THE GOD SENDS DOWN HIS ANGRY PLAGUES . . . .' (28·0 × 20·2 cm.) (Possibly related drawings are in the Huntington and University College, London [2].)
17. 'THE GOOD RACE' (34·0 × 22·7 cm.) (Mr. Christopher Powney has a drawing for it.)
18. 'PLEIADES.' 'WHEN, ATLAS BORN, THE PLEIAD STARS ARISE' (35·6 × 25·2 cm). (A sketch is in Princeton.)
19. 'PLEIADES.' '. . . WHEN THEY SINK . . . TIS TIME TO PLOUGH' (35·5 × 25·4 cm).
20. 'THE HAPPY MAN.' (27·7 × 21·5 cm.) (In some copies [BM, GEB, RA], the plate is misnumbered 37; presumably this is one of the plates Jeffreys was paid for 'altering' to '20', as in BMPR, Bodley, GEB, RA.)
21. 'THEOGONY' (35·4 × 25·0 cm).
22. 'HESIOD AND THE MUSES.' (35·6 × 25·3 cm.) (A sketch is in the Huntington, and another is in Princeton.)
23. 'JUPITER AND THE MUSES.' (35·5 × 25·2 cm.)
24. 'NIGHT LOVE EREBUS CHAOS' (18·3 × 23·5 cm).
25. 'VENUS.' 'THE WAFTING WAVES FIRST BORE HER . . .' (35·2 × 20·8 cm). (A proof before letters is in the Morgan.)
26. 'VENUS.' 'HER APHRODITE GODS AND MORTALS NAME.' (35·3 × 21·0 cm.) (A proof is in the BMPR.)
27. 'VENUS.' 'HER HONORS THESE . . . .' (35·6 × 25·2 cm.)
28. 'SEA DIVINITIES.' (35·6 × 15·2 cm.)
29. 'TYPHAON ECHIDNA GERYON.' (35·5 × 25·2 cm.) (A sketch is in the Fogg.)
30. 'ASTRÆUS AND AURORA.' (22·6 × 28·0 cm.)
31. 'SATURN AND HIS CHILDREN.' (21·6 × 15·2 cm.)
32. 'INFANT JUPITER.' (17·0 × 18·3 cm.) (Mr. Christopher Powney has a draft for it.)
33. 'THE BRETHREN OF SATURN DELIVERED.' (23·4 × 18·2 cm.)
34. 'GODS AND TITANS.' (22·8 × 25·4 cm.) (A proof before letters is in the BMPR.)

35. 'GIANTS AND TITANS.' (22·5×27·7 cm.)
36. 'FURIES   CERBERUS   PLUTO RROSERPINE   HARPIES
/ DEATH' (33·9×22·8 cm). (A proof before letters is in the Morgan.
The pencil inscription on the Bodley proof has the same orthographic
irregularity in 'RROSERPINE'.)
37. 'IRIS.' (20·8×25·3 cm.)

There is a paper label on the cover, and an engraved half-title, both
made from the same copperplate, which read: 'THE / THEOGONY
WORKS & DAYS & THE / DAYS OF HESIOD / ENGRAVED FROM
THE COMPOSITIONS / OF IOIIN FLAXMAN R·A· SCVLPTOR. /
LONDON.' There may be some connection between the mistaken repetition of 'Days' in the title and the misnumbering of pl. 20; there is no
separate work called 'The Days', and the *Works* and *Theogony* are in the
wrong order here.

The publishers apparently sent out an announcement of publication
(similarly inaccurate) which appeared in the *Edinburgh Review* (XXVIII
[March 1817], 261) and the *New Monthly Magazine* (VII [1 April 1817], 246):
'Compositions in Outline from Hesiod's Theogony, Works [Weeks *in ER*]
and Days, and the Days. Engraved by J. Blake, from Designs by John
Flaxman, R.A. fol. 2l. 12s. 6d.' (After 'R.A.', the *ER* has 'Printed to corre-
spond with the Outlines from Homer, &c.') The repeated mistake of 'J.'
Blake presumably originated with the publisher.

The 200 copies printed sold slowly, and no reviews are known. In June
1838 there were still 18 copies left, and these were divided equally between
Longmans and Flaxman's executrix, his sister-in-law Maria Denman.
According to the Longmans records (Divide Ledger III, f. 103),

1838
March 7   To Coppers & Copyright [*of Flaxman's Hesiod*]
           Sold by Miss M. Denman to H. G. Bohn—for   50   0   0

Bohn clearly reprinted the work, for he offered reduced-price copies in
his 1841 catalogue (no. 554).

B. Bell clearly acquired the plates themselves and may have reprinted
them repeatedly without a new title-page. Certainly the unwatermarked
paper on which many copies are printed looks suspiciously as if it were made
in the late nineteenth century. Bell & Daldy apparently sold the plates for
copper in a fit of patriotism in the First World War (R. Todd, 'Blake's
Dante Plates', *TLS*, 29 Aug. 1968, p. 928).

C. Bell's 1881 edition consists of lithographs reduced to *c.* 21 × 13 cm.

457. A. THE / ILIAD OF HOMER / ENGRAVED FROM THE COM-
POSITIONS / OF IOHN FLAXMAN R·A· SCVLPTOR, / LONDON. /
[Vignette] / LONDON: Printed for LONGMAN, HURST, REES, AND
ORME, Paternoster Row, R. H. EVANS, Pall Mall, W. MILLER, Albe-
marle Street, & I & A. ARCH, Cornhill, March 1. 1805. (BM, BMPR,
Bodley, California [Los Angeles], Chicago Art Institute, Clarke [Los
Angeles], Columbia, Dalhousie, GEB [4], Huntington, Illinois, LC, Liverpool

Public, Metropolitan [N.Y.], Michigan, Montreal Art Gallery, National Library of Ireland, National Library of Scotland, Newberry, Philadelphia Museum, Princeton, Royal Academy, John Rylands Library, Soane Museum, Syracuse, Toronto, Trinity College [Cambridge] [2], Trinity College [Hartford, Conn.], V&A, Western Ontario, Westminster Public)

B. COMPOSITIONS FROM / THE ILIAD OF HOMER, / DESIGNED BY / JOHN FLAXMAN, R.A., SCULPTOR. / ENGRAVED AT ROME BY THOMAS PIROLI. / [Bell emblem] / LONDON: / BELL AND DALDY, YORK STREET, / COVENT GARDEN. / 1870.

C. FLAXMAN'S CLASSICAL OUTLINES. / NOTES ON THEIR LEADING CHARACTERISTICS, / WITH A BRIEF MEMOIR OF THE ARTIST / BY / JOHN C. L. SPARKES, / . . . LONDON. / . . . MDCCCLXXIX [1879].

D. COMPOSITIONS / OF / JOHN FLAXMAN, R.A. / SCULPTOR. / BEING DESIGNS IN ILLUSTRATION OF THE ILIAD OF HOMER. / LONDON: / GEORGE BELL AND SONS . . . / 1880.

E. *The Iliad of Homer.* Engraved from the Compositions of Iohn Flaxman R.A. Scvlptor, London. London [*c.* 1890].

In 1793 in Rome, Flaxman made designs for the *Iliad* (now in University College), *Odyssey*, and Aeschylus for Mr. Hare-Naylor, which were engraved by Piroli. On 12 March 1803 Longman bought 'Flaxmans Homer's Iliad Whole with Plates [*from*] Mr Hare Naylor' for £120 (Longman Copy Register Vol. I), and in Longman's *Annual Review*, I (1803), II (1804) was announced 'New editions [*of these works*] with additional Plates'. Five plates (pl. 1–2, 5, 14, 37) were added to the *Iliad*, the first three engraved by Blake and the last two by Parker. The *Iliad* was published in April 1805 at £2. 2s. for the whole, and 'For the accommodation of those who purchased the former Edition of the Iliad, the additional Plates for that work will be sold separately. Price 10s. 6d.' (*Edinburgh Review*, VI [July 1805]).

The production records are preserved by Longman, Green & Co. (Impression Books No. 3, ff. 21, 160, and No. 4, f. 52):

Flaxman's Iliad	April &c.—1805			
Engraving 5 New Plates [*at* £5. 5s. @]		26	5	,,
Writing Engraver		19	12	6
5 New Drawings		15	15	—
Printing 280 sets 40 plates [*by Gordon at 6s. per 100*]		33	12	—
Labels		,,	10	,,
Paper 11 Rms [*Medium Plate at*] 88/- [@]		48	8	—
Binding		30	5	—
		174	7	6
(35 plates Cost £120)				
1806	100 Sets 4 Rms [*at* £4. 5s. *per ream*]	17	0	0
June	Working	12	3	6
	Binding	10	16	—
		39	19	0

50 printed before cost £10. 10 0
5 New plates

Printing	50 Setts [*of five each*] ————————————	,,	15	,,
Paper	¼ Rm ————————————————	1	2	,,
	doing up ———————————————	[*erased*]		
	Advertising ———————————	27	0	0
	Dº farther ——— /21/ 23. 16. 7½			

Flaxmans Iliad   June 1808

	Working 50 Setts ————————————	6	0	0
	————— Titles —————————	3 —		

1808   Flaxmans Iliad
Novʳ   Working 50 Setts [*printed by*] Cox & Barnett &

Cover [*i.e., label*], 2/6 ———————	6	2	6
Paper ffor do —— L & D [*2 reams at £5 @*] ——	10 — —		

Nov. 09   Working 50 & Titles ————————   6   3 —
Paper [*for June & Nov. printings*] —————   20   7   3
Sewing   [*blank*]

To summarize the Longman records (Copy Register Vols. II, III, IV, Impression Book V, ff. 55, 140, 183, VII, f. 179, IX, f. 4), Flaxman's *Iliad* was printed as follows:

Date	Number of copies
April 1805	280
June 1806	100
June & Nov. 1808	100
Nov. 1809	50
Jan. 1810	50
19 Jan. 1813	50 'on thin paper'
20 July 1814	50
25 March 1815	50
July 1822	50
Jan. 1829	50
1805–32	830

There are, then, at least ten printings 1805–29, and evidently others later, with nothing to distinguish them from one another on the title-page. The watermark is little help, for some (V&A) are watermarked 1805 and many (RA, Soane, GEB) are unwatermarked.

The *Iliad* was 'Sold [*to*] Mʳ [*William*] Sotheby [*for*] £100 Decʳ 3 1832' (Copy Register IV), who published his four-volume translation of the *Iliad* and *Odyssey* in 1834 with Flaxman's designs engraved in reduced size by H. Moses.

The plates, like those for Hesiod, evidently passed into the hands of H. G. Bohn, who offered reduced-priced copies in his 1841 catalogue.

All the 1793 plates except the title-page have Piroli's name on them, though in 1793 Piroli's name had appeared only on the title-page. Blake's plates are signed '*Blake sculp.*' but not dated.

1. '*Plate* 1.' 'HOMER INVOKING THE MUSE.' 'ACHILLES WRATH TO GREECE THE DIREFUL SPRING, / OF WOES UNNUMBERD

HEAVENLY GODDESS SING! / Popes Homers Iliad.' (Plate-mark: 35·3×25·2 cm.) (Sketches are in Harvard and the Fogg, and a proof before letters is in the BMPR.)

2. '*Plate* 2.' 'MINERVA REPRESSING THE FURY OF ACHILLES.' 'WHILE HALF UNSHEATH'D APPEAR'D THE GLITTERING BLADE, / MINERVA SWIFT DESCENDED FROM ABOVE. / Pope's Homers Iliad B. I Line 260.' (35·2×25·1 cm.) (Sketches are in the Chicago Art Institute, the Huntington [4], the Royal Academy, the collection of Mr. Christopher Powney, and proofs before letters are in the Morgan and the BMPR.)

3. '*Plate* 5.' 'THETIS ENTREATING JUPITER TO HONOR ACHILLES.' 'THUS THETIS SPOKE BUT JOVE IN SILENCE HELD / THE SACRED COUNCILS OF HIS BREAST CONCEAL'D. / Pope's Homers Iliad B. I. Line 662.' (35·3×25·2 cm.) (Sketches are in the Huntington and the Royal Academy, and a proof is in the BMPR.)

B. The 1870 edition is part of a reprint of all Flaxman's Greek designs, with a title-page: THE CLASSICAL COMPOSITIONS / OF / JOHN FLAXMAN, R.A. / SCULPTOR, / COMPRISING / THE ILIAD AND ODYSSEY OF HOMER, AND THE TRAGEDIES OF AESCHYLUS, / ENGRAVED AT ROME BY PIROLI; / AND THE THEOGONY, AND WORKS AND DAYS OF HESIOD, / ENGRAVED BY WILLIAM BLAKE. / [Bell emblem] / LONDON: / BELL AND DALDY, YORK STREET, / COVENT GARDEN. / 1870. Bell evidently sold the plates for copper about 1915 (see Hesiod, no. 456).

C. The designs in the 1879 edition are reduced to *c.* 27×18 cm.

D. Those in the Bell 1880 edition are reduced to *c.* 20×12 cm.

E. The undated edition is also a much-reduced facsimile.

For information about the pre-1805 history of Flaxman's *Iliad* designs, see G. E. Bentley, Jr., *The Early Engravings of Flaxman's Classical Designs* (1964).

458. A LETTER / TO / *THE COMMITTEE* / FOR RAISING / THE NAVAL PILLAR, / OR / MONUMENT, / UNDER THE PATRONAGE OF HIS ROYAL HIGHNESS / *THE DUKE OF CLARENCE.* / — / BY JOHN FLAXMAN, *SCULPTOR.* / — / *LONDON:* / PRINTED FOR T. CADELL, JUN. AND W. DAVIES, IN THE STRAND; T. PAYNE, / MEWS-GATE; AND R. H. EVANS (SUCCESSOR TO MR. EDWARDS), / NO. 26, PALL-MALL; / BY G. WOODFALL, NO. 22, PATERNOSTER-ROW. / — / 1799. (Bodley, BM, BMPR, Harvard, Huntington, Liverpool Public, Newberry, Princeton, Royal Institute of British Architects, Soane Museum, V&A)

There are three plates, all undated, and only the first is signed ('Blake sculp'). However, Blake's responsibility for the two unsigned plates as well is demonstrated by his receipt (now in the Haverford College Library): 'Receivd Decr 14 1799 of Mr Flaxman the Sum of Eight pounds Eight shillings for Engraving Three Plates For the Statue of Britannia & Twelve Shillings & Eight pence for Copper Willm Blake'.

1. The 'Frontispiece' to the pamphlet represents 'BRITANNIA BY DIVINE PROVIDENCE TRIUMPHANT', '*A Colossal Statue 230 feet high; proposed to be erected on Greenwich hill*' (framing line: 15·0 × 18·9 cm).
2. 'Plate 2' illustrates six kinds of monuments: 'Obelisk', 'Column', 'Meta', 'Arch', 'Pharos', and 'Temple' (18·8 × 9·7 cm) at p. 6.
3. 'Plate 3' at p. 13 gives 'A View of Greenwich Hospital with the Statue of Britannia on the Hill' (15·1 × 18·8 cm).

Blake's three plates after Flaxman were sold at Flaxman's sale on 1 July 1828, lot 9170 (see no. 540). Four sketches for Britannia triumphant are in Princeton, a finished design in form and inscription very like Blake's engraving is in the V & A (reproduced and described by J. Physick, *Designs for English Sculpture* [1969], 165, 167), Flaxman's wax model was exhibited at the Royal Academy in 1801, lot 1037, and is now in the Soane Museum, and the design was incorporated in the monument for Lord North paid for in 1799 and executed in 1805 in Wroxton, Oxfordshire (see Physick, p. 41 n.), the model for which is in University College, London.

F USELI, John Henry

459. LECTURES / ON / PAINTING, / DELIVERED AT THE ROYAL ACADEMY / MARCH 1801, / By HENRY FUSELI, P.P. / WITH ADDITIONAL OBSERVATIONS AND NOTES. / [Vignette engraved by F. Legat] / LONDON: / PRINTED FOR J. JOHNSON, ST. PAUL'S CHURCH-YARD. / 1801. / — / Luke Hansard, Printer, near Lincoln's-Inn Fields. (BM, GEB, McGill, Michigan, Princeton, Westminster Public, West Sussex Record Office, Yale)

The only plate besides the title-page-vignette is:

1. On p. 151 is '*Ancore imparo.* / *M: Angelo Bonarroti.*' '*Blake: sc*' (plate size: 13·5 × 7·2 cm). (Fuseli's wash drawing reported by Keynes [1921] has not been traced, but his pen-and-ink sketch—reproduced in *Blake Newsletter*, V [1972], 175—and a proof without letters except for signature are in the collection of Mr. Robert N. Essick.)

The rest of Fuseli's lectures were published in 1820, with one plate of Fuseli by R. W. Sievert.

G AY, John

460. A. FABLES / By / *JOHN GAY,* / With a Life of the Author / AND / *embellished with Seventy Plates.* / [Vignette] / Vol. I [II]. / — / LONDON / *PRINTED FOR JOHN STOCKDALE, PICCADILLY* / 1793. (BMPR, GEB, Iowa State, Princeton, Southampton, Syracuse, Toronto)

B. 1793 (i.e. 1811). (BM, Bodley, GEB, Princeton [2], Yale)

(Copies of unrecorded date: Berg [NYP], Buffalo, California [San Diego], Columbia, Connecticut College for Women [3], Emory, Harvard [5], Huntington, Illinois, McGill, Michigan, Morgan, Newberry, New York, Smith,

Spencer [NYP], Texas, Toronto Public, Trinity College [Hartford, Conn.],
Wellesley, West Sussex Record Office, Westminster Public)

A. *Engravings*: Gay's *Fables* were originally published at two different times,
Vol. I in 1727 with an elegant plate for each fable after W. Kent or J. Wootton, and Vol. II in 1738 with fine plates after H. Gravelot. These illustrations
were repeatedly reprinted and silently copied. The 1793 Stockdale edition
contained 71 plates (including the title-pages), 12 of them signed '*Blake*[:]
sc[:]', no. 1–2, 4, 6–7 (reversed) silently copied from Kent's designs, no. 3, 5,
8–9, all reversed, after Wootton, and no. 10–12, reversed, after Gravelot.
The design-sizes of Blake's plates are 9·4 × 7·7 cm, except for trifling variants
in width (9·8 on no. 3, 6; 9·6 on no. 8–9; 9·1 cm on no. 7) and height
(7·5 cm on no. 3–4). There are proofs of Blake's plates in the BMPR, and
six unfinished proofs were shown in the 1891 Boston exhibition.

Blake's plates were at Vol. I:

1. P. 1, for Fable i, 'The Shepherd and the Philosopher'.
2. P. 29, Fable vi, 'The Miser and Plutus'.
3. P. 59, Fable xiii, 'The Tame Stag' (Blake has reduced Wootton's men to
   children).
4. P. 73, Fable xvi, 'The Pin and the Needle'.
5. P. 99, Fable xxii, 'The Goat without a Beard'.
6. P. 109, Fable xxiv, 'The Butterfly and the Snail'.
7. P. 125, Fable xxviii, 'The Persian, the Sun, and the Cloud'.
8. P. 133, Fable xxx, 'The Setting-Dog and the Partridge'.
9. P. 181, Fable xli, 'The Owl and the Farmer'.
10. Vol. II, p. 1, Fable i, 'The Dog and the Fox'.
11. P. 105, Fable xii, 'Pan and Fortune'.
12. P. 145, Fable xvi, 'The Ravens, the Sexton, and the Earth-Worm'.

Publication: According to an advertisement on the wrappers of *The British
Critic* for Oct. 1793, the first edition was issued in two forms: (a) in royal
octavo, on superfine wove paper, at 12*s.*, and (b) in a neat octavo on wove
demy paper at 7*s.* 6*d.* None of the fables in 1793 (GEB) is on watermarked
paper, but some of the plates are watermarked 'W C & Co'.

In the 'List of Subscribers' at the end of Vol. II appears 'Blake Mr.', and
the likelihood that this is the poet is increased to near certainty by the fact
that six of the other seven engravers for this edition (Messrs. Audinet,
Granger, Lovegrove, Mazell, Skelton, and Wilson) also appear in this list
similarly shorn of their Christian names.

B. For the second edition [of 1811], all the same plates (including the title-
pages) were used at the same places, but the type was entirely reset, following A word for word, line for line, and page for page, but eschewing the
long ſ of A. B has no list of subscribers, is about an inch shorter than A,
and was printed by T. Bensley (there is no indication of a printer in A).
In the later edition, the plates are worn, the lights are lighter, and the darks
are by contrast darker.

There are four kinds of paper used in 1811 (GEB). The most common is watermarked 'J WHATMAN 1809', and this, with '2 BALSTON 1810' is found on the fables themselves. The plates are watermarked 'H SMITH 1810' and, very faintly, '1811'. Therefore the earliest possible date for B is 1811.

At the end of some copies of Gay's *Fables* (1793), Vol. II (GEB, BMPR) is an advertisement dated 2 Feb. 1793 for 'A Splendid Edition of Barlow's Aesop's Fables . . . [*which*] Speedily will be Published [*by Stockdale*] . . . embellished with ONE HUNDRED and FOURTEEN beautiful Copper Plates, from Barlow's Designs, and engraved by Hall, Mazell, Eastgate, Grainger, Wilson, Audinet, Medland, Skelton, Cromeck, Blake, Leney, Corner, Lovegrove, &c. &c.' The work referred to is *The Fables of Aesop* [tr. Samuel Croxall], With a Life of the Author: And Embellished with one Hundred & twelve Plates. [2 vols.] London Printed for John Stockdale, Piccadilly, 4th June 1793. There are 30 engravings and 4 unsigned plates; 21 of the engravers who signed plates are not mentioned in the advertisement, and 4 of the engravers listed there (Blake, Cromek, Hall, and Wilson) did not sign plates. (An advertisement for Gay's *Fables*, similar to the one above, was printed with the Aesop, but neither it nor the advertisements for Stockdale's Gay and Aesop printed with Hunter's *Journal* of July 1793 mention Blake.)

An edition of Gay's *Fables* 'Printed by Darton & Harvey, for F. & C. Rivington . . . & E. Newbery' (1793) (BM & GEB) contains two plates to a page which very closely copy (often reversed) those in the 1793 Stockdale edition; most notable in this respect is the strikingly Blakean shepherd imitated from Blake's first engraving.

[GOUGH, Richard]

461. SEPULCHRAL MONUMENTS, / IN / GREAT BRITAIN. / APPLIED TO ILLUSTRATE / THE HISTORY OF / FAMILIES, MANNERS, HABITS, AND ARTS, / AT THE / DIFFERENT PERIODS / FROM THE NORMAN CONQUEST TO THE SEVENTEENTH CENTURY. / WITH / INTRODUCTORY OBSERVATIONS. / [2 vols. bound in 5 Parts.] PART I. VOL. I. / CONTAINING THE FOUR FIRST CENTURIES. / La Sculpture peut aussie fournir les Monumens en quantité: *la plupart sur les* TOMBEAUX. / MONTFAUCON. / [vignette] / LONDON, / PRINTED BY J. NICHOLS, FOR THE AUTHOR; / AND SOLD BY T. PAYNE AND SON. / MDCCLXXXVI [1786].

[Vol. I, Part II, and Vol. II (which is called 'Part II. Containing the Fifteenth Century' on the title-page, but 'Vol. II' on the plates), Parts I, II, and III were all published in 1796 by T. Payne at the Mews-Gate; and G. G. and J. Robinson, Pater-Noster-Row.] (BM)

There are 276 plates in all, not counting very small, inset plates. Of the 76 in Vol. I (Parts I & II), the vast majority (64) were signed by James Basire, to whom Blake was apprenticed from 1772 to 1779. According to Blake's friend B. H. Malkin, Blake was sent as an apprentice to sketch

The monuments of Kings and Queens in Westminster Abbey . . . particularly that of King Henry the Third, the beautiful monument and figure of Queen Elinor, Queen Philippa, King Edward the Third, King Richard the Second and his Queen

... [*and*] Aymer de Valence's monument ... But I do not mean to enumerate all his drawings ... in Westminster Abbey ... [*and in*] other churches in and about London.
[B. H. Malkin, *A Father's Memoirs of his Child* (1806), xx–xxi—see *Blake Records* (1969), 422, 423.]

These drawings and engravings commissioned from Basire by Richard Gough are now in the Bodleian Library. They have been examined in particular by Sir Geoffrey Keynes, who reports (*Blake Studies* [1971], 17–18) that the drawings Malkin mentions[1] are all on the same J WHATMAN paper, three are unsigned, and the rest are signed 'Basire [*or* B] del [*or* d, D]', plus '1777' on two of them. In addition, there are drawings on the same paper, and apparently by the same hand, of Edmund Crouchback (Earl of Lancaster), John of Eltham, William of Windsor, the monument of the children of Edward III, and the effigy of Aveline wife of Edmund Crouchback, the last two of which were not engraved. All these drawings are presumably by Blake. (Of these drawings, Aveline, Queen Anne, and Richard II are reproduced in Keynes above, and Edward III in *Blake Records*.)

Malkin says nothing of who engraved the plates, but it seems likely that Blake engraved some of these, as well as others in the book which are unidentifiable.[2] All the plates after Blake's designs but pl. XXIII are signed with variants of '*Basire del & sc*'. They are:

PART I

1. '*Pl. XX. p. 57*', two views of the '*Monument of Henry III.—*' (Plate-size: 28·2 × 39·7 cm.)
2. '*Pl. XXII. p. 57.*' '*Portrait of Henry III. from his Monument.*' (28·7 × 39·7 cm.)
3. '*Pl. XXIII. p. 63.*' Two views of the '*Monument of Eleanor Queen of Edward I. 1290.*' '*Basire del et Sculp. 1783.*' (29·6 × 40·9 cm.) (The date 1783 must refer to the engraving rather than the drawing.)
4. '*Pl. XXIII*. p. 63*', '*Portrait of Queen Eleanor from her Monument.*' (28·9 × 40·2 cm.)
5. '*Pl. XXV. p. 68*', '*Monument of Edmund Crouchback, Earl of Lancaster. 1296.*' (28·9 × 43·8 cm.)

[1] There are two drawings each of the monuments of Eleanor, of Richard II and Anne, and of Edward III, but the monument of Philippa mentioned by Malkin is not included in the series reported by Keynes.
[2] Blake may have sketched other views of the same monuments which were later engraved as:

(a) '*Pl. XXVI. p. 68*', '*Edmund Crouchback*' (top view, with a vignette of a horse and rider). Signed, like the others, '*Basire del & sc*'. (28·3 × 44·9 cm.)
(b) '*Pl. XXX. p. 85.*' '*Aymer de Valence Earl of Pembroke.*' (Top view, with a vignette of a horse and rider.) (27·1 × 44·9 cm.)
(c) '*Pl. XXXII. p. 94 [i.e. 95]*', '*Figures on the North Side of Aymer de Valence Earl of Pembroke's Monument.*' And '*Figures at the Side of John of Eltham's Monument.*' (27·5 × 42·5 cm.)
(d) '*Pl. XXXIII. p. 95*', top view of '*John of Eltham.*' (25·7 × 40·9 cm.)

Blake's part in these plates must remain more dubious, however, partly because the sketches are on different paper and partly because at least one other engraved view of a monument he sketched (pl. XXI of the '*North view of the Tomb of Henry III*') is signed '*S. Carter del*'.

PART II

6. '*Pl. XXIX. p. 85.*' '*Monument of Aymer de Valence, Earl of Pembroke. 1308.*' (27·5 × 42·3 cm.)

7. '*Pl. XXXI. p. 94 [i.e. 95]*', profile '*Monument of John of Eltham, 1334.*' (Sideways: 26·7 × 42·6 cm.)

8. '*Pl. XXXIV. p. 96.*' Two views of '*William of Windsor and his Sister Blanche de la Tour 1340.—*' (Sideways: 29·3 × 44·4 cm.)

9. '*Pl. XLVIII, p. 123.*' '*Monument of Philippa Queen of Edward III. 1369.*' (29·1 × 41·2 cm.)

10. '*Pl. XLIX. p. 125.*' '*Portrait of Queen Philippa from her Monument.*' (28·7 × 40·8 cm.)

11. '*Pl. LIV [i.e. LV]. p. 139.*' '*Monument of Edward III. 1377*' (29·2 × 44·9 cm).

12. '*Pl. LV [i.e. LVI]. p. 139.*' '*Portrait of Edward III. from his Monument.*' (28·4 × 39·9 cm.)

13. '*Pl. LXI. p. 163.*' Profile '*Monument of Richard II & his Queen Anne 1395 and 1399*' (28·2 × 40·8 cm.)

14. '*Pl. LXII. p. 163 [i.e. 165].*' Top view of '*Figures of Richard II. & his Queen Anne.*' (28·7 × 42·2 cm.)

15. '*Pl. LXIII. p. 165.*' '*Portrait of Richard II. from his Monument.*' (28·5 × 40·4 cm.)

16. '*Pl. LXIV. p. 167*', '*Portrait of Anne Queen of Richard II. from her Monument.*' (28·5 × 40·4 cm.)

The Bodleian collection includes three to five proofs of each of the plates attributed here to Blake and hundreds of drawings for Gough's book. Assuming that Blake made extensive sketches for this work in Westminster Abbey (as Malkin says he did), these Bodleian materials for Gough may be one of the most extensive collections known of Blake's drawings—most of them unidentifiable.

GREGO, Joseph

462. MRS. Q— / AND / 'WINDSOR CASTLE' / *WITH A NOTE ON THE PLATES BY* JOSEPH GREGO / AND / MEMOIRS OF THE LIFE OF THE CELEBRATED / MRS. Q— / By EDWARD EGLANTINE, Esq. / London / KEGAN PAUL, TRENCH, TRÜBNER & CO., LIMITED / DRYDEN HOUSE, 43, GERRARD STREET, W. / 1906. (Texas)

The copperplate of

1. 'Mrs Q', i.e. Harriet Quentin, mistress of the Prince Regent, 'Drawn by Huet Villiers', 'Engraved by W. Blake', 'London, Published 1st June 1820 by I Barrow, Weston Place, St Pancras' (plate-size: 21·5 × 27·5 cm) survived until at least the early twentieth century and was reprinted in this 27-page work, along with its companion 'Windsor Castle' engraved by G. Maile after J. Barrow. The Grego book was Printed by Gilbert and Rivington Ltd., but Wm Clowes & Sons Ltd. (of Dorland House, 14 & 16 Lower Regent Street, London) which took over Gilbert & Rivington in 1907, report that the firm's records were destroyed by German bombs in 1941, and cannot trace the copperplate.

HAMILTON, G.

463. THE / ENGLISH SCHOOL / A SERIES OF / THE MOST AP-
PROVED PRODUCTIONS / IN / PAINTING AND SCULPTURE; /
Executed by British Artists / FROM THE DAYS OF HOGARTH TO THE
PRESENT TIME. / SELECTED, ARRANGED, AND ACCOMPANIED
WITH DESCRIPTIVE AND / EXPLANATORY NOTICES IN
ENGLISH AND FRENCH. / *By G. Hamilton.* / *Engraved in Outline upon*
Steel. / — / *Vol.* *1[-4].* / — / LONDON. / BOSSANGE, BARTHÉS AND
LOWELL, / 14, GREAT MARLBOROUGH STREET. / — / [Vol. I–II:]
1831 [Vol. III–IV:] 1832. (Princeton)

A duplicate title-page reads: ÉCOLE / ANGLAISE, / RECEUIL / DE
TABLEAUX, STATUES ET BAS-RELIEFS / *des plus célèbres Artistes*
anglais, / DEPUIS LE TEMPS D'HOGARTH JUSQU'A NOS JOURS, /
Gravé à l'eau-forte sur acier; / ACCOMPAGNÉ / DE NOTICES DESCRIP-
TIVES ET HISTORIQUES, / EN FRANCAIS ET EN ANGLAIS, / *Par*
G. Hamilton, / *et publié sous sa direction.* / — / *Vol.* *1[-4].* / — / A PARIS. /
CHEZ M. HAMILTON, GRANDE RUE DES BATIGNOLLES, N° 50, /
PRÈS LA BARRIÈRE DE CLICHY; / ET CHEZ AUDOT, LIBRAIRE,
RUE DES MAÇONS-SORBONNE, N° 11. / — / 1831 [–1832].

There are minor variants in the title-pages; the Toronto copy of Vol. I
(only) was published by 'CHARLES TILT, 86, FLEET STREET', and
the Princeton Vol. II is simply 'TO BE HAD AT THE PRINCIPAL
BOOKSELLERS / AND PRINTSHOPS'; in the French Vols. II–IV
Audot's address is altered to 'RUE DU PAON, N°. 8' and in Vols. III–IV
is added '/ ET A LA LIBRAIRE ÉTRANGÈRE, RUE NEUVE-
S.-AUGUSTIN, N°. 55'. An advertisement in Vol. I explains that the
publishers tried to issue one of the 'numbers every fortnight', apparently
beginning in July 1830, and 'to include specimens of every eminent artist
that has appeared within the last hundred years'. There are 6 plates to a
number, 12 numbers to a volume, 48 numbers and 288 plates in all. If the
plates and parts appeared on the schedule described in the advertisement,
the numbers in Vol. I appeared July 1830–10 March 1831; in Vol. II, 24
March–18 Aug. 1831; in Vol. III, 7 Sept. 1831–9 Feb. 1832; in Vol. IV,
23 Feb.–27 July 1832.

Each plate is followed by an English description on one side of the leaf
and a French one on the other. Both Blake's plates were designed by '*Blake*'
and engraved by '*Normand fils.*' (who engraved all the plates).

1. At Vol. III, no. 181, issued with number 31 on 30 Nov. 1831, represents
   'DEATH'S DOOR. / LA PORTE DU TOMBEAU.' (Engraved surface:
   8·6 × 14·4 cm.) The description says that Blake's 'productions, though
   often disfigured by conceit and extravagance, and sometimes unintel-
   ligible, occasionally present much grace'.
2. At Vol. IV, no. 271, issued with number 46 on 29 June 1832, represents
   'DEATH OF THE STRONG WICKED MAN. / MORT D'UN
   RÉPROUVÉ.' (8·6 × 11·3 cm.) The description says the design is 'fearful
   and extravagant'.

HARTLEY, David

464. A. OBSERVATIONS / ON / MAN, / HIS FRAME, HIS DUTY, AND HIS EXPECTATIONS. / IN TWO PARTS. / PART. I. / CONTAINING OBSERVATIONS ON THE / *FRAME OF THE HUMAN BODY AND MIND,* / AND ON THEIR / *MUTUAL CONNEXIONS AND IN-FLUENCES.* / PART. II. / CONTAINING OBSERVATIONS ON THE / *DUTY AND EXPECTATIONS OF MANKIND.* / By DAVID HARTLEY, M.A. / Reprinted from the Author's Edition in 1749. / TO WHICH ARE NOW ADDED, / NOTES AND ADDITIONS / TO THE SECOND PART; / Translated from the German of The Rev. / HERMAN ANDREW PISTORIUS, / RECTOR OF POSERITZ / IN THE ISLAND OF AGEN. / ALSO / A SKETCH OF THE LIFE AND CHARACTER [by his son, David Hartley], / AND A / *HEAD OF THE AUTHOR.* / = / LONDON: / PRINTED FOR J. JOHNSON, Nº. 72, ST. PAUL'S CHURCH-YARD. / — / MDCCXCI [1791]. (BM, LC, West Sussex Record Office)

B. OBSERVATIONS / ON / MAN, / HIS FRAME, HIS DUTY, / AND HIS / EXPECTATIONS. / *IN TWO PARTS.* / PART THE FIRST: / CONTAINING / OBSERVATIONS ON THE FRAME OF THE / *HUMAN BODY AND MIND,* / AND ON THEIR / MUTUAL CON-NEXIONS AND INFLUENCES. [*And in the second volume*: PART THE SECOND: / CONTAINING OBSERVATIONS ON THE / DUTY AND EXPECTATIONS OF / *MANKIND.*] / = / *LONDON:* / FIRST PRINTED IN MDCCXLIX. / Reprinted by J. JOHNSON, ST. PAUL'S CHURCH-YARD. / MDCCXCI [1791]. (Bodley, GEB)

In *The St. James's Chronicle* for 5–7 April 1791 (a single issue) (Yale) is an announcement that Hartley's *Observations on Man* 'With a Head of the Author, engraved by Mr. BLAKE' '*will be published*' '*On Wednesday, the 13th instant*'. Johnson entered the supplementary matter published with his edition of Hartley's *Observations* (i.e. Vol. III of B) in the Stationers' Register on 19 April 1791.

In the 'Bookseller's Advertisement' (where Blake is mentioned), the work is described as consisting of three volumes, the third being Herman Andrew Pistorius, *Notes and Additions to Dr. Hartley's Observations on Man*, Translated, To which is Prefixed a Sketch of the Life and Character of Dr. Hartley, London, 1791. The only difference in the two editions appears to be in the binding and title-pages. According to the long review by QQ in Joseph Johnson's *Analytical Review*, April 1791, pp. 361–76, B in three volumes sold for '18s. in boards', while A is described as '*The same printed on Royal Quarto Paper, with a Head of the Author, engraved by Blake.* Pages 756. Price 1l. 7s. in boards. ib. [The Head is sold alone, pr. 2s. 6d.]' (The separate head does not appear in Keynes's *Separate Plates* [1956] no. 669.)

1. The only engraving on both editions is the frontispiece, representing '*David Hartley, M.A. From a Painting by Shackelton*', '*Blake sc:*', '*Published by J. Johnson, in S!. Paul's Church-Yard, March 1.ˢᵗ 1791.*' (Oval size: 11·2 × 15·0 cm.) (A proof before letters is in the BMPR, and others lacking Blake's name are in the Rosenwald Collection and Princeton.)

HAYLEY, William

465. BALLADS, / BY / *WILLIAM HAYLEY, ESQ.* / FOUNDED ON / ANECDOTES RELATING TO ANIMALS, / WITH / *PRINTS*, / DE-SIGNED AND ENGRAVED / By WILLIAM BLAKE. / = / Chichester: Printed by J. Seagrave; / FOR RICHARD PHILLIPS, BRIDGE-STREET, / BLACKFRIARS, LONDON. / — / 1805. (BM, BMPR, Bodley, Connecti-cut College for Women, Cornell, Fitzwilliam, GEB, Harvard [3], Liverpool Public, McGill, Morgan, National Library of Scotland, New York Univer-sity, Newberry, Princeton [2], St. John's Seminary [Camarillo, Calif.], Smith College, Southampton, Texas, Toronto, Trinity College [Hartford, Conn.], V&A, Wellesley College, West Sussex Record Office, Westminster Public)

All 5 plates have the imprint '*Pub.ᵈ* [or *Pub'd*] *June 18, 1805, by R Phillips N[°] 6 Bridge Street Black Friers.*' '*Blake inv & s[c]*'. Pl. 1–3 are new engravings of designs for the 1802 Ballads.

1. The frontispiece is '*The Dog*,' (plate-size: *c.* 9·0 × 14·6 cm; design size: 7·1 × 11·3 cm).
2. At p. 22 is '*The Eagle*,' (plate-size: *c.* 9·4 × 14·7 cm; design size: 7·0 × 10·7 cm).
3. P. 100, '*The Lion*' (plate-size: *c.* 9·0 × 14·5 cm; design size: 6·9 × 10·9 cm).
4. P. 123, '*The Hermits Dog*' (plate-size: *c.* 9·0 × 14·8 cm; design size: 7·5 × 10·7 cm).
5. P. 204, '*The Horse*' (plate-size: *c.* 9·0 × 14·8 cm; design size: 7·2 × 10·7 cm). (A proof before signature is in the collection of Mr. Raymond Lister. A tempera version on copper belongs to Mr. Paul Mellon.)

Blake composed an Advertisement for the 1805 *Ballads* in his letter of 25 March 1805, but it was not printed in the book. The work was described as 'in the press' in the *Monthly Magazine* for 1 April 1805 (p. 261), despite the dates on Blake's plates, and there were advertisements for the book at 6*s.* mentioning Blake's engravings in the *Monthly Magazine* (1 July 1805, p. 583), in W. Bent's *Monthly Literary Advertiser* (Aug. 1805, p. 26), and in an undated Phillips Short List (in the John Johnson Collection in Bodley). It was reviewed in *The Eclectic Review* (1805) (no. 1736), *The Monthly Magazine*, LXX (1805, Supplement [31 Jan. 1806], pp. 614–15), and in *The Poetical Register* (1807) (no. 840).

There is more than one issue, for one Princeton copy has a comma on the title-page after 'BLAKE', instead of the full stop, and the plates of '*The Eagle*' and '*The Dog*' are more extensively worked than in the other Princeton copy.

A copy of the 1805 *Ballads* in the collection of Mrs. Landon K. Thorne is inscribed to 'Mr. Weller, / With grateful Remembranc[e] / from / William Blake'. Another copy in the collection of the late Professor S. Foster Damon has plates coloured (in the opinion of the owner and of Sir Geoffrey Keynes) by Blake.

All five plates are reproduced in R. R. Easson & R. N. Essick, *William Blake: Book Illustrator* (see 1972, under Catalogues).

466. DESIGNS / TO / *A SERIES of BALLADS,* / WRITTEN / By WIL-LIAM HAYLEY, Esq. / And founded on / ANECDOTES RELATING TO ANIMALS, / *Drawn, Engraved, and Published,* / BY / WILLIAM BLAKE. / With the Ballads annexed, by the Author's Permission. / — / *Chichester:* / Printed by J. SEAGRAVE, and sold by him and P. HUMPHRY; and by R. H. EVANS, / Pall-Mall, London, for W. BLAKE, Felpham. / 1802. (All 4 Ballads: Huntington, Keynes [Fitzwilliam], LC, Princeton, Trinity College [Hartford, Conn.]; Ballad 1: Bodley, Westminster Public; Ballads 1–2: BMPR., GEB, Keynes; Ballad 2: Keynes; Ballads 1–3: National Library of Wales)

Hayley said the Ballads were written and 'printed for the emolument' and amusement of Blake (*Blake Records* [1969], 88, 92–3), and in his Preface he explained that the manuscript and drawings were first circulated privately and then printed and published monthly. Fifteen numbers were proposed, but only the first four appeared in June–Sept. 1802. They were sold largely through Hayley's friends (see *Blake Records,* 95–111, 114–18, 173), who generally found 'a flagrant deficiency of taste among my neighbours' in their reluctance to buy (110). Blake thought them 'likely to be Profitable' (30 Jan. 1803), but they were probably a clear loss. Hayley said that Blake eventually 'suspended their publication, that He might proceed, without any Interruption, in his plates for the Life of Cowper' (114), and the last number was in Sept. 1802. The project was revived with somewhat greater success in 1805, with the *Ballads* published by Phillips.

Each Ballad was issued separately in a blue paper cover. On the cover of the first was printed: A SERIES OF BALLADS. / = / *Number 1.* / = / The ELEPHANT. / = / BALLAD THE FIRST. / *Price 2s. 6d.* Thereafter, besides the changes in title and number, the price was dropped and replaced by: CHICHESTER: Printed by J. Seagrave, and sold by him and P. Humphry; and by R. H. Evans, Pall-Mall, London, for W. Blake, Felpham. 1802.

Blake is referred to in Hayley's Preface, pp. i–ii, iv.

1. The frontispiece to the Preface apparently represents Adam and the beasts:

   > *Their strength, or speed, or vigilance, were giv'n*
   > *In aid of our defects. In some are found*
   > *Such teachable and apprehensive parts,*
   > *That man's attainments in his own concerns*
   > *Match'd with th'expertness of the brutes in theirs*
   > *Are oft times vanquish'd and thrown far behind.*
   > > *Cowpers Task*
   > > *Book VI.*

   Pl. 1–5 are '*Publishd June 1, 1802 by W Blake Felpham*', and 1, 3–4, 6–8 are signed '*Blake d & s*'. (The plate-mark of pl. 1 is 16·2 × 17 cm, a proof before imprint is in the BMPR, and another before engraved signature is in the collection of Sir Geoffrey Keynes.)

2. On Preface p. iv is a view of Chichester signed '*W B d & s*' (14·5 × 5·6 cm).

Each Ballad has a full-page frontispiece and smaller engravings on the rst and last pages of text.

3. The frontispiece to 'THE ELEPHANT. *Ballad the First*' represents an elephant lifting a man (11·2 × 16·3 cm). (A sketch for it is in a set of extra-illustrated Royal Academy catalogues in the Royal Academy.)

4. On p. 1 is an engraving of a tiger stalking a man on a roof (11·2 × 8 cm).

5. On p. 9 is an engraving '*From an Antique Gem*' representing an elephant, with an oval to show the '*Size of the Gem*', '*Blake sc*' (11·2 × 8·2 cm). (Hayley used this gem to seal his letters with—there are several examples in the Fitzwilliam Museum.)

6. The frontispiece to Ballad the Second, The Eagle, represents a cliff with an eagle, a baby, and its mother, and, like pl. 7–8, is '*Publishd July 1. 1802 by W Blake Felpham*' (11·4 × 16·1 cm). (Trial sketches are in the BMPR and the Rosenwald Collection, and the finished watercolour is in the collection of Mrs. Landon K. Thorne. The same design was re-engraved for the 1805 *Ballads*.)

7. On p. 11 is a design of an eagle about to steal a child (11·1 × 8 cm).

8. On p. 26 is the baby rejoicing by the dead eagle, signed '*Blake i[n]v*' (11·2 × ?7·7 cm).

9. The frontispiece of the Third Ballad, The Lion, represents two Negroes shooting a lion (14·1 × 16·9 cm); it is signed '*Blake in & sc*' like pl. 10 and '*Publish'd Augˢᵗ 5: 1802 by W Blake Felpham*' like pl. 10–11. (A sketch is on the verso of that for 'The Elephant' in the Royal Academy, and a proof before letters is in the Morgan. The design was re-engraved for the 1805 *Ballads*.)

10. On p. 27 is a design of a Negro woman and child with bows and arrows (11·2 × 8 cm).

11. On p. 39 is engraved a lion '*From an Antique*' (9·3 × 6·7 cm), signed '*T. H. [i.e. Thomas Hayley] del:*', '*Blake sc*'.

12. The frontispiece of a dog leaping into a crocodile's jaws to save his master for the Fourth Ballad, The Dog, was, like no. 13–14, '*Publish'd Septʳ 9: 1802 by W Blake Felpham*' and signed '*Blake inv & sc*' (14 × 16·7 cm). (The manuscript of the Fourth Ballad is in the Rosenwald Collection. The design was re-engraved for the 1805 *Ballads*.)

13. On p. 41, the engraving represents Edward bidding adieu to Lucy and Fido (11·2 × 8 cm); it is signed '*Blake inv s*'.

14. Facing p. 52 is a full-page design of Lucy caressing a marble statue of Fido in the moonlight (10·7 × 15·4 cm); it is signed '*Blake in: s*'. (A proof is on the verso of the 'Riddle MS'.)

The printer Joseph Seagrave supplied Blake with the printed but unsewn sheets of each Ballad on paper watermarked '1802', and Blake and his wife printed his engravings on the appropriate pages at his own press. Blake then sold the individual Ballads for his own profit as best he could (the Rosenwald copy belonged to his old partner 'J Parker'). At first he was energetically assisted by Hayley and Hayley's friends, but eventually the project subsided. Consequently Blake was probably left with large numbers of the sheets Seagrave had supplied him with. Since paper was expensive, and Blake's means were limited, he frugally used these printed sheets for anything he could think of. Generally he tore off the printed part, leaving the very generous double inner margin which could be used for scratch paper. Blake used these blank leaves in a number of ways. Some examples are:

1. The verso of the title-page with a transcript of Sheridan's 'When 'tis night' (Sir Geoffrey Keynes);

2. Pp. iii–iv, 37–8 used as wrappers for the *Job* sketches (Fitzwilliam);

3. Pp. 9 10 with a sketch called 'Chaining of Orc' (BMPR: 1874-12-12-117);

4. P. 9 with a sketched figure in flight, back of a nude woman (BMPR: 1867-10-12-192);

5. P. 9 with studies of a human leg (Rosenwald);

6. P. 9 with a sketch of Catherine Blake (Tate);

7. Pp. 19–20 &c. used for 'The Ballads [Pickering] MS' (Morgan);

8. Pp. 19–20, 25–6 with a Dante drawing (reproduced in *Blake's Pencil Drawings*, ed. G. Keynes [1956]), with the catchword from p. 20 ('With') and three letters from p. 26 ('[bre]ast') (Morgan);

9. Pp. 19–20, 25–6 with a figure seated under a tree (BMPR: 1867-10-12-193);

10. Pp. 19–20, 25–6 with a running man (very like the one in the Goyder design below) before a Gothic church, with the catchword 'With' from p. 20 and 't' showing through from p. 26 (Mr. George Goyder);

11. Pp. 21–4 with a sketch of a man with his hands raised in horror as he looks up at a circle containing a church, above which a man (much like the one in the Goyder design above), upside-down, runs to the left, and at the bottom left is the catchword 'It' from p. 22, with the catchword 'Run' showing through from p. 24 (Mr. George Goyder);

12. Pp. 22, 24: A sketch (?1805) for 'The Death of the Strong Wicked Man' (on p. 24, catchword 'Run') for Blair's *Grave*, with a sketch (?1805) for 'The Ascension' (?1805–6) on the verso (p. 22, 'It') in the V&A;

13. Pp. 22, 24: A sketch (?1805) for 'A widow embracing the turf . . .' for Blair's *Grave* (1808) in the BMPR (1867-10-12-198);

14. Pp. 25–6 with a sketch for Dante (*c.* 1826), perhaps for 'The Circle of the Lustful' (reproduced in *Drawings*, ed. G. Keynes [1970], no. 87) showing the 't,' of 'breast,' on p. 26 (Rosenwald Collection, National Gallery);

15. Pp. 27–8 bearing a sketch of 'Satan' like that in *Job* (1826) pl. 5 (reproduced in *Drawings* [1970], no. 75) showing '[tr]uth.' (Sir Geoffrey Keynes);

16. Pp. 29–32 with a sketch for *Jerusalem* (1804–?20) pl. 14 (BMPR: 1874-12-12-150);

17. Pp. 31–2 with a sketch of a man with a halo(?) holding balls of light (?or emptying jars) in his outstretched hands as he floats between two winged men, one at the right evidently writing, showing '[drea]d;' from p. 32 (untraced; described in *The Blake Collection of W. Graham Robertson*, ed. K. Preston [1952], no. 87; my friend Professor Karen

Mulhallen showed me a photograph of it and told me about pp. 19–20 [Goyder], 25–6, 27–8 above);

18. Pp. 37–8 in the binding of *America* (O) (Fitzwilliam);
19. Pp. 41–4 with several sketches, including one for 'Adam and Eve finding the Body of Abel' (BMPR: 1929-7-13-272);
20. Pp. 41–8 (the inner margin) used in Blake's *Notebook* pp. 117–20 (BM MSS).

Probably numerous other sketches and drafts are on paper from these Ballads sheets.

The 1802 Ballads were reviewed in *The Poetical Register* (1803), 440, without reference to Blake, and in *The Annual Review*, IV (1806), 575, by Southey, who accused Hayley and Blake of rampant 'MEDIOCRITY'.

For the 'extreme complexity' of 'the make-up', see N. J. Barker, 'Some Notes on the Bibliography of William Hayley: Part III', *Transactions of the Cambridge Bibliographical Society*, III (1962), 342–3 and in R. R. Easson & R. N. Essick, *William Blake: Book Illustrator* (see 1972, under Catalogues, where all twelve plates are reproduced).

467. AN / ESSAY / ON / SCULPTURE: / IN A SERIES OF EPISTLES / *TO JOHN FLAXMAN, ESQ. R.A.* / WITH NOTES. / [5-line motto] / = By WILLIAM HAYLEY, Esq. / = / *LONDON:* / Printed by A. Strahan, Printers Street; / FOR T. CADELL JUN. AND W. DAVIES, IN THE STRAND. / 1800. (BM, BMPR [Nancy Flaxman's copy], Bodley, Fitzwilliam, GEB, Huntington, King's College [Cambridge], McGill, National Library of Ireland, National Library of Scotland, Princeton, Trinity College [Hartford, Conn.], V&A, West Sussex Record Office)

In the Strahan Ledgers (BM Add. MSS 48811, f. 100) under June 1800 is the account of Cadell & Davies:

Hayley on Sculpture 46 1/2 Sheets. Nº 750 ⎫			
fine work at £1:9:0 [*should be* £67.3.6] ⎬	68	8	6
Extra for 24 1/2 Sheets Appendix, and Corrections	11	11	6

There are three engravings (not counting the unsigned ornaments at the head of each epistle), all '*Publishd June 14. 1800 by Cadell & Davi[e]s Strand*'. None is signed by an engraver, but all may confidently be assigned to Blake:

1. '*To face the Title*': 'PERICLES. / *from a Bust in the Possession of Charles Townley Esq.*' (22·3 × 16·1 cm). On 6 May 1800 Blake said he had sent Hayley 'A Proof of Pericles'.
2. '*To face Page 126*': 'THE DEATH OF DEMOSTHENES. / *He views this Outrage with indignant Eyes / and at the Base of Neptunes Statue dies. / Epistle 5 Verse 61 [i.e. 63–4].*' 'T. H[ayley]. invenit', 'W. Blake sc.' (16·1 × 12·5 cm.) (Mr. Walter Fancutt owns a proof printed in Red. Sir Geoffrey Keynes owns Hayley's own copy of the *Essay*, with MS corrections, in which is inserted Thomas Hayley's pencil sketch for 'The Death of Demosthenes'.)
3. '*To face Page 163*' (the last page of the epistles): '*THOMAS HAYLEY, / the Disciple of / John Flaxman. / from a Medallion [by Flaxman].*' 'Blake. sc.'

(plate-size: 22·4 × 16·1 cm). Blake sent a proof of this plate to Hayley on 1 April 1800, Hayley asked for extensive corrections on 17 April, Blake sent another proof on 2 May, but Hayley still thought it 'miserably unjust' in the published form (*Blake Records* [1969], 73; cf. pp. 62–8).

468. A. THE / LIFE, / AND / *POSTHUMOUS WRITINGS*, / OF / WILLIAM COWPER, Esǫr. / WITH AN / INTRODUCTORY LETTER, / TO THE / *RIGHT HONOURABLE EARL COWPER.* / = / By WILLIAM HAYLEY, Esǫr. / [5-line motto] / = / VOL. I [–III]. / = / Chichestei. / *Piinted by J. Soagravo*; / FOR J JOHNSON, ST. PAUL'S CHURCH-YARD, LONDON. / — / [Vol. I–II:] 1803 [Vol. III:] 1804. (BM, GEB [2], King's College [Cambridge])

B. SECOND EDITION [of Vols. I–II]. / = / Chichester: / PRINTED BY J. SEAGRAVE; / FOR J. JOHNSON, ST. PAUL'S CHURCH-YARD, LONDON. / — / 1803. (Bodley, GEB, Huntington, McGill, South Carolina) (1803 copies of unrecorded edition: California [Los Angeles], Clarke Library [Los Angeles], Connecticut College for Women, Fitzwilliam, Illinois, Michigan, NYP, Newberry, Princeton [3], Toronto [2], Trinity College [Hartford, Conn.], Wellesley, Yale).

All 6 plates were engraved by Blake, and all 4 in Vols. I–II were *'Publish'd Novemb. 5, 1802 by J. Johnson S. Paul's Church Yard'*.

VOLUME I

1. The frontispiece represents 'WILLIAM COWPER. / Carmine Nobilem / Hor:', *'From a Portrait in Crayons Drawn from the Life by Romney in 1792 Engravd by W Blake 1802'* (design size: 14·3 × 18·4 cm).
2. At p. 4 is: 'Mrs COWPER / Mother of the Poet', '*D. Heins Pinx*', '*W Blake sculp*'. (12·9 × 15·7 cm.) (The charming original miniature is in the possession of Miss Mary Barham Johnson.)

VOLUME II

3. The frontispiece represents 'William Cowper— / *Author of "The Task"* ', '*T Lawrence R A: ad vivum del: 1793*'; '*W. Blake sculp 1802*' (16·5 × 22·9 cm).
4. On p. 415, the bottom of the page, is an engraving signed '*Blake d & sc*', representing 'the Weather-house', 'The Peasants Nest', and 'Cowper's tame Hares', 'Puss Tiney & Bess', with a quotation from *The Task*, Book I, line 200 (11·6 × 15·7 cm).

VOLUME III

5. The frontispiece represents '*A View of S. Edmund's Chapel, / in the Church of East Dereham, / Containing the Grave of William Cowper Esq*', 'Francis Stone del:', '*W Blake. sculp*'; this and the next plate were '*Publish'd by J Johnson S. Pauls 25 March 1804*' (14·25 × 20·0 cm).
6. At p. 416 (or opposite the frontispiece—there are no directions to the binder in Vol. III) is '*A Sketch* [with inscription] *of the Monument / Erected in the Church of East Dereham in Norfolk / In Memory of William Cowper Esqre / Etch'd by W Blake from the original Model / by John Flaxman Esqr Sculptor to his Majesty*' (15·2 × 17·2).

B. There was no 'Second Edition' of the third volume.

The original of Romney's Cowper is in the National Portrait Gallery, London. Romney's sketch from which Blake worked is in the Rosenwald Collection, and Lawrence's sketch is in the Cowper Museum (Olney, Buckinghamshire) (according to Ryskamp, 'Lawrence's Portrait of Cowper'). Ryskamp also points out ('Blake's Cowperian Sketches') that Blake's own pencil sketch is in the Widener Collection at Harvard. An early proof of one plate is in the Rosenwald Collection, and Keynes (1921) reports that he owns a proof of Blake's pl. 6.

For the likelihood that Blake was also given a set of the biography of Cowper for which he had made engravings, see no. 727.

Blake's plates were not re-used in the editions of New York, 1803 (GEB, re-engraved by P. Maverick), 1806 (BM, re-engraved by Caroline Watson), 1809 (BM), 1812 (BM), 1824 (BM), 1835 (BM, two editions), or 1836 (BM).

469. THE / LIFE / OF GEORGE ROMNEY Esq. / [10 lines of motto] / — / By WILLIAM HAYLEY, Esq. / — / Chichester: / PRINTED BY W. MASON, / FOR T. PAYNE, PALL-MALL, LONDON. / — / 1809. (BM, Fitzwilliam, GEB, Huntington, King's College [Cambridge], Liverpool Public, Mellon [Yale], National Library of Scotland, New York University, Princeton, University of New Brunswick, Westminster Public, West Sussex Record Office)

The manuscript of pp. 1–168, 329–32, dated 22 Oct. 1807, is in the Rosenwald Collection of the Library of Congress.

Of the 12 plates, all bear the imprint 'Published April 14.th 1809 by Thomas Payne, Pall Mall', all are signed, 7 are by Caroline Watson, and 1 is by Blake, namely:

1. At p. 84 is 'Sketch of a Shipwreck after Romney.' 'Engraved by Blake' (design size: 17·6 × 13·2 cm). (Blake's sketch is in the BMPR, reproduced in the Letters [1968], at p. 112.)

In 1803 and 1804 Blake refers constantly to his progress in engraving a portrait of Romney (7, 26 Oct., 13 Dec. 1803, 27 Jan., 23 Feb., 16 March, 4 May, 22 June, 28 Sept., 23 Oct., 18, 28 Dec. 1804), but this print did not appear with Hayley's biography. (Blake's sketch for the Romney engraving was sold at Sotheby's, 29 April 1862, lot 178, and has since disappeared. Ruthven Todd, ed. Gilchrist's Life of William Blake [1942], p. 380, traced a copy in the Rosenwald Collection, but there is no other record of it in this collection and it cannot be found there.)

470. A. Little TOM the Sailor. / [48 lines of verse] / Printed for & Sold by the Widow Spicer of Folkstone / for the Benefit of her Orphans / October 5, 1800. (BMPR, Glasgow, Philadelphia Museum [defective], Princeton)

B. Bound in The Century Guild Hobby Horse, I [1886], at p. 121.

C. Issued with Muir's 'Edition of the Writings of Wm. Blake', no. 249 i.

D. Issued separately.

E. Little Tom the Sailor. London, 1917.

A. This etched broadsheet ballad was written by Hayley on 22 Sept. 1800 (four days after Blake's arrival in Felpham) and was 'successfully devoted to relieve the necessities of a meritorious poor Woman . . . whose heroic sea Boy was the Hero of the Ballad', according to Hayley's autobiography (*Blake Records* [1969], 74). Catherine Blake printed it in dark Brown ink on wove paper watermarked '1797' or unwatermarked, 'a few in colours [*i.e. watercoloured*] and some in black', as Blake said in his letter of 26 Nov. 1800. The printing shows numerous minor defects.

Blake's four plates engraved in relief on pewter consist of:

1. The headpiece of the boy in a storm at sea (11×16 cm);
2. The text of the poem ($10 \cdot 6 \times 22 \cdot 0$ cm);
3. The tailpiece of the mother at her cottage ($11 \times 15 \cdot 8$ cm), signed '*W Blake Inv & sc*';
4. The colophon ($12 \times 3 \cdot 5$ cm)

A sketch for 'Little Tom' in the V&A is reproduced in *Pencil Drawings by William Blake*, ed. G. Keynes (1927), pl. 25.

Five copies in private hands are traced in G. Keynes, 'Blake's *Little Tom the Sailor*', *Book Collector*, XVII (1968), 421–7.

B is described in a note by H. H. Gilchrist, no. 1683.

C is the same plate issued by Muir and D is the same plate presumably sold by its printer, Emery Walker.

B–D are extremely persuasive facsimiles, printed on paper with chainlines or watermarked 'POUNCY' (Morgan), 'JOHN DICKINSON', or (according to Keynes, above) 'P le Bas' or 'L B & Cie'. The printing is careful, there are no plate-marks, there is a spot of light over the head of the angel (perhaps following an untraced copy of the original), the double loop and tassel of the 'P' of 'Printed' is missing, as is the flourish from the 'S' of 'Spicer'.

E is a facsimile by the mendacious Richard C. Jackson, with Hayley's poem printed from conventional type.

471. A. THE / TRIUMPHS / OF / TEMPER. / *A POEM*: / IN SIX CANTOS. / — / By WILLIAM HAYLEY Esq. / — / O voi ch'avete gl'intelletti sani / Mirate la dottrina, che si asconde / Sotto' il velame degli versi strani. / Dante, Inferno, Canto 9. / — / THE TWELFTH EDITION, CORRECTED. / *With New Original Designs*, / By MARIA FLAXMAN. / = / CHICHESTER: / *Printed by J. Seagrave*; / FOR T. CADELL AND W. DAVIES, STRAND, / LONDON. / — / 1803. (BM [2], BMPR, Bodley, GEB [2, one large paper], Harvard, Huntington, Liverpool Public, McGill, Morgan, National Library of Scotland, Newberry, New York University, Princeton [3], Smith, Texas, Trinity College [Hartford, Conn.], West Sussex Record Office, Westminster Public)

B. THE THIRTEENTH EDITION, CORRECTED. / *With New Original Designs*, / By MARIA FLAXMAN. / = / CHICHESTER: / *Printed by*

J. SEAGRAVE; / FOR T. CADELL AND W. DAVIES, / Strand, LONDON. /
. . . . . . / 1807. (GEB, Harvard, Trinity College [Hartford, Conn.])

A. All 6 plates have '*Maria Flaxman inv & del.*', '*W Blake sculp* [*or sc*]', and
'*Publish'd May 1, 1803, by Cadell & Davies, Strand*'.

1. At p. 2 is '*Canto I. Verse 29*' (plate-size: 10·1 × 15·9; design surface:
   7·6 × 11·0 cm).
2. At p. 48: '*Canto II^d Verse 471*' (9·8 × 15·3; 7·7 × 10·5 cm).
3. At p. 60: '*Canto III Verse 201*' (10·0 × 16·4; 7·9 × 10·4 cm).
4. At p. 96: '*Canto IV Verse 328*' (10·1 × 15·8; 7·4 × 10·3 cm).
5. At p. 104: '*Canto V. Verse 43*' (10·0 × 16·4; 7·9 × 9·9 cm).
6. At p. 154: '*Canto VI Verse 294*' (9·8 × 16·7; 7·9 × 10·2 cm).

The position of the plates is variable, for there are no directions to the
binder; sometimes they face the pages they illustrate (as in BM, Bodley, and
one GEB), and sometimes they face the first page of each canto, pp. 2, 24,
50, 81, 103, 149 (as in another GEB).

Miss Flaxman's drawings were exhibited at the Royal Academy in 1800,
and sold, with Hayley's MS of the *Triumphs of Temper*, at the Flaxman sale
at Christie's, 26–7 Feb. 1883, lot 295; the MS was sold again with the Moss
collection at Sotheby's, 2–9 March 1937, lot 284b.

Hayley gave a copy to Catherine Blake (see no. 730), and another copy
'From the Author' with the plates coloured, apparently by Blake, is in the
collection of Mr. George Goyder.

B. There were two thirteenth editions. In one (BM, Bodley, GEB), nothing
is said of Maria Flaxman's designs on the title-page, and the plates in fact
are those originally engraved after Stothard by Sharp, Neagle, and Heath
for the sixth edition (1788). In the other Miss Flaxman is named on the
title-page, and Blake's plates appear at pp. 1, 24, 49, 82, 103, 139, facing the
first page of each canto. The succeeding edition (Chichester, 1812) had no
plates at all.

HENRY, Thomas

472. MEMOIRS / OF / ALBERT DE HALLER, M.D. / MEMBER OF
THE / SOVEREIGN COUNCIL OF BERNE; / PRESIDENT OF THE
UNIVERSITY, / AND OF / THE ROYAL SOCIETY OF GOTTINGEN;
/ FELLOW of the ROYAL SOCIETY of LONDON, &c. / Compiled,
chiefly, from the ELOGIUM spoken before the / ROYAL ACADEMY OF
SCIENCES AT PARIS, / And from the *Tributes* paid to his Memory / BY
OTHER FOREIGN SOCIETIES. / By THOMAS HENRY, / *Fellow* of the
Royal Society, Member of the *Medical Society* / of *London*, and of the *Literary* and
Philosophical / *Society* of *Manchester*. / — / WARRINGTON, / Printed by
W. EYRES, for J. JOHNSON, N°. 72, / St. Paul's Church-Yard, LONDON.
MDCCLXXXIII [1783]. (BM, Bodley, Princeton)

1. The only plate is the frontispiece, which represents 'ALBERT DE HALLER.'
   and is signed '*Dunker. d.*', '*Blake. sc*' (plate-mark: ?8·5 × 13·1 cm).

Henry wrote to Joseph Johnson on 13 April 1783 asking him:

Pray hasten the head of Haller— The Book is finished, and very neat; and the Season is advancing rapidly. The heads [*i.e. prints*] might come in Clerke's parcel, or in Newton's.

> (Quoted from a reproduction of the MS in Bodley, generously pointed out to me by Professor Gerald P. Tyson.)

HOARE, Prince

473. ACADEMIC CORRESPONDENCE, / 1803. /   / CONTAINING / EXTRACTS, NO. II., FROM A CORRESPONDENCE WITH THE / ACADEMIES OF VIENNA AND ST. PETERSBURG, / ON THE PRESENT CULTIVATION OF THE ARTS OF / PAINTING, SCULP-TURE, AND ARCHITECTURE; / A SUMMARY REPORT OF THE TRANSACTIONS OF / THE ROYAL ACADEMY OF LONDON, / FROM THE CLOSE OF THE EXHIBITION, 1802, TO THE SAME PERIOD, 1803. / AND / A DESCRIPTION OF / PUBLIC MONU-MENTS, / VOTED / BY THE PARLIAMENT OF GREAT BRITAIN, / TO THE MEMORY OF DISTINGUISHED / NAVAL AND MILITARY OFFICERS, SINCE THE YEAR 1798. / = / Communes utilitates in medium afferre; tum artibus, tum opera, tum facultatibus devincire / hominum inter homines societatem. CICERO DE OFF. / = / PUBLISHED BY DESIRE OF THE ACADEMY, / BY / PRINCE HOARE, / MEMBER OF THE ACADEMIES OF FLORENCE, AND CORTONA, AND SECRETARY FOR FOREIGN CORRESPONDENCE / TO THE ROYAL ACADEMY OF LONDON. / = / London: / — / PRINTED FOR ROBSON, OLD BOND-STREET: PAYNE, MEWS-GATE; / HAT-CHARD, PICCADILLY, AND BARKER, GREAT RUSSEL-STREET. / — / 1804. (BM, Bodley)

1. The only engraving, the frontispiece signed '*J Flaxman R A. del:*', '*W Blake. sc:*', represents two views of a '*Fragment of an Antique Statue of Ceres, found in the Ruins of Eleusis and now placed in the Public Library at Cambridge*' (plate size: 18·1 × 19·8 cm).

Flaxman describes the statue in the volume. He had recommended Blake as an engraver to Hoare on 25 Dec. 1803, Hoare had not received a 'proof of Mr Blake's Etching' by 4 Jan. 1804, but Blake sent Hayley a copy of the work on 23 Feb. 1804 (*Blake Records* [1969], 136, 139).

S. Q. complained in the *Literary Gazette* (1 Feb. 1804) that Blake's plate was not 'worthy of the subject, and of the country'.

474. AN / INQUIRY / INTO THE / REQUISITE CULTIVATION / AND / PRESENT STATE / OF THE / ARTS OF DESIGN / IN / *ENG-LAND*. / — / BY / PRINCE HOARE. / — / *LONDON:* / PRINTED FOR RICHARD PHILLIPS, NO. 6, BRIDGE- / STREET, BLACKFRIARS, / BY B. McMILLAN, BOW-STREET, COVENT-GARDEN. / — / 1806. [*Price 7s. in Boards.*] (BMPR, Bodley, GEB, National Library of Scotland, Trinity College [Hartford, Conn.], Westminster Public)

1. The only plate, the frontispiece, represents a woman with a scroll labelled 'THEORY' and entitled above '*The Graphic Muse.*' Below is inscribed:

> ....*To explore*
> *What lovelier forms in Natures boundless store*
> *Are best to Art allied* ....

'*Sketched from the* Picture by Sir Joshua Reynolds *on the ceiling of the Library of* the Royal Academy.' '*Sʳ Joshᵃ Reynolds pinxᵗ*', '*Blake. sc*', '*Pubᵈ Febᵞ 21. 1806, by R. Phillips. Nᵒ 6. Bridge Street Blackfriars.*' (Plate size: 17·3 × 11·0 cm.) Reynolds's painting is still in the Royal Academy. Blake's engraving is described as an 'elegant outline' in the *Monthly Magazine* review (July 1806 supplement, p. 607). Flaxman's account of 'the bust of CERES' is on p. 25.

HOGARTH, William

475. A. THE / ORIGINAL WORKS / OF / WILLIAM HOGARTH. / = / SOLD BY JOHN AND JOSIAH BOYDELL, / AT THE SHAKSPEARE GALLERY, / PALL-MALL, AND NO. 90, CHEAPSIDE, / LONDON. 1790. (Library Company of Philadelphia; Metropolitan Museum, N.Y.)

B. THE / ORIGINAL / AND / GENUINE WORKS / OF / WILLIAM HOGARTH. / = / 'HOGARTH may be indisputably regarded as the first Moral Painter of / 'this or any other country; for, to his honour be it recorded, the / 'almost invariable tendency of his *Dramatic Histories* is the promotion / 'of Virtue, / 'and diffusion of such a spirit as tends to make men / 'Industrious, Humane, and Happy.' / 'His matchless works, of fame secure, / 'Shall live our country's pride and boast, / 'As long as Nature shall endure, / 'And only in her wreck be lost!' / *See Hogarth Illustrated, in Three Vols. by John Ireland.* / = / LONDON: / = / PUBLISHED BY BOYDELL AND COMPANY, No. 90, CHEAPSIDE. / PRINTED BY W. BULMER AND CO. CLEVELAND-ROW, ST. JAMES'S [?1795]. (NYP)

C. THE WORKS / OF / WILLIAM HOGARTH, / FROM THE / ORIGINAL PLATES RESTORED / BY JAMES HEATH, EsQ. RA; / WITH / THE ADDITION OF MANY SUBJECTS NOT BEFORE COLLECTED: / TO WHICH ARE PREFIXED, / A BIOGRAPHICAL ESSAY ON / 𝕿𝖍𝖊 𝕲𝖊𝖓𝖎𝖚𝖘 𝖆𝖓𝖉 𝕻𝖗𝖔𝖉𝖚𝖈𝖙𝖎𝖔𝖓𝖘 𝖔𝖋 𝕳𝖔𝖌𝖆𝖗𝖙𝖍, / AND / EXPLANATIONS OF THE SUBJECTS OF THE PLATES, / BY JOHN NICHOLS, EsQ. FSA. / — / 𝕷𝖔𝖓𝖉𝖔𝖓: / PRINTED FOR BALDWIN, CRADOCK, AND JOY, PATERNOSTER ROW, / BY J. NICHOLS AND SON, PARLIAMENT STREET. / — / 1822. (GEB, Harvard, Morgan, NYP, Princeton)

D. THE WORKS / OF / WILLIAM HOGARTH, / FROM THE / ORIGINAL PLATES / RESTORED BY JAMES HEATH, EsQ., R.A.; / WITH / THE ADDITION OF MANY SUBJECTS NOT BEFORE COLLECTED: / TO WHICH IS PREFIXED, / A BIOGRAPHICAL ESSAY / ON THE / GENIUS AND PRODUCTIONS OF HOGARTH, / AND / EXPLANATIONS OF THE SUBJECTS OF THE PLATES, / BY JOHN NICHOLS,

EsQ. F.S.A. / — / **London;** / PRINTED FOR BALDWIN, CRADOCK AND JOY, PATERNOSTER ROW, / BY NICHOLS AND SON, PARLIAMENT STREET. / — / 1822 [i.e. ?1826] (NYP & Toronto Public)

E. *The Works of William Hogarth,* from the Original Plates Restored by James Heath, Esq. R.A.; with The Addition of Many Subjects Not Before Collected: to which are prefixed, A Biographical Essay on the Genius and Productions of Hogarth, and Explanations of the Subjects of the Plates, By John Nichols, Esq. F.S.A. London: Printed for Baldwin and Cradock, Paternoster Row, by G. Woodfall, Angel Court, Skinner Street. [1830?] (Princeton)

F. [1835?] (Princeton, Cornell, & Harvard)

G. [1838?] (Toronto Public & BM)

H. *Die Werke* / von / William Hogarth. / Nach den / Original=Platten auf 118 Blättern / photolithographiert von Carl Haack in Wien, / nebst / einen biographischen Essay über den Genius und die / Schöpfungen Hogarth's, / sowie / Erklärungen der einzelnen Bilder / von John Nichols Esq. F.S.A. / Bearbeitet von Emil Charles Barschall. / . . . Brünn und Wien, / Verlag untr. Karafiat T. 1878. (BM)

I. *'The Beggar's Opera' by Hogarth and Blake,* a Portfolio Compiled by Wilmarth S. Lewis & Philip Hofer. Cambridge & New Haven, 1965.

A. There are 103 plates, of which no. 103 is Gay's 'BEGGAR'S OPERA, ACT III.' '"*When my hero in Court appears, &c.*"' '*From the Original Picture, in the Collection of his Grace the Duke of Leeds.*' '*Painted by Wm Hogarth.*' '*Engraved by W^{m}* 'Blake.' '*Size of the picture* $\frac{1}{24}$ . . *by* $\frac{1}{30}$ . . *long.*' '*Publish'd July 1st 1790, by J. and J. Boydell, Cheapside, & at the Shakspeare Gallery Pall Mall London*' (design size: 40·1 × 54·2 cm.).

In the table of contents (as it were) for the volume is listed: '*103. Beggars Opera, — [£] 0 15 0*', and a footnote states: 'N.B. The Prints marked * were never before inserted in this Collection.' The prints were offered for sale separately (£18. 13. 0 for the lot), and the book was priced at £15. 15. 0.

B. In the [1795] issue were 107 plates, and Blake's plate, no. 101, has the same imprint as before. The price of his plate was reduced to 10/6 (the range was 1/- to 15/-, with most of them about 3/-), but the volume as a whole advanced to £21. Most of the plates (66) were engraved by Hogarth himself, and a note states that the Boydells are 'the sole Proprietors of the ORIGINAL WORKS of that celebrated Artist', which they have not allowed any other engraver to touch.

C. The 1822 edition was issued in twenty-four monthly parts, each with a separate dated title-page, running from 1 April 1820 to 1 March 1822. The part with Blake's plate bore the following title:

The Original and Genuine Works of William Hogarth, from the plates lately in the Possession of Messieurs Boydell; with others engraved by eminent artists, under the superintendance of James Heath, Esq. R.A. accompanied by explanations of the various subjects By John Nichols, Esq. F.A.S.L.E. & P. N° IV. Contents. July 1, 1820. 1. Beggar's Opera. 2. The Rake's Progress,

Plate I. 3. The Distressed Poet. 4. The Beggar's Opera Burlesqued. Just View of the Stage. [*These two are bracketed together.*] 5. England. Third Sheet of Descriptions. London: Printed for Baldwin, Cradock, and Joy, Paternoster Row. 1820. To be completed in twenty-four numbers, Price £1. 1s. until January 1, 1821; afterwards £1. 5s. Each Number to contain, on an average, Five Plates; with occasional Sheets of Letter-Press. Printed by Nichols and Son, 25, Parliament Street, Westminster. (Harvard)

In this 1820–2 issue there are 119 prints, and Blake's is usually bound as no. 19, as close as possible to the description of it. The biographical essay is pp. iii–x, and the running explanation of the plates (52 pp.) points out that Hogarth made three paintings of the same *Beggar's Opera* subject, and that these provide the only known representations of the interior of Lincoln's Inn Theatre. The performers and actors in the engraving are carefully identified. Many of the plates for this edition were engraved by Cook, and many of the rest seem to have been otherwise harmed by him. A colophon at the foot of the last page of text (p. 52) states that the work was printed in 'London: From The Press of John Nichols and Son, 25, Parliament-Street'.

D. The [1828?] edition has the same title-page as C, but the type has been reset. The essay is now pp. iii–xi, and the explanation of the plates is only 42 pp. Blake's plate is still no. 19, but there are 116 plates in all, as compared with 119 in C. The colophon (p. 42) says that the edition was 'Printed by Jas. Wade, 18, Tavistock-street, Covent Garden, London.' The dating of this and the following editions is almost pure guess-work. I know no authority who has distinguished C from D, or E from F, and these (E & F) from G. In catalogues, E, F, and G are normally dated '[1835–1837]' on the basis of evidence unknown to me.

E., F., G. The order and dating of E, F, and G are highly arbitrary. In all of them the title-page reads identically; all have 116 plates; and in all Blake's engraving (with the inscription still unchanged) is the nineteenth. The remarkable difference is in the printers indicated in the colophons on p. 42. In E it is 'Printed by Jas. Wade, Tavistock-street, Covent Garden, London', the same inscription that appeared on p. 42 of the [1828?] edition. In F it is 'G. Norman, Printer, Maiden Lane, Covent Garden'; and in G it is 'G. Woodfall, Angel Court, Skinner Street, London', as on the *title-page* of all three issues. Perhaps the title-page refers primarily to the printer of the engravings.

H. Plate 17 in the German edition of 1878 is an exact size-replica of Blake's, including the signatures and caption.

I. The portfolio contains a pull from Blake's copperplate and reproductions of Hogarth's sketch, his six oils of the subject (Blake's plate was based on the painting now owned by Mr. Paul Mellon), of Blake's etched proof, and of the second state of his engraving.

All these volumes are, of course, enormous folios.

The Blake plate was also issued separately, and four states of it have been recorded (see [John Bowyer Nichols, ed.] *Anecdotes of William Hogarth*, London 1833, pp. 174, 323, with more details given in Keynes, *Separate Plates*, no. 669) and Ronald Paulson, *Hogarth's Graphic Works* (1965). The first is the etching, with the imprint: 'Painted by Willm Hogarth 1729.' 'Etch'd by Willm Blake 1788', 'Publish'd October 29: 1788: by Ald^m Boydell & Co. Cheapside.' Keynes records four copies, and a fifth is in the New York Public Library with a note by James D. Smillie (1833–1909): 'Price 3.^d'; 'This print I bought at an auction in Edinburgh when I was about ten years old'. The second state is said to be the finished proof before writing, but neither Keynes nor Nichols records a copy; Professor Robert Essick acquired one in 1974. The third state is inscribed as in the book form, except that the size is omitted and the letters are open (Keynes records one copy). The fourth state is the same with the letters filled up, and the size added. Keynes records four copies and mentions that it was also published 'in a large volume of prints after Hogarth published by Boydell in 1790'. Clearly the final state is relatively common, and should probably be divided into at least five sub-states. If nothing else, the impressions steadily degenerate with time, par-ticularly after the plate fell into the restoring hands of James Heath.

There are no reliable bibliographies of books with engravings after Hogarth, and I can take the history of his printed *Works* no further. The copperplates, however, can be traced in somewhat more detail, with the help of A. W. Tuer, *Bartolozzi and his Works*, London, [1881?], Vol. I, p. 12, and Paulson, I. 71. Hogarth's plates passed at his death to his widow, from her to his cousin Mary Lewis, and from her to Boydell. Later the owners of the plates (Baldwin & Cradock?) put them up as security for a loan of £2,000 from the banking firm of Salt & Co. Salt & Co. steadily bungled their attempts to sell the plates. They offered the plates at Hodgson's about 1833, but bought them in at £475. H. G. Bohn bought the plates in 1835 for £250 and had them repaired by Ratcliff of Birmingham for about £250 more. Bohn printed from the plates (though I have seen no issue of the *Works* with his name on the title-page), and sold them, when he retired [about 1864], to Chatto & Windus for £500. Chatto & Windus continued publication (though once again I have seen no edition of the *Works* with their imprint), and eventually sold the plates to Quaritch. Quaritch had the plates repaired (for at least the fourth time now) and printed from them (I have seen no examples of this printing). The plate by Blake is now in the possession of Philip Hofer of Harvard.

HUNTER, John

476. A. AN / HISTORICAL JOURNAL / of the TRANSACTIONS at / PORT JACKSON AND NORFOLK ISLAND, / *with the Discoveries which have been made in* / NEW SOUTH WALES AND IN THE SOUTHERN OCEAN, / since the publication of / PHILLIP'S VOYAGE, / *compiled from the Official Papers*; / Including the JOURNALS of Governors PHILLIP and KING, and of Lieut. BALL; / AND THE / VOYAGES / *From the first Sailing of the Sirius in 1787, to the Return of that* / Ship's Company to England in 1792. / [Vignette] / By IOHN HUNTER, Esqr / POST CAPTAIN IN HIS MAJESTY'S NAVY. / — / *Illustrated with seventeen Maps, Charts, Views, &* / *other embellishments,* / Drawn on the Spot by / *Captains Hunter, & Bradley,* / *Lieutenant Dawes, & Governor King.* / LONDON. / *Printed for John Stockdale,*

Piccadilly, / January 1. 1793. (BM, Bodley [2], Mitchell Library [Sydney] [6], National Library of Australia [3], National Library of Scotland, Turnbull [2])

B. *AN* / HISTORICAL JOURNAL / *of the Transactions at* / *PORT JACK-SON, AND NORFOLK ISLAND* / *Including the Journals of Governors* / PHILLIP AND KING, / *Since the Publication of Phillip's Voyage,* / *With an Abridged Account of the New Discoveries* / *In the South Seas,* / *BY* IOHN HUNTER, *ESQ.ᴿ* / *Post Captain in His Majesty's Navy.* / [Vignette] / To which is prefixed A Life of the Author, / *and Illustrated with a Map of the Country, by Lieuᵗ Dawes.* / And other Embellishments. / *London, Printed for John Stockdale, Piccadilly, Janʸ 1. 1793.* (BM, GEB, Mitchell Library [Sydney], National Library of Australia, Princeton, Turnbull)

C. *An Historical Journal of Events at Sydney and at Sea 1787–1792* by Captain John Hunter, with further accounts by Governor Arthur Phillip, Lieutenant P. G. King, and Lieutenant H. L. Ball (Originally published 1793). Ed. John Bach. Sydney, London, & Melbourne, 1968.

A. There are 17 plates, including four unsigned ones, in the quarto edition which Stockdale entered at Stationers' Hall a week after the date on the engraved title-page, 8 Jan. 1793. There is only one plate by Blake, namely:

1. At p. 414 is 'A FAMILY OF NEW SOUTH WALES', '*From a Sketch by Governor King*', '*Blake Sculpᵗ*', '*Publish'd by I. Stockdale, Piccadilly Novʳ 15. 1792*' (20·7 × 24·6 cm). The wash drawing from which Blake's engraving was probably made is in the Mitchell Library in the Sydney Public Library (Australia) and is reproduced in no. 2717.

The 17 plates are named by M. T. and described as 'well engraved' in *The Analytical Review,* XV (April 1793), 386. Blake's plate was copied with minute fidelity by G. Vogel in *Abbildung eineger Landschaften von Neu=Sud= Wales* (Nurnberg, 1794) (Turnbull).

B. The octavo condensation was evidently issued some time later than A, for its 'Advertisement' is dated 'July 5, 1793'. It has only 4 engravings, including the newly engraved title-page and Blake's plate at p. 372, which is unchanged, though of course it is now folded to make it fit the new format.

C. In Bach's edition of A, Blake's plate is reproduced at p. 261.

JOB: see BIBLE: *Job*

JOSEPHUS, Flavius

477. A. THE GENUINE AND COMPLETE / WORKS / OF / FLAVIUS JOSEPHUS, / The celebrated Warlike, Learned and Authentic / JEWISH HISTORIAN. / CONTAINING / I. The Antiquities of the Jews in Twenty Books; with / their Wars, memorable Transactions, authentic and / remarkable Occurrences, their various Turns of / Glory and Misery, of / Prosperity and Adversity, &c. / from the Creation of the World. / II. The Wars of the Jews with the Romans, from their / Commencement to the final Destruction of Jeru- / salem by Titus in the Reign of Vespasian. In Seven / Books. / III. The Book of Josephus against Apion, in Defence / of the Jewish Antiquities.

In Two Parts. / IV. The Martyrdoms of the Maccabees. / V. The Embassy of Philo from the Jews of Alex- / andria to the Emperor Caius Caligula. / VI. The Life of Flavius Josephus, written by himself. / VII. The Testimonies of Josephus concerning Our / Blessed Saviour, St. John the Baptist, &c. clearly / vindicated. / The Whole translated from the Original in the Greek Language, and diligently revised and compared with the Writings of / cotemporary Authors of different Nations on the Subject; all tending to prove the Authenticity of the Work. / To which will now be *first* added, / A CONTINUATION of the HISTORY of the JEWS, / From *Josephus* down to the present Time, including a Period of more than 1700 Years. / Containing an Account of their Dispersion into the various Parts of Europe, Asia, Africa and America, their different / Persecutions, Transactions, various Occurrences, and present State throughout the known World. / ALSO / Various Copious INDEXES, particularly of the Countries, Cities, Towns, Villages, Seas, / Rivers, Mountains, Lakes, &c. / Together with Marginal References to the various important Occurrences recorded in the Work. / Also Notes Historical, Biographical, Classical, Critical, Geographical and Explanatory; and every other / striking Matter recorded in the Works of the celebrated JOSEPHUS. / Likewise TABLES of the Jewish Coins, Weights, Measures, &c. used in the Time of the AUTHOR. / With a great Variety of other interesting and authentic Particulars never given in any Work of the like Kind either in the English / or any other Language. / — / By GEORGE HENRY MAYNARD, LL.D. / — / Embellished with a great Number of beautiful Copper Plates, descriptive of the most distinguished Transactions related in the Work, from / original Drawings of the ingenious Messrs. *Metz, Stothard,* and *Corbould,* Members of the Royal Academy, and other eminent Artists. / The Whole engraved by the most capital Performers, particularly *Grignion, Collier, Heath, Tookey, Taylor,* &c. / = / LONDON: Printed for J. COOKE, No. 17, *Paternoster-Row.* [?1785–6] (BM, Southampton)

B. THE WHOLE GENUINE AND COMPLETE / WORKS / . . . / Rivers, Mountains, Lakes, &c. / Likewise TABLES of the Jewish Coins, Weights, Measures, &c. used in the Time of the AUTHOR. / With a great Variety of other interesting and authentic Particulars never given in any Work of the like Kind / either in the English or any other Language. / — / By GEORGE HENRY MAYNARD, LL.D. / Illustrated with MARGINAL REFERENCES, and Notes Historical, Biographical, Classical, Critical, / Geographical and Explanatory, / By the Rev. EDWARD KIMPTON, Vicar of *Rogate* in *Sussex,* / And Author of the Compleate UNIVERSAL HISTORY of the HOLY BIBLE. / — / Embellished . . . / = / LONDON: Printed for J. COOKE, No. 17, *Pater-noster-Row.* / And sold by all other Booksellers in *Great Britain.* [?1791] (BM, Princeton Theological Seminary)

C. By the King's Royal License and Authority. / — / THE WHOLE GENUINE AND COMPLETE / WORKS / . . . / = / LONDON: Printed for J. COOKE, No. 17, *Pater-Noster-Row* [?1795]. (GEB)

D. . . . / LONDON: Printed for C. COOKE, No. 17, PATERNOSTER-ROW [?1799]. (GEB)

E. THE / WHOLE GENUINE AND COMPLETE / WORKS / OF / *FLAVIUS JOSEPHUS,* / THE LEARNED AND AUTHENTIC / JEWISH HISTORIAN, / AND / CELEBRATED WARRIOR. / CONTAINING / I. The Antiquities of the Jews, in Twenty Books; with their Wars, memorable Transactions, remarkable Occurrences, / their various Turns of Glory and Misery, Prosperity and Adversity, from the Creation of the World. / II. The Wars of the Jews with the Romans, from their Commencement to the final Destruction of Jerusalem by / Titus, in the Reign of Vespasian. In Seven Books. / III. The Book of Josephus against Apion, in Defence of the Jewish Antiquities. In Two Parts. / IV. The Martyrdoms of the Maccabees. / V. The Embassy of Philo from the Jews of Alexandria, to the Emperor Caius Caligula. / VI. The Life of Flavius Josephus, written by himself. / VII. The Testimonies of Josephus concerning Our Blessed Saviour, St. John the Baptist, &c. clearly vindicated. / *Translated from the Original in the Greek Language,* / And diligently revised and compared with the Writings of cotemporary Authors, of different Nations, on the Subject. / All tending to prove the Authenticity of the Work. / TO WHICH IS ADDED / VARIOUS USEFUL INDEXES, / Particularly of the COUNTRIES, CITIES, TOWNS, VILLAGES, SEAS, RIVERS, MOUNTAINS, LAKES, &c. / which are related in the HISTORY. / ALSO A / CONTINUATION / OF THE / HISTORY OF THE JEWS, / From JOSEPHUS down to the present Time, / INCLUDING A PERIOD OF MORE THAN ONE THOUSAND SEVEN HUNDRED YEARS. / CONTAINING / An Account of their Dispersion into the various Parts of Europe, Asia, Africa, and America; their different / Persecutions, Transactions, various Occurrences, and present State throughout the known World. / WITH / A great Variety of other interesting and authentic Particulars, collected from various valuable Works, recording / the principal Transactions of the Jews since the Time of JOSEPHUS. / — / By GEORGE HENRY MAYNARD, LL.D. / — / Illustrated with MARGINAL REFERENCES, and NOTES, Historical, Biographical, Classical, Critical, / Geographical, and Explanatory, / By the Rev. EDWARD KIMPTON, / Vicar of ROGATE, in SUSSEX, and Morning Preacher at ST. MATTHEW's, BETHNAL-GREEN, / And Author of the Compleat UNIVERSAL HISTORY of the HOLY BIBLE. / — / Embellished with upwards of Sixty beautiful Engravings, taken from original Drawings of Messrs. *Metz, Stothard,* and *Corbould,* Members of the Royal Academy, and / other eminent Artists; and engraved by *Grignion, Collier, Heath, Tookey, Taylor,* &c. / = / LONDON: PRINTED FOR C. COOKE, No. 17, PATER-NOSTER ROW; AND SOLD BY THE BOOKSELLERS OF / BATH, BRISTOL, BIRMINGHAM, CANTERBURY, CAMBRIDGE, COVENTRY, CHESTER, DERBY, / EXETER, GLOUCESTER, HEREFORD, HULL, IPSWICH, LEEDS, LIVERPOOL, / LEICESTER, MANCHESTER, NEWCASTLE, NORWICH, NOTTINGHAM, / NORTHAMPTON, OXFORD, READING, SALISBURY, SHERBORN, / SHEFFIELD, SHREWSBURY, WORCESTER, WINCHESTER, / YORK; AND BY ALL OTHER BOOKSELLERS / IN ENGLAND, SCOTLAND, / AND IRELAND. [?1800] (BM, Bodley, & GEB)

A. The editions of Josephus exhibit all the internal stigmata of works issued in 61 sixpenny parts of 3 signatures and a plate each visible in Kimpton's *History of the Bible* (?1781) (q.v.), where the plates were first used. Three dates added to the plates of Josephus (29 Oct. 1785 on no. 2 at p. 381, 31 Dec. 1785 on no. 11 at p. 398, 14 Jan. 1786 on no. 13 at p. 125) indicate that A was issued on Saturdays from 22 Oct. 1785 to 23 Dec. 1786. This and later editions were probably sold both in weekly numbers (over more than a year) and bound together in one or two volumes, as Kimpton's *History* was.

The problems of date and priority are vexatious. It seems clear that A was the earliest edition, as it is the only one which does not have Kimpton's continuations and additions. In A–D, the Continuation of the History of the Jews is '*first* added', but in E no priority is claimed—'Also a Continuation . . .' suggesting that E succeeds the others. Further, Charles Cooke (1760–1816) succeeded to the business of his father (1731–1810), and this fact, though undated, clearly places D–E as the latest of the series.

B may be the edition listed in the *London Catalogue* (1791) at £1. 17*s*.

C. A date of 1795 for C is almost purely hypothetical.

D, which was reset, may be the edition listed in the *London Catalogue* (1799) also at £1. 17*s*.

E, which was not reset except for the title-page, may be dated about 1800.

Eleven of the 61 plates are not signed by the engraver. The engravers mentioned on the title-page were not so distinguished for the number of engravings they undertook, for though Grignion did 16, Tookey did only 6, Heath 4, Collier (and Collyer) 3, and Taylor signed none at all. The plates are the same as those in Kimpton's *History*, except that each has an elaborate new border misleadingly labelled at the top '*Engraved for* MAYNARD'S *Josephus*' (only the *border* was engraved for Josephus), the previous signatures (within the borders) and titles are gone and new ones are written under the borders, and the engravings are more worn and sometimes slightly darkened by the engraver.

Blake's 3 plates are:

1. At p. 12 is 'The PARTING of LOT and ABRAHAM, / *after seperating their Flocks, &c.*', '*Metz delin.*', '*Blake sculp.*' (Plate-size 14·2 × 28·6 cm.) The 'Directions to the Binder' indicate that it was issued with part 32 [on 27 May 1786].

2. At p. 64 is '*The* BATTLE *of* AIN [*i.e. Ai*], *& the* DESTRUCTION *of the* CITY, *by the Army of* JOSHUA.', '*Stothard delin.*', '*Blake sculp.*' (Plate-size: 17·6 × 28·9 cm.) According to the 'Directions', it was issued with part 26 [on 15 April 1786]. (The warriors are left-handed; an engraving of the same scene in the Rosenwald Collection shows them right-handed—see p. 590.)

3. At p. 76 is 'THE FUGITIVE SHECHEMITES / *Burnt and Suffocated in the Holds of their Retreat. / by order of King Abimelech.*', '*Metz delin.*', '*Blake sculp.*' (Plate-size: 17·7 × 28·9 cm.) In the 'Directions', it is no. 23 [issued 25 March 1786].

4. An unpublished plate in the BMPR inscribed in pencil '*The Return of the Jewish Spies from Canaan*', '*Stothard del*', '*Blake sc*' (design size: 10·9 × 16·7 cm) (reproduced in *Blake Newsletter*, V [1972], 242) may have been intended for Kimpton or for Josephus.

Josephus was extraordinarily popular with English readers for two centuries and more. After at least 10 editions in the seventeenth century, there were further printings in 1702, 1709, 1716, 1725, 1733, 1736, 1737, 1740, 1741, 1755, 1762, 1770, 1773, 1777–8, 1784, 1785?, 1792, 1793, and 1800 and of these at least those of 1733, 1736, 1737, 1740, 1741, and 1777–8 were issued in parts (see R. M. Wiles, *Serial Publication in England before 1750* [1957]).

KIMPTON, Edward

478. A NEW AND COMPLETE / UNIVERSAL HISTORY / OF THE / HOLY BIBLE, / INCLUDING THE / OLD AND NEW TESTAMENT; / AND COMPRISING / All the TRANSACTIONS recorded in the SACRED WRITINGS, / FROM THE / CREATION OF THE WORLD, / TO THE / *Full Establishment of Christianity*. IN WHICH / The several Parts of Scripture are pleasingly related, and satisfactorily illustrated; Obscure / Passages rendered clear; Seeming Inconsistencies reconciled; the various Significations of the / most expressive Appelatives elucidated; False Translations amended; Former Errors corrected; / and Difficult Texts made clear to every Capacity. / TO WHICH ARE ADDED / An ample and comprehensive DISPLAY of the CONNECTION between the / SACRED WRITERS and PROFANE AUTHORS: Also / Particular Accounts of the LIVES and TRANSACTIONS of the most eminent PATRIARCHS, / PROPHETS, and other Servants of GOD, who, by an inspired Grace, have distinguished / themselves in the Display of Divine Wisdom. / ILLUSTRATED WITH NOTES

Historical	Literal	Systematical	Reconciliatory
Theological	Critical	Chronological	Biographical
Civil	Natural	Argumentative	Practical
Commercial	Military	Philological	AND
Geographical	Political	Explanatory	Moral

The Whole calculated to enlighten the Understanding, purify the Heart, and promote the Knowledge of / those SACRED SCRIPTURES, by which we may obtain Happiness here, and eternal Salvation hereafter. / — / By the Reverend EDWARD KIMPTON, / Vicar of ROGATE in *Sussex*, Morning Preacher of *St. Matthew's*, *Bethnal-Green*, and late of / CHRIST's COLLEGE, *Cambridge*; / Assisted by many learned GENTLEMEN, who have made the Sacred Writings their peculiar Study. / — / Embellished with a great Number of beautiful COPPER-PLATES, descriptive of the most distinguished Transactions related in / the SACRED WRITINGS; From Original Drawings of the ingenious Messrs. METZ. STOTHARD and SAUNDERS, / Members of the Royal Academy; and other eminent Artists. The Whole engraved by the most Capital Performers, / particularly GRIGNION, COLLIER, HEATH, COOK, BLAKE, WHITE, TAYLOR, &c. / — /

[6-line motto] / = / LONDON: / Printed for J. COOKE, No. 17, PATER-
NOSTER ROW [?1781]. (BM, GEB, Princeton Theological Seminary)

A prospectus in the John Johnson Collection of Ephemera in Bodley
(b279) announces that 'The Whole of [*Kimpton's HISTORY*] . . . being just
printed off, may be had complete neatly bound in Calf and lettered, Price
1l. 16s. or in Sixty Weekly Numbers [*of 3 folio signatures each on Saturdays*],
Price Six-Pence each, one or more at a Time.' Each Number 'will be embellished with one or more Grand Copper-Plates' 'and each Plate [*is*]
curiously ornamented with Borders emblematical of the respective Subjects',
comprising 'the most inimitable Set of Prints ever given in a Work of a
similar Nature in this Kingdom'. The first issue of the work was presumably
in similar numbers.

Three of the 61 plates are signed '*Blake sc*', all the plates are undated, and
most are, like Blake's, headed '*Engraved for Kimpton's History of the Bible*'
above a heavy ornamental border. Blake's plates are:

1. At p. 19 is 'GENESIS, XIII. 11.' 'The PARTING of LOT and ABRA-
   HAM, *after seperating their Flocks, &c.*' '*C.M. Metz del*' (plate-size: 17·6 ×
   29·0 cm). In the 'Directions to the Binder' this is pl. 9.
2. At p. 110 in 'JOSHUA, VIII. 20.' '*The* BATTLE *of* AI, *with the* DE-
   STRUCTION *of the* CITY, *by the Army of* JOSHUA.' '*Stothard del*'
   (plate-size: 17·5×28·7 cm). In the 'Directions', this is pl. 13. A proof
   is in the BMPR.
3. At p. 131 is 'JUDGES IX–46.' 'THE FUGITIVE SHECHEMITES
   Burnt and Suffocated in the Holds of their Idol Berith, by order of King Abimelech.'
   '*C. M. Metz del.*' (plate-size: 17·6 × 28·8 cm). It is pl. 2 in the 'Directions'.
4. A different engraving of 'The Battle of Ai' survives in a unique pull in
   the Rosenwald Collection without letters but showing the warriors fighting right-handed rather than left-handed as in the published version.
   According to R. Todd ('Stothard [Thomas] *The Battle of Ai*', *Paul Grinka
   Catalogue Five* [1972]), this engraving is 'undoubtedly also by Blake'
   and must have been the one he intended to publish, for it corresponds
   more closely to Stothard's drawing in the Rosenwald Collection than
   does the engraving in the book, in which the sky seems to have 'been left
   unfinished'. Todd reproduces both engravings and the drawing.

The plates in Kimpton's *History* were also used in Kimpton's three editions
of Josephus, and, since the four editions are all undated, the problems of
date and priority are particularly intricate. A number of facts suggest that
the plates appeared first in Kimpton's *History*: (1) Though the acknowledgement of copyright in Josephus specified that John Cooke has engaged 'the
most able Artists to design and engrave a more beautiful set of Copper
Plates than was ever given in a Work of the like Kind in the English Language', this is specifically and explicitly contradicted by the inscription on
the *History* plates themselves: '*Engraved for Kimpton's History of the Bible*'.
(Perhaps Cooke would have defended himself by pointing out that the
Josephus statement does not actually say for what 'Work' the engravings
were commissioned—and John Cooke was the publisher of both works.)

(2) The plates in the *History* are considerably sharper and brighter than those in Josephus. For example, in 'The Battle of Ai' there is more shading on the horse's shoulder and neck in Josephus than in the *History*. (3) Blake was singled out as a 'Capital Performer' in the *History*, but not in Josephus. (4) None of the plates is dated in Kimpton, though two are in Josephus.

This gives priority but no date. Unfortunately, Kimpton's career tells us nothing. (Born 1744, at Cambridge 1765–8, Morning Preacher at St. Matthew's, Bethnal-Green, and Vicar of Rogate, Surrey, 1771–1811, died 1811, according to *Alumni Cantabrigienses*, ed. J. A. Venn, Part II, Vol. IV [1951].) A better indication is that Blake did not sign his own engravings until he had finished his apprenticeship in 1779, so his plates are probably 1779 or later. Better yet are puffs, for two works 'lately published' by Cooke, carefully planted in Kimpton's *History* (pp. 80, 217, 438; 470, 691)—C. T. Middleton's *New and Complete System of Geography* (LC has editions of 1777–8, 1778–9) and Henry Southwell's *New Book of Martyrs* (BM dates its copy ?1780). The 60 numbers of the *History* probably started or finished about 1781.

Blake's first and third plates have a different ornamental frame, and are signed in a different place, in the *History* than in Josephus. In Blake's second plate the border and inscription are the same in all printings.

A new edition in 1813 (Princeton Theological Seminary) had no plates.

THE LADY'S POCKET BOOK

479. § [*The Lady's Pocket Book*. London: Published for James Dodsley and Joseph Johnson. 1782.] (*UNTRACED*)

No copy of *The Lady's Pocket Book* (1782) has been traced, so we can only speculate about it. The prime evidence is two plates on one leaf in the BMPR:

1. '*The Morning Amusements of her Royal Highness the Princess Royal & her 4 Sisters.*' 'Stothard del.', 'Blake sc.', 'Published by J. Johnson, S! Paul's Church Yard, Nov! 1. 1782'. (Design size: 12·6×9·6 cm.) (Proofs are also in the Royal Academy [before title] and the Rosenwald Collection.)
2. '*A Lady in the full Dress, & another in the most fashionable Undress now worn.*' 'T. S. del', 'W.B. sc' (design size: 6·5×9·6 cm). (A proof with only Blake's name is in the Royal Academy.)

Gilchrist (1942, p. 44) says that these plates appeared in 'Dodsley's' *Lady's Pocket Book*, but Dodsley is hard to reconcile with Johnson's name in the imprint. Perhaps they published the book jointly. In any case the Dodsley must be James (1724–97) rather than his better-known brother Robert (1703–64).

If Dodsley was the publisher, *The Lady's Pocket Book* must have been a descendant of *The Ladies New Memorandum Book* for 1758 which Robert Dodsley advertised in the *London Chronicle* for 22–4 Nov. 1757 (see R. Strauss, *Robert Dodsley* [1910], 336–7). According to this advertisement, the work was published 'in a Size fit for the Pocket, Price 1s,' and contained twenty-four country dances for 1758, fifty-two pages for entering engagements, a daily table of expenses, rules to be observed at Bath, 'Maxims for the Ladies concerning the Art of Pleasing', an essay on female economy, bills of fare for every month in the year, 'Ready Messes for Supper', directions for playing piquet, a list of the holidays in public offices, and 'Some general Things proper to be known and remembered'.

The title and type of book were commonplace, and I have traced (1) *Ladies' Pocket-Book* (1778); (2) *Ladies Own Memorandum Book* (1778, 1784); (3) *Ladies most elegant . . . Lottery Pocket Book* (1778); (4) *Ladies Complete Pocket Book* (Newbury, 1778); (5) *Ladies' Annual Journal or Complete Pocket Book* (1778, 1784); (6) *The Ladies Diary* (1779); (7) *Ladies Complete Pocket Book* (Newcastle: W. M. Harding, 1781); (8) *Ladies most elegant and complete Pocket Book* (Newbury, 1789); and (9) *Young Lady's Pocket Library* (1790). The title was casually used, and Stothard signed a receipt of 11 April 1795 for 'sixteen guineas [*for*] two drawings for Lady's [Pocket Book *del*] Maggazien' (Princeton).

Such an ephemeral publication was likely to be preserved only by the sentimental relatives of the lady who had entered her engagements in it, and to be recorded in library catalogues under the name of the original owner rather than the title of the memorandum book itself. It would be a matter of very considerable interest to discover a complete copy of *The Lady's Pocket Book*, with Blake's long-ignored plate in it. Probably the most promising line of further search would be to get in touch with the owners of the 104 diaries of 1782 listed by W. Matthews, *British Diaries* (1950). The first dozen I have contacted, however, could give no information about *The Lady's Pocket Book*.

LAVATER, John Caspar

480. A. APHORISMS ON MAN: / TRANSLATED [by J. H. Fuseli] / FROM THE ORIGINAL MANUSCRIPT / OF / THE REV. JOHN CASPAR LAVATER, / CITIZEN OF ZURIC. / — / ——— è cœlo descendit γνωθι σεαντον. / Juv. Sat. IX. / — / LONDON: / PRINTED FOR J. JOHNSON, / ST. PAUL'S CHURCH-YARD. / — / MDCCLXXXVIII [1788]. (BM, GEB)

B. APHORISMS ON MAN. / . . . Juv. Sat. IX. / — / SECOND EDITION. / = / London, / PRINTED BY T. BENSLEY, / FOR J. JOHNSON, ST. PAUL'S CHURCH-YARD, / — / M,DCC,LXXXIX [1789]. (BM, GEB)

C. . . . THIRD EDITION. / — / London, / PRINTED FOR J. JOHNSON, ST. PAUL'S CHURCH- / YARD. / — / M,DCC,XCIV [1794]. (GEB, LC)

A. The only plate, the frontispiece, representing a seated man looking up, is signed 'Blake sc', and was probably designed by Fuseli, to whom the book is dedicated. (Fuseli's sketch, now in the collection of Mr. Robert N. Essick, is reproduced in *Blake Newsletter*, V [1972], 173.)

B. There is no change in the plate in the second and third editions (1789 & 1794). There were no plates in the 'Third Edition' of Dublin, 1790, or the 'Fifth Edition' of Newburyport, 1793.

According to the 'Advertisement', 'It is the intention of the editor to add another volume of APHORISMS ON ART, WITH CHARACTERS AND EXAMPLES, not indeed by the same author [*but by Fuseli*], which the reader may expect in the course of the year.' Consequently the half-title reads simply 'Aphorisms. Vol. I.' Fuseli's *Aphorisms* were destroyed by a fire at the printer's, and were not published until Knowles's edition of Fuseli's works appeared in 1831.

In the Rosenwald Collection of the Library of Congress are proofs of Blake's plate in three different states.

Blake made extensive marginal comments in his own copy of the first edition (1788) of this work; see no. 735.

481. A. ESSAYS / ON / PHYSIOGNOMY, / DESIGNED TO PRO-MOTE / THE KNOWLEDGE AND THE LOVE OF MANKIND. / BY / JOHN CASPAR LAVATER, / CITIZEN OF ZURICH, AND MINISTER OF THE GOSPEL. / ILLUSTRATED BY MORE THAN / EIGHT HUNDRED ENGRAVINGS ACCURATELY COPIED; / AND SOME DUPLICATES ADDED FROM ORIGINALS. / EXECUTED BY, OR UNDER THE INSPECTION OF, / THOMAS HOLLOWAY. / TRANSLATED FROM THE FRENCH / BY / HENRY HUNTER, D.D. / MINISTER OF THE SCOTS CHURCH, LONDON-WALL. / — / *GOD CREATED MAN AFTER HIS OWN IMAGE.* / — / [3 vols., but bound in 5 parts.] VOLUME I. / [Vignette] / LONDON: PRINTED FOR JOHN MURRAY, No. 32, FLEET-STREET; H. HUNTER, D.D. CHARLES'S-/SQUARE; AND T. HOLLOWAY, NO. 11, BACHE'S-ROW, HOXTON. M DCC LXXXIX [1789]. VOLUME II [bound in 2 parts]. . . . H. HUNTER, D.D. BETHNAL- / GREEN ROAD . . . MDCCXCII [1792]. VOLUME III [bound in 2 parts]. / [Vignette] / LONDON. PRINTED FOR MURRAY AND HIGHLEY, NO. 32, FLEET-STREET; H. HUNTER, D.D. / BETHNAL-GREEN ROAD . . . MDCCXCVIII [1798, i.e. 1799]. (Boston Museum, BM, Fitzwilliam, GEB, LC, Wellesley, Westminster Public)

B. . . . [3 vols. bound in 5 parts.] VOLUME I [II] [III]. / [Vignette] / LONDON: PRINTED FOR JOHN MURRAY, NO. 32, FLEET-STREET; H. HUNTER, D.D. BETHNAL- / GREEN ROAD; AND T. HOLLOWAY, NO. 11, BACHE'S-ROW, HOXTON. MDCCXCII [1792]. (Princeton)

C. . . . ILLUSTRATED BY / ENGRAVINGS, ACCURATELY COPIED; / . . . [3 vols. bound in 5 parts] VOLUME I [II] [III]. / [Vignette] / LON-DON: PRINTED BY T. BENSLEY, BOLT COURT, FLEET STREET, / FOR JOHN STOCKDALE, PICCADILLY. / 1810. (Raymond Lister)

In all three printings, the two parts of Volumes II and III are bound separately, but are continuously paginated, and the second Parts do not have separate title-pages.

A. The book was issued in 41 sumptuous folio parts intended to be at intervals of six weeks at 12s. to subscribers, the first in Jan. 1788 and the last in March 1799. Naturally, 'The Vignettes belonging to each *Number* . . . accompany the letter-press, in the proper places' (as the back-cover to Part III announced), but the larger plates did not necessarily accompany the sheets they illustrated, and, as the same Part III announcement stated, the only undertaking was that 'Care will be taken to bring forward the larger plates, so as to enable Subscribers to complete every Volume as it is printed' (Berg Collection, NYP). Each part-title announced the engravings which were issued with it. Blake's 'Democritus' plate was issued with the third number, which was described as follows on the cover:

N⁰· III. *LONDON, May*, 1788. / [PRICE TWELVE SHILLINGS TO SUBSCRIBERS.] / NUMBER III. / LAVATER'S / ESSAYS ON PHYSI-OGNOMY: / CONTAINING / THREE SHEETS OF LETTERPRESS; / AND / THE FOLLOWING ENGRAVINGS FINELY EXE-CUTED: / . . . / 7. DEMOCRITUS, FINISHED. / . . . / — / LONDON: / PRINTED FOR JOHN MURRAY, NO. 32, FLEET-STREET; HENRY HUNTER, D.D. / THE TRANSLATOR, CHARLES'-SQUARE; AND THOMAS HOLLOWAY, THE / ENGRAVER, NO. 11. BACHE'S-ROW, NEAR CHARLES'-SQUARE, HOXTON. / SOLD ALSO BY / G. NICOL, BOOKSELLER TO HIS MAJESTY, PALLMALL; J. AND J. BOYDELL, CHEAPSIDE; J. WALTER, CHARING-CROSS; AND J. SEWELL, NO. 32, CORNHILL. (Berg Collection, NYP)

It will be noticed that the publishers are not the same as on the general title-page, nor are they quite the same on the cover of the last number.

Blake's plate at p. 127 was issued with Part V in the summer of 1788. Blake's last two plates were issued with the eighth Part in Feb. 1789, the cover of which differed from the third only in the number of the part, the date, 'FOUR SHEETS OF LETTER-PRESS', and 16 named engravings, including no. '2. A HAND WITH A TORCH, FINISHED' and the head Blake engraved in profile identified as no. '11. SPALDING, DITTO [*i.e. in* OUTLINE].' (Berg Collection. I am grateful to Dr. D. V. Erdman for assistance with the description of the parts in the Berg Collection.)

Not counting small unsigned designs and mere outlines, there are 523 pages with engravings on them. Of these, 256 are unsigned—34 in Vol. I, 100 in Vol. II, 121 in Vol. III. Blake's four engravings are all in the first volume:

1. Vol. I, p. 127 is a vignette of two markedly Blakean old men planting trees, signed '*Blake Sc*' (plate-mark: 8·5 × 6·1 cm).
2. Vol. I, at p. 159 is 'DEMOCRITUS.' '*Rubens delin.*', '*Blake sculp.*', '25' (plate-size: 27·0 × 22·5 cm). (A reduced engraving of Blake's plate of 'Democritus' is in the Rosenwald Collection of the Library of Congress.)
3. Vol. I, on p. 206 is an arm and hand holding a candle, with moths nearby, signed '*Blake Sc*' (plate-size: 14·3 × 6·9 cm).
4. Vol. I, on p. 225, a head in profile, is signed '*Blake sculp*' (plate-size: 18·0 × 15·4 cm).

B. The 1792 issue was presumably for late subscribers, with the title-page of Volume III antedated. The Blake plates are not changed.

C. The 1810 Stockdale printing seems to be a new edition, on paper water-marked '1806', with a label giving the 'PRICE 30 GUINEAS'. The plates are unchanged.

The work was very profitable and popular, but though there were several translations (by Holcroft [1789 ff., twenty editions], by C. Moore [1791 ff.], Samuel Shaw [1792], and George Grenville [1797]), Blake's plates were apparently not printed after 1810. The 537 coppers were sold at auction by Mr. Saunders on 29 Jan. 1818 (according to a prospectus, BM 11902.c.26).

MALKIN, Benjamin Heath

482. A / FATHER'S MEMOIRS / OF / HIS CHILD. / BY / *BENJ. HEATH MALKIN, ESQ*. / M.A. F.A.S. / = / Great loss to all that ever him did see; / Great loss to all, but greatest loss to me. / ASTROPHEL. / = / LON-DON: / PRINTED FOR LONGMAN, HURST, REES, AND ORME, / PATERNOSTER ROW; *BY T. BENSLEY, BOLT COURT, FLEET STREET.* / 1806. (BM, Bodley, Boston Museum, Columbia, Fitzwilliam, GEB, Harvard, Michigan, New York University, Princeton [2], Smith, Syracuse, Trinity College [Hartford, Conn.], Wellesley, Westminster Public, West Sussex Record Office, Yale [2])

The first version of this biography appeared in the *Monthly Magazine*, XIV (1 Nov. 1802), 329–31, and 'S. P.' asked for further memoirs in the 1 Dec. 1802 issue (p. 409).

The expenses of the book entered in the records of Longman, Green, and Co. (Impression Book No. 3, f. 14) are:

Malkins Memoirs of his Child	1000- Jan 1806		
Printing 30 sheets -- 2/[*illeg*]/0 Bensley	30	16	—
Corrections 36/- Labels 7/6 ----	2	3	6
Hotpressing ---------------------------	5	5	—
Paper [*?30 reams at ?2.10s per ream*]			
Royal (M^r Ms own)	?75		
	113	4	6

(The last two figures are in pencil.) Further records (Commission & Divide Ledger, f. 187, Jan. 1806) are for copper and engraving of 'Fac Simile Plates', £1. 0. 6; working plates and maps, £22. 11. 3; advertising, £14. 18. 7. Later records (Commission Ledgers, Vol. I, f. 30) indicate that Malkin took at least 47 copies for himself; that '450 [*copies were*] Wasted [*producing*] 12 Rms [*at*] 12/- [*each for £*]7 4 0 [*credit, with*] 60 left Aug 1811'; and that seventeen more were sold by June 1815.

There are four plates, three of them (at pp. 33, 54, 95) after the child T. W. Malkin; though they are unsigned, we may be confident that they, like the fourth plate, were engraved by Cromek. Blake's only plate is:

1. The frontispiece of an angel taking a child to heaven from its mother, inscribed: '*Wm Blake inv^t*', '*R H Cromek sc*', '*London Published by Longman C^o February 1st 1806*' (plate size: 21·7 × 14·5 cm). Inset into this design is an oval portrait (7·7 × 6·0 cm) of the two-year-old child, painted,

according to the introductory letter (p. xliv), by [Richard Morton] Paye. (Two proofs before letters are in the BMPR. Gilchrist [1942, p. 226] asserted very positively that Blake originally engraved his own design for the frontispiece, but that this was later erased and re-engraved by Cromek.)

Malkin's important account of Blake in the introductory letter to Thomas Johnes, M.P., dated 4 January 1806 (pp. xviii–xli), is reprinted in Symons (1907), in *Blake Records* (1969), and in Wittreich (1970).

Blake's opinion of Master Malkin's artistic talents is quoted on pp. 33–4.

Malkin's *Memoirs* were reviewed in *The British Critic, The Literary Journal, The Monthly Magazine*, and *The Monthly Review* (nos. 836, 823, 955, 2238, 832).

THE MONTHLY MAGAZINE

483. THE / MONTHLY / MAGAZINE, / AND / *BRITISH REGISTER*, / [IV, no. xxiii (Oct. 1797)] ... / *LONDON:* / PRINTED FOR R. PHILLIPS; / AND / SOLD BY J. JOHNSON, No. 72, ST. PAUL's CHURCH-YARD. (BM, Bodley, Michigan, National Library of Scotland)

As an illustration to an anonymous article entitled 'Memoirs of the Life and principal Works of the late Joseph Wright, Esq. of Derby' (pp. 289–94) in a section called 'Original Anecdotes and Remains of Eminent Persons' is an engraving

1. '*For the Monthly Magazine, Sept. 1797.*' 'The late Mʳ WRIGHT of Derby.' '*Blake: s*' (design size: 6·0 × 8·7 cm).

MORA, Jose Joaquin de

484. MEDITACIONES / POETICAS. / — / POR / JOSE JOAQUIN DE MORA. / — / LONDRES: / LO PUBLICA R. ACKERMANN, No. 101, STRAND; / Y EN SU ESTABLECIMIENTO EN MEGICO: / ASIMISMO / EN COLOMBIA, EN BUENOS AYRES, CHILE, PERU, Y GUATEMALA. / 1826. (GEB, Liverpool, Texas)

The preface (pp. ii–iii) explains that the poems of Mora were especially written to interpret (in their own way) the magnificent designs of 'Guillermo Black'. Ackermann, the publisher, had purchased Schiavonetti's etchings of Blake's designs for Blair's *Grave* (1808) and published them again in 1813. The frontispiece is titled 'GUILLERMO BLAKE', '*T. Phillips, R.A. Pinxᵗ* ', '*L. Schiavonetti, V.A. Sculpᵗ*' Schiavonetti's and Blake's names remain on the plates as previously, but the pages references and imprints have been removed and the latter replaced, on pl. 2–7, 9–12 below, with '*Pub. por R. Ackermann, Londres, y en Megico.*' The plates seem only slightly worn. Each title has been altered, and the new title is also, with one exception, the title of Mora's poem on the facing page. The plates are:

1. The duplicate title-page, 'MEDITACIONES / POETICAS, / por / *Jose Joaquin de Mora.*' '*L. Schiavonetti. sculp*'. The frontispiece and title-page have been reduced to *c.* 23·6 × 36·6 cm.
2. At p. 1, 'LA ETERNIDAD Y EL ESPACIO' (pl. 2).

3. At p. 4, 'EL SEPULCRO' (pl. 4).
4. At p. 7, 'LA MUERTE DEL IMPIO' (pl. 5).
5. At p. 10, 'LA MUERTE DEL JUSTO' (pl. 10)
6. At p. 13, 'LA SEPARACION' (pl. 6).
7. At p. 17, 'LA PUERTA DE LA MUERTE' is the title for pl. 11, but the poem is called 'La Puerta del Sepulchro'.
8. At p. 19, 'EL VALLE DE LA MUERTE' (pl. 7).
9. At p. 21, 'LA CAVERNA' (pl. 9).
10. At p. 24, 'LA RESURRECCION' (pl. 12).
11. At p. 26, 'EL JUICIO' (pl. 8).
12. At p. 30, 'LA REUNION' (pl. 3).

THE NOVELIST'S MAGAZINE, Vol. VIII

485. A. THE / Novelist's Magazine. / VOL. VIII. / *CONTAINING* / Don Quixote. / [vignette] / *LONDON*: / Printed for Harrison and Cº / Nº 18 Paternoster Row / 1782. (BM, Bodley, Boston Public, Buffalo Public, GEB, Indiana, Iowa, Newberry, Princeton, Swansea, Wisconsin, Yale)

B. *LONDON:* / Printed for Harrison and Co. / No. 18, Paternoster Row. / 1784. (GEB, Minnesota, New York, Rice Institute)

C. . . . Cº / Nº . . . . / 1792. (Brooklyn College, Minnesota)

Publication: In all volumes of the *Novelist's Magazine* there are both general title-pages (as above) and individual title-pages for each novel in that volume. Further, the dates on the two title-pages do not always correspond, so that the individual title-page (below) may be *either earlier or later* than the general title-page, and in Vol. IX this happens frequently. Consequently, the general title-page above affirms nothing reliably about the date of the work that follows, and the location of copies refers, for the *general* title-page, to title-page alone. Each volume is broken down into its component novels, and the location of each individual dated title-page is given. The two lists, of general and of individual title-pages, do not quite tally with each other because (*a*) often one of the two title-pages is missing, and (*b*) my information, often derived at a distance from generous librarians, is not always complete.

According to Thomas Rees (*Reminiscences of Literary London 1779 to 1853* [1896], 21, 22), Harrison was one of the first publishers to divide works of magnitude into small portions and issue them periodically in fascicles:

His first speculation of the sort was 'The Novelist's Magazine'. . . . They were printed in octavo, in double columns, stitched up in small numbers, and published weekly, at sixpence each. . . . Its popularity may be estimated by the fact that, at one time 12,000 copies of each number were sold weekly.

This is most useful information, for none of the dozens of sets examined by or for me preserves original wrappers, labels, binding, or any external indication that it was not sold to begin with in the form in which it has survived—as complete volumes of the *Novelist's Magazine* or as separate novels. Each *Novelist's Magazine* volume has about 16 plates, but they are not evenly distributed through the text as we might expect if they were issued at intervals corresponding, however roughly, to the dates on the engravings.

(In GEB's Vol. VIII, for instance, the plates are at pp. 34, 48, 89, 93, 120, 126, 256, 334, 360, 407, 431, 475, 527, 535, 586.) Further, the dates and numbers on the plates do not correspond with their positions in the books. In Vol. VIII the dates cover 9 March to 22 June 1782, but the plate at p. 34 is dated 25 May, and that at p. 527 is 6 April. Each volume (in a multi-volume novel such as IX) starts a new series of signatures, but the first signature is B, not A, and in most cases the first few pages of the new novel are the unidentified remainder of the signature of the previous novel. The division into fascicles was obviously an arbitrary one, having nothing to do with internal divisions (such as chapters) indicated by the author, for a new chapter or novel often begins on the verso of the last page of the preceding one. (In later volumes of the *Novelist's Magazine*, including Vol. VIII–XI, however, new 'Volumes' within the *Novelist's Magazine* volume normally begin on the recto of a fresh page.)

The only physical evidence I have discovered to indicate the original issue in fascicles is a pattern of supplementary stab holes in two sets (Boston Public & GEB), which seem to run consistently through 5 gatherings. These stab holes do not include (1) the general title-pages or (2) the engravings. This suggests that there were 5 sheets or gatherings to a fascicle. The plates (at least for Vol. VIII–XI) are regularly dated a week apart, so the fascicles were clearly issued at weekly intervals. The proportion of plates to gatherings is consistently about one to five (16 for 74 gatherings in Vol. VIII, 18 for 84 in Vol. IX, 28 for 141 in Vol. X–XI).

When all the fascicles had been issued at 6*d.* apiece, a general title-page was printed and issued with the last fascicle and engraving, and the individual owner had the fascicles bound as seemed best to him or to his binder (there are no directions to the binder). Thus at a rate not beyond a journey-man's pocket could be obtained over the years 1780–8 some 60 novels in 23 volumes, including some of the best novels of the century—*Vicar of Wakefield, Roderick Random, Tom Jones, Gil Blas, Robinson Crusoe, Tristram Shandy, Peregrine Pickle, Ferdinand Count Fathom, Gulliver's Travels, Sir Launcelot Greaves, Sir Charles Grandison, Clarissa Harlowe, Humphry Clinker, Pamela, Rasselas*—as well as some works not so well remembered, such as *Memoirs of a Magdalen* and *The History of Miss Betsy Thoughtless*.

However, there is still a further problem in understanding the *Novelist's Magazine*. Since the issue was in fascicles, there was always the danger that some buyers might avoid some works and rejoin the series when a more attractive title was offered. Thus whole novels were left on the publisher's hands after the issue in fascicles, and many novels from the series today are to be found with no overt indication that they were originally part of the *Novelist's Magazine*. Some of the novels in the series went out of print before the others. For instance, in Vol. IX, *A Sentimental Journey* was apparently out of print by 1785, but *Gulliver's Travels* lasted until 1792. When buyers wanted a complete Vol. IX, therefore, they were likely to get a mixed bag of dates.

New dates on the title-pages indicate new editions, not just reissues of the old type-settings.

The Individual title-page in Vol. VIII reads:

A. THE / HISTORY / AND / ADVENTURES / OF THE RENOWNED / DON QUIXOTE. / TRANSLATED FROM THE SPANISH / OF / MIGUEL DE CERVANTES SAAVEDRA. / TO WHICH IS PREFIXED, / SOME ACCOUNT OF THE AUTHOR'S LIFE. / BY DR. [Tobias] SMOLLETT. / IN FOUR VOLUMES. / [Ornament] / LONDON: / Printed for HARRISON and Co. No. 18, Paternoster-Row. / M DCC LXXXII [1782]. (BM, Bodley, Buffalo Public, GEB, Illinois, Swansea)

B. . . . M DCC LXXXIV [1784]. (BM, Bodley, Brooklyn College, GEB, Minnesota)

C. . . . No 18 Paternoster Row. / M DCC XCII [1792]. (Princeton, Minnesota)

Engravings: Proofs of all the *Novelist's Magazine* are in Princeton in an extra-illustrated copy of Mrs. Bray's *Stothard*. None of Blake's plates below has an engraved title, and in all the imprint formula is 'Published as the Act directs ⌊,⌋ by Harrison & Co. . . .' Since there are no directions to the binder, there are minor variations in the location of the plates.

In Vol. VIII there are 16 plates, all inscribed '*Stothard del.*' and 'DON QUIXOTE', but only two have '*Blake sculp.*':

1. 'Plate IX.' at p. 256 represents a group of men looking at a hat-shaped basin which one is holding up; it is dated 'May 4, 1782.' (Design size, exclusive of ornamental border: 7·0 × 11·7 cm.)
2. 'Plate XV.' (p. 586) showing Don Quixote dictating his will from his deathbed is dated 'June 15, 1782.' (7·0 × 11·7 cm.)

THE NOVELIST'S MAGAZINE, Vol. IX

486. A. THE / Novelist's Magazine. / VOL. IX. / *CONTAINING* / Sentimental Journey, / Gulliver's Travels, / David Simple, / Sir Launcelot Greaves, / The Peruvian Princess, / and Jonathan Wild. / [Vignette] / *LONDON:* / Printed for Harrison and Co / No 18 Paternoster Row / 1782. (Bodley, Boston Public, Buffalo Public, Cambridge, GEB [2 copies], Illinois, Newberry, Rice Institute, Wisconsin, Yale)

B. *LONDON*: / Printed for Harrison and Co. / No. 18, Paternoster-Row. 1785. (Minnesota, New York)

C. *AND* Jonathan Wild. / . . . Co / No . . . / 1793. (Brooklyn College)

The individual title-pages read:

i. A. A / SENTIMENTAL JOURNEY / THROUGH / FRANCE AND ITALY, / BY / MR. YORICK. / IN TWO VOLUMES. / BY THE REV. MR. [Laurence] STERNE. / [Ornament] / LONDON: / Printed for HARRISON and Co. No. 18, Paternoster-Row. / M DCC LXXXII [1782]. (Buffalo Public, Cambridge, GEB, NYP, Princeton)

B. M DCC LXXXV [1785]. (Bodley, Brooklyn College, GEB, Minnesota)

C. No 18, Paternoster Row. / M DCC XCII. (Minnesota)

ii. A. TRAVELS / INTO SEVERAL / REMOTE NATIONS / OF THE /

WORLD. / BY / LEMUEL GULLIVER, / FIRST A SURGEON, AND THEN A CAPTAIN OF SEVERAL SHIPS. / IN TWO VOLUMES. / BY DEAN [Jonathan] SWIFT. / . . . / M DCC LXXXII [1782]. (Bodley, Buffalo Public, Cambridge, GEB [2], Minnesota, NYP, Princeton)

B. N° 18, Paternoster Row / M DCC XCII [1792]. (Brooklyn)

iii. A. THE / ADVENTURES / OF / DAVID SIMPLE: / CONTAINING / AN ACCOUNT OF HIS TRAVELS / THROUGH / THE CITIES OF LONDON AND WESTMINSTER, / IN THE / SEARCH OF A REAL FRIEND. / BY MISS [Sarah] FIELDING. / IN TWO VOLUMES. / . . . Paternoster-Row. / M DCC LXXXII [1782]. (Bodley, Buffalo Public, Cambridge, GEB [2], NYP, Princeton)

B. Paternoster Row / M DCC LXXXVIII [1788]. (Brooklyn College, Minnesota)

C. N° 18 . . . . / M DCC XCII [1792]. (Minnesota)

iv. A. THE / ADVENTURES / OF / SIR LAUNCELOT GREAVES. / BY DR. SMOLLETT, / IN TWO VOLUMES. / . . . Paternoster-Row. / M DCC LXXXII [1782]. (Bodley, Buffalo Public, Cambridge, GEB [2], NYP, Princeton)

B. Paternoster Row / M DCC LXXXVII [1787]. (Brooklyn College, Minnesota)

v. A. LETTERS / OF / A PERUVIAN PRINCESS: / WITH / THE SEQUEL. / TRANSLATED FROM / THE FRENCH OF MADAME [Francoise Huguet] DE GRAFIGNY, / BY FRANCIS ASHWORTH, ESQ.[1] / IN TWO VOLUMES. / . . . Paternoster-Row. / M DCC LXXXII [1782]. (Bodley, Buffalo Public, Cambridge, GEB [2], NYP, Princeton)

B. TRANSLATED . . . BY FRANCIS ASHMORE, ESQ.[1] / . . . Paternoster Row. / M DCC LXXXVII [1787]. (Brooklyn College, Minnesota)

C. N° 18. . . . / M DCC XCII [1792]. (Minnesota)

vi. A. THE / HISTORY / OF / JONATHAN WILD THE GREAT. / BY HENRY FIELDING, ESQ. / . . . Paternoster-Row. / M DCC LXXXII [1782]. (Bodley, Buffalo Public, Cambridge, GEB [2], NYP, Princeton)

B. Paternoster Row. / M DCC LXXXVIII [1788]. (Brooklyn College, Minnesota)

In a note at the end of Vol. XI, 'The Proprietors of the NOVELIST'S MAGAZINE' explain that they have been careful to print in every case 'the original Number of Volumes'. Each novel, however, like *A Sentimental Journey*, is continuously paginated. In Vol. IX all eleven 'Volumes' are normally bound as one.

There are 18 plates, 'Published' at weekly intervals following immediately after Vol. VIII, and though they are not in strict chronological order, the

---

[1] I can neither account for the alteration of the translator's name from Ashworth to Ashmore nor state confidently which one is correct, but as Ashmore translated Voltaire's *Zadig* and *The Sincere Huron* in the same series (Vols. II & XXI), it seems probable that Ashworth is merely a mistake.

first four novels as a whole are. For instance, all the plates for *David Simple* are in August, and all those for *Sir Launcelot Greaves* are in September. All the plates were inscribed '*Stothard del.*', but only 3 have '*Blake Sculp.*' or '*sculp.*':

1. 'Plate II.' of 'SENTIMENTAL JOURNEY' (Vol. II, p. 52) illustrates the chapter called 'The Grace', in which the peasant family dance after dinner; it was published 'July 6, 1782.' (Design size exclusive of ornamental frame: 7·3 × 11·7 cm.)
2. 'Plate I.' of 'DAVID SIMPLE' (Vol. I, p. 66) represents two women and a man attending the bed of a sick person; it was 'Published . . . Aug. 10, 1782.' (7·0 × 11·6 cm.)
3. 'Plate III.' of 'LAUNCELOT GREAVES' (Vol. I, p. 45) portrays an unruly rabble at a hustings; it was 'Published . . . Sept. 21. 1782.' (7·3 × 11·9 cm.)

It is simply coincidence that Blake's three plates are lettered 'I', 'II', and 'III', for a new numbering system begins in every novel.

THE NOVELIST'S MAGAZINE, Vol. X–XI

487. A. THE / Novelist's Magazine. / VOL. X. / *CONTAINING* / The First, Second, Third, and Fourth, / Volumes [*and* VOL. XI. / *CONTAINING* / The Fifth, Sixth, and / Seventh Volumes, /] of / Sir Charles Grandison. / [Vignette] / *LONDON*: / Printed for Harrison and C? / N? 18, Paternoster Row. / 1783. (BM, Bodley, Boston Public, Brooklyn College, Buffalo Public, GEB [2], Illinois, Indiana, Newberry, Princeton, Rice Institute, Swansea, Toronto, Wisconsin, Yale)

B. Harrison and Co. / No. 18, Paternoster Row. / 1785. (Bodley, Minnesota, New York)

C. § 1793.

There is a separate title-page for Vol. X:

A. THE / HISTORY / OF / SIR CHARLES GRANDISON. / IN / A SERIES OF LETTERS. / BY MR. SAMUEL RICHARDSON. / IN SEVEN VOLUMES. / [Ornament] / LONDON: / Printed for HARRISON and Co. No. 18, Paternoster-Row. / M DCC LXXXIII [1783]. (BM, Bodley, Buffalo Public, GEB, Swansea)

B. Paternoster Row. / M DCC LXXXV [1785]. (Bodley, Brooklyn College, Northwestern, Toronto)

C. N? 18, Paternoster Row. / M DCC XCIII [1793]. (GEB)

D. THE / History / OF / *SIR CHARLES* / GRANDISON, / and / *The Honourable Miss Byron*: / in which are included / MEMOIRS OF A NOBLE ITALIAN FAMILY, / IN / A Series of Letters. / — / By SAMUEL RICHARDSON EsQ. / Author of 'PAMELA and CLARISSA HARLOWE.' / — / *FORMERLY PUBLISHED IN SEVEN VOLUMES*: / Now Comprised in Two Large Octavo Volumes / EMBELLISHED WITH ELEGANT COPPER-PLATES. / — / Vol. I. / — / London: / Printed for HARRISON and Co., Paternoster-Row [?1800]. (Charles Ryskamp)

There are 28 plates in Vol. X–XI, published at weekly intervals (except for the last), but not bound in chronological order. All are inscribed '*Stothard del.*' and 'GRANDISON' and have roughly the same ornamental border, but only three are '*Blake sculp.*', all in Vol. X:

1. 'Plate XXIII.' (at Vol. III, p. 328 in BM and Bodley A and Brooklyn College B; bound at the back with the other plates in GEB C) represents Emily's maid opening the bedroom door to Hariet Byron. It was 'Published . . . Apr. 5, 1783.' (Design size exclusive of the ornamental border: 7·1 × 11·9 cm.)
2. 'Plate VI.' (at Vol. III, p. 351) shows Salmonet on the floor, Sir Charles with Salmonet's sword, and O'Hara in a clumsy fencing posture, while their lady flees out the door. It was 'Published . . . Dec. 7, 1782.' (7·1 × 11·9 cm.)
3. 'Plate XII.' (Vol. III, p. 442) depicts Sir Charles entering a room in which Clementina is standing holding a book and the Marchioness is holding a handkerchief to her eyes. It was 'Published . . . Jan. 18, 1783.' (7·1 × 11·6 cm.)

E. The undated edition appears to lack pl. 1–2.

OLIVIER [J.]

488. FENCING / FAMILIARIZED: / OR / A NEW TREATISE / ON THE / ART of SMALL SWORD. / ILLUSTRATED BY ELEGANT EN-GRAVINGS, / Representing all the different Attitudes on which the / Principles and Grace of the Art depend; / Painted from Life, and executed in a most elegant and / masterly Manner. / A NEW EDITION, / Revised, Corrected, and Augmented by an original Set of Prints. / BY MR. OLIVER, / Educated at the Royal Academy of Paris, and Professor / of Fencing, N° 8, Serle-street, Lincoln's Inn Fields. / *Sine Regula, sine Delectatione.* / LONDON: / Printed for JOHN BELL, at the British Library, Strand. / M DCC LXXX [1780]. (BM, Bodley, GEB, Harvard, Princeton)

A French title-page, which sometimes supplements or supplants the English one above, reads:

L'ART DES ARMES / SIMPLIFIÉ: / OU / Nouveau Traité sur la Maniere de / Se servir de l'Epée. / ENRICHI DE FIGURES EN TAILLE DOUCE, / Représentant toutes les differentes Attitudes d'où dependent / les Principes et la Grace de cet Art, peintes d'après Nature; / Executées superieurement et de la Maniere la plus élégante. / NOUVELLE EDITION, / Reveue, Corrigée, et Augmentée de plusieurs Planches. / PAR MR. OLIVIER, / Eléve de l'Academie Royal de Paris, et Maitre en fait / d'Armes, N° 8, Serle-street, Lincoln's Inn Fields. / *Sine Regula, Sine Delectatione.* / A LONDRES: / Chez J. BELL, Libraire, près d'Exeter Change dans le Strand. / M DCC LXXX [1780].

There are English and French texts side by side. The claim on the title-page about an 'original Set of Prints' is somewhat misleading, since, though all the engravings are new, the same actions are depicted in the earlier edition [1771]. All but the first of the fourteen plates fold out. Blake's only plate is:

1. At p. 44: '*4ᵉ. Position de l'allongement du Coup de quatre.*' '*J. Roberts delᵗ ad vivum.*' '*W Blake sculp*' (design size: ?20·5 × 15·0 cm).

The work may have sold slowly, for it seems to have been offered as a remainder almost ten years later; in *The World* for 1 Jan. 1787 and in *The Oracle* for 1 June 1789 were advertisements for Olivier's *Fencing Familiarized* 'with AN ORIGINAL SET OF PLATES', sold by Bell and by Olivier at Bell-yard, Carey-street, Lincoln's Inn, Temple Bar at 10s. 6d. (S. Morison, *John Bell, 1745–1831* [1930], 28). There is no other evidence for a printing of the book after 1780.

Rees, Abraham

489. THE / CYCLOPÆDIA; / OR, / *UNIVERSAL DICTIONARY* / OF / Arts, Sciences, and Literature. / BY / ABRAHAM REES, D.D. F.R.S. F.L.S. *S. Amer. Soc.* / WITH THE ASSISTANCE OF / EMINENT PRO-FESSIONAL GENTLEMEN. / — / ILLUSTRATED WITH NUMEROUS ENGRAVINGS, / *BY THE MOST DISTINGUISHED ARTISTS.* / — / PLATES. VOL. I / AGRICULTURE–ASTRONOMICAL INSTRU-MENTS. [VOL. II. / BASSO-RELIEVO–HOROLOGY.] [VOL. III./ HYDRAULICS–NAVAL ARCHITECTURE.] [VOL. IV / NAVIGA-TION–WRITING BY CYPHER.] / — / *LONDON*: / Printed for LONG-MAN, HURST, REES, ORME, & BROWN, SCATCHERD AND LETTERMAN, J. CUTHELL, / CLARKE AND SONS, LACKINGTON HUGHES HARDING MAVOR AND JONES, J. AND A. ARCH, / CADELL AND DAVIES, S. BAGSTER, J. MAWMAN, BLACK KINGS-BURY PARBURY AND ALLEN, / R. SCHOLEY, J. BOOTH, J. BOOKER, SUTTABY EVANCE AND FOX, BALDWIN CRADOCK AND JOY, / SHERWOOD NEELY AND JONES, OGLE DUNCAN AND CO., R. SAUNDERS, HURST ROBINSON AND CO., / J. DICKINSON, J. PATERSON, E. WHITESIDE, WILSON AND SONS, AND BRODIE AND DOWDING. / 1820. (BM [3], Bodley, Chicago, John Crerar, National Library of Scotland, Princeton, Southampton, Trinity College [Hartford, Conn.])

The *Cyclopaedia* was published at more or less regular intervals from Jan. 1802 until Aug. 1820 in 79 fascicles, two of which make up a volume (except for the last volume, which has three). The illustrations for the articles were issued pretty much as they were completed, sometimes with the article itself, sometimes in later fascicles, and sometimes with the six collections of plates in 1812, 1813, 1814, 1815, 1818, and 1819. For instance, the fascicle con-taining the article on 'Armour' was published on 2 May 1803, but Plate I illustrating it (dated 1 Sept. 1802) had been issued with fascicle 3 on 2 Sept. 1802; Plate II (9 Jan. 1804) appeared with fascicle 6 on 1 Feb. 1804; Plate III (1 June 1803) with fascicle 5 in Aug. 1803; and Plate 'IV & V' (10 Dec. 1818) with fascicle 78 in Sept. 1819. (Cf. B. Daydon Jackson, 'The Dates of Rees's Cyclopaedia', *The Journal of Botany, British and Foreign*, XXXIV

[1896], 307–11; Mr. J. S. G. Simmons kindly supplemented Jackson's description by an examination of the apparently unique surviving set of the *Cyclopaedia* in the original parts, now in the Oxford University Department of Botany. The preceding dates for the fascicles were supplied by Jackson, and confirmed by GEB, largely on the basis of publishers' advertisements or the latest dated engraving in any given fascicle, except for no. 2–4. For these, Mr. Simmons found a printed publisher's slip bearing the date Sept. 1819 pasted on the inner front board of Vol. XXXIX, Pt. 2 [fascicle 78]. The paper lettering label on the spine of Part F of the plates states that it was distributed with Vol. XXXIX, Pt. 2, so that F and fascicle 78 both probably appeared in September 1819.)

Up to 1809, 5,000 copies were printed of each fascicle, and then second editions were published (*Monthly Literary Advertiser*, 10 March 1809). Longmans preserve the publishing records, and the Strahan Printing Ledgers in the British Museum (Add. MSS 48816, ff. 91, 188, 190; 48817, ff. 88, 103) indicate that from 1810 on 6,250 copies were printed of each fascicle.

Blake engraved seven plates for 'Armour', 'Basso-Relievo', 'Miscellany' (i.e. 'Gem Engraving'), and 'Sculpture'. They may be preserved with the fascicles with which they were issued, but normally they are collected in Vols. I–IV of the 'Plates', with title-pages dated 1820. The articles which the engravings illustrate are unsigned, but according to the *Annual Biography and Obituary for the Year 1828* (no. 997), 'To Dr. Rees's Cyclopaedia Mr. Flaxman contributed the articles, "Armour," "Basso-Relievo," "Beauty," "Bronze," "Bust," "Composition," "Cast," and "Ceres."' Flaxman acknowledged the 'Basso Relievo' essay in 1804, and Tatham attributed the 'Sculpture' article to him (*Blake Records* [1969] 138, 238). He was advertised as the author of the articles on architecture, sculpture, and statuary in W. Bent's *List of New Publications* for April 1803, p. 14.

Blake's plates were issued between 1816 and 1819, as follows:

VOLUME I

1. 'ARMOUR', *'PLATE IV & V'*, representing 10 figures in chain and plate mail, was inscribed *'Blake sc'* and *'Published as the Act directs, Dec.ʳ 10, 1818, by Longman, Hurst, Rees, Orme & Brown, Paternoster Row.'* (Design size: 17 × 24 cm.) This plate was issued with fascicle 78 in Sept. 1819; the three other plates for Armour were engraved by Milton.

VOLUME II

2. 'BASSO RELIEVO', *'PLATE IV'*, represents 5 *'PAGAN ALTARS'*, a *'Basso-relievo round a Capitol in the Cathedral of Carrara'*, and *'Basso-relievo of Zethus, Antiope & Amphion.'* (Plate-size: *c.* 19·9 × 26·7 cm.) It is inscribed *'Blake sc.'*, dated 11 Nov. 1818, and was issued with fascicle F (of the plates) in Sept. 1819. The article itself was published on 1 Feb. 1804, with one plate (by J. Parker after Flaxman) dated 2 Jan. 1804. Two more plates for the article on Basso-Relievo, engraved by Bond and dated 1 Dec. 1807, were issued with fascicle 18 on 1 March 1808.

VOLUME III

3. 'MISCELLANY', '*GEM Engraving*', '*PLATE XVIII*', exhibits 18 figures '*Drawn by Farey*', '*Engraved by W. Blake & W. Lowry*', and published in '*1819*' (design size: *c.* 16·2×21 cm). The two large figures are probably the ones engraved by Blake. The article on 'Gem Engraving' was published on 8 Oct. 1810, and Blake's plate illustrating it was issued with fascicle F in Sept. 1819. Wilson Lowry engraved most of the 27 'Miscellany' plates.

VOLUME IV

4. 'SCULPTURE', '*PLATE I*', represents' '*Hercules of Dædalus, from a small Bronze*'; '*Cupid of Praxiteles, British Museum &c.*'; '*Minerva of Dipœnus & Scyllis, in the Villa Albani*'; '*Venus of Praxiteles, Perriers Statues*'; '*Jupiter Olympius. See Pausanias Ancient Statues, Coins & Gems*'; and '*Minerva of the Acropolis in Athens. See Hunter's Coins.*' (Design size: *c.* 18·5×26·7 cm.) It is signed '*Blake sc*' and was published 1 Feb. 1816. (Blake's sketch is in the Rosenwald Collection.) The article on Sculpture was issued in March 1816, and this plate appeared with fascicle 67 in Oct. 1816. (*N.B.* Two plates designed by H. Howard, engraved by R. H. Cromek, dated 1 Nov. 1804, and also called Plates I–II, were published with fascicle 8 on 1 Feb. 1805, eleven years before the article itself appeared.)

5. 'SCULPTURE', '*PLATE II*', depicts '*Hercules Farnese*', '*Dirce*', and '*Phocion*', is signed '*Blake, sculp*' and dated 1 Jan. 1816, and was issued with fascicle 68 in Oct. 1816. (Design size: *c.* 14·5×25·0 cm.)

6. 'SCULPTURE', '*PLATE III*', shows '*Venus de Medicis*', '*Apollo Belvedere*' and '*Laocoon*', is signed '*Blake del et sc.*' and dated 1 Oct. 1815, and was issued with fascicle 66 in July 1816 (design size: *c.* 15·0×25·5 cm). (Blake's sketch for this Laocoon is reproduced in *Blake's Pencil Drawings*, ed. G. Keynes [1956], pl. 30, and a proof in the BMPR on the verso of a proof of Hesiod pl. 26 has an anecdote about the sketch—see *Blake Records* [1969] 238. This engraving of Laocoon is quite different from Blake's separate engraving and his independent drawings of the same subject.)

7. 'SCULPTURE', '*PLATE IV*', represents '*Durga Slaying Mahishasura, a Hindoo group*', '*An Etruscan Patera, in the British Museum*', '*A Colossal Statue, at Thebes*', '*A Chinese Statue*', and two views of '*Persian Sculpture, at Persepolis*' (design size: *c.* 18×21·7 cm). The plate, dated 1 March 1816 and signed '*Blake sculp*', was published with fascicle 69 in Feb. 1817. (A proof before letters on the verso of Hesiod pl. 25 is in the Morgan. For an argument 'that Flaxman provided Blake with a drawing' for the Thebes statue, see Roe, 'The Thunder of Egypt' no. 2565 10, p. 193.)

REMEMBER ME!

490. A. REMEMBER ME! / A / *New Years Gift* / OR / CHRISTMAS PRESENT, / 1825. / — / London. / I. Poole. 8. Newgate Street. / Fenner sc. Pater Noster Row. [1824] (Cambridge, Keynes [6], NYP [Berg], Princeton, Wolf)

B. . . . 1826 . . . [1825]. (Edwin Wolf 2nd)

Remember Me! was evidently organized by Dr. R. J. Thornton, who signed the 'Introduction', and whose daughter Sylvia contributed a story. It is a gift book, the bottom of the engraved frontispiece engraved with: 'A TRIBUTE OF REGARD / Presented by / *Your Affectionate Friend* . . . .' A prospectus (in the John Johnson Collection in Bodley) announced its publication '*In* NOVEMBER 1824' as 'A NEW ANNUAL', and mentioned Blake's plate.

Not counting the nine plates of flowers tinted by T. Dales, there are six engravings, one unsigned, and one by Blake:

1. At p. 32 is '*Hiding of Moses.*', illustrating the unsigned description of 'The Hiding of Moses' (pp. 32–5) in which Blake is mentioned; it is signed '*Blake del et sculpt.*' (design size: 7·0 × 9·9 cm.) (The watercolour is in the Huntington; a proof lettered '*W. Blake invin. & sculp.*' in the Rosenwald Collection is 1·1 cm wider than the published version and shows houses by the Nile to the left of the design which were later cut off.)

Keynes (*Blake Studies* [1971], 144) reports a considerable variety of original printed covers, mostly from copies in his own collection:

1. Cream boards, Brown endpapers (no slip case).
2. Cream boards, Pink endpapers, bright Green case.
3. Brown paper sides, slate Grey endpapers and case.
4. Pink boards, slate Grey endpapers, Pink case with Roan strip and gilt lettering on one 'spine'.
5. Bright Green boards, Brown endpapers, Red case.
6. Pale Green boards, Orange endpapers, Red case.
7. Green straight-grained morocco, gilt, gilt edges, marbled endpapers.

B. There appears to be no difference between A and B except for the '1826' on the title-page of B and the 'Kalendar and Album 1826' rather than '1825'. There is no change in the Introduction in B (though A had announced that the Introduction was to be continued the next year), nor in the essay in which Blake is praised. Apparently the sale of *Remember Me!* was not so great as had been hoped, and instead of publishing a sequel for 1826 they simply altered the title-page of that for 1825 and pretended it was a new work. The second issue presumably appeared in November 1825. The 1826 work also omits the blank pages with ruled frames (for notes) and the miscellaneous facts on pp. 361–72.

[RITSON, Joseph, ed.]

491. A / SELECT / COLLECTION / OF / ENGLISH SONGS. / IN THREE VOLUMES. / VOLUME THE FIRST [SECOND] [THIRD]. / [Ornament] / —APIS MATINÆ / MORE MODOQUE / GRATA CARPENTIS THYMA PER LABOREM / PLURIMUM. / HOR. / LONDON: / Printed for J. JOHNSON in St. Pauls Church-yard. / MDCCLXXXIII [1783]. (BM, Bodley, Boston Museum, GEB, Harvard [2], McGill, Morgan, National Library of Scotland, Princeton, Rosenbach Foundation (2), Wellesley, Yale)

Only 9 of the 16 plates are signed by an engraver, and of these 7 (nos. 1–2, 5–9) are inscribed '*Blake sc*' and '*Stothard del*'. In addition, unfinished proofs of no. 3 in the Balmanno Collection of Stothard materials in BMPR, and in GEB, are inscribed in ink 'Stothard d.', 'Blake Sc', and a proof of no. 4 in the Balmanno Collection is similarly inscribed, though both no. 3 and 4 are unsigned in the book as printed. The Blake plates have no titles and are on pages with letterpress text. They are found at:

VOLUME I

1. p. 1, a courtier kneeling before his mistress, for Anon., 'Ah Chloris! could I now but sit' (plate-size: 10·2 × 7·6 cm).
2. p. 85, a woman sitting on a rock by the shore looking at a floating corpse, perhaps for William Shenstone, 'Jemmy Dawson' (10·2 × 7·6 cm).
3. p. 86, an adolescent cupid playing a harp for three women, for Dryden's 'Address to Britain' in his *King Arthur* (8·7 × 6·7 cm).
4. p. 108, a young man running from a woman, for Carew's 'Disdain Returned' (8·4 × 6·0 cm).
5. p. 156, four couples dancing round a maypole, evidently for Anon., 'A Cobbler there was . . .' (10·2 × 7·4 cm).
6. p. 157, Cupid holding a candle for a woman to sketch by, for Charles Sedley's 'As Amoret with Phillis sat' in Etherege's *Man of Mode* (10·1 × 7·7 cm).
7. p. 170, two cupids flying from a melancholy woman, for Goldsmith's 'When lovely woman stoops to folly' [in *She Stoops to Conquer*] (10·2 × 7·6 cm).
8. p. 171, a couple sitting in a bower, for Barton Booth's 'Sweet are the charms of her I love' (10·2 × 7·6 cm).

VOLUME II

9. p. 1, six men drinking at a table (a related scene is in 'Laughing Song', *Innocence* [1789], pl. 15), for Anon., 'The Honest Fellow' (10·2 × ?7·4 cm).

In the 1813 edition, crude, new, unsigned woodcuts were substituted for these copperplates.

SALZMANN, C. G.

492. A. ELEMENTS / OF / MORALITY, / FOR THE / USE OF CHILDREN; / WITH AN / INTRODUCTORY ADDRESS TO PARENTS. / = / Translated from the GERMAN of the / Rev. C. G. SALZMANN [by Mary Wollstonecraft]. / = / ILLUSTRATED WITH FIFTY COPPER PLATES. / IN THREE VOLUMES. / — VOL. I [II] [III]. / — / LONDON: / PRINTED BY J. CROWDER, / FOR J. JOHNSON IN ST. PAUL'S CHURCH-YARD. / — / M,DCC,XCI [1791]. (Harvard, Huntington, LC, New York, Princeton, Texas, Toronto Public, Trinity College [Hartford, Conn.], Westminster Public, Yale)

B. . . . THE THIRD EDITION. / = / . . . M,DCC,XCII [1792]. (BM, GEB)

C. . . . THE FOURTH EDITION . . . M,DCC,XCIX [1799]. (NYP, Trinity College [Hartford, Conn.])

D. . . . A NEW EDITION. / IN THREE VOLUMES. / ILLUSTRATED WITH PLATES. / VOL. I. / LONDON: / PRINTED FOR J. JOHNSON, IN ST. PAUL'S / CHURCH-YARD. / — / 1805. (GEB [Vol. I only])

E. ELEMENTS OF MORALITY / FOR THE / USE OF CHILDREN. / — / ILLUSTRATED WITH ENGRAVINGS. / = / IN TWO VOLUMES. / VOL. I [II] / = / LONDON· / PRINTED FOR JOHN SHARPE, JUVENILE LIBRARY, / LONDON MUSEUM, PICCADILLY [?1815]. (Connecticut College for Women)

Joseph Johnson entered the first edition of Salzmann's *Elements of Morality* at Stationers' Hall on 12 July 1790 and deposited the usual nine copies. It was described on the title-page as 'ILLUSTRATED WITH COPPER-PLATES' (BM), but in fact there were no plates. The second edition was the first with plates (A above, 1791), and the third and fourth 'editions' were just reissues of the second edition with the same plates. That of John Sharpe (E) has the same press-figures as the 1793 edition (below) and is presumably also just a new issue of the sheets with a new title-page. In other editions of London, 1793 (BM), Providence, 1795 (Library Company of Philadelphia), Philadelphia, 1796 (Library Company of Philadelphia), Baltimore, 1811, Edinburgh & London, 1821 (Bodley), the plates are different or omitted. An advertisement in Enfield's *Speaker* (1791) offered Salzmann's *Elements of Morality* with 50 plates at 10s. 6d. or without plates at 6s., and some copies at least of the 1799 issue have no plates.

The 'Advertisement' is signed by 'Mary Wolstonecraft'. All 51 plates are unsigned except the one facing Vol. I, p. 84, which has 'W. E [*or P.?*]: C fec¹'; the latter part of this signature is an acknowledgement that the plates are copied from those by David Chodowiecki in the original German edition of the book. The signed plate is quite different from the others. The English plates are dated 1 Oct. 1790 (15 in Vol. I, 3 in Vol. II), 1 Jan. 1791 (15 in Vol. II), and 15 March 1791 (18 in Vol. III). The volumes of the 1791 edition came out at different times, for Vol. I was reviewed in Joseph Johnson's *Analytical Review*, IX (Jan.–April 1791), 101–3, with the comment:

> The prints are far superior, both with respect to design and engraving, to any we have ever seen in books designed for children; and that prints, judiciously introduced, are particularly calculated to enforce a moral tale, must be obvious to every one who has had any experience in education.

The plates are unsigned, and the grounds for assigning the engraving to Blake are stylistic and uncertain; the chief analogue is the plates he engraved for Mary Wollstonecraft's *Original Stories* (1791). The first writer to attribute them to Blake was Gilchrist (1863), who may have had information from Blake's friends (he does not give his evidence). A. G. B. Russell (*Engravings* [1912], 156–8) claims for Blake the engravings numbered 2, 5–6, 8 perhaps, 9, 12–13 perhaps, 14 (p. 136) probably, 15 perhaps, 26 perhaps, 33 perhaps, 37, 39 perhaps, and 47 perhaps. Keynes (1921) accepts no. 2, 5–6, 8–9, 12–13, 15, 26, 37, 39, and 47 from this list, rejects no. 14 and 33, and adds no. 32, 36, 41, and 50. Though discouraged by the necessity of deciding on such meagre evidence, and loath to complicate the issue still further, I have some confidence in attributing to Blake no. 2, 8–9, 12–13, 26, 32, 36–7, and 41; accept, though less cheerfully, no. 5–6, 15, 33, 39, 47, and 50; and reject firmly no. 14.

The hypothetical Blake plates were '*Publish'd by J. Johnson, Oct.ʳ 1. 1790*' (no. 1–8), '*Jan.ʸ 1, 1791*' (no. 9–10), and '*March 15, 1791*' (no. 11–17) and are to be found:

VOLUME I

1. At p. 15: '*Pl. 2, Vol. I.*' '*Health is dearer to me than a whole Sack full of Gold.*' (Design size: 7·0 × 12·4 cm.)
2. At p. 28: '*Pl. 5, Vol. I.*' '*Stop! Stop!*' (7·0 × 12·4 cm.)
3. At p. 41: '*Pl. 6. Vol. I.*' '*There he is! There comes our dear Father.*' (7·0 × 12·4 cm.)
4. At p. 60: '*Pl. 8, Vol. I.*' The dog '*Pompey is dead!*' (7·0 × 12·4 cm.)
5. At p. 81: '*Pl. 9, Vol. I.*' '*Patience can soften every pain.*' (7·3 × 12·7 cm.)
6. At p. 124: '*Pl. 12, Vol. I.*' '*Is there any Hope [for the injured man]?*' (7·1 × 11·9 cm.)
7. At p. 130: '*Pl. 13, Vol. I.*' '*Your Compassion has saved my life.*' (7·3 × 12·4 cm.)
8. At p. 144: '*Pl. 15, Vol. I.*' '*If we love others, they will love us in return.*' (7·1 × 13·0 cm.)

VOLUME II

9. At p. 86: '*Pl. 26, Vol. II.*' '*Through Perseverance we may do many things, which we thought impossible.*' (7·0 × 11·4 cm.)
10. At p. 177: '*Pl. 32, Vol. II.*' '*We loathe a Slanderer as we do a Viper.*' (6·5 × 12·0 cm.)

VOLUME III

11. At p. 12: '*Pl. 33, Vol. III.*' '*Welcome dear Henry, & good Catherine.*' (6·8 × 12·2 cm.)
12. At p. 37: '*Pl. 36, Vol. III.*' '*He who can torment a little helpless animal, has certainly a bad heart.*' (6·9 × 12·2 cm.)
13. At p. 50: '*Pl. 37, Vol. III.*' '*A wicked man is more to be pitied than a cripple.*' (6·8 × 12·1 cm.)
14. At p. 76: '*Pl. 39, Vol. III.*' '*See how much good a Single man can do!*' (7·0 × 12·3 cm.)
15. At p. 93: '*Pl. 41, Vol. III.*' '*How happy it is that there are rich men in the world.*' (6·8 × 11·8 cm.)
16. At p. 164: '*Pl. 47, Vol. III.*' '*O God! Thou art Just!*' (7·0 × 11·3 cm.)
17. At p. 195: '*Pl. 50, Vol. III.*' '*My Spirit is immortal, and goes to God.*' (7·5 × 12·7 cm.)

E. The date of E derives tentatively from the advertisement for it (in two volumes, with 50 plates) in T. L. Peacock, *Sir Hornbook* (John Sharpe, 1815) —according to Miss Eleanor Nicholes.

493. GYMNASTICS / FOR / YOUTH: / OR A / PRACTICAL GUIDE /
TO / *HEALTHFUL* AND *AMUSING EXERCISES* / FOR THE USE OF
SCHOOLS. / AN ESSAY TOWARD THE NECESSARY IMPROVE-
MENT / OF / EDUCATION, / CHIEFLY AS IT RELATES TO THE
BODY; / FREELY TRANSLATED FROM THE GERMAN / OF /
C. G. SALZMANN, / MASTER OF THE ACADEMY AT SCHNEP-
FENTHAL, / AND AUTHOR OF ELEMENTS OF MORALITY. / — /
ILLUSTRATED WITH COPPER PLATES. / London: / PRINTED FOR
J. JOHNSON, ST. PAUL'S CHURCH-YARD, / By Bye and Law, St.
John's Square, Clerkenwell. / = / 1800. (BM, BMPR, Bodley, Boston
Athenaeum, Columbia, Harvard, Huntington, Library Company of Phila-
delphia, NYP, New York University, Princeton, Toronto, V & A, West
Sussex Record Office, Westminster Public, Yale)

Thos. Windsor, 'Mr. Ralph Thomas's "Swimming"', *N & Q*, CX (1904),
382–4, suggests without evidence that the *Gymnastics* was really written by
Johann C. F. Guts-Muth; I have no information to confirm or contradict
this allegation.

The plates bear the name of neither designer nor engraver. They may have
been copied, and considerably altered and improved, from the different
proofs, some reversed, in the BMPR. Blake's responsibility for the engravings is based chiefly on stylistic grounds; it is denied by Thomas (no. 2835)
and by A. G. B. Russell (no. 603, p. 195) and affirmed by Keynes (1921)
and, though not happily, by GEB. All ten plates are *'Publish'd by J. Johnson,
in S.t Pauls Church Yard London. Feb.y 1. 1800.'* They represent:

1. *'Frontispiece Pl. I'*, a set of diagrams (design size: 23·7 × 19·0 cm, a fold-
   out plate).
2. *'Pl. 2, p. 196'*, *'The Leap in Height, with & without a Pole.'* (6·8 × 11·4 cm.)
3. *'Pl. 3, p. 218'*, *'The Leap in Length, with & without a Pole.'* (6·8 × 11·5 cm.)
4. *'Pl. 4, p. 226'*, *'Running, & Leap-frog.'* (6·7 × 11·4 cm.)
5. *'Pl. 5, p. 237'*, *'Throwing & Shooting at a Mark.'* (6·8 × 11·4 cm.)
6. *'Pl. 6, p. 247'*, *'The different kinds of Wrestling.'* (6·5 × 11·4 cm.)
7. *'Pl. 7, p. 264'*, *'Climbing.'* (6·8 × 11·4 cm.)
8. *'Pl. 8, p. 286'*, *'Preservation of Equilibrium.'* (6·8 × 11·4 cm.)
9. *'Pl. 9, p. 314'*, *'Trundling a Hoop &c.'* (6·8 × 11·4 cm.)
10. *'Pl. 10, p. 339'*, *'Bathing & Swimming.'* (6·9 × 11·3 cm.)

GEB has three proofs.

Ralph Thomas (no. 2835) says that the English plates are copied after the
original German ones, with the costumes changed from German to English.
(I have not seen the German edition.)

The book was shipped to America and was there copied (probably from
the copy in The Library Company of Philadelphia) in Philadelphia and
'Printed by William Duane, No. 106, Market Street. 1802.' (Michigan,
Columbia, Library Company of Philadelphia.) This in turn was again
'Printed for P. Byrne, No. 72 Chesnut-Street [Philadelphia]. 1803.' (Harvard,
Library Company of Philadelphia, Yale.) In these two Philadelphia editions,
Blake's copperplates are carefully but crudely copied by a U.S. engraver.

SCOTT, John

494. A. THE / POETICAL WORKS / OF / JOHN SCOTT ESQ: /
[Portrait] / LONDON / Printed for J. Buckland, / MDCCLXXXII [1782].
(BM [2 copies], Bodley, Boston Museum, LC, Princeton [2], Trinity College
[Hartford, Conn.], Wellesley, Westminster Public, Yale [Samuel Johnson's
copy])

B. THE SECOND EDITION. / LONDON / Printed for J. Buckland, /
MDCCLXXXVI [1786]. (GEB, Friends House [London], LC, National
Library of Scotland, Trinity College [Hartford, Conn.])

C. *The Second Edition.* / = / LONDON: / Printed for ALEXANDER CLEUGH,
14, Ratcliff-Highway; / AND / JOHN DOLFEE, 19, John-Street, Minories. /
1795. (GEB)

A. There are 14 plates, including the title-page, none of them dated, and
4 signed '*Stothard del.* [or *d*]' and '*Blake sc*':
1. On p. 21 is 'ECLOGUE IV' (9·9 × 7·8 cm).
2. At p. 23 is:

> *There is, who deems all climes, all seasons fair*
> *Contentment, thankful for the gift of life.*

The number '3' on the plate signifies that it is the third full-page design
(11·4 × 8·3 cm).
3. At p. 247 is number '7' (11·4 × 8·4 cm):

> *Warriors! let the Wretches live!*
> *Christians! pity and forgive.*

4. On p. 335 is an altar inscribed 'SACRED TO SIMPLICITY' (8·7 ×
9·3 cm).

In the Rosenwald Collection of the Library of Congress are proofs before
lettering of these engravings. *The European Magazine*, (II), 195, said 'the
plates . . . are designed and executed with skill and elegance'.

B and C. In the 'Second Edition' printed in 1786 and reissued in 1795 (with
a printed title-page substituted for the engraved one of 1786), the plates
were moved as follows: 2. p. 25; 3. p. 249; 4. p. [338, misnumbered '322'].

SEALLY, John, & Israel LYONS.

495. A. A COMPLETE / Geographical Dictionary, / OR / UNIVERSAL
GAZETTEER; / OF / ANCIENT and MODERN GEOGRAPHY: / CON-
TAINING A FULL, PARTICULAR, AND ACCURATE / Description of
the known World; / IN / EUROPE, ASIA, AFRICA, and AMERICA; /
COMPRISING / A COMPLETE SYSTEM OF GEOGRAPHY, / ILLUS-
TRATED WITH CORRECT MAPS AND BEAUTIFUL VIEWS OF
THE PRINCIPAL CITIES, &c. / AND CHRONOLOGICAL TABLES
OF THE SOVEREIGNS OF EUROPE. / — / THE GEOGRAPHICAL

PARTS / By JOHN SEALLY, A.M. / MEMBER OF THE ROMAN ACADEMY; AUTHOR OF THE HISTOIRE CHRONOLOGIQUE, SACRÉE ET PROFANE; / ELEMENTS OF GEOGRAPHY AND ASTRONOMY, &c. &c. / Interspersed with Extracts from the *private Manuscripts* of one of the Officers who accompanied Captain Cook in his Voyage to the / SOUTHERN HEMISPHERE. / THE ASTRONOMICAL PARTS FROM THE PAPERS / Of the late Mr. ISRAEL LYONS, of Cambridge; / ASTRONOMER IN LORD MULGRAVE'S VOYAGE TO THE NORTHERN HEMISPHERE. / — / VOL. 1 [11]. / — / *By the King's Royal License and Authority.* / — / LONDON: / Printed for JOHN FIELDING, Numb. 23, Pater-noster-Row. [?1784] (Yale)

B. . . . Printed for SCATCHERD and WHITAKER, Ave-mary Lane. / MDCCLXXXVII [1787]. (BM & GEB.)

A. The undated first edition was almost certainly issued originally in parts of five folio signatures apiece. Every signature is clearly labelled with the part in which it appeared—e.g. 'Vol. II.—No. 52'—and the last part is No. 95. The 32 'views' are dated alternately with the 34 maps at quite regular weekly intervals, with a few gaps, from 29 Sept. 1781 to 24 May 1783, though this chronological order has nothing to do with the alphabetical order in which they are bound. The last plate is dated 23 Dec. 1783, some seven months later than the next previous plate. Probably the parts were issued regularly for 90 weeks and then were unaccountably held up. The earliest probable publication date for the whole is 1784.

The address 'To the Public' remarks on the 'large Collection of most superb Views, superior to any ever offered to the Public, the greatest Part of which have never appeared in any English Publication' (I. iv), implying that they had appeared in a work published on the Continent. As Ivanyi pointed out in *TLS* (1955), the designs for Lyons and Presburg derive from engravings in [Pierre d'Avity], *Archonotologia Cosmica*, tr. Johann Ludwig Gottfried (1638; 1649), I. 114, 381. (D'Avity's original work, *Les Estats, Empires, Royaumes, et Principautez du Monde* [1614, 1625], had no plates.) The original for Osnaburg is not known.

All the plates were published for Fielding (the publisher of the first but not of the second edition), and all but six of the views were signed by the engravers, though none has the name of the designer. There are no page numbers, but the plates are in alphabetical order. Blake's plates are all in Vol. II, viz.:

1. '*LYONS*.' '*Blake sc*', '*Publish'd May 4 1782 by J. Fielding, N° 3 Paternoster Row.*' (Plate-size: 25·1 × 18·7 cm.)

2. '*OSNABURG in WESTPHALIA.*' '*Blake Sc*', '*Published Jany 12, 1782, by I. Fielding, N° 23, Pater-noster Row.*' (25·3 × 18·2 cm.)

3. '*PRESBURG in HUNGARY.*' '*Blake Sc*', '*Published April 6, 1782, by I. Fielding, N° 23, Pater-noster Row.*' (24·2 × 17·9 cm.)

B. In the second edition of 1787, there seem to be only 28 plates and 31 maps, but Blake's plates in Volume II are unchanged.

THE SEAMAN'S RECORDER

496. THE / SEAMAN'S RECORDER; / OR, AUTHENTIC AND INTERESTING / 𝔑arratibes / OF / POPULAR SHIPWRECKS, / AND / OTHER CALAMITIES / INCIDENT TO A LIFE OF MARATIME [*sic*] ENTERPRISE. [*3 vols.; Vol. I*] / = / LONDON: / PUBLISHED BY J. EEDES, NEWGATE STREET. / — / 1824. [Vol. II (& III). / = / LONDON: / PUBLISHED BY J. GIFFORD, QUEEN'S HEAD PASSAGE, / PATERNOSTER-ROW. / — / 1825.] (LC [defective], McGill, Provincial Library [Victoria, British Columbia] [defective])

B. [Vol. I only:] THE / SEAMAN'S RECORDER, / OR, / AUTHENTIC AND INTERESTING / Narrative[*s*] / OF / REMARKABLE SHIPWRECKS. / VOL. I. / = / LONDON: / PRINTED FOR THE PROPRIETOR, / AND PUBLISHED BY JACQUES & WRIGHT, / PATERNOSTER ROW; / AND SOLD BY SHERWOOD & CO. AND ALL BOOKSELLERS. / — / 1827. (Mariners' Museum [Newport News, Va.] [defective], Southampton Public [defective])

A multi-volume publication may not have been contemplated initially, for the first title-page gives no hint of accompanying volumes. By the time Vols. II & III were printed in 1825, the stock of Vol. I may have been in short supply, necessitating the resetting of Vol. I in 1827. This may have been a hasty and ill-planned undertaking, for the only two copies of 1827 traced are jumbled and confusing, with plates missing, in the wrong places, in proof states, and so on. (The Mariners' Museum copy also has an extra set of title-pages reading: The / SAILORS CHRONICLE, / OR, INTERESTING NARRATIVES, / OF / SHIPWRECKS. / VOL. I [II] [III]. / [*Vignette*] / LONDON: / PUBLISHED BY G. VIRTUE 26 IVY LANE / AND BATH STREET BRISTOL [n.d.]. These may be a spurious later addition.)

The work seems to have changed hands regularly, for not only is a different publisher mentioned with each new year on the title-pages, but there are imprints with yet others, in the outer margins of the plates, where they would normally be trimmed off, e.g. 'Printed by S. Cave, Islington Green [*this colophon appears in this form in all three volumes*].—Published by W. Crawford, Cheapside, London.—Price Twopence' (I [1824], 327), or 'Printed for J. Gifford & Co., by S. Cave at the Publication Office, opposite Dolly's Chop House, Paternoster Row.—No. 21' (III, 300).

The 78 plates include 50 anonymous woodcuts and 22 by William C. Walker (1791–1867). The most ambitious plates are the 6 copperplates signed '*Blake sc*' (nos. 1, 3, 5–6), '*Blake del et sc.*' (no. 2), or '*Blake Sc*' (no. 4) (all are reproduced in no. 1164), which are as follows:

1. Volume I, frontispiece, '*Loss of the Abergavenny*' (plate-mark: 20·4 × ?13·0 cm; design size: 17·7 × 11·4 cm), illustrating the anonymous 'Narrative of the Loss of The Earl of Abergavenny East Indiaman, Captain John Wordsworth [*the poet's brother*], Which drove on the Shambles, off

the Bill of Portland, and sunk in twelve Fathoms Water, Feb. 5, 1805' (I, 399–403), which in turn is derived from Anon, *An Authentic Narrative of the Loss of the Earl of Abergavenny* (Printed for John Stockdale, Piccadilly, and Blacks and Parry, Leadenhall Street, Feb. 1805).

2. Volume II, frontispiece, a representation of a monument [put up in 1817 in St Paul's Cathedral by Flaxman] which is inscribed 'Erected at the Public expence, to the Memory of Vice Admiral Horatio Viscount Nelson K.B.' *'London Published by T. Gifford'* (plate-mark invisible; design size: 8·8 × 14·7 cm); no Narrative is specifically about Nelson.

3. Volume II, a second frontispiece, a fold-out plate representing the *'Shipwreck of Lord Royston and Suite, on Memel Bar, with a View of M.ʳ Greathead's Life Boat.'* (plate-mark: 22·7 × 18·3 cm; design size: *c.* 20·8 × 14·7 cm), illustrating the 'Affecting Narrative [*by* One of the passengers Mr. Halliday] of The Loss of the Agatha, Which was stranded on the Suder Hacken, near Memel, the 7th of April, 1808, by which unfortunate event, thirteen Persons lost their lives. Captain Koop, Commander' (II, 145–7).

4. Volume II, at p. 1, is a fold-out plate of *'Lord Byron in a Storm.'* (plate-mark: 20·5 × 15·1 cm; design size: 20·0 × 11·1 cm), illustrating the anonymous and apocryphal account of 'Lord Byron in a Storm. An Account of Lord Byron's Voyage to Sicily, Corsica, and Sardinia, In the Year 1821; *Compiled from notes made during the Voyage by passengers, and extracts from the journal of his Lordship's yacht Mazeppa*, CAPTAIN BENSON, R.N. Commander' (II, 1–4), which in turn is derived from Anon., *Narrative of Lord Byron's Voyage to Corsica and Sardinia* (1824), 22–33. The design represents Byron and Shelley on deck in a great storm.

5. Volume II, p. 93, a fold-out plate entitled *'M.ʳ Woodard discovers Millar lying at the waters edge, murdered by the Malay's.'* (plate-mark: 21·8 × 14·2 cm; design size: 18·5 × 12·4 cm), illustrating the 'Account of the Sufferings and Escape of Captain Woodard and Four Seamen, who lost their ship, while in a boat at Sea [*in March 1793*], and afterwards endured a captivity of two years and a half, amongst the Malays' (II, 93–115), based on *The Narrative of Captain David Woodard and Four Seamen* (1804).

6. Volume II, at p. 164 is a plate of the *'Loss of the Hindostan by Fire'* (plate-mark: 19·8 × ?; design size: 17·9 × 10·2 cm), illustrating the 'Narrative of the Loss of The Hindostan Storeship. Commanded by Captain J. Le Gros. Which was burned in the Bay of Roses, April 2, 1804. *Extracted, per Favour, from the Log-Book*' (II, 164–9).

Sir Geoffrey Keynes finds that the 'plain incompetence' of these plates makes it 'quite inconceivable' that the poet could have executed them ('Blake's Engravings for Gay's Fables', *Book Collector*, XXI [1972], 60). His case will be stronger when there is clear evidence that another engraver named Blake was signing plates in the 1820s.

SHAKESPEARE, William

497. A. THE / DRAMATIC WORKS / OF / SHAKSPEARE / REVISED BY GEORGE STEEVENS. / [9 vols.] VOL. I[–IX]. / LONDON: /

PRINTED BY W. BULMER AND CO. / 𝔖𝔥𝔞𝔨𝔰𝔭𝔢𝔞𝔯𝔢 𝔓𝔯𝔦𝔫𝔱𝔦𝔫𝔤-𝔒𝔣𝔣𝔦𝔠𝔢, / FOR JOHN AND JOSIAH BOYDELL, GEORGE AND W. NICOL; / FROM THE TYPES OF W. MARTIN. / MDCCCII [1802, i.e. 1803]. (Birmingham Public [2], Folger [2], GEB, LC, Princeton [2], South Carolina, Texas, Toronto)

B. THE / DRAMATIC WORKS / OF / [Vignette] / WILLIAM SHAKSPEARE; / WITH / GLOSSARIAL NOTES, / A SKETCH OF HIS LIFE, AND AN ESTIMATE OF HIS WRITINGS; / NEWLY ARRANGED AND EDITED [by Charles Henry Wheeler]. / [Vignette] / LONDON: MOON, BOYS, & GRAVES, PRINTSELLERS TO THE KING, PALL MALL. 1832. (Folger)

A. The heroic project of Alderman Boydell to found a School of English History Painting and a School of English Engraving was announced in a prospectus (in the Folger) of 1 Dec. 1786:

MR. ALDERMAN BOYDELL, JOSIAH BOYDELL, / AND GEORGE NICOL, / PROPOSE TO PUBLISH BY *SUBSCRIPTION* / A MOST MAGNIFICENT AND ACCURATE EDITION / OF THE / PLAYS OF SHAKSPEARE, IN EIGHT VOLUMES / Of the largest QUARTO SIZE, on the finest ROYAL ATLAS PAPER, / to be fabricated for that Purpose by Mr. WHATMAN. / The LETTER-PRESS will be executed by Mr. HUGHS, with a Set of / NEW TYPES cast by Mr. CASLON. / The TEXT to be regulated, and the LITERARY PART of the Undertaking conducted, / BY GEORGE STEEVENS, ESQ. / — / TO ACCOMPANY THIS WORK / MESSIEURS BOYDELL / INTEND TO PUBLISH BY SUBSCRIPTION / A SERIES. OF LARGE AND CAPITAL PRINTS / After PICTURES to be immediately painted . . . [*and*] ENGRAVED[.]

The prospectus goes on to name the painters and engravers who will be employed, and to say that the edition will appear in eighteen parts with four plates to a part.

Surprisingly little of this description applies to the completed work. According to the Advertisement of A, the publishers discovered that the state of printing was such that, in order to be sure the work would surpass in splendour all former publications, they had to found a manufactory to supply ink; to found a foundry to make type; and to found a printing-house to print the book. Though they stuck to the plan to issue 18 parts, the work was eventually bound in nine volumes rather than eight, and, instead of 72 plates, 99 were published. The published book embodied the work of only about half the announced painters (seven out of thirteen) and engravers (seven out of twelve), while five-sixths of the work was done by painters and engravers apparently not considered in 1786.

The first part appeared with the general title-page: THE / DRAMATIC WORKS / OF / SHAKSPEARE. / REVISED / BY GEORGE STEEVENS. / LONDON: / = / PRINTED BY W. BULMER AND CO. / Shakspeare Printing=Office, / FOR JOHN AND JOSIAH BOYDELL, AND GEORGE NICOL; / *From the Types of W. Martin.* / 1791. (Folger, John Johnson Collection of Ephemera in Bodley)

According to a printed announcement (in the Folger), the second part was about ready to be issued in June 1791. Thereafter the parts were issued with labels but without title-pages. The second part bore the following label:

No II. / SHAKSPEARE. / = / AS YOU LIKE IT. / ROMEO AND JULIET. / = / *Printed by* W. BULMER & CO. *Shakspeare Printing-Office,* / *Cleveland-Row, St. James's.* (Folger and Johnson Collection)

This must have appeared at least by the end of 1792, for Steevens's corrected proofs for *Titus* (in the Folger), which was issued in Part V, are dated Sept. and Oct. 1793. Part II was probably issued with no more than three *Romeo and Juliet* plates (the Folger and Johnson copies have none), for in the 1803 issue of *Romeo* (A above) three plates are dated between 2 Jan. and 2 Feb. 1792, and the other three from 1797 to 1799. (In 1803, *As You Like it* is in Volume III and *Romeo and Juliet* in Volume IX.) Among these (1792) was a plate designed by Opie and engraved by Simon representing Juliet discovered unconscious on her bed.

By 1803 the book was finished; five of the plates and the dedication are dated 4 June 1803 (George III's birthday), and an advertisement in *The British Critic* for April 1803 announced the last number for 4 June. For those who so desired, the parts were bound up with the above title-page dated '1802'. As is appropriate for the issue in parts, each play is separately paginated, but, rather surprisingly, there are no signatures to the gatherings at all. Of the 99 plates in the book's final form, a number, including Blake's only plate, must have been first 'Published' some time after the part in which they should be bound had appeared. The price of the whole was £37. 16s.

In Volume IX, after p. 100 of *Romeo and Juliet,* is Simon's engraving of the Opie painting of Juliet, and immediately following it is a plate with the inscription:

1. 'Variation. / SHAKSPEARE. / *Romeo and Juliet,* / ACT IV. SCENE V.' '*Painted by J. Opie.*' '*Engrav'd by W. Blake.*' '*Pub^d March 25, 1799, by John and Josiah Boydell, at the Shakspeare Gallery Pall Mall, & N° 90, Cheapside.*'
   (Plate size: over 43 × 31 cm; design size: 23·7 × 16·6 cm.)

Blake's plate differs from that engraved by Simon in having two more figures in the left foreground but no jar in the centre, three more figures gathered about Juliet, etc. The central figures of the two engravings are very similar, but all the rest is different. Blake's plate, in fact, is from the same design as the one engraved for the *Collection of Prints* (see below).

For those who wished to possess the plates alone, the publishers issued a separate work entitled *Boydell's Graphic Illustrations of the Dramatic Works, of Shakspeare* [?1803], where Blake's engraving also appears.

The plates in the *Dramatic Works* and the *Graphic Illustrations* are approximately 43 × 29 cm and should not be confused with the much larger engravings (*c.* 68 × 51 cm) which were issued in connection with this same stupendous enterprise, entitled *Collection of Prints, from Pictures Painted for the Purpose of Illustrating the Dramatic Works of Shakspeare*, published in two volumes by John and Josiah Boydell in 1803 (Bodley). This latter includes new engravings from 93 of the same 163 pictures which the Boydells had commissioned, but Blake made no plate for it.

Apparently these publications proved far less remunerative than had been anticipated. The work was still being offered in Boydell lists of Dec. 1810 and April 1812 (in the Johnson Collection), and the Boydells had to sell all their pictures by way of a lottery to stave off bankruptcy. Later, an undated prospectus announced that over 5,000 copperplates of the Boydells, including those for Hogarth (no. 475) and Shakspeare (the second of which cost not less than £100,000) were to be sold in the spring of 1818 (BM: 1879 b. 1, Vol. I).

B. The second edition of Shakspeare to contain the Boydell plates is a very curious one. In the year it was published, the following octavo work appeared:

THE / DRAMATIC WORKS OF / WILLIAM SHAKSPEARE; / WITH / GLOSSARIAL NOTES, / A SKETCH OF HIS LIFE, / AND AN ESTIMATE OF HIS WRITINGS; / 𝔑ewly 𝔄rrangeb anb 𝔈biteb, / BY CHARLES HENRY WHEELER. / [2-line motto] / — / LONDON: FISHER, SON, & CO. 38, NEWGATE-STREET. / — / 1832. (Folger)

Moon, Boys, & Graves (the successors to the Boydells) were anxious to avoid the expense of an entire new type-setting when they republished the Boydell plates, so they took the type for the Fisher edition, rearranged the formes for folio printing, and printed a new impression as a folio, with four of the octavo 'pages' on each folio page. The purpose of this arrangement was to make the book-size large enough to accommodate the enormous Boydell engravings. Blake's plate in B, with the inscription unchanged, faces pp. 251–4.

For all the facts about the Folger copies, I am indebted to the patient generosity of Mr. Giles Dawson.

The Boydells' Shakespeare publications should not be confused with *The Plays of William Shakspeare* (1805), for which Blake made engravings after Fuseli.

498. B. THE / PLAYS / OF / WILLIAM SHAKSPEARE, / Accurately printed from the Text of the corrected Copy left by the late / GEORGE STEEVENS, Esq. / WITH / A SERIES OF ENGRAVINGS, / FROM ORIGINAL DESIGNS OF / HENRY FUSELI, Esq. R.A. Professor of Painting: / AND A SELECTION / OF EXPLANATORY AND HISTORICAL NOTES, / From the most eminent Commentators; / *A History of the Stage, a Life of Shakspeare, &c.* / BY ALEXANDER CHALMERS, A.M. / = / IN TEN VOLUMES. / = / VOLUME VII. / CONTAINING / KING RICHARD III. / KING HENRY VIII. / TROILUS AND CRESSIDA. [VOLUME X. / CONTAINING / ROMEO AND JULIET. / HAMLET. / OTHELLO.] / — / *LONDON:* / Printed for F. C. and J. Rivington; J. Johnson; R. Baldwin; H. L. / Gardner; W. J. and J. Richardson; J. Nichols and Son; T. Payne; R. / Faulder; G. and J. Robinson; W. Lowndes; G. Wilkie; Scatcherd and / Letterman; T. Egerton; J. Walker; W. Clarke and Son; J. Barker and Son; / D. Ogilvy and Son; Cuthell and Martin; R. Lea; P. Macqueen; Lackington, / Allen and Co.; T. Kay; J. Deighton; J. White; W. Miller; Vernor and / Hood; D. Walker; C. Law; B. Crosby and Co; R. Pheney; Longman, Hurst, / Rees, and Orme; Cadell and Davies;

J. Harding; R. H. Evans; S. Bagster; / J. Mawman; Blacks and Parry; J. Badcock; J. Asperne; and T. Ostell. / — / 1805. (BM, Folger)

C. IN NINE VOLUMES. / = / VOLUME VI. / CONTAINING / KING HENRY VI. PART III. / KING RICHARD III. / KING HENRY VIII. / TROILUS AND CRESSIDA. [VOLUME IX. / CONTAINING / ROMEO AND JULIET. / HAMLET. / OTHELLO.] . . . 1805. (Folger, GEB)

D. CHALMERS, A. M. / — / A NEW EDITION. / . . . / *LONDON:* / Printed for J. Nichols and Son; F. C. and J. Rivington; J. Stockdale; / W. Lowndes; G. Wilkie and J. Robinson; T. Egerton; J. Walker; / W. Clarke and Son; J. Barker; J. Cuthell; R. Lea; Lackington and / Co.; J. Deighton; J. White and Co.; B. Crosby and Co.; W. Earle; / J. Gray and Son; Longman and Co.; Cadell and Davies; J. Harding; R. H. Evans; J. Booker; S. Bagster; J. Mawman; Black and Co.; / J. Richardson; J. Booth; Newman and Co.; R. Pheney; R. Scholey; J. Asperne; J. Faulder; R. Baldwin; Cradock and Joy; J. Mackin- / lay; J. Johnson and Co.; Gale and Curtis; G. Robinson; and Wilson / and Son, York. / — / 1811. (Folger)

E. IN NINE VOLUMES. / . . . / 1805 [i.e. 1812]. (Folger)

The publication history of Chalmers's *Shakspeare* is distressingly intricate, and many of the conclusions below are little more than hypotheses. There seem to have been seven or more ways in which these plays appeared: (1) as separate plays, in 1804 and 1805; with illustrations; (2) in ten volumes in 1805 with illustrations; (3) in nine volumes in 1805 with illustrations; (4) in nine volumes in 1805 with*out* illustrations; (5) in nine volumes in 1811 with illustrations; (6) in nine volumes in 1811 with*out* illustrations; (7) in nine volumes in 1812 (though with 1805 still on the title-page) with illustrations. Naturally only the five with illustrations concern us much here.

A. The first issue was clearly in parts, one play per part, though I have not seen such an issue. The evidence for such an issue is decisive:

1. In the first place, a Prospectus of 1 Dec. 1802 (in the British Museum, pressmark 11902 c 26) advertised the work in numbers, 'each number to contain ONE PLAY, and an ENGRAVING: and the whole to be comprised in about THIRTY-EIGHT, but not exceeding FORTY NUMBERS, making EIGHT VOLUMES, OCTAVO', the first number to appear on 1 Jan. 1803 'and the succeeding numbers every fortnight' (they averaged one every two-and-a-half weeks, irregularly) at 2*s*. or, on Extra Royal woven paper, hot pressed, with first impressions of the plates, at 4*s*.

2. In the second place, several references in Blake's letters particularly point to periodical issue of the plates. On 26 Oct. 1803 he told Hayley: 'I have to work after Fuseli for a little Shakespeare'. On 23 Feb. 1804 he wrote again: 'I have enclosd for you the 22 Numbers of Fuselis Shakespeare that are out' (according to the dates on the plates, 27 of the engravings were completed by this time, the 22nd on 1 Dec. 1803). Blake said on 28 Sept. 1804: 'I send . . . 5 Numbers of Fuselis Shakespeare' (at this time all the engravings had been dated). Finally, on 18 Dec. 1804 Blake mentioned 'the concluding [*10*] numbers' of 'Fuseli's *Shakespeare*' 'which I now send'.

Blake was paid 25 guineas each for his plates, according to his letter of 22 June 1804.

3. In the third place, each play was evidently printed separately (not with the others), for each play begins (at the half-title) with a new signature, and sometimes the signature consists of only one or two leaves. Chalmers's preface, dated Nov. 1804, states that 'The Editor's intentions . . . have been explained in the Prospectus which has accompanied every play'. Owners of the whole collection naturally did not want 37 examples of the same Prospectus bound into the work, and probably the Prospectus was normally thrown away on receipt—certainly I have not seen one. Clearly each play was issued separately with a Prospectus during 1804 and 1805.[1]

The undertaking apparently began in late 1802, for on 3 Jan. 1803 'Fuseli told me [*Joseph Farington*] . . . He is also engaged in making a complete set of drawings for an edition of Shakespeare for a body of Booksellers' (*The Farington Diary*, ed. J. Greig [1923], II. 72).

B. There are two almost identical issues in 1805, the first large, considerably more elegant, in ten volumes with Fuseli's plates. The thirty-eight signed plates (which are the same in all the illustrated editions) include two by Blake, viz.:

1. At Vol. VII, p. 235 is '*Act. IV.* KING HENRY VIII. *Sc. II.*' 'Katharine, Griffiths & Patience. / *Kath. Spirits of peace, where are ye? Are ye all gone?*' '*Fuseli. inv*', '*Blake. sculp*', '*Publish'd May 12. 1804, by F & C. Rivington, S? Paul's Church Yard.*' (Design size: 9·5 × 15·9 cm.) Proofs of Blake's two plates before all letters except the artist's and engraver's names are in the BMPR [2 sets] and the Rosenwald Collection of the Library of Congress, and Charles Ryskamp has a set of all the proofs of Fuseli's *Shakspeare* in the same state.

2. At Vol. X, p. 107 is '*Act 1* [*i.e.*, *V*]. ROMEO and JULIET. *Sc. 1.*' '*Enter Apothecary. / Romeo. Come hither Man—I see, that thou art poor; / Hold, there's forty ducats:—*', '*H. Fuseli. R.A. inv.*', '*W. Blake. sc*', '*Publish'd by C & F Rivington London Jan 14, 1804.*' (Design size: 9·2 × 17·2 cm.)[2]

(*N.B.* There are no directions to the binder for placing the plates in any of these editions, and practice varied considerably. The volumes, of course, do not change, but the place within the volume does, and the pages given represent only one set, and are not to be thought of as standard.)

Apparently each of the issues was printed in fairly large numbers, and the wear on the plates was very great. Even the prints in the issue in parts (A) were affected, for Blake wrote to Hayley in some distress on 28 Dec. 1804

---

[1] W. Jaggard, *Shakespeare Bibliography* (1911) says that this work was originally issued in 'Forty parts, forming 10 vols.'; I do not know his evidence that there were *forty* parts. Jaggard also lists *Dramatic Works of Shakespeare*, Revised by G. Steevens, With plates from designs by Henry Fuseli (London: J. & J. Boydell . . . 1803), 2 vols., Folio, Birmingham Public Library. This is a curious misdescription of Boydell's *Collection of Prints* (see under no. 497); there is no work such as Jaggard describes in Birmingham Public Libraries.

[2] The extraordinary stuffed crocodile hanging from the ceiling is a common way of identifying an apothecary's shop; see Hogarth's eighth illustration to *Hudibras*, printed for instance, in no. 475.

of the 'shamefully worn-out impression' in 'your copy' of the part containing 'the Print of Romeo & the Apothecary'.

C. In the smaller, humbler, nine-volume illustrated issue of 1805 there were stop-press changes in each sheet, and the pagination, naturally, is new. Blake's two plates are at Vol. VI, p. 263 and the frontispiece of Vol. IX. The only excuse I can think of for printing a nine-volume and a ten-volume illustrated edition simultaneously is that the nine-volume issue could be sold somewhat more cheaply. The nine-volume set was advertised at £4. 14. 6, with plates (£3. 3s. without plates) and the ten-volume set at £10. 10s. in the *London Catalogue of Books* for 1805, 1811, 1814, 1818, and 1822.

The only difference in the unillustrated nine-volume 1805 issue is in the omission of the plates and in the excision from the title-pages of everything about the plates ('A Series of Engravings . . . Professor of Painting: and') (Folger).

D. The nine-volume 1811 edition, both illustrated and unillustrated, is a completely new printing of the entire work, which was announced in the *Monthly Literary Advertiser* for December 1810. The differences in the illustrated and unillustrated title-pages are exactly like those in C above, the unillustrated variant omitting everything concerning the engravings ('A Series of Engravings . . . Professor of Painting: and'). The binding, however, seems to have been very careless. Of the three sets at the Folger, one announces no plates and has none; one has no plates but advertises them; and one has all the plates, and proclaims them on all the title-pages but the first. These are clearly simply accidental variants. Of Blake's plates, the first is much worn, but the second is not much worn.

E. The nine-volume [1812] edition requires the most intricate explanation. Apparently the first printing of the plays was relatively small, but part way through the publishers decided to increase significantly the size of the printing. They therefore printed considerably more of Volumes VII–IX— and of the preliminary matter (171 pp.) and *The Tempest* from Volume I. Apparently the original printing lasted them through about 1810, but by then they could see that the demand was steady enough to justify an entirely new printing. They therefore set the whole edition anew in 1811, and printed more of Volumes II–VI and part of Volume I than of the others. These they combined with the old sheets printed in 1805, and bound with the 1805 title-pages.

E was published in April 1812 at £5. 8s., according to the *Repository of Arts*, VII (April 1812), and a printed label dated 1812 is on the copy in the original boards in the Folger. The most curious feature of E is that though it includes matter from the 1811 edition the title-pages are from 1805, despite the fact that the list of publishers was different in 1811 than it had been in 1805.

E, then, consists of the preliminary matter (171 pp.) and *The Tempest* in Vol. I, and Vols. VII–X, plus all the 'illustrated' title-pages from the 1805 edition; and the rest of Vol. I and Vols. II–VI from the 1811 edition. Blake's plates are in Vols. VI and IX as before, but by now of course they are terribly worn, and it is unlikely that they could have been used again without being thoroughly recut.

Though there were editions of what might be called Chalmers's *Shakspeare* in 1818, 1823, 1826, 1837, 1844, 1851, [1864] and 1886 (*inter alia*), Blake's plates were not reprinted in them.

STEDMAN, J. G.

499. A. NARRATIVE, / *of a five years' expedition, against the* / Revolted Negroes of Surinam, / *in GUIANA, on the WILD COAST* of / SOUTH AMERICA; / *from the year 1772, to 1777*: / *elucidating the History of that Country, and* / describing its Productions, *Viz.* / *Quadrupedes, Birds, Fishes, Reptiles, Trees, Shrubs, Fruits, & Roots*; / *with an account of the INDIANS of Guiana, & NEGROES of Guinea,* / By CAPT.ᴺ J. G. STEDMAN. / *illustrated with 80 elegant Engravings, from drawings made by the Author.* / VOL. I [II]. / [Vignette and six-line motto from] / *Valerius Flaccus.* / London. Printed for J. Johnson, Sᵗ Paul's Church Yard, & J. Edwards, Pall Mall. 1796. (BM, Bodley, Boston Public, John Carter Brown, Columbia, Fitzwilliam, GEB, Huntington, LC, Library Company of Philadelphia, National Library of Scotland, NYP, Newberry [2], Princeton, South Carolina, Southampton, Trinity College [Hartford, Conn.], Yale)

B. Vol. I [II]. / *Second edition corrected.* / . . . / London. Printed for J. Johnson, Sᵗ Paul's Church Yard, & Th. Payne, Pall Mall. 1806. (BM, Bodley, Boston Public, Brown, Harvard, McGill, NYP, Newberry, Peabody, Southampton, V & A, Wellesley, Westminster Public)

C. 1813. (BM, Bodley, Harvard, LC, NYP)

D. EXPEDITION TO SURINAM / being the narrative of a five years expedition / against the revolted negroes of Surinam in Guiana / on the wild coast of South America / from the year 1772 to 1777 / elucidating that country and describing its productions / with an account of Indians of Guiana / and negroes of Guinea / by CAPTAIN JOHN STEDMAN / newly edited and abridged / by CHRISTOPHER BRYANT / and illustrated with engravings / selected from the earliest edition / themselves made after drawings by the author / The Folio Society. London. 1963.

E. Louis Collis. *Soldier in Paradise*: The Life of Captain John Gabriel Stedman 1744–1797. London, 1965.

F. *Narrative of a Five Years' Expedition Against the Revolted Negroes of Surinam in Guiana on the Wild Coast of South America from the Years 1772 to 1777. Elucidating the History of that Country & Describing its Productions, Viz. Quadrupedes, Birds, Reptiles, Trees, Shrubs, Fruits, & Roots; with an Account of the Indians of Guiana and Negroes of Guinea by Captain J. G. Stedman, Illustrated with 80 Elegant Engravings from Drawings Made by the Author.* [2 vols.] Barre, Massachusetts, 1971. The Imprint Society.

A. The book was long in printing, partly perhaps because of Stedman's consistent 'studying to be singular, in as much as can be'. At an early stage Blake was engaged to engrave some of Stedman's designs, and about 1 Dec.

1791 Stedman received 'above 40 Engravings from London, some well Some very ill. . . . I wrote to the Engraver *B*lake to thank him twice for his excellent work'. He and Blake thereafter became close friends.

Stedman and Johnson his publisher evidently disagreed about the proofs of the book. On 5 June 1795 Stedman took 'home My Spoilt M. Script & repair all plates' (*Blake Records* [1969], 45, 49). Johnson had probably been alarmed by the eccentricities of Stedman and his book, and

it became necessary to furnish him with assistance. And we have been told, that Mr. Johnson applied for that purpose to the doctor [*Wm Thomson (1746–1817)*], who on this occasion acted the important part of *literary dry-nurse*. . . .

> (Anon., 'William Thomson, LL.D.', *Annual Biography and Obituary*, II [1818], 110; cf. *Gentleman's Magazine*, LXXXVII, i [June 1817], 647, which says Thomson was Stedman's 'editor'.)

Stedman was outraged by this interference, though he apparently thought the changes were by Johnson, for he never mentions Thomson. On 24 June 1795 Stedman said he 'receive[d] the 1⸴ vol. of My book quite mard⌊,⌋ oaths & Sermons inserted &c . . . am put to the most extreme trouble and expence . . . . I reconcile Johnson and cansel best part of first volume' (*Blake Records*, 49). On 17 Jan. 1796 he wrote:

My book was printed full of lies and nonsense, without my knowledge. I burnt two thousand vols. and made them print it over again, by which they lost 200 guineas.

(S. Thompson, *John Gabriel Stedman* [1966], 75)

In August 'I visit M⸱ Blake for 3 days who undertakes to do business for me when I am not in London—I leave him all my papers [*?for the book*]'. In Jan. and Feb. 1796 Stedman sent his copy of the preliminaries, index, &c., directly to Hansard the printer, and 'I charged *H*ansard not to trust the above papers with Johnson who I would now not Save from the gallows . . . so cruelly was I treated—and I declare him a Scound[r]ell without he gives me Satisfaction' (*Blake Records*, 49–51). In the Feb. 1796 issue of Joseph Johnson's *Analytical Review* (Vol. XXIII), it was listed, with 80 plates 'executed by Bartolozzi, Blake, Holloway, Benedetti, &c. &c.', with other works which 'In a short Time will be published'. However, it was not until May 1796 that Hansard could report to Stedman that

all, all, all is well, and printed to my mind and wishes. I am pleased, but Johnson, the demon of hell, again torments me by altering the dedication to the Prince of Wales &c., &c., he being a d—mn'd eternal Jacobin scoundrel. . . . The whole or most of my publication, of which I send away, the last cancels so late as the middle of May 1796, having been in hand no less than 7 or 8 long years.

(*Blake Records*, 51.)

Engravings: The 86 plates are dated Dec. 1792, Dec. 1793, Dec. 1794, and Dec. 1795, and 41 have no engraver's name. Presumably all were drawn by Stedman, as the title-page states, though only two have his name on them. Thirteen are signed '*Blake Sculp!*'; besides these, GEB & Keynes (1921) are confident that Blake also engraved no. 7, 12, 14 below which are not signed. Blake's plates are inscribed '*London, Published Dec⸱ 2ᵈ 1793, by*

J. Johnson, S.ᵗ Paul's Church Yard', except for no. 2, 13, 16 dated '*Dec.ʳ 1ˢᵗ 1792*' and no. 12 dated '*Decʳ 1ˢᵗ 1794*'. The leaves are trimmed, even in large-paper copies (Princeton), so that the plate-marks do not show. Blake's plates are:

VOLUME I, at

1. p. 80: '*A Coromantyn Free Negro, or Ranger, Armed.*' '7' (Design size: 13·7 × 17·9 cm.)
2. p. 110: '*A Negro hung alive by the Ribs to a Gallows.*' '11' (13·2 × 18·0 cm).
3. p. 132: '*A private Marine of Col. Fourgeoud's Corps.*' '13' (13·6 × 18·7 cm).
4. p. 166: '*The Mecoo & Kishee Kishee Monkeys.*' '18' (13·6 × 18·8 cm).
5. p. 174: '*The skinning of the Aboma Snake, shot by Cap. Stedman.*' '19' (13·7 × 18·3 cm). (*The British Critic*, VIII [Nov. 1796], 540, complained that 'the snake in the plate must be greatly out of proportion to the man. In the narrative it is expressly affirmed to have been about the thickness of the boy Quace; but in the plate it far exceeds that of the man David.')
6. p. 200: '*Group of Negros, as imported to be sold for Slaves.*' '22' (13·3 × 18·2 cm).
7. p. 227: '*The Sculls of Lieu.ᵗ Leppar; & Six of his Men.*' '25' (13·1 × 18·6 cm).
8. p. 326: '*Flagellation of a Female Samboe Slave.*' '35' (13·4 × 18·2 cm).

VOLUME II, at

9. p. 10: '*The Quato & Saccawinkee Monkeys.*' '42' (13·4 × 18·5 cm).
10. p. 56: '*A Surinam Planter in his Morning Dress.*' '49' (13·6 × 18·3 cm).
11. p. 74: '*Limes, Capsicums, Mammy Apple &c.*' '52' (13·4 × 18·4 cm).
12. p. 104: '*March thro' a swamp or Marsh, in Terra-firma.*' '55' (13·4 × 18·4 cm).
13. p. 280: '*Family of Negro Slaves from Loango.*' '68' (13·4 × 18·1 cm).
14. p. 296: '*The Execution of Breaking on the Rack.*' '71' (13·4 × 18·1 cm).
15. p. 348: '*The celebrated Graman Quacy.*' '76' (13·4 × 18·5 cm).
16. p. 394: '*Europe supported by Africa & America.*' '80' (15·3 × 18·4 cm).

In all three editions, 'Blake (Mr. Wm) London' appears in the subscription list.

Both text and plates made a strong impression on reviewers. The *Analytical Review*, XXIV (Sept. 1796), 237, said 'The numerous plates . . . are neatly engraved, and are, we have great reason to believe, faithful and correct delineations of objects described in the work.' The *Critical Review* (Jan. 1797) pp. 52–60, praised the engravings as being 'in a style of uncommon elegance', and the *London Review* (Jan.–April 1797), pp. 20–5, 116–18, 175–80, 253–6, singled out Blake's fifth plate as 'a very good print' (p. 118). The *British Critic*, VIII (Nov. 1796), 536–40, thought the book admirable, though

The plates are very unequal; some would do honour to the most elegant, whilst others would disgrace the meanest, performances. The representations of the negroes suffering under various kinds of torture, might well have been omitted, both in the narrative and as engravings, for we will not call them embellishments to the work.

Copies of all three editions are often found coloured; those in which Gold is used may have been coloured early.

Keynes (*Blake Studies* [1971], 103) says that, besides the ordinary copies

(as above) of *c.* 21·5×26·6 cm, there are copies on large paper of *c.* 23 ×
29·5 cm with the imprint in Vol. I as '*London / Printed by J. Johnson &c.*' (the
Vol. II imprint is corrected as above) and 'the plates admirably coloured by
hand'.

B. The edition of 1806 is about a centimetre shorter than the first edition,
and consequently the bottoms of some of the plates have been trimmed off.
Blake's plates appear unchanged at Vol. I, pp. 87, 116, 140, 174, 182, 209,
237, 339; and Vol. II, pp. 10, 58, 76, 107, 291, 307, 361, and 409.

C. The printing of 1813 is clearly simply a reissue of that of 1806, with the
date on the title-page changed and the name of Johnson (who died in 1809)
erroneously repeated. Blake's plates are in the same places as in the 1806
edition.

D. The 1963 is condensed and 'modernized' (p. viii), with reproductions of
no. 1, 3, 5, 8, 10, 12–13, 15 by Blake.

E. Collis's Life reproduces no. 1, 3–6, 10, 13, 15 by Blake.

F. In the 1971 edition, Rudolph [A. J.] van Lier's 'Introduction' (Vol. I,
pp. v–xv) and 'Notes' (Vol. II, pp. 443–80) are almost entirely about
Surinam. The reproductions omit the imprints on the 80 plates and omit the
engraved title-pages entirely.

The plates were not re-used in the editions of Halle (1797) or Paris (1799,
reprinted 1960), nor apparently in those of Leyden (1799), Lausanne (1799),
Amsterdam (1800), Stockholm (1800), London (?1809), Milan (1818), and
Boston (1838).

STUART, James, & Nicholas REVETT

500. THE · ANTIQVITIES · OF / ATHENS · / MEASVRED · AND ·
DELINEATED / BY · JAMES · STVART · F.R.S. AND · F.S.A. / AND ·
NICHOLAS · REVETT. / PAINTERS · AND · ARCHITECTS. [Ed.
Willey Reveley.] / — / VOLVME · THE · THIRD. / — / [Vignette] /
LONDON / PRINTED · BY · JOHN · NICHOLS · MDCCXCIV [1794].
[Vols. I, II, and IV are dated 1762, 1787, and 1816.] (BM [2], BMPR,
Bodley, Princeton)

In this enormous volume of illustrations of Athens there are 23 small,
unsigned plates; 48 maps, plans, and diagrams; and 36 plates on a heroic
scale, 9 unsigned and 4 signed '*Blake. Sculp^t*'. Blake's plates are of 'The
sculpture on the frieze of the posticus, representing the battle of the Centaurs
and Lepithae', in the Temple of Theseus and are inscribed '*W. Pars delin^t*'
and '*Pub^d as the Act directs, April 3^d 1791—*', as follows:

1. 'Vol. III. Chap. I. Pl. XXI.' (Plate-size: 43·5×21·8 cm.)
2. 'Vol. III. Chap. I. Pl. XXII.' (43·5×21·9 cm.)
3. 'Vol. III. Chap. I. Pl. XXIII.' (43·5×21·8 cm.)
4. 'Vol. III Chap I Pl XXIV' (43·4×21·6 cm.)

None of Blake's plates bears a title.

In May 1808 George Cumberland wrote in his notebook: 'Got Blake to
engrave for Athens' (*Blake Records* [1969], 136), of which he had just acquired

the first three volumes. However, none of the plates in Volume the Fovrth, London: Printed by T. Bensley, for J. Taylor, High-Holborn, 1816, is signed by Blake. (Not counting some 31 unsigned diagrams, there are 71 plates in Vol. IV, 14 of them unsigned. None is very Blake-like; the most possible seem to be for Chap. VI, Pl. V, VII.) Cumberland may have meant that he procured the original commission for Blake's plates in Vol. III. Blake corresponded with Willey Reveley about the commission in Oct. 1791. Flaxman praised Blake's engravings as being executed 'in a very masterly manner' (*Blake Records*, 189).

The original engravings were not used again in the later editions of 1808–22 (in French), 1825–30, 1829–33 (in German), 1837, 1849, 1881, 1905.

VARLEY, John

501. A TREATISE / ON / ZODIACAL PHYSIOGNOMY; / ILLUS-TRATED BY / ENGRAVINGS OF HEADS AND FEATURES; / AND ACCOMPANIED BY / TABLES OF THE TIME OF RISING OF THE TWELVE SIGNS / OF THE ZODIAC; / AND / CONTAINING ALSO NEW AND ASTROLOGICAL EXPLANATIONS OF / SOME RE-MARKABLE PORTIONS OF / ANCIENT MYTHOLOGICAL HIS-TORY. / — / By JOHN VARLEY. / — / LONDON: / PUBLISHED BY THE AUTHOR, 10½, GREAT TICHFIELD STREET; / AND SOLD BY / LONGMAN AND CO., PATERNOSTER ROW. / — / 1828. / [ENTERED AT STATIONERS' HALL.] (BM [defective], Trinity College [Hartford, Conn.] [2])

The cover, bearing substantially the same information, adds the '*PRICE FIVE SHILLINGS*' and the fact that the pamphlet was '*TO BE COM-PLETED IN FOUR PARTS.*' No more parts were published. The work was announced for publication in *The Literary Gazette* on 11 Oct. 1828 (see no. 971) and was reviewed in the same journal on 27 Dec. 1828 (see no. 1038). How-ever, it was not 'ENTERED AT STATIONERS' HALL' until 16 May 1829, some six months later. Perhaps Varley had intended to wait until the whole work was published before he entered it, and he may not have been persuaded from the slowness of its sale not to publish any more parts until May 1829.

There are six plates of astrological designs, mostly heads designed by Varley and engraved by John Linnell, the last five bound at the end.

1. No. 4, *c.* 15·1×24·2 cm, is signed, like the next two plates, 'J. Varley. inv.', 'J. Linnel sc.'; it represents ten heads, including a male 'Cancer.' (after a design very like a self-portrait originally in the Blake–Varley Sketchbook [see no. 401] and now owned by Mr. F. Bailey Vanderhoef, Jr., with a duplicate in the collection of Mr. Leonard Baskin) and a left profile of a female 'Gemini.' (evidently after the head on p. 80 of the Blake–Varley Sketchbook).
2. No. 5, *c.* 15·6×23·7 cm, represents a right profile of the female 'Gemini', a female 'Cancer' (not by Blake), and 'Ghost of a Flea [*with open mouth*]. from Blake's vision.' (from the Blake–Varley Sketchbook).

3. No. 6, *c.* 15·1 × 23·8 cm, represents a female 'Taurus' (not by Blake), 'Ghost of a Flea [*with mouth closed*]. from Blakes. vision.' (from the Blake–Varley Sketchbook), and 'Reverse of the coin of Nebuchadnezzar; after Blake.' A separate drawing of both sides of the 'Coin of Nebuchadnezzar seen by Mr Blake in a vision' (see Keynes [1921]) was sold with the Linnell Collection at Christie's, 15 March 1918, lot 163. The Coin is not referred to in the text of the *Zodiacal Physiognomy*; perhaps its description was reserved for the later, unpublished parts.

Sir Geoffrey Keynes owns an unpublished print, 16·0 × 25·5 cm, engraved by Linnell and evidently intended for the *Zodiacal Physiognomy*, representing the obverse of the 'Coin of Nebuchadnezzar' and the head of 'Cancer' which was reworked for pl. 4 above (see no. 687).

On pp. 54–5 is an account of Blake's vision of the flea, in which a promise (not fulfilled) is made to 'give in this work' 'a view of his whole figure' (evidently to be copied from the Blake–Varley Sketchbook). This account is reprinted in Symons (1907) and Wilson (1927, 1948), as well, of course, as in *Blake Records* (1969).

502. Prospectus for *Zodiacal Physiognomy*, 1828. (BM pressmark 1879 b. 1, Vol. IV)

'In a Memoir of the late William Blake, under the article "Cancer," will be found an account of some of his remarkable Visions, with engravings from some of the most curious of them, including portraits of King Edward the First, Nebuchadnezzar, &c. &c.' In fact, neither of these portraits appeared in the only Part published.

Vetusta Monumenta

503. *VETVSTA* / MONVMENTA: / QVAE AD / RERVM BRITANNI-CARVM / MEMORIAM CONSERVANDAM / SOCIETAS ANTI-QVARIORVM / LONDINI / SVMPTV SVO EDENDA CVRAVIT. / VOLVMEN SECVNDVM. [London, ?1789.] (BM, Bodley, Princeton)

Blake's name appears on none of the plates in *Vetusta Monumenta*, but it is very likely that he had a hand in some of them. His master James Basire, who was the chief engraver of the Society of Antiquaries, sent Blake from 1774 to 1779 to make drawings of 'all the old monuments in Westminster Abbey, as well as . . . other churches in and about London', and according to Malkin (1806), Blake was also engaged 'occasionally, especially in winter, in engravings from those drawings' (*Blake Records* [1969], 423, 422). Malkin identifies Blake's part in the plates signed by Basire for Gough's *Sepulchral Monuments* (1786), and Blake almost certainly made at least the drawings for the journal of the Society of Antiquaries as well. The most likely candidates are those in the separately titled section: AN / ACCOUNT / OF SOME / ANCIENT MONUMENTS / IN / WESTMINSTER ABBEY. / By Sir JOSEPH AYLOFFE, Bart. / V.P.A.S.L. F.R.S. SOC. ANTIQ. CASSEL. SOD. HONORAR. / Read at the Society of Antiquaries March 12, 1778. / — / [ornament] / = / LONDON, / PRINTED BY J. NICHOLS / PRINTER TO THE SOCIETY OF ANTIQUARIES. /

M.DCC.LXXX [1780]. In his text, Ayloffe says that the 'accurate drawings [*were*] taken under the inspection of Mr. Basire' in 1775 (p. 4). All the plates below are signed 'PLATE I[–VII]'; 'VOL. II, PLATE XXIX[–XXXV]'; '*Sumptibus Societatis Antiquar. Londini*'; '*J. Basire del. et Sc.*'; '*Publish'd as the Act directs, April 23, 1780*'; and the size is 31·3 × 38·1 cm (there are very minor variants in all these details).

1. '*The front of the Monument of AVELINE, FIRST WIFE OF EDMUND CROUCHBACK | EARL OF LANCASTER, on the North Side of the Altar in Westminster Abbey.*'
2. '*The Figure of AVELINE COUNTESS OF LANCASTER, cumbent on her | Monument on the North Side of the Altar in Westminster Abbey.*'
3. '*A. The UNDER VAULTING of one side of the Canopy of the Monument of AVELINE | COUNTESS OF LANCASTER.*
   B. *ACANTHUS on the front of the Canopy of the same Monument.*
   C. *PAINTING on the Compartment over the top of the same Canopy.*
   D. *ORNAMENT on the Spandrels in the pediment of the Canopy.*'
4. '*The North front of the Monument of KING SEBERT, on the South Side of the | Altar in Westminster Abbey.*'
5. '*The figures supposed to be those of KING SEBERT (1) and KING HENRY III. (2) | as painted on the North front of the Monument of King Sebert in Westminster Abbey.*'
6. '*HEADS & ORNAMENTS on the North Side of the Monument of KING SEBERT, in Westminster Abbey*'.
7. '*The Monument of ANN OF CLEVES, FOURTH WIFE OF KING HENRY VIII, on the South Side of the Altar in Westminster Abbey.*'

There are wash drawings, mostly signed Basire (or B) del 1775 of no. 1–7 (plus duplicates of no. 3 and 5) in the Royal Society of Antiquaries, others of no. 1–6 (plus a duplicate of no. 5) in Bodley, and proofs of no. 1–3, 6 (2) in Bodley.

Vetusta Monumenta was issued in irregular parts consisting of a series of sumptuous engravings accompanied by descriptive text such as Ayloffe's for *Westminster Abbey*. From time to time volume title-pages were issued; the first (1747) covered plates from 1718; the second covers plates as late as 1789; and the third is dated 1796. Clearly, the most important publishing unit was the separate part, like Ayloffe's.

VIRGIL

504. THE / *PASTORALS* / OF / VIRGIL, / WITH A COURSE / OF / ENGLISH READING, / ADAPTED FOR SCHOOLS: / IN WHICH ALL / THE PROPER FACILITIES / ARE GIVEN, ENABLING YOUTM TO ACQUIRE / THE LATIN LANGUAGE, / IN / *THE SHORTEST PERIOD OF TIME.* / Illustrated by 230 Engravings. / = / BY / ROBERT JOHN THORNTON, M.D. / MEMBER OF THE UNIVERSITY OF CAMBRIDGE, &c. &c. / — / THIRD EDITION. / — / VOL. I [II]. / *LONDON*: / Stereotyped and Printed by J. M'Gowan, Great Windmill Street. / Published by F. C. & J. Rivingtons; Longman and Co.; Sherwood / and Co.; Whittaker and Co. / Cadell and Co.; Arch and Co.; Black / and Co.;

J. Richardson; Asperne; Souter; Sir Richard Phillips and / Co.; Rodwell and Co.; Gosling; Cox; Highly; Bumpus; Sharp; / and may be had of all Booksellers in the United Kingdom; or of Mr. / Harrison, 13, Little Tower Street, Agent for Dr. Thornton. / 1821. / *N.B. The Price of Thornton's Pastorals of Virgil, is* 15*s. bound.* / A full Allowance to the Trade and Schoolmasters. (BM, BMPR, Cincinnati Art Museum, Fitzwilliam, GEB, Harvard [2], Huntington, McGill, Metropolitan [N.Y.], Morgan, NYP, Princeton [2], Trinity College [Hartford, Conn.], V & A, Wellesley, Westminster Public, Yale)

The first edition of Thornton's Virgil in 1812 had no plates; woodcuts for it were issued separately in 1814, without text; the woodcuts were united with the second edition of the text in 1819. This was clearly a successful venture, and other engravers, including Blake, were commissioned to provide yet more plates for the Third Edition. Blake made six engravings on copper (no. 1–4, 26–7 below), one design for another engraver (no. 25), and twenty woodcuts after his own designs (no. 5–24).

When Blake had produced his cuts, which were, however, printed with an *apology*, a shout of derision was raised by the wood-engravers. 'This will never do,' said they; 'we will show what it ought to be'—that is, what the public taste would like

and no. 18–20 below were re-cut by another hand (Henry Cole in *The Athenaeum* [1843], no. 1406). According to Gilchrist (1863, I. 273, 275), the other plates were only saved by the 'warm admiration' of them expressed to Thornton by Sir Thomas 'Lawrence, James Ward, Linnell, and others', but even so Blake's 'blocks, moreover, proved in the first instance too wide for the page and were, irrespective of the composition, summarily cut down [*about 0·5 to 1·0 cm*] to the requisite size by the publishers'. The book was entered at Stationers' Hall on 12 Feb. 1821 as the 'Property of Willm Harrison', though 'Published by F. C. & J. Rivington'.

Blake is said to have had a hand in 27 of the 232 plates in the two volumes; 196 plates are not signed by a designer, and 193 have no engraver. Blake's plates 1–4, 26–7 are signed '*Blake, del. et Sculp.*', '*London, Published by Dr Thornton, 1821*'.

1. Vol. I, p. 3: '*Theocritus, / A Grecian Poet of Sicily Flourished 273 years before the Birth of Christ, and quitting his native country, governed by Hiero, King of Syracuse, went over to King Ptolemy in Egypt, by whom he was greatly patronized. / Vide Idyllium, 17.*' (Design size: 9·8 × 7·1 cm.)

2. p. 4: '*Publius Virgilius Maro. / Poetarum Latinorum Princeps. / Born 69 years before the Birth of Christ; was 7 years older than Augustus; lost his Estate, at 30; recovering it was nearly killed by Arius, the Centurion; some think he began his Eclogues, at 31; which took him 3 years. Commenced his Georgies, at 34, which occupied him 7 years; at 41 began his Æneid, which employed him 11 years; at 52, Virgil died, 19 years before the Christian Æra.*' (Design size: 10·0 × 6·8 cm.)

3. Immediately following it is: '*Octavius Augustus Cæsar. / Was Nephew to Julius Cæsar, and 18 years old when Cæsar was assassinated; joins Antony, and Lepidus, and defeats Brutus and Cassius, at the Battle of Phillippi, 41 years*

B.C. — *Antony marries Octavia, Sister to Augustus, whom he deserts for Cleo-patra, Queen of Egypt, whom Cæsar defeats in a naval battle at Actium, 31 years before Christ; /Shuts the Temple of Janus, the world having been created 3948 years, when a new Æra commences, the Birth of Christ; — dies 14 years after that period, at 76, having reigned 44 years.*' (Design size: 12·4 × 8·4 cm.)

4. Following this is a plate of five portraits '*From Antique Coins*', with names under the portraits, and identifications at the foot: '*POLLIO was a Poet, a General, & a great favourite to Augustus, & was twice Consul. | GALLUS was made Præfect of Egypt, a Poet, who slew himself having ruled Tyrannically, | AGRIPPA a famous General to Augustus, commanded in all his battles, & was married to Julia daughter to Augustus. | VARUS was of noble extraction, Father to Maia, Virgil's wife, was also a Poet, and Governor of Gisalpine Gaul. | MECÆNUS was prime Minister to Augustus, & died 7 Years after the birth of Christ.*' (Design size: 13·1 × 8·4 cm)

5. 'To face page 13': 'ILLUSTRATIONS / OF / IMITATION OF ECLOGUE I [*by Ambrose Philips*]. FRONTISPIECE' (design size: 6·0 × 8·3 cm). Below the plate is: 'THENOT AND COLINET. / — / The Illustrations of this English Pastoral are by the famous BLAKE, the illustrator of *Young's* Night Thoughts, and *Blair's* Grave; who designed and engraved them himself. This is mentioned, as they display less of art than genius, and are much admired by some eminent painters.'

None of the next 19 'ILLUSTRATIONS OF IMITATION OF ECLOGUE I' (each *c.* 7·6 × 3·2 cm) is signed, but no. 18–20 were engraved by a journeyman engraver. No. 6, 9, 12–13, 15–16 are labelled 'COLINET', no. 7, 10–11, 14, 17, 'THENOT', no. 8 'COLI-NET and THENOT'.

6–9. Four plates on one leaf 'To face page 14'. (Blake's design for pl. 7 was also cut by another hand in a woodblock not published until 1843 in the *Athenaeum*—see no. 1406.)

10–13. Four plates on one leaf 'To face page 15'.

14–17. Four plates on one leaf 'To face page 16'.

18–20. Three plates on one leaf entitled 'First [Second, *and* Third] Comparison'.

21–4. 'To face page 18'. 'THENOT. To illustrate lines 1, 2.' Three more blocks on the same page are labelled simply '3, 4, 5, 6.', '7, 8, 9.', '10.'

25. 'To face page 21': 'ILLUSTRATION OF ECLOGUE I / INTRODUCTORY.' 'THE GIANT POLYPHEME, FROM A FAMOUS PICTURE BY N. POUSSIN.' '*Blake, del.*' '*Byfield sculps.*' (Design size: 11·6 × 7·8 cm; either the inscription is in error or Blake took over work commenced by Linnel, for in his Journal for 18 Oct. 1820 Linnell wrote: 'Began a small Drawing on a wood Block of Polypheme (from N. Poussin) for Dᖟ Thornton₍ₗ,₎ to receive a guinea for it'.)

26. Vol. II, p. 229: '*Caius Julius Caesar, | Assassinated 44 years before the Christian Æra | Virgil: æt. 26*' (Design size: 12·4 × 8·3 cm.)

27. p. 360: '*Epicurus. | A Grecian Philosopher, Flourished 264 years before Christ, His philosophy was transfused into Latin, by the great Roman Poet Lucretius, who*

flourished 105 years before Christ, and wrote his 'De Rerum Naturâ' on the Nature of Things. He placed the summum bonum on Tranquility of Mind, arising from Virtue, and the Contemplation of Nature. | He is said to have been born 342 B.C. Died 270 B.C. æ: 72.' (Design size: 10·1 × 7·0 cm.)

There are proofs of the untrimmed blocks in the BMPR (no. 2–5, 6–9, on 2 sheets); in Mr. Hofer's collection (no. 2–5); in that of Mrs. G. Ramsay Harvey (no. 2–5); and in the Fitzwilliam Museum, with the *Island in the Moon* (no. 6–9). Before the commercial printing, Blake's blocks were cut down. In a manuscript 'List of John Linnell Senior's Letters and Papers' (in the Ivimy MSS), John Linnell, Jr., wrote of the seventeen Virgil woodblocks:

These blocks after the Publisher [*i.e. Thornton*] had used them, (J. L. bought of him [*16 Sept. 1825*] for 2 guineas) E Calvert printed them for J. L. & self, &c (certain number of imprints of the set) (J. L. jun. & brother printed a few of the blocks, but did not finish the set)⌊.⌋

There are, consequently, a large number of 'proofs' of the finished blocks to be found, *inter alia*, in the BMPR, Cincinnati Art Museum, Fitzwilliam, Harvard, Huntington, LC, Dr. David McC. McKell, Morgan, Princeton Art Museum, V & A, Wellesley, and Yale, and a set of seven coloured prints (reproduced by James G. Ingli in *Apollo* [1974], 194–5) is in the possession of Herbert Palmer's daughters Mrs. Joanna M. Lees and Mrs. Sybil M. Johns. The woodblocks which Linnell acquired stayed in the family until they were sold at Christie's, 2 Dec. 1938, lot 60, for £504 to the National Art Collections Fund for the BMPR. In the same sale (lot 61) were the electrotypes from which the 1937 facsimile was printed.

The sketches for no. 6–8, 10, 12–15, 17–18, 20–1, plus a design not engraved, are reproduced in *Pencil Drawings* (1927) and the Virgil facsimile (1937), and no. 11 in the Philadelphia catalogue (1939).

Plates 5–21 are reproduced in R. R. Easson & R. N. Essick, *William Blake: Book Illustrator* (see 1972, under Catalogues), no. 8 was printed from the woodblock in Henry Cole's *Athenaeum* article (1843), and no. 9–10, 13 in Gilchrist, *Life of William Blake* (1863, 1880).

Blake's Virgil drawings were made in a sketchbook which was broken up after 1924, and separate sketches may now be found, *inter alia*, in the collections of Harvard, Sir Geoffrey Keynes, Princeton Art Gallery, and Yale. For the designs themselves, see no. 510.

In general, when Blake's Virgil is mentioned, the designs on the woodblocks are intended.

505. *William Blake: XVII Designs to Thornton's Virgil* Reproduced from the Original Woodcuts of MDCCCXXI. Portland, Maine, 1899 (vDVE).

Introduction (pp. xi–xx), notes (pp. 55–9).

506. *William Blake: Being all His Woodcuts* Photographically Reproduced in Facsimile with an Introduction by Laurence Binyon. London & N.Y., 1902. Little Engravings Classical & Contemporary, Number II.

The 'Introduction' is 3 pp.

507. *William Blake's Illustrations to Thornton's Pastorals of Virgil* in Ambrose Phillips' Imitation of Virgil's First Eclogue 1821. Enlarged Fac-similes in Platinotype from the scarce original edition by Frederick Evans. [London], 1912.

Twelve sets of the plates were issued separately in 1919 (see no. 509).

508. 'XVII Woodcut Designs to Thornton's Virgil by William Blake.' *Bibelot*, XX (1914), 405–13.

Blake's woodcuts are printed beside the 1821 translation and an 'Introduction' by Laurence Binyon.

509. *William Blake's | Illustrations | to the | Pastorals of Virgil.* | Platinotype Enlargements / from the original edition / of 1821 / by Frederick H. Evans. / [London] 1919 (vKP).

A re-issue of the 1912 plates without the text, in 12 sets.

510. *The Illustrations of William Blake for Thornton's Virgil* with the First Eclogue and the Imitation by Ambrose Philips. The Introduction by Geoffrey Keynes. London, 1937.

Besides facsimiles of the printed plates, there are 8 proof plates from the first state and 16 reproductions of the pencil designs. Inserted in a small portfolio is a set of the prints printed one to a page. The 'Introduction' (pp. 7–19) is revised and reprinted in Keynes's *Blake Studies* (1949, 1971).

WEDGWOOD CATALOGUE

511. [*Wedgwood's Catalogue of Earthenware and Porcelain.* ?1816–43] (BMPR).

Blake corresponded from 29 July to 13 Dec. 1815 with Wedgwood about his eighteen plates containing 189 figures of pottery, and on 11 Nov. 1816 he was paid £30 for his labour (*Blake Records* [1969], 239–41, 578). The catalogue was presumably issued for the use of Wedgwood salesmen in 1816 and thereafter, but beyond this it is difficult to speak with confidence, for the issues of the Wedgwood catalogues are a daunting bibliographical jungle.

The catalogues were issued without title or imprint, and all copies known to me are in loose sheets, which tend to get jumbled. Blake's plates were gradually replaced in successive catalogues, until the last one disappeared in the issue of *c.* 1843, which contained thirty-four plates. Unfortunately I cannot say how many issues there were or which Blake plates appeared in a given issue.

The BMPR has a set of Blake's 18 plates (from the Linnell Collection), plus duplicates of pl. 8–9, 14, 16 (pl. 9, 14 are proofs before number or signature, marked for correction). Sir Geoffrey Keynes has a 34-plate version, and other sets are in the Wedgwood Museum, Barlaston, Stoke-on-Trent. Mrs. Robert D. Chellis has pl. 6–7 printed on one sheet and inscribed by Tatham: 'Mr Flaxman introduced Blake to Mr Wedgwood. The Designs of the Pottery were made by Mr. Flaxman [*this seems doubtful*] and engraved by Blake for some work.' Pl. 2–8, 10–18 are reproduced in Wolf Mankowitz, *Wedgwood* (1953; 1966), plates 14–29. According to Sir Geoffrey Keynes (*Blake Studies* [1971], 65), 8 of Blake's Wedgwood copperplates survive, one of them with a central figure removed and a bedpan substituted. (Sir Geoffrey tells me that he saw them on the premises of the Wedgwood firm at Etruria, but they are not now in the firm's museum, according to the Museum Curator.)

All the plates are headed 'WEDGWOOD', and each object represented is numbered. The plate-sizes are: *c.* 16·8×22·7 cm (pl. 1–5, 7, 11–18); 18·0×22·5 cm (pl. 6); *c.* 16·9×23·6 cm (pl. 8–10). Blake's plates are signed '*Blake d & sc*':

1. '*P 1*', no. 1–2, 422, 425–6, 440.
2. '*P 2*', no. 3–4.
3. '*P 3*', no. 7, 12–13.
4. '*P 4*', no. 14, 17, 64, 75.
5. '*P 5*', no. 1, 40, 44, 51, 69, 89, 113, 119, 121.
6. '*P 6*', no. 112, 114–15, 120, 160, 888–9, 891.
7. '*P 7*', no. 146, 152, 154, 164, 346–7, 753–4, 757, 1319.
8. '*P 8*', no. 185, 190–3, 198, 1219–20, 1222, 1227–8.
9. '*P 9*', no. 258, 260, 265–8, 281–2, 302, 304–6, 308–9, 313–15.
10. '*P 10*', no. 734, 736, 781, 783–4, 789–93, 802–3.
11. '*P 11*', no. 331–2, 335, 337, 340–1, 643–4, 921, 923.
12. '*P 12*', no. 916–17, 944–5, 999, 1043–4, 1046–7.
13. '*P 13*', no. 850–1, 853–4, 856, 870–1.
14. '*P 14*', no. 543–5, 553, 576, 579–81, 587.
15. '*P 15*', no. 430–1, 650–3, 660, 669, 813, 815.
16. '*P 16*', no. 1457, 1459, 1461, 1467–9, 1481, 1486, 1538, 1553–4, 1556, 1561, 1565–6.
17. '*P 17*', no. 739, 747, 1421, 1429, 1433, 1446, 1463, 1510, 1516–17, 1519, 1533, 1535, 1551.
18. '*P 18*', no. 1494, 1496, 1567, 1575–6, 1579–80, 1584, 1593–4, 1598, 1606, 1609, 1611, 1636.

Hughes (no. 1904) says that the 1815 catalogue was for the Continental market, that it was to be accompanied by price-lists in the languages of different countries, and that the plates were sent loose in reply to queries and were rarely bound.

WHITAKER, John

512. A. Vol. 1 [2] / THE SERAPH, / A Collection of / SACRED MUSIC, / *Suitable to Public or Private Devotion;* / Consisting of the most celebrated / Psalm and Hymn Tunes, / With Selections from the Works of / HANDEL, HAYDN, MOZART, PLEYEL, / AND FAVORITE ENGLISH AND ITALIAN COMPOSERS: / adapted to Words from / *Milton, Young, Watts, Wesley,* / *Merrick, Cowper, Henry Kirke White, D.ʳ Collyer, &c.* / To which are added / Many Original Pieces, / *Composed and the Whole arranged for* / Four Voices / With an Accompaniment for the / *Piano Forte or Organ and Violoncello.* / By / JOHN WHITAKER. / [vignette] / *London* / *Printed by Button, Whitaker and Comp.ʸ* / 75, S.ᵗ *Paul's Church Yard.* [?1818–28] / Ent. Sta. Hall. Price 1. 11. 6 each Vol. (BM, Cambridge [Vol. II, no. 1 only])

B. ... *Whitaker and Comp*ᵞ ... [?1819–28] (GEB, Michigan)

C. *Printed for Jones & C*ᵒ *| 3, Acton Place Kingsland Road* ... [?1825–28] (Cambridge)

The title-page of Vol. II (reported here) differs, at least in B, from that in Vol. I in omitting commas after 'Composed' and 'Organ' and substituting italics for roman capitals in the imprints.

Whitaker's *Seraph* consists of 8 numbers of 60 pages (240 pages to a volume), each printed from a copperplate and inscribed with some variant of 'Seraph Nᵒ 1 Vol: 1.' The first part evidently appeared early in 1818, for John Whitaker's integral 'Advertisement' is dated 1 Feb. 1818, and his note 'To Vocal, and Instrumental Performers' is dated 28 Feb. 1818. A review of the first number in the *Repository of Arts* for April 1818 (p. 229) said: 'Messrs. Button, Whitaker, and Co. the publishers, intend to complete it in sixteen monthly numbers, each at [5s.] ... to contain sixty pages of music ....' (Note that this is twice the present size and a cost of £4 versus the £3. 3s. on the title-pages.) Probably they were not able to keep to their schedule of a part a month. Occasional watermarks in the GEB copy—Vol. I, no. 2 (1819), I, 3 (1817, 1821), I, 4 (1821), II, 1 (1823, 1825), II, 2 (1823, 1827), II, 3 (1823), II, 4 (1823, 1828)—suggest that it was issued from 1819 to 1828. Over the years the work changed hands, and the new publishers altered the title-pages to indicate the new ownership. Button, Whitaker & Co. of 75 St Paul's were followed at the same address by Whitaker & Co. from 1819 to Dec. 1824 (C. Humphries & W. C. Smith, *Music Publishing in the British Isles* [1954]), and Jones & Co. was at Acton Place from 1825 to 1828 (ibid.). Evidently, therefore, Button, Whitaker & Co. issued the first number[s] in 1818; Whitaker issued subsequent numbers from 1819 to 1824, changing the title-pages accordingly; and Jones & Co. issued most of the numbers in Vol. II from 1825 to 1828, also changing the title-pages. Jones & Co. offered the work 'In about 60 nos. at 6d. or 30 Parts, at 1s. each' (total £1. 10s.) in an ad. bound, e.g., with Darwin's *Botanic Garden* (1824) (NYP).

The only designs in the volume are on the engraved title-pages, the second of which is inscribed in A:

1. 'Drawn by the late W. Blake Esqʳ R.A.', 'Engᵈ by P. Jones. 290, Holborn.' (Design size: *c.* 14·5 × 17·5 cm.) In B–C, the engraver's address is altered to '36. Theobolds Rᵈ' In C, an identification was added below the design: '*Conscience & the recording Angel.* / Youngs Nᵗ. Thoughts —See Page 1. Vol. 2, of this Work.' At the top of Vol. II, p. 1 is an 'Explanation of the Frontispiece. Conscience; as a recording Angel, veiled, in the act of noting down the sin of intemperance in a Bacchanalian.' This is followed by a psalm, 'Conscience. From Young's Night Thoughts.' The design is copied from *Night Thoughts* (1797) p. 27. Presumably the Vol. II title-page (called a 'Frontispiece' here) was issued with Vol. II, no. 1 (which refers to it) about 1824. At that date Blake was not, of course, 'late', and he was never 'R.A.'

THE WIT'S MAGAZINE

513. THE / WIT's MAGAZINE; / OR, / LIBRARY of MOMUS. / BEING A / COMPLETE REPOSITORY / OF / MIRTH, HUMOUR, AND ENTERTAINMENT. / MIRTH! WITH THEE I MEAN TO LIVE. / MILTON. / VOL. I. / [Ornament] / LONDON: Printed for HARRISON and Co. Nº 18, Paternoster-Row. / M DCC LXXXIV [1784]. (BM, BMPR, Bodley, GEB, Harvard, Huntington, McGill, National Library of Scotland, Princeton, Swansea, Trinity College [Hartford, Conn.], Wellesley, Westminster Public)

Each monthly number, entitled simply 'The Wit's Magazine', has a fold-out frontispiece illustrating one of the issue's articles or poems. Blake engraved plates for the first five numbers of Vol. I in 1784, all of them signed '*Blake sculp.*' Under each month's title-page from January through May is a puff pointing out the Blake engraving. Thomas Holcroft 'was the Editor' 'of the four first numbers' of 'The Wits' Magazine' (according to the preface to Holcroft's *Tales in Verse* [1806]); Blake's tenure ceased just after Holcroft's.

Blake's plates are for:

1. The Jan. 1784 number, 'The Temple of Mirth.' '*Stothard del.*' 'Published as the Act directs by Harrison & Cº Febʸ 1. 1784.' (Design size: 22·8 × 17·5 cm.) (A proof before lettering is in the BMPR, and another proof is in the collection of Mr. Robert N. Essick.)

Note. There are *two* quite separate plates of this design; the duplication was first observed, and generously pointed out to me, by Professor Robert Essick, to whose fraternal assistance I owe most details of the differences noted below. Each version was issued with copies of *The Wit's Magazine*, the first with copies in the BMPR and Huntington, the second with three copies in the BM and one in Bodley. Though the design in pl. 1 and 2 is essentially the same, the differences are quite plain, and there can be no doubt that there are two copperplates rather than two versions of one plate. Some of the more striking differences are as follows:

	Plate 1	Plate 2
Two busts at left labelled	'VOLT', 'STE'	'STERNE', 'SWIFT'
Squares on floor have	Wavy lines	Cross hatches and dark circles in centre
Left man has	No watch fob	Watch fob
In second row to left of Mirth are	Three men	Two men
Niches for busts are	Lighted (?windows) which go to ceiling	Not lighted, arched over busts
Horse in picture is seen	Full face	In profile
Picture frames descend to	Just Mirth's elbow	Well below her elbow
Second person to right of Mirth has	White wig, hand to face	Lank black hair, no hand
Last woman on right has	Dark hat (?with feathers), plain skirt	Pale hat, with bow, striped skirt
Right man has	White wig, buttons on coat	Grey hair, no buttons
General effect is	Lighter, clearer, somewhat unfinished	Darker, more shadowed, more details

The question of priority is very difficult; perhaps pl. 1 was earlier. The prints give no clear clue to me as to why a replacement was made; perhaps the earlier one was damaged. Since both bear Blake's name, presumably he engraved them both.

2. The lettering is as in pl. 1 (except that the comma after 'directs' is omitted), but the design size is 22·7 × 17·1 cm. (A proof before signature is in the Huntington.)

3. The Feb. 1784 number, 'TYTHE IN KIND; OR THE SOW'S RE-VENGE.' Pl. 2–5 are signed *'Collings del.'* (23·9 × 19·3 cm.) Pl. 2 is dated 'March 1. 1784'; it illustrates the poem 'Tythe in Kind; or The Sow's Revenge' by 'F——' on pp. 71–2.

4. Blake's engraving called 'THE DISCOMFITED DUELLISTS' for the March 1784 issue is dated 'April 1, 1784' (24·0 × 19·3 cm). It is for an essay by 'H——' (?Holcroft) entitled 'Preservative against Duelling' on pp. 89–92.

5. Blake engraved a plate for the April 1784 issue entitled 'THE BLIND BEGGAR'S HATS' and dated 'May 1. 1784' (22·7 × 18·9 cm). It illustrates a poem called 'The Beggars Hats; or, The Way to Get Rich. A Tale. By Mr. Holcroft' on pp. 151–3.

6. Blake's plate for the May 1784 issue called 'MAY-DAY IN LONDON' is dated 'June 1, 1784' (23·7 × 19·0 cm). It illustrates a poem called 'May-Day. An Epistle from Sammy Sarcasm in Town, to his Aunt in the Country. By Mr. [*Samuel*] Collings' on p. 191.

WOLLSTONECRAFT, Mary

514. A. ORIGINAL STORIES / FROM / *REAL LIFE*; / WITH / CON-VERSATIONS, / CALCULATED TO / REGULATE the AFFECTIONS, / AND / FORM the MIND / TO / TRUTH and GOODNESS. / — / *LONDON*: / PRINTED FOR J. JOHNSON, NO. 72, ST. / PAUL'S CHURCH-YARD. / — / 1791. (BM, BMPR, Bodley, Columbia, Harvard [2], Huntington, Illinois, New York, Newberry, Pforzheimer, Princeton, Rosenbach, Smith, Texas, Toronto Public, Trinity College [Hartford, Conn.], Wellesley, West Sussex Record Office, Westminster Public, Yale)

B. . . . FORM THE MIND TO TRUTH AND / GOODNESS. / BY / MARY WOLLSTONECRAFT. / — / A NEW EDITION. / — / *LONDON*: / PRINTED FOR J. JOHNSON, NO. 72, ST. PAUL'S / CHURCH-YARD. / — / 1796. (BM, Bodley, GEB)

C. MARY / WOLLSTONECRAFT'S / ORIGINAL / STORIES / WITH FIVE ILLUSTRATIONS / BY / WILLIAM BLAKE / WITH AN INTRO-DUCTION / BY / E. V. LUCAS / LONDON / HENRY FROWDE / 1906.

A. Johnson entered the original unillustrated edition of the *Original Stories* at Stationers' Hall on [2] April 1788.

Blake's ten drawings (not including pl. 5) for the *Original Stories* (now in the Rosenwald Collection) were reproduced in W. Godwin, *Memoirs of Mary Wollstonecraft* (1927), no. 1708. All six plates in the 1791 edition are

'Published by J. Johnson, Sept.ᵣ 1ˢᵗ 1791', but only the first has any signature, namely *'Blake d. & sc'*. The plates are at:

1. *'Frontispiece'*, *'Look what a fine morning it is.—Insects, Birds, & Animals, are all enjoying existence.'* (Plate-mark: *c.* 9·3 × 14·7 cm.) (Blake's 'Nurse's Song' [*Songs* (1794) pl. 38] has a related design.)
2. *'P. 24'*, *'The Dog strove to attract his attention.—He said, Thou wilt not leave me!'* (*c.* 9·2 × 15·7 cm.) (*For Children* [1793] pl. 15 has a related design.)
3. *'P. 74.'* *'Indeed we are very happy!—'* (9·8 × 15·0 cm).
4. *'P. 94.'* *'Be calm, my child, remember that you must do all the good you can the present day.'* (9·5 × 15·9 cm.)
5. *'P. 114.'* *'Trying to trace the sound, I discovered a little hut, rudely built.'* (9·4 × 15·7 cm.)
6. *'P. 173.'* *'Œconomy & Self-denial are necessary, in every station, to enable us to be generous.'* (*c.* 9·6 × 15·6 cm.)

B. In the 1796 edition the plates were darkened, especially the clothes; pl. 4, 6 were moved to pp. 84, 153; and all six plates including the first were given some variant of *'Blake inv. & sculpt'*, but the dates were not changed. The plates were probably optional in both 1791 and 1796 editions, for an advertisement bound with the GEB Enfield *Speaker* (1799) offered *Original Stories*, 'Price 2s. 6d. with Cuts bound, or 2s. without Cuts.'

C. The edition of 1906 reproduces pl. 1, 3–6.

The editions of Dublin, 1792 and 1799, had no plates, and the plates in the editions of Chiswick, 1820 and London [1835] have no relation to Blake's.

The six plates are reproduced in R. R. Easson & R. N. Essick, *William Blake: Book Illustrator* (see 1972 under Catalogues).

YOUNG, Edward

515. THE COMPLAINT, / AND / THE CONSOLATION; / OR, / NIGHT THOUGHTS, / BY / EDWARD YOUNG, LL.D. / = / —fatis centraria fata respendens. / VIRG. / = / [Nights I–IV out of 9] LONDON: / PRINTED BY R. NOBLE. / FOR R. EDWARDS, No. 142, BOND-STREET, / MDCCXCVII [1797]. (Auckland Public, Adelaide, *Anon., Ashmolean, BM, BMPR, Bodley, Boston Museum, *Boston Museum of Fine Art, Boston Public, California [San Diego], Cincinnati Art Museum, Fitzwilliam, GEB, **Harvard [5], *Huntington [3], Illinois, **LC [2], London [2], Los Angeles County Museum, McGill [2], **Mellon [2], *Morgan, National Gallery of Canada, National Library of Scotland, Newberry, NYP [Berg], NYP [3], New York, Pforzheimer, *Princeton [2], Rosenbach Foundation, *Rylands, St. David's College [Lampeter, Cardiganshire], St. John's Seminary [Camarillo, Calif.], *Soane Museum, State Library of Victoria [Melbourne], Syracuse, *Texas [3], *Thorne [2], Toronto Public, Trinity College [Hartford, Conn.], Turnbull Library, V&A, Wellesley, Westminster Public, Yale [2] [Asterisks indicate coloured copies])

Fuseli told Joseph Farington on 24 June 1796 that

Blake has undertaken to make designs to encircle the letter press of each page of 'Youngs night thoughts.⌐'⌐ [*Richard*] Edwards the Bookseller, of Bond Sᵗʳ employs him, and has had the letter press of each page laid down on a large half sheet of paper. There are ab! 900 pages.—Blake asked 100 guineas for the whole. Edwards said He could not afford to give more than 20 guineas [*?for the drawings*] for which Blake agreed.[1] Fuseli understands that Edwards proposes to select ab! 200 from the whole and to have that number engraved [*by Blake*] as decorations for a new edition.

[*Blake Records* (1969), 52.]

Thomas Edwards (Richard's brother) said that the drawings 'occupied nearly two years' (1821 catalogue) or 'more than two years' (1826) of Blake's time, indicating that they must have been started about 1794. In his 'Advertisement' dated 22 Dec. 1796, Richard Edwards said that he chose to have Young illustrated in order 'to make the arts . . . subservient to the purposes of religion'. 'Of the merit of Mr. Blake' in the designs, he considered it 'to be unnecessary to speak', beyond saying that 'the original conception, and the bold and masterly execution of this artist cannot be unnoticed or unadmired'.

Sheets of 1794 J WHATMAN paper were set round the leaves of early editions of the separately published Nights, on one 'blank leaf' of which was 'the Author's [*Young's*] signature'; this leaf was later cut off by 'The Bookbinder from inattention' (according to the 1821 advertisement). These 537 preparatory drawings have been preserved as a unit since Blake sold them to Edwards and were presented in 1929 by W. A. White to the British Museum Print Room. The pages were numbered consecutively in Brown ink and the lines ticked (to indicate which to illustrate) before they were mounted, for the outer leaves sometimes overlap these numbers and ticks. Often the lines ticked are not the same as those starred as illustrated in the published edition. Some lines are underlined, and there are a few corrections or annotations to the text in crayon. Many, though not all, of the published designs are marked 'Engraved' or 'Engraved reversed'. No. 63, two naked men with sheep illustrating 'Know'st thou, *Lorenzo!* what a Friend contains', is marked 'Engraved', and no. 107, for '*Age and disease; Disease tho' long my Guest' is marked 'Engraved revers^d', though neither was engraved. (Thirty of the BMPR designs are reproduced in Keynes, no. 395. All 43 plates are reproduced in R. R. Easson & R. N. Essick, *William Blake: Book Illustrator* [see 1972 under Catalogues].)

A few sketches have survived outside the BMPR collection. There are sketches of the Christ in pl. 18 on *Vala* pp. 16, 58, 116. Another *Night Thoughts* design, inaccurately 'supposed for the Grave of Blair . . . by Fredk Tatham', was in the Graham Robertson Collection (no. 664). A sketch for pl. 32, called (probably not by Blake) 'Let Loose the Dogs of War', from the Ruskin collection, is reproduced in no. 1960. A design for 'The Thought of Death alone, the fear destroys' is in the Cleveland Museum. In the Huntington Library is a curious design on vellum (reproduced in the Huntington catalogue, no. 646) which is a mirror image of one of the unengraved designs in the BMPR; it may have been made for Edwards to

---

[1] This scarcely bears out Edwards's claim in his 'Advertisement' that he 'has shrunk from no expence in the preparing' of the edition. J. T. Smith called it a 'despicably low' price (*Blake Records* 46).

use in his shop window as an advertisement. Gilchrist (1863), chap. xxiv, refers to a drawing in the Butts Collection called 'The Soul departing from the dying Narcissa', which must have been intended for *Night Thoughts* Night VIII, where Young describes the death of Narcissa.

A prospectus for 'EDWARDS's MAGNIFICENT EDITION OF YOUNG's NIGHT THOUGHTS' (?Spring 1797) announced that 'EARLY in JUNE' the first part would be published with forty engravings (eventually forty-three) 'by BLAKE':

These engravings are in a perfectly new style of decoration, surrounding the text which they are designed to elucidate.

The work is printed in atlas-sized quarto, and the subscription for the whole, making four parts, with one hundred and fifty engravings, is five guineas;—one to be paid at the time of subscribing, and one on the delivery of each part.—The price will be considerably advanced to non-subscribers.

[Copy in the John Johnson Collection in Bodley; see *Blake Records*, 59.]

In fact, only the first part appeared, with four out of nine Nights. (A single engraving for Night V is offered in Francis Edwards's catalogue *William Blake* [1930]; I have not traced the print.) The edition may have been a small one, for the book had become excessively scarce by 1810, according to Crabb Robinson (*Blake Records*, 441).

Proofs of most of the plates are known, some of them before letters and in varying states; Mr. Philip Hofer has pl. 1 (two copies), 2, 6–7, 10, 11 (3), 12, 13 (2), 14–16, 18–20, 25, 31–4, 39, and Blake wrote his *Vala* on proofs of pl. 1, 3, 4 (2), 5 (2), 7 (2), 8–10, 12–21, 22 (2), 23–4, 26–33, 34 (3), 35–6, 37 (2), 38–9, 40 (2), 41–3.

The work contained an 'ADVERTISMENT' dated 22 Dec. 1796 (pp. iii–viii), presumably by Richard Edwards, in which Blake is mentioned (pp. vii–viii); it is followed by a 2-page 'EXPLANATION of the ENGRAVINGS', perhaps by Fuseli.

The paper was only marginally larger than the copperplate, and even in untrimmed copies (e.g. Bodley), parts of the platemarks may not appear. When the bottom margin is defective, the date and part of the design may be missing. In the following list, the information on imprints is therefore often a composite from several copies.

Pl. 1–20, 26, 32 bear the imprint: '[*London,*] *Pubᵈ June* 27[*ᵗʰ*] *1796, by R. Edwards,* [*Nᵒ*] *142 New Bond Street* [or *Strᵗ*]'; pl. 25 is dated 1 Jan. 1797; pl. 22 '*Jan: 4, 1797*'; pl. 23, 27 '*Mar: 22, 1797*'; pl. 31, 33, 36, 39, 42 '*June 1st. 1797*'; and pl. 21, 24, 28–30, 34–5, 37–8, 40–1, 43 have no imprint. On pl. 4–5, 7, 9–10, 12–33, 35–43 Blake used a monogram:

which he apparently used for no other commercial engravings, though he did use it for his drawings and for the separate plate called 'The Man Sweeping the Interpreter's Parlor'.

The pages are enormous, and the engravings *surround* the text, though most of the design is in the bottom and outer margins. For most of the plates, a line of text has been starred to indicate that it is the subject of the illustration. The plates are:

1. The title-page for 'NIGHT the FIRST / ON / LIFE, / DEATH / AND / IMMORTALITY.' (Plate-size: ?32·8 × 39·5 cm.) (The water-colour is also on Night I, title-page.)

2. P. 1: l. 4 is starred: 'Sleep . . . *Swift on his downy pinion flies from woe' (?32·4 × 39·6 cm). (No line is marked in the water-colour, Night I, p. 3, reversed.)

3. P. 4: '*What, though my soul fantastick measures trod / O'er fairy fields' (*c*. 32·0 × 40·2 cm). (No line is marked in the water-colour, Night I, p. 9, reversed.)

4. P. 7: '*. . . Death's . . . restless iron tongue / Calls daily for his millions' (*c*. 33·4 × 41 cm). (No line is marked in the water-colour, Night I, p. 13.)

5. P. 8: '*Death! great proprietor of all!' (*c*. 31·6 × 41 cm). (No line is marked in the water-colour, Night I, p. 15.)

6. P. 10: '*Disease invades the chastest temperance' (?31·8 × 41·1 cm). (No line is marked in the water-colour, Night I, p. 19, reversed.)

7. P. 12: '*Its [*heaven's*] favours here are trials, not rewards' (*c*. 32·3 × 41·5 cm.) (No line is marked in the water-colour, Night I, p. 22, reversed.)

8. P. 13: '*The present moment terminates our sight' (?32·3 × 40·6 cm). (No line is marked in the water-colour, Night I, p. 26, reversed.)

9. P. 15: '*The longest night though longer far, would fail [e'er I forgot Philander]' (?33·5 × 41·8 cm). (No line is marked in the water-colour, Night I, p. 29.)

10. P. 16: '*Oft bursts my song beyond the bounds of life' (?32·6 × 41·0 cm). (No line is marked in the water-colour, Night I, p. 30.)

11. P. 17: The title-page of '*NIGHT the SECOND* / ON / TIME, / DEATH / AND FRIENDSHIP.' (?32·7 × 39·7 cm.) (The water-colour is also on Night II title-page.)

12. P. 19: '*This midnight centinel, with clarion shrill, / . . . shall awake the dead' (33·1 × 41·0 cm). (The same line is marked on the water-colour, Night II, p. 5.) (The design was used again for the title-page for Blair's *Grave* [1808].)

13. P. 23: '*We censure nature for a span too short' (?33·0 × 39·4 cm). (The water-colour on Night II, p. 11 has two apparently irrelevant lines marked: '*Who murders Time, He crushes in the Birth' and '*Like Children babling, nonsense in their sports'.)

14. P. 24: '*Time, in advance, behind him hides his wings (*c*. 33·0 × 41·4 cm). (The same line is marked in the water-colour, Night II, p. 12.)

15. P. 25: No line is marked, because the relevant line ('*Behold him, when past by, what then is seen But his broad Pinions . . . ?', water-colour, Night II, p. 13) is on p. 24 of the 1797 text. (32·9 × 40·9 cm.)

16. P. 26: 'Measuring his motions by revolving spheres' (*c*. 32·9 × 41·5 cm). (The same line is marked in the water-colour, Night II, p. 16.)

17. P. 27: '*O treacherous conscience!' (33·0 × ?41·0 cm). (No line is marked

in the water-colour, Night II, p. 19.) (The design was engraved again for Whitaker's *Seraph* [?1818], no. 512.)

18. P. 31: '*Tis greatly wise to talk with our past hours' (*c.* 32·1 × 40·4 cm). (The same line is marked in the water-colour, Night II, p. 25.)

19. P. 33: '*Like that, the dial speaks; and points to thee [Assyrian, flush'd with wine]' (*c.* 32·7 × 40·7 cm). (No line is marked in the water-colour, Night II, p. 27.)

20. P. 35: '*Teaching, we learn' (*c.* 32·5 × 40·5 cm). (The line marked on the water-colour, Night II, p. 31, is: '*Speech* ventilates our Intellectual fire'.)

21. P. 37: '*Love, and love only, is the loan for love' (*c.* 32·4 × 41·0 cm). (The same line is marked in the water-colour, Night II, p. 35.)

22. P. 40: '*Angels should paint it [The death-bed of the just]' (?32·7 × 40·8 cm). (The line marked in the water-colour, Night II, p. 38, '*Man's highest Triumph! Man's profoundest Fall! The *Deathbed* of the Just!', is on p. 39 of the 1797 text.)

23. P. 41: No line has an asterisk in the 1797 text; the line marked in the water-colour, Night II, p. 43, is '*One radiant Mark; the Deathbed of the Just'—this line does not appear in the 1797 text, which omits the last 58 lines of the water-colour text. (32·5 × 40·9 cm.)

24. P. 43: 'NIGHT / THE / THIRD, / NARCISSA' (?32·7 × 41·0 cm). (The water-colour is also on Night III title-page.)

25. P. 46: '*Where sense runs savage broke from reason's chain' (?32·3 × 40·8 cm). (No line is marked in the water-colour, Night III, p. 6.)

26. P. 49: Perhaps the star should be at 'the sun . . . check'd his beam' (*c.* 33·0 × 41·7 cm). (No line is marked in the water-colour, Night III, p. 12, reversed.)

27. P. 54: '*The Vale of death! that hush'd cimmerian vale' (on p. 53; the same line is marked in the water-colour, Night III, p. 19) (*c.* 32 × 39·7 cm).

28. P. 55: '*Ungrateful, shall we grieve their hovering shades' (33·0 × 39·6 cm). (The line marked on the water-colour, Night III, p. 21, is '*Are Angels sent on Errands full of Love'.)

29. P. 57: '*Trembling each gulp, lest death should snatch the bowl' (?32·5 × 40·6 cm). (The line marked in the water-colour, Night III, p. 24, is 'Still-streaming Thorough fairs of dull Debauch'.)

30. P. 63: '*This KING OF TERRORS is the PRINCE OF PEACE' (?32·6 × 41·3 cm). (The line marked in the water-colour, Night III, p. 33, is '*Death, the great Counsellor, who Man inspires'—in the 1797 text this line appears on p. 62.) On the scroll in the design is mirror-writing in Hebrew which has been translated (*Blake's Sublime Allegory*, ed. S. Curran & J. H. Wittreich, Jr. [1973], 162) as 'Lord You are Death, YHVH The fire was with the fire You . . . lust'.

31. P. 65: Night the Fourth, '*The* / *Christian* / *Triumph*' (?33·0 × 39·7 cm). (The water-colour for this engraving is the frontispiece for the whole series.)

32. P. 70: '*Till death, that mighty hunter, earths them all' (?32·8 × 40·7 cm). (The same line is marked in the water-colour, Night IV, p. 8.) (Blake's

drawing ?after this engraving in the Nelson Gallery–Atkins Museum of Kansas City is reproduced by Jessup in *The New Reasoner* [1957], 65–8.)

33. P. 72: '*sense and reason shew the door . . . and point me to the dust' (?32·8×39·6 cm). (The same line is marked in the water-colour, Night IV, p. 10.)

34. P. 73: '*Draw the dire steel [*from Christ's hand?*]—ah no!' (*c.* 31·5× 39·7 cm). (The same line is marked in the water-colour, Night IV, p. 12, reversed.)

35. P. 75: The 1797 text has no line marked, but the water-colour, Night IV, p. 16, reversed, has two lines marked: '*The Sun beheld it—No, the shocking Scene Drove back his Chariot' and '**Sun*! did'st thou fly thy Maker's Pain' (*c.* 32·8×39·7 cm).

36. P. 80: '*shall I question loud / The thunder, if in that the ALMIGHTY dwells?' (Design size: 32×37·7 cm.) (The same line is marked in the water-colour, Night IV, p. 24.)

37. P. 86: '*His hand the good man fastens on the skies' (design size: 31·5×38·1 cm). (The same line is marked in the water-colour, Night IV, p. 32.)

38. P. 87: 'O how omnipotence / *Is lost in love! thou great PHILANTHRO-PIST!' (Plate-size: ?32·5×39·5 cm.) (The same line is marked in the water-colour, Night IV, p. 34, reversed.)

39. P. 88: '*But for the blessing wrestle not with heaven!' (*c.* 31·0×41·6 cm). (The same line is marked in the water-colour, Night IV, p. 36.)

40. P. 90: '*That touch, with charm celestial heals the soul' (?32·4×39·8 cm). (The same line is marked in the water-colour, Night IV, p. 39, reversed.) (The design is repeated from *No Natural Religion* [?1788] pl. b1 and, reversed, from *Songs* [1789] pl. 18.)

41. P. 92: '*When faith is virtue, reason makes it so' (?32·4×39·6 cm). (In the water-colour, Night IV, p. 42, the line marked is '*Reason* the Root, fair *Faith* is but the Flow'r'.)

42. P. 93: '*If angels tremble, 'tis at such a sight [A Christian who the blessed cross wipes off]' (?32·8×39·5 cm). (In the water-colour, Night IV, p. 44, two lines are marked: '**Christian* is the highest Stile of Man. *And is there, who the blessed Cross wipes off . . . .')

43. P. 95: '*The goddess bursts in thunder and in flame' (?33·0×39·7 cm). (The same line is marked in the water-colour, Night IV, p. 47.)

N.B. In the 1797 text, on p. 20 is '*I know thou say'st it, says thy Life the same?' (as in the water-colour for Night II, p. 6) and on p. 61 is '*Age and disease; disease, though long my guest' (as in the water-colour for Night III, p. 32), as if they were to be engraved, but no engravings of these scenes appear in the 1797 pages.

(Twenty-two engravings are reproduced in Butterworth, no. 516, and fourteen in Socupault, no. 2726.)

The centres of the *Night Thoughts* plates left blank (except for p. 65) for the typeset text could have been cut out to form 42 of the 52 or more copper-plates needed for *Jerusalem* (1804–?20).

Night Thoughts centres 15·4 to 17·5 cm wide by 20·7 to 25·0 cm high
Jerusalem plates   13·8 to 17·1 cm wide by 20·1 to 22·7 cm high
No contemporary reviews are known, and the work clearly met with a discouraging reception. Crabb Robinson reported that Hazlitt 'saw no merit in them as designs'; Cunningham said that the 'nudity' of the figures 'alarmed fastidious people: the serious and the pious'; and Bulwer-Lytton described the designs as 'balanced between the conception of genius and the ravings of positive insanity', perhaps because Young's 'mere metaphors [*were*] illustrated and made corporeal'. Contemporary owners included Caroline Bowles [Southey], T. F. Dibdin, ?Wm Ensom, Wm Godwin, Crabb Robinson, Louis Schiavonetti, Robert Scott, Sir John Soane, Wm Thane, and Joseph Thomas (*Blake Records*, 229, 487, 402, 398 n. 2, 243, 239, 41 n. 3, 229, 227 n. 1, 193, 413 n. 1, 227 n. 1, 166).

E. J. Ellis (*The Real Blake* [1907], 83) has suggested that the designs were left as little more than outlines so that they could be coloured by hand; certainly a number were so coloured. Mr. Martin Butlin tells me that the colouring seems to be in two distinct styles, the first of about 1797, and the second of about 1805, similar in effect to the coloured copies of Hayley's *Triumphs of Temper* (1803, owned by Mr. George Goyder) and *Ballads* (1805, owned by the late Professor S. Foster Damon). The ascriptions of colouring dates below derive from Mr. Butlin.

CENSUS OF COLOURED COPIES[1]

COPY A: BINDING: Bound for Milnes by J. Leighton in half reddish-Brown morocco, sago Brown cloth sides, with Milnes's crest, 'a garb or';* 42·1 × 33 cm;* lacks the 'Explanation of the Engravings' leaf.*
HISTORY: (1) Sold anonymously for Thomas Butts at Sotheby's, 26 March 1852, lot 59 (not described as coloured), for £2. 1s. to R.M.M.; (2) Sold by the Earl of Crewe (the son of Richard Monckton Milnes) at Sotheby's, 30 March 1903, lot 13, for £170 to Edwards; (3) Acquired by Algernon Methuen, lent to the National Gallery exhibition (1913), no. 73, and sold posthumously at Sotheby's, 19 Feb. 1936, lot 505, for £580 to Robinson; (4) Acquired by A. E. Newton, lent to the Philadelphia exhibition (1939), no. 90, and sold posthumously at Parke-Bernet, 16 April 1941, lot 139, for $1,750 to Sessler; (5) Sold by Sessler's to a client, from whom it passed by inheritance to (6) An *Anonymous* collection.

COPY B: BINDING: Coloured about 1805; bound in contemporary full straight-grain Red morocco, with broad gilt borders, Red and Blue marbled paper fly-leaves, covers damaged with knife-cuts and ink-stains, leaves intact but slightly soiled;* 41·7 × 33 cm.*
HISTORY: (1) Possibly once the property of Richard Edwards;* (2) Bought in 1910 from a London bookseller by Lt.-Col. W. E. Moss,* lent to the Manchester exhibition (1914), lot 150, and sold at Sotheby's, 2 March

---

[1] The foundation of this census is a typescript by W. E. Moss (*c.* 1942) in Bodley, published in the *Blake Newsletter* (1968), no. 22, and supplemented in no. 27. An asterisk (*) indicates that I have not verified information from Col. Moss.

1937, lot 261, for £800 to Rosenbach; (3) Acquired by Mr. LESSING J. ROSENWALD.

COPY C: BINDING: Coloured about 1797; bound in half leather and canvas, with a pencil(?) signature 'W. Blake' at the bottom left corner of p. 7 and 'as pattern' at the foot of p. 95;* lacks the 'Explanation' leaf.

HISTORY: (1) A nineteenth(?)-century inscription on the fly-leaf indicates that it belonged to 'Ottomar[?] Findlaw [or Fiedler] / 360'; (2) Apparently acquired 'from a Dresden collector'* by St. Goar, a bookseller of Frankfurt, who sold it in April 1925 to (3) E. N. Adler,* who in turn sold it in 1940 to Lincolns, Ltd., London;* (4) Acquired by Dr. Fazekas of the Czech diplomatic staff, who sold it through a London agent (according to a note with the volume) to (5) J. H. Lutcher Stark, who gave it to (6) The UNIVERSITY OF TEXAS.

COPY D: BINDING: Coloured about 1797; bound in contemporary Brown calf over Blue and reddish-Yellow marbled boards, rebacked with reddish-Brown leather.[1]

HISTORY: (1) Perhaps this is the copy in 'calf extra, marble leaves', sold posthumously with the Bibliotheca Splendissima of Mrs. Bliss by Saunders & Hodgson, 26 April 1826, lot 371, for £4. 4s.; (2) Sold by Francis Barlow Robinson at Sotheby's, 19 Feb. 1884, lot 423, for £22 to Bennett; (3) Owned by W. P. Bennett; (4) Acquired by John Ruskin and sold at Sotheby's, 24 July 1930, lot 109*; (5) Acquired by John Gribble, who inserted his bookplate and sold it at Parke-Bernet, 16 April 1945, lot 28 (erroneously described as imperfect), for $400; (6) Sold by Paul Francis Webster at Parke-Bernet, 28 April 1947, lot 5; (7) Acquired by Mrs. Gerard B. Lambert, who gave it on 25 Jan. 1960[1] to (8) PRINCETON.

COPY E: BINDING: (1) Bound in half morocco uncut, in 1887 and 1894; (2) Rebound by 1905 (if the History conjecture is correct) by the Guild of Women Binders, Hampstead, in elaborate crushed levant morocco, still uncut; the 'Explanation' leaf is cut down and inlaid, and the engraving was never printed on p. 24.

HISTORY: (1) Perhaps this is the copy (in half morocco, uncut, with the 'Explanation' leaf) sold anonymously at Christie's, 1 June 1887, lot 256, and (2) Offered in John Pearson's Catalogue 79 (?1894), lot 154, for £68; (3) Sold (uncut) for R. A. Potts at Sotheby's, 20 Feb. 1913, lot 64;[2] (4) Perhaps this is the copy acquired by Lionel Philips (bound by the Guild of Women Binders, as above), who inserted his bookplate dated 1905; (5) Acquired through J. Sawyer in Feb. 1973 for £2,500 by The UNIVERSITY OF ALBERTA.

COPY F: BINDING: Bound in half Brown morocco, sides and fly-leaves of the same 'frog-spawn' marbled paper.*

HISTORY: (1) Acquired by Sir John Soane (1753–1837), who added his bookplate and left it to (2) The SIR JOHN SOANE MUSEUM, London.

---

[1] According to Mr. Paul R. Wagner, Curator of Special Collections, Princeton University Library.

[2] Moss is apparently wrong in saying that it was (?also) sold by Potts at Sotheby's on 18 June 1912.

COPY G: BINDING: Bound in half Red levant morocco by Riviere, t.e.g.

HISTORY: (1) Acquired by Thomas Gaisford (1779–1855), who added his bookplate and with whose library it was sold at Sotheby's, 23 April 1890, lot 192;* (2) Acquired by Bernard Buchanan Macgeorge, described in his private catalogues (1892, 1906), and sold by him at Sotheby's, 1 July 1924, lot 118, for £125 to Quaritch; (3) Offered by Quaritch in Catalogue 388 (Oct. 1924), lot 226, and Catalogue 401 (May 1926), lot 218 for £175; (4) *UNTRACED*.

COPY H: BINDING: Coloured about 1805, perhaps Blake's model, bound in 1901 by Annie S. Mcdonald of the Guild of Women Binders, Edinburgh, in undressed morocco* with embossed designs on the upper cover and Blake's head on the lower;* title inlaid.*

HISTORY: (1) Perhaps acquired by W. Rae Macdonald* (it has a bookplate of 'H. M.'[1]) or J. M. Gray;* (2) Offered by Tregaskis at an unknown date for £25; (3) Offered by Ellis & Elvey in catalogue 120 for £45[1]; (4) Owned by William Sargent;[1] (5) Sold at Sotheby's, 4 June 1908, lot 734, for £24 to Stirling;* (6) Evidently it passed from Stirling in 1919 to (7) The MUSEUM OF FINE ARTS, BOSTON.

COPY I: BINDING: Coloured about 1797; bound in Brown morocco, panelled, by F. Bedford;* an inserted leaf of vellum[2] contains pp. 3–4 and a watercolour drawing (on p. 3)[3] and a proof of Blake's 'Satan' after Fuseli was with it.*

HISTORY: (1) Evidently once owned by 'Pearson '86 / rsi-:', according to the note on the fly-leaf;* (2) Sold for T. G. Arthur at Sotheby's, 17 July 1914, lot 848;* (3) Bought from G. D. Smith in Oct. 1914 by the HUNTINGTON LIBRARY.

COPY J: BINDING: Coloured about 1797.

HISTORY: (1) Acquired by Samuel Boddington (*fl.* 1830), who added his bookplate; (2) Acquired by Herschel V. Jones, who added his bookplate and sold it at Anderson Galleries, 2 Dec. 1918, lot 186, to Gabriel Wells for (3) W. A. White (according to Mr. Butlin); (4) Acquired (probably with the rest of White's Blake collection on 1 May 1929 through Rosenbach) by Mr. LESSING J. ROSENWALD.

COPY K: BINDING: Bound in full contemporary Green straight-grain morocco, gilt and blind-tooled, rubbed, the binding very slightly broken; 41·6×32·1 cm.*

HISTORY: (1) Acquired by Oliver Henry Perkins, who added his bookplate; (2) Acquired by G. C. Smith, Jr., described in his anonymous catalogue (1927), lot 21, and sold posthumously at Parke-Bernet, 2 Nov. 1938, lot 45, for $675 to Rosenbach for (3) *Mrs. Landon K. Thorne.*

---

[1] According to Mr. Butlin.

[2] A copy printed on vellum without the plates was sold by A. G. Dew-Smith at Sotheby's, 27–30 June 1906, lot 587, for 12*s.* to Rewin.

[3] See R. R. Wark, 'A Minor Blake Conundrum', *HLQ* XXI (1957), 83–7.

COPY L: BINDING Coloured about 1805; (1) In a modern calf binding, rather broken at the joints according to Belle Da Costa Greene (Morgan's Librarian);* (2) Bound about 1919 in New York by Miss M. D. Lahey.*

HISTORY: (1) Acquired by the PIERPONT MORGAN LIBRARY.

COPY M: BINDING: 'BOUND BY RIVIERE & SON' in dark Blue crushed levant morocco, g.e., 41·5 × 32·2 cm.

HISTORY: (1) Acquired 'many years' before Aug. 1870 by John Bingley Garland, according to a note of that date on a fly-leaf by Garland; (2) Offered in Ellis & Elvey Catalogue 100 (1903), from which Quaritch bought it for £45 and sold it (according to a transcript on a sheet with the volume of 1 April 1903) to (3) W. A. White, who added his name and the date (20 April 1903) on a fly-leaf, apparently lent it anonymously to the Grolier Club exhibition (1905), no. 41 and gave it on 3 March 1913 (according to the same inscription) to his daughter (4) Frances W. Emerson, who lent it to the Fogg exhibition (1938)[1] and to the Philadelphia exhibition (1939), lot 91, and sold it posthumously at Sotheby's, 19 May 1958, lot 6, for £850 to Fleming, who sold it to (5) The BIBLIOTHECA BODMERIANA, Cologny-Geneva, Switzerland.

COPY N: BINDING: Brown paper back, marbled boards, uncut (c. 42·7 × 33·6 cm);* lacks the leaves with pp. 45–6, 71–72;* a copy of the Prospectus is laid in.*

HISTORY: (1) Acquired by A. E. Newton, who lent it to the Philadelphia exhibition (1939), lot 90, and sold it posthumously at Parke-Bernet, 16 April 1941, lot 138, for $400 to Sessler; (2) Acquired by Wilmarth Lewis, who gave it in 1967 to (3) Mr. *Paul Mellon.*

COPY O: BINDING: '*Bound by* C. HERING, 10. S.t Martin's street', heavily gilt, with the royal arms, g.e., the inside cover marked 'Bibliotheca Spenceriana', with duplicate uncoloured title-pages in Nights I–IV.

HISTORY: (1) The copy acquired by George John Spencer (1758–1834), third Earl Spencer, whose portrait Blake etched in 1813, went with his library in 1892 to (2) The JOHN RYLANDS LIBRARY, Manchester.

COPY P: BINDING: Coloured about 1805; bound in old half Brown calf, brownish Black marbled paper sides and endpapers, 41·2 cm high.[2]

HISTORY: (1) Perhaps this is the copy (bound in half russia, t.e.g.) sold for Charles Dew of Salisbury at Sotheby's, 25 June 1892, lot 1002;* (2) Offered by Quaritch in a letter of 24 May 1900[2] for £42 to (3) Miss Amy Lowell, who bought it and bequeathed it to (4) HARVARD.

COPY Q: BINDING: Coloured about 1797, perhaps Blake's original; bound in contemporary half calf, the upper cover detached (according to the 1958 catalogue).

HISTORY: (1) Inscribed 'This Copy was coloured for me by Mr Blake /

---

[1] According to the 1958 catalogue.
[2] According to Miss Carolyn Jakeman, Houghton Library.

W. E.' perhaps by William Ensom (1796–1832), who made a prize portrait of Blake in 1815, or by William Esdaile (1758–1837) as Sir Geoffrey Keynes and Mr. Martin Butlin think; (2) An erased inscription, '   Milne[?] / The Rectory / Farnham[?]', presumably represents another owner; (3) Perhaps this is the copy (in original boards, uncut, back defective) sold at Hodgson's, 2 July 1914, lot 528, for £46 to Dobell; (4) Acquired (for £5[1]) by a Lady in Geneva, who sold it anonymously at Sotheby's, 3 March 1958, lot 47, for £680 to Traylen, evidently for Stonehill, who sold it to (5) Mr. *Paul Mellon.*

COPY R: BINDING: Coloured about 1797; inscribed in a contemporary hand 'This copy col[rd] by W. Blake';[2] bound in half calf and marbled boards and marbled endpapers, uncut[2] (42·5 cm high[2]), the spine repaired;[2] two fly-leaves at each end are watermarked J WHATMAN / 1808.[2]

HISTORY: (1) Acquired by John S. Harford, Jr. (1785–1866), who added his book-plate; (2) It was bought between 1913 and 1915 for the Widener Collection of HARVARD.

COPY S: BINDING: Bound for the New York Public Library in Maroon buckram.[3]

HISTORY: (1) Acquired by Robert Lenox Kennedy,[3] after whose death in 1887 it was bought with the Lenox Library by (2) The NEW YORK PUBLIC LIBRARY, where it is now in the Prints Division.

DRAWINGS

The drawings were long ignored, despite Fuseli's opinion that they '*alone* ... would be sufficient to immortalize his name ... as that of an Artist of the very highest order' (1826 advertisement). They were put 'in 2 vols. Atlas Folio, each leaf surmounted with a border and sumptuously bound in red morocco, gilt edges' and offered by Richard Edwards's brother Thomas of Halifax in 1821 for £300, but in the 10 May 1826 and 24 May 1828 sales the price was reduced to fifty pounds or guineas, at which it still found no purchaser (*Blake Records*, 269, 330, 368; before 1810 Edwards had refused a handsome offer for them—p. 442). In 1874 an engraving of one of the designs was made by G. I. F. Tupper, and 'A few copies only are struck off for private distribution' 'as a SPECIMEN' for James Bain, evidently to advertise the drawings for sale (copy in the Rosenbach Foundation). They were eventually sold for £750 through Dodd to W. A. White and formed the first part of his great Blake collection, until they went in 1929 to the British Museum Print Room.

The 537 water-colour designs in the British Museum Print Room are available in colour microfilm from The EP Group of Companies [formerly Micro Methods], Bradford Road, East Ardsley, Wakefield, Yorkshire.

[1] The information about price derives from Mr. Anthony Hobson of Sotheby's (according to G. Keynes, *Blake Studies* [1971], 56 n.).
[2] According to Miss Mary C. Johnson, Assistant, Widener Memorial Rooms.
[3] According to Miss Elizabeth E. Roth, Prints Division, NYP.

A515. *Night Thoughts*, or The Complaint and The Consolation Illustrated by William Blake, Text by Edward Young, Edited with an Introduction and Commentary, by Robert Essick [&] Jenijoy La Belle. N.Y., 1975.

Reproduction of the text and plates of the 1797 edition 'at 65% of original size', plus 'Introduction to the Dover Edition' (pp. iii–iv), a useful 'Commentary on Blake's Illustrations' (pp. v–xviii), and a brief 'Bibliography: Studies of Blake's *Night Thoughts* Designs' (pp. xix–xxi).

Section B

COLLECTIONS AND SELECTIONS

516. *Butterworth, Adeline M. *William Blake, Mystic*: A Study, together with Young's Night Thoughts: Nights I & II, with Illustrations by William Blake and frontispiece Death's Door, from Blair's 'The Grave'. Liverpool & London, 1911.

'William Blake, Mystic: A Study' is on ff. 1–14 (rectos only). The bulk of the book is a reduced reproduction of the 23 engravings and complete poetical text of Nights I–II (pp. 1–42, including pages without design), plus a print of the 'Explanation of the Engravings' for Nights I–II of Young's poem and a plate of the Blair design. (Nights III–IV of Young are not reproduced.)

517. A. *William Blake's Engravings*. Ed. Geoffrey Keynes. London, 1950. B. §N.Y. 1972.

'Introduction' (pp. 7–22); there are 142 plates, including Virgil, *Job*, and *For Children*.

PART IV
CATALOGUES AND BIBLIOGRAPHIES

Catalogues and bibliographies of Blake's literary and graphic works are organized in this Part *by date* rather than alphabetically by author. Since the majority of these works were issued anonymously, it seems most convenient to arrange them chronologically.

The chief omission here is in sale and auction catalogues. I have tried to include everything before 1831; thereafter I have chosen only the most important sales, defined as those containing five or more works in Illuminated Printing. Since the focus of this work is Blake Books, the coverage of sales of Blake's designs is less systematic. I have included all catalogues of exhibitions devoted entirely or largely to Blake, but I have ignored the 'Bibliographies' which it used to be the fashion to tack on to literary books on Blake. Catalogues of private libraries, such as those of B. B. Macgeorge or C. B. Tinker, are included when they include any original Blakes, but those of institutional libraries are included only when they include major Blake collections.

519. 1780. *The Exhibition of the Royal Academy, M.DCC. LXXX.* The Twelfth. London: Printed by T. Cadell, Printer to the Royal Academy. (BM and Huntington)

Blake exhibited the 'Death of Earl Goodwin'.

N.B. For many of the Royal Academy exhibitions there were apparently several editions of the catalogues issued, in which the numbering of the entries was not always uniform (see A. Graves, *The Royal Academy of Arts* [1905], I). However, no attempt has been made to trace the various editions of the Royal Academy catalogues in which Blake's works are recorded.

520. 1784. *The Exhibition of the Royal Academy, M.DCC.LXXXIV.* The Sixteenth. London: Printed by T. Cadell, Printer to the Royal Academy. (BM and Huntington)

Blake exhibited 'A breach in a city, the morning after a battle' and 'War unchained by an angel, Fire, Pestilence, and Famine following'.

521. 1785. *The Exhibition of the Royal Academy. M.DCC.LXXXV.* The Seventeenth. London: Printed by T. Cadell, Printer to the Royal Academy. (BM and Huntington)

Blake exhibited 'Joseph making himself known to his brethren', 'Joseph's brethren bowing before him', 'Joseph ordering Simeon to be bound' and 'The Bard, from Gray'.

522. A. 1788, 1801, 1803, 1814. *The Theatrical Remembrancer*, Containing A Complete List of All the Dramatic Performances in the English Language; their several Editions, Dates, and Sizes, and the Theatres where they were originally performed: together with an Account of those which have been acted and are unpublished, and a Catalogue of such Latin Plays as have been written by English Authors, from the earliest Production of the English Drama to the End of the Year MDCCLXXXVII. To which are added Notitia Dramatica, Being a Chronological Account of Events relative to the English Stage. London: Printed for T. and J. Egerton, at the Military Library, Whitehall, 1788. (BM)

B. [J.] *Barker's Continuation of Egerton's Theatrical Remembrancer* . . . From MDCCLXXXVII to MDCCCI . . . The Whole arranged, &c. by Walley Chamberlain Oulton. London: Printed and Published by Barker & Son . . . [1801]. (BM)

C. [J.] *Barker's Complete List of Plays* . . . to 1803. . . . Printed and Published by Barker & Son [1803]. (BM)

D. *The Drama Recorded*; or, Barker's List of Plays, Alphabetically Arranged, Exhibiting at One View, The Title, Size, Date, and Author, with their various Alterations, from the earliest Period, to 1814; to which are added, Notitia Dramatica, or, A Chronological Account of Events Relative to the English Stage. London: Printed and Published by J. Barker, (Dramatic Repository,) Great Russell Street, Covent-Garden. 1814. (BM)

A. In the chronological list (p. 258) is 'W. BLAKE. "King Edward the Third." Drama. 8vo. 1783. Printed in a Pamphlet, called, "Poetical Sketches."'

B–C. In the index of titles in both 1801 and 1803 is 'King Edward III. D[*rama*]. 12 mo. 1783 *Murdock*' (p. 225), clearly a conflation from the 1788 *Theatrical Remembrancer*, where the entry after Blake's 'King Edward the Third' is John Murdock, *Double Disguise*, 12 mo, 1783.

D. On p. 48 is '[EDWARD III]—Dr[*ama*]. Poet. Sk.——— 1783 *Blake*'. (Poetical Sketch is the description of the work, not the title of Blake's book, *Poetical Sketches*.)

523. 1791. Jer. Dav. Reuss. *Alphabetical Register of All the Authors* actually living in Great-Britain, Ireland and in the United Provinces of North-America, with A Catalogue of their Publications. From the Year 1770 to the Year 1790. Berlin and Stettin, printed for Frederic Nicolai 1791. P. 40. (Chicago)

Under the Blakes is '——— [W. . . .] King Edward the third. Drama. 1783', apparently referring to the dramatic fragment so entitled in Blake's *Poetical Sketches*. Blake does not appear in the 1804 edition of Reuss (Princeton).

524. 1794. *Poetic Description of Choice and Valuable Prints*, Published by Mr. Macklin, at the Poets' Gallery, Fleet Street. London: Printed by T. Bensley. 1794. (Princeton)

The plates include 'The Fall of Rosamond', 'Robinhood and Clorinda',

'Morning Amusements', 'Evening Amusements', engraved by Blake (pp. 62, 68, 70).

525. 1799. *The Exhibition of the Royal Academy, M,DCC.XCIX.* The Thirty-First. London: Printed by J. Cooper, Printer to the Royal Academy. [Price Sixpence.] [*sic*] (BM & Princeton)

Blake exhibited 'The last supper'.

526. A. ?1800. §*A Catalogue of Prints Published by J. R. Smith*, (No. 31) King-Street, Covent-Garden. London, [?1800].

B. John Raphael Smith. *A Complete Catalogue of Plates Published by Him.* Giving Titles, Prices, Exact Sizes, and Names of the Artists and Engravers. A Facsimile of the Only Copy Known. [Ed. E. E. Legatt.] London, 1914.

Items 195–6 are Blake's engravings of 'Industrious Cottager' and 'The Idle Laundress' after 'G. Morland' at 4*s.* each. The date must be between 12 May 1788, when the plates were first published by Smith, and 1 Jan. 1803, when they were republished by H. Macklin.

527. 1800. *The Exhibition of the Royal Academy, M.DCCC.* The Thirty-Second. London: Printed by B. McMillan, Bow-street, Covent-Garden, Printer to the Royal Academy. [Price Sixpence] [*sic*] (Princeton)

Blake exhibited 'The loaves and fishes'.

528. 1803. *An Alphabetical Catalogue of Plates* engraved by the most esteemed artists After the Finest Pictures and Drawings of the Italian, Flemish, German, French, English, and other schools, which compose the stock of John and Josiah Boydell, Engravers and Printsellers, No. 90, Cheapside, and at the Shakspeare Gallery, Pall Mall; preceded by An Account of Various Works, Sets of Prints, Galleries, &c. forming part of the same stock. London: Printed by W. Bulmer and Co. Cleveland-Row, St. James's. 1803. (NYP)

On page 21 is listed Hogarth plate '104 The Beggars Opera [size in inches] 22 18 Blake [£]0 10 6', though Blake is not mentioned under Opie.

529. 1807 5 Dec. *Bibliotheca Reediana*: A Catalogue of the Curious & Extensive Library of the late Isaac Reed, Esq. of Staple Inn. Deceased . . . Which Will be Sold by Auction, By Messrs King and Lochee, At their Great Room, No. 38, King-Street, Covent-Garden, on Monday, Nov. 2, 1807, and 38 following Days, (Sundays excepted.) (BM, Bodley, Harvard)

On the 30th day (5 Dec., p. 303), under Poetry, lot '6577 Blake's Poetical Sketches [F]— 1783' was sold (according to the marked copy in Bodley) for 6*s.* 6*d.* to Heber.

530. 1808. *The Exhibition of the Royal Academy, M.DCCCVIII.* The Fortieth. London: Printed by B. McMillan, Bow-Street, Covent Garden, Printer to the Royal Academy. [Price Sixpence.] [*sic*] (BM & Princeton)

Blake exhibited 'Jacob's Dream' and 'Christ in the Sepulchre'.

1809. For Blake's own catalogue of his exhibition, see no. 32.

531. 1812. *A Catalogue of the Fifth Annual Exhibition by the Associated Painters in Water Colours.* At the Society's Rooms, No. 16, Old Bond Street. Admittance,

One Shilling; catalogue, sixpence. London: Printed by J. Moyes, Greville Street, Hatton Garden. 1812. (Tate)

Blake is listed as a member of the society, and as the contributor of entries numbered 254 (Chaucer's Pilgrims), 279 (The Spiritual Form of Pitt), 280 (The Spiritual Form of Nelson) and 324 (specimens of *Jerusalem*).

532. 1813 26 April. Books. *A Catalogue of the Valuable and Elegant Library, the property of Mrs. E. Iremonger*, Of Upper Grosvenor-Street; including some of the Best Authors in History, and Belles Lettres; in the French, Italian, German, and English Languages; many of them enriched by valuable MS. notes and observations; and the whole in the finest possible preservation. Which will be Sold by Auction, by King & Lochée, At their Great Room, No. 38, King-street, Covent-Garden, On Monday, April 26, 1813, And Two following Days, at Twelve o'Clock. May be viewed on Thursday preceding the Sale, and Catalogues, then had at the Room. J. Barker, Printer, Great Russell-Street, Covent-Garden. (BM)

Lot '165 Blake (Will.)—Songs of Innocence and Experience [*?D*], 8*vo. elegantly bound*—1789' was sold on the first day. This is the copy from which Crabb Robinson transcribed Blake's poems for his article on Blake (*Blake Records* [1969], 232).

533. A. 1819. *PART I[–XI].—VOLUME I.*[1]/ BIBLIOTHECA BRITAN-NICA; / OR, / A GENERAL INDEX / TO THE / Literature of Great Britain and Ireland, / ANCIENT AND MODERN; / INCLUDING / SUCH FOREIGN WORKS / AS HAVE BEEN TRANSLATED INTO ENGLISH, OR PRINTED / In the British Dominions. / AS ALSO, A COPIOUS SELECTION FROM THE WRITINGS OF THE MOST DISTINGUISHED / AUTHORS OF ALL AGES AND NATIONS. / IN TWO PARTS [later DIVISIONS]. / In the First, the Authors are arranged Alphabetically, and of each, / as far as possible, a short Biographical Notice is given; to / which is subjoined a Chronological List of his Works, their / various Editions, Sizes, Prices, &c.; and in many instances the / Character of the Work. / In the Second, the Subjects are arranged Alphabetically, and / under the Works, and principal parts of Works, treating / of that Subject, are arranged in Chronological Order. This / Part also includes the Anonymous Works which have appeared / in this Country. / = / BY ROBERT WATT, M.D. / LATE PRESIDENT OF THE FACULTY OF PHYSICIANS AND SURGEONS OF GLASGOW; / PHYSICIAN TO THE GLASGOW ROYAL INFIRMARY; LECTURER ON THE THEORY AND PRACTICE OF MEDICINE; / MEMBER OF THE MEDICO-CHIRURGICAL SOCIETY OF LONDON; LATE PRESIDENT OF THE / PHILOSOPHICAL, LITERARY, AND MEDICAL SOCIETIES OF GLASGOW; AUTHOR / OF CASES OF DIABETES; TREATISE ON CHINCOUGH, &c. / = / 'The chief glory of every people arises from its Authors.' —JOHNSON. / 'Catalogorum accuratior notitia ita necessaria

---

[1] Parts II–III are headed '*VOLUME I.—PART II [–III]*'; Parts IV–XI omit the reference to VOLUME entirely.

est Polyhistori, ut Mapparum / Geographicarum cognitio Peregrinatur.'—
MORSON. / GLASGOW: / *Printed for the Author, at the University Press:* /
AND PUBLISHED BY ARCHIBALD CONSTABLE & CO. EDIN-
BURGH; / LONGMAN, HURST, / REES, ORME, & BROWN, LON-
DON: / AND ANDREW & JOHN M. DUNCAN, GLASGOW. / — / 1819.
[Part IV is 1820; Parts V–VI are] EDINBURGH: / *Printed by Abernathy &*
Walker; / PUBLISHED BY ARCHIBALD CONSTABLE & CO. EDIN-
BURGH; AND LONGMAN, HURST, / REES, ORME, & BROWN,
LONDON. / — / 1821. [Part VII is 1822, Parts VIII–X are 1823, and Part
XI 1824.] (Toronto)

B. BIBLIOTHECA BRITANNICA; / OR / A GENERAL INDEX / TO /
BRITISH AND FOREIGN LITERATURE. / BY ROBERT WATT,
M.D. / IN TWO PARTS:—AUTHORS [2 vols.] AND SUBJECTS [2
vols.]. / VOLUME I [II].—AUTHORS [VOLUME III (IV).—SUB-
JECTS]. / — / EDINBURGH: / PRINTED FOR ARCHIBALD CON-
STABLE AND COMPANY EDINBURGH; / AND LONGMAN,
HURST, REES, ORME, BROWN, & GREEN; AND / HURST,
ROBINSON, & CO., LONDON. / — / 1824. (BM, Bodley, Chicago,
GEB, Princeton, Toronto)

C. N.Y. [1963].

The compiler, Robert Watt (1774–12 March 1819), saw part of the work
through the press but died before any of it was published. The eleven Parts
were issued to subscribers with the Part-titles printed on the Pink boards,
at a guinea each, and some of them were announced in the 'Quarterly List
of New Publications' in the *Edinburgh Review*, XXXII (July 1819), 250
(Part I); XXXII (Oct. 1819), 509 (Part II); XXXIII (Jan. 1820), 247
(Part III); XXXVI (Feb. 1822), 568 (Part VI); XXXIX (Jan. 1824), 505
(Part X); XL (March 1824), 272 (Part XI). With Part XI were printed the
dedication, errata, &c., and four half-titles and titles (as in B above).
Naturally most copies were rebound in volume-form, and the original
boards were thrown away. Surviving copies rarely contain any indication as
to whether they were issued in Parts, as in A, or collected in volume-form,
as in B.

The Blake entry, a bibliography in Vol. I, Part I, is simply borrowed from
Watkins, no. 2929.

534. § [1821. *Catalogue of Thomas Edwards, Bookseller.* Halifax, 1821.]

According to T. W. Hanson (no. 1782), Blake's *Night Thoughts* drawings
were offered for £300 in 'Thomas Edwards's [Halifax] catalogue 1821', but
unhappily Mr. Hanson could not remember where he saw the copy he quotes,
and I have not located any copy in a determined search. The title above
is, therefore, hypothetical.

535. A. 1821. Friedrich Adolf Ebert. *Allgemeines Bibliographisches Lexikon.*
[2 vols.] Leipzig: F. A. Brockhaus. [Vol. I] 1821, [II] 1830. Vol. I, pp. 199,
605; Vol. II, p. 1097. (BM, LC)

B. *A General Bibliographical Dictionary*. [Tr. Arthur Browne.] In Four Volumes. Oxford, 1837. Vol. I, p. 196.

C. § Hildesheim, 1965 [in German].

The brief entry under Blake is taken directly from Crabb Robinson's essay (no. 2538), which is cited. The engraving of Flaxman's Hesiod drawings is said to be 'by J. Blake', and the account of the 1797 Young is taken largely from Robinson.

B is simply a translation of A, and adds no new material.

536. 1824. *A Catalogue of Books*, in various languages, And in Every Department of Literature, now selling, at the Prices Affixed to Each Article, by Rivingtons and Cochran, 148, Strand, (near Somerset-House.) London: Printed by R. Gilbert, St. John's-Square. Catalogues to be had at the place of sale, and of Messrs. C. and J. Rivington, St. Paul's Church-Yard, and Waterloo-Place, Pall-Mall. Of Mr. Parker, Oxford; Messrs. Deighton and Sons, Cambridge; Messrs. W. and D. Laing; Mr. Black; and Messrs. W. and C. B. Tait, Edinburgh; Mr. Ogle, Glasgow; Mrs. Watson; and Mr. Tims, Dublin; MM. de Bure, Paris; and MM. Luchtmans, Leyden. 1824. (Princeton)

This offers (11795) Blake's *Song's* (U) 'bound by Charles Lewis', which was later sold by Thomas Edwards on 24 May 1828. Rivington also specifies Blake as the engraver of *The Grave* (292; 11795), Lavater's *Aphorisms* (13139) and Hayley's *Ballads* (12817).

537. 1826 26 April. *Bibliotheca Splendissima*: A Catalogue of a Select Portion of The Library of Mrs. Bliss, Deceased, Removed from her Residence at Kensington. Saunders & Hodgson, April 26–29, 1826. (BM)

Lots 10–11, 371 are *For Children* (A) (8s.), *Songs* (P) (£1), and a coloured *Night Thoughts* (£4. 4s.).

538. 1826 10 May. *A Catalogue of the very Valuable, Extensive and Genuine Collection of Books, (Selected from the Stock in Trade) of Mr. Thomas Edwards, Bookseller of Halifax*, (who is retiring from business) comprising The Best Works in Divinity, Poetry, and the Belles Lettres; the best editions of the most esteemed works in History, Biography, Topography, Antiquities, Voyages and Travels, Enriched with very choice and early Impressions of the Plates; many costly and highly beautiful Works (English and Foreign) in Natural History and Botany, Accurately and beautifully coloured from Nature: Encyclopaedias; Superb Copies of the Galleries, and other Works Illustrative of Art, recently published in this Country, many of them early Subscription Copies, and selected with great attention to the Embellishments; also, several splendid Works Richly Illustrated with Plates; some very fine Books of Prints And a Few Illuminated Missals, (Both printed and Manuscript) of great interest and Beauty, which will be Sold By Auction, By Messrs. Thomas Winstanley & Co. At the Exchange Rooms, Manchester, On Monday the 1st of May next, and following days (Saturday and Sunday excepted.) The whole may be viewed on Friday the 28th and Saturday the 29th of April, when Catalogues may be had at the place of Sale, price two shillings and sixpence, and to prevent intrusion and damage to this valuable property, no person whatever will be admitted to the view without a Catalogue. Halifax: Printed by N. Whitley, for Thomas Edwards, Bookseller. Pp. 65–6. (Harvard, Bodley)

Lot no. 1076, Blake's *Night Thoughts* drawings, is described in considerable eulogistic detail.

539. 1828 24 May. *A Catalogue of the Splendid and Valuable Collection of Books, Manuscripts, and Missals, the property of Thomas Edwards, Esq.* (Late of Halifax, Yorkshire.) Comprising . . . Young's Night Thoughts, with Original Drawings by Blake . . . Which Will Be Sold By Auction, by Messrs. Stewart, Wheatley, & Adlard, at their Great Room, 191, Piccadilly, On Thursday, May 15th, 1828, and eight following days, (Sunday excepted). (BM, Bodley)

On the last day (24 May), lot 940, Boswell's copy of *Songs of Innocence [and of Experience]* (U) was sold to Clarke for £2. 13*s*., but lot 1130, Blake's 'sublime' *Night Thoughts* drawings, which were 'alone sufficient to immortalize' him, were withdrawn at £52. 10*s*.

540. 1828 1 July. *A Catalogue of a Valuable Assemblage of Engravings*, by Ancient and Modern Masters, including . . . Various Carvings, and a fine Collection of Vocal Italian Music, bound and unbound; and various other interesting articles of virtu, the property of the late John Flaxman, Esq. R.A. Dec. Which Will be Sold by Auction, By Mr. Christie, at his Great Room, No. 8, King Street, St. James's Square, on Tuesday, July the 1st, 1828, at one o'clock. (BMPR)

There are two Blake items, lots
'61 A singularly grand drawing of the Last Judgment, by Blake';
'85 A COPY OF GRAY'S POEMS, illustrated by W. Blake, with his
    Portrait by Mr Flaxman'.

541. 1830 13 Jan. *Catalogue of a Select and Elegant Library, the Property of a Collector* [Robert Balmanno] . . . . To which is added, The Topographical Portion of the Library of a Gentleman. Which Will Be Sold By Auction, By Mr. Sotheby and Son, Wellington Street, Strand, On Wednesday, January the 13th, and Three following Days, at Twelve o'Clock. To be viewed on Monday the 11th, and Catalogues (price 1s. 6d.) had at the place of sale. (BM)

On the first day lot '41 Blake's Phantasies, Songs of Innocence and of Experience [BB], on 55 PLATES, *brown calf, elegant, very rare v.y.*' was sold to Glynn for £1.

542. 1830 21 May. *A Catalogue of the First Part of the Valuable Collection of Original Drawings, by distinguished modern artists, the property of the late Sir Thomas Lawrence* . . . which (by order of the executor) Will be Sold by Auction, By Mr. Christie, at his Great Room, King Street, St. James's Square, On Thursday and Friday, the 20th and 21st of May, 1830. (Yale)

Lots 234 and 235 are Blake's 'Wise and Foolish Virgins' and 'The Dream of Queen Catherine'.

543. 1832 12 Dec. *Catalogue of the Select and Choice Collection of Engravings, Water-Colour Drawings, Picture-Books, and Books of Prints and Other Effects, of the late William Ensom, Esq* . . . Which will be Sold by Auction, by Mr. Sotheby and Son . . . 12th of December, 1832, and following day. (BM, BMPR)

Lot 86 is a 'Portrait of W. Blake, R.A. [*sic*] *in pen and ink* . . . . For this drawing Mr. Ensom obtained the Silver Medal from the Society of Arts, which, together with the two vouchers of the society, will be given with the drawing.' (This is the evidence on which is based the *DNB* statement that Ensom's 1815 drawing was a portrait of Blake. The portrait has not been traced further.)

544. 1833 18 and 20 July. *Catalogue of the Splendid, Choice, and Curious Library of P. A. Hanrott, Esq.* Part the First . . . which will be Sold by Auction, by Mr. Evans, at his House, No. 93, Pall-Mall, On Tuesday, July 16, and Eleven following Days, (Sunday excepted). (BM)

This enormous library was sold eventually in more than 11,000 lots for more than £22,000. The Blake items on the third day consisted of lot 630, *America, Europe,* and *Jerusalem,* which were sold for £4, and on the fifth day *Songs,* and the *Gates of Paradise,* lots 893 and 894, went for £2. 1s. od. and £1. 16s. od. respectively.

545. 1833. *Autographs of Illustrious Personages, English and Foreign*; comprising an Extraordinary Assemblage of Letters, of greater extent and equal interest, yet wholly distinct from, the former catalogue; Among these are . . . Letters of Celebrated Authors, Poets, and Painters . . . constituting the most diversified and largest collection ever submitted for selection. Now selling, at the very low prices affixed, by Thomas Thorpe, N°. 38, Bedford Street, Covent Garden, London . . . . 1833. (Thomas Thorp [no relation], 170 High Street, Guildford, Surrey)

Among the 1,623 lots in no. '140 William Blake, Artist, Autograph Dedication of his Visions to the Queen, in Verse [*see no. 207*], 4s.' This MS has not been traced further.

546. 1834 17–19 June. *A Catalogue of the Beautiful Original Sketches, and some finished Pictures, with a large collection of Drawings and Studies, in Colours and Indian Ink, of that Charming Artist, Thomas Stothard, Esq. R.A., Deceased* . . . Which will be Sold by Auction, by Messrs. Christie, Manson, and Christie . . . On Tuesday, June 17, 1834, and two following days.

At some time after 1880 an unknown hand wrote in Robert Blake's sketchbook (now in the Huntington): 'This Sketch-book belonged to *Robert Blake,* brother of *William Blake,* the Artist & Poet, and was purchased some years since among the Collection of the late Thomas Stothard R.A. at one period a personal friend of the brother's.' The only sale of Stothard's effects of which I know is the one above in June 1834. Though more than 1,500 items are listed, this sketchbook is not specified among them. It is possible, however, that it was included among the numerous lots labelled merely 'Various'.

547. 1834 8 Dec. Bibliotheca Heberiana. *Catalogue of the Library of the late Richard Heber, Esq.* Part the Fourth, Removed from his House at Pimlico. Which will be Sold by Auction, by Mr. Evans, at his House, No. 93, Pall Mall. On Monday, December 8, and Fourteen following days, Sundays excepted. (Princeton)

Among the 54,534 lots sold over 208 days, lot '99 Blake's (W.) Poetical Sketches, *red morocco*, 1783' sold for 2s.

548. A. 1834 ... 1890. Lowndes, William Thomas. *The Bibliographer's Manual of English Literature.* [4 vols.] London, 1834.

B. Revised and enlarged [by H. G. Bohn]. [11 vols.] London, 1857–61, [1864–65].

C. § [5 vols.] London, 1869.

D. In Four Volumes. London, 1871.

E. § [6 vols.] London, 1883.

F. [6 vols.] London, 1890.

In A (1834) Blake is merely mentioned under Blair and Young as having designed plates for their works, but in B (1857) he is given a separate section to himself as well as being mentioned under Blair, Malkin, and Young. The succeeding editions (1869, 1871, 1883, and 1890) follow the second edition.

549. 1835 6 May. *A Catalogue of the collection of Books on Art, Antique Bronzes, Terra Cottas and Coins, the property of George Cumberland, Esq.*; Comprising the Works of Bartoli, Vasari, Winkelmann, and other Italian Works on Art; a few Books of Prints and Engravings; Some Silver and Brass coins of Greek Cities; small bronzes of antique and early Italian work, A few Fragments of Terra Cotta and Marbles; and a cabinet of Tassie's casts from gems: Which will be Sold by Auction, by Messrs. Christie & Manson, at their great room, King Street, St. James's Square, On Wednesday, May the 6th, 1835. (Christie)

Lot '60 Blake's America [*copy F*], Visions [*B*], Europe [*D*], and Song of Los [*D*], bound together, the plates coloured. Blair's Grave; and Blake's designs by Schiavonetti' was bought by Butts for £3. 18s., and lot '61 Blake's Book of Job. Book of Thel [*A*], &c. coloured; and Gates of Paradise' went to W. Bohn for £3. 13s. 6d. This provides interesting information about what Cumberland owned. According to Keynes & Wolf (1953), Cumberland owned *Thel* when it was bound with *Urizen* [F] and the *Marriage* [A], but the above lot 60 would indicate that these works were bound together after Cumberland sold them, and consequently that Cumberland did not own either *Urizen* or the *Marriage. Experience* (F), inscribed 'G. Cumberland' must have remained in the family (the first sales record is in 1929), since it does not appear in this sale. The four volumes bound together were not, as Keynes and Wolf (1953), say (under *America*), 'Originally bought from Blake by Thomas Butts', as this sale lot entry 60 demonstrates.

550. 1836 13 June. *Catalogue of Curious Autograph Letters and Early Historical Documents Relating to England . . .* R. H. Evans, 13–18 June 1836. (BMPR)

Among the papers of the Earl of Buchan is Blake's letter of 18 Jan. 1808 (lot 312).

551. 1837 21 July. *Catalogue of the Valuable Collection of Books of Prints, and Works Connected with Literature and the Fine Arts, the property of the late William Young Ottley, Esq. . . . Sotheby. . . . July 21[–22], 1837.*

According to the Priced copy in the BMPR, lot '306 Jerusalem: The Emanation of the Giant Albion, *one hundred engravings from wood, printed by W. Blake* 1804' was bought by Bohn for £3. 18s.

A551. 1838 24 April. *A Catalogue of the Valuable and very Interesting Collection of Pictures; Modern Drawings, and Books of Prints; Made During a Series of Years by James Vine, Esq, Deceased . . .* Christie & Manson . . . April 23, 1838, and Three Following Days. (Christie's)

Lots 296–9 on the Second Day include Blake's *Job*, *Milton* (D) and *Thel* (O) together, *Jerusalem* (J), and *Songs* (V), all half bound; all of them went to Bohn, who offered them in his 1841 catalogue. (The 1838 catalogue was generously pointed out to me by my friend Professor Janet Warner.)

552. A. 1839 ff. Jacques-Charles Brunet. *Manuel du Libraire et de L'Amateur de Livres.* Quatrième Édition. [5 vols.] Bruxelles, 1839.

B. Paris, 1842–4. Vol. I (1842).

C. [6 vols.] Paris (1860–5). Vol. I (1860).

A–B cites only a copy of the *Songs* in Rivington's catalogue (1824), but C adds a description of five other works apparently added from Lowndes (see 1834).

553. 1840. *Catalogue of the Printed Books and Manuscripts bequeathed by Francis Douce, Esq. to the Bodleian Library.* Oxford, 1840. P. 32.

Douce's Blake bequest consisted of *Thel*, the *Descriptive Catalogue*, and Hayley's *Ballads* (1802).

554. 1841. *A Catalogue of Books.* Henry G. Bohn York Street Covent Garden. London, 1841. (GEB, Princeton)

Lots 172–8 consist of *Job* (2), *Thel* (£1. 5s.), Blair's *Grave*, *Jerusalem* (£5. 5s.), *Songs*, *Milton*, and *Thel*, the last two bound together and the last three unpriced. None of these works appears in Bohn's 1831 *Catalogue* (Princeton), and significant information is added to the description of *Milton* and *Thel* in his 1847 *Catalogue*. (The Blakes were purchased by Bohn at the 1838 Vine sale.)

555. 1846 15 June. *Catalogue of the Library of the late William Upcott . . .* Which will be sold by auction, (Under the Direction of the Court of Chancery), By Messrs. Evans, at their rooms, No. 106, New Bond Street, On Monday, June 15th, and Four following Days. (BM)

The Blake lots included no. 65, *Experience*, at £1. 14s., and 277, *America* and *Europe* at £7. 2s. 6d.

556. 1847. *Henry G. Bohn's Catalogue of Books.* [4 parts.] London, 1847, 1850,

1866, 1867. Vol. I [containing Natural History. Books of Prints. Science. Language. Bibliography. Oriental & Northern Literature. Old English Historians. Early Voyages, &c. Games, Etc. 1847]. (Princeton)

Blake's *Job*, Dante, *America*, *Thel*, and *Milton* are offered, the last two bound together and 'finished in colours, in the style of Drawings, expressly for his principal patron, Mr. Vine of the Isle of Wight', though they were not so described in Bohn's 1841 catalogue. Keynes & Wolf quote rather different information about *Milton* and Vine from an 1843 Bohn catalogue; this is an error, for there appears to be no 1843 Bohn catalogue.

557. A. 1848 5 Feb. Anon. 'Charles Lamb's Library in New York.' *Literary World*, III (5 Feb. 1848), 10–11.

B. *Catalogue of Charles Lamb's Library* for Sale by Bartlett & Welford, Booksellers and Importers, 7 Astor House, New York [Feb. 1848].

C. Anon. 'Books of Charles Lamb's Library in America.' *The Historical Magazine and Notes and Queries*, IX (1865), 45–9.

D. 'Catalogue of Charles Lamb's Library. . . .' Pp. 297–307 of Mary and Charles Lamb, *Poems, Letters, and Remains*: Now First Collected, with Reminiscences and Notes. Ed. W. Carew Hazlitt. London, 1874.

E. [?W. Carew Hazlitt.] 'Charles Lamb's Library in New York.' *Publisher's Weekly*, LI (15 May 1897), 817–20.

F. *A Descriptive Catalogue of the Library of Charles Lamb*. N.Y. (The Dibdin Club), 1897. Pp. 10.

The 54th lot, including *Descriptive Catalogue* (S), was sold for $4.50.

B is an offprint of A which was used as a catalogue of the sale (a copy is in Harvard). Hazlitt (1897) says the catalogue 'was made by Charles Welford . . . with an introduction by Evert D. Duyckinck', but the Dibdin Club reprint says the introducer was George L. Duyckinck.

558. A. 1848 21 Oct. Cooley, Keese & Hill (191 Broadway, N.Y.) Catalogue of A Private Library [of James T. Annan].

B. *A Descriptive Catalogue of the Library of Charles Lamb*. N.Y. (The Dibdin Club), 1897. P. 16.

Lot 376, Lamb's copy of *Descriptive Catalogue* (S) bound with eleven other works, was sold for $4.25 to Campbell.

559. 1852 26 March. *Catalogue of a Valuable Collection of Engravings & Drawings, from the portfolio of an Amateur*, comprising . . . works of that able but eccentric artist, William Blake, with many of his best drawings . . . Together with the Collection formed by the late Thomas Moule, Esq. . . . S. Leigh Sotheby & John Wilkinson . . . 26 of March, 1852, and following day. (BM)

Lots 50–61 are Blake books and lots 147–67 are Blake water-colours. The anonymous Blake owner was Thomas Butts.

560. 1853 29 June. *Catalogue of a Collection of Pictures, Drawings and Works of Art*, The Property of Thomas Butts, Esq. Removing from his Residence,

Grafton Street; including . . . A Collection of Pictures and Drawings, By the late William Blake, Distinguished for originality of Design, and facility of Pencil, Amongst which are subjects from Sacred History, Illustrations from Milton, &c., and forming a curious and, perhaps, matchless Assemblage of the Works of this highly gifted Artist. Which will be sold by Auction, by Messrs. Foster and Son At the Gallery, 54, Pall Mall, On Wednesday, the 29th of June, 1853, at one o'clock precisely. (BMPR)

'Drawings & Pictures by the late Wm. Blake, Whose genius and talents are familiar to the Public by his Illustrations to the Poem of "The Grave," "Young's Night Thoughts," &c.' (pp. 6–8, lots 70–144) included 110 paintings and drawings, and two books.

561. 1854 8 March. Pall Mall. Ancient and Modern Pictures, Part by direction of the Executors. *Catalogue of A Collection of Italian, Dutch, Flemish & English Pictures*, including . . . A Few Drawings by the late Mr. W. Blake . . . which will be sold by auction, by Messrs. Foster and Son, At the Gallery, 54, Pall Mall, On Wednesday, the 8th of March, 1854. (V&A)

The 19 Blake drawings (lots 13–18) sold for £4. 3s. 0d. According to F. Lugt, *Repertoire des catalogues de ventes publiques* (La Haye, 1953), lot 21763, the seller was Butts.

562. 1854 7–30 June. *A Catalogue of the very extensive, highly important Stock of Engravings, Water-Colour Drawings, and Books of Prints, of Mr. [Joseph] Hogarth, of the Haymarket* . . . Which will be sold by Auction, by Southgate and Barrett . . . June 7ᵗʰ[–30th], 1854. (BM)

Seventy-eight Blake pictures were sold in lots 237, 643, 1095, 1521, 1922, 2363, 2784, 3270, 3705, 4180, 4624, 5068, 5082, 5509, 7112, and 7553.

563. 1857. *Catalogue of the Art Treasures of the United Kingdom* Collected at Manchester in 1857. London, 1857. Lots 130, 130a.

'Oberon and Titania on a Lily' and 'Vision of Queen Catherine' lent by William Russell and C. W. Dilke.

A563. 1857. *A Handbook to the Water Colours, Drawings, and Engravings, in the [Manchester] Art Treasures Exhibition*, Being a Reprint of Critical Notices Originally Published in 'The Manchester Guardian.' London, 1857. Pp. 12–13.

A comparison of Blake and Richard Dadd: 'Both were mad . . . [*but*] Blake's fancies were lovely, rather than terrible' (p. 12); it also quotes 'To the Muses' and gives details of Blake's life from Cunningham. I have not traced the original notice in the *Manchester Guardian*.

564. 1859 . . . 1922. Jean George Théodore Graesse. *Trésor de livres rares et précieux* ou Nouveau Dictionnaire bibliographique. [7 vols.] Dresde, Genève, Londres, Paris, 1859–1900. Vol. I [1859], p. 436.

B. § Berlin, 1922.

Graesse lists 17 works by Blake, with dealers and prices.

565. 1862 29 April. *Catalogue of A Valuable Collection of Engravings, Drawings* *and Pictures, chiefly from the cabinet of An Amateur*; comprising . . . Original Drawings and Sketches by W. Blake . . . S. Leigh Sotheby & John Wilkinson . . . 29th day of April, 1862.

The 'Original Drawings and Sketches [*&c*], By W. Blake' are lots 158–202. The 'Amateur' may be Frederick Tatham.

566. 1862. *International Exhibition 1862.* Official Catalogue of the Fine Art Department. London, 1862

The Blake entries are no. 221, 965–8; Blake and Stothard are compared on p. 46.

A566. 1862. *Illuminated Guide to the International Exhibition.* London [1862]. The Blake entries are no. 965–8.

567. 1863 1 May. *Catalogue of the Splendid Collection of Water-Colour Drawings, Formed by that distinguished Patron of Art, Elhanan Bicknell, Esq., deceased* . . . Christie, Manson & Woods . . . April 29, 1863, And Two following Days.

Lots 377–89 are 'Drawings in Indian Ink, by W. Blake', largely for *Tiriel*.

568. [1864?] § [Sale catalogue of Francis Harvey, 30 Cockspur Street, London.]

On pp. 3–6 (known to me only from a fragment in the Anderdon Collection in the BMPR) are 22 Blake lots, including the 'Pickering [Ballads] Manuscript' and at least 24 drawings.

569. 1866 17–18 May. Sotheby mixed sale.

Lots 17–18, 21–5 in the Robert Arthington Library are important Blake books.

570. 1875. § J. W. Bouton, *Original Drawings in Watercolor and India Ink by the Celebrated William Blake.* N.Y., 1875.

The water-colours in this sale catalogue identified in the American Art Association catalogue of 2 May 1923, lot 15, and perhaps all the water-colours, were by J. C. Hotten.

571. 1876. Burlington Fine Arts Club *Exhibition of the Works of William Blake.* London, 1876.

William B. Scott, 'Introductory Remarks' (pp. 3–11); 333 entries.

572. 1878 20 May. *Catalogue of A Valuable Collection of Autograph Letters, forming The Hayley Correspondence*, comprising Thirty-Four Characteristic Letters in the Autograph of William Blake [and thousands of other Hayley MSS] . . . which will be sold by auction, by Messrs. Sotheby, Wilkinson & Hodge . . . On Monday, the 20th of May, 1878, and Two following Days . . . .

The Blake lots (1–34) include 16 letters which have still not been traced, and some for which the excerpts printed here are the only or the best text available.

573. 1880 1–5 April. Christie sale of George Smith.

Lots 164–8 are important Blake items.

574. 1880 16 July. *Catalogue of the Collection of Drawings and Engravings of George Smith* . . . Christie, Manson & Woods . . . July 16, 1880.
Lots 98–123 are Blakes.

575. A. 1880. § [Boston] Museum of Fine Arts *Exhibition of Drawings, Water Colors, and Engravings by William Blake.* Arranged in the First Print Room. Boston, 1880.
B. Second Edition. Boston, 1880.
Anon., 'William Blake' (pp. 3–6) says that the exhibition was 'occasioned by the temporary deposit here of a number of pictures by Blake belonging to Mrs. Alexander Gilchrist'; 160 entries.

576. 1881. Anon. 'William Blake.' *Bulletin of the Boston Public Library*, IV (1881), 335–6 (vMKN).
A short list of the holdings of the Boston Public Library, including reviews.

577. 1882 20 March. *Catalogue of Engravings and Etchings, the property of the late Rt. Hon. the Earl of Beaconsfield* . . . comprising among other rarities A Series of the Works of William Blake . . . Sotheby, Wilkinson & Hodge . . . the 20th day of March, 1882.
The important Blake lots are 56–63.

578. 1882 4 July. The Hamilton Palace Libraries. *Catalogue of The first Portion of The Beckford Library*, removed from Hamilton Palace. Which will be sold by auction by Messrs. Sotheby, Wilkinson & Hodge, . . . On Friday, the 30th day of June, 1882, and Eleven following Days.
Lots 950–7 in the fourth day's sale are important Blake items.

579. 1883 29 Nov. The Hamilton Palace Libraries. *Catalogue of The Fourth and Concluding Portion of The Beckford Library*, removed from Hamilton Palace. Which will be sold by auction by Messrs. Sotheby, Wilkinson & Hodge . . . On Tuesday, the 27th of November, 1883, and Three following Days.
In the supplement, no. 764 consists of *Thel, Urizen*, and *The Marriage* bound together.

580. 1885 27 Jan. Alfred Aspland sale at Sotheby's.
The Blake drawings are lots 62–104.

581. 1885 21 April. W. B. Scott sale at Sotheby's, 20–4 April 1885.
The Blake lots are 160–86*, mostly drawings.

582. 1886. *The Rowfant Library.* A Catalogue of the Printed Books, Manuscripts Autograph Letters, Drawings and Pictures, collected by Frederick Locker-Lampson. [Compiled by A. W. Pollard and B. J. Lister.] London, 1886.
The important Blake collection is on pp. 138–41. (The *Appendix* [1900] has no Blake.)

583. 1887. *Catalogue of the Library and a Brief List of the Engravings and Etchings Belonging to Theodore Irwin*, Oswego, N.Y. N.Y., 1887.

Lot 180 is the extra-illustrated Kitto Bible containing *America* pl. 3 and *For the Sexes* pl. 12.

584. 1887. *A General Catalogue of Books* offered to the public at the affixed prices by Bernard Quaritch. London, 1887.

Lots 10249–52, 13842–6 include two important books, *c.* 103 engravings (with the 'Order' of the *Songs*), and 67 drawings.

585. 1890 23 April. *Catalogue of a portion of the Important Library of Thomas Gaisford, Esq.* . . . [including an] Important Series of Works Illustrated by W. Blake . . . which will be sold by auction, by Messrs. Sotheby, Wilkinson & Hodge . . . On Wednesday, the 23rd of April, 1890, and Seven following Days . . . .

Blake's works were sold as lots 184–95.

586. 1891 7 Feb.–15 March. [Boston] Museum of Fine Arts Print Department *Exhibition of Books, Water Colors, Engravings, Etc. by William Blake.* February 7 to March 15, 1891. Boston, 1891.

'Introductory Note' (pp. iii–iv); 234 entries.

587. 1892 14 July: *Catalogue of Engravings, Modern Etchings & Drawings, the property of the late William Bell Scott, Esq.* . . . also several important oil paintings and drawings in water-colour by William Blake . . . Which will be sold by Auction by Messrs. Sotheby, Wilkinson & Hodge, July 14, 1892.

Lots 134–8, 177–81, 235–8 are Blakes.

588. 1892 8 Dec. Anon. *Examples of the English Pre-Raphaelite School of Painters,* Including Rossetti, Burne-Jones, Madox-Brown and Others, Together with a Collection of the Works of William Blake. To be exhibited in Philadelphia at the [Pennsylvania] Academy of the Fine Arts, December Eighth, MDCCCXCII.

Entries 115–205 are by Blake, mostly from the collection of H. H. Gilchrist.

589. A. 1892, 1906. *A Catalogue of The Library of Bernard Buchanan Macgeorge.* Privately Printed. Glasgow, 1892.

B. *Catalogue of the Library of Bernard B. Macgeorge.* Printed for Private Use. Glasgow, 1906.

The works by Blake include 13 (1892) or 14 (1906) important ones.

590. 1893 24 April. *'Catalogue of a Collection of Books, Engravings and Drawings illustrative of the Work of the Poet and Painter, William Blake. Lent by Mr. Edward J. Shaw.'* Pp. 21–32 of the *Catalogue of the Second Loan Exhibition of Pictures, Sculpture, etc. in the Art Gallery and Museum,* (at the Free Library), Goodall Street, Walsall, To be Opened on Monday, 24th April, 1893.

'E. J. S[haw]', 'William Blake' (pp. 22–4); the 77 entries are chiefly photographs, critical books, &c.

591. 1893. [Royal Academy] *Exhibition of Works by The Old Masters,* and by

Deceased Masters of the British School; including a Collection of Water
Colour Drawings, &c., by William Blake, Edward Calvert, Samuel Palmer,
and Louisa, Marchioness of Waterford. Winter Exhibition Twenty-Fourth
Year. Pp. 41–5.
 Blake's 29 entries are all Dante drawings.

592. 1894. [Royal Academy] *Exhibition of Works by The Old Masters*, and by
Deceased Masters of the British School; including Special Collections of
the Works of Thomas Stothard, R.A., of William Blake, and of John Pettie,
R.A. Winter Exhibition Twenty-Fifth Year. Pp. 62 4.
 The Blake entries (47–67) are all sketches for *Job*.

593. 1898. Binyon, Laurence. 'Blake, William.' Pp. 124–31 of Vol. I, of
*Catalogue of Drawings by British Artists and Artists of Foreign Origin Working in
Great Britain*, Preserved in the Department of Prints and Drawings in the
British Museum. [4 vols.] London, 1898 [Vol. II, 1900, III, 1902, IV, 1907].
 There are 94 Blake entries.

594. 1899 July. *Descriptive Catalogue of the Gluck Collection of Manuscripts and
Autographs in the Buffalo Public Library*. Buffalo, July 1899.
 The two Blakes include 'Original water-colour' for *Europe* pl. 4.

595. 1899. *Catalogo dei Libri posseduti da Charles Fairfax Murray*. [2 vols.]
 Lots 141–4 are important Blakes.

596. 1903 30 March. *Catalogue of a Choice Selection of the Original Productions
of William Blake*, the Property of the Rt. Hon. The Earl of Crewe, which
will be sold by Sotheby, Wilkinson & Hodge, March 30th, 1903.
 Lots 1–18 are Blakes.

597. 1903 24 June *Catalogue of Drawings by William Blake*, the property of
Captain Butts, Grandson of Thomas Butts, Muster Master General [*sic*] . . .
[and of a descendant of Alexander Gilchrist]: which will be sold by auction
by Messrs. Sotheby, Wilkinson & Hodge, June 24th, 1903.
 Lots 1–42 are Blakes.

598. 1904 Jan. *Exhibition of Works by William Blake*. January, 1904. Carfax
& Co., Ltd. London [1904].
 Archibald G. B. Russell, 'The Art of William Blake' (pp. i–iii); 'Note' on
techniques (p. 9); 41 entries.

599. 1905 26 Jan.–25 Feb. *Catalogue of Books, Engravings, Water-Colors &
Sketches by William Blake* Exhibited at the Grolier Club from January 26 to
February 25 1905.
 Anon., 'Introductory Note' (pp. vii–xvii); the 148 works lent anonymously
are mostly from the collections of W. A. White, M. J. Perry, and Hoe.

600. 1906 14 June–31 July. *Carfax* [& Co., Ltd.] *Exhibition of Works by
William Blake*. 14 June to 31 July 1906.
 'Appendix: Extracts from Blake's Descriptive Catalogue referring to some
of the Pictures now re-exhibited' (pp. 25–40); 106 entries.

601. 1908 2–4 June. *Catalogue of Choice and Rare Books and Illuminated and Other Manuscripts,* including selections from the Library of the Rt. Hon. The Earl of Fringall, . . . Original Drawings by Wm. Blake . . . which will be sold by Sotheby, Wilkinson & Hodge, June 2–4, 1908.

'Original Drawings by William Blake' form lots 513–33.

602. 1911 25 April. *Catalogue of The Library of Robert Hoe of New York.* Illuminated Manuscripts, Incunabula, Historical Bindings, Early English Literature, Rare Americana, French Illustrated Books, Eighteenth Century English Authors, Autographs, Manuscripts, Etc. Part I—A to K to be sold by auction beginning on Monday, April 24, 1911 by The Anderson Auction Company.

The important Blakes are no. 389–97.

603. A. 1912. *The Engravings of William Blake.* By Archibald G. B. Russell. London, 1912.

B. *Boston & N.Y., 1912.

C. *N.Y., 1968.

Russell's pioneer work, now largely superseded by Keynes's *Separate Plates* (no. 533) and this volume, is yet valuable for its independent conclusions. There are 32 illustrations, a 'Catalogue of the Engravings' (51–201) and a reprint of Fuseli's comments on *The Grave* (211–12).

604. A. 1913 Oct.–Dec. Archibald G. B. Russell. *Catalogue of Loan Exhibition of Works by William Blake* [at] The National Gallery, British Art, October to December, 1913. London, 1913.

B. Second Edition. 1913.

'Blake (William), 1757–1827' (pp. 3–6); 156 Blake entries, plus 30 by Romney, Fuseli, and others.

605. 1914 Feb.–March. The Manchester Whitworth Institute *Catalogue of a Loan Collection of Works by William Blake.* February to March, 1914.

R. Bateman, 'Preface' (p. 3); [A. G. B. Russell] 'Blake (William), 1757–1827' (pp. 4–7); the catalogue descriptions are repeated from the National Gallery exhibition, but 61 of the 176 Blake entries are newly loaned; no. 177–208 are 'Contemporaries and Pupils'.

606. 1914 April. City of Nottingham Art Museum, Nottingham Castle. *Catalogue of a Loan Exhibition of Works by William Blake* (1757–1827). April, 1914.

G. H. Wallis, 'Preface' (p. 2); [A. G. B. Russell], 'Blake (William), 1757–1827' (pp. 3–7); 138 Blake entries, plus 40 'Contemporaries and Pupils'. The exhibition and catalogue are borrowed from the Manchester Whitworth Institute.

607. 1914 22 May–4 July. National Gallery of Scotland. *Catalogue of Loan Exhibition of Works by William Blake and David Scott* May 22nd to July 4th 1914.

James L. Caw, 'Preface' (p. 2); A. G. B. R., 'William Blake, 1757–1827' (pp. 3–6), and the 139 Blake works are from the 1913 National Gallery Blake exhibition.

608. 1918 15 March. *Catalogue of the John Linnell Collection of Highly Important Works by William Blake* Obtained direct from the Artist . . . which (by Order of the Trustees) Will be Sold by Messrs. Christie, Manson & Woods . . . March 15, 1918.

'The John Linnell Collection of Works by William Blake' is lots 148–215, over 360 items.

609. 1918 2 Dec. *Catalogue of The Library of Herschel V. Jones* [A–H]. The Anderson Galleries.

The important Blake entries are no. 181–9.

610. 1918. *Old Books*: Catalogue No. 282 of E. Parsons & Sons (45 Brompton Road, London), 1918.

Items 443–73 include 27 drawings 'From the Collection of John Linnell'.

611. 1919 17–22 Nov. §*Soetsu (Muneyoshi) Yanagi. *William Blake no Fukusei Hanga Tenraikai Mokuroku* [*An Annotated Catalogue of an Exhibition of Reproductions from the Works of William Blake* at the Russian Gallery, Tokyo, Nov. 7–11, 1919, and The Imperial University Y.M.C.A. Hall, Kyoto, Nov. 18–22, 1919.] Shirakabasha [The White Birch Society]. Tokyo, 1919.

Twenty-six pages of Japanese annotations about 74 works reproduced.

612. 1919 5 Dec.–1920 10 Jan. *William Blake: An Exhibition* [in] The Grolier Club. N.Y., 1919.

'Introduction' (pp. v–vi); 61 entries.

613. A–B. 1920 15 March, 26 April. *The Library of the Late H. Buxton Forman* [Parts I–II]. The Anderson Galleries, March 15, April 26, 1920.

The Blakes are lots 35–72 in Part I, 47–65 in Part II, some of them important.

614. 1920. *Archibald G. B. Russell. 'The Graham Robertson Collection.' *Burlington Magazine*, XXXVII (1920), 27–39.

A catalogue of 98 Blake pictures.

615. 1921 26 April. *Catalogue of Rare Books By William Blake* . . . the property of Mrs. Alexander Mackay Deceased . . . Christie Manson & Woods, April 26, 1921.

There are ten important Blake entries.

616. 1921. *Catalogue of an Exhibition of Original Water-Colour Drawings by William Blake to Illustrate Dante.* With an Introductory Essay by Martin Birnbaum. N.Y., 1921.

Birnbaum's essay on 'Illustrators of Dante with Special Reference to Blake and Flaxman' (pp. 3–13) has little to say about Blake. The catalogue contains 21 entries, for twenty Dante drawings and a set of the Flaxman Dante drawings.

617. A. *1921. Geoffrey Keynes. *A Bibliography of William Blake.* N.Y., 1921.

*B. N.Y., 1921 [i.e. 1969].

There are 66 reproductions (including all of *All Religions are One*) and 973 entries. The Blake references are reprinted from no. 719, 941, 970, 988, 989, 1058, 1101, 1198, 1372, 1765A, 2017.

B is a photographic reprint of A.

Keynes's massive and monumental bibliography vastly increased our knowledge and understanding of Blake. The undertaking and the difficulties were enormous and the accomplishment splendid. Only gradually, as new information and techniques have become available, has the work been superseded in half a dozen separate books, mostly by Keynes. The 1921 Bibliography is still of very great importance for independent judgements. It was largely translated, reprinted, and somewhat extended, by Bunsho Jugaku in his *William Blake Shoshi* (1929).

618. 1921. Anon. 'Kuan-yu Po-lai-k'o ti Yen-chiu Shu-mu [A Bibliography of Studies of Blake].' *Hsiao-shuo Yueh-pao,* XVIII, no. 8 (Aug. 1927) (vADH).

In Chinese.

619. A. 1921, 1929. *Catalogue of the Johnsonian Collection of R. B. Adam.* With Introduction by Dr. Charles Grosvenor Osgood of Princeton University. Privately Printed, March, 1921. Buffalo, N.Y., 1921.

B. *The R. B. Adam Library Relating to Dr. Samuel Johnson and his Era.* [3 vols.] London & N.Y., 1929. Vol. III, pp. 29–30.

Blake's letter of 7 Oct. 1803 is largely quoted in each catalogue, without provenance.

620. 1923 July. *Drawings in Pencil & in Pen & Wash* by J. M. W. Turner, R.A. John Flaxman, R.A. Samuel Palmer William Blake and Others. The Cotswold Gallery. London [July], 1923.

There are two Blakes in a total of 27.

621. 1923 12–14 Nov. *The Library of John Quinn.* Part One [A–C]. To be sold by his Order. The Anderson Galleries.

Items 711–69 (pp. 64–70) are minor works connected with 'William Blake', though one is a copy of the 1813 *Grave* said to have been given by Blake to William Thane.

622. 1923. *A Catalogue of Early and Rare Editions of English Poetry Collected and Presented to Wellesley College by George Herbert Palmer.* Boston, 1923.

Includes *Poetical Sketches* and *Descriptive Catalogue.*

623. 1924 1 July. *Catalogue of the Well-Known and Valuable Library of the late Bernard Buchanan MacGeorge, Esq. . . . Sotheby, Wilkinson & Hodge . . .* 1st of July, 1924, and Three following Days . . . 7th of July, and Two following Days . . . .

The important Blake collection included lots 108–34.

624. 1924. *Works by William Blake Lent to the Fogg Art Museum.* [Cambridge, 1924.]

A typescript in the BMPR lists 128 unnumbered entries.

625. 1925 29–31 July. Sotheby sale.

'Drawings, Engraved Works, Etc. by William Blake. The Property of E. J. Shaw, Esq., J.P. of Walsall' were lots 141–68.

626. 1926 20 Oct.–31 Dec. **Catalogue of an Exhibition of Drawings, Etchings & Woodcuts by Samuel Palmer and other Disciples of William Blake* October 20–December 31, 1926. With an Introduction and Notes by A. H. Palmer. Victoria and Albert Museum Department of Engraving, Illustration and Design. London, 1926.

A. H. Palmer, 'Samuel Palmer, Painter and Etcher' (pp. 1–20), contains a reference to Blake in a letter from Richmond of 1828 (p. 9).

627. A. 1926. *The Engraved Designs of William Blake.* By Laurence Binyon. London & N.Y., 1926.

B. § N.Y., 1967.

'Catalogue of Blake's Engraved Designs' (pp. 35–140); 82 plates.

628. 1927. Anon. 'A Blake Bibliography.' *Methodist Review*, CX (1927), 806–7 (vMKN).

Sixteen standard items.

629. 1927. § *Blake 100-nen Kinen Tenraikai Kaiga Mokuroku* [*Exhibition Catalogue of the Paintings Celebrating Blake's Centenary*]. Tokyo, 1927.

630. 1927. ***[Soetsu Yanagi, Makoto Sangu, Bunsho Jugaku, compilers.] 100-*nenki Kinen Blake*: Sakuhin Bunken Tenrankai Shuppin Mokuroku Oite Onshi Kyoto Hakubutsukan [*Commemoration of Blake's Centenary*: Bibliography and Exhibition Catalogue at Onshi Kyoto Scientific Museum]. Kyoto, 1927.

The 340 entries in Japanese are mostly of books and articles after 1863 and photographs.

631. 1927. *William Blake.* The Description of a Small Collection of His Works In the Library of A New York Collector. N.Y., 1927.

Anon., 'William Blake' (pp. 3–4) is a general account of Blake's life. There are 89 entries in the catalogue. The collector, who is not identified in the catalogue, was G. C. Smith.

632. A. 1927. **Burlington Fine Arts Club *Catalogue: Blake Centenary Exhibition.* London, 1927.

B. 1927.

L. B[inyon], 'Introductory Note' (pp. 11–15 in A, pp. 7–11 in B); the 91 entries are 'in most cases reprinted (with some alterations) from the Catalogue' made by A. G. B. Russell for the National Gallery (1913); G. L. K[eynes], 'Books and Prints, Chiefly in Illuminated Printing: Introduction' (pp. 54–6 in A, pp. 50–2 in B); the chief difference between A and B is that there are 49 plates in A.

633. 1927. *Loan Exhibition*: Illustrations to the Book of Job: Being a set of 22 Original Water Colour Drawings believed to be by William Blake. [Auckland, 1927.]

The recently discovered 'New Zealand' set, lent by 'the Martin family, of Ellerslie' to 'The Council of the Auckland Society of Arts'.

A633. 1928 1 Dec.–28 Feb. 1929. **William Blake*: The Complaint or Night Thoughts [Drawings exhibited at The City of Birmingham Museum and Art Gallery] Dec. 1st, 1928–Feb. 28th, 1929. [Birmingham, 1928].

This is the first of a series of exhibitions (the rest of which I have not traced) of the Blake designs for *Night Thoughts* given in 1928 to The British Museum. A. E. Whitley's untitled essay (pp. 3–7) is about Blake's career and the *Night Thoughts* drawings; there is no catalogue of the exhibition.

634. 1929.*Bunsho Jugaku. *William Blake Shoshi* [*Bibliography*]. Tokyo, Kyoto, Kobe, 1929.

The 1474 entries and 117 plates for this bibliography, published for the Grolier Society [of Japan], adapt and extend the Keynes *Bibliography* (1921) published for The Grolier Club of New York. The text is largely in Japanese.

635. 1929. Bunsho Jugaku. 'Blake Shoshi Hoi [A Supplement to (his) *Blake Bibliography*].' *Eigo Seinen: The Rising Generation*, LXI (1929), 177.

636. 1930 17 Feb.–1 March. **Illustrated Books and Original Drawings of William Blake, Drawings, Etchings, Lithographs by Muirhead Bone* Loaned by Lessing J. Rosenwald February 17 to March 1, 1930 [to] The Print Club of Philadelphia.

The Blake entries are nos. 1–29.

637. 1930 22 Oct.–5 Dec. *Loan Exhibition of Works of William Blake* [in the] Fogg Art Museum October 22 to December 15 1930. Cambridge, 1930.

A mimeographed list of an extraordinarily rich exhibition.

638. [1930?] *William Blake*: Original Drawings, Engraved Work, Poetical Works, Books About Blake, Etc., Etc., Mainly from the Collection of Dr. Grenville Macdonald offered by Francis Edwards, Ltd. London [1930?]

98 items, a few originals.

639. 1936 16–28 March. *A Descriptive Hand-List* of a Loan Exhibition of Books and Works of Art by William Blake, 1757–1827, chiefly from the Collection of Mr. Lessing J. Rosenwald Assembled by Mrs. George M. Millard at the Little Museum of La Miniatura 645 Prospect Crescent Pasadena. March 16 to March 28, 1936.

'William Blake, Mystic. English Poet, Painter and Engraver 1757–1827' (pp. 5–7) is signed A. M. [for Mrs. Millard?]; 93 Blake entries.

640. A. 1936 12 May–31 July. **[C. H. Collins Baker.] An Exhibition of*

William Blake's Water-Color Drawings of Milton's 'Paradise Lost' May 12—July 31, 1936 [in the] Henry E. Huntington Library and Art Gallery. San Marino, California, 1936.

B. § Second Edition, 1936.

C. *Third Edition, 1938.

Baker, 'William Blake 1757–1827' (pp. 3–7); 13 drawings are reproduced and described.

641. 1936. Lowery, Margaret Ruth. 'A Census of Copies of William Blake's *Poetical Sketches*, 1783.' *Library*, 4th Ser., XVII (1936), 354–60.

642. A. 1937 15 Jan.–April. *Dodgson, Campbell. *Acquarelles de Turner Oeuvres de Blake*. Association Franco-Britannique Art et Tourisme. Bibliothèque Nationale, 15 janvier—15 février 1937.

B. *Austellung von Englischen Graphiken und Aquarellen: W. Blake und J. M. W. Turner*. Staatliche Graph. Sammlung Albertina Verein der Museums- freunde in Wien. Marz–April 1937.

Julien Cain, 'Avant-Propos' (pp. i–iii in A); Laurence Binyon, 'Turner et Blake' (pp. v–xiii in A, tr. Franz Ottman as 'Blake und Turner', pp. 1–14 of B); 94 Blake entries in A, 65 in B.

643. 1937 2 March. *Catalogue of the Very Well-Known and Valuable Library The Property of Lt.-Col. W. E. Moss* . . . comprising A Most Important and Extensive Collection of the Works of William Blake and of Books and MSS. relating to him . . . Sotheby & Co, March 2–5, 8, 9, 1937.

The important Blake lots are numbered 138–284F.

644. 1938 2–3 Nov. *William Blake*: The Renowned Collection of First Editions Original Drawings, Autograph Letters and an Important Painting in Oils [*and*] Samuel L. Clemens . . . Collected by the late George C. Smith, Jr. Public Sale November 2 and 3. Parke-Bernet Galleries Inc.

There are 104 Blake entries.

645. 1938 2 Dec. *Catalogue of Water Colour Drawings Printed Drawings and Wood Blocks by William Blake* Sold by Order of the Surviving Trustee of the late John Linnell, Esq., Senior, The Executor of the late Miss S. H. Pease and Miss Enid Morse . . . Christie, Manson & Woods, December 2, 1938.

The Blake lots, 55–63, include the Virgil woodblocks and the *Job* accounts and receipts.

646. A. 1938, 1957, 1969. *C. H. Collins Baker. *Catalogue of William Blake's Drawings and Paintings in the Huntington Library*. San Marino [Calif.], 1938.

B. *Enlarged and Revised by R. R. Wark. San Marino, 1957.

C. Reprinted 1969.

The 'Introduction' to A is pp. v–viii; R. R. Wark, 'Preface to the Second Edition' is p. v of B; there are 51 entries in A and 46 in B; the reproductions (38 in B) include 6 for Milton's 'Nativity Ode', 8 for *Comus*, and 13 for *Paradise Lost*. In B, R. R. Wark, 'A Blake Chronology Correlated with the

Principal Objects in the Blake Collection in the Huntington Library' is on pp. 1–8, and the 'Introduction to the Catalogue' by Baker & Wark is on pp. 9–12.

647. 1939. *[Edwin Wolf 2nd & Elizabeth Mongan.] *William Blake 1757–1827*: A Descriptive Catalogue of an Exhibition of the Works of William Blake Selected from Collections in the United States. Philadelphia Museum of Art.

A. Edward Newton, 'Introduction' (pp. v–xviii); 283 entries; 86 splendid plates; one of the most important Blake exhibitions.

648. 1940. Keynes, G. L. 'William Blake (1757–1827).' Vol. II, pp. 347–50 of *The Cambridge Bibliography of English Literature*. [5 vols.] Ed. F. W. Bateson. Cambridge [England], 1940.

Supplemented by Keynes in 1957.

649. 1940. Manson, J. B. 'William Blake and His Followers.' Pp. 32–40 of *The Tate Gallery*. London, 1940 (vMKN).

650. 1941 16–18 April. **Rare Books Original Drawings Autograph Letters and Manuscripts* Collected by the late A. Edward Newton . . . [Part i] For Public Sale . . . at the Parke-Bernet Galleries Inc.

The Blake entries are lots 115–86.

651. A. 1941 21 Oct.–14 Dec. *Water Colours by William Blake for Bunyan's The Pilgrim's Progress*. Loan Exhibition October 21 to November 8, 1941, at the Galleries of M. Knoedler and Company, 14 East 57th Street, New York.

B. . . . Loan Exhibition November 18 to December 14 1941 Cleveland Museum of Art.

S. Foster Damon, Introduction (3 pp.); 29 items.

652. 1942 14 Jan. **The Splendid Library of Mr and Mrs Anton G. Hardy* including The Important Painting in Tempera 'Faith, Hope, and Charity' By William Blake. Parke-Bernet Galleries, January 14th 1942.

The Blake lots are no. 19–50, mostly minor.

653. 1942 2–28 Feb. **William Blake Exhibition*. The Winnipeg Art Gallery from February 2 to February 28.

An 8-page catalogue, mostly of facsimiles and engravings.

654. 1944 June. *Blake to Beardsley*: A Century of English Illustrators. Fogg Museum of Art, June 1944. [Cambridge, Mass., 1944.]

The anonymous title essay is on 5 unnumbered pages. There are 8 Blake entries (no. 13–20).

655. 1945 Oct. *Frederick R. Goff. 'Catalog of Fine Books and Manuscripts Selected for Exhibition at the Library of Congress from the Lessing J. Rosenwald Collection October 1945.' *Quarterly Journal of the Library of Congress*, III (1945), 5–51.

The descriptions of the Blake items (pp. 43–9) are taken from the Philadelphia catalogue (1939). 'The Formation of the Rosenwald Collection' is described by the collector (pp. 53–62, the Blakes on pp. 54–5).

656. 1947 Oct.–Nov. *Exhibition of Water Colors and Drawings by William Blake* [in the] Fogg Museum of Art, October–November, 1947. [Cambridge, Mass.]

The 66 entries in this mimeographed list are chiefly for Job and Dante drawings.

657. A. 1947. **William Blake, 1757–1827.* Paris–Antwerp–Zurich. Organized by The British Council. Tate Gallery [London], 1947.

B. **William Blake, 1757–1827.* Catalogue de l'Exposition organisée par la Galérie René Drouin et The British Council. Paris, 1947.

C. **William Blake (1757–1827).* Exposition organisée par The British Council. Musée royal des Beaux-Arts—Anvers. Brussels.

D. **Ausstellung der Werke von William Blake [1757–1827].* Kunsthaus Zurich, 1947. The British Council.

Eric Maclagen, 'Introduction' (p. 5 in A, p. 11 in B, p. 5 in C, half a page in D); Jasper Ridley, 'Foreword' (p. 6 in A; not translated in B–D); Archibald G. B. Russell, 'William Blake' (pp. 7–9 in A, pp. 25–8 in B, pp. 6–10 in C, 3 pp. in D); the catalogue is based on Russell's of 1913 (no. 604); there are 84 entries and 27 plates in A, 43 entries (tr. Simone Boisecq) and 18 plates in B, 42 Blake entries and 36 plates in C, and 41 Blake entries and 42 plates in D. Additionally, in B there was a puff by André Gide (p. 13), Philippe Soupault, 'William Blake Poète et Graveur' (pp. 15–17), Jean Wahl, 'William Blake Paien, Chrétien et Mystique' (pp. 19–23), and Geoffrey Keynes, 'Bibliographie' (pp. 39–42). In D, M. Wartmann, 'Vorwort des Direktors des Kunsthauses' is half a page.

658. 1949 7 April–6 June. Bournemouth Arts Club. *An Exhibition of Original Works by William Blake (1757–1827) from the Graham Robertson Collection.* Bournemouth, 1949.

Anon. [?Kerrison Preston], 'Introduction to Graham Robertson and his Blake Collection' (pp. 2–3); 53 entries. The exhibition was at Bournemouth 7–21 April, Southampton 25 April–5 May, and Brighton 11 May–6 June.

659. 1949 22 July. [Keynes, Geoffrey.] *Catalogue of Original Works by William Blake* the property of the late Graham Robertson, Esq. which will be sold by Christie, Manson & Woods, Ltd., July 22, 1949.

Geoffrey Keynes, 'Preface' (pp. 3–4); 90 Blakes.

660. 1949 16 Dec.–1950 14 Jan. *A Newly Discovered Painting by William Blake lent by The National Trust.* The Arts Council of Great Britain 4 St. James's Square, S.W.1 16th December, 1949–14th January, 1950.

Three pages of text about the Arlington Court Picture are 'Condensed' from Keynes's *Country Life* article, no. 2034.

661. 1949. [W. G. Constable.] *Catalogue of Paintings and Drawings in Water Color [in the] Museum of Fine Arts Boston.* Boston, 1949.

'Blake, William' is pp. 19–33, with 33 entries.

662. 1950 15 July–30 Sept. *Exhibition of Works by William Blake* 15th July–

30th September, 1950. The Lady Lever Art Gallery, Port Sunlight, Cheshire (vKP).

There is a brief 'Introduction' by Kerrison Preston to this loan exhibition of 'carefully chosen' but 'comparatively unknown and mostly subsidiary' paintings and drawings.

663. 1951. *The Tempera Paintings of William Blake*: A Critical Catalogue. Arts Council of Great Britain. London, 1951.

Philip James, 'Foreword' (p. 3); Geoffrey Keynes, 'Introduction' (pp. 5–11); there are 30 Blake entries in this exhibition catalogue.

664. 1952. *The Blake Collection of W. Graham Robertson* described by the Collector. Ed. Kerrison Preston. London, 1952. The William Blake Trust.

Kerrison Preston's 'Introduction' (pp. 9–12), 140 entries and 64 plates.

665. 1953. Mary Chamot. 'Blake, William.' Pp. 13–18 of *The Tate Gallery British School*. A Concise Catalogue. London, 1953.

72 Blake entries.

666. A. 1953. *William Blake's Illuminated Books*: A Census compiled by Geoffrey Keynes & Edwin Wolf 2nd. N.Y., 1953.

B. §N.Y., 1969.

Geoffrey Keynes, 'Preface' (pp. vii–xix); the Census brings up to date the comparable section of Keynes (1921). The 1969 issue is a photographic reprint.

667. 1954. *William Blake The Romantic Poets The Nineteenth Century*. The Brick Row Book Shop Catalogue No. 41. N.Y., 1954.

Lots 1–70 are minor Blakes.

668. 1954. *The Rosenwald Collection*. A Catalogue of Illustrated Books and Manuscripts, of Books from Celebrated Presses, and of Bindings and Maps, 1150–1950 The Gift of Lessing J. Rosenwald to the Library of Congress. [Compiled by Marion Schild, ed. Frederick R. Goff.] Washington, D.C., 1954.

The extremely important collection of 'The Works of William Blake' covers pp. 186–96, items 993–1055.

669. 1956. Geoffrey Keynes. *Engravings by William Blake*: The Separate Plates: A Catalogue Raisonée. Dublin, 1956.

'Preface' (pp. xi–xiii); 44 entries (not counting varying states and impressions); 45 plates; an extremely important catalogue.

670. 1957 2–28 Feb. *William Blake Exhibition*. The Winnipeg Art Gallery from February 2 to February 28 [1957?] The Winnipeg Auditorium.

73 entries, almost all of them reproductions.

671. 1957 25 April–18 May. [Victor Rienaecker.] *William Blake (1757–1827) Bicentenary Celebrations*. Paintings, Drawings and Facsimiles. Whitworth Art Gallery. April 25–May 18 1957. Manchester.

Margaret Pilkington, 'Foreword' (p. 3); 75 entries.

672. 1957 July 15. Collection of the late Col. Gould Weston sold at Christie's. Lots 16–29 are important Blake drawings.

673. 1957 Oct.–Nov. *Exhibition of Water Colors and Drawings by William Blake.* Fogg Museum of Art October–November, 1957. [Cambridge.]
Mimeographed descriptions.

674. 1957 18 Oct.–1 Dec. *[Elizabeth Mongan.] *The Art of William Blake.* Bicentennial Exhibition October 18th–December 1st, 1957. National Gallery of Art, Smithsonian Institution. Washington [D.C., 1957].
John Walker, 'Foreword', is pp. 3–4. Elizabeth Mongan, 'The Art of William Blake' (pp. 7–10) is reprinted in the 1961 Iowa exhibition. There are 163 entries and 22 plates.

675. 1957 Nov.–Dec. City and County of Kingston upon Hull Ferens Art Gallery *Bicentenary Exhibition of Works by William Blake (1757–1827).* November–December 1957. Hull.
Sir Anthony Blunt, 'Foreword' (pp. 3–4), is extracted from the Tate catalogue (no. 679); 13 Blake entries.

A675. 1957 20 Nov.–1958 27 Feb. *William Blake 1757–1827.* Exhibition in the Buvelot and Childers Galleries November 20th 1957–February 27th 1958. [Victoria, Australia, 1957.]

676. 1957 23–4 Nov. *Makoto Sangu. *William Blake Seitan 200-nen Kinen*: Blake Bunken Tenjikai Shuppin Mokuroku: *Catalogue of an Exhibition of Blakeana* held in Commemoration of the Bicentenary of Blake's Birth at Hosei University, Tokyo, 23–4 November, 1957. Tokyo, 1958.
There are 214 entries in Japanese and English chiefly editions of Blake's works and books about him.

677. 1957 23 Nov.–22 Dec. *Blake 1757–1827.* Bicentenary Exhibition 23rd November–22nd December 1957 Battersea Central Library [London].
'Foreword' by J. Bronowski (1 p.); 107 entries of reprints, facsimiles, etc.

1957 Huntington Catalogue; see 1938 Huntington Catalogue.

678. 1957. G. L. Keynes. 'William Blake (1757–1827).' Pp. 425–8 of Vol. V (Supplement: A.D. 600–1900. Ed. George Watson) of *The Cambridge Bibliography of English Literature.* Ed. F. W. Bateson. [5 vols.] Cambridge [England], 1957.
A supplement to the 1940 *CBEL.*

679. A. 1957, 1971. *Martin [R.F.] Butlin. *William Blake (1757–1827)*: A Catalogue of the Works of William Blake in the Tate Gallery with An Introduction by Anthony Blunt and A Foreword by John Rothenstein. London, 1957.
B. **William Blake*: a complete catalogue of the works in the Tate Gallery . . . 1971.
Rothenstein's 'Foreword' (pp. 1–5 in A, pp. 5–7 in B) is on the formation of the collection. Blunt's 'The Art of William Blake', is pp. 7–23 in A, pp. 9–19 in B. There are 86 entries in A, 87 in B, plus 40 plates in A, 109 in B.

B. Norman Reid's 'Preface' (p. 5) says that in the new edition the essays by Blunt and Rothenstein have had only 'minor revisions' but that Butlin's catalogue is 'completely revised'.

680. 1957. *William Blake and his Circle*. British Museum Bicentenary Exhibition.

There are about 199 Blake entries in this mimeographed list.

681. 1957. **William Blake's Illustrations to the Bible*. A Catalogue compiled by Geoffrey Keynes. London, 1957. The William Blake Trust.

George Goyder, 'Introduction' (pp. x–xi). There are 208 entries in this 'list [of] all the tempera and water-colour paintings Blake is known to have made in illustration of the Bible'. All the paintings presently locatable (174) are reproduced in tiny dimensions, with a few also of enormous size and lovely colour.

682. A. 1958 19 May. **Catalogue of the Celebrated Collection of Books Illuminated & Illustrated by William Blake* The Property of the late Mrs. William Emerson which will be sold by Sotheby & Co. 19 May 1958.

B. 1958.

'Introduction' (p. 5) is signed Sotheby & Co; 15 Blake entries and 12 plates; there was also another (otherwise identical) edition without the plates.

683. 1959. *The Tinker Library*. A Bibliographical Catalogue of the Books and Manuscripts collected by Chauncey Brewster Tinker. Compiled by Robert F. Metzdorf. New Haven, 1959.

Items 259–88 are by Blake.

684. A. 1960, 1962. Kerrison Preston. *Notes for a Catalogue of the Blake Library at The Georgian House Merstham*. Cambridge [England], 1960.

B. Second Edition revised. Cambridge, 1962.

A. There are some 472 entries, including books, MSS, and pictures by Blake and books, pamphlets, and articles about him. 'Notes for a Catalogue' are on p. 5.

B. The revision in the Second Edition seems to consist of an 'Additional' section of works acquired after 1960.

685. **1961 17 Nov.–8 Dec. *Blake*: An Exhibition Arranged by the Iowa Print Group in the New Gallery, Department of Art, School of Fine Arts, University of Iowa, November 17 to December 8, 1961.

Elizabeth Mongan, 'The Art of William Blake' (7 pp.) is reprinted from the National Gallery exhibition (1957). All 40 entries listed are from the Rosenwald Collection.

686. 1964. **G. E. Bentley, Jr., & Martin K. Nurmi. *A Blake Bibliography*: Annotated Lists of Works, Studies, and Blakeana. Minneapolis, 1964.

Revised in the present work. 'Blake's Reputation and Interpretaters' (pp. 3–30); GEB, 'Blake's Chronology' (pp. 31–8); MKN, 'Note on Musical

Settings' (pp. 363–5). There are 2,197 entries, which do not include original descriptions of contemporary copies of Blake's own works.

687. 1964. *Geoffrey Keynes. *Bibliotheca Bibliographici*: A Catalogue of the Library Formed by Geoffrey Keynes. London, 1964.

The important collection of Blake works and Blakeana comprehends especially no. 467–783. Of these, no. 467–500, 506–9, 511–14, 516–20, 522–3, 551–2, 555, 558–60, 563–77, 579, 582–4, 588–610, 612–727 are to go to the Fitzwilliam Museum, according to the Fitzwilliam Catalogue (1970) which reprints the more important entries here.

688. A. 1964. *An Exhibition of the Illuminated Books of William Blake Poet · Printer · Prophet* Arranged by The William Blake Trust. A Commemorative Handbook with a study by Geoffrey Keynes and a foreword by Lessing J. Rosenwald. Clairvaux, 1964. The William Blake Trust.

B. *Geoffrey Keynes. *A Study of the Illuminated Books of William Blake Poet · Printer · Prophet*. London & Paris, 1965.

C. *London & Paris, 1970.

A. 'Foreword' (pp. 7–8); 'The Illuminated Books' (pp. 11–55) (a general explanation, not a catalogue of the exhibition), and 27 colour plates.

B. The second work seems to differ from the first only in the omission of Mr. Rosenwald's 'Foreword', the relocation of the plates so that the unchanged study of 'The Illuminated Books' is pp. 11–27, the addition of some 34 new plates, and cursory bibliographical descriptions of each book reproduced.

The 'Foreword' is adapted in no. 698.

689. 1965 27 Feb.–29 March. *[Albert S. Roe.] *William Blake*: An Annotated Catalogue [of an exhibition at the] Andrew Dickson White Museum of Art, Cornell University, February 27–March 29, 1965.

The travelling Blake Trust exhibition.

690. 1965 25 Sept.–24 Oct. *William Blake 1757–1827*. September 25—to—October 24 1965. Smithsonian Exhibition—Blake Trust [in] The Winnipeg Art Gallery.

The same works as in Cornell, plus a few ephemera from Winnipeg collections.

691. 1965 Nov.–1966 Feb. [Robert R. Wark.] *William Blake and His Circle*: Two Exhibitions at the Henry E. Huntington Library and Art Gallery November 1965 through February 1966.

Preface (p. 1); 'Introduction' (pp. 2–5); 30 Blake entries and 24 of his contemporaries (Romney, Fuseli, Flaxman, etc.).

692. 1965. William White. 'A Blake Bibliography: Review With Additions.' *Bulletin of Bibliography and Magazine Notes*, XXIV (1965), 155–6.

50 entries added to Bentley & Nurmi (1964), mostly reviews of works published after its terminal date.

693. 1967. *Preston Blake Library.* Westminster City Libraries. [London, 1967.]
A leaflet describing the collection; see no. 664.

694. 1968 9 Jan.–21 April. *Frederick Cummings. 'William Blake 1757–
1827.' Pp. 157–66 of Frederick Cummings, Allen Staley, Robert Rosenblum,
Romantic Art in Britain: Paintings and Drawings 1760–1860. The Detroit
Institute of Arts 9 January–18 February 1968. Philadelphia Museum of Art
14 March–21 April 1968. Philadelphia, 1968.
8 drawings exhibited and reproduced.

695. A. 1968. Geoffrey Keynes. 'Blake's *Little Tom the Sailor.*' *Book Collector*,
XVII (1968), 421–7.
B. *Revised and reprinted in his *Blake Studies* (1971).
Bibliographical description and census of copies.

696. 1968. *Charles Ryskamp. '*Songs of Innocence and of Experience* and Miss
Caroline Newton's Blake Collection.' *Princeton University Library Chronicle*,
XXIX (1968), 150–5.
Details of an exhibition of Blakes from the Princeton and Newton
collections in Nov. and Dec. 1967.

697. 1969 29 April–18 May. [Elizabeth Johnston.] '*For Friendship's Sake*':
William Blake and William Hayley. City Art Gallery Manchester 29th April
to 18th May 1969. Organized for the Manchester Cathedral Arts Festival.
[Manchester.]
G. L. Conran, 'Foreword' (p. 2); 'Arguments Towards a Conjectural
Arrangement of Blake's "Heads of the Poets"' (by Miss Johnston?) (pp. 3–5);
and 47 works (six by Blake) which provide context and 'iconographical
sources' for Blake's 'Heads of the Poets', which were evidently also exhibited.
Mr. Wells's booklet on the 'Heads' was 'published concurrently'.

698. 1969 14 May–21 June. *William Blake: Poet · Printer · Prophet*; an exhibition of illuminated books arranged by the William Blake Trust and a selection of watercolours and drawings formerly in the collection of W. Graham
Robertson (the exhibition is supported by the North West Arts Association)
14 May to 21 June 1969 [in] Whitworth Art Gallery, University of Manchester.
Francis W. Hawcroft, 'Foreword' (pp. 2–3); Lessing J. Rosenwald,
'Introduction' ('adapted from the Foreword' in no. 688) (pp. 6–7); and
Kerrison Preston, 'The Blake Collection of W. Graham Robertson' (p. 32);
41 entries.

699. 1969 21 Aug.–30 Sept. *William Blake: A Loan Exhibition*. National
Library of Scotland, Edinburgh.
William Beattie, 'Note' (p. 2); Geoffrey Keynes, 'The Blake Trust'
(pp. 3–4, reprinted with minor changes but without acknowledgement by
Keynes in the 1971 Blake Trust Gray exhibition catalogue), Isabel Henderson,
'Introduction' (pp. 5–6). 'The exhibition has been organized primarily to
bring to general notice the work . . . of the William Blake Trust' (p. 3).

700. 1969 Dec.–1970 Feb. * *William Blake Engraver*: A Descriptive Catalogue of an Exhibition by Charles Ryskamp with an Introductory Essay by Geoffrey Keynes. Princeton University Library. Princeton, 1969.

Preface by Charles Ryskamp (pp. vii–x); 'Introduction' by Sir Geoffrey Keynes (pp. 1–18); 129 entries, described with great care.

1969 Huntington Catalogue; see 1938 Huntington Catalogue.

1969. Robert N. Essick. 'A Finding List of Reproductions of Blake's Art.' See no. 1217 42.

701. A. 1969, 1972. [Phyllis Goff.] *William Blake*: Catalogue of the Preston Blake Library Presented by Kerrison Preston in 1967 [to the] Westminster City Libraries. London, 1969.

B. *William Blake*: Supplement to the Catalogue of the Preston Blake Library, Westminster City Libraries. [London], 1972.

A. Kerrison Preston, 'Foreword' is on one unnumbered page, K. C. Harrison, 'City Librarian's Preface' on another. There are 700 entries. For an earlier catalogue of the same library, see no. 684.

702. 1969. *[Mary MacFarlane.] *William Blake 1757–1827*. [*An exhibition* Circulated by the Extension Services of the National Gallery of Canada, Ottawa 1969–1970.] Ottawa, 1969.

'William Blake' (pp. [1–4]); 33 prints exhibited. The catalogue is in French and English.

703. 1970. * *William Blake*: Catalogue of the Collection in the Fitzwilliam Museum Cambridge. Ed. David Bindman. Cambridge, 1970.

David Piper, in the 'Foreword' (p. vii), explains that the catalogue was compiled about 1953 by Sir Geoffrey Keynes, 'added to by many hands, notably those of Mr Carlos van Hasselt, Mr J. W. Goodison, Mr Malcolm Cormack and Mr Martin Butlin', and then 'entirely recast' by Mr David Bindman. 'The History of the Fitzwilliam Blake Collection' is on p. 1. There are 64 entries. The 'Appendix' (pp. 65–84) reprints Keynes's *Bibliotheca Bibliographici* (1964), no. 467–500, 506–9, 511–14, 516–20, 522–3, 551–2, 555, 558–60, 563–77, 579, 582–4, 588–610, 612–56, 721–6, and announces that Sir Geoffrey has 'promised to bequeath to the Museum these' plus no. 657–76, 678–720. The 74 plates include the designs for the Story of Joseph (3), *Paradise Regained* (12), and the reduced ones for *Job* (24). The publication of the catalogue was accompanied by an exhibition of all 64 Fitzwilliam Blakes, extended by works described in a flyer: *William Blake* (1757–1827) [12] Additional items on exhibition, 13 January—28 March 1971.

1971, Summer–Autumn. See Robert Essick, 'finding list of reproductions of blake's art', *Blake Newsletter*, V, No. 1–2 (1971).

A703. 1971 15 June. *Christie sale of Important English Drawings and Watercolours.

Lots 141–72 are the *detached* leaves of the Blake–Varley sketchbook, with 20 plates.

704. 1971 17 Oct.–18 Dec. *Imagination and Vision*: Prints and Drawings of William Blake [exhibited in] The Art Gallery, Illinois State University October 17 to November 7, 1971 [and] the University of Kansas Museum of Art November 28 to December 18, 1971. [?Lawrence, Kansas], 1971. Miscellaneous Publications of the [University of Kansas] Museum of Art No. 84.

Charles C. Eldredge, 'Foreword' (2 pp.), Vernon H. Minor, 'William Blake (1757–1827)' (5 pp.), [Pamela D. Kingsbury] 'Catalogue' of 18 items (21 pp.).

705. A. 1971 Dec.–1972 Spring. *William Blake's Water-Colour Designs for the Poems of Thomas Gray* with an Introduction and Commentary by Geoffrey Keynes Kt. London, 1971.

B. *William Blake's Water-Colours Illustrating the Poems of Thomas Gray* with an Introduction and Commentary by Sir Geoffrey Keynes. Chicago & Paris, 1972.

A is 'a Commemorative Catalogue to accompany the exhibition arranged by the William Blake Trust . . . at the Tate Gallery, London [*Dec. 1971–Jan. 1972*] and at . . . Yale University [*Spring 1972*] and at other [*unspecified*] museums' (p. iv), as well as 'an introductory handbook' to the (then still-unpublished) Blake Trust facsimile of Blake's water-colours (p. viii). The text of A consists of Geoffrey Keynes, 'The William Blake Trust' (pp. vii–viii, reprinted with minor changes but without acknowledgement from his essay in the 1969 Edinburgh exhibition catalogue), Arnold Fawcus, 'Acknowledgements' (p. ix), Keynes's 'Introduction' (pp. 1–6) and 'Commentary' (pp. 41–71), the last mostly descriptive. The 137 plates (including the covers) comprehend the 116 Gray designs in black-and-white mostly reduced 4-to-a-page plus 19 large ones in colour.

B is like A except for the omission of the Keynes essay on 'The William Blake Trust' and small revisions to the 'Acknowledgements' (pp. ix–x).

706. 1971. *The Blake Collection of Mrs. Landon K. Thorne*: Catalogue by G. E. Bentley, Jr., Introduction by Charles Ryskamp. The Pierpont Morgan Library. N.Y., 1971.

Ryskamp's 'Introduction' is pp. 5–7; GEB, 'The Great Collections of Blake's Books' is pp. 11–15 and 'Postscript' (excerpts from Blake's '*Notebook* and conversations') is pp. 64–5. There are 35 entries in 'The Catalogue' (pp. 17–62) and 32 reproductions. The detailed bibliographical entries are adapted from *Blake Books* (then not yet published). The catalogue was published concurrently with an 'Exhibition of Mrs. Thorne's Collection: 19 November 1971 to 22 January 1972 [*at*] The Pierpont Morgan Library'.

707. 1971. D. V. Erdman, 'Blake 1757–1827.' Chap. 9 (pp. 144–66) of *English Poetry*: Select Bibliographical Guides [to Chaucer, Spenser, Donne, Herbert, Milton, Marvell, Dryden, Pope, Blake, Wordsworth, Coleridge, Byron, Shelley, Keats, Tennyson, Browning, Arnold, Hopkins, Yeats, Eliot]. Ed. A. E. Dyson. Oxford, 1971.

A workmanlike survey of Texts, Criticism, Biographies, and Bibliographies.

708. 1971. G. E. B[entley, Jr.]. 'William Blake 1757–1827.' Vol. II, cols.
615–36 of *The New Cambridge Bibliography of English Literature*. Ed. George
Watson. Cambridge, 1971.
Substituted for the Keynes lists of 1940 and 1957.

1972 Spring. 'A Handlist of Works by William Blake in The Department of
Prints & Drawings in The British Museum.' See *Blake Newsletter*, V (1972),
223–58.

709. 1972. *Roger R. Easson & Robert N. Essick. *William Blake: Book
Illustrator*: A Bibliography and Catalogue of the Commercial Engravings.
Volume I: Plates Designed and Engraved by Blake. Normal, Illinois, 1972.
    The *'raison d'être'* of this important work 'is the complete reproduction of
Blake's commercial book illustrations [*excluding Job and Dante*], but we have
also provided notes on the prints [*by Essick*] and bibliographic descriptions of
the books in which they appear' [by Easson] (p. vii), chiefly from copies in the
U.S. and Canada. The plates of Vol. I include the *Royal Universal Family
Bible* (1), Commins's *Elegy* (1), Mary Wollstonecraft's *Original Stories* (6),
Young's *Night Thoughts* (43), Hayley, 'Little Tom' (4), Hayley, *Designs to
A Series of Ballads* (12), Hayley, *Life . . . of William Cowper* (1), Hayley,
Ballads (5), Chaucer, *Prologue* (2), Virgil (17), and *Remember Me!* (1). Vols.
II–III will include all the books for which Blake made the designs *or* the
engravings.

710. 1972. 1 Nov.–1973 31 Jan. *[Gleeson, Larry] *The Followers of William
Blake*: An Exhibition at the Henry E. Huntington Library and Art Gallery
November 1, 1972 through January 31, 1973.
    Robert R. Wark, 'Preface' (p. 1); Larry Gleeson, 'The Followers of
William Blake' (pp. 3–10); [Larry Gleeson], 'The Catalogue' (pp. 11–33)
includes 1 Blake, 8 Palmers, 7 Richmonds, 10 Calverts, 8 Linnells, 1 Walter,
and 1 Finch.

A710. 1974 21 April–13 May. **William Blake*: The Apocalyptic Vision.
Preface and Catalogue by Harvey Stahl, Introduction by Bruce Daryl Barone
[to An Exhibition at Reid Hall] Manhattanville College [April 21 to May
13, 1974]. Purchase, N.Y., 1974.
    Harvey Stahl, 'Preface' (1 unnumbered page), Bruce Daryl Barone, 'In-
troduction' (6 pp.); each of the 27 designs exhibited is reproduced.

PART V

BOOKS OWNED BY BLAKE

Part V consists of books from Blake's library which can presently be located or which are known fairly clearly to have been his,[1] though his copies are *UNTRACED*. Works which he annotated are described in more detail than the others.

Blake is known to have owned as well unidentified editions of:

1. 'Sessi [*i.e. Allessandro*] Vellutello's Dante' which he used for his Dante drawings, according to the *Literary Gazette*; there were editions of 1551, 1554, 1564, 1571, 1578, 1596.
2. 'Mr. [*Henry Francis*] Cary's translation' of Dante, according to the same *Literary Gazette* article; there were editions of London, 1814, 1819, and Philadelphia, 1822.
3. Edmund 'Burkes treatise', i.e. *A Philosophical Enquiry into the Origins of our Ideas of the Sublime and Beautiful* which Blake annotated 'when very Young', according to his marginalia to Reynolds's *Works*; there were eight editions by 1776.
4. Edward 'Bysshes Art of Poetry', which Catherine Blake 'had in her hand' in Aug. 1807 when the Blakes used it for a kind of magic-game, according to Blake's account in his *Notebook*, pp. 88–9; there were editions of 1702, 1705, 1708, 1710, 1714 (2 vols.), 1718 (2 vols.), 1724, 1725, 1737, 1739 (2 vols.), 1762 (2 vols.), but the Blakes were evidently using a one-volume edition.
5. 'Locke on Human Understanding', i.e. his *Essay Concerning Human Understanding*, read and annotated by Blake 'when very Young', according to his marginalia to Reynolds's *Works*; there were 16 editions by 1768.
6. '*Works of Peter Pindar*' (i.e. John Wolcot), 12 mo, with 'Blake's signature on the fly leaf', 'Sold by Mr. Arthur Rogers of Newcastle-upon-Tyne in March 1926', according to Keynes (no. 2020); there were editions of 1794–1801 (5 vols.), 1809 (4 vols.), 1812 (5 vols.), and 1816 (4 vols.).

The Appendix lists books bearing the name William Blake which did *not* belong to the poet.

---

[1] According to Anon., 'Felpham and the Poet-Painter Blake. The Thirty-fourth Meeting of the William Blake Society . . .', *The Observer and West Sussex Recorder*, 27 May 1914, 'books with Blake's Autograph' and copies of *Jerusalem* ('an original decorated copy') and the title-pages of *America* and *Europe* were lent for display on the occasion by R. C. Jackson, but no copies of these works can now be traced to Jackson, and neither the reporter nor the donor is likely to inspire much confidence.

AESCHYLUS

711. THE / TRAGEDIES / OF / ÆSCHYLUS / TRANSLATED / By R. POTTER. / THE SECOND EDITION, CORRECTED, / WITH NOTES. IN TWO VOLUMES. / VOL. I [II]. / LONDON: / PRINTED FOR W. STRAHAN; AND T. CADELL / IN THE STRAND. / MDCCLXXIX [1779].

BINDING: In original paper boards, with no labels or writing on the exteriors except for '1' and '2'.

HISTORY: (**1**) Acquired by Blake, signed 'William Blake' on the half-title of Volume I and the title-page of Volume II; (**2**) Probably acquired at his death in 1827 by his widow Catherine, and at her death in 1831 by (**3**) Frederick Tatham (who acquired the rest of her property); Tatham probably gave or sold it to Blake's devoted disciple (**4**) 'Samuel Palmer 1833', who wrote his name and the date on the front endpapers of Volumes I and II and gave it to (**5**) His son Herbert, who gave it on 15 July 1890 to (**6**) F. G. Stephens (a note pasted in Vol. I says the work was 'given me, July 15, 1890, by Herbert Palmer, son of Samuel Palmer, and containing the autographs of William Blake and Samuel Palmer, to whom they belonged. F. G. Stephens'); (**7**) Acquired by 'Iohn Drinkwater 1920', who wrote his name and the date on the recto of the first fly-leaf of Volume I and added his bookplate on the fly-leaf of Volume II; (**8**) Acquired by Gabriel Wells,[1] from whose estate it was acquired in 1947 by (**9**) A. S. W. Rosenbach,[1] whose successor (**10**) John Fleming offered it in his catalogue (1961), no. 182, for $345, from which it was bought by (**11**) Mrs. Landon K. Thorne, who gave it in February 1972 to (**12**) The PIERPONT MORGAN LIBRARY.

ALIGHIERI; see DANTE.

BACON, Francis

712. ESSAYS / MORAL, ECONOMICAL, / AND / POLITICAL. / BY / *FRANCIS BACON,* / BARON OF VERULAM, / AND / VISCOUNT ST. ALBANS. /=/ LONDON: / PRINTED BY T. BENSLEY / FOR J. EDWARDS, PALL MALL, AND T. PAYNE, / MEWS GATE. / — / 1798.

COLLECTION: Sir Geoffrey Keynes.

DATE OF ANNOTATION: ?1798.

The tenor of the comments, particularly the frequent comparison of Bacon's advice to Christ's, suggests a date not long after publication for Blake's annotations.

DESCRIPTION: The first endpaper is inscribed 'Samuel Palmer / 1833'.
All the notes are in pencil. There are no notes on pp. 240–70.

BINDING: Bound in Green cloth over original boards (now rather tatty); some pages have pulled free.

HISTORY: (**1**) Acquired by 'Samuel Palmer / 1833' (according to the note

---

[1] As Mr. Fleming wrote to me.

on the first endpaper); (2) 'About 1900' (as A. G. B. Russell told Keynes, *Bibliography* [1921]), it belonged to Lionel Isaacs; (3) Acquired from Goodspeed's of Boston (according to the buyer's letter of 30 Oct. 1947 with the volume) by Josiah K. Lilly, Jr., who passed it on in 1947 to (4) *Geoffrey Keynes*, who signed the first fly-leaf and described it in his catalogue (1964), no. 720.

713. *The Tvvo Bookes of Francis Bacon.* Of the proficience and aduancement of Learning, diuine and humane. To the King. At London, Printed for Henrie Tomes, and are to be sould at his shop in Graies Inne Gate in Holborne. 1605.

In his copy of Reynolds's *Works* Blake wrote: 'when very Young . . . I read . . . Bacon's Advance of Learning on Every one of these Books I wrote my Opinions', and in his letter of 23 Aug. 1799 he quoted accurately from Bacon's 'Advancem^t of Learning, Part 2, P. 47 of first Edition'. However, Blake's annotated copy of the first edition is *UNTRACED*.

BARRY, James

714. *An Account of a Series of Pictures*, in the Great Room of the Society of Arts, Manufactures, and Commerce, at the Adelphi. London: Printed for the Author. 1783. (Keynes)

The copy of this book, with a pencil drawing of Barry by Blake and which presumably belonged to Blake, is in the collection of Sir *Geoffrey Keynes*.

BERKELEY, George

715. *SIRIS:* / A CHAIN OF / Philosophical Reflexions / AND / INQUIRIES / Concerning the VIRTUES of / *TAR WATER*, / And divers other *Subjects* connected together / and arising one from another. / — / By G. L. B. O. C.[1] / — / *As we have opportunity let us do good unto all men.* / Gal. vi. 10. / *Hoc opus hoc studium parvi properemus et ampli.* / HOR. / ≡ / DUBLIN: Printed by MARG^T. RHAMES, / For R. GUNNE, Bookseller in *Capel-street*, / M DCC XLIV [*1744*].

COLLECTION: Trinity College, Cambridge.

DATE OF ANNOTATION: *c.* 1820.

The concern in the notes for the divinity of imagination and the conflict between it and mathematics suggest a date close to that of 'The Everlasting Gospel' (?1818) parts k, l and to that of 'Laocoon' (?1820) in which very similar ideas are expressed.

DESCRIPTION: The fly-leaf is inscribed 'From the Author', i.e. from Berkeley. Blake's annotations are in ink. In the middle of p. 51 is a pencil comment in another hand: 'the same Effects were produced by oxygen gass—vital air'.

HISTORY: (1) 'In 1833' it belonged to Samuel Palmer (according to Keynes [1957] who cites no evidence); (2) Sold by Tregaskis 'About 1909' (according to Keynes, *Bibliography* [1921]) to (3) W. E. Moss; (4) Acquired by Lord

---

[1] That is, George, Lord Bishop of Cloyne.

Rothschild, who gave it in 1969 to (5) TRINITY COLLEGE, Cambridge. Blake's annotations are printed in *The Rothschild Library*: A Catalogue of the Collection of Eighteenth-Century Books and Manuscripts formed by Lord Rothschild (Cambridge, 1954), I. 70–1.

BLAIR, Robert

716. THE / GRAVE, / A POEM. / BY / ROBERT BLAIR. / — / ILLUSTRATED BY / Twelve Etchings / EXECUTED FROM / ORIGINAL DESIGNS. / — / LONDON: / *PRINTED BY T. BENSLEY, BOLT COURT,* / FOR THE PROPRIETOR, R. H. CROMEK, Nº 64, NEWMAN STREET; / AND SOLD BY / CADELL AND DAVIES, J. JOHNSON, T. PAYNE, J. WHITE, LONGMAN, HURST, REES, AND / ORME, W. MILLER, J. MURRAY, AND CONSTABLE AND CO. EDINBURGH. / 1808.

According to his letter to George Cumberland of 14 Aug. 1808 (*Blake Records* [1969], 198), Cromek 'sent him [*Blake*] 2 Copies' of this book for which Blake had made the designs, 'but he has not had the common politeness to thank me for them'. Blake's two copies are *UNTRACED*.

CENNINI, Cennino

717. DI CENNINO CENNINI / TRATTATO / DELLA PITTURA / MESSO IN LUCE LA PRIMA VOLTA / CON ANNOTAZIONE / DAL CAVALIERE / GIUSEPPE TAMBRONI / SOGIO ONORARIO DELL'ACCADEMICA DI S. LUCA / DELLA I. R. DELLE BELLE ARTI DI VIENNA / DELL'ARCHELOGICA DI ROMA / DELLA R. DI SCIENZE LETTERE ED ARTI DI PARIGI EC. / — / ROMA / CO' TORCHJ DI PAOLO SALVIUCCI / 1821 / *Con Approvazione.*

COLLECTION: *UNTRACED*; see below.

DATE OF ANNOTATION: ?1822.

From Linnell's comment (below) it is clear that Blake must have been reading Cennini's book soon after it was published in 1821.

DESCRIPTION: The text derives from E. J. Ellis, *The Real Blake* (1907), 420, who says merely that Blake's comments are 'In the margin of a copy of Cennini's book on fresco painting'.[1] On 10 Dec. 1862 Linnell wrote to Anne Gilchrist:

I believe that the first copy of Cennino Cennini seen in England was the copy I obtained from Italy & gave to Blake who soon made it out & was gratified to find that he had been using the same materials & methods in painting as Cennini describes —particularly the Carpenters glue[.].[2]

---

[1] Erdman (p. 803) argues that the notoriously inaccurate Ellis intended not Cennini's *Trattato della Pittura* but Benvenuto Cellini's *Trattato dell'Oreficeria.*

[2] MS with the Ivimy MSS. Keynes (*Bibliography of William Blake* [1921], 54) says that Blake transcribed an extract from Cennini in a sketch-book (watermarked 1824) used by George Richmond. (The sketch-book, also used by Palmer, C. H. Tatham, and Calvert was described, without reference to the Blake passage, in the Sotheby catalogue of 28 July 1920, lot 162. Sir Geoffrey tells me that the book contained as well a sketch by Blake of a Vision of Hercules inked over by Richmond.)

BINDING: Unknown because untraced.

HISTORY: (1) 'The first copy of Cennino seen in England was the copy I [*John Linnell*] obtained from Italy and gave to [(2)] Blake' (according to Linnell's letter of 10 Dec. 1862 to Anne Gilchrist, with the Ivimy MSS), who made notes in it which were seen by E. J. Ellis and reported in his *Real Blake* (1907); (3) *UNTRACED*.

CHATTERTON, Thomas

718. *POEMS,* / SUPPOSED TO HAVE BEEN WRITTEN AT BRISTOL, / BY THOMAS ROWLEY, AND OTHERS, / IN THE FIFTEENTH CENTURY. / THE THIRD EDITION; / TO WHICH IS ADDED / AN APPENDIX, / CONTAINING SOME OBSERVATIONS UPON THE / LANGUAGE OF THESE POEMS; / TENDING TO PROVE, / THAT THEY WERE WRITTEN, NOT BY ANY ANCIENT / AUTHOR, / BUT ENTIRELY BY THOMAS CHATTERTON. / LONDON: / Printed for T. PAYNE and SON, / at the MEWS-GATE. / — / M DCC LXXVIII [1778]. (Keynes)

The copy with 'William Blake' written on the title-page and the authenticating signature of 'Samuel Palmer' on the inside cover is in the collection of Sir *Geoffrey Keynes*.

CHEVRIER, François Antoine

719. *The Political Testament of the Marshal Duke of Belleisle.* London: Printed for P. Vaillant, and D. Wilson, in the Strand. 1762. (Charles Feinberg)

'W. Blake' in a hand very much like the poet's is on the half-title of the copy in the possession of Mr. *Charles Feinberg* of Detroit.

CUMBERLAND, George

720. = / THOUGHTS ON OUTLINE, SCULPTURE, AND THE SYSTEM / THAT GUIDED THE ANCIENT ARTISTS IN COMPOSING THEIR / FIGURES AND GROUPES: / ACCOMPANIED WITH FREE RE-MARKS ON THE PRACTICE OF / THE MODERNS, AND LIBERAL HINTS CORDIALLY INTENDED / FOR THEIR ADVANTAGE. / TO WHICH ARE ANNEXED TWENTY-FOUR DESIGNS OF CLASSICAL SUBJECTS INVENTED ON THE PRINCIPLES RE- / COMMENDED IN THE ESSAY BY GEORGE CUMBERLAND. / = / AINSI IO SON PITTORE. / = / LONDON. PRINTED BY W. WILSON, ST. PETER'S-HILL, DOCTORS'-COMMONS: AND SOLD / BY MESSRS. ROBIN-SON, PATERNOSTER-ROW; AND T. EGERTON, WHITEHALL. MDCCXCVI [1796].

In an undated diary reference (*Blake Records* [1969], 55), Cumberland noted that he had given away 19 bound copies of his *Thoughts on Outline*, including one to 'Mr Blake', who had engraved some of the designs. The date of the gift was probably Aug. 1796, for James Townly, who also appears in Cumberland's list, thanked the donor on 2 Sept. 1796 (BM Add. MSS 36498, f. 123), as did Blake on 23 Dec. 1796. Blake's copy is *UNTRACED*.

Dante Alighieri

721. A / TRANSLATION / OF THE / INFERNO / OF / *DANTE ALI-GHIERI,* / IN ENGLISH VERSE. / WITH / HISTORICAL NOTES, AND THE LIFE OF *DANTE.* / TO WHICH IS ADDED, / A SPECIMEN OF A NEW TRANSLATION / OF THE / ORLANDO FURIOSO / OF / *ARIOSTO.* / — / By HENRY BOYD, A.M. / = / DUBLIN: / PRINTED BY P. BYRNE. 1785.

COLLECTION: Sir Geoffrey Keynes.

DATE OF ANNOTATION: ?1800.

In the subscription list is 'William Hayley, Esq. 7 sets'. Hayley may have given Blake a set soon after Blake moved to Felpham to work with him in Sept. 1800. Blake's concern for political liberty in his comments is consistent with a date of 1800.

DESCRIPTION: The first endpaper is inscribed by A. H. Palmer, 'Samuel Palmer's copy' and

This volume as far back as I can remember, stood upon one of my father's bookshelves by the side of books annotated or illustrated by Blake. Among them was the now well-known copy of Lavater's 'Aphorisms' . . . Bacon's Essays with Blake's notes were there, Hayley's Ballads, and a Copy of Thornton['*s Virgil.*]

Up to p. 131, Blake's comments are in ink; thereafter they are in pencil. There is an erasure on p. 209. In addition to Blake's annotations, there are a number of corrections to the text[1] as follows: p. 193, 'His look' to 'Her look'; p. 207, 'wand'ring son' to 'wand'rings on'; pp. 312, 316, 'noisome frogs' to 'noisome fogs'; p. 313, 'Hide' to 'Hid'; p. 360, 'her' to 'his'; p. 326, in the sentence 'Epicurus . . . thought the Louban air of fleeting breath' the strange noun was changed to 'Soul an'.

BINDING: Bound in early nineteenth-century cloth.

HISTORY: (1) It was 'Samuel Palmer's copy' (according to the note on the first endpaper), from whom it was inherited by his son (2) A. H. Palmer, who wrote other notes on the endpaper, and bequeathed it to his son (3) Bryan Palmer, who sold it in 1957 to (4) Sir *Geoffrey Keynes,* according to Keynes's catalogue (1964), no. 722.

Duché, Jacob

722. *Discourses on Various Subjects.* [2 vols.] London: Printed by J. Phillips, George-Yard, Lombard-Street; And Sold by T. Cadell, in the Strand; H. Payne, Pall-Mall; C. Dilly, in the Poultry; and J. Phillips. 1779.

The likelihood that the 'Mr. William Blake' among the subscribers is the poet is increased by the facts that his friend William Sharp both engraved the plates for and subscribed to this work. Sharp also apparently took care of the publishing details of the book, for he signed a draft to pay Mr. Hoquet on

---

[1] There is no Errata list. Erdman (p. 801) says the corrections are 'not [*by*] Blake', but he does not say how he knows. In addition, he says that on p. 187 Blake added the Italian above the English text: 'Nel mezzo del cummin de nostra vita'.

demand £12. 12s. 0d. 'on account of printing, for Mʳ Duchee' (Princeton), 21 Dec. 1779. However, if Blake owned a copy, it is *UNTRACED.*

FALCONER, William, a Sailor

723. *The Shipwreck*, A Poem. The Text Illustrated by Additional Notes, and Corrected from the First and Second Editions, with A Life of the Author, by James Stanier Clarke. London. Printed for William Miller, Old Bond Street, By T. Bensley, Bolt Court, 1804.

On 4 May 1804 Blake thanked Hayley 'sincerely for Falconer, an admirable poet, and the admirable prints to it by Fittler'. This is the first edition in which appeared the five vignettes and three large plates 'by J. Fittler, R.A.S. Marine Engraver to His Majesty; from Paintings by N. Pocock, Esq.' to illustrate the popular poem of this 'second Homer' (p. xxvi). Blake clearly valued the book, for he derived from it 'some excellent hints in engraving', but his copy is *UNTRACED.* Hayley's interest in the book presumably derived from his friendship with the editor, J. S. Clarke.

GAY, John

724. FABLES / By / *JOHN GAY,* / With a Life of the Author / AND / *embellished with Seventy Plates.* / [Vignette] / Vol. I [II]. / — / LONDON / *PRINTED FOR JOHN STOCKDALE, PICCADILLY* / 1793.

The likelihood that the 'Blake Mr.' in the subscription list is the poet is increased to near certainty by the fact that six of the other seven engravers for this edition (Messrs. Audinet, Granger, Lovegrove, Mazell, Skelton, and Wilson) also appear in the same list similarly shorn of their Christian names. However, Blake's copy (if he had one) is *UNTRACED.*

GORDON, William

725. *The History of the Rise, Progress, and Establishment of the Independence of the United States of America*: Including an Account of the Late War; and of the Thirteen Colonies, from their Origin to that Period. In Four Volumes. London: Printed for the Author; and sold by Charles Dilly, in the Poultry; and James Buckland, in Pater-noster-Row. 1788. [Entered at Stationer's Hall] (LC and Cleveland Public Library.)

'William Blake esq' is listed among the British subscribers, and the poet's known interest in America at this time makes him a strong possibility. If he owned a copy, however, it is *UNTRACED.*

HAY, Alexander

726. *The History of Chichester*; interspersed with Various Notes and Observations on the Early and Present State of the City, The most Remarkable Places in its Vicinity, And the County of Sussex in General: with an Appendix, Containing the Charters of the City, at three different Times; also an Account of all the Parishes in the County, their names, patronage, appropriations, value in the king's books, first-fruits, &c. Dedicated, by Permission, To William Hayley, Esqr. Chichester: Printed and sold by J. Seagrave;

the Booksellers in the County, and by Longman and Co. Paternoster-Row, London. 1804.

The dedicatee evidently wrote to Blake that he was sending as a present one of the 'four copies, large paper', for which he had subscribed, for on 18 Dec. 1804 Blake replied: 'I have not yet received the *History of Chichester*. I mention this not because I would hasten its arrival before it is convenient, but fancy it may have miscarried.' Probably the book had only just been published, for the preface is dated Sept. 1804, and the delay was due to Seagrave rather than to Hayley. Blake presumably received a copy in time, but if so it is *UNTRACED*.

HAYLEY, William

727. THE / LIFE, / AND / *POSTHUMOUS WRITINGS*, / OF / WILLIAM COWPER, EsQR. / WITH AN / INTRODUCTORY LETTER, / TO THE / *RIGHT HONOURABLE EARL COWPER*. / = / By WILLIAM HAYLEY, EsQR. / [5-line motto] / = / VOL. I[–III]. / = / Chichester: / *Printed by J. Seagrave*; / FOR J. JOHNSON, ST. PAUL'S CHURCH-YARD, LONDON. / — / [Vol. I–II:] 1803, [Vol. III:] 1804.

On 4 May 1804 Blake asked Hayley to 'Accept, also, of my thanks for Cowper's third volume, which I got, as you directed, of Mr. Johnson.' Hayley had clearly told his publisher to give Blake a copy of Vol. III of his biography, for which Blake had engraved two plates; it would be surprising if Blake had not been given the first two volumes as well, for which he had made four plates. However, if he did receive them, they are *UNTRACED*.

728. *The Triumph of Music*; A Poem: In Six Cantos. Chichester Printed by and for J. Seagrave; and sold by T. Payne, Mew's Gate—J. Johnson, St. Paul's Church-Yard—R. H. Evans, Pall-Mall—and Longman, and Co. Paternoster Row, London. 1804.

Hayley's interminable poem about a girl named Venusia and the moral effect of music is diplomatically referred to by Blake on 18 Dec. 1804: 'Your beautiful and elegant daughter *Venusea* grows in our estimation on a second and third perusal.' (There is no such work as that cited by Keynes, 1957, p. 853: '*Venusia*, a long poem by Hayley, published by Henry Seagrave, Chichester, 1804.') We may be confident that Hayley gave him *The Triumph of Music*, though his copy is *UNTRACED*.

729. *The Triumphs of Temper*; A Poem: In Six Cantos. The Tenth Edition, Corrected. London: Printed for T. Cadell, jun. and W. Davies, in the Strand. 1799.

J. T. Smith, *Nollkens and his Times* (1828), II. 465–6, records a poem which Hayley wrote in the copy of his *Triumphs of Temper* which he gave to Blake in 1800, and Gilchrist (1942), 125, identifies this as the 'tenth edition'. Hayley's draft of the poem is now in Trinity College (Hartford, Conn.), but Blake's copy of the *Triumphs of Temper* (1799) is *UNTRACED*.

730. THE / TRIUMPHS / OF / TEMPER. / *A POEM*: / IN SIX CANTOS. / — / By WILLIAM HAYLEY EsQ. / — / O voi ch'avete gl'intelletti sani /

Mirate la dottrina, che si asconde / Sotto'il velame degli versi strani. / DANTE, Inferno, Canto 9. / — / THE TWELFTH EDITION, COR-RECTED. / *With New Original Designs*, / BY MARIA FLAXMAN. / = / CHICHESTER: / *Printed by J. Seagrave*; / FOR T. CADELL AND W. DAVIES, STRAND, / LONDON. / — / 1803. (BM)

A large-paper copy in the British Museum (11656 c 8) is inscribed 'To / Mrs Blake / from the Author / 1803'. On p. 51, the last six lines are bracketed in pencil; on p. 53 the last three lines of a footnote on Dante are bracketed in pencil, and some lines are underscored; and on pp. 54–5 are brackets spanning the pages. There is an inlaid frontispiece of Hayley after Romney published 30 April 1797 by Bellamy at the Monthly Mirror Office.

HOMER

731. *The Whole Works of Homer*; Prince of Poetts In his Iliads, and Odysses. Translated according to the Greeke, By Geo: Chapman. At London printed for Nathaniell Butter. William Hole sculp: [1616].

On 18 May 1829 Mrs. Blake sold her husband's copy of the 'Illiad & Oddisy' to John Linnell for £1. 11s. 6d. (*Blake Records* [1969], 584), and A. T. Story, *The Life of John Linnell* (1892), i. 78, identifies it as the 1616 Chapman edition. Blake's copy is now *UNTRACED*.

(The sentence of marginalia conjecturally quoted from it by Keynes in his edition of Blake's *Letters* [1956] turned out later [Keynes (1957), 412] to be an annotation to Boyd's translation of Dante's *Inferno*.)

732. THE / ILIAD AND ODYSSEY / OF / HOMER, / TRANSLATED INTO / ENGLISH BLANK VERSE, / BY W. COWPER, / OF THE INNER TEMPLE, ESQ. / IN TWO VOLUMES. / VOL. I [II.] / CON-TAINING THE ILIAD [ODYSSEY, AND / THE BATTLE OF THE FROGS AND MICE]. / LONDON: / PRINTED FOR J. JOHNSON, N° 72 ST. PAUL'S CHURCH-YARD. / M DCC XCI [1791].

Among the subscribers are 'W. Blake, Esq' and 'Mr. W. Blake, Engraver'. The latter must be the poet, but, if so, his copy is *UNTRACED*.

HURDIS, James

733. POEMS / BY / THE REV. JAMES HURDIS, D.D. / LATE FELLOW OF MAGDALEN COLLEGE, / AND PROFESSOR OF POETRY IN THE UNIVERSITY / OF OXFORD. / — / IN THREE VOLUMES. / — / VOL. I [II] [III]. / — / OXFORD, / At the University Press for J. PARKER; / Messrs. RIVINGTON, St. Paul's Church Yard, and Messrs. / LONGMAN and Co. Pater-Noster Row, London. / 1808.

'Mr. Blake' appears in the subscription list (Vol. I, p. xxx) and may well be the poet. William Hayley, Blake's erstwhile patron, had been a good friend to Hurdis, had advised on editing his poems, subscribed for them, and urged Blake's London friend Joseph Johnson to 'exert his zeal' in finding subscribers (Hayley, *Memoirs* [1823], ii. 157–9). It seems likely that either Johnson or Hayley asked Blake to subscribe; however, if he did his copy is *UNTRACED*.

LA MOTTE FOUQUÉ, Frederic Heinrich Carl Baron de

734. SINTRAM / AND HIS COMPANIONS: / A ROMANCE. / FROM THE GERMAN / OF / FREDERIC / BARON DE LA MOTTE FOUQUÉ, / AUTHOR OF UNDINE, &c. / [Tr. Julius C. Hare] LONDON: / C. and J. OLLIER, VERE STREET, BOND STREET; / AND WILLIAM BLACKWOOD, EDINBURGH. / 1820 (BM, GEB)

Crabb Robinson wrote in his diary for 7 Dec. 1826: 'He produced *Sintram* by Fouqué— ⌜"⌝This is better than my things!"' (*Blake Records* [1969], 337) Robinson's implication is that Blake owned a copy of this enormously popular work, but if so it is *UNTRACED*.

LAVATER, John Caspar

735. APHORISMS ON MAN / TRANSLATED [by J. H. Fuseli] / FROM THE ORIGINAL MANUSCRIPT / OF / THE REV. JOHN CASPAR LAVATER, / CITIZEN OF ZURIC. / — / ——è cœlo descendit γνωθι σεαυτον / Juv. Sat. IX. / — / LONDON: / PRINTED FOR J. JOHNSON, / ST. PAUL'S CHURCH-YARD. / — / MDCCLXXXVIII [1788].

COLLECTION: Huntington Library.

DATE OF ANNOTATION: 1788.

From the facts that Blake engraved the frontispiece for this edition of Lavater's *Aphorisms*, and that his friend Fuseli made the translation, it may be confidently concluded that Blake read and annotated the volume in the year of publication.

DESCRIPTION: On the title-page Blake wrote '*Willm Blake*' below 'LAVA-TER' and drew a heart around the two names in ink, and at the top of p. 1 he wrote 'Will. Blake' in the same ink as the notes. The notes on some paragraphs (e.g. 11, 39, 97, 98, 163, 410), the change from pencil to ink, and the change in pen-points indicate that Blake went through the book making comments several times.

Offsets: Faint impressions left by the ink before it dried appear in the normal way on the following facing pages: 42–3, 118–19, 156–7, 162–3, 170–1, 172–3, 174–5, 180–1, 188–9, 190–1, 204–5, 218–19, 220–1, 222–3, and the notes on these pages may have been made after the book was bound. Other offsets, however, were transferred from pages which do not at present face one another, and therefore the notes must have been made when the sheets were unbound. These are: 97 (G1r)–100 (G2v); 115 (H2r)–120 (H4v); 135 (I4r)–82 (F1v); 224 (O8v)–208 (N8v); *upside-down*: 64 (D8v)–66 (E1v), 139 (I6r)–209 (O1r); 207 (N8r)–134 (I3v). Clearly the sheets were stacked on each other, higgledy-piggledy, when the ink of the annotations was still fresh and before the sheets were bound.

Erasures: There are illegible erasures by ¶ 70, 342, 452, 533, 612 ('?for . . . persons'), 638.

Xs: There are Xs in the margin[1] beside ¶ 21, 32, 36, 37, 39, 54, 70, 71,

---

[1] Erdman (pp. 573–90) gives these as if they were by Blake. He says as well that the horizontal line in the margin beside ¶ 25 and the daggers by ¶ 289, 343 are by Blake. He seems sure that the pencil comments to ¶ 20, 503 are 'by two different writers', but Keynes (1957) and I think they are by Blake.

86, 92, 96–8, 121, 141, 150–1, 163–4, 168, 219, 226, 261, 276, 308, 338, 385–6, 389, 410, 414, 440, 444, 449, 460, 465, 486, 514, 518, 526, 543, 577, 588, 602 (?under the writing), 607, 619, 624, 638.

Pencil and Pen: Blake's comments on ¶ 10, 285, 287, 502, and 532 are in pencil; the rest are in ink. A dull pen is superseded by a conspicuously sharper one in ¶ 68, 71 (at the full stop), 124, 309 (at 'mark'), 334, 409 (after 'Noble'), 526, 539 (at 'a mans female').

Corrections: The substantive misprints identified in the printed Errata list have been corrected.

Notes by Others: After Blake's comment on ¶ 21, 'See 384'[1] is written in a yellowed ink; after ¶ 280 is '115'; and after ¶ 384 is 'See 20 & 21'[1] in the same ink. ¶ 165 has parallel lines beside it in the margin in an ink somewhat different from that of Blake's comments. At the top of p. 220 (¶ 633) an unknown hand has written in pencil: 'Not an Apho[*rism*]'.

BINDING: (1) Bound after Blake had made notes in the margins, in sheep-skin; (2) After this became broken, it was 'BOUND BY W. R. SMITH' in Ochre morocco, t.e.g., for Robert Hoe in the late nineteenth century.

HISTORY: (1) Blake made his notes when the sheets were not bound[2] and showed them 'to Fuseli; who said one could assuredly read their writer's character in *them*';[3] (2) Acquired by Robert Hoe, who added his bookplate, and wrote a note now pasted in: 'This copy which was Blake's, had to be rebound; it was in broken sheepskin, and more than dirty. All the writing by Blake on the [*back*] fly leaves is carefully preserved. R. H.'; sold posthumously with Hoe's Library at Anderson Galleries, 25 April 1911, lot 396, for $1,525 to (3) The HUNTINGTON LIBRARY.

PERCY, Bishop Thomas, ed.

736. RELIQUES / OF / ANCIENT ENGLISH POETRY: / CONSISTING OF / Old Heroic BALLADS, SONGS, and other / PIECES of our earlier POETS, / (Chiefly of the LYRIC kind.) / Together with some few of later Date. / VOLUME THE FIRST [SECOND] [THIRD]. / [Vignette] / LONDON: / Printed for J. DODSLEY in Pall-Mall. / M DCC LXV [1765] (Wellesley)

The Wellesley copy is inscribed by John Linnell's wife 'Mary Ann Linnell / The gift of Mr W– Blake'. The trifling alterations in the text in pencil and in ink are probably not by the poet.

REYNOLDS, Joshua

737. THE / WORKS / OF / SIR JOSHUA REYNOLDS, KNIGHT; / LATE PRESIDENT OF THE ROYAL ACADEMY: / CONTAINING / HIS DISCOURSES, IDLERS, / A JOURNEY TO FLANDERS AND HOL-LAND, / AND HIS COMMENTARY ON DU FRESNOY'S ART OF /

---

[1] See note 1 on p. 690.

[2] As shown by offsets from p. 64 to p. 66, from p. 97 to p. 100, from p. 115 to p. 120, from p. 135 to p. 82, from p. 224 to p. 208, from p. 139 to p. 209 (upside-down), and from p. 207 to p. 134 (upside-down).

[3] Gilchrist *Life of William Blake* (1863), i. 62. He also showed them to John Linnell, who transcribed them into a copy of the 1794 edition now in Yale.

PAINTING; / PRINTED FROM HIS REVISED COPIES, / (WITH HIS LATEST CORRECTIONS AND ADDITIONS,) / *IN THREE VOLUMES.* / TO WHICH IS PREFIXED / AN ACCOUNT OF THE LIFE AND WRITINGS OF THE / AUTHOR, / By EDMOND MALONE, Esǫ. / ONE OF HIS EXECUTORS. / THE SECOND EDITION CORRECTED. / — QUASI NON EA PRÆCIPIAM ALIIS, QUÆ MIHI IPSI DESUNT. CICERO. / — / VOLUME THE FIRST. / — / *LONDON:* / PRINTED FOR T. CADELL, JUN. AND W. DAVIES, IN THE STRAND. / 1798.

Collection: British Museum.

Dates of Annotation: ?1801–2, 1808–9.

Blake's annotations to Reynolds were probably written at two distinct periods, perhaps first about 1801–2 and second in 1808–9.[1]

Twice in his letters he cites the opinions of Sir Joshua, and on each occasion he had been making a prolonged and careful study of theories of colouring. On 22 Nov. 1802 he told Butts:

> I have now given two years to the intense study of those parts of the art which relate to light & shade & colour . . . . All Sʳ J Reynolds's discourses to the Royal Academy will shew, that the Venetian finesse in Art can never be united with the Majesty of Colouring necessary to Historical beauty⌊.⌋

Perhaps during these two years (1801–2) Blake made the series of pencil comments in his copy of Reynolds's *Works.* These pencil notes seem rather more temperate and less personal than those he made later.

In May 1809 Blake told Ozias Humphry: 'you demand of me to Mix two things that Reynolds has confessed cannot be mixed. . . . Florentine & Venetian Art cannot exist together⌊.⌋' For some time he had been brooding over his wrongs at the hands of Cromek and the scant public patronage he had attracted and preparing 'an account of my various Inventions in Art'.[2] Probably at this time (1808–9) he went through Reynolds's *Works* once again, confirming many of the old pencil comments in ink, and making a great many new ones. The ink notes are distinguished from those written originally in pencil by their virulence, by the personal rancour they display against 'Sʳ Joshua & his Gang of Cunning Hired Knaves' (title-page verso), and by their concern for Venetian colour. These differences are also reflected in various forms in Blake's *Descriptive Catalogue* (1809), in his 'Public Address' (?1810–11), and in several poems in the *Notebook* apparently written just before or during the composition of the two former, particularly one replying directly to Reynolds's last Lecture.

Even if the two dates, 1801–2 and 1808–9, are accepted, it is possible that a few of the annotations were made between 1802 and 1808 or after 1809.

---

[1] Blake probably heard some of the lectures delivered from the time when he became a student at the Royal Academy in 1779, and he could also have read them as they were individually printed before the collected editions of 1797 and 1798. The references to Fuseli's Milton Gallery (1799–1800) on the title-page verso and pp. i, 3 suggest a date after 1800.

[2] As he told Cumberland on 19 Dec. 1809. The reference in ink on p. 4 to the British Insttiution must be after that society was founded in 1805. A note on p. 159 was incorporated in the *Descriptive Catalogue* (1809), ¶ 3, and another on p. 2 in *Jerusalem* (1804–?20) pl. 43, l. 35.

Some of the ink comments may have been made before 1808, and some of the pencil comments (e.g. on pp. 144, 147) were certainly made after the ink notes on the same pages.

DESCRIPTION: The three volumes are now in uniform modern bindings heavily trimmed on all sides,[1] but only the first volume (containing Malone's 'Life' and Reynolds's first eight Discourses) has Blake's annotations or any indication of his ownership. Some of the poems in Blake's *Notebook* were directly stimulated by Discourses in the second volume of Reynolds's *Works*, but there is no direct evidence that Blake owned and annotated any volume except the first.[2] The comment on p. xlvii is so far into the inner margin that it must have been written before the sheets were bound.

Pencil and Ink: The first notes seem to have been made in *pencil only* on pp. ix, xxxiv, xlvii, lx, xcvi, civ (erasure), cxx, 13, 30, 48, 61, 65, 67, 75 bottom, 92 (all but the top three words), 93 bottom, 98 bottom, 99, 100 top and bottom, 133 bottom, 144 top, 147 top seven words, 152 top, 158, 159 top, 180, 209, 256, 260, 262, 264, 266–7, 272, 274–5, 277, 281, 284, 285 (that is, from 256 on except for pp. 279, 286).

Later many *pencil notes were darkened in ink* on the title-page verso, Contents [i], [iii]–[v], i–ii, xiv–xix, xxix, xlii, lvii, lxxxix–xc, xcviii–xcix, ciii–civ, cxi, [2]–5 top, 9, 26, 32 top four words, 35, 37, 40, 41 top, 47, 52, 55–6, 58, 60, 62–4, 71, 74–5 top, 78–80, 83 bottom, 89–90, 92 top three words, 93[3]–5, 98 (all but the poem), 100 (middle only), 106, 109–10, 114, 118–20, 123–7, 129, 132–3 (all but the last four words), 134, 144 (the pencil begins with 'by Men'), 147 (but not the top seven words), 152 (but not the top), 157 (but not the last sentence), 159 (all but the first paragraph, the numbers, and the second 'born', for which read '. . .'), 165–7, 172, 176, 178–9, 196, 208 bottom, 245 bottom, 251 bottom. Sometimes of course he changed the text a little when confirming it in ink.

The notes *in ink only*[4] are in effect additions to the title-page, iii, viii, xlix, l, liii, lxx, lxxii, cix, 5 bottom, 7, 11, 14–18, 22–3, 25, 29, 32 (all but the top four words), 33–4, 42–3, 50, 54, 57, 82, 83 top, 86–7, 92 bottom, 93 bottom, 98 bottom, 99, 100 bottom, 101–4, 111–12, 116–17, 121, 128, 131, 133 bottom, 135, 137–9, 141–2, 144 top, 147 top, 149, 152 top, 153–5, 157 bottom, 159 some, 161, 163, 188, 194–5, 197–204, 208 top, 214–15, 232, 242, 244–5 top, 251 top, 279, 286. For a discussion of the implications of these writing variations, see the *DATE* above.

Erasures: There are erasures on pp. civ footnote, 30, 36, 38, 75, 87.

A misprint ('reserved' for 'reversed') is corrected on p. 273.

Comments in other hands are written after Blake's on pp. 83, 134.

BINDING: All three volumes are bound in uniform modern leather, heavily trimmed, though only Vol. I has any overt connection with Blake.

---

[1] A number of letters and words from Blake's marginalia were cropped off in the process.

[2] The reference (title-page verso) to 'my Remarks on these Books', plural, might suggest that he annotated Vols. II and III as well. If so, they were separated from Vol. I by 1865, when the above set entered the British Museum.

[3] The pencil passage on p. 93 is inked over only as far as 'Form'.

[4] Erdman (p. 801) treats all these 'notes in ink only . . . as additions'.

HISTORY: (1) Acquired on 27 April 1865 by the BRITISH MUSEUM.

SHENSTONE, William

738. THE / POETICAL WORKS / OF / WILL. SHENSTONE. / WITH / *THE LIFE OF THE AUTHOR,* / AND / A DESCRIPTION OF THE LEASOWES. = / Cooke's Edition. / = / [21 lines of verse] / = / EMBELLISHED WITH SUPERB ENGRAVINGS. / = / London: / Printed for C. COOKE, No. 17, Paternoster-Row; / And sold by all the Booksellers in / Great Britain and / Ireland [1795]. [A duplicate title-page reads:] THE / POETICAL WORKS / OF / WILL. SHENSTONE. / CONTAINING HIS / [Column 1:] ELEGIES, / LEVITIES, OR PIECES / OF HUMOUR, / [Column 2:] PASTORALS, / ODES, / SONGS AND BALLADS, [end of columns] / MORAL PIECES, &c. &c. / = / [17 different lines of verse] / = / London: / PRINTED AND EMBELLISHED / Under the Direction of / C. COOKE [1795]. (Keynes)

The date of this copy derives from the three plates dated 1794 and 1795; the work was evidently issued with the same title-pages but different plates, for of the 4 plates in the Toronto copy, one is dated 1798 and one 1800.

The signature of the poet, 'Wm Blake / 1799', appears on the fly-leaf of the copy obtained in 1971 by Sir Geoffrey Keynes.

SPURZHEIM, J. G.

739. OBSERVATIONS / ON THE / DERANGED MANIFESTATIONS / OF / THE MIND, / OR / INSANITY. / = / BY / J. G. SPURZHEIM, M.D. / LICENTIATE OF THE COLLEGE OF PHYSICIANS OF LONDON, PHYSICIAN TO THE / AUSTRIAN EMBASSY, AUTHOR OF THE 'PHYSIOGNOMICAL SYSTEM / OF DRS. GALL AND SPURZHEIM,' ETC. / — / WITH FOUR COPPER PLATES. / — / 'NOTHING TENDS MORE TO THE CORRUPTION OF SCIENCE THAN / TO SUFFER IT TO STAGNATE.' / = / LONDON: / PRINTED FOR BALDWIN, CRADOCK, AND JOY, / 47, PATERNOSTER-ROW. / — / 1817.

COLLECTION: *UNTRACED*; see below.

DATE OF ANNOTATION: ?1818.

Blake's long interest in phrenology was probably stimulated anew by Spurzheim's book shortly after it was published in June 1817. Not long thereafter, he began producing his Visionary Heads for Varley, which are clearly related to the phrenological theories of Spurzheim, Lavater, and others.

DESCRIPTION: The only direct information about Blake's notes to Spurzheim is to be found in *The Works of William Blake,* ed. E. J. Ellis & W. B. Yeats (1893), i. 154–5:

A fragment of paper, seemingly torn off to make a hasty memorandum of the incident, is preserved by the Linnell brothers among the sheets of the Vala MS.[1] It is

---

[1] The Spurzheim note is not now with the *Vala* MS in the British Museum.

in Blake's handwriting, and bears no sign of having been of the nature of a letter. . . .
It is a note made while reading Spurzheim, in a copy[1] where marginal pencillings
were either not permitted, or insufficient. The words are as follows:—'Methodism,
&c. 154. . . .' And to a previous page, 106, he has, on the same piece of paper,
'Corporeal disease . . . .'

The passages from Spurzheim to which Blake evidently refers are not given
by Ellis & Yeats.

BINDING: Binding unknown because untraced; Blake's notes were on a
loose scrap of paper.

HISTORY: (1) Seen by Ellis & Yeats, who quoted it in 1893; (2) *UNTRACED*.

STEDMAN, J. G.

740. NARRATIVE, / *of a five years' expedition, against the* / Revolted Negroes
of Surinam, / *in GUIANA, on the WILD COAST of* / SOUTH AMERICA; /
from the year 1771, to 1777: / *elucidating the History of that Country, and* / describing its Productions, *Viz.* / *Quadrupedes, Birds, Fishes, Reptiles, Trees, Shrubs,
Fruits, & Roots;* / *with an account of the INDIANS of Guiana, & NEGROES of
Guinea.* / By CAPT.ᴺ J. G. STEDMAN. / *illustrated with 80 elegant Engravings, from drawings made by the Author.* / VOL. I [II]. / [Vignette and 6-line
motto from] / *Valerius Flaccus.* / London. Printed for J. Johnson, S.ᵗ Paul's
Church Yard, & J. Edwards, Pall Mall. 1796.

The 'Blake (Mr. Wm.) London' who appears in the subscription list is
almost certainly the poet, who engraved 16 plates for the work, but his copy
is *UNTRACED*. (The same subscription list appears in the editions of
1806, 1813, but clearly the subscribers received only the first edition.)

SWEDENBORG, Emanuel

741. A / TREATISE / CONCERNING / HEAVEN AND HELL, / AND
OF THE / Wonderful Things therein, / AS / HEARD AND SEEN, / BY
THE HONOURABLE AND LEARNED / EMANUEL SWEDENBORG,
/ Of the SENATORIAL ORDER of NOBLES in the Kingdom of SWEDEN. / — /
TRANSLATED FROM THE ORIGINAL LATIN [by William Cookworth & Thomas
Hartley]. / — / THE SECOND EDITION. / — / Where there is no Vision,
the people perish. Prov. xxix. 18. / The invisible things of Him from the
creation of the world are clearly / seen, being understood by the things that
are made. Rom. i. 20. / He that hath ears to hear, let him hear. Luke xiv.
35. / = / London: Printed by R. HINDMARSH, No. 32, Clerkenwell-
Close; / And Sold by T. EVANS, AND T. BUCKLAND, Paternoster-Row; / J.
DENIS and SON, New-Bridge-Street, Fleet-Street; / I. CLARK, Manchester;
T. MILLS, Wine-Street, Bristol; / S. HAZARD, Bath; and by all the other
Booksellers in Town / and Country. / M.DCC.LXXXIV [1784].

COLLECTION: Harvard.

DATE OF ANNOTATION: ?1788.

The reference to a book of 1787 provides the earliest date for Blake's

[1] Perhaps the copy Blake saw was Linnell's, bought from Spurzheim on 14 June 1817,
according to Linnell's Ledger (in the Ivimy MS).

marginalia. The latest is probably 1790, when such eager interest as the comments suggest was modified by disillusionment. 1788 is a plausible guess between the two.

DESCRIPTION: On the title-page is the signature 'William Blake'. Another hand has made a note on the half-title on which in turn Blake comments vigorously, indicating that Blake was not the first annotator.[1]

HISTORY: (1) Acquired by an unknown owner, who made notes on the title-page; (2) Acquired by Blake, who wrote his name on the title-page and commented on the previous owner's notes; (3) Acquired by 'Louise Kennedy / 1897' (according to the note on the fly-leaf); (4) Given by Mrs. Mildred Kennedy in March 1960 to (5) HARVARD.

742. THE / WISDOM / OF / *ANGELS*, / CONCERNING / DIVINE LOVE / AND / DIVINE WISDOM. / — / TRANSLATED FROM THE ORIGINAL LATIN / OF THE / *Hon. EMANUEL SWEDENBORG* [by Dr. N. Tucker]. / — / LONDON: / PRINTED BY W. CHALKLEN, GROCERS COURT, POULTRY. / M.DCC.LXXXVIII [1788].

COLLECTION: British Museum.

DATE OF ANNOTATION: ?1789.

The relatively uncritical nature of Blake's comments suggests that they were written before his disillusionment with Swedenborg about 1790, while the reference to what 'was asserted in the society' (p. 429), which Blake and his wife joined in April 1789,[2] implies a date after the spring of 1789.

DESCRIPTION: A note on the half-title says 'the Volume came' from 'Mr Tatham'. Blake's comments are in pencil, many of them, particularly those on the fly-leaf, very dim indeed.[3] The annotations continue through the volume quite steadily except for gaps between pp. 58 and 131, between 146 and 181, between 233 and 268, and between 295 and 410.

HISTORY: (1) Acquired by Frederick Tatham, probably from Catherine Blake at her death in 1831; (2) 'The Ms. notes [*are*] by Blake the Artist— acc[*ordin*]g to [?] Mr Tatham (an architect) a friend of Blake, from whose possession the Volume came. / Jan. 1, 1839' (according to the note in an unknown hand on the half-title); (3) Sold with the A. G. Dew-Smith Library at Sotheby's, 29 Jan. 1878, lot 15, for £6 to Ellis; (4) Acquired by the BRITISH MUSEUM, perhaps for the '10/–/–' inscribed on the cover.

743. THE / WISDOM / OF / *ANGELS* / CONCERNING THE / DIVINE PROVIDENCE. / — / TRANSLATED FROM THE LATIN / OF THE / *Hon. EMANUEL SWEDENBORG* [by Dr. N. Tucker]. / — / Originally Published at AMSTERDAM, Anno 1764. / = / *LONDON*: / Printed and Sold by R. Hindmarsh, / PRINTER TO HIS ROYAL HIGHNESS THE PRINCE OF WALES, / No. 32, *CLERKENWELL-CLOSE*, / And may be had by

---

[1] ¶¶ 333–4 are quoted by Erdman (p. 591) because they were 'scored' as 'by [*a*] fingernail', but he does not say how he knows the fingernail was Blake's.

[2] *Blake Records* (1969), 35.

[3] Erdman (p. 597) prints ¶ 336 because he assumes that the cross beside it is by Blake.

giving Orders to any of the Booksellers / in Town or Country. / M.DCC.XC [1790].

COLLECTION: Sir Geoffrey Keynes.

DATE OF ANNOTATION: ?1790.

Blake was clearly sympathetic to Swedenborg's New Jerusalem Church when he joined it in April 1789[1] and sharply critical when he wrote the *Marriage* (?1790–3). The vigour of Blake's indignation with Swedenborg's 'Cursed Folly' (p. 434) in the *Divine Providence* implies a recent disillusionment and a date for Blake's marginalia shortly after the book's publication in 1790.

DESCRIPTION: 'William Blake' appears on the half-title. All the notes are in pencil. The original boards and label are still present, though rather battered. The leaves are not trimmed.

BINDING: Bound in the original boards, rather battered.

HISTORY: (1) Acquired (probably for the published price of 7s. 6d.) by 'William Blake', who wrote his name on the half-title; (2) Acquired by Samuel Palmer, who added his monogram and probably put on the Gold label with '147'; (3) Perhaps it was this work (Swedenborg's 'Wisdom of Angels') which was lent by Mr. J. R. Kirby to the Burlington Fine Arts Club exhibition (1876), no. 333; (4) Acquired by James Spiers (according to J. Hyde, *Bibliography of the Works of Emmanuel Swedenborg* [1906]); (5) In 1920 it belonged to C. H. Whittington (according to Keynes [1921]); (6) Acquired by *Geoffrey Keynes*, who wrote his name on the first fly-leaf, and described it in his catalogue (1964), no. 724.

TATHAM, Charles Heathcote

744. *ETCHINGS, / REPRESENTING THE BEST EXAMPLES / OF / ANCIENT ORNAMENTAL / ARCHITECTURE;* / DRAWN FROM THE ORIGINALS / IN / ROME, / AND OTHER PARTS OF ITALY, / DURING THE YEARS 1794, 1795, and 1796. / BY CHARLES HEATHCOTE TATHAM, ARCHITECT; / MEMBER OF THE ACADEMY OF SAINT LUKE AT ROME, / AND THE INSTITUTE AT BOLOGNA. / [Motto from Pliny] / LONDON: / PRINTED FOR THE AUTHOR, / AND SOLD BY / THOMAS GARDINER, BOOKSELLER, PRINCES STREET, CAVENDISH SQUARE. / MDCCXCIX [1799]. (BM, Cleveland Public)

The 'Mr. William Blake' who appears in the subscription list (p. 9) may with some confidence be identified as the poet, for *America* (B) is inscribed 'From the author to C H Tatham Oct[r] 7 1799'. Blake's copy is *UNTRACED*.

745. *THREE DESIGNS / FOR THE / NATIONAL MONUMENT, /* PROPOSED TO BE ERECTED / IN COMMEMORATION / OF THE / LATE GLORIOUS VICTORIES / OF THE / BRITISH NAVY. / = /

---

[1] *Blake Records* (1969), 35.

BY CHARLES HEATHCOTE TATHAM, ARCHITECT, / MEMBER OF THE ACADEMY OF ST. LUKE AT ROME, / AND OF THE INSTITUTE AT BOLOGNA. / = / *London:* / PRINTED BY J. BARFIELD, WARDOUR-STREET, / PRINTER TO HIS ROYAL HIGHNESS THE PRINCE OF WALES; / FOR / T. GARDINER, PRINCES-STREET, CAVENDISH-SQUARE. / — / M, DCCCII [1802]. (BM)

The likelihood that the 'Mr. William Blake' in the subscription list is the poet is increased by the facts that he knew Tatham personally and had engraved Flaxman's designs for the same monument in 1799. Blake's copy is *UNTRACED*.

THOMAS, Joseph

746. RELIGIOUS EMBLEMS, / BEING A SERIES OF / *ENGRAVINGS ON WOOD*, / EXECUTED BY / THE FIRST ARTISTS IN THAT LINE, / FROM / DESIGNS / DRAWN ON THE BLOCKS THEMSELVES / BY / *J. THURSTON, ESQ.* / THE / DESCRIPTIONS / WRITTEN BY / *THE REV. J. THOMAS, A.M.* / CHAPLAIN TO THE EARL OF CORKE AND ORRERY. / = / LONDON: / *PRINTED BY T. BENSLEY, BOLT COURT, FLEET STREET;* / AND SOLD BY R. ACKERMANN, RE-POSITORY OF ARTS, / No 101, STRAND. 1809. (Bodley)

The 'William Blake, Esq.' in the List of Subscribers may well be the poet, for Thomas had been a generous patron to him, but his copy is *UNTRACED*.

THORNTON, Robert John

747. THE / LORD'S PRAYER, / NEWLY TRANSLATED / *FROM THE ORIGINAL GREEK*, / WITH CRITICAL AND EXPLANATORY NOTES, / BY / ROBERT JOHN THORNTON, M.D. / OF TRINITY COLLEGE, CAMBRIDGE, AND MEMBER OF THE ROYAL LONDON COLLEGE / OF PHYSICIANS. / WITH A FRONTISPIECE / FROM A DESIGN BY HARLOW, / OF THE ACADEMY OF ST. LUKE, AT ROME, AND OF THE ACADEMY OF FLORENCE. / *ADDRESSED TO THE BIBLE SOCIETIES* / *FOR DISTRIBUTION.* / — / *Stereotyped and printed by J. M'Gowan and Son, 16, Great Windmill Street, Haymarket.* / PUBLISHED BY SHERWOOD AND CO., PATERNOSTER ROW; COX, ST. THOMAS STREET, BOROUGH; AND DR. THORNTON, / 52, GREAT MARL-BOROUGH STREET; AND SOLD BY ALL BOOKSELLERS, 1s. 6d. INCLUDING A PRINT / FROM THE FAMOUS PAINTER HARLOW, BY COOK. / — / 1827.

COLLECTION: Huntington Library.

DATE OF ANNOTATION: 1827, between 31 March, the imprint on the frontispiece, and 12 Aug. when Blake died.

DESCRIPTION: The little pamphlet is stitched through the original Blue paper wrappers (with the original label) *and* through modern cardboard covers. The two leaves with the title-page and the 'Reasons for a New Translation of the Whole Bible' are misbound behind the other four leaves.

Blake's comments were evidently of some interest to Blake and his friends.[1] All but that on p. 2 were first written in pencil, and later all were confirmed in ink (except for those on pp. 3 and 10). Those on p. 10 were carefully transcribed by someone—not Blake—on the inside of the back Blue wrapper. These transcriptions were apparently made at different times, for one sentence at the bottom of the title-page verso is in Brown ink, and one in Black. The faintness of the pencil and the overwriting in ink have made some of the words exceedingly difficult to read.

BINDING: Stitched through the original Blue paper wrappers *and* through modern cardboard covers, the leaves with the title-page and the 'Reasons for a New Translation of the Whole Bible' misbound behind the other leaves.

HISTORY: (1) Apparently given by Blake to Linnell, who had it by 1828 (*Blake Records* [1969], 369), and with whose Collection it was sold at Christie's, 15 March 1918, lot 204, to G. D. Smith, who sold it to (2) The HUNTINGTON LIBRARY.

[WALPOLE, Horace]

748. A / CATALOGUE / OF THE / ROYAL AND NOBLE / AUTHORS OF ENGLAND, / WITH / LISTS OF THEIR WORKS. / *IN TWO VOLUMES.* / = / [2-line motto] / = / A NEW EDITION, / — / VOL. FIRST [SECOND]. / — / EDINBURGH: / PRINTED FOR LAWRIE AND SYMINGTON, / PARLIAMENT-SQUARE. / = / 1792. / =

Blake's set is in the Widener Collection at Harvard, with 'William Blake' on the fly-leaf of each volume, and '1795' and '6/6' by the name in the first volume, apparently in the same hand.

WATSON, Richard

749. AN / APOLOGY / FOR THE / BIBLE, / IN A / SERIES OF LETTERS, / ADDRESSED TO / *THOMAS PAINE,* / Author of a Book entitled, The Age of Reason, Part the Second, / being an Investigation of True and of Fabulous Theology. / — / By R. WATSON, D.D. F.R.S. / LORD BISHOP OF LANDAFF, AND REGIUS / PROFESSOR OF DIVINITY IN THE UNIVERSITY OF CAMBRIDGE. / — / EIGHTH EDITION. / — / LONDON: / Printed for T. EVANS, in Paternoster-Row. / — / 1797. / — / Price One Shilling, or Fifty Copies for Two Pounds, stitched. / *Entered at Stationers' Hall.*

COLLECTION: Huntington Library.

DATE OF ANNOTATION: 1798.

The reference to 'this year 1798' (title-page verso) gives the date unequivocally.

DESCRIPTION: At the top of the title-page is the signature of 'S. Palmer'.

---

[1] On 29 Aug, 1828 Samuel Palmer wrote to Linnell: 'My Father . . . would be very much amused by a sight of Mr. Blake's annotations on Dr. T.s Lord's Prayer' (*Blake Records* [1969], 369).

The front and back of the text are very dirty. On the early pages the margins are regularly filled to overflowing with Blake's comments. The notes to the Preface and pp. 31, 34, 95 are in pencil, the rest in ink.

BINDING: 'BOUND BY F. BEDFORD' in Blue morocco.

HISTORY: (1) Acquired by 'S. Palmer', who wrote his name on the title-page; (2) Sold with the T. G. Arthur Library at Sotheby's, 15 July 1914, lot 44, to (3) The HUNTINGTON LIBRARY.

[WESLEY, John and Charles]

750. *Hymns for the National Fast, Feb. 8, 1782.* London: sold at the New Chapel, in the City-Road; and at the Rev. Mr. Wesley's Preaching-Houses in Town and Country. [1782].

Sir Geoffrey Keynes acquired from Christie's on 8 Dec. 1958 a copy of this work, in which 'W Blake 1790' is written on the first leaf of the text. The top margin, and the signature, have been trimmed. Keynes and I regard the signature as authentic.

WINKELMANN, Abbe [J. J.]

751. *Reflections on the Painting and Sculpture of the Greeks*: with Instructions for the Connoisseur, and An Essay on Grace in Works of Art. Translated from The German Original By Henry Fusseli [i.e. Fuseli]. London, Printed for the Translator, and Sold by A. Millar, in the Strand. 1765.

On the fly-leaf of a copy of this work in the possession of Sir Geoffrey Keynes is written 'William Blake, Lincoln's Inn'. Fortunately 'the signature resembles later examples so closely that there can be no doubt of its authenticity'. (Keynes no. 2020.) Were the handwriting less conclusive we might be left in some doubt, for a 'William Blake' was admitted to Lincoln's Inn 8 June 1790 and was called to the bar in 1798; and a William J. Blake was admitted 28 Nov. 1826 and was called to the bar in 1831 (*The Records of the Honourable Society of Lincoln's Inn*, 1896–1902, vol. i, p. 536; vol. iv, p. 242; vol. ii, p. 112; vol. iv, p. 253). Further, we might have expected a member of one of the law societies to write 'Lincoln's Inn', but it is a little odd that the apprentice did not write 'Great Queen Street', where he lived as an apprentice to Basire, 1772–9, or at least 'Lincoln's Inn *Fields*', the nearest well-known square. The address given by the apprentice-poet appears to be rather a swagger-gesture.

WORDSWORTH, William

752. THE EXCURSION, / BEING A PORTION OF / THE RECLUSE, / *A POEM.* / = / BY / WILLIAM WORDSWORTH. / = / LONDON: PRINTED FOR LONGMAN, HURST, REES, ORME, AND BROWN, / PATERNOSTER-ROW. / 1814.

COLLECTION: No copy of *The Excursion* with Blake's notes is known; see below.

DATE OF ANNOTATION: 1826.

On 18 Feb. 1826 'He [*Blake*] gave me [*Crabb Robinson*] copied out by himself Wordsworths preface to his Excursion'.[1] Blake had remarked on this passage when he first met Robinson on 10 Dec. 1825,[2] and shortly thereafter 'I [*Robinson*] lent him the copy of Wordsworths poems which occasiond this Extract'.[3] The loan was between 10 Dec. 1825, when Robinson met Blake, and 18 Feb. 1826. Blake's notes are almost certainly of 1826.

DESCRIPTION: Crabb Robinson's copy of *The Excursion* which Blake read has not been traced, but Blake gave a copy of his notes to Crabb Robinson on 18 Feb. 1826, and this copy has been preserved.[4] The unwatermarked leaves on which Blake's ink notes are written are of slightly different size (11·8 × 21·4 cm for the first, 11·2 × 19·8 cm for the second), and there are no stab holes in them. The four sides are quite filled.

BINDING: The volume with Blake's annotations has not been traced, but Blake's copy of his notes is bound with Crabb Robinson's letters of 1864–7, ff. 101–2.

HISTORY: (1) 'I lent him [*Blake*] the copy of Wordsworths poems which occasioned this Extract [*in the handwriting of Blake.*] / H. C. Robinson' (according to the note on the folder in which Robinson kept Blake's transcript); (2) Robinson's copy is *UNTRACED*; Blake's transcript was given with Robinson's papers to DR. WILLIAMS'S LIBRARY, London.

753. POEMS / BY / WILLIAM WORDSWORTH: / INCLUDING / LYRICAL BALLADS, / AND THE / MISCELLANEOUS PIECES OF THE AUTHOR. / WITH ADDITIONAL POEMS, / A NEW PREFACE, AND A SUPPLEMENTARY ESSAY. / = / IN TWO VOLUMES. / = / VOL. I. / — / LONDON: / PRINTED FOR LONGMAN, HURST, REES, ORME, AND BROWN, / PATERNOSTER-ROW. / — / 1815.

COLLECTION: Cornell.

DATE OF ANNOTATION: 1826.

Crabb Robinson lent his set of Wordsworth's *Poems* (1815) to Blake between 10 Dec. 1825, when he first met him, and 26 Jan. 1826, when Blake transcribed a portion of the Michelangelo sonnet in Upcott's Autograph Album. Blake probably made his notes soon after he received the volume.

DESCRIPTION: Both volumes are inscribed at the tops of the title-pages 'H. C. Robinson', though in Vol. I the name is largely trimmed off. Blake's notes are entirely in Vol. I.

In a letter of 10 Aug. 1848 (now in Dove Cottage, Grasmere), Crabb Robinson wrote: 'I had lent him when he died the 8vo Edit in 2 Vols: of W. Ws poems— They were sent me by his widow with pencil marginalia which I inked over' lest they should be lost, except for the passage on p. 375 which he could not decipher.

---

[1] *Blake Records* (1969), 321.   [2] *Blake Records* (1969), 312.
   [3] This is Crabb Robinson's note on the folder in which he kept Blake's transcript. Robinson transcribed it in his Diary for 18 Feb. 1826 and in his letter to Dorothy Wordsworth of 19 Feb.
   [4] In Dr. Williams's Library, ff. 101–2 in the volume containing Robinson's letters 1864–7.

HISTORY: (1) 'H. C. Robinson' wrote his name on the title-pages, lent the volumes to Blake in 1826, retrieved them the next year after his death, darkened Blake's notes in ink, and transcribed them in his Reminiscences (*Blake Records* [1969], 545–6); (2) They were apparently given by Robinson to his friend Edwin Wilkins Field (1804–71), whose bookplates they bear; (3) Sold by Pickering & Chatto in the summer of 1956 to (4) CORNELL.

YOUNG, Edward

754. *The Complaint; or, Night Thoughts* on Life, Death, and Immortality. To which are added, A Glossary, A Paraphrase on Part of the Book of Job, and A Poem on the Last Day. A New Edition, corrected. London: Printed for T. Longman, & Dodsley; C. Dilly; F. and C. Rivington; W. Otridge and Son; T. Cadell, Jun. and W. Davies, and Hookham and Carpenter. 1796.

Keynes (no. 617) says that 'I have notes' of a copy of Young's *Night Thoughts* ('London, 1796') 'from Blake's Library'. Sotheby's sold a copy of *Night Thoughts* printed in *Glasgow*, 1796 with the 'autograph and Note of W. Blake the artist' (26 April 1893, lot 781). It seems likely that Keynes has misinterpreted his note of this sale, rather than that Blake owned *two* 1796 editions of *Night Thoughts* or that Keynes was correcting an erroneous Sotheby reference. In any case, Blake's copy of Young's *Night Thoughts* is *UNTRACED*.

APPENDIX

BOOKS OWNED BY THE WRONG WILLIAM BLAKE

BASTIEN, J.-F.

755. *La Nouvelle Maison Rustique*, ou Économie Rurale, Pratique et Générale de tous les biens de campagne. Nouvelle Édition, entièrement refondue, considérablement augmentée, et mise en ordre, d'après les expériences les plus sûres, les auteurs les plus estimés, les mémoires et les procédés de cultivateurs, amateurs et artistes, chacun dans les parties qui les concernent: avec 60 figures. [3 vols.] A Paris, chez Deterville, libr., rue du Battoir, n° 16, près celle de l'Éperon. [Et chez] Desray, libraire, rue Hautefeuille, n° 36, près s.-André-des Arcs. An VI.—M.DCC.XCVIII [1798]. (Yale)

The inscription 'Wm Blake' in old Brown ink in a not unBlake-like hand at the top of each title-page of the copy in Yale is somewhat unlikely to be by the poet. There seem to be no marginalia.

BIBLE: New Testament

756. THE / New Testament / Adapted to the / CAPACITIES of CHILDREN. / To which is added, An / HISTORICAL ACCOUNT / OF THE / LIVES, ACTIONS, TRAVELS, SUFFERINGS, / and DEATH / Of the / APOSTLES and

EVANGELISTS. / VIZ. / [two columns:] St. PETER. / St. PAUL. / St. JAMES the Great. / St. JOHN. / St. ANDREW. / St. PHILIP. / St. THOMAS. / St. BARTHOLO-MEW. / St. MATTHEW. / St. JAMES the Less. / St. SIMON. / St. JUDE. / St. MAT-THIAS. / St. BARNABAS. / St. MARK. / St. LUKE. / St. STEPHEN. / WITH / A PREFACE setting forth the Nature and / Necessity of the Work. / ADORNED with CUTS; / Designed by the celebrated RAPHAEL, / And Engraved by Mr. WALKER. / — / *LONDON:* / Printed for J. NEWBERY, at the Bible and Sun in / St. Paul's Church-yard. MDCCLV [1755]. (V & A)

The inscription 'Wm Blake's Book' in the Victoria & Albert copy of this work does not appear to be in the hand of the poet.

BOWLES, Revd. W. L.

757. *Sonnets, and Other Poems.* Sixth Edition. To which is added, Hope, An Allegorical Sketch on Recovering Slowly from Sickness. Printed for C. Dilly, Poultry, and T. Cadell, Jun. and W. Davies, Strand, London; and R. Cruttwell, Bath, 1798.

According to Keynes (1921), who owned the book in 1921, 'William Blake' is written on the half-title, and at the top of the title-page is 'Jeremiah & M. E. Awdry, Decbr 29, 1799.' Keynes later decided, however (no. 2020), that the owner must have 'been some other Blake.'

CHATTERTON, Thomas

758. Rowley's *Poems*, quarto, 1782.

Keynes reports (no. 2020) that a copy of this work sold at Sotheby's, 3 March 1926 bore 'W. Blake' on the title-page, 'but the signature was unlike Blake's usual hand and I regarded it as of very dubious authenticity'.

COLLIER, W.

759. *Poems on Various Occasions*; with Translations from Authors in Different Languages. Dedicated, by Permission, To His Royal Highness Prince William of Gloucester. In Two Volumes. London: Printed by G. Sidney, Black-horse Court; for Cadell and Davies, Strand; and Robson, New Bond Street. 1800. (BM).

Despite the fact that William Hayley and some of his intimate friends appear in the 'List of Subscribers' for this book, the likelihood that the 'W. Blake' in it is the poet is reduced to zero by the fact that he appears in a clear family group having nothing to do with the poet—'Mr. Blake Mrs. Blake Mr. W. Blake Miss F. Blake Miss C. Blake'.

[DENON, V.]

760. VOYAGE / DANS / LA BASSE ET LA HAUTE / ÉGYPTE, / PENDANT / LES CAMPAGNES DU GÉNÉRAL BONOPARTE. / PAR VIVANT DENON. / [Monogram; 2 vols.] / A PARIS, / DE L'IMPRI-MERIE DE P. DIDOT L'AÎNÉ, / AU PALAIS DES SCIENCES ET ARTS. / AN X. M.DCCCII [1802].

The name 'Blake (W.)' among the nearly 300 'NOMS DES SOUS-SCRIPTEURS' to these huge volumes is probably that of a man of means and not that of the poet.

[DOSSIE, Robert.]

761. *The Handma[id] to the Art[s.]* [2 vols.] Vol. the First. Teaching I. A perfect knowledge of the Materia Pictoria, or, the nature, use, preparation, and composition of all the various substances employed in Painting, as well vehicles, dryers, &c. as colours; including those peculiar to enamel and painting on glass. II. The means of delineation, or the several Devices employed for the more easily and accurately making Designs from Nature, or Depicted Representations; either by off-tracing, calking, reduction, or other means; with the methods of taking casts, or impressions, from figures, busts, medals, leaves, &c. III. The various manners of Gilding, Silvering, Bronzing, with the preparation of the genuine Gold and Silver powders, and imitations of them, as also of the fat oil, gold sizes, and other necessary compositions;—the art of Japanning, as applicable not only to the former purposes, but to coaches, snuff-boxes, &c. in the manner lately introduced;—and the method of Staining Different Kinds of Substances, with all the several colours. The whole being calculated, as well for conveying a more accurate and extensive knowledge of the matters treated of to professed artists, as to initiate those who are desirous to attempt these arts, into the method of preparing and using all the colours, and other substances employed in painting in oil, miniature, crayons, encaustic, enamel, varnish, distemper, and fresco, as also in gilding, &c. [Vol. the S(econd.) Teachi(ng,) I. The preparation of inks, cements, and sealing-wax, of every kind. II. The art of engraving, etching, and scraping mezzotintos; with the preparation of aqua fortis, varnishes, or other grounds, &c. in the best manner now practised by the French; as also the best manner of printing copper-plates; an improved method of producing washed prints, and of printing in chiaro obscuro, and with colours, in the way practised by Mr. Le Blon. III. The nature, composition, and preparation of glass of every sort; as also the various methods of counterfeiting gems of all kinds, by coloured glass, pastes, doublets, or the use of foils. IV. The nature and composition of *porcelain*, as well according to the methods practised in China, as in the several European m[anu]factures; with the best manner of burning, glazing, painting, and gilding the ware. V. Preparation of transparent and coloured glazings, for stone or earthen-ware. VI. The manner of preparing and moulding papier mache, and whole paper, for the forming boxes, frames, festoons, &c. and of varnishing, painting, and gilding the pieces of each kind; with the method of making the light Japan-ware. To which is added an Appendix; containing Several supplemental articles belonging, in some manner, to heads before treated of, either in this or the first volume; particularly, the method of marbling paper, or taking off paintings from old and transferring them to new cloths; of weaving tapestry, both by the high and low warp; and of manufacturing paper hangings of every kind.] The Second

Edition, with considerable Additions and Improvements. London: Printed for J. Nourse, Bookseller in Ordinary to his Majesty. 1764. (NYP)

A set in the New York Public Library is inscribed on the front fly-leaf of Vol. I: 'These Books are Mine!! Let None Presume to Make Them Thine! William Blake'; the fly-leaf at the front of Vol. II reads: 'Touch NOT Wm Blake'; on the back fly-leaf of Vol. I is: 'From cover to cover I know you by heart I no longer need you I'm Master of Art. Willm Blake'; the back fly-leaf of Vol. II is inscribed: 'I've mingled with the mind of men And delved in logic's lore! I've studied Lines and spiral curves And Poet's rhymes Galore The more I search The more I find Epitomized in My own MIND. Willm Blake'. The author of *Songs of Innocence* is not known to have exhibited elsewhere such puerility of verse, or this careful, bold print-writing, or what appears to be early-nineteenth-century Black ink. The author may be either one of the hosts of William Blakes or, as the New York Public thinks, a forger.

SEVERN, James

762. § *The Wandering Night of Dunstanborough Castle and Miscellaneous Poems.* Alnwick, 1823.

A copy of this work inscribed on the fly-leaf 'W. Blake 1823' was sold at Sotheby's, 9 Dec. 1957, lot 109a, but, according to Keynes (no. 2020), 'in my opinion the signature is not the right one'.

SOTHEBY, William

763. *Tragedies.* The Death of Darnley. Ivan. Zamorin and Zama. The Confession. Orestes. London: Printed for John Murray, Albemarle-Street; by W. Bulmer and Co. Cleveland-Row, St. James's. 1814.

Keynes (1921) reports that he owns a copy inscribed 'Wm Blake Esqr. From the Author.' However, as he pointed out later (no. 2020), Sotheby's copy of Virgil's *Georgica Hexaglotta* (1827) (sold by Sotheby's in 1954) has the inscription 'For William Blake Esqre from William Sotheby with his kind regards—London June 25th 1828', and this date is ten months after the poet's death. These two works did not, then, belong to the poet. It may be the same 'Wm. Blake, Esq.' who appears in the subscription list of *The Tribute*: a collection of Miscellaneous Unpublished Poems, by Various Authors. Edited by Lord Northampton. London: John Murray, Albemarle Street; and Henry Lindsell, Wimpole Street, 1837 and who signed the fly-leaf with 'William Blake' in the copy in the Berg Collection of the New York Public Library.

YEARSLEY, Ann, A Milkwoman of Bristol

764. *Poems, on Several Occasions.* London: Printed for T. Cadell, in the Strand. 1785.

'William Blake Esq.' is among about 1,120 others in the subscription list, but the homerific at the end suggests it is not the poet.

PART VI

BIOGRAPHY AND CRITICISM
BOOKS AND ARTICLES ABOUT BLAKE

A

765. A. 'The Fairy's Funeral.' *New-York Mirror*, XI (21 June 1834), 406.
MacNish's anecdote about Blake's having attended a fairy's funeral is repeated and then given in 'poetical dress'.

766. A., B. C. 'William Blake.' *N&Q*, CVII [9th Ser. XI] (1903), 285 (vMKN).
On the Crewe collection.

767. A., H. 'Londra: Le mostre di William Hogarth e di William Blake.' *Emporium*, CXIV (1951), 283–7 (vMKN).

768. *A., M. 'William Blake's "Nelson".' *Burlington Magazine*, XXVI (1915), 139–40.
Acquired by the National Gallery [and later transferred to the Tate].

769. A. Abbott, Claude Colleer. *The Life and Letters of George Darley, Poet and Critic*. London, 1928. Pp. 97, 165. B. Oxford, 1967. Pp. 97, 165.
Abbott quotes a letter from Darley about Cunningham's Blake biography and Darley's obituary of Seguier.

770. Abrams, M. H. 'The Circuitous Journey: From Blake to D. H. Lawrence.' Chapter 5, pp. 253–324 (esp. 'Unity Lost and Integrity Earned: Blake and Coleridge', pp. 256–77) of his *Natural Supernaturalism*: Tradition and Revolution in Romantic Literature. N.Y., 1971. Also *passim*.
The general theme is 'the secularization of inherited theological ideas' (p. 12).

771. Adams, Frederick B., Jr. *'Blake Water-Colors for Poems by Milton.' Pp. 56–60 of his *First Annual Report to the Fellows of the Pierpont Morgan Library*. N.Y., 1950.
On their acquisition.

772. —— 'William Blake 1757–1827.' Pp. 69–70 of his *Fourth Annual Report to the Fellows of the Pierpont Morgan Library*. N.Y., 1953.
Acquisition of *No Natural Religion*.

773. Adams, Frederick B., Jr. 'William Blake 1757–1827.' Pp. 74–5 of his *Fifth Annual Report to the Fellows of the Pierpont Morgan Library.* N.Y., 1954.
Acquisition of more *No Natural Religion* plates.

774. Adams, Hazard. 'Blake and Gulley Jimson: English Symbolists.' *Critique,* III (1959), 3–14 (vMKN).
Traces parallels in their careers, art, and aesthetic theories.

775. —— 'Blake and the Muse.' *Bucknell Review,* XV (1967), 112–19.
About dictation and the 'creative process' in Blake.

776. A. —— *Blake and Yeats: The Contrary Vision.* Ithaca [N.Y.], 1955. Cornell Studies in English Volume XL. B. N.Y., 1968.
A revision of a dissertation, no. 778.

777. —— 'The Blakean Aesthetic.' *JAAC,* XIII (1954), 233–48 (vMKN).
Analyses it in relation to vision. See also no. 1267.

778. A. —— 'Reading Blake's Lyrics: "The Tyger".' *Texas Studies in Literature and Language,* II (1960), 18–37. B. Reprinted in no. 1724.
An intelligent case for the view 'that in effect Blake's early poems strive to express the same system that the later prophetic books approach'.

779. —— 'The Structure of Myth in the Poetry of William Blake and W. B. Yeats.' Univ. of Washington Ph.D., 1954 (vMKN). See *DA,* XIV (1954), 105–6 and Adams, no. 776.

780. —— *William Blake*: A Reading of the Shorter Poems. Seattle, 1963. Chap. iv was reprinted in Frye (no. 780), pp. 44–5 in Paley (no. A2439 11), and pp. 58–74, in Weathers (no. 2937).
The book is particularly useful for the sections on the 'Ballads (or Pickering) MS' and the 'Bibliographical Appendix' (pp. 299–332) with a checklist of critical opinions on Blake's lyrics.

781. *A-Dayot, Magdeleine. 'William Blake et Turner à la Bibliothèque nationale: premier exhibition organisée par "Art et tourisme".' *Art et les Artistes,* n.s. XXXII (1937), 125–9 (vMKN).
See the Paris exhibition.

782. A. Adcock, A. St. John. 'Blake and Flaxman.' Chapter VII, pp. 118–39, of *Famous Houses and Literary Shrines of London.* With Seventy-Four Illustrations by Frederick Adcock and 16 Portraits. London & N.Y., 1912. B. *Famous Houses and Literary Shrines of London.* With Fifty-Nine Illustrations by Frederick Adcock. London, Toronto, N.Y., 1929. Pp. 89–104.

783. *Adhémar, Jean. 'Turner et Blake à la Bibliothèque Nationale.' *L'Illustration,* CXCVI (1937), 137 (vMKN).
See the Paris exhibition.

784. Adlard, John. 'The Annandale Druids: A Blake Crux.' *N&Q,* CCXII [N.S. XIV] (1967), 19–20.
Why are the Druids put in *Annandale* in *Milton* pl. 35, l. 11?

785. Adlard, John. 'Blake and "Electrical Magic".' *Neophilologus*, LIII (1969), 422–3.
About the effect of John Birch upon Catherine Blake and *Milton*.

786. —— 'Blake and *Rasselas*.' *Archiv für das Studium der neueran Sprachen und Literaturen*, CCI (1964), 47.

787. —— 'Blake and the "Geeta".' *English Studies*, XLV (1964), 460–2.
Faint parallels from the *Marriage* and *Milton*.

788. —— 'Blake and Thomas Taylor.' *English Studies*, XLIV (1963), 353–4.

789. —— 'Blake's Crystal Cabinet.' *MLR*, LXII (1967), 28–30.
The cabinet-mind metaphor may come from Locke; the poem 'arose from Blake's despair at ever making *Milton* the poem he hoped it might be' (p. 29).

790. —— 'The Cock, the Lion, and the Spectres in Blake.' *Archiv für das Studium der neueren Sprachen und Literaturen*, CCIV (1968), 432–3.
The question of the cock and the lion is not one of antipathy (*pace* Damon), but of contrariety.

791. —— 'Drunkenness at the Mills in Blake's "Milton".' *N&Q*, CCX [N.S. XII] (1965), 183–4.
Connected with the printer Seagrave.

792. —— 'Mr. Blake's Fairies.' *Neuphilologische Mitteilungen*, LXV (1964), 144–60.
A survey.

793. —— 'Tasso and the Cock and the Lion in Blake's *Milton*.' *Symposium*, XX (1966), 5–6.
Analogies with *Paradise Lost* and Tasso's *Mondo Creato*.

794. Adler, Jacob H. 'Symbol and Meaning in "The Little Black Boy".' *MLN*, LXXII (1957), 412–15.
The symbols do double duty.

795. *Aitken, Charles. 'Recent Acquisitions for Public Collections—XI: Satan Smiting Job with Sore Boils, Job ii, 7—By William Blake—National Gallery, British Art.' *Burlington Magazine*, xxxiv (1919), 165.

796. *Akesson, Elof. 'William Blake.' *Sydsvenska nagbladet Snallposten*, 2 Dec. 1957.

797. *Albani, Maria. 'William Blake.' *Nuova Antologia*, 5 S., CLIII (1911), 603–15.

798. Alfassa, Paul. 'L'Exposition Blake et Turner.' *Revue de Paris*, XLIV (1937), 665–78 (vMKN). See no. 642.

799. —— *'Un Peintre-Poète Visionnaire. William Blake.' *Revue de l'Art*

Ancien et Moderne [Paris], XXIII (1908), 219–36, 281–98 (vMKN).
A general article, mostly on Blake's art.

800. Allen, L. H. *William Blake*. A Centenary Address Delivered before the Australian English Association Sydney. Sydney, 1927.
A brief (38 pp.) introduction to Blake's mind and myth.

801. Allentuck, Marcia. 'Addendum to Bentley and Nurmi: Stillman on Blake.' *Publications of the Bibliographical Society of America*, LXIV (1970), 463.
W. J. Stillman, *The Old Rome and the New* (1897), 215, has one pejorative sentence about Blake.

802. —— 'Blake, Flaxman, and Thomas: A New Document.' *Harvard Library Bulletin*, XX (1972), 318–19.
The document is Flaxman's letter (now in the Folger) to Hayley of 31 July 1801, with a postscript to Blake.

803. Allingham, William. 'Some Chat about William Blake.' *Hogg's Weekly Instructor*, N.S. II (1849), 17–20.
This survey-essay is sympathetic and understanding but not very original.

804. A. *William Allingham: A Diary*. Ed. H. Allingham & D. Radford. London, 1907. Pp. 53. B. *William Allingham's Diary*. [Ed. H. Allingham & D. Radford.] Introduction by Geoffrey Grigson. Carbondale, Illinois, 1967. Pp. 53, 350.
Blake references for 16–18 Aug. 1849.

805. A. Alper, Benedict S. 'The Mysticism of William Blake, a Psychological Re-Examination.' *Poet-Lore*, XLIV (1938), 344–50. B. Reprinted in *Poetry Review*, XXIX (1938), 115–21 (vMKN).

806. Altizer, Thomas J. J. *The Gospel of Christian Atheism*. Philadelphia, 1966. *Passim*.
'*A* theological analysis based upon the Christian visions of Blake, Hegel, and Nietzsche' (p. 23); Blake unveils 'the Christian God as Satan' (p. 97).

807. —— **The New Apocalyse*: The Radical Christian Vision of William Blake. [Lansing], Michigan, 1967.
'It is the thesis of this book that William Blake is the most original prophet and seer in the history of Christendom, that he created a whole new form of vision . . . and that an understanding of his revolutionary work demands a new form of theological understanding.' (P. xi) ('*A* few crucial pages' from the MS of the book were published in 1965 in no. 808.)

808. A. —— 'William Blake and the Role of Myth in the Radical Christian Vision.' *Centennial Review*, IX (1965), 461–82. B. §Reprinted in pp. 171–91 of *Radical Theology and the Death of God*. Ed. Thomas J. J. Altizer & William Hamilton. Indianapolis, 1966. C. Harmondsworth, 1968. Pelican A957. Pp. 169–88. D. Tr. Shin Ohara as 'William Blake — Kagekina Kiristokyo-teki Genso to Shinwa no Yakuwari.' Pp. 259–90 of his translation of the book as *Kami no Shi no Shingaku* [*Theology and the Death of God*]. Tokyo, 1969 (vHK).

'*A* theological analysis of . . . [*Blake's*] prophetic poetry, employing Hegel as a dialectical guide to Blake's vision and attempting to lay the groundwork for a new form of Christian theology', consisting of 'a few crucial pages from my manuscript' book on Blake (C, p. 169).

809. *Ames, Winslow. 'William Blake as Artist.' *Magazine of Art*, XXXII (1939), 69–73 (vMKN).
Blake's techniques and subject-matter, 'essentially man and woman.'

810. §Anada, A. '"Eien no Fukuin": William Blake Kenkyu ["The Everlasting Gospel": A Study of William Blake].' *Jochi Daigaku Gaikokugo Gakubu Kiyo* [*Bulletin of Sophia University Faculty of Foreign Languages*], No. 1 (1967).

811. *Anderson, Jørgen. 'Et hjørne af Paradiset.' *Bogvennen* [Copenhagen], Ny række VII (1952), [77]–87. English summary on p. 92.

812. Anderson, William Davis, '"Awake Ye Dead": A Study of Blake's *The Book of Urizen, The Four Zoas*, and *Jerusalem.*' *DA*, XXVIII (1967), 1386A. Texas Ph.D. (1966).

813. Anon. [Untitled] *The Art Journal*, LVIII [N.S. XLVIII] (1896), 30 (vMKN).
Notice of formation of Blake Society.

814. —— [*Cincinnati*] *Enquirer*, 9 Jan. 1941.
On H. G. French's talk on Blake; does not refer to his *Innocence*.

815. —— *Morning Chronicle and Daily Advertiser*, 28 April 1785 (BM).
Review of the Royal Academy Exhibition mentions Blake in a selective list of exhibitors. Normally George Cumberland had reviewed the Royal Academy Exhibitions for this paper under the signature of Candid, but in April 1785 he was on the Continent.

816. —— *Sunday Express* [London], 9 Nov. 1919.
Note on Blake.

817. —— *Sussex Weekly Advertiser*, 10 Oct. 1803 (Sussex County Record Office).
A brief paragraph of news concerning the true bill returned by the Grand July indicting Blake for treason.

818. —— *Sussex Weekly Advertiser*, or Lewes Journal, 16 Jan. 1804, p. 3. (Brighton Public Library)
'Charles Blake, an engraver, at Felpham, was tried on a charge exhibited against him by two soldiers, for having uttered seditious and treasonable expressions, such as "D—n the King, d—n all his subjects, d—n his soldiery, they are all slaves; when Bonaparte comes, it will be cut throat for cut throat, and the weakest must go to the wall; I will help him, &c. &c." After a very

long and patient hearing he was by the Jury acquitted, which so gratified
the auditory, that the Court was, in defiance of all decency, thrown into
an uproar by their noisy exultations.'

819. Anon. *'A la Bibliothèque Nationale. Deux Artistes anglais [Blake and
Turner] précurseurs de l'Art moderne.' *Beaux-Arts*, 8 Jan. 1937, p. 1 (vMKN).

820. —— 'America Celebrates Blake: All-Native Loans to a Great Philadelphia Show.' *Art News*, XXXVII (18 Feb. 1939), 8, 19–20 (vMKN).

821. —— 'America Pays Homage to Britain's Only Mystic.' *Art Digest*,
XIII (15 Feb. 1939), 12 (vMKN).
   At the Philadelphia exhibition.

822. —— *'Art Find of the Year.' *Newsweek*, 6 Jan. 1941, pp. 54–5 (vMKN).
   The water colours for *Pilgrim's Progress*.

823. —— 'Art. II. *A Father's Memoirs of his Child. By* Benjamin Heath
Malkin . . .' *Literary Journal*, 2 S., II (July 1806), 27–35.
   Concludes by quoting the 'Laughing Song' as an example of ' "modern
nonsense" '.

824. —— 'Art. III. *Nollekens and his Times*: . . . by John Thomas Smith . . . .'
Eclectic Review, III (Dec. 1828), 536–7. (Bodley)
   'Amid much out-of-the-way rubbish [*in Blake's poetry*], there are gleams of
high conception and vigorous expression.'

825. —— 'Art. IV. Names and Addresses, of the principal Artists residing
or practising in the Metropolis, with the Line of Art they profess.' *Annals of
the Fine Arts*, I (Dec. 1816), 421–50. (Yale)
   According to the Preface (p. iv) to the first volume, 'The Lists of Artists,
their professions and addresses, have been collected [for each December
issue], from the catalogues of all the various exhibitions, from private information, and from every other possible source.' In this list (p. 443), under
Line Engravers though not under Painters, is 'Blake, William, South Molton-
street'. The entry appears in exactly the same form in the next three volumes
of the journal (no. 833–5) but not in the last (1820) volume. The periodical
was conducted by James Elmes.

826. —— 'Art. V.—*Vie des Révélations de la Soeur Nativité, Religieuse converse
au Couvent des Urbanistes de Fougères: écrites sous la Dictée; suivies de sa Vie
intérieure, écrite aussie d'après ellemême par le Rédacteur de ses Révélations* [the
Abbé Genet], *et pour y servir de suite*. Paris, 1817. 3 tom. 12mo.' *Quarterly
Review*, XXXIII (March 1826), 375–410. (Princeton)
   Sister Nativity saw angels blowing the last trump. 'Among Blake's strange
designs for Blair's poem of the Grave, is one representing the reunion of the
body and the soul; the highest genius alone could have conceived it, and
only madness have dared to attempt the execution. Sister Nativity's vision
is cold in comparison with his vivid and passionate delineation.' (P. 390)

827. Anon. 'Art. VI.—*Works of Mrs. Child* . . .' *North American Review*, XXXVII (July 1833), 138–64.
A quotation from her *Good Wives* about the Fairy's Funeral and about Blake's deathbed.

828. —— 'Art. VIII. British Artists and Writers on Art.' *British and Foreign Review*, VI (1838), 610–57.
'William Blake's estimate of himself as a man of genius, (visions inclusive,) was a just one. If he saw no faults in his works, it has been a pleasant occupation for others to discover them for him.' (P. 626)

829. —— 'Art. X.—*Lives of the Most Eminent British Painters, Sculptors, and Architects.* By Allan Cunningham, Esq. 2 vols. 12mo. London: J. Murray. 1830.' *Monthly Review*, XIII (March 1830), 453–4.
A very cursory account of Blake describes him as 'an extraordinary lunatic'.

830. —— 'Art. XI. *Illustrations of the Bible.* By John Martin . . . .' *Westminster Review*, XX (April 1834), 452–65.
'His [*Martin's*] pictures are opium dreams, a phantasmogoria of landscape and architecture, as Fuseli's and Blake's designs were of human beings.' (P. 464)

831. —— 'Art. XI. *Leonora. A Tale, translated from the German of Gottfried Augustus Bürger.* By J. T. Stanley, Esq. F.R.S. &c. A new Edition. 4to. 16 pages, with a Frontispiece and two Vignettes, by Blake. Price 7s. 6d. sewed. Miller. 1796.' *Analytical Review*, XXIV (Nov. 1796), 472. (Cambridge)
This one-paragraph review concludes: 'This edition is embellished with a frontispiece, in which the painter has endeavoured to exhibit to the eye the wild conceptions of the poet, but with so little success, as to produce an effect perfectly ludicrous, instead of terrific.'

832. —— 'Art. XIV. *A Father's Memoirs of his Child*, by Benjamin Heath Malkin . . . .' *Annual Review* . . . for 1806, V (1807), 379–81. (Bodley)
'The poems are certainly not devoid of merit . . .'

833. —— 'Art. XVII. Names and Residences of the principal living Artists residing or practising in the Metropolis, with the Line of Art they profess, corrected up to the 1st of January, 1820.' *Annals of the Fine Arts*, IV [for 1819] (1 Jan. 1820), 641–67. (Yale)
The Blake entry appears, exactly as before (see no. 825), on p. 661. In the same volume appeared Keats's 'Ode to a Nightingale' and in the same number was his 'Ode on a Grecian Urn'.

834. —— 'Art. XIX. Names and Residences of the principal living Artists residing or practising in the Metropolis, with the Line of Art they profess, corrected up to the 1st. January, 1818.' *Annals of the Fine Arts*, II [for 1817] (1 Jan. 1818), 566–95. (Detroit Public Library)
The Blake entry appears, exactly as before (see no. 825), on p. 588. A total of 205 London engravers were listed under five different 'lines'.

835. Anon. 'Art. XXII. Names and Residences of the principal living Artists residing or practising in the Metropolis, with the Line of Art they profess, corrected up to the 1st of January, 1819.' *Annals of the Fine Arts*, III [for 1818] (1 Jan. 1819), 651–680. (Yale)

The Blake entry appears, exactly as before (see no. 825), on p. 674.

836. —— 'Art. 40. *A Father's Memoirs of his Child. By Benjamin Heath Malkin, Esq. M.A. F.A.S.* Royal 8vo. 172 pp. 10s. 6d. Longman and Co. 1806.' *British Critic*, XXVIII (Sept. 1806), 339.

About half this rude review is devoted to a denigration of Blake, who 'seems chiefly inspired by . . . Divine Nonsensia'.

837. —— 'Art. XLII. *Elements of Morality for the Use of Children; with an Introductory Address to Parents.* Translated from the German of the Rev. C. G. Salzmann. Illustrated with Fifty Copper Plates. In Three Volumes. Vol. I. 200 p. and 16 plates. Price 3s. sewed. Johnson. 1791.' *Analytical Review*, IX (Jan. 1791), 101–3. (Cambridge)

The last paragraph of this short review reads: 'The prints are far superior, both with respect to design and engraving, to any we have ever seen in books designed for children; and that prints, judiciously introduced, are particularly calculated to enforce a moral tale, must be obvious to every one who has had any experience in education.' Mary Wollstonecraft is identified as the translator in a footnote, and Volumes II and III were reviewed in Volume XI (Oct. 1791), 217–20.

838. —— 'Art Exhibitions. Blake Engravings and Colour Prints.' *The Times*, 30 April 1924.

At the British Museum Print Room.

839 —— 'Art Stream Reversed.' *New York Evening Post*, 13 Aug. 1928 (vMKN).

On the return of the Young drawings to Britain.

840. —— 'Ballads, by William Hayley, Esq. founded on Anecdotes Relating to Animals, with Prints, designed and engraved by William Blake. Small 8vo. pp. 212.' *Poetical Register* for 1805 (London, 1807). (BM)

Blake is mentioned only in the title, and not in the 54-word review.

841. —— 'The Bibliographer.' *Boston Evening Transcript*, 8 Feb. 1905.
Account of the Grolier Club Blake exhibition.

842. —— 'Biographical Index of Deaths, for 1827. Compiled in part from original papers, and in part from contemporary publications.' *Annual Biography and Obituary for the Year 1828*, XII (1828), 416–18. (Toronto)

Though this obituary cites both the *Literary Gazette* (no. 107) and *The Gentleman's Magazine* (no. 989), in fact it is taken with only the smallest stylistic changes from the latter.

843. —— 'Bits of Biography. No. I. Blake, the Vision Seer, and Martin the York Minster Incendiary.' *Monthly Magazine*, XV (March 1833), 244–9. (Smith College)

The Blake section (pp. 244–5) of this piece of sensational journalism claims to be an eye-witness account of Blake's interview with Edward III. The minutiæ of the story are unique, and the dialogue may not be invented. (The Blake section is reprinted in Wilson, no. 2981.)

844. Anon. 'Blake and Birmingham.' *Connoisseur*, LXXXIII (1929), 59 (vMKN).
Night Thoughts drawings exhibited.

845. —— *'Blake and Scott.' *Boston Evening Transcript*, 4 June 1913 (vMKN).

846. —— 'Blake Art Brings $2,100. Tempera Painting [of 'Faith, Hope & Charity'] Sold at Auction of the Hardy Collection.' *New York Times*, 15 Feb. 1942.

847. —— 'Blake at Philadelphia.' *New York Times*, 12 Feb. 1939.
The Blake exhibition.

848. —— 'Blake at the Philadelphia Museum.' *Magazine of Art*, XXXII (1939), 46 (vMKN).
The Blake exhibition.

849. —— 'Blake at the Tate.' *TLS*, 23 July 1964.
Notice of the exhibition.

850. —— *'Blake at 200.' *Time Magazine*, 23 Dec. 1957, p. 52.

851. —— 'Blake at the Tate Gallery.' *Athenaeum*, No. 4487 (1913), 462 (vMKN).

852. —— 'A Blake Bequest.' [London] *Daily Express*, 4 Aug. 1903.
About 50 works to the Hampstead Subscription Library.

853. —— 'Blake Bicentenary in America.' *TLS*, 17 May, 1957, p. 412 (vMKN).
An account of the exhibition at the National Gallery.

854. A. —— §'Blake Books Here.' [Princeton] *Town Topics*, 9 Nov. 1967.
B. Reprinted in 'Blake at Princeton.' *Blake Newsletter*, I (1967), 6–7.
Account of the 1967 exhibition.

855. —— 'Blake Centenary. Celebrations in London.' *The Times*, 13 Aug. 1927.

856. —— 'Blake Centenary. Memorial at Bunhill Fields.' *The Times*, 9 Aug. 1927.

857. —— 'Blake Collection sold for $66,807.' *New York Times*, 3 Nov. 1938.
At the G. C. Smith sale, no. 644.

858. —— 'Blake, Cromek and Hoppner.' *TLS*, 7 Oct. 1926, p. 680.
Prints a letter from Hoppner to Hoare, 1808.

859. Anon. *'Blake Displayed Less Art than Genius.' *Art Digest*, XI (1 Sept. 1937), 25 (vMKN).
In Thornton's Virgil, no. 504.

860. —— 'Blake Drawings and Prints. The Linnell Collection.' *The Times*, 28 Feb. 1918.
News account of imminent sale, no. 608.

861. —— 'Blake Drawings for Public Galleries. Big Total at Linnell Sale. *The Times*, 16 March 1918.
See no. 608.

862. —— *'Blake Drawings for the Nation.' *The Times*, 28 July 1928, p. 16.
The *Night Thoughts* drawings.

863. —— *'Blake Drawings in a Shakespeare Folio.' *The Times*, 9 Dec. 1954.
Merely three reproductions.

864. —— 'The Blake Drawings in the Quaritch Collection.' *Critic*, XVI (1 March 1890), 110.
Appreciative comment on Blakes evidently in their stock.

865. —— 'Blake Drawings Realize £500.' *Art News*, XXVI (12 Jan. 1929), 24 (vMKN).
The Job series from New Zealand.

866. —— 'Blake Engravings Discovered.' *Evening Standard*, 11 Nov. 1937.
The Virgil blocks.

867. —— 'The Blake Exhibition.' *Spectator*, CXI (1913), 715–16 (vMKN).
At the National Gallery, no. 604.

868. —— 'The Blake Exhibition at Cambridge.' *TLS*, 19 Feb. 1954, p. 128 (vMKN).
From Keynes's collection.

869. —— 'Blake Exhibition Opens Today in Philadelphia.' *Boston Evening Transcript*, 11 Feb. 1939 (vMKN).

870. —— 'Blake Exhibition Opens Today in Philadelphia.' *Philadelphia Transcript*, 10 Feb. 1939.

871. —— 'Blake Exhibition Scheduled.' *Art Digest*, XVI (15 Oct. 1941), 7 (vMKN).

872. —— *'Blake from Bucharest.' *Manchester Guardian*, 24 Oct. 1958, p. 7.
A Rumanian postage stamp with a portrait of Blake.

873. —— *'Blake from Swinburne to Whitman.' *Walt Whitman Newsletter*, IV (1958), 115 (vMKN).
Facsimile of the title-page of no. 2795 which Swinburne sent Whitman, with a note.

874. Anon. 'Blake, Guillaume.' Vol. VI [1854], pp. 178–9 of *Nouvelle Biographie Universelle*. Ed. [Ferdinand] Hoefer. [46 vols.] Paris, 1852–66.

An ordinary summary of Blake's life, notable only for its determination to be wrong about the date of Blake's death.

875. —— 'Blake Illustrations of Shakespeare.' *Shakespeare Quarterly*, VI (1955), 106 (vMKN).

A note on acquisitions.

876. —— 'Blake in facsimile.' *Guardian*, 15 July 1964, p. 8.

Account of the Blake Trust exhibition.

877. —— 'The Blake Society.' *Christian Science Monitor*, 19 May 1921, p. 3.

A 'Special' report on its meeting.

878. —— 'The Blake Society.' *The Times*, 13 Aug. 1912, p. 7 (vMKN).

Wright advocated a concordance and a bibliography.

879. —— 'Blake Society at Hampstead.' *Hampstead and Hightgate Express*, 17 Aug. 1912, pp. 4–5.

Description of meeting.

880. —— 'A Blake Treasure from U.S. Given to Britain.' *Manchester Guardian*, 16 April 1957, p. 5.

On Mrs. Emerson's gift of the Notebook to the British Museum.

881. —— 'A Blake Triumph. 7,300 GS. for "The Divina Commedia".' [London] *Daily Telegraph*, 16 March 1918.

882. A. —— 'Blake, William.' Vol. II, p. 142 of *Chambers's Encyclopaedia*. London and Edinburgh, 1861. B. London and Edinburgh, 1874 Vol. II, p. 142. See also 1734, 1236.

883. —— 'Blake, *William*.' Vol. IV [1854], p. 153 of *The Encyclopaedia Britannica, or Dictionary of Arts, Sciences, and General Literature*. Eighth Edition. With Extensive Improvements and Additions; and Numerous Engravings. [22 vols.] Edinburgh [1853–60]. (Toronto Public Library)

This brief but spectacularly inaccurate paragraph is especially remarkable for the statement that 'Blake . . . was born in Ireland'. How did the author reach this conclusion, which was independently re-invented by Ellis & Yeats some forty years later (see no. 369)?

Blake is mentioned somewhat more temperately in the same volume under Robert Blair.

This is the first edition of the *Encyclopaedia Britannica* in which Blake appears. Unfortunately the present managers of the *Encyclopaedia Britannica* in Chicago have no records extending back to this date, so we can only guess at the authorship. In the next (Ninth) edition of the *Britannica* the Blake piece was entirely rewritten by J. C. Carr (no. 1344)

884. —— 'Blake, William.' Vol. I, cols. 716–77 of *The English Cyclopaedia. A New Dictionary of Universal Knowledge. Biography*. Conducted by Charles Knight. London, 1856. (Toronto)

The *English Cyclopaedia* consisted of four parts, with separate volume numbers: *Geography*, four volumes (1854–5); *Natural History*, four volumes (1854–6); *Biography*, six volumes (1856–8); and *Arts and Sciences*, eight volumes (1859–61). The respectful notice of Blake, which finds that some qualities in his poetry 'cannot easily be surpassed' but that he suffered from 'a species of chronic insanity' in his visions, seems to be derived entirely in its facts from Cunningham, no. 143.

885. Anon. 'Blake, William (1757–1827).' Vol. V, pp. 292–3 of *Bol'shaia Sovetskaia Entsiklopediia*. Ed. S. I. Vavilov. 2nd Ed. Moscow, 1950 (vMKN).
A general account.

886. —— 'BLAKE, WM.' P. 30 of 'Dictionary of British Biography: A Series of Original Memoirs' in *The British Empire*: Historical, Biographical, and Geographical. By Sir Archibald Alison . . . [& 19 others]. London & Glasgow, 1856.
A sentence.

887. —— 'Blake's Colour Printed Drawings. Gift to Tate Gallery.' *The Times*, 15 Dec. 1939, p. 11 (vMKN).
From Graham Robertson.

888. —— *'Blake's Cottage, Felpham.' *Sussex County Magazine*, I (1927), 518, 519, 540.
Modern drawings of Blake's handsome cottage.

889. —— 'Blake's Designs for Gray. Light on their History.' *The Times*, 5 Nov. 1919, p. 15. See also no. 1747.

890. —— §*'Blake's Divine Comedia.' *Coronet*, II (June 1937), 95–8.
Coloured Dante engravings.

891. —— *'Blake's Engravings After the Designs of Other Artists.' *The Times*, 18 July 1964, p. 11.
General impression of his career.

892. —— 'Blake's Engravings for the Book of Job.' *Minneapolis Institute Bulletin*, XXIII (1934), 29–30 (vMKN).
To be exhibited.

893. —— 'Blake notebook is split up for sale.' *Guardian*, 12 May 1971, p. 9.
The Blake–Varley sketchbook (no. 401) 'has recently been broken up' and the leaves will be sold at Christie's, 15 June 1971, 'which is perhaps a pity'.

894. —— *'Blake's Pilgrim.' *Survey Graphic*, XXX (1941), 698–9 (vMKN).
Seven *Pilgrim's Progress* illustrations.

895. —— *'Blake's "Riposo", a Note.' *Burlington Magazine*, XXIV (1914), 184–5 (vMKN).

896. —— 'Blake's Songs of Innocence and Experience.' *British Museum Quarterly*, VII (1932), 65–6 (vMKN).
On the acquisition of copy X.

897. Anon. 'Blake's "Songs of Innocence and of Experience".' *TLS*, 13 Aug. 1931, p. 624.
Notes on sales. See also no. 1363.

898. —— 'Blake's Water Colors.' *Boston Evening Transcript*, 15 July 1939 (vMKN).

899. —— *'Boston Adds to Its William Blake Grays.' *Art Digest*, II (Dec. 1927), 5 (vMKN).

900. —— 'Boston Letter.' *Critic*, XVIII (14 Feb. 1891), 85.
About the 'admirable' Boston Blake exhibition.

902. —— *'British Museum's Acquisitions: Woodblocks by William Blake.' *The Times*, 16 Jan. 1939.
17 Thornton woodblocks.

903. —— 'British School of Engraving.—No. II.' *Library of the Fine Arts*, IV (July 1832), 1–16.
Blake is referred to briefly in the accounts of Sharp (p. 5) and Schiavonetti (p. 13).

904. —— 'Bunyan: A Rediscovery.' *Art News*, XL (1–14 Nov. 1941), 26.
Blake's drawings for *Pilgrim's Progress*.

905. —— 'Bust of Blake Unveiled In Abbey's Poets' Corner.' *New York Times*, 25 Nov. 1957.

906. —— 'Camargo Society. Vaughan Williams's "Job".' *The Times*, 6 July 1931.
At the Cambridge Theatre last night.

907. —— 'The Carfax Gallery. A Memorable Blake Exhibition.' [London] *Daily News*, 8 Jan. 1904.

908. —— *'*The Creation of Eve* by William Blake.' *Burlington Magazine*, X (1907), 290–1 (vMKN).

909. —— 'A Creative Visionary. Some Reflections on the Need of the Blake Society.' [London] *Daily Graphic*, 5 Aug. 1912.

910. —— *'Dante Gabriel Rossetti and William Blake.' *New York Times Magazine*, 30 Nov. 1919, p. 10 (vMKN).
Plans for the exhibition at the Grolier Club.

911. A. —— *'Death and Immortality.' *The Illustrated Exhibitor and Magazine of Art*, I (12 June 1852), 369–71. *B. Pp. 15–16 of *The Ladies' Drawing Room Book*. N.Y., [1852].
An inaccurate conventional account.

912. —— 'Death of Blake, the Painter.' *Arthur's Home Magazine*, III (March 1854), 220.
'One of the most touching scenes in the history of art.'

913. Anon. *'Death's Door.' *Littell's Living Age*, LIX [3 S., III] (4 Dec. 1858), 784.

A quotation from the 1858 *Grave* (no. 4356) illuminates A. L. Dick's engraving of Blake's 'Death's Door' design at p. 721.

914. —— *'Death's Door. By William Blake.' *Howitt's Journal*, II (20 Nov. 1847), 321–2.

Reproduction, with a note.

915. —— 'Deaths . . . Mr. William Blake, an excellent, but eccentric, artist.' *Annual Register* [for 1827], LXIX (1828) [Chronicle], 253–4. (BM)

This obituary is taken almost word for word, but without acknowledgement and with extensive omissions, from that in the *Gentleman's Magazine*, no. 989, which in turn was chiefly derived from that in the *Literary Gazette*, no. 1071.

916. —— 'Deaths.' *Monthly Magazine*, N.S. IV (Sept. 1817), 330. (Toronto)

The relevant entry in its entirety is: '68, Mr. W. Blake, engraver.' The full obituary appears in no. 1052.

917. —— *'Dialogue with a Flea.' *Time Magazine*, 21 April 1967, p. 72.

Rediscovery of the Blake–Varley sketchbook (no. 401).

918. A. —— §'Dinner by the Amateurs of the Vegetable Diet (Extracted from an Old Paper).' *London Magazine and Theatrical Inquisitor*, IV (1821), 31–5. B. Reprinted in *The Unextinguished Hearth*: Shelley and his Contemporary Critics. Ed. Newman Ivey White. Durham, North Carolina, 1938. Pp. 263–9. C. N.Y., 1968.

Curran & Wittreich (Addenda no. A 1437) allege that the 'Mr. B, of Bible-celebrity', author of a 'treatise on "Antedeluvian Cherubim"', is Blake.

919. —— 'Discovery of Supposed Blake Paintings.' *The Times*, 24 March 1928.

Jobs found in the New Zealand home of Mrs. Hickson and her sister Mrs. Martin, daughters of the late Albin Martin.

920. —— 'Discovery of the Missing Leaves of the Beaconsfield Blakes.' *Burlington Magazine*, IV (1904), 298 (vMKN).

921. —— 'Discovery of William Blake's Grave.' [London] *Morning Post*, 29 June 1941.

On Jenkins's article in *Nineteenth Century*, no. 1457.

922. —— 'Drawings by Blake in the Ashmolean.' *Oxford Magazine* (21 June 1918), 341–2.

Three Dante drawings.

923. —— *'Drawings by William Blake: Lately Acquired by the Tate Gallery.' *Illustrated London News*, 11 April 1942, p. 449 (vMKN).

924. —— 'Edward Calvert Woodcuts.' *Christian Science Monitor*, 19 May 1921, p. 6.

On Blake and Calvert, by one who assisted Samuel Calvert in compiling the Memoir of his father (no. 1333).

925. Anon. *'"Elihu": An Engraving from the "Inventions to the Book of Job." By William Blake (1757–1827).' *Christian Science Monitor*, 12 May 1955 (vMKN).

926. A. ——— 'Eminent Living Artists.' THE / LITERARY POCKET-BOOK / OR, / COMPANION / FOR THE / LOVER OF NATURE AND ART. 1819. / — / (*To be continued annually.*) / LONDON: / PRINTED FOR C. AND J. OLLIER, VERE-STREET, / BOND-STREET, / (where communications will be received.) / SOLD ALSO BY G. AND W. B. WHITTAKER, AVE-MARIA- / LANE; W. WHITELEY, NEWGATE-STREET; / MUNDAY AND SLATTER, OXFORD; AND / R. NEWBY, CAMBRIDGE [1819] P. 167. (BM) B. . . . 1820 . . . SOLD ALSO BY MUNDAY AND SLATTER, OXFORD; / R. NEWBY, CAMBRIDGE; BELL AND BRADFUTE, EDIN- / BURGH; AND ALL OTHER BOOK-SELLERS / AND STATIONERS [1820]. p. 169. (BM) C. . . . 1822. . . . AND SOLD BY / SUTTABY, EVANCE, AND FOX, STATIONERS' COURT; / PEACOCKS AND BAMPTON, SALISBURY SQUARE; T. / AND J. ALLMON, PRINCES-STREET, HANOVER-SQUARE; /BELL AND BRADFUTE, EDINBURGH; MILLIKEN, DUB- / LIN; AND ALL OTHER BOOKSELLERS AND STATIONERS [1822]. P. 148. (BM) D. . . . 1823. . . . SOLD ALSO BY / SUTTABY, EVANCE, AND FOX, STATIONERS' COURT; / PEACOCKS AND BAMPTON, SALISBURY SQUARE; BELL / AND BRADFUTE, EDINBURGH; / MILLIKEN, DUBLIN; / AND ALL OTHER BOOKSELLERS AND STATIONERS [1823]. P. 156. (BM)

After 'Blake, W.' is 'poetry' in 1819, 'poetical subjects' in 1820, and 'visions' in 1822–3; the entry does not appear in 1821.

The editor of the diary was Leigh Hunt, and the compiler of the lists of Eminent Living Artists may have been Blake's friend Thomas Griffiths Wainewright, who claimed to have had a hand (otherwise untraceable) in 'the Literary Pocket Book' (see J. Curling, *Janus Weathercock* [1938], 345, 113).

927. ——— 'England Gets Blake Drawings.' *Art News*, XXVII (30 Nov. 1929), 13 (vMKN).

Mrs. Emerson returned the drawings for *Night Thoughts* to England.

928. ——— *'England's Glory in Blake.' *Literary Digest*, LXXXII (2 Aug. 1924), 31–2 (vMKN).

Clemence Dane's high opinion of Blake.

929. ——— 'Enthusiasm of an Artist.' *Atkinson's Saturday Evening Post*, 28 Feb. 1835, p. 2.

An account of the death-bed finishing of 'The Ancient of Days', from Cunningham.

930. Anon. 'The Ethics of William Blake Applied to Our Own Time.' *Current Literature*, LXVIII (1920), 227–8 (vMKN).
See also no. 2526, on which this comments.

931. —— *The Exhibition of the Royal Academy, M.DCCCVII.* The Thirty-Ninth. London: Printed by B. McMillan, Bow-Street, Covent-Garden, Printer to the Royal Academy. [Price Sixpence.] [*sic*] [1807]. (Princeton)
In the Anti-Room was no. '274 Portrait of Mr. Blake—T. Phillips, A[ssociate].'

932. —— 'An Exhibition of the Works of William Blake.' *Publishers' Weekly*, XCVI (1919), 1611.
A survey of the Grolier Club exhibition.

933. —— ***'Exhibition of Water Colors and Drawings by William Blake, 1757–1827 October 7–December 6.' *Bulletin of the Fogg Museum of Art*, X (1947), 210.
A brief notice.

934. —— 'Exhibition of Work by Blake in Capital [*Washington*].' *New York Times*, 25 Oct. 1964. See no. 688.

935. —— 'Exhibition of Works by William Blake.' [London] *Daily Telegraph*, 19 Jan. 1904.
The Carfax Exhibition, no. 598.

936. —— 'An Exploded Idol.' *Saturday Review*, XII (1876), 492–3.
About the 'grotesque' works by Blake (who was 'hopelessly mad') at the Burlington Fine Arts Club.

937. —— ***'L'exposition Blake et Turner.' *Beaux-Arts*, 15 Jan. 1937, p. 6 (vMKN).

938. —— 'The Family Library, No. X. The Lives of the most eminent British Painter, Sculptors, and Architects. By Allan Cunningham. Vol. II. London, 1830. J. Murray.' *London Literary Gazette*, 6 Feb. 1830, pp. 85–6.
Seventeen paragraphs of the Blake biography are quoted because they are 'so curious a sketch of a very extraordinary mind'.

939. —— 'Felpham and the Poet-Painter Blake. The Thirty-Fourth Meeting of the William Blake Society of Arts and Letters. Interesting Speech by the President.' *Observer and West Sussex Recorder*, 27 May 1914.
Mostly a report of President R. C. Jackson's speech.

940. —— 'A Fine Tribute to the Art of William Blake.' *New York Tribune*, 11 May 1913, Part VI, p. 6 (vMKN).

941. —— ***'Finest possible Blakes.' *Connoisseur*, CXLIII (Feb. 1959), 52 (vMKN).
Urizen facsimile.

942. Anon. 'Four English Painters.' *The Times*, 21 Aug. 1947, p. 5; see also 'Four Great British Artists', p. 7 (vMKN).
Trivial notices of the Blake exhibition (1947).

943. —— '£4,000 for Books in 10 Minutes.' [London] *Daily Mail*, 2 July 1924.
Sotheby sold *Songs, Marriage, Europe*, and other Blakes for £4,000.

944. —— *'From Blake's sketchbook.' *The Times*, 7 Aug. 1969, p. 5.
'On indefinite loan' at the Tate (sold 1971).

945. —— *The Gallery of Portraits: with Memoirs.* Under the Superintendence of the Society for the Diffusion of Useful Knowledge. [7 vols.] London, [Vols. I–II] 1833, [III] 1834, [IV–V] 1835, [VI] 1836, [VII] 1837. Vol. I, p. 28.
The biography of Flaxman, which is derived from Cunningham, merely mentions his 'intimacy with Blake and Stothard'.

946. —— *'Gems from Blake at the National Gallery.' *Art Digest*, XVII (17 May 1943), 20 (vMKN).

947. —— 'Genius of William Blake.' *Art Digest*, XIII (1 Jan. 1939), 11 (vMKN).
Seen at the Philadelphia exhibition.

948. —— 'Gifts to British Museum. Blake's Poems.' *The Times*, 17 Dec. 1932.
The Carey *Songs*.

949. —— 'Gifts to the British Museum: Miniature Portraits by Blake.' *The Times*, 12 Oct. 1942, p. 6 (vMKN).
Of the Butts family.

950. —— *'Graham Robertson Blake Pictures To Be Sold.' *Illustrated London News*, 9 July 1949, p. 67 (vMKN).

951. —— 'The Grave; a Poem by Blair, illustrated by Twelve Etchings, executed by Louis Schiavonetti, from the original Inventions of William Blake. 1808.' *The Monthly Magazine*, XXVI (1 Dec. 1808), 458. (Princeton)
This brief review remarks on the 'correctness' of the drawing and the 'wildness' of design in Blake's work.

952. —— '*The Grave, a Poem, illustrated by Twelve Etchings, executed by Louis Schiavonetti, from the Original Inventions of William Blake.* 4to. pp. 50. £2. 12s. 6d. 1808, Cromek. Cadell and Davis.' *Antijacobin Review and Magazine*, XXXI (Nov. 1808), 225–34. (Princeton)
This long, slashing review excoriates Blake's designs as 'absurd effusions', the 'offspring of a morbid fancy', which 'totally failed' to achieve their purpose, and suggests that the next time Blake turns his hand to poetry, 'his friends would do well to restrain his wanderings by the strait waistcoat'.

953. —— 'The Grave of William Blake.' *The Times*, 29 June, 1911.
On Jenkins's article, no. 1957.

954. Anon. *'Great Examples of English Painting: Masterpieces of Four Artists at the Tate.' *Illustrated London News,* 23 Aug. 1947, p. 219 (vMKN).
On the Tate exhibition (1947).

955. —— 'Half-Yearly Retrospect of Domestic Literature.' *Monthly Magazine,* Supplementary Number, XXII (25 Jan. 1807), 621–46. (BM)
The reviewer of Malkin steps aside (p. 633) to assert that Blake's poetry 'does not rise above mediocrity'.

956. —— *'Homage to William Blake.' *Guardian,* 27 June 1968, p. 6.
Unveiling of sculpture of Blake by Jn W. Mills at William Blake House, Marshall Street, London.

957. —— 'Honouring a Poet–Painter. First Meeting of the Newly-Founded Blake Society.' [London] *Daily Graphic,* 13 Aug. 1912.
A news report.

958. —— 'Hôpital des fous à Londres.' *Revue Britannique,* 3ᵉ Série, IV (July 1833), 179–87.
This astonishing account (pp. 183–6) of Blake and Martin in Bethlehem madhouse is clearly pirated and jumbled from no. 843. (The Blake reference is reprinted in Keynes [1921] and in Wilson, no. 298.)

959. —— *'Illustrated Second Folio Shakespeare for B.M.' *Museums Journal,* LIV (1954–5), 268.

960. —— *'Illustrations to the Divine Comedy of Dante.' Pp. 40–4 of *National Art-Collections Fund: Sixteenth Annual Report 1919.* London, 1920.
Acquired at the Linnell sale.

961. —— *'Including Blake Water-Colours: Illustrations from the British Museum's Newly-Acquired Second Folio.' *Illustrated London News,* 25 Dec. 1954, p. 1163 (vMKN).
Six by Blake reproduced.

962. —— *'Interest in Blake's Art Receives Impetus.' *Art Digest,* VIII (15 May 1934), 17 (vMKN).
The impetus comes from the Philadelphia show.

963. —— 'International Exhibition, 1862. Pictures of the British School.' *Art Journal,* N.S. I (1 July 1862), 149–52.
Three sentences comparing Stothard's 'Canterbury Pilgrims' with Blake's: 'of the two, Blake shows himself the more shadowy and visionary.' (P. 152)

964. A. —— 'International Exhibition. The English Water-Colour Pictures.' *Athenaeum,* no. 1803 (17 May 1862), 663. B. §*What Do You Think of the Exhibition?* A Collection of the Best Descriptions and Criticisms from the Leading Journals Concerning the International Exhibition. Ed. Robert Kempt. London, 1862. Pp. 179–81.
One sentence about Blake: 'Blake's transcendental fancies are freely seen.'

965. Anon. 'The Inventions of William Blake, Painter and Poet.' *London University Magazine*, II (March 1830), 318–23. (Bodley)

This astonishing essay is the most perceptive and enthusiastic analysis of Blake as a poet to appear before the 1860s. For an interesting suggestion that the author was C. A. Tulke, see D. Dorfman, *Blake in the Nineteenth Century* (1964), 42 n.

966. —— 'Juno Dispatching and Receiving the Winds [*by Flaxman*]. *People's Journal*, III (1847), 172–3.

'Blake and Stothard . . . were doubtless instrumental in moulding his [*Flaxman's*] genius.' (P. 172)

967. —— 'Lambeth dreamer and poet William Blake—mystic and master.' *Brixton Free Press*, 25 July 1913.

968. —— 'The Last of the Supernaturalists.' *Fraser's Magazine*, II (March 1830), 217–35. (Bodley)

This extremely long, pretentious, and empty article is attributed confidently to Carlyle by J. A. S. Barrett (no. 1128), and to John Abraham Heraud, or William Maginn, by T. M. H. Thrall, *Rebellious Fraser's* (1934), p. 268. The vacuity of the article makes the question one of little importance to Blake scholarship.

969. —— 'The Life and Works of Thomas Stothard, R.A.' *Gentleman's Magazine*, N.S. XXXVII (1852), 146–50.

An anonymous review of Mrs. Bray's life of Stothard (no. 1273) includes Cromek's letter to Blake of May 1807 (pp. 149–50), together with incidental derogatory references to Blake's picture from Chaucer.

970. —— 'Literary Gossip.' *Athenaeum*, No. 4494 (1913), 705 (vMKN).

Account of a meeting of the William Blake Society of Art and Letters.

971. —— 'Literary Novelties.' *Literary Gazette*, 11 Oct. 1828, p. 654. (Toronto)

'Mr. Varley (the water-colour artist) announces for publication a Treatise on Zodiacal Physiognomy [*no. 501*]! This is a work of really too absurd a nature to be tolerated in the present age. . . . Let him leave the study of astrology for the study of leaves—nor extend the effect of skies beyond the landscape. Then, indeed, will we commend his knowledge of "natural philosophy." But seriously speaking, the madness of poor Blake (sublime as in some remains of him which we possess, it was) is too serious a subject to be jested with.'

For evidence that W. P. Carey was the author of the regular feature, 'Literary Novelties', see the *Literary Gazette* obituary of Blake, no. 1071. Carey was also probably the anonymous reviewer of Varley two months later in no. 1038.

972. —— 'Liverpool and Blake.' *Liverpool Courier*, 27 Nov. 1906, p. 6 (vMKN).

A review article on Gilchrist and other books, noting the contribution of Liverpool to Blake studies.

973. Anon. '*The Lives of the Most Eminent British Painters, Sculptors, and Architects.* By Allan Cunningham. Vol. II. London: Murray.' *Athenaeum*, 6 Feb. 1830, pp. 66–8. (BM)

Extensive quotations from Cunningham demonstrate that Blake was an 'extraordinary man' both for his artistic visions and for the felicity of his marriage.

The authorship of this anonymous review is not indicated in the marked editorial files of the *Athenaeum*, now in the London office of the *New Statesman*.

974. —— '*The Lives of the most eminent British Painters, Sculptors, and Architects.* By Allan Cunningham. *Vol. II.* Murray. 1830.' *Gentleman's Magazine*, C (Feb. 1830), 141–3. (Bodley)

'*Blake* . . . appears to have been an amiable enthusiast, on the wrong side of the line of demarcation as it respected his sanity.'

975. —— 'Lives of the Painters. By Allan Cunningham. Messrs. Harpers.' *American Monthly Magazine*, III (1831), 155–74 (vMKN).

Introduces anecdotes concerning Blake (pp. 164–71) from Cunningham with the remark: 'The following anecdotes give one of the most singular pictures of a mind we have ever met:—'.

976. —— 'Long Lost Blake Found.' *Art Digest*, III, No. 19 (Aug. 1929), 30 (vMKN).

'Faith, Hope, and Charity.'

977. —— 'Lord Crewe's Collection of Blake's Works.' *Athenaeum*, No. 3928 (1903), 185.

The sale at Sotheby's.

978. —— 'Lost Legacies of Genius.' [Auckland] *Sun*, 24 March 1927.

Concerns the recently found 'New Zealand' set of *Job*.

979. —— 'Mad Artists.' 'William Blake. Born 1737, died 1827.' *Journal of Psychological Medicine and Mental Pathology*, N.S. VI (1880), 40–6.

Because 'there was scarcely a phase in the constitution of his mind which was not modified by perversion', 'we cannot restrain our pity and sympathy' for Blake and his 'incomprehensible, and his mystical and allegorical writings'.

980. —— '*Major's Cabinet Gallery of Pictures; with Historical and Critical Descriptions and Dissertations*, by Allan Cunningham. No. 1.' *Athenaeum*, No. 254 (8 Sept. 1832), p. 582.

This review gives *in toto* the 'capital anecdote of Blake' from Cunningham.

981. —— 'The Matter of Originality.' *Nation* [New York], CXXIII (1926), 141 (vMKN).

982. —— 'Memoir of Flaxman the Sculptor.' *New Jerusalem Magazine*, V ([Boston] Dec. 1831), 153–60. (LC)

Blake is mentioned in the passage quoted from Cunningham on pp. 153–4.

983. Anon. 'Memoirs of William Blake.' *New Jerusalem Magazine*, V ([Boston] Jan. 1832), 192–9.

These excerpts from Cunningham (no. 1431) are given 'for the sake of the contrast between him [Blake] and Flaxman', Flaxman being 'a model of order and rationality', that is, a receiver of Swedenborgian truth, while Blake was a man of 'unregulated enthusiasm' and 'wild phantasy' who could not understand 'these [Swedenborgian] truths'.

984. —— 'Memorial to William Blake. Unveiling in Crypt of St. Paul's.' *The Times*, 7 July 1927.

A news report.

985. —— 'Memorial to Wm. Blake.' *Daily Telegraph*, 28 Sept. 1899.

986. —— *Minutes of the First Seven Sessions of the General Conferences of the New Church* signified by the New Jerusalem in the Revelation, together with those of other Contemporary Assemblies of a similar Character. Reprinted from the Original Editions. London, 1885. P. xx.

In the list of those attending the First Session, 13–17 April 1789, appear the names of 'W. Blake. C. Blake'. The 'Original Editions' meant the manuscript minutes, which are in New Church College, Woodford Green, Essex, for the attendance list was not printed in the *Minutes of a general Conference of the Members of the New Church signified by the New Jerusalem in the Revelation* (*April 13–17, 1789*), London (Hindmarsh), 1789. (Bodley)

987. —— 'Monthly Retrospect of the Fine Arts.' *Monthly Magazine*, XI (April 1801), 245–6. (Bodley)

For his engraving of Stothard's 'Fall of Rosamond' Macklin paid Blake £80.

988. —— *'Mr. Blake.' *Time*, 27 Feb. 1939, pp. 50–1.

989. A. —— 'Mr. William Blake.' *Gentleman's Magazine*, XCVIII (Oct. 1827), 377–8. (BM) B. Reprinted in A. Symons, *William Blake*, 1907, no. 2804.

Most of this long obituary notice was lifted silently from the *Literary Gazette* (no. 1071); was as silently reprinted in the *New Monthly Magazine* (no. 990) and in *Annual Register* (no. 915); and was copied with acknowledgements in *The Annual Biography and Obituary for the Year 1828* (no. 842).

990. —— 'Mr. William Blake.' *New Monthly Magazine*, XXI [Part III, Historical Register] (1 Dec. 1827), 535–6. (Toronto)

Except for minor stylistic changes in the first and last sentences, this obituary is pirated almost word for word from that in the *Gentleman's Magazine*, no. 989.

991. —— 'Model of a Painter's Wife.' *Literary Port Folio*, I (13 May 1830), 150. (Harvard)

This is simply an unacknowledged reprint of all but the first paragraph of the Blake section in the review of Cunningham in the *Athenaeum* (no. 973).

N.B. There is some confusion about the title of this short-lived journal.

The first page of each number carries the title *Literary Port Folio*, but the running title is consistently *Philadelphia Port Folio*.

992. Anon. 'Monthly List of New Publications.' *Athenaeum Magazine*, IV (Sept. 1808), 253. (Princeton)

'The Grave, a Poem; illustrated by Twelve Etchings, executed by Louis Schiavonetti, from the original inventions of William Blake. Royal 4to. 2l. 12s. 6d. in boards.'

993. —— *'Mysticism of William Blake Seen at the Fogg Art Museum.' *Art Digest*, V (1 Nov. 1930), 21 (vMKN).

994. —— 'Le mysticisme de William Blake.' *Beaux-Arts*, 12 Feb. 1937, p. 2 (vMKN).

995. —— 'Nativity of Mr. Blake, The Mystical Artist.' *Urania*; or, the Astrologer's Chronicle, and Mystical Magazine, Edited by Merlinus Anglicus, Jun. the astrologer of the nineteenth century, assisted by the metropolitan society of occult philosophers. No. 1. London: Printed by A. Sweeting, Aldersgate Street; Published by Cowie and Strange, 24, Fetter Lane; and sold by Sherwood, Jones, and Co. Paternoster Row, and all Booksellers. 1825. Pp. 70–2. (Bodley)

The nativity includes valuable praise for and comment about the subject. Keynes (1921) says [evidently on the evidence of the initials R. C. S. on two nativities] that *Urania* was edited by R. C. Smith and that Smith may have written this article. He is probably right, for *The Astrologer of the Nineteenth Century* (1825), which was edited under the same pseudonym [by Robert C. Smith (1795–1832), according to the *National Union Catalogue*], gives the birth date of 19 March 1795 for him in the nativity of 'The Editor of the Present Work' (p. 435).

996. —— 'Newly Discovered Blakes Seen in New York.' *Art Digest*, XVI (1 Nov. 1941), 24 (vMKN).

The *Pilgrim's Progress* designs.

997. —— 'No. II. John Flaxman, Esq. R.A. Professor of Sculpture at the Royal Academy.' *Annual Biography and Obituary for the Year 1828*, XII (1828), 20–51. (Toronto)

Blake is mentioned briefly as Flaxman's friend and engraver (pp. 21, 23) in this long, tardy obituary.

998. —— 'Nollekens and his Times.' *Athenaeum*, No. 56 (19 Nov. 1828), 881–2. (Bodley)

A summary of Smith's account (no. 2723).

999. —— *'A Note on Four Watercolors by William Blake.' *International Studio*, LXXIV (1921), xxxvii–xxxviii (vMKN).

1000. —— 'Notes and News.' *Academy*, 6 June 1874, pp. 645–7.

Gives new information about Blake's *Night Thoughts* drawings (p. 645), particularly from 'An advertisement [*which*] appeared in March in some of the London papers, inserted by Mr. H. W. Birtwhistle, of Halifax'. (*Pace* Miss Hoover, *Blake Newsletter*, V [1972], 170, it is not signed by W. M. Rossetti.)

1001. Anon. 'Notes of the Month.' *Gentleman's Magazine*, N.S. XXXVII (Feb. 1852), 165.
Sale of *Songs* and *Urizen* (G) at Sotheby's, 21 Jan. 1852.

1002. —— 'Notes on Books, &c.' *N&Q*, LXII [6th Ser., III] (1881), 200.
Note on Colnaghi's purchase of the original plate of Blake's Canterbury Pilgrims and impressions made from it.

1003. —— 'Notes on Sales.' *TLS*, 15 July 1920, p. 460.
A note on Dibdin's reference to D'Israeli's Blake collection.

1004. —— 'On Some Strange Mental Feats.' *Cornhill Magazine*, XXXII (1875), 157–75.
Blake (pp. 167–8) could draw 300 portraits in a year without sitters but his ability to see absent people led him to insanity. See also no. 2516 and Palmer, no. 2355, who show the account to be absurd.

1005. —— *'An Original Drawing by William Blake.' *Portfolio* [Old Print Shop, N.Y.], IV (1945), 148–52.
Offers drawing for *America* pl. 7 for $400.

1006. —— 'The Paintings of William Blake.' *Academy*, LXX (1906), 600–1 (vRN).

1007. —— 'Paintings Shown of William Blake.' *New York Times*, 21 Oct. 1941 (vMKN).

1008. —— 'Past and Present.' *New England Magazine*, VI (March 1834), 235–6.
A passing reference to Blake's visions.

1009. —— 'Personal Relics of William Blake.' *Pall Mall Gazette*, 24 March 1910.
Butts's desk sold at Sotheby's.

1010. —— 'Pictor Ignotus.' *Once a Week*, IX (1872), 438–42.
A general account.

1011. —— 'Pictor Ignotus.' *Sharpe's London Magazine*, N.S. XXXI (1876), 19–28.
An attempt to 'lay forth a slight sketch' of Blake, based on Gilchrist.

1012. —— *'Pictures by William Blake.' *Art Journal*, LXVI (1904), 349–51.
A general article stimulated by the Carfax exhibition.

1013. —— 'Pilgrim's Progress by Blake Discovered.' *Art Digest*, XV (1 Jan. 1941), 24 (vMKN).

1014. Anon. *'The Plate.' *Littell's Living Age*, LIX [3rd Ser., III] (18 Dec. 1858), 912.
A quotation from the 1858 *Grave* (no. 435F) illuminates Dick's engraving of Blake's 'Soul exploring' design at p. 849.

1015. —— 'Plays by Picasso and William Blake.' *The Times*, 17 Feb. 1950, p. 10 (vMKN).
A reading of *The Island in the Moon* at Steiner Hall.

1016. —— 'Poetry and Painters.' *Illustrated Magazine of Art*, I (Jan. 1853), 48.
Blake's engravings for Young are admired in passing.

1017. —— 'The Poetry of Sacred and Legendary Art [*by Mrs Jameson*].' *Blackwood's Edinburgh Magazine*, LXV (Feb. 1849), 183.
Admiring reference to Blake.

1018. A. —— 'The Poetry of William Blake.' *Academy*, LXI (1901), 15–16.
B. Reprinted in *Current Literature*, XXXII (1902), 110–11 (vMKN).

1019. —— 'Prints of Wm. Blake Seen in Philadelphia.' *New York Times*, 18 Oct. 1936 (vMKN).

1020. —— 'The productions of time.' *Guardian* 25 Jan. 1968, p. 8.
Blake's South Molton Street House 'is to be turned into a betting shop'.

1021. —— 'A Prophecy of America. From the Correspondence of —— —— and ***.' *Poet Lore*, V (1893), 93–6 (vMKN).
A rather ordinary appreciation, despite the odd title.

1022. —— 'Que nous réserve W. Blake?' *Boréal Express*, IV (1961), 21.
An article purporting to give a French-Canadian view of Blake in 1792.

1023. —— *'Queen Elizabeth Loans Pictures to Show.' *Washington Post*, 16 Oct. 1957.
The Washington Blake Bicentennial exhibition.

1024. —— *'Ranking Blake with Shakespeare.' *Current Opinion*, LXXVII (1924), 350–1 (vMKN).

1025. —— 'Rare Books Sold in New York. High Prices for Blake Drawings.' *The Times*, 14 May 1941.
A. E. Newton sale.

1026. —— *'Resurrected Art of William Blake.' *Literary Digest*, LVI (12 Jan. 1913), 25–6 (vMKN).
Blake's supposed portrait of Lamb and self portrait. See also no. 1058, 2539.

1027. —— 'Revue de la critique. La Critique française et William Blake.' *Navire d'Argent*, I (1925), 437–40 (vMKN). See no. 2276.

1028. —— 'St. Paul's Cathedral, London.' *Illustrated Magazine of Art*, I (Feb. 1853), 109–11.
A casual reference to the charity children in St. Paul's justifies the quotation of 'Holy Thursday' from *Songs of Innocence*, on p. 111.

1029. Anon. 'Sale of Works by William Blake.' *The Times*, 14 Jan. 1904.
The Hodgson sale, 14 Jan. 1904.

1030. —— 'The Sale Room. 'Nathaniel Horne Portrait. William Blake Drawings.' *The Times*, 27 July 1929.
Morse sale at Christie's yesterday.

1031. —— 'A Seer in Lambeth.' *Pall Mall Gazette*, 27 Nov. 1909.
On associations with Lambeth and his visions at Hercules Buildings.

1032. —— 'The Simple and Fantastic Genius of Blake.' *Current Literature*, XLII (1907), 169–73 (vMKN).
Comment occasioned by the publication of editions of Swinburne and Gilchrist.

1033. —— 'Sussex and Adjacencies. Chichester.' *Sussex Chronicle & Chichester Advertiser*, No. 22 (2 June 1802), 172.
A notice of 'the first number of Mr. Hayley's . . . Ballads, to the engravings of Mr. Blake', in a weekly news column.

1034. —— 'Swedenborg and Blake.' *New Church Weekly*, XL (1917), 413 (vMKN).
Report of H. N. Morris's address on 'Blake and Swedenborg' at the sixth annual meeting of the Blake Society, Tuesday, 11 Sept. 1917.

1035. —— *'The Tempera Painting of William Blake.' *Connoisseur*, CXXVIII (1951), 46–7 (vMKN).

1036. *'A Tintoretto Cleaned; and William Blake.' *Illustrated London News*, 4 May 1957, p. 739 (vMKN).
Exhibition at the British Museum.

1037. —— 'Translations of Burger's Leonora.' *British Critic*, VIII (Sept. 1796), 277. (BM)
The critic pauses in the midst of a brief review of four translations of *Leonora* to execrate the 'detestable taste' shown in Blake's design for J. T. Stanley's second version.

1038. —— 'A Treatise on Zodiacal Physiognomy: illustrated by Engravings of Heads and Features; and accompanied by Tables of the Time of Rising of the Twelve Signs of the Zodiac; and containing also New and Astrological Explanations of some remarkable Portions of Ancient Mythological History. By John Varley. No. 1. Large 8vo. pp. 60. To be comprised in four Parts. Longman and Co.' *Literary Gazette*, 27 Dec. 1828, pp. 822–4. (Toronto)
The Blake section from Varley's book is given at the end (p. 824) of a mocking review designed to prove 'that our friend Varley is the only man alive who understands the true principles of human nature, which we take to be a proper mixture of credulity, insanity, and unconscious obedience to incomprehensible influences'.

1039. Anon. 'Two Works by Blake.' *Bodleian Library Record*, I (1940), 178–9; also listed under 'Notable Accessions' on p. 192.
Innocence (L) and *Job* illustrations.

1040. —— *'U.S. Gift of Blake [*Note*-]Book. British Museum Acquisition.' *Daily Telegraph*, 15 April 1957.

1041. —— 'Varieties, Literary and Philosophical.' *Monthly Magazine*, XXV (1 June 1808), 353. (Princeton)
'Mr. Cromek will very shortly present to the public Mr. William Blake's Illustrations of Blair's Grave, etched by Mr. Louis Schiavonetti.'

1042. —— *'Vessels of Immortal Life.' *Time*, 21 April 1952, pp. 32–4.
A paragraph occasioned by the *Jerusalem* facsimile.

1043. —— *'Vision of Easter: Blake Retells Sacred Story in Mystic Art and Words.' *Life*, 19 April 1954, pp. 60–4, 66–8.

1044. —— 'The Visionary Painter.' Pp. 120–6 of *The Brilliant, 1851*. Ed. T. S. Arthur. N.Y., 1850.
A biographical account taken largely from Cunningham.

1045. —— 'Visions of Blake the Artist.' [Philadelphia] *Casket*, V (May 1830), 231–2. (Cleveland Public)
An extract of paragraphs 36–9 and 41 from Cunningham (no. 1431), the first two of which were reprinted in the *New-England Weekly Review* (no. 1046).

1046. —— 'Visions of Blake the Artist.' *New-England Weekly Review*, [Hartford, Conn.] 3 May 1830, p. 1. (Connecticut Historical Society)
These two paragraphs from Cunningham are inaccurately derived from the first two quoted in [Philadelphia] *Casket* (no. 1045).

1047. —— *'Visions of William Blake.' *New York Times Magazine*, 13 Oct. 1957, pp. 46–7 (vMKN).

1048. —— 'William Blake.' *Art Journal*, 1907, pp. 75–7.
A general article.

1049. —— *'William Blake.' *Bulletin of the Minneapolis Institute of Arts*, XX (1931), 66–7.
Brief note on *Job*.

1050. —— 'William Blake.' *Literary Chronicle And Weekly Review*, 1 Sept. 1827, 557–8. (Bodley)
An obituary.

1051. —— *'William Blake.' *Littell's Living Age*, LIX [3rd Ser., III] (11 Dec. 1858), 848.
A quotation of the Blake biography in the 1858 *Grave* (no. 435G) explains A. L. Dick's engraving of Phillips's portrait of Blake at p. 785.

1052. —— 'William Blake.' *Monthly Magazine*, n.s. IV (Oct. 1827) 435. (Toronto)

Except for a sentence about Varley, and wrong dates for Blake's birth and death, this is entirely taken from the *Literary Gazette* obituary (no. 1071), though the phraseology is consistently debased.

1053. Anon. *'William Blake.' *Pennsylvania Museum Bulletin*, XXIX (1934), 75–6 (vMKN).
An account of the Rosenwald exhibition.

1054. —— *'William Blake.' *Times Educational Supplement*, 17 May 1957, pp. 682–3 (vMKN).
Reproduces the popular pictures.

1055. —— 'William Blake, 1827–1927.' *Nation* [New York], CXXV (1927), 221–2 (vMKN).

1056. —— 'William Blake Anniversary Marked in Soviet Union.' *Soviet Weekly*, XXXI (19–26 Dec. 1957), 12.
'Blake was a progressive, romantic poet', according to his translator, Samuel Marshak.

1057. —— 'William Blake à Philadelphia.' *Beaux-Arts*, 24 March 1939, p. 3.
Note on the exhibition.

1058. —— *'William Blake a Portrait Painter.' *Graphic*, 27 April 1918, p. 524 (vMKN).
Reproduces portraits of Lamb, Leigh Hunt, Byron, Shelley, Pope, and Keats alleged to be by Blake but obviously not. See also no. 1026, 2539.

1059. —— 'William Blake. A True Englishman. The New National Anthem.' *The Times*, 12 Aug. 1927, pp. 11–12.

1060. —— 'William Blake Art Will Assist Relief.' *New York Times*, 19 Oct. 1941, Section D, p. 1 (vMKN).
On the Knoedler Gallery exhibition for the Refugees of England, Inc.

1061. —— *'William Blake as the Pontiff of a New Spiritual Dispensation.' *Current Literature*, XLIII (1907), 646–7 (vMKN).
Notes current interest.

1062. —— (***.) 'William Blake et la Révolte contre la Loi Morale.' *Messages* [Cahiers Chroniques], Cahier II (1942), 28–36 (vMKN).
Mostly quotations from 'The Everlasting Gospel' and *The Marriage*.

1063. —— **William Blake Bicentenary Celebrations*. [London], 1957. Programme for service in Westminster Abbey, 24 Nov. 1957.

1064. —— 'William Blake: Centenary Memorial in St Paul's.' *Herald*, 23 March 1926.
A news report.

1065. —— 'William Blake. Exhibition at the Tate Gallery.' *The Times* 16 Oct. 1913, p. 12 (vMKN).

1066. Anon. *'William Blake, Mystic.' *New York Times*, 6 Nov. 1938 (vMKN).

1067. —— *'William Blake, Painter and Poet.' *Scribner's Monthly*, XX (1880), 225–40 (vMKN).

1068. —— *'William Blake, Poet, Painter, Engraver, and Printseller.' *Printseller*, I (1903), 333–9 (vMKN).
A general article.

1069. —— *'William Blake, Poet, Painter to Be Honored in Century.' *Springfield Union Herald Republican*, 28 Aug. 1927 (vMKN).

1070. —— *William Blake: Poet, Printer, Prophet.' *Connoisseur*, CLVI (1964), 199.
Review of exhibition.

1071. A. —— 'William Blake: The Illustrator of The Grave, &c.' *Literary Gazette*, 18 Aug. 1827, pp. 540–1. (LC) B. Reprinted in A. Symons, *William Blake*, 1907, no. 2804.
This very enthusiastic obituary was reprinted, with omissions and minor alterations, in the *Monthly Magazine* (no. 1052), and almost *in toto* in the *Gentleman's Magazine* (no. 989), which in turn was silently reprinted, with minor changes, in the *New Monthly Magazine* (no. 990) and in the *Annual Register* (no. 915), and with acknowledgements in the *Annual Biography* (no. 842).
According to the editor of the *Literary Gazette* (*The Autobiography of William Jerdan*, London, 1852, Vol. II, p. 176), 'William Carey was the chief contributor' to the early numbers of the magazine, and was probably primarily in charge of the sections on Art. Since Carey was a known Blake enthusiast, it seems likely that he was the author of this eloquent obituary.

1072. —— §'William Blake. The Proposed Memorial.' *Christian Globe*, 20 April 1899.

1073. —— 'William Blake triomphe.' *Mercure de France*, CXXIX (1918), 575 (vMKN).
News note concerning purchases.

1074. —— *'William Blake Vorläufer und Prophet.' Pp. 8–9 of *England im Übergang*. Ed. Hugo Debrunner. Zurich, 1948.
An introduction with translations of poems.

1075. —— 'William Blake Was a Unique Genius.' [Toronto] *Mail and Empire*, Aug. 1927.
A centenary article.

1076. —— 'William Blake Water Colors at the [Boston] Museum.' *Boston Evening Transcript*, 13 April 1937 (vMKN).

1077. —— 'William Blake Water-Colors for Pilgrim's Progress.' *Hobbies, the Magazine for Collectors*, [XLV], No. 12 (Feb. 1941), 36–7 (vMKN).

1078. Anon. 'William Blake Wood-cuts. 17 Blocks Bought for the Nation.'
The Times, 3 Dec. 1938.
Thornton blocks bought at Christie's.

1079. —— 'William Blake's Dante Illustrations.' *Christian Science Monitor*,
31 Oct. 1921 (vMKN).

1080. —— 'William Blake's Homes in Lambeth and Sussex.' *Spectator*,
CXVI (1916), 571–2 (vMKN).

1081. —— *'William Blake's Masterpiece. Reproductions for the Only
Copy of "Jerusalem" Hand-Coloured by the Poet Himself.' *Illustrated London
News*, 4 Nov. 1950, Supplement iv (vMKN).

1082. —— 'Wonderful Blake Drawings.' *Daily Telegraph*, 5 Feb. 1918.
News account of the imminent Linnell Sale, no. 608.

1083. —— 'Works of Hans Christian Andersen.' *Blackwood's Edinburgh
Magazine*, LXII (Oct. 1847), 387–407.
The 'Introduction' to *Innocence* (transcribed from Cunningham) is used to
'preface our notice of the life and works of Andersen', who is said to be 'a
man of somewhat kindred nature' to Blake (p. 389).

1085. Ansari, Asloob Ahmad. *Arrows of Intellect*: A Study in William Blake's
Gospel of the Imagination. Aligarh (India), 1965.

1086. Anshutz, H. L., & D. W. Cummings. 'Blake's THE SICK ROSE.'
Explicator, XXIX (1970), no. 32.
'Has it been noticed that William Blake's "The Sick Rose" seems to be his
reaction to Matthew Prior's "A True Maid"?' (Yes, in 1946 by Meyerstein.)

1087. Arensberg, W. C. 'The Lyrics of William Blake.' *Harvard Monthly*,
XXVIII (1899), 145–51 (vMKN).

1088. Armah, Ayi Kwei. 'The Romantic Response to the Industrial
Revolution: A Sociological Study of the Works of William Blake, 1757–1827
and William Wordsworth, 1770–1850.' Harvard, Ph.D., 1963.

1089. [Arms, G. W., J. P. Kirby, L. G. Locke, and J. E. Whitesell.] The
Editors. 'Blake's Stanzas from *Milton*.' *Explicator*, I (1943), item 38.
An orthodox explication referring to the Bible.

1090. Arnold, Eric. 'Keats, Blake and Bridges.' *TLS*, 14 May 1931, p. 390.
Bridges expresses Blake's and Keats's poetic faith.

1091. A. §Arvine, Kazlitt. 'Blake, the Poet, Painter, and Engraver.' *Cyclopaedia of Anecdotes of Literature and the Fine Arts*. Boston, 1851. P. 250. B. Boston,
1852. P. 250.
This account is from Cunningham as is that on 'Blake' under 'Eccentricities', p. 487.

1092. Ashelford, T. H. 'The Grave of William Blake.' *The Times*, 2 Aug. 1926.
   'A suitable memorial ought to be erected over his grave.'

1093. *Ashton, Dore. 'Fuseli and Blake: Two Against the Grain.' *Art Digest*, XXVIII (15 Jan. 1954), 8–9 (vMKN).

1094. Astorg, Bertrand d'. *Introduction au Monde de la Terreur*. Paris, 1945. Pp. 33–41.

1095. *Atkinson, George H. 'William Blake, Engraver, At Princeton.' *this week* Magazine of the [Trenton] *Times Advertiser*, 4 Jan. 1970, p. 5.
   Review of the 'really superb' exhibition (no. 700).

1096. Atkinson, J. Beavington. 'Exhibition of Works of William Blake, Burlington Club.' *Portfolio*, VII (1876), 69–71.

1097. Audard, Jean. 'William Blake et la Révolution.' *Messages*, I (1939), 15–19.

1098. Auden, W. H.; Kathleen Raine; W. H. Auden. '"A Mental Prince".' *Observer*, 17, 24 Nov., 1 Dec. 1957, pp. 12, 23, 6.
   Miss Raine complains that Auden wrote his bicentenary appreciation of Blake (p. 12) 'without having read or understood the bulk of his writings' (p. 23); Auden's temperate reply (p. 6) appears to confute her.

1099. Aynard, Joseph. 'William Blake, poète.' *Journal des Débats*, XXX (1923), 626–8 (vMKN).

1100. *Ayre, Robert. 'William Blake's Engravings At the Redpath Library', *Montreal Star*, 6 July 1957.
   An appreciation of *Job*.

B

1101. B., D. J., and E. J. Rose. 'Blake's TO THE ACCUSER WHO IS THE GOD OF THIS WORLD, 8.' *Explicator*, XX (1962), query 3; XXII (1964), item 37.
   D. J. B. asks the meaning of the last line and Rose answers.

1102. B., W. 'Blake's "Tyger."' *N&Q*, CXIV [10th Ser., VI] (1906), 226 (vMKN).
   The source said to be Buchanan's 'Baptists'.

1103. Babenroth, A. Charles. 'William Blake.' Chap. VI, pp. 262–98 of *English Childhood*: Wordsworth's Treatment of Childhood in the Light of English Poetry from Prior to Crabbe. N.Y., 1922.

1104. Bacon, M. E. 'Blake and Gray: A Case of Literary Symbiosis.' *Culture*, XXIX (1968), 42–50.
   'Blake's poem "To Mrs Ann Flaxman" is not only parallel to, but ultimately dependent upon, Gray's "Elegy"', she says (p. 50).

1105. Bacon, M. E. 'Blake's IMITATION OF POPE: A COMPLIMENT TO THE LADIES and A PRETTY EPIGRAM FOR THE ENTERTAINMENT OF THOSE WHO PAID GREAT SUMS IN THE VENETIAN AND FLEMISH OOZE.' *Explicator*, XXVIII (1970), item 79.

'Blake's imitation of Pope was intended to ridicule not the style of Pope but the man.'

1106. —— 'Blake's THE TYGER.' *Explicator*, XXVI (1967), item 35.

The previously remarked connection of the tyger with Orc is reinforced by the 'hitherto unnoticed' fact that on the page in the *Notebook* on which 'The Tyger' is drafted (p. 108) is a sketch which may represent Orc for *America* pl. 12.

See also Mary Ellen [Bacon] Reisner.

1107. Bagdasarianz, Waldemar. *William Blake*: Versuch einer Entwicklungsgeschichte des Mystikers. Erster Teil: bis 1795. Zurich und Leipzig, 1935. Swiss Studies in English, Vol. II. (No more parts were issued.)

1108. Bagenal, Hope. 'On the Mysticism of Wordsworth and Blake.' *Durham University Journal*, n.s. IV (1943), 79–87.

Chiefly deals with attitudes to or from childhood.

1109. Ba Han, Maung. *The Evolution of Blakean Philosophy*. Rangoon, [1926].

A pastiche of commonplaces (94 pp.).

1110. Ba-Han, Maung. *William Blake His Mysticism*. Bordeaux, 1924.

Blake's mysticism consists in 'his insistence on the supreme value of the "self"' (p. 237).

1111. Baine, Rodney M. 'Blake's THE LITTLE VAGABOND.' *Explicator*, XXVII (1968), item 6.

'Dame Lurch' in ll. 11–12 is probably a school-teacher.

1112. A. —— 'Blake's "Tyger": The Nature of the Beast.' *SP*, XLVI (1967), 488–98. B. Reprinted in Weathers (no. 2937).

'*A* reading of "The Tyger" in the context of [*the*] *Songs* . . . and of its analogues or sources reveals it as the shocked and fascinated reaction of an observer imaginatively visualizing the creation of brutal cruelty in nature and in man . . .' (p. 488).

1113. Baird, Sister Mary Julian. 'Blake, Hopkins and Thomas Merton.' *Catholic World*, CLXXXIII (1956), 46–9.

The influence of Blake and Hopkins on Merton.

1114. Baker, C. H. Collins. 'Blake at the Tate Gallery.' *Saturday Review*, 8 Nov. 1918, pp. 582–3.

Blake was 'an inferior artist, but a fine technician' (p. 582).

1115. —— *'Recent Acquisitions in Art.' *HLQ*, X (1946–7), 105–18.

Includes designs for *The Grave* and Phillips's portrait.

1116. A. Baker, C. H. Collins. *'The Sources of Blake's Pictorial Expression.' *HLQ*, IV (1940–1), 359–67. B. Reprinted in R. N. Essick, ed., *The Visionary Hand* (1973), no. A1583.

Among them Brown's *Ars Pictoria* and a gallery catalogue of 1792.

1117. —— *'William Blake, Painter.' *Huntington Library Bulletin*, X (1936), 135–48 (vMKN).

A good general lecture.

1118. Baker, Carlos H. 'William Blake—Soldier of Christ.' *Theology Today*, XIV (1957), 80–8 (vMKN).

1119. *Baker, Ernest Hamlin. 'Old Master Clinic: Wise and Foolish Virgins by William Blake.' *American Artist*, V, No. 7 (Sept. 1941), 22–3 (vMKN).

The composition analysed.

1120. Balakian, Anna. 'The Literary Fortune of William Blake in France.' *MLQ*, XVII (1956), 261–72.

Includes bibliography of Blake in France.

1121. Baldi, Wanda. *La Figure e l'Arte di William Blake*. Salerno, 1951.

1122. Baldwin, Stanley, J. Ramsay MacDonald, Pamela Grey of Falloden, W. R. Inge, Edward Elgar, Owen Seaman, Thomas Hardy, Charles Aitken, Laurence Binyon, Muirhead Bone, George Clausen, Laurence Housman, Selwyn Image, John Masefield. 'A Blake Memorial in St. Paul's.' *The Times*, 20 March 1926, p. 13.

Appeal for a fund.

1123. Banner, Delmar Harmood. 'William Blake and Sir Joshua Reynolds.' *Nineteenth Century*, CI (1927), 620 (vMKN).

Reply to Herbert Wright.

1124. *Barker, Virgil. 'A Traveler's Notes on Art: The Blakes in the Tate Gallery.' *Arts*, XII (1927), 83–98.

1125. *Barnard, Eunice Fuller. 'To a Poet-Mystic Belated Honors Come.' *New York Times Magazine*, 7 Aug. 1927, pp. 8–9, 18 (vMKN).

1126. Barnes, Walter. 'William Blake.' Pp. 86–102 of *The Children's Poets*. Yonkers-on-Hudson, 1924 (vMKN).

An essay (negligible) on pp. 86–96, selected poems on pp. 97–102.

1127. Barr, D. J. 'William Blake's Use of the Bible.' *N&Q*, CCVII (1962), 312.

Very small corrections of Tolley, no. 2863.

1128. Barrett, James A. S. 'Carlyle on Blake and Vitalis.' *TLS*, 26 April 1928, p. 313.

Barrett ascribes to Carlyle the authorship of 'The Last of the Supernaturalists', no. 968.

1129. Basan, P. F., et H. L. DICTIONNAIRE / DES / GRAVEURS / ANCIENS ET MODERNES, / Depuis l'origine de la Gravure; / PAR

P. F. et H. L. BASAN, père et fils, / GRAVEURS. / SECONDE ÉDITION, / Précedée d'une Notice historique sur l'Art de la / Graveur, Par P. P. CHOF-FARD; suivie d'un / Précis de la Vie de l'Auteur, et ornée de soixante / Estampes par différens Artistes célèbres, dont 18 / Sujets nouveaux. / TOME PREMIER [SECOND]. / — / A PARIS, / Chez J. J. BLAISE, Libraire, quai des Augustins, / No. 61. / — / 1809. I, 70 (Bodley)

'BLAKE, (W.), a gravé à Londres en 1784 &c, divers sujets à la manière pointillée, d'après différens artistes Anglais.' (The first edition of 1767 of course omits the Blake reference.)

1130. A. Basler, Roy P. *Sex, Symbolism, and Psychology in Literature*. New Brunswick [N.J.], 1948. Pp. 19–24. B. Reprinted as 'The Tyger: A Psychological Interpretation' in Weathers (no. 2937).

'Blake understood . . . the duality ruling the realm of the psyche' (p. 24).

1131. Bassalik-de Vries, J. C. E. *William Blake in his Relation to Dante Gabriel Rossetti*. Basel, 1911.

Mrs. Bassalik-de Vries's brief (56 pp.) Zurich Ph.D. dissertation is not notably accurate.

1132. A. Bataille, Georges. 'William Blake.' Pp. 81–107 of *La Littérature et le Mal*: Emily Bronte—Baudelaire—Michelet—Blake—Sade—Proust—Kafka—Genet. Paris, 1957. B. Tr. Isao Yamamoto as *Bungaku to Aku* [*Literature and Evil*]. Tokyo, 1959. Pp. 82–117 (vHK).

The most moving writers in English are John Ford, Brontë, and Blake (p. 83 of A).

1133. —— 'William Blake ou la Vérité du Mal.' *Critique*, IV (1948), 771–7, 976–85 (vMKN).

Ostensibly a review article on Witcutt, but includes discussion of 'The Tyger'.

1134. Bateman, Arthur B. 'Spiritual Genius of William Blake.' *London Quarterly [and Holborn] Review*, CXLVIII (1927), 34–45 (vMKN).

A centenary article.

1135. Bateson, Frederick W., & [Sir] Geoffrey Keynes. 'Selections from Blake.' *TLS*, 26 April 1957, p. 257; 10 May 1957, p. 289 (vMKN).

Bateson objects to the review of his edition of *Selected Poems*; Keynes points out that both Bateson and the reviewer are wrong in saying that there was no final order for the *Songs*, which were given a fixed order in seven out of eight copies after 1815.

1136. Battenhouse, Henry M. 'William Blake.' Pp. 50–5 of *English Romantic Writers*. Great Neck, N.Y., 1958.

A student guide.

1137. *Battye, John Christopher. 'William Blake: Revolutionary or Rebel?' art and artists*, IV (Aug. 1969), 24–5.

'He was, plainly and simply, a rebel' (p. 25).

1138. *Bazin, G. 'Blake et Turner à la Bibliothèque Nationale.' *L'Amour de l'Art*, XVIII (1937), 30–1.

1139. *Beaumont, Elie de. *William Blake.* N.p., 1959. Curiosa Typografica II.

1140. *Beaumont, Germaine. 'Deux visionnaires anglais: Blake et Turner à la Bibliothèque Nationale.' *Nouvelles Littéraires*, 23 Jan. 1937, p. [1] (vRG). Impressionistic praise of Blake's art.

1141. Beeching, H. C. 'Blake's Religious Lyrics.' *E&S*, III (1912), 136–52. Blake wrote his *Songs* to impress his ideas of true religion upon children.

1142. *Beer, John. 'Blake at the Fitzwilliam.' *Cambridge Review*, XCII (1971), 110–13. Review of the exhibition (see no. 703).

1143. —— *Blake's Humanism.* Manchester & N.Y., 1968. 'Blake's humanism is idiosyncratic' (p. 23).

1144. —— *Blake's Visionary Universe.* N.Y., 1969. An attempt to deal with Blake's struggle 'to create artistic myth on the grand scale' (p. 53), particularly in *Vala* and *Jerusalem*. There are 78 plates.

1145. Bell, C. C.; J. Wickham Legg; Celer et Audax, F. C. Birkbeck Terry; C. C. Bell; Celer et Audax; Celer et Audax. 'Blake's "Holy Thursday".' *N&Q*, LXXXIII [7th Ser., XI] (1891), 386, 475, 514, LXXXIV [7th Ser., XII] (1891), 58, LXXXVI [8th Ser., II] (1892), 214, XCIV [8th Ser., IX] (1896), 394. The day referred to is Ascension Day or Maundy Thursday.

1146. Bell, C. F., and Geoffrey Keynes. 'Blake and Flaxman.' *TLS*, 31 March 1945, p. 151. The Flaxman receipt for £100 from Blake was misattributed to the poet by Lowery (no. 2150), instead of to Robert Blake of 14 Essex Street. See also Erdman, no. 1560.

1147. *Benoit, François. *Un Maître de l'Art: Blake le Visionnaire.* Lille & Paris, 1906. Competent and brief; 62 plates.

1148. —— *'A Master of Art.' *Annals of Psychical Science*, VII, No. 37 (Jan. 1908), 3–22 (vDS). Considers Blake under the heads of 'Visionary', 'Seer', and 'Mystic'.

1149. Benson, Arthur Christopher. 'William Blake.' Pp. 147–79 of *Essays.* London, 1896.

1150. *Benson, Preston. 'World's Greatest Love Stories, 39: The Adam & Eve Lovers.' *The Star*, 21 Aug. 1958 (vKP). A rubbishy evening newspaper article on the Blakes.

1151. Bentley, Gerald E., Jr. 'Additions to Blake's Library.' *BNYPL*, LXIV (1960), 595–605.

More suggestions about the contents of Blake's library, using criteria less strict and more varied than those of Sir Geoffrey Keynes (no. 2020).

For other articles in this 'William Blake Issue', see no. 1309.

1152. Bentley, Gerald E., Jr. 'A. S. Mathew, Patron of Blake and Flaxman.' *N&Q*, CCIII (1958), 168–78.

A good many new facts added to Margoliouth's, throwing more light on Mathew and Flaxman than on Blake.

1153. —— 'Blake and Percy's Reliques.' *N&Q*, CCI [N.S. III] (1956), 352–3.

Discusses and traces the lines which Blake quotes from Thomas Tickell's 'Lucy and Colin' (which had in fact been previously identified) to Percy's *Reliques* (1765).

1154. —— 'Blake and Swedenborg.' *N&Q*, CXCIX [N.S. I] (1954), 264–5.

The selective list of books of the Bible on *Jerusalem* pl. 48 duplicates exactly the books approved as having 'the internal Sense' by the 1789 meeting to organize the New Church, at which Blake was present and voted.

1155. —— 'Blake and Young.' *N&Q*, CXCIX [N.S. I] (1954), 529–30.

An apparent echo of *Night Thoughts* in *For the Sexes*.

1156. *—— 'Blake, blāk, William.' Vol. IV, pp. 55–6 of *The Encyclopedia Americana* International Edition. N.Y., 1967.

Standard account, rewritten in the encyclopedia's editorial office.

1157. —— 'Blake, Hayley, and Lady Hesketh.' *RES*, N.S. VII (1956), 264–86.

The nature of the relationship established from their letters.

1158. —— *Blake Records.* Oxford, 1969.

'The purpose of the *Blake Records* is to collect and publish as many as possible of the references to Blake made by his contemporaries' (p. xxiv), including the biographical essays by Malkin, Crabb Robinson, J. T. Smith, Cunningham and Tatham, with separate sections on Blake's Residences, Accounts, and Engravings. There are 67 illustrations, including all the plates for Blair's *Grave*.

1159. —— 'Blake Scholars and Critics: [I] The Texts [(II) Commentators and Exhibitions].' *University of Toronto Quarterly*, XXXIX (1970), 274–87, XL (1970), 86–101.

Review of 19 works, chiefly factual corrections of the *Letters* (1968), *Gates* (1968), *Concordance* (1967), and Miss Raine's *Blake and Tradition* (1968).

1160. —— 'Blake's Annotations to Swedenborg's *Heaven and Hell*.' *University of Toronto Quarterly*, XXXIV (1965), 290–3.

Blake's copy is in Harvard.

1161. —— *'Blake's Engravings and his Friendship with Flaxman.' *SB*, XII (1959), 161–88.

Blake's relationship with Flaxman traced through manuscript references, some of them new.

1162. Bentley, Gerald E., Jr. 'Blake's Hesiod.' *Library*, 5th Ser., XX (1965), 315–20.
Dates, prices, and proofs of Blake's work on Flaxman's *Hesiod* designs, 22 Sept. 1814 to 21 Feb. 1817.

1163. *—— 'Blake's *Job* Copperplates.' *Library*, 5th Ser. XXVI (1971), 234–41.
Plates for an abortive *Job* facsimile are in McGill; *copper for Blake's *Job* pl. 14, 16 had previously been used in H. L. Duhamel du Monceau's *Practical Treatise of Husbandry* (1759, 1762); copperplates in *America*, *Marriage*, *Europe*, *Songs*, *Urizen*, and *Jerusalem* were apparently etched on both sides.

1164. —— *'Byron, Shelley, Wordsworth, Blake, and *The Seaman's Recorder*.' *Studies in Romanticism*, IX (1970), 21–36.
Six previously unrecorded journeyman plates by Blake of 1824–5.
Sir Geoffrey Keynes 'defend[s] his [*Blake's*] reputation against . . .[*this*] mistaken attribution' in 'Blake's Engravings for Gay's *Fables*', *Book Collector*, XXI (1972), 60.

1165. —— 'A Collection of Prosaic William Blakes.' *N&Q*, CCX [N.S. XII] (1965), 172–8.
Some 23 London contemporaries of the poet who bore his names.

1166. —— 'The Date of Blake's Pickering Manuscript *or* The Way of a Poet with Paper.' *SB*, XIX (1966), 232–43.
The paper is from the 1802 *Ballads*, and the date of the fair copy is probably between 1807 and 1824.

1167. A. —— 'The Date of Blake's *Vala* or *The Four Zoas*.' *MLN*, LXXI (1956), 487–91. B. Pp. 96–100 of *A Mirror for Modern Scholars*: Essays in Methods of Research in Literature. Ed. Lester A. Beaurline. N.Y., 1966.
Evidence that 'all of *Vala* from the fourth Night on was written or transscribed in its present state after May, 1802'.

1168. —— 'The Failure of Blake's *Four Zoas*.' *Texas Studies in English*, XXXVII (1958), 102–13.
Some detailed conclusions from a study of the manuscript as to how and why the poem went wrong.

1169. —— 'A Footnote to Blake's Treason Trial.' *N&Q*, CC [N.S. II] (1955), 118–19.
A manuscript letter from Blake's lawyer demonstrates that his fee for defending Blake was paid by Hayley.

1170. —— *'A New Blake Document: The "Riddle" Manuscript.' *Library*, 5th Ser., XXIV (1969), 337–43.
Description, significance, and history of a previously unknown 'trifle'.

1171. —— 'A Piper Passes: The Earliest Parody of Blake's "Songs of Innocence".' *N&Q*, CCIX [N.S. XI] (1964), 418–19.

1172. Bentley, Gerald E., Jr. 'Postscript.' *BNYPL*, LXII (1958), 202.
A pendant to no. 439, attempting to date Blake's early prose fragments with some precision.

1173. —— *'The Printing of Blake's *America.*' *Studies in Romanticism*, VI (1966), 46–57.
Printing variants in the second Preludium plate 'help to indicate in what order the copies of *America* were printed over a period of forty years'.

1174. —— *'The Promotion of Blake's *Grave* Designs.' *University of Toronto Quarterly*, XXXI (1962), 340–53.
New prospectuses illuminate the causes of Blake's rage at Cromek.

1175. —— 'Thomas Butts, White Collar Maecenas.' *PMLA*, LXXI (1956), 1052–66.
Collects all the old and a number of new facts (chiefly financial) about Butts, the most interesting of which is that Butts was not as his family and the critics had always said, Muster Master General, but merely a clerk in that office. His patronage of Blake claimed an impressive part of his limited salary.

1176. —— *'The Thorne Blake Collection at the Pierpont Morgan Library, New York.' *Apollo*, XCIV (1971), 416.
Notice of the exhibition.

1177. —— 'Two Contemporary Facsimiles of *Songs of Innocence and of Experience.*' *Publications of the Bibliographical Society of America*, LXIV (1970), 450–63.
Made by 1825.

1178. —— 'An Unknown Early Biography of Blake.' *TLS*, 16 March 1962, p. 192.
By Thomas Dodd, *c.* 1835, largely derived from Cunningham.

1179. —— 'William Blake and "Johnny of Norfolk".' *SP*, LIII (1956), 60–74.
Blake's friendship with Cowper's cousin John Johnson traced through letters to and from Hayley.

1180. —— 'William Blake and the Alchemical Philosophers.' Oxford B.Litt. Dissertation, 1954.
Diffuse and inconclusive.

1181. —— 'William Blake as a Private Publisher.' *BNYPL*, LXI (1957), 539–60.
Discusses, largely on the basis of manuscript references, some of them new, the methods and failures of the publication, in 1802 and 1805, of Hayley's *Ballads* with Blake's plates and for Blake's benefit. See also no. 1308 for other articles in this Blake issue.

1182. Bentley, Gerald E., Jr. 'William Blake's Protean Text.' Pp. 44–58 of *Editing Eighteenth-Century Texts*: Papers given at the Editorial Conference, University of Toronto, October 1967. Ed. D. I. B. Smith. Toronto, 1968.
Some samples of the problems facing an editor of Blake.

1183. Berger, Pierre. 'L'État Actuel des études sur Blake d'après quelques livres récents.' *Revue Anglo-Américaine*, IV (1926), 55–70 (vMKN).
Composite review-article.

1184. A. —— 'William Blake: Visions et doctrines de William Blake.' *Mercure de France*, CXCVII (1927), 5–27. B. 'William Blake.' *Indépendance belge*, 27 Aug. 1927.
A centenary essay, abstracted in B.

1185. A. —— *William Blake, Mysticisme et Poésie.* Paris, 1907. §B. Paris, 1936. C. *William Blake Poet and Mystic.* Tr. Daniel Conner. London, 1914. D. N.Y., 1915. E. N.Y., 1968. F. §Folcroft, Pennsylvania, 1973.
The translation omits the appendices, 'Éditeurs et Critiques', 'Remarques sur la Versification de Blake', and 'Fragments inédits', the last being marginalia since republished.

1186. A. Bernbaum, Ernest. 'William Blake.' Pp. 69–82 of *Guide Through the Romantic Movement* (Vol. I of *Anthology and Guide Through the Romantic Movement.* 5 vols.). N.Y., 1930. B. 'Blake.' Pp. 42–52 of *Guide Through the Romantic Movement.* Second Edition Revised and Enlarged. [Published separately.] N.Y., 1949.
A rather hasty and dogmatic survey of Blake's life, style, thought, and bibliography.

1187. Bertram, Anthony. 'Blake: An Aesthetic Approach.' *Nineteenth Century*, XCIX (1926), 442–9 (vMKN).
Blake as artist was a mystical expressionist not to be understood rationally.

1188. Bier, Jesse. 'Put a Lion in Your Tank.' *Carleton Miscellany*, X, No. 2 (Spring 1969), 86–94.
In their quarrel about 'The Tyger', Robinson and Grant have conspired to ignore Bier's 'Blake's Fortune-Cookie: "The Tyger" Reconsidered and Resolved', *Enco Products New Bulletin*, XLI (1959), 14–182.

1189. A. —— 'A Study of Blake's "The Tyger".' *Bucknell University Studies*, I, No. 2 (June 1949), 35–46. B. Reprinted in Weathers (no. 2937).
An analysis with references to Moby Dick, Donne, and Yin-Yang mysticism.

1190. A. Billington, Michael. 'Blake Revitalized.' *The Times*, 22 July 1971. B. Reprinted in *Blake Newsletter*, V (1972), 209, with a review by Morton D. Paley.
Review of Mitchell's *Tyger*.

1191. Bindman, David. 'The dating of Blake's Marginalia to Reynolds.' *Burlington Magazine*, CVIII (1966), 522.

The 'Society [of "The Rich Men of England"] to Sell and Not to Buy Pictures' is a clear 'reference to the founding of the British Institution for the Encouragement of the Arts in 1805.'

1192. Bindman, David. *'Heads from Blake's head.' *Guardian*, 26 May 1971, p. 16.
About the Blake–Varley sketch-book, for sale in June.

1193. —— *'William Blake and the Victorians.' *Cambridge Review*, XCII (1971), 113–15.

1194. A. Binyon, Laurence. 'The Art of Blake.' *Independent Review*, II (1904), 407–14. B. Reprinted in *Littell's Living Age*, CCXLI (1904), 487–92. C. *Eclectic Magazine*, CXLIII (1904), 129–34 (vMKN).
An informed general article.

1195. A. —— *'Blake.' Pp. 79–93 of *English Water-Colours*. London, 1933. The Library of English Art. B. *Second Edition, London, 1944. Pp. 71–83. . . . E. 1962.

1196. —— (L. B.) 'Blake's *Songs of Innocence and Experience*.' *British Museum Quarterly*, VII (1933), 55–6.
On the acquisition of a copy from Miss Cary. A 'Correction', VIII (1934), 53–4, notes that Miss Cary's copy came through Mrs. Charles Warren 'who may well have got it direct from Blake'.

1197. —— *'Blake's Woodcuts.' *Burlington Magazine*, XXXVII (1920), 284–9 (vMKN).
On the Virgil Illustrations.

1198. —— 'Blake's Work as a Painter.' *Putnam's Monthly*, III (1907–8), 410–17 (vMKN).
A judicious introduction.

1199. —— 'English Poetry in Its Relation to Painting and the Other Arts.' *Proceedings of the British Academy*, VIII (1918), 3–24.
A general lecture, partly about Blake.

1200. A. —— *'The Engravings of William Blake and Edward Calvert.' *Print Collector's Quarterly*, VII (1917), 305–32 (vMKN). B. Reprinted in R. N. Essick, ed., *The Visionary Hand* (1973), no. A1583. See also no. 1205.

1201. A. —— *The Followers of William Blake*: Edward Calvert, Samuel Palmer, George Richmond & their Circle. London & N.Y., 1925. B. *N.Y., 1968.
The brief text (29 pp.) is just a summary of Blake's effect on The Ancients. The *raison d'être* of the book is the 92 plates of pictures chiefly by disciples. The 8 fine colour plates in 1925 degenerated to monotone in 1968.

1202. A. —— *'Lecture IV.' Pp. 147–95 of his *Landscape in English Art and Poetry*. Tokyo [1930]. B. London, 1931.
Rowlandson and Blake (pp. 165–95) 'are the two chief figure painters of the English water-colour school' (p. 147).

1203. Binyon, Laurence. *‘A Rediscovered Blake.’ *Burlington Magazine*, LIV (1929), 284–5.
'Charity.'

1204. —— §‘William Blake.’ *British Institute of Paris*, April 1938, pp. 7–12.
Extract of a Sorbonne lecture.

1205. —— *‘William Blake und Edward Calvert.’ *Die Graphischen Künste*, XXV (1902), 96–101 (vMKN).
A valuable article. See also no. 1200.

1206. *Birnbaum, Martin. ‘William Blake and Other Illustrators of Dante.’
Pp. 67–79 of *Jacovleff and Other Artists*. N.Y., 1946.

1207. Birrell, T. A. ‘The Figure of Satan in Milton and Blake.’ Pp. 379–93 of *Satan*. London & N.Y., 1951.

1208. Birss, J. H. ‘Herman Melville and Blake.’ *N&Q*, CLXVI (1934), 311 (vMKN).
Melville owned Gilchrist's *Life* 1680 and may have been influenced by Blake.

1209. Bishop, Morchard [pseudonym for Oliver Stoner]. ‘Blake and Buckingham.’ *TLS*, 2 April 1964, p. 277.
‘Busy, Busy, Busy I bustle along . . .’ is from *The Rehearsal*, v.

1210. —— *Blake's Hayley*. The Life, Works, and Friendships of William Hayley. London, 1951.
This excellent work contains a number of quotations from contemporary accounts of Blake.

1211. Blackstone, Bernard. *The Consecrated Urn*: An Interpretation of Keats in Terms of Growth and Form. London, N.Y., Toronto, 1959. *Passim*.
Faint analogies adduced to prove that Blake was an important influence on Keats.

1212. A. —— *English Blake*. Cambridge, 1949. B. *Hamden, Conn., 1966.
A useful, rather miscellaneous book; the most stimulating section is on the *Island in the Moon*. A new Foreword in B says that no ‘major modifications’ were needed.

1213. ——‘“Poetical Sketches” and “Hyperion”.’ *The Cambridge Journal*, VI (1952), 160–8.
Blackstone persuades himself that he has found ‘conclusive evidence’, though in the nature of ‘affinities of atmosphere’, that Keats ‘knew *Poetical Sketches* and was powerfully influenced by them’.

1214. —— ‘The Traveller Unknown.’ Pp. 51–89 of his *The Lost Travellers*. A Romantic Theme with Variations. London, 1962. See also *passim*.
A general critical account of Blake.

1215. Blagg, Helen M. ‘The Social Teaching of William Blake.’ *Commonwealth*, X (1905), 270–4 (vMKN).

1216. Blake, Vernon. 'William Blake, Painter and Poet.' *Architectural Review*, LXII (1927), 59–60 (vMKN).

1217. *Blake Newsletter*. Ed. Morton D. Paley.

[Vol. I], No. 1 (June 1967): Brief notes and news.

[Vol. I], No. 2 (Sept. 1967):
1. G. E. Bentley, Jr. 'Blake Apocrypha.' Pp. 4–5. (A doggerel poem on Hayley mis-attributed to Blake.)
2. John E. Grant. 'Recognizing Fathers.' Pp. 7–9. (Rebuttal of Connolly & Levine, no. 1416.)
3. Michael J. Tolley. 'Remarks on "The Tyger".' Pp. 10–13. (Disagreement with Paley, no. 2350; with a reply by Paley on pp. 13–14.)

[Vol. I], No. 3 (Dec. 1967), 'Damoniana' issue, dedicated to S. Foster Damon on his 75th birthday:
4. S. Foster Damon, 'How I discovered Blake.' Pp. 2–3. (Apparently reprinted from no. 1449.)
5. M. D. Paley. 'Blake at Princeton.' Pp. 6–7. (Exhibition of the collections of Princeton and Miss Caroline Newton.)
6. Kathleen Raine. 'The Crested Cock.' Pp. 9–10. (*Milton*, pl. 28, l. 24 derived from Thomas Taylor, Plato, and Proclus; the note is apparently independent of no. 790.)
7. E. J. Rose. 'The Meaning of Los.' Pp. 10–11. ('I think "los" means . . . "look" or "behold" in the traditionally shortened form of the interjection "lo".')
8. David V. Erdman. 'Errata Emendata: Second Printing: Erdman–Bloom P & P of WB.' Pp. 11–13. (About 50 new corrections for no. 304.)
9. W. H. Stevenson. 'Two Problems in *The Four Zoas*.' Pp. 13–16. (The first problem, dealt with here, is: 'Where does the Second Night begin?')
10. M. D. Paley. '*Europe* iii: 18.' Pp. 16, 18. (Not 'where' as in Keynes [1927 ff.] and Erdman–Bloom, but 'when' as in Sampson [1905] and Keynes [1925].)
11. Thomas E. Connolly & George R. Levine. 'Recognizing Mother,' Pp. 17–18. (Reply to 'Grant's cavalier dismissal of us' above; see no. 23, 30, below.)

[Vol. I], No. 4 (March 1968):
12. W. H. Stevenson. 'Two Problems in *The Four Zoas* (continued).' Pp. 6–8. ('I conclude that Blake had decided to keep [*Night*] VIIb somehow.')
13. David V. Erdman. 'Blake's Terrible Ease!' P. 8. (Correction of 4 lines of 'When Klopstock England defied' in his edition, no. 304.)
14. Michael J. Tolley. 'Some Analogues or Sources.' P. 9. (Report of Wittreich's article, and a suggestion about R. C. Rogers, *Cain's Lamentations over Abel* [c. 1811–25].)
15. John Howell, 'An Early, Hand-Made Facsimile of the *Songs of Innocence and of Experience*.' Pp. 10–11. (Made about 1821.)
16. David V. Erdman. 'On the Newly Rediscovered Blake Letter.' P. 12. (Two corrections to no. 95.)

Vol. II, No. 1 (June 1968):

17. Alvin Rosenfeld. 'A Yiddish Poem on Blake.' P. 9. (By Reuben Iceland [1884–1953].)
18. Michael J. Tolley. 'Three Bibliographical Additions.' P. 10. (The Sparrow Bible, a 1936 Sawyer catalogue, and an essay on Gray's 'Bard'.)
19. G. E. Bentley, Jr. 'All the Evidence That's Fit to Print.' Pp. 11–13. (On R. C. Jackson's articles, no. 1934–41.)
20. Joseph Anthony Wittreich, Jr. 'A Bibliographical Note.' Pp. 13–14. (A reference in *Blackwood's*.)

Vol. II, No. 2 (Sept. 1968):

21. Joseph Anthony Wittreich, Jr. 'A Note on Blake and Milton.' Pp. 17–18. (Echoes in *The Marriage*.)
22. W. E. Moss. 'The Coloured Copies of Blake's "Night Thoughts".' Pp. 19–23. (History and census of 17 copies.)
23. John E. Grant. 'Mother of Invention, Father in Drag or Observations on the Methodology that Brought About These Deplorable Conditions and What Then is to be Done.' Pp. 29–32. (A continuation of the dispute with Connolly and Levine, no. 11, above.)

Vol. II, No. 3 (Dec. 1968):

24. Robert P. Kolker. 'Blake in the Institute.' Pp. 36–7. (Report of the English Institute [1968] papers on Blake.)
25. Martin Butlin. 'William Rossetti's Annotations to Gilchrist's *Life of William Blake*.' Pp. 39–40. (In Harvard; see no. 45, below.)
26. John Buck. 'Miss Groggery.' Pp. 40–1. (A tiger described in Anon., *An Historical Description of the Tower of London* [1768].)
27. G. E. Bentley, Jr. 'A Census of Coloured Copies of Young's *Night Thoughts*.' Pp. 41–5. (A supplement to Moss above.)
28. Frederic Cummings. 'Blake at Detroit and Philadelphia.' Pp. 46–8. (Correction of a review of no. 694 by Anne T. Kostelanetz in the June 1968 issue.)
29. David V. Erdman. '*J[erusalem]*. 95: 2–20.' P. 49. (Another correction of the Kostelanetz review.)
30. John E. Grant. 'Mothers and Methodology.' Pp. 50–4. (A continuation of the quarrel with no. 11, above.)

Vol. II, No. 4 (April 1969):

31. Michael J. Tolley. 'Blake's Debt to Pope.' Pp. 62–4. (Ten parallels in Blake and Pope.)
32. G. E. Bentley, Jr. 'Sterne and Blake.' Pp. 64–5. (Passages in *Sentimental Journey* and *America* show 'in some respects a striking coincidence of minds'.)
33. Morton D. Paley. 'Thomas Johnes, "Ancient Guardian of Wales".' Pp. 65–7. (*Jerusalem* 41 [46], ll. 3–4 'can only apply to Johnes of Hafod'— or may do so.)
34. David V. Erdman. 'Every Thing Has Its Vermin.' P. 68. (The Columbia

copy of Malkin has a note by 'Jabez Legg 1809' stating that Malkin gives 'a little too much about Mr. Blake'.)

35. John Adlard. '*Milton* 29: A Retort to William Frend?' P. 73. (In Frend's *Evening Amusements* [1814]; a remote connection.)

36. G. E. Bentley, Jr. 'A Fugitive or Apocryphal Blake Engraving.' P. 74. (The BMPR acquired in 1859 a print then catalogued as 'The World before the Flood' by Blake from *The Minor's[?] Pocket Book*, and then mislaid it; see no. 81 below.)

37. G. E. Bentley, Jr. 'A Supplement to G. E. Bentley, Jr., and Martin K. Nurmi, *A Blake Bibliography* (1964).' Supplement, pp. 1–29.

Vol. III, No. 1 (June 1969):

38. Joseph Anthony Wittreich, Jr. 'A Note on Blake and Fuseli.' Pp. 3–4. (In a lecture of 1803, Fuseli 'defines epic poetry as "sublime allegory"'.)

39. Stuart Curran & Joseph Anthony Wittreich, Jr. 'Some Additions to *A Blake Bibliography*.' Pp. 4–6. (Eight items.)

40. David V. Erdman. 'Dating Blake's Script: the 'g' hypothesis.' Pp. 8–13. (Blake formed his 'g' with an unconventional, leftward serif from 'the middle of 1791' until between 'Nov 5 1802 . . . and March 25 1804' or until 18 June 1805, and used a rightward serif before and after these dates; see no. 43–4.)

41. W. H. Stevenson. 'Blake and William Frend.' Pp. 19–20. ('Frend's idea seems to be drawn from Blake, rather than vice versa', as Adlard suggested above.)

Vol. III, No. 2 (Sept. 1969):

42. Robert N. Essick. 'A Finding List of Reproductions of Blake's Art: Part I: The Illuminated Books.' Pp. 24–41. (An exceedingly useful index of individual plates; see below no. 49, 56. Revised in the issue for Summer and Autumn 1971.)

43. David V. Erdman. 'Dating Blake's Script: a postscript.' P. 42. (Correction of a 'crucial mistake' above.)

44. G. E. Bentley, Jr. 'Blake's Sinister "g", from 1789–93 to ?1803.' Pp. 43–5. (A 'dating more precise than 1789–93 to ?1803 will be highly speculative without better evidence than we have at present'.)

Vol. III [No. 3] (Dec. 1969):

45. Joseph Anthony Wittreich, Jr. 'Further Observations on William Rossetti's Annotations to Gilchrist's *Life of Blake*.' Pp. 48–51. (Quotes annotations apparently made after 1868 and before autumn 1873; see no. 25, above.)

46. Michael J. Tolley. 'The Auckland Fuselis.' Pp. 51–2. (Excerpts from P. A. Tomory, *A Collection of Drawings by Henry Fuseli* [1967].)

47. Victor Skretkowicz, Jr. 'J. Deffett Francis: The Swansea Blakes.' (They include seven prints from *America*, *Europe*, and *Jerusalem*.)

48. David Bindman. 'J. S. Deville's Life Mask of William Blake.' Pp. 55–7. (History and description.)

49. Robert N. Essick. 'A Finding List of Reproductions of Blake's Art.' Pp. 64–70. ('Addenda to Part I', p. 64, 'Part II: Illustrations to Blake's

Non-illuminated Writings', pp. 64–70; see no. 42, 56. Revised in the issue for Summer and Autumn 1971.)

Vol. III, No. 4 [part i] (May 1970):

50. Mark L. Reed. 'Blake, Wordsworth, Lamb, Etc.: Further information from Henry Crabb Robinson.' Pp. 76–84. ('"Lamb used to call him a 'Mad Wordsworth'".')

51. Paul F. Betz. 'Wordsworth's First Acquaintance with Blake's Poetry.' Pp. 84–9. (Wordsworth's transcript of Blake's poems in Malkin were made between 12 Feb. and 25 Aug. 1807.)

52. Thomas L. Minnick. 'Blake Items in the Library of Isaac Reed.' P. 89. (*Poetical Sketches* and Hayley's *Ballads* [1802].)

53. Kathleen Raine. '*Blake and Tradition*.' Pp. 89–90. (Contrary to Daniel Hughes's review in the December 1969 number, 'Keynes does . . . agree with my interpretation of the Arlington Court Tempera'.)

54. Mary Lynn Johnson. 'The Devil's Syntax and the O.E.D.' Pp. 94–6. ('How should we parse "Damn. braces: Bless relaxes"?')

55. John E. Grant. 'Discussing the Arlington Court Picture Part I: A Report on the Warner-Simmons Theory.' Pp. 96–105. (See no. 69, below.) (Analysis and criticism of an oral interpretation at the 1969 MLA meetings.)

Vol. III, No. 4, part ii (May 1970):

56. Robert N. Essick. 'A Finding List of Reproductions of Blake's Art Part III: Illustrations in Series to Other's Writings [pp. 1–23]; Part IV: Paintings, Drawings, and Engravings not part of any series [pp. 1–21]; Supplement: Blakeana [pp. 1–3].' (See no. 42, 49, above.) Revised in the issue for Summer and Autumn 1971.

Vol. IV, No. 1 (Aug. 1970):

57. Michael J. Tolley. '*Jerusalem* 12: 25–29—Some Questions Answered.' Pp. 3–6. (Topographical.)

58. Charles L. Cherry. 'William Blake and Mrs. Grundy: Suppression of *Visions of the Daughters of Albion*.' Pp. 6–10. (Chiefly about Macmillan's prudery.)

59. Francis Wood Metcalf. 'Toward a More Accurate Description of the *Tiriel* Manuscript.' Pp. 10–11. (The numeration is for sections, not, as Bentley [no. 204] supposes, for folios.)

60. Thomas L. Minnick. 'Blake and "Cowper's Tame Hares".' Pp. 11–12. (The plate in Hayley's Cowper [no. 468] *is* signed, *pace* Bentley & Nurmi [no. 686].)

61. John E. Grant. 'Discussing the *Arlington Court Picture* Part II: Studying Blake's Iconography for Guidance in Interpreting the Picture.' Pp. 12–25. (See no. 55, above and no. 69, below.)

62. Irene H. Chayes. 'Blake and Tradition: "The Little Girl Lost" and "The Little Girl Found".' Pp. 25–8. (Criticism of the 'critical method' in Raine [no. 2403 1].)

Vol. IV, No. 2 (Autumn 1970):

63. *David Bindman. 'An Unpublished Blake Pencil Drawing of the

Lambeth Period.' Pp. 38–40. (Recto for *Urizen* [or *Visions* pl. 2?], verso for *Song of Los* pl. 2.)

64. Michael Phillips. 'Blake's Corrections in *Poetical Sketches*.' Pp. 40–7. (A census of changes in eight [out of eleven] corrected copies.)

Vol. IV, No. 3 (Winter 1971):

65. *Robert Essick. 'The Blakes at UCLA.' Pp. 75–8. (*Three drawings, including 'Donald the Hammerer' and one perhaps for 'Enoch'.)

66. Edward J. Rose. 'The 1839–Wilkinson Edition of Blake's *Songs* in Transcendental America.' Pp. 79–81. (Copies in Harvard belonged to Emerson and to Emily Dickinson's tutor Thomas Wentworth Higginson.)

67. *Morton D. Paley. 'Blakes at Buffalo.' Pp. 81–6. (The State University of New York has *Europe* pl. 18 [print], *'Discus Thrower' [not by Blake], a *sketch [not by Blake] after *America* pl. 3, and Blake's 'Beggar's Opera' plate after Hogarth, and the Buffalo and Erie County Library has *Europe* pl. 4.)

68. Allen Ginsberg. 'To Young or Old Listeners: Setting Blake's *Songs* to Music, and a Commentary on the *Songs*.' Pp. 98–103. (Reprinted from the 'liner' of MGM 'Verve' FTS-3083 record of 'Songs of Innocence and Experience by William Blake, tuned by Allen Ginsberg, With Peter Orlovsky, variously accompanied'.)

69. John Beer. 'A Reply to John Grant [*no. 55, above*].' Pp. 103–6.

70. Janet Warner. 'James Vine.' Pp. 106–7. (Biographical facts about Blake's patron.)

71. G. E. Bentley, Jr. 'An Apocryphal Blake Engraving: *The Minor's Pocket Book* (1814).' Pp. 107–8. (The BMPR print described in no. 36, above, is not by Blake.)

Vol. IV, No. 4 (Spring 1971):

72. *John E. Grant. 'Blake's Designs for *L'Allegro* and *Il Penseroso*, With Special Attention to *L'Allegro* 1, "Mirth and Her Companions": Some Remarks Made and Designs Discussed at MLA Seminar 12: "Illuminated Books by William Blake," 29 December 1970 [Part I].' Pp. 117–34. (Reproduction and description of the 12 *L'Allegro* and *Il Penseroso* designs; continued in no. 88.)

73. *Judith Rhodes. 'Blake's Designs for *L'Allegro* and *Il Penseroso*: Thematic Relationships in Diagram.' Pp. 135–6 and cover.

74. *Roger R. Easson. 'Blake and the Contemporary Art Market.' Pp. 137–9. (Reflections on the prices of three Blake drawings currently for sale at an average of $20,000 apiece.)

75. John Beer. 'A Reply to Irene Chayes [*no. 62, above*].' Pp. 144–7. (Rejoined in no. 89 below.)

76. Louis Middleman. '"Bring out number, weight & measure in a year of dearth".' P. 147. (It is 'built on a close translation of the Aramaic writing on the wall [Daniel 5: 25–8], 'mene, mene, tekel, upharsin,' or 'numbered, numbered, weighed, divided".') (Corrected in no. 90, below.)

77. John Adlard. '"The Garden of Love".' Pp. 147–8. (The 'Priests . . .

binding with briars my joys and desires' allude to the briars which were wound over graves to keep the soil in place.)

78. Michael Phillips. '"Blake's Corrections in *Poetical Sketches*": A Forthcoming Supplement and the Britwell Court Library Copy.' Pp. 148–9. (Mostly a description by Mr. Douglas C. Ewing of the Britwell Court copy which the Morgan acquired: see also his no. 64 above.)

79. Ruthven Todd. 'The Bohn Catalogue and James Vine.' P. 149. (The Keynes & Wolf description of an '1843' Bohn catalogue is a misprint for '1848'.)

Vol. V, No. 1–2 (Summer & Autumn 1971), a single issue:

80. *robert essick. 'finding list of reproductions of blake's art.' Pp. 1–160. '*A* revised and considerably expanded version' of the 'Finding List' which appeared in the 1969–70 issues [p. 1]; it consists of: 'introduction' [pp. 1, 3–4]; I. 'engraved and illuminated books [*by Blake*]' [pp. 9–42]; II. 'manuscripts, illustrations to manuscripts, letters, and printed works [*in conventional typography by Blake*]' [pp. 43–51]; III. 'illustrations [*designed or engraved by Blake*] in series [*to writings of other men*]' [pp. 52–108]; IV. 'paintings, [*separate*] drawings, and [*separate*] engravings not in series' [pp. 109–44]; V. 'portraits of blake and minor blakeana' [pp. 145–51].

Vol. V, No. 3 (Winter 1971–2):

81. John Beer. 'Blake's "Donald the Hammerer".' Pp. 165–7. (Demonstration that the 'Donald the Hammerer' drawing at UCLA [see Essick, no. 65, above] is based on Sir Walter Scott's 'History of Donald the Hammerer' in Edward Burt's *Letters from a Gentleman in the North of Scotland* [1818, 1822].)

82. Suzanne R. Hoover. 'Fifty Additions to Blake Bibliography: Further Data for the Study of His Reputation in the Nineteenth Century.' Pp. 167–72. (16 are for 1796–1862; the rest are mostly reviews.)

83. *Ruthven Todd. 'Two Blake Prints and Two Fuseli Drawings with some possibly pertinent speculations.' Pp. 173–81. (Fuseli's drawings for the frontispiece to Lavater's *Aphorisms* and for the last plate in his own *Lectures* belong to Ernest Seligmann.)

84. Thomas L. Minnick. 'A New Rossetti Letter.' Pp. 181–2. (Of summer 1862, mentioning 'Blake business' with Mrs. Gilchrist.)

85. Jerome J. McGann. 'Staging *The Marriage of Heaven and Hell*.' Pp. 182–3. (Account of a production at the University of Chicago in May 1970.)

86. Robert N. Essick. '"What is the price of Experience do men buy it for a Song"; Blake at Auction 1971.' Pp. 183–4. (Prices and buyers at sales of 29 March, 19 Oct., 15 June, and 9 Nov. 1971.)

87. *Morton D. Paley and Deirdre Toomey. 'Two Pictorial Sources for *Jerusalem* 25.' Pp. 185–90. (Paley's, subtitled 'I The Martyrdom of St. Erasmus', traces Blake's design to a painting by *Nicholas Poussin showing Erasmus being disembowelled; Miss Toomey's, subtitled 'II Le Tre Parche', traces the three women to an *anonymous engraving after Il Rosso Fiorentino.)

88. *John E. Grant. 'The Meaning of Mirth and Her Companions in

Blake's Designs for *L'Allegro* and *Il Penseroso*. Part II: Of Some Remarks Made and Designs Discussed at the MLA Seminar 12: "Illuminated Books by William Blake," 29 December 1970.' Pp. 190–202. (Partly concerned with labelling the figures in 'Mirth' as 'Kitty', 'Batty', and 'Assy', continuation of no. 72, above.)

89. Irene H. Chayes. 'A Rejoinder to John Beer [*no. 75, above*].' Pp. 211–13.

90. Edward W. Tayler & Everett C. Frost. 'The Source of "Bring out number, weight & measure in a year of dearth".' P. 213. (Middleman [no. 76] has misconstrued the handwriting on the wall; Blake's phrase is a commonplace, both Tayler and Frost agree.)

91. Martin Butlin. 'An Extra Illustration to *Pilgrim's Progress*.' Pp. 213–14. (The drawing known as 'A Warrior with Angels' in the Rosenwald Collection illustrates Bunyan—see Wills, no. 110.)

92. Marney Ward. 'Copy N of the *Songs*.' P. 214. (It lacks pl. 28, 54, not pl. 28, 34 as Keynes & Wolf say.)

93. John Adlard. 'Blake's Indenture and "The Little Vagabond".' P. 214. ('Taverns', 'Meat', 'Apparel' in the former reminds him of 'Barrel', 'drink and Apparel' in the latter.)

94. Mary Ellen Reisner. 'The Locations of Copy U of *Songs of Innocence* and copy d of *Songs of Innocence and of Experience*.' P. 214. (*Pace* Keynes & Wolf, the former is not at Harvard and the latter not at Yale; see Grant's erroneous 'Correction' in no. 101 and Mrs. Reisner's reply in no. 123.)

Vol. V, No. 4 (Spring [i.e. Dec.], 1972):

95. *'A Handlist of Works by William Blake in The Department of Prints & Drawings of The British Museum' [drafted by Richard Morgan, edited] with Supplementary Notes by G. E. Bentley, Jr. Pp. 223–58. (The text includes Drawings [pp. 226–33, mostly for Young's *Night Thoughts*], Miscellaneous Engravings [pp. 234–43], Illuminated Books [pp. 244–50], Reproductions [pp. 251–3], 'Engraved Portraits of William Blake' [p. 255], reference works [pp. 255–6], and 'Works by Blake in Other Departments of the British Museum' [p. 256]. The 28 designs include 8 *Night Thoughts* drawings. A correction appears in no. 151.)

Vol. VI, No. 1 (Summer 1972 [i.e. Feb. 1973]):

96. *Suzanne R. Hoover. 'Pictures at the Exhibitions.' Pp. 6–12. (About catalogue descriptions and reviews of Blakes in the Manchester Art-Treasures Exhibition [1857] and the London International Exhibition [1862].)

97. *William A. Gibson & Thomas L. Minnick. 'William Blake and Henry Emlyn's *Proposition for a New Order in Architecture*: A New Plate.' Pp. 12–16. (One—?or seven—plates by Blake in editions of 1781, 1784—?and 1794.)

98. Francis Wood Metcalf. 'Reason and "Urizen": The Pronunciation of Blakean Names.' Pp. 17–18. (Evidence from scansion about 'Urizen' and 'Urthona'.)

99. Raymond Lister. 'A Fragmentary Copy of *Songs of Innocence and of Experience*.' P. 19. (Brief description of his copy of *Innocence* [X].)

100. *Martin Butlin. 'William Blake in the Herbert P. Horne Collection.' Pp. 19–21. (4 designs on 2 sheets in the Uffizi, described in *L. Ragghianti Collobi, *Disegni inglesi della Fondazione Horne in Firenze* [1966]. A 'Correction' by Butlin appears in Vol. VI, No. 2, p. 42.)

101. John E. Grant. 'On Mary Ellen Reisner's "Locations of Copy U of *Songs of Innocence* and Copy d of *Songs of Innocence and of Experience*" from *Blake Newsletter* *19* [no. 94].' p. 22. (Her information is neither new nor accurate.)

102. John Beer & Irene Chayes. 'Brief Ripostes [see no. 62, 75, 89].' Pp. 22–4. (Beer speaks of her kindness and Mrs. Chayes of his misrepresentation.)

103. Ruthven Todd. 'A Recollection of George Richmond by his Grandson.' P. 24 ('When Blake died, George closed his eyes: "to keep the vision in".')

Vol. VI, No. 2 (Fall 1972 [i.e. July 1973]):

104. Martin Butlin. 'A "Minute Particular" Particularized: Blake's Second Set of Illustrations to *Paradise Lost*.' Pp. 44–6. (A demonstration that the second, Butts, series 'consisted of twelve watercolors', *pace* J. A. Wittreich, Jr. in *Calm of Mind* [1971].)

105. *Deirdre Toomey. 'The States of Plate 25 of *Jerusalem*.' Pp. 46–8. (An attempt to show that it 'exists in three states', which is bibliographically, or rather chalcographically, unconvincing, as Essick demonstrates in no. 133 below.)

106. *G. E. Bentley, Jr. 'A "New" Blake Engraving in Lavater's *Physiognomy*.' Pp. 48–9. (A signed vignette at Vol. I, p. 127.)

107. Dennis M. Welch. '*America* and Atlantis: Blake's Ambivalent Millenialism.' P. 50.

108. *Rodney M. Baine. 'Blake and Defoe.' Pp. 51–2. (Blake apparently made several drawings for *Robinson Crusoe*.)

109. *Raymond Lister. 'Two Blake Drawings and a Letter from Samuel Palmer.' Pp. 53–4. (A design for the woodblock of 'Isaiah foretelling the destruction of Jerusalem' and Palmer's note about it.)

Vol. VI, No. 3 (Winter 1972–3 [i.e. Nov. 1973]):

110. *James T. Wills. 'An Additional Drawing for Blake's Bunyan Series.' Pp. 62–7. (The history and position in the series of the Rosenwald design first described by Butlin in no. 91, above.)

111. G. E. Bentley, Jr. 'The Inscriptions on Blake's Designs to *Pilgrim's Progress*.' Pp. 68–70. (Transcribed and attributed mostly to Tatham.)

112. Ruthven Todd. 'The Rev. Dr. John Trusler (1735–1820).' P. 71. (His interest in 'a script type' was like Blake's.)

113. Robert F. Gleckner. 'Blake and Fuseli in a Student's Letter Home.' P. 71. (In Anon., *Letters from an Irish Student in England to His Father in Ireland* [1809].)

114. James King. 'A New Piece of Tayloriana.' P. 72. (Working notes for Taylor's *Arguments of Celsus* [1830] now in McMaster.)

115. *Roland A. Duerksen. 'A Crucial Line in *Visions of the Daughters of Albion*.' Pp. 72–3. (The frontispiece refers to 'terror and meekness' who 'dwell' 'Bound back to back in Bromion's caves', pl. 2, l. 5.)

116. John Adlard. 'The Age and Virginity of Lyca.' P. 73. (She is 7 because Hierocles describes 'seven [*as*] being a virgin'.)

117. Martin Butlin. 'The Inscription on *Evening Amusement*.' P. 74. (More details given from a newly discovered copy now in Butlin's collection.)

Vol. VI, No. 4 (Spring 1973 [i.e. Feb. 1974]):

118. *Janet Warner. 'Blake and English Printed Textiles.' Pp. 84–92. ('*It* seems possible that Blake's inspiration for his floral designs was found in eighteenth century embroidery patterns and textile designs' [p. 85].)

119. Joel Morkan. 'Blake's "Ancient Forests of Europe".' P. 93. (The association of forests with repressive chivalry in *The French Revolution* ll. 93, 101 has a sound historical basis.)

120. F. B. Curtis. 'The Geddes Bible and the Tent of the Eternals in *The Book of Urizen*.' Pp. 93–4. (Faint parallels with A. Geddes, *The Holy Bible* [1792].)

121. Donald H. Reiman. 'A Significant Early Review of Blake.' Pp. 94–5. (Of Hayley's *Ballads* [1802] in the *European Magazine* [1802].)

122. G. E. Bentley, Jr. 'The Accuracy of the Blake Trust Gray Catalogue.' Pp. 95–6. ('*S*ome serious minor defects in the . . . reproductions'; a reply by Keynes is in no. 132 and a rejoinder by Bentley in no. 150.)

123. Mary Ellen Reisner. '*Songs of Innocence* Copy U.' P. 96. (*Pace* Grant [no. 101], her note in no. 94 was correct in referring to *Innocence* [U]; the book itself *is* in Harvard after all.)

124. Thomas E. Connolly. '*Songs of Innocence* Copy U.' P. 96. (*Innocence* [U] is in Harvard.)

Vol. VII, No. 1 (Summer 1973 [i.e. April 1974]):

125. *Martin Butlin. 'Five Blakes from a 19th-Century Scottish Collection.' Pp. 4–8. (Drawings of *c.* 1779–1805 related to *Jerusalem*, Malkin [*Europe* and *Vala*].)

126. *Geoffrey Keynes. 'William Blake & Bart's.' Pp. 9–10. (Sir James Earle, like Sir Geoffrey the Senior Surgeon at St. Batholomew's Hospital, London [Bart's], was the author of *Practical Observations on the Operation for the Stone* [1793] with plates by Blake and probably the designer [previously misattributed] of Blake's separate plate of *Edmund Pitts [*c.* 1793].)

Vol. VII, No. 2 (Fall 1973 [i.e. May 1974]):

127. E. J. Rose. 'Night Thoughts.' P. 30. (Brief description of a newly discovered coloured copy [T] acquired by the University of Alberta.)

128. *John Wright. 'Toward Recovering Blake's Relief-Etching Process.' Pp. 32–9. (A technical discussion concluding that 'there is a range of relatively simple techniques for making . . . relief-etched designs in the composite art form' [p. 39].)

129. *John E. Grant & Mary Lynn Johnson. 'Illuminated Books in the

Cincinnati Art Museum.' Pp. 40–3. (Descriptions of *Thel* [N], *Inno cence* [S], and *Songs* [S], correcting Keynes & Wolf.)

Vol. VII, No. 3 (Winter 1973–4 [i.e. Aug. 1974]):

130. *Robert N. Essick. 'Blake in the Marketplace, 1972–73.' Pp. 52–9. (Blakes in the catalogues of picture and book dealers and auction-houses.)

131. *Andrew Wilton. 'A Fan Design by Blake.' Pp. 60–3. (Authentication and analysis of a BMPR design whose connection with Blake was previously doubted.)

132. Geoffrey Keynes. 'The Blake Trust Gray Catalogue and the Blake Trust Facsimiles.' Pp. 64–6. (Reply to Bentley, no. 122 above, with a rejoinder in no. 150.)

133. Robert N. Essick. '*Jerusalem* 25: Some Thoughts on Technique.' Pp. 64–6 [*sic*]. (A much-needed correction of the chalcographic description of Toomey, no. 105, above.)

134. Leonard Trawick. 'Nature and Art in *Milton*: Afterthoughts on the 1973 MLA Seminar.' Pp. 67–8.

Vol. VII, No. 4 (Spring [i.e. Nov.] 1974):

135. *Robert N. Essick. 'Blake, Linnell, & James Upton: An Engraving Brought to Light.' Pp. 76–9. (Discovery, reproduction, and illuminating analysis of the only known copies of the Blake–Linnell engraving of the Upton portrait.)

136. Roy J. Pearcy. 'Blake's Tyger & Richard Crashaw's Paraphrase of Thomas of Celano's *Dies Irae*.' Pp. 80–1. (Suggestive general parallels.)

137. *Peter Alan Taylor. 'Blake's Text for the *Enoch* Drawings.' Pp. 82–6. (Proves conclusively that the standard analyses of Blake's Enoch designs by Brown and Keynes are based on the 1912 Charles translation, not the 1821 Laurence translation; reproduces all *six* of Blake's Enoch designs, including one newly identified.)

138. Robert M. Ryan. '"Poisonous Blue".' Pp. 87, 89. (The phrase in *Jerusalem* pl. 68, l. 9 probably refers to Prussian blue rather than to woad.)

139. Joel Morkan. 'Milton's *Eikonoklastes* & Blake's Mythic Geography: A Parallel.' Pp. 87, 89. (Vague parallels in the comparison of Ireland and Israel.)

140. Thomas E. Connolly. '*Songs of Innocence*, Keynes (1921) Copy U, Keynes–Wolf (1953) Copy U.' Pp. 88–9. (Records some new bibliographical details.)

141. *Peter Roberts. 'On Tame High Finishers of Paltry Harmonies: A Blake Music Review & Checklist.' Pp. 90–9. (Opinions about musical settings of Blake's poetry.)

Vol. VIII, No. 1–2 (Summer–Fall [i.e. Nov.] 1974), a single issue:

142. *'John Todhunter's Lectures on Blake, 1872–1874.' Ed. Ian Fletcher. Pp. 4–14. (Four lectures at Alexandra College, Dublin, printed from the MSS in the University of Reading.)

143. Michael J. Tolley. 'John Todhunter: A Forgotten Debt to Blake.' Pp. 15–16. (Several of his poems derive from Blake.)

144. *Francis A. Carey. 'James Smetham (1821–1889) and Gilchrist's *Life of Blake.*' Pp. 17–25. (His marginal sketches in a copy of Gilchrist [1863].)

145. *Suzanne R. Hoover. 'The Public Reception of Gilchrist's *Life of Blake.*' Pp. 26–31. (Comment on 17 reviews of Gilchrist [1863] before 1865.)

146. *Morton D. Paley. 'The Critical Reception of *A Critical Essay.*' Pp. 32–7. (Comment on 9 reviews of Swinburne's book.)

147. *Malcolm Kingsley Macmillan. 'Dialogue between Blake and Wordsworth Written in Rome before 17 April 1889 and Left Unfinished.' Pp. 38–41. (Amusing fiction.)

Blake Newsletter, Vol. VIII, No. 3 (Winter 1974–5 [March 1975]):

148. *John E. Grant & Robert E. Brown. 'Blake's Vision of Spenser's *Faerie Queene*: A Report and an Anatomy.' Pp. 56–85. (A remarkably fine factual description; the 30 reproductions of Blake's 'Characters of Spenser's Faerie Queene' include a splendid one in colour.)

149. Morris Eaves. 'Reproducing *The Characters of Spenser's Faerie Queene.*' Pp. 86–7. (About the colour plate reproduced here.)

150. G. E. Bentley, Jr. 'The Accuracy of the Blake [Trust] Reproductions.' Pp. 88–9. (A conclusion to the exchanges in no. 122, 132.)

151. Robert N. Essick. 'Corrections of the BMPR Handlist [*no. 95*].' P. 90.

152. Mary V. Jackson. 'Additional Lines in *VDA.*' Pp. 91–3. (Disagreement with Duerksen, no. 115; see no. 153–4.)

153. E. B. Murray. '"Bound Back to Back in Bromion's Cave".' P. 94. (See no. 115, 154.)

154. Roland A. Duerksen. 'Bromion's Usurped Power—Its Source, Essence, and Effect: A Replication.' Pp. 95–6. (See no. 115, 152–3.)

1218. *Blake Studies.* Ed. Kay Long [later Easson] & Roger R. Easson.

Vol. I, No. 1 (Autumn 1968):

1. Karl Kiralis. '"London" in the Light of *Jerusalem.*' Pp. 5–15. (The 'people of London . . . are miserable because of the various means to an organized way of society'.)

2. Edward J. Rose. 'Blake's *Milton*: The Poet as Poem.' Pp. 16–38. ('The purpose of this essay is to discuss *Milton* as a creative "state" by examining how Blake uses the figure of Milton as a symbol' [p. 16]. See no. 17 below.)

3. *Clyde R. Taylor. 'Iconographical Themes in William Blake.' Pp. 39–85. (An exploration of 'core images, compositional strategies, and connotations' [p. 40], particularly in eight pictures. For complaints about the article, see no. 11, 16, below.)

4. Joseph Anthony Wittreich, Jr. 'William Blake and Bernard Barton: Addendum to *BNB* Entry No. a852 [*no. 686 above*].' Pp. 91–4. (Barton's comments on Blake [previously given in Story's *Linnell* (1892) and elsewhere].)

5. Ruthven Todd. 'Gilchrist Redivivus.' Pp. 95–7. (His plans for a new edition of no. 1680.)

6–7. Untitled abstracts of dissertations by Anne T. Kostelanetz (Columbia), pp. 102–3, and James Denise McGowan (Rutgers), pp. 103–4.

Vol. I, No. 2 (Spring [i.e. Oct.] 1969):

8. John Adlard. 'A "Triumphing Joyfulness": Blake, Boehme and the Tradition.' Pp. 109–22. (A brief attempt to establish 'Once and for all . . . whether Blake's philosophy [*chiefly as found in MILTON*] . . . belongs to the theosophical tradition' of Boehme, Paracelsus, the Kabbala, Hinduism, Platonism, Thomas Taylor, *et al.* [p. 109].)

9. Raymond Lister. 'W. B. Yeats as an Editor of William Blake.' Pp. 123–38. (Though 'As editors of Blake, Yeats and Ellis were failures', Yeats's commentary 'on Blake's symbolism had . . . some [*contemporary*] value' [p. 137].)

10. *Karl Kiralis. 'William Blake as an Intellectual and Spiritual Guide to Chaucer's *Canterbury Pilgrims*.' Pp. 139–90. (Includes a discussion [pp. 167–74] of which edition of Chaucer Blake used. For corrections, see no. 33, 35, below.)

11. John E. Grant. 'You can't Write about Blake's Pictures Like That.' Pp. 193–202. (In no. 3, above, 'most of Taylor's authoritative pronouncements are wrong' [p. 193].)

12. Eugene DeGruson. 'Bentley and Nurmi Addendum: Haldeman–Julius' Blake.' Pp. 203–5. [Bibliographical details about no. 288].)

13–15. 'Dissertations Abstracts', viz.:

13. Patrick J. Callahan. 'Historical and Critical Problems in William Blake's *America*.' Pp. 206–7. (Nebraska.)

14. Peter Alan Taylor. 'A Reading of Blake's *Milton*.' Pp. 208–9. (Connecticut.)

15. Alan Watson. 'William Blake's Illustrated Writings.' Pp. 210–11. (New Mexico; deals with works through *Urizen*.)

16–18. Untitled 'Correspondence', viz.:

16. Martin Butlin. P. 212. (Clyde R. Taylor's 'article [*no 3, above*] is vitiated by the fact that he does not seem to have looked at some of the pictures he discusses'.)

17. Karl Kiralis. Pp. 213–14. ('I must agree and disagree with Rose' in no. 2, above.)

18. Raymond Lister. Pp. 214–15. ('*A* small but important correction to Miss Désirée Hirst's generous review' of his book [no. 2137] in the first issue of *Blake Studies*.)

Vol. II, No. 1 (n.d. [late 1970]):

19. Warren Stevenson. '"The Tyger" as Artefact.' Pp. 5–19. (A summary of 'criticism of "The Tyger" during the past decade or so' [p. 7]; this is apparently a chapter from his thesis; it was slightly altered and printed as Chapter VIII of his *Divine Analogy* [1972].)

20. Susan C. Fox. 'The Structure of a Moment: Parallelism in the Two Books of Blake's *Milton*.' Pp. 21–35. (Seems to be mostly précis.)

21. Eve Teitelbaum. 'Form as Meaning in Blake's *Milton*.' Pp. 37–64. (Seems to be largely a summary, as an 'attempt to ponder' 'the Rintrah–Palamabron–Satan myth' (p. 37).

22. Stuart Curran. '"Detecting" the Existential Blake.' Pp. 67–76. ('In *The Glass Cage* [*Colin*] Wilson has performed the not inconsiderable feat of integrating Blake with the existential human condition of modern man through the curious medium of a detective story.')

23. Michael J. Tolley. 'Blake's Blind Man.' Pp. 77–84. ('Essentially a critique' of Hagstrum, above.)

24. Jean H. Hagstrum. 'Rebuttal.' Pp. 84–6. ('Tolley's reply has not persuaded me to repent.')

25. Michael J. Tolley. 'Reply.' Pp. 86–8. (Reply to Hagstrum on Tolley on Hagstrum.)

26. Robert Newman Essick. 'The Art of William Blake's Early Illuminated Books.' Pp. 89–90. (California [San Diego] Ph.D. précis: 'A study of the iconography of the early illuminated books [*c.* 1789–93] and the *Tiriel* drawings' dealing with Blake's 'reintegration of word and visual image'.)

Vol. II, No. 2 (Spring [May] 1970):

27. William S. Doxey. 'William Blake and William Herschel: The Poet, The Astronomer, and "The Tyger".' Pp. 5–13. (A tenuous 'astronomical interpretation which questions the nature of the universe' [p. 6].)

28. Roland A. Duerksen. 'The Life-in-Death Theme in *The Book of Thel*.' Pp. 15–22. (A reading.)

29. Christopher Keane. 'Blake and O'Neill: A Prophecy.' Pp. 23–34. ('Blake prophesied in "The Tyger" what Eugene O'Neill realized in *The Hairy Ape*' [p. 22].)

30. G. E. Bentley, Jr. 'William Blake, Samuel Palmer, and George Richmond.' Pp. 43–50. (Chiefly Richmond's marginal notes in his copy of Gilchrist [1863].)

31. Joseph Anthony Wittreich, Jr. 'Blake in the Kitto Bible.' Pp. 51–4. (In the Huntington; includes *Job*, *America* pl. 3, and *For Children* pl. 12.)

32. Marcia Allentuck. 'William Blake and William Bell Scott: Unpublished References to Blake's Late Nineteenth Century Reputation.' Pp. 55–6. (Pedestrian letters of 1876, 1879.)

33–6. Untitled 'Correspondence', viz.:

33. Geoffrey Keynes. Pp. 63–4. (Corrections of Kiralis, no. 10, above.)

34. Joseph Holland. P. 64. (Encloses a poem by Percy MacKaye on Blake.)

35. Robert Essick. Pp. 65–6. (Corrections of Kiralis, no. 10, above.)

36. Marcia Allentuck. Pp. 66–7. (John Linnell, Jr., letter of 1882 about his father and Blake.)

Vol. III, No. 1 (Fall 1970):

37. Karl Kroeber. 'Graphic–Poetic Structuring in Blake's *Book of Urizen*.' Pp. 7–18. ('*A* definition of formal principles of interaction between verse and pictures', p. 7.)

38. John Howard. 'An Audience for *The Marriage of Heaven and Hell.*' Pp. 19–
    52. ('*It* addresses an audience composed of members of the New Jeru-
    salem Church and of the Joseph Johnson circle', p. 20.)
39. Eli Pfefferkern. 'The Question of the Leviathan and the Tiger.' Pp. 53–
    60. ('*The* technique used by Blake in mystifying [*sic*] the nature of the
    Tiger is akin to that used by Melville in describing the Leviathan',
    p. 59.)
40. Thomas E. Connolly. 'A Blakean Maze.' Pp. 61–8. (Discovers that the
    Keynes [1921] and Keynes & Wolf [1953] descriptions of the four BM
    copies of the *Songs* are 'inaccurate'.)
41. Morris Eaves. 'A List of the Entries in Damon's *Blake Dictionary.*'
    Pp. 69–85. (A kind of Table of Contents for no. 1445.)

Vol. III, No. 2 (Spring 1971):
42. *Michael J. Tolley. 'Some Blake Puzzles—Old and New.' Pp. 107–28.
    (The puzzles are connected with newly revealed sketches on the versos
    of three BMPR drawings.)
43. *John E. Grant. 'Addenda and Some Solutions to Tolley's Blake
    Puzzles.' Pp. 129–35. (Associates the new BMPR sketches with two
    designs in Harvard and others in *All Religions are One*, the last of which
    Tolley is 'uneasy about' [p. 128].)
44. William Royce Campbell. 'The Aesthetic Integrity of Blake's *Island in
    the Moon.*' Pp. 137–47. ('*An Island* not only objectifies acutely and [*sic*]
    discomforts and absurdities Blake felt in his striving for financial and
    social success, but also reflects a high degree of aesthetic skill' [p. 138].)
45. *Robert N. Essick. 'Blake's Newton.' Pp. 149–62. (An analysis of the
    colour-print.)
46. James Hazen. 'Blake's Tyger and Milton's Beasts.' Pp. 163–70. (Perhaps
    'the animal imagery of *Paradise Lost* is an important source of Blake's
    poem' [p. 165].)
47. Gail Kmetz. 'A Reading of Blake's *The Gates of Paradise.*' Pp. 171–85.
    (An earnest 'reading' of *For the Sexes.*)
48. Rodger L. Tarr. '"The Eagle" versus "The Mole": The Wisdom of
    Virginity in *Comus* and *The Book of Thel.*' Pp. 187–94. (*Thel* 'seems to
    have been written, on one level at least, as an answer to and a refutation
    of Milton's championship of chastity, hence virginity [*sic*], in *Comus*'
    [p. 188].)
49. Marcia Allentuck. 'Dorothy Richardson on William Blake and the
    Broadside: An Unrecorded Appraisal.' Pp. 195–6. (In one sentence of
    'The Status of Illustrative Art', *Adelphi*, III [1925], 54–7, Dorothy
    Richardson mentioned 'Blake, the father in England of the decorative
    book [*sic*] . . . [*who*] produced in his best work . . . a cosmic extension of
    the coloured broadside'.)

Vol. IV, No. 1 (Autumn 1971):
50. Edward J. Rose. 'Blake's Metaphorical States.' Pp. 9–31. (Concerns
    what 'Blake is trying to achieve with the metaphorical processes he calls
    states or classes' [p. 9].)

51. Brian John. 'William Blake's "Hereford, Ancient Guardian of Wales".' Pp. 33–41. (Suggests 'John Davies of Hereford *ca.* 1565–1618)' as a 'candidate' [p. 34].)
52. Peter Alan Taylor. 'Providence and the Moment in Blake's *Milton.*' Pp. 43–60.
53. Jean Hall. 'Blake's *Everlasting Gospel.*' Pp. 61–72. (Another reading.)
54. G. J. Finch. '"Never Pain to Tell Thy Love"—Blake's Problem Poem.' Pp. 73–9. (The poem 'was the victim [*sic*] of Blake's complex response to the problems of sexual love' [p. 79].)
55. *H. B. de Groot. 'R. H. Horne, Mary Howitt and a Mid-Victorian Version of "The Ecchoing Green".' Pp. 81–8. (An article in the *British and Foreign Review* [1838] and Blake's poem in *Pictorial Calendar of the Seasons* [1854] are pointed out.)
56. Walter Pache & Ursula Salacki. 'Blake and Ovid.' Pp. 89–92. (A serpentine passage in 'I saw a chapel all of gold' is derived, by progressively less plausible evidence, from Ovid's *Fasti*, Virgil's *Aeneid*, and Livy's *Ab Urbe Condita.*)

Vol. IV, No. 2 ('Spring 1972' [i.e. Jan. 1973]):
57. Kay Parkhurst Easson & Roger R. Easson. 'Editorial Comments.' P. 7. ('The five essays in this number [*?Wittreich-Rose*] were first presented at the first symposium of The American Blake Foundation, October 21, 1971 at Illinois State University, Normal, Illinois.')
58. *'Robert N. Essick. 'A Preliminary Design for Blake's *Grave.*' Pp. 9–13. (A *variant of 'The Soul exploring'?)
59. Joseph Anthony Wittreich, Jr. '"Sublime Allegory": Blake's Epic Manifesto and the Milton Tradition.' Pp. 15–44. (On the connection of epic theory and prophecy.)
60. *Irene Tayler. 'Blake's *Comus* Designs.' Pp. 45–80. ('Blake saw the lady's encounter with Comus as the product of that frightened girl's fantasy' [p. 46]; the essay, reproducing the 8 Huntington *Comus* designs, 'forms part of' her 'somewhat fuller study' in *Blake's Sublime Allegory*, ed. Curran & Wittreich.)
61. *Morris Eaves. 'A Reading of Blake's *Marriage of Heaven and Hell*, Plates 17–20: On and Under the Estate of the West.' Pp. 81–116.
62. Stuart Curran. 'Blake and the Gnostic Hyle: A Double Negative.' Pp. 117–33. (A carefully documented argument that Blake derived much—e.g. 'hyle . . . the Greek word for matter'—from the Gnostics, mostly via Priestley and other eighteenth-century dissenters.)
63. Edward J. Rose. 'Good-Bye to Orc and All That.' Pp. 135–51. ('*My* primary purpose is to examine Orc as a symbol of thwarted creativity' [p. 135].)
64. John E. Grant. 'The Visionary Perspective of Ezekiel.' Pp. 153–7. (Another attempt 'to set the record straight' [p. 153], this time about 'Ezekiel's Vision'.)

Vol. V, No. 1 (Fall 1972):
65. Kay Parkhurst Easson & Roger R. Easson. 'Editorial Comments.' P. 5.

('The essays that comprise this number of *Blake Studies*, edited by Joseph Anthony Wittreich, Jr., were selected to provide the focus for discussion in the MLA Blake Seminar' in New York, 30 December 1972.)

66. Joseph Anthony Wittreich, Jr. 'Blake and Tradition: A Prefatory Note.' Pp. 7–11. ('The essays printed in this issue of *Blake Studies* . . . relate Blake to central traditions of western culture, its literature and its art . . .')

67. Florence Sandler. 'The Iconoclastic Enterprise: Blake's Critique of "Milton's Religion".' Pp. 13–57. ('*In* his critique of "Milton's Religion" and of the Christianity of his day . . . [*in MILTON, Blake*] shares to a considerable extent the criticisms of traditional religion proposed by the men of the Enlightenment' [p. 47].)

68. *Robert N. Essick. 'Blake and the Traditions of Reproductive Engraving.' Pp. 59–103. (A major article on the relation between Blake's etching-engraving technique and his graphic intentions.)

69. *Thomas H. Helmstadter. 'Blake and the Age of Reason: Spectres in the *Night Thoughts*.' Pp. 105–39. (A discussion of 'portrayals of Reason . . . in the contexts of science and religion' in *Night Thoughts* designs no. *73, 124, 163, 218, *267, *360, *444, *460, *509 [p. 106].)

70. Leslie Tannenbaum. 'Blake's Art of Crypsis: *The Book of Urizen* and Genesis.' Pp. 141–64. (*Urizen* is 'a sustained satiric interpretation', an inverted condensation of Genesis [p. 143].)

Vol. V, No. 2 [March 1975]:

71. *John E. Grant. 'The Fate of Blake's Sun-Flower: A Forecast and Some Conclusions.' Pp. 7–64. (A 57-page analysis of a 50-word poem, with a useful 'Appendix: Blake's Iconography of the Sun-flower' [pp. 41–9].)

72. George Mills Harper. 'The Odyssey of the Soul in Blake's *Jerusalem*.' Pp. 65–80. ('It is my purpose here to seek for the end of Blake's "golden string".' P. 65.)

73. *Ben F. Nelms. '"Exemplars of Memory and of Intellect": *Jerusalem* Plates 96–100.' Pp. 81–95. (A reading.)

Vol. VI, No. 1 (Fall 1973 [i.e. Jan. 1974):

74. Kay Parkhurst Easson & Roger R. Easson. 'Editorial Comments.' Pp. 3–5. (Explanation that the papers were the subject of the MLA Blake Seminar, 29 Dec. 1973.)

75. Karl Kroeber. 'Perspectives on Blake's *Milton*: A Prefatory Note.' Pp. 7–9. ('Blake business booms . . . half a million dollars is spent annually supporting people and activities connected with Blake scholarship.')

76. Mary Lynn Johnson. '"Separating What Has Been Mixed": A Suggestion for a Perspective on *Milton*.' Pp. 11–17. ('The major principle of unity in *Milton* . . . is the conversion of sets of twos (apparent opposites) into threes (genuine contraries separated from an unreal negation).')

77. Thomas W. Herzing. 'Book I of Blake's *Milton*: Natural Religion as an Optical Fallacy.' Pp. 19–34. ('Book I of *Milton* . . . shows sensate nature

to be a Satanic delusion and Natural Religion to be essentially an optical fallacy' [p. 34].)

78. Jeffrey Mitchell. 'Progression from the *Marriage* into the Bard's Song of *Milton*.' Pp. 35–44. ('The *Marriage* is ambiguous . . . [*as to whether* contraries *must* be enemies] but in the Bard's song, the proper relation between contraries grows clearer' [p. 44].)

79. *W. J. T. Mitchell. 'Style and Iconography in the Illustrations of Blake's *Milton*.' Pp. 47–71. (An attempt 'to explore the basic characteristics of form and content in the designs for *Milton*, and to suggest an explanatory framework in which those pictures may be seen as related, integral parts of the vision which informs this book' [p. 47]; there are 21 reproductions; the first half of this 'study' is in Curran & Wittreich's *Blake's Sublime Allegory* [1973].)

80. David V. Erdman. 'The Steps (of Dance and Stone) that Order Blake's Milton.' Pp. 73–87. (The author says he sees *Milton* [D] 'increasingly . . . as a two-part dance opera' [p. 73]; certainly he discusses feet in the designs a good deal.)

1219. *Blake to* [*and*] *Whitman*. Ed. Bunsho Jugaku and Soetsu Yanagi. Vol. I ([Tokyo], 1931), Vol. II (1932).

The Blake items consist of:

1. Bunsho Jugaku. 'Blake Kenkyu eno Josetsu [Introduction to the Study of Blake].' Vol. I, pp. 29–38.

2. Bunsho Jugaku, tr. *Poetical Sketches*. Vol. I, pp. 39–44, 72–81, 120–4, 171–81, 205–22, 273–83, 312–20.

3. *Minoru Umegaki. 'Blake no "Kyantaberi Junreize" [Blake's "Canterbury Pilgrims"].' Vol. I, pp. 51–66.

4. *Shotaro Oshima. 'Blake no Shizen Sozo: Doshin Sencho Joshi wo Chushin to shite [Blake's Imagination on Nature: "Auguries of Innocence"].' Vol. I, pp. 99–104, 147–62. (Reprinted in his *Blake and Celtic Literature* [1933], pp. 85–99.)

5. Bunsho Jugaku. 'Shohin Shishu no Blake [Blake in *Poetical Sketches*].' Vol. I, pp. 262–7, 365–74.

6. *Shotaro Oshima. 'Blake to [and] Celticism.' Vol. I, pp. 291–305, 344–57, 404–12. (Reprinted in his *Blake and Celtic Literature* [1933], pp. 1–46.)

7. *Bunsho Jugaku, tr. 'Blake Shoki no Sanbun [Blake's Earlier Prose].' Vol. I, pp. 375–82. ('Joseph of Arimathea', 'Then she bore Pale desire', 'Woe cried the Muse'.)

8. *Minoru Umegaki. 'Blake no Saisho no Saishokubon [Blake's First Illuminated Printing].' Vol. I, pp. 387–93.

9. Bunsho Jugaku, tr. 'Blake "Tsuki no Naka no Shima" [Blake's *Island in the Moon*].' Vol. I, pp. 413–17, Vol. II, pp. 69–80, 172–82, 222–9.

10. C. H. Herford, 'William Blake.' Tr. Bunsho Jugaku. Vol. I, pp. 435–47, Vol. II, pp. 29–39. (See no. 1837.)

11. *Bunsho Jugaku. 'Sashie Shokai [Explanation of Pictures].' Vol. I, p. 474. ('Winter' and 'Evening' reproduced.)

12. *Minoru Umegaki. 'Blake no Hanga no Giho [Blake's Engraving Technique].' Vol. I, pp. 483–9, 531–43, Vol. II, pp. 3–11, 58–63.
13. T. S. Eliot. 'Blake Ron [Study].' Tr. Mitsuharu Hashizume. Vol. I, pp. 500–6. (See no. 1544.)
14. Lytton Strachey. 'Blake no Shi [The Poetry of Blake].' Tr. Bunsho Jugaku. Vol. II, pp. 99–115.
15. Minoru Umegaki. 'Blake Saishokubon no Shotai to Seihan no Nendai [The Lettering Style and Engraving Date of Blake's Illuminated Books].' Vol. II, pp. 122–8.
16. *Mitsuharu Hashizume. 'Blake no Sen no Kannen no Toyo Tenkai [The Oriental Development of Blake's Conception of Line].' Vol. II, pp. 147–55, 195–209, 243–52.
17. Bunsho Jugaku, tr. '"Shohin Shishu" no Ippon ni Kakareshi Blake no shi 3-pen [Three Poems in Blake's *Poetical Sketches*].' Vol. II, pp. 272–3.
18. Bunsho Jugaku, tr. 'Lavater no "Ningen Ron" ni ataetaru Blake no Chogo [Blake's Marginalia to Lavater's *Aphorisms*].' Vol. II, pp. 273–8, 318–26, 367–74, 403–23.
19. *Bunsho Jugaku. 'Blake no Kakei [Blake's Family Tree].' Vol. II, pp. 339–49.
20. Bunsho Jugaku. 'Binyon Fusai tono Ichiya [An Evening with the Binyons].' Vol. II, pp. 356–66. (Talking about Blake.)
21. *Bunsho Jugaku. 'Osanaki Blake [The Childhood of Blake].' Vol. II, pp. 387–93.
22. Clarence Bicknell, tr. [into Esperanto]. 'La Sekreto de Amo ["Never Seek to Tell thy Love"].' Vol. II, p. 393.
23. *Bunsho Jugaku. 'Shugyochu no Blake [Blake's Apprenticeship].' Vol. II, pp. 435–45.
24. Bunsho Jugaku, tr. 'Swendenborg no "Shin'ai to Shinchi toni kansuru Tennin no Shokaku" ni ataetaru Blake no Chogo [Blake's Marginalia to Swedenborg's *Divine Love and Divine Wisdom*].' Vol. II, pp. 454–70.
25. *Middleton Murry. 'William Blake to Kakumei [William Blake and Revolution].' Tr. Bunsho Jugaku. Vol. II, pp. 483–91. (See no. 2263.)
26. Bunsho Jugaku, tr. 'Blake no Chunenki no Shibun [Blake's Middle-Aged Prose].' Vol. II, pp. 500–7. ('Shizen Shukyo wa sonsezu [*No Natural Religion*]', 500–2; 'Arayuru Shukyo wa Itsu nari [*All Religions are One*]', 502–3; 'Tiriel', 504–7.)

1220. §Blanchot, Maurice. 'Le Mariage du Ciel et de l'Enfer.' *Journal des Débats, Politiques et Littéraires*, CLIV, No. 672 (25 March 1942).

1221. Bland, David. *A History of Book Illustration*. The Illuminated Manuscript and the Printed Book. London, 1958. Pp. 242–6.

1222. A. *Bliss, Douglas Percy. 'Blake and the Modern English Wood-Engravers.' Pp. 203–26 of his *A History of Wood-Engraving*. London, Toronto, N.Y., 1928. B. London, 1964.
Deals chiefly with Blake's successors.

1223. Blois, Raymond Earl. 'The American Reputation and Influence of

William Blake.' Boston University Ph.D., 1941. Abstracted as a 3 page leaflet by the Boston University Graduate School.

1224. §Blondel, Jacques. 'William Blake: THE CHIMNEY SWEEPER; de l'innocence à la violence.' *Langues Modernes*, LX (1966), 162–7.

1225. —— *William Blake: émerveillement et profanation.* Paris, 1968. Archives des Lettres Modernes no. 95. Archives anglo-américaines 13.
'Émerveillement et profanation sont donc les deux pôles d'une expérience et d'une création' (p. 4).

1226. Bloom, Harold. 'Blake and Yeats.' Chap. 5 (pp. 64–82) of his *Yeats*. N.Y., 1970. Also *passim*.

1227. A. —— *Blake's Apocalypse*: A Study in Poetic Argument. London, 1963. B. Garden City, N.Y., 1963. C. Garden City, N.Y., 1965. D. §Ithaca [N.Y.], 1970.
Paraphrastic explications.

1228. —— 'Blake's *Jerusalem*: The Bard of Sensibility and the Form of Prophecy.' *Eighteenth-Century Studies*, IV (1970), 6–20.
'Blake's *Jerusalem* has the form of' 'a series of firebursts, one wave of flame after another', and its 'structure takes Ezekiel's book as its model' (p. 6).

1229. A. —— 'Dialectic in *The Marriage of Heaven and Hell*.' *PMLA*, LXXIII (1958), 501–4. B. Pp. 76–83 of *English Romantic Poets*: Modern Essays in Criticism. Ed. M. H. Abrams. N.Y., 1960.
Involutions in its meaning and method.

1230. —— *Shelley's Mythmaking.* New Haven, 1959. Yale Studies in English Vol. 141. *Passim*.
Blake is used analogically to illuminate Shelley.

1231. A. —— 'Visionary Cinema.' *Partisan Review*, XXXV (1968), 557–70. B. Reprinted in no. 2565 2.
'*T*he rough outlines of a visionary cinema in Blake, Wordsworth and Shelley' (p. 557), though the connection with cinema seems very tenuous.

1232. A. —— 'William Blake.' Pp. 1–119 of *The Visionary Company*. A Reading of English Romantic Poetry. N.Y., 1961. B. Garden City, N.Y., 1963. Pp. 1–130. C. The section on *The Four Zoas* reprinted in Frye, no. 1643. D. Revised and Enlarged Edition [of *The Visionary Company*]. Ithaca [N.Y.] & London, 1971. Pp. 5–123, 471.
A responsible introduction to individual works.

1233. Bloomfield, Paul. 'William Blake and his Albion.' *Journal of the Royal Society of Arts*, LXXXVIII (1940), 844–6.
Blake is an inspiration in our time of trial.

1234. Blunden, Edmund. 'William Blake.' Pp. 77–99 of his *Sons of Light*: A Series of Lectures on English Writers. [Tokyo], 1949.

1235. A. *Blunt, Anthony [Frederick]. *The Art of William Blake.* N.Y., 1959. B. London, 1959. C. Second Printing, 1969. D. Chap. iv is reprinted in Frye, no. 1643.

The book forms the best 'general introduction to his art', though Blunt has 'made no attempt to convert the lectures into a full-dress monograph'. It is therefore suggestive rather than definitive. There are 153 reproductions.

1236. ——— 'Blake, William.' Vol. II, pp. 354–5 of *Chambers Cyclopaedia.* London, 1950. See no. 1734 which it replaced.

1237. ——— *'Blake's "Ancient of Days": The Symbolism of the Compasses.' *JWCI*, II (1938), 53–63 (vMKN).

An admirable article tracing the iconography.

1238. ——— (A. B.) *'Blake's "Brazen Serpent".' *JWCI*, VI (1943), 225–7 (vMKN).

An interpretation of the water colour in the Boston Museum of Fine Arts.

1239. ——— (A. B.) *'Blake's Glad Day.' *JWCI*, II (1938), 65–8 (vMKN).

The source is in Scamozzi's *Idea dell' Architettura Universale,* 1615.

1240. A. ——— *'Blake's Pictorial Imagination.' *JWCI*, VI (1943), 190–212 (vMKN). B. *Pp. 193–215 of *England and the Mediterranean Tradition*: Studies in Art, History, and Literature. Ed. The Warburg and Courtauld Institutes. London, 1945.

Blake's indebtedness to classical, medieval, renaissance, mannerist, oriental, and primitive art.

1241. *Boase, T. S. R. *English Art 1800–1870.* Oxford, 1959. The Oxford History of English Art. Vol. X. Pp. 58–64.

A sound general survey.

1242. ———*'An Extra-Illustrated Second Folio of Shakespeare.' *British Museum Quarterly,* XX (1955), 4–8.

With six watercolours by Blake in it.

1243. Bodgener, J. Henry. 'Blake's Vision and Imagination: A Bicentenary Appreciation.' *London Quarterly and Holborn Review,* CLXXXII (1957), 292–8.

On how to approach Blake.

1244. 'Blake's Vision of the Divine Man.' *Congregational Quarterly,* XXXVI (1958), 59–64.

A conventional survey.

1245. A. Bodkin, Maude. *Archetypal Patterns in Poetry*: Psychological Studies of Imagination. London, 1934. Pp. 317–21. B. London, N.Y., Toronto, 1948.

1246. Bogen, Nancy. 'Blake on "The Ohio".' *N&Q*, CCXIII [N.s. XV] (1968), 19–20.

Miss Bogen believes that Blake's enthusiasm for the Ohio river was aroused by Gilbert Imlay's *Topographical Description of the Western Territory of North America* (1792).

1247. Bogen, Nancy. 'Blake's Debt to Gilray.' *American Notes & Queries*, VI (1967), 35–8.
Some more associations between *Europe* pl. 4 and Fox and Burke (see no. 1576).

1248. ——'An Early Listing of William Blake's *Poetical Sketches*.' *English Language Notes*, III (1966), 194–6.
In John Egerton's *Theatrical Remembrancer* (1788, 1801, 1803).

1249. —— 'A New Look at Blake's *Tiriel*.' *BNYPL*, LXXIV (1970), 153–65.
'Bryant's *New System* may provide the answer' to the questions as to 'when and where . . . this story take[s] place' (p. 155); some of the same points are made in Mary Hall's article, which follows this one.

1250. —— 'The Problem of William Blake's Early Religion.' *Personalist*, XLIX (1968), 509–22.
'Blake, then, may have begun life as an Anglican—but then again, perhaps not.' (P. 516.)

1251. —— 'William Blake, the Pars Brothers, and James Basire.' *N&Q*, CCXV [N.S. XVII] (1970), 313–14.
Pars may perhaps have recommended Basire as a master to Blake.

1252. —— 'William Blake's "Island in the Moon" Revisited.' *Satire Newsletter*, V (1968), 110–17.
An excellent article correcting Erdman's identifications of characters in his *Prophet Against Empire*.

1253. Boldereff, Frances M. *A Blakean Translation of Joyces Circe*. Woodward, Pennsylvania, 1965.

1254. A. Bolt, S. F. 'William Blake (1): The Songs of Innocence.' *Politics and Letters*, I (1947), 9–14 (see no. 2177 for part 2). B. Reprinted in Bottrall, no. 1261.
An excellent close examination of the text of the poems.

1255. Bolton, Arthur T., ed. *The Portrait of Sir John Soane, R.A.* (1753–1837) Set forth in Letters from his Friends (1775–1837). London, 1927.
Tatham's letter to Soane offering Blake material is on pp. 485–6.

1256. Bone, Stephen. 'Divided Heritage: Blake the artist at the British Museum.' *Manchester Guardian*, 30 April, 1957, p. 5.
On the British Museum Blake exhibition, no. 680.

1257. Bonte, C. H. 'Assembling Blake Show: Display Opening At Art Museum.' *Philadelphia Inquirer*, 1 Jan. 1939.

1258. Bonte, C. H. 'Blake Exhibit at Museum. Artist and Seer And also Poet.' *Philadelphia Inquirer*, 12 Feb. 1939.

1259. Bottrall, Margaret. 'Blake and the Coming of the Kingdom.' *The Wind and the Rain*, VI (Summer 1949), 26–42.
'Blake's vision . . . is profoundly Christian' (p. 41).

1260. A. —— *The Divine Image*: A Study of Blake's Interpretation of Christianity. Roma, 1950. Edizioni di Storia e Letteratura. B. §N.Y., 1965.
An anxious attempt to prove that 'Blake's Christianity was essentially and soundly Christian'.

1261. —— ed. *William Blake: Songs of Innocence and Experience*: A Casebook. London, 1970.
The volume includes A. E. Dyson, 'General Editor's Preface' (pp. 9–10), Margaret Bottrall, 'Introduction' (pp. 11–23), 'Part One: Blake: Aphorisms [*p. 27*] and Extracts from Letters [*pp. 28–30*]'; 'Part Two: Contemporary Impressions' consisting of brief excerpts from letters by Coleridge (no. 1407), Lamb (no. 2097, 15 May 1824), Linnell (no. 2769, 3 April 1830), Caroline Bowles & Southey (no. 2730), Edward Quillinan (no. 2534), Samuel Palmer (no. 1680, 1855), and small fragments of essays or journals by Malkin (no. 482), Crabb Robinson (no. 2536), Cunningham (no. 433 [?A]), Tatham (no. 2823), Garth Wilkinson (no. 171), and from *London University Magazine* (no. 965); 'Part Three: Comments and Critiques 1863–1907', brief excerpts from Gilchrist (no. 2769 A), James Thomson (no. 2837 A), Swinburne (no. 2795 A), Smetham (no. 2716 A), W. M. Rossetti (no. 299 A), D. G. Rossetti (no. 2474 B), Yeats (no. 3047 A), Arthur Symons (no. 2795 A); and 'Part Four: Recent Studies', apparently complete essays by T. S. Eliot (no. 1544 A), F. S. Bolt (no. 1254 A, with a brief '*Author's Postscript 1967*'), Mankowitz (no. 2177 A), Bowra (no. 1269 A), Frye (no. 1642), Gleckner (no. 1703), Nurmi (no. 2297 A), and parts of Wicksteed (no. 2954 A), [F.] J. Harvey Darton, *Children's Books in England* [: Five Centuries of Social Life], Cambridge, 1932 [pp. 182–7], Raine (no. 2482), and Bateson (no. 318 A).

1262. *Bourdillon, F. W. 'An "Imaginary Portrait" by William Blake.' *Country Life*, XLII (16 Feb. 1918), 172.
Likeness of a devil in Dante plate 2 to the German emperor.

1263. Bourniquel, Camille. 'William Blake et les Monstres.' *Esprit*, XVI, (1947), 163–6.

1264. *Boutang, Pierre. *William Blake*. N.p., 1970. Essai et Philosophie nᵒ 4.
An extensive gloss on selected poems; *For the Sexes* is reproduced.

1265. Bowden, William R. 'Blake's "*Introduction*" to *Songs of Innocence*.' *Explicator*, XI (1953), item 41.
Sensible correction of Justin, no. 1981.

1266. Bowen, Robert O. 'Blake's *The Tiger*, 7–8.' *Explicator*, VII (1949), item 62 (vMKN).
Suggests the Daedalus–Icarus myth as a source.

1267. Bowman, Marcia Brown. 'William Blake: A Study of His Doctrine of Art.' *JAAC*, X (1951), 53–66.
'*H*is mysticism provided the foundation of his art' (p. 54).

1268. A. Bowra, C. M. 'The Romantic Imagination.' Pp. 1–24 of *The Romantic Imagination*. Cambridge [Mass.], 1949. B. London, 1950. C. §1950. D. 1957. E. §1961. F. 1963.
An excellent general introduction to the imagination of Blake and others.

1269. A. —— 'Songs of Innocence and Experience.' Pp. 25–50 of *The Romantic Imagination*. Cambridge [Mass.], 1949. B. London, 1950. C. §1950. D. 1957. E. 1961. F. 1963. G. Reprinted in Bottrall (no. 1261).

1270. Boyce, George Price. 'Extracts from Boyce's Diaries: 1851–1875.' *The Old Water-Colour Society's Club Nineteenth Annual Volume* (1941), pp. 9–71.
At Gilchrist's in 1861 'looking over some books of Blake's' (p. 40).

1271. Boyle, C. S. *Blake, Rossetti and Walt Whitman*. Trivandrum [India], 1904. Pp. 1–46 (vKP).
Three small lectures.

1272. Brain, Russell. 'Newton and Blake.' *Friends' Quarterly*, XIV (1963), 206–17.
A very general comparison of their theological ideas.

1273. *Bray, Mrs. [A. E.] *Life of Thomas Stothard, R.A.* With Personal Reminiscences. London, 1851. Pp. 20–1.
Stothard's daughter-in-law tells for the first time of the arrest of Stothard, Blake, and Ogleby as spies on a sailing trip about 1780. The anecdote did not appear in the first version of the book in *Blackwood's Edinburgh Magazine*, XXXIX (1836), 669–88, 753–68.

1274. Brennan, Joseph X. 'The Symbolic Framework of Blake's "The Tyger".' *College English*, XXII (1961), 406–7 (vMKN).
The tiger starts out as really dreadful and gets more so through the poem; unconvincing.

1275. *Brenner, Anita. 'Blake: The modern before the moderns.' *New York Times Magazine*, 12 Feb. 1939, pp. 12–13, 23 (vMKN).

1276. Brereton, Geoffrey. 'Imagination Enthroned: Blake and Romanticism.' Chap. ix (pp. 172–88) of his *Principles of Tragedy*: A Rational Examination of the Tragic Concept in Life and Literature. London, 1968.
'Blake provides a fair and striking illustration of the new view of man' (p. 172).

1277. Breslar, M. L. R., Alan Stewart, and T. F. Dwight. 'Blake and His Friend Butts.' *N&Q*, CXXVII [11th Ser., VII] (1913), 428, 492–3; CCXXVIII [11th Ser., VIII] (1913), 35.

A query concerning the identity of Butts, and replies.

1278. Breton, Georges le. 'William Blake et le néo-platonisme.' *Mercure de France*, CCCXLVIII (1963), 494–9.

A résumé of Harper's book (no. 1793).

1279. A. Brierre de Boismont, A[lexandre Jacques Francois]. *Des Hallucinations ou Histoire Raisonnée des apparitions, des visions, des songes, de l'extase, du magnétisme et du somnambulisme.* Seconde édition entièrement refondue. Paris, Londres, Lyon, Strasbourg, Saint-Pétersbourg, Madrid, New-York, Montpellier, Toulouse, Florence, 1852. Pp. 94–6. B. *Hallucinations*: or, The Rational History of Apparitions, Visions, Dreams, Ecstacy, Magnetism, and Somnambulism. First American, from the Second Enlarged and Improved Paris Edition. Philadelphia, 1853. Pp. 85–7. C. *A History of Dreams, Visions, Apparitions, Ecstasy, Magnetism, and Somnambulism.* First American, from the second enlarged and improved Paris edition. Philadelphia, 1855. Pp. 85–7. D. *On Hallucinations*: A History and Explanation of Apparitions, Visions, Dreams, Ecstasy, Magnetism, and Somnambulism. Tr. Robert T. Hulme. London, 1859. Pp. 83–5. E. *Des Hallucinations* ou Histoire Raisonée des apparitions, des visions, des songes, de l'extase, des rêves, du magnétisme et du somnambulisme. Troisième Édition entièrement refondue. Paris, London, N.Y., Madrid, 1862. Pp. 89–91.

This account of Blake's visions is taken from the mendacious article in the *Revue Britannique* (no. 958).

I have not seen the first Paris edition of 1845, but probably Blake appeared in it as well.

1280. *Briggs, Ada E. 'Mr. Butts, the Friend and Patron of Blake.' *The Connoisseur*, XIX (1907), 92–6.

A biographical account.

1281. §*Brion, Marcel. 'Un Poète anglais méconnu. Le génie visionnaire de William Blake.' *Comoedia*, 23 April 1927.

1282. —— *'Vie de William Blake.' *Navire d'argent*, I (1925), 386–407.

1283. *Britten, Benjamin. *Songs & Proverbs of William Blake* for Baritone and Piano: Op. 74. London & N.Y., 1965.

Seven proverbs and a song each.

1284. Broers, Bernarda Conradina. *Mysticism in the Neo-Romanticists*. Amsterdam, [1923]. Pp. 29–38.

1285. *Bromhead, H. W. 'An Illustrator of Blake.' *Art Journal*, [LXII] (1900), 237–9 (vMKN).

She was Celia Levetus.

1286. *Bronowski, Jacob. 'The Mystical Quest of William Blake.' *Literary Guide*, LXIX (June 1954), 4–7.
A general article.

1287. —— 'A Prophet for Our Age: William Blake: 1757–1827.' *Nation*, CLXXXV (1957), 407–11 (vMKN).
A good centenary essay.

1288. A. —— *William Blake, 1757–1827*: A Man Without a Mask. London, 1943 [i.e. 1944]. B. London, 1944. §C. London, 1945. D. London & N.Y., 1947. E. *Revised and reissued as a Penguin Book, 1954. F. *1961. G. *1964. H. N.Y., 1967. I. *Revised and reissued as *William Blake and the Age of Revolution*. N.Y., 1965. J. *N.Y. & Evanson (Ill.), 1969. Harper Colophon Books.
One of the most illuminating books on Blake, dealing chiefly with the social and political background of his time.
In I, misleadingly called 'FIRST EDITION' on the title-page verso, a new chapter has been added ('Introduction: The Turbulent Age', pp. 3–17), and some more recent works are cited in the Notes, but otherwise few changes seem to have been made.

1289. —— 'William Blake: Soi to Sozo [Invention and Imagination].' *Nyu Epokka: New Epoch*, I (Aug. 1949), 60–3.
In Japanese.

1290. —— 'William Blake the Visionary.' *Radio Times*, 30 Aug. 1946, p. 4.
Introductory.

1291. Brooke, Stopford A. 'William Blake.' Pp. 1–54 of *Studies in Poetry*. London, 1907.

1292. Brooke-Rose, Christine. *A Grammar of Metaphor*. London, 1958. *Passim*.
Blake is one of fifteen poets used throughout as examples in this grammatical study of the nature of poetical metaphor.

1293. Brooks, Phillip. 'Notes on Rare Books.' *New York Times Book Review*, 30 Oct. 1938, p. 35 (vMKN).
On the sale of the George C. Smith, Jr., collection.

1294. Brown, Allan R. 'Blake Plates.' *Literary Review*, III (1923), 822.
Previously unnoticed plates in Stuart & Revett, no. 500.

1295. —— *'Blake's Drawings for the *Book of Enoch*.' *Burlington Magazine*, LXXVII (1940), 80–5.
The drawings, which are said to be from 1821 to 1827, are here discussed and reproduced.

1296. —— 'Unrecorded Engravings of Blake.' *Colophon*, III (1938), 457–8.
They appear in Kimpton's *History of the Bible*.

1297. Brown, E. K. 'The Question of Egotism: Blake.' *Transactions of the Royal Society of Canada*, Ser. 3, XXV (May 1931), Section II, pp. 99–107.

'Blake's doctrines show themselves to be those of a mind, clearly conscious of its penchant to egotism and determined to establish and maintain continuously sound and notably complete relations with the world without.'

1298. Brown, John E. 'Neo-Platonism in the Poetry of William Blake.' *JAAC*, X (1951), 43–52.

Blake's particular kind of mysticism is said to be Plotinian.

1299. Bruce, Harold Lawton. 'Blake, Carlyle, and the French Revolution.' *The Charles Mills Gayley Anniversary Papers*, University of California Publications in Modern Philology, Volume XI. Berkeley California, 1921, pp. 165–76.

A rather impressionistic comparison of the works by Blake and Carlyle called *The French Revolution*.

1300. —— 'William Blake and Gilchrist's Remarkable Coterie of Advanced Thinkers.' *MP*, XXIII (1926), 285–92.

There is no evidence for Blake's membership in the Paine, Godwin, Wollstonecraft circle, *pace* Gilchrist.

1301. —— 'William Blake and His Companions from 1818 to 1827.' *PMLA*, XXIX (1924), 358–67.

General account of R. C. Smith, Varley, Calvert, Finch, Richmond, Tatham, Palmer, Robinson, and Linnell.

1302. —— A 'William Blake in a Brown Coat.' *TLS*, 27 Aug. 1925, p. 557.

A contemporary reference by Sophia de Morgan, no. 1472.

1303. —— *'William Blake in "The City of Assassinations".' *Arts*, VII (1925), 141–52.

A survey of Blake's art and his aesthetic ideas.

1304. A. —— *William Blake in This World*. London, 1925.   B. *N.Y., 1925.

1305. Bryan, Michael. *A Biographical Dictionary of Painters and Engravers*, from the revival of the art under Cimabue, and the alleged discovery of engraving by Finiguerra, to the present time: with the Ciphers, Monograms, and Marks, Used by Each Engraver. A new edition, revised, enlarged, and continued to the present time, comprising above one thousand additional memoirs, and large accessions to the lists of pictures and engravings, also new plates of ciphers and monograms, By George Stanley. London, 1849.

Blake first appears in this edition, having been omitted from that of 1816. This account, largely from Cunningham, is enlarged by Mrs. M. Heaton, no. 1822, and E. J. Oldmeadow, no. 2321.

1306. *Buchanan, Walter. 'A New Portrait of William Blake.' *Country Life*, LXII (1927), 390.

By Richmond, *c.* 1857–9.

1307. A. Buckley, Vincent. 'Blake's Originality.' *Melbourne Critical Review*, No. 7 (1964), 3–21. B. Reprinted as Chapter VI (pp. 117–43) of his *Poetry and the Sacred*. London, 1968.

'Blake's greatness lies' in his 'amazing originality' and not in his use of obscure traditions (A, p. 3; B, p. 117).

1308. **Bulletin of the New York Public Library*, 'William Blake Issue', LXI (1957), 531–63. Articles by Bentley (no. 1181), Gleckner (no. 1703), and Larrabee (no. 2102).

1309. —— *'William Blake Issue', LXIV (1960), 565–605. Articles by Bentley (no. 1151), Erdman (no. 1571, 1573), Gleckner (no. 1697), Kempcr (no. 1995), and Keynes (no. 2026).

1310. *Bullett, Gerald. 'Blake.' Chap. vii (pp. 161–85) of his *The English Mystics*. London, 1950.

An introduction with 'a few salient features, not a detailed portrait' (p. 180), with little reference to mysticism.

1311. Bullough, Geoffrey. 'William Blake: *The Book of Thel*.' Pp. 108–23 of *Versdichtung der Englischen Romantik*: Interpretationem Unter Mitarbeit zahlreicher Fachgelehrter. Ed. Teut Andreas Riese und Dieter Reisner. Berlin, 1968.

A reading in English.

1312. *Burke, Joseph. 'The Eidetic and the Borrowed Image: an Interpretation of Blake's Theory and Practice of Art.' Chap. 13 (pp. 110–27) of *In Honour of Daryl Lindsay*: Essays and Studies. Ed. Franz Philipp & June Stewart. Melbourne, London, Wellington, N.Y., 1964.

'Eidetic images are phenomena that take up an intermediate position between sensations and images' (p. 115).

1313. A. [Bulwer Lytton, Edward.] 'Conversations with an Ambitious Student in Ill Health.' *New Monthly Magazine*, XXIX (Dec. 1830), 511–19. (Cambridge) B. *The Student*, A Series of Papers. In Two Volumes. London, 1835. Vol. II, pp. 152–5. C. Second Edition. In Two Volumes. London, 1835. Vol. II, pp. 152–5. D. E. L. Bulwer. *L'Étudiant*. [2 vols.] Paris, 1835. Vol. II, pp. 159–61. E. *Miscellaneous Prose Works*. [4 vols.] Leipzig, 1868. Vol. IV, 'Essays Written in Youth. First Published under the Title of The Student in 1832 [*sic*].' Pp. 73–5. F. *Miscellaneous Prose Works*. [3 vols.] London, 1868. Vol. II, pp. 261–2.

The 'Papers' that made up *The Student* appeared over a long period in *The New Monthly Magazine*. The issue above, which contained a dialogue about Blake's engravings for Young's *Night Thoughts* (pp. 518–19), was rechristened 'The New Phaedo, or Conversations on Things Human and Divine, with One Condemned' in the collected volumes. Reprinted in Keynes (1921).

1314. A. —— 'A Strange Story.' *All the Year Round*, VI (18 Jan., 1862), 386. B. *A Strange Story*. In Two Volumes. London, 1862. Vol. II, pp. 167–8.

C. Sir E. Bulwer Lytton. Second Edition. Mobile, Ala, 1863. P. 260. D. [E. Bulwer Lytton.] Third Edition. In Two Volumes. London, 1862. Vol. II, Pp. 167–8. E. London, 1863. P. 355. F. *A Strange Story; and the Haunted and the Haunters*. London & N.Y., 1864. P. 227. G. London & N.Y., 1865. P. 242. H. *A Strange Story*. Library Edition—in Two Volumes. Novels of Sir Edward Bulwer Lytton. Romances. Vols. VI and VII. Edinburgh & London, 1866. Pp. 154–5. I. The Knebworth Edition. London & N.Y., 1875. P. 307. J. *A Strange Story and The Haunted and the Haunters*. Lord Lytton's Novels. Vol. XXII. London & N.Y., 1878. P. 355. K. *A Strange Story*. The Pocket Volume Edition of Lord Lytton's Novels. London, Glasgow & N.Y., 1887. P. 287. L. The Caxton Novels. London, Glasgow, Manchester, & N.Y., 1892. P. 128. M. Bulwer's Novels. London, Glasgow, & Manchester, [1892]. N. The New Knebworth Edition. London, Manchester, & N.Y., 1895. P. 381.

The passing comparison of a young madwoman's drawings to those of Blake appears in chapter xxiv of the early two-volume editions (B & D), and in the renumbered chapter lxiv of the one-volume editions (C, E–N) and in Dickens's journal (A). The Blake quotation does not change in the slightest in any of these editions (it is reprinted in Keynes [1921]).

1315. Bunston, Anna. 'Blake's Songs of Battle.' *Country Gentleman and Land & Water*, LXV (2 Oct. 1915), 15.

Excerpts from *Poetical Sketches* are used to demonstrate Blake's militant patriotism.

1316. Burdett, Osbert. *William Blake*. London, 1926. English Men of Letters.

A shallow, trite, and untrustworthy book which concludes, among other things, that Blake's symbols and myth are aberrations, and show him 'deserted by his poetic genius'.

Bu-re-i-ku ko Ho-i-tsu-to-ma-n (1931–2); see *Blake to Whitman*, the new form for transliteration of this Japanese journal.

1317. Burger, M. W. [i.e. J. Thore]. *Histoire des Peintres de toutes les Écoles: École Anglaise*. Paris, 1863.

'William Blake' is no. 26 in the English school and no. 355 in the whole series. The essay is 4 pp.

1318. Burgoyne, E. J. 'London Statues and Memorials.' *N&Q*, CXVIII [10th Ser., X] (1908), 258.

On the Blake memorial at the Tate Central Library, Brixton.

1319. Burman, L. A. 'Blake's Prophetic Books.' *University Libertarian*, No. 6 (April 1957), 11–13 (vMKN).

1320. Burns, Robert. RELIQUES / OF / ROBERT BURNS; / CONSIST-ING CHIEFLY OF / ORIGINAL LETTERS, POEMS, / AND / CRITI-CAL OBSERVATIONS / ON / *SCOTTISH SONGS*. / — / COLLECTED AND PUBLISHED BY / R. H. CROMEK. / — / [5-line motto] / = / LONDON: / PRINTED BY J. M'CREERY, / FOR T. CADELL, AND W. DAVIES, STRAND. / — / 1808. (GEB, Toronto).

At the end are four integral leaves advertising Stothard's Chaucer print and 'BLAKE'S ILLUSTRATIONS OF BLAIR'.

1321. Burrow, Charles Kennett. 'Poet, Visionary, and Artist. William Blake's Work at the Carfax Gallery.' *T.P.'s Weekly*, 15 Jan. 1904.
Admiring review of the exhibition.

1322. Burrows, Carlyle. 'Blake Drawings on View.' *Christian Science Monitor*, 8 Nov. 1941 (vMKN).

1323. A. [Bury, Lady Charlotte.] *Diary Illustrative of the Times of George the Fourth*, Interspersed with Original Letters from the Late Queen Caroline, the Princess Charlotte, and from Various Other Distinguished Persons. Ed. John Galt. In Four Volumes. London, [Vols. I & II] 1838, [Vols. III & IV] 1839. Vol. III, Pp. 345–8. B. *The Court of England under George IV*. Founded on a Diary Interspersed with Letters Written by Queen Caroline and various other Distinguished Persons. In Two Volumes. London, 1896. Vol. II, pp. 190–1. C. *The Diary of a Lady-in-Waiting*. Being the Diary Illustrative of the Times of George the Fourth. Ed. A. Francis Steuart. Two Volumes. London & N.Y., 1908. Vol. II, pp. 213–15.
An interesting account of Blake at a dinner party given in 1818? by Lady Caroline Lamb, Byron's *bête noire*. The blanks in the text are filled in in the third edition (C), but otherwise there are no changes of substance. The Blake account is reprinted in A. Symons, *William Blake* (1907).

1324. *Butlin, Martin. 'The Bicentenary of William Blake.' *Burlington Magazine*, C (1958), 40–4.

1325. —— 'The Blake Collection of Mrs. William T. Tonner.' *Bulletin Philadelphia Museum of Art*, LXVII (1972), 5–31.
An account of the late Mrs. Tonner's *11 designs given to the Philadelphia Museum, with a 'Foreword' by Evan H. Turner, pp. 3–4.

1326.* ——'Blake's "God Judging Adam" rediscovered.' *Burlington Magazine*, CVII (1965), 86–9.
The Tate colour-print long known as 'Elijah in the Chariot of Fire' is in fact the long-lost design which Blake called 'God Judging Adam'.

1327. —— *'Blake's "Vala, or the Four Zoas" and a new Water-colour in the Tate Gallery.' *Burlington Magazine*, CVI (1964), 381–2.
Review of no. 212 and its connection with a *drawing of Los and Orc.

1328. —— *'William Blake—The Bi-Centenary of a Visionary.' *Pictures and Prints*, No. 63 (Winter 1957), 6–9 (vKP).

1329. §Buzzini, Louis. 'William Blake.' *Figaro littéraire*, 13 Aug. 1927.

C

1330. C., A. K. 'The Destructive Sword: An Analysis of Blake's Attitude to War.' *Poetry Review*, VII (1916), 125–32.
Blake shows a 'confusion of ideas' about war (p. 126).

1331. C., O., and F. G. Stephens. 'William Blake, the Poet and Artist.' *N&Q*, CII [5th Ser., IV] (1875), 129, 316 (vMKN).
Query concerning Blake's madness and a reply.

1332. [Caldwell, Revd. W. B.?) 'Did Blake Meet Swedenborg?' *New Church Life*, XLVIII (1928), 162–3.
Editorial points out that Pryke's case (no. 2463) is not proved.

1333. [Calvert, Samuel.] *A Memoir of Edward Calvert Artist* by his Third Son. London, 1893. Pp. xvii, 17, 19–36, 49, 50, 59, 155.
Important quasi-contemporary references to Blake.

1334. *Cammell, Charles Richard. 'Blake.' Pp. 72–89 of his *The Name on the Wall*. London, 1960.
About Blake's birthplace.

1335. Campbell, William Royce. 'The Views of Blake and Shelley on Man in Society.' *DA*, XXVII (1968), 3632–3633A. Oregon Ph.D. (1967).
Especially on history, revolution, and reform.

1336. Candid [i.e. George Cumberland]. *Morning Chronicle and London Advertiser*, 27 May 1780. (BM)
A review of the Royal Academy annual exhibition ends with a criticism of 'the death of Earl Goodwin, by Mr. Blake'. On 6 May 1780 Cumberland wrote to his brother Richard sending his two articles on the exhibition, signed Candid (BM, Add. MSS 36492, ff. 338–41). In time four articles appeared, on 4, 20, 22, and 27 May.

1337. A. Carey, William [Paulet]. *Critical Description and Analytical Review of 'Death on the Pale Horse,' Painted by Benjamin West, P.R.A.* with Desultory References to the Works of Some Ancient Masters, and Living British Artists. Respectfully Addressed to the Most Noble The Marquis of Stafford. London, Dec. 31, 1817. Pp. 9, 128–36. (BM) B. *Critical Description and Analytical Review of Death upon the Pale Horse, Painted by Benjamin West, P.R.A.* Dedicated to the Marquis of Stafford. Philadelphia: Published by Robert Desilver, 110 Walnut Street. April 27, 1836. P. 20.
The first passing reference to Blake is preserved in both editions, but B omits the long eulogy of Blake's designs for Blair's *Grave*. (The Blake sections are reprinted in Keynes [1921].)

1338. A. —— CRITICAL DESCRIPTION / OF THE PROCESSION / OF / CHAUCER'S PILGRIMS / TO / CANTERBURY, / PAINTED BY / THOMAS STOTHARD, ESQ. R.A. / RESPECTFULLY ADDRESSED, BY PERMISSION, / TO JOHN LEIGH PHILIPS, ESQ. / — / '*I have known many gentlemen, in whom the wish* to see / nothing but beauties in the Ancients, *was accompanied / by something like a resolution* to discern nothing in the / Moderns but defects.'—Page 45. / — / BY WILLIAM CAREY. / = / LONDON, / PUBLISHED BY T. CADELL AND W. DAVIES, FOR / R. H. CROMEK, 64, NEWMAN-STREET. 1808. / PRICE TWO SHILLINGS. Pp. 10–11. (BM, Bodley) B. Respectfully Addressed, by Permission, to General Dowdeswell. Second Edition with Additions. London:

Published at 35, Mary-la-Bonne Street, Piccadilly. 1818. Price Three Shillings. Pp. v, 18. (BM, GEB)

The praise of Cromek in A (1808) for having commissioned Blake's designs for Blair's *Grave* is repeated, unchanged, in a footnote (p. 8) in B (1818) and in Keynes (1921) and is restated in different terms on p. v.

In a letter to James Montgomery of 16 Dec. 1808 (in Sheffield City Library), Cromek said the pamphlet 'is admirably calculated to promote the success of the Subscription for the Print. . . . I will send you a few . . . as I mean to visit Sheffield with the Picture in the course of the next Summer: I wish you to *give* them, not to *sell* them.'

1339. Carey, William [Paulet]. DESULTORY / EXPOSITION / OF AN / ANTI-BRITISH SYSTEM / OF / *Incendiary Publication, &c.* / INTENDED TO / SACRIFICE THE HONOR AND INTERESTS / OF / THE BRITISH INSTITUTION, / 𝕿𝖍𝖊 𝕽𝖔𝖞𝖆𝖑 𝕬𝖈𝖆𝖉𝖊𝖒𝖞, / *And the whole Body of the* / BRITISH ARTISTS AND THEIR PATRONS, / TO THE / *Passions, Quackeries, and Falsehoods* / OF CERTAIN / DISAPPOINTED CANDIDATES / FOR / Prizes at the BRITISH GALLERY and ADMISSION, as ASSOCIATES / into the ROYAL ACADEMY. / — / *Respectfully addressed to the* / BRITISH INSTITUTION, THE / 𝕬𝖗𝖙𝖎𝖘𝖙𝖘 𝖆𝖓𝖉 𝕬𝖒𝖆𝖙𝖊𝖚𝖗𝖘 𝖔𝖋 𝖙𝖍𝖊 𝕴𝖓𝖎𝖙𝖊𝖉 𝕶𝖎𝖓𝖌𝖉𝖔𝖒, / BY / WILLIAM CAREY. / = / 𝕷𝖔𝖓𝖉𝖔𝖓 / PRINTED BY W. GLINDON, RUPERT STREET, HAYMARKET, / FOR THE AUTHOR; / AND PUBLISHED AT 37, MARYLEBONE STREET, PICCADILLY. / — / 1819. (BM) Pp. 22, 32.

Carey quotes some of his words on Blake from his book on West's 'Death on the Pale Horse' (no. 1337).

1340. —— 'Remarks on Blake's Designs Illustrative of Blair's Grave, (From *"Critical Description of* West's *Death on the Pale Horse*,) By Mr. William Carey.' *The Repository of Arts, Literature, Fashions, Manufactures, &c.,* 2nd Ser., V (1 May 1818), 278–80. (NYP)

1341. —— SOME / MEMOIRS / OF THE / PATRONAGE AND PROGRESS / OF THE / FINE ARTS, / *IN ENGLAND AND IRELAND,* / DURING THE REIGNS OF / GEORGE THE SECOND, GEORGE THE THIRD, AND / HIS PRESENT MAJESTY; / WITH / ANECDOTES OF LORD DE TABLEY, / OF OTHER PATRONS, AND OF EMINENT ARTISTS, / AND / OCCASIONAL CRITICAL REFERENCES TO / BRITISH WORKS OF ART. / — / BY WM. CAREY, / H.M.R.C.S.A. & H.M.R.I.I. / Author of — Thoughts on the best means of checking the prejudices against British Works of / Art, 1801; . . . Letter to a Connoisseur / in London, 1809; . . . &c. &c. / — / LONDON: / PUBLISHED FOR THE AUTHOR, / BY SAUNDERS AND OTTLEY, CONDUIT STREET; HARDING AND LEPARD, / PALL MALL, EAST; SAMS, ST. JAMES'S STREET; / *And at the Author's House,* 37, *Marylabonne Street, Piccadilly.* / — / 1826. (Pennsylvania)

'CROMEK, with a taste and spirit worthy of the best age of art in Italy, published the inestimable prints engraved by the *elder* SCHIAVONETTI, for *Blair's Grave*, from the inspired conceptions of that exalted enthusiast BLAKE.' (p. 132.)

1342. Carey, William [Paulet]. *Variae*. Historical Observations on Anti-British and Anti-Contemporanian Prejudices. Important critical coincidences of Lord Byron in 1820; of Thomas Campbell, Esq. in 1818, with William Carey in 1809; of Sir Walter Scott in 1821, with the same in 1805. Thoughts on the Shakespeare Gallery, and British Artists, with other Desultory Essays, including A Predictive Announcement Of Chantrey, the sculptor's present celebrity, published in the Sheffield Iris, in 1805; and of Gibson, the sculptor's celebrity, published in 1810. Published for the Author, by James Macauley Carey, 37, Mary-le-bone Street, Piccadilly, London, 1822. (Keynes)

'William Blake' is one of forty-six artists who signed a letter recommending Carey as the curator of an art collection.

This same letter is printed, in a very slightly different form, in 8 pp. of 'Documents', printed by 'Clarke, Printer, Dublin', which Carey evidently kept by him to recommend himself. It was probably not published in any ordinary sense, and the only copy at present known is bound in GEB's copy of Carey's *Critical Description of the Procession of Chaucer's Pilgrims*, 1818 (no. 1338), which Carey inscribed to William Becher, M.P., and dated 19 Aug. 1823.

1343. *Carner, Frank. 'A Printing House in Hell: William Blake's Theory of Art.' *Artscanada*, XXVI (Aug. 1969), 24.

1344. A. Carr, J. Comyns. 'Blake, William.' *Encyclopaedia Britannica*. Edinburgh, 1875 [ninth edition]. Vol. III, pp. 804–7. B. Cambridge, 1910 [eleventh edition]. Vol. IV, pp. 36–8. C. London & N.Y., 1926 [thirteenth edition]. Vol. IV, pp. 36–8. Revised by Geoffrey Keynes in the fourteenth edition: see no. 2012.

No attempt has been made to carry the various issues of the *Encyclopaedia Britannica*, but it may be useful to know that the tenth and twelfth editions were simply supplements to the preceding editions.

1345. A. —— 'William Blake.' *Belgravia*, XXIX (1876), 366–79. B. Reprinted as 'William Blake, Poet and Painter.' Pp. 35–76 of his *Essays on Art*. London, 1879.

'*He* never became in any full sense of the word a painter' (p. 367 of A).

1346. A. —— (J.C.C.) *'William Blake.' *Cornhill Magazine*, XXXI (1875), 721–36. B. *Living Age*, CXXVI (1875), 67–77.

Concerns Blake 'only as an artist' (p. 735), chiefly the *Night Thoughts* drawings.

1347. A. Carruthers, Robert. 'William Blake.' Vol. II, pp. 57–8 of [Robert] *Chambers's Cyclopaedia of English Literature*. Third Edition. Revised by Robert Carruthers. In Two Volumes. London & Edinburgh, 1876. B. Fourth Edition. London & Edinburgh, 1892. See no. 1513 which replaced this article.

The article is unsigned, but it is presumably by Carruthers, as there is no Blake entry in the editions of 1844 and 1858–60.

1348. Carter, John, and Kerrison Preston. 'The Stirling Copy of "Jerusalem".' *TLS*, 7 May 1954, p. 304; 14 May, 1954, p. 319 (vMKN).

Carter objects to imputation of sharp practice in a review of Keynes & Wolf (no. 666) in the Stirling copy's going to America; Preston says Americans are fine and generous.

1349. *Cary, Elisabeth Luther. *The Art of William Blake*: His Sketch-Book, His Water-Colours His Painted Books. N.Y., 1907.

The 51 plates include the 8 *Comus* designs from the Boston series; the text is pp. 1–56.

1350. —— *'Blake's "Night Thoughts" Drawings to British Museum.' *New York Times*, 19 Aug. 1928 (vMKN).

1351. —— *'Notes on William Blake: Number One: The Manuscript Book.' *Scrip*, II (1907), 273–83 (vMKN).

1352. —— *'Notes on William Blake: No. 2: Blake's Water-colors in the Print Room, Boston Museum.' *Scrip*, II (1907), 396–9 (vMKN).

1353. —— *'Notes on William Blake: No. 3: Some Characteristics of His Designs.' *Scrip*, III (1907), 1–15 (vMKN).

1354. —— *'Notes on William Blake: No. 4: His Literary Sympathies.' *Scrip*, III (1907), 67–79 (vMKN).

1355. —— 'Reproducing Blake's "Book of Job".' *New York Times*, 27 Oct. 1935 (vMKN).

1356. —— *'William Blake and his Water-color Drawings in the Museum of Fine Arts, Boston.' *Print Collector's Quarterly*, V (Feb. 1915), 38–58 (vMKN).

1357. —— 'William Blake and Two of His Young Followers.' *New York Times*, 22 April 1934.

1358. —— *'William Blake as an Illustrator.' *Critic [and Literary World]*, XLVI (1905), 214–16 (vMKN).

1359. —— *'The Years Bring New Honors to Blake.' *New York Times Magazine*, 20 Oct. 1935 (vMKN).

1360. Casier, Esther. 'William Blake: A Study in Religious Sublimation.' *Catholic World*, CLXII (1946), 518–25 (vMKN).

Attempts to trace religious sublimation throughout the major works, with thin results.

1361. Casimir, Paul H. 'Blake's *Marriage of Heaven and Hell*.' *Contemporary Review*, CLXXXIII (1953), 351–5 (vMKN).

A general appreciation.

1362. *Cassou, Jean. 'Poésie——William Blake——Voie Libre.' *Nouvelles Littéraires*, IX (12 July 1930), 12.

1363. Cater, W. 'Blake's Songs.' *TLS*, 3 Sept. 1931, p. 664 (vMKN).
Copies offered by Quaritch (1875–7, 1880).

1364. Caudwell, H. *The Creative Impulse in Writing and Painting*. London, 1951.
Pp. 39–42 and *passim*.

1365. Cave, Roderick. 'In Blake's Tradition: the Press of Ralph Chubb.'
American Book Collector, XI (1960), 8–17.

1366. Cazamian, Louis. *Symbolisme et Poésie*: L'Exemple anglais. Neuchatel,
1947. Pp. 76–85.
Translations and discussions.

1367. Cecchi, Emilio. 'William Blake, poeta, profeta e pittore'. *La Nuova Parola*, IX (1906), 381–9.

1368. Cestre, Charles. *La Révolution française et les Poètes anglais (1789–1809)*.
Dijon & Paris, 1906. *Revue Bourguignonne*, tome XVI. Pp. 204–15.

1369. §Chao, Ching-shen. 'Ying-kuo Shih-jen Po-lai-k'o Pai-nien Chi-nien
[The Centenary of the English Poet Blake].' *Wen-hsueh Chou-pao*, V, no. 11
(1927[?]).
In Chinese.

1370. A. —— §'Ying-kuo Ta-shih-jen Polai-k'o Pai-nien chi-nien [The
Centenary of the Great English Poet Blake].' *Pei-hsin Pan-yueh-k'an*, II, no. 2
(1927). B. Reprinted in *Hsiao-shuo Yueh-pao*, XVIII, no. 8 (Aug. 1927)
(vADH).
In Chinese.
—See also the pseudonym Po-tung.

1371. A. Chase, Lewis Nathaniel. 'The Fame of William Blake.' *South Atlantic Quarterly*, VII (1908), 93–9 (vMKN). B. Reprinted as a separate
pamphlet, pp. 1–9.
A very sketchy history of Blake's reputation.

1372. Chatto, William A. *Gems of Wood Engraving*, from the Illustrated
London News With A History of the Art, Ancient and Modern. London,
1849. P. 28.
The paragraph about Blake's etching technique did not appear in the
version printed in the *Illustrated London News* from 20 April to 6 July 1844.

1373. §Chayes, Irene Hendry. 'The Circle and the Stair: Patterns of Romantic Theme and Form in the Poetry of Blake, Wordsworth, Coleridge, Shelley,
and Keats.' Johns Hopkins Ph.D., 1960.

1374. A. —— *'Little Girls Lost: Problems of a Romantic Archetype.'
BNYPL, LXVII (1963), 579–92. B. Reprinted in Frye, no. 1643.
Deals with Blake, Wordsworth, Keats, Coleridge, and others.

1375. Chayes, Irene Hendry. 'Plato's *Statesman* Myth in Shelley and Blake.' *Comparative Literature*, XIII (1961), 358–69 (vMKN).
The myth in *Prometheus Unbound* and in 'The Mental Traveller'.

1376. Cheney, John Vance. 'William Blake.' Pp. 169–87 of *That Dome in Air*: Thoughts on Poetry and Poets. Chicago, 1895.
'It is a waste of time to look for a system in the work of such a mind' (p. 171).

1377. —— *'William Blake.' *California Illustrated Magazine*, IV ([San Francisco] 1893), 446–54.

1378. *Cheney, Sheldon. 'A Mystic in the Age of Enlightened Scepticism: William Blake.' Pp. 309–77 of *Men Who Have Walked with God*: Being the Story of Mysticism through the Ages Told in the Biographies of Representative Seers and Saints with Excerpts from their Writings and Sayings. N.Y., 1945.
An impressionistic, exclamatory account.

1379. —— *'Three Strange Englishmen [Constable, Turner, and Blake].' Chap. III (pp. 47–74) of *The Story of Modern Art*. N.Y., 1941.
Blake is especially pp. 66–74.

1380. Chesterton, G. K. 'On Blake and his Critics'. Pp. 128–33 of *Avowals and Denials*. A Book of Essays. London, 1934.
A review of Murry, no. 2262.

1381. A. —— *William Blake*. London & N.Y., 1910. B. *London, 1920. The Popular Library of Art.
This book is inaccurate, emphatic, and misleading. There are 32 plates.

1382. —— 'William Blake and Inspiration.' Pp. 78–81 of *A Handful of Authors*. Ed. Dorothy Collins. N.Y., 1953 (vMKN).
Blake and other poets do not write from 'inspiration', but do their own work.

1383. A. Child, Mrs. D. L. [Lydia Maria Francis]. 'Good Wives. No. 1.— Mrs. Blake, wife of William Blake.' *Ladies Pocket Magazine*, Part 2 (1833), 1–5. B. 'Mrs. Blake, Wife of William Blake.' Pp. 128–33 of *Good Wives*. Boston, 1833. C. §Reprinted in pp. 125–28 of L. Maria Child, *Biographies of Good Wives*. N.Y. & Boston, 1846. D. Third Edition, Revised. N.Y. & Boston, 1847. Francis & Co.'s Cabinet Library of Choice Prose and Poetry. E. *Biographies of Good Wives*. London & Glasgow, 1849, Pp. 123–8. F. Boston & N.Y., 1850. G. §Boston & N.Y., 1855. H. *Married Women: Biographies of Good Wives*. N.Y., 1871. Pp. 124–8.
This account (with an unattributed engraving of 'The Fairy Funeral' in A) is simply extracted from Cunningham.

1384. Chillag, Robert Charles. 'Image and Meaning in William Blake's Poetry.' Northwestern Ph.D., 1954. See *DA*, XIV (1954), 2343.

1385. Chislett, William. 'The Influence of William Blake on William

Butler Yeats.' Pp. 88–95 of Part II of *The Classical Influence in English Literature of the Nineteenth Century* and Other Essays and Notes. Boston, 1918.

1386. Chislett, William. 'The New Christianity of William Blake.' Pp. 69–88 of Part II of *The Classical Influence in English Literature of the Nineteenth Century* and Other Essays and Notes. Boston, 1918.

1387. A. —— 'William Vaughn Moody and William Blake.' *Dial*, LIX (1915), 142 (vMKN). B. Pp. 107–9 of Part II of *The Classical Influence in English Literature of the Nineteenth Century* and Other Essays and Notes. Boston, 1918.
A letter to the editor, noting similarities in their dualist conceptions of God.

1388. §Chou, Tso-jen. 'Ying-kuo Shih-jen Po-lai-k'o-ti Ssu-hsiang [The Philosophy of the English Poet Blake].' *Shao-nien Chung-kuo*, I, no. 8 (1920).
In Chinese.

1389. Christoffel, Ulrich. 'William Blake.' Pp. 5–17 of *Malerei und Poesie*: die symbolische Kunst des 19. Jahrhunderts. Wien, 1948.

1390. Cirlot, Juan-Eduardo. 'La ideología de William Blake.' *Papeles de Son Armadans*, XLIII (1966), 166–75.

1391. A. Clark, Thomas. 'The Art of Poetry VIII: Allen Ginsberg.' *The Paris Review*, 37 (Spring 1966), 13–55. B. Reprinted as 'Allen Ginsberg.' Chap. xii (pp. 279–320) of *Writers at Work*: The *Paris Review* Interviews. 3rd Ser. Intro. Alfred Kazin. N.Y. [1967].
Ginsberg describes visions of God, 'the moment[s] that I was born for', which were induced by reading Blake's *Songs* (B, pp. 299–307).

1392. Clark, Thomas M. 'William Blake, Painter and Poet.' *Old and New*, VI (1873), 67–82.
A general summary.

1393. Clarke, John. 'Joyce and the Blakean Vision.' *Criticism*, V (1963), 173–80.
Purpose is 'to note some of the Blakean patterns, symbols, and allusions in *Ulysses*, but more importantly . . . to show that, in spite of Joyce's apparent resemblance, and even indebtedness to Blake, they are, in fact, operating in mutually exclusive spheres'.

1394. §Clarke, John C. 'The Psychology of Blake's Visionary Mythopoeia.' Western Reserve Ph.D., 1963 (according to L. F. McNamee, *Dissertations in English and American Literature* [1968]).

1395. *Clarke, John Henry. *From Copernicus to William Blake*. London, [1928].
A lecture of 49 pp.

1396. A. —— *The God of Shelley and Blake*. London, 1930. B. N.Y., 1966, 21 pp.

1397. A. Clarke, John Henry. *William Blake (1757–1827) on The Lord's Prayer*. London, 1927. B. *N.Y., 1971.

A virulently anti-Semitic fragment about true religion and also about Blake.

1398. Clarke, William F. 'The Significance of William Blake in Modern Thought.' *International Journal of Ethics*, XXXIX (1929), 217–30.

A very general article on whether we can 'in our need today, utilize his message'.

1399. *Clausen, George. 'The Blake Memorial in the Free Public Library, Lambeth.' *Magazine of Art*, XXVII (1903), 306–7.

A relief of a Young illustration, with a medallion bust after Phillips.

1400. A. Clayton, Ellen C. *English Female Artists*. In Two Volumes. London, 1876. Vol. II, p. 406. B. Ruskin's letter is reprinted in *The Letters of John Ruskin*. Volume I, 1827–1869. (Vol. XXXVI of *The Works of John Ruskin*. Ed. E. T. Cook and Alexander Wedderburn. Library Edition.) London & N.Y., 1909. P. 110.

Ruskin praises Blake's *Job* in a letter to Mrs. Blackburn, an English Female Artist.

1401. *Cleaver, James. 'William Blake and Thomas Bewick.' Chapter VII, pp. 95–107, of *A History of Graphic Art*. London, 1963.

1402. A. Clutton-Brock, Alan Francis. *Blake*. London, 1933. Great Lives Series. B. §N.Y., 1970.

A trivial, inaccurate book which is appreciative of the lyrics, but finds that Blake was mad, and that his prophecies 'cannot, *ipso facto*, be poetry'.

A 1402. —— 'Blake's Jerusalem.' *Speaker*, n.s. XI (1904), 38–9.

1403. A. —— 'A Literary Causerie. The Poetry of William Blake.' *The Academy*, LXXI (1906), 524–6(vRN). B. *The Living Age*, CCLI (1906), 809–13 (vMKN). C. Reprinted as 'The Poetry of William Blake.' Pp. 63–73 of his *Essays on Literature & Life*. London, 1926.

1404. A. —— 'On Blake as a Prophet.' *London Mercury*, I (1920), 283–90. B. Reprinted in pp. 74–91 of *Essays on Literature & Life*. London, 1926.

Blake confused art and prophecy.

1405. Coates, Robert M. 'The Art Galleries: William Blake at the Frick.' *New Yorker*, 9 Jan. 1960, pp. 69–72.

Review of the exhibition of Bunyan drawings.

1406. *[Cole, Henry.] 'Fine Arts. *The Vicar of Wakefield. With thirty-two Illustrations*. By W. Mulready, R.A. Van Voorst.' *Athenaeum*, 21 Jan. 1843, p. 165.

Blake is praised in an aside for the felicity with which he executed his own conceptions, particularly the Virgil woodcuts.

The author ('Cole') is identified in the marked editorial file of the *Athenaeum* now in the London office of the *New Statesman*. The research for the article is probably referred to in an undated letter to Linnell from Charles Went-worth Dilke (the editor of the *Athenaeum*) which A. H. Palmer copied into an Exercise Book with the Ivimy MSS: 'I shall be most happy to have another morning with Blake. Mr Cole writes to me that he has named next Tuesday morning & to breakfast with you.' Presumably Dilke and Cole were coming to see the Virgil woodblocks in Linnell's possession, one of which was borrowed to print a plate for the article.

1407. A. Coleridge, Samuel Taylor. *Letters of Samuel Taylor Coleridge*. Ed. Ernest Harley Coleridge. In Two Volumes. London, 1895. Vol. II, pp. 685–8. B. *Unpublished Letters of Samuel Taylor Coleridge*. Ed. Earl Leslie Griggs. [2 vols.] London, 1932. Vol. II, p. 233. C. *The Letters of Samuel Taylor Coleridge*. Selected & with an Introduction by Kathleen Raine. London, 1950. The Grey Walls Letters Series. Pp. 230–3. D. *Collected Letters of Samuel Taylor Coleridge*. Ed. Earl Leslie Griggs. [6 vols.] Oxford, 1959. Vol. IV, pp. 833–4, 836–8.

The Blake reference in the letter of 6 Feb. 1818 (printed in B and D) is rather casual, but the commentary on Blake's *Songs* in the letter of [12 Feb. 1818] (in A, C, and D) is of very great importance.

1408. A. Collins, Joseph. 'The Sanity of William Blake.' *Bookman* [N.Y.], LXI (1925), 553–5. B. *The Doctor Looks at Biography*: Psychological Studies of Life and Letters. N.Y., 1925. Pp. 154–8 (vMKN).

This quasi-review of Bruce (no. 1304) says Blake is interesting less for his work than for his biography.

1409. A. Collins, Mortimer. 'William Blake, Seer and Painter.' Vol. II, pp. 179–97 of his *Pen Sketches by a Vanished Hand*. Ed. Tom Taylor and Mrs. Mortimer Collins. In Two Volumes. London, 1879.

A dull general essay.

1410. Collis, Maurice. 'A Display of British Genius.' *Time and Tide*, XXVII (1947), 932.

Criticism of the Tate exhibition of Blake, Constable, Hogarth, and Turner.

1411. A. *Collobi, Licia Ragghianti. 'Hogarth Romney Füssli Flaxman Blake nella Raccolta Horne a Firenze.' *Critica d'Arte*, XI, no. 62 (1964), 33–42.

*Four Blake designs are discussed on pp. 39–42.

1412. Colodne, Carl, John E. Grant, and Stephen A. Larrabee. 'Blake.' *New York Times Book Review*, 5 Jan. 1958.

Objecting severally to statements in a review of Keynes's *Writings* (no. 370B) by Horace Gregory (24 Nov. 1957) that Blake's 'War Song to Englishmen' is 'one of the greatest of English patriotic poems' and evidence of Blake's 'intense nationalism' (Colodne and Larrabee) and that Coleridge and Wordsworth plagiarized Blake (Grant).

1413. A. Colvin, Sidney. 'Children in Italian and English Design. Pt. II. Blake.' *The Portfolio*, II (1871), 138–43 (vMKN). B. Reprinted as *'The

English. Blake (1757–1827).' Pp. 21–9 of *Children in Italian and English Design*. London, 1872.

1414. *Combe, Jacques. 'William Blake.' *Arts Plastiques*, I (1947), 157–64.

1415. *Comstock, H. 'Blake's Illustrations for Bunyan's Pilgrim's Progress.' *Connoisseur*, CIX (1942), 67–8 (vMKN).

1416. *Connolly, Thomas E., & George R. Levine. 'Pictorial and Poetic Design in Two Songs of Innocence.' *PMLA*, LXXXII (1967), 257–64.

In 'The Little Boy lost' and 'found' the 'God . . . like his father in white' who 'by the hand led' the child in the text is shown in the design as 'the mother holding the child's hand' (p. 263). For discussions of this thesis, see no. 2000, 1217 2, 11, 30.

1417. Corrigan, Matthew. 'Metaphor in William Blake: A Negative View.' *JAAC*, XXVIII (1969), 187–99.

'The metaphoric principle was incompletely realized and used throughout most of Blake's poetry' (p. 198).

1418. *Cortissoz, Royal. 'A Memorable Discourse on the Genius of William Blake.' *New York Herald Tribune*, 17 Jan., 1934, p. 10.

Enthusiastic commentary on a lecture concerning *Job* by Binyon.

1419. A. Coveney, Peter. 'Blake's *Innocence* and *Experience*.' Chap. 2 (pp. 15–29) of his *Poor Monkey*: The Child in Literature. London, 1957. B. *Chap. 2 (pp. 52–67) of [the same work:] *The Image of Childhood*: The Individual and Society: A Study of the Theme in English Literature. Revised Edition. Introduction by F. R. Leavis. Harmondsworth & Baltimore, 1967. Peregrine Books Y62.

For Blake, children were 'a symbol of innocence, without which, as a religious artist, he could not have worked' (B, p. 52).

1420. Cox, Kenyon. 'William Blake.' Pp. 127–32 of his *Old Masters and New*: Essays in Art Criticism. N.Y., 1905 (vDVE).

Without merit.

1421. Cram, W. A. 'William Blake.' *Radical*, III (1868), 378–82 (vMKN).

Nobody understands Blake.

1422. *Craven, Thomas. 'Blake.' Pp. 359–68 of *Man of Art*. N.Y., 1931.

A popular introduction.

1423. A. —— *'Blake.' Chap. 10 (pp. 67–72) of his *Famous Artists and their Models*. N.Y., 1949. B. *N.Y., 1962. Pp. 67–72.

A shoddy popular account, scarcely alluding to his 'models'.

1424. *[Crawford, David Alexander Edward Lindsay, 27th Earl of Crawford.] *Address by Lord Crawford at the Unveiling Ceremony*. [London, 1927.]

A four-page speech given at the unveiling of the *'Blake Memorial in St. Paul's Cathedral by Henry Poole, R.A.' on 6 July 1927.

1425. [Crawfurd, Oswald.] 'William Blake: Artist, Poet, and Mystic.' *New Quarterly Magazine*, II (1874), 466–501.

This restrained but perceptive essay is valuable chiefly for its paraphrase of a Blake letter which cannot be traced today.

1426. *Croft-Murray, E. 'The Graham Robertson Blakes.' *British Museum Quarterly*, XVI (1951), 11–12 (vMKN).

'Jacob's Ladder', 'The Sacrifice of Jephthah's Daughter', and 'The Judgement of Paris' in the British Museum.

1427. A. Cromek, R. H. 'Account of Mr. Schiavonetti.' *Examiner*, No. 131 (1 July 1810), 412–14. (Toronto) B. 'Biographical Memoirs of the Late Lewis Schiavonetti.' *Gentleman's Magazine*, LXXX (Supplement to Jan.–June 1810), 662–5. (Toronto)

The purpose of these two identical obituaries (neither of which acknowledges the other) is apparently to puff Cromek's publications (though his ownership of them is not mentioned). Alternatively it may be just coincidence that three of Schiavonetti's eight 'principal performances' singled out for praise, including the portrait of Blake and Blake's designs for *The Grave*, were published by the author of the obituary.

1428. Crompton, Louis W. 'Blake's Nineteenth Century Critics.' Chicago Ph.D., 1954.

A sound, thorough study.

1429. —— 'William Blake: Man Without a Mask.' *Commonweal*, LXVI (1957), 492–4.

A general appreciation of his reputation.

1430. Cumberland, G. 'Hints on various Modes of Printing from Autographs.' *Journal of Natural Philosophy*, XXVIII (Jan. 1811), 56–9.

A passing comment that '*Blake* . . . alone excels in that art' of reading or writing backwards.

1431. A. Cunningham, Allan. *The Cabinet Gallery of Pictures*, selected from The Splendid Collections of Art, public and private, which adorn Great Britain; with Biographical and Critical Descriptions. [2 vols.] London, [Vol. I] 1833, [Vol. II] 1834. Vol. I, pp. 11–13. (BM) B. *The Gallery of Pictures* by The First Masters of the English and Foreign Schools, with biographical and critical dissertations. [2 vols.] London: George Virtue, Ivy Lane. [1835?] Vol. I, pp. 115–16. (GEB)

This work was first issued in parts as *Major's Cabinet Gallery of Pictures*; with Historical and Critical Descriptions and Dissertations, by Allan Cunningham (see no. 1431). The first part, with the delightful anecdote about Blake and the archangel Gabriel which Cunningham had omitted from his *Lives*, was reviewed in the *Athenaeum* on 8 Sept. 1832, the second part on 13 Oct., the third on 17 Nov. 1832, the fifth on 5 Jan. 1833. . . . I have not seen the issue in parts.

B. I have found no indication of date in B, and the possibilities are almost any time between 1832 and 1850. The Blake anecdote, unchanged, is still introduced gratuitously into a description of Guercino's 'Christ in the Sepulchre', but it is now the last, rather than the first, section of Volume I. (It is reprinted in Keynes [1921].)

1432. Cunningham, Allan. *Poems and Songs.* With an introduction, glossary, and notes by Peter Cunningham. London, 1847. P. ix. (Bodley)

Allan Cunningham hoped 'that his fame would rest hereafter' in part on his accounts of Flaxman, Burns, and 'the wild but noble imaginations of Blake'.

1433. A. —— *'William Blake.' Vol. II, pp. 140–79 of *The Lives of the Most Eminent British Painters, Sculptors, and Architects.* Three Volumes [eventually six]. London: John Murray, Albemarle Street. [Vol. I] 1829, [II & III] 1830, [IV] 1831, [V] 1832, [VI] 1833. The Family Library. (BM) B. *The Second Edition. London: John Murray, Albemarle Street. [Vols. I–III] 1830, [IV] 1831, [V] 1837, [VI] 1838. The Family Library. Vol. II, pp. 143–88. (BM & GEB) C. *The Lives of the Most Eminent British Painters and Sculptors.* In Three Volumes. New=York: Printed by J. & J. Harper, 82 Cliff St. Sold by Collins & Hannay, Collins & Co., G. & C. & H. Carvill, White, Gallaher, & White, E. Bliss, & C. S. Francis;—Albany, O. Steele, and Little & Cummings;—Philadelphia, John Grigg, Carey & Lea, Towar & Hogan, E. L. Carey & A. Hart, T. Desilver, jr., and U. Hunt;—Boston, Richardson, Lord, & Holbrook, Carter & Hendee, and Hilliard, Gray, & Co.;—Baltimore, W. & J. Neal, J. Jewett, and Cushing and Sons. 1831. Harper's Family Library. Vol. II, pp. 124–55. (Toronto) D. N.Y., 1837. Harper's Stereotype Edition. Vol. II, pp. 124–55. E. §N.Y., 1839. Harper's Stereotype Edition. Vol. II, pp. 124–55. F. §In Three [eventually five] Volumes. N.Y., 1842. Harper's Stereotype Edition. Vol. II, pp. 124–55. G. N.Y., 1844. Harper's Stereotype Edition. Vol. II, pp. 124–55. H. §In Three Volumes. N.Y. 1846. Harper's Stereotype Edition. Vol. II, pp. 124–55. I. *The Lives of the Most Eminent British Painters.* Revised Edition. Annotated and Continued to the Present Time by Mrs. Charles Heaton. [2 vols.] London, [Vol. I] 1879, [II] 1880. Vol. II, pp. 392–432. J. *Great English Painters.* [Five] Selected Biographies from Allan Cunningham's 'Lives of Eminent British Painters'. Ed. William Sharp. London, 1886. The Camelot Classics. Pp. 275–311. K. London, [1898]. Pp. 275–311.

A, C, D, E, F, G, and H. The first edition is markedly shorter than the second, but it was nevertheless reprinted in the issues of N.Y., 1831, 1837, 1839, 1842, 1844, 1846 and in A. Symons, *William Blake*, 1907 (no. 2804).

On 11 Feb. 1961 Sir John Murray, K.C.V.O., D.S.O., 50 Albemarle Street, London, generously wrote that 'there were 7,000 copies printed of Volumes I and II: 14,000 of Volumes III and IV, and the remaining stock seems to have been sold off to Tegg later'. (In Volumes V & VI of the Second Edition after 'John Murray, Albemarle Street' is added: 'and sold by Thomas Tegg and Son, Cheapside.') The firm also preserves a mass of letters from Allan Cunningham covering a wide variety of subjects.

B, I, J, and K. The considerably more important second and longer version was reprinted in the editions of 1880, 1886, and 1893, and in *Blake Records* (1969), and reproduced in facsimile in Wittreich (1970).

A and B. The original boards of the first two editions are labelled 'Lives of British Artists', 'The Family Library', 'A Volume Published Every Alternate Month'. In this 'Family Library' series, Cunningham's *Lives* form Vols. IV, X, XIII, XIX, XXVII, XXXVIII, and the life of Blake is in Vol. X.

C, D, E, and H. The three-volume editions of N.Y., 1831, 1837, 1839, and 1846 are called volumes 17–19 of Harper's Family Library.

F and G. The five-volume editions of N.Y., 1842 and 1844 are called volumes 18–22 of the Family Library.

I. The only edition with editorial pretensions is that of Mrs. Heaton (I), who says, reassuringly and honestly: 'My task—one of correction, and addition of new matter—has all been accomplished in notes. I have in no instance interfered with the original text except in the correction of mere verbal errors.' (P. v.)

In the Huntington Library is a peculiar mixed set of Cunningham's *Lives*, in which Volumes III and IV are of the first edition; Volumes I and V are called the 'Third Edition' and dated respectively 1854 and 1848 [*sic*]; the last volume is not ascribed to any edition but is dated 1846; and the title-page of the second volume is missing, though the contents are the same as in the second edition. I know nothing further of this odd 'Third Edition'.

There are four casual references to Blake in the biographies of Flaxman (Second Edition, Vol. III [1830], pp. 277, 283, 308) and of Lawrence (Vol. VI [1833], p. 193) and a wonderful anecdote about Blake and the Virgin Mary in that of Fuseli (Second Edition, Vol. II [1830], p. 333).

Cunningham's life of Blake is largely an amalgam of previously published anecdotes, but it is suavely and deftly written, and until Gilchrist's biography in 1863 it was by far the best-known account of Blake.

1434. Cunningham, Allan. 'Züge aus dem Leben des Künstlers Blake.' [Tr. anon.] *Zeitgenossen*, Reihe III, Zweiter Band, Nr. XIII. XIV ([Leipzig] 1830), 170–8 (vDS). (NYP)

A translation of paragraphs 8–10, 23–4, 36–9, 41–4, 47–9 of Cunningham's life of Blake with no editorial matter except two negligible footnotes.

1435. Cunningham, George Godfrey, ed. *Lives of Eminent and Illustrious Englishmen*, from Alfred the Great to the Latest Times, On an Original Plan. 8 vols. Glasgow, Edinburgh, & London, 1838. Vol. VIII, p. 310.

The account of Flaxman (VIII. 310–12) quotes Allan Cunningham's description of Flaxman with Blake (no. 1433).

1436. Cunningham, Peter. 'New Materials for the Life of John Flaxman, R. A.' *The Builder*, XXI (17, 24 Jan. 1863), 37–8, 60.

Maria Denman's comments (now in the National Library of Scotland) on Allan Cunningham's accounts of Flaxman (no. 1433) assert, among other things, that Mr. Mathew did not join Flaxman in publishing Blake's *Poetical Sketches*.

1437. Curran, Stuart. 'The Mental Pinnacle: *Paradise Regained* and the Romantic Four-Book Epic.' Pp. 133–62 of *Calm of Mind*: Tercentenary Essays on *Paradise Regained* and *Samson Agonistes* in Honor of John S. Diekhoff. Ed. Joseph Anthony Wittreich, Jr. Cleveland & London, 1971.

A study of *Endymion*, *Jerusalem* (pp. 145–55), and *Prometheus Unbound*, which asserts that 'When the richness of narrative and symbolic patterns' in *Jerusalem* 'is reduced', 'we are left with the plot of *Paradise Regained*' (p. 155).

1438. Curry, H. Wilson. 'William Blake: Poet of Divine Forgiveness.' *Expository Times*, LXXX (1969), 371–4.

Admiring general article.

1439. Curtis, F. B. 'Blake and the "Moment of Time": An Eighteenth Century Controversy in Mathematics.' *PQ*, LI (1972), 460–70.

Blake makes 'an original poetic interpretation of the mathematical connotations' of the Newtonian term 'moment', after 1800 and especially in *Milton* (p. 460).

1440. Curtis, George W. 'Jenny Lind.' *Union Magazine*, II (April 1848), 155–9 (vMKN).

'Like Correggio, Jenny Lind recalled in their best meaning, the verses of Blake: "Piping down the valleys wild . . . ."'

D

1441. D., C. 'Prints and Drawings: Recent Accessions.' *British Museum Quarterly*, IV (1929), 47–50 (vMKN).

Designs for *Night Thoughts*.

1442. D'Agostino, Nemi. 'William Blake.' *English Miscellany*, VIII (1957), 55–108.

An introductory essay in Italian.

1443. *Dalton, J. 'The Art of William Blake: Towards a New Aesthetic.' *Apollo*, LXVI (1957), 50–5 (vMKN).

1444. Daly, Michael Joseph. 'The Marriage Metaphor and the Romantic Prophecy: A Study of the Use of the Epithalamium in the Poetry of Blake, Wordsworth, and Coleridge.' *DAI*, XXIX (1969), 2254 A. University of Southern California Ph.D., 1968.

1445. A. *Damon, S. Foster. *A Blake Dictionary*: The Ideas and Symbols of William Blake. Providence, Rhode Island, 1965. B. 1965 [i.e. Second Printing, 1967]. C. *N.Y., 1971. Dutton Paperbacks.

This enormous work is particularly useful in identifying Blake's allusions to people in the Bible and places in Britain.

A table of contents (missing from the book) is supplied in no. 1218 41.

1446. Damon, S. Foster. 'Blake: Psychologist.' *Saturday Review of Literature*, I (1926), 357–8 (vMKN).
Partly a review.

1447. —— §'Blake's Illuminated Books now on Exhibition at Fogg.' *Harvard Crimson*, LXXVI, No. 93 [i.e. No. 94] (23 Jan. 1920), 7.

1448. —— *'Exhibition of Blake's Books.' *Harvard Alumni Bulletin*, XXII (1920), 359–61.
The Grolier Club exhibition came to Harvard.

1449. A. —— 'How I came to discover Blake.' *Faith and Freedom*, IX (1956), 137–44. B. Mimeographed. [?1957] C. Reprinted in the *Blake Newsletter*, I, iii (1967), no. 1217 4.
Personal reminiscences given at a Blake dinner.

1450. —— *A Note on the Discovery of a New Page of Poetry in William Blake's Milton*. Illustrated by Facsimile Reproductions from the Original in the Possession of a Member of the Club of Odd Volumes. Boston, 1925.
The new page is reproduced and transcribed.

1451. —— 'Some American References to Blake before 1863.' *MLN*, XLV (1930), 365–70.
Blake references in Arthur, Dendy, Durfee, *The Harbinger* (no. 279), Henry James, Macnish, *The New Jerusalem Magazine* (no. 268, 983), *The New York Mirror* (no. 165), and Whittier.

1452. —— 'The Unwritten Music of a Great Man.' *Harvard Musical Review*, II (1913), 3–8, 38–9 (vDS).

1453. A. —— 'William Blake.' *Freeman*, VI (31 Jan. 1923), 191–2 (vMKN). B. Reprinted in his *Philosophy and Symbols* (1924) as the Introduction.
A plea for a sane appreciation of Blake.

1454. —— §'William Blake.' *Rhode Island Historical Collection*, Jan. 1934.

1455. A. —— *William Blake, His Philosophy and Symbols*. Boston, London, Bombay, Sydney, 1924. B. *N.Y., 1947. C. Gloucester [Mass.], 1958. D. London, 1969.
A and B are identical except for title-page. The Introduction was originally printed in *The Freeman* (no. 1453) and pp. 225–36, with slight modifications and entitled 'William Blake's Doctrine of Job', are reprinted in the 1947 and 1950 *Jobs*.
William Blake, His Philosophy and Symbols is the first thoroughly scholarly book about Blake, and as such it is of great importance. It is particularly valuable for the parallels it draws between Blake's works and an immense variety of recondite mythologies, and for the careful, book-by-book explication of Blake's works.

1456. *Dandieu, Arnaud. 'Le Centenaire de William Blake.' *Nouvelles Littéraires*, 20 Aug. 1927, p. 3.

1457. §Dane, Clemence. 'Blake at the Tate Gallery.' *Time and Tide*, 10 Sept. 1920.

1458. A. Daniel-Rops [i.e. Jules Charles Henri Petiot]. 'Poésie et Prophétie.' *Revue de Paris*, LII (1945), 29–39 (vMKN). B. Reprinted in his translation of the *Marriage* (no. 116).

1459. —— 'Un Prophète de nos Terreurs: William Blake.' Pp. 27–33 of *Chants pour les Abîmes*. Paris, 1949 (vDVE).

1460. —— 'William Blake: Une Apocalypse pour notre temps.' *Nouvelle Relève*, V ([Montreal] 1946), 392–412 (vMKN). Reprinted in his translation of the *Marriage* (no. 116).
General article which, among other things, compares Blake with Rimbaud.

1461. [Darley, George.] 'Mr. William Seguier.' *Athenaeum*, 18 Nov. 1843, p. 1028.
In this highly critical obituary, Seguier is reported to have 'been "taught" by the celebrated William Blake—how different the master and the pupil!' Strangely enough, the difference is taken to reflect credit upon the master.
The authorship of the obituary is given by Abbott (no. 769), who quotes it.

1462. *Daugherty, James. *William Blake*: with reproductions of drawings by William Blake. N.Y., 1960.
This short biography for children reprints the twenty-one *Job* drawings and the 'Canterbury Pilgrims' engraving.

1463. Davenport, A. 'Blake's Minute Particulars.' *N&Q*, CXCIII (1948), 7 (vMKN).
Boswell a source for the phrase.

1464. Davies, E. Jeffries, Frank Penny, and John Sampson. 'Blake and London.' *TLS*, 8 Sept. 1927, p. 608; 15 Sept. 1927, p. 624; 22 Sept. 1927, p. 647 (vMKN).
On place-names in *Jerusalem*.

1465. Davies, Hugh Sykes, ed. 'Blake.' Pp. 17–43 of *The Poets and their Critics*. [2 vols. Vol. II:] Blake to Browning. London, 1962.
An anthology of some twenty snippets of Blake criticism from 1800 to 1957.

1466. A. Davies, J. G. *The Theology of William Blake*. Oxford, 1948. B. Hamden, Conn., 1965.
Davies attempts to assert Blake's religious orthodoxy, but he is illuminating on Blake's relations with the Swedenborgians, particularly in demonstrating the impossibility of the legend that Blake's father and family belonged to the New Church.

1467. Davies, Randall. 'Blake and the Modernists.' *New Statesman*, II (Nov. 1913), 117 (vMKN).
The 'Modernists' here are post-impressionists.

1468. Davies, Randall. *'William Blake.' *The Old Water-Colour Society's Club Twenty-Second Annual Volume*, 1944, pp. 1–11 (vMKN).

The *Examiner* review of 1809, a letter from Palmer to Gilchrist, and two excerpts from articles by Davies and Binyon.

1469. Davis, John Lowell. 'Blake and Boehme.' Univ. of Cincinnati Ph.D., 1931 (vMKN).

1470. *Debrunner, Hugo. 'Blake als Künstler und Mensch.' Pp. 13–20 of *England im Übergang*. Ed. Hugo Debrunner. Zurich, 1948.

A summary of Blake's life and work.

1471. De Casseres, Benjamin. 'William Blake.' Pp. 74–87 of *Forty Immortals*. N.Y. 1926 (vDVE).

1472. deFord, Miriam Allen. 'Blake, William.' Pp. 55–8 of *British Authors of the Nineteenth Century*. Eds. Stanley J. Kunitz & Howard Haycraft. N.Y., 1936.

1473. *de Groot, H. B. 'The Ouroboros and the Romantic Poets: A Renaissance Emblem in Blake, Coleridge and Shelley.' *English Studies*, L (1970), 553–64.

Blake uses the traditional symbol of the snake with its tail by its mouth to 'represent the natural and the earth-bound' rather than the eternal (p. 562).

1474. Delattre, H.-F. 'L'Exposition Blake et Turner à la Bibliothèque Nationale.' *Études Anglaises*, I (1937), 183–4 (vMKN).

See no. 642A.

1475. De Luca, Vincent A. 'Ariston's Immortal Palace: Icon and Allegory in Blake's Prophecies.' *Criticism*, XII (1970), 1–19.

A challenging argument about interruptions to the narrative in *Milton* and *Jerusalem* by 'numinous constructions of which Ariston's palace [*in AMERICA*] has been the type' (p. 13).

1476. De Morgan, Sophia Elizabeth. *Threescore Years and Ten*: Reminiscences of [i.e. by] the late Sophia Elizabeth De Morgan, to which are added letters to and from her Husband the late Augustus De Morgan, and others. Ed. Mary A. De Morgan. London, 1895. Pp. 66–8.

An interesting childhood memory of Blake by the daughter of the Cambridge radical, William Frend.

1477. Dendy, Walter Cooper. *On the Phenomena of Dreams, and Other Transient Illusions*. London, 1832. Pp. 123–4.

A passing reference to Blake as a 'wild' visionary who had visions of William Wallace and Edward I.

1478. A. —— *The Philosophy of Mystery*. London, 1841. P. 90. B. §N.Y., 1845.

A casual reference to Blake's visionary eccentricities.

1479. De Selincourt, Basil. 'Parallelism of Religion and Art. A Comment on William Blake.' *Hibbert Journal*, V (1907), 397–406 (vMKN).

Blake as a guide for 1907; religion and art involve the whole man.

1480. A. —— **William Blake*. London & N.Y., 1909. B. N.Y., 1971.

There are 40 plates.

1481. De Selincourt, E. 'Blake.' Pp. 131–56 of *Oxford Lectures on Poetry*. Oxford, 1934. B. Reprinted in no. 285.

1482. Destéfano, José Rafael. 'William Blake.' Pp. 101–9 of *Baudelaire y otras rutas de la nueva literatura*. Buenos Aires, 1945 (vDVE).

1483. Devree, Howard. 'Blake Exhibition in Philadelphia.' *New York Times*, 11 Feb. 1939. See no. 647.

1484. A. Dibdin, T. F. THE / Library Companion; / OR, / THE YOUNG MAN'S GUIDE, / AND / THE OLD MAN'S COMFORT, / IN THE / CHOICE OF A LIBRARY. / — / BY THE / REV. T. F. DIBDIN, F.R.S., A.S. / [Vignette inscribed:] BOOK OPENETH BOOK. / [2 vols.] / — / LONDON: PRINTED FOR / HARDING, TRIPHOOK, AND LEPARD, / FINSBURY-SQUARE; / AND J. MAJOR, FLEET-STREET. / MDCCCXXIV [1824]. Vol. II, p. 334. (BM) B. [One vol.] [1824]. P. 734. (BM & GEB) C. . . . BY THE / REV. T. F. DIBDIN, M.A., F.R.S. / *Member of the Academies of Rouen and Utrecht.* / — / SECOND EDITION. / . . . MDCCCXXV [1825]. P. 742. (GEB)

The relationship between A and B is explained in an advertisement that appeared in the *Literary Gazette* for 31 July 1824, p. 495: 'On Monday 9th August will be published [*Dibdin's LIBRARY COMPANION*], in 1 very large 8vo. vol. to be divided into 2 at the Purchaser's option, for which purpose two Sets of Title-pages will be delivered . . .'. 'A few Copies are struck off on large Paper to arrange with the other Works of the Author.' The large and small paper copies in one volume are paginated straight through, while the two-volume sets are separately paginated. An advertisement in the *Repository of Art* for 1 May 1825 announces a similar arrangement in the Second Edition, but I have not seen the issue in two volumes.

The reference to Blake is an intriguing and enigmatic account of his engravings and of the Blake collection of 'My friend Mr. D'Israeli'. (For another version, see Dibdin, no. 1485.) The Blake accounts in A and B are identical; in C a comma is added. Dibdin's marginalia in his own copy of B in the BM do not refer to Blake.

1485. —— *Reminiscences of a Literary Life*. [In Two Parts.] London, 1836. Pp. 784–9.

A striking account of a visit from Blake and D'Israeli's Blake collection (reprinted in Keynes [1921]).

1486. A. Dickinson, Kate Laetitia. *William Blake's Anticipation of the Individualistic Revolution*. N.Y., 1915 (vMKN). B. §Folcroft, Pennsylvania, 1969.

A 56-page New York Univ. thesis, privately printed.

1487. Dickson, Arthur. 'Blake's *The Clod and the Pebble* and Masefield's *Cargoes.*' *Explicator*, II (1943), item 12 (vMKN).
Two kinds of love.

1488. A. *Digby, George Wingfield. *Symbol and Image in William Blake.* Oxford, 1957. B. Oxford, 1967.
The book consists of three essays (based on lectures) on 'The Gates of Paradise' (pp. 5–53), 'The Arlington Court Picture: Regeneration' (pp. 54–93), and 'On the Understanding of Blake's Art' (pp. 94–127). These suggestive attempts to apply modern psychological distinctions to Blake's art are most effective in the first chapter. The 77 plates include all of *For the Sexes: The Gates of Paradise.*

1489. —— *'William Blake and Education.' *Athene* [London], VIII, No. 4 (Autumn 1957), 6–10.

1490. *Digby, G. W., and Kathleen Raine. 'Understanding Blake's Art.' *TLS*, 24, 31 Jan. 1958, pp. *37, 45, 61 (vMKN).
Digby, in rebuttal to a review of his book (no. 1488), gives an exegesis of the *Arlington Court picture, noting differences between his conception of it and that of Kathleen Raine (see no. 2486). Miss Raine replies, arguing for the importance of neoplatonic sources.

1491. Dike, Donald. 'The Difficult Innocence: Blake's Songs and Pastoral.' *ELH*, XXVIII (1961), 353–75 (vMKN).
A rather rambling article, mostly on the *Songs*.

1492. §Dilke, Charles Wentworth. *Charles Wentworth Dilke (1789–1864): Papers of a Critic.* Ed. Sir C. W. Dilke. 2 vols. London, 1875. Vol. I, p. 51.

1493. *Dixon, William Mcneile. 'Civilization and the Arts.' *Fortune*, XXVII (April 1943), 112–15, 120, 123–4, 126, 128, 130, 132, 134, with 'A Note on Blake' on p. 134.
Blake is used to support an argument concerning the importance of the arts.

1494. —— *English Poetry from Blake to Browning.* London, 1894. Pp. 32–6.
A trifle.

1495. Dix[s]on, William. 'Notes on Australian Artists.' *The Royal Australian Historical Society Journal and Proceedings*, V (1919), 225–48.
'William Blake' (229–31) is really about W. S. Blake and the painter of the picture of Sydney which he engraved.

1496. Dobell, B[ertram], and S. Butterworth. 'William Blake and S. T. Coleridge.' *N&Q*, CXIII [10th Ser., V] (1906), 89, 135.
Query concerning mention of Blake and Coleridge in *London University Magazine* of 1830 (no. 965), with reply.

1497. A. [Dodge, Mary Abigail]. 'Pictor Ignotus.' *Atlantic Monthly*, XIII

(1864), 433–47 (vMKN). B. Reprinted as pp. 358–98 of Gail Hamilton (her pseudonym), *Skirmishes and Sketches*. Boston, 1865 (vMKN).

A biographical account based entirely on Gilchrist.

1498. Doherty, F. M. J. 'Blake's "The Tyger" and Henry Needler.' *SP*, XLVI (1967), 566–7.

An intriguing possibility that a poem by Needler 'is evidently the covert target of Blake's'.

1499. Doi, Kochi. 'Blake no [and his] Lyca Poems.' *Eibungaku Kenkyu: Studies in English Literature* (Compiled by The English Seminar of The Tokyo Imperial University), IX (1929), 210–21.

1500. —— 'Blake no Choshi "Milton" [Blake's Long Poem *Milton*].' *Eibungaku Kenkyu: Studies in English Literature*, XXIII (1943), 153–72.

1501. —— *'Blake no "Yobu-ki" kaisetsu [Interpretation of Blake's "Job"].' Pp. 102–8 of his *Eibungaku no Kankaku* [*Senses of English Literature*]. Tokyo, 1935 (vHK).

1502. —— 'Punctuation of William Blake's Songs.' *Eibungaku Kenkyu: Studies in English Literature* Compiled by The English Seminar of The Tokyo Imperial University, XX (1940), 466–85.

1503. —— '"Songs of Experience" Shiken [A Personal View of *Songs of Experience*].' Pp. 35–49 of *Okakura Sensei Kinen Ronbunshu*: Okakura Sensei Kanreki Shukugakai [*Essays for Professor Okakura* in Commemoration of his Sixtieth Birthday]. Ed. Miyoshi Ichikawa. Tokyo, 1928.

1504. A. —— *'William Blake no Shocho-shugi [Symbolism of William Blake].' *Kaizo* [*Reformation*], April 1927, pp. 148–60. B. 'Blake no Shocho [Blake's Symbolism].' Pp. 35–101 of his *Eibungaku no Kankaku* [*Senses of English Literature*]. Tokyo, 1935 (vHK).

1505. *Doin, Jeanne. 'William Blake (1757–1827).' *Gazette des Beaux-Arts*, 4ᵉ Série, VII (1912), 113–30 (vMKN).

Blake a mystic with great freedom in his work.

1506. Donaghey, Brian. 'An Unrecorded Printing of Blake's *Illustrations to the Book of Job?*' *Biblionews and Australian Notes & Queries*, 2nd Ser., II (1967), 40–3.

Prints on paper watermarked T H SAU[NDER]S 1900 in the Queensland University Library are 'impressions from the original plates', '*not* a facsimile' [in fact, a set of the 1902 facsimile].

1507. Dooley, William Germain. 'Blake's Progress.' *Boston Evening Transcript*, 28 Dec. 1940 (vMKN).

1508. *Dorfman, Deborah. 'Blake in 1863 and 1880: The Gilchrist *Life*'. *BNYPL*, LXXI (1967), 216–38.

Background, authorship, and revisions of Gilchrist's *Life*.

1509. —— *Blake in the Nineteenth Century*: His Reputation as a Poet From

Gilchrist to Yeats. New Haven & London, 1969. Yale Studies in English Volume 170.

A useful survey, concentrating on Gilchrist (no. 1680 A–B) and Ellis & Yeats (no. 369), with an appended list of 'Appearances of Blake's Writings' in print, 1806–93 (pp. 229–90).

1510. Doughty, Oswald. 'The Rise of Mysticism and Idealism. Blake.' Chapter VII (pp. 378–430) of *English Lyric in the Age of Reason*. London, 1922.
A general but intelligent account of Blake.

1511. §Douglas, Dennis, 'Blake and the Grotesque.' *Balcony*, VI (1967), 9–16.

1512. —— 'Blake's "Europe": A Note on the Preludium.' *Aulla*, No. 23 (May 1965), 111–16.
Sources in Thomas Taylor and Boehme.

1513. Douglas, James. 'William Blake.' Vol. II, pp. 717–20, of [Robert] *Chambers's Cyclopaedia of English Literature*. Ed. David Patrick. [3 vols.] London and Edinburgh, 1901, 1902, 1903. See also no. 994.

1514. Downing, Richard, and J. B. Beer. 'Blake and Augustine.' *TLS*, 18 June 1970, p. 662; 2 July 1970, pp. 726–7.
Downing's allegations of an influence from Augustine's *Confessions* on Blake are corrected and extended by Beer.

1515. Doxey, William S. 'William Blake and the Lunar Society.' *N&Q*, CCXVI [N.S. XVIII] (1971), 343.
In 1778 the Lunar Society met once in London.

1516. —— 'William Blake, James Basire, and the *Philosophical Transactions*: An Unexplored Source of Blake's Scientific Thought?' *BNYPL*, LXXII (1968), 252–60.
A list of 123 Basire engravings in the *Philosophical Transactions* for 1772–8, in which Blake might have had a hand.

1517. Drake, Constance M. 'An Approach to Blake.' *College English*, XXIX (1968), 541–7.
The approach is 'to deal with each poem on its own merits' (p. 543), e.g. in 'The Little Girl Lost' and 'The Tyger'.

1518. *Drucker, G. M. Michael. 'William Blake.' *Arts (Beaux Arts)*, No. 108 (28 March 1947), 1, 5.
Discusses the exhibition at René Drouin Gallery.

1519. *Dudley, Laura Howland. 'Blake Exhibition.' *Fogg Art Museum Notes*, II (1931), 285–304.
An exhibition 22 Oct.–15 Dec. 1930.

1520. Dufty, J. G. 'William Blake.' *Morning Light*, XXVI (1903), 109.
Corrects the very brief report (p. 100) of his lecture called 'William Blake, Poet and Artist'.

1521. Dufty, J. G. 'William Blake.' *Morning Light*, XXVI (1903), 140.
A plea for help with Dufty's researches on Blake and Swedenborg.

1522. Dumbaugh, Winnifred. *William Blake's Vision of America*. Pacific Grove, California, 1971.
A brief (43 pp.), derivative, inaccurate account.

1523. A. Duncan-Johnstone, L. A. *A Psychological Study of William Blake*. London, December 1945. The Guild of Pastoral Psychology, Guild Lecture No. 40. B. §1958.
This brief (22 pp.) lecture explains the psychology of Blake's myth in Jungian terms, with parallels from the Kabbala, the Gnostics, and others.

1524. A. [Durfee, Job.] 'Theoptes.' *The Panidèa*: or, An Omnipresent Reason Considered as the Creative and Sustaining Logos. Boston, 1846. P. 63 fn. B. *The Complete Works of the Hon. Job Durfee, LL.D.*, Late Chief Justice of Rhode-Island; with A Memoir of the Author. Edited by his Son [Thomas Durfee]. Providence & Boston, 1849. P. 391 fn.
This incidental reference to Blake is taken from Cunningham.

1525. Durr, R. A. *Poetic Vision and the Psychedelic Experience*. Syracuse [N.Y.], 1970. *Passim.*

1526. §Durrant, G. H. 'Blake's "My Pretty Rose Tree".' *Theoria*, XXX (1968), 1–5.

1527. Durstine, Jean Marie. 'William Blake's Theory of Art and Its Application to His Poetry.' Indiana Ph.D. Cf. *DA*, XXVI (1965), 2748–9.
'The chaotic form of the prophecies' results from Blake's theory of art.

1528. Dyce, Alexander. *The Reminiscences of Alexander Dyce*. Ed. Richard J. Schrader. [Columbus, Ohio], 1972. Pp. 134–5.
An anecdote of Blake and Taylor, by a contemporary.

1529. Dyson, A. E. 'The Little Black Boy: Blake's Song of Innocence.' *Critical Quarterly*, I (1959), 44–7 (vMKN).
A sound, though not very original, reading of the poem.

E

1530. E., J. 'Blake's Engravings for Night Thoughts.' *More Books*, XV (1940), 64 (vMKN).
A brief note on the engravings in Boston Public Library.

1531. —— 'Blake's Illustrations for the Book of Job.' *More Books*, XV (1940), 290.
Acquisitions by Boston Public Library.

1532. Eames, Mrs. Elizabeth J. 'Love's Last Work.' *Southern Literary Messenger*, IX (Sept. 1843), 559–60.
This inferior poem about an Italian painter making a sketch of his wife while on his death-bed makes no mention of Blake but may conceivably have

been inspired by Cunningham's account of such a scene in Blake's life, or patterned after the poem by Mrs. Hemans.

1533. Earp, T. W. 'Blake as an Art Critic.' *New Statesman*, XXIX (1927), 597 (vMKN).

1534. §Easson, Roger R. 'The Rhetoric and Style of Apocalypse in William Blake's Jerusalem.' University of Tulsa Ph.D., 1970.

1535. *Eaton, Anne Thaxter. 'Illustrated Books for Children Before 1800.' *Illustrators of Children's Books 1744–1945*. Compiled by Bertha E. Mahoney, Louise Payson Latimer, & Beulah Folmsbee. Boston, 1947. Pp. 21–4.
One of the few works on children's books in which Blake is discussed, even cursorily.

1536. Eberly, Ralph D. 'Blake's *The Little Black Boy*.' *Explicator*, XV (1957), item 42 (vMKN).
A distressing misreading of the poem, missing the irony.

1537. —— 'Blake's *The Tyger*, 17–18.' *Explicator*, VIII (1949), item 12 (vMKN).
Says the tears temper 'the still-glowing Tiger metal'.

1538. *Eglington, Guy. 'Blake Illustrates Gray.' *International Studio*, LXXIX (1924), 39–47 (vMKN).

1539. A. —— *'Dante Alighieri and Blake.' *International Studio*, LXXX (1924), 239–48 (vMKN). B. 'Dante and Blake.' Pp. 106–20 of *Reaching for Art*. Boston & London, 1931.

1540. Ehrstine, John W. 'William Blake's "King Edward the Third".' *Research Studies* [of] Washington State University, XXXVI (1968), 151–62.
'Blake is using historical characters . . . to indicate the eternal aspects of tyranny' (p. 40); the essay is partly drawn from no. 1540.

1541. *Eigo Seinen: The Rising Generation*, LXVII (Tokyo, 1927). 'Blake Number (1) [(2) (3) (4) (5)].'
1. *Kochi Doi, tr. *The Marriage of Heaven and Hell*. Pp. 256–8, 291–2, 330–1, 372–3, 403–4.
2. Isamu Saito, tr. 'Blake Tenshinranman no Takusen ["Auguries of Innocence"].' Pp. 258–9, 290–1, 334–5, 370–1.
3. Makoto Sangu, tr. *Poetical Sketches* poems. Pp. 260–2, 292–3.
4. Sofu Taketomo. 'William Blake.' Pp. 254–5, 295–7, 332–3, 376–8, 409–10. (An essay in Japanese.)
5. Yoshisaburo Okakura. 'Totomajiri [Innocence].' Pp. 262–3, 337, 369.
6. Yoshisaburo Okakura. 'Maigo [Lost Boy].' P. 294.
7. *Bunsho Jugaku. 'Blake Shinwa no Rinkaku [Outline of Blake's Myth].' Pp. 299–301, 338–9, 374–5.
8. *Makoto Sangu. ' "The Grave" series Kaisetsu [Interpreted].' Pp. 301–2.
9. *Shigeo Inoue. 'Blake: "Songs of Experience" no Ankoku to Komyo ni

tsuite [On Darkness and Light in *Songs of Experience.*]' Pp. 302–6, 335–6, 367–8.

10. Makoto Sangu. '"When the morning Stars sang together" Kaisetsu [Interpreted].' P. 342.
11. Makoto Sangu. 'Blake no Eikyo [Blake's Influence].' Pp. 366–7.
12. Tenrai Shigeno. 'Blake no Tora [Blake's "The Tyger"].' Pp. 402–3.
13. Yoshisaburo Okakura. 'Shijin to Sennin [Poet and Prophet].' Pp. 405–6.
14. Konosuke Hinatsu. 'Yameru Bara ni tsuite [On "The Sick Rose"].' Pp. 407–8.
15. *Makoto Sangu. 'Blake Kenkyu Tosho Kaidai [Bibliographical Introduction to Blake Studies].' Pp. 411–13.

1542. *Eigo Seinen: The Rising Generation*, CIII ([Tokyo,] 1957). 'William Blake: Special Section.' Ed. Bunsho Jugaku.
1. *Bunsho Jugaku. 'William Blake and Japan.' Pp. 518–19.
2. *Yasushi Takeshima. 'A Study on "The Blossom".' Pp. 520–2.
3. Ichiro Koizumi. 'Blake to [and] Reynolds.' Pp. 523–5.
4. Bunsho Jugaku. 'Blake Honbun no kaishaku ni tsuite [How to Interpret Blake's Works].' P. 525. (Concerns punctuation.)
5. Jiro Ogawa. 'Blake to [and] Wordsworth.' Pp. 526–7.
6. Narumi Umetsu. '20-sai-dai Kohan no Blake [Blake in his Later Twenties]—*An Island in the Moon* no naka no *Songs of Innocence* no Mittsu no Genkei wo Chushin ni [On Three Original *Songs of Innocence* included in *An Island in the Moon*].' Pp. 528–31.
7. *Kenjiro Okamoto. 'Blake to Gendai Geijutsu [Blake and Modern Art].' Pp. 531–3.
8. Makoto Sangu. 'Shoki Blake Gakusha no Koto-nado [Reminiscences of the Early Stage of Blake Study in Japan].' P. 534.
9. Kazumi Yano. 'Blake Inyu-shi Oboegaki [Notes on Some Early Introducers of Blake in Japan].' Pp. 535–6.

1543. Eliot, T. S. 'The Mysticism of Blake.' *The Nation & Athenaeum*, XLI (1927), 799 (vMKN).
Reviews recent books on Blake.

1544. A. —— (T. S. E.) 'The Naked Man.' *Athenaeum*, No. 4685 (13 Feb. 1920), 208–9. B. Revised as 'Blake'. Pp. 137–43 of Eliot's *The Sacred Wood*: Essays on Poetry and Criticism. London, 1920. C. §1928. D. §1932. E. Reprinted as 'William Blake'. Pp. 317–22 of his *Selected Essays*. London, 1932. F. §*The Sacred Wood*. London, 1934. G. Reprinted as pp. 76–80 of his *Points of View*. London, 1941. H. §*The Sacred Wood*. London, 1945. I. §1948. J. 1950. K. 1960. L. §Translated into Japanese by Shigeo Tsuji in *Oberon*, No. 9 ([Tokyo], March 1935), 30–4. M. Also translated into Japanese in no. 1219 13. N. *Il boscosacro*. Tr. Luciano Ancheschi. Milano, 1946. Pp. 229–37. O. Reprinted in Bottrall, no. 1261.
This essay, which began as a review, discovers that Blake was a traditionalist, but not often enough.

1545. *Elistratova, Anna Arkad'evna. 'Bleik.' Chap. I (pp. 45–106) of *Nasledie Angliiskogo Romantizma i Sovremennost'*, Moscow, 1960.

1546. —— *Vil'yam Bleik, 1757–1927*. (Vsesoyuz. obsihchestvo po rasprostraneniyu polit. i nauchnikh znanii. Seriya 6, No. 21.) Moskva, 1957.

1547. *Ellis, Edwin J. *The Real Blake*. A Portrait Biography. London, 1907.

Ellis reprints the marginalia to Swedenborg's *Divine Love* (pp. 109–15), to Lavater's *Aphorisms* (pp. 122–51), to Reynolds's *Works* (pp. 371–96), and Blake's *Descriptive Catalogue* (pp. 274–92), his 'Public Address' (pp. 302–12), and his 'Vision of the Last Judgment' (pp. 317–27), the last two from Blake's *Notebook*.

About a quarter of the book consists of quotations from Blake (some previously unpublished). The remainder is a kind of hit-or-miss interpretation and a history of Blake which is frequently grossly distorted. The most stunning inventions are the 'facts' that Blake was really Irish, not English, and that his name was really O'Neill, not Blake. Small fragments of the MS are in Reading University Library.

1548. —— 'William Blake.' *Occult Review*, IV (1906), 26–35, 87–95.

A fragmentary and only moderately inaccurate introduction to Blake.

1549. Ellmann, Richard. *The Identity of Yeats*. London, 1954. *Passim*, especially pp. 25–9 and 91–8.

1550. —— *Yeats: The Man and the Masks*. London, 1949. *Passim*.

1551. Elton, Oliver. 'William Blake.' Vol. I, pp. 137–71 of *A Survey of English Literature 1780–1830*. In Two Volumes. London, 1912.

1552. A. *England, Martha Winburn. 'Blake and the Hymns of Charles Wesley [Part I: Wesley's Hymns for Children and Blake's *Songs of Innocence and of Experience*;] [Part II: Wesley's *Hymns for the Nation* and Blake's *Milton*;] [Part III: Enthusiasm without Mysticism;] [Part IV: *Short Hymns* and *Jerusalem*].' *BNYPL*, LXX (1966), 7–26, 93–112, 153–68, 251–64. *B. Pp. 44–112 of Martha Winburn England & John Sparrow. *Hymns Unbidden*: Donne, Herbert, Blake, Emily Dickinson and the Hymnographers. N.Y., 1966.

A very wide-ranging discussion of their kinship. Only very minor changes were made in B.

1553. A. —— *'The Satiric Blake: Apprenticeship at the Haymarket? Part I [*and* Part II, Conclusion].' *BNYPL*, LXXIII (1969), 440–64, 531–50. B. The original, shorter form, is reprinted in *Visionary Forms Dramatic*, ed. D. V. Erdman & J. E. Grant (1970).

'My hypothesis is that Blake . . . modeled [AN ISLAND IN THE MOON] on [*Samuel Foote's*] *Tea' in the Haymarket*, but 'all is hypothesis . . . qualified by varying degrees of probability' (p. 440). Part II consists of nine appendices concerning Foote, Hayley's plays, theatrical language, Handel, Milton, James Harris's *Daphnis and Amaryllis*, 'Blake's Street Cries', 'The Roast Beef of Old England', and 'London Theatrical Seasons, 1782–1784'.

1554. Engsberg, Richard Carl. 'Two by Two: Analogues of Form in Poetry and Music.' *DAI*, XXX (1969), 278A; New York University Ph.D.
Gives special attention to Pope, Blake, Wordsworth, Browning, and Yeats.

1555. Enright, D. J. 'William Blake and the Middle Way.' Pp. 112–18 of his *Literature for Man's Sake*: Critical Essays. Tokyo, 1955.
Apparently a review of Jugaku's study of Blake's *Notebook*.

1556. Enscoe, Gerald E. 'The Content of Vision: Blake's "Mental Traveller".' *Papers on Language & Literature*, IV (1968), 400–13.
Another reading, psychological and paraphrastic.

1557. Erdman, David V. 'The Binding (et cetera) of *Vala*.' *Library*, XIX [for 1964] (1968), 112–29.
A review attacking no. 212.

1558. —— 'Blake and Godwin.' *N&Q*, CXCIX [N.S. I] (1954), 66–7 (vMKN).
Possibly Blake lent Godwin money.

1559. —— '"Blake" Entries in Godwin's Diary.' *N&Q*, CXCVIII (1953), 354–6 (vMKN).
'*No* one named Blake loomed very large in Godwin's acquaintance.'

1560. —— 'Blake, Flaxman, and the £100.' *PQ*, XXVII (1948), 279–81.
Erdman demonstrates again (see also no. 1146) that the note to Flaxman with £100 from Blake, which M. R. Lowery had associated with William Blake, was in fact made by a lawyer Robert Blake.

1561. A. —— **Blake: Prophet Against Empire*. A Poet's Interpretation of the History of his Own Times. Princeton, 1954. **B.** *Revised Edition. Garden City (N.Y.), 1969.
A massive, extraordinarily original and thorough analysis of the part played by radical politics in Blake's life, art, and writing. There are 22 reproductions in A, 25 in B. Chapter x of A is reprinted in Frye, no. 1643, and part of Chapter xiii in B in Paley, no. A2439. In B, a good deal of 'New material has generally been added in the notes' (p. ix).

1562. A. —— 'Blake; the Historical Approach.' Pp. 197–223 of *English Institute Essays 1950*. Ed. Alan S. Downer. N.Y., 1951. **B.** Reprinted in no. 1724. **C.** Reprinted as pp. 147–73 of *Explication as Criticism*: Selected Papers from the English Institute 1941–1952. Ed. W. R. Wimsatt, Jr. N.Y. & London, 1963.
A good brief demonstration of how Blake's historical allegory works.

1563. —— *'Blake, William.' Vol. II, pp. 601–2, of *New Catholic Encyclopaedia*. N.Y., St. Louis, San Francisco, Toronto, London, & Sydney, 1967.

1564. —— 'Blake's Early Swedenborgianism: A Twentieth-Century Legend.' *Comparative Literature*, V (1953), 247–57.
Erdman demolishes most effectively all the suggestions and statements that

Blake or his family was in any way associated with Swedenborgianism before about 1789.

1565. Erdman, David V. 'Blake's *Jerusalem*: Plate 3 Fully Restored.' *SB*, XVIII (1965), 281–2.

1566. —— 'Blake's Landlord.' *BNYPL*, LXIII (1959), 61 (vMKN).
Reports Paul Miner to have discovered that the Thomas Taylor who was Blake's landlord was a tailor.

1567. —— *'Blake's "Nest of Villains".' *Keats–Shelley Journal*, II (1953), 61–71.
Explains the significance of Blake's dealings and quarrels with the periodicals of his time.

1568. —— 'Blake's Transcript of Bisset's "Lines Written on hearing the surrender of Copenhagen".' *BNYPL*, LXXII (1968), 518–21.
Highly speculative suggestion that James Bisset (?1762–1832) was the author of the poem Blake transcribed in his *Notebook*.

1569. —— *'Blake's Vision of Slavery.' *JWCI*, XV (1952), 242–52.
The illuminating relationships between Blake's *Visions* and Stedman's *Narrative* which Blake illustrated.

1570. —— 'The Dating of William Blake's Engravings.' *PQ*, XXXI (1952), 337–43.
Arguments to date 'Joseph of Arimathea', 'Albion Rose', and 'The Accusers'.

1571. [——] 'Desire under the Oak.' *BNYPL*, LXIV (1960), 565–6.
Speculation on a Blake anecdote mentioned in the same issue (no. 1181).

1572. —— 'Lambeth and Bethelehem in Blake's Jerusalem.' *MP*, XLVIII (1951), 184–92.
The way in which mundane features of Blake's neighbourhood acquired heroic and symbolic significance in his later Prophecies.

1573. —— *'Reliques of the Contemporaries of William Upcott, "Emperor of Autographs".' *BNYPL*, LXIV (1960), 581–7.
Reproduction of the page with Blake's autobiographical comment and charming drawing, and discussion of the circumstances under which he made them.

1574. —— *'The Suppressed and Altered Passages in Blake's *Jerusalem*.' *SB*, XVII (1964), 1–54.
An important examination of bibliographical cruxes.

1575. —— '"Terrible Blake in His Pride": An Essay on *The Everlasting Gospel*.' Pp. 331–56 of *From Sensibility to Romanticism*: Essays Presented to Frederick A. Pottle. Ed. Frederick W. Hilles & Harold Bloom. N.Y., 1965.
An attempt 'to reduce or isolate' the editorial difficulties 'by a careful examination of the manuscript fragments' of the poem (p. 333).

1576. Erdman, David V. *'William Blake's Debt to James Gillray.' *Art Quarterly,* XII (1949), 165–70.
In the first two plates of *Europe* and the 'Preludium' to *America.*

1577. 'William Blake's Debt to Joel Barlow.' *American Literature,* XXVI (1954), 94–8.
Barlow's *Vision of Columbus* is an obvious source of Blake's *America.*

1578. —— 'William Blake's Exactness in Dates.' *PQ,* XXVIII (1949), 465–70.
'Blake's dates are precise if accurately interpreted.'

1579. —— With the assistance of John E. Thiesmeyer and Richard J. Wolfe. Also G. E. Bentley, Jr., Palmer Brown, Robert F. Gleckner, George Mills Harper, Karl Kiralis, Martin K. Nurmi, and Paul M. Zall. *A Concordance to the Writings of William Blake.* [2 vols.] Ithaca, N.Y., 1967.
This wonderfully accurate and useful work is based upon the Keynes edition of Blake's *Writings* (1957; later editions are also valid) (no. 370B). There are appendices of 'Word Frequencies (Verse and Prose)' (II. 2181–2244) and 'Corrections and Additions to the Keynes Text' (II. 2245–2317), based upon very extensive examination of most of the original manuscripts and samples of the original printed works.

1580. —— & John E. Grant, ed. **Blake's Visionary Forms Dramatic.* Princeton, [N.J.] 1970 [i.e. 1971].
The work consists of a 'Preface' (pp. vii–x) by D. V. E.; 'From Fable to Human Vision: A Note on the First Illustration' for *L'Allegro* no. 6 (pp. xi–xiv) by J. E. G.; 141 plates and figures, including all *America* (K) and pl. a–c; and 20 critical essays:

A. Martha W. England, 'Apprenticeship at the Haymarket?' Pp. 3–29. (The original, *shorter* form of her 1969 essay, no. 1553, on the *Island.*)
B. William F. Halloran. '*The French Revolution*: Revelation's New Form.' Pp. 30–56. (The poem is 'a visual and dramatic prophecy, an imaginative recasting of Revelation from a different perspective' [p. 35].)
C. W. J. T. Mitchell. 'Blake's Composite Art.' Pp. 57–81. (Blake's text and design are 'organized expressions of the polarized phenomena of space and time' [p. 62].)
D. Jean H. Hagstrum. 'Blake and the Sister-Arts Tradition.' Pp. 82–91. (*Pace* Mitchell, Blake remained 'profoundly indebted to the pictorialist masters of his youth' [p. 82].)
E. David V. Erdman. '*America*: New Expanses.' Pp. 92–114. ('*The* visualizable picture . . . can be apocalyptically threefold or fourfold' [p. 94].)
F. Michael J. Tolley. '*Europe*: "to those ychain'd in sleep".' Pp. 115–45. (In *Europe*, Blake 'related it [the contemporary situation] to the great biblical pattern of history. Milton's poem on the Nativity provided him with a framework and a stimulus' [p. 145].)
G. Robert E. Simmons. '*Urizen*: The Symmetry of Fear.' Pp. 146–73.

(Shows 'the symmetry of *Urizen*, and . . . why that symmetry is fearful' [p. 146].)

H. Janet A. Warner. 'Blake's Use of Gesture.' Pp. 174–95. (Deals with 'the consistency and the variety' of Blake's repeated 'visual images', which form 'a highly sophisticated pictorial language' and particularly with 'the gesture of outstretched arms' [pp. 174, 175].)

I. Eban Bass. '*Songs of Innocence and of Experience*: The Thrust of Design.' Pp. 196–213. (Considers the designs not 'as illustrations' but 'as compositions' [p. 199].)

J. Irene H. Chayes. 'The Presence of Cupid and Psyche.' Pp. 214 43. ('Concerned with Blake's most direct uses of Apuleius' fable' [p. 215].)

K. John Sutherland. 'Blake and Urizen.' Pp. 244–62. ('Blake had deeply ambivalent feelings about . . . Urizen' [p. 244].)

L. George Quasha. 'Orc as a Fiery Paradigm of Poetic Torsion.' Pp. 263–84. (In *America*, Orc is 'the creative force of the universe alembicated by human vision-in-action' [pp. 266–7].)

M. Irene Tayler. 'Metamorphoses of a Favorite Cat.' Pp. 285–303. (Blake's Gray designs form 'a singularly clear paradigm of Blake's method in his larger works' [p. 303]. The essay is reprinted with trifling changes in her *Blake's Illustrations to the Poems of Gray* [1971], 55–70, with no indication in either book of the duplication.)

N. John E. Grant. 'Envisioning the First *Night Thoughts*.' Pp. 304–35. (Factual description and speculative interpretation of the 35 designs for Night I.)

O. Ben F. Nelms. 'Text and Design in *Illustrations of the Book of Job*.' Pp. 336–58. (Concerned chiefly with pl. 11.)

P. Brian Wilkie. 'Epic Irony in *Milton*.' Pp. 359–72. ('Blake's *Milton* is a vicarious palinode' [p. 361].)

Q. Helen T. McNeil. 'The Formal Art of *The Four Zoas*.' Pp. 373–90. (The 'high rant and bone-crushing agony' of *The Four Zoas* 'follow a hectic, disruptive pattern' [pp. 390, 381].)

R. Henry Lesnick. 'Narrative Structure and the Antithetical Vision of *Jerusalem*.' Pp. 391–412. (The designs on pl. 4, 26, 50–3, 75–8, 99–100 suggest 'the structural antithesis [*which*] reflects the truly paradoxical nature of Blake's vision' [p. 391].)

S. Kenneth R. Johnston. 'Blake's Cities: Romantic Forms of Urban Renewal.' Pp. 413–42. ('*A* study of the cumulative development of Blake's urban imagery, emphasizing the connection between mythic cities and historical cities' [p. 413].)

T. Edward J. Rose. '"Forms Eternal Exist For-ever": The Covenant of the Harvest in Blake's Prophetic Poems.' Pp. 443–62.

The title of the essays collected here is taken from Irene Tayler's dissertation (no. 2825), apparently without indication of her priority.

1581. §*Esaka, Yukiko. '"Mushin no Uta" to "Keiken no Uta" ["Songs of Innocence" and "Songs of Experience"].' *Sylvan*, No. 1 (20 Oct. 1955), 22–7.

1582. Esdaile, K. A. 'An Early Appreciation of William Blake.' *Library*, V (1914), 229–56.

Includes an annotated translation of Crabb Robinson's article. (See also no. 2198, written under her maiden name, McDowell.)

1583. Essick, Robert Newman. 'The Art of William Blake's Early Illuminated Books.' University of California (San Diego) Ph.D., 1969.

A useful study of the illuminations through the *Visions* (1793).

1584. Evans, B. Ifor. 'Thomas Gray and William Blake.' Pp. 99–108 of *Tradition and Romanticism*. London, 1940.

Minor.

1585. [Evans, E. P.] 'William Blake, Poet and Painter.' *Hours at Home*, XI (1870), 55–65 (vMKN).

1586. A. §Evans, Frederick H. *James John Garth Wilkinson: An Introduction.* 1912. B. Reprinted by Dr. Garth Wilkinson's youngest daughter Mrs. Frank Claughton Mathews. [Edinburgh] 1936. Pp. 11–20.

About Wilkinson's edition of the *Songs* (1839).

1587. Evenden, John. 'Blake's Dante Plates.' *TLS*, 12 Sept. 1968, p. 1023.

The drypoint title discovered by Todd (no. 2849) is visible in Binyon's *Engraved Designs* reproduction.

F

1588. F., Nu-shih C. [Miss C. F.] 'Mei-kuo Po-lai-k'o [Blake of America].' *Shih*, II, No. 1 (April 1923).

1589. Fairchild, H. N. 'Blake.' Chap. III, pp. 66–137, of *Religious Trends in English Poetry*. Vol. III: 1780–1830. Romantic Faith. N.Y., 1949.

Fairchild emphasizes, with no very marked reluctance, Blake's religious heterodoxy, and stresses the biographical and sexual elements in his poetry.

1590. —— 'Unpublished References to Blake by Hayley and Lady Hesketh.' *SP*, XXV (1928), 1–10.

References from manuscript letters.

1591. A. *Fairholt, F. W. 'Tombs of English Artists. No. 7.—William Blake.' *Art Journal*, [IV] (1 Aug. 1858), 236. B. Reprinted in pp. 94–100 of **Homes, Works, and Shrines of English Artists*. London, 1873.

1592. B. Farington, Joseph. *The Farington Diary*. Ed. James Greig. [8 vols.] London, [Vol. I] 1922, [II] 1923, [III and IV] 1924, [V] 1925, [VI] 1926, [VII] 1927, [VIII] 1928. Vol. I, pp. 141–2, 151–2, Vol. III, p. 127. C. §London, [I] 1922, [II] 1923, [III and IV] 1924, [V] 1925, [VI] 1926, [VII] 1927, [VIII] 1928. D. §London, [I and II] 1923, [III and IV] 1924, [V] 1925, [VI] 1926, [VII] 1927, [VIII] 1928.

The Blake references printed by Greig are remarkably important and inaccurate. The manuscript of the diary is now in the Royal Library at Windsor Castle; a typescript of the entire diary has been deposited in the

British Museum; and the EP Group of Companies [formerly Micro Methods] has produced a microfilm of the manuscript.

MKN did not see the original form of Greig's edition as it appeared in the *Morning Post.*

1593. Fausset, Hugh I'anson. 'William Blake.' Chap. VI, pp. 152–64 of *Studies in Idealism.* London & N.Y., 1923.

1594. *Fawcus, Arnold. 'William Blake, republican and anti-imperialist.' *Connoisseur*, CLXXII (1969), 78–80.

A 'necessarily simplified piece' about *America* and *Europe*, condensed from Keynes and Erdman.

1595. —— *'The Work of the "Insane" Genius.' *Picture Post*, LXIX, No. 13 (24 Dec. 1955), 30–1.

A colourful popular appreciation.

1596. Federmann, Arnold. 'Fusslis Freundschaft mit Blake.' Pp. 60–2 of *Johann Heinrich Füssli Dichter und Maler 1741–1825.* Zurich und Leipzig, 1927. Monographien zur Schweizer Kunst Erster Band.

1597. —— 'Johann Heinrich Füssli und William Blake.' *Neue Zürcher Zeitung*, No. 1326 (18 Aug. 1926), 1.

1598. Fehr, Bernhard. 'Füssli und Blake.' Pp. 116–21 of *Orell Füssli Almanach*, 1928 (vW Kenney).

Fuseli and Blake had many things in common, but Fuseli loved the world, while Blake denied it and emphasized the spiritual.

1599. —— 'Füssli und Blake.' Pp. 119–23 of *Von Englands Geistigen Beständen* aüsgewählte aufsätze. Frauenfeld, 1944.

1600. —— 'William Blake.' Pp. 51–60 of *Die Englische Literatur des 19. und 20. Jahrhunderts.* Potsdam, 1931.

1601. —— 'William Blake und die Kabbala.' *Englische Studien*, LIV (1920), 139–48.

An important pioneering study.

1602. *Feinblatt, Ebria. 'Blake's Illustrations for "The Book of Job".' *Los Angeles County Museum of Art Bulletin*, II, Nos. 1–2 (Summer 1948), 19–26 (vMKN).

The recently acquired prints discussed.

1603. —— *'Recent Accessions: Prints and Drawings.' *Los Angeles County Museum Bulletin*, VI, No. 2 (Spring 1954), 10–14 (vMKN).

The 'Canterbury Pilgrims'.

1604. *[Fell, H. Granville.] 'Dispersal of the Graham Robertson Blakes at Christie's.' *Connoisseur*, CXXIV (1949), 52–3 (vMKN).

1605. §Ferenz, Czeslaw. 'Empedokles i Blake.' *Kwartalnik Neofilologiczny* [Warsaw], VI (1959), 333–8.

1606. Finch, Wallace H. 'God's Face at the Window.' *Religion in Life*, III (1934), 281–90 (vMKN).

1607. Fisch, Harold. *Jerusalem and Albion*: The Hebraic Factor in Seventeenth-Century Literature. London, 1964. Pp. 11–15, 274–80, and *passim*.
Blake is used as an analogy.

1608. A. Fisher, Peter F. 'Blake and the Druids.' *JEGP*, LVIII (1959), 589–612. B. Reprinted in no. 1724.
Suggests that much of Blake's information about Druidism came through Edward Williams, particularly his *Poems, Lyrical and Pastoral* (1794).

1609. —— 'Blake's Attacks on the Classical Tradition.' *PQ*, XL (1961), 1–18.
Chiefly on Blake's attacks on the abuses of the classical tradition.

1610. —— 'The Doctrine of William Blake in the Background of the Eighteenth Century. Part I: The Doctrine in its Larger Historical Setting.' Toronto Ph.D., 1949.
Part II does not form part of the thesis, and was reserved 'for inclusion in the book which I hope to produce'.

1611. A. —— *The Valley of Vision*: Blake as Prophet and Revolutionary. Ed. Northrop Frye. Toronto, 1961. University of Toronto Department of English Studies and Texts, No. 9. B. Toronto, 1971.
A study of Blake's context as an intellectual revolutionary.

1612. A. Fiske, Irving. *Bernard Shaw's Debt to William Blake*. With Foreword and Notes by G. B. S. London, 1951. Shavian Tract No. 2. B. Reprinted as 'Bernard Shaw and William Blake'. Pp. 170–8 of *G. B. Shaw*: A Collection of Critical Essays. Ed. R. J. Kaufmann. Englewood Cliffs (N.J.), 1966. Twentieth Century Views.
In the Foreword to A, Shaw writes: 'This essay . . . I rank among the best, perhaps the very best, about myself.'

1613. *A FitzGerald Friendship*: Being Hitherto Unpublished Letters from Edward FitzGerald to William Bodham Donne. Ed. Mrs. Catherine Bodham Johnson and Neilson Campbell Hannay. London, 1932. P. 6.
FitzGerald refers to Blake in a letter to Donne of 23 Oct. 1836.

1614. A. —— *Letters and Literary Remains of Edward FitzGerald*. Ed. William Aldis Wright. In Three Volumes. London & N.Y., 1889. Vol. I, p. 21. B. *Letters of Edward FitzGerald*. [Ed. William Aldis Wright.] In Two Volumes. London, 1894. Vol. I, pp. 25–6. C. *Letters and Literary Remains of Edward FitzGerald*. [Ed. William Aldis Wright.] In Seven Volumes. London & N.Y., 1902. Vol. I, p. 26. D. *Letters of Edward FitzGerald*. Ed. J. M. Cohen. London, 1960. Centaur Classics. Pp. 5, 6.
A letter to W. B. Donne of 25 Oct. 1833 (also reprinted in Keynes [1921]).

1615. Flake, Otto. 'William Blake.' *Gegenwart*, LXXI (1907), 374–6 (vMKN).
A general article.

1616. Flatto, Elie. 'The Social and Political Ideas of William Blake.' *DA*, XXVII (1967), 3870 A.

1617. *Fletcher, Angus. 'A Note on Blake's Illustrations for *Comus*.' Pp. 253–6 of his *The Transcendental Masque*: An Essay on Milton's *Comus*. Ithaca [N.Y.] & London, 1971.

Brief comparison of the early (Huntington) series of designs to *Comus* with the later (Boston Museum) series, which are reproduced in colour on facing pages.

1618. A. Fletcher, Ian. 'The Ellis–Yeats–Blake Manuscript Cluster.' *Book Collector*, XXI (1972). B. Reprinted in pp. 90–112 of *To Geoffrey Keynes*: Articles contributed to The Book Collector to Commemorate his Eighty-Fifth Birthday. London, 1972.

Fragments of the Ellis & Yeats edition of Blake's *Works* (1893) and of Ellis's *Real Blake* (1907) are in Reading University Library.

1619. Fletcher, John Gould. 'Blake's Affinities with Oriental Thought (I) [(2)].' *Eigo Seinen: The Rising Generation*, LXV (1931), 197–8, 233–5.

Chiefly concerned with 'Hindu epics'.

1620. —— 'Was William Blake a Taoist?' *Eigo Seinen: The Rising Generation*, LXV (1931), 273–4, 294–6.

Blake's 'principles of life . . . were akin to the purest principles of Taoism' (p. 296).

1621. —— 'William Blake.' *North American Review*, CCXVIII (1923), 518–28 (vMKN).

Blake was 'more radical and more logical in his revolt' than any other Romantic.

1622. —— 'Yale Discovers Blake.' *Poetry*, XX (1917), 315–20 (vMKN).

Ostensibly a review of Pierce, no. 323.

1623. *Flint, Carissa D. 'New Acquisitions in the Print Department.' *Bulletin of the Chicago Art Institute*, XXVIII (1934), 26–7 (vMKN).

The Virgil woodcuts.

1624. Follansbee, Eleanor. *Heavenly History*: An Account of Heavenly Architecture After Dante, Milton, Swedenborg and Blake With a Complete History of the Genesis and Hierarchy of the Blessed Angels and Sundry Apocrypha. Chicago, 1927.

A brief work about angels, devils, heaven, and hell (*not* about 'Heavenly Architecture'), with very desultory phrases about Blake.

1625. *Fontaine*, XI [XVIIIᵉ année], No. 60 (May 1947), 217–76, 'William Blake 1757–1827' issue, with articles by R. Fry, le Breton, E. Souffrin, A. C. Swinburne, A. Symons, and translations from Blake (pp. 251–76).

1626. *Forbes-Robertson, John. 'William Blake, 1757–1827.' Pp. 402–5 of his *The Great Painters of Christendom* from Cimabue to Wilkie. London, Paris, N.Y. [?1885].

'*H*is art, as art, [*is*] anything but sound and instructive' (p. 402).

1627. Ford, Boris. '"From Blake to Byron".' *TLS*, 31 Jan. 1958, p. 61 (vMKN).
Not about Blake; Ford merely objects to the review of his book (see no. 1752).

1628. Ford, C. Lawrence. 'Glowworms and Fireflies.' *N&Q*, CVI [9th Ser., X] (1902), 365–6.
A metaphor in 'A Dream' reappears coincidentally in W. H. Hurlbut, *Pictures of Cuba* (1955).

1629. Forseth, Roger Daniels. 'The Function of Imagery in the Lyric: Pope to Wordsworth.' Northwestern Ph.D., 1956; cf. *DA*, XVII (1957), 852–3 (vMKN).
Blake crucial in the development.

1630. Forster, E. M. 'An Approach to Blake.' *Spectator*, CXLVIII (1932), 474 (vMKN).
A review, which says 'read him, don't talk about him', but also remarks that Blake 'gets a bore' in his later works.

1631. Forster, John. *Walter Savage Landor*: A Biography. In Two Volumes. London, 1869. Vol. II, pp. 322–3.
A reference of 1836. (Reprinted in Keynes [1921].)

A1632. *Freeman, John. 'Blake's Innocence and Experience Rationalized.' *Bookman*, LXXV, No. 445 ([London] Oct. 1938), 17–19 (vMKN).

1632. *——. 'William Blake The Centenary of a Great English Poet.' *Bookman*, LXXII (1927), 249–53.
A general centenary essay.

1633. Freiberg, Stanley Kenneth. 'The Artist's Year: A Study of the Meaning of Time in the Life and Works of William Blake.' Wisconsin Ph.D., 1957. Cf. *DA*, XVII (1957), 848.

1634. —— 'The Fleece-Lined Clock: Time, Space, and the Artistic Experience in William Blake.' *Dalhousie Review*, XLIX (1969), 404–15.
'Viewed by the imagination, the clock, . . . ringed with peacock's eyes, . . . opens into Beulah and beyond.' (P. 415.)

1635. *Freund, Frank E. Washburn. 'William Blake der Dichter, Mystiker und Künstler.' *Hochland*, II (1913), 673–707.
An introductory essay with translations of poems.

1636. Fridlander, David. 'Notes et Glossaire sur la Mythologie de William Blake.' *Messages*, I (1939), 56–63.

1637. *Friedländer, Walter. 'Notes on the Art of William Blake: A Romantic Mystic Completely Exhibited.' *Art News*, XXXVII (18 Feb. 1939), 9–10 (vMKN).
In Philadelphia.

1638. Frosch, Thomas Richard. 'The Awakening of Albion: The Renovation of the Body in William Blake's *Jerusalem*.' *DAI*, XXX (1969), 1561 A; Yale Ph.D.

'*A* literalistic reading of Blake's imagery of the fall and resurrection of the human body . . . .'

1639. Fry, Roger E. 'Blake et le Symbolisme pictural.' *Fontaine*, XI (1947), 245–9. See no. 1625.

1640. A. —— **Reflections on British Painting*. London, 1934. Pp. 82–8. B. *Reprinted in pp. 1'/3–6 of *French, Flemish and British Art*. London, 1951.

1641. A. —— *'Three Pictures in Tempera by William Blake.' *Burlington Magazine*, IV (1904), 204–11. B. *Reprinted as pp. 140–4 of *Vision and Design*. London, 1920. C. §1925. D. London [1928]. The Phoenix Library. Pp. 214–20. E. §1929. F. 1937. Pelican Books. Pp. 176–81. G. Cleveland & N.Y., 1963. Pp. 214–20.

1642. A. Frye, Northrop. 'Blake After Two Centuries.' *University of Toronto Quarterly*, XXVII (1957), 10–21 (vMKN). B. Pp. 55–67 of *English Romantic Poets*: Modern Essays in Criticism. Ed. M. H. Abrams. N.Y., 1960. C. Pp. 138–50 of Frye's *Fables of Identity*: Studies in Poetic Mythology. N.Y., 1963. D. Reprinted in Bottrall, no. 1261.

An excellent general article.

1643. —— ed. *Blake*: A Collection of Critical Essays. Englewood Cliffs, N.J., 1965. Twentieth Century Views.

The volume includes Frye's 'Introduction' (pp. 1–7) and William J. Keith, 'The Complexities of Blake's "Sunflower": An Archetypal Speculation' (pp. 56–64), plus reprints of essays by Frye (no. 1644, 1648), Chayes (no. 1375), Gleckner (no. 1703), Grant (no. 1725), Hagstrum (no. 1771), Nurmi (no. 2298), and of chapters from books by Adams ('"The Crystal Cabinet" and "The Golden Net"', Chap. vi of no. 780), Bloom ('States of Being: *The Four Zoas*', from no. 1232), Blunt ('The First Illuminated Books', Chap. iv of no. 1235), and Erdman (Chap. x of no. 1561, retitled here 'Blake's Vision of Slavery').

1644. A. —— 'Blake's Introduction to Experience.' *HLQ*, XXI (1957), 57–67. B. Reprinted in no. 1643. C. Reprinted in no. 2327.

An admirable exegesis leading the reader into the Prophecies.

1645. A. —— 'Blake's Treatment of the Archetype.' Pp. 170–96 of *English Institute Essays 1950*. Ed. Alan S. Downer. N.Y., 1951. B. Reprinted in no. 1724 and 2327.

An excellent article.

1646. A. —— **Fearful Symmetry*: A Study of William Blake. Princeton, 1947. B. *1949. C. *1958. D. Boston, 1962. E. 1965. F. 1967. G. *Princeton, 1969.

A magisterial analysis of Blake's poetry and thought, remarkable alike for its brilliance and its complexity. The 1969 edition has a new Preface on three unnumbered pages.

1647. A. Frye, Northrop. 'The Keys to the Gates.' Pp. 1–40 of *Some British Romantics*: A Collection of Essays. Ed. James V. Logan, John E. Jordan & Northrop Frye. [Columbus, Ohio,] 1966. B. Chap. 11 (pp. 175–99) of his *The Stubborn Structure*: Essays in Criticism and Society. London, 1970. C. Reprinted on pp. 233–54 of *Romanticism and Consciousness*: Essays in Criticism and Society. Ed. Harold Bloom. N.Y., 1970.

'A documentation of' the 'feeling that the keys to poetic thought are in' Blake (A, p. 8).

1648. A. —— *'Poetry and Design in William Blake.' *JAAC*, X (1951), 35–42. B. Reprinted in no. 1724. C. Reprinted in no. A1538.

The relationship between text and designs.

1649. —— 'Quest and Cycle in *Finnegans Wake*.' *James Joyce Review*, I (1957), 39–47.

'*T*he major parallels between Blake's myth of Albion and Joyce's myth of Finnegan' (p. 39).

1650. A. —— 'The Road of Excess.' Pp. 3–20 of *Myth and Symbol*: Critical Approaches and Applications by Northrop Frye, L. C. Knights, and others. Ed. Bernice Slote. Lincoln (Nebraska), 1963. B. Chap. 10 (pp. 166–74) of his *The Stubborn Structure*: Essays in Criticism and Society. London, 1970. C. Reprinted on pp. 119–32 of *Romanticism and Consciousness*: Essays in Criticism and Society. Ed. Harold Bloom. N.Y., 1970.

An examination of 'the actual connecting links between my study of Blake and my study of the theory of criticism' (A, p. 3).

1651. —— 'William Blake.' Pp. 1–31 of *The English Romantic Poets and Essayists*. A Review of Research and Criticism. Ed. Carolyn Washburn Houtchens and Lawrence Huston Houtchens. N.Y., 1957.

An important article on Blake scholarship.

1652. —— 'Yeats and the Language of Symbolism.' *University of Toronto Quarterly*, XVII (1947), 1–17 (vMKN).

Distinguishes Yeats's symbolism from Blake's.

1653. Fryer, Eugénie Mary. 'Blake—The Boy of the London Streets.' Pp. 108–16 of *A Book of Boyhoods*. New York, 1920 (vMKN).

A silly fictionalized account of Blake as a little boy.

1654. Fukuura, Noritake. 'Blake "Muku to Keiten no Uta" Kanken—sono Niritsu Haihan [A Short Study of W. Blake's *Songs of Innocence and of Experience*].' *Hokkaido Eigo Eibungaku: The English Literature in Hokkaido*, VIII (1962). 26–34.

1655. —— 'Blake no Ichikosatsu—"The Tyger" no Shocho [A Study of W. Blake—Symbol of "The Tyger"].' *Hokkaide Eigo Eibungaku: The English Literature in Hokkaido*, No. 13 (1968), 1–10.

1656. *Furst, Herbert. 'Darwin or Blake?' *Apollo*, V (1927), 105–6.
Which is most important?

1657. §Furuya, Senzo. 'Blake no "Chikon no Uta" niokeru Honmonteisei no
Mondai [On Textual Emendation of "Introduction" from *Songs of Experience*].'
Nihon Daigaku Eibungakkai Kaiho [*Nihon University English Literary Society
Transactions*], IV, No. 1 (Dec. 1939), 7–10.

1658. Fuseli, H. *The Mind of Henry Fuseli*. Selections from his Writings with
an Introductory Study by Eudo C. Mason. London, 1951. Pp. 41–58.
The relationship between Blake and Fuseli.

G

1659. Gardner, Charles. 'The Religion of William Blake.' *Church Quarterly
Review*, CV (1927), 141–8 (vMKN).
A combination of Whitefield, Wesley, Lavater, Swedenborg.

1660. A. —— *Vision & Vesture*: A Study of William Blake in Modern
Thought. London, Paris, Toronto, 1916. B. London & Toronto, 1929.
C. N.Y., 1929.
The half of the book dealing with 'Modern Thought' (c. pp. 106–215)
virtually abandons Blake.

1661. —— 'William Blake.' *Spectator*, CXXXIX (1927), 246–7.
A biographical résumé, stressing Swedenborg; L. G. (pp. 349–50) objects
to the references to Swedenborg.

1662. A. —— *William Blake the Man*. London & N.Y., 1919. B. §N.Y.,
1970.
A conventional 'attempt to trace the mental and spiritual growth of
William Blake as disclosed in his works' (p. 7).

1663. A. *Gardner, Stanley. *Blake*. London, 1968. Literature in Perspective.
B. §N.Y., 1969. Arco Literary Techniques.
An elementary, 'straightforward' work 'taken up wholly with the poetry'
'mainly . . . before 1794' (p. 5).

1664. A. —— *Infinity on the Anvil*: A Critical Study of Blake's Poetry.
Oxford, 1954. B. 1965.
In this slim (152 pp.) volume Gardner effectively analyses the dramatic
conflicts in Blake's early poetry (to 1794), but finds his later Prophecies
'barren of poetry'. The work was drafted in no. 1665. Pp. 123–30 are
reprinted in Weathers (no. 2937).

1665. —— 'Infinity on the Anvil: A Study of the Poetic Symbolism of
William Blake.' Oxford D.Phil., 1957 (according to L. F. McNamee,
Dissertations in English and American Literature [1968]).
Printed as no. 1664.

1666. §Garnett, Richard. 'Blake & Messrs. W. H. Smith and Son.' [London]
Daily Chronicle, 1896.

'A letter from Dr. Richard Garnett on their refusal to supply *The Savoy*' (Keynes [1921]).

1667. Garnett, Richard. 'Gleanings from the Cumberland Papers: Blake and Poolo.' *Hampstead Annual*, 1904–1905, pp. 110–23.

Includes the discovery of eight plates by Blake in Cumberland's *Thoughts on Outline*.

1668. —— *'John Linnell and William Blake at Hampstead.' *Hampstead Annual*, 1902, pp. 9–21.

Forced to produce a speech on short order, Garnett compiled this pastiche largely from A. T. Story (no. 2769), and then brazenly published it.

1669. —— *William Blake, Painter and Poet*. London & N.Y., 1895. The Portfolio Monographs on Artistic Subjects No. 22.

A moderately good, brief (80 pp.), general account, with an interesting report of an interview with Tatham in 1860 (pp. 71–2); there are 26 plates.

1670. Gauger, Hildegard. 'William Blake. Zur 200 Wiederkehr seines Geburtstags.' *Neuren Sprachen*, N.S. VI (1957), 297–300 (vMKN).

1671. *Gaunt, William. *Arrows of Desire*: A Study of William Blake and his Romantic World. London, 1956.

This superficial book deals so heavily and unoriginally in background material, chiefly people who may have known Blake, that the ostensible subject is often invisible. Critically the author is capable of describing Urizen as 'a universal spoil-sport'.

1672. —— *'Blake and the current of imaginative art.' Chap. X (pp. 139–48) of his *A Concise History of English Art*. N.Y., 1964.

1673. —— 'The followers of Blake.' Chap. XI (pp. 149–53) of his *A Concise History of English Art*. N.Y., 1964.

1674. —— 'William Blake.' *Konstrevy*, 1951, pp. 170–3.

1675. —— *'William Blake Sketchbook Found: Series of "Visionary Heads".' *The Times*, 7 April 1967, pp. 1, 9.

History of the sketchbook, with excerpts.

1676. —— *'William Blake the John Bull who saw visions.' *Réalités*, L (Jan. 1955), 38–43.

Brief general account of 'a typical Englishman' inspired.

1677. Geisler, Bruce L. 'Concept of Forgiveness in Blake's "Gates of Paradise" and Major Prophetic Poems: The Predicament of a Protestant Mystic in The Context of The Romantic Revolt.' *Insight* (Bulletin of the Society of English Literature and Linguistics of Notre Dame Women's University [in Kyoto]), No. 2 (1970), 16–35 (vHK).

1678. A. Gibson, John. *Life of John Gibson, R.A. Sculptor*. Ed. [E.] Lady Eastlake. London, 1870. P. 42. B. *The Biography of John Gibson, R.A., Sculptor, Rome*. [Ed.] T. Matthews. London, 1911. P. 39.

The incidental contemporary reference to Blake appears in slightly different forms in these two editions of Gibson's autobiography.

1679. Gilbert, A. H. 'A Note on Shelley, Blake, and Milton.' *MLN*, XXXVI (1921), 505–6.
Shelley is more likely to have derived ideas from Milton than from Blake.

1680. A. *Gilchrist, Alexander. *Life of William Blake, 'Pictor Ignotus.'* With Selections from his Poems and Other Writings. Illustrated from Blake's Own Works, in Facsimile by J. W. Linton, and in Photolithography; with a Few of Blake's Original Plates. In Two Volumes. London & Cambridge, 1863. B. *Life of William Blake, with Selections from his Poems and Other Writings. A New and Enlarged Edition Illustrated from Blake's Own Works with Additional Letters and a Memoir of the Author. In Two Volumes. London, 1880. C. *The Life of William Blake. Ed. with an Introduction by W. Graham Robertson and Numerous Reproductions from Blake's Pictures Many Hitherto Unpublished. London & N.Y., 1907. D. *1922. E. *1928. F. *Life of William Blake. Ed. Ruthven Todd. London & N.Y., 1942. Everyman's Library 971. G. *1945. H. N.Y., 1969.

A. In the 1863 edition, Vol. I is the *Life*, and Vol. II, pp. 1–176 the 'Selections'. There are 66 plates, including the *Job* engravings and 16 plates from electrotypes of the copperplates of the *Songs* (see no. 185). In Vol. II there are appendices of '[Ten] Letters from Blake [to Butts]', pp. 178–98, and 'Annotated Lists of Blake's Paintings, Drawings, [Writings] and Engravings', pp. 199–264.

The problem of authorship in Gilchrist's historic biography is intricate. After Gilchrist's death in 1861, the Pre-Raphaelite Brotherhood formed a kind of syndicate to finish the book. Besides those mentioned below as writing for the book, Burne-Jones was at one point suggested by Dante Gabriel Rossetti as a possible copyist of Blake's designs; and by 26 Aug. 1862 Rossetti could report to Anne Gilchrist that 'Mr. Swinburne . . . has made, next to your husband, the most diligent searches of anyone into the most recondite side of Blake.' (*Anne Gilchrist*—no. 1681—pp. 87 and 127. Swinburne began research as preparation to review Gilchrist, but his labours turned into a whole book, no. 2795.)

According to the 1863 preface (p. v), the first eight chapters were in print when Gilchrist died. The chief changes necessary were minor stylistic revisions, and the writing of the last chapter by Dante Gabriel Rossetti from some rough notes left by Gilchrist. After the publication of the book, Mrs. Gilchrist was most anxious to maintain that it was in substance and intent the work of her husband, and she made various slightly misleading statements to that effect. For instance, on 2 May she asserted that 'He left it *completed*—all the insertions put together would not (apart from quotations) occupy half-a-dozen pages' (*Rossetti Papers*—no. 2577—p. 25). However, when D. G. Rossetti's works were collected (no. 2572), the section from Gilchrist's book came to over thirty pages.

Besides these contributions of others to her husband's book, Mrs. Gilchrist apparently also ignored the very substantial 'Selections' and 'Annotated

Lists', in fact, all Vol. II. Much of the 'editing' of Blake's writings was not done by Gilchrist, either. Dante Gabriel was responsible, and unrepentant, for the 'rather unceremonious shaking up of Blake's rhymes. I really believe that is what ought to be done' (*Anne Gilchrist*, p. 94). As a consequence, the poetry which Gilchrist's readers found was often considerably more conventional and reasonable than Blake left it.

William Michael Rossetti drew up most of the original and revised 'Annotated Lists', but 'Mr William Haines . . . [*was responsible for*] compiling the list of Blake's engravings' (*Rossetti Papers*, pp. 20–1), and the list of engravings was not altered in the 1880 or 1907 editions.

B. In the 1880 edition, 34 new letters to Haylcy and the letters to Butts formerly in the appendix were worked into the text. The Selections (Vol. II, pp. 1–200) and the Annotated Lists (Vol. II, pp. 207–87), except those for the engravings, were revised and expanded. There are 64 plates in this edition, including the reproductions from the *Job* engravings and from the *Songs*.

There were a number of additions at the end of Volume II, as follows:
Frederick James Shields. 'Descriptive Notes of the Designs to Young's "Night Thoughts".' Pp. 289–307.
James Smetham, 'Essay on Blake.' Pp. 311–51, reprinted from no. 2716, omitting many of the quotations and references appropriate only to its original form as a review of Gilchrist.
Samuel Palmer, 'Francis Oliver Finch. In Memoriam.' Pp. 353–6.
[Anne Gilchrist.] 'Memoir of Alexander Gilchrist.' Pp. 359–76.

On 9 Feb. 1961, S. Moore of Macmillan & Co. Ltd. wrote to me that the only records the firm preserves of Gilchrist's biography are the facts that (1) the 1863 edition was 2,000 copies offered for £1. 12s. 0d. until 1871, when they were reduced to 18s.; (2) the 1880 edition consisted of 1,500 copies at £2. 2s. 0d.

C–E. In the 1907 edition there were no major revisions of the text: 'the principal aim has been to retain the book intact' (p. ix). The text is that of 1880 with the letters in the text. The issues of 1922 and 1928 are merely reprints.

Robertson's 'Introduction' is pp. v–xi, and he has added a final chapter on 'The Colour Plates' (pp. 404–12). There are 52 plates in this edition. The 'Annotated Lists', pp. 415–90, are reprinted from the edition of 1863, with some changes by Robertson and a 'Supplementary List' (pp. 491–6), apparently compiled from the 1880 edition. *A Descriptive Catalogue* is printed on pp. 497–526.

F. In the 1942 reprint of Vol. I of the 1880 edition, there are meticulous footnotes (pp. 367–96), verifying many of the facts and quotations; in particular, the quotations from Crabb Robinson were corrected. The Supplementary Chapter was shortened, and an independent 'Bibliographical List' (pp. 397–404) was added which is particularly useful for books with engravings by or after Blake (pp. 398–400). Todd's 'Introductory Note' is pp. vii–ix.

The illustrations are Blake's designs for Thornton's Virgil, printed from electrotypes of the originals.

G. The notes for the 1945 edition were slightly expanded and revised. This edition is certainly the cheapest and probably the best biography of Blake which has appeared.

H. is a facsimile of the 1880 edition.

Gilchrist's biography is of enormous historical and intrinsic importance for the study and understanding of Blake. 1863 marks the beginning of critical, scholarly, widespread, and sympathetic understanding of the man as poet, artist, and thinker. For the first time Gilchrist presented the facts and the works to a public at last willing and able to understand part of them.

Intrinsically, the merit of the book is such that it can never be outdated. Gilchrist gleaned information from many people who had been intimate friends of Blake, and consequently almost everything he says *may* be based on a first- or second-hand oral authority which can never be recovered. Further, he was a careful and accurate searcher in old books and records, and when the footnotes he omitted are supplied (as in F & G) he is discovered to be commendably reliable. Victorian and blinkered as he was in some respects, he was yet astonishingly far-seeing, and his biography is one with which every serious student of Blake should be familiar.

1681. Gilchrist, Anne. *Anne Gilchrist: Her Life and Writings.* Ed. Herbert Harlakenden Gilchrist. Preface by William Michael Rossetti. London, 1887. Pp. viii, 54, 57–9, 74, 87, 94, 112–13, 122–38, 141–3, 145, 255–62, 282.

Some of the references to Blake which occur in the correspondence relating to the *Life* are of considerable importance.

1682. A. ——— 'Blake, William.' Vol. V, pp. 180–4 of *The Dictionary of National Biography*. Ed. Leslie Stephen & Sidney Lee. [66 vols.] London, 1885–1901 (Vol. V, 1886). B. Vol. II, pp. 642–6 of *The Dictionary of National Biography*. Ed. Leslie Stephen & Sidney Lee. [22 vols.] London, 1908. C. §London, 1921–2. D. §London, 1937–8. E. London, 1949–50.

1683. *Gilchrist, Herbert H. 'Nescio Quae Nugarum. No. III. "The Ballad of Little Tom the Sailor".' *Century Guild Hobby Horse*, I (1886), 158–9.

A note about the facsimile of Blake's plate at p. 121.

1684. Gill, Frederick C. 'Blake—The Poet of Shattered Mankind.' *London Quarterly and Holborn Review*, CLXIV (1939), 185–99 (vMKN).

1685. ——— *The Romantic Movement and Methodism*. London, 1937. Pp. 146–59 especially.

1686. A. Gillet, Louis. 'Un mystique anglais: William Blake.' *Journal des Débats, Politiques et Littéraires*, CXXV (1913), 1. B. *Revue des Deux Mondes*, 8e Sér., XXXVIII (1937), 190–205 (vMKN).

On Blake's art.

1687. Gillham, D. G. 'Blake: Visions of the Daughters of Albion.' *Wascana Review*, III (1968), 41–59.
A paraphrastic commentary.

1688. —— *Blake's Contrary States*: The 'Songs of Innocence and of Experience' as Dramatic Poems. Cambridge, 1966.
Reprint and criticism of each Song, with references to Hobbes, Burke, Bolingbroke, Paine, and Wordsworth.

1689. Gimblett, Charles. 'William Blake—Some Random Reflections.' *London Quarterly and Holborn Review*, CLXVII (1942), 289–93 (vMKN).
Suggests, among other things, an affinity between Blake and Kirkegaard.

1690. Giovannini, Margaret. 'Blake's "*Introduction*" to *Songs of Innocence*.' *Explicator*, VII (1949), item 5 (vMKN).
The meaning is clear.

1691. Gleckner, Robert F. 'Blake and the Senses.' *Studies in Romanticism*, V (1965), 1–15.
A responsible analysis.

1692. —— 'Blake and Wesley.' *N&Q*, CCI [N.s. III] (1956), 522–4.

1693. —— 'Blake and Yeats.' *N&Q*, CC [N.s. II] (1955), 38.
Yeats's 'A Coat' influenced by passage in Blake.

1694. —— 'Blake's *My Pretty Rose Tree*.' *Explicator*, XXIII (1955), item 43.
A reading.

1695. —— 'Blake's Religion of the Imagination.' *JAAC*, XIV (1956), 359–69.
Jesus is shown to be a symbol of the imagination.

1696. —— 'Blake's Seasons.' *Studies in English Literature 1500–1900*, V (1965), 533–51.
The background of Blake's poems in *Poetical Sketches*.

1697. —— 'Blake's *Thel* and the Bible.' *BNYPL*, LXIV (1960), 573–80.
Finds 'substantial evidence of Biblical usage in the poem'.

1698. —— 'Blake's *Tiriel* and the State of Experience.' *PQ*, XXXVI (1957), 195–210.
Tiriel is Blake's first attempt to express his concept of 'Experience' after the completion of the *Innocence*.

1699. —— 'Irony in Blake's "Holy Thursday I."' *MLN*, LXXI (1956), 412–15. Reprinted in no. 2327.
Sets the poem in context.

1700. —— 'Joyce and Blake: Notes Toward Defining a Literary Relationship.' Chap. x (pp. 188–225) of *A James Joyce Miscellany*. Third Series. Ed. Marvin Magalaner. Carbondale (Ill.), 1962.

'Blake was seldom out of Joyce's thoughts when writing *Finnegan's Wake*' (p. 189).

1701. Gleckner, Robert F. '"The Lamb" and "The Tyger"—How Far with Blake?' *English Journal*, LI (1962), 536–43.

1702. —— *The Piper and The Bard*: a study of William Blake. Detroit, 1959.
An intelligent critical study which grew from no. 1705.
Innocence (pp. 3–14), *Experience* (pp. 15–30), *Tiriel* (pp. 131–42), *Thel* (pp. 157–61), *Marriage* (pp. 175–85), and *Visions* (pp. 198–204) are carefully printed with Blake's punctuation from the original engraved or (in the case of *Tiriel*) MS copies, though Gleckner does not specify *which* copy of a given engraved work (say *Thel*) he is reproducing.

1703. A. —— *'Point of View and Context in Blake's Songs.' BNYPL*, LXI (1957), 531–8. 'William Blake Issue.' B. Pp. 68–75 of *English Romantic Poets*: Modern Essays in Criticism. Ed. M. H. Abrams. N.Y., 1960. C. Reprinted in Frye, no. 1643. D. Reprinted in Bottrall, no. 1261.
Careful considerations of point of view and context are crucially important to any understanding of Blake's *Songs*.

1704. —— 'William Blake and the Human Abstract.' *PMLA*, LXXVI (1961), 373–9.
Study of Blake's composition of 'The Human Abstract'.

1705. —— 'William Blake, The Piper and the Bard.' Johns Hopkins Ph.D., 1954 (according to L. F. McNamee, *Dissertations in English and American Literature* [1968]).
The work was printed in no. 1702.

1706. *Goddard, Harold C. *Blake's Fourfold Vision*. Wallingford Pennsylvania, 1956. Pendle Hill Pamphlet No. 86.
A 33-page lecture originally delivered in 1935, which puts Blake in company with Dante, Shakespeare, Dostoevsky, and Beethoven.

1707. Godden, G. W., C. H. Collins Baker, and Cyril Bruyn Andrews. 'A Religious Blake.' *TLS*, 27 Nov. 1919, p. 696; 4 Dec. 1919, p. 714 (Baker and Andrews) (vMKN).
Comments on a review of Gardner (*TLS*, 23 Oct. 1919, p. 585), with further comments on Blake's portrayal of Christ.

1708. *Godwin, William. *Memoirs of Mary Wollstonecraft*. Ed. W. Clark Durant. London & N.Y., 1927.
Blake is discussed by Durant (pp. 207–14), and 10 of his drawings for Mary Wollstonecraft's *Original Stories* are reproduced.

1709. Goldman, Arnold. 'Blake and the Roscoes.' *N&Q*, CCX [N.S. XII] (1965), 178–82.
Influence of Blake on William Stanley Roscoe.

1710. *Gordon, Jan. 'Some British Precursors of Modernism.' *Studio*, CXXIII (1942), 89–100.

Blake is one of the more British precursors; *passim*.

1711. *Gorely, Jean. 'William Blake's Engravings for a Wedgwood Catalogue.' *Old Wedgwood*, No. 4 (Aug. 1937), 60–5.

The Blake–Wedgwood relationship as 'another notable instance of the integration of art and industry'.

1712. Gorlier, Claudio. 'Il Blake di Ungaretti.' *Paragone*, No. 196 (1966), 142–6.

1713. A. §Gosse, Edmund. 'Blake and Gray.' *Sunday Times*, 16 Aug. 1925. B. Reprinted in pp. 343–50 of his *More Books on the Table*. London, 1923.

1714. —— 'Swinburne and Kirkup.' *London Mercury*, III (1920), 156–65.

The chief value of this article is in the history of Swinburne's book on Blake (no. 2795), and in the quotation of a letter from Seymour Kirkup to Swinburne describing his memories of Blake.

1715. *Gould, F. Carruthers. 'Blake's Prophetic Portrait.' *Country Life*, XLII (23 Feb. 1918), 199. See no. 1262.

A drawing adapted from Blake's Dante devils to represent Admiral Tirpitz and the German Crown Prince.

1716. Gould, John. *Biographical Sketches of Eminent Artists*: comprising Painters, Sculptors, Engravers, and Architects, from the earliest ages to the present time; Interspersed with Original Anecdotes. To which is added An Introduction, containing a brief account of various schools of Art. London, 1834. Pp. 48–9.

An account derived from Watkins & Shoberl and, silently, from the *Gentleman's Magazine* (no. 989).

1717. Gould, Thomas. 'Four Levels of Reality in Plato, Spinoza, and Blake.' *Arion*, VIII (Spring 1969), 20–50.

The visions of Spinoza and of Blake (pp. 40–50) are parallel to Plato's but not derivative.

1718. Gowing, Emelia Aylmer. 'William Blake.' *Belgravia*, LXXVII (1892), 357–77 (vMKN).

1719. Goyder, George. 'The Significance of William Blake (1757–1957).' *Prism*, Nov. and Dec. 1957, pp. 14–16 (vKP).

1720. *Grafly, Dorothy. 'Blake's Art Exhibition Amazing. Makes U.S. Mecca for His Work.' *Philadelphia Record*, 12 Feb. 1939.

1721. —— 'A William Blake Exhibition.' *Christian Science Monitor*, 18 Feb. 1939 (vMKN).

1722. Granger, Frank. 'What did Blake mean by Sculpture?' *TLS*, 17 June 1926, p. 414.

He meant engraving.

1723. A. *Grant, John E. 'The Art and Argument of "The Tyger".' *Texas Studies in Literature and Language*, II (1960), 38–60. B. Reprinted in revised form in no. 1724.

A contentious reading.

1724. —— ed. *Discussions of William Blake*. Boston, 1961. Discussions of Literature [series].

Grant's 'Introduction' is pp. vii–xi. The following comments on Blake are reprinted: 778, 1407, 1562, 1608, 1645, 1647, 1723, 2020 (an extract only), 2055, 2091 (15 May 1824), 2296, 2783, 2896. Of these, no. 778, 1562, 1723, 2055 were revised by their authors, while no. 1645 is printed with revisions and omissions by the editor and no. 2296 is reprinted in part.

1725. —— 'Illuminations.' *TLS*, 2 Nov. 1967, p. 1045.

Correction of the review (14 Sept.) of *Milton* (no. 110), with the reviewer's largely irrelevant reply.

1726. A. —— *'Interpreting Blake's "The Fly".' *BNYPL*, LXVII (1963), 593–615. B. Reprinted in Frye, no. 1643.

An academic argument.

1727. —— 'Misreadings of "The Fly".' *Essays in Criticism*, XI (1961), 481–7 (vMKN).

A critique of Kirschbaum (no. 2061).

1728. ——*'Redemptive Action in Blake's *Arlington Court Picture*: Observations on the Simmons–Warner Theory.' *Studies in Romanticism*, X (1971), 21–6.

An analysis 'fundamentally different' from the 'Simmons–Warner Theory' (no. 2703), based upon the '"Whirlwind of Lovers" as a Key' (p. 22).

1729. —— and Fred C. Robinson. 'Tense and the Sense of Blake's "The Tyger".' *PMLA*, LXXXI (1966), 596–603.

The meaning of 'Dare' and 'twist' discussed by Grant (pp. 596–8, 600–2) and Robinson (pp. 602–3) as outgrowths of no. 1724, 2532; see also Bier (no. 1188).

1730. ——, Our Reviewer; Geoffrey Keynes. 'Illuminations.' *TLS*, 2, 9 Nov. 1967, pp. 1045, 1069.

Grant corrects a review (of 14 Sept., p. 820) [by Kathleen Raine] in fact and interpretation; the reviewer replies with an attack on all Blake scholars; Keynes points out that the Blake Trust *Milton* is a 'facsimile', not just a reproduction.

1731. *Grassby, Percy. 'William Blake as Printer and Engraver: A Note.' Six pp. inserted in the 1924 Craftsman Number of the *American Printer*.

Blake must have written his Illuminated Works normally with a pen; transferred them in mirror images to the copper; and printed from the copper, thus reversing the images again.

1732. A. §Gray, B. Kirkman. 'Notes on a Blake Exhibition.' *Inquirer*, Feb.

1904. B. Reprinted in pp. 201–5 of his *A Modern Humanist*: Miscellaneous Papers of B. Kirkman Gray. Ed. Henry Bryan Binns. With an Appreciation by Clementina Black. London, 1910.

Review of the Carfax exhibition (1904).

1733. *Gray, Basil. 'Blake: Original Design and the Illuminated Book.' Chapter V, pp. 70–89 of his *The English Print*. London, 1937 (vKP).

1734. A. Gray, J. M. 'Blake, William.' Vol. II, pp. 209–10 of *Chambers's Encyclopaedia*. London, Edinburgh & Philadelphia, 1888. B. 1895. C. 1901. D. 1908. E. 1923.

Only the smallest changes, chiefly in the bibliography, were made in these editions.

Cf. no. 882 A, B which this replaced, and no. 1236, by which in turn it was replaced.

1735. §Gray, Pamela, and Edward J. Shaw. 'Was Blake Mad?' *Sunday Times*, 11 July 1926.

1736. [Greatheed, Samuel.] 'Art. VIII. *Ballads*; by William Hayley, Esq. founded on Anecdotes relating to Animals, with Prints designed and engraved by William Blake. Small 8vo. pp. 216. Price 10s. 6d. Phillips. 1805.' *Eclectic Review*, I (Dec. 1805), 923. (BM)

The unsigned review includes a brief appreciation of the engravings. Greatheed was one of the editors of the *Eclectic Review*, and is known to have received and tried to sell Hayley's Ballads for Blake (*Blake Records* [1969], 108–9).

1737. Grebanier, Bernard D. N. 'William Blake (1757–1827).' Pp. 352–7 of *The Essentials of English Literature*. Volume Two. The Nineteenth Century to the Present. Great Neck, N.Y., 1948.

Trivial.

1738. Green, Julien. 'William Blake, Prophet.' *Virginia Quarterly Review*, V (1929), 220–32.

A general account.

1739. —— 'William Blake, Prophète 1757–1827.' Pp. 41–66 of *Suite Anglaise*. Paris, 1927. Les Cahiers de Paris, 2e série, Cahier VII (vMKN).

1740. Green, Ruth N. 'Literary Critical Theory of William Blake.' Boston Ph.D., 1941 (according to L. F. McNamee, *Dissertations in English and American Literature* [1968]).

1741. Greenberg, Alvin. 'The Real World of Blake's Manuscript Lyrics.' *Bucknell Review*, XIII (1965), 26–46.

The *Notebook* and 'Pickering Manuscript' poems refer 'to a real and comprehensive public world' (p. 26), and not to Blake's private mythology.

1742. Greenfield, Meg. 'The Prophetic Visions of William Blake.' *Reporter*, XVIII (9 Jan. 1958), 38–40, 42, 44 (vMKN).

Ostensibly a review of Keynes (no. 370B), this essay is in reality a general summary of Blake's life and thought which never mentions Keynes.

1743. Greenwood, Ormerod. 'William Blake as Prophet.' Being the Text of the Addresses given in *Lift Up Your Hearts* series, Feb. 15–20, 1954, No. 6. [London, 1954.]
Well-meant banalities for radio broadcast.

1744. Gregory, Horace. 'A Reply.' *New York Times Book Review*, 5 Jan. 1957.
In response to the (sound) protests in no. 1412, Gregory complains that his critics were 'wilfully misinformed'.

1745. *Greig, T. P. 'Graham Robertson Blake Drawings.' *Connoisseur*, CXXIX (1949), 65 (vMKN).

1746. Grierson, H. J. C. 'Blake and Macpherson.' *TLS*, 7 April 1945, p. 163.
Comment on Keynes, no. 2023.

1747. —— 'Blake's Designs for Gray. Discovery in Hamilton Palace.' *The Times*, 4 Nov. 1919, p. 15.
Letter containing the text of 'To Mrs. Anna Flaxman' and 'Around the Springs of Gray . . .'; cf. no. 889.

1748. —— *Lyrical Poetry from Blake to Hardy.* London, 1928. Hogarth Lectures on Literature.
See especially pp. 23–9 of Chapter II, 'Eighteenth-Century Lyric—Blake, Wordsworth, and Coleridge.'

1749. ——, John Sampson, Geoffrey Keynes, G. B., Thomas J. Wise. 'A Textual Point in Blake.' *TLS*, 9 Oct. 1919, p. 548 (Grierson); 16 Oct. 1919, p. 572 (Sampson); 23 Oct. 1919, p. 591 (Keynes and G. B.); 30 Oct. 1919, p. 611 (Wise); 12 Feb. 1920, pp. 105–6 (Keynes again) (vMKN).
In 'Mad Song' l. 7, 'beds' should be 'birds'.

1750. A. ——, & J. C. Smith. 'Blake.' Chap. xxiii (pp. 292–305) of *A Critical History of English Poetry*. London, 1944. B. Second (Revised) Edition. London, 1947. C. §1950. D. 1956. E. §1962.

1751. Grigson, Geoffrey. 'Between Blake and Rossetti.' *Listener*, 13 June 1940, p. 1125 (vMKN).
Discusses painters from Blake to Rossetti.

1752. —— 'English Painting from Blake to Byron.' Pp. 258–72 of *From Blake to Byron*. Ed. Boris Ford. Harmondsworth, 1957. Volume V of The Pelican Guide to English Literature.
About trends in art during Blake's lifetime.

1753. —— 'Painters of the Abyss.' *Architectural Review*, CVIII (1950), 215–20 (vMKN).
Chiefly on Mortimer, Barry, and Fuseli, but of value for Blake too.

1754. Grigson, Geoffrey. 'Palmer and William Blake.' Chapter iii, pp. 18–34 of his *Samuel Palmer The Visionary Years*. London, 1947. See also *passim*.
A detailed and responsible account of the relations between the two men.

1755. —— *'A Trio of Underestimated Virtues—I.' *Listener*, LIV (1955), 700–1.
Virtue I is independence, illustrated by Blake. Of possible interest to students of independence.

1756. *Grønbech, Vilh. *William Blake*, Kunstner Digter Mystiker. Kobenhavn, 1933.
There are 43 plates.

1757. Groslee, Nancy Moore. 'Mutual Amity: *Paradise Lost* and the Romantic Epic.' *DAI*, XXX (1969), 723A; Yale Ph.D.
Deals especially with Blake, Shelley, and Keats.

1758. Grove, Myrtle [pseudonym]. 'A Sussex Fairy's Funeral: Its True History.' *Sussex County Magazine*, I (1927), 394, 399.
An adaptation of Blake's anecdote; 'I'm sure that all Sussex fairies sing his songs to this day. I often hear them. Don't you?'

1759. *Guenne, J[acques]. 'Blake, Turner à la Bibliothèque Nationale.' *Art Vivant*, No. 209 (Feb.–March 1937), 35 (vMKN).

1760. *Guerber, Louise. 'Water Colors of William Blake.' *Bulletin of the Metropolitan Museum of Art*, XXIII (1928), 103–7 (vMKN).
For *Night Thoughts*.

1761. Guilly, René. 'Blake, Lapicque, les Fauves.' *Revue Internationale*, III (1947), 358–62 (vMKN).
On the British Council exhibition, no. 657.

1762. Guthrie, James. 'Blake's Cottage.' *Daily News*, 1 July 1911.
Announces that 'a movement is on foot to acquire and preserve' Blake's cottage. (The project was not carried out.)

1763. —— 'William Blake at Felpham.' *Christian Science Monitor*, 4 April 1937 (vMKN).

1764. A. Guthrie, William Norman. 'William Blake: Poet and Artist.' *Sewanee Review*, V (1897), 328–48. B. Reprinted as pp. 268–95 of Guthrie's *The Vital Study of Literature* and Other Essays. Chicago, 1912.
This general essay invites the reader to 'Call me a foolish lover' of Blake, but makes some interesting suggestions about the sources of Blake's symbolic names.

1765. A. —— 'William Blake: *The Mystic*.' *Sewanee Review*, V (1897), 438–56. B. Reprinted as pp. 296–321 of Guthrie's *The Vital Study of Literature* and Other Essays. Chicago, 1912.
This and the preceding general essay began as review of Ellis & Yeats (no. 369).

H

1766. Hacket, J. T. *The Student's Assistant in Astronomy and Astrology* containing observations on the real and apparent motions of superior planets.— The geocentric longitude of the Sun and Superior Planets, calculated for 44 years to come. Geocentric Longitude of the Planet Herschel for 100 years during the 18th Century. The Moon's Node on the first day of every month, from 1836 to 1880. Heliocentric and Geocentric longitude of all the planets' ascending and descending Nodes. Longitude, Latitude, and magnitude of one hundred and forty-four fixed stars, for past and future years. Eclipses of the Sun visible in England. Also a discourse on the harmony of Phrenology, Astrology, and Physiognomy. London, 1836. P. 119.

In 'A List of a few Names [65] of the Patrons and Admirers of the science and doctrine of Astrology' (pp. 118–20) appears 'Mr. Blake, Nov. 28, 7 h. 45' p.m. 1757'. The names start with Aristotle, and most have only the year of birth attached to their name, but some (such as Kepler, Milton, Sir Richard Steele) do not even have the birth-year.

1767. Hagiwara, Tsutomu. 'William Blake Dansho—"Mayotta Shojo" wo Chushin ni [On Blake's Poems—"The Little Girl Lost"].' *Bunkyo Joshi Tankidaigaku Kiyo [Bunkyo Women's Junior College Bulletin]*, I (1968), 77–84 (vHK).

1768. Hagstrum, Jean H. 'Blake's Blake.' Pp. 169–78 of *Essays in History and Literature* Presented by Fellows of The Newberry Library to Stanley Pargellis. Ed. Heinz Bluhm. Chicago, 1963.

An examination of how Blake figures in his own works 'as an artistic symbol, as a speaking voice, as a self-portrait' (p. 169).

1769. —— 'The rhetoric of fear and the rhetoric of hope.' *Tri-Quarterly*, No. 11 (1968), 109–23.

A comparison of Samuel Johnson and Blake.

1770. —— **William Blake Poet and Painter.* An Introduction to the Illuminated Verse. Chicago & London, 1964.

On the relationship of text and design.

1771. A. —— 'William Blake rejects the enlightenment.' *Studies on Voltaire and the Eighteenth Century*, Ed. Theodore Besterman. Geneva, 1963. Vol. XXV [Transactions of the First international congress on the Enlightenment (Vol.) II], pp. 811–28. B. Reprinted in Frye, no. 1643.

A sound summary.

1772. —— **'William Blake's "The Clod & the Pebble".'* Pp. 381–8 of *Restoration and Eighteenth-Century Literature*: Essays in Honor of Alan Dugald McKillop. Ed. Carroll Camden. Chicago, 1963. Rice University Semicentennial Publications.

The conclusion of the poem is ambivalent.

1773. —— **'"The Wrath of the Lamb": A Study of William Blake's Conversions.'* Pp. 311–30 of *From Sensibility to Romanticism*: Essays Presented

to Frederick A. Pottle. Ed. Frederick W. Hilles & Harold Bloom. N.Y., 1965.
The implications of 'the return of Christ to Blake's poetry and art' (p. 325).

1774. Hall, Mary Starritt. 'Blake's *Tiriel*: A Visionary Form Pedantic.' *BNYPL*, LXXIV (1970), 166–76.
'Many puzzling aspects of *Tiriel* can be explained by tracing Blake's careful reconstruction of the legends of the Titans' as found in Bryant (166); some of the same points are made more plausibly in Nancy Bogen's article, which precedes this one.

1775. —— 'Materialism and the Myths of Blake.' *DA*, XXIX (1968), 1208A. Princeton Ph.D. (1968).
'Much of Blake's . . . mythology seems to have been drawn from historical studies of myth, and was intended as objective, scholarly evidence for the metaphysical position he was developing.'

1776. Halliburton, David G. 'Blake's *French Revolution*: The *Figura* and Yesterday's News.' *Studies in Romanticism*, V (1965), 158–68.
An analysis of Blake's poem.

1777. Halloran, William F. 'William Blake's *The French Revolution*: A Note on the Text and a Possible Emendation.' *BNYPL*, LXXII (1968), 3–18.
A plausible argument that ll. 110–20 should follow l. 104.

1778. *Hamblen, Emily S. *The Book of Job Interpreted*: Illustrated with the [22 engraved] Designs of William Blake. N.Y., 1939.

1779. A. —— *Interpretation of William Blake's Job* Its Ancient Wisdom and Mystic Ways. N.Y., n.d. [c. 1939]. B. N.Y., 1965.
Miss Hamblen describes each plate in her own inimitably wise and mystic way, though there are no reproductions.

1780. —— *On the Minor Prophecies of William Blake*. With an Introduction by S. Foster Damon. London, Toronto, N.Y., 1930.
S. Foster Damon's 'Introduction' is pp. vii–x. Miss Hamblen had two unusual advantages in writing her book: she had 'deliberately avoided reading any of those recent writers who also have attempted a complete inquiry [into Blake]', and she had been assisted by visitations from the dead. The result is as might be expected.

1781. Hamilton, Kenneth M. 'William Blake and the Religion of Art. *Dalhousie Review*, XXIX (1949), 167–81.
Blake was not misled into starting a new religion of philosophy, because he withdrew into the realm of art.

1782. A. Hanson, T. W. 'Edwards of Halifax. Book Sellers, Collectors and Book-Binders.' *Halifax Guardian*, Dec. 1912 and Jan. 1913. B. '"Edwards of Halifax." A Family of Book-Sellers, Collectors and Book-Binders.' *Papers, Reports, &c. Read before the Halifax Antiquarian Society, 1912*. Halifax, [1913]. Pp. 142–200.

In this very full paper Hanson quotes, by the way, the Edwards catalogues of 1821 (no. 534) and 1826 (no. 538) in which Blake's *Night Thoughts* drawings were offered unsuccessfully for sale (A, 4 Dec. 1912; B, p. 171).

1783. Hanson, T. W. 'Richard Edwards, Publisher.' *TLS*, 8 Aug. 1942, p. 396.
Summarizes the career of the publisher of Blake's *Night Thoughts* engravings, and Blake's relations with him.

1784. *Hardie, Martin. 'The Coloured Books of William Blake.' Vol. III, pp. 260 9 of *The Collector*, ed. Ethel Deane. London, 1907.

1785. —— *'William Blake.' Chap. VIII, pp. 72–86 of *English Coloured Books*. London, [1906]. The Connoisseur's Library.

1786. —— *'William Blake and Henry Fuseli.' Chap. xi (pp. 192–204) of his *Water-colour Painting in Britain*. [Volume] I: The Eighteenth Century. Ed. Dudley Snelgrove, Jonathan Mayne, & Basil Taylor. London, 1966.
A general account, with the premiss that 'Blake [is] the greatest imaginative artist of the British school' (p. 192).

1787. A. Harding, D. W. 'William Blake.' Pp. 67–84 of *From Blake to Byron*. Ed. Boris Ford. Harmondsworth, 1957. Volume V of The Pelican Guide to English Literature. B. Reprinted as 'Experience and Symbol in Blake.' Chap. II, pp. 31–52 of his *Experience into Words*: Essays on Poetry. London, 1963.
A general and somewhat inaccurate account of Blake.

1788. Harper, George Mills. 'Apocalyptic Vision and Pastoral Dream in Blake's *Four Zoas*.' *South Atlantic Quarterly*, LXIV (1965), 110–24.

1789. —— 'Blake's Lost Letter to Hayley, 4 December 1804.' *SP*, LXI (1964), 573–85.

1790. —— 'Blake's *Nebuchadnezzar* in "The City of Dreadful Night".' *SP*, L (1953), 68–80 (vMKN).
In Canto xviii, Thomson rejects Blake's 'Golden string'.

1791. —— 'Blake's Neo-Platonic Interpretation of Plato's Atlantis Myth.' *JEGP*, LIV (1955), 72–9.
Blake's interpretation traced through Thomas Taylor.

1792. —— 'The Neo-Platonic Concept of Time in Blake's Prophetic Books.' *PMLA*, LXIX (1954), 142–55.
Said to come from Thomas Taylor.

1793. —— *The Neoplatonism of William Blake*. Chapel Hill, [N.C.] 1961.
Occasionally persuasive arguments that Blake was extensively and deeply indebted to Plato and to his eighteenth-century disciple Thomas Taylor.

1794. —— 'The Source of Blake's "Ah! Sun-Flower".' *MLR*, XLVIII (1953), 139–42.
In Taylor's translation of the *Hymns of Orpheus*, says Harper.

1795. Harper, George Mills. 'Symbolic Meaning in Blake's "Nine Years".'
MLN, LXXII (1957), 18–19.
Suggests Taylor's *Phaedrus* as a source.

1796. —— 'Thomas Taylor and Blake's Drama of Persephone.' *PQ*, XXXIV
(1955), 378–94.
The premiss, as in Harper's other articles, is that 'The fountain-head of
much of Blake's Greek mythology was Thomas Taylor.' In particular here,
Thel and *Visions* are found to 'represent Blake's interpretation of the Persephone myth', with sources or parallels for *Thel* (1789) discovered in Taylor's
works of 1790, 1792, and 1804.

1797. —— 'William Blake and Thomas Taylor: A Study in the Romantic
Revival of Platonism.' University of North Carolina Ph.D., 1951.

1798. *Harris, Eugenia. *The Poetry of William Blake*. [N.Y.] 1966. Monarch
Notes and Study Guides.
The biographical account (pp. 5–12) of Blake's 'Courtship and Marriage',
'Married Life', and 'Other Problems' is frequently accurate, the accounts
of individual poems (pp. 30–105) less so, particularly in the 'Minor' '*Prophetic
Lays*' *Milton* and *Jerusalem*.

1799. *Harris, Mary P. 'Imagination in English Painting: William Blake:
Mystic, Poet and Artist.' Chap. IX (pp. 73–82) of her *The Cosmic Rhythm of
Art and Literature*. Adelaide, Australia [?1948].
An enthusiastic, conventional summary.

1800. Harris, Rendel; C. E. Lawrence; Alfred Tressider Sheppard; Thomas
Wright; and George H. McNeal. 'The Blake Memorial.' *TLS*, 26 Aug. 1926,
p. 564; 2 Sept. 1926, p. 580; 9 Sept. 1926, p. 596; 16 Sept. 1926, p. 616; 23
Sept. 1926, p. 632.
A series of letters on the location of the proposed memorial.

1801. Harrold, William. 'Blake's "Tyger" and Vaughan's "Cock-Crowing".'
N&Q, CCXII [N.s. XIV] (1967), 20–1.
Plausible similarities.

1802. Harvey, Herbert. 'Les artistes étranges: William Blake.' *La République
des Lettres*, 2ᵉ Sér., III (1877), 65–8, 133–7.
The first article is biographical, the second about 'Le mariage du ciel et
de l'enfer'.
Georges Lafourcade argues in *Swinburne*: A Literary Biography (1932),
pp. 239–43, that Harvey is a pseudonym for Swinburne: 'The internal
evidence is tremendous.'

1803. Hashizume, Mitsuharu. 'Blake ni okeru Bi [Blake's Idea of Beauty].'
Doshisha Bungaku [*Literary Magazine of the Doshisha Literary Society*], No. 16
(1933), 138–61 (vHK).

1804. —— 'Shisoka to shite no Blake no Ichimen [An Aspect of Blake as a

Thinker].' *Doshisha Bungaku* [*Literary Magazine of the Doshisha Literary Society*], V (1932), 307–16 (vHK).

1805. Hashizume, Mitsuharu. §'Wakaki Hi no Blake eno Genso [An Image of Young Blake].' *Doshisha Bungaku* [*Literary Magazine of the Doshisha Literary Society*], No. 8 (1930), 13–22.

1806. —— 'Hokoku-Blake Kenkyu no Tenkai to sono Iso [The Development and Phases of Blake Studies in Japan].' *Shomotsu* [*Books*], I, No. 2 (Nov. 1933), 25–31; No. 3 (Dec. 1933), 56–60; II, No. 1 (Jan. 1934), 85–90, 99.

1807. *Hataya, Masao. *William Blake*. Blake 100–nen Kinenshuppan [Publication to Commemorate Blake's Centenary]. Tokyo, 1927. 216 pp.

1808. Havens, Raymond Dexter. 'Blake and Browning.' *MLN*, XLI (1926), 464–6.
Robinson's account of Blake may have influenced 'Karshish'.

1809. —— '"Hand" in Blake's "Sons of Albion".' *N&Q*, CXCIV (1949), 505 (vMKN).
Printer's-sign hand at the end of Leigh Hunt's articles.

1810. —— 'The Influence Outside of Blank Verse: Ossian, Blake, Shelley, Byron.' Pp. 215–33 of *The Influence of Milton on English Poetry*. Cambridge [Mass.] and London, 1922. See especially pp. 217–28.

1811. Hawkins, John. *I am, my dear Sir* . . . A Selection of Letters written mainly to and by John Hawkins, F.R.S., F.G.S. 1761–1841 of Bignor Park, Sussex, & Trewithen, Cornwall. Ed. Francis W. Steer. [Chichester] 1959. P. 4.
A reference to Blake in a letter from Hayley to Hawkins of 11 Aug. 1800.

1812. Haya, Ken'ichi. 'Honto no "Kami" no Sugata—Blake no imi [The True Figure of "God"—The Meaning of Blake].' *Oberon*, No. 32 (March 1970), 15–19 (vHK).

1813. Hayashi, Asa. 'Blake no Kami ni tsuite—*Songs of Innocence* oyobi *Songs of Experience* wo megurite [On Blake's God—Centring on *Songs of Innocence* and *Songs of Experience*].' *Tezukayama Gakuin Tankidaigaku Kenkyu Nenpo: Annual Report of Scientific Studies* [of] Tezukayama Gakuin Junior College, XII, No. 2 (1954), 62–9.

1814. Hayley, William. MEMOIRS / OF THE / LIFE AND WRITINGS / OF / WILLIAM HAYLEY, ESQ. / THE FRIEND AND BIOGRAPHER OF / COWPER, / WRITTEN BY HIMSELF. / WITH EXTRACTS FROM HIS / PRIVATE CORRESPONDENCE / AND UNPUBLISHED POETRY. / AND / MEMOIRS OF HIS SON / THOMAS ALPHONSO HAYLEY, / THE YOUNG SCULPTOR. / — / EDITED BY JOHN JOHNSON, LL.D. / RECTOR OF YAXHAM WITH WELBORNE, IN NORFOLK. / — / IN TWO VOLUMES. / VOL. I [II]. / — / LONDON: / PRINTED FOR HENRY COLBURN AND CO. CONDUIT-STREET, /

AND SIMPKIN AND MARSHALL, STATIONERS-HALL-COURT. /
1823. Vol. II, pp. 22–3, 32, 37–8, 42, 46–7, 123–7, 131–5, 138–9, 141–2.
(BM, GEB, Princeton)

The 'Memoirs of Thomas Alphonso Hayley, the Young Sculptor' in Vol. II
are paginated separately after the last 222 pages of William Hayley's
autobiography. The manuscript corresponding to Vol. I, pp. 1–100, 210–
349, and Vol. II, pp. 1–76 is in Yale; that for Vol. II, pp. 77–193 is in the
Fitzwilliam; no manuscript has been located for Vol. I, pp. 101–209, and
Vol. II, pp. 194–222, or for the biography of Thomas Alphonso Hayley.

The important Blake references appear in the *William* Hayley sections of
Vol. II.

1815. *Hayter, S. W. *New Ways of Gravure*. N.Y., 1949. Pp. 85, 143–4, 207.

An interesting account of the attempts by Ruthven Todd and Joan Mirò
to reproduce Blake's method of printing.

1816. A. Hazlitt, William. *Lectures on the English Poets*. Delivered at the Surrey
Institution. London: Printed for Taylor and Hessey, 93, Fleet Street. 1819.
P. 50. (BM) B. Second Edition. London: Printed for Taylor and Hessey,
93, Fleet Street. 1819. P. 50. (BM & GEB) C. Third Edition. Ed. by his Son
[William Carew Hazlitt]. London, 1841. P. 48. D. *Lectures on the English
Poets, and the English Comic Writers*. Ed. William Carew Hazlitt. London,
1870. P. 33. E. *Lectures on the English Poets and on the Dramatic Literature of the
Age of Elizabeth Etc.* Ed. A. R. Waller and Arnold Glover. London & N.Y.,
1902. P. 24. Vol. V of *The Collected Works of William Hazlitt*. F. *Lectures on
the English Poets*. London & N.Y., [1908]. P. 39. The New Universal Library.
G. *Lectures on English Poets & The Spirit of the Age*. London & N.Y., [1910].
Everyman's Library. H. *Lectures on the English Poets*. London, Edinburgh,
Glasgow, Copenhagen, N.Y., Toronto, Melbourne, Cape Town, Bombay,
Calcutta, Madras, Shanghai, 1924. P. 38. The World's Classics. I. London,
1929. P. 38. J. *Lectures on the English Poets* and *A View of the English Stage*. Ed.
P. P. Howe after the Edition of A. R. Waller and Arnold Glover. London &
Toronto, 1930. P. 24. Vol. V of *The Complete Works of William Hazlitt*.
K. *Lectures on the English Poets. The Spirit of the Age*. London & N.Y., 1955.
P. 24. Everyman's Library, No. 459.

The statement: 'Chaucer, it has been said, numbered the classes of men,
as Linnaeus numbered the plants', clearly refers to the almost identical
statement in Blake's *Descriptive Catalogue*.

1817. A. [——] *The Plain Speaker*: Opinions on Books, Men, and Things.
In Two Volumes. London, 1826. Vol. I, pp. 223–4. (BM) B. Second Edition.
Ed. by his Son [William Carew Hazlitt. 2 vols.] London, 1841. Vol. I, p. 184.
C. A New Edition. Ed. William Carew Hazlitt. London, 1870. Pp. 129–30.
D. Ed. William Carew Hazlitt. London, 1902. Pp. 129–30. E. Ed. A. R.
Waller and Arnold Glover. London & N.Y., 1903. P. 95. Vol. VII of *The
Collected Works of William Hazlitt*. F. London, [1928]. P. 95. Everyman's
Library, No. 814. G. Ed. P. P. Howe after the Edition of A. R. Waller and
Arnold Glover. London & Toronto, 1931. P. 95. Vol. XII of *The Complete
Works of William Hazlitt*.

In 'Essay IX. On the Old Age of Artists', Blake is mentioned in a list including Flaxman, Cosway, and other artists as 'a profound mystic'.

1818. Healey, George Harris, and [Sir] Geoffrey Keynes. 'Blake and Wordsworth.' *TLS*, 5 April 1957, p. 209; 12 April 1957, p. 225 (vMKN).

Healey says that Blake's annotations to Wordsworth's *Poems* (now at Cornell) have never been published in full; Keynes replies that they *were* printed, and gives information about the ownership of the book.

1819. A. Hearn, Lafcadio. 'Blake—The First English Mystic.' Vol. I, Chapter VI (pp. 51–71) of *Interpretations of Literature*. Ed. John Erskine. [2 vols.] London, 1916. B. *Reprinted in pp. 115–40 of his *Some Strange English Literary Figures* of the Eighteenth and Nineteenth Centuries In a Series of Lectures. Ed. R. Tanabé. Tokyo, 1927. C. *Freeport (N.Y.), 1965. Essay Index Reprint Series.

An 1899 lecture concluding that 'his chief glory' is that the Victorian poets 'learned a great deal from him' (p. 140).

1820. A. —— *'William Blake.' Pp. 3–21 of his *Some Strange English Literary Figures* of the Eighteenth and Nineteenth Centuries In a Series of Lectures. Ed. R. Tanabé. Tokyo, 1927. B. *Freeport (N.Y.), 1965. Essay Index Reprint Series.

An 1899 lecture dealing with 'poetry only', some of which is 'absolutely incomprehensible' because Blake was 'insane' all his life (pp. 6–7).

1821. Heath, Carl. 'Blake as a Humanitarian.' *Humane Review*, VII (1907), 73–83.

Blake was clearly a humanitarian, because he liked animals, and talked about sweet lambs and little children.

1822. A. Heaton, Mrs. M. 'Blake, William.' Vol. I of Michael Bryan. *Dictionary of Painters and Engravers, Biographical and Critical*. Ed. Robert Edmund Graves. [3 vols.] London, [Vol. I] 1886, [II & III] 1889. B. Ed. R. E. Graves and Walter Armstrong. [2 vols.] London, 1898. Vol. I.

A revised version of the article in the 1849 edition of Bryan's *Dictionary* (no. 1305). The entry was again rewritten by E. J. Oldmeadow.

1823. [Heinecken, Carl Heinrich von.] DICTIONNAIRE / DES / AR-TISTES, / DONT NOUS AVONS / DES ESTAMPES, / AVEC / UNE NOTICE DÉTAILLÉE / DE LEURS / OUVRAGES GRAVES. / — / [4 vols.] . . . / A LEIPSIG, / CHEZ JEAN-GOTTLOB-IMMANUEL BREITKOPF. / 1778[–1790]. (Bodley)

'W. BLAKE. / Graveur en Angleterre.' (Vol. III [1789], p. 3)

1824. Heinrich, G. 'Der englische Gott in der Dichtung von William Blake.' *Deutsche allgemeine Zeitung*, No. 381 (1939) (vRG).

1825. *Hellman, George S. '"The Judgment of Solomon" by William Blake.' *Print Collector's Quarterly*, XXIX (1942), 105–18.

The attribution to Blake is refuted by Blunt (no. 1240).

1826. Helms, Loyce Randel. 'Artful Thunder: A Literary Study of Prophecy.' *DAI*, XXIX (1969), 3612A. Washington Ph.D., 1968.

'I am trying to establish Blake's conscious and unconscious debt and relationship to the genre of prophecy', especially in *Milton* and *Jerusalem*.

1827. —— 'Orc: The Id in Blake and Tolkien.' *literature and psychology*, XX (1970), 31–5.

Orc as an 'id projection' in Blake and Tolkien.

1828. *Helmstadter, Thomas H. 'Blake and Religion: Iconographical Themes in *Night Thoughts.*' *Studies in Romanticism*, X (1971), 199–212.

Religious images in Blake's drawings.

1829. —— 'Blake's *Night Thoughts*: Interpretations of Young.' *Texas Studies in Literature and Language*, XII (1970), 27–54.

'Blake's disagreement with Young' is shown in designs *7, *64, *81–*82, *333, *349, *404, *490 (p. 29).

1830. A. Hemans, Mrs. [Felicia Dorothea]. 'The Painter's Last Work.— A Scene.' *Blackwood's Edinburgh Magazine*, XXXI (Feb. 1832), 220–1. B. 'The Painter's Last Work—A Scene.' *Philadelphia Album and Ladies Literary Port Folio*, VI (31 March 1832), 97. C. *Godey's Lady's Book*, V (July 1832), 30. D. *Scenes and Hymns of Life*, with Other Religious Poems. Edinburgh & London, 1834. Pp. 157–64. E. *The Poetical Works of Mrs. Felicia Hemans*. Philadelphia, 1836. Pp. 371–2. F. *Works of Mrs Hemans*, with a Memoir by her Sister [Mrs. Hughes. 7 vols.] Edinburgh & London, 1839. Vol. VII, pp. 210–15. G. *The Poetical Works of Mrs. Felicia Hemans*. Philadelphia, 1842. Pp. 371–2. H. *The Complete Works of Mrs. Hemans*. Ed. by her Sister [Mrs. Hughes]. In Two Volumes. N.Y. & Philadelphia, 1847. Vol. II, pp. 490–2. I. *The Poems of Felicia Hemans*. Edinburgh & London, 1849. Pp. 595–6. J. *Poems of Felicia Hemans*. Edinburgh & London, 1865. Pp. 595–6. K. *The Complete Works of Mrs. Hemans*. Ed. by her Sister [Mrs. Hughes. 2 vols.] N.Y., 1866. Vol. II, pp. 490–2. L. *Poems of Felicia Hemans*. Edinburgh & London, 1872. Pp. 595–6. M. *The Poetical Works of Felicia Hemans*. Introduction by William Michael Rossetti. London, Melbourne & Toronto, 1912. Pp. 520–2. N. *The Poetical Works of Felicia Dorothea Hemans*. London, Edinburgh, Glasgow, N.Y., Toronto, Melbourne, & Bombay, 1914. Pp. 610–13. Oxford Edition. O. *The Poetical Works of Mrs. Hemans*. London, Edinburgh, & N.Y., [1920?]. Pp. 579–81.

A footnote to the first printing says that this poem was 'Suggested by the closing scene in the life of the painter Blake; as beautifully related by Allan Cunningham'. In this first printing the setting is in Italy, but in the collected editions the scene and nomenclature were transferred to England, and 35 lines were substituted for the last 9. The poem has greater merit than one might anticipate.

1831. Hendry, J. F. 'The Social Philosophy of William Blake.' *Life and Letters Today*, XXXIX (1943), 156–63.

1832. Henn, T. R. *The Lonely Tower*: Studies in the Poetry of W. B. Yeats. London, 1950. *Passim*.

1833. —— *'Two kinds of obscurity: Blake's *The Sick Rose*: and a passage from T. S. Eliot's *The Waste Land*.' Chap. IV (pp. 38–48) of his *The Apple and the Spectroscope*, being Lectures on Poetry designed (in the main) for Science Students. London, 1951.

Elementary but good.

1834. Heppenstall, Rayner. 'Blake and Mr. Murry [A Reprint].' Chap. ix (pp. 162–75) of his *Middleton Murry*: A Study in Excellent Normality. London, 1934.

1835. Heppner, Christopher A. E. 'The Problem of Form in Blake's Prophecies.' Toronto Ph.D., 1970.

1836. §Herbert, Jack. 'William Blake and the Interpretation of Poetry and Painting.' Cambridge University M. Litt., 1959.

1837. A. Herford, C. H. 'William Blake.' *Hibbert Journal*, XXVI (1927), 15–30 (vMKN). B. Reprinted in *Bulletin of the John Rylands Library*, XII (1928), 31–46. C. The latter also reprinted in a separate pamphlet, pp. 1–16. D. Translated into Japanese by Bunsho Jugaku, no. 1219 10.

A small general article.

1838. Hess, M. Whitcomb. 'William Blake: 1757–1957.' *Christian Century*, LXXIV (1957), 1376–7 (vMKN).

Centenary essay warning against Blake's 'tangential Christianity'.

1839. Heuer, Helmut. *Die Amerikavision bei William Blake und Franz Kafka*. Munchen, 1959.

A 139-page Munich dissertation, Teil A (pp. 1–89) about Blake.

1840. Hewlett, Henry G. 'Imperfect Genius: William Blake.' *Contemporary Review*, [Part I] XXVIII (1876), 756–84; [Part II] XXIX (1877), 207–28.

A sound attack upon Blake's religious and social heresies, and upon his incoherence and inconsistency.

1841. A. Higham, Charles. 'Blake and the "Swedenborgians".' *New Church Weekly*, XXXVIII (1915), 168 (vMKN). B. *N&Q*, CXXXI [11th Ser., XI] (1915), 276–7.

Concerning the Blakes' relations with the New Church.

1842. —— 'Swedenborg annotated by William Blake.' *New-Church Weekly*, XLI (1918), 73.

Describes Blake's notes to *Divine Love and Divine Wisdom*.

1843. Hildick, Wallace. 'William Blake.' Pp. 160–75 of his *Word for Word*: A Study of Authors' Alterations with Exercises. London, 1965.

On the *Notebook*.

1844. Hill, Archibald A. 'Imagery and Meaning: A Passage from Milton, and from Blake.' *Texas Studies in Literature and Language*, XI (1969), 1093–1105.
About mixed metaphors in Milton's 'Lycidas' and Blake's 'London'.

1845. Hill, Charles G. 'André Gide and Blake's *Marriage of Heaven and Hell*.' *Comparative Literature Studies*, III (1966), 21–32.
A study of 'Blake's role in Gide's development' (p. 30).

1846. *Hill, Julian. 'William Blake.' Pp. 169–84 of his *Great English Poets*. London, 1907.
An enthusiastic biographical account.

1847. Hinatsu, Konosuke. '[Blake on "The Sick Rose"].' Pp. 81–95 of his *Igirisu Roman Shocho Shifu Kanjo* [*English Romantic and Symbolic Poetry*]. Part I. Tokyo, 1940 (vHK).

1848. Hind, A. M. 'Two Undescribed Engravings by William Blake.' *British Museum Quarterly*, IX (1935), 103–4 (vMKN).
'The Child of Nature' and 'The Child of Art'.

1849. —— 'Wood Blocks by William Blake.' *British Museum Quarterly*, XIV (1940), 37 (vMKN).
Those for Thornton's Virgil in the British Museum.

1850. §Hirabayashi, Takeo. 'William Blake no Shiso to Shikei ni kansuru Ichikosatsu: *Songs of Experience* ro "Introduction" oyobi "Earth's Answer" wo chuchin ni [A Study of William Blake's Imagination and his Poetic Forms, with Special Reference to "Introduction" and "Earth's Answer" from *Songs of Experience*].' *Nihon Daihon Eibungakkaiho* [*Nihon University English Literary Society Transactions*], IV, No. 1 (Dec. 1939), 5–7.

1851. Hirata, Ienari. 'Blake no Jojo Shishu to "Aware" [Blake's Lyric Poems and "Pathos"].' *Jinbun Kagaku*: Wakayama Daigaku Gakugeigakubu Kiyo: *Humanities*: Bulletin of Liberal Arts College, Wakayama University, No. 4 (1954), 83–100.

1852. A. Hirata, Tokuboku. 'William Blake—100-nen-ki ni saishite [On the Centenary of his Death].' Pp. 315–21 of his *Eibungaku Sansaku* [*Strolls in English Literature*]. Tokyo, 1933. B. 1941 (vHK).

1853. Hirsch, E. D., Jr. *Innocence and Experience*: An Introduction to Blake. New Haven & London, 1964. Pp. 265–70 are reprinted in Paley (no. A2439) and pp. 244–52 in Weathers (no. 2937).
A psychological-biographical critique of the *Songs*, of somewhat uncertain scholarship.

1854. —— 'The Two Blakes.' *RES*, N.S. XII (1961), 373–90.
Ambivalent qualities in the poet.

1855. A. *Hirst, Désirée. *Hidden Riches*. Traditional Symbolism from the Renaissance to Blake. London, 1964. B. *N.Y., 1964.
On alchemical and mystical symbolism, largely.

1856. Hirst, Désirée. 'New Light on William Blake.' *The Month*, XIX (1958), 33–7.
A survey of recent scholarship.

1857. —— 'On the Aesthetics of Prophetic Art.' *British Journal of Aesthetics*, IV (1964), 248–52.
'Blake has, perhaps, most fully worked out the philosophy of this mode of art.'

1858. —— *'Problem of a Blake Painting.' *Country Life*, 9 Feb. 1950, p. 456.
Suggests a Kabbalistic interpretation for 'The Spiritual Condition of Man'.

1859. —— 'A Study of Blake's *Milton*.' Oxford B.Litt., 1953.
A provocative study of Blake's mythological sources.

1860. —— 'William Blake. A Mental Prince.' *Blackfriars*, XXXVIII (1957), 418–25 (vKP).
A survey of recent Blake scholarship.

1861. Hobbes, James R. *The Picture Collector's Manual*, adapted to the professional man, and the amateur; being a Dictionary of Painters, containing fifteen hundred more names than in any other work, together with an Alphabetical Arrangement of the Scholars, imitators, and copyists of the various masters. And A Classification of Subjects, shewing the names of those who painted in the several departments of art, thus affording, in all uncertain cases, a clue by which the judgment may be guided, the opinion strenthened, and the doubt removed. In Two Volumes. London, 1849. Vol. I, p. 41.
This brief and inaccurate account of Blake praises his 'strange and wonderful pictures, the first of which he called the Songs of Innocence . . .'.

1862. Hobday, Canon. 'Paine, Blake and Burns.' *University Forward*, IX (Nov. 1943), 28–31 (vKP).

1863. A. Hobsbaum, Philip. 'A Rhetorical Question Answered: Blake's Tyger and its Critics.' *Neophilologus*, XLVIII (1964), 151–5. B. Reprinted in Weathers (no. 2937).
'It is quite evident that the critics are not trying to understand the poem at all.' (P. 154.)

1864. Hodgart, Patricia, & Theodore Redpath. 'William Blake (1757–1827).' Pp. 125–49 of their *Romantic Perspectives*: The work of Crabbe, Blake, Wordsworth, and Coleridge as seen by their contemporaries and by themselves. N.Y., 1964.
Extracts from J. T. Smith, Alan Cunningham, Coleridge, Crabb Robinson, Gilchrist, Blake, and Lamb.

1865. Hofer, Philip. *'Blake Exhibition in America.' *Burlington Magazine*, LXXIV (1939), 82–5 (vMKN).
In Philadelphia.

1866. A. —— *'Drawings by William Blake for "The Book of Job".'

Connoisseur, CXVII (1936), 183–8. B. Summarized in *N&Q*, CLXX (1936), 271 (vMKN).
Gives an account of the facsimile.

1867. Hofer, Philip. **An Illustration by William Blake* for the 'Circle of the Traitors' Dante's Inferno, Canto XXXII. A Monograph. Meriden [Conn.], 1953.
On the changes made from sketches to proofs; 6 pages.

1868. *Hoff, Ursula. 'The Bi-Centenary of William Blake (1757–1957).' *Quarterly Bulletin of the National Gallery of Victoria, Australia*, XI, No. 4 (1957), 5–7 (vKP).

1869. —— *'William Blake's Illustrations to Dante's Divine Comedy.' Pp. 91–7 of *Masterpieces of the National Gallery of Victoria*. Ed. Ursula Hoff. Melbourne & London, 1949.

1870. Hoki, Kanji. 'Blake to sono Jojo Shishu (1) [(2)] [(3)]: Blake and His Lyrical Poems (1) [(2)] [(3)].' *Kenkyu Kiyo*: Jinbun-Shakai-Kagaku Hen (Kagoshima Daigaku Kyoikugakubu): *Bulletin* of the Faculty of Education, University of Kagoshima (Cultural and Social Science), XIV (1962), 18–28; XV (1963), 20–30; XVI (1964), 34–46.

1871. [Holbrook, Josiah.] *A Familiar Treatise on the Fine Arts, Painting, Sculpture, and Music*. Boston, 1833. Pp. 96–7.
Blake is introduced to 'young readers' in three paragraphs as 'a man whose fancy over-mastered his reason'.

1872. Holden, [W.] *Holden's Triennial Directory 1799*. Corrected to the end of April 1799. London, 1799. (BM)
Blake is listed, with his address, at p. 63.

1873. Holland, John, and James Everett. *Memoirs of the Life and Writings of James Montgomery*. [7 vols.] London, [Vol. I] 1854, [Vols. II, III, IV] 1855, [V, VI, VII] 1856. Vol. I, p. 38.
An expression of a curiously prudish reaction to Blake's illustrations for *The Grave* (reprinted in Keynes [1921]).

1874. A. Hollander, John. 'Blake and the Metrical Contract.' Pp. 293–310 of *From Sensibility to Romanticism*: Essays Presented to Frederick A. Pottle. Ed. Frederick W. Hilles & Harold Bloom. N.Y., 1965. B. Revised and expanded as 'Romantic Verse Form and the Metrical Contract.' Pp. 181–200 of *Romanticism and Consciousness*: Essays in Criticism. Ed. Harold Bloom. N.Y., 1970.
On contemporary metrical conventions, with allusions to Blake.

1875. Holloway, John. *Blake: The Lyric Poetry*. London, 1968. Studies in English Literature No. 34.
An interesting brief (70 pp.) introduction.

1876. Hondo, Masao. 'William Blake: Doku aru Ki ["A Poison Tree"].' *Eigo Kenkyu: The Study of English*, No. 6 (1960), 42–3.

1877. Hone, Joseph. *W. B. Yeats 1865–1939.* London, 1942. *Passim.*

1878. Hönnighausen, Lothar. 'Aspekte des Blake-Verständnisses in der Äesthetik des neunzehnten Jahrhunderts: Blake und die Präraphaeliten.' *Zeitschrift für Kunstgeschichte*, XXXIII (1970), 41–53.

1879. Hood, Thurman Los. 'An Allusion to Blake.' *Nation* [London], XCIII (1911), 240 (vMKN).
In Browning's 'Transcendentalism'.

1880. —— *'Browning and Blake.' *Trinity Review* [Hartford, Conn.], N.S. II (March 1948), 42–50.

1881. A. H[ooper], L[ucy]. 'The Fairy's Funeral.' *Long Island Star*, 27 Nov. 1833, p. 1. B. *The Poetical Remains of the late Lucy Hooper.* Ed. John Keese. N.Y., Philadelphia & Boston, 1842. Pp. 174–6.
The poem is based upon Cunningham's anecdote of Blake. The poem is not the same as 'The Fairy's Funeral', 1834, no. 765.

1882. Hopkins, Alfred G. 'William Blake's House at Lambeth.' *TLS*, 29 Nov. 1918, p. 584 (vMKN).
Anecdotes.

1883. Hopkins, Robert H. 'Postscript: Blake and Charles Lamb.' *BNYPL*, LXVIII (1964), 257–8.
Historical background of Lamb's 'Praise of Chimney Sweepers', as a postscript to Nurmi (no. 2298); not about Blake.

1884. A. Hopkirk, Peter. 'Blake dismembered to boost profit. Scholars shocked by practice of breaking up hand-printed books and drawings for sale.' *The Times*, 19 May 1971. B. Reprinted in *Blake Newsletter*, IV (1971), 112–13.
About *Urizen* (C) (see no. 38) and the Varley–Blake sketchbook (see no. A703).

1885. *Horne, Herbert P. 'Blake's Sibylline Leaf on Homer and Virgil.' *Century Guild Hobby Horse*, II (1887), 115–16.
A critique illustrated by a [Muir] facsimile.

1886. —— *'The Life Mask of William Blake.' *Century Guild Hobby Horse*, II (1887), 29–30.
Discussion of George Richmond's copy of the life mask, on which there were 'many of Blake's hairs adhering to the plaster until quite recently'.

1887. [Horne, Richard Henry] 'British Artists and Writers on Art.' *British and Foreign Review*, VI (1838), 610–57.
'William Blake's estimate of himself as a man of genius (visions inclusive,) was a just one. If he saw no faults in his works, it has been a pleasant occupation for others to discover them for him.' (P. 626.) The authorship is established by Mr. H. B. de Groot in no. 1218 55.

1888. Horton, William T. 'Was Blake Ever in Bedlam? A Strange Discovery.' *Occult Review*, XVI (1912), 266–9.
Horton says Yes, but the truth is, No!

1889. Horwood, Harold. 'E. J. Pratt and William Blake: An Analysis.' *Dalhousie Review*, XXXIX (1959), 197–207 (vMKN).
Pratt mentions Blake only once but is similar to him in some respects.

1890. A. Hosmer, William H. C. 'Blake's Visitants.' *Graham's Magazine*, XXIX (Sept. 1846), 151. B. Reprinted in *The Poetical Works of William H. C. Hosmer*. [2 vols.] N.Y., 1854. Vol. II, pp. 317–18.
This dull poem is based on Cunningham's account of Blake.

1891. A. Hoste, M. R. 'William Blake.' *Literature* [London], V (26 Aug. 1899), 207–8. B. [N.Y.], n.s. [II], (15 Sept. 1899), 226–7 (vMKN).

1892. Housman, A. E. *The Name and Nature of Poetry*. The Leslie Stephen Lecture Delivered at Cambridge 9 May 1933. Cambridge, 1933. Pp. 41–5.
Blake even more than Shakespeare creates 'pure unmingled poetry, poetry independent of meaning'.

1893. *Housman, Laurence. 'Blake as an Impressionist.' *Universal Review*, VI (1890), 209–22 (vMKN).
The word 'impressionist' used loosely.

1894. A. —— 'Messengers.' *Nineteenth Century*, CV (1929), 269–85 (vRG). B. Reprinted as 'The Messengers.' Pp. 47–86 of his *Cornered Poets: A Book of Dramatic Monologues*. London, 1929.
A slightly amusing reconstructed dialogue about Blake and the impertinent soldier at Felpham in 1803.

1895. Houville, Gérard d'. 'A l'Exposition Blake et Turner.' *Revue des Deux Mondes*, 8ᵉ Sér. XXXVII (1937), 663–6 (vMKN).
At the Paris exhibition.

1896. Howard, John Douglas, Jr. 'The Child-Hero in the Poetry of Blake, Shelley, Byron, Coleridge, and Wordsworth.' *DA*, XXVIII (1968), 2647A. Maryland Ph.D.
'Blake sees the child's power as two kinds of innocence.'

1897. —— 'Swedenborg's *Heaven and Hell* and Blake's *Songs of Innocence*.' *Papers on Language & Literature*, IV (1968), 390–9.
An inconclusive discussion of 'how *Heaven and Hell* helps in interpreting *Songs of Innocence*' (p. 391).

1898. Howard, N. R. 'What is Art? Here's a Slant.' *Cleveland News*, 8 Jan. 1952 (vMKN).
Report of a lecture by Dr. Robert Hemphill, who finds elements of Blake's designs in psychotics.

1899. A. Howes, Frank. 'Job.' Pp. 45–65 of his '*The Musical Pilgrim*': The Dramatic Works of Ralph Vaughan Williams. London, N.Y., Toronto,

1937. B. Pp. 299–314 of his *The Music of Ralph Vaughan Williams*. London, N.Y., Toronto, 1954.

The music for the ballet based on Blake's Job designs is 'one of the greatest creations of its composer' (A, p. 45; B, p. 299).

1900. Howes, Frank. 'The Music of Job.' Pp. 35–45 of Joan Lawson, James Laver, Geoffrey Keynes, Frank Howes. *Job and The Rake's Progress*. London, 1949. Sadler's Wells Ballet Books, No. 2.

Music for the ballet based on Blake's designs.

1901. Hsing, P'eng-chu. 'Po lai k'o [Blake].' *Hsin-yueh Yueh-k'an*, II, No. 8–10 (Oct.–Dec. 1927) (vADH).

In Chinese.

1902. §Hsu, Hsia-ts'un. 'I-ko Shen-mi-ti Shih-jen-ti Pai-nien-chi [The Centenary of a Mystic Poet].' *Hsiao-shuo Yueh-pao*, XVIII, No. 8 (Aug. 1927).

In Chinese.

1903. Huang, Roderick. 'William Blake's "The Tyger": A Re-Interpretation.' *Humanities association bulletin*, XVIII, No. 2 (1967), 31–5.

'The tiger . . . cannot be the work of an immortal hand or eye, but is rather the work of the mortal hand' (pp. 31–2).

1904. *Hughes, G. Bernard. 'Blake's Work for Wedgwood.' *Country Life*, CXXVI (3 Sept. 1959), 194–6.

A careful account of the 1815 catalogue, no. 511.

1905. Hüllen, Werner. 'Zwei Interpretationen aus "The Songs of Innocence and Experience" von William Blake.' *Neuren Sprachen*, N.S. V (1956), 394–401 (vMKN).

On 'The Tyger' and 'The Lamb'.

1906. Hume, Robert D. 'The Development of Blake's Psychology: The Quest for an Understanding of Man's Position in the World.' *Revue des Langues Vivantes: Tijdschrift voor Levende Talen*, XXXV (1969), 240–58.

A simplistic attempt 'to explain concisely the questions and answers with which Blake dealt' (p. 240).

1907. Humma, John B. 'From Transcendental to Descendental: The Romantic Thought of Blake, Nietzsche, Lawrence.' *DAI*, XXX (1970), 4454A (Southern Illinois).

1908. A. Huneker, James G. ' "Mad, Naked Blake".' Pp. 277–90 of his *Egoists: A Book of Supermen*. London, 1909. B. London & N.Y., 1924 (vMKN).

Admiration for Blake, largely based on Symons, no. 2804.

1909. A. Hungerford, Edward B. 'Blake's Albion.' Pp. 35–62 of *Shores of Darkness*. N.Y., 1941. B. §Cleveland & N.Y., 1963.

A suggestive and illuminating discussion of the way Blake and the other Romantics used in their works the often wonderfully perverse conclusions of contemporary antiquarians and mythologists. (Two or three sentences are altered in B.)

1910. [Hunt, Leigh.] 'Miscellaneous Sketches upon Temporary Subjects, &c.' *Examiner*, 28 Aug. 1808, p. 558. (BM)

'Blake' is listed as one of the Officers of Painting in 'The Ancient and Redoubtable Institution of Quacks'.

1911. [Hunt, Robert.] 'Mr. Blake's Exhibition.' *Examiner*, 17 Sept. 1809, pp. 605–6. (BM)

A violent attack on Blake.

1912. —— (R.H.) 'Blake's Edition of Blair's Grave.' *Examiner*, 7 Aug. 1808, pp. 509–10. (BM)

An important mocking review.

1913. Hutin, Serge. 'Blake et Boehme.' Chap. viii, pp. 163–70 of his *Les Disciples anglais de Jacob Boehme* aux XVIIe et XVIIIe siècles. Paris, 1960.

This sensible if summary introduction to the problem of the relationship of Blake and Boehme concludes properly: 'Il a *lu* Boehme, il n'est jamais devenu son "disciple".'

1914. Hyder, Clyde K. 'A Swinburne Allusion to Blake.' *PMLA*, LX (1945), 618 (vMKN).

Merely that.

I

1915. *I., W. M., Jr. 'The Department of Prints: Accessions.' *Bulletin of the Metropolitan Museum of Art*, XII (1917), 107–11 (vMKN).

Job and the Calvert copy of *Songs*. The author is W. N. Ivins, Jr.

1916. *Ikegaya, Toshito. 'Blake no Saishoku Ban [Blake's Illuminated Printing].' *Jissen Bungaku* (Jissen Bungakukai) [*Jissen English Literature*(Jissen English Association)], No. 38 (1969), 74–66 [*sic*].

1917. Ingamells, John. 'An Image Shared by Blake and Henri Rousseau.' *British Journal of Aesthetics*, III (1963), 346–52.

The image of a lion watching over a girl in the desert.

1918. Ireland, William W. 'William Blake.' Pp. 130–4 of his *Through the Ivory Gate*: Studies in Psychology and History. Edinburgh & London, 1889.

Blake's paintings reveal insanity.

1919. *Ironside, Robin. 'The Followers of William Blake.' *Magazine of Art*, XL (1947), 309–14 (vMKN).

Brief general account.

1920. —— *'William Blake and his Circle.' Pp. 81–6 of his *English Neoclassical Art*: Studies in Inspiration and Taste. London, 1966.

A competent survey.

1921. Isaksson, Folke. 'William Blake.' *Bonniers Litterara Magasin*, XXV (1956), 184–5.

1922. Itakura, Tamotsu. 'On William Blake's Idea in Proverbs of Hell.'

Eibungaku Kenkyu (Tachikawa Daigaku Eibungakkai): *Studies in English Literature* [of] The Tachikawa College English Literary Society, I (1954), 9–18.
In Japanese.

1923. Ivanyi, G. G. 'Blake sc.' *TLS*, 23 Dec. 1955, p. 777.
Identifies the Blake engravings in Seally & Lyons.

1924. Ives, Herbert [i.e. Herbert Jenkins]. 'A "Boom" in Blake And The Coming To Him Of A Posthumous Fame.' *Book Monthly*, IV (1906), 96–9.

1925. A. —— *'The Most Perfect Wife on Record. Catherine Blake. Born April 25th, 1762. Died October 18th, 1831.' *Bibliophile*, III (1909), 91–8.
B. Reprinted as 'The Most Perfect Wife on Record'. Pp. 33–50 of Jenkins's *William Blake* (1925).
An anecdotal tribute to Catherine.

1926. —— 'A Poet as Teacher.' *Outlook*, XXVI (1910), 646–7.
Blake's religion.

1927. A. ——. 'The Trial of William Blake for High Treason.' *Nineteenth Century*, LXVII (1910), 849–61. B. Reprinted as pp. 51–80 of Jenkins's *William Blake* (1925).
The great merit of this article derives from the invaluable documents it reprints.

1928. A. —— 'William Blake as a Teacher.' *Fortnightly Review*, XCIII (1910), 569–74. B. Reprinted as pp. 97–110 of Jenkins's *William Blake* (1925).
A general article on Blake's message. 'A portion' was reprinted in *The First Meeting of The Blake Society* (1912), no. 3016.

1929. A. —— 'William Blake at Felpham.' *Monthly Review*, XXI (1905), 123–9 (vMKN). B. Reprinted as pp. 21–32 of Jenkins's *William Blake* (1925).

1930. *Ivins, William M., Jr. 'The Blake Exhibition at the Grolier Club.' *Arts and Decoration*, XII (Jan. 1920), 183, 218.

1931. §Iwasaki, Soji. 'Ikyoshugi ni tsuite no Dansho: Blake, Yeats, Stevens [On Paganism in Blake, Yeats, Stevens].' *Mulberry* (Aichi Kenritsu Daigaku Eibungakkai [The English Literary Society, Aichi Prefectural University]), No. 19 (1969), 27–32.

J

1932. A. Jackson, John [& William A. Chatto]. *A Treatise on Wood Engraving, Historical and Practical*. With Upwards of Three Hundred Illustrations, Engraved on Wood By John Jackson. London, 1839. Pp. 715–17. B. **A* *Treatise on Wood Engraving Historical and Practical* with upwards of three hundred illustrations engraved on wood By John Jackson. The Historical Portion by W. A. Chatto. Second Edition with a new chapter on the artists of the present day By Henry G. Bohn and 145 additional wood engravings. London, 1861. Pp. 631–3. §C. *Detroit, 1969.

The authorship of this work is discussed with some heat by Chatto in *A Third Preface to 'A Treatise on Wood Engraving, Historical and Practical;'* Exposing the Fallacies contained in the First, Restoring the Passages Suppressed in the Second, and containing an account of Mr. John Jackson's Actual Share in the Composition and Illustration of that Work. In a Letter to Stephen Oliver. By Wm. A. Chatto, Author of the First Seven Chapters of the work, and the writer of the Whole as Originally Printed. London, Printed for the Author, 1839. The account of Blake's engraving process in Chapter VIII is apparently by Jackson.

B. The only change in the Blake account in the second edition (1861) is the addition of a very minor footnote.

C. The 1969 edition is a reprint of B.

1933. Jackson, Mary Vera. 'A Study of the Use of Poetic Myth in the Work of William Blake from 1783 to 1794.' *DAI*, XXX (1970), 5410–11A (Washington University Ph.D.).

1934. Jackson, Richard C. 'The Portraiture of William Blake.' *Brixtonian*, 18 Jan. 1901, p. 3; 25 Jan. 1901, p. 3 [with a note, 'To be continued', but no further articles traceable].
Short biographical sketch with a plea for recognition of Blake.

1935. —— 'Vision of William Blake: Ode on his 156th Birthday.' *South London Observer*, 21 Nov. 1913.
Includes a short essay.

1936. —— 'William Blake: An Unlooked for Discovery.' *South London Observer*, 22, 29? June 1912.
Blake's vine and fig tree in Lambeth were given him by Romney.

1937. —— 'William Blake at the Tate Gallery. Resident in Lambeth from 1793–1800.' *South London Press*, 31 Oct. 1913.
Comments on pictures.

1938. —— 'William Blake—England's Michael Angelo. Some noble thoughts of our poet-painter brought into the light of day for his 156th birthday (November 28, 1913).' *South London Observer*, 26 Nov. 1913.
A eulogy.

1939. —— 'William Blake, Hampstead, and John Linnell.' *South London Observer*, Summer 1912 (2 parts, a week apart). [This and the next two articles are reported from clippings in the Tate Gallery marked June–August 1912.]
Mentions that the writer owns Blake's chairs, dishes, and clock.

1940. —— 'William Blake's Lambeth "Dulce Domum".' *South London Observer*, Summer 1912.

1941. —— 'William Blake's Residence at Lambeth.' *South London Observer*, Summer 1912.
A quarrel with the London County Council as to which house was the poet's.

1942. Jacobson, Dan. 'Don't do it.' *Listener*, 13 Feb. 1969 p. 218.
A television programme about Blake narrated by Dr. Bronowski was, in parts, 'acutely embarrassing', 'sycophantic', 'solemn and gratuitous'.

1943. *Jakobson, Roman. 'On the Verbal Art of William Blake and Other Poet-Painters.' *Linguistic Inquiry*, I (1970), 3–23.
*'Infant Joy' shows 'impressive grammatical balance' (p. 7).

1944. §Jakovsky, Anatole. 'Le Mariage du Ciel et de l'Enfer.' *Vie des Arts*, No. 4 (1947), 4–6.

1945. Jaloux, Edmond. Chapter XIX (pp. 149–60) of his *Johann-Heinrich Füssli*. Montreux, 1942.
A superficial study of the relationship concludes that 'Füssli ait orienté Blake' (p. 158).

1946. —— 'William Blake.' *Revue de Littérature Comparée*, XXIX (1955), 305–10 (vMKN).
Text of a 1937 lecture.

1947. A. James, D. G. 'The Gospel of Hell.' Part I, pp. 1–63, of *The Romantic Comedy*. Oxford, London, N.Y., Toronto, 1948. B. Oxford, 1963.
The theme of the book as a whole is the Romantics' distressing heterodoxy and originality. James finds that 'Blake's mind was extremely confused', that 'endless perversity' marks his life and thought, and that his works arise from and illustrate 'intellectual and imaginative disorder'. Certainly there is confusion to be found here.

1948. [Jame]S., [Henr]Y. 'William Blake's Poems.' *Spirit of the Age*, I (25 Aug. 1849), 113–14.
In a letter to the editor, the novelist's father admires 'The Little Vagabond' (reprinted) for its humanitarianism though not for its poetry and goes on to use the poem as a text for a discussion of worship.

1949. A. James, Laura DeWitt. *William Blake: The Finger on the Furnace*. N.Y., 1956. B. **William Blake & the Tree of Life*. Berkeley [Calif.] & London, 1971.
'Much of the underlying pattern of Blake's Prophetic and Symbolic Poems . . . is surprisingly harmonious with qabalistic lore' (B, p. 62). There is no indication in the 'new edition' of its relationship to that of 1956.

1950. James, R. A. Scott. 'William Blake: His Critics and Interpreters.' *Speaker*, n.s. IV (1907), 585–6.

1951. A. *Jameson, Mrs. [Anna Brownell]. *Sacred and Legendary Art*. [2 vols.] London, 1848. Vol. I, pp. 50–1.   B. *Second Edition, Complete in One Volume. London, 1850. P. 51.   C. *Third Edition. [2 vols.] London, 1857. Vol. I, p. 85. . . .   E. *Fifth Edition. London, 1866. Vol. I, p. 85. . . . G. *Seventh Edition. London, 1874. Vol. I, p. 85. . . . I. *Ninth Edition. London, 1883. Vol. I, p. 85.   J. *Ed. Estelle M. Hurrl. Boston & N.Y., 1896. Vol. I, p. 80.   K. *London, N.Y., Bombay, 1900. Vol. I, p. 85   L. *London, N.Y., Bombay, 1905. Vol. I, p. 85.

The Blake reference is admiring but unimportant. Since the only change of significance in London editions from 1857 to 1905 was in the number of illustrations, no attempt was made to locate intervening editions.

1952. Jameson, Grace. 'Irish Poets of Today and Blake.' *PMLA*, LIII (1938), 575–92. (vMKN).
The influence of Blake on A E and Yeats is rather superficially considered.

1953. Jamot, P. 'Turner et Blake.' *Études* CCXXXIX (1938), 592–603 (vRG).

1954. A. Jealous, Walter K. 'Hampstead in the time of Blake.' *Hampstead and Highgate Express*, 17 Aug. 1912, p. 5. B. Reprinted in *The First Meeting of the Blake Society* (1912), no. 3016.
Mostly about other people in Hampstead.

1955. Jeffares, A. Norman. *W. B. Yeats Man and Poet*. London, 1949. *Passim*.

1956. Jeffrey, Lloyd N. 'Blake's *The Little Black Boy*.' *Explicator*, XVII (1958), item 27 (vMKN).

1957. A. Jenkins, Herbert (Herbert Ives) [*sic*]. 'The Grave of William Blake.' *Nineteenth Century*, LXX (1911), 163–9. B. Reprinted in pp. 81–96 of Jenkins's *William Blake* (1925).
Blake's unmarked grave in Bunhill Fields must be more or less under a path.

1958. *Jenkins, Herbert G. *William Blake*: Studies of his Life and Personality. Ed. C. E. Lawrence. London, 1925.
C. E. Lawrence, 'Introduction', is pp. 5–15.
This is a collection of Jenkins's articles on Blake (no. 1924–5, 1927–9, 1957), four of which were published over the name of Herbert Ives.

1959. —— 'William Blake's Grave.' *Manchester Guardian*, 10 July 1911.
Praise of Catherine.

1960. Jessup, W. P. 'The Making of "London".' *New Reasoner*, I (1957), 65–8.
The theme of commercial degradation in 'London'.

1961. A. Johnson, Charles. 'William Blake and his Circle.' *History of British Art*. London, 1932. B. 1934.

1962. A. Johnson, Lionel. 'The Works of William Blake.' *Academy*, No. 1112 (1893), 163–5. B. Reprinted as 'William Blake' in pp. 81–90 of his *Post Liminum*. Ed. Thomas Whittemore. London, 1911.
A review of Ellis & Yeats, no. 369.

1963. Johnson, Mary Lynn. 'Beulah, "Mne Seraphim," and Blake's *Thel*.' *JEGP*, LXIX (1970), 258–78.
'Thel's problem is down to earth' (p. 271).

1964. *Johnstone, William. 'Recrudescence—Blake.' Pp. 154–84 of his *Creative Art in England* From the Earliest Times to the Present. London, 1936.

'*A* study of the character of the most intense and creative English work' (p. 15), dealing with Blake only on pp. 156, 158, 160, 168.

1965. Jones, Myrddin. 'Blake's "To Spring": A Formative Source?' *N&Q*, CCXV [N.s. XVII] (1970), 314–15.

The angel-sun probably derives from Psalm 19.

1966. Jones, William Powell. 'The Idea of the Limitations of Science From Prior to Blake.' *Studies in English Literature*, 1, No. 3 (Summer 1961), 97 114.

'The purpose of this paper is to illustrate, in a rough chronological scheme, the highlights in English poetry after 1700 of the central idea that science, with all its glorious achievements proving the wisdom of God in nature, was unable to provide certain answers.' The article in general, and the Blake section (pp. 111–14), are, of course, no more than suggestive.

1967. *Jongh, Nicholas de. 'William Blake.' *Guardian*, 1 Oct. 1970, p. 12.

David Hare's play, *What Happened to Blake?*, is 'a mad charade'.

1968. A. Joyce, James. 'James Joyce "William Blake".' Ed. Ellsworth Mason. *Criticism*, I (1959), 181–9 (vMKN). B. '[William Blake.]' Pp. 214–22 of *The Critical Writings of James Joyce*. Ed. Ellsworth Mason and Richard Ellmann. N.Y., 1959.

The central fragment of Joyce's Blake lecture, given in Italian in A, in English in B.

1969. Jugaku, Bunsho. 'Art of William Blake.' *Muse*, V (1927), 14–17.

Mostly a bibliography, in Japanese.

1970. A. —— **A Bibliographical Study of William Blake's Note-Book*. Tokyo, 1953. B. *N.Y., 1971.

Edmund Blunden's 'Foreword' is 1 p. and the meticulous transcript (based on the 1935 facsimile) of 'William Blake's Note-Book Tentatively Arranged in Chronological Order' occupies pp. 67–170.

1971. —— 'A Bibliographical Study of Blake's "Note-Book".' *TLS*, 30 July 1954, p. 487 (vMKN).

Objects to a review; the reviewer apologizes for some of the things he said.

1972. A. —— *'Blake no Garon [Blake's Theory of Painting].' *Bi* [*The Beauty*], XXIII (1929), 55–84. B. *Blake no Garon. Kyoto, 1929. Toyo Geijutsu Sasho 21 [Oriental Art Series 21]. 29 pp. C. Reprinted in pp. 85–114 of his *Blake Ronshu* (1931).

1973. —— §'Blake no Kirisuto Kan [Blake's Vision of Christ].' *Osaka Asahi Shinbun* [*Osaka Asahi Newspaper*], 25 Aug. 1935.

1974. —— 'Blake no Notebook [Blake's Notebook].' *Genso: Pensée*, No. 9 (Jan. 1948), 20–3; No. 10 (Feb. 1948), 26–9; No. 11 (March 1948), 26–9.

Cf. his book on the same subject.

1975. Jugaku, Bunsho. *Blake Ronshu [Commentary].* Ed. Soetsu Yanagi & Mitsuharu Hashizume. Kyoto, 1931. 114 pp.

The Prologue is by Yanagi. Jugaku's text reprints his articles on Blake and his Age, at Felpham, his Myth, and his Theory of Painting (no. 1541 7, 1972, 1978).

1976. —— 'Blake Seitan 200–nen [The Bicentenary of the Birth of Blake].' *Eigo-Seinen: The Rising Generation,* CII (1956), 578–9.

1977. —— 'Blake wo Yakushitsutsu [On Translating Blake].' *Shomotsu Tenbo [Observation of Books],* VI (1936), 347–51.

1978. A. —— 'Felpham no Blake [Blake at Felpham].' *Eigo Kenkyu: The Study of English,* XXII (1930), 1148–51, 1280–4. B. Reprinted in his *Blake Ronshu* (1931), pp. 41–60.

1979. —— 'Hihyo no Reigi [Courtesy of Criticism].' *Eigo Seinen: The Rising Generation,* CIII (1957), 405.

Objects to reference to his Blake work by Michio Yoshitake in *Golden Treasury.* See Yoshitake for a reply.

1980. —— *William Blake.* Tokyo, 1934. Kenkyusha Eibeibungaku Hyoden-sosho [Kenkyusha Critical Biographies of Anglo-American Literature, Vol. 31]. 125 pp.

A biography in Japanese.

1981. Justin, Howard. 'Blake's "*Introduction*" to *Songs of Innocence.*' *Explicator,* XI (1952), item 1 (vMKN).

An over-ingenious interpretation.

K

1982. Kamishima, Kenkichi. 'Blake no Tora [Blake's "The Tyger"].' *Kikan Eibungaku: English Quarterly,* IV (1967), 121–8.

1983. Kano, Hideo. 'Blake no Kyoshin [Blake's Fanaticism].' Pp. 79–169 of his *Yuutsu to Kyoshin* [Melancholy and Fanaticism]. Tokyo, 1948.

Gray is dealt with in the other half of the book.

1984. Kaplan, Fred. '"The Tyger" and its Maker: Blake's Vision of Art and the Artist.' *Studies in English Literature 1500–1900,* VII (1967), 617–27.

'The poem is about the relationship between the artist as creator and the work of art as creation' (p. 617).

1985. Karnaghan, Anne Webb. 'Blake Exhibition at Boston Museum.' *Art News,* XXVIII, No. 13 (28 Dec. 1929), 11 (vMKN).

1986. ——*'Blake Manuscripts Shown at Museum.' *Boston Evening Transcript,* 11 Dec. 1929.

1987. Kashiwagi, Toshikazu. ' "The Four Zoas" ni okeru Blake [Blake in *The Four Zoas*].' *Koyasan Daigaku Ronso: Journal of Koyasan University*, III (1968), 1–14.

1988. A. Kassner, Rudolph. 'William Blake.' Pp. 14–56 of *Die Mystik die Künstler und das Leben*: Uber Englische Dichter und Maler im 19. Jahrhundert. Leipzig, 1900. B. Revised and reprinted as pp. 61–89 of *Englische Dichter*. Leipzig, 1920.

1989. Katsura, Fumiko, 'Blake no Uchu-Sozo-Shinwa—*The Book of Urizen* wo Chushin ni [Blake's Myth of the Creation of the Universe—Especially in *The Book of Urizen*].' *Shikai: The Outlook*, No. 13 (1970), 16–28.

1990. —— 'Blake Shinwa Oboegaki—The Four Zoas wo megutte [Notes on Blake's Mythology—On the Four Zoas].' *Kiyo: Shitennoji Joshidaigaku: Review of Shitennoji Women's College*, No. 2 (1970), 32–46.

1991. A. Kazin, Alfred. 'An Introduction to William Blake.' Pp. 36–88 of *The Inmost Leaf*: A Selection of Essays. N.Y., 1941 (vMKN). B. Reprinted in no. 306.

1992. Keeble, S. E. 'Imagination and William Blake.' *London Quarterly [and Holborn] Review*, CXXVII (1917), 215–26.
' "Jerusalem" . . . means . . . the Imagination.'

1993. Keen, Geraldine. 'Sketches of Blake's visions for auction.' *The Times*, 10 May 1971, p. 14.
About the Blake–Varley sketchbook for auction 15 June.

1994. Kellner, Leon. 'William Blake.' *Oestereich Rundschau*, X (1907), 450–4.

1995. *Kemper, F. Claudette. 'The Interlinear Drawings in Blake's *Jerusalem*.' *BNYPL*, LXIV (1960), 588–94.
A gallant but unconvincing attempt to draw consistent conclusions about the drawings within the text of Blake's prophecy.

1996. —— 'Blake, Wicksteed, and the Wicked Swan.' *N&Q*,n.s. VII (1960), 100–1 (vMKN).
The swan on *Jerusalem* pl. 11 is not a 'bitter indictment of London nightlife', but a positive symbol drawn from alchemy.

1997. *Kenchoshvili, Iracli. 'Geniosi, Poeti da Mkhatvari [A Genius, a Poet, and an Artist].' *Akhalgazrda Stalineli*, XXXVIII (13 Dec. 1957)
A brief summary in Georgian.

1998. —— 'William Blake.' *Mnat'obi*, III (1958), 163–5. [The title is transliterated from the Georgian.]

1999. A. Kennedy, Wilma. 'A Mystic's Conception: By William Blake.' Pp. 73–88 of *The English Heritage of Coleridge of Bristol 1798*: The Basis in Eighteenth-Century English Thought for His Distinction between Imagina-

tion and Fancy. New Haven [Conn.] & London, 1947. B. §Hamden, [Conn.] 1959.
A responsible study of the anticipations (not sources) of Coleridge's anti-fanciful concept of the imagination.

2000. Keogh, J. G.; Thomas E. Connolly, & George R. Levine. 'Two Songs of Innocence.' *PMLA*, LXXXIV (1969), 137–40.
Two statements concerning the unreliability of the article by Connolly & Levine in no. 1416, and two rejoinders.

2001. *Kerenyi, Karl, Alfons Rosenberg und Hugo Debrunner. 'Ein Gespräch.' Pp. 12–13 of *England im Übergang*. Ed. Hugo Debrunner. Zurich, 1948.
A discussion of the 'Newton' colourprint.

2002. Kermode, Frank. *Romantic Image*. London, 1957. *Passim*.
Small but frequent references to Blake.

2003. Kessel, Marcel. 'A Comparative Study of Blake and Wordsworth as Mystical Writers.' Cornell Ph.D., 1929 (according to L. F. McNamee, *Dissertations in English and American Literature* [1968]).

2004. Kettle, Arnold. 'The Mental Traveller.' *Arena*, No. 3 (1949), 46–52, 93, 94 (vKP).
A Marxist interpretation of Blake's poem.

2005. —— 'William Blake—No Chains.' *Mainstream*, X, No. 11 (Nov. 1957), 9–23 (vMKN).
Blake as a revolutionary, with a discussion of 'Fayette'.

2006. Keynes, Geoffrey Langdon. 'The Bibliography of Blake.' *TLS*, 23 March 1922, p. 196 (vMKN).
Attempts to answer the criticism that 250 copies of his *Bibliography* are not enough.

2007. —— 'Blake and Wesley.' *N&Q*, CCII (1957), 181.
Evidence that Blake owned a copy of Wesley's *Hymns for the Nation* (1782).

2008. —— 'Blake Drawings.' *TLS*, 17 Dec. 1925, p. 883 (vMKN).
Two drawings in Figgis (no. 408) are not by Blake.

2009. —— *'A Blake Engraving in Bonnycastle's *Mensuration*, 1782.' *Book Collector*, XII (1963), 205–6.
Bibliographical details.

2010. A. —— *Blake Studies*: Notes on his Life and Works in Seventeen Chapters. London, 1949. B. *Blake Studies*: Essays on his life and work. Second Edition. Oxford, 1971.
Blake Studies is a collection of essays (17 in 1949, 29 in 1971), most of which first appeared elsewhere. 'None of the papers is here reproduced exactly as it

first appeared; all have been revised and most of them extended' (1949, p. xiii); further revisions were made in 1971. The work consists of:

Title	1949 Chapter	1949 Pages	1971 Chapter	1971 Pages	Originally printed as no.
'William and Robert.'	I	3–12	I	1–7	2046
'Blake's *Notebook*.'	II	13–20	II	8–13	123
'The Engraver's Apprentice.'	IV	41–9	III	14–30	
'*Poetical Sketches*.'	III	23–39	IV	31–45	2023
'Engravers Called Blake.'	V	50–5	V	46–9	2027
'Blake's Illustrations to Young's *Night Thoughts*.'	VI	56–66	VI	50–8	395
'Blake and the Wedgwoods.'	VII	67–75	VII	59–65	2043
'*A Descriptive Catalogue*.'	VIII	76–83	VIII	66–73	2050
'William Blake with Charles Lamb and his Circle.'	IX	84–104	IX	74–89	Read at the Lamb Society, 9 Oct. 1943
'William Blake and Sir Francis Bacon.'			X	90–7	2044
'William Blake and John Gabriel Stedman.'			XI	98–104	2041
'"Little Tom the Sailor".'			XII	105–10	695
'Blake's Miniatures.'			XIII	111–12	2022
'Blake's Trial at Chichester.'			XIV	113–14	2024
'New Lines from *Jerusalem*.'	XI	110–18	XV	115–21	2033
'Blake's Copper-plates.'	X	105–9	XVI	122–9	2013
'Blake's Visionary Heads and The Ghost of a Flea.'			XVII	130–5	2026
'Thornton's *Virgil*.'	XV	157–66	XVIII	136–42	510
'*Remember Me!*'	XVII	186–90	XIX	143–6	
'Blake's Copy of Dante's *Inferno*.'			XX	147–54	2014
'Blake's Library.'			XXI	155–62	2020
'*The Pilgrim's Progress*.'	XVI	167–85	XXII	163–75	377
'The History of the *Job* Designs.'	XII	119–34	XXIII	176–86	374
'Blake's *Job* on the Stage.'	XIV	146–56	XXIV	187–94	2029
'The Arlington Court Picture.'			XXV	195–204	2025
'The Blake–Linnell Documents.'	XIII	135–45	XXVI	205–12	2032
'William Blake and John Linnell.'			XXVII	213–20	2042
'John Linnell and Mrs. Blake.'			XXVIII	221–9	2030
'George Cumberland and William Blake.'			XXIX	230–52	2039

The 1949 edition has a rather patchy 'Bibliography of the writings of Geoffrey Keynes on Blake' (pp. 193–9); there are 48 plates in A, and 81 reproductions in B.

2011. Keynes, Geoffrey Langdon. 'Blake, Tulk, and Garth Wilkinson.' *Library*, 4th Ser., XXVI (1945), 190–2.
The edition (no. 172) described by Sampson (no. 2627) was printed by C. A. Tulk, as the recently acquired BM copy demonstrates.

2012. —— 'Blake, William.' *Encyclopaedia Britannica*. London & N.Y., 1929. Vol. III, pp. 694–6.
A replacement for the article by J. Comyns Carr. No attempt has been made to record issues of the *Encyclopaedia Britannica*, but it may be useful to note that there were printings in 1929, 1930, 1932, 1936, 1937, 1938, 1939, 1940, 1941, 1942, 1943 . . . *inter alia*.

2013. A. —— 'Blake's Copper Plates.' *TLS*, 24 Jan. 1942, p. 48. B–C. *Revised and reprinted in his *Blake Studies* (1949, 1971).
Describes Blake's engraving techniques.

2014. A. —— 'Blake's Copy of Dante's "Inferno".' *TLS*, 3 May 1957, p. 277. B. *Revised and reprinted in his *Blake Studies* (1971).
The annotations in the recently discovered book.

2015. A. —— *'Blake's Engravings for Gay's Fables.' *Book Collector*, XXI (1972), 59–64. B. Reprinted as pp. 47–52 of *To Geoffrey Keynes*: Articles Contributed to The Book Collector to Commemorate his Eighty-Fifth Birthday. London, 1972.
A comparison of Blake's plates with those of the same designs by preceding engravers.

2016. —— 'Blake's "Holy Thursday" in Anne and Jane Taylor's *City Scenes*.' *Book Collector*, IX (1960), 75–6.

2017. 'Blake's Illuminated Books.' *Books*, No. 314 (1957), 231–3 (vKP).

2018. —— 'Blake's "Jerusalem".' *TLS*, 16 June, 1950, p. 373 (vMKN).
An announcement that subscription dates for the facsimile edition have been extended.

2019. —— 'Blake's Letters to Hayley.' *TLS*, 25 March 1955, p. 181.
Lists lost letters.

2020. A. —— 'Blake's Library.' *TLS*, 6 Nov. 1959, p. 648. B. *Revised and reprinted in his *Blake Studies* (1971).
A list of the books Blake is known to have owned, with a letter from Tatham of 8 June 1864 about Blake's reading.

2021. —— 'Blake's Milton.' *TLS*, 13 Dec. 1923, p. 875.
Bibliographical information.

2022. A. —— 'Blake's Miniatures.' *TLS*, 29 Jan. 1960, p. 72. B. *Revised and Reprinted in his *Blake Studies* (1971).

Quotes a letter from Hayley to David Parker Coke of 13 May 1801 referring to a miniature by Blake which has not been traced.

2023. A. Keynes, Geoffrey Langdon. 'Blake's Poetical Sketches.' *TLS*, 10, 17 March 1945, pp. 120, 132. B–C. *Revised and reprinted in his *Blake Studies* (1949, 1971).

Describes the circumstances of publication, corrections and punctuation, and gives a census of copies (22). For a comment by Grierson, see no. 1746.

2024. A. —— 'Blake's Trial at Chichester.' *N&Q*, CCII [N.s. IV] (1957), 484–5. B. *Revised and reprinted in his *Blake Studies* (1971).

Two new documents, the indictment of Blake and the recognizance entered into by his accusers to ensure their presence at the trial, suggest that the 'Hutton' of Blake's later Prophecies is the Lt. George Hulton who was responsible for the appearance of the two privates.

2025. A. —— *'Blake's Vision of the Circle of the Life of Man.' Pp. 202–8 of *Studies in Art and Literature for Belle Da Costa Greene*. Ed. Dorothy Miner. Princeton, 1954. B. *Revised and reprinted in his *Blake Studies* (1971).

A history and interpretation of the Arlington Court Picture, the interpretation radically revised in 1971.

2026. A. —— *'Blake's Visionary Heads & the Ghost of a Flea.' *BNYPL*, LXIV (1960), 567–72. B. *Revised and reprinted in his *Blake Studies* (1971).

Amplifies and illustrates the source suggestion made by Singer (no. 2706).

2027. A. —— 'Engravers Called Blake.' *TLS*, 17 Jan. 1942, p. 36. B–C. *Revised and reprinted in his *Blake Studies* (1949, 1971).

On W. S. Blake.

2028. —— 'A Gift to the Nation. Blake Drawings from the U.S.A. "Ninepence Each".' *The Times*, 28 July 1928, p. 13 (vMKN).

The 537 water-colour drawings for *Night Thoughts*, from Frances White Emerson to the BM.

2029. A. —— *'Job.' Pp. 24–34 of Joan Lawson, James Laver, Geoffrey Keynes, Frank Howes. *Job and The Rake's Progress*. London, 1949. Sadler's Wells Ballet Books, No. 2. B. *Revised and reprinted in his *Blake Studies* (1949, 1971.)

2030. A. —— *'John Linnell and Mrs. Blake.' *TLS*, 20 June 1958, p. 348. B. Revised and reprinted in his *Blake Studies* (1971).

Evidence from the Ivimy MSS about disputes between Tatham and Linnell over Blake's property.

2031. —— 'The Macgeorge Blakes.' *TLS*, 26 June 1924, p. 403 (vMKN).

A description of his Blakes to be sold at Sotheby's.

2032. A. —— 'New Blake Documents: History of the Job Engravings.' *TLS*, 9 Jan. 1943, p. 24. B–C. *Revised and reprinted in his *Blake Studies* (1949, 1971).

A summary of the financial history of *Job*, from Linnell's receipts and account books.

2033. A. Keynes, Geoffrey Langdon. 'New Lines from Blake's "Jerusalem".' *TLS*, 10 July 1943, p. 336. B–C. *Revised and reprinted in his *Blake Studies* (1949, 1971).

An early proof of pl. 1 reveals lettering Blake later obscured; a census of copies of *Jerusalem* is included.

2034. A. —— *'A Newly Discovered Painting by William Blake.' *Country Life*, 11 Nov. 1949, p. 1427. B. 'Condensed' in no. 660.

The Keynes article reproduces and comments on the Arlington Court picture.

2035. —— 'The Nonesuch Blake.' *TLS*, 8 Nov. 1957, p. 673 (vMKN).

In his 1927 and 1957 editions of Blake's *Writings*, 'off his own tail' in *The Marriage* should read 'off of his own tail'.

2036. —— 'The Nonesuch Milton.' *Nation & Athenaeum*, XXXIX (1926), 697.

Blake's 'Satan, Sin, and Death' is very close to Hogarth's.

2037. —— 'On Editing Blake.' *English Studies Today*, ed. G. I. Duthie, 3rd Ser. (1964), 137–53.

A history of his texts of Blake.

2038. —— '*Religio Bibliographici*.' *Library*, VIII (1953), 63–76.

Includes a history of Keynes's *Bibliography* (1921).

2039. A. —— *'Some Uncollected Authors XLIV: George Cumberland 1754–1848.' *Book Collector*, XIX (1970), 31–65. B. *Revised and reprinted in his *Blake Studies* (1971).

A list of Cumberland's books and a study 'particularly of his relations with William Blake' (A, p. 31); the checklist is omitted in B.

2040. —— *'William Blake.' Vol. IV, p. 247 of *Collier's Encyclopedia*. N.p., 1966.

2041. A. —— 'William Blake and John Gabriel Stedman.' *TLS*, 20 May 1965, p. 400. B. *Revised and reprinted in his *Blake Studies* (1971).

Résumé of the Blake passages in Stedman's diary, no. 2749.

2042. A. —— 'William Blake and John Linnell.' *TLS*, 13 June 1958, p. 332. B. *Revised and reprinted in his *Blake Studies* (1971).

Blake references in Linnell's journal.

2043. A. —— 'William Blake and Josiah Wedgwood.' *TLS*, 9 Dec. 1926 p. 909. B–C. *Revised and reprinted in his *Blake Studies* (1949, 1971).

The relationship illustrated by some letters.

2044. A. —— 'William Blake and Sir Francis Bacon.' *TLS*, 8 March 1957, p. 152. B. *Revised and reprinted in his *Blake Studies* (1971).

The newly discovered copy of the *Essays* with Blake's annotations.

2045. A. —— 'William Blake and the Portland Vase.' *TLS*, 3 July 1930, p. 554. B–C. *Revised and reprinted in his *Blake Studies* (1949, 1971).

On the basis of a letter from Joseph Johnson to Erasmus Darwin of 23 July 1791, we can be confident that Blake engraved the plate of the Portland Vase for Darwin's *Botanic Garden* (1791).

2046. A. Keynes, Geoffrey Langdon. 'William Blake's Brother.' *TLS*, 6, 13 Feb. 1943, pp. 72, 84. B–C. *Revised and reprinted in his *Blake Studies* (1949, 1971).
An account of Robert.

2047. A. —— 'William Blake's "Laughing Song": A New Version.' *N&Q*, CXXII [11th Ser. II] (1910) 241–2. B. Separately printed in Edinburgh, 1969.
First printed here (1910) from *Poetical Sketches* (F).

2048. —— 'William Blake's Notebook: An American Generosity to the British Museum.' *The Times*, 16 April 1957, p. 11 (vMKN).

2049.* —— & Gwendolen Raverat. *Job A Masque for Dancing* Founded on Blake's Illustrations to the Book of Job. Music by R. Vaughan Williams. Pianoforte arrangement by Vally Lasker. London, N.Y., Leipzig, Amsterdam, [1931?].
The Masque was first performed at the Norwich Festival in 1930 and is now a regular part of the repertoire of the Royal Ballet.

2050. A. —— & Ruthven Todd. 'William Blake's Catalogue: A New Discovery.' *TLS*, 12 Sept. 1942, p. 456. B–C. *Revised and reprinted in Keynes's *Blake Studies* (1949, 1971).
A description and census of the catalogue, and report of the discovery of the flyer 'Exhibition of Paintings in Fresco' (1809).

2051. King, Anne R. 'Hopkins' "Windhover" and Blake.' *English Studies*, XXXVII (1956), 245–52.
The second water-colour for 'L'Allegro' said to be the source.

2052. King, James. 'The Meredith Family, Thomas Taylor, and William Blake.' *Studies in Romanticism*, XI (1972), 153–7.
Provides 'definitive evidence' from the Commonplace Book of William George Meredith (1804–31) that 'Taylor gave Blake lessons in geometry'.

2053. Kinugasa, Umejiro. 'Honpo Blake Bunken Senku no Ben [Some Notes on the Earliest Japanese Blakeana].' *Eigo Seinen: The Rising Generation*, LXXXI (1939), 309.

2054. Kiralis, Karl. 'Blake.' *New York Times Book Review*, 24 March 1957, p. 43.
Refutes Alfred Kazin's charge (made in a review of Keynes's edition of the *Letters*, *New York Times Book Review*, 27 Jan. 1957), that Blake's later letters show 'cringing pieties'.

2055. A. —— 'A Guide to the Intellectual Symbolism of William Blake's Later Prophetic Writings.' *Criticism*, I (1959), 190–210. B. Reprinted in no. 1724.
A solid, useful article.

2056. Kiralis, Karl. 'James Hogg and William Blake.' *N&Q*, CCIV [N.s. VI] (1959), 12–14.

Kiralis suggests, with suitable hesitation, that the 'great original' 'W——m B——e' in Hogg's *The Private Memoirs and Confessions of a Justified Sinner*, 1824, may be the poet-engraver. Interesting but thin.

2057. —— 'Joyce and Blake: A Basic Source for "Finnegan's Wake".' *Modern Fiction Studies*, IV (1958–9), 329–34.

2058. —— 'A Possible Revision in Blake's *Jerusalem*.' *Art Bulletin*, XXXVII (1955), 203–4.

First design in *Paradiso* may be a sketch for *Jerusalem* pl. 97.

2059. A. —— 'The Theme and Structure of William Blake's *Jerusalem*.' *ELH*, XXIII (1956), 127–43. B. Reprinted 'in altered form' in Pinto, *Divine Vision* (no. 2402), pp. 139–62.

The structure is one of 'interfolded growth'.

2060. Kirsch, Robert R. 'Blake: Portrait of a Mystic.' *Los Angeles Times*, 3 Feb. 1966.

General article in a regular column ('The Book Report') on the occasion of Erdman's text.

2061. Kirschbaum, Leo. 'Blake's "The Fly".' *Essays in Criticism*, XI (1961), 154–62, with an 'Editorial Postscript' by F. W. Bateson, pp. 162–3.

Kirschbaum gives a stanza-by-stanza explication, with an appendix on the revisions of the poem. Bateson concludes that in 'The Fly' Blake struggles 'against the grain to recapture the naïve wisdom of Innocence'.

2062. Kline, Alfred Allan. 'The English Romantics and the American Republic: An Analysis of the Concept of America in the Work of Blake, Burns, Wordsworth, Coleridge, Byron and Shelley.' *DA*, XIV (1954), 112. Columbia Ph.D.

2063. —— 'Blake's *A Song of Liberty*.' *Explicator*, XV (1956), item 4.

The influence of Paine gives 'keys' to the poem.

2064. *Knoblauch, Adolf. *William Blake*: Ein Umriss seines Lebens und seiner Gedichte. Berlin, 1925. Shöpfung Beiträge zu einer Weltgeschichte religiösen Kunst Band 7.

There are 24 pl. and 20 pp.

2065. Knockshim. 'Blake Modai [Blake's Problem].' *Eigo Seinen: The Rising Generation*, LXIV (1931), 429.

Comment on Punch's assertion.

2066. A. Knowles, John. *The Life and Writings of Henry Fuseli, Esq. M.A. R.A.* In Three Volumes. London, 1831. Vol. I, pp. 172, 290–3. B §1970.

Minor Blake references, including Fuseli's recommendation of Blake's designs for Blair's *Grave*.

854 VI. CRITICISM Kobayashi, no. 2067

2067. *Kobayashi, Akio. 'William Blake to sono Keishiki ni tsuite [William Blake's Poetic Diction].' *Arubiyon: Albion*, No. 7 (1955), 46–52.

2068. §Kobayashi, Haruo. '[Revolutionary Ideas of Blake].' *Eibungaku Kenkyubushi [Magazine of the Society for the Study of English Literature* in Aoyamagakuin University], No. 1 (Feb. 1934), 22–9.

2069. Kodama, Hisao. 'Blake's Innocence and Experience: A Reconsideration.' *Kiyo*: Kyoritsu Joshidaigaku Tankidaigakubu: *Collected Essays* by Members of the Faculty [of] Kyoritsu Women's Junior College, No. 4 (1960), 69–84.
'I doubt if there were any sudden visitation of disillusionment in Blake's mental career' (p. 71).

2070. *Koizumi, Ichiro. 'William Blake ni okeru Ningenzo [The Human Image Seen by William Blake].' *Kiristokyo Bunka: Christianity and Culture*, No. 47 (1950), 43–52.

2071. —— 'Blake no Marginalia ni tsuite [Blake and his "Marginalia"].' *Tokyo Joshidaigaku Ronshu: Essays and Studies by Members of Tokyo Women's Christian College*, II (1951), 319–23.

2072. Kolker, Robert Phillip. 'The Altering Eye: William Blake's Use of Eighteenth-Century Poetics.' *DAI*, XXX (1969), 1987A (Columbia Ph.D.).
Blake 'carries Augustan humanism as far as it will go'.

2073. Kono, Rikyu. 'Shi to Shinwa—William Blake no Baai: Myth and Poetry—A Note on William Blake.' *Muroran Kogyodaigaku Kenkyuhokoku* (Bunka-hen): *Memoirs of the Muroran Institute of Technology* (Cultural Science), VI (1968), 307–32.
'His myth seems to have suffered from want of control', because 'the working of the unconscious mind cannot be expressed objectively, insidely, and logically' (p. 308). An abstract is in English, the essay in Japanese.

2074. —— 'W. Blake no Yogenshi *Milton* ni tsuite: A Study of Blake's poem *Milton*—Blake no Milton wa naze kakoshinakereba naranakattaka [Why Milton in Blake's poem must descend].' *Muroran Kogyodaigaku Kenkyuhokoku: Memoirs of the Muroran Institute of Technology* (Cultural Science), VI (1967), 55–78.
The article is in Japanese, but it is abstracted in English.

2075. —— 'William Blake no Imagination ni tsuite no Ichikosatsu: A Study of William Blake's Imagination.' *Muroran Kogyodaigaku Kenkyuhokoku: Memoirs of the Muroran Institute of Technology*, V (1965), 1029–44.
The abstract is in English, the essay in Japanese.

2076. Kono, Toshihisa [i.e. Rikyu]. 'William Blake no Kami to Hito ni tsuite [Blake's doctrine of God and Man].' *Hokkaido Eigo Eibungaku: The English Literature in Hokkaido*, XII (1967), 19–29.

2077. Korteling, Jacomina [geboren te Deventer]. *Mysticism in Blake and Wordsworth*. Amsterdam, 1928.

Mysticism is defined so broadly that we find that 'the poets, the artists in general, partake of the nature of mystics'. Her understanding of Blake's 'prettily expressive' poetry is not much more illuminating.

Kostelanetz, Anne; see also under her married name, Mellor.

2078. Kostelanetz, Anne Tidaback. 'The Human Form in the Poetry and Art of William Blake.' *DAI*, XXX (1969), 1987–8A (Columbia Ph.D.).

2079. Kreiter, Carmen S. 'Evolution and William Blake.' *Studies in Romanticism*, IV (1965), 110–18.
Excellent on the biogeneric symbolism and background in *Urizen*.

2080. *Kremen, Kathryn R. 'Blake's Fourfold Resurrection and Christianity of the Imagination.' Chap. 3 (pp. 129–259) of her *The Imagination of the Resurrection*: The Poetic Continuity of a Religious Motif in Donne, Blake, and Yeats. Lewisburg [Pa.], 1972. Also *passim*.
A reading of the theological passages in Blake, with 20 poorly reproduced plates. (The work was originally a Brandeis Ph.D. of 1970.)

2081. Kudo, Naotaro. 'William Blake no Ie—Seitan Ni 200-nen ni chinande [William Blake's Birthplace—In Commemoration of the Bicentenary of his Birth].' *Gakuto* [*Lamplight of Learning*], LIV, No. 10 (Oct. 1957), 42–4.

2082. Kuhn, Albert J. 'Blake on the Nature and Origins of Pagan Gods and Myths.' *MLN*, LXXII (1957), 563–72.
This article with some new suggestions about Blake's antiquarian sources shows no great familiarity with other scholarship on the subject.

2083. A. *Kumashiro, Soho (Shinsuke). *Eien no Ningenzo* [*The Image of the Eternal Man*]: Wakai Hitobito no tame no Blake: Hito to Shi to E [Blake for Young People: The Man, his Poems, and his Paintings]. Tokyo, 1960. 266 pp. B. *Blake Kenkyu* [*A Study of Blake*]: Hito to Shi to E [The Man, his Poems, and his Paintings]. Tokyo, 1966. (vHK) C. Tokyo, 1969. 266 pp.
The 37 plates include all of *For Children*.

2084. —— 'Job-ki Ezu no Migi to Hidari [Right and Left in "The Illustrations of the Book of Job"].' *Chuo Daigaku Bungakubu Kiyo: Journal of the Faculty of Literature of Chuo University*, No. 7 (1956), 35–49.
About Blake.

2085. —— 'Sen to Bisaiinshi [A Line and Minute Particulars].' *Chuo Daigaku Bungakubu Kiyo: Journal of the Faculty of Literature of Chuo University*, No. 4 (1955), 33–52.
About Blake.

2086. *Kup, Karl. 'The Engraved Work of William Blake 1757–1827.' *American Artist*, XI, No. 8 (Oct. 1947), 25–9, 49 (vMKN).

2087. Kuriyama, Minoru. 'Blake to Coleridge no yogen no koe [The Prophecy Voices of Blake and Coleridge].' *Jimbun Kenkyu: Studies in the*

Humanities (The Journal of the Literary Association of Osaka City University), XV (1964), 224–34.

2088. Kuriyama, Minoru. §'William Blake—"Songs of Experience" e no Shishin no Tenkai [William Blake—The Development of his Poetic Mind Leading to Songs of Experience].' *Jimbun Kenkyu* [*Studies in the Humanities*: The Journal of The Literary Association of Osaka City University], IX (1958), 117–34.

2089. *Kuroda, Masatoshi. 'Blake's Illustrations to the *Divine Comedy*.' *The Muse*, V (1927), 5–13.

A Japanese journal.

L

2091. *L[a] F[arge], H[enry]. 'Blake's Best Book.' *Art News*, LI (March 1952), 36–7 (vMKN).

Jerusalem described.

2092. Lafourcade, Georges. *La Jeunesse de Swinburne* (*1837–1867*). [2 vols.] Paris, 1928. Vol. II, pp. 320–6.

An excellent detailed account of the genesis of Swinburne's essay on Blake (1868).

2093. —— 'William Blake et le Marquis de Sade.' *Confluences*, 3ᵉ anne (1943), 556–62.

2094. A. Lamb, Charles. *Letters of Charles Lamb*. Ed. Thomas Noon Talfourd and W. Carew Hazlitt. In Two Volumes. London, 1886. Bohn's Standard Library. Vol. II, pp. 176–7. B. *The Letters of Charles Lamb*. Ed. Alfred Ainger. [2 vols.] London & N.Y., 1888. Vol. II, pp. 104–6. C. *The Letters of Charles Lamb*. Ed. Alfred Ainger. Volume III (Vol. XI of *The Life and Works of Charles Lamb*. In Twelve Volumes). London, 1900. Pp. 148–50. D. *The Letters of Charles Lamb*. Ed. William MacDonald. Vol. II (Vol. XII of *The Works of Charles Lamb*. In Twelve Volumes). London, 1903. Pp. 87–9, 212. E. *The Letters of Charles Lamb*. Ed. Alfred Ainger. [2 vols.] London & N.Y., 1904. Vol. II, pp. 105–7. F. **The Works of Charles and Mary Lamb*. Ed. E. V. Lucas. [7 vols.] London, 1905. Vol. VII, pp. 642–3, 779. G. *The Letters of Charles Lamb*. Ed. Russell Davis Gillman. London & N.Y., 1907. Pp. 339–40, 388. H. *The Letters of Charles Lamb*. [2 vols.] London & N.Y., [1909]. Everyman's Library. Vol. II, pp. 87–9, 212. I. *The Letters of Charles and Mary Lamb 1821–1842*. Ed. E. V. Lucas. (Vol. VI of *The Works of Charles and Mary Lamb*.) London, 1912. Pp. 690–1, 833. J. *The Letters of Charles and Mary Lamb*. Ed. E. V. Lucas. [3 vols.] London, 1935. Vol. II, pp. 424–6; Vol. III, p. 178. K. *The Complete Works and Letters of Charles Lamb*. N.Y., 1935. The Modern Library. Pp. 881–2. L. *The Letters of Charles Lamb*. Arranged by Guy Pocock in 2 Volumes from the Edition of E. V. Lucas. London & N.Y., 1945. Everyman's Library No. 343. Vol. II, pp. 116–17, 246. M. *The Letters of Charles Lamb*. Selected and edited by George Woodcock. London, 1950. Pp. 154–5, 186.

The two letters with Blake references are dated 15 May 1824 and 11 Oct. 1828. In every case above where there is only one page reference (A, B, C, E, K), only the 1824 letter is printed. Of the two letters, the first (now in the Huntington) is important for Blake, and was apparently first printed by Allan Cunningham; the second is only a passing reference to Blake.

2095. *Lande, L. M. *Sackcloth and Light*: A Study of Blake's Job. Montreal, 1948 (vKP).
All the *Job* plates are reproduced.

2096. *Landry, Hilton. 'The Symbolism of Blake's Sunflower.' *BNYPL*, LXVI (1962), 613–16.

2097. A. Lang, Andrew. *The Library*. With a Chapter on Modern English Illustrated Books by Austin Dobson. London, 1881. Pp. 125–33. B. London, 1881. Pp. 125–33. C. N.Y., 1892. Pp. 125–33.
The section on Blake is in Dobson's chapter.

2098. Langridge, Irene. *William Blake*: A Study of his Life and Art Work. London, 1904.
A shallow and inept attempt to 'sketch again his artistic personality', based upon 'our public collections in London' (p. v), with 50 plates. Chap. xi (pp. 159–75) is on 'Work in the [*Carfax*] Exhibition of 1904' and Chap. xii (pp. 176–94) on 'Engravings and Drawings in the [*British Museum*] Print Room' and in the National Gallery [now the Tate] (pp. 189–94).

2099. *Larrabee, Stephen A. 'Blake.' Chapter V, pp. 99–119 of *English Bards and Grecian Marbles*. The Relationship between Sculpture and Poetry especially in the Romantic Period. N.Y., 1943.

2100. —— 'An Interpretation of Blake's "A Divine Image".' *MLN*, XLVII (1932), 305–8 (vMKN).

2101. —— 'John Gibson Visits William Blake.' *TLS*, 3 April 1937, p. 256.
Visit mentioned in Matthews's life of Gibson (no. 1678B).

2102. —— 'Some Additional American References to Blake 1830–1863.' *BNYPL*, LXI (1957), 561–3.
16 new items; see also no. 1451, 2156, 2158–9, 2162–3 for American references.

2103. Larson, Gary Dean. 'The Role of God in Blake's Later Vision: The Fall and the Apocalypse.' *DA*, XXVIII (1968), 5059A–60A. Emory Ph.D., 1967.
'God undergoes a fourfold transformation, moving through the fall to the apocalypse.'

2104. La Valley, Albert J. *Carlyle and the Idea of the Modern*: Studies in Carlyle's Prophetic Literature And Its Relation to Blake, Nietzsche, Marx, and Others. New Haven [Conn.] & London, 1968.
Blake serves as an occasional analogy.

2105. *Leach, Bernard. 'Notes on William Blake.' *Shirakaba* [*The White Birch*], V (April 1914), 462–71.

2106. Leavis, F. R. 'Blake and *Ash Wednesday*.' Pp. 140–2 of *Revaluation*: Tradition & Development in English Poetry. London, 1936.

2107. Le Blanc, Ch., ed. *Manuel de l'Amateur d'Estampes*, Contenant 1° Un Dictionnaire des Graveurs de toutes les nations . . . [2 vols.] Paris, 1854–1857. Vol. I (1854), p. 354.

2108. *Lee, Sherman E. 'Los, Urthona and Blake's Illustrations to Dante.' Pp. 151–7 of *Art and Thought* Issued in honour of Dr. Ananda K. Coomaraswamy on the occasion of his 70th birthday. Ed. Bharatha Iyer. London, 1947 (vMKN).
Blake is not a Romantic but participates in the Perennial Philosophy.

2109. Lefcowitz, Barbara Freedgood. 'The Shaping Flame: Self, Nature and Madness in the Poetry of Christopher Smart and William Blake.' DAI, XXXI (1970), 4125–6A. Maryland Ph.D.
'*T*heir poetry seems strongly to counter the possibility of madness.'

2110. Legge, J. G. 'The *Examiner* and William Blake.' *London Mercury*, XX (1929), 70–1.
Legge does little more than draw attention to the Hunts' *Examiner* articles on Blake, largely by means of excerpts.

2111. *L., M. C. 'William Blake, London 1757–1827, Poet, Painter and Engraver.' *Bulletin of the Minneapolis Institute of Arts*, VIII (1919), 57–60, and cover.
A general essay inspired by the exhibition of *Job*.

2112. —— 'William Blake, London, 1757–1827, Painter and Engraver.' *International Studio*, LXIX (Dec. 1919), 2–4 (vMKN).

2113. Lelj, Caterina. *William Blake*. Milano, 1938.
17 unnumbered pages, 2 × 2 in.

2114. Lemaitre, Henri. 'Blake Re-Visited.' *Études Anglaises*, XII (1959), 151–5 (vMKN).
An assessment (in French) of current scholarship.

2115. —— §'Les Illustrations pour le Livre de Job par William Blake.' University of Paris Ph.D., 1953.

2116. Lemonnier, Léon. 'Blake.' Chapter XII (pp. 204–30) of *Les Poètes anglais du XVIIIe siecle*. Paris, 1947. Le Livre de l'Étudiant.

2117. Leporini. 'Wien. Ausstellung Blake und Turner.' *Pantheon*, XIX (1937), 130 (vMKN).

2118. Lescure, Jean. 'Présentation.' *Messages*, I (1939), 3–10.

2119. —— 'William Blake, ou la réalité de l'Imaginaire.' *Art et Style*, No. 7 (1947), 80–1 (vMKN).

2120. A. Leslie, C. R. *A Hand-Book for Young Painters*. London, 1855. P. 58.
B. *Handbook for Young Painters*. Second Edition. London, 1870. P. 57.
A passing and inaccurate reference to Blake's visions.

2121. A. —— *Memoirs of the Life of John Constable, Esq. R.A.* Composed
Chiefly of his Letters. London, 1843. P. 123. B. Second Edition. London,
1845. P. 307. C. *Life and Letters of John Constable, R.A.* Ed. Robert C. Leslie.
London, 1896. P. 348. D. *John Constable*. Tr. Léon Bazalgette. Paris, 1905.
P. 304. E. *Memoirs of the Life of John Constable, Esq., R.A.* Introduction by
Benedict Nicolson. London, 1949. The Chiltern Library. P. 298. F. *Memoirs
of the Life of John Constable*. London, 1951. P. 280.
Only minute mechanical changes in the Blake anecdote were made in the
second edition and perpetuated in those that followed it.

2122. Lesnick, Henry G. 'Blake's Antithetical Vision: A Study of the
Structure of *Jerusalem*.' *DAI*, XXX (1969), 1987A; Columbia Ph.D.

2123. —— *'The Function of Perspective in Blake's *Jerusalem*.' *BNYPL*,
LXXIII (1969), 49–55.
The men in *Jerusalem* pl. 1 and in 'Death's Door' 'stand at different sides of
the same Gate' (p. 53).

2124. Lethaby, W. R. 'Blake in the Abbey.' *TLS*, 1 Sept. 1927, p. 592.
Attribution to Blake of drawings for Gough.

2125. Leyris, Pierre, and Pierre Boutang. 'A propos de William Blake.' *Le
Monde*, 19 Feb. 1971, p. 15 (tr. Lee Johnson as 'About William Blake.'
Blake Newsletter, IV [1971], 72–3), 5 March 1971, p. 14.
Leyris attacks an enthusiastic review of Boutang's book by André Dalmas
(*Le Monde*, 20 Nov. 1970, p. 17; tr. Lee Johnson, *Blake Newsletter*, IV [1971],
70–1), and Boutang replies.

2126. Lindberg, Bo. 'William Blake.' *Finsk Tidskrift*, X (1971), 424–39.
A popular account in Finnish, with a translation of 'The Mental Traveller'.

2127. —— *'William Blake's Visions and the Unio Artistica.' Pp. 141–67
of *Mysticism*: Based on Papers read at the Symposium on Mysticism held at
Abo on the 7th–9th September, 1968. Ed. Sven S. Hartman & Carl-Martin
Edsman. Stockholm, 1972. Scripta Instituti Donneriani Aboensis V.
Blake's eidetic visions in *Job* convert the *unio mystica* to *unio artistica*: 'When
they [the classical mystics] say "God" Blake very often says "Art"' (p. 167).

2128. *Lindsay, Daryl. 'William Blake.' *Art in Australia*, 4th Ser., No. 1
(March–May 1941), 38–46.

2129. Lindsay, Jack. 'Donne and Blake.' *TLS*, 24 July 1937, p. 544.
'I do not think the influence of Nonconformity on William Blake has been
sufficiently realized.'

2130. A. —— 'William Blake: A Man without a Mask.' *Our Time*, III
(June 1944), 10–12. B. Reprinted in *Little Reviews Anthology 1945*. Ed. Denys
Val Baker. London, 1945. Pp. 187–95 (vKP).

A defence of what Lindsay takes to be Bronowski's theme (no. 1288), that Blake was a pre-Marx Marxist.

2131. A. Lindsay, Jack. *William Blake*: Creative Will and the Poetic Image. London, 1927. B. Second Edition, Enlarged. London, 1929. C. §Folcroft, Pennsylvania, 1969.

A highly personal and impressionistic 'effort to define the condition of mind his work represents and to expose its psychological machinery'. It begins: '*William Blake, William Blake* the earth chanted through the rhythm of his swinging body'.

2132. *Lindsay, Lionel. 'William Blake, The Artist.' *Art in Australia*, 3rd Ser., No. 4 (May 1923), 3 pages.

A general essay.

2133. A. Lipa, Charles Buell. 'The Critical Theory of William Blake.' Cornell Ph.D., 1940. B. Digested in pp. 33–6 of *Cornell University Abstracts of Theses*. Ithaca [N.Y.], 1941.

2134. *Lister, Raymond. *Beulah to Byzantium*: A Study of Parallels in the Works of W. B. Yeats, William Blake, Samuel Palmer & Edward Calvert Being No. II of the Dolmen Press Yeats Centenary Papers. [Dublin] 1965.

A lecture.

2135. —— *British Romantic Art*. London, 1973. *Passim*.

An introduction to the themes of Romantic British paintings, in which Blake's writings are frequently quoted.

2136. —— *'William Blake.' Pp. 13–21 of his *Edward Calvert*. London, 1962.

Blake's influence on Calvert and The Ancients is fruitfully discussed both in the second chapter above and *passim*.

2137. —— * *William Blake*: An introduction to the Man and to his Work. With a Foreword by G. E. Bentley, Jr. London, 1968.

A responsible introduction for the general reader. The 'Foreword' is pp. vi–vii and there are 32 plates.

2138. [Lister, Thomas Henry.] 'Art. III. *Lives of the most Eminent British Painters, Sculptors, and Architects*. By Allan Cunningham. 6 vols. 12 mo. London: 1830–1–2–3.' *Edinburgh Review*, LIX (April 1834), 48–73.

A passing reference affirms that 'the able, but, alas! insane' Blake 'could scarcely be considered a painter' (p. 53; cf. p. 64). The author is identified in *The Wellesley Index to Victorian Periodicals 1824–1900*, ed. W. E. Houghton (1966) I, 476.

2139. Littlewood, S. R. 'Laureate of Childhood. Birthplace of William Blake—a Bi-Centenary Suggestion.' *Referee*, 24 Dec. 1924.

Buy it for the Nation.

2140. §Lo-jui, Meng-chia. 'Shih-jen Pai-lei-k'o Chih Sheng-p'ing [The Life of the Poet Blake].' *Wen-i Yueh-k'an*, IV, No. 4 (19   ).

In Chinese.

2141. §Long, Kay Parkhurst. 'Unity in William Blake's Songs of Innocence and of Experience: A Review and Discussion.' University of Tulsa Ph.D., 1970.

See also Kay Parkhurst Easson (in the Index), her married name.

2142. Looker, Samuel J. 'William Blake as Lyric Poet and Humanist.' *Socialist Review*, XV (1918), 359–64.

2143. *Lord, John. *William Blake private printer.* N.p., 1972. [Brewhouse Press] Broadsheet number Ten.

8 pages of competent, unoriginal text.

2144. A. §Lossing, Benson J. *Outline History of the Fine Arts.* N.Y., 1840. Pp. 301–3. B. N.Y. 1843. Pp. 301–2.

A brief discussion of Blake's engraving technique.

2145. Lovell, Ernest J., Jr. 'The Heretic in the Sacred Wood; or, The Naked Man, the Tired Man, and the Romantic Aristocrat: William Blake, T. S. Eliot, and George Wyndham.' Pp. 75–94 of *Romantic and Victorian*: Studies in Memory of William H. Marshall. Ed. W. Paul Elledge & Richard L. Hoffman. Rutherford, Madison, Teaneck, 1971.

Concerns 'The contradictory nature of Eliot's remarks on Blake' (p. 75).

2146. Lowenstein, Amy. 'Annals of the Poor: Social Fact and Artistic Response in Gray, Goldsmith, Cowper, Crabbe, Blake, Burns.' *DAI*, XXIX (1969), 4006–7A. New York University Ph.D.

Their responses 'to the situation of the laboring poor'.

2147. Lowery, Margaret Ruth. 'Blake and the Flaxmans.' Pp. 281–9 of *The Age of Johnson*: Essays Presented to Chauncey Brewster Tinker. [Ed. Frederick W. Hilles.] New Haven (Conn.) & London, 1949.

Chiefly about the designs to Gray which Blake gave to the Flaxmans, and which Miss Lowery dates about 1782 despite the fact that the text of the poems which the designs surround was published in 1790.

2148. —— 'William Blake and the "Divine Imagination".' *Northwest Missouri State College Studies*, XIV, No. 1 (1950), 105–31 (vMKN).

An exceedingly general, low-level introduction.

2149. —— 'William Blake's Poetical Sketches 1783.' Yale Ph.D., 1935.

Presumably printed in her *Windows of the Morning* (1940).

2150. A. —— *Windows of the Morning*: A Critical Study of William Blake's *Poetical Sketches*, 1783. New Haven [Conn.] & London, 1940. Yale Studies in English Volume 93. B. §N.Y., 1970.

This pioneering study of the sources of Blake's earliest poetry (presumably based on her thesis) finds them chiefly in the eighteenth century and uses a large number of previously unnoticed contemporary references to Blake in the correspondence of his friends.

2151. Lowther, G. 'Blake and Smetham.' *Academy*, 31 Aug. 1909.

Praises Smetham's writings on Blake.

2152. A. Lucas, F. L. 'Blake, Shelley, Dionysus.' Pp. 116–29 of *Literature and Psychology*, London, Toronto, Melbourne, Sydney, Wellington, 1951. B. Ann Arbor (Mich.), 1957. Pp. 116–30 (vMKN).

2153. Luke, Hugh J., Jr. 'Review Essay: William Blake: *Pictor Notus.*' *Papers on Language & Literature*, II (1966), 274–82.
Review of current scholarship.

2154. A. [Lynd, R.] 'John O'London.' 'The Fame of Blake.' *John O'London's Weekly*, LVI (1947), 601. B. Reprinted in Lynd's *Books and Writers*. London, 1952. Pp. 62–6.
A review of Saurat's anthology (no. 367) in letters to Gog and Magog.

M

2155. M., P. 'William Blake. I.—Blake the Author [II (III).—Blake the Artist.]' *Light Blue*, II (1867), 146–51, 216–26, 286–94.
A sympathetic summary, incorporating ideas evidently of Linnell and Palmer, and occasioning the first publication of three poems from the *Island in the Moon* ('This city and this country . . .' on p. 162 and 'Phoebe drest like Beauty's queen' and 'Leave, Oh leave me to my sorrow' on p. 240).

2156. Mabbott, Thomas Ollive. 'Blake in America.' *N&Q*, CXLII [12th Ser., X] (1922), 128 (vMKN).
Notes publication of poems from *Poetical Sketches* in *The Harbinger* (1848) no. 344.

2157. —— 'Blake's *A Poison Tree.*' *Explicator*, VI (1948), item 19 (vMKN).

2158. —— 'Blake's American Fame.' *TLS*, 23 Feb. 1933, p. 127 (vMKN).
Notes references before 1850: a poem about Blake in the *New York Mirror*, 1834 (no. 765), a sketch in the *New Jerusalem Magazine*, Jan. 1832 (no. 983), and an article in *Atkinson's Saturday Evening Post*, 1835 (929).

2159. —— 'Blake's Designs for Blair's "Grave", American Edition.' *N&Q*, CXLVIII (1925), 98.
Describes a copy of the N.Y. 1847 edition of *The Grave* with Blake's illustrative plates.

2160. —— 'Blake's "Tyger"—"When the Stars threw down their spears".' *N&Q*, CLXXXIX (1945), 211–12 (vMKN).
The line is explicable in an astrological context.

2161. —— 'The Hour of Blake's Birth.' *N&Q*, CXCIII (1948), 7.
7.45 p.m., according to Hacket.

2162. —— '[3] More American References to Blake before 1863.' *MLN*, XLVII (1932), 87–8.
Points out Blake references in no. 280, 1440, 1890.

2163. Mabbott, Thomas Ollive. 'More Early American Publications of Blake.' *N&Q*, CLXV (1933), 279.
See no. 242, 273.

2164. —— 'William Blake's Allamanda.' *N&Q*, CXC (1946), 16 (vMKN).
From French *allemande*.

2165. —— 'William Blake's "Urizen".' *N&Q*, CLXXIX (1945), 161–2.
From 'your-eyes-on'.

2166. —— (T. O. M.) and Geoffrey Keynes. 'The Text of Blake's "A Fairy Stepd upon my Knee".' *N&Q*, CLXIV (1933), 388–9; CLXV (1933), 302.
T. O. M. corrects Swinburne's transcription of the poem from a facsimile of the manuscript in a sale catalogue; Keynes corrects the text and points out that he had already printed a careful version.

2167. *Mabille, Pierre. 'William Blake.' *Cahiers d'Art*, XX (1947), 117–27 (vMKN).

2168. A. *MacDonald, Greville. 'The Sanity of William Blake.' *Saint George*, XI (1908), 1–31 (vMKN). B. *The Sanity of William Blake*. London, 1908.
The thesis of this amusing lecture is that Blake had an especially sane kind of insanity in an unbalanced world. 'If his words be madness, then is there no hope left for us.'

2169. —— *'William Blake: His Critics and Masters.' *The Vineyard*, No. 8, 9 (1911), 558–71, 626–42.
A responsible amateur approach to Blake.

2170. A. —— 'William Blake, the Practical Idealist.' *Vineyard*, V (1912), 98–110. B. 'Abbreviated Paper on William Blake, Practical Idealist.' Pp. 17–24 of *The First Meeting of The Blake Society* (1912), no. 3015.
'Blake's practical gift . . . [*is*] manifest . . . in his sublime optimism' (B, p. 24).

2171. Mackay, Charles. *Through the Long Day*, or, Memorials of a Literary Life during Half a Century. [2 vols.] London, 1887. Vol. I, p. 389.
Theodore von Holst (1810–44) 'often suggested to my mind, as I looked upon him, what his erratic predecessor, Blake, must have appeared in the eyes of his contemporaries, when the semi- or demi-semi fits of his highly poetical lunacy were upon him'.

2172. Mackenzie, Basil William Sholto. 'The Death of William Blake.' *University College Hospital Magazine*, XIII (1928), 197–9 (vMKN).
Mostly excerpts from Blake's letters concerning his health, with commentary and explanations of the symptoms by the author.

2173. *Maclagen, Sir Eric. 'Drawings and Paintings of William Blake.' *Listener*, 2 Oct. 1947, pp. 569–70 (vMKN).
In the British Council exhibition.

2174. A. Macnish, Robert. *The Philosophy of Sleep.* N.Y., 1834. Pp. 227–8. B. §1836. C. Glasgow & London, 1838. Pp. 258–60. D. Glasgow, London, & Edinburgh, 1845. Pp. 296–8. E. Glasgow & London, 1859. Pp. 152–3.
Cunningham's accounts of Blake's visions are cited as evidence that Blake mistook 'the chimeras of an excited brain for realities'.

2175. Macphail, J. H. 'Blake and Switzerland.' *MLR*, XXXVIII (1943), 80–7.
Blake and Swedenborg, Charles Bonnet, Taylor, and Lavater.

2176. Maillet, Albert. 'Blake et Nietzsche.' *Revue des Lettres Modernes*, No. 76–7 (1962–3), 73–89.
Parallels and differences.

2177. A. Mankowitz, Wolf. 'William Blake (2): The Songs of Experience.' *Politics and Letters*, I (1947), 15–23 (for part 1, see no. 1254). B. Reprinted in Bottrall, no. 1261.
An admirable *explication de texte*.

2178. Margoliouth, Herschel Maurice. 'The Bicentenary of William Blake's Baptism. An Address given in St. James's Church by Mr. H. M. Margoliouth on December 11th, 1957.' *St. James's Church Piccadilly Parish Magazine*, Jan. 1958, pp. 9–16.
Chiefly concerned to demonstrate that Blake believed essentially in the tenets of the Apostles' Creed.

2179. A. —— 'Blake's Drawings for Young's Night Thoughts.' *RES*, N.S. V (1954), 47–54. B. *Reprinted 'in altered form' in Pinto, *Divine Vision* (no. 2402), pp. 191–204.
A description of the drawings and of the scholarship and reproductions of them.

2180. —— 'Blake's Mr. Mathew.' *N&Q*, CXCVI (1951), 162–3.
Points out, for the first time in any study of Blake, that the obscure and untraceable 'Henry Mathew' who helped to publish the *Poetical Sketches* can be given life and history if identified as Anthony Stephen Mathew.

2181. —— 'Blake's "Sons of Albion".' *N&Q*, CXCIV (1949), 94–5.
Identifies the twelve 'sons of Albion' in *Jerusalem* with Blake's contemporaries, chiefly those ranged against him at his trial for sedition.

2182. —— 'The Marriage of Blake's Parents.' *N&Q*, CXCII (1947), 380–1.
Records for the first time the marriage of Blake's parents in St. George's Chapel on 15 Oct. 1752.

2183. —— 'Notes on Blake.' *RES*, XXIV (1948), 303–16.
Presents a number of persuasive 'Biblical References' (pp. 303–12) and literary sources for Blake's treatment of 'Human Sacrifice' (pp. 312–16).

2184. A. —— *William Blake.* London, N.Y., Toronto, 1951. Home University Library. B. *No city [U.S.A.], 1967.

This little book combines in a curious way the excellent historical scholarship shown in Margoliouth's articles on Blake with a strong tendency to popular over-simplification, as in the statement that Blake was 'not so very far from being an orthodox Christian'. Its chief lasting merit is the attempt to trace the development of the myth in the study of individual poems.

2185. Margoliouth, Herschel Maurice. *'William Blake: Historical Painter.' *Studio*, CLIII (1957), 97–103.
Distinguishes between 'what Blake called Historical as opposed to Portrait Painting, imaginative as opposed to representational'.

2186. —— 'William Blake's Family.' *N&Q*, CXCIII (1948), 296–8.
Points out the tenuousness of Ellis & Yeats's story of Blake's Irish ancestry.

2187. §Marken, Ronald. '"Eternity in an Hour"—Blake and Time.' *Discourse*, IX (1966), 167–83.

2188. Marriott, Charles. 'Blake's "Jerusalem".' *TLS*, 24 Jan. 1942, p. 43.
Query concerning the legend that Joseph of Arimathea brought the infant Christ to the English village of Priddy.

2189. §Maruyama, Satoru. '[The Progress of XVIIIth Century English Lyrical Poetry, a Supplement.]' *Yokohama Daigaku Ronso* [*Yokohama Municipal University Society Bulletin*], IX (1958), 77–114.

2190. A. Masefield, John. 'William Blake.' Pp. 280–304 of his *Recent Prose*. London, 1926. B. 1932. C. N.Y., 1933. Pp. 257–78 (vMKN).
A general speech.

2191. [——] *Words on the Anniversary of the Birthday of William Blake.* [London, 1957.]
A 4-page mimeographed address read by Professor Pinto at the ceremony in Westminster Abbey.

2192. Mathews, Godfrey W. 'William Blake.' *Proceedings of the Literary and Philosophical Society of Liverpool*, No. LXVIII (1926), 71–96.
An amateur summary of Blake's life and work.

2193. Matsushita, Senkichi. '"Glee" (Yorokobi no Uta) to Iu Kotoba no Fukkatsu ni tsuite [The Revival of the Word "Glee", meaning "Joy" (or "Song of Joy")], no. 1— Blake no *Muku no Uta* no Baai [In Blake's *Songs of Innocence*].' *Eibungaku Hyoron* [*Review of English Literature*], of the English Department, College of Liberal Arts, Kyoto University, XXV (March 1970), 45–72 (vHK).

2194. Maunder, Samuel. *The Biographical Treasury.* A Dictionary of Universal Biography; intended as A Companion to 'The Treasury of Knowledge.' London, 1838. P. 96.
'BLAKE, William, a highly gifted but very eccentric artist and writer; author of "Europe," a prophecy; "America," a prophecy; "Songs of Experience;" and an infinity of admirable engravings. Born, 1759; died, 1827.'

2195. *Mayer, David, III. 'William Blake and the Juvenile Drama.' *Theatre Notebook*, XVII (1963), 143–4.
Not persuasive.

2196. *McBride, Henry. 'Dante Drawings by William Blake.' *New York Herald*, 16 Oct. 1921 (vMKN).

2197. *McDonald, Robert. 'William Blake's Canterbury Pilgrims.' *Print Collector's Quarterly*, XXV (1938), 185–99.
On distinguishing the several states.

2198. *McDowell, Katherine A. '*Theory*, or *The Graphic Muse*, Engraved by Blake after Reynolds.' *Burlington Magazine*, XI (1907), 113–15 (vMKN).
For a frontispiece for Hoare's *Inquiry*. (See also no. 1582, written under her married name, Esdaile.)

2199. McElderry, B. R., Jr. 'Coleridge on Blake's Songs.' *MLQ*, IX (1948), 298–302 (vRN).
Coleridge's grading of the songs; see no. 1407.

2200. McGlynn, Paul D. 'Blake's THE CHIMNEY SWEEPER (From SONGS OF INNOCENCE).' *Explicator*, XXVII (1968), item 20.
The poem describes 'a dramatically ironic situation'.

2201. McGowan, James Denise. 'Rising Glories: A Study of William Blake's *Poetical Sketches*.' *DAI*, XXIX (1969), 2221A. Rutgers Ph.D., 1968.
In *Poetical Sketches*, 'the sequence of poems . . . seems in fact quite controlled' and is 'probably meaningful'.

2202. *McKenzie, D. F. 'Blake's *Poetical Sketches* (1783).' *Turnbull Library Record*, I, No. 3 (March 1968), 4–8.
Bibliographical description of copy F, with reproductions of the MS additions in ink.

2203. —— 'William Allingham's Notebook of Poems by Blake.' *Turnbull Library Record*, I, No. 3 (March 1968), 9–11.
Allingham transcribed poems from *Poetical Sketches*, the *Songs*, and the Notebook 'in the 1850's'.

2204. Mechlin, Leila. 'Blake's Art Seen.' *Washington Evening Star*, 6 Nov. 1937 (vMKN).

2205. Mégroz, R. L. *Dante Gabriel Rossetti*. Painter of Heaven in Earth. London, 1928. Pp. 235–41.

2206. —— 'William Blake A Radiant Man.' *Aryan Path*, XXVIII (1957), 484–7.
A highly simplified introduction for an Indian audience.

2207. Meissner-Weichert, Hildegund. 'William Blakes Konzeption des ewigen Evangeliums: Ein Beitrag zum Verstaendnis seiner prophet. Buecher.' Freiburg Dissertation, 1955 (according to L. F. McNamee, *Dissertations in English and American Literature* [1968]).

2208. Melchiori, Giorgio. 'L'Influenza di Michelangelo: II—William Blake.' Pp. 91–110 of *Michelangelo nel settocento inglese*. Un Capitolo di Storia del Gusto in Inghilterra. Roma, 1950. Lettere di Pensiero e d'Arte.

2209. —— *The Whole Mystery of Art*: Pattern into Poetry in the Work of W. B. Yeats. London, 1960. *Passim*.

2210. A. §Melikian, Souren. 'Les Poèmes peints du prophète Blake.' *Réalités*, No. 260 (Sept. 1967), 72–8. *B. Tr. as 'William Blake: singer of fearful symmetry.' *Realites*, No. 206 (Jan. 1968), 78–83.
A general article.

2211. *Mellor, Anne Kostelanetz. 'Blake's Designs for *The Book of Thel*: An Affirmation of Innocence.' *PQ*, L (1971), 193–207.
An unconvincing argument that 'Her return to Har, then, is a positive personal action' (p. 205). (See also under the author's maiden name, Anne Kostelanetz.)

2212. *Mellow, James R. 'William Blake: Put-Upon Painter of the Patient Job.' *New York Times*, 19 July 1970, Section 2, p. 17, cols. 1–6.
Autobiographical interpretation of the 21 *Job* water-colours exhibited at the Morgan.

2213. *Melville, Lewis. 'Blake as a Book Illustrator.' *Booklover's Magazine*, VI (1907), 238–43 (vMKN).

2214. *Merchant, W. Moelwyn. 'Blake's Shakespeare.' *Apollo*, LXXIX (1964), 318–25.
A survey of Blake's Shakespeare illustrations with 22 reproductions.

2215. —— *Shakespeare and the Artist*. London, N.Y., & Toronto, 1959. Pp. 81–6.
The only book to deal with Blake's Shakespeare-inspired designs with any detail or thoroughness.

2216. *Messages*, I ([Paris] 1939). Ed. Jean Flory.
The whole issue was devoted to Blake, with articles by Audard, Fridlander, Keynes (a bibliography), Lescure, Read, Saurat, Stutfield, and Vague.

2217. Messiaen, Pierre. 'William Blake, Poète lyrique.' *Revue Bleue Politique et Littéraire*, LXXV (1937), 125–7.
An introduction to Blake, with translations of poems, on the occasion of the exhibition at the Bibliothèque Nationale.

2218. —— 'William Blake (1751–1827).' *Revue de l'Enseignement des Langues Vivantes*, LVI (1939), 145–9.
An introduction to Blake, in French, with several poems translated.

2219. Meyerstein, E. H. W. '"A True Maid" and "The Sick Rose".' *TLS*, 22 June 1946, p. 295.
Suggests Prior's poem as a source of Blake's.

2220. A. Miles, Josephine. 'The Language of William Blake.' Pp. 141–69 of *English Institute Essays 1950*. Ed. Alan S. Downer. N.Y., 1951. B. Reprinted as 'The Sublimity of William Blake'. Chapter V, pp. 78–99 of *Eras & Modes in English Poetry*. Berkeley & Los Angeles [Calif.], 1957.

This pioneering study of Blake's poetic vocabulary points out that Blake used rather conventional words and did not alter his choice very significantly in his later poetry.

2221. A. *Milner, Marion [i.e. Joanna Field]. 'Psycho-Analysis and Art.' Chap. iv (pp. 77–101) of *Psycho Analysis and Contemporary Thought*. Ed. John Sutherland. London, 1958. The International Psycho-Analytical Library No. 53. B. N.Y., 1959.

Includes an earnest psycho-analysis of Blake's *Job* plates, esp. pp. 84–99.

2222. A. Milnes, Richard Monckton, Lord Houghton. *Life, Letters, and Literary Remains, of John Keats*. In Two Volumes. London, 1848. B. Complete in One Volume. N.Y., 1848. P. 190. C. *The Life and Letters of John Keats*. A New Edition. In One Volume. London, 1867. P. 245. D. §London & N.Y., 1906. New Universal Library. E. §London, Toronto, N.Y., 1927. Everyman's Library. F. London, 1931. World's Classics. P. 206.

A and B are said to be edited by R. M. Milnes, while the rest are 'By Lord Houghton', though E gives both names. The allusion to Blake is a very casual one; the omitted stanza of 'Melancholy' (with its 'bark of dead men's bones') is said to be 'as grim a picture as Blake or Fuseli could have dreamed or painted'.

2223. A. Milsand, J. 'Un Précurseur du XIXᵉ Siècle: W. Blake, le Peintre, le Poète et le Visionnaire.' *Revue Moderne*, XLIV (1868), 5–41. B. Reprinted as pp. 305–46 of his *Littérature anglaise et philosophie*. Dijon, 1893.

A survey of an unknown.

2224. Mims, Edwin. 'William Blake: Rebel & Prophet.' Pp. 119–44 of *The Christ of the Poets*. N.Y. & Nashville [Tenn.], 1948 (vDVE).

2225. *Miner, Paul. 'The Apprentice of Great Queen Street.' *BNYPL*, LXVII (1963), 639–42.

Attribution to Blake of drawings from monuments in Westminster Abbey.

2226. —— '"Newton's Pantocrator".' *N&Q*, CCVI [N.S. VIII] (1961), 15–16.

Argues that Blake took his phrase from Newton's *Mathematical Principles of Natural Philosophy*, tr. A. Motte (1729), ii. 389–92. See also no. 2402 7.

2227. —— 'The Polyp as a Symbol in the Poetry of William Blake.' *Studies in Literature and Language*, II (1960), 198–205.

An examination of the 'tenuous threads [in Blake's poetry] which help to explicate and define the genesis of the polyp as a nucleating symbol.'

2228. —— '"The Tyger": Genesis & Evolution in the Poetry of William Blake.' *Criticism*, IV (1962), 59–73.

Traces the development of Blake's feline symbolism and its relevance to 'The Tyger'.

2229. Miner, Paul. 'William Blake: Two Notes on Sources. (1) Blake's Use of Gray's "Fatal Sisters" (2) A Source for Blake's Enion?' *BNYPL*, LXII (1958), 203–7.

Gray's influence on *Vala* Night VIII, *Milton*, and *Jerusalem*; a source for Enion in Drayton's *Poly-Olbion*.

2230. —— 'William Blake's "Divine Analogy".' *Criticism*, III (1961), 46–61.

Discusses the Biblical bases and analogues (chiefly in the Pentateuch) for Blake's concept that 'the act of coitus becomes a propitiatory offering, a sacrifice of the selfhood' (p. 50).

2231. —— *'William Blake's London Residences.' *BNYPL*, LXII (1958), 535–50.

The traditional chronology revised on evidence from the Rate Books.

2232. *Misciatelli, Piero. 'Un Poeta Pittore: William Blake.' *Vita d'Arte* [Sienna], IV (1909), 470–82.

2233. *Mitchell, William John Thomas. 'Poetic and Pictorial Imagination in Blake's *The Book of Urizen.' *Eighteenth-Century Studies*, III (1969), 83–107.

'In the painting, as in the poetry, anything can be a metaphor for anything else' (p. 107).

2234. —— 'Blake's Composite Art: The Relationship of Text and Design in the Illuminated Poetry of William Blake.' *DA*, XXIX (1969), 1874A. Johns Hopkins Ph.D.

Traces a 'dialectic' relationship in *Thel*, *Urizen*, and *Jerusalem*.

2235. Mizuta, Iwao. 'Yeats ni okeru Blake no Eikyo—Hitotsu no Josetsu [The Influence of Blake on Yeats—An Introduction].' *Yamaguchi Daigaku Bungakukai shi* [*Magazine of Yamaguchi University Literary Association*], III (1952), 61–72.

2236. M[onroe], H[arriet]. 'Christmas and William Blake.' *Poetry*, XXXI (1927), 148–55 (vMKN).

A centenary tribute characterizing his verse as 'dewey' and his voice as 'flutelike'.

2237. Montgomery, John. 'Felpham and the Poets.' *Sussex County Magazine*, XXI (1947), 124–6 (vWKenney).

Narrates the events bringing Blake to Felpham, and remarks that Hayley's residence and Blake's cottage are still there.

2238. [Moody, Christopher Lake.] 'Art. 37. *A Father's Memoirs of his Child.* By Benj. Heath Malkin, Esq. M.A. F.A.S. Royal 8vo. 10s. 6d. Boards. Longman and Co 1806.' *Monthly Review*, n.s. LI (Oct. 1806), 217. (BM)

'In the long dedication to Mr. Johnes of Hafod, a biographical notice is inserted of Mr. William Blake the artist, with some selections from his poems, which are highly extolled: but if Watts seldom rose above the level of a mere versifier, in what class must we place Mr. Blake, who is certainly very inferior to Dr. Watts?'

The authorship is established by Benjamin Christie Nangle (*The Monthly Review Second Series 1790–1815* [1955], p. 259) on the basis of the editor's marked copy (now in the Bodleian) in which this piece is attributed to 'Mo[od]y'.

2239. *Moore, C. H. 'Amedee Pichot's Discovery of Blake.' *Études Anglaises*, XVI (1963), 54–8. See no. 2392.

2240. A. *Moore, T. Sturge. 'Blake and his Aesthetic.' Pp. 193–216 of his *Art and Life*. London, 1910. B. Summarized in Anon. 'The Vital Import of Esthetics as Illustrated by Flaubert and Blake.' *Current Literature*, XLIX (1910), 325–8 (vMKN).

2241. A. —— 'William Blake, Poet and Painter.' *Quarterly Review*, CCVIII (1908), 24–53. B. Revised as *'Visionary Art.' Pp. 217–41 of his *Art and Life*. London, 1910.
A general review of Blake and fifteen books about him.

2242. Moore, Virginia. 'Blake as a Major Doctrinal Influence.' Pp. 84–102 of *The Unicorn*: William Butler Yeats' Search for Reality. N.Y., 1954.

2243. —— 'Religion and William Butler Yeats.' Columbia Ph.D., 1952; cf. *DA*, XII (1952), 427 (vMKN).
Chapter iv is on Blake's influence.

2244. A. §More, Paul Elmer. 'William Blake.' *New York Evening Post*, 1905. B. Reprinted as pp. 212–38 of his *Shelburne Essays*. Fourth Series. N.Y. & London, 1906.
A review of Sampson.

2245. Morley, Christopher. 'An Alphabet of the Abyss.' *Saturday Review of Literature*, IV (6 Aug. 1927), 23.
Centenary impressions; *Experience* has 'a whole alphabet of the abyss'.

2246. Morley, Edith. 'Blake and Wordsworth.' *TLS*, 28 May 1925, p. 368.
Not really about Blake: merely corrects errors in her edition of Crabb Robinson.

2247. Morris, H. N. 'Blake and Swedenborg.' *Quest*, XI (1919), 69–82.
This rather assertive address to the Blake Society on Blake's debt to Swedenborg depends rather upon the faith of a believer than on the facts of scholarship.

2248. A. —— 'William Blake, Artist and Poet.' *New Church Young People's Magazine*, V (1909), 160, 181, 204. B. Reprinted as 'William Blake', pp. 75–104 of his *Flaxman Blake Coleridge and other men of Genius Influenced by Swedenborg* together with Flaxman's Allegory of the 'Knight of the Blazing Cross'. London, 1915.
Strikingly inaccurate.

2249. Morris, Lloyd R. 'William Blake: The First of the Moderns.' *Forum* [*and Century*], LI (1914), 932–9 (vMKN).
General article.

2250. Morse, B. J. 'Dante Gabriel Rossetti and William Blake.' *Englische Studien*, LXVI (1932), 364–72 (vMKN).

2251. Morton, A. L. *The Everlasting Gospel*: A study in the sources of William Blake. London, 1958.
Morton 'was able to trace the essentials of all Blake's main ideas in these seventeenth century' pamphleteers, chiefly Ranters, Muggletonians, and other extreme dissenters. His thesis, briefly developed (64 pp.), is that Blake participates in a radical politico-religious tradition that was most vocal and extreme in the seventeenth century, and his 'sources' illustrate illuminating currents of thought rather than books Blake read.

2252. A. Moulton, Charles Wells, assisted by a corps of able contributors, eds. 'William Blake.' Vol. V, pp. 56–64 of *The Library of Literary Criticism of English and American Authors*. [8 vols.] Buffalo, 1902. B. N.Y., 1935. Vol. V, pp. 56–64.
A collection of observations on various literary figures, Blake among others.

2253. Mowbray, Charlotte. 'Tatham's Life of Blake.' *N&Q*, CXIII [10th Ser., V] (1906), 108–9.
What and where is Tatham's life of Blake?

2254. §Moyer, Patricia. 'William Blake, Critic of Literature and Art.' Nottingham University Ph.D., 1964.

2255. Moynihan, Florence. 'Francis Thompson and Blake.' *Catholic Educational Review*, XV (1918), 306–8.
'Of the various influences present in Francis Thompson's poems that of Blake seems paramount.'

2256. Mueller, Kurt. 'William Blake als Vorlaeufer der englischen Romantik.' Marburg Ph.D., 1922 (according to L. F. McNamee, *Dissertations in English and American Literature* [1968]).

2257. Mulchahy, T. I. 'William Blake, Poet and Painter.' *Irish Monthly*, L (1922), 519–26.

2258. Munby, A. N. L. 'Letters of British Artists of the XVIIIth and XIXth Centuries—Part I.' *Connoisseur*, CXVIII (1946), 24–8, 64.
Reproduces Flaxman's letter to Blake of 7 Oct. 1801 (among other material not relevant to Blake).

2259. M[unsterberg], M[argaret]. 'The Dante Engravings of William Blake.' *More Books*, XVII (1942), 223.
On their acquisition by the Boston Public Library.

2260. Murray, Helen G. 'So This Is Blake.' *Christian Century*, XLIX (1932), 1199–1200 (vMKN)
Blake has moments of realism.

2261. A. Murry, John Middleton. '"To Redeem the Contraries".' *Adelphi*, N.S. VII (1934), 361–9 (vMKN). B. Reprinted as 'Blake and Keats', pp. 215–26 of *Looking Before and After*. London, 1948. C. Revised and reprinted as 'Keats and Blake'. Pp. 241–53 of *The Mystery of Keats*. London & N.Y., 1949. D. Reprinted as pp. 292–304 of *Keats*. [4th edition.] London, 1955.

Keats's 'Beauty is Truth' may be understood by understanding Blake's 'Divine Imagination' (B).

2262. A. —— *William Blake*. London, 1933. B. London & Toronto, 1936. The Life and Letters Series No. 76. C. N.Y., Toronto, London, 1964.

Murry carefully eschews Blake's other interpreters, and, perhaps therefore, is able to conclude that he is both a 'Christian' and 'a great Communist'. A good deal of the author gets between the reader and Blake, but Murry's enthusiasm, and his fair treatment of Blake's development, make this a useful if unreliable book.

2263. A. —— 'William Blake and Revolution.' *New Adelphi*, N.S. IV (1932), 536–43. B. Tr. Bunsho Jugaku in no. 1219 25.

Deals with the comprehensive freedom perceived by Blake and by all revolutionaries.

2264. Muses, C. A. 'Blake and Boehme.' *Jacob Boehme Society Quarterly*, I, No. 6 (Winter 1953–4), 15.

A brief note.

2265. Musgrove, A. J. 'Blake Exhibition Is Gallery Treat.' *Winnipeg Tribune*, 14 Feb. 1942.

On the Blake exhibition at the Winnipeg Gallery, no. 653.

N

2266. N., N. 'William Blake at the Tate Gallery.' *Nation*, XCVII (1913), 573–4 (vRN).

2267. A. Nagler, Dr. G. K. 'Blake, William.' Vol. I [1835], pp. 519–22, of *Neues allgemeines Künstler-Lexicon oder Nachrichten von dem Leben und den Werken der Maler, Bildhauer, Baumeister, Kupferstecher, Formschneider, Lithographen, Zeichner, Medailleure, Elfenbeinarbeiter*, etc. [25 vols.] Munchen, 1835[–51]. B. Vol. I [1904], pp. 539–43 of the edition of Linz, 1904–14, 25 vols.

An ambitious though necessarily derivative account of Blake. He is also mentioned under Flaxman (A, IV. 365).

2268. *Nanavutty, Piloo. 'Blake and Emblem Literature.' *JWCI*, XV (1952), 258–61.

Some emblematic sources for Blake's designs.

2269. —— 'Some Eastern Influences on William Blake's Prophetic Books.' Cambridge Ph.D., 1939. See *Cambridge University Abstracts of Dissertations, During the Academical Year 1938–1939* (1940), 73.

'The purpose of this dissertation has been to investigate further the Gnostic, Cabbalistic, and Hindu influences on William Blake's Prophetic Books.'

2270. Nanavutty, Piloo. *'A Title Page in Blake's Illustrated Genesis Manuscript.' *JWCI*, X (1947), 114–22.
An interpretation, showing that creation implied conflict and a liberation of the spirit through suffering.

2271. —— and Mark Perugini. 'Puzzling Names in Blake.' *TLS*, 3, 10 July 1937, pp. 496, 512.
On possible sources of Or-Udan, Vala, Ahania.

2272. Nathan, Norman. 'Blake and Nontheism.' *PMLA*, LXXV (1960), 147.
Rejects the classification by Bloom (no. 1129) of Blake as a 'nontheist'.

2273. —— 'Blake's "Head Downwards".' *N&Q*, CXCV (1950), 302–3 (vMKN).
Christ treated like a Jewish criminal, executed with the head downwards.

2274. —— 'Blake's Infant Sorrow.' *N&Q*, n.s. VII (1960), 99–100 (vMKN).
Corrects Wickstead's interpretation (no. 2954).

2275. —— *Prince William B.* The Philosophical Conceptions of William Blake. N.Y., 1949 (vMKN).
An abridgement of a New York University Ph.D. (1947) of little merit.

2276. *La Navire d'Argent*, I ([Paris] Sept. 1925); issue devoted to Blake, with articles by Anon. (1027), Swinburne, and Symons.

2277. Nekrasova, Ekaterina Alekseevna. 'Iz Istorii Angliiskoi Knizhnoi Grafiki [The History of Graphic Writing] (William Blake).' Pp. 229–35 of *Iskusstvo Knigi* [*The Culture of the Book*], Moscow, 1961.

2278. —— *Tvorchestvio Vil'iama Bleika.* Moscow, 1962. 72 pp., 48 plates.

2279. Nelson, John Walter. 'Blake's Minor Prophecies: A Study of the Development of His Major Prophetic Mode.' Ohio State University Ph.D., 1970.

2280. Nemerov, Howard. 'Two Ways of Imagination.' *Carleton Miscellany*, V (Fall 1964), 18–41.
Natural beauty in the *Prelude* versus imagined beauty in *Jerusalem*.

2281. *Newberry, John S. 'William Blake's Original Line-Engravings in the Philadelphia Exhibition.' *Print Collector's Quarterly*, XXVI (1939), 67–81 (vMKN).

2282. Newsom, Barbara. 'Tracing the Origins of *Heartbreak House*: William Blake's Influence on Shaw.' *Independent Shavian*, VIII (1969–70), 31.
Report of an assertive 'talk' concerning 'strong parallels between . . . *Heartbreak House* and Blake's *Four Zoas*'.

2283. A. *Newton, Alfred Edward. 'A Sane View of Blake.' Pp. 196–221 of *A Magnificent Farce and Other Diversions of a Book Collector*. Boston, 1921. B. 1921. C. 1921. D. London & Boston, [1922].

An amusing personal essay about the pleasure of buying Blake's works.

2284. —— *'Works of William Blake.' *Pennsylvania Museum Bulletin*, May 1926, pp. 162–5.

Description of an exhibition.

2285. *Nicoll, Allardyce. *William Blake & his Poetry*. London, 1922. Poetry & Life Series.

A popular, ill-informed biography which accepts the preposterous O'Neil genealogy and concludes that the 'longer prophecies are entire failures', 'a chaos of heterogeneous pages'.

2286. A. Nicoll, W. Robertson, & Thomas J. Wise. 'The Trial of William Blake for Sedition.' Vol. I, pp. 2–17 of their *Literary Anecdotes of the Nineteenth Century*. [2 vols.] London, [Vol. I] 1895, [Vol. II] 1896. B. Reprinted as a separate, anonymous pamphlet.

Reprints the Information of Scofield (pp. 5–6) and The Speech of Counsellor Rose (pp. 11–17).

2287. A. Nicolson, Marjorie Hope. 'Epilogue: The Poetic Damnation of Newton.' Pp. 165–74 of her *Newton Demands the Muse*: Newton's *Opticks* and the Eighteenth Century Poets. Princeton [N.J.], 1946. History of Ideas Series No. 2. B. Hamden, Connecticut, 1963. Archon Books. C. Princeton, 1966.

An 'easy résumé' 'of Blake's "Newtonianiasm"' (p. 165 n).

2288. Nishida, Noboru. 'Blake no Seijitsu—Kare no Innocence yori Experience eno Iko no Ichikosatsu [A Consideration on Blake's "Peculiar Honesty" through his Innocence and Experience].' *Yamagata Daigaku Kiyo* (Jinbun Kagaku): *Bulletin of the Yamagata University* (Cultural Science), II (1952), 153–68.

2289. Nitchie, Elizabeth. 'Blake's *The Tyger*.' *Explicator*, I (1943), item 34 (vMKN).

Relates the fifth stanza to *Vala*.

2290. A. *Norman, Hubert J. *Cowper and Blake*. A Paper Read at the 13th Annual Meeting of the Cowper Society. With a Summary of the other Papers read on that occasion. [Ed. T. Wright?] Olney, [1913]. B. §Folcroft, Pennsylvania, 1972.

All but the titular essay are exclusively on Cowper. Norman's essay (pp. 18–57) is merely conversational about both his subjects.

2291. A. —— *'William Blake.' *Journal of Mental Sciences*, LXI (1915), 198–244. *B. Reprinted as *William Blake*. London, 1915.

A detailed argument that Blake's condition may 'be classified as one of maniacal-depressive insanity' (B, p. 44).

2292. Norton, Charles Eliot. *Letters of Charles Eliot Norton* with Biographical Comment by His Daughter Sara Norton and M. A. DeWolfe Howe. [2 vols.] Boston & N.Y., 1913. Vol. I, p. 376.
A charming anecdote about Mr. Blake in Paradise from Seymour Kirkup in 1870.

2293. Novak, Jane. 'Verisimilitude and Vision: Defoe and Blake as Influences On Joyce's Molly Bloom.' *Carrell*, VIII (1967), 7–20.
Based on Joyce's lecture, but not much on Blake.

2294. *Noyes, Alfred. 'William Blake.' *Bookman*, XXX (1906), 201–11.
A general article, stimulated by the reissue of Swinburne's book (no. 2795), with 20 plates.

2295. Nurmi, Martin Karl. 'Blake's Doctrine of Contraries: A Study in Visionary Metaphysics.' University of Minnesota Ph. D., 1954; cf. *DA*, XIV (1954), 977–8 (vMKN).

2296. A. —— *Blake's Marriage of Heaven and Hell*: A Critical Study. Kent, Ohio, 1957. Kent State University Bulletin Research Series III. B. §N.Y., 1972.
The *Marriage* 'is a shapely masterpiece' (p. iii). Extracts are reprinted in Grant's anthology.

2297. A. —— 'Blake's Revisions of *The Tyger*.' *PMLA*, LXXI (1956), 669–85. B. Reprinted in Bottrall (no. 1261), and Weathers (no. 2937).
A study of the evolution of the poem in the Notebook.

2298. A. —— 'Fact and Symbol in "The Chimney Sweeper" of Blake's *Songs of Innocence*.' *BNYPL*, LXVIII (1964), 249–56. B. Reprinted in Frye, no. 1643.
A careful study of the background of the poem.

2299. —— 'Joy, Love, and Innocence in Blake's "Mental Traveller".' *Studies in Romanticism*, III (1964), 109–17.
A reading.

2300. Nutt, Thomas. 'Lord Crewe's Blake Collection.' *Critic*, XLII (1903), 463–4.
Mentions a MS poem, 'W. Blake—on the publication of Klopstock's "Messiah"' [transcribed by Swinburne].

O

2301. O., C., and F. G. Stephens. 'William Blake, the Poet and Painter.' *N&Q*, XL [5th Ser., IV] (1875), 129, 316.
Query concerning Blake's alleged stay in a madhouse, prompted by

Richardson (no. 2516; see also no. 1004), and a reply (see also no. 2355, which shows the story to be ridiculous).

2302. *O'C[onnor], J., Jr. 'Drawings and Engravings by William Blake.' *Carnegie Magazine*, X (1936), 43–4 (vMKN).

2303. Ogawa, Jiro. 'Blake and Imagination.' *Eigo Seinen: The Rising Generation*, C (1954), 283–4.

2304. —— 'Blake ni yoru Bungakuteki Jinseikan [(My) View of Life Inspired by Blake].' *Eigo Seinen: The Rising Generation*, XCV (1949), 169–70.

2305. —— *Mushin to Keiken no Uta Kenkyu*: A Study on William Blake's *Songs of Innocence and of Experience*. Kyoto, 1950. 298 pp.
Thesis in Japanese.

2306. —— 'Notes on Some Poems of William Blake's Rossetti MS.' *Eibungaku Kenkyu: Studies in English Literature*, XXXII (1956), 185–97.

2307. —— 'A Study of William Blake's "Songs of Innocence and of Experience".' *Hiroshima Daigaku Bungakubu Kiyo: The Hiroshima University Studies Literary Department*, No. 11 (1957), 197–231; No. 13 (1958), 232–52; No. 14 (1958), 253–72.
The first part is called 'Thematic Structure'; the rest are on individual songs of *Innocence*.

2308. —— *'William Blake no Shi [William Blake's Poem].' *Youth's Companion*, Sept. 1948, pp. 34–7.
The poem is 'Infant Sorrow'.

2309. —— 'William Blake no Shi Kenkyu [A Study of a Poem of William Blake].' *Eigo Seinen: The Rising Generation*, XCIV (1948), 336–8.
The poem is 'Lafayette'.

2310. O'Higgins, Elizabeth. 'Blake's Joy of the Yew.' *Dublin Magazine*, XXXI, No. 1 (Jan.–March 1956), 21–9.
Concludes that Blake composed first in Irish and then translated into English. Ostensibly it is about the Irishness of 'Infant Joy'.

2311. —— 'The Fairy in the Streaked Tulip of Suibhne Geilt, Cennfaeladh O Neill, and William Blake.' *Dublin Magazine*, XXVII (July–Sept. 1952), 17–29; XXVII (Oct.–Dec. 1952), 7–19.
'Recognition of Blake's Irish origin has led to a new understanding of some old problems in Irish literature.' (Part I, p. 17.)

2312. —— 'Irish Words in William Blake's Mythology.' *Dublin Magazine*, XXV (Oct.–Dec. 1950), 27–33; XXVI (Jan.–March 1951), 25–39.
'Blake's names are in general the rendering of Irish sounds into English spelling.' (XXV, 27.)

2313. —— 'William Blake, Son of the Sandal.' *Dublin Magazine*, XXVII (April–June 1952), 4–12.

The sandal episode in *Milton* is said to follow the ritual of inauguration of O'Neill in Ulster.

Ojima, Shotaro; see Oshima, Shotaro.

2314. *Okamoto, Kenjiro. *Blake*. Tokyo, 1970. Critical Biographies of the Artists Series (vHK).
There are 53 plates.

2315. —— *'Blake.' Pp. 171–98 in his *Eikoku no Kaiga* [*English Pictorial Arts*]. Tokyo, 1953.
In Japanese.

2316. —— *'Blake-sono Ichi [Blake's Position].' *Mizue* [*Water-colour Paintings*], No. 606 (1956), 31–8.

2317. —— §*'William Blake no Ucho-Kankaku-teki Sekai.' *Mizue* [*Water-colour Paintings*], No. 763 (Aug. 1968), 3–21.
33 plates.

2318. Okui, Kiyoshi. 'Hana 2-rin—Blake Kenkyu no Jo [A Rose and a Sun-Flower—A Preface to the Study of Blake].' *Toyo Daigaku Kiyo: Journal of the Toyo University*, No. 12 (1958), 75–84.

2319. —— '"Muku no Uta" ["Songs of Innocence" (1) ([2])].' *Hakusan Eibungaku* [*Hakusan English Literary Magazine*], No. 1–2 (1958), 45–57, 87–106 (vHK).
Part 1 is subtitled 'Scrooge no Kofuku [Surrender of Scrooge]' and Part 2 'Blake Shoko [An Essay on Blake]'.

2320. Oldcastle, John. 'Artist and Wife.' *Magazine of Art*, IV (1881), 478–81 (vMKN).
On Catherine Blake.

2321. A. Oldmeadow, E. M. 'Blake, William.' Pp. 140–2 (Vol. I) of [M.] *Bryan's Dictionary of Painters and Engravers*. Ed. George C. Williamson. [5 vols.] London, 1904. B. 1920 [other volumes in the latter edition are dated: II, 1920; III, 1919; IV and V, 1921].
A revised version of M. M. Heaton's article.

2322. Oliphant, Mrs. [Margaret O.] *The Literary History of England* in the End of the Eighteenth and Beginning of the Nineteenth Century. In Three Volumes. London, 1882. Vol. II, pp. 285–94 (vDVE).

2323. Olivero, Federico. 'Sulla Tecnica Poetica di William Blake.' Pp. 1–28 of Olivero's *Studi sul Romanticisma Inglesa*. Bari [Italy], 1914.

2324. §Olivier, T. 'The Voice of the Bard in Blake's "Songs of Experience".' *Theoria*, XXXIII (1969), 71–6.

2325. 'Olybrius.' 'Blake's *The Clod and the Pebble*.' *Explicator*, I (1943), item 32 (vMKN).
Four meanings sometimes and two always in Blake's poems.

2326. O'Malley, Frank. 'The Wasteland of William Blake.' *Review of Politics*, IX (1947), 183–204 (vDS).

2327. O'Neill, Judith, ed. *Critics on Blake*: Readings in Literary Criticism. London, 1970. Readings in Literary Criticism 7.

'Introduction' (pp. 7–8) parts of letters and MSS of Blake, Coleridge, Lamb, and Crabb Robinson; fragments of essays and books by Anon. (*London University Magazine* [1830]), Blunt (1959), William Carey (1827), Cunningham (1830), Damon (1924), Digby, T. S. Eliot, Erdman (*Prophet*), Fischer (1961), Gilchrist, Hungerford, Hunt (1809), R. D. Laing (*The Divided Self* [1965], 162), Malkin, J. M. Murry (ed. *Visions*), Percival, Martin Price, Herbert Read (*The Contrary Experience* [1963], 161), Schorer (1946) J. T. Smith (1845), Swinburne (1868), Symons (1907), Wickstead (*Job*), and Yeats (ed. *Poems* [1893]); and genuine, whole essays by Frye (no. 1644), Gleckner (no. 1699), and Sutherland (no. 2782).

2328. Oppenheimer, Jane M. 'A Note on William Blake and John Hunter.' *Journal of the History of Medicine and Applied Sciences*, I (1946), 41–6.

Jack Tearguts in the *Island* was John Hunter, founder of experimental surgery.

2329. Orchard, M. *A Commentary & Questionnaire on Songs of Innocence and Songs of Experience*. London, Bath, Melbourne, Toronto, N.Y., 1927. Commentaries and Questionnaires on English Literature.

For children, with questions at the end (pp. 18–32).

2330. *Ordish, T. Fairman. 'Blake and London (with Special Reference to Lambeth).' *London Topographical Record*, IX (1914), 35–47.

A Blake Society Address with a correction of the story by Tatham (no. 2823) about Astley.

2331. Ortiz Behety, Luis. *William Blake, o La transfiguración*. Buenos Aires, 1942. 61 pp. (vDVE).

2332. A. *Oshima, Shotaro. *Blake to Celt Bungaku Shiso: Blake and Celtic Literature*. Tokyo, 1933. 113 pp. B. Revised and included in 'Blake to Celt no Shinpishiso [Blake and Celtic Mysticism]', Chap. IV, pp. 159–208 of his *Igirisu Bungaku to Shiteki Sozo*—Celt Minzoku no Rinshitsu no Tenkai [*English Literature and Poetic Imagination*: The Development of Celtic Racial Characteristics and Culture]. Tokyo, 1953.

A. The text of the first version is in Japanese except for 'William Blake and Macpherson's "Ossian"' (pp. 85–99), presumably reprinted from no. 2333.

B. In the second version, there is in addition 'Celt Bungaku to Eibungaku no Shiteki Sozo [Poetic Imagination in Celtic and English Literature]' (Chap. II), including Part I: 'Blake no "Doshinsenchojoshi" [Blake's "Auguries of Innocence"]', pp. 42–7, and Part II, 'Blake no Sozo to sono Ruihi [Imagination in Blake and other Poets]', pp. 47–52.

2333. —— 'Some Notes on William Blake and Macpherson's "Ossian".'

Eibungaku Kenkyu: Studies in English Literature Compiled by The English Seminar of The Tokyo Imperial University, X (1930), 535–49.
 Apparently reprinted in no. 2332.

2334. Osmond, Percy H. 'Byrom, Brooke, and Blake.' Chap. VIII (pp. 250–90) of his *The Mystical Poets of the English Church.* London & N.Y., 1919.
 'It is a little annoying to find people wasting time in the elucidation of his [*Blake's*] mystifying myths' (p. 285).

2335. Ostriker, Alicia S. *Vision and Verse in William Blake.* Madison & Milwaukee, 1965. Chap. 5 is reprinted in Paley's anthology.
 A sensitive and responsible commentary on Blake's prosody.

2336. —— 'William Blake: A Study in Poetic Technique.' Wisconsin Ph.D., 1963 (according to L. F. McNamee, *Dissertations in English and American Literature* [1968]).

2337. Owen, A. L. 'All Things Begin and End in Albion's Ancient Druid Rocky Shore.' Pp. 224–40 of Owen's *The Famous Druids.* A survey of three centuries of English literature on the Druids. Oxford, 1962.
 No scholar is better equipped than Owen to recount the eccentric development of neo-Druidism, or to demonstrate that 'Blake's borrowings from the literature on the Druids shows how widely he had read in it, and how ingeniously he applied his borrowings' (pp. 228–9).

2338. Owlett, F. C. 'Blake as a Romantic sees him.' Pp. 29–35 of *Chatterton's Apology* with a Short Essay on Blake and a Note on Cowper. N.p. [England], 1930.
 Minor.

2339. §Ozaki, Yasushi. 'Jojo Shijin to Shite no W. Blake no Koso [The Einbildungskraft of W. Blake as a Lyric Poet].' *Seinangakuin Daigaku Ronshu* [*Seinangakuin University Review*], III (1951), 1–35; IV (1952), 71–86.

P

2340. P. Letter on the Tabarde Inn in *Gentleman's Magazine,* LXXXII (Sept. 1812), 217. (Bodley)
 'A well-painted Sign [*sic*] by Mr. Blake represents Chaucer and his merry Company setting out on their journey.'

2341. P., C. K. 'Blake's THE CLOD AND THE PEBBLE.' *Explicator,* I (1942), query 11 (vMKN).
 Trivial.

2342. P., F. 'The World's Window.' *Vancouver World,* 12 April 1918, p. 4; *17 April 1918, p. 4; 15 Dec. 1919, p. 4.
 Blake discussed.

2343. Paden, W. D., & Gerhard H. W. Zuther. 'Blake's "Jerusalem", Plate 28: A Further Correction.' *N&Q,* CCX [N.S. XII] (1965), 182–3.
 To Erdman's description (no. 1574).

2344. Paley, Morton David. 'Blake in Nighttown.' Chap. ix (pp. 175–87) of *A James Joyce Miscellany*. Third Series. Ed. Marvin Magalaner. Carbondale (Ill.), 1962.

Blake and Joyce had the same sources.

2345. —— *'Cowper as Blake's Spectre.' Eighteenth Century Studies*, I (1968), 236–52.

'There is much to suggest that the model for the Spectre of *Jerusalem* 10 was . . . William Cowper.'

2346. —— 'Energy and the Imagination: A Study of the Development of Blake's Thought.' *DA*, XXVIII (1967), 689A–690A. Columbia Ph.D., 1964.

2347. ——*Energy and the Imagination*: A Study of the Development of Blake's Thought. Oxford, 1970.

As Blake's myth develops, Orc (energy) diminishes in importance and Los (imagination) becomes central.

The book incorporates revised versions of Paley's articles on 'The Mental Traveller', *Ahania*, and 'The Tyger', and apparently his doctoral dissertation as well.

2348. A. —— 'The Female Babe and "The Mental Traveller".' *Studies in Romanticism*, I (1962), 97–104. B. Incorporated in his *Energy and Imagination* (1970).

2349. A. —— 'Method and Meaning in Blake's *Book of Ahania*.' *BNYPL*, LXX (1966), 27–33. B. Incorporated in his *Energy and Imagination* (1970).

2350. A. —— 'Tyger of Wrath.' *PMLA*, LXXXI (1966), 540–51. B. Reprinted in anthologies of Paley and Weathers and incorporated in his *Energy and Imagination* (1970).

'How would an ideal contemporary reader . . . have regarded "The Tyger"' chiefly in relation to Old Testament typology and the Sublime? See the rebuttal by Tolley and the reply by Paley, no. 1217 3.

2351. A. Palgrave, Francis Turner. *Handbook to the Fine Art Collections in the International Exhibition of 1862*. London & Cambridge, 1862. Pp. 65–6. B. Second Edition, Revised and Completed. London & Cambridge, 1862. Pp. 65–6.

Though showing 'penetrative imagination', 'it is hardly as art that his strange creations appeal to us'.

2352. Palgrave, Gwenllian F. *Francis Turner Palgrave*: His Journals and Memories of his Life. London, N.Y., Bombay, 1899. Pp. 26–7, 80, 111, 116, 146–7, 152.

Impressions of Blake's works, some before 1863.

2353. A. Palmer, A. H. *The Life and Letters of Samuel Palmer*, Painter & Etcher. London, 1892. Pp. 8–10, 13, 15, 16, 21, 23–8, 170, 241–8, 251. B. 1970.

Apparently first-hand accounts of Blake.

2354. Palmer, A. H. *Samuel Palmer*, A Memoir. Also a Catalogue of his Works, including those exhibited by The Fine Art Society 1881, and an account of the Milton Series of Drawings, by L. R. Valpy. London, 1882. Pp. 2–3.

A contemporary reference to Blake.

2355. Palmer, Samuel. 'Fictions Concerning William Blake.' *Athenaeum*, No. 2498 (11 Sept. 1875), pp. 348–9.

Palmer couples his authority with that of Linnell to demolish the silly idea (specifically of Dr. Richardson, but cf. no. 2516, 2301) that Blake spent 30 years in a madhouse.

2356. —— *Samuel Palmer's Sketch-Book*. An Introduction and Commentary by Martin Butlin with a preface by Geoffrey Keynes. [London?] 1962.

A reference to Blake.

2357. —— *Samuel Palmer's Valley of Vision*. Forty-eight plates With an introduction & notes by Geoffrey Grigson and a selection from Samuel Palmer's writings. London, 1960. Pp. 3–9, 17–18.

A previously unpublished note about Blake from Palmer's sketchbook is printed on p. 17.

2358. *Parr, James. 'Songs of Imprudence.' *Humanities association bulletin*, XVII (1966), 97–110.

Ingeniously illustrated parodies of the *Songs*, with a 'foreword' by Wilfred Watson (p. 98).

2359. Parris, Leslie. 'William Blake's Mr. Thomas.' *TLS*, 5 Dec. 1968, p. 1390.

'*A* fair amount can be discovered about Thomas, and he emerges as one of Blake's more considerable patrons.'

2360. *Parsons, Coleman O. 'Blake's "Tyger" and Eighteenth-Century Animal Pictures.' *Art Quarterly*, XXXI (1968), 296–312.

A useful survey shows that in the design of 'The Tyger' Blake is not 'even abreast of the most effective practice of his day' (p. 307).

2361. —— 'Tygers Before Blake.' *Studies in English Literature 1500–1900*, VIII (1968), 573–92.

The background of 'The Tyger' in eighteenth-century natural history, in philosophical speculation, and in *Job*.

2362. Partington, Charles F. *The British Cyclopaedia of Biography*: Containing the Lives of Distinguished Men of All Ages and Countries, with Portraits, Residences, Autographs, and Monuments. Complete in Two Volumes. London, [Vol. I] 1837, [Vol. II] 1838. (Part of his *British Cyclopaedia of Arts and Sciences*, 10 vols., 1835–8.) Vol. I, p. 223.

A conventional brief paragraph.

2363. Partington, Wilfred. 'Some Marginalia.' *TLS*, 28 Jan. 1939, p. 64.

Quotes some important notes about Blake from his copy of J. T. Smith's life of Blake, probably by Joseph Hogarth, a contemporary of Blake's.

2364. Partington, Wilfred. 'A William Blake Discovery and Its Lesson.' *Bookman* [New York], LXXIV (1932), 669–71.

The discovery, a copy of Nollekens containing Blake anecdotes, probably by Joseph Hogarth. See also Partington, no. 2363.

2365. Partridge, Eric. *Eighteenth Century English Romantic Poetry.* (Up till the publication of the 'Lyrical Ballads', 1798.) Paris, 1924. Pp. 49–52, 109–18.

2366. A. —— 'Inter-Relationships in Blake's Songs.' *MLN*, XXXVIII (1923), 220 2 (vMKN) B Reprinted as pp. 36–8 of *A Critical Medley.* Paris, 1926.

Poems correspond with each other.

2367. §Paterson, E. H. 'Simple Thoughts on William Blake.' *Theoria*, No. 28 (1967), 63–5.

A continuation of the discussion in Pechey, no. 2372.

2368. A. [Patmore, Coventry.] 'Blake.' *St. James Gazette*, 31 March, 1887, p. 7. B. Reprinted as pp. 97–102 of Patmore's *Principle in Art, etc.* London, 1889. C. Second Edition. London, 1890. Pp. 97–102.

In this review of the 1874 edition of Rossetti's Blake, Patmore manages to find that the 'red republican' Blake exhibited his 'near madness' by writing 'delirious rubbish', 'mere drivel'. Patmore thinks Blake better as an artist than as a poet, but not much.

2369. Paton, Lucy Allen. 'A Phase of William Blake's Romanticism.' *Poet Lore*, V (1893), 481–8 (vMKN).

According to Pater's definition.

2370. Paul, C. Kegan. *William Godwin*: His Friends and Contemporaries. [2 vols.] London, 1876. Vol. II, p. 284.

The 'Mr William Blake' whom Lady Caroline Lamb thought 'would have a pleasure' in assisting to bail Godwin out of his chronic bankruptcy in 1823 was almost certainly not the poet, though Paul is noncommittal.

2371. *Pearson, Edwin. *Banbury Chap Books* and Nursery Toy Book Literature [of the XVIII. and early XIX. Centuries] [*sic*] with Impressions from Several Hundred Original Wood-Cut Blocks, By T. & J. Bewick, Blake, Cruikshank, Craig, Lee, Austin, and Others. London, 1890.

Blake merely reproduced.

2372. Pechey, G. K. 'Blake's *Tyger*.' *Theoria*, No. 26 (1966), 81–92.

The discussion is continued in Paterson.

2373. *Peckham, Morse. 'Blake, Milton, and Edward Burney.' *Princeton University Library Chronicle*, XI (1950), 107–26.

Burney's influence on Blake's illustrations to *Paradise Lost*.

2374. Pederson, Glenn Malvern. 'Blake's Urizen as Hawthorne's Ethan Brand.' *Nineteenth-Century Fiction*, XII (1958), 304–14.

Parallels to show the similar psychology of the authors.

2375. Pederson, Glenn Malvern. 'The Religion of William Blake: Interpreted from the Fall and Regeneration of Albion, Divine Man in the Myth of Blake.' Univ. of Washington Ph.D., 1954. Cf. *DA*, XIV (1954), 830 (vMKN).

2376. Pedrini, Lura Nancy Gregory. 'Serpent Imagery and Symbolism in the Major English Romantic Poets: Blake, Wordsworth, Coleridge, Byron, Shelley, Keats.' Texas Ph.D., 1958. See *DA*, XX (1959), 2277 (vMKN).
   Apparently abstracted in no. 2377.

2377. —— and Duilio T. Pedrini. 'Serpent Imagery and Symbolism in the Major English Romantic Poets: Blake, Wordsworth, Coleridge, Byron, Shelley, Keats.' *Psychiatric Quarterly Supplement*, XXXIV (1960), 189–244; XXXV (1961), 36–99 (vMKN).
   Useful as a collection of serpent passages, but offers little that is new for Blake.

2378. *Penrose, Boies. 'William Blake.' *Art in America and Elsewhere*, XXVII (1939), 97–8 (vMKN).
   At the Philadelphia Museum.

2379. A. *Percival, Milton O. *William Blake's Circle of Destiny*. N.Y., 1938. B. N.Y., 1964. C. §1970.
   This illuminating study of Blake's mythology and symbolism is particularly useful for the Blakean sources and analogies it points to in alchemical, Biblical, and Kabbalistic literature.

2380. A. P[éricaud], Val. 'Blake (Guillaume).' Vol. IV (1843) of *Biographie Universelle* Ancienne et Moderne, ou histoire, par ordre alphabétique, de la vie publique et privée de tous les hommes qui se sont fait remarquer par leurs écrits, leur actions, leur talents, leur vertus, ou leurs crimes. Nouvelle Édition, Publiée sous la diréction de M. [Joseph-François] Michaud. [45 vols.] Paris, 1843–58. B. Paris, 1880. Vol. 10, pp. 403–4.
   This is one long paragraph, apparently taken from the *Gentleman's Magazine* (no. 989).
   This work first came out in 52 vols. (1810–28), but Blake does not appear in it (Vol. IV. 1811). A 30-volume biographical supplement, completed in 1862 (which I have not seen), may include the Blake entry above.

2381. Perry, T[homas] S[ergeant]. 'William Blake.' *Atlantic Monthly*, XXXV (1875), 482–8 (vMKN).

2382. Perspex [Horace Shipp]. 'Current Shows and Comments. Blake the Anti-Academic.' *Apollo*, LXV (1957), 199–200.
   Blake at the BM.

2383. —— 'Current Shows and Comments. Manners and Modes.' *Apollo*, XLVI (1947), 77–8 (vMKN).
   Review of the Tate exhibition.

2384. Perugini, Mark E. 'Blake's Prophetic Books.' *TLS*, 29 July 1926, p. 512.

'Bne Seraphim' in the *Conjuror's Magazine* is the source for 'Mne Seraphim' in *Thel*.

2385. Perugini, Mark E. *'An Eighteenth Century Occult Magazine: and a Query as to William Blake.' *Bibliophile*, II (1908), 86–9.

The *Conjuror's Magazine*, where 'Bne Seraphim' and 'Tiriel' occur. Perugini answered his own query in *TLS* in 1926.

2386. —— §'William Blake Memorial.' *Sunday Times*, 24 Sept. 1899.

2387. Petter, Henri. *Enitharmon: Stellung und Aufgabe eines Symbols in dichterischen Gesamtwerk William Blakes. Bern, 1957. Swiss Studies in English, 42. Band.

A 1956 doctoral dissertation, 160 pp.

2388. A. *Pevsner, Nikolaus. 'Blake and the Flaming Line.' *Listener*, LIV (1955), 833–5. B. *Reprinted as Chapter 5 (pp. 117–47) of *The Englishness of English Art*, an expanded and annotated version of the Reith Lectures broadcast in October and November 1955. London, 1956.

Places Blake firmly in the English tradition of linear, two-dimensional art.

2389. *Philipp, Franz. 'An Afterthought to Blake's *Antaeus*.' *Annual Bulletin of the National Gallery of Victoria*, VII (1965), 25.

Blake's Dante drawing is similar to Tibaldi's 'Conception of St John'.

2390. §Phillips, Claude. 'Blake at the Tate Gallery.' *Daily Telegraph*, 1913.
(Keynes [1921] item 624).

2391. §Phillips, Michael Curtis. 'The *Poetical Sketches* of William Blake: A definitive text, the reputation of the poems from 1783 to the present, and an interpretation of their meaning.' University of Exeter Ph.D., 1969.

2392. A. [Pichot, Amédée.] 'Artiste, Poète et Fou. (La Vie de Blake.)' *Revue de Paris*, LVI (1833), 164–82. B. Mostly reprinted, with small additions, in Amédée Pichot. 'Le Visionnaire Blake.' *Revue Britannique*, V (1862), 25–47.

In the second article, Pichot wrote (p. 25): 'J'avais écrit et publié, dans l'ancienne *Revue de Paris*, une Vie de William Blake'. Cunningham's Life 'm'avait presque seul fourni les documents anecdotiques', and 'Je reproduis donc ici [1862, pp. 27–47] en grande partie mon ancienne notice', mostly word for word. The translation from Cunningham is what might charitably be called loose. Facts are distorted, dialogue is invented, and in general Cunningham served chiefly as a stimulus to Pichot's imagination.

2393. §Pickering, B. M. *William Blake and his Editors*. London, 1874.

A 4-page pamphlet, apparently objecting to W. M. Rossetti's review (*Academy*, VI [5 Sept. 1874], 255) of the Shepherd edition of Blake's *Poems* (Pickering, 1874); the pamphlet was in turn corrected by W. M. Rossetti.

2394. Pierce, Frederick E. 'Blake and Klopstock.' *SP*, XXV (1928), 11–26.

Weak parallels which even Pierce admits leave Blake's debt to Klopstock not 'absolutely proved'.

2395. Pierce, Frederick E. 'Blake and Seventeenth Century Authors.' *MLN*, XXXIX (1924), 150–3.
  Source-hunting in Browne and Drayton.

2396. ——'Blake and Thomas Taylor.' *PMLA*, XLIII (1928), 1121–41.
  Vague parallels listed.

2397. —— 'Etymology as Explanation in Blake.' *PQ*, X (1931), 395–9.
  Far-fetched derivations of names.

2398. —— 'The Genesis and General Meaning of Blake's *Milton.*' *MP*, XXV (1927), 165–78.
  This inconclusive article deals chiefly with the ways in which information about Milton could have come to Blake via Hayley.

2399. —— 'Taylor, Aristotle, and Blake.' *PQ*, IX (1930), 363–70.
  Inconclusive parallel quotations.

2400. —— 'Two Notes on Blake.' *MLN*, XLI (1926), 169–70.
  Suggests Paracelsus as source for *Vala*, VIII, 500–1; and points out the parallelism of Blake and Bronson Alcott.

2401. A. Pilkington, Matthew. *A General Dictionary of Painters*; containing Memoirs of the Lives and Works of the most eminent Professors of the Art of Painting, from its revival by Cimambue, in the year 1250, to the present time. A New Edition, corrected and revised, with an introduction, historical and critical, and twenty-six new lives of artists of the British School, by Allan Cunningham. London, 1840. Pp. xcii–xciii, 52–3. B. *A General Dictionary of Painters*; containing Memoirs of the Lives and Works of the most eminent Professors of the Art of Painting, from its revival by Cimambue, in the year 1250, to the present time. With an introduction, historical and critical, by Allan Cunningham. A New Edition, corrected and revised, by R. A. Davenport. London, 1852. Pp. xci & 48. C. *A General Dictionary of Painters*; containing Memoirs of the Lives and Works of the most eminent Professors of the Art of Painting, from its revival by Cimambue, in the year 1250, to the present time. With an introduction, historical and critical, by Allan Cunningham. A New Edition, with Supplement. London, 1857. Pp. xci & 48.

A. Presumably, since this is the first edition Cunningham edited, and since Blake does not appear in the editions of 1805, 1810, 1824, and 1829, Cunningham wrote the sections on Blake in the introduction and the biographies.

B. The only changes are in spelling and style.

C. The Blake sections are simply reprinted from the edition of 1852.
  The accounts of Blake are summary but responsible.

2402. A. *Pinto, Vivian de Sola, ed. *The Divine Vision*: Studies in the Poetry and Art of William Blake born November 28th, 1757; with an introductory poem by Walter de la Mare. London, 1957. B. *N.Y., 1968.

The contents of this volume, sponsored and published by the Blake Bicentenary Committee, are:

1. Kathleen Raine. 'The Little Girl Lost and Found and The Lapsed Soul.' Pp. 17–49 and 50–63. (Blake drew so heavily upon ancient traditions, particularly Neoplatonism, that in some of his works 'Not one symbolic figure or theme is of Blake's own invention'. To come down to cases, *Songs of Innocence* [1789] is heavily derivative from Thomas Taylor's *Dissertation* [1790]. The essay was revised and reprinted in Vol. I, Chap. 5 [pp. 126–65] of her *Blake and Tradition* [1968].)
2. V. D. S. Pinto. 'William Blake, Isaac Watts, and Mrs. Barbauld.' Pp. 66–87. (A revision of no. 2404.)
3. S. Foster Damon. 'Blake and Milton.' Pp. 89–96. (A summary of Milton's influence.)
4. Northrop Frye. 'Notes for a Commentary on *Milton*.' Pp. 97–137.
5. Piloo Nanavutty. 'William Blake and Hindu Creation Myths.' Pp. 163–82. (The chief value of the essay lies in its survey of where Blake might have found information about India.)
6. *Piloo Nanavutty. 'She Shall be Called Woman.' Pp. 183–9. (An attempt to demonstrate that Blake's drawing called 'She Shall be Called Woman' is a companion piece to 'The Angel of the Divine Presence', 1803.)
7. *Martin K. Nurmi. 'Blake's "Ancient of Days" and Motte's Frontispiece to Newton's *Principia*.' Pp. 205–16. ('If Motte was not a "source" (a negative one), he ought to have been.')

There are also reprints 'in altered form' of articles by Kiralis (no. 2059) and Margoliouth (no. 2179).

2403. Pinto, Vivian de Sola. 'In Our Era of Chaos William Blake Points the Way.' *Aryan Path*, XXVIII (1957), 488–95.

Pinto informs his Indian audience that 'the teaching of William Blake' is the right antidote to 'inhuman' Communism.

2404. A. —— 'Isaac Watts and William Blake.' *RES*, XX (1944), 214–23. B. Summarized in *N&Q*, CLXXXVII (1944), 155. C. Revised in no. 2402 2.

Inconclusive suggestions on an important subject.

2405. —— 'A Neglected Poem of William Blake.' Pp. 19–31 of *Critical Essays on English Literature* Presented to Professor M. S. Duraiswami on the occasion of his Sixty-first birthday. Ed. V. S. Seturaman. Bombay, Calcutta, Madras, New Delhi, 1965.

A 'personal-autobiographical, historical-mythological, and philosophic-religious' 'Commentary' on 'To the Jews' (*Jerusalem*, pl. 27).

2406. —— *'William Blake: The Visionary Man.' *Journal of the Royal Society of Arts*, CVI (1958), 74–89.

A very generalized introductory lecture.

2407. —— and Others. 'William Blake Memorial.' *The Times*, 15 Oct. 1957, p. 11.

An appeal for funds by the Bicentenary Committee.

2408. §*Pioli, G. 'William Blake artista dell'invisibile (1757–1827).' *Bilychnus*, XXXI (1928), 325–38.

2409. *Piper, David. 'Blake.' Pp. 123–9 of his *Painting in England 1550–1800*: An Introduction. Cambridge, 1965.

2410. Piper, J. 'English Painting at the Tate.' *Burlington Magazine*, LXXXIX (1947), 285.
About the Tate exhibition.

2411. Pirkhover, A. M. 'Zur Bildersprache von Blake und Yeats.' *Anglia*, LXXV (1957), 224–33 (vMKN).
Notes parallels.

2412. *Pitfield, Robert Lucas. 'William Blake and His Tree Full of Angels.' *Medical Life*, XXXVIII, No. 6 [N.S. No. 129] (1931), [335]–6.
A psychological study of Blake with an account of his health and death.

2413. Plowman, Max. 'Blake: A Textual Point.' *TLS*, 29 March 1928, p. 243 (vMKN).
'Binds' not 'bends'; see no. 2415.

2414. —— 'Blake and Hayley.' *TLS*, 30 April, 1925, p. 300.
The poem read to Hayley was probably *The Four Zoas*.

2415. —— 'Blake: "Binds", not "Bends".' *TLS*, 11 June 1931, p. 467. See no. 2413.

2416. —— 'Blake Drawings.' *TLS*, 1 April 1926, p. 249.
Who rubbed out parts of the drawings in *The Four Zoas* MS?

2417. —— 'Blake's Bible of Hell.' *TLS*, 6 Nov. 1924, p. 710 (vMKN).
Suggests that it may be *The Four Zoas*.

2418. —— 'Blake's "Infant Sorrow".' *TLS*, 18 Nov. 1926, p. 819.
'In a Mirtle Shade' is the end of 'Infant Sorrow'.

2419. —— *Bridge into the Future*. Letters of Max Plowman. Ed. D. L. P. [Dorothy Plowman] London, 1944. *Passim*.
Many letters, especially those to Geoffrey Keynes, discuss Blake.

2420. —— 'The Incomplete "Marriage of Heaven and Hell".' *TLS*, 22 Oct. 1925, p. 698.
The 'Song of Liberty' is integral.

2421. —— A. **An Introduction to the Study of Blake*. London & Toronto, 1927. B. *London, 1952. C. Second Edition with a new introduction by R. H. Ward. London, 1967.
A well-meant general account of the poet. R. H. Ward, 'Max Plowman and Blake' in C is pp. vii–xviii.

2422. —— 'The Key to Blake.' *Aryan Path*, V (1934), 462–6 (vMKN).
The key proposed is the 'experiencing consciousness'.

2423. A. Plowman, Max. 'William Blake and the Imagination of Truth.'
New Adelphi, N.S. III (1930), 177–83. B. Reprinted as pp. 102–8 of *The Right
to Live*. [Ed. Dorothy L. Plowman.] London, 1942.

Discusses Blake as a model of resistance to the 'science of circumstance'
(psychology, etc.).

2424. —— and Geoffrey Keynes. 'A Text of Blake.' *TLS*, 16, 23 Oct. 1924,
pp. 651, 667 (vMKN).

Plowman inquires whether anyone is producing a text of Blake, and
Keynes replies that he is.

2425. Plunkett, Margaret Louise. 'The Political Philosophy of William
Blake.' *South Atlantic Quarterly*, XXX (1931), 27–39.

This ineffective article concludes that Blake was naïve and uninformed
about politics and that his 'mature political thought was next-door-neighbor
to anarchy'.

2426. Pointon, Marcia R. 'William Blake and Milton (1801–1825).' Pp. 135–
66 of her *Milton & English Art*. Manchester, 1970.

A useful survey, including 25 Blake plates and a list of 'Blake's Illustrations
to *Paradise Lost*' (pp. 261–3).

2427. Pollard, Arthur. 'Five Poets on Religion 2. Cowper and Blake.'
Church Quarterly Review, CLX (1959), 436–45.

'Blake . . . show[s] enthusiasm in its final form' (p. 444).

2428. Poncella, Segundo Serrano, 'Blake sin profícia.' *Asomante*, XXIII
(1967), 7–24.

2429. Ponsonby, Arthur, Millicent G. Fawcett; Herbert Ham; Dorothea
Ponsonby. 'Blake and Parry.' *The Times*, 16, 18, 20 Aug. 1927, 22 Oct. 1941.

Arthur Ponsonby says Parry wrote the music to Blake's 'Jerusalem' lyric;
M. G. Fawcett says some credit should go to the National Union of Women's
Suffrage Societies, of which she was president in 1918; Ham quotes C. L.
Graves's life of Parry for the genesis of the music; Dorothea Ponsonby says
the 'Jerusalem' music is by Parry (her father), as pointed out in *The Times*
for 16 Aug. 1927.

A2429. Popham, A. E. 'Proofs of William Blake's Europe.' *British Museum
Quarterly*, XI (1937), 184–5.

In the BM.

2430. A. Porter, Miss Jane. *The Scottish Chiefs*. Revised, Corrected, and
illustrated with A New Retrospective Introduction, Notes, &c., by the
author. [2 vols.] London: George Virtue, [1841]. Vol. II, pp. 466–70. (Yale
& GEB). B. London & N.Y., [1900]. Pp. 556–8.

The first edition of *The Scottish Chiefs* of 1810 had an appended 'Note
respecting the personal Conformation of Sir William Wallace and King
Robert Bruce'. When the copyright passed back into Miss Porter's hands,
she added a 'Postscript to the above Appendix, added May, 1841' (466–70).

In the Postscript she related the story which Blake, 'a young painter' [age 61], had told 'a friend of the author of the book', evidently Varley, of his visions of Wallace and Edward I which he saw 'Soon after' 1810 (actually in Oct. 1819, according to Linnell's Journal). Miss Porter's version of the story is original but inaccurate.

Though some of the subsequent editions of this very popular novel advertised that they contained 'the latest alterations and additions of the author', the account of Blake's visionary drawing is *not* in the editions of Dublin, 1841; London, 1854; London, [1855]; Halifax, 1862; London, [1870]; London, [1879]; London & N.Y., [1880]; London & N.Y., 1882; London & Newcastle-upon-Tyne, [1883?]; London, 1904; London, 1921; Dublin, 1937 (in Irish).

A copy of this work as originally issued in its twenty monthly parts (1840–1) is in the Arents Collection of the New York Public Library. The MS of the Note on Blake was offered at Sotheby's, 28 June 1966, lot 460, but withdrawn by the Robinson Trustees.

2431. Porteus, Hugh Gordon. 'William Blake (1757–1827).' Pp. 465–79 of *From Anne to Victoria: Essays by Various Hands.* Ed. Bonamy Dobrée. London, 1937.

2432. *Portmann, Paul. 'Gott erschafft Adam.' *Du*, XV (April 1955), 28.
Reproduction and brief discussion of 'Elohim Creating Adam'.

2433. *Portner, Leslie Judd. 'Queen's Treasures in Blake Show.' *Washington Post*, 20 Oct. 1957.

2434. Pottle, Frederick A. 'Blake's *The Tyger*, 17–18.' *Explicator*, VIII (1950), item 39.
Believes that the tears are the dew.

2435. Po-tung [pseudonym of Chao, Ching-shen]. 'San Lun Po-lai-k'o [Three Things about Blake].' *Wen-hsueh Chou-k'an*, VI, No. 22 (19).
In Chinese.

2436. P[ovey], K[enneth]. 'Blake and "the Bard of Oxford".' *Sussex County Magazine*, I (1927), 391.
Identifies the character so named in the letters of Hayley and Blake as an Oxford undergraduate named E. G. Marsh.

2437. Povey, Kenneth. 'A Blake Reference.' *N&Q*, CLI (1926), 368 (vMKN).
In Sandell.

2438. —— 'Blake's "Genesis".' *TLS*, 3 Oct. 1952, p. 645.
Blake was the transcriber but not the author.

2439. —— 'Blake's "Heads of the Poets".' *N&Q*, CLI (1926), 57–8.
Corrects some misidentifications of Blake's paintings.

2440. A. Povey, Kenneth, 'The Case of Rex v Blake.' *Nation*, XLIII (1928), 526–7. B. **Sussex County Magazine*, III (1929), 314–17.
A sound, intelligent reconstruction of what happened.

2441. —— ***'William Blake in Sussex.' *Sussex County Magazine*, I (1927), 385–90.
A summary of Blake's relations with Hayley.

2442. —— and R. Stewart-Brown. '"The Lady of Lavant".' *TLS*, 21, 20 Oct. 1906, pp. 722, 746.
Povey says Blake's friend Henrietta Poole died in 1827, not in 1807 as in Gilchrist (p. 722); Stewart-Brown adds facts about her mother, who died in 1807.

2443. A. Powell, A. E. [Mrs. E. R. Dodds.] 'Blake.' Chap. III (pp. 52–72) of her *The Romantic Theory of Poetry*: An Examination in the light of Croce's Æsthetic. London, 1926. B. N.Y., 1962.

2444. Powell, Frederick York. 'Blake's Etchings.' *The Academy*, VII (1875), 66.
Source of Nebuchadnezzar in *The Marriage* is Richard Blome's *Bible Commentary* (1703), pl. 146.

2445. *Powell, Mary. 'Engravings by William Blake.' *Bulletin of the City Art Museum of St. Louis*, XXIX, Nos. 1–2 (Nov. 1944), 16–20 (vMKN).
Acquisition of the Dante and *Job* engravings.

2446. *Powell, Richard. 'Phila. Displays "Exiled" Art of Blake, World's "First Surrealist" Painter.' *Philadelphia Ledger*, 15 Feb. 1939.

2447. §Powys, John Cowper. 'William Blake.' Pp. 43–60 of his *Essays on de Maupassant, Anatole France, William Blake*. Girard, Kansas, 1916. Little Blue Book No. 450.

2448. —— 'William Blake.' Pp. 255–75 of *Suspended Judgments*: Essays on Books and Sensations. N.Y., 1916.
A general essay.

2449. *Prasse, Leona E. 'Department of Prints and Drawings.' *Fifteenth Annual Report of the Cleveland Museum of Art*, 1930, pp. 34–7, in *Cleveland Museum of Art Bulletin*, XVIII (1931) (vMKN).
Concerns Blake holdings.

2450. Praz, Mario. 'Blake Occultista.' Pp. 251–8 of *Studi e Svaghi Inglesi*. Florence, 1937.
Mostly deals with Saurat, no. 2654.

2451. *Preston, Kerrison. *Blake and Rossetti*. London, 1944.
A product of amateur enthusiasm.

2453. —— 'Fragments from Blake's Jerusalem.' *Apollo*, LXVII (1958), 3–7.
The four part-pages are not the result of mutilations by Ruskin but coloured

proofs from the collection of Tatham—later that of Col. Gould Weston [Preston, &c.]

2454. Preston, Kerrison. *'A Note on Blake Sources.' *Apollo*, LXXXIV (1966), 384–7.
Rembrandt, Bonasone, Bronzino.

2455. —— **Notes on Blake's Large Painting in Tempera The Spiritual Condition of Man*. The Graham Robertson Collection. N.p., 1949.

2456. —— 'Understanding Blake's Art.' *TLS*, 10 Jan. 1958, p. 19 (vMKN).
A correction of a review of Digby's book.

2457. —— and Geoffrey Keynes. 'Blake's America.' *TLS*, 5, 19 March 1964, pp. 195, 238.
Preston corrects a review (6 Feb., p. 111) of the facsimile of the 'Andrew [i.e. Paul] Mellon' copy of *America* by listing previous 'facsimiles'; Keynes points out that the Blake Trust *America* 'is a true facsimile', not just a reproduction like most previous ones.

2458. *Preston, Stuart. 'Visions of William Blake.' *New York Times Magazine*, 13 Oct. 1957, pp. 46–7.
A popular summary.

2459. —— 'William Blake's Clear Visions: Frick Shows Drawings for Bunyan Allegory: Illustrator Saw World in Cloak of Dreams.' *New York Times*, 28 April 1964.
Review of exhibition.

2460. Price, J. B. 'William Blake, the Visionary.' *Contemporary Review*, CLXXXI (1957), 346–50.
An inaccurate general article.

2461. A. Price, Martin. 'Blake: Vision and Satire.' Chap. XIII (pp. 390–445) of his *To the Palace of Wisdom*: Studies in Order and Energy from Dryden to Blake. Garden City, N.Y., 1965. Anchor Books. B. Reprinted as 'The Standard of Energy.' Pp. 255–73 of *Romanticism and Consciousness*: Essays in Criticism. Ed. Harold Bloom. N.Y., 1970. C. Pp. 389–401 of A are reprinted in Paley's anthology.
A responsible survey, dealing particularly with the problem of order.

2462. *Priestley, J[ohn] B[oynton]. 'William Blake.' *Saturday Review of Literature*, XLI (13 Aug. 1927), 33–5 (vMKN).
A centenary article.

2463. Pryke, J. S. 'Blake and Swedenborg.' *New Church Life*, XLVIII (1928), 311.
Pryke admits Blake may not have met Swedenborg, but he is still sure that (but not how) he was influenced.

2464. —— 'William Blake and the imagination.' *New Church Life*, XLVIII (1928), 137–51.

Blake should have accepted Swedenborg's concept of the imagination but, tragically, did not.

2465. *Pulley, Honor M. 'Pity.' Chap. xii (pp. 63–7) of her *The Ritual Mask on the Will to Live* being a speculation as to the origin and function of the Poetic Image of God. London, 1928.

About Blake's 'picture of Pity' (p. 63).

2466. Punch. 'Blake no Shogai no "Itaita Shisa" [Blake's "Misery"].' *Eigo Seinen: The Rising Generation*, LXIV (1930), 139.

Commented on later by Knockshiui.

Q

2467. Q., S. '*Academic Correspondence* . . . .' *Literary Journal*, III (1 Feb. 1804) 93–5.

A complaint that in Prince Hoare's book, 'Surely . . . the Royal Academy of England might have offered an engraving worthy of the subject, and of the country' (pp. 94–5).

2468. Queen, R. Wendell. 'Concerning William Blake and Other Matters.' *Quest*, XIII (1922), 507–26.

2469. Quennell, Peter. 'Religion of Blake.' *New Statesman*, 12 Oct. 1929, pp. 11–13 (vMKN).

2470. —— *Romantic England*: Writing and Painting 1717–1851. London, 1970. Pp. 231–47 & *passim*.

2471. Quinn, Kerker. 'Blake and the New Age.' *Virginia Quarterly Review*, XIII (1937), 271–85 (vMKN).

Notes on a number of modern poets showing Blake's influence or coincidental similarities to him.

R

2472. R., G. M. 'Blake's THE TIGER.' *Explicator*, I (1942), query 3 (vMKN).

Unimpressive.

2473. *R., L. E. 'Blake's "Book of Job".' *Bulletin of the Rhode Island School of Design*, X, No. 2 (April 1922), 10 (vMKN).

2474. Radford, Ernest. 'William Wynne Ryland and Blake.' *Art Journal*, 1896, pp. 237–8.

Mostly about Ryland.

2475. Raimbach, Abraham. *Memoirs and Recollections of the Late Abraham Raimbach, Esq. Engraver* including a Memoir of Sir David Wilkie, R.A. Ed. M. T. S. Raimbach. London, 1843. [Not Published.] [*Sic*] P. 36 fn.

Abraham merely mentions 'the insane genius Blake' in a short note on James Parker.

2476. Raine, Kathleen. *Blake and England.* Founders' Memorial Lecture Girton College 20 February, 1960. Cambridge, 1960.
A general lecture with reference to Blake's Englishness.

2477. ——— 'Blake and Tradition.' *Encounter*, VII, No. 38 (Nov. 1956) 51–4.
Blake is a great traditionalist who sometimes overloads his work with allusions—but Miss Raine does not present the evidence to support her conclusions.

2478. ——— **Blake and Tradition.* The A. W. Mellon Lectures in the Fine Arts, 1962, The National Gallery of Art, Washington, D.C. [2 vols.] Princeton, [N.J.] 1968. Bollingen Series XXXV, 11.
A learned and tendentious work, incorporating previous articles (no. 2481–2, 2486–7, 2490) 'some very extensively' 'revised' (p. xi); 196 plates.

2479. ——— 'Blake and Traditional Symbolism. A Bi-Centenary Address by Kathleen Raine, November 9th.' *Charles Lamb Society Bulletin*, No. 140 (Jan. 1958), pp. 185–7.
This appears to be a secretary's notes of what Miss Raine said, the chief conclusion being 'that virtually all of his symbols were derived from tradition', including Norse, Indian, and 'Aleleusical' mythologies.

2480. ——— **'Blake, Maker of Myths.'* *Man, Myth & Magic*: An illustrated encyclopaedia of the supernatural Published weekly, No. 10 (1970), 278–85.
The poet was 'a creator of myths'.

2481. A. ——— **'Blake's "Cupid and Psyche".'* *Listener*, LVIII (1957), 832–5. B. Revised and reprinted in Vol. I, Chap. 7 (pp. 180–203) of *Blake and Tradition* (1968).
Luvah and Vala in Vala Night IX are said to be from Apuleius.

2482. A. ——— 'Blake's Debt to Antiquity.' *Sewanee Review*, LXXI (1963), 352–450. B. Revised and reprinted in *Blake and Tradition* (1968).
An abridged version of the 1962 Mellon lectures, later reconstituted in *Blake and Tradition*.

2483. ——— 'A Case for the Razor?' *TLS*, 5 Feb. 1960, p. 81.
Miss Raine protests that neither she nor Blake was a Jungian.

2484. ——— 'A Dryden Quotation.' *TLS*, 13 Sept. 1957, p. 547.
Miss Raine wonders vainly where in Dryden Blake's notebook quotation 'At length for hatching ripe he breaks the shell' comes from [answer: his translation of Chaucer].

2485. ——— **'Note sur Blake créateur des mythes.'* [Tr. George Lavieille.] *Cahiers d'Art*, XX (1947), 128–34 (vMKN).

2486. A. ——— **'The Sea of Time and Space.'* *JWCI*, XX (1957), 318–37. B. Revised and reprinted in Vol. I, Chap. 3 (pp. 69–98) of *Blake and Tradition* (1968).

Miss Raine proves to her own satisfaction that the sources of the Arlington Court picture are Homer as interpreted by Thomas Taylor and the Platonists and concludes that 'Blake ceases to be obscure when we discover his sources'.

2487. A. Raine, Kathleen. 'Some Sources of *Tiriel.*' *HLQ*, XXI (1957), 1–36. B. Reprinted in Vol. I, Chap. 2 (pp. 34–66) of *Blake and Tradition* (1968).
Chiefly Cornelius Agrippa and Aeschylus.

2488. —— 'Thomas Taylor, Plato, and the English Romantic Movement.' *Sewanee Review*, LXXVI (1968), 230–57.
Blake is a prime example in the argument that 'the English Romantic movement' drew its inspiration from the Platonic writings translated by Thomas Taylor (pp. 230–1).

2489. —— 'A Traditional Language of Symbols.' *Listener*, LX (1958), 559–60.
'Yeats's poem ["Resurrection"] and Blake's ["The Mental Traveller"] mutually explain one another₁.」'

2490. A. —— 'Who Made the Tyger?' *Encounter*, II, No. 9 (June 1954), 43–50. B. Revised and reprinted in Vol. II, Chap. 16 (pp. 3–31) of *Blake and Tradition* (1968).
Using occult sources, Miss Raine finds that the answer to the question posed in 'The Tyger' 'is, beyond all possible doubt, No' in A, but 'the answer is . . . a no and yes' in B (p. 30).

2491. A. —— *William Blake*. London, N.Y., Toronto, 1951. Bibliographical Series of Supplements to 'British Book News'. §B. 1958. *C. Revised 1965. D. *Revised 1969. E. Tr. Ichiro Koizumi. Tokyo, 1956. Eibungaku Handbook—Sakka toto Sakuin Series [Handbooks of English Literature—'Authors and their Works' Series]. 41 pp.
A very brief introductory pamphlet, not remarkable for accuracy.

2492. A. —— *William Blake*. London, 1970. The World of Art Library: Artists. B. §N.Y., 1971.
A frequently accurate biographical account, with emphasis on Blake's art and 156 plates.

2493. A. —— 'Yeats's Debt to Blake.' *Dublin Magazine*, V (1966), 27–47. B. Slightly revised as 'Yeats's Debt to William Blake.' Chap. 4 (pp. 66–87) of her *Defending Ancient Springs*. London, N.Y., Toronto, 1967.
A lecture on their 'affinity of thought'.

2494. ——, Anon.; Edgar Foxall. 'Blake and Tradition.' *TLS*, 8, 22 Jan. 1970, pp. 34, 85.
In response to a review of her book (no. 2478), Miss Raine says that Blake cannot be made to 'fit the pattern of "humanism"'; the reviewer and Mr. Foxall point out that Miss Raine's supporting evidence is misquoted.

2495. ——, William Empson, Geoffrey Keynes; W. W. Robson; Philip Sherrard, G. W. Digby; John Wain. 'Kidnapping Blake.' *Spectator*, CXCIX

(13, 20, 27 Dec. 1957), 833 (Raine, Empson, Keynes), 869–70 (Robson), 894 (Raine); CC (3, 10 Jan. 1958), 18 (Sherrard, Digby), 47 (Wain).

Robson's review of Pinto's *Divine Vision*, Keynes's *Complete Writings*, and Digby's *Symbol and Image* (6 Dec. 1957, pp. 806–8) provokes Miss Raine to protest at comments on her essay for Pinto, Empson defends her, and Keynes defends his edition; Robson temperately points out further errors in Miss Raine's essay and replies to Empson and Keynes; Miss Raine tries to reply to Robson's 'quibbles' and 'blind passion' [by further misquotations]; Sherrard attacks Robson and Digby defends Raine; and Wain defends Robson.

2496. Rasmussen, Egil. 'Blakes revolusjonaere forkynnerperiode.' *Edda*, XXXIII (1933), 290–333.

2497. Rawson, C. J. '"Ida's Shady Brow": Parallels to Blake.' *N&Q*, CCX [N.S. XII] (1965), 183.

2498. A. Read, Herbert. *The Meaning of Art.* London, 1931. Pp. 109–15. B. Reprinted as pp. 160–8 of the Second Edition. London, 1936. C. Tr. by Geoffrey Stutfield and Jean Lescure as 'Le Poète Graphique.' *Messages*, I (1939), 35–8. D. Reprinted in *The Meaning of Art.* Penguin Books, 1949. Pp. 120–5. E. Reprinted in *The Meaning of Art.* London, 1951. Pp. 167–74.
Unimportant for Blake.

2499. —— *'William Blake.' *Country Life*, 9 July 1927, pp. 66–8.
Review of the Burlington exhibition.

2500. A. Redgrave, Richard & Samuel. *A Century of Painters of the English School.* In Two Volumes. London, 1866. Vol. I, pp. 440–8. B. §Second Edition. London, 1890. Pp. 164–7. C. London [1893]. Pp. 164–7. D. [Ed. Ruthven Todd.] London, 1947. Pp. 181–5.
A superficial account of Blake, emphasizing his madness, irascibility, and genius.

2501. Redgrove, H. Stanley. 'Blake and Swedenborg: A Study in Comparative Mysticism.' *Occult Review*, XXXVIII (1923), 288–96.

2502. —— 'Blake's Annotations on the Divine Providence.' *New Church Magazine*, XLIV (1925), 38–44.

2503. Reed, Edward Bliss. *English Lyrical Poetry.* New Haven (Conn.) & London, 1912. Pp. 378–85.
Trifling.

2504. Reid, T. Wemyss. *The Life, Letters, and Friendships of Richard Monckton Milnes, First Lord Houghton.* In Two Volumes. London, Paris, Melbourne, 1890. Vol. I, pp. 220–1; Vol. II, pp. 222–3.
Contemporary references of some importance.

2505. Reisner, Mary Ellen. 'Blake's IMITATION OF POPE: A COMPLIMENT TO THE LADIES and A PRETTY EPIGRAM FOR THE ENTERTAINMENT OF THOSE WHO PAID GREAT SUMS IN THE

VENETIAN AND FLEMISH OOZE.' *Explicator*, XXVIII (1970), No. 79.
'Blake's imitation of Pope', which 'is very poor', ridicules 'not the style of Pope but the man'.

2506. Reisner, Mary Ellen. 'The Rainbow in Blake's "Visions of the Daughters of Albion".' *N&Q*, CCXVI [N.s. XVIII] (1971), 341–3.
The sketch on *Notebook* p. 30 is 'probably a study for the circle of dancing figures' in *Visions* pl. 2.

2507. —— 'The Wages of Art: Blake and his Public.' *Culture*, XXXI (1970), 327–37.
A general essay on why Blake was neglected.

2508. Reisner, Thomas A. 'Cain: Two Romantic Interpretations.' *Culture*, XXXI (1970), 124–43.
On Byron's *Cain* (pp. 124–37) and on Blake's *Ghost of Abel* (pp. 137–43).

2509. §René, Jean. 'Peintres d'hier et d'aujourd'hui: William Blake et André Lhôte.' *Comoedia*, 15 Feb. 1928.
Defends Blake.

2510. Renwick, W. L. *English Literature 1789–1815*. Oxford, 1963. The Oxford History of English Literature.
The facts in the Blake section (pp. 115–26) are often astonishingly wrong.

2511. A. Revol, Enrique Luis. 'William Blake.' *Cursos y Conferencias*, XXXIII (1948), 307–48. B. Amplified as 'William Blake, el hombre primitivo.' Pp. 11–80 of his *Caminos del Exceso*: William Blake y el Marques de Sade. Cordoba [Argentina], 1964. Colección de Ensayos y Estudios.
Sade is dealt with in a separate essay as 'el hombre moderno' (pp. 81–105).

2512. *Rexroth, Kenneth. 'Classics Revisited—LXIII: The Works of Blake.' *Saturday Review of Literature*, 30 March 1968, p. 17.
'The *Prophetic Books* are certainly the greatest, the most comprehensive and profound, group of philosophical poems in the English language.'

2513. Rhodes, Jack Lee. 'A Study in the Vocabulary of English Romanticism: *Joy* in the Poetry of Blake, Wordsworth, Coleridge, Shelley, Keats, and Byron.' *DA*, XXVII (1967), 3434A. Texas Ph.D.
'Blake's use of *Joy* is distinguished primarily by the wide variety of contexts and associations in which he places the term.'

2514. Rhodes, S. A. 'William Blake and Pierre Jean Jouve.' *Romanic Review*, XXIV (1933), 147–9 (vMKN).
An exposé, showing that Jouve passed off a translation of the first four lines of 'Auguries of Innocence' as his own work.

2515. A. *Rice, Howard C., Jr. 'Lesser Known Examples of Blake's Engraving Skill.' *Princeton Alumni Weekly*, LXXI (29 Sept. 1970), 38–44. B. *University*: A Princeton Quarterly, No. 76 (Fall 1970), 2, 26–32.
Plates from the Princeton exhibition.

2516. [Richardson, Dr.] 'Hallucinations.' *Chambers' Journal*, Ser. 4, No. 439 (1872), 324–7 (vMKN).

Blake mentioned on p. 326. See Anon., no. 1004, and Palmer, no. 2355, who refutes it. See also no. 2301.

2517. Richmond, George, & William Blake Richmond. *The Richmond Papers* from the correspondence and manuscripts of George Richmond, R.A., and his son Sir William [Blake] Richmond, R.A., K.C.B. Ed. A. M. W. Stirling. London, 1926. Pp. 8, 23–8, 50, 99, 101, 134, 321.

There are important references to Blake on pp. 8 and 24–7, but it is difficult to ascertain whether they are first, second, or third hand.

2518. Richmond, William Blake. 'Blake's Grave.' *The Times*, 6 July 1911, p. 7 (vMKN).

Suggestion, by a namesake, to move Blake's grave to Westminster Abbey.

2519. Richter, Helene. 'Blake und Hamann.' *Archiv für das Studium der neuren Sprachen und Literaturen*, CLVIII (1930), 213–21; CLIX (1931), 37–45 195–210 (vRG).

2520. —— **William Blake.* Strassburg, 1906.

2521. Rienaecker, Victor. 'William Blake and Spiritual Democracy.' *Aryan Path*, XXVIII (1957), 496–9.

It is 'vital' for us to understand Blake because he was so 'close to the human problem' of his day.

2522. *Riese, Teut Andreas. 'William Blake: *The Little Girl Lost* und *The Little Girl Found*.' Pp. 80–107 of *Versdichtung der Englischen Romantik*: Interpretationem Unter Mitarbeit zahlreicher Fachgelehrter. Ed. Teut Andreas Riese und Dieter Riesner. Berlin, 1968.

2523. *Rinder, Frank. 'William Blake: For Few or All?' *Country Life*, XLIII (1918), 249–52 (vRG).

Particularly on Blake's art.

2524. *Ritchie, Andrew C. 'William Blake.' Chap. IV, pp. 38–47, of his *English Painters Hogarth to Constable*. Lectures Delivered April 9, 10, 11, 16, 17, 1940 at the Johns Hopkins University. Baltimore, 1942.

This introduction concludes that at his best 'Blake is certainly in a class with the greatest imaginative artists of all time.'

2525. §Rixecker, E. 'William Blake's psychologisches Darstellung der Imagination.' Marburg Ph.D., 1939. 78 pp.

2526. Roberts, Richard. 'The Ethics of William Blake.' *Hibbert Journal*, XVII (1919), 660–71.

Doctrine of 'the intrinsic worth and social character of the Minute Particular—the individual man'.

2527. —— *'William Blake Comes Back.' *Methodist Review*, CX (1927) 673–84 (vMKN).

2528. *Robertson, Alec. 'El Greco, Blake, and Van Gogh.' Pp. 96–113 of his *Contrasts: The Arts & Religion*. London, 1945.

2529. Robertson, [W.] Graham. *Letters from Graham Robertson*. Ed. Kerrison Preston. London, 1953. *Passim*.

Some absorbing glances in the back door of Blake-collecting and scholarship.

2530. —— *Letters to Francis White Emerson from W. Graham Robertson*. Privately Printed [Cambridge, 1948.] *Passim*.

Charming gossip and notes about Blake pictures and enthusiasts.

2531. Robinson, Donald; P. Stapells, John Usher. 'Satanic mills.' *Observer*, 27 Sept. 1970, p. 17; 4 Oct. 1970, p. 19.

In the famous phrase 'Blake was in fact referring to the universities', not to the 'Lancashire textile mills', or to 'unimaginative mechanism', or to 'the churches'.

2532. Robinson, Fred C. 'Verb Tense in Blake's "The Tyger".' *PMLA*, LXXIX (1964), 666–9.

The verb 'dare' 'could only have been intended as a past tense'. See no. 1729.

2533. A. Robinson, Henry Crabb. *Blake, Coleridge, Wordsworth, Lamb, Etc.* being Selections from the Remains of Henry Crabb Robinson. Ed. Edith J. Morley. Manchester, London, N.Y., 1922. Pp. 1–27. B. Manchester, 1932. Pp. 1–27.

A fresh transcript of Crabb Robinson's important memoirs of Blake.

2534. —— *The Correspondence of Henry Crabb Robinson with The Wordsworth Circle*, (1808–1856) the Greater Part now for the First Time Printed from the Originals in Dr. Williams's Library, London. Ed. Edith J. Morley. In Two Volumes. Oxford, 1927. Vol. I, p. 153; Vol. II, pp. 675–6.

References to Blake in letters of 20 Feb. 1826 and 27 July 1848.

2535. A. —— *Diary, Reminiscences, and Correspondence of Henry Crabb Robinson*, Barrister-at-Law, F.S.A. Ed. Thomas Sadler. In Three Volumes. London, 1869. Vol. I, pp. 299, 338, 385, 472; Vol. II, pp. 301–10, 314, 316–18, 321–5, 330, 370–1, 379–83; and Vol. III, p. 319. B. Second Edition. London, 1869. C. In Two Volumes. Boston, 1869. Vol. I, pp. 191, 192, 238, 247, 303; Vol. II, pp. 24–30, 33–5, 37–40, 43, 69, 74–7, 372. D. In Two Volumes. Third Edition. With Corrections and Additions. London & N.Y., 1872. Vol. I, pp. 156–7, 176, 201, 247; Vol. II, pp. 7–11, 14–19, 22, 42, 47–9, and 292.

These contemporary accounts of Blake, chiefly dating from 1825 to 1827, are of the very first importance. The Blake references are largely and independently reprinted by Symons, by Gilchrist (independently retranscribed by Todd) in *Blake Records*, and by Morley (no. 2536) from the MS in Dr. Williams's Library, London.

2536. —— *Henry Crabb Robinson on Books and their Writers*. Ed. Edith J. Morley. [3 vols.] London, 1938. Vol. I, pp. 15, 20, 25, 31, 40–1, 85, 117,

324–33, 335, 337, 342–5, 353, 355, 356, 361, 394; in Vol. II, pp. 498, 549–50, 625, 669, 675, 676, 705, 706, 717, 752, 799, 809–10.

2537. Robinson, Henry Crabb. *The Diary of Henry Crabb Robinson*: nA Abridgement [from E. J. Morley's edition]. Ed. Derek Hudson. London & N.Y., 1967.

2538. [——] 'William Blake, Kunstler, Dichter und religiöser Schwärmer.' [Tr. Dr. Nikolaus Heinrich Julius.] *Vaterlandisches Museum*, I (Jan. 1811), 107–31. (BM & Dr. Williams's Library)

In his journal for 1810 Robinson noted that he had written an account of Blake for what he called *Vaterländische Annalen*, which 'was translated by Dr. Julius', and on 28 April 1811 he received a copy, which is now in Dr. Williams's Library, signed at the end 'H. C. R.' (No pages had been opened except for Robinson's article when I first saw the volume.)

This important account of Blake is reprinted in Wright and *Blake Records* (no. 3009, 1158) and translated in Esdaile (no. 1582) and *Blake Records*.

2539. *Robinson, J. E. 'An Unknown Collection of Portraits by William Blake; the Genius of the Pre-Raphaelite Movement.' *Arts and Decoration*, VIII (1918), 100–5, 130 (vMKN).

The portraits of the poets, not by Blake.

2540. Robinson, J. J. 'A Creeping Jesus.' *TLS*, 27 Aug. 1925, p. 557.

Blake probably heard the epithet in Felpham, where it is still in use (Blake uses the phrase in his *Notebook* p. 53).

2541. Rochoz, Hans von. 'William Blake und unsere Erziehungsarbeit.' *Neuphilologische Monatsschrift*, IV (1933), 199–206.

2542. Rodway, Allan. 'Blake.' Pp. 115–39 and *passim* of his *The Romantic Conflict*. London, 1963.

2543. A. *Roe, Albert S. *Blake's Illustrations to the Divine Comedy*. Princeton, [N.J.] 1953. B. §Second Printing. Princeton, 1967.

'Appendix A' is a table of page correspondences for the fourth edition of Keynes's *Poetry and Prose* (no. 303) and later editions (p. 205). 'Appendix B' is a table locating the Dante drawings (p. 206) and 'Appendix C' is a list of exhibitions which included the Dante drawings (p. 206). The 112 plates include all the Dante drawings and engravings.

This is a very sound study of the ways in which Blake's own ideas and Giant Figures influenced his illustrations to Dante.

2544. —— *'A Drawing of the Last Judgment.' *HLQ*, XXI (1957), 37–55.

That in the Rosenwald Collection, Library of Congress, analysed.

2545. *Roger-Marx, Claude. 'A propos de l'exposition Blake; les vision-naires.' *Beaux-Arts*, 29 Jan. 1937, pp. 1–2 (vMKN).

2546. Romney, Ch[arles]. 'Blake (William).' Vol. III [1852], pp. 265–6 of *Dictionnaire de la conversation et de la lecture* Inventaire raisonné des notions générales les plus indispensables à tous Par une Société de Savants et de

Gens de Lettres Sous la Direction de M. W. Duckett. Seconde édition entièrement refondue corrigée, et augmentée de plusieurs milliers d'articles tout d'actualité. [16 vols.] Paris, 1852–60.

A rather long (8 paragraphs) and conventionally inaccurate account of Blake.

I have not seen the editions of 1833–51 (68 vols.) or 1839–51 (52 vols.), and can only guess, therefore, as to whether the Blake article was part of the augmentation or appeared in the original edition.

2547. §Rønning, Helge. 'Revolusjonsdikteren William Blake.' *Samtiden*, LXXVI (1967), 263–72.

2548. Rood, Mary. 'In Defence of Blake.' *Commonweal*, XI (1929), 114 (vMKN).

Defence against the suggestion (in a review by Cortlandt van Winkle, *Commonweal*, X [1929], 649) that Blake was a philosopher.

2549. Roos, Jacques. 'William Blake.' Pp. 25–194 of *Aspects Littéraires du Mysticisme Philosophique et l'Influence de Boehme et de Swedenborg au début du Romanticisme: William Blake. Novalis Ballanche*. Strasbourg, 1951.

Roos traces with some competence but in no great detail the 'puissant souffle de mysticisme' carried by Boehme and Swedenborg.

2550. Roscoe, E. S. 'The Career and Works of Flaxman.—I [II].' *The Magazine of Art*, IV (1881), 368–74, 468–74.

Includes comments about Flaxman by Blake reported by Samuel Palmer (473–4).

2551. Rose, Edward J. 'Blake's Fourfold Art.' *PQ*, XLIX (1970), 400–23.

Examines 'the relation of Blake's body symbolism to his dramatized critique of his theory of art' (p. 400).

2552. —— 'Blake's Hand: Symbol and Design in Jerusalem.' *Texas Studies in Literature and Language*, VI (1964), 47–58.

Deals with 'the relationships between the symbolism of the hand and the figure of Hand in both Blake's designs and his verse' (p. 46). It apparently originated in his thesis.

2553. —— 'Blake's Human Insect: Symbol, Theory, and Design.' *Texas Studies in Literature and Language*, X (1968), 215–32.

'The purpose of this essay is . . . to discuss the fly . . . or the worm . . . as man' (p. 215).

2554. —— *'Blake's Illustrations for *Paradise Lost*, *L'Allegro*, and *Il Penseroso*: A Thematic Reading.' *Hartford Studies in Literature*, II (1970), 40–67.

'Blake's illustrations for these three poems are . . . a commentary on Milton' (p. 40). The reproductions include all those for *Paradise Lost* (Huntington set), *L'Allegro*, and *Il Penseroso*.

2555. —— 'Circumcision Symbolism in Blake's *Jerusalem*.' *Studies in Romanticism*, VIII (1968), 16–25.

'"Uncircumcision" is a symbolic synonym for all that must be removed from man' (p. 20).

2556. Rose, Edward J. *'"Mental Forms Creating": "Fourfold Vision" and the Poet as Prophet in Blake's Designs and Verse.' *JAAC*, XXIII (1964), 173–83.
Apparently the article derives from his thesis.

2557. —— 'Mental Forms Creating: A Study in Blake's Thought and Symbols.' Toronto Ph.D., 1963.
'The thesis contends that Blake's metaphors, images, and symbols describe the creative process' (p. ii). Nos. 2552, 2556, 2560 appear to be derived from it.

2558. —— '"A Most Outrageous Demon": Blake's Case Against Rubens.' *Bucknell Review*, XVII (1969), 35–54.
Organizes Blake's opinions of Rubens to 'show how they are related to Blake's poetic theory of the artist' (35).

2559. —— 'The Structure of Blake's *Jerusalem*.' *Bucknell Review*, XI (1963), 35–54.

2560. —— 'The Symbolism of the Opened Center and Poetic Theory in Blake's *Jerusalem*.' *Studies in English Literature 1500–1900*, V (1965), 587–606.
About 'the way in which eternal time becomes historical time' and vice versa (p. 587), apparently derived from his thesis.

2561. —— *'Visionary Forms Dramatic: Grammatical and Iconographical Movement in Blake's Verse and Designs.' *Criticism*, VIII (1966), 111–25.
'The purpose of this discussion is to examine the meaning of visual and verbal direction [right–left or east–west] in Blake's language, symbolism, and designs' (p. 111).

2562. Rose, Hugh James. *A New General Biographical Dictionary*. In Twelve Volumes. London, 1850. Vol. IV, p. 284.
Blake is dismissed with a brief and curiously inaccurate paragraph.

2563. *Rosenberg, Alfons. 'Die Bedeutung der Menschengestalt bei William Blake.' Pp. 10–12 of *England im Übergang*. Ed. Hugo Debrunner. Zurich, 1948.

2564. Rosenblum, Robert. 'The International Style of 1800: A Study in Linear Abstraction.' New York University Ph.D., 1956.
A work of major importance, in which Blake is considered on pp. 99–114.

2565. *Rosenfeld, Alvin H., ed. *William Blake*: Essays for S. Foster Damon. Providence, [R.I.] 1969.
There are 33 plates and Blake essays by:

1. Hazard Adams, 'Blake and the Postmodern.' Pp. 3–17, 425–6. ('Postmodernism . . . is a criticism that seeks to answer the demands of modern art', with its 'principle immediate source' in 'the Blakean critical theorizing of Northrop Frye' [p. 7].)
2. Harold Bloom, 'The Visionary Cinema of Romantic Poetry.' Pp. 18–35, 427. (Reprinted from no. 1231.)

3. Harold Fisch, 'Blake's Miltonic Moment.' Pp. 36–56, 427–9. ('This moment . . . occurs when Los takes over from Orc as the god of Time and Prophecy.' [P. 44.])

4. Geoffrey H. Hartman, 'Blake and the "Progress of Poesy".' Pp. 57–68, 429–31. Reprinted in pp. 193–205 of his *Beyond Formalism*: Literary Essays 1958–1970. New Haven & London, 1970. (In *Poetical Sketches*, 'Blake's season poems are about poetry' [A p. 58].)

5. Daniel Hughes, 'Blake and Shelley: Beyond the Uroboros.' Pp. 69–83, 431–2. (An exploration of the use by Blake and Shelley of the image of 'the snake with its tail in its mouth' [p. 71].)

6. Vivian de Sola Pinto, 'William Blake and D. H. Lawrence.' Pp. 84–106, 432–4. (A 'tentative and fragmentary attempt' to explore 'the points of contact' between Blake and Lawrence [p. 84].)

7. Martin Butlin, 'The Evolution of Blake's Large Color Prints of 1795.' Pp. 109–16, 434–8. (An important technical analysis.)

8. Anne T. Kostelanetz, 'Blake's 1795 Color Prints: An Interpretation.' Pp. 117–30, 438–9. (On iconography; reprinted in Chapter 4 of her *Blake's Human Form Divine* [1974].)

9. Morton D. Paley, 'Blake's *Night Thoughts*: An Exploration of the Fallen World.' Pp. 131–57, 439–43. (A survey of the drawings.)

10. Albert S. Roe, '"The Thunder of Egypt".' Pp. 158–95, 443–58. (A suggestive essay on Blake's use of Egyptian art, with sections on Blake and Jacob Bryant [pp. 169–75] and Erasmus Darwin [pp. 159–69].)

11. Asloob Ahmad Ansari, 'Blake and the Kabbalah.' Pp. 199–220, 459. (An attempt 'to uncover a few strata of significance common to' Blake and 'the innumerable translations of the *Zohar* that were in vogue in the eighteenth century' [pp. 199–200].)

12. Northrop Frye, 'Blake's Reading of the Book of Job.' Pp. 221–34. (A 'conjectural reconstruction of the reader's "vision" of Job that preceded the final re-creation in the engravings' [p. 221].)

13. George Mills Harper, 'The Divine Tetrad in Blake's *Jerusalem*.' Pp. 235–55, 459–61. (A persuasive demonstration that Blake used 'the divine numbers in an amazingly complex system' [p. 254].)

14. Paul Miner, 'Visions in the Darksom Air: Aspects of Blake's Biblical Symbolism.' Pp. 256–92, 461–77. (An impressive demonstration that 'Hundreds of biblical allusions and references are found in Blake's poetry' [p. 257].)

15. Piloo Nanavutty, '*Materia Prima* in a Page of Blake's *Vala*.' Pp. 293–302, 477–8. (An 'alchemical analysis' of *Vala* p. 26.)

16. Martin K. Nurmi, 'Negative Sources in Blake.' Pp. 303–18, 478–80. (An attempt 'to show how Blake formed certain of his visionary ideas [limits, vortexes, and the mundane shell] partly in reaction against philosophical enemies' such as Newton, Descartes, and Thomas Burnet [pp. 303, 317–18].)

17. Robert F. Gleckner, 'Blake's Verbal Technique.' Pp. 321–32, 480–1. (An attempt 'to see to what extent "Every word" seems to have been "studied and put into its fit place"' [p. 321].)

18. John E. Grant, 'Two Flowers in the Garden of Experience.' Pp. 333–67, 481–91. (A 'detailed interpretation of . . . "My Pretty Rose Tree" and "The Lilly" . . . [*and*] other important concurrences of this flower imagery throughout Blake's literary and pictorial work' [p. 333].)
19. Jean H. Hagstrum, '"The Fly".' Pp. 368–82, 491–4. (A correction of Grant, Kirschbaum, and Hirsch [no. 1727, 2061, 1853].)
20. Kathleen Raine, 'A Note on Blake's "Unfettered Verse".' Pp. 383–92, 494.
21. David V. Erdman, 'A Temporary Report on Texts of Blake.' Pp. 395–413, 494–8. (A 'most impersonal report' concerning the 'substantive text' 'of the many new editions of Blake, out recently or promised soon' [p. 395].)
22. Geoffrey Keynes, 'The William Blake Trust.' Pp. 414–20. (An intimate history.)

2566. R[osenwald], V[ictor]. 'BLAKE (*Guillaume*).' Vol. VI, pp. 178–9 of *Nouvelle biographie universelle*. Paris, 1853.
Digested from Cunningham and Nagler.

2567. *Ross, Robert. 'The Place of William Blake in English Art.' *Burlington Magazine*, IX (1906), 150–67.
Blake is 'an exquisite accident' whose 'place . . . is still undetermined' (pp. 161, 150).

2568. —— 'Swinblake: A Prophetic Book, with Home Zarathrusts.' *Academy*, LXXI (1906), 307–9.
An amusing review of Swinburne.

2569. Rossetti, Dante Gabriel. *Dante Gabriel Rossetti: His Family-Letters.* With a Memoir by William Michael Rossetti. [2 vols.] London, 1895. Vol. I, pp. 109–10, 415.
The account of the acquisition of the 'Rossetti Manuscript' is Vol. I, pp. 109–10.

2570. —— *Letters of Dante Gabriel Rossetti.* Ed. Oswald Doughty [Vols. I, III] & John Robert Wahl [Vols. II & IV]. [4 vols.] Oxford, [Vols. I–II] 1965. Vol. I, pp. 96–7, 279, 380; Vol. II, pp. 396, 417–18, 420, 424, 438–41, 445, 451–9, 461–83, 487–9, 493–4.
Chiefly references to the preparation of Gilchrist's life of Blake.

2571. —— *Letters of Dante Gabriel Rossetti to William Allingham 1854–1870.* Ed. George Birckbeck Hill. London, 1897. Pp. 158–9, 237, 261–2.
Minor references to Blake.

2572. B. —— 'William Blake.' Vol. I, pp. 443–77 of *The Collected Works of Dante Gabriel Rossetti.* Ed. William M. Rossetti. In Two Volumes. London, 1886. C. *The Works of Dante Gabriel Rossetti.* Ed. William M. Rossetti. London, 1911. Pp. 587–605.
These excerpts first appeared in Gilchrist's biography of Blake (no. 1680), with which Rossetti assisted. His brother William wrote: 'Nothing else of any

substantial bulk or importance was written by my brother for Gilchrist's book.' (P. 526 of the 1886 edition.)

2573. Rossetti, William Michael. 'Blake at the Burlington Club.' *Academy*, IX (1876), 248 (vRN).

2574. A. —— *Letters of William Michael Rossetti* Concerning Whitman, Blake, and Shelley to Ann Gilchrist and her Son Herbert Gilchrist. Ed. Clarence Gohdes and Paull Franklin Baum. Durham [N.C.], 1934. Duke University Publications Pp. 3–17, 20, 22 fn., 25, 72, 85–9, 93, 95, 96, 110, 112, 117, 118, 122–33. B. §N.Y., 1968.

A number of these letters referring to Blake were written before the publication of Gilchrist's life, but few are of much importance.

2575. —— 'The Blake Catalogue.' *Academy*, IX (1876), 364–5.
Review of Burlington House exhibition.

2576. —— 'The Poems of William Blake.' *Academy*, VI (10 Oct. 1874), 407.
Correction of Pickering's 'fly-sheet' *William Blake and his Editors* (1874).

2577. —— *Rossetti Papers* 1862 to 1870. A Compilation. London, 1903. Pp. 6, 15–16, 18–25, 27, 40–3, 63–4, 169–72, 177, 178, 180–2, 221, 229, 234, 344.

The references on pp. 6, 15–16, 18–25, 27, 41–2, 171–2, 177–8 are to letters before 1863, or written by Seymour Kirkup, who knew Blake.

2578. —— *Some Reminiscences of* [i.e. by] *William Michael Rossetti*. [2 vols.] London, 1906. Vol. II, pp. 302–8, 378.

Reminiscences of Blake's Notebook, Gilchrist, Linnell, and Tatham, of small importance.

2579. —— 'William Blake.' *Athenaeum*, No. 3309 (1891), 407–8 (vMKN).
References to Blake in Lady Charlotte Bury's *Diary*.

2580. *Rossiter, Henry Preston. 'Blake to Bunyan: Rediscovered Drawings for Pilgrim's Progress.' *Art News*, XXXIX (4 Jan. 1941), 9, 17–18 (vMKN).
Comment on them.

2581. *—— (HPR). 'Drawing by Blake, Restored.' *Bulletin of the* [Boston] *Museum of Fine Arts*, XLVI (1948), 69–71.
Before and after pictures and description of the cleaning of 'Abraham & Isaac'.

2582. Roston, Murray. *Prophet and Poet*: The Bible and the Growth of Romanticism. London, 1965.

This 'study of Hebraism and Classicism against an eighteenth-century background' (p. 13) deals usefully with Blake on pp. 159–70.

2583. Rothery, Agnes. 'Mad Poets in the Spring.' *Virginia Quarterly Review* III (1927), 250–63 (vMKN).

John Clare, Blake, Mangan, and Dowson discussed in an article which loosely associates Spring and imaginative enthusiasm.

2584. §Roudalphi, Marthe-Augusta-Paulette. 'William Blake: Rapports de l'Art et de la Pensée.' University of Paris Ph.D., 1948.

2585. A. Rudd, Margaret E. *Divided Image*: A Study of William Blake and W. B. Yeats. London, 1953. B. §N.Y., 1970.

The thesis of this influence-study (drafted in her thesis) is that Blake was a mystic and Yeats a magician. Unfortunately Miss Rudd does not understand Blake very well.

2586. A. ——— *Organized Innocence*: The Story of Blake's Prophetic Books. London, 1956. B. *Westport, Connecticut, 1973.

This naïve, rather incoherent book sets out to prove that the 'very wonderful story' of *The Four Zoas, Milton,* and *Jerusalem* (which 'form one long narrative') is in intimate detail 'Blake's own psychological drama'. It may have been Miss Rudd's refusal to consult *any* Blake scholarship during the writing of her book which allows her to conclude, *inter alia,* that '*The Four Zoas* has a simple, almost naive, coherence'.

2587. ——— 'William Blake and W. B. Yeats: A Study of Poetry and Mystical Vision.' Reading Ph.D., 1951 (according to L. F. McNamee, *Dissertations in English and American Literature* [1968]).

The work was printed as no. 2585.

2588. Rudens, S. P. 'The God of William Blake.' *Reflex*, IV, No. 5 (May 1929), 36–41 (vMKN).

2589. Ruggles, Alice McGuffey. 'The Kinship of Blake, Vachel Lindsay, and D. H. Lawrence.' *Poet Lore*, XLVI (1940) 88–92 (vMKN).

Lawrence admired Blake.

2591. Rusk, William Sener. 'A Preceptorial in Comparative Aesthetics: Maitani and Blake.' *Education*, LIII (1933), 549–53 (vMKN).

A compressed transcript of it.

2592. A. Ruskin, John. *The Elements of Drawing*; in Three Letters to Beginners. London, 1857. P. 342. B. 1857. P. 342. C. 1859. P. 342. D. 1860. P. 352. E. 1861. P. 352. F. 1892. Pp. 344–5. G. 1895. Pp. 344–5. H. London & Orpington, 1898. Pp. 344–5. I. London, 1900. Pp. 344–5. J. *The Elements of Drawing The Elements of Perspective and The Laws of Fésole.* London & N.Y., 1903. Vol. XV of *The Works of John Ruskin.* Library Edition. Ed. E. T. Cook and Alexander Wedderburn. P. 223. K. *The Elements of Drawing.* London, 1904. Pp. 344–5. L. London & N.Y., [1907]. The Universal Library Series. P. 261. M. *The Elements of Drawing & the Elements of Perspective.* London & N.Y. [1907]. Everyman's Library. P. 199. N. *The Elements of Drawing.* London [1920?]. P. 261.

Blake's *Job* is praised in an Appendix of 'Things to be Studied'.

2593. ——— *The Letters of John Ruskin.* Volume I 1827–1869. London & N.Y., 1909. Vol. XXXVI of *The Works of John Ruskin.* Ed. E. T. Cook and Alexander Wedderburn. Pp. 32–3, 110 (cf. no. 1400).

2594. A. Ruskin, John. *Modern Painters*. Volume III. Containing Part IV. Of Many Things. London, 1856. Pp. 103, 259. B. §1867. Pp. 103, 259. C. 1873. Pp. 103, 259. D. Orpington, 1888. Pp. 103, 259. E. N.Y., 1888. Pp. 98, 254. F. Orpington & London, 1897. Pp. 106, 260. G. Orpington & London, 1898. Pp. 106, 260. H. London & N.Y., 1904. (Vol. V of *The Works of John Ruskin*. Ed. E. T. Cook and Alexander Wedderburn. Library Edition.) Pp. 137–8, 323. I. London & N.Y., 1906. Everyman's Library. Pp. 95, 242. J. London & N.Y. [1907?]. The Universal Library Edition. Pp. 108–9, 277. K. London [1920]. Pp. 108–9, 277.

There are casual references to Blake in Chap. VIII, paragraph eight, and Chap. XVI, paragraph ten.

The history of the other volumes of *Modern Painters* is complicated and irrelevant.

2595. —— *The Seven Lamps of Architecture*. London & N.Y., 1903. (Vol. VIII of *The Works of John Ruskin*. Library Edition. Ed. E. T. Cook and Alexander Wedderburn.) P. 256 fn.

The editors print a section on the reputations of the two geniuses of the nineteenth century, Turner and Blake, which was omitted from the first (1849) and all subsequent editions.

2596. *Russell, Archibald G. B. 'The Blake Centenary.' *Apollo*, V (1927), 258–61 (vMKN).

On the Burlington exhibition.

2597. —— 'Blake, William.' Vol. IV, pp. 84–8 of *Allgemeines Lexicon der Bildenden Künstler* von der antike bis zur gegenwart. Ed. Ulrich Thieme und Felix Becker, Leipzig, 1910.

2598. —— *'On Dreams.' *Bibby's Annual*, Summer 1907, p. 76 (vMKN).

Blake's *'Vision of Jacob's Ladder' used to illustrate prophetic-symbolic dream.

2599. A. [——] 'The Visionary Art of William Blake.' *Edinburgh Review*, CCIII (1906), 161–79. B. Archibald G. B. Russell. *Die Visionäre Kunst Philosophie des William Blake*. Tr. Stefan Zweig. Leipzig, 1906.

A summary-review of the Blake catalogues of 1809, 1876, 1880, 1891, 1904, plus Robertson's edition of Gilchrist.

2600. Russell, G. W. 'Blake.' Pp. 116–18 of his *Living Torch*. London, 1937 (vDVE).

A trifle.

2601. —— 'Blake's Designs.' Pp. 121–2 of *Living Torch*. London, 1937 (vDVE).

A trifle.

2602. —— 'Blake's Prophetic Books.' Pp. 118–21 of *Living Torch*. London, 1937 (vDVE).

A trifle.

2603. *Rutter, Frank. 'Pictorial Art of William Blake.' *Bookman*, LXXII (1927), 253–5.

A general essay, which concludes that Blake is 'the greatest of our symbolists'.

2605. Ryskamp, Charles. 'A Blake Collection for Princeton.' *Princeton University Library Chronicle*, XXI (1960), 172–5.

A description of the Lambert Collection.

2606. —— *'The Blake Collection of Mrs. Gerald B. Lambert Presented to Library.' *Princeton Alumni Weekly*, LX (12 Feb. 1960), 3–4.

General article on Blake.

2607. —— 'Blake's Cowperian Sketches.' *RES*, n.s. IX (1958), 48–9.

Two in Harvard College Library.

2608. —— *'Blake's Drawing of Cowper's Monument.' *Princeton University Library Chronicle*, XXIV (1962), 27–31.

2609. —— *Lawrence's Portrait of Cowper.' *Princeton University Library Chronicle*, XX (1959), 140–4.

The recently discovered pencil-and-wash sketch, probably by Lawrence, discussed and reproduced.

S

2610. *S., E. I. 'Seven Angels Pouring Out the Vials of the Wrath of God Upon the Earth.' *Bulletin of the Worcester Art Museum* [Mass.], XIII (1922), 13–16 (vMKN).

2611. S., P. H. 'Last Urizen.' *The Times*, 8 May 1971, p. 12.

What will happen to *Urizen* (C), bought by a dealer (29 March 1971) for £24,000?

2612. *Sage, E. 'Hayley and Blake at Felpham.' Pp. 174–88 of *Memorials of Old Sussex*. Ed. Percy D. Mundy. London, 1909.

A general sentimental piece.

2613. Saintsbury, George. 'Blake.' *Nation and Athenaeum*, XLI (1927), 634–5.

A centenary appreciation.

2614. A. —— 'Burns, Blake, and the Close of the Eighteenth Century (with an Excursus on *Ossian*).' Chap. I, pp. 3–42 (esp. pp. 8–29), of Vol. III ('From Blake to Mr. Swinburne') of *A History of English Prosody*. London, 1910. B. London, 1923. Vol. III, Chap. I ('Burns and Blake'), esp. pp. 8–29.

Includes the first printing of thirteen lines from the *French Revolution* (1791).

2615. A. —— *A History of Criticism and Literary Taste in Europe*. [3 vols.] Edinburgh & London, 1904. Vol. III, pp. 266–9. B. *A History of English*

Criticism: Being the English Chapters of A History of Criticism and Literary Taste in Europe revised, adapted and supplemented. London & Edinburgh, 1911. Pp. 376–9. C. London & Edinburgh, 1949. Pp. 376–9.

2616. A. Saintsbury, George. 'Things About Blake.' *Dial*, LXXXII (1927), 451–60 (vMKN). B. Reprinted as pp. 233–9 of *A Last Vintage*. Ed. John W. Oliver, Arthur Melville Clark, and Augustus Muir. London, 1950.
A review of Burdett, no. 1316.

2617. Saito, Kuniji. 'Shijin oyobi Gaka to shiteno William Blake [William Blake as a Poet and Painter].' *Meiji-Gakuin Daigaku Ronso* [*Meiji-Gakuin University Studies*], No. 155 (1970), 33–47 (vHK).

2618. Saito, Takeshi. 'Blake Zakkan [Talk on Blake].' *Gakuto* [*Lamplight of Learning*], LIV, No. 11 (Nov. 1957), 4–7.

2619. —— 'Kitan-naki Kansha: William Blake wo ronzu [Unreserved Thanksgiving: A Comment on William Blake].' *Bunmei Hyoron* [*Civilization Criticism*], II (1915), 214–21 (vHK).

2620. *Sakazaki, Otsuro. 'Blake—Eiko ni michita Seinaru Maboroshi ni Mugen no Kachi wo [Give Infinite Value to his Glorious and Divine Vision].' *Bijutsu Techo* [*Fine Arts Handbook*], No. 333 (Oct. 1970), 121–47 (vHK).

2621. Salmon, Arthur L. 'William Blake: Poet, Painter and Seer.' *Sun*, IV (1891), 547–51.

2622. *Salomon, Richard G. 'A Fuseli Drawing in the Huntington Library.' *HLQ*, XV (1952), 305–8 (vMKN).
Thought to be by Blake, but shown to be a drawing of Siegfried overcoming Alberich by Fuseli.

2623. Salvat, Michel. 'Les Éléments chrétiens dans la pensée de William Blake.' *Vie des Peuples*, XIV (1924), 330–59.

2624. Sampson, Edward C. 'Blake's *A Poison Tree*.' *Explicator*, VI (1947), item 19 (vMKN).
The apple is the Biblical one.

2625. Sampson, John. 'Blake Parodies 1895–1913.' Pp. 13–22 of *In Lighter Moments*: A Book of Occasional Verse and Prose. Liverpool & London, 1934.
'Songs of Idiocy and Insanity': 'I wander past each village pub . . .'.

2626. —— 'On a Manuscript Poem Attributed to William Blake.' *TLS*, 23 March 1922, p. 195 (vMKN).
An analysis of the 'Genesis' in Blake's hand, which Sampson believes to be by Hayley (see Povey, no. 2438).

2627. —— & S. Butterworth. 'Blake's Songs: An Early Private Reprint.' *N&Q*, CXIV [10th Ser. VI] (1906), 421–2, 473, 511; CXV [10th Ser. VII] (1907), 56.
Concerning the 1839 edition (no. 171).

2628. Sandell, Joseph. *Memoranda of Art and Artists*, Anecdotal and Biographical. London, 1871. P. 31.
Sandell quotes a letter from Flaxman soliciting work for Blake.

2629. Sangu, Makoto. 'Blake Inyu Zatsuwa [Talk on Blake].' *'Shikai'*: Nihon Shijin Kurabu: *The Shika*: Bulletin of the Japan Poet's Club, No. 61 (1960), 127–9.

2630. —— 'Blake no Kindaisei—sono Toyo-fu ni tsuite [Modernity in Blake—with Special Reference to his Orientalism].' *Eibungakushi* (Fukkan) Hosei Daigaku Eibungakuikai: *Studies in English Literature*, (Revival) Hosei University, No. 1 (1958), 3–4.

2631. —— 'Blake no Kotoba [Blake's Proverbs].' *Shinshicho* (Dai Sanji) [*Shinshicho Review*], 3rd Ser., No. 7 (1914), 95–7.

2632. —— 'Blake no Shimpisetsu [Blake's Mysticism].' *Mirai [Future]*, II (1915), 42–9.

2633. —— **Blake Ronko [Blake Studies]*. Tokyo & Osaka, 1929. 210 pp., 45 plates.
Reprints his 'Nihon Blake-gaku Kaiko'.

2634. —— 'Eikoku de atta Blakeans no Omoide [Memoir of Blakeans Whom I Met in England].' *Eibungaku Kenkyu: Studies in English Literature* Compiled by The English Seminar of The Tokyo Imperial University, VII (1927), 372–89.

2635. —— ***'Honshitsu-bi no Hyogen to shite no Shocho [Symbolism as an Expression of True Beauty].' *Shinshicho* (Dai Sanji) [*Shinshicho Review*], 3rd Ser. I (1914), 8–16.
Mostly about Blake.

2636. A. —— 'Nihon Blake-gaku Kaiko [Memoirs of Blake Studies in Japan].' *Eigo Kenkyu: The Study of English*, XXII (1929), 630–7, 683–9. B. Reprinted in pp. 169–93 of his *Blake Ronko* (1929).

2637. A. —— 'Shijin to shite no Blake [Blake as a Poet].' *Suzuran [Lily of the Valley]*, II (1923), 2–16. B. Reprinted in pp. 291–322 of his *Shigaku ni Noboru [Ascent of Poetic Mountain]*. Tokyo, 1925.

2638. —— 'Shoshi ni moreta Meiji-ki no Honpo Blake-bunken [Japanese Blakeana in the Meiji Era Not Included in Bibliographies].' *Eigo Seinen: The Rising Generation*, LXXXI (1939), 180–1.

2639. —— 'Toyofu no Gaka Shijin: William Blake Seitan 200-nen ni atatte [Oriental Poet and Painter: Commemoration of William Blake's Bicentenary].' *'Shikai'*: Nihon Shijin Kurabu: *The Shika*: Bulletin of the Japan Poet's Club, No. 52 (1958), 1–2.

2640. —— ***'William Blake.' Pp. 340–9 of *Igirisu Bungaku-hen Ge-kan [English Literature Part II]*. Ed. Giryo Sato. Tokyo, 1930. Sekai Bungaku Koza 4 [Lectures on World Literature Vol. IV].

2641. Sangu, Makoto. 'William Blake no Shiso [William Blake's Thought].' Pp. 181–215 of his *Shigaku ni Noboru [Ascent of Poetic Mountain]*. Tokyo, 1925.

2642. Sankey, Benjamin. 'A Preface to Blake.' *Spectrum*, IV (1960), 108–12 (vMKN).

Blake is said to have attracted the wrong kind of critics, who do not remember that most of his poetry is not very good in their zeal to expound his system, which they take too seriously.

2643. Sansom, Clive, W. P. Witcutt, and Kerrison Preston. 'Blake's Pun.' *TLS*, 22 July, 5, 19 Aug., 2 Sept. 1944, pp. 355, 379, 403, 427 (vMKN).

Urizen from 'horizon'.

2644. Sartain, John. 'William Blake and John Varley.' Chap. VIII (pp. 108–16) of *The Reminiscences of a Very Old Man 1808–1897*. N.Y., 1899.

Second-hand but important quasi-contemporary accounts of Blake on pp. 110, 112, and 114.

2645. *Sato, Kensho. 'William Blake no Shiika ni Okeru Imagination [Imagination in the Poems of William Blake].' *Eibungaku Kenkyu: Studies in English Literature* Compiled by The English Seminar of The Tokyo Imperial University, VII (1927), 390–412.

2646. A. Sato, Kiyoshi. 'Blake no [and his] Colour Print, Drawing sono Ta [and so on].' *Eibungaku Kenkyu: Studies in English Literature* Compiled by The English Seminar of The Tokyo Imperial University, VII (1927), 455–66. B. Reprinted in pp. 261–83 of his *Eishi no Seizui [The Essence of English Poetry]*. Tokyo, 1930 (vHK).

2647. A. —— §'Blake no Geijutsukan [Blake's Views on Art].' *Shisei*, No. 6 (1955), 31–4. B. Vol. III, pp. 268–71 of *Sato Kiyoshi Zenshu [Collected Works]*. Tokyo, 1964.

2648. A. —— 'Blake no "Milton" ni tsuite [On Blake's *Milton*].' *Eibungaku Kenkyu: Studies in English Literature* Compiled by The English Seminar of The Tokyo Imperial University, VII (1927), 349–71. B. Reprinted as 'Blake no "Milton" [Blake's *Milton*]' in pp. 32–64 of his *Eishi no Seizui [The Essence of English Poetry]*. Tokyo, 1930 (vHK).

2649. —— 'Blake no Shukyoshi [Blake's Religious Poems].' *Youth's Companion*, No. 9 [Japan] (Sept. 1947), 38–41.

2650. ——'Blake to [and] Shelley.' *Eigo Seinen: The Rising Generation*, CII (1956), 435.

2651. Saurat, Denis. 'Blake.' Pp. 166–9 (under 'Literary Values') of *Gods of the People*. London, 1947.

2652. A. —— *Blake and Milton*. Bordeaux, 1920. B. N.Y., 1924. C. London, 1935. D. N.Y., 1965.

A useful introduction to the relationships, parallels, and differences of the two poets.

2653. Saurat, Denis. 'Blake and Milton.' *TLS*, 11 Jan. 1936, p. 35 (vMKN).
A rejoinder to a review.

2654. A. —— *Blake & Modern Thought*. London, 1929. B. N.Y., 1964.
A provocative study of Blake and eighteenth-century thought, conducted
on the productive principles that 'there was not an absurdity in Europe at
the end of the 18th century that Blake did not know' and that 'Blake's ideas
considered as a whole are perfectly coherent and reasonable'. Saurat's
generalizations are very useful, and when he chooses his scholarship is good,
but he chooses infrequently.

2655. —— 'Blake et la Pensée moderne.' *Messages*, I (1939), 20–3.

2656. —— 'Blake et les Celtomanes.' *MP*, XXIII (1925), 175–88.
Demonstrates that Blake's odd ideas about the Druids were commonplace
among his contemporaries, and suggests that he was deliberately writing for
an initiated audience.

2657. —— 'Blake, la Pensée moderne et les Gnostiques.' *Yggdrasil*, No. 5
(Aug.–Sept. 1936), 3–6, and No. 6 (23 Oct. 1936), 1–7.
A study of Blake's eighteenth-century sources.

2658. A. —— 'Les Éléments religieux non chrétiens dans la poésie moderne.'
Revue de Littérature Comparée, III (1923), 337–58 (vMKN). B. Reprinted as
pp. 15–61 of *La Littérature et L'Occultisme*. Paris, 1929. C. Tr. by Dorothy
Bolton as *Literature and Occult Tradition*. London, 1930. D. §N.Y., 1930.
Blake is discussed *passim* in the books cited here.

2659. —— 'Male and Female in Blake.' Pp. 134–7 of his *Gods of the People*.
London, 1947.

2660. —— 'Spiritual Attitudes in Spenser, Milton, Blake and Hugo.'
Comparative Literature Studies, XIV (1944), 8–12, 23–7.
Blake saw further than the others, and his visions are beautiful, but he did
not understand what he saw.

2661. —— *William Blake*. Paris, 1954.
On Blake as an occultist, in French.

2662. Schaupp, Roscoe Frederick. 'Blake's "Correction" of Milton in Poem
and Picture.' Ohio State University Ph.D., 1934; cf. *Abstracts of Dissertations,
Ohio State University*, No. 15 (1934), 171–80 (vMKN).

2663. *Schmutzler, R. 'Blake and Art Nouveau.' *Architectural Review*, CXVIII
(Aug. 1955), 90–7 (vMKN).
Blake, Rossetti, and Japan the most important influences on Art Nouveau.

2664. A. Schorer, Mark. 'Blake as a Religious Poet.' *Sewanee Review*, LIV
(1946), 241–9. B. Incorporated in his *William Blake* (1946).

2665. —— *'How the Eighteenth Century Died to Music.' *Reading and
Collecting*, II (1937), 7–8 (vMKN).
Historical account of the *Poetical Sketches*.

2666. Schorer, Mark. *'Magic as an Instrumental Value: Blake and Yeats.'
Hemispheres, [Éditions de la Maison Française, N.Y.], II, No. 5 (Spring 1945)
Special Number, 49–54 (vMKN).

Blake and Yeats, 'unwilling to submit their individuality to nature as
science had discovered it', turned 'to those methods which science had
discarded', among them magic. Substantially the same discussion is in
Schorer's *William Blake* (1946), pp. 52–7.

2667. A. —— 'The Mask of William Blake.' *Yale Review*, XXXI (1942),
747–63. B. Incorporated in *William Blake* (1946).

Blake is complex and intelligent, not just inspired as he himself claimed.

2668. A. —— 'Mythology (For the Study of Blake).' *Kenyon Review*, IV
(1942), 366–80. B. Incorporated in his *William Blake* (1946).

Blake reorganized Christian myth for his poetry.

2669. A. —— 'Swedenborg and Blake.' *MP*, XXXVI (1938), 157–8.
B. Incorporated in his *William Blake* (1946), 104–22.

A sound, suggestive examination of the elements in Swedenborg's thought
which appealed to Blake.

2670. —— 'William Blake and the Cosmic Nadir.' *Sewannee Review*, XLIII
(1935), 210–21 (vMKN).

Blake and Bacon, Newton, Locke.

2671. —— 'William Blake as a Radical.' University of Wisconsin Ph.D.,
1936; cf. *Summaries of Doctoral Dissertations, University of Wisconsin*, I (1937),
288–90 (vMKN).

Presumably revised in *William Blake* (1946).

2672. A. —— *William Blake*: The Politics of Vision. N.Y., 1946. *B. N.Y.,
1959. Vintage Books.

A. The book incorporates no. 2644, 2666–9, 2671; it includes contemporary records of Blake (pp. 18–19). The work is an important examination
of the radical element in Blake's poetry and society.

B. The 1959 edition was reduced in bulk by about 10 per cent but was not
revised.

2673. —— & Charles P. Parkhurst, Jr. 'Blake, William.' Pp. 494–5 of
Vol. III of *Collier's Encyclopedia*. N.Y., [1953].

2674. Schulz, Max F. 'Point of View in Blake's "The Clod & The Pebble".'
Papers on Language & Literature, II (1966), 217–24.

The point of view is that of the Bard; an answer to Hagstrum.

2675. *Schuyler, James, compiler. 'Grandeur of ideas is founded on precision of ideas.' *Art News*, LVI (Oct. 1957), 30–1, 63.

A 'collage' of Blake's designs and opinions on art.

2676. Scott, William Bell. *Autobiographical Notes of the Life of William Bell
Scott*. Ed. W. Minto. [2 vols.] London, 1892. Vol. I, pp. 21–2.

An account of the effect of Blair's *Grave* with the Blake illustrations. (The manuscript of the book is in Princeton, N.J.)

2677. Scott, William Bell. 'The Blake Catalogue.' *Academy*, IX (1876), 385 (vMKN).
Of the exhibition (1876).

2678. —— *Memoirs of David Scott, R.S.A.* Containing his Journal in Italy, Notes on Art and Other Papers: with seven illustrations. Edinburgh, 1850. P. 238.
David Scott refers in passing to Blake's purity of design and deficiency in execution.

2679. —— **'A Varley-and-Blake Sketch-Book.' *Portfolio*, II (1871), 103–5.

2680. Scott-James, R. A. 'The Master Mystic.' Chap. xii (pp. 174–88) of his *Modernism and Romance*. London & N.Y., 1908.
A general account of Blake and his critics.

2681. A. [Scudder, Horace Elisha.] 'Looking at a Picture.' Pp. 9–21 of *Stories from My Attic*. Boston, 1869 (vDVE). B. Boston, 1896. C. N.Y., 1897.
An insignificant appreciation.

2682. *Scudder, H. E. 'William Blake. Painter and Poet.' *Scribner's Monthly* [*Century*], XX (1880), 225–40 (vMKN).
A general article mostly on Blake's art.

2683. §Sekimoto, Eiichi. 'Shijin Blake [Blake the Poet].' *Shiro* [*The Castle*], VIII (Dec. 1957), 9–13.

2684. —— 'Blake Kenkyu Josetsu [An Introduction to the Study of W. Blake].' *Meiji-Gakuin Ronso: The Meiji-Gakuin Review*, No. 23 (1951), 75–91.

2685. Seligo, Irene. 'Der Prophet in seinem Vaterlande: William Blake.' Pp. 232–74 of *Zwischen Traum und Tat: Englische Profile*. Frankfort, a.M., 1938 (vMKN).
Much on Swedenborgian influence.

2686. Senior, John. 'Hermetic Vessels: Blake and Hugo.' Pp. 52–73 of his *The Way Down and Out*. The Occult in Symbolist Literature. Ithaca [N.Y.], 1959.
An excellent suggestive essay on Blake's occultism.

2687. Serra, Beatrice. 'Un Pioniere dei Lirici Inglesi del sec. XIX: William Blake.' *Revista d'Italia*, XIX (1926), 983–1007.

2688. Serra, Cristóbal. 'El rapto de un visionario: W. Blake.' *Papeles de son Armadans*, XLVI [No. cxxxvi] (1967), ii–ix.

2689. Sethna, K. D. 'Blake's Tyger: A New Interpretation.' Pp. 170–213 of *Critical Essays on English Literature* Presented to Professor M. S. Durai-swami on the occasion of his Sixty-first birthday. Ed. V. S. Seturaman. Bombay, Calcutta, Madras, New Delhi, 1965.

A grammatical 'analysis of the poem's internal pattern' indicates that 'it is an original reconstruction of the Christian parable of rebellion in heaven' (p. 210).

2690. *Sewter, A. C. 'William Blake and the Art of the Book.' *Manchester Review*, VIII (1959–60), 360–73.
A general lecture on the way Blake illustrated his own works.

2691. *Seymour, Charles. 'Blake's Esthetic and His Century.' *Parnassus*, XI (Feb. 1939), 10–13 (vMKN).

2692. Seymour-Smith, Martin. *Poets through their letters*. London, 1969. Pp. 250–8.
Excerpts from letters interspersed with comments.

2693. Sharrock, Roger. 'Godwin on Milton's Satan.' *N&Q*, n.s. IX (1962), 463–5.
Perhaps Godwin preceded Blake as a Satanist.

2694. Shaw, Edward J. 'William Blake, as Painter.' *Midland Magazine*, V, Supplement (1880), 252–61.

2695. Shepherd, Richard Herne. 'Blake's Songs of Innocence.' *Academy*, VII (1875), 636.
Letter describing Pearson's copy.

2696. Shepherd, T. B. *Methodism and the Literature of the Eighteenth Century*. London, 1940. Pp. 243–7.
'The greatest poet of the Evangelical Revival was William Blake.'

2697. Sherwood, Margaret. 'William Blake and Catherine.' *North American Review*, CCII (1915), 576–91 (vMKN).

2698. *Shields, Frederic J. 'Blake's Work Room and Death Room and Rossetti's Sonnet.' *Manchester Quarterly*, XXIX (1910), 93–8 (vDS).
With half-tone reproduction of Shields's drawing of the room.

2699. Shima, Fujiro. 'Blake ni tsuite [On Blake].' *The Muse*, V (1927), 2–3.

2700. Sholl, Anna McClure. 'William Blake.' *Catholic World*, CXXV (1927), 653–7 (vMKN).
Centenary article.

2701. Shook, Margaret Lulu. 'Visionary Form: Blake's Prophetic Art and the Pictorial Tradition.' *DA*, XXVII (1967), 4265A.

2702. A. *Short, Ernest H. *Blake*. London, 1925. British Artists. §B. N.Y., 1970.
A surprisingly informative little book, concentrating, naturally, on Blake's art.

2703. *Simmons, Robert, & Janet Warner. 'Blake's *Arlington Court Picture*: The Moment of Truth.' *Studies in Romanticism*, X (1971), 3–20.
'The composition and details of the picture itself' indicate that it represents

'the moment . . . [*of*] the full recognition' of 'the philosophical and psychological fall of man' (pp. 3, 20). (For an attempted rebuttal of 'the Simmons–Warner Theory', see Grant, no. 1217 55.)

2704. *Simon, Howard. 'William Blake 1757–1827.' Pp. 68–80 of his *500 Years of Art in Illustration* From Albrecht Dürer to Rockwell Kent. Cleveland & N.Y., 1945.

2705. Simons, Joan O. 'Teaching Symbolism in Poetry'. *College English*, XXIII (1962), 301–2.
How to teach freshmen, with 'Ah, Sun-flower' as an example.

2706. *Singer, Charles. 'The first English microscopist: Robert Hooke (1635–1703).' *Endeavor*, XIV (1955), 12–18.
Blake's 'Ghost of a Flea' was influenced by Hooke's drawing of a microscope observation of a flea's head and neck in *Micrographia* (1665). See also no. 2026.

2707. A. *Singer, June K. *The Unholy Bible*: A Psychological Interpretation of William Blake. N.Y., 1970. B. N.Y., Evanston, San Francisco, London, 1973.
M. Esther Harding, 'Introduction', is pp. xi–xvi. The book is an examination by a Jungian analyst of Blake's mythological works, chiefly (pp. 39–176) of *The Marriage* (pl. 1–24 of which are reproduced [from copy C] and reprinted), which is the product of Catherine's refusal any 'longer [*to*] allow him any sexual intimacy' (p. 45) and of 'his naive conviction that what he wrote was dictated by an unseen voice' (p. 10).

2708. *Siple, Ella S. 'Art in America.' *Burlington Magazine*, LXXX (1942) 77–8 (vMKN).
Exhibition of *Pilgrim's Progress* series at the Knoedler Gallery.

2709. Sitwell, Edith, ed. *The American Genius*: An Anthology of Poetry with Some Prose. London, 1951. Pp. viii–xi of the introduction.
On the kinship of Blake and Whitman.

2710. —— 'Applicable to Blake.' Pp. 53–4 of *A Poet's Notebook*. London, 1943.

2711. —— ed., *The Pleasures of Poetry*: A Critical Anthology. Second Series: The Romantic Revival. London, 1931. Pp. 17–40.
The analysis in the 'Introduction' of the verse-sounds in Blake's poetry (pp. 69–110) is excellent.

2712. —— 'Whitman and Blake.' *Proceedings of the American Academy of Arts and Letters and the National Institute of Arts and Letters*, Series 2, No. 1 (1951), 52–8.

2713. —— 'William Blake.' Pp. 111–21 of *Edith Sitwell's Anthology*. London, 1940.
An anthology of notes Edith Sitwell wrote on Blake from time to time for herself.

2714. Skelton, John. 'William Blake.' Pp. 260–7 of his *Essays in History and Biography* including The Defence of Mary Stuart. Edinburgh & London, 1883.
An admiring general essay.

2715. *Sketchley, R. E. D. 'Some British Illustrators of the Bible: Blake's "Illustrations to the Book of Job".' *Art Journal*, XLII (1903), 114–18 (vMKN).
A commentary. Includes sonnet by Rossetti inspired by sketch of Blake's work room, reproduced here.

2716. A. [Smetham, James.] 'Art. I. *Life of William Blake* . . . .' *The London Quarterly Review*, XXXI (1869), 265–311. B. Reprinted as 'William Blake.' Essay II, pp. 98–194, of *The Literary Works of James Smetham*. Ed. William Davies. London & N.Y., 1893. C. Reprinted, with many of the quotations from and references to Gilchrist's life omitted, in the 1880 edition of Gilchrist.
Originally a review of Gilchrist.

2717. A. *Smith, Bernard. 'European Vision and the South Pacific.' *JWCI*, XIII (1950), 65–100. B. *European Vision and the South Pacific 1768–1850*. A Study in the History of Art and Ideas. Oxford, 1960.
The Blake engraving in Hunter is identified, and in B the sketch from which it was probably made is reproduced.

2718. Smith, David J. 'Blake's THE DIVINE IMAGE.' *Explicator*, XXV (1967), item 69.
'*T*he poem is a syllogism' that the divine is in all men.

2719. Smith, Henry Justin. 'The Poetry of William Blake.' *The Century Illustrated Magazine*, N.S., XXXVIII (1900), 284–91 (vMKN).
Undergraduate prize essay.

2720. Smith, J. C. 'A Blake Head Piece.' *TLS*, 20 April 1933, p. 276 (vMKN).
Plate 5 of *Marriage* to be seen upside down for the Devil's view of it.

2721. Smith, James. *Lights and Shadows of Artist Life and Character*. London, 1853. Pp. 7, 249–53.
Anecdotes from Cunningham.

2722. A. Smith, John Thomas. *A Book for a Rainy Day*: or, Recollections of the Events of the last Sixty-Six Years. London, 1845. Pp. 81–2. B. Second Edition. London, 1845. Pp. 81–3. C. *A Book for a Rainy Day*: or, Recollections of the Events of the Years 1766–1833. Third Edition, Revised. London, 1861. Pp. 83–4. D. Ed. Wilfred Whitten. London, 1905. Pp. 96–7.
There is no change of substance in this important Blake account in any of these editions. The Blake section is reprinted in A. Symons, *William Blake* (1907) and in *Blake Records* (1969).

2723. A. —— 'William Blake.' Vol. II, pp. 454–88, of NOLLEKENS / AND HIS TIMES: / COMPREHENDING A / LIFE OF THAT CELEBRATED SCULPTOR; / AND MEMOIRS OF SEVERAL / CONTEMPORARY ARTISTS, / FROM THE TIME OF / ROUBILIAC,

HOGARTH, AND REYNOLDS, / TO THAT OF / FUSELI, FLAXMAN, AND BLAKE. / BY / JOHN THOMAS SMITH, / KEEPER OF THE PRINTS AND DRAWINGS IN THE BRITISH MUSEUM. / IN TWO VOLUMES. / VOL. I [II]. / LONDON: / HENRY COLBURN, NEW BURLINGTON STREET. / 1828. See also Vol. I, pp. iv, 156. (BM, GEB)

B. SECOND EDITION. / . . . BURLINGTON-STREET. / 1829. (BM)

C. *Nollekens and his Times*, And Memoirs of Contemporary Artists from the Time of Roubiliac Hogarth and Reynolds to that of Fuseli Flaxman and Blake. Ed. Wilfred Whitten. In Two Volumes. London & N.Y., 1920. Vol. I, p. vii; Vol. II, pp. 366–95.

The lineation of the title of B differs slightly from A in ways not recorded above.

There are no changes of substance in any of these important accounts of Blake. The biography is reproduced in facsimile in Wittreich (1970) and reprinted in Symons (1907) and *Blake Records* (1969).

2724. Smith, W. 'William Blake's "Book of Thel".' *N&Q*, LII [5th Ser. IV] (1875), 449–50 (vMKN).

Query concerning two omitted lines in the Bodleian copy.

2725. Smith, William Marion. 'Four Songs on Texts by William Blake. [Original Composition.]' *DA*, XXVIII (1967), 254A. Florida State Ph.D., 1966.

Set for soprano and orchestra.

2726. A. §*Soupault, Philippe. *William Blake*. 40 planches hors-texte en héliogravure. Paris, 1928. B. Tr. J. Lewis May. With forty illustrations. London, 1928. Masters of Modern Art.

The plates include all the engravings for the *Grave*, and 14 for Young's *Night Thoughts*. The essay is factually unreliable but it criticizes Blake's art usefully.

2727. —— *'William Blake.' *Connaissance des Arts*, No. 31 (15 Sept. 1954), 54–9 (vWKenney).

An appreciation, stressing his unique qualities.

2728. —— §'William Blake: Les Années de combat (1788–1811).' *Chantecler*, 14 Jan. 1928.

About engravings.

2729. [Southey, Robert.] '*Art. XVII.*—Ballads. By *William Hayley, Esq.* Founded on Anecdotes relating to Animals, with Prints, designed and engraved by *William Blake*. 8vo. pp. 212.' *The Annual Review*, and History of Literature; for 1805, IV (1806), 575. (BM)

The review bitingly mocks both artist and poet.

2730. Southey, Robert. *The Correspondence of Robert Southey with Caroline Bowles*. Ed. Edward Dowden. London & Dublin, 1881. Pp. 191, 193–4.

References to Blake in letters of Caroline Bowles (27 April 1830) and Southey (8 May 1830).

2731. A. [Southey, Robert.] *The Doctor, &c.* London, [Vols. I–III] 1834, [Vol. IV] 1837, [Vol. V] 1838, [Vols. VI & VII] 1847. Vol. VI, pp. 116–27, Vol. VII, pp. 161–2. B. Robert Southey. *The Doctor, &c.* Ed. John Wood Warter. Complete in One Volume. London, 1848. Pp. 473–6 and 578–9. C. *The Doctor, &c.* Ed. John Wood Warter. New Edition, Complete in One Volume. London, 1849. Pp. 473–6 and 578–9.

These references (chaps. clxxxi and ccxiv) are important for the suggestion that William Owen was the source of Blake's knowledge of Welsh history and literature.

2732. A. —— ed. *The Works of William Cowper, Esq.* Comprising His Poems, Correspondence, and Translations. With a Life of the Author. [15 vols.] London, [Vol. I] 1835, [Vols. II–XV] 1836. Vol. III, p. 238. B. Reprinted In Eight Volumes. London, 1853. Vol. II, p. 160.

A letter from William Hayley to Lady Hesketh, referring to Blake, appears at the end of the biography.

2733. A. Speaight, George. *Juvenile Drama*: The History of the English Toy Theatre. London, 1946. Pp. 93–5. B. *The History of the English Toy Theatre.* London, 1969. Pp. 72–3.

The 'W. B.' who signed the engraving *The Broken Sword* in West's New Theatrical Characters is not the poet.

2734. Spicer, Harold Otis. 'Biblical Sources of William Blake's *America.*' *Ball State University Forum*, VIII, iii (1967), 23–9.

'The Guardian Prince of Albion is [*both*] Goliath . . . [*and the archangel*] Michael' (pp. 25, 26).

2735. —— '*The Chariot of Fire*: A Study of William Blake's Use of Biblical Typology in the Minor Prophecies.' Wisconsin Ph.D., 1962; cf. *DA*, XXIII (1962), 2141.

2736. Spilling, James. 'Blake, Artist and Poet.' *New Church Magazine*, VI (1887), 253–9.
Insignificant.

2737. —— 'Blake the Visionary.' *New Church Magazine*, VI (1887), 204–11.
A brief historical sketch in which Blake's ambivalent attitude toward Swedenborg is quoted as conveyed by Blake to Tulk to Wilkinson to Spilling.

2738. A. Spooner, Shearjashub. *Anecdotes of Painters, Engravers Sculptors and Architects, and Curiosities of Art.* In Three Volumes. N.Y., 1853. Vol. I, pp. 3–4; Vol. II, p. 79. §B. N.Y., 1854. C. N.Y., 1880. Vol. I, pp. 3–4, Vol. II, p. 79.
The facts about Blake are taken from Cunningham.

2739. A. —— *A Biographical Dictionary of Painters, Engravers, Sculptors and Architects*, from Ancient to Modern Times. N.Y., 1853. P. 106. B. §Boston, 1865. . . . D. *A Biographical History of the Fine Arts*: Being Memoirs of the Lives and Works of Eminent Painters, Engravers, Sculptors and Architects, from

the Earliest Ages to the Present Time. [2 vols.] Fourth Edition. N.Y., 1867.
Vol. I, p. 106.
  The brief and inaccurate reference of 1853 grew to four simple paragraphs
by 1867.

2740. Spurgeon, Caroline F. E. *Mysticism in English Literature*. Cambridge,
1913. Cambridge Manuals of Science and Literature. Pp. 129–47 and *passim*.

2741. Stahly, F. 'William Blake. Galerie René Drouin.' *Werk*, XXXIV (May
1947), 59–60 (vMKN).

2742. —— A. *'William Blake: The Visionary in Book-Craft.' *Graphis*, IV
(1948), [English] 2–7, [German] 7–10, [French] 10–13 (vMKN).

2743. Standing, Percy Cross. 'Was Blake a Poet?' *Catholic World*, LXXXI
(1905), 445–50 (vMKN).
  The answer is no, and 'The Tyger' is 'arrant drivel'.

2744. Statham, H. H. 'The Blake Drawings at the Burlington Fine Arts
Club.' *Macmillan's Magazine*, XXXIV (1876), 55–68 (vMKN).
  A commentary on the exhibition.

2745. Stavrou, Constantine M. 'A Reassessment of *The Marriage of Heaven
and Hell*.' *South Atlantic Quarterly*, LIV (1955), 381–5.
  Brief general article.

2746. —— 'William Blake and D. H. Lawrence.' *University of Kansas City
Review*, XXII (1956), 235–40.
  Their similarities briefly noted.

2747. —— 'William Blake & D. H. Lawrence: A Comparative Study in the
Similarity of Their Thought.' Buffalo Ph.D., 1952; cf. *DA*, XII (1952),
430–1 (vMKN).

2748. A. *Stedman, Edmund C. 'William Blake, Poet and Painter.' *Critic*,
I (1881), 3, 5 (vMKN). B. Reprinted as 'William Blake, Painter and Poet.'
Pp. 21–8 of *Essays from "The Critic."* [Ed. Anon.] Boston, 1882. C. Re-
printed as pp. 102–6 of *Genius and Other Essays*. N.Y., 1911 (vDVE).
  A general article.

2749. Stedman, John Gabriel. *The Journal of John Gabriel Stedman 1744–1797
Soldier and Author Including an authentic account of his expenidtion to
Surinam, in 1772*. Ed. Stanbury Thompson. London, 1962. Pp. 336, 352,
360, 363, 381–4, 389–92, 395, 397.
  Contemporary references to Blake.

2750. Stein, Kenneth. 'Blake's Apocalyptic Poetry: A Study of the Genre of
Blake's Prophetic Books.' *DAI*, XXX (1969), 2500A, Brandeis Ph.D.
  A study 'of their indebtedness to the apocalyptic books of the Bible and
the intertestamental era'.

2751. Steiner, Henry-York. 'The Emanation and its Spectres: William

Blake's Theory of Poetry.' Oregon Ph.D., 1963; cf. *DA*, XXIV (1964), 4684.
'Blake's poetry was Romantic in nature.'

2752. Stenberg, Theodore T. 'Blake's Indebtedness to the "Eddas".' *MLR*, XVIII (1923), 204–6.
Mostly names.

2753. Stephens, F. G. Masterpieces of Mulready. *Memorials of William Mulready.* London & Cambridge, 1867. P. 44.
Stephens's account of an occasion on which Varley took Blake to Lady Blessington's house appears to be unique.

2754. —— 'Samuel Palmer.' *Portfolio*, 1872, pp. 162–9.
Quotes a letter from Palmer of 1871 which refers in passing to Blake (p. 164).

2755. Stevenson, Stanley Warren. 'Artful Irony in Blake's "The Fly".' *Texas Studies in Literature and Language*, X (1968), 77–82.
Stresses 'the mental context'.

2756. —— 'The Creative Motif in Romantic Poetry and Theory with Particular Reference to the Myth of Blake and the Poetic Theory of Blake and Coleridge.' Northwestern Ph.D., 1958; cf. *DA*, XIX (1958), 1368–9.

2757. Stevenson, W. H. 'Blake's "From Cratetos": A Source and a Correction.' *N&Q*, CCXIII [N.s. XV] (1968), 21.
'The epigram [on *NOTEBOOK p. 64*] is a translation of two iambic lines attributed to Crates of Thebes.'

2758. —— 'Blake's *Jerusalem*.' *Essays in Criticism*, IX (1959), 254–64 (vMKN).
Blake could not handle larger structures.

2759. —— 'Circle, Centre and Circumference in Blake.' *Ibadan Studies in English*, 1 (Spring 1970), 1956–65.

2760. —— 'The Shaping of Blake's "America".' *MLR*, LV (1960), 497–503.
An attempt to show Blake's poetic method 'as we can deduce it from the fragments and the completed version of *America*', and to date the composition in 1792.

2761. —— 'A Study of Blake's *Song of Liberty, Visions of the Daughters of Albion, America* and *Europe*.' Oxford B.Litt. thesis, 1956.

2762. —— 'William Blake, Dr. Priestley and the Gnostics.' *N&Q*, CCII [N.s. IV] (1957), 122.
Blake could have encountered Gnostic ideas in Priestley's *A History of the Early Opinions Concerning Jesus Christ* (1780).

2763. —— 'Yeats and Blake: The Use of Symbols.' Pp. 219–25 of *1865 W. B. Yeats 1965*: Centenary Essays on the Art of W. B. Yeats. Ed. D. E. S. Maxwell & S. B. Bushrui. Ibadan, 1965.

'The root of the matter is that Yeats was a disciplined thinker, and Blake was not, although he was the profounder of the two.' (P. 219.)

2764. Stoddard, Richard Henry. 'William Blake.' Pp. 164–81 of *Under the Evening Lamp*. London, 1893.
A general appreciation.

2765. Stokoe, Frank. 'William Blake.' *Plume*, XV (1903), 325–33.
An introduction to Blake chiefly from Yeats's introduction (no. 293), with translations of poems.

2766. Stone, George Winchester. 'Blake's "The Tyger".' *Explicator*, I (1942), item 19 (vMKN).
The poem is about the wonder of God and the evil of the tiger.

2767. Stone, M. W. 'William Blake and the Juvenile Drama.' *Theatre Notebook*, I (1946), 41.
The plates for West's New Theatrical Characters, though signed 'W.B. ft', were neither designed nor engraved by the poet. Cf. no. 2872.

2768. Story, Alfred T. 'Blake and Linnell.' Pp. 259–68 of *James Holmes and John Varley*. London, 1894. Cf. also *passim*.
This general anecdotal history does not contain new material.

2769. —— *The Life of John Linnell*. In Two Volumes. London, 1892.
Blake appears throughout the first volume; in particular, there are apparently first-hand accounts of Blake in Vol. I, pp. 148–51, 158–63, 168–77, 179, 192, 194, 223–5, 228, 231, 241, 243–7, 281.

2770. —— *'The Royal Academy Old Masters Exhibition: William Blake and His Disciples.' Art Journal, [XLV] (1893), 43–4 (vMKN).

2771. A. —— 'William Blake.' *Temple Bar*, CVI (1895), 525–37. B. *Littell's Living Age*, CCVIII (1896), 177–85 (vMKN). C. *Eclectic Magazine*, CXXVI (1896), 319–27 (vMKN).
A general account, stimulated by the Royal Academy exhibition.

2772. A. —— *William Blake*: His Life Character and Genius. London & N.Y., 1893. B. §N.Y., 1970.
Despite the author's access to extensive original materials, this brief pedestrian biography adds no independent facts to the poet's life.

2773. —— *'William Blake, Poet and Painter.' Literary Collector, III (1901), 33–8.
A general account.

2774. —— 'William Blake, Seer and Painter.' *Temple Bar*, XVII (1866), 95–105.
This general and not conspicuously accurate account of Blake begins as a review of Gilchrist.

2775. Stothard, Robert T. 'Stothard and Blake.' *Athenaeum*, No. 1886 (19 Dec. 1863), p. 838.

'I cannot admit Mr. Gilchrist's assertion that there was any apparent ill-will between my father and Blake'; nor, apparently, that there were grounds for ill-will in the cases of the Blair and Chaucer illustrations. (Stothard's letter is reprinted in Keynes [1921].)

2776. A. Strachey, G. Lytton. 'The Poetry of Blake.' *Independent Review*, IX (1906), 215–26 (vMKN). B. Reprinted (pp. 209–22) in *Books and Characters* French and English. London, 1922. C. Reprinted (pp. 179–90) in *Books & Characters* French and English. London, 1924. D. Reprinted (pp. 139–50) in *Literary Essays*. London, 1948. E. Tr. into Japanese by Bunsho Jugaku in no. 1219 14.

Eulogistic reviews of the Sampson editions, no. 275, 300.

2777. Strong, L. A. G. *The Sacred River*: An Approach to James Joyce. London, 1949. Pp. 83–9.

Three writers who most deeply influenced Joyce: Shakespeare, Swift, and Blake.

2778. Struck, Wilhelm. *Der Einfluss Jacob Boehmes auf die englische Literatur des 17. Jahrhunderts*. Berlin, 1936. Neue Deutsche Forschungen Abteilung englische Philologie. Band 6. Pp. 252–3.

A revision of a §Rostock dissertation.

2779. Stutfield, Geoffrey. 'L'Imagination chez Blake.' *Messages*, I (1939), 28–34.

2780. Sudo, Nobuo. 'William Blake no Kirisutokyo [William Blake's Inter-pretation of Christianity].' *Meiji-Gakuin Ronso: the Meiji-Gakuin Review*, No. 50 (1958), 1–21.

2781. *Summers, Montague. 'The Toy Theatre.' *The Connoisseur*, C (1937), 295–301 (vMKN).

Illustrations for scripts supposed to be by Blake (but are not).

2782. *Sutherland, Graham. 'A Trend in English Draughtsmanship.' *Signature*, III (1936), 7–13.

Analyses Blake's style and the modern trend which has developed from it.

2783. A. Sutherland, John H. 'Blake's "Mental Traveller".' *ELH*, XXII (1955), 136–47. B–C. Reprinted in Grant and O'Neill.

An analysis.

2784. —— 'William Blake and Nonviolence.' *Nation*, CCVIII (1969), 542–4.

'Blake surely preferred "Mental" to "Corporeal War".'

2785. *Sutton, Denys. 'Blake and His Era.' *New York Times*, 1 Sept. 1957 (vMKN).

2786. Sutton, Eric A. 'Swedenborg and Blake.' *New-Church Magazine*, April–June 1929, 77–85.

Neither Blake nor his critics have understood Swedenborg.

2787. Suzuki, Teiji. 'Hyogen to sono Haigo no Sekai—William Blake no Baai [Literary Expression and its Background—The Case of William Blake].' *Kyoyo Shogaku Kenkyu* (Waseda Seikeigakubu) [*Studies in Liberal Arts* (Waseda University Department of Politics and Economics)], No. 5 (1957), 3–22.

2788. —— 'William Blake: His Literary Expression.' *Eibungaku* (Waseda Eibungakkai) [*English Literature* (Waseda University English Literary Society)], VI (1953), 19–30.

2789. —— §'William Blake no Shogai [The Life of William Blake].' *Toei* [*The Toei*], No. 2 (July 1933), 1.

2790. Swainson, W. P. *William Blake*, Seer, Poet, & Artist. London, [1908]. Christian Mystics No. 8.
Trivial.

2791. *Sweeney, John L. 'The Winthrop Collection: Imaginative Design: Blake to the Pre-Raphaelites.' *Art News*, XLII (1–14 Jan. 1944), 19, 35–6.
The Greville Winthrop gift to Harvard included over fifty Blake pictures.

SWINBURNE, Algernon Charles. See also Herbert HARVEY, a possible pseudonym.

2792. Swinburne, Algernon Charles. 'Blake ou le Feu.' *Fontaine*, XI (1947), 222–35.

2793. —— 'La Génie et la Foi de William Blake: Nietzsche et Blake.' [Tr. Raymond Brugère.] *Navire d'Argent*, I (Sept. 1925), 383–5.

2794. —— *The Swinburne Letters*. [6 vols.] Ed. Cecil Y. Lang. New Haven [Conn.], [Vols. I–II] 1959, [III–IV] 1960, [V–VI] 1962. *Passim.*
Most of the references are to Swinburne's book on Blake.

2795. A. —— **William Blake*: A Critical Essay. London, 1868, B. *Second Edition. London, 1868. C. *London, 1906. D. *N.Y., 1906. E. London, 1925. F. 'William Blake.' Vol. XVI, pp. 49–350 of *The Complete Works of Algernon Charles Swinburne*. Ed. Sir Edmund Gosse and Thomas James Wise. Prose Works Vol. VI. London & N.Y., 1926. G. §*William Blake* N.Y., 1967. H. Ed. Hugh J. Luke. Lincoln, Nebraska, 1970.
There are one or two first-hand accounts of Blake from Kirkup (notably on p. 81 fn. of A), which are, however, given at greater length in no. 1714, 2054.
This book, Swinburne's most ambitious critical work, reveals frequent pithy insights into Blake's early writings, and is often frankly ecstatic about Blake's ideas. Swinburne found the Prophecies a mere 'sea of words'—a remarkable judgement considering his own poetic practice. A 2-page 'Note Added by the Author in 1906' apparently printed only at the end of F suggests that Blake's defects are explained by his Celtic blood, his greatness by his English upbringing.
H. In the 1970 edition, Luke's 'Introduction' is pp. vii–xix and his 'Notes' on sources pp. 309–19. The text is that of 1868, with the 1906 note.

2796. Swingle, L. J. 'Answers to Blake's "Tyger": A Matter of Reason or of Choice?' *Concerning Poetry*, II (Spring 1969), 61–71.

'*It* simply is not rationally possible . . . to produce answers' in 'The Tyger' (p. 61).

2797. *Swingler, Randall, and Paul Hogarth. 'William Blake Engraver: Born 28 November 1757.' *New Reasoner*, I (1957), 'Blake Bicentenary Supplement', i–xii.

This Blake Supplement is chiefly an introduction to Blake as an artist.

2798. Symons, Arthur. 'Blake et Nietsche.' *Fontaine*, XI (1947), 236–44.

2799. —— 'Blake's "Nest of Villains" Unearthed.' *Athenaeum*, No. 4177 (1907), 618 (vMKN).

Identifies the *Examiner* as Robert Hunt.

2800. A. —— 'The Family of William Blake.' *Athenaeum*, No. 4096 (1906), 515–16. B. Incorporated in his *William Blake* (1907).

2801. —— 'A French Blake: Odilon Redon.' *Art Review*, I (1890), 205–6.

There is a 'wonderful' though coincidental 'kinship' between Blake and Redon, who draws 'almost with the eyes of Blake'.

2802. —— 'La Place de William Blake.' Tr. George Luciani. *Navire d'Argent*, I (1925), 371–82.

2803. —— 'Some Notes on Blake. (From the Cumberland Papers.)' *Saturday Review*, CII (1906), 231–2.

2804. A. —— *William Blake*. London, 1907. B. Reprinted in Volume IV of *The Collected Works of Arthur Symons*. London, 1924. C. §1928. D. §N.Y., 1970. E. §Introduction tr. into Japanese by Kazumi (Hojin) Yano in *Mizugame* [*Water-Pitcher*], II (1915), No. 3–4, 7–8.

The latter part of A (not reprinted in B–C) includes reprints of:

1. H. C. Robinson, Reminiscences, transcribed anew by Symons (pp. 253–306), reproduced in facsimile in Wittreich (1970).
2. Malkin, *Memoirs* (pp. 309–29).
3. Charlotte Bury, *Diary* (pp. 333–5).
4. [R. C. Smith], *Urania* (pp. 339–41).
5. *Literary Gazette* obituary (pp. 345–8).
6. *Gentleman's Magazine* obituary (pp. 349–50).
7. Varley, *Zodiacal Physiognomy* (pp. 353–4).
8. J. T. Smith, *Nollekens* (pp. 357–87).
9. J. T. Smith, *A Book for a Rainy Day* (pp. 387–8).
10. Cunningham, *Lives* (pp. 391–433), first edition.

It also incorporates no. 2800.

E. The 1970 edition is a reprint of that of 1907.

2805. —— 'William Blake (1757–1827).' Pp. 37–51 of *The Romantic Movement in English Literature*. London, 1909.

2806. Szerb, Antal. *William Blake.* Szeged [Hungary], 1928. Széphalom-Könyvatár, No. 10.
In Hungarian, 21 pp.

T

2807. §Tai, Liu-ling. 'Lun Pu-lai-k'o-ti "Lun-tun" [On Blake's "London"].'
Chung-shan Ta-hsueh Hsuen Pao, No. 3 (Dec. 1957).
In Chinese.

2808. §Takemori, Osamu. 'Blake "Kami no aru Image" [Blake: "Divine Image"].' *Eibungaku Techo [English Literature Notebook]*, No. 5 (1961), 16–19.

2809. —— §'Blake no Tanshi Futatsu [Blake's Two Short Poems].'
Kikan Eibungaku [English Literature Quarterly], III (1966), 143–61.

2810. —— §'William Blake—Tanshi "Ah Sun-Flower" wo Chushin to shite [about his short poem "Ah! Sun-Flower"].' *Kokoro [Mind]*, XVII (1964), No. 4, 37–44; No. 5, 47–53; No. 6, 41–50; No. 7, 34–43; No. 8, 48–51.

2811. —— 'William Blake "Tora" ["The Tyger"].' *Eibungaku Hyoron: Review of English Literature* [of the] English Department, College of Liberal Arts, Kyoto University, VIII (1961), 71–90.

2812. —— 'William Blake "Yameru Bara" Kaishaku [William Blake: Interpretation of "The Sick Rose"].' *Kokoro [Mind]*, XXI, No. 4 (April 1968), 50–8, No. 5 (1968), 61–9.

2813. —— *'Kakusha Blake [Blake as Enlightened Man].' *Eigo Eibungaku Kenkyu*, Fukui Daigaku, Gaikokugo Dai-1, Dai-2 Kenkyushitsu [*English Studies*, Fukui University Department of Foreign Languages, First and Second Seminars], No. 1 (Aug. 1951), 1–94.

2814. —— 'Shelley no "Ode to the West Wind" ni taisuru Blake no Eikyo ni tsuite [Blake's Influence on Shelley's "Ode to the West Wind"].' *Eigo Seinen: The Rising Generation*, CII (1956), 388–90.

2815. —— 'Songs of Innocence no Kenkyu [A Study of *Songs of Innocence*].' *Eigo Eibungaku Kenkyu*, Fukui Daigaku Gaikokugo Dai-1 Dai-2 Kenkyu-shitsu [*English Studies*, Fukui University Department of Foreign Languages, First and Second Seminars], No. 3 (March 1953), 1–51; No. 4 (Oct. 1953), 1–50.

2816. —— *William Blake no Kenkyu*—'Mushin to Keiken no Uta' wo Chushin to Shite [*A Study of William Blake*—Chiefly on *Songs of Innocence and of Experience*]. Tokyo, 1961. 222 pp.
The Preface to this dissertation is by Bunsho Jugaku.

2817. —— 'William Blake "Songs of Experience" no Kenkyu [A Study of William Blake's *Songs of Experience*].' *Jinbun Kagaku*: Fukui-daigaku Gakugeiga-kubu Kiyo [*The Humanities*: Fukui University Faculty of Arts Periodical],

No. 4 (1955), 12–25; No. 5 (1956), 61–78; No. 6 (1957), 51–62; No. 8 (1958), 15–25; No. 9 (1959), 43–56.
Continued from no. 2815.

2818. Taniguchi, Shigeru. 'The Circle of Destiny no Keisei: *The Four Zoas* Night I no Bunseki [The Formation of the Circle of Destiny: An Analysis of *The Four Zoas*, Night I].' Pp. 83–112 of *So Takeyuki Kyoju Kanrekikinen Bunshu* [*Essays and Studies in Honour of the Sixtieth Birthday of Professor So Takeyuki*]. Kashiwa [Japan], 1969.

2819. —— '*The Four Zoas* Night II ni okeru Cycle Images ni tsuite [Cycle Images in *The Four Zoas* Night II].' *Reitaku Daigaku Kiyo* [*Reitaku University Bulletin*], IX (1969), 86–98.

2820. —— '*The Four Zoas* ni okeru Kozo to Giko no Ichikosatsu—Night the First wo Chushin to shite [A Survey of the Structure and Technique in *The Four Zoas*—Centring on Night the First].' *Reitaku Daigaku Kiyo* [*Bulletin of Reitaku University*], X (1970), 53–67.

2821. —— ' "The Marriage of Heaven and Hell" ni okeru Blake no Evil ni tsuite [On Blake's Evil in *The Marriage of Heaven and Hell*].' *Reitaku Daigaku Kiyo* [*Reitaku University Bulletin*], IV (1964), 1–6.

2822. A. [Tartt, W. M.] ' "Pictor Ignotus;" A Biography.' *New Monthly Magazine*, CXXX (1864), 309–19. B. Revised as ' "Pictor Ignotus." ' Vol. II, pp. 192–215, of Tartt's *Essays on some Modern Works*, chiefly biographical. In Two Volumes. London, 1876.
   A highly unsympathetic review of Gilchrist (no. 1680), in passing attributes some doggerel about Hayley and Miss Seward to Blake (the mistaken attribution without the verses themselves is repeated in B).

2823. Tatham, Frederick. 'Life of Blake.' [*c.* 1832] (MS in the Mellon Collection.) Printed with *The Letters of William Blake* (1906) and in *Blake Records* (1969).

2824. Tayler, Irene. **Blake's Illustrations to the Poems of Gray*. Princeton, [N.J.], 1971.
   Persuasive commentary on Blake's 116 designs, all of which are reproduced in monochrome, with a duplicate in colour and Flaxman's sketch of Blake. The section on the 'Ode on the Death of a Favourite Cat' is also printed (with no indication of the duplication in either volume) in the Erdman–Grant *Blake's Visionary Forms Dramatic*. Mrs. Tayler's book was originally a dissertation entitled 'Visionary Forms Dramatic'.

2825. —— 'Visionary Forms Dramatic: William Blake's Illustrations to the Poetry of Thomas Gray.' *DA*, XXIX (1968), 881A. Stanford Ph.D., 1967.
   Slightly revised for her book.

2826. Taylor, Clyde Russel. 'William Blake and the Ideology of Art.' Wayne State Ph.D. Cf. *DA*, XXIX (1968), 277A.

2827. Taylor, Tom. *Handbook of the Pictures in the International Exhibition of 1862.* London, 1862. Pp. 73–6.

In general, 'Blake's [*pictorial*] work is rather tame and lumpish', though he 'was a poet of rare originality and sweetness'.

2828. Theobald, John. 'Blake's Idea of God.' *Personalist*, XXXVII (1956), 161–7.

Blake offers 'human self-confidence'.

2829. —— 'Blake's Ideas of Good and Evil.' *Personalist*, XXXVII (1956), 264–73.

Blake offers a 'vigorous world affirmation'.

2830. —— 'Was Blake a Mystic?' *Personalist*, XXXVII (1956), 47–59 (vMKN).

2831. Thomas, Dylan. '*Dictator in Freedom*, Tract Four. By Alfred Hy. Haffenden.' *Adelphi*, N.S. IX (1935), 317–18 (vMKN).

Blake 'lives because he had a glorious vocabulary, a divine inquiry, the key to the files of a Mystic Rogue's Gallery, and possibly epileptic vision,' 'not because he was a wise man with a message . . . .'

2832. Thomas, George Powell. 'Blake's Last Picture.' Pp. 103–7 of his *Poems.* London, 1847.

A poem on Blake's deathbed, based on Cunningham.

2833. A. Thomas, [Philip] Edward. 'William Blake.' Pp. 3–17 of his *A Literary Pilgrim in England.* London, 1917. B. N.Y., 1917. C. London, 1928. The Travellers' Library. Pp. 11–23. D. 1937. The New Library No. 9.

A general biographical account.

2834. Thomas, Ralph. 'Gilchrist's "Life of William Blake".' *N&Q*, LXII [6th Ser. II] (1880), 77 (vMKN).

Sergeant Thomas's collection of Theodore von Holst's sketches (Gilchrist [1863], I. 380) sold.

2835. —— 'William Blake.' *N&Q*, XCV [8th Ser. XI] (1897), 302–3; XCVI [9th Ser. I] (1898), 454–5; CXIII [10th Ser. V] (1906), 86; CXIX [10th Ser. XI] (1909), 287.

1897–8, 1906, 1909 say Salzmann's *Gymnastics* plates are not by Blake; 1898 says (inaccurately) that the poet made plates for West's juvenile theatre; and 1906 says that the plates in Lamb's *Tales from Shakespeare* are not designed by Blake.

2836. §Thompson, J. B. 'Blake's "My Pretty Rose Tree"—An Interpretation.' *Theoria*, No. 24 (1965), 33–7.

2837. A. Thomson, James. 'The Poems of W. Blake.' *National Reformer*, N.S. VII (1866), 22–3, 42–3, 52–4, 70–1 (vMKN). B. Reprinted in pp. 101–27 of *Shelley*, A Poem: with other Writings relating to Shelley, to which is added an Essay on The Poems of William Blake. London, 1884. C. Reprinted in pp. 240–69 of his *Biographical and Critical Studies*. [Ed. Bertram Dobell.]

London, 1896. D. Pp. 214–34 of *The Speedy Extinction of Evil and Misery*: Selected Prose of James Thomson (B. V.). Ed. William David Schaefer. Berkeley & Los Angeles [Calif.], 1967.

A review of Gilchrist (1863), of historical interest.

2838. A. [Thomson James.] 'B. V.' 'A Strange Book. I[–IV].' *The Liberal*, I (1879), 404–14, 463–72, 500–11, 543–56. B. Reprinted in pp. 289–371 of Thomson's *Biographical and Critical Studies*. [Ed. Bertram Dobell.] London, 1896. Also *passim*.

An account of J. J G. Wilkinson's *Improvisations from the Spirit* (1857), which has many verses 'startlingly akin to some of Blake's' (see B, pp 304–17, 321–3).

2839. Thornbury, Walter. 'The Prophet in Carnaby Market—Blake the Visionary.' Vol. II, chap. ii, pp. 26–44 of *British Artists from Hogarth to Turner*: being a Series of Biographical Sketches. In Two Volumes. London, 1861.

Some of the information in this sketch, notably on pp. 28 and 33, may be second-hand from 'the father of my old friend, Leigh, the artist', whom Blake visited frequently.

2840. Thorslev, Peter L., Jr. 'Some Dangers of Dialectic Thinking, with Illustrations from Blake and his Critics.' Pp. 43–74 of *Romantic and Victorian*: Studies in Memory of William H. Marshall. Ed. W. Paul Elledge & Richard L. Hoffman. Rutherford, Madison, Teaneck, 1971.

A warning against the 'Either–Or' syndrome, the 'absolutizing of abstractions', and 'the Both–And Syndrome' (p. 50).

2841. *Tiebze, Hans. 'William Blake.' *Kunst*, LIX (1929), 356–60 (vMKN).

2842. Tilloch, Alexander. 'Mr. Alexander Tilloch, of Cary-street, London . . .' testimonial, '*London, 5th April, 1797*' (Mrs. George Galt).

A testimonial bearing the poet's signature, quoted in *Blake Records* (1969), p. 58.

2843. A. Tillyard, E. M. W. 'The Two Village-Greens.' Pp. 7–16 of *Poetry Direct and Oblique*. London, 1934. Cf. also pp. 168–72. B. Revised and reprinted as pp. 11–15 of *Poetry Direct and Oblique*. London, 1945. Cf. also pp. 64–6.

A comparison of Goldsmith's *Deserted Village* and Blake's 'Ecchoing Green'.

2844. A. Timbs, John. 'William Blake, Painter and Poet.' Vol. II, pp. 66–72 of *English Eccentrics and Eccentricities*. In Two Volumes. London, 1866. B. Reprinted in pp. 339–50 of the one-volume edition of London, 1875.

2845. A. *Tinker, Chauncey B. 'Blake: Dreams of Milton.' *Art News*, XLIX (March 1950), 22–5, 64. B. Reprinted in *Il Penseroso* (1954), no. 393.

A description of the drawings for 'L'Allegro' and 'Il Penseroso' recently acquired by the Pierpont Morgan Library.

2846. —— *Blake: "The Gates of Paradise".' Pp. 100–20 of *Painter and*

Poet: Studies in the Literary Relations of English Painting. Cambridge [Mass.], 1938.

A lecture of no great importance.

2847. Tinker, Chauncey B. (C. B. T.) *'"The Resurrection" by William Blake.' *Bulletin of the Associates in Fine Arts at Yale University*, IV (1930), 95–7 (vRG).

2848. Todd, Ruthven. 'An Accidental Scholar.' *London Magazine*, N.S. VIII (Jan. 1969), 42–51.

About his editions of Gilchrist (1942, 1945).

2849. A. —— 'Blake's Dante Plates.' *TLS*, 29 Aug. 1968, p. 928. B. Corrected and amplified in 'Blake's Dante Plates—Revised Version.' *Book Collecting & Library Monthly*, No. 6 (1968), 164–71.

A cleaning of the Dante copperplates has made possible a printing of 25 new sets 'considerably superior to the earlier [*contemporary*] ones'.

2850. —— 'Fuseli and Blake: Companions in Mystery.' *Art News*, LII (Feb. 1954), 26, 57–8.

'The interchange of ideas and motives between Fuseli and Blake was about equal' on both sides.

2851. —— '"The Pilgrim's Progress."' *TLS*, 31 Jan. 1942, p. 55.

The drawings were sold at Sotheby's 29 April 1862 (lot 187) to M. Milnes (Lord Houghton) and probably came from Tatham's collection.

2852. —— *'Stothard (Thomas) *The Battle of Ai*.' Pp. 17–19 of *Paul Grinke Catalogue Five*. [London, 1972.]

In Blake's published *engraving in Kimpton's *History of the Holy Bible* (?1781), showing the warriors fighting left-handed, the sky seems to have 'been left unfinished'; the more finished but unsigned and unpublished *pull (Rosenwald Collection) is 'undoubtedly also by Blake'—it is more finished, is right-handed, and corresponds in this respect to Stothard's newly discovered *drawing.

2853. A. —— *'The Techniques of William Blake's Illuminated Printing.' *Print*, VI (1948), 53–65. B. *Print Collector's Quarterly*, XXIX (Nov. 1948), 25–36.

Describes experiments to reproduce Blake's methods.

2854. —— 'The Two Blakes.' *TLS*, 10 Feb. 1945, p. 72.

The signatures of both W. S. Blake and William Blake on Tilloch's testimonial.

2855. —— 'William Blake.' *TLS*, 5 April 1941, p. 172 (vMKN).

Asks for letters for new edition of Gilchrist.

2856. A. —— *'William Blake and the Eighteenth-Century Mythologists.' Pp. 29–60 of his *Tracks in the Snow*. Studies in English Science and Art. London, 1946. B. N.Y., 1947.

Informative study of Blake's indebtedness to currents of thought among contemporary antiquarians.

2857. Todd, Ruthven. *William Blake The Artist*. London & N.Y., 1971. Studio Vista/Dutton Pictureback [*sic*].

118 plates interspersed with staccato chronological text 'about the manner in which William Blake lived as an artist' (p. 7).

2858. Tolley, Michael J. 'The Auckland Blakes.' *Biblionews and Australian Notes & Queries*, 2nd Ser. II (1967), 6–16.

Bibliographical descriptions of *America* (N) and *Europe* (I).

2859. —— 'Blake's "Edens Flood" Again.' *N&Q*, CCXIII [N.S. XV] (1968), 11–19.

More Biblical allusions in 'The Everlasting Gospel', a sequel to and partial correction of no. 2863.

2860. —— '*The Book of Thel* and *Night Thoughts*.' *BNYPL*, LXIX (1965), 375–85.

A source study.

2861. [——] 'The Everlasting Gospel.' *N&Q*, CCVII (1962), 394.

Corrects misprints in no. 2863.

2862. —— 'On The Cutting Edge of Blake Scholarship.' *Adelaide University Graduates' Union Monthly Newsletter and Gazette*, Dec. 1968, pp. 4–5.

Autobiographical.

2863. —— 'William Blake's Use of the Bible in a Section of "The Everlasting Gospel".' *N&Q*, CCVII (1962), 171–6. See no. 2859, 2861.

2864. Trawick, Leonard M. 'The Present State of Blake Studies.' *Studies in Burke and His Time*, XII (1970–1), 1784–1803.

A survey of all Blake scholarship, concentrating on books published after 1966.

2865. Trinick, John. 'William Blake.' Pp. 92–101 of his *The Fire-Tried Stone* (signum atque signatum): An Enquiry into the Development of a Symbol. Marazion (Cornwall) & London, 1967.

Blake 'belongs . . . to the line of the Hermetic Philosophers' (p. 93).

2866. Trobridge, George. 'Blake and Swedenborg.' *Morning Light*, XXVI (1903), 119.

At the Burlington Fine Arts Club Exhibition many years previously (?1876), he saw written on a Blake sketch a 'list of works to be studied', headed by Swedenborg's *Worship and Love of God*. This list has not been subsequently recorded.

2867. Trollope, T. Adolphus, Anon. [the editor]; C. F. S. Warren, W. E. Buckley. 'Blake's "Songs of Innocence".' *N&Q*, XCII [7th Ser. VIII] (1889), 146–7, 216.

Anon. (p. 147) and Buckley (p. 216) say their copies of the 1866 *Songs* contain lacunae not found by Trollope in his copy (pp. 146–7).

2868. Tsu-Cheng. 'Lo-t'o-ts'ao: Chi-nien Ying-kuo Shen-mi Shih-jen

Pai-lei-k'o [Camel Grass: A Commemoration of Blake, the English Mystic Poet].' *Yu-ssu*, No. 148, 150; 153 (Sept.; Oct. 1927) (vADH).
In Chinese.

2869. Tsuchiya, Shigeko. 'Blake "Jerusalem" [On Blake's *Jerusalem*].' *Eibungaku* (Waseda Daigaku Eibungakkai): *English Literature* (Waseda University English Literary Society), No. 26 (1965), 5–13.

2870. —— §'Blake no Yogensha-ishiki [Blake's Prophetic Consciousness].' *Critica*, X (1964), 20–32.

2871. —— §'Vision no Shijin Blake [Blake, the Poet of Vision].' *Eibungaku Techo* [*English Literature Notebook*], (1961), 1–7.

2872. Turner, Godfrey. 'A Penny Plain; Twopence Coloured.' *Theatre*, XVII [N.S. VIII] (1886), 177–82 (vMKN).
Attributes the engravings for advertisements for the toy theatre to Blake.

U

2873. Umegaki, Minoru. 'Blake no Jojoshi [Blake's Lyrical Poems].' *Doshisha Bungaku* [*Literary Magazine of the Doshisha Literary Society*], No. 14 (1932), 317–34; No. 15 (1932), 40–65 (vHK).

2874. —— §'Blake no Shukyo-shiso [Blake's Religious Thoughts].' *Doshisha Bungaku* [*Literary Magazine of the Doshisha Literary Society*], No. 2 (1928), 13–25.

2875. —— 'Blake no "Yogensho" Kenkyu Josetsu [An Introduction to the Study of Blake's Prophetic Books].' *Doshisha Bungaku* [*Literary Magazine of The Doshisha Literary Society*], No. 12 (1931), 91–135 (vHK).

2876. —— *'Blake Saku "Milton" no kansu [The Number of Books in Blake's *Milton*].' *Eigo Seinen: The Rising Generation*, LIX (1928), 420.

2877. —— §'Blake to Shizen [Blake and Nature].' *Doshisha Bungaku* [*Literary Magazine of the Doshisha Literary Society*], No. 18 (1935), 54–64.

2878. —— §'Tsuki ni aru Shima—Blake no Shoki no Kohon ni tsuite [On *An Island in the Moon*, Blake's Early Manuscript].' *Doshisha Bungaku* [*Literary Magazine of the Doshisha Literary Society*], No. 9 (1930), 22–31.

2879. *Umetsu, Narumi. 'Blake.' Pp. 18–38 of *Eibungakushi, Koza Dai-6-kan, 18-seiki, 2 1701–1797* [*Lectures on the History of English and American Literature, Vol. VI, Eighteenth Century Part II, 1701–1797*]. Tokyo, 1961.
Umetsu's essay is in Japanese.

2880. —— 'Blake Nyumon [An Introduction to the Study of Blake].' *Kiyo*: Nagoya Daigaku Kyoyogakubu: *Research Bulletin*, Published by The Department of General Education, Nagoya University, No. 6 (1962), 39–54.

2881. —— 'Lamb no Blake Hihyo [Lamb's Comments on Blake].' *Kindai no Eibungaku*: Fukuhara Rintaro Sensei Kanreki Kinen Rombunshu [*Modern English Literature*: Essays and Studies by the Friends and Former Students of

Professor Rintaro Fukuhara in Commemoration of his Sixty-First Birthday].
Tokyo, 1955.

2882. Umetsu, Narumi. 'Mushi sareta Sakusha no Ito—Blake no Ichi Tanshi
wo megutte [Writer's Intention Neglected—One Poem by Blake].' *Eigo
Seinen: The Rising Generation,* CXIII (1967), 440–2.
   About 'Never seek to tell thy love' and 'I asked a thief'.

2883. —— *'Songs of Innocence* no Hitotsu no Bungakushiteki Ichi [*Songs of
Innocence*: Its Place in the History of English Devotional Poetry].' *Athenaeum,*
V ([Tokyo] 1962), 34–50.

2884. —— **A Study of William Blake: Songs of Innocence and of Experience*:
Blake Kenkyu [Studies]. Tokyo, 1963. 383 pp.
   A doctoral thesis in Japanese.

2885. —— 'Wakaki Blake no Yashin [The Ambition of the Young Blake].'
Eigo Seinen: The Rising Generation, CI (1955), 353–4.

2886. —— §'William Blake no Geijutsu [The Art of William Blake].' Vol. IX
(England Part 2: National Gallery, etc. Ed. Shigeki Goto), pp. 213–19 of
Genshoku, Sekai no Bijutsu: The Great Museums of the World. Tokyo, 1970.
   There are 22 Blake plates.

2887. —— *'William Blake no Shi [A poem of William Blake].' *Eigo Kenkyu:
The Study of English,* LIV, No. 3 (March 1965), 24–5.
   On 'The Sick Rose'.

2888. *Underwood, Eric. 'Gaka toshite no Blake [Blake as a Painter].'
Tr. Kazuo Iwata. *Nyu Epokka: New Epoch,* I (April 1949), 45–7.

2889. 'Urbanus, Sylvanus.' 'Table Talk. William Blake.' *Gentleman's
Magazine,* n.s. LII (1894), 429–31 (vMKN).
   The lyrics are ravishing, the prophecies incomprehensible.

2890. Usami, Michio. '"Songs of Innocence and Experience" Shoron [A
Short Paper].' *Nagoya Kogyo Daigaku Gakuho* [*Nagoya Institute of Technology
Publication*], No. 11 (1959), 263–70.

2891. Ussher, Arland. 'The Thought of Blake.' *Dublin Magazine,* XXIII
(April–June 1948), 23–32.
   Blake exhibited Irish qualities, but 'he seems not to have given his Irish
origins a thought' (p. 23).

2892. §Ustvedt, Yngvar. 'William Blake. Et 200-års minne.' *Samtiden,*
LXVIII (1959), 126–32.
   Blake anticipated the spiritual revolution of our time (in Norwegian).

V

2893. Vacher, Francis. 'Blake's Manner.' Pp. 99–100 of his *Engravers &
Engraving*: Being an Inaugural Address, delivered at the commencement of

the Session [of the 'Birkenhead Literary & Scientific Society. Session xxxi, 1887–88'.] Manchester [1888].
Very minor.

2894. Vagne, Jean. 'Panorama.' *Messages*, I (1939), 11–14.
Part of the special Blake issue.

2895. Valdés, Mario J. 'Archetype and Re-creation: A Comparative Study of William Blake and Miguel de Unamuno.' *University of Toronto Quarterly*, XL (1970), 58–72.
A careful article on Blake's influence.

2896. A. Van Doren, Mark. *Introduction to Poetry*. N.Y., 1951. Pp. 110–15. B. Reprinted in Grant's anthology.
On 'The Little Black Boy'.

2897. A. Van Rensselaer, Mariana G. [Mrs. Schuyler Van Rensselaer]. 'The Works of William Blake.' *American Architect and Building News*, VIII (1880), 215–16, 223–4 (vMKN). B. Expanded and rewritten from a new point of view as 'William Blake. 1757–1827.' Pp. 113–38 of Mrs. Schuyler Van Rensselaer. *Six Portraits: Della Robbia, Correggio, Blake, Corot, George Fuller, Winslow Homer*. Boston & N.Y., 1899.

2898. *Van Sinderen, Adrian. *Blake: The Mystic Genius*. Syracuse [N.Y.], 1949.
Van Sinderen's annual 'Christmas Book' for 1949 reproduces in colour the plates and text for Blake's *L'Allegro* and *Il Penseroso* designs; the text is negligible.

2899. Vedder, Elihu. *The Digressions of V*. Written for his Own Fun and that of his Friends. London, Boston & N.Y., 1911. Pp. 409–17.
Trivial.

2900. Vengerova, Z. 'Rodonachal'nik angliiskovo simvoiizma [Forefather of English Symbolism].' *Severnyi Vestnik* [St. Petersburg], IX (1896), 81–99.
A brief biographical sketch and criticism.

2901. §Vernon, Madeleine. 'A propos du centenaire de William Blake: William Blake et ses contemporains.' *Figaro*, 24 Dec. 1927.

2902. *Veronesi, Giulia. 'William Blake.' *Emporium*, CVI (Sept. 1947), 68–70 (vMKN).

2903. Vickery, John B. 'William Blake and Eudora Welty's "Death of a [Travelling] Salesman".' *MLN*, LXXVI (1961), 625–32.
Very slim.

2904. Vickery, Willis. *Three Excessively Rare and Scarce Books and Something of Their Author*. Cleveland, [Ohio], 1927.
Blake's *Poetical Sketches*, his *Songs*, and his *Grave* which Vickery owns (40 pp.).

2905. A. Vivante, Leone. 'Blake.' Chap. v, pp. 135–54, of *La Poesia Inglese*, ed il suo contributo alla conoscénza dello spirito. Florence, 1947. B. Reprinted as 'William Blake 1757–1827.' Chap. v, pp. 86–97 of *English Poetry and its contribution to the knowledge of a creative principle.* With a preface by T. S. Eliot. London, 1950.

2906. ———— 'Sulla Poesia di William Blake.' *Poesia*, VI (1947), 110–22 (vMKN).

2907. Vogler, Thomas A. 'Blake: Mental Fight.' Chap. 3 (pp. 39–59) of his *Preludes to Vision*: The Epic Venture in Blake, Wordsworth, Keats, and Hart Crane. Berkeley, Los Angeles [Calif.], London, 1971. Also *passim*.

An intelligent close reading of *Milton* as a 'prelude' to *Jerusalem*.

W

2908. *Wackrill, H. R. *The Inscription over the Gate*. London, 1937.

A quasi-autobiographical account of 'what exactly it is in Blake's work [*especially the Tate designs*] that makes it so irresistibly fascinating' (p. 107).

2909. Wahl, Jean. 'Magie et Romantisme: Notes sur Novalis et Blake.' *Hermes* [Brussels], 2nd Ser. No. 2 (June 1936), 7–13 (vSFDamon).

2910. A. ———— & René Tavernier. 'Notes sur William Blake suivies de poèmes.' *Confluences*, 2e année (1942), 391–400. B. Jean Wahl. 'Notes sur William Blake.' *Poésie, Pensée, Perception*. Paris, 1948. Pp. 217–30.

A. 'Notes' on pp. 391–4, 'Le Tigre' tr. J. Wahl with comment, pp. 394–7; 'Introduction' to *Innocence*, 'Le Thème du mariage du ciel et de l'enfer', and 'La Voix du mal' tr. R. Tavernier, pp. 397–400.

B. Only Wahl's part was reprinted in 1948.

2911. Wain, John, F. W. Bateson, and W. W. Robson. '"Intention" and Blake's *Jerusalem*.' *Essays in Criticism*, II (1952), 105–14 (vMKN).

A critical controversy.

2912. A. [Wainewright, Thomas Griffiths.] 'Mr. [*Janus*] Weathercock's Private Correspondence, Intended for the Public Eye.' *London Magazine*, I (Sept. 1820), 300. (BM) B. *Essays and Criticisms by Thomas Griffiths Wainewright*, now first collected with some account of the author by W. Carew Hazlitt. London, 1880. Pp. 109–10.

A jocular reference to Blake's *Jerusalem*.

2913. Walling, William. 'The Death of God: William Blake's Version.' *Dalhousie Review*, XLVIII (1968), 237–50.

Cf. Altizer.

2914. A. Wallis, John P. R. 'Blake.' Pp. 181–202 of Volume XI (The Period of the French Revolution) of *The Cambridge History of English Literature*. Ed. A. W. Ward and A. R. Waller. Cambridge, 1914. B. Cambridge, 1932. C. Cambridge, 1953.

2915. Wallis, John P. R. 'Blake's Milton.' *TLS*, 11 March 1926, p. 182 (vMKN).
On the bad Quaritch facsimile, no. 369.

2916. —— 'Blake's Symbolism and Some of its Recent Interpreters.' Pp. 1–42 of *Primitiae: Essays in English Literature by Students of the University of Liverpool*. Liverpool, 1912.

2917. A. Walter, Jakob. *William Blakes Nachleben in der englischen Literatur des neunzehnten und zwanzigsten Jahrhunderts*. Schaffhausen, 1925. B. Schaffhausen, 1927.
A Zurich Ph.D. dissertation.

2918. Wang, Alfred Shih-pu. 'The Images in Blake's Minor Prophecies.' *DA*, XXVIII (1968), 3652A. Tulane Ph.D.
Blake dramatizes 'the interdependence of Innocence and Experience' in *Thel, Visions, Tiriel, Marriage*, and 'The Mental Traveller'.

2919. W[ard], C[olin]. 'The Apotheosis of William Blake.' *Freedom: The Anarchist Weekly*, 7 Dec. 1957, pp. 3–2 [*sic*] (vMKN).

2920. Ward, Mrs. M. J. 'Blake and Jung.' *John O' London's Weekly*, LVI (1947), 390 (vDS).
A letter.

2921. Wardle, J. 'Blake's Leutha.' *English Language Notes*, V (1967), 105–6.
Derived from Leucothea, goddess of dawn.

2922. —— '"Europe" and "America".' *N&Q*, CCXIII [N.s. XV] (1968), 20–1.
'*T*he frontispiece to "Europe" clearly derives from that of King Lear in James Barry's picture', and the *America* plates 'bear a contrapuntal relation to the text'.

2923. Ware, Audrey. 'Blake, The[y] Say, Was Mad.' Pp. 25–9 of *The Atlantic Prize Essays—Prize Stories—Prize Poems*. Boston, [1951]. Prize Papers 1950–1951 Atlantic Contests for College Students (vMKN).
Miss Ware, who won third honourable mention, discusses the four-fold vision.

2924. *Wark, Robert R. 'Blake's "Satan, Sin and Death".' Chap. VII (pp. 79–91) of his *Ten British Pictures 1740–1840* [in] The Huntington Library. San Marino [Calif.], 1971.
A general account of Blake's picture for *Paradise Lost*.

2925. —— *'A Minor Blake Conundrum.' *HLQ*, XXI (1957), 83–7 (vMKN).
Unsolved. A vellum page of *Night Thoughts*, but with different typography and text from that of the published edition and with a coloured illustration which is a mirror image of the drawing in the British Museum.

2926. Warschavsky, Sidney. 'W. B. Yeats as Literary Critic.' Columbia Ph.D., 1957; cf. *DA*, XVII (1957), 1559–60 (vMKN).

2927. Wasser, Henry H. 'Notes on The *Visions of the Daughters of Albion* By William Blake.' *MLQ*, IX (1948), 292–7.

Unconvincing argument that the *Visions* is the story of Mary Wollstonecraft and Fuseli.

2928. Waters, Louis Addison, Jr. 'The Idea of Nature in the Poetry of William Blake.' *DA*, XXI (1961), 265–6.

A Columbia Ph.D. showing seven stages in Blake's treatment of Nature: (1) Innocence; (2) Sex; (3) Energy; (4) Imagination; (5) Experience; (6) Deceit; (7) Restraint.

2929. [Watkins, John, and Frederick Shoberl.] A / BIOGRAPHICAL DICTIONARY / OF THE / LIVING AUTHORS / OF / GREAT BRITAIN AND IRELAND; / COMPRISING / 𝕷iterary 𝕸emoirs and 𝕬necdotes of their 𝕷ibes; / AND / A CHRONOLOGICAL REGISTER OF THEIR PUBLICATIONS, / WITH THE NUMBER OF EDITIONS PRINTED; / INCLUDING / *NOTICES OF SOME FOREIGN WRITERS WHOSE WORKS HAVE BEEN / OCCASIONALLY PUBLISHED IN ENGLAND.* / 𝕴llustrated by / A VARIETY OF COMMUNICATIONS / FROM PERSONS OF THE FIRST EMINENCE IN THE / WORLD OF LETTERS. / = / LONDON: / PRINTED FOR HENRY COLBURN; / PUBLIC LIBRARY, CONDUIT STREET, HANOVER SQUARE. / 1816. (BM & GEB)

The running heads of 'LITERARY CALENDAR' with dates of '1814' and '1815' suggest that the work was first issued in parts, though I have not seen a copy in that form. According to a persuasive witness (B. Corney, *N&Q*, XI [1855], 34), the *Biographical Dictionary* was compiled as far as F by Watkins and from there on by Shoberl. The GEB copy is heavily revised in MS apparently by William Upcott.

There are references to Blake under William Hayley, W. Blake, and William Blake, the bibliography from the last of which is reprinted in Watt (no. 533).

2930. Watson, Alan McCabe. 'William Blake's Illustrated Writings: The Early Period.' *DAI*, XXX (1969), 1538A; New Mexico Ph.D.

'*T*he writer has simply tried to see them [*Blake's illustrations*] suggest to the imagination when confronting them at close quarters.'

2931. *Watson, Jane. 'Blake Illustrations for Pilgrim's Progress.' *Magazine of Art*, XXXIV (1941), 40 (vMKN).

2932. Watson-Williams, Helen. 'The Blackened Wall: Notes on Blake's *London* and Eliot's *The Waste-Land*.' *English*, X (1955), 181–4.

'Blake's poem *London* may have played its influential part in the creation of *The Waste Land*.'

2933. Watsuji, Tetsuro. 'Shocho-shugi no Senkusha William Blake [William Blake as a Forerunner of Symbolism].' *Teikoku Bungaku* [*Teikoku Literature*], XVII, No. 2 (1911), 1–13.

2934. *Watt, A. 'Notes from Paris: Three Master Water-Colourists: Blake, Turner, Guys.' *Apollo*, XXV (1937), 154–6 (vMKN).
In the Paris exhibition.

2935. Watts, A. 'Blake's Ode to the Tiger.' *Literary World*, 7 Aug. 1885, p. 134.
On the spears and tears.

2936. Watts, Alaric Alfred. *Alaric Watts*: A Narrative of His Life. In Two Volumes. London, 1884. Vol. II, pp. 6–7.
Admiration for Blake in a letter of 1830 from Mary Howitt.

2937. *Weathers, Winston, ed. *William Blake: The Tyger*. Columbus (Ohio), 1969. The Merrill Literary Casebook Series.
The volume includes 'General Instructions For A Research Paper' (pp. v–xii), Weathers's 'Introduction' (pp. 1–5), *'The Tyger', and excerpts or whole essays by S. Foster Damon (no. 1455 pp. 276–8), Roy P. Basler (no. 1130 pp. 20–4), Jesse Bier (no. 1189), Stanley Gardner (no. 1664 pp. 123–30), Martin K. Nurmi (no. 2297A), Hazard Adams (no. 780, pp. 58–74), E. D. Hirsch, Jr. (no. 1853 pp. 244–52), Philip Hobsbaum (no. 1863), Morton D. Paley (no. 2350), Rodney M. Baine (no. 1112), and Kay Parkhurst Long, 'William Blake and the Smiling Tyger' (pp. 115–21, 'written especially for this volume'; '"The Tyger" is a kind of nonsense verse').

2938. Webb, Clement C. J. 'Blake and Jeremy Taylor.' *TLS*, 11 April 1929, p. 296.
Suggests a source for the opening lines of 'Auguries of Innocence'.

2939. A. Wedmore, Frederick. 'William Blake.' *Temple Bar*, LXII (1881), 52–63 (vMKN). B. Reprinted in *Littell's Living Age*, CXLIX (1881), 557–63 (vMKN). C. Reprinted in *Eclectic Magazine*, XXXIV (1881), 104–12 (vMKN).

2940. §Wei, Chao-chi. 'Wei-lien Po-lai-k'o Pai-nien-Chi [The Centenary of the Death of William Blake].' *I-pan*, IV (Jan. 1928).
In Chinese.

2941. Weisinger, Nina Lee. 'José Joaquin de Mora's Indebtedness to William Blake.' *Bulletin of Hispanic Studies*, XXVIII (1951), 103–7.
Sound but summary.

2942. *Weisstein, Ulrich. 'Blake at the National Gallery.' *Arts*, XXXII (Jan. 1958), 42–5 (vMKN).

2943. Wellek, René. 'William Blake.' *Listy pro umeni a kritiku* [*Journal for Art and Criticism*], I (1933), 236–41.
In Czech.

2944. *Wells, William. *William Blake's 'Heads of the Poets'* for Turret House, the Residence of William Hayley, Felpham. [Manchester, 1969.]
The 'Foreword' by G. L. Conran is on p. 1, the study of 'Blake's "Heads of

the Poets"' on pp. 2–10, a 'Bibliographical Note' on p. 11, Elizabeth Johnston, 'Postscript' (concerning the 'plan of Hayley's Library' in the Osborn
Collection) on pp. 12–13, and the 'Catalogue of the "Heads of the Poets"' on
pp. 15–28. The 48 plates include all those of the 'Heads of the Poets', plus
their sources, most of which Blake copied very carefully.

The work was issued 'concurrently' with the 1969 Manchester catalogue
of the exhibition built round the 'Heads' (see no. 697).

2945. Wenger, A. Grace. 'Blake's THE FOUR ZOAS, Night the Ninth.'
Explicator, XXVII (1969), item 59.

The threshing of the nations is plausibly traced to Isaiah 41 : 15–16.

2946. Werblowsky, R. J. Zwi. 'Appendix A. From William Blake, *The
Marriage of Heaven and Hell*.' Pp. 107–10 of his *Lucifer and Prometheus*: A Study
of Milton's Satan. With an Introduction by Professor C. G. Jung. London,
1952.

An explication of how 'much of the argument of the preceding study is
anticipated in this quotation' from the *Marriage*.

2947. *Whistler, Laurence. 'The William Blake Trust's facsimile of
"America, A Prophecy".' *Connoisseur*, CLVI (1964), 182–3.

Blake's books are 'twinkling'.

2948. White, Hal Saunders. *A Primer of Blake*. Ames [Iowa], 1951 (vDVE).

An enthusiastic brief introduction to Blake.

2949. White, Helen C. 'The Mysticism of William Blake.' Wisconsin Ph.D.,
1924 (according to L. F. McNamee, *Dissertations in English and American
Literature* [1968]). Revised and printed as no. 2950.

2950. A. —— *The Mysticism of William Blake*. Madison, 1927. University of
Wisconsin Studies in Language and Literature, Number 23. B. N.Y., 1964.
(See no. 2949.)

A close comparison of Blake's works and life with the mystical tradition
leads to the conclusion that he 'is not a great mystic in any sense that means
anything'.

2951. §White, Wayne. 'William Blake: Mystic or Visionary?' *College
Language Association Journal*, IX (1966), 284–8.

2952. W[hitesell], J. E. 'Blake's *The Little Black Boy*.' *Explicator*, V (1948),
item 42 (vMKN).

Trivial.

2953. [Whittier, John Greenleaf.] *The Supernaturalism of New England*.
London, 1847. Pp. 25–6. Wiley & Putnam's Library of American Books.

Refers in passing to 'the mad painter, Blake' and his account of the fairy's
funeral.

2954. Wicksteed, Joseph H. *Blake's Innocence and Experience*: A Study of the
Songs and Manuscripts 'Shewing the Two Contrary States of the Human
Soul'. London, Toronto, N.Y., 1928.

A naïve, highly personal, and often useful study, with reproductions of all the etchings and manuscript drafts (in the *Notebook* and *The Island*).

2955. Wicksteed, Joseph H. **Blake's River of Life*: Its Poetic Undertones. Bournemouth [?1951].

A brief (24 pp.) philosophical discussion of Blake's picture called *'The River of Life'.

2956. —— 'Blake's Songs of Innocence.' *TLS*, 18 Feb. 1932, p. 112 (vMKN).

The sources for two songs in *Innocence* (1789) are in Salzmann's *Elements of Morality* (1791).

2957. A. —— **Blake's Vision of the Book of Job*: With Reproductions of the [engraved] Illustrations. London & N.Y., 1910. B. *Second Edition, Revised and Enlarged. London & N.Y., 1924. C. §*N.Y., 1971.

This pioneering study of Blake's iconography is of great historical and intrinsic importance despite Wicksteed's assertiveness and his determination to make all his facts fit his interpretation. The first edition (1910, reprinted in 1971) was considerably improved in the Second Edition (1924), which reprinted in Appendix G (pp. 229–32) an extract from Wicksteeds 'The Method of William Blake'.

2958. A. 'The Method of William Blake.' *Quest*, III (1912), 422–42. B. Extracts reprinted in *Blake's Vision of the Book of Job* (1924), pp. 229–32.

2959. —— 'The So-Called "Madness" of William Blake.' *Quest*, III (1911), 81–99.

2960. —— *'William Blake's Eternal River.' *Vistas*, I (1946), 30–7.

2961. —— **William Blake's Jerusalem*. Foreword by Geoffrey Keynes. London, 1954. See the *Jerusalem* facsimiles (1951–5), which this was written to accompany.

The 'Foreword' is pp. ix–x. A highly personal book which persistently reads *Jerusalem* as mere autobiography, often stimulating and rarely conclusive; 28 plates.

2962. Widmer, Kingsley. 'The Marriage of Heaven and Hell.' Chap. 3 (pp. 35–47) of his *The Literary Rebel*. Carbondale & Edwardsville [Ill.], 1965. 'Blake, I am arguing, really is a rebel' (p. 42).

2963. Wilde, Oscar. 'La Renaissance anglais de l'art.' *Mercure de France*, CV (1913), 286–313 (vMKN).

Blake is mentioned as being part of it.

2964. Wildenstein, G. 'William Blake et la peintre mystique française du XIXe siècle.' *Actes Congrès Londres*, 1939, p. 61.

Blake and David had the same sources.

2965. A. *Wilenski, R. H. 'Blake 1757–1827.' Chap. XV, pp. 229–60 of *English Painting*. London [1933]. B. *Second Edition. London, 1943. Pp. 228–59. C. *Third Edition (Revised). London, 1954. Pp. 228–59.

This essay is divided into three sections, 'Blake's Life', 'Blake's Character', and 'Blake's Art', of which the third is reliable and suggestive. (Twenty-three plates in A, 24 in B and C.)

2966. A. Wilenski, R. H. **An Outline of English Painting* from the Middle Ages to the Period of the Pre-Raphaelites. London, 1933. Criterion Miscellany No. 41. Pp. 55–61. B. *An Outline of English Painting*. London, 1946. Pp. 45–52. C. 1969.
An introductory account of Blake.

2967. —— **'William Blake as Artist.' *Apollo*, IV (1926), 258–62.
Blake had little imagination.

2968. Wilkinson, Andrew M. 'Blake's Songs.' *The Use of English*, XIII (1962), 233–41.
An elementary discussion, partly drawn from his edition, no. 188.

2969. —— 'Illuminated—or Not? A Note on Blake's *Songs of Innocence and of Experience*.' *MLR*, LVII (1962), 387–91.

2970. Wilkinson, Clement John. *James John Garth Wilkinson*; a Memoir of his Life, with a Selection from his Letters. London, 1911. Pp. 25–31, 35, 52.
References to Blake of 1838, 1839, and 1848.

2971. Wilkinson, James John Garth. *The Human Body and its Connexion with Man*. Illustrated by the Principal Organs. London, 1851. P. 376.
Reprints 'The Divine Image' from *Innocence*.

2972. A. Will, Frederick. 'Blake's Quarrel with Reynolds.' *JAAC*, XV (1957), 340–9 (vMKN). B. Reprinted as Part II, Chap. II, pp. 32–48 of his *Intelligible Beauty in Aesthetic Thought* from Winckelmann to Victor Cousin. Tubingen, 1958.

2973. Williams, Aneurin. 'P. Jones, Engraver.' *N&Q*, CLI (1926), 28 (vMKN).
Query concerning engravings after Blake in Whitaker's *Seraph*.

2974. A. Williams, Charles. 'Blake and Wordsworth.' *Dublin Review*, CCVIII (1941), 175–86 (vMKN). B. Summarized in *N&Q*, CLXXX (1941), 289 (vMKN). C. Reprinted as pp. 59–67 of *The Image of the City and Other Essays*. Ed. Anne Ridler. London, N.Y., Toronto, 1958.
Blake may be approached through Wordsworth, especially through *The Prelude*.

2975. **Williamson, Audrey. 'Blake in Ballet.' *Theatre*, No. 10 (Autumn 1948), 14–18 (vKP).
A study of the *Job* ballet.

2976. Williamson, Margaret. 'Dealers Get Book Rarities; Blake Item Goes for $4,400.' *Christian Science Monitor*, 18 April 1941 (vMKN).
Water-colour for 'When the Morning Stars . . .'.

2977. Willmore, Edward. 'William Blake and Modern Problems.' *University Magazine and Free Review*, VIII (1897), 204–13.

2978. Wilson, H. C. 'Blake's Criticism and Painting of the Canterbury Pilgrims.' University of Washington Ph.D., 1941; cf. *Abstracts of Theses* [Washington], V (1941), 98–9 (vMKN).

2979. *Wilson, J. Macartney. 'The Book of Job.' Vol. II [Joshua to Job], pp. 137–44 of *The Old Testament in Art*. Ed. W. Shaw Sparrow. [3 vols.] London [?1906]. The Art & Life Library.

A design-by-design commentary on Blake's twenty-one plates reproduced.

2980. Wilson, Mona. 'Blake and Bedlam.' *TLS*, 15 Dec. 1927, p. 961 (vMKN).

Concerns the *Monthly Magazine* article (1833), no. 843; see Wilson, no. 2981.

2981. A. —— *The Life of William Blake*. London, 1927. B. London, 1932. C. *London, 1948. D. §1951. E. *N.Y., 1969. F. §N.Y., 1970. *G. Ed. Geoffrey Keynes. London, Oxford, N.Y., 1971. Oxford Paperbacks.

A. There are 24 plates in the first edition, which was printed and bound to range with the Keynes *Writings* (1925) (no. 370A), plus six appendices, viz.: I. 'Notes on Illustrations' (pp. 313–17); II. George Cumberland. 'New Mode of Printing' (pp. 318–19); III. 'Blake's Calligraphy' (pp. 320–1); IV. 'The "Rossetti MS."' (pp. 322–32); V. 'Extracts from Varley's "Zodiacal Physiognomy" [no. 501] and "Urania" [no. 995]' (pp. 333–5); VI. 'Extract from "Revue Britannique" [no. 958]' (pp. 336–7).

B. In the second edition all the notes and appendices were omitted.

C. The third edition was revised, the notes and appendices were restored, and some notes and appendix material were added, the most important change being the addition to Appendix VI of extracts from 'Bits of Biography [no. 843]' (pp. 349–50).

F. The 1970 edition is a reprint of that of 1948.

G. In the Keynes edition, quotations have been verified, references checked, numerous new footnotes added, and Appendices III, V, and VI retained.

Miss Wilson's biography scrupulously used contemporary accounts of Blake, a number of which had not appeared in print before. This is a very full, accurate, and reliable work, and is sometimes called the 'standard' biography of Blake.

2982. A. —— 'The Twilight of the Augustans.' *Empire Review*, XLV (1927), 509–17. B. *Living Age*, CCCXXXIII (1927), 338–43 (vMKN). C. *Essays and Studies*, XX (1935), 75–86.

An excellent general essay on Blake and the critical tradition of Johnson, the Wartons, *et al.*

2983. —— *'La Vida de William Blake.' *Ars revista mensual*, I, 4 (April 1942), 37–49.

2984. Wilson, Patrick Seymour. 'A Study of the Proper Names mentioned in Blake's Poetry and Prose.' 3 vols. Victoria University of Wellington (New Zealand) Ph.D., 1952.

2985. *Wind, Edgar. 'Blake and Reynolds.' *Listener*, 28 Nov. 1957, pp. 879–80.
In defence of Reynolds.

2986. Winslow, Olga Elizabeth. 'William Blake and the Century Test.' *South Atlantic Quarterly*, XXV (1926), 25–44 (vMKN).
Centennial appreciation.

2987. Wirz, Ernst. 'William Blake und Heinrich Füssli.' *Neue Zürcher Zeitung*, No. 201 (7 Feb. 1926), 3.

2988. A. Witcutt, W. P. *Blake: A Psychological Study.* London, 1946. B. §Port Washington (N.Y.), 1966.
A brief, factually unreliable, but promising argument that Blake can be profitably illuminated by Jung.

2989. —— 'The Structure of the Psyche: A Psychological Examination of the Poetry of Blake.' *Wind and The Rain*, III (Summer 1945), 14–21 (vMKN).
Blake is a Jungian 'intuitive introvert'.

2990. —— *'Wm. Blake and Modern Psychology.' *John O'London's Weekly*, LVI, No. 1307 (4 April 1947), 317–18 (vDS).

2991. Withers, P. 'Blake, Shields and Rossetti.' *TLS*, 18 Aug. 1927, p. 561.
Shields's drawing evoked Rossetti's sonnet.

2992. Withrow, Helena H. 'The Chimney-Sweep in American Verse.' *N&Q*, CLX (1931), 98.
'The Little Sweep' in Henry Cogwell Knight (1788–1835), *The Cypriad* (Boston, 1809), is either the only original piece in the book or it comes from Blake.

2993. Witke, Joanne. '*Jerusalem*: A Synoptic Poem.' *Comparative Literature*, XXII (1970), 265–78.
An intriguing argument that 'Just as the canonical gospels consist of four, so *Jerusalem* has four chapters' (p. 275).

2994. Wittreich, Joseph Anthony, Jr. 'Blake's Philosophy of Contraries: A New Source.' *English Language Notes*, IV (1966), 105–10.
Milton's *Reason of Church-Government* is a possibility.

2995. —— 'Blake's THE LITTLE GIRL LOST, Stanzas 9–11.' *Explicator*, XXVII (1969), item 61.
Faint parallels with Dante's *Inferno* Canto I, *Comus*, and *Paradise Lost*.

2996. —— 'Dylan Thomas' Conception of Poetry: A Debt to William Blake.' *English Language Notes*, VI (1969), 197–200.
A brief general survey.

2997. Wittreich, Joseph Anthony, Jr. ed. *Nineteenth-Century Accounts of William Blake* by Benjamin Heath Malkin, Henry Crabb Robinson, John Thomas Smith, Allan Cunningham, Frederick Tatham, William Butler Yeats: Facsimile Reproduction with Introductions and Headnotes. Gainesville, Florida, 1970. Scholars Facsimiles and Reprints.

Facsimiles of excerpts from Malkin's *Memoirs*, Crabb Robinson in Symons, Smith's *Nollekens*, Cunningham's *Lives* (2nd Edition), Tatham in Russell's *Letters* (no. 88), and Yeats, introduction to *Poems* (1905), no. 293C. The headnotes are perfunctory, there is no new annotation or index, and the texts of Robinson and Tatham are taken from inferior transcripts.

2998. —— 'The "Satanism" of Blake and Shelley Reconsidered.' *SP*, LXV (1968), 816–33.

'*An* attempt to set the record straight' about 'what Blake and Shelley *really* said' about Milton's satan.

2999. *—— 'William Blake: Illustrator-Interpreter of *Paradise Regained*.' Pp. 93–132 of *Calm of Mind*: Tercentenary Essays on *Paradise Regained* and *Samson Agonistes* in Honor of John S. Diekhoff. Ed. Joseph Anthony Wittreich, Jr. Cleveland & London, 1971.

A diffuse essay on the ways in which the critical and illustrative traditions concerning Milton's brief epic affected Blake's illustrations; the essay is supported by reproductions of Blake's 12 *Paradise Regained* drawings (Fitzwilliam), by an admirably detailed 'Appendix A: Illustrators of *Paradise Regained* and Their Subjects (1713–1816)' (pp. 309–29) and by 'Appendix B: A Catalogue of Blake's Illustrations to Milton' (pp. 331–42).

3000. Wolf, Edwin, 2nd. 'Blake Exhibitions in America on the Occasion of the Bicentenary of the Birth of William Blake.' *Book Collector*, VI (1957), 378–85.

Notes also the owners of many works.

3001. —— 'The Blake–Linnell Accounts in the Library of Yale University.' *Papers of the Bibliographical Society of America*, XXXVII (1943), 1–22.

Important transcriptions and discussion.

3002. —— with John F. Fleming. *Rosenbach* A Biography. Cleveland & N.Y., 1960. Pp. 54, 64, 74, 75, 79, 81, 99, 102, 104, 112, 314, 315, 320, 379, 441, 462, 463, 493, 519, 524, 565–7.

A biography of the man whom its subject modestly took to be 'the world's greatest bookseller' who probably sold more important Blake books than any other has or will.

3003. Wolfe, Thomas P. 'The Blakean Intellect.' *Hudson Review*, XX (1967–8), 610–14.

Concerns the 'exhilaration of the unimpeded intellect' (p. 612).

3004. A. *Wolf-Gumpold, Kaethe. *William Blake*: Versuch einer Einführung in sein Leben und Werk. Stuttgart, 1964. B. *William Blake*: Painter:

Poet: Visionary; An Attempt at an Introduction to his Life and Work. Tr. Ernest Rathgeber in collaboration with Peter G. Button. London, 1969.

Ernst Rathgeber, 'Geleitwort' (A, pp. 7–12); when Blake was born, 'a light like a reflection of the sun lit up the city of London as soon as he opened his radiant eyes' (B, p. 12).

3005. *Woods, Humphrey. 'William Blake: Poet and Visionary.' *Coming Events in Britain*, XXII (Oct. 1967), 33–5.
Surviving Blake houses which can still be seen.

3006. Woodworth, Mary K. 'Blake's Illustrations for Gray's Poems.' *N&Q*, CCXV [N.S. XVII] (1970), 312–13.
Commissioned before November 1797.

3007. Wormhoudt, Arthur. 'Blake's Introduction to Songs of Innocence.' *Explicator*, VII (1949), item 55 (vMKN).
Blake exalting the artist over Christ.

3008. *Wright, Cyril E. 'William Blake's Notebook.' *British Museum Quarterly*, XXI (1959), 88–90.
On Mrs. Emerson's gift to the British Museum, with a record of previous owners.

3009. Wright, Herbert G. 'Henry Crabb Robinson's "Essay on Blake".' *MLR*, XXII (1927), 137–54.
Background, summary, and reprint.

3010. —— 'William Blake and Sir Joshua Reynolds: A Contrast in Theories of Art.' *Nineteenth Century*, CI (1927), 417–31.
A commentary on Blake's marginalia to Reynolds.

3011. —— & Mona Wilson. 'Blake and the Welsh Triads.' *TLS*, 5, 12 March 1931, pp. 178, 199.
Wright suggests William Owen or Edward Williams as the source of Blake's knowledge; Miss Wilson says Owen is the more likely.

3012. Wright, J. C. 'A Word on William Blake.' *Quest*, XVII (1926), 393–6.

3013. *Wright, Thomas. *Blake for Babes*: A popular illustrated Introduction to the Works of William Blake. Olney, 1923.
A trifling, amusing dialogue with a six-year-old (37 pp.).

3014. —— 'A Blake Museum for London.' *The Times*, 6 Sept. 1912, p. 8 (vMKN).
A proposal from the Blake Society (never realized).

3015. —— 'Blake's Grave.' *TLS*, 20 Jan. 1927, p. 44 (vMKN).
On its location in Bunhill Fields.

3016. [—— ed.?] *The First Meeting of The Blake Society*: Papers Read before The Blake Society at the First Annual Meeting, 12th August, 1912. Olney [1912].

The volume includes J. Foster Howe, 'The Chairman's Address' (pp. 8–9), Thomas Wright, 'The Secretary's Address' (pp. 10–16), Greville MacDonald, 'Abbreviated Paper on William Blake, Practical Idealist' (pp. 17–24) (for the full version, see no. 2170), Herbert Jenkins, 'The Teaching of William Blake' (pp. 25–34) (partly reprinted from no. 1928, q.v.), Walter K. Jealous, 'Hampstead in the time of Blake' (pp. 35–42) (also printed in no. 1954), George H. Leonard, 'The Art of William Blake' (pp. 43–8), F. C. Owlett, 'Blake's Burden' (pp. 49–53) (a general assessment), Thomas Wright, 'Appendix: The Engravings of William Blake' (pp. 56–8) (review of Russell [1912], no. 603).

3017. A. Wright, Thomas. *The Life of William Blake*. With 135 Illustrations. In Two Volumes. Olney, 1929. B. §N.Y., 1969. C. §* Newport Pagnell, 1972.

Many contemporary references (notably in the correspondence of John Johnson and William Hayley) which first appeared in this book have since been corrected and republished elsewhere. The work is a curious combination of original, fruitful research and garbled facts which make it frequently suggestive and rarely reliable.

In Vol. II are appendices of 'Decorations in Blake's Works' and 'Blake's Paintings, Colour Prints, Sketches and Engravings [in subject chronological order]', the second of which is novel and useful.

3018. —— 'Plates Engraved by Blake.' *TLS*, 10 Nov. 1927, p. 818 (vMKN).
Wonders where to find a copy of Allen's *History*.

3019. —— 'William Blake.' *Reader*, II (1926–7), 27–31.
Ostensibly a review of Sloss & Wallis, no. 309.

3020. Wyss, Hedy A. 'William Blake Kunsthaus, 20. Juni bis 20. Juli 1947.' *Werk*, XXXIV, heft 8 (Aug. 1947), 90.
Notice about the Vienna exhibition, no. 657.

Y

3021. Yamaguchi, Hideo. 'Blake's "Europe" to [*and*] Shelley's "Ode to the West Wind".' *Eigo Seinen: The Rising Generation*, CII (1956), 436–7.

3022. Yamanaka, Takeshi. 'A Study of William Blake's "A Song of Liberty".' *Kenkyu Ronbunshu*: Saga Daigaku Kyoikugakubu [*Faculty Journal* of Saga University Department of Education], XII (1964), 25–52.

3023. *Yamato, Yasuo. 'Blake no "Yoru" to "Tora" [Blake's "Night" and "The Tyger"].' *Youth's Companion*, Nov. 1949, pp. 36–9.

3024. —— 'William Blake.' Pp. 51–9 of his *Eibungaku ni okeru Romanshugi* [*Romanticism in English Literature*]. Tokyo, 1951. Kenkyusha Shin Eibeibungaku Gogaku Koza [New Kenkyusha Lectures on British and American Literature and Linguistics Volume VIII].
In Japanese.

3025. Yamazaki, Susumu. 'Blake ni okeru Ningenkeisei no ichikosatsu

[Formation of Blake's Personality].' *Himejikodai Kenkyuhokoku*, Ippan Kyoiku-kankei [*Himeji Technical College Research Report*, General Education Studies], IX (1960), 31–45.

3026. [Yanagi, Soetsu (Muneyoshi)]. 'Blake Tenrankai [Blake Exhibition].' *Shirakaba* [*The White Birch*], X (1919), 180.
News paragraph about the recent exhibition.

3027. Yanagi, Soetsu (Muneyoshi). 'Kotei no 2-shijin [Two Affirmative Poets].' *Shirakaba* [*The White Birch*], V (1914), 150–76.
The poets are Blake and Whitman.

3028. —— 'Watakushi no Blake-ron ni tsuite [About my Book on Blake].' *Bunmei Hyoron* [*Civilization Criticism*], II (1915), 423–5 (vHK).
A rebuttal of Takeshi Saito's review ('Kitan-naki Kansha: William Blake wo ronzu', *Bunmei Hyoron*, II [1915], 275–7), followed on pp. 426–7 by Saito's reply.

3029. —— *William Blake*. Tokyo, 1914. 756 pp.
A commentary, with 60 plates. (For errata, see his 'William Blake Seigohyo ni tsuite'.)

3030. —— *'William Blake—1757–1827.' *Shirakaba* [*The White Birch*], V, No. 4 (April 1914), 1–137.
In Japanese.

3031. —— 'William Blake Seigohyo ni tsuite [On the Errata in My book on William Blake].' *Shirakaba* [*The White Birch*], VI, No. 2 (1915), 173 (vHK).

3032. §Yasuda, Masayoshi. 'Blake Kenkyu [Studies].' Pp. 71–90 of *Toyoda hakase Koki Kinen eibei bungaku Ronso* [*Essays and Studies on British and American Literature in Honour of the Seventieth Birthday of Dr Minoru Toyoda*]. Ed. 'The Q.A. Society' in Kyoshi University. Fukuoka, 1956.

3033. —— 'Blake no Jesus-kan [Blake's View of Christ],' *Kwanseigakuin Daigaku Keizaigakubu Bungaku Gogaku Ronshu* [*Kwanseigakuin University Economics Department, Essays in Languages and Literatures*], No. 4 (1967), 67–86 (vST).

3034. —— §'Blake no Koto [William Blake: A Short Essay].' *Kyodai* [*The Brothers*, Revival], I, No. 2 (May 1957), 19.

3035. —— 'Four Zoas kara Milton e (1) [From Four Zoas to Milton (1)].' *Kwanseigakuin Daigaku Eibeibungaku: Journal of the Society of English and American Literature, Kwanseigakuin University*, 11th Ser. VI, No. 6 (Nov. 1961), 15–32, 90.
The English résumé on p. [90] says that this, the first of three parts, 'treats of the internal changes of Blake in which the Death of Jesus on the Cross and his Resurrection was introduced into *Vala, the Four Zoas* for the first time'.

3036. —— 'Innocence no Kozo to Jisso [Structure and Essence in Innocence].' *Kwanseigakuin Daigaku Ronko* [*Kwanseigakuin University Studies*], (1969), 115–26.
About Blake.

3037. Yanagi Soetsu (Muneyoshi). §' "The Marriage of Heaven and Hell" Oboegaki [Notes on *The Marriage of Heaven and Hell*].' *Kwanseigakuin Kotobu Ronso* [*Kwanseigakuin High School Studies*], No. 2 (1958), 50–62; No. 3 (1959), 28–43.

3038. —— ' "Mushin no Uta" ni okeru Chichi to Haha [Father and Mother in *Songs of Innocence*].' *Kwanseigakuin Daigaku Ronko* [*Kwanseigakuin University Studies*], No. 14 (1967), 153–65.

3039. —— ' "Songs of Innocence" ni okeru Kami no Sekai [World of God in *Songs of Innocence*].' *Kwanseigakuin Daigaku Ronko* [*Kwanseigakuin University Studies*], No. 15 (1968), 131–43.

3040. —— ' "Tora" ni arawareta Shiron [Poetic Diction in "The Tyger"].' *Kwanseigakuin Daigaku Ronko* [*Kwanseigakuin University Studies*], X (1963), 111–25.

3041. —— 'William Blake ni okeru Eien no Mondai—Urizen Oboegaki [Some Notes on William Blake's *Urizen, the First Book*].' *Eibei Bungaku* (Kwanseigakuin Daigaku): *Journal of the Society of English and American Literature* [of] *Kwanseigakuin University*, 7th Ser. IV (1959), 47–60.

3042. —— 'William Blake no Kodoku Oboegaki [Notes on William Blake's Solitude].' *Kwanseigakuin Daigaku Ronko* [*Kwanseigakuin University Studies*], VIII (1961), 161–77.

3043. —— 'William Blake no Shinko [William Blake's Faith].' *Kwanseigakuin Daigaku Ronko* [*Kwanseigakuin University Studies*], XII (1965), 115–28.

3044. —— 'William Blake no Shiron Oboegaki—Poetical Sketches ni tsuite [Note on William Blake's Poetics—on *Poetical Sketches*].' *Kwanseigakuin Daigaku Ronko* [*Kwanseigakuin University Studies*], IX (1962), 223–39.

3045. —— 'William Blake no Unmeikan [William Blake's View of Destiny].' *Kwanseigakuin Daigaku Ronko* [*Kwanseigakuin University Studies*], XIII (1966), 119–32.

3046. —— 'William Blake no Yogensha no Jikaku no Keisei [William Blake's Awakening as a Prophet].' *Eibei Bungaku*: Kwanseigakuin Daigaku [*English and American Literature:*] The Society of British and American Literature [of] Kwanseigakuin University, II (1957), 85–103.

3047. A. *Yeats, William Butler. 'Academy Portraits, XXXII.—William Blake.' *The Academy*, LI (1897), 634–5. B. Reprinted as 'William Blake and the Imagination.' Pp. 168–75 of his *Ideas of Good and Evil*. London, 1903. C. N.Y., 1903. D. Second Edition. London, 1903. E. Third Edition. London & Dublin, 1907. F. Reprinted as pp. 131–7 of *Ideas of Good and Evil*, which in turn is Vol. VI of *The Collected Works in Verse & Prose of William Butler Yeats*. Stratford on Avon, 1908. G. Reprinted as pp. 111–15 of *Essays and Introductions*. London, 1961. H. Tr. Makoto Sangu as 'William Blake to Sozo.' *Mirai* [*Future*], II (1944), 123–30. I. *Zen'aku no Kannen* [*Ideas of Good and Evil*]. Tr. Makoto Sangu. Tokyo, 1915.

Blake is 'an inexhaustible fountain of beauty' (E, p. 172).

3048. Yeats, William Butler. *The Letters of W. B. Yeats*. Ed. Allan Wade. London, 1954. *Passim.*
Interesting minor references to Blake.

3049. —— *W. B. Yeats Letters to Katharine Tynan*. Ed. Roger McHugh. Dublin & London, 1953. *Passim.*

3050. —— 'William Blake.' *Bookman* X (1896), 21 (vMKN).
Review of Garnett's book.

3051. A. —— *'William Blake and his Illustrations to the Divine Comedy.' Savoy*, Nos. 3–5 (1896), subtitled 'His Opinions upon Art', No. 3, pp. 41–57; 'His Opinions on Dante', No. 4, pp. 25–41; 'The Illustrations of Dante', No. 5, pp. 31–6. B. Reprinted as pp. 176–225 of his *Ideas of Good and Evil*. London, 1903. C. N.Y., 1903. D. Second Edition. London, 1903. E. Third Edition. London & Dublin, 1907. F. Reprinted as pp. 138–75 of *Ideas of Good and Evil*, which in turn is Vol. VI of *The Collected Works in Verse & Prose of William Butler Yeats*. Stratford on Avon, 1908. G. Reprinted in pp. 116–45 of *Essays and Introductions*. London, 1961.
Though he is sometimes 'a too literal realist of imagination', 'the only designs that compete with Blake's are those of Botticelli and Giulio Clovio' (E, pp. 147, 176–7).
Parts of Yeats's essay were translated into Japanese by Makoto Sangu and printed in *Mirai*, Nos. I & II (1914), 123–30. The manuscript of the essay is in Harvard.

3052. —— 'The Writings of William Blake.' *Bookman*, IV (1893), 146–7 (vMKN).
Hard review of Housman's edition, no. 302.

3053. —— & J. Churton Collins. 'Mr. Churton Collins on Blake.' *TLS*, 30 May, 13 June 1902, pp. 157, 173.
Flashes of critical acerbity (in a quarrel about other matters, pp. 132, 139–40, 148–9), as to whether 'The Tyger' ll. 16–20 are, as Collins claimed (p. 149), 'nonsense pure and absolute', or whether, as Yeats thought (p. 157), they and 'The Lamb' may be taken as 'a touchstone' of poetical taste; Collins complains (p. 173) that he was quoted out of context.

3054. §Yen, Yu-heng. 'Shen-mi Shih-jen Wei-lien Po-lai-k'o [The Mystic Poet William Blake].' *Nan-k'ai Ta-hsueh Chou-k'an*, no. 61 (19).
In Chinese.

3055. Yoshida, Michiko. 'William Blake no Shi ni araware ta Divine Image e no Ichikosatsu [A Study of the Divine Image in William Blake's Works].' *Hokuseigakuen Tankidaigaku Kiyo: Journal of Hokusei Gakuen Women's Junior College*, No. 5 (1959), 14–31.

3056. §Yoshida, Suzuko. 'Blake no Saisho no Jojoshishu [Blake's First Lyric Poems].' *Dosokai Gakuyukai Kiho [The Alumni Bulletin of Doshisha Girls' College and Doshisha Girls' High School]*, No. 58 (15 Dec. 1933), 98–102.

3057. Yoshida, Suzuko. §'Blake Saku "Musen no Urakata' no Josetsu ni tsuite [On Blake's "Auguries of Innocence"].' *Dosokai Gakugukai Kiho* [*The Alumni Bulletin of Doshisha Girls' College and Doshisha Girls' High School*], No. 57 (1932), 95–9.

3058. —— §'"Musen Mumyo no Uta" ni arawareta Blake no Shiso no Benshoho-teki Hatten [Dialectic Development of Blake's Ideas in *Songs of Innocence and of Experience*].' *Dosokai Gakuyukai Kiho* [*The Alumni Bulletin of Doshisha Girls' College and Doshisha Girls' High School*], No. 58 (15 Dec. 1933), 102–7.

3059. Yoshioka, Motoko. 'Blake in His Age.' *Toyo Eiwa Jogakuin Tanki-Daigaku* [*Toyo Eiwa Junior College Studies*], No. 6 (1967), 9–19 (vHK).
In Japanese.

3060. Yoshitake, Michio. '"Hihyo no Reigi" wo yonde—Jugaku Hakushi eno Tegami [On Reading "Courtesy of Criticism"—A Letter to Dr. Jugaku].' *Eigo Seinen: The Rising Generation*, CIII (1957), 569.
Quarrel partly about 'The Tyger'; see Jugaku's article.

3061. §Yoshiwara, Fumio. 'The World of Imagination and Religion in William Blake.' *Vision*, No. 1 (1967), 26–34.

3062. Young, Mildred Binns. *Woolman and Blake*: Prophets for Today. Lebanon, Pennsylvania, 1971. Pendle Hill Pamphlet 177.
Brief (32 pp.) and distant parallels between Blake and the U.S. Quaker John Woolman (d. 1772).

3063. §Yuan, K'o-chia. 'Pu-lai-k'o-ti Shih: Wei-lien Pu-lai-k'o Tan-sheng Erh-pai Chou-nien Chi Nien [Blake's Poetry: In Commemoration of the Second Centenary of the Birth of William Blake].' *Wen-hsueh Yen-chiu*, No. 4 (Dec. 1957).
In Chinese.

Z

3064. §Zweig, Stefan. 'William Blakes Auferstehung.' *Beilage der Neuen Freien Presse* [Vienna], 27 Jan. 1907.

ADDENDA

Note: The following Addenda appear in the order of, and with the numbers they would bear in, the body of the work. For example, no. 1984. B is the second printing or edition of no. 1984. A work which should have appeared between no. 1932 and no. 1933 is numbered A1932, a second work which should have appeared there is B1932, and so on. Most of the several hundred works here appeared since 1972.

PART I. EDITIONS OF BLAKE'S WRITINGS

SECTION A. *Individual Works*

6. . . . *America* (D) was bequeathed in 1975 by the late Miss Caroline Newton to **(9)** PRINCETON.

. . . *America* (G) **(5)** His son the present Lord Cunliffe, who had the works disbound in June 1966 for the Blake Trust facsimile of *Europe* (1967) and *Jerusalem* (1974), lent *America* and *Europe* anonymously to the National Library of Scotland exhibition (1969), no. 43, 48, and placed *Europe* in 1971 in **(6a)** GLASGOW UNIVERSITY LIBRARY.

16. *The Book of Los* (A) was reproduced in colour filmstrip by EP Microform Ltd.

32. *Descriptive Catalogue* (S) BINDING: It was trimmed to 11·0 × 18·5 cm and 'half [*or rather three-quarter*] bound / (not letterd)' (according to Charles Lamb's instructions on the title-page) in calf over marbled boards (p. 60 torn) with a manuscript table of contents by Lamb listing the works bound after the *Descriptive Catalogue*, viz.

(2) [John Wilmot, Earl of Rochester], *Poems on Several Occasions* (n.d., after 1679), lacking the title-page and all preliminaries, pp. 1–162, with Lamb's notes on pp. 54, 104, 154;

(3) [Henry Carey], *Chrononhotonthologos*; The Most Tragical Tragedy That ever was Tragedized, The Fifth Edition (London: J. Shuckburgh, 1753), pp. 1–30;

(4) Anne [Finch] Countess of Winchelsea, *Poems on Several Occasions* (London: W. Taylor & Jonas Browne, 1714), pp. i–viii, 1–390, with Lamb's notes on the title-page and p. 202;

(5) [Metastasio, adapted by T. A. Arne], *Artaxerxes*, An English Opera, The Music composed by Tho. Aug. Arne, A New Edition (London: W. Lowndes, 1813), pp. 1–22, signature trimmed from the title-page, perhaps 'A Ryle 1813', note by Lamb on the Dramatis Personae page;

(6) Sempronia, a letter '*To the Editor of the British Lady's Magazine.* | ON NEEDLE-WORK' (n.d.; *The British Lady's Magazine* flourished 1815–18), pp. 259–64 (only pp. 259–60 are 'On Needle-Work');

(7) [Robert Southey], *Wat Tyler*, edition pirated in *The Republican*, No. 5 (London, Saturday, 29 March 1817), pp. 65–80, price 2*d.*;

(8) [Charles Lamb], 'CONFESSIONS OF A DRUNKARD' (running head: 'CONTRIBUTE TO MORAL EXCELLENCE'), perhaps printed in *The Philanthropist*, IX (1813),[1] 201–15, revised by Lamb, the running-heads deleted;

(9) Edward Young, *The Force of Religion*: or, Vanquish'd Love, A Poem (London: E. Curll & J. Pemberton, 1714), pp. i–viii, 1–38, pencil sketches on title-page verso;

(10) [Thomas] Southerne, *The Spartan Dame*, A Tragedy (London: W. Chetwood & T. Jauncy, 1719), pp. i–viii, 1–70;

(11) [Ambrose] Philips, *The Briton*, A Tragedy (London: R. Lintot, 1722), pp. i–xiv, 1–64;

(12) [John Galt], *The Witness*, A Tragedy, lacking all preliminaries, printed in *The New British Theatre*, ed. John Galt, Vol. I (1814),[2] 1–42.[3]

HISTORY: (1) Blake made the standard corrections on the title-page and p. 64, and his brother James sold it with three other copies on 23 April 1810 to (2) Henry Crabb Robinson,[4] who may have added the inscription at the top of the title-page (now almost entirely trimmed off) when he gave it to (3) Charles Lamb,[4] who had it bound with other works (as above) and bequeathed it (1834) with the rest of his library to (4) Edward Moxon,[5] who, after the death of Lamb's sister Mary (1847), destroyed all but about sixty volumes (according to the 1848 catalogues) and sold the rest for £10 to the New York store of (5) Bartlett & Welford, which sold them piecemeal in Feb. 1848;[6] the 54th lot described as 'Tracts Miscellaneous, 1 thick volume, 12 mo . . .', including *Descriptive Catalogue* (S) went for $4.50; (6) The volume of miscellaneous Tracts was sold anonymously (?by James T. Annan) through Cooley, Keese, & Hill, of New York, 21 Oct. 1848, lot 376, for $4.25 to Campbell; (7) It was given by an old lady, probably in the 1930s, to (8) Mr. Baker, a book dealer of Cambridge, Massachusetts, who left it to (9) His widow, of Long Island; (10) It was acquired about 1970 by Mr. Michael Papantonio of Seven Gables Book Shop (the authority

---

[1] The essay was also printed in Basil Montague, *Some Enquiries into the Effects of Fermented Liquors* (1814) and *The London Magazine* (Aug. 1824).

[2] The work was first called 'The Rejected Theatre' (because the plays had not been acted), and by signature A is 'VOL. *I. Rej. Th.* No. I'.

[3] For information about this volume, I am indebted to Mr. Thomas Lange of The Pierpont Morgan Library, Mr. Michael Papantonio, and Professor Richard Ludwig of Princeton.

[4] *Blake Records* (1969), 537, 578.

[5] According to Crabb Robinson's Diary for 27 April 1848 (Dr. Williams's Library).

[6] The Bartlett & Welford list was printed in Anon., 'Charles Lamb's Library in New York', *Literary World*, iii (5 Feb. 1848), 10–11, and offprinted for the commercial use of the firm.

for the twentieth-century history here), who sold it to (**11**) Mr. *Robert Taylor* of Princeton.

33. *Europe* (K) is reproduced in the Hamburger Kunsthalle katalog (1975), no. B710.

38. *The First Book of Urizen* (D) was reproduced in colour filmstrip by EP Microform Ltd.

Pl. 4: BINDING: A loose, unwatermarked leaf 22·4 × 28·9 cm, printed in Orange, slightly askew, with one Red framing-line, the background somewhat clumsily coloured Grey.

HISTORY: (**1**) Perhaps the plate was intended for copy G of *c*. 1815, which lacks pl. 4 but was, like this plate, printed (not colour-printed) in Orange— a slightly different shade; it may have been omitted because of its printing defects; (**2**) Acquired in England about 1923 by a California collector of illustrated books, whose (**3**) Son sold it in 1972 to (**4**) An *Anonymous Collection*.

Pl. 9: *Urizen* pl. 9 was bequeathed in 1975 by the late Miss Caroline Newton to (**6**) PRINCETON.

43. *For Children: The Gates of Paradise* pl. 15: A reversed design for it in the Royal Collection, Windsor, is labelled 'The spirit of a just man newly departed appearing to his mourning family.'

45. . . . *For the Sexes* (H) was bequeathed in 1975 by the late Miss Caroline Newton to (**6**) PRINCETON.

75. *Jerusalem* (B) is reproduced in the Hamburger Kunsthalle katalog (1975), no. B710.

98. *The Marriage of Heaven and Hell* (H) was reproduced in the 1975 facsimile.

Marriage pl. 11 was bequeathed by the late Miss Caroline Newton in 1975 to (**6**) PRINCETON.

A109. §**The Marriage of Heaven and Hell* [H]. With an Introduction and Commentary by Sir Geoffrey Keynes. London & N.Y., 1975.
   A. Fawcus, publisher's note (p. viii), Keynes, 'Introduction' (6 pp.), commentary interspersed with the colour facsimile.

136. The Small Book of Designs (A) and Large Book of Designs (A) were reproduced in microfilm by EP Microform Ltd.

137. *The Song of Los* (B) was reproduced in the Blake Trust facsimile (1975).

A137. *The Song of Los* [B]. London, 1975. The William Blake Trust. Geoffrey Keynes, 'Commentary and Bibliographical History' (5 pp.).

139. *Songs of Innocence and of Experience* (T) was reproduced in the 1975 facsimile.

Songs (j) . . . was bequeathed by the late Miss Caroline Newton in 1975 to **(6)** PRINCETON.

C191. **Lieder der Unschuld und Erfahrung* [*Songs* copy T] Herausgegeben und mit einem Nachwort versehen von Werner Hofmann. Frankfort am Main, 1975.
    Persuasive facsimile (pp. 9 6ą), German translation of it (pp. 65–103), and Hofmann's 'Nachwort' (pp. 105–15).

200. *There is No Natural Religion* (M) is reproduced in the Hamburger Kunsthalle katalog (1975), no. B710.

213. *Visions of the Daughters of Albion* (C) . . . **(5)** The present Lord Cunliffe, placed it in 1971 in **(6)** GLASGOW UNIVERSITY LIBRARY.

SECTION B. *Collections and Selections*

A219. §*The Angel*. London, 1951.

A240. §*The Clouded Hills*: Selections from William Blake. Ed. Catharine Hughes. N.Y., 1973. Mysticism and Modern Man Series.

260. 'Holy Thursday' from *Innocence* in Jane & Ann Taylor, *City Scenes*.
    According to Christine Duff Stewart's exhaustive and admirable *The Taylors of Ongar*: An Analytical Bio-Bibliography (1975), the correct description probably should be:
  A. Darton, Harvey & Darton, 1818. (Essex County Library, Guildhall Library, Toronto Public)
      Collation: A–C^{12}.
  B. Darton, Harvey & Darton, 1818. (V & A)
      Collation: A–B^{12} C^8.
  C. Harvey & Co., 1818. (Florida State)
  D. Darton, Harvey & Darton, 1823. (Bodley, California [Los Angeles])
  E. Harvey & Darton, 1828. (BM, Columbia, GEB, Guildhall Library [coloured])
      With a new plate for the Charity Children.
  F. Harvey & Darton, n.d. [*c.* 1845]. 82 Pp. (BM, Columbia, Essex County Library, Guildhall Library, V & A, Western Ontario)

A260. *Holy Thursday* from Songs of Innocence [*and* From Songs of Experience]. Designed, illustrated and printed by Paul Peter Piech. Bushey Heath [1971]. Taurus Poems No. 18.

A261. **The Illuminated Blake*. Ed. D. V. Erdman. . . . B. §**Oxford, 1975.
    B. The second printing has some minor corrections.

A296. *The Poems of William Blake.* Ed. Aileen Ward. With Illustrations from Blake's Illuminated Books. Cambridge [England], for Members of The Limited Editions Club, 1973.

'Introduction' (pp. xv–xxii), 'Notes on the Poems' (pp. 273–82), the text is that of Keynes, emended 'In a few places' from that of Erdman (1965). This is scarcely more than a pretty piece of bookmaking.

A305. *Poezje Wybrane*: Wybrał, przelzyl i wstepem opatrzył. Warzawa, 1972. Biblioteka poetów.

Zygmunt Kubiak, 'William Blake' (in Polish) is on pp. 5–21, the Polish translations on pp. 23–142.

B311. *Proverbs of Hell* with Illustrations by Paul Peter Piech. Bushey Heath [1973].

Excerpts from the *Marriage*.

318. A. *Selected Poems of William Blake.* Ed. F. W. Bateson. . . . G. London, 1974.

A333. *Songs of Innocence and of Experience*: Selected Plates Reproduced in [Colour] Facsimile from Originals in the Huntington Library Selected and introduced by James Thorpe. San Marino, California [1975].

Thorpe's 'Introduction' is pp. 3–4. The 'slightly enlarged' facsimile is of pl. 1, 3–4, 8, 15, 24–25, 28–30, 38–39, 48–49 from copy E, pl. 32, 42 from N, with transcripts on facing pages.

370. A. *Blake: Complete Writings* with variant readings. Ed. Geoffrey Keynes. . . . I. London, Oxford, New York, 1974.

New 'minor corrections' were made in the editions of 1969, 1971, 1972, and 1974.

PART II. REPRODUCTIONS OF DRAWINGS AND PAINTINGS

SECTION A. *Illustrations of Individual Authors*

377. Bunyan, John. *Pilgrim's Progress* . . . Ed. G. B. Harrison (1941); the 29 Blake designs are reproduced in colour microfilm by EP Microform Ltd.

389. A. Milton, John. *On the Morning of Christ's Nativity.* Milton's Hymn with [six] Illustrations by William Blake and a Note by Geoffrey Keynes. . . . B. Folcroft, Pennsylvania, 1971.

A reprint of the 1923 edition.

PART III. COMMERCIAL BOOK ENGRAVINGS

SECTION A. *Illustrations of Individual Authors*

435. A. Blair, Robert. *The Grave.* . . . . H. A Poem. Illustrated by Twelve Etchings from the Original Inventions of William Blake. A New Edition. N.Y., 1903.

482. Malkin, B. H. *A Father's Memoirs of his Child* (1806), the copy presented by Malkin to Thomas Johnes, to whom the printed introductory letter about Blake is addressed, is in the possession ot Major Herbert Lloyd-Johnes.

The account of Blake is reprinted in G. E. Bentley, Jr., ed., *William Blake*: The Critical Heritage (1975), no. B1181.

498. A. Shakspeare, William. *Plays* . . . F. THE / PLAYS / OF / WILLIAM SHAKSPEARE, / ACCURATELY PRINTED / FROM THE TEXT OF THE CORRECTED COPIES / LEFT BY THE LATE / GEORGE STEEVENS, Esq., AND EDMUND MALONE, Esq. / WITH / MR. MALONE'S VARIOUS READINGS; / A SELECTION OF / EXPLANATORY AND HISTORICAL NOTES, / FROM THE MOST EMINENT COMMENTATORS; / A HISTORY OF THE STAGE, AND A LIFE OF SHAKSPEARE; / BY / ALEXANDER CHALMERS, F.S.A. / — / VOLUME I. / JOHNSON'S PREFACE. / ACCOUNT OF THE ENGLISH STAGE. / POPE'S PREFACE. / TEMPEST [&c.]. / . . . / — / LONDON: / PRINTED FOR LONGMAN AND CO. / MDCCCXXXIX [1839]. (American Blake Foundation, defective.)

According to information kindly provided by Professor Roger Easson, the work is printed by 'C. and R. Baldwin, Printers, / New Bridge-street, Blackfriars', and the gatherings seem to be the remnants of the 1811 edition, with a new title-page. The plates, including Blake's, seem to be much worn.

515. Young, Edward. *Night Thoughts* (1797), coloured copies: COPY T: BINDING: A tall copy (32·0 × 41·6 cm) in rough condition, waterstained and foxed, with many tears, pp. 25–6, 39–40, 61–4, 75–6, 83–4, 87–8, 93–6 crudely mended with strips of paper tape at the edges (once, p. 25, partly over the water-colouring), lacking the leaf of explanations, pp. 73–4 replaced with quite different paper and type; coloured lightly and beautifully in Blake's early style on Night I title-page and pp. 1, 4, 7–8, 10, 13, 15, 19, 23–7, 31, 33, 35 (omitting pp. 12, 16–17, 36–72); bound in late nineteenth-century(?) pebbled grain black three-quarter calf, gilt; the pages trimmed but not gilt.

HISTORY: (1) The title-page was embossed twice with the oval stamp of the 'EXAMINING OFFICER·IPSWICH' of 'M.U.I.O.O.F.' (Manchester Unity Independent Order of Odd Fellows),[1] perhaps indicating that

---

[1] The Examining Officer's duties were to examine and relieve members of the Society travelling in search of work, who carried such an embossed stamp as this with them.

the volume once belonged to an Examining Officer of the Ipswich branch of the Society such as James Ball (the 1892 Officer); (2) Acquired by the London dealer E. Seligmann, who sold it for £5 in May 1953 to (3) *Mr. & Mrs. H. P. Cook.*

SECTION B. *Collections and Selections*

A517. William Blake. **Selected Engravings.* Ed. Carolyn Keay. London & N.Y., 1975.
Reproduction of 169 plates, some of them simply redrawn; the 'Introduction' is pp. 5–7.

PART IV. CATALOGUES AND BIBLIOGRAPHIES

B710. 1974 15 March–1 June. Anon. 'William Blake and His Followers: Selected Books, Prints and Drawings from the Collection of Charles A. Ryskamp.' *Gazette of The Grolier Club*, N.S., No. 20–1 (June–Dec. 1974), 81–9.
Thirty-four minor Blake items, a few very rare.

C710. A. 1975 6 March–27 July. **[David Bindman.] William Blake 1757–1827. [An exhibition in* Hamburger Kunsthalle 6. März bis 27. April 1975.] [Tr. Detlef Dörrbecker, Eleonora Reichert, & Georg Syamken.] [Munich & Hamburg, 1975.] B. **William Blake 1757–1827*: Städelsches Kunstinstitut und Städtische Galerie Frankfurt am Main [15. Mai bis 27. July 1975]. [Munich & Frankfort, 1975.]
A. This splendid catalogue consists of:
   (1) *Werner Hofmann, 'Vorwort' (pp. 7–9);
   (2) *Werner Hofmann, 'Die Erfüllung der Zeit' (pp. 11–30);
   (3) *Johannes Kleinstueck, 'Blake als Dichter' (pp. 31–7);
   (4) *Siegmar Holsten, 'Historisches Dokumentation' and 'Biographische Dokumentation' (pp. 38–83);
   (5) Henry Crabb Robinson, 'William Blake, Künstler, Dichter, und religiöser Schwärmer' from *Vaterländisches Museum* (pp. 75–83);
   (6) *David Bindman, 'Die Kunst William Blakes' (pp. 103–11);
   (7) *David Bindman, 'Katalog' of *225 entries (pp. 112–239), with 527 plates including all of *No Natural Religion* (M), *Europe* (K), *Jerusalem* (B), Blake's designs for *Paradise Lost* (Fitzwilliam set), 16 woodcuts for Virgil, and engravings for Mary Wollstonecraft's *Original Stories* (1791), Blair's *Grave* (1808), *Job*, and Dante.
B. The Frankfurt edition seems to differ chiefly in the substitution of Klaus Gallwitz, 'Vorwort' (pp. 9–10).

PART VI. BIOGRAPHY AND CRITICISM

Books and Articles about Blake

A769. Abrams, Lois. 'William Blake: The Lineaments of History.' *DAI*, XXXIV (1974), 4223A. Brandeis Ph.D., 1973.

A770. §Abukh, S. B. 'Blake, William.' Vol. I, p. 521 of [*Literary Encyclopedia*]. Moscow, 1929.

In Russian, with a bibliography.

B770. Adams, Eric. *Francis Danby*: Varieties of Poetic Landscape. New Haven & London, 1973. *Passim.*

There are frequent allegations, only slightly supported by evidence, that the paintings of Danby (1793–1861) show 'clear echoes of Blake' (p. 35).

C771. Adams, Hazard. 'Blake and the Philosophy of Literary Symbolism.' *New Literary History*, V (1973), 135–46.

A787. §Adlard, John. 'Blake's "The Little Girl Lost and Found".' *Archiv*, CCX (1973), 330–4.

Sources in Agrippa and Swedenborg.

A791. §—— 'Los Enters London.' *English Studies*, LIV (1973), 227–30.

A792. ——*The Sports of Cruelty*: Fairies, Folk-Songs, Charms and Other Country Matters in the Work of William Blake. London, 1972.

A very original, uneven work.

A802. Allentuck, Marcia. 'Fuseli's Translations of Winckelmann: A Phase in the Rise of British Hellenism with an aside on William Blake.' Pp. 163–85 of *Studies in the Eighteenth Century*, II: Papers presented at the Second David Nichol Smith Memorial Seminar Canberra 1970. Ed. R. F. Brissenden. Canberra, 1973.

A learned essay on the background and nature of Fuseli's translations; the paragraph on Blake (p. 185) is of dubious relevance and significance.

B802. A. Allibone, S. Austin. *A Critical Dictionary of English Literature, and British and American Authors*, Living and Deceased, from the earliest accounts to the Middle of the Nineteenth Century [Vols. II & III of A, and all vols. of B & C are extended 'to the Latter Half of the Nineteenth Century']. [3 vols. Vol. I] Philadelphia & London, 1859; [Vol. II] Philadelphia, 1870; [Vol. III] Philadelphia & London, 1871. Vol. I, p. 203. B. Philadelphia & London, 1877. Vol. I, p. 203. C. Philadelphia [Vol. I], 1891. Vol. I, p. 203.

The account of Blake (bibliographical and critical) does not change from edition to edition.

A814. Anon. *Illustrated London News*, VI, No. 158 (10 May 1845), 291 (vFrances Butlin).

A summary of J. M. W. Turner's career concludes that 'He is the very William Blake of living landscape painters', evidently because of his 'systematic defiance of every kind of principle in art or appearance in nature'.

A841. Anon. 'Big Price for a Book.' *The Times*, 11 June 1901.

Sotheby sold the Calvert–F. S. Ellis *Songs* for £700 to A. Jackson.

A883. *Anon. 'Blake, William.' *Enciclopedia Universale Fabbri* [Part] 35. Milano, 1970.

A916. Anon. *'Designs to a Series of Ballads written by William Hayley, Esq. and founded on Anecdotes relating to Animals, drawn, engraved, and published, by William Blake. With the ballads annexed by the Author's Permission. Two Numbers.* 4to. Printed at Chichester.' *European Magazine,* XLII (Aug. 1802), 125–6.

'The artist has executed his share of the undertaking much to his credit . . . .'

965. Anon. 'The Inventions of William Blake, Painter and Poet' (1830). . . . The *Blake Records* (1969) version is reprinted in G. E. Bentley, Jr., ed., *William Blake*: The Critical Heritage (1975), no. A1181.

968. Anon. 'The Last of the Supernaturalists' (1830) . . . . The *Blake Records* (1969) version is reprinted in G. E. Bentley, Jr., ed., *William Blake*: The Critical Heritage (1975), no. A1181.

A969. Anon. 'Literary and Miscellaneous Information.' *Athenaeum Magazine,* III (June 1808), 567. (Princeton).

'Mr. Cromek will very shortly present to the public Mr. Wm. Blake's celebrated Illustrations of Blair's Grave, etched by Mr. Louis Schiavonetti.'

989. Anon. 'Mr. William Blake.' *Gentleman's Magazine* (1827); for a suggestion that the revisions were by William Upcott, see no. A1171 below.

A990. Anon. 'Mr. William Blake . . . .' *The Star Chamber,* I (3 May 1826), 73.

A miscellany of cultural news including the information that 'Mr. William Blake . . . has completed his designs for the Book of Job . . . full of wildness and singularity of conception.' (This reference was generously pointed out to me by Professor William S. Ward.)

The anonymous author may be Benjamin Disraeli, who contributed a poem to *The Star Chamber* and who is indeed thought to have edited it (British Museum catalogue); the reference to Blake's 'earlier productions' is easily explicable in terms of his father's important Blake collection.

A1035. Anon. 'Tigre! Tigre! burning bright.' *TLS,* 26 July 1974, p. 796.

Editorial 'TLS Commentary' praising the Leyris translation.

A1065. §*[Anon.] '[William Blake in the world of vision. The Drawings of Famous Writers.]' *Kurier Iunesko,* VIII (1957), 52 pp. in Russian.

A1081. Anon. 'William Blake's "Songs".' *The Times,* 17 March 1909.

Sotheby sold a copy of the *Songs* to Dobell for £166.

A1086. *Antin, David. 'Fuseli, Blake, Palmer.' Chapter viii (pp. 109–23) of *The Grand Eccentrics*: Five centuries of artists outside the main currents of art

history. Ed. Thomas B. Hess. N.Y., 1966. *Art News Annual*, XXXII. B. *The Grand Eccentrics*. Ed. Thomas B. Hess & John Ashbery. N.Y., 1971. Pp. 109–27.
A brief, general account.

B1086. *Archer, William. 'The Drama is Pasteboard.' *Art Journal*, N.S., 1887, pp. 105–8, 141–4 (vMKN).
'I am disposed to doubt' the part played by William Blake in making engravings for the toy theatre.

A1091. Ashe, Geoffrey. 'Albion in Transition' and 'The Immortal City'. Chapters 9 (pp. 147–67) and 10 (pp. 168–85) of his *Camelot and the Vision of Albion*. London, 1971. Also *passim*.
'Through Blake's intuitions a whole series of themes can be seen to link up illuminatingly with the mystique of Camelot' (p. 14), and Ashe therefore rehearses Blake's Albion myth.

A1098. §*Ault, Donald A. 'Visionary Physics: Blake's Response to Newton.' University of Chicago Ph.D., 1968.
The basis of his book, below.

B1098. *——*Visionary Physics*: Blake's Response to Newton. Chicago & London, 1974.
Derived from his thesis, above.

C1098. Avni, Abraham. 'Blake's "Tiriel"—The Meaning of "Ijim".' *N&Q*, CCXIX [N.S. XXI] (1974), 60–1.
'Ijim' means 'jackals' in Hebrew.

A1102. §Babchina, T. 'William Blake.' *Literature un Maksla* [*Literature and Art*] (30 Nov. 1957).
In Latvian.

A1112. Baine, Rodney. 'Thel's Northern Gate.' *PQ*, LI (1972), 957–61.
'Thel's northern gate affords no evidence that Blake knew Taylor's *Porphyry*', as Damon, Harper, and Raine have argued, for it is 'more likely to be merely a recollection from Pope's familiar translation of *The Odyssey*' (pp. 961, 958).

A1113. Baird, [?Sister Mary] Julian. 'Swinburne, Sade, and Blake: The Pleasure–Pain Paradox.' *Victorian Poetry*, IX (1971), 49–75.
An 'attempt to define his [*Swinburne's*] intellectual combination of Sade with the set of ideas which he had drawn from Blake' (p. 50).

A1122. Ballin, Michael G. 'D. H. Lawrence and William Blake: A Critical Study in Influence and Analogy.' Toronto Ph.D., 1972. See *DAI*, XXXIV (1974), 5745A.
Concerned mostly with analogies in Lawrence.

B1122. §Balmont, K. D. '[The Father of Contemporary Symbolists (William Blake 1757–1827)].' Vol. I, pp. 43–8 of Balmont's [*Mountain Tops*]. Moscow, 1904.
In Russian.

C1122. Bandy, Melanie Flossie. 'The Idea of Evil in the Poetry of Blake and Shelley: A Comparative Study.' *DAI*, XXXII (1972), 5218A. New Mexico Ph.D.
'This analogical study' discovers 'striking similarities'.

A1123. Barach, Frances K., ed. 'William Blake 1757–1827.' Vol. II, pp. 271–95, of *The Critical Temper*: A Survey of Modern Criticism on English and American Literature from the Beginnings to the Twentieth Century. In Three Volumes. Ed. Martin Tucker. N.Y., 1969.
Thirty-eight fragments.

A1129. [Basan, F.] SUPPLÉMENT / AU / DICTIONNAIRE / DES / GRAVEURS / ANCIENS ET MODERNES / De F. BASAN, graveur. / Suivi d'une table alphabétique des maitres, / cités dans cet ouvrage. / [ornament] / A BRUXELLES, / Chez Jos. ERMENS, imprimeur libraire, / marché aux charbons. / — / 1791. Pp. 24–5. (Toronto)
The *Supplément* to his *Dictionnaire des Graveurs Anciens et Modernes* depuis l'Origine de la Gravure [2 vols.] (Paris, 1767) has a brief entry for Blake which was repeated verbatim in the *Dictionnaire* of 1809 (see no. 1129).

A1142. §Beer, John B. 'Blake, Mr. Tolley and the Scholarly Imagination.' *Southern Review*, IV (1971), 247–55.

A1146. §Bengerova, Z. 'Rodonachal'nik angliiskovo simvolizma [Forefather of English Symbolism].' *Severnyi Vestnik*, IX (St. Petersburg, 1896), 81–99.
The Russian article contains a brief biographical sketch and criticism and is said to be based on Ellis & Yeats.

B1146. §—— 'William Blake.' Vol. I, pp. 153–82 of Bengerova's [*Literary Characteristics*]. 1897.
In Russian.

A1151. Bentley, Gerald E., Jr. *A Bibliography of George Cumberland (1754–1848)* Comprehending his Published Books (1780–1829) and Articles (1769–1847) and his Unrecorded Works in Manuscript including a Novel (?1800), a Play (?1800), a Biography (?1823), a long Poem (1802–3), and Works on Art (?1788, ?1816, ?1820). N.Y. & London, 1975. Garland Reference Library of the Humanities (Vol. 11).
Includes references to Blake in Cumberland's writings, especially a recommendation of him to Horne Tooke as a 'true son of Freedom' (pp. 89, 92) and an account of '*Blakes* Instructions to Print Copper Plates' (pp. 95–6).

A1152. Bentley, Gerald E., Jr. 'Blake and Cromek: The Wheat and the Tares.' *MP*, LXXI (1974), 366–79.

New documents about *The Grave*, chiefly a prospectus (Nov. 1805) and a letter from Cromek (April 1807) dating 'To the Queen'.

1158. —— *Blake Records* (1969). 'Forgotten Years: References to William Blake 1831–62', pp. 220–69 of G. E. Bentley, Jr., ed., *William Blake*: The Critical Heritage (1975), no. A1181, forms, as it were, Part VII of *Blake Records*.

A1170. —— 'Ozias Humphry, William Upcott, and William Blake.' *Humanities Association Review / La Revue de l'Association Canadienne des Humanités*, XXVI (1975), 116–22.

Some new inferences about their relationship.

A1177. *—— 'A Unique Prospectus for Blake's *Grave* Designs.' *Princeton University Library Chronicle*, XXXV (1974), 321–4.

A summary account of the earliest known prospectus newly discovered.

A1181. *——, ed. *William Blake*: The Critical Heritage. London & Boston, 1975.

The hundreds of critical references to Blake of 1761–1862 largely extracted from *Blake Records* (1969) include the accounts of Malkin in his *Memoirs* (1806), by Crabb Robinson in *Vaterländisches Museum* (1811), by Allan Cunningham in his *Lives* (1830), by Anon. in *London University Magazine* (1830), by Anon. in *Fraser's Magazine* (1830), and by Frederick Tatham in MS (?1832). Part VI, 'Forgotten Years: References to William Blake 1831–62' (pp. 220–69) forms, as it were, Part VII of *Blake Records* (p. 221 n. 3). There are 20 plates.

A1190. *Bindman, David. *'The Artistic Ideas of William Blake.' London Ph.D., 1971 (vRNE).

B1190. —— 'Blake's Job.' *TLS*, 29 March 1974, p. 341.

Pace Fawcus, the New Zealand Job drawings seem 'on stylistic grounds' to be 'careful and uninspired copies'.

1192. B. *—— 'Blake's heads.' *Guardian Weekly*, CIV (5 June 1971), 22.

Notice of the Blake–Varley sketchbook to be sold at Christie's on 15 June.

1217. *Blake Newsletter*.

    73. Judith Rhodes. 'Blake's Designs for *L'Allegro* and *Il Penseroso*: Thematic Relationships in Diagram' (1971). . . . B. Reprinted in R. N. Essick, ed., *The Visionary Hand* (1973).

Vol. VIII, No. 4 (Spring [June] 1975):

    155. Joanne Witke. 'Report: 1974 MLA Blake Seminar.' Pp. 105–6.

('Unfortunately, only one author of the essays selected for discussion was present'; they were printed in *Blake Studies*, Vol. VIII, No. 1.)
156. Donald Ault. [Ibid.] P. 106.
The bulk of the issue is taken up with 'Reviews' (pp. 108–44).

N.B. Blake Newsletter, I, no. I–III and no. 4 were reprinted in 1975.

1218. *Blake Studies*.
68. R. N. Essick. 'Blake and the Traditions of Reproductive Engraving' (1972). . . . B. Reprinted in R. N. Essick, ed., *The Visionary Hand* (1973).
72. J. E. Grant. 'Blake's Designs for *L'Allegro* and *Il Penseroso*' (1971). . . . B. Reprinted in R. N. Essick, ed., *The Visionary Hand* (1973).

Vol. VII, No. 1 [Dec. 1974]:
81. Edward J. Rose. 'Preface: Perspectives on *Jerusalem*.' Pp. 7–9. (The subject of the 1974 MLA Blake seminar.)
82. E. B. Murray. 'Jerusalem Reversed.' Pp. 11–25. (Concerned with 'The image of reversed movement . . . as a self-referential key to the meaning of *Jerusalem*' [p. 12].)
83. Mollyanne Marks. 'Self-Sacrifice: Theme and Image in *Jerusalem*.' Pp. 27–50.
84. *Irene H. Chayes. 'The Marginal Design on *Jerusalem* 12.' Pp. 51–76. (Based on the premiss that in 'the righthand margins [*of JERUSALEM*] . . . everything . . . pertains . . . to error' [p. 52].)

§Vol. VII, No. 2 [Jan. 1976]:
85. *Martin Butlin. 'A New Portrait of William Blake.'
86. David M. Wyatt. 'The Woman Jerusalem: Pictura vs Poesis.'
87. B. H. Fairchild, Jr. 'Melos and Meaning in Blake's Lyric Art.'
88. Hazard Adams. 'Blake, Jerusalem, and Symbolic Form.'
89. J. Walter Nelson. 'Blake's Diction—An Amendatory Note.'
90. Désirée Hirst. 'Once More Continuing "The Tyger".'

1228. A. Bloom, Harold. 'Blake's *Jerusalem*: The Bard of Sensibility and the Form of Prophecy' (1970). . . . B. Reprinted as Chapter 5 (pp. 65–79) of his *The Ringers in the Tower*: Studies in the Romantic Tradition. Chicago & London, 1971.

1229. A. —— 'Dialectic in *The Marriage of Heaven and Hell*' (1958). . . . C. Reprinted as Chapter 4 (pp. 55–62) of his *The Ringers in the Tower*: Studies in the Romantic Tradition. Chicago & London, 1971.

1231. A. —— 'Visionary Cinema' (1968). . . . B. Reprinted as 'The Visionary Cinema of Romantic Poetry' in Rosenfeld (no. 2565). C. Reprinted as Chapter 3 (pp. 37–55) of Bloom's *The Ringers in the Tower*: Studies in the Romantic Tradition. Chicago & London, 1971.

1236. A. Bl[unt], A. F. 'Blake, William (1757–1827)' (1950). . . . B. Vol.

I, pp. 352–3 of *Chambers's Encyclopaedia* New Revised Edition. Oxford, London, Edinburgh, N.Y., Toronto, Paris, Braunschweig, Sydney, Wellington, Tokyo, 1967.

1237. A. Bl[unt], A. F. 'Blake's "Ancient of Days": The Symbolism of the Compasses' (1938). . . . B. Reprinted in R. N. Essick, ed., *The Visionary Hand* (1973).

1265. A. Bowden, William R. 'Blake's "*Introduction*" to *Songs of Innocence*' (1953). . . . B. Reprinted in no. A1587 6.

1266. A. Bowen, Robert O. 'Blake's *The Tyger*, 7–8' (1949) . . . B. Reprinted in no. A1587 17.

A1272. Brantlinger, Patrick. 'Classic and Romantic: An Augury of Innocence.' *College English*, XXXIII (1972), 702–11.
A short story about a student who has visions of Blake.

A1278. *Brett, Guy. 'Blake, Blake, burning bright.' *The Times*, 8 Dec. 1971, p. 18.
About the Tate exhibition of Blake's water-colours for Gray.

A1282. Brisman, Leslie. 'Blake and the Eternals' Time.' Pp. 192–212 of his *Milton's Poetry of Choice and Its Romantic Heirs*. Ithaca & London, 1973.

A1283. Brockington, A. Allen. *Mysticism and Poetry* On a Basis of Experience. London, 1934. Pp. 84–101, *passim*.
'Obedience to the Spiritual Imperative [His name for it is "Dictation"] is the key to Blake' (pp. 84–5).

A1284. Bromberg, Pamela Starr. 'Blake and the Spectre of Milton.' *DAI*, XXXIV (1973), 2548–9A. Yale Ph.D.
'*A*ttempts to study Blake's poetic relationship with Milton'.

1295. A. Brown, Allan R. 'Blake's Drawings for the *Book of Enoch*' (1940). . . . B. Reprinted in R. N. Essick, ed., *The Visionary Hand* (1973).

A1298. Browning, Robert, & Elizabeth Barrett Barrett. *The Letters of Robert Browning and Elizabeth Barrett Barrett 1845–1846*. Ed. Elvan Kintner. Cambridge (Mass.), 1969. Vol. II, p. 861.
A letter from Browning of 9 July 1846, which in passing compares B. R. Haydon, who had recently committed suicide, with Blake, who lived with poverty 'in power and glory'.

A1304. Brunskill, Ann. *Aphrodite*: A Mythical Journey in Eight Episodes with [8] Etchings by Ann Brunskill. Accompanying Poems by William Blake (and others). London[?], 1970.

A1306. Bucke, Richard Maurice. 'William Blake.' Chapter II (pp. 159–64) of Part IV ('Instances of Cosmic Consciousness') of his *Cosmic Consciousness: A Study in the Evolution of the Human Mind*, Philadelphia, 1905.

'*He* had the Cosmic Sense, which he called "Imagination"' (p. 159). (I have not seen the 1901 edition.)

B1306. §Buckley, Vincent. 'Blake's Later Lyrics.' *Quadrant*, LXXXIV (1973), 34–47.

1312. A. Burke, Joseph. 'The Eidetic and the Borrowed Image: an Interpretation of Blake's Theory and Practice of Art' (1964). . . . B. Reprinted in R. N. Essick, ed., *The Visionary Hand* (1973).

1326. A Butlin, Martin. 'Blake's "God Judging Adam" Rediscovered' (1965). . . . B. Reprinted in R. N. Essick, ed., *The Visionary Hand* (1973).

A1328. §Butter, Ph.H. 'Blake's *Book of Urizen* and Boehme's "Mysterium Magnum".' Pp. 35–49 of *Le Romanticism anglo-américain: Mélanges offerts à Louis Bonnerat*. Paris, 1971.

A1332. §Callahan, Patrick J. 'Historical and Critical Problems in William Blake's *America*.' Nebraska Ph.D., 1969.

A1335. *Canaday, John. 'One Good Reason for Living in New York.' *New York Times*, 9 Jan. 1972, p. 23.

Review of the Thorne Blake exhibition at the Morgan.

B1335. §Cancenian, L. 'William Blake (1757–1827).' *Studii si cercetări de istorie literară și folclor*, III–IV (Bucuresti, 1958), 471–89.

In Rumanian.

A1346. Carroll, Lewis [Charles Lutwidge Dodgson]. *The Diaries of Lewis Carroll*. Ed. R. L. Green. 1953. Vol. I, p. 206.

On 19 Oct. 1863 Dodgson 'got him [*Macmillan*] to print me some of Blake's *Songs of Innocence* on large paper'; presumably these were made from the electrotypes of *Innocence* used in Gilchrist's '*Pictor Ignotus*' (1863).

A1372. §Chaubey, Sushil Kumar. 'Child in Blake's Poetry.' University of Lucknow Ph.D., 1951 (according to *Humanities*: A Bibliography of Doctoral Dissertations 1857–1970 [New Delhi, 1975], no. 114).

B1372. —— 'Study of Blake's influence on his successors together with a consideration of his ideas in the Marriage of Heaven and Hell.' University of Lucknow D.Litt., 1969 (according to *Humanities* [1975], no. 115).

C1372. Chayes, Irene H. 'Blake and the Seasons of the Poet.' *Studies in Romanticism*, XI (1972), 225–40.

'*A* modified reading' of the seasons poems in *Poetical Sketches* (p. 226) as 'a history of the growth of the poet' (p. 240).

A1379. §Cherry, Charles L. 'The Apotheosis of Desire: Dialectic and Image in *The French Revolution, Visions of the Daughters of Albion,* and the *Preludium* of *America.*' *Xavier University Studies,* VIII (1969), 18–31.

A1388. Christian, Diane. '"The Eternal Body": A Study of the Structural Metaphor in the Work of William Blake.' *DAI,* XXXIV (1974), 7183–4A. Johns Hopkins Ph.D., 1974.

A1390. Clark, Kenneth. 'Blake.' Chapter 6 (pp. 146–76) of his *The Romantic Rebellion*: Romantic versus Classic Art. Toronto, 1973.
    The opinionative, inaccurate, general Blake chapter (with 27 Blake plates) is part of a lecture series turned television series turned book; for the previous lecture, see his *Blake and Visionary Art* (1973).

B1390. —— *Blake and Visionary Art.* Glasgow, 1973. W. A. Cargill Memorial Lectures in Fine Art 2.
    A lecture on 'How good an artist was Blake?' (p. 3), largely incorporated in his *Romantic Rebellion.*

1395. A. *Clarke, John Henry. *From Copernicus to William Blake.* . . . B. *Folcroft, Pennsylvania, 1969.
    A lecture of 49 pages.

A1405. Cohen, Sandy. 'Is William Blake's Concept of Marriage Kabbalistic?' *N&Q,* CCXVIII [N.S. XX] (1973), 100–1.
    A remarkably vague query.

A1416. Cook, Albert. 'Blake's *Milton.*' *Costerus,* VI (1972), 27–33.
    Mostly on the verse form.

A1429. Cross, Colin. 'A Direct Line to Heaven.' *Observer* [magazine], 21 Nov. 1971, pp. 23, 25–6.
    A general account of Blake, in conjunction with exclamatory accounts and reproductions of Blake's Gray designs entitled variously 'William Blake: Discovery of a Masterwork' (on the cover) and 'Blake Revealed' (pp. 19–22).

A1430. Cumberland, George. 'To the Editor of the Monthly Magazine.' *Monthly Magazine,* XV (1 March 1803), 101–4. (Bodley)
    In a defence of his *Thoughts on Outline* (1796), Cumberland mentions in passing 'a mind full of images, (such as the fruitful one of our own Blake)', (p. 102).

1433. A. Cunningham, Allan. 'William Blake' in his *Lives* (1830). . . . L. The second edition is reprinted in G. E. Bentley, Jr., ed., *William Blake*: The Critical Heritage (1975), no. A1181.

A1437. *Curran, Stuart, & Joseph Anthony Wittreich, Jr., ed. *Blake's Sublime Allegory*: Essays on *The Four Zoas, Milton, Jerusalem.* Madison, 1973.

Besides the 'Preface' (pp. xiii–xvii) by S. C. & J. A. W., the contents consist of:

1. Jerome J. McGann. 'The Aim of Blake's Prophecies and the Uses of Blake Criticism.' Pp. 3–21. ('*To* the degree that one regards Blake's art as an object of analysis and interpretation . . . Blake has been misused, even . . . misread' [p. 4].)

2. Joseph Anthony Wittreich, Jr. 'Opening the Seals: Blake's Epics and the Milton Tradition.' Pp. 23–58. (Concerned centrally with 'the fusion of epic and prophecy', particularly in Milton and Revelation [p. 27].)

3. Ronald L. Grimes. 'Time and Space in Blake's Major Prophecies.' Pp. 59–81. ('Blake's medium is intended to be a point of coincidence between space [artistic engravings] and time [poetic lines]' [p. 81]. The essay is modified in Chapter Two of his dissertation [1970] published as *The Divine Imagination* [1972].)

4. Edward J. Rose. 'Los, Pilgrim of Eternity.' Pp. 83–99. ('*The* figure of Los embodies' 'his ideas about art and perception', which are 'the subject of his work', 'for Los is the act of perceiving' [p. 83].)

5. Jean H. Hagstrum. 'Babylon Revisited, or the Story of Luvah and Vala.' Pp. 101–18. (A study of 'Blake's concept of sexuality' [p. 115].)

6. *Morton D. Paley. '*The* Figure of the Garment in *The Four Zoas, Milton* and *Jerusalem.*' Pp. 119–39. ('Sometime during the composition of *The Four Zoas*', imagery of weaving and clothing 'took on a more technical meaning in Blake's symbolism, with results . . . of even greater importance to *Milton* and *Jerusalem*' [p. 139].)

7. *John E. Grant. 'Visions in *Vala*: A Consideration of Some Pictures in the Manuscript.' Pp. 141–202. ('*Raises* a number of interesting questions and makes some valid interpretational points' [p. 142], partly on the basis of some pictorial 'details that have not previously been noticed' and of the methods of a 'visionary . . . sexologist' [p. 144].)

8. Mary Lynn Johnson & Brian Wilkie. 'On Reading *The Four Zoas*: Inscape and Analogy.' Pp. 203–32. (A 'reading' of 'the first six Nights only' [p. 205].)

9. *Irene Tayler. 'Say First! What Mov'd Blake? Blake's *Comus* Designs and *Milton*.' Pp. 233–58. ('Ololon is a fulfilled version of the lady of *Comus*' [p. 258]; this essay is a fulfilled version of one she first printed in *Blake Studies* [1972], as pp. 235–51 here.)

10. James Rieger. '"The Hem of Their Garments": The Bard's Song in *Milton*.' Pp. 259–80. ('We must try as cryptologists to penetrate this sublime rag of language and nature' [p. 280].)

11. W. J. T. Mitchell. 'Blake's Radical Comedy: Dramatic Structure as Meaning in *Milton*.' Pp. 281–307. ('*Milton* is a radical comedy because it returns to the root situation, London of the 1800s' [p. 282]; the second half of this study appeared in *Blake Studies*, VI, 1 [1973].)

12. Roger R. Easson. 'William Blake and His Reader in *Jerusalem*.' Pp. 309–27. ('*Jerusalem* may be read as a poem about the experience of reading *Jerusalem*' [p. 309].)

13. Stuart Curran. 'The Structures of *Jerusalem*.' Pp. 329–46. (*Jerusalem* discloses seven structures, in two to seven parts each, to express '*the* sublime allegory of Christ's life and death' [p. 346].)

14. Karl Kroeber. 'Delivering *Jerusalem*.' Pp. 347–67. ('Today the poem needs to be delivered not from oblivion but from its interpreters', particularly Frye [p. 347].)

The 38 plates include all 8 Huntington *Comus* designs.

1445. A. *Damon, S. Foster. *A Blake Dictionary*. . . . C. *N.Y., 1971. Dutton Paperbacks. D. §London, 1973.

1462. A. *Daugherty, James. *William Blake*: with reproductions of drawings by William Blake. . . . D. Fourth Printing, 1969.

A1466. Davies, James Mark Quentin. 'Blake's Designs for *Paradise Lost*: A Critical Analysis.' *DAI*, XXXIII (1973), 6866–7A. Iowa Ph.D.

'The series are not literal illustrations but astute critical commentaries on the shortcomings of Milton's epic . . . .'

A1468. Davis, John Lindsey. 'Blake and the Rhetoric of Humour.' *DAI*, XXXV (1974), 2936A. Texas Ph.D., 1974.

A1469. Dearnaley, G. 'Editorial: William Blake and Modern Technology Assessment.' *Physics in Technology*, no. 2 (1974), 73–8.

Blake knew what contemporary scientists were doing and anticipates some aspects of modern technology, specifically microelectronics.

B1469. Deboo, Kitayun Erachshaw. 'The Principle of Cyle in James Joyce's *Ulysses* and William Blake's *The Mental Traveller*.' *DA*, XXVIII (1967), 623A. State University of New York at Buffalo Ph.D. (1967).

'The parallel . . . is in the psychic states'.

A1478. A. [De Quincey, Thomas.] 'Sketches of Life and Manners, from the Autobiography of an English Opium-Eater.' *Tait's Edinburgh Magazine*, VII (March 1840), 166. B. Thomas De Quincey. *Literary Reminiscences*; from The Autobiography of an English Opium-Eater. In Two Volumes. Boston, 1851. Vol. II (Vol. VI of *DeQuincey's Writings* [ed. J. T. Fields]), p. 164. C. §Reprinted in Boston, 1873. D. *Literary Reminiscences*; from The Autobiography of an English Opium-Eater. N.Y., 1878. The Works of Thomas De Quincey. Riverside Edition. Vol. III, p. 529. E. *The Collected Writings of Thomas De Quincey*. New and Enlarged Edition. Ed. David Masson. Vol. II: Autobiography and Literary Reminiscences. Edinburgh, 1889. P. 400. F. *Reminiscences of the English Lake Poets*. London & N.Y., n.d. [?1911]. G. §Revised edition, ed. J. E. Jordan. 1961.

'Death was indeed to him [*Charles Lloyd*], in the words of that fine mystic, Blake the artist, "a golden gate"—the gate of liberation from the captivity of half a life' (1840, p. 166). The quotation from Blake's dedication 'To the Queen' for Blair's *Grave* appears in a section of Reminiscences of 'Charles L—' (1840), 'Loyd' (1851, chap. xviii), or, properly, Lloyd (1878 ff.); it is called 'Society of the Lakes: Charles Lloyd' in chap. viii, 1887, and ?1911.

The Blake reference was generously pointed out to me by my friend Professor Vincent DeLuca.

1480. A. *De Selincourt, Basil. *William Blake.* . . . C. §Port Washington, N.Y., 1971.

1487. A. Dickson, Arthur. 'Blake's *The Clod and the Pebble* and Masefield's *Cargoes.*' . . . B. Reprinted in no. A1587 2.

A1491. Dilgard, Cynthia Corlew. 'The Structure of *Jerusalem*.' *DAI*, XXXIV (1973), 2553–4A. Vanderbilt Ph.D.

A1492. Di Salvo, Jackie. 'William Blake on the Unholy Alliance: Satanic Freedom and Godly Repression in Liberal Society.' *Wordsworth Circle*, III (1972), 212–22.

About Blake's 'unique realization of the political significance [*i.e.* the ideology of bourgeois society] of *Paradise Lost*' (pp. 212, 213).

A1497. Doggett, John Rentz. 'A Reading of William Blake's *The Book of Urizen*.' *DAI*, XXXV (1974), 2936A. Texas Ph.D., 1974.

The reading, of 144 pp., is 'confined to *Urizen* itself'.

A1505. Domke, Charlotte Frances Townsend. 'Progeny of Fire: A Study of Blake's Satanic Images.' *DAI*, XXXII (1972), 5733–4A. Texas Ph.D.

A1506. Donaghue, Denis. 'The Peremptory Imagination.' Pp. 59–84 of his *Thieves of Fire*. London, 1973. The T. S. Eliot Memorial Lecture.

Lectures forming 'notes for a typology of the imagination' (p. 15), the second of which deals with Blake.

A1509. Doskow, Minna Levine. 'Structure and Meaning in William Blake's *Jerusalem*.' *DAI*, XXXIII (1972), 2322–3A. Maryland Ph.D.

'*Jerusalem* displays a thematic rather than a narrative unity.'

A1512. §Douglas, Dennis. 'The Eclecticism of Blake's "Europe".' Pp. 40–2 of *Proceedings of the Ninth Congress of the Australasian Universities' Language and Literature Association*. Ed. Marion Adams. Melbourne [1964].

A1516. Doyno, V. 'Blake's Revision of "London".' *Essays in Criticism*, XXII (1972), 58–63, with an 'Editorial Comment' by F. W. Bateson on pp. 61–2.

A1518. Druian, Michael Gregory. 'Visual Imagination in Blake's *Jerusalem* and Goethe's *Faust II.*' *DAI*, XXXIV (1973), 1238A. Oregon Ph.D.
'The mode of operation of imagination is primarily visual'.

A1523. Dunlap, Ann Bush. 'Blake's "The Mental Traveller" and the Critics.'
DAI, XXXIV (1974), 6586–7A. New Mexico Ph.D., 1973.

A1529. §Dzene, L. '[The Joyful and Anxious Artist].' *Tsinia* [*Battle*] (28 Nov. 1957),
In Latvian.

A1535. Eaves, Morris Emery. 'Blake's Artistic Strategy.' *DAI*, XXXIII (1972), 1165–6A. Tulane Ph.D.
Blake's text cannot be separated from his designs.

1536. A. Eberly, Ralph D. 'Blake's *The Little Black Boy*' (1957). . . . B. Reprinted in no. A1587 8.

1537. A. —— 'Blake's *The Tyger*, 17–18' (1949). . . . B. Reprinted in no. A1587 18.

A1537. Edwards, Thomas R. 'Blake: The Mythologist as Agitator.' Part I (pp. 141–59) of Chapter iv ('The Revolutionary Imagination') of his *Imagination and Power*: A Study of Poetry on Public Themes. London, 1971.

A1540. Ehrstine, John W. *William Blake's Poetical Sketches*. [Pullman, Washington], 1967.
Text of the *Poetical Sketches* and a rather pedestrian attempt 'to read them as poems . . . in the context of Blake's organic thought' (p. 2). Part of it is reprinted 'in different form' in no. 1540.

A1546. §Elistratova, A. '[A Collection of Works on the Bicentennial Jubilee of William Blake].' *Vopressi Literaturi* [*Literary Sketches*], XII (1959), 222–31.
A review, in Russian, of the literature on the work of the poet.

B1546. §*—— '[The Poet and his Time].' *Inosrtrannaia* [*Foreign*] *Literatura*, X (1957), 189–92.
For the bi-centennial celebration of the birth of William Blake, in Russian, with a portrait.

1547. A. *Ellis, Edwin J. *The Real Blake*: A Portrait Biography. . . . B. N.Y., 1970.

A1556. Epstein, E. L. 'Blake's "Infant Sorrow"—An Essay in Discourse Analysis.' Pp. 231–41 of *Current Trends in Stylistics*. Ed. Braj B. Kachru & Hubert F. W. Stahlke. Edmonton & Champaign, 1972. Papers in Linguistics Monograph Series 2.
The poem illustrates 'dynamic asymmetry' (p. 232).

1570. A. Erdman, David V. 'The Dating of William Blake's Engravings' (1951). . . . B. Revised and reprinted in R. N. Essick, ed., *The Visionary Hand* (1973).

A1583. Essick, Robert N., ed. **The Visionary Hand*: Essays for the Study of William Blake's Art and Aesthetics. With an Introduction by Robert N. Essick. Los Angeles, 1973.

The volume includes Essick's 'Introduction' (pp. 1–4), and Jenijoy La Belle, 'Words Graven with an Iron Pen: The Marginal Texts in Blake's *Job*' (pp. 527–50; the marginal Biblical quotations provide 'a formal parallel' to the theme of the engravings [p. 548]), plus reprints of fragments from J. T. Smith (no. 2723), Gilchrist (no. 1680), Rees, *Cyclopaedia* (no. 489), Robert Dossie, *The Handbook to the Arts* (no. 761), and reprints of whole essays by George Cumberland, 'New Mode of Printing', *A New Review*, VI (1784), 318–19 (pp. 11–12, plus a letter from Cumberland on the subject, pp. 13–14), *Todd (no. 2853), *Binyon (no. 1200), *Blunt (no. 1237), *A. R. Brown (no. 1295), *C. H. C. Baker (no. 1116), *Nanavutty (no. 2270), Frye (no. 1647), Erdman (no. 1570), Adams (no. 777), *Roe (no. 2544), *Merchant (no. 2214), *Burke (no. 1312), *Butlin (no. 1324), Rose (no. 2558), *Mitchell (2233), *Helmstadter (no. 1829), *Grant (no. 1217 72), *Rhodes (no. 1217 73), *Simmons & Warner (no. 2703), Grant (no. 1728), and *Essick (no. 1218 68), those by Todd, Erdman, Hemlstadter, and Mitchell being revised (p. xv). There are 166 plates.

B1583. *—— & Morton D. Paley. 'The Printings of Blake's Designs for Blair's *Grave*.' *Book Collector*, XXIV (1975), 535–52.

A careful description of the states of the plates and editions of the text, proving brilliantly that the small paper '1813' folio was printed for John Camden Hotten in 1870.

C1583. §Evanoff, Alexander. 'The Visions of William Blake.' *Antigonish Review*, II (1971), 11–18.

Interpretation of Blake must take account of his spiritualism.

A1586. Evans, James C. 'The Apocalypse as Contrary Vision: Prolegomena to an Analogical Reading of *The Four Zoas*.' *Texas Studies in Language and Literature*, XIV (1972), 313–18.

The '"Circle of Destiny" aptly describes the basic structure of *The Four Zoas*' (p. 315).

A1587. *The Explicator Cyclopedia.* [3 vols.] Volume II: Traditional Poetry Medieval to Late Victorian From THE EXPLICATOR Volumes I–XX (1942–1962). Ed. Charles Wild Walcutt & J. Edwin Whitesell. Chicago, 1968.

Under Blake are:

[1] Olybrius. 'THE CLOD AND THE PEBBLE.' (Pp. 33–4)

[2] Arthur Dickson. 'Blake's THE CLOD AND THE PEBBLE and Masefield's CARGOES.' (P. 34)

[3] Arthur Wormhoudt. '"INTRODUCTION" to SONGS OF INNO-CENCE.' (Pp. 34–5)

[4] Margaret Giovannini. [Ibid.] (Pp. 34–5)

[5] Howard Justin. [Ibid.] (Pp. 35–6)

[6] William R. Bowden. [Ibid.] (Pp. 36–7)

[7] J. Edwin Whitesell. 'THE LITTLE BLACK BOY.' (Pp. 37–8)

[8] Ralph D. Eberly. [Ibid.] (Pp. 38–9)

[9] Lloyd N. Jeffrey. [Ibid.] (Pp. 39–40)

[10] Robert F. Gleckner. 'MY PRETTY ROSE TREE.' (Pp. 40–1)

[11] T. O. Mabbott. 'A POISON TREE.' (P. 41)

[12] Edward C. Sampson. [Ibid.] (P. 41)

[13] Allan Kline. 'A SONG OF LIBERTY, 5–6.' (Pp. 41–2)

[14] Louis G. Locke. 'Stanzas from MILTON.' (P. 42)

[15] George W. Stone, Jr. 'THE TIGER.' (P. 43)

[16] Elizabeth Nitchie. [Ibid.] (Pp. 43–4)

[17] Robert O. Bowen. [Ibid.] (P. 44)

[18] Ralph D. Eberly. [Ibid.] (P. 44)

[19] Frederick A. Pottle. [Ibid.] (P. 44)

(For the original printings, see under the authors' names above.)

A1591. §Faktorovich, D. 'William Blake.' *Zviazda* (Minsk, 28 Nov. 1957). In Belorussian.

A1593. *Fawcus, Arnold. 'Blake: Lost and Found: *Horizon* presents for the first time in America [*sic*], one of the major art rediscoveries of recent years: Blake's illustrations for the poems of Thomas Gray.' *Horizon*, XIV (1972), 112–20.

A one-page description by the publisher of the Gray facsimile, complete with price ('$1,378') and address of the publisher, plus 8 plates in colour.

B1593. *—— 'Blake's Illustrations for the Book of Job.' *TLS*, 15 March 1974, pp. 271–2.

An inconclusive attempt to 'set at rest' the doubts that the New Zealand Job 'drawings are by Blake's hand'. For a contradictory view, see Bindman, 'Blake's Job', no. B1190.

C1593. *—— 'Unknown watercolours by William Blake.' *Illustrated London News*, CCLIX (Dec. 1971), 45–6, 49–51.

About the Gray designs to be exhibited at the Tate and the 'perhaps dangerously accurate' Blake Trust facsimile [made by Mr. Fawcus's Trianon Press].

A1594. *—— 'William Blake's watercolour designs illustrating Gray's poems—and Mr. Paul Mellon.' *Connoisseur*, CLXXIX (Jan. 1972), 10–14.

Explication of the *7 plates on the occasion of the Tate exhibition.

A1616. Flaxman, John. *Oeuvres de Flaxman.* Receuil de ses Compositions Gravées par Reveil, avec analyse de la Divine Comédie du Dante et Notice sur Flaxman. Sujets Divers. Paris, 1847. P. 3.

'Ses amis principaux furent Blacke et Stothard. Dans les compositions sauvages du premier il vit plus d'élévation poétique . . . .'

A1631. Franci, Giovanna. *William Blake: Innocenza-Esperenza*: dalla Simmetrica alla Dialletica. Convergenze I. [Bologna], 1973.
Sixteen pages.

A1637. Frosch, Thomas R. *The Awakening of Albion*: The Renovation of the Body in the Poetry of William Blake. Ithaca & London, 1974.

A study of 'the conviction that the transformation of man needed to include what can be described as a resurrection of his body through a remaking of its sensory organization [*sic*]' (p. 9). The work first appeared as a dissertation (no. 1638).

A1638. §Frost, Everett C. 'The Prophet Armed: William Blake's *Marriage of Heaven and Hell*.' University of Iowa Ph.D., 1971.
Printed as a book, above.

A1643. Frye, Northrop. 'Blake, William.' Vol. I, pp. 319–20 of *The Encyclopedia of Philosophy*. Ed. Paul Edwards. N.Y. & London, 1967.

*1646. A. *—— *Fearful Symmetry*: A Study of William Blake. . . .

Chapter I (pp. 14–29, 435–7) is adapted by the editor and printed as 'Blake's Case Against Locke', Chapter vi (pp. 119–35) of *English Literature and British Philosophy*: A Collection of Essays, ed. S. P. Rosenbaum, Chicago & London, 1971.

1648. A. —— 'Poetry and Design in William Blake' (1951). . . . D. Reprinted in R. N. Essick, ed., *The Visionary Hand* (1973).

A1656. Fulbright, James Stephen. 'William Blake and the Emancipation of Women.' *DAI*, XXXIV (1974), 7132A. Missouri Ph.D., 1973.

A 118-page essay on Blake's ideas of 1778–93 and his relations with such 'close friends' as James Barry and Mary Wollstonecraft.

B1656. Furst, Lilian R. *Romanticism in Perspective*: A Comparative study of aspects of the Romantic movements in England, France and Germany. London, Melbourne, Toronto, N.Y., 1969. *Passim.*

Blake appears chiefly in the section on 'Imagination'.

A1658. *Gage, John. 'Blake's *Newton*.' *JWCI*, XXXIV (1971), 372–7.

A densely packed article arguing particularly that 'Blake's rainbow was essentially Newtonian' (p. 375).

1669. A. Garnett, Richard. *William Blake, Painter and Poet*. . . . B. §Folcroft, Pennsylvania, 1972.

A1672. Gaunt, William. 'The English style.' *The Times*, 21 Jan. 1971, p. 9.
Mostly about the Blake exhibition at the Fitzwilliam.

1680. A. *Gilchrist, Alexander. *The Life of William Blake*. . . . C. Ed. with an Introduction by W. Graham Robertson and Numerous Reproductions from Blake's Pictures Many Hitherto Unpublished. . . . I. Folcroft, Pennsylvania, 1972. J. *Life of William Blake* with Selections from his Poems and Other Writings. A New and Enlarged Edition Illustrated from Blake's Own Works With Additional Letters and a Memoir of the Author. New Introduction by W. A. G. Doyle-Davidson. Vol. I [only]. Wakefield, Yorkshire, 1973.
I is a facsimile of the 1907 edition.
J is a reprint of Vol. I (1880) only; the 'Introduction' (pp. v–xiii) is about Gilchrist and his book.

A1683. §Gilenson, B. A. 'Blake, William.' Vol. I, pp. 639–40 of [*A Short Literary Encyclopaedia*]. Moscow, 1962.
In Russian, with a bibliography.

1687. A Gillham, D. G. 'Blake: *Visions of the Daughters of Albion*' (1968). . . .
B. Adapted in Chapter ix of his *William Blake* (1973).

1688. —— *Blake's Contrary States* (1966).
The work is the basis of his *William Blake* (1973).

A1688. *—— *William Blake*. Cambridge [England], 1973. British Authors: Introductory Critical Series.
Another introduction for 'the student' and 'the general reader', especially foreign ones, consisting mostly of assertive paraphrases of the *Songs* (Chapters i–vi 'based on' his *Blake's Contrary States* [1966]), *Thel* (viii), and *Visions* (ix, 'an adaptation' of his *Wascana Review* article [1968]), plus a paragraph or more each for some of 'Blake's longer works' (Chapter vii).

A1689. A. Ginsberg, Allen. 'Blake Notes: *To Young or Old Listeners*.' *Caterpillar*, 14 (Jan. 1971), 126–32. B. Reprinted as 'To Young or Old Listeners: Setting Blake's *Songs* to Music, and a Commentary on the Songs.' *Blake Newsletter*, IV (1971), 98–103.
A reprint of the jacket information on MGM Record of '*Songs of Innocence and Experience* by William Blake, tuned by Allen Ginsberg' (FTS/3083). (An account of his setting the *Songs* to music is on pp. 289–94 of Alison Colbert, 'A Talk with Allen Ginsberg', *Partisan Review*, XXXVIII [1971], 289–309.)

1690. A. Giovannini, Margaret. 'Blake's "*Introduction*" to *Songs of Innocence*.'. . .
B. Reprinted in no. A1587 4.

1694. A. Gleckner, Robert F. 'Blake's *My Pretty Rose Tree*' (1955). . . . B. Reprinted in no. A1587 10.

1702. A. —— *The Piper and The Bard*: a study of William Blake. . . . B. §1960.

1706. A. *Goddard, Harold Clarke. *Blake's Fourfold Vision*. . . . C. 1973. D. 'Blake's Twofold Vision.' Pp. 85–107 of *Alphabet of the Imagination*: Literary Essays of Harold Clarke Goddard. Ed. Eleanor Goddard Worther & Margaret Goddard Holt. With an Introduction by Leon Edel and a Special Foreword by Neville Coghill. Atlantic Highlands, New Jersey, 1974.
    A reprint of his 1936 lecture.

A1709. Goldstein, Laurence Alan. 'The Mercy of Eternity: Aspects of Regeneration in *The Prelude* and *Milton*.' *DAI*, XXXI (1971), 6548A. Brown Ph.D., 1970.

A1721. Grammaticus. 'Act of Courage.' *Weekly News* [Auckland], 23 April 1962, p. 35 (vMT).
    On the *Milton* Preface and Joseph of Arimathea's legendary visit with Jesus to Cornwall.

A1723. Grant, John E. 'Blake's "Illustrations of the Book of Job".' *TLS*, 30 Nov. 1973, p. 1484.
    Description of a set of *Job* engravings (1826) in an anonymous collection 'no doubt' coloured by Blake himself [but their claimed similarity to the New Zealand set of Job drawings, which Lindberg (*Blake's* . . . *Job* [1973]) has shown to be not by Blake, might lead to doubt].

1728. A. —— 'Redemptive Action in Blake's *Arlington Court Picture*: Observations on the Simmons–Warner Theory' (1971). . . . B. Reprinted in R. N. Essick, ed., *The Visionary Hand* (1973).

1748. A. Grierson, H. J. C. *Lyrical Poetry from Blake to Hardy*. . . . B. Second Impression, 1950.

A1755. Grimes, Ronald L. *The Divine Imagination*: William Blake's Major Prophetic Visions. Metuchen, N.J., 1972. ATLA [American Theological Library Association] Monograph Series No. 1.
    'I have interpreted Blake . . . in terms of his most comprehensive image and in terms of his imagic goal. . . . one's assessment of Blake's vision depends on his [*sic*] understanding of the Jesus of vision' (p. 164). The work is a Columbia University and Union Theological Seminary Ph.D. in religion (1970); Chapter ii 'is a modification' of his essay in *Blake's Sublime Allegory*, ed. Curran & Wittreich (1973).

B1755. —— 'The Dynamics of Vision in the Major Prophetic Works of William Blake.' *DAI*, XXXIII (1973), 5816–17A. Columbia Ph.D. in religion.

A1758. *Grunfield, Frederic V. 'Quotations from Chairman Blake.' *Horizon*, XIV (1972), 106–11.
A popular account, with a few Blake aphorisms.

A1765. §Gutner, M. N. 'Blake.' Vol. I, pp. 613–22 of [*A History of English Literature*]. Second Edition. Moscow & Leningrad, 1945.
In Russian.

1770. A. *Hagstrum, Jean H. **William Blake Poet and Painter*. . . . C. §Third Impression, 1969.

A1773. Haight, Richard Paul. 'Pope's *Dunciad* and Blake's *Jerusalem*: An Epic Eighteenth Century Dialogue.' *DAI*, XXXII (1972), 6375A. Ohio State Ph.D.
On their 'thematic and structural complementarities and antagonisms'.

A1776. Halloran, William F. 'Blake's *Tiriel*: Snakes, Curses, and a Blessing.' *South Atlantic Quarterly*, LXX (1971), 161–79.
'An overview of the poem' (p. 161).

1780. A. Hamblen, Emily S. *On the Minor Prophecies of William Blake*. With an Introduction by S. Foster Damon. . . . B. §1968. C. §1972.

A1781. Hampton, Nigel. 'William Blake's "Art of Poetry": A Critical Supplement to Five Minor Prophecies.' *DAI*, XXXII (1972), 5875A. Connecticut Ph.D.
The five prophecies are *Thel*, *Visions*, *Urizen*, *Ahania*, and *The Book of Los*.

A1785. *Hardie, Martin. 'William Blake and Henry Fuseli.' Chapter xi (pp. 192–204) of his *Water-colour Painting in Britain*. [Volume] I: The Eighteenth Century. Ed. Dudley Snelgrove, Jonathan Mayne, & Basil Taylor. London, 1966.
A general account, with the premiss that 'Blake [is] the greatest imaginative artist of the British school' (p. 192).

A1787. Harding, Eugene J. 'Jacob Boehme and Blake's "The Book of Urizen".' *Unisa English Studies*, VIII (June 1970), 3–11.
'Blake knew the writings of Jacob Boehme well enough to use his ideas on the power of the imagination, his idea of contraries, his seven natural properties, and his notion of an androgynous Adam' (p. 3).

A1799. Harris, R. W. 'The New Jerusalem and William Blake.' Chapter viii (pp. 149–69) of his *Romanticism and the Social Order 1780–1830*. London, 1969.
A general account of Blake's life.

A1801. Hartley, William Joseph. 'The Golden String: William Blake's Epistemology.' *DAI*, XXXIV (1974), 5102A. Vanderbilt Ph.D.

'The purpose of this dissertation is to discuss Blake's development of a theory of knowing which would permit man to see past his fallen state on to the state of the Eternals', especially in a few of the early prophecies.

A1802. §Hashizume, Mitsuharu. '[Blake in his Last Moments].' *Kufuku Sei* [*The Festival of the Empty Stomachs*], No. 1 (15 Sept. 1929), 19–29.

A1807. §Haya, Kenichi. 'Honto no Kami no Sugata—Blake no Imi [Figure of the True God—Blake's Meaning].' *Oberon*, XXXII (1970), 15–19.

1814. A. Hayley, William. *Memoirs of the Life and Writings of William Hayley.* Ed. John Johnson. . . . B. §1971.

A1826. Helms, [Loyce] Randel. 'Blake at Felpham: A Study in the Psychology of Vision.' *Literature & Psychology*, XXII (1972), 57–66.
About 'the psychological mechanisms at work' in *Milton* (p. 62).

1829. A. Helmstadter, Thomas H. 'Blake's *Night Thoughts*: Interpretation of Edward Young' (1970). . . . B. Revised and reprinted in R. N. Essick, ed., *The Visionary Hand* (1973).

1835. Heppner, Christopher A. E. 'The Problem of Form in Blake's Prophecies.' Toronto Ph.D., 1970; see *DAI*, XXXII (1971), 433A.

A1837. Herzing, Thomas W. 'Ceaseless Mental Fight: William Blake and Eighteenth-Century Thought.' *DAI*, XXXIII (1973), 4345–6A. Wisconsin Ph.D.
On Blake's fight with eighteenth-century thought.

A1846. Hilles, Frederick W. 'Reynolds among the Romantics.' Pp. 267–83 of *Literary Theory and Structure*: Essays in Honor of William K. Wimsatt. Ed. Frank Brady, John Palmer, & Martin Price. New Haven & London, 1973.
Comparison of the marginalia of Blake, B. R. Haydon, and Hazlitt; 'basically the three are in agreement' (p. 282).

A1849. Hipple, Walter. 'General and Particular in the Discourses of Sir Joshua Reynolds.' *JAAC*, XI (1953), 231–47 (vMKN).
Blake is a point of departure; it is mostly on Reynolds.

1863. A. Hobsbaum, Philip. 'A Rhetorical Question Answered: Blake's Tyger and its Critics.'. . . C. Reprinted in Hobsbaum's *A Theory of Communication*. London, 1970. Pp. 67–71; see also pp. 119–24 and *passim*.

A1875. Holloway, John. 'Blake—The Lyric Poetry.' *Unisa English Studies*, VIII (March 1970), 33–41.

B1875. Holmberg, Carol E. 'A Study of William Blake's Fourfold Perspective Process as Interpreted by William Butler Yeats.' *DAI*, XXXIII (1971), 2666A. Minnesota Ph.D.

The Yeats source seems to be exclusively 'The Necessity of Symbolism' (1893).

A1881. §Hoover, Suzanne S. 'William Blake in the Wilderness: The Early History of his Reputation.' Columbia Ph.D., 1966.

B1881. Hope-Wallace, Philip. 'Tyger.' *Guardian*, 21 July 1971, p. 7.

Adrian Mitchell's 'extravaganza' is 'a real celebration'.

A1887. Horovitz, Michael, 'Blake and the Voice of the Bard in our time.' *Books*, No. 10 (Winter 1972), 18–24.

A defence of 'the Children of Albion', with Blake as a prophet.

B1887. —— 'The Need for the Non-literary.' *TLS*, 29 Dec. 1972, p. 1583.

An extensive quarrel with the statement by Roy Fuller (10 Nov. 1972) that 'the views of "the Children of Albion" about Blake stem from a reading of him that is quite incomplete', referring to *Poetry of the Children of Albion Underground in Britain*, ed. Michael Horovitz (1969), republished as *Children of Albion*: Poetry of the 'Underground' in Britain (1970), especially Horovitz's 'Afterwords' (pp. 316–77, 315–76).

A1907. §Humma, John B. 'Poe's "Ligeia:" Glanville's Will or Blake's Will?' *Mississippi Quarterly*, XXVI (1973), 55–62.

1912. [Hunt, Robert.] (R. H.) 'Blake's Edition of Blair's Grave.' *The Examiner*, 7 Aug. 1808, pp. 509–10. (BM)

An important, mocking review; it was announced in the issue for 31 July 1808 (p. 494).

A1932. Jackson, Mary Vera. 'Prolific and Devourer: From Nonmythic to Mythic Statement in *The Marriage of Heaven and Hell* and *A Song of Liberty*.' *JEGP*, LXX (1971), 207–19.

A reading.

A1941. Jackson, Wallace. 'William Blake in 1789: Unorganized *Innocence*.' *MLQ*, XXXIII (1972), 396–400.

Criticism of critics of *Innocence*; 'far too much has been claimed for its complexity' (p. 404); 'There is no ruling principle of organization' in *Innocence*.

A1944. Jakubec, Doris. ' "La rose malade" de William Blake.' *Études de Lettres*, Series 3, V, 2–3 (1972), 51–9.

On Pierre-Louis Matthey's translation.

A1946. James, Carol. 'Eldridge Builds Art At Golgonooza: Blakeian Spirit Motivates.' *The Messenger* [Athens, Ohio], 25 Nov. 1973, p. C–1.

About Aethelred Eldridge and his 'Church of the Blake Recital' at Mill-field, Ohio. [Eldridge publishes *News from Golgonooza*, mimeographed sheets which began appearing approximately monthly in summer 1973, illustrated with his own designs or Blake's, with text of a consistently sub-lunar obscurity, e.g. '"Naked Beauty Displayed" is nothing, more or less, than the old Moses swallowing hard.']

B1946. James, David Edmund. 'Written Within and Without: Form and Structure in Blake's *Milton*.' *DAI*, XXXII (1972), 4614A. Pennsylvania Ph.D.

A1947. *James, G. Ingli. 'Blake's Woodcuts Illuminated.' *Apollo*, XCIX (1974), 194–5.

Colour reproductions of Blake's Virgil prints.

B1947. —— 'Blake's woodcuts, plain and coloured.' *TLS*, 18 May 1973, p. 564.

Eight Virgil engravings were probably printed by Linnell and 'exquisitely coloured' by his children. (For a minor sequel, see Stone & Ingli.)

1949. A. James, Laura DeWitt. *William Blake: The Finger on the Furnace* (1956).

Part was reprinted in *Tree* (1970), below.

A1949. —— 'Sweet Science.' *Tree*, I (Winter 1970), 83–95.

Reprinted from her *Finger on the Furnace*.

A1953. A. §Jannoud, Claude. Review of William Blake, *Works*. Ed. Pierre Leyris. Vol. I —— in *Le Figaro*, 29 June 1974, p. 8. B. Tr. Katharyn R. [Kremen] Gabriella. *Blake Newsletter*, VIII, 4 (1975), 121.

1956. A. Jeffrey, Lloyd N. 'Blake's *The Little Black Boy*' (1958). . . . B. Reprinted in no. A1587 9.

A1960. Jewkes, W. T. 'Blake's Creation Myths as Archetypes of Art.' Pp. 127–41 of *Directions in Literary Criticism*: Contemporary Approaches to Literature. Ed. Stanley Weintraub & Philip Young. University Park [Pennsylvania] & London, 1973.

Comparison with other creation myths.

B1960. John, Brian. 'William Blake: The Poet as Mental Prince.' Chap. 1 (pp. 15–74) of his *Supreme Fictions*: Studies in the Work of William Blake, Thomas Carlyle, W. B. Yeats, and D. H. Lawrence. Montreal & London, 1974.

'The vitalism central later to Carlyle, Yeats, and Lawrence is expressed most plainly in *The Marriage*' (p. 35).

A1963. *Johnson, Mary Lynn. 'Emblem and Symbol in Blake.' *HLQ*, XXXVII (1974), 151–70.

A learned and useful 'scouting expedition' for analogies in emblem literature with 'Aged Ignorance' from *The Gates of Paradise* and the flower poems from *Experience*.

A1964. *Jones, Ben. 'Blake on Gray: Outlines of Recognition.' Pp. 127–35 of *Fearful Joy*: Papers from the Thomas Gray Bicentenary Conference at Carleton University [18–20 May 1971]. Ed. James Downey & Ben Jones. Montreal & London, 1974.

Some reflections on a few Blake designs for Gray.

A1965. Jones, Warren. 'Blake's Large Color-Printed Drawings of 1795.' *DAI*, XXXIII (1973), 6873A. Northwestern Ph.D.

A1971. A. §Jugaku, Bunsho. '[Blake and His Age].' *Miotsukushi* [*The Sea-mark*], No. 2 (Jan. 1930), 34–46. B. Reprinted on pp. 1–39 of his *Blake Ronshu* (1931).

In Japanese.

A1975. —— 'Blake Saishoku bon no Yurai [The Origin of Blake's Book of Illustrations].' *Shomotsu no Shumi* [*Taste for Books*] (7 vols.) (19), Vol. I.

A1976. §Jugaku, Bunsho. 'Blake to [and] Kagaku.' *Arubiyon: Albion*, No. 47 (19).

A1977. —— 'Dante to [and] Blake.' *Eigo Seinen: The Rising Generation*, CXIX (1973), 322–3.

A1980. Juninus. 'On Splendour of Colours, &c.' *The Repository of Arts, Literature, Commerce, Manufactures, Fashions, and Politics*, II (June 1810, Supplement), 404–9. (Toronto Public)

'Blake's plates from Blair's *Grave*, lately engraved, are excellent studies for a young artist. Blake has lately received much deserved commendation from Fuseli. Perhaps, this engraver has more genius than any one in his profession in this country. If he would study the ornamental requisites more, he would probably attain much higher celebrity than he has already acquired.' (Pp. 404–9.) (This reference was pointed out to me by my friend Professor Janet Warner.)

1981. A. Justin, Howard. 'Blake's "*Introduction*" to *Songs of Innocence*.' . . . B. Reprinted in no. A1587 5.

A1981. Juszczak, W. '"Laokoon" William Blake's.' *Miesiecznik Lit.*, XI (Warszawa, 1970), 58–67.

In Polish.

1984. A. Kaplan, Fred. '"The Tyger" and its Maker: Blake's Vision of Art and the Artist' (1967). . . . B. Reprinted as 'Blake's Artist.' Chapter 2 (pp. 17–28) of his *Miracles of Rare Device*: The Poet's Sense of Self in Nineteenth-Century Poetry. Detroit, 1972. See also 'From Blake to Browning', Chapter 1 (merely the introduction to the book, pp. 11–16).

A1988. §Katahama, Toshihiko. '[William Blake and France].' *Sedai* [*The Generation*], No. 7 (June 1937), 26.

A1990. §Kauvar, Elaine Mozer. 'Blake's Botanical Imagery.' Northwestern Ph.D., 1971.

B1990. Kay, Wallace G. 'Blake, Baudelaire, Beckett: The Romantics of Nihilism.' *Southern Quarterly*, IX (1971), 253–9.
A peculiar view of Nihilism; for example, 'Loss of Innocence' (i.e. 'loss of value') in 'The Voice of the Ancient Bard' is nihilism (p. 255).

A1994. Kellog, Seth. 'Tragic Generation: A Commentary on Some Works of William Blake and on the Book of Genesis.' *DAI*, XXXIV (1973), 3346–7A. Massachusetts Ph.D.
'*A* critical reading [*sic*] of some works by William Blake and of the Book of Genesis as Blake read it.'

A2004. *Kettle, Arnold (for the Course Team). *William Blake (1757–1827)*. Bletchley, Bucks., 1972. Arts: A Second Level Course: The Age of Revolution. [The Open University] Units 21–22.
Fifty-three pp. of lessons on the *Songs* and *Marriage*, co-ordinated with broadcasts on television by Graham Holderness and on radio by A. L. Morton and Northrop Frye.

2010. A. *Keynes, Geoffrey. *Blake Studies*: Notes on his Life and Works in Seventeen Chapters. B. §N.Y., 1971. C. *Blake Studies*: Essays on his life and work. Second Edition. Oxford, 1971.
B is a reprint of the 1949 edition, while C was greatly expanded.

2063. A. Kline, Alfred Allan. 'Blake's *A Song of Liberty*.'. . . B. Reprinted in no. A 1587 13.

A2063. Klotz, G. 'Prophetie einer neuen Menschliechkeit.' *Aufbau*, Jg. 14, N. 4 (Berlin, 1958), 419–45.

B2063. Knights, L. C. 'Early Blake.' *Sewanee Review*, LXXIX (1971), 377–92.
'My purpose is . . . to call attention to . . . eight Songs' in *Poetical Sketches* (p. 378).

A2071. Kolesnikov, B. I. '[The Works of Robert Burns and Early English

Romanticism (William Blake)].' Pp. 190–206 of his [*Tradition and Innovation in Scottish Poetry, 14th–18th Centuries*]. Moscow, 1970.
In Russian.

A2076. Koper, Peter Thomas. 'Authentic Speech: An Essay with investigations of the Rhetoric of Samuel Johnson, Edmund Burke, and William Blake.' *DAI*, XXXIV (1974), 6594–5A. Texas Christian Ph.D., 1973.
A 136-page study concentrating, in the Blake section, on the *Marriage*.

2077. A. Korteling, Jacomina. *Mysticism in Blake and Wordsworth.* . . . B. N.Y., 1966.

A2080. Kremen, Kathryn Rebecca. 'The Imagination of the Resurrection: The Poetic Continuity and Conversion of a Religious Motif in Donne, Blake, and Yeats.' *DAI*, XXXI (1971), 5366A. Brandeis Ph.D.
'Chapter III (the dissertation's center) considers Blake's unifying mythology of the Four Zoas' resurrection as an appropriation of the imagination.' Revised as no. 2080. See also Kathryn R. [Kremen] Gabriella.

B2080. Kroeber, Karl. *Romantic Narrative Art.* Madison, Wisconsin, 1960. Pp. 68–77.
Chiefly paraphrase of *Tiriel* and 'The Mental Traveller'.

A2082. §Kumashiro, Soho. *Blake wo tadashiku yomu* [*Correct Reading of Blake*]. Tokyo, 1972.

A2098. §Lapidus, N. '[William Blake—Poet and Artist].' *Sov. Bellorussia* (28 Nov. 1957).
In Russian.

A2105. Leary, D. J. 'Shaw's Blakean Vision: A Dialectic Approach to *Heartbreak House*.' *Modern Drama*, XV (1972), 89–103.
'I make use of the writings of William Blake . . . to suggest Shaw's connection with the whole mythopoetic context of English art' (p. 89).

A2106. Leavis, F. R. 'Introductory: "Life" is a Necessary Word.' Chapter i (pp. 11–37) of his *Nor Shall My Sword*: Discourses on Pluralism, Compassion and Social Hope. London, 1972.
Blake (pp. 11–27) and D. H. Lawrence as inspiration for 'essential human creativity' (p. 19).

A2108. Lefcowitz, Barbara F. 'Blake and the Natural World.' *PMLA*, LXXXIX (1974), 121–31.
An attempt 'to examine in some detail Blake's diverse responses to the object world'; 'Generally, Blake's descriptive passages view nature as energy' (pp. 121, 122).

B2108. § Lefcowitz, Barbara F. 'Omnipotence of Thought and the Poetic Imagination: Blake, Coleridge, Rilke.' *Psychoanalytic Review*, LIX (1972), 417–32.

A2115. §Lemaitre, Henry. 'William Blake, vision et poésie.' Pp. 45–54 of *Le Romanticism anglo-américain*: Mélange offert à Louis Bonnerat. Paris, 1971.

A2124. Levitt, Annette Esther Shandler. 'The Poetry and Thought of William Blake in Joyce Cary's *The Horse's Mouth*.' *DAI*, XXXI (1971), 4778–9A. Pennsylvania State Ph.D.
'*U*ltimately he [*Cary*] re-creates for us the entire Blake myth-complex.'

B2124. *Leyris, Pierre. 'Le voyant contres les spectres.' *Le Monde*, 8 Oct. 1971, pp. 20–1.
A general account.

A2125. ——, and Geoffrey Keynes. 'Blake.' *TLS*, 28 April, 5 May 1972, pp. 496, 521.
Leyris suggests that in the 'Song' beginning 'Fresh from the dewy hill, the merry year' in *Poetical Sketches*, the terminal word in l. 1 would make better sense if it were 'dawn' rather than 'year'; Keynes replies that such a change 'is surely unnecessary for the sense'.

A2126. *Lindberg, Bo. *William Blake's Illustrations to the Book of Job*. Åbo [Finland], 1973. Acta Academiae Aboensis, Ser. A: Humaniora: Humanistika Vetenskaper, Socialvetenskaper och Juridik, Teologi, Vol. xlvi.
A major work, built round a *catalogue raisonné* (pp. 183–352) of every Blake design related to the Biblical Job, including the sources and interpretation of each, with 144 small illustrations comprehending all the 22 engravings, some proofs, and most of the Fitzwilliam sketches. The arguments about the date of the Butts water-colours, the authenticity of the New Zealand drawings, and the meaning of 'The Spiritual Form of Pitt' and of 'Nelson' are particularly novel and important.

B2126. *—— 'William Blake's Nebuchadnezzar och mänskodjuret.' *Taidehistoriallisia Tutkimuksis—Konsthistoriska Studier 1* ([Helsinki] 1974), 10–18.
On the sources and analogues of Blake's Nebuchadnezzar designs.

2131. A. Lindsay, Jack. *William Blake*: Creative Will and the Poetic Image. . . . D. N.Y., 1971.

A2133. *Lipking, Lawrence. 'Blake and The Book.' Pp. 64–9 of Chapter 7 ('The Art of Reynolds' *Discourses*') of his *The Ordering of the Arts in Eighteenth-Century England*. Princeton, 1970.

A2141. *Longstreet, Stephen. 'Blake.' Pp. 154–64 of his edition of *A Treasury of the World's Great Prints*: A collection of the best-known woodcuts, etchings, engravings and lithographs by twenty-three great artists. N.Y., 1961.

The text is a conventional summary.

2157. A. Mabbott, Thomas Ollive. 'Blake's *A Poison Tree*' (1948). . . . B. Reprinted in no. A1587 11.

A2167. Macandrew, Hugh. 'Selected Letters from the Correspondence of Henry Fuseli and William Roscoe of Liverpool.' *Gazette des Beaux-Arts*, VI Période, LXII (1963), 204–20.

Fuseli praises Blake's plate of 'Annubis in the first part of the Botanic Garden' in a letter of 17 Aug. 1798 (p. 218).

A2176. *Majdiak, Daniel, & Brian Wilkie. 'Blake and Freud: Poetry and Depth Psychology.' *Journal of Aesthetic Education*, VI (1972), 87–98.

Urizen shows a 'strikingly full anticipation of psychoanalytic theory' (p. 87).

B2176. Mandell, Robert. 'The Emergence of Los within Blake's Archetypal Dialectic.' *DAI*, XXXIII (1973), 4354A. Wisconsin Ph.D.

'Where does Los begin and how does he evolve?'

A2177. *Marek, F. 'William Blake neboli realismus obraznosti.' *Nový život*, XI (Praha, 1957), 1208–12.

In Czech.

A2187. *Marks, Claude, 'William Blake 1757–1827.' Pp. 207–15 of his *From the Sketchbooks of the Great Artists*. London, 1972.

A general account.

B2187. Marks, Mollyanne Kauffman. 'Despair and Desire: A Study of William Blake's *Jerusalem* and its Relation to Poetic Tradition.' *DAI*, XXXII (1972), 6987A. Yale Ph.D.

'Blake was deliberately working within a tradition of "true poetry"' in all his poetry.

A2194. §Maxwell-Mahon, W. D. 'The Prophetic Mind: An Aspect of the Poetry of Blake and Yeats.' *Unisa English Studies*, II (March 1964), 11–16.

A2195. *Mayoux, Jean-Jacques. 'La vision se détourne du visible: William Blake.' Pp. 179–89 of Chapter 6 of his *La Peinture anglaise de Hogarth aux Pré-raphaélites*. Geneva, 1972.

A2204. Medawar, P. B. 'Blake as Rake?' *TLS*, 30 June 1972, p. 749.

Incidental reference to Blake in a skirmish about a review.

A2208. §Melchiori, Giorgio. 'William Blake and Michelangelo.' *Art and Ideas*, [23] (1961), 114–32.

A2211. *Mellor, Anne Kostelanetz. *Blake's Human Form Divine.* Berkeley, Los Angeles, London, 1974.

Assertive discussion of 'The conflict between . . . his philosophical rejection of the human body and his aesthetic glorification of the human figure' (p. xvii), mostly by means of readings and paraphrases of word and design. The 87 plates include all of *For Children* (B). The work was originally a dissertation (no. 2078), and parts of Chapters 2, 4, and 8 originally appeared in her articles in *PQ* (no. 2211), the Damon festschrift, ed. Rosenfeld (no. 2565), and in *SEL* (no. B2211).

B2211. *—— 'The Human Form Divine and the Structure of Blake's *Jerusalem.*' *Studies in English Literature 1500–1900,* XI (1971), 595–620.

Jerusalem Chapters 2–4 define the 'three basic errors, or sins which can separate man from his own divinity', abuse of body, of mind, and of imagination (p. 597); the article is reprinted in Chapter 8 of her *Blake's Human Form Divine* (1974), no. A2211.

2214. A. Merchant, W. Moelwyn. 'Blake's Shakespeare' (1964). B. Reprinted in R. N. Essick, ed., *The Visionary Hand* (1973).

A2218. §Metsar, L. 'William Blake.' *Edasi* [*Forward*] (1 Dec. 1957).
In Estonian.

A2219. Middleman, Louis Isaac. 'William Blake and the Form of Error: Satiric Craft in the Engraved Minor Prophecies.' *DAI,* XXXV (1974), 2947A. Pittsburgh Ph.D., 1974, 169 pp.

A2231. Minnick, Thomas Ludwig. 'On Blake and Milton: An Essay in Literary Relationship.' *DAI,* XXXIV (1973), 2641A. Ohio State Ph.D.
'*A* case study in the varieties of literary relationship'.

A2232. Mitchell, Adrian. *Tyger*: A Celebration based on the life and work of William Blake. Music by Mike Westbrook. London, 1971.

A vigorous, loud, modernizing of Blake. A record of it was issued: §*Tyger*: A Celebration of William Blake. By Adrian Mitchell. Music by Mike Westbrook. RCA Original Cast Recording. SER 5612. London: RCA Limited, 1971.

B2232. *—— *Tyger*: A celebration of William Blake. Music by Westbrook. The National Theatre at the New Theatre. First performance: 20 July 1971. [London, 1971.]

The theatre programme includes 'Quotes about Blake' and 'Quotes by Blake'.

C2232. Mitchell, Jeffrey David. 'Blake's *Milton* as a Problem of Conscience.' *DAI,* XXXV (1974), 1113–14A. Columbia Ph.D., 1974, 146 pp.

2233. A. Mitchell, W. J. T. 'Poetic and Pictorial Imagination in Blake's *The Book of Urizen*' (1969). . . . B. Revised and reprinted in R. N. Essick, ed., *The Visionary Hand* (1973).

A2235. *Monkhouse, Cosmo. 'Figure Painters: Stothard, Blake, Cattermole, &c.' Chap. vii (pp. 77–90) of his *The Earlier English Water-Colour Painters*. London, 1890.

A2239 Moore, Donald Keith. 'An Annotated Edition of William Blake's *Europe*.' *DAI*, XXXIV (1973), 282A. State University of New York at Stony Brook Ph.D.

B2239. *—— 'Blake's Notebook Versions of *Infant Sorrow*.' *BNYPL*, LXXVI (1972), 209–19.
  A supplement to Appendix I of Erdman's edition of the *Notebook* (1973).

A2251. Moss, John G. 'Structural Form in Blake's "Visions of the Daughters of Albion".' *Humanities Association Bulletin*, XXII, 2 (Spring 1971), 9–18.
  An impressive argument that *Visions* 'is meticulously arranged as a forensic [*Ciceronian*] oration' (p. 12).

A2270. A. Nanavutty, Piloo. 'A Title Page in Blake's Illustrated Genesis Manuscript' (1947). . . . B. Reprinted in R. N. Essick, ed., *The Visionary Hand* (1973).

A2275. Natoli, Joseph Philip. 'A Study of Blake's Contraries with Reference to Jung's Theory of Individuation.' *DAI*, XXXIV (1973), 3351–2A. State University of New York at Albany Ph.D.

A2278. §Nekrasova, Ekaterina Alekseevna. 'William Blake.' *Isskustvo*, VIII (1957), 58–9.
  In Russian.

B2278. §—— 'William Blake.' *Sov. Kultura* (28 Nov. 1957).
  In Russian.

C2278. §*—— [*The Works of William Blake*]. Moscow: Moscow University Press, 1962.
  In Russian, with 182 pp., 25 illustrations, bibliography on pp. 177–82.

D2278. *Nelson, Cary. 'Blake's *Jerusalem*: a fourfold vision of the human body.' Chap. vi (pp. 129–59) of his *The Incarnate Word*: Literature as verbal space. Urbana, Chicago, London, 1973.
  About womb-shapes in Blake.

2279. A. Nelson, John Walter. 'Blake's Minor Prophecies: A Study in the

Development of his Major Prophetic Mode.' *DAI*, XXXI (1971), 3154A.
Ohio State Ph.D., 1970.
Analyses of *America* through *Ahania*.

A2280. Neubauer, John. 'The Sick Rose as an Aesthetic Idea: Kant, Blake, and the Symbol in Literature.' Pp. 167–79 of *Irrationalism in the Eighteenth Century*. Ed. Harold E. Pagliaro. Cleveland & London, 1972. Studies in Eighteenth-Century Culture: Proceedings [of] The American Society for Eighteenth Century Studies Vol. II.
'The theoretical statement by Kant and the poetic practice of Blake illuminate each other' (p. 175).

B2280. *Neve, Christopher. 'Blake as Printer and Printed.' *Country Life*, CXLV (5 June 1969), 1448–9.
Review of the exhibition at the Whitworth Gallery.

2289. A. Nitchie, Elizabeth. 'Blake's *The Tyger*.'. . . B. Reprinted in no. A1587 16.

A2289. Norman, Geraldine. 'Reversal in values of works by Blake.' *The Times*, 10 Nov. 1971, p. 17.
About the sale at Christie's, 9 Nov. 1971.

A2299. *Nurmi, Martin K. *William Blake*. London, 1975.
A brief 'introduction to Blake's poetry' (p. 9).

A2301. O'Brien, Michael William. 'Between Language and Voice: A Study of Aesthetic Experimentation in Blake, Whitman, Cummings, and Concrete Poetry.' *DAI*, XXXIV (1974), 6985A. Illinois Ph.D., 1973.
A 177-page essay concentrating in the Blake section on the *Songs*.

A2304. §Ogawa, Jiro. *Blake 'Rossetti Kohon' Shoki no Shi [Blake's Rossetti Manuscript'—Early Poems]*. Tokyo, 1973.

2325 A. Olybrius. 'Blake's *The Clod and the Pebble*.'. . . . B. Reprinted in no. A1587 1.

A2331. §Osetrov, G., & R. Trusov. '[William Blake in the Monographs of a Kishinev Student].' *Sov. Moldavia* (21 July 1968).
In Russian, on the work of T. N. Vasilieva.

A2342. Pache, Walter. 'Blake's seltsame Poesien: Bildzitat und Bildwirkung in Thomas Manns *Doktor Faustus*.' *arcadia*, VIII (1973), 138–55.

A2349. Paley, Morton D., ed. *Twentieth Century Interpretations of Songs of Innocence and of Experience*: A Collection of Critical Essays. Englewood Cliffs, N.J., 1969.

The work consists of Paley's 'Introduction' (pp. 1–9) and

(1) Alicia Ostriker, 'Metrics: Pattern and Variation' (pp. 10–29, from her *Vision and Verse in William Blake* [1965], 55–78);

(2) S. Foster Damon, 'The Initial Eden' (pp. 30–5, from his *William Blake* [1924], 39–42);

(3) Martin Price, 'The Vision of Innocence' (pp. 36–48, from his *To the Palace of Wisdom* [1964], 389–401);

(4) David V. Erdman, 'Infinite London' (pp. 49–57, from his *Blake: Prophet Against Empire* [1969], chap. 13);

(5) Northrop Frye, 'Blake's Introduction to Experience' (pp. 58–67, a reprint of his essay in *HLQ* [1957]);

(6) Morton D. Paley, 'Tyger of Wrath' (pp. 68–92, a reprint of his essay in *PMLA* [1966]);

(7) Joseph H. Wicksteed, 'The Blossom' (pp. 93–5, from his *Blake's Innocence and Experience* [1928] [125–8]);

(8) Robert F. Gleckner, 'Spring' (pp. 96–8, from his *The Piper & The Bard* [1959], 94–7);

(9) Harold Bloom, 'Holy Thursday' (pp. 98–9, from his *Blake's Apocalypse* [1963], 44–5);

(10) Mark Schorer, 'Experience' (pp. 99–100, from his *William Blake* [1946], 237–8);

(11) Hazard Adams, 'The Two Nurse's Songs' (pp. 100–4, from his *William Blake* [1963], 252–5);

(12) Martin K. Nurmi, 'Blake's Revisions of *The Tyger*' (pp. 104–6, from his essay in *PMLA* [1956], 681–3);

(13) E. D. Hirsch, Jr., 'The Human Abstract' (pp. 107–10, from his *Innocence and Experience* [1964], 265–70).

A2350. *Paley, Morton D., & Michael Phillips, ed. *William Blake*: Essays in honour of Sir Geoffrey Keynes. Oxford, 1973.

There are 82 plates and Blake essays by

(1) *Michael Phillips. 'Blake's Early Poetry.' Pp. 1–28. ('I wish to show what was particularly personal' about *Poetical Sketches* [p. 2.].)

(2) *David Bindman. 'Blake's "Gothicised Imagination" and the History of England.' Pp. 29–49. (Interesting analysis of Blake's early History Paintings.)

(3) *Robert N. Essick. 'The Altering Eye: Blake's Vision in the *Tiriel* Designs.' Pp. 50–65. (An analysis of the *Tiriel* designs.)

(4) F. R. Leavis. 'Justifying One's Evaluation of Blake.' Pp. 66–85. (A lecture with the premiss that 'Blake is a major value, and one of peculiar importance for our time' [p. 66], largely based on T. S. Eliot's essay.)

(5) Josephine Miles. 'Blake's Frame of Language.' Pp. 86–95. ('As a whole, one can generalize from the *Concordance* much as I did earlier' in 1964 [p. 87].)

(6) *Michael J. Tolley. 'Blake's Songs of Spring.' Pp. 96–128. (A study of references to spring throughout Blake's work.)

(7) *Jean H. Hagstrum. 'Christ's Body.' Pp. 129–56. (Studies changes in Blake's way of depicting Christ.)

(8) G. Wilson Knight. 'The Chapel of Gold.' Pp. 157–61. ('An interpretation of "I saw a chapel all of gold", with the especial purpose of indicating what I mean . . . by the "interpretation of poetry"' [p. 157].)

(9) *David V. Erdman 'with' Tom Dargan & Marlene Deverell-Van Meter. 'Reading the Illuminations of Blake's *Marriage of Heaven and Hell*.' Pp. 162–207. (An often tendentious 'attempt to point out every bird, beast, tree, rock, orb, and human form we see and to do so in terms meaningful on many symbolic levels' [p. 163].)

(10) *Janet Warner. 'Blake's Figures of Despair: Man in his Spectre's Power.' Pp. 208–24. (The 'symbolic meaning' in Blake's pictures of despair, as part of his visual 'language of art' [p. 208].)

(11) *Morris Eaves. 'The Title-page of *The Book of Urizen*.' Pp. 225–30. (An odd visual analysis.)

(12) *John Beer. 'Blake, Coleridge, and Wordsworth: Some Crosscurrents and Parallels 1789–1805.' Pp. 231–59. ('Parallel themes and preoccupations' [p. 232], especially concerning Godwin, Darwin, Fuseli, and Egypt.)

(13) *Morton D. Paley. 'William Blake, The Prince of the Hebrews, and The Woman Clothed with the Sun.' Pp. 260–93. (Interesting parallels between Blake, Richard Brothers, and Joanna Southcott as prophets.)

(14) *Martin Butlin. 'Blake, the Varleys, and the Patent Graphic Telescope.' Pp. 294–304. (It is 'likely' 'That John Varley and Linnell made use of Cornelius Varley's Patent Graphic Telescope in making copies from Blake's Visionary Heads' [p. 304].)

(15) Raymond Lister. 'References to Blake in Samuel Palmer's letters.' Pp. 305–9. (Minor references 1839–81.)

(16) *Suzanne R. Hoover. 'William Blake in the Wilderness: A Closer Look at his Reputation 1827–1863.' Pp. 310–48. (A summary of the facts scattered elsewhere.)

(17) G. E. Bentley, Jr. 'Geoffrey Keynes's Work on Blake: *Fons et Origo*, and a Checklist of Writings on Blake by Geoffrey Keynes, 1910–72.' Pp. 349–75. (The evaluation is pp. 349–55, the annotated checklist pp. 356–76.)

A2370. *Paulson, Ronald. 'The Spectres of Blake and Rowlandson.' *Listener*, 2 Aug. 1973, pp. 140–2.
'If we assembled all Rowlandson's drawings and arranged them in a kind of chronology, they would form a cycle strangely like Blake's' [but not very].

A2386. Peschel, Enid Rhodes. 'Themes of Rebellion in William Blake and Arthur Rimbaud.' *French Review*, XLVI (1973), 750–61.
The article, which traces vague parallels between Blake and Rimbaud, precedes, and is similar to, her essay on 'Violence and Vision'.

B2386. Peschel, Enid Rhodes 'Violence and Vision: A Study of William Blake and Arthur Rimbaud.' *Revue de littérature comparée*, XLVI (1972), 376–95.

The two poets are said to be similar; the essay is a sequel to the one on 'Themes of Rebellion'.

C2386. §Peterson, Jane E. 'The *Visions of the Daughters of Albion*: A Problem of Perception.' *PQ*, LII (1973), 252–64.

A2389. §Philippide, A. 'Insemiari despre William Blake.' Pp. 116–39 of *Studii si portrete literare*. Bucaresti: Ed. pentru lit., 1963.

In Rumanian.

A2391. §Pialing. V. 'William Blake.' *Sov. Estonia* (28 Nov. 1957).

In Russian.

2392. A. [Pichot, A.] 'Artiste, Poète et Fou' (1830). . . . C. Translated anonymously as 'Artist-Poet-Sumasshedshii: zhizn' Vil'yama Bleka [Artist-Poet-Madman: life of William Blake].' *Teleskop* [*Telescope*: A Journal of Contemporary Enlightenment], XXII ([Moscow] 1834), 69–97.

C. This is the first article on Blake in Russian.

A2400. Pierce, Hazel May Beasley. 'A Critical Study of William Blake's *Europe*.' *DAI*, XXXI (1971), 5372–3A. Nebraska Ph.D.

A2412. Pittman, Philip McM. 'Blake, Rossetti, and Reynolds. A Detail.' *N&Q*, CCXIX [N.S., XXI] (1974), 215–16.

Rossetti knew Blake's attitudes to Reynolds by 1847–8 because of the comments in Blake's *Notebook*, which he owned.

2434. A. Pottle, Frederick A. 'Blake's *The Tyger*, 17–18' (1950). . . . B. Reprinted in no. A1587 19.

2447. A. §Powys, John Cowper. 'William Blake.' Pp. 43–60 of his *Essays on de Maupassant, Anatole France, William Blake*. Girard, Kansas, 1916. Little Blue Book No. 450. B. Gerard, 1923. Five Cent Pocket Series No. 450. Ed. E. Haldeman-Julius. C. *William Blake*, 1974.

'The strange and mysterious figure of William Blake seems continually to appear at the end of almost every vista of intellectual and aesthetic interest down which we move in these latter days. . . . *H*is astonishing genius dominates our modern taste . . . .'

B was transferred to the American Library Service as publishers, and C has text on pp. 3–7.

A2462. *Primeau, Ronald. 'Blake's Chimney Sweeper as Afro-American Minstrel.' *BNYPL*, LXXVIII (1975), 418–30.

Some exceedingly loose 'connections between Blake . . . [*and*] modern Afro-American [i.e. *Negro*] literature' (p. 418).

A2466. §Puras, K. '[The Poet-Artist.]' *Kombiaunimo Tiesa* (29 Nov. 1957). In Lithuanian.

A2476. Raine, Kathleen. 'Blake and the Education Of Childhood.' *Southern Review*, VIII (1972), 253–72.
She finds a 'valid alternative [*to nihilism*] in the philosophy of . . . Blake' (p. 272).

A2482. *—— 'Blake's Last Judgment.' *Ampleforth Journal*, LXXVI (1971), 70–84.
Discursive account of Blake's ideas on the subject.

A2496. §Rasmussen, Egil. *William Blake*: En psykologisk studie. Oslo, 1969.

B2496. Rawlinson, D. H. 'An Early Draft of Blake's "London".' Chapter 6 (pp. 45–51, 160–1) of his *The Practice of Criticism*. Cambridge, England, 1968.
On how to read poetry.

C2496. —— 'Relevance and Irrelevance in Response: Another Blake Poem ["The Human Abstract"].' Chapter 7 (pp. 52–61, 161–2) of his *The Practice of Criticism*. Cambridge [England] 1968.

A2497. §Rawson, Wyatt. 'William Blake—Psychic, Visionary and Prophet.' *Light*, XC (1970), 188–94.

B2497. Ray, William Ernest. 'William Blake and the Critical Development of William Butler Yeats.' *DAI*, XXXII (1971), 2652A. North Carolina Ph.D.
'Blake remained centrally important to Yeats throughout his critical career'.

A2503. §Reid, Anthony. 'Ralph Chubb, the Unknown: Part I: His Life, 1892–1960.' *Private Library*, 2 S, III (Autumn 1970), 141–56.
Parallels between the career and art of Chubb and Blake.

A2508. Reisner, Thomas A., & Mary Ellen Reisner. 'A Blake Reference to Goldsmith's "Citizen of the World".' *N&Q.*, CCXIX [N.s., XXI] (1974), 264–5.
Speculation that the dog as a counsellor in *Visions* pl. 5 and *Vala* Night II derives from the unspeakable 'man with dogs' heads [*who*] taught Grammar and Music' in Ptolemaic Egypt.

A2510. §Reubart, A., *et al.*, ed. *Blake through Student Eyes*. Oakland, California, 1971.
Student papers and poems on Blake for courses taught at Mills College, 1970 and 1971.

A2520. §Rienaecker, Victor. *William Blake*: A Natural Visionary. London, 1957.

A2522. Riffaterre, Michael. 'The Self-sufficient Text.' *diacritics*, III, 3 (1973), 39–45.
'My purpose is to analyse a poem ["The Sick Rose"] using internal evidence only' (p. 39).

A2522. Rinder, Frank. 'Seer or Madman? The Blake Exhibition.' *The Times* 19 June 1906.

A2525. Roberts, Mark. 'Blake and the Damnation of Reason.' Chapter 3 (pp. 82–122) of his *The Tradition of Romantic Morality*. London, 1973.
About 'the nature of Blake's break with the moral orthodoxy of the eighteenth century' (p. 118).

2538. A. Robinson, Henry Crabb. 'William Blake, Künstler, Dichter und religiöser Schwärmer' (1811). . . . B. Reprinted in the Hamburger Kunsthalle katalog (1975), no. B710. C. The translation in *Blake Records* (1969) is reprinted in G. E. Bentley, Jr., *William Blake*: The Critical Heritage (1975), no. A1181.

A2545. §*Rogov, V. 'William Blake.' *Kultura i Zhizn* [*Culture and Life*], XII (1957), 76–7.
In Russian, for the bicentennial of his birth, with a portrait.

A2554. Rose, Edward J. 'Blake's TO THE ACCUSER OF THIS WORLD.' *Explicator*, XXII (1964), no. 37.
An assertive answer to a query of D. J. B. in *Explicator*, XX (1962), Query 3.

2558. A. —— '"A Most Outrageous Demon': Blake's Case Against Rubens' (1969). . . . B. Reprinted in R. N. Essick, ed., *The Visionary Hand* (1973).

A2558. —— 'The Spirit of the Bounding Line: Blake's Los.' *Criticism*, XIII (1971), 54–76.
'The purpose of this essay . . . is to discuss Los as the iconographical word within the word (Blake's prophecies) and as the eye of the body of art (Blake's visual art) that circumscribes and determines the outline of the body . . .' (p. 54).

A2561. —— 'Wheels within Wheels in Blake's *Jerusalem*'. *Studies in Romanticism*, XI (1972), 36–47.
On wheel imagery; '*Jerusalem* in symbol and theory, like the Bible, is defined symbolically by the tropology that it is' (p. 47).

A2563. Rosenberg, Marc. 'Style and Meaning in *The Book of Urizen*.' *Style*, IV (1970), 197–212.

A careful argument that 'Blake's style corresponds in a significant manner with his explicitly stated ideas' (p. 197).

A2584. Rousselot, Jean. 'William Blake ou: le perception de l'infini par la voie des sens.' Pp. 15–27 of his *Présences contemporaines*: Rencontres sur les chemins de la Poésie. Paris, 1958.
Concerns particularly the ideas in the *Marriage*.

B2584. §Rozenberg, Paul. *Le romanticism anglais*: Le défie des vulnérables. Paris, 1973.

A2602. Russell, John. 'Blake the craftsman.' *Sunday Times*, 12 Dec. 1971, p. 27.
Review of Blake's Gray designs exhibited at the Tate Gallery.

A2611. *Sabri-Tabrizi, G. R. *The 'Heaven' and 'Hell' of William Blake*. N.Y., 1973.
'The main aim of this book is to present the whole of Blake in a coherent and comprehensible way', with emphasis upon Blake's 'consistent materialism' and his 'social context' (p. vii).

2624. A. Sampson, Edward C. 'Blake's *A Poison Tree*' (1947). . . . B. Reprinted in no. 1587 12.

A2643. Sanzo, Eileen Barbara. 'William Blake and the Technological Age.' *Thought*, XLVI (1971), 577–91.
'Through his creation of an industrial mythology, he speaks for the modern industrial age' (p. 578).

B2643. —— 'William Blake: Poet of the City in the Industrial Age.' *DAI*, XXXIII (1972), 764–5A. New York University Ph.D.
'The study attempts to show how industry and its cities shaped his language' particularly in *Vala*, *Milton*, and *Jerusalem*.

C2643. §Sarnov, B. '[Each Time is an Exception].' *Literaturnaia Gazeta*, LXI (26 May 1966).
On the mastery of S. I. Marshak, the translator of Blake's poetry; in Russian.

A2662. *Schiff, Gert. 'Füssli und Blake.' Vol. I, pp. 279–91 of his *Johann Heinrich Füssli 1741–1825*. [2 vols.; Vol. I:] Text und Oeuvrekatalog [Vol. II: Abbildungen]. Zürich & Munchen, 1973. Oeuvrekatalogue Schweizer Künstler Band 1/2 Schweizerischer Institut für Kunstwissenschaft, Zurich. Also *passim*.

A2663. *Schneiderman, Stuart. 'Blake's Prophecy: The Opening of the Western Gate.' *The Western Gate* [a periodical 'published occasionally' in Buffalo] (1970), 7 unnumbered pages.

The raising up of the tongue 'in its function of speech-maker . . . is the opening of the Western Gate'.

A2675. Scott, Janis Marie McAtee. 'The Stubborn Structure of the Language: A Study of the Syntax of William Blake.' *DAI*, XXXIV (1974), 5148–9A. Mississippi Ph.D., 1973.

A 147-page 'computer-assisted statistical study . . . written in COBOL for use on the Dec 10 system'.

A2692. §Shaginian, M. S. 'William Blake.' Pp. 214–16 of his *Inostrannaia Literaturnaia [Foreign Letters]*. Moscow, 1964. . . . C. §Third Edition. Moscow, 1971.

B2692. —— '[William Blake: For the Bicentennial of his Birth].' *Izvestia* (28 Nov. 1957).

In Russian.

C2692. *Sharp, Dennis. 'Blake into Print.' *riba journal,* LXXI (Feb. 1972), 80.

Two paragraphs about the Tate Blake–Gray exhibition.

A2694. §Shaw, Edward J. 'Was Blake Mad?' *Sunday Times* [London], 11 July 1926.

B2694. Shea, James P. 'Blake's Archetypal Tyger: A More Comprehensive View.' *DAI*, XXXV (1974), 2243A. Marquette University Ph.D., 1974.

This 143-page effort to give 'a more comprehensive view [*of 'The Tyger'*] . . . than any of Blake's critics have thus far put forth' does not seem more comprehensive, in the abstract.

A2702. Siemens, Reynold. 'Borders in Blake's "The Little Girl Lost-Found".' *Humanities Association Bulletin*, XXII, 2 (Spring 1971), 35–43.

Lyca is on the borders of heaven.

2703. A. Simmons, Robert, & Janet Warner. 'Blake's *Arlington Court Picture*: The Moment of Truth' (1971). . . . B. Reprinted in R. N. Essick, ed., *The Visionary Hand* (1973).

B2703. §—— 'Blake's "How Sweet I Roam'd": From Copy to Vision.' *Neohelicon*, I, 3–4 (1973), 295–304.

A2714. Skelton, Susan. 'Blake, Novalis and Nerval: The Poetics of the Apocalypse: A Study of Blake's *Milton*, Novalis' *Hymnen an die Nacht* and *Heinrich von Ofterdingen* and Norval's *Aurelia*.' *DAI*, XXXIV (1974), 7247A. Southern California Ph.D., 1973.

A 153-page essay arguing merely that they 'share essentially the same assumptions. . . .'

A2717. Smith, Catherine Findley. 'Pictorial Language in *The Four Zoas* by Blake.' *DAI*, XXXIII (1973), 5142A. North Caroline Ph.D.

It 'is a verbal organization of images of sight, sound, and movement'.

A2721. *Smith, Janet Adam. 'From Horn-Book to Blake.' Pp. 7–14 of her *Children's Illustrated Books*. With 4 Plates in Colour and 33 Illustrations in Black & White. London, 1948.

One paragraph on Blake.

A2733. Speirs, John. 'Blake, Coleridge, Keats and Shakespeare.' Chapter i (pp. 11–48) of his *Poetry Towards Novel*. London, 1971.

Blake's 'Shakespearian use of language' places him 'somewhere between Shakespeare and . . . Dickens and Lawrence' (p. 20; see pp. 12–20 and *passim*).

A2737. §Spins, C. William. 'Blake's Spectre.' Pp. 34–5 of *Studies in Relevance*: Romantic and Victorian Writers in 1972. Ed. Thomas M. Harwell. Salzburg, 1973.

A2743. Starr, Pamela. 'Blake and the Spectre of Milton.' *DAI*, XXXIV (1973), 2548–9A. Yale Ph.D.

'This dissertation attempts to study Blake's poetic relationship with Milton' in the *Marriage, Europe, Vala*, and *Milton*.

2756. Stevenson, Stanley Warren. 'The Creation Motif in Romantic Poetry and Theory with Particular Reference to the Myth of Blake and the Poetic Theory of Blake and Coleridge.' *DA*, XIX (1958), 1368–9A. Northwestern Ph.D.

The typescript is evidently reproduced in his *Divine Analogy* (1972); Stevenson's essay on 'The Tyger' in *Blake Studies* (1969), reprinted in *Divine Analogy*, evidently originated in the thesis.

A2756. —— *Divine Analogy*: A Study of the Creation Motif in Blake and Coleridge. Salzburg, 1972. Salzburg Studies in English Literature: Romantic Reassessment [No.] 25.

Part I (pp. 1–189) is on 'Blake's Myth of Creation and Re-Creation', Part II (pp. 190–355) on 'Creative Imagination in the Poetic Theory and Practice of Blake and Coleridge'. The book is, apparently, a reproduction from typescript of his thesis; Chapter viii, '"The Tyger" as Los's Artefact', reprints in slightly altered form his essay in *Blake Studies*, II, 1 (1969).

A2759. Stevenson, W. H. 'On the Nature of Blake's Symbolism.' *Texas Studies in Literature and Language*, XV (1973), 445–60.

In Blake's symbols, the image takes 'over from the idea' in a very personal (not abstract) way (p. 449).

2766. A. Stone, George Winchester, Jr. 'Blake's *The Tyger*' (1942). . . . B. Reprinted in no. A1587 15.

A2767. Stone, Reynolds, and G. Ingli James. 'Blake's Woodcuts.' *TLS*, 8 June 1973, pp. 617, 645.

Stone asks: 'Was Dr Thornton really such a philistine as Mr Ingli James [TLS, *18 May 1973*, q.v.] suggests', and James replies Yes.

A2780. *Sullivan, Edward Joseph. 'Blake.' Chapter xix (pp. 145-7) of his *The Art of Illustration*. Illustrated. London, 1921. Universal Art Series.

A perfunctory introduction.

A2782. Sutherland, John. 'Blake: A Crisis of Love and Jealousy.' *PMLA*, LXXXVII (1972), 424-31.

'William Bond' illustrates 'clearly a dramatic change of mind' about 'sexual love' (p. 426).

A2811. §Takemori, Osamu. 'William Blake's "To Tirzah": an Interpretation.' *Studies in English Literature* (English Literary Society of Japan), XLII (March 1971), 179-98 (in Japanese), 325-6 (English synopsis).

A2817. §Tandon, Jagdish Narain. 'The influence on the poetry of William Blake [*sic*].' University of Agra Ph.D., 1963-7 (according to *Humanities*: A Bibliography of Doctoral Dissertations Accepted by Indian Universities 1857-1970 [New Delhi, 1975], no. 116).

A2821. Tannenbaum, Leslie Warren. 'Dark Visions of Torment: Symbol and Structure in William Blake's *The Book of Urizen*.' *DAI*, XXXIII (1973), 6328A. Wisconsin Ph.D.

2823. B. Tatham, Frederick. 'Life of Blake' (?1832). Reprinted in G. E. Bentley, Jr., ed., *William Blake: The Critical Heritage* (1975), no. A1181.

A2824. *Tayler, Irene. 'Two Eighteenth-Century Illustrators of Gray.' Pp. 119-26 of *Fearful Joy*: Papers from the Thomas Gray Bicentenary Conference at Carleton University [18-20 May 1971]. Ed. James Downey & Ben Jones. Montreal & London, 1974.

An attempt 'to suggest something of Gray's ability to elicit from his illustrators [*Blake and Richard Bentley*] highly sensitive and personally revealing responses' (p. 123), derived, partly verbatim, from her book (1971), pp. 55-70 (p. 126).

A2826. §Taylor, Gary [James]. 'Blake's "Proverb 67" (from *The Marriage of Heaven and Hell*).' *Explicator*, XXXII (1973), item 8.

B2826. —— 'A Critical Edition of *The Marriage of Heaven and Hell* with Annotations.' *DAI*, XXXIII (1972), 2345-6A. Arkansas Ph.D.

Includes a facsimile of copy I and an anthology of criticism of the *Marriage*.

2839. Thornbury, W. 'The Prophet. . . .' *British Artists* (1861).

Blake is also mentioned incidentally and derivatively under Stothard

(II, 135) and David Scott (II, 181–2, including 6 lines of his dedication of the designs to Blair's *Grave*).

2846. A. Tinker, Chauncey Brewster. *'Blake: "The Gates of Paradise".' Pp. 100–20 of his *Painter and Poet* (1938). . . . B. *Freeport, N.Y., 1969. Essay Index Reprint Series.
A lecture of no great importance.

2853. A. Todd, Ruthven. 'The Techniques of William Blake's Illuminated Printing' (1948). . . . C. Revised and reprinted in R. N. Essick, ed., *The Visionary Hand* (1973).

A2857. §Toki, Koji. 'Blake to "Fukugo Geijutsu" [Blake and "Composite Art"].' *Eigo Seinen: The Rising Generation*, CXIX (1973), 204–5.

B2857. §—— 'Icons of Albion.' *English Quarterly: Apollon-sha*, VIII ([Kyoto] 1971), 222–34 (in Japanese).

A2862. §Tolley, Michael J. 'References to the Bible and Milton in Blake's "Europe".' Pp. 40–2 of *Proceedings of the Ninth Congress of the Australian Universities' Language and Literature Association*. Ed. Marion Adams. Melbourne [1964].

A2871. §Tsuchiya, Shigeko. 'Who is Milton-Blake?' *English Quarterly: Apollon-sha*, VIII ([Kyoto] 1971), 144–57 (in Japanese).

A2888. §Unruh, Donald John. 'Jerusalem: The Primitive Christian Vision of William Blake.' University of Southern California Ph.D., 1970.

A2894. Vaish, Yogi Nandan. 'William Blake.' *My Magazine of India*, XXXVII (1966), 30–2, 81.
An ignorant general introduction.

A2898. §Vasilieva, T. N. '[Blake in Correspondence with his Friends and Contemporaries].' Pp. 3–51 of [*Problems in Romanticism and Realism in Foreign Literatures of the 18th–20th Centuries*]. Kishinev, 1972.
In Russian.

B2898. §—— '[The Epigrams of William Blake].' *Literaturovedch* [*Literary Studies*: Scholarly Annals of Kishinev State University], LXXXVIII (1967), 103–14.
In Russian.

C2898. §—— '[The Later Poems of William Blake: Brothers of Heaven, "The Everlasting Gospel"].' Pp. 298–300 of [1964 *Papers of the Faculty and Associates of the State University of Kishinev*]. Kishinev, 1965.
In Russian.

D2898. §Vasilieva, T. N. '[The Lyrics of William Blake].' [*Philological Studies*], XXXVI ([Kishinev: Kishinev University Press] 1959), 97–117.
In Russian.

E2898. §—— '[*Milton*, The Poem by William Blake].' *Literaturovedch* [*Literary Studies*], LX ([Kishinev: Kishinev University Press] 1962), 137–61.
In Russian.

F2898. §—— '[The Poems of William Blake (Prophetic Books 18th–19th Centuries)].' [*Scholarly Annals of Kishinev State University*], CVIII (1969), 23–316.
In Russian, with a chronological table of the life and work of Blake.

G2898. §—— '[The Satire of Blake's *Island in the Moon*].' *Literaturovedch* [*Literary Studies*], LXXVI ([Kishinev: University of Kishinev Press] 1964), 95–190.
In Russian.

H2898. §—— '[W. Blake and the French Revolution, 1789–93].' [*Philological Studies*], LI ([Kishinev: Kishinev University Press] 1960), 101–12.
In Russian.

I2898. §—— 'W. Blake [Prophetic Books (90's)].' [*Philological Studies*], XLVII ([Kishinev: Kishinev University Press] 1962), 167–90.
In Russian.

A2908. *Wagenknecht, David. *Blake's Night*: William Blake and the Idea of Pastoral. Cambridge, Mass., 1973.
A laborious analysis of Spenserian pastoral elements in Blake's early work and Miltonic ones in the later poems; it 'first saw the light as a doctoral thesis' (p. vii).

B2908. —— 'William Blake and the Idea of Pastoral.' University of Sussex D.Phil., 1972 (vDW).
The dissertation is essentially the same as the book.

C2908. ——, and Our Reviewer. '"Blake's Night".' *TLS*, 15 March 1974, p. 265.
Wagenknecht protests that the review of 15 Feb. 'totally misrepresents my book', and Our Reviewer unrepentantly exhibits 'exasperation' and 'disappointment'.

A2918. *Ward, Aileen. 'The Forging of Orc: Blake and the Idea of revolution.' *Tri-Quarterly*, XXIII–XXIV (1972), 204–27.
Blake's use of the word 'revolution' is conservative.

A2923. *Wark, Robert R. 'Blake, William.' Vol. I, pp. 333–5 of *McGraw-*

Hill Dictionary of Art. Ed. Bernard S. Myers. N.Y., Toronto, London, Sydney, Johannesburg, 1969.

2929. [Watkins, John, & Frederick Shoberl.] *Biographical Dictionary* (1816).
For a suggestion that the author of the Blake section was William Upcott, see no. A1171.

A2929. Watkinson, Raymond. '"White on Black".' *TLS*, 13 Sept. 1974, p. 980.
About the artistic capacities of William Blake (poet) and William Staden Blake (writing engraver).

B2929. §Watson, Alan [McCabe]. 'Blake's Frontispiece to the Visions of the Daughters of Albion.' *Transactions of the Johnson Society of the Northwest*, VI (1973), 70–8.

A2942. §Welch, Dennis Martin. 'Blake, Nehemiah, and Religious Renewal.' *Christian Scholar's Review*, II (1973), 308–10.
'The Little Vagabond' echoes Nehemiah 8: 9–10, 12.

B2942. —— 'William Blake's Apocalypses: A Theo-Psychological Inter-pretation.' *DAI*, XXXIII (1973), 736A. University of Southern California Ph.D.
Attempts 'to show how Blake sought to permanently escape history'.

A2950. White, Mary Elizabeth. 'Woman's Triumph: A Study of the Changing Symbolic Values of the Female in the Works of William Blake.' *DAI*, XXXIII (1972), 2348A. University of Washington Ph.D.

2952. A. Whitesell, J. Edwin. 'Blake's *The Little Black Boy*' (1948). . . .
B. Reprinted in no. A1587 7.

A2952. Whitley, William T. *Art in England 1821–1837.* Cambridge [England], 1930. Pp. 33–4.
A transcript of the Royal Academy record of its gift to Blake.

2954. Wicksteed, Joseph H. *Blake's Innocence and Experience.* . . . Pp. 149–70 are mostly reprinted in *Experience* (?1947).

A2967. Wilkes, John Edwin. 'Aeolian Visitations and the Harp Defrauded: Essay on Donne, Blake, Wordsworth, Keats, Flaubert, Heine and James Wright.' *DAI*, XXV (1974), 1129A. California (Santa Cruz) Ph.D., 1973.
The Blake section is a 'close reading' of 'Blake's seasons poems'.

B2967. Wilkie, Brian. 'Blake.' Vol. II, pp. 12–15 of *The McGraw-Hill Encyclopedia of World Biography*: An International Reference Work in Twelve Volumes Including an Index. N.Y., San Francisco, St. Louis, Johannesburg,

Kuala Lumpur, London, Mexico [sic], Montreal, New Delhi, Panama [sic], Rio de Janeiro, Singapore, Sydney, Toronto, 1973.

A2969. Wilkinson, Andrew Maylor. *William Blake and the Great Sin*: An Inaugural Lecture delivered in the University of Exeter 22 April 1974. Exeter, 1974.
'The "great sin" is education' (p. 5).

B2969. Wilkinson, Carolyn. 'Perception, Action, and Character: The Structure of Blake's *Jerusalem.*' *DAI*, XXXV (1974), 1630–9A. Michigan State Ph.D., 1974.

A2972. *William Blake—200 years.* Sudbury, Suffolk [1957].
Four pages of poems by Jack Beeching, Thomas McGrath, Maurice Carpenter, Gordon Harris, and Jack Lindsay.

A2974. Williams, Harry. 'Dylan Thomas' Poetry of Redemption: Its Blakean Beginnings.' *Bucknell Review*, XX, iii (Winter 1972), 107–20.
Redemption through annihilation traced through Thomas's notebooks.

B2974. —— 'The Tyger and the Lamb.' *Concerning Poetry*, V, 1 (1972), 49–56.
In 'The Tyger' stanza 5, Los is the lamb and the tyger.

A2977. *Wills, James T. 'William Blake's Designs for Bunyan's *Pilgrim's Progress.*' Toronto Ph.D., 1975.
A careful survey of Bunyan *illustrations (1680–1824) and analysis of Blake's Bunyan *designs, concluding that Christian's journey is circular; there are 193 plates.

B2977. Wilner, Eleanor Rand. 'The Eye of the Storm: An Inquiry into the Role of Imagination in Maintaining Human Order and Mediating Social and Personal Change.' *DAI*, XXXIV (1973), 3362–3A. Johns Hopkins Ph.D.
'The second chapter contains a reading [sic] of the poets William Blake, Thomas Lovell Beddoes, and William Butler Yeats.'

A2984. Wiltshire, John. 'Blake's Simplicity.' *Cambridge Quarterly*, V (1971), 211–22.
Blake exhibits 'the apparent simplicity of a precisely formulated thought' (p. 211).

A2992. Witke, Joanne. 'Blake's Tree of Knowledge Grows out of the Enlightenment.' *Enlightenment Essays*, III (1972), 71–84.
On Berkeley and Hume.

A2993. §*Wittreich, Joseph Anthony, Jr. *Angel of Apocalypse*: Blake's Idea of Milton. Madison, 1975.

A2995. *Wittreich, Joseph Anthony Jr. '"Divine Countenance": Blake's Portrait and Portrayal of Milton.' *HLQ*, XXXVIII (1975), 125–60.
'*A* discussion of Blake's idea of Milton and his employment of tradition'.

B2995. —— 'Domes of Mental Pleasure: Blake's Epics and Hayley's Epic Theory.' *SP*, LXIX (1972), 101–29.
Hayley's epic theory is parallel to Blake's practice.

2999. —— 'William Blake: Illustrator-Interpreter of *Paradise Regained*' (1971).
Corrected by Butlin in *Blake Newsletter*, VI, 2 (1972 [1973]).

3007. A. Wormhoudt, Arthur. 'Blake's *Introduction* to *Songs of Innocence*' (1949). . . . B. Reprinted in no. A1587 3.

A3007. *Worrall, David. 'William Blake and Erasmus Darwin's *Botanic Garden*.' *BNYPL*, LXXVIII (1975), 397–417.
Stimulating speculation as to 'Darwin's influence' on 'Blake's works of 1791–95'.

B3007. *Wright, Andrew. *Blake's Job*: A Commentary. Oxford, 1972.
Reproduction of the 22 engravings with about a page of conventional commentary for each (pp. 2–51), plus 'Appendix I: The Biblical Texts and Blake's Alterations' (pp. 53–64).

3017. A. *Wright, Thomas. *The Life of William Blake*. . . . C. Two Volumes in One. Chicheley [England], 1972.

A3021. §Yamamoto, Matsuyo. '[On Blake and his *Songs of Innocence*].' *Yufubana* [*The Unwithering Flower*], No. 11 (March 1942), 33–9.
In Japanese.

A3046. §Yasuda, Masayoshi. *William Blake Kenkyu* [*Study of William Blake*]. Tokyo, 1973.
In Japanese.

A3063. Ziegelman, Lois Abrams. 'William Blake: The Lineaments of History.' *DAI*, XXXIV (1974), 4223A. Brandeis Ph.D.
'The aim of this thesis is to trace the course of Blake's reflections on the meaning of history.'

B3063. §Zubkova, S. 'William Blake.' *Uchitelskaia Gazeta* [*Teachers' Journal*] (28 Nov. 1957).
In Russian.

INDEX

This is primarily an index of proper names. Most references are to pages, but those beginning with 'no.' (e.g. 'no. B769') refer to individual entries in the section of Addenda.

The index has been prepared under somewhat unusual conditions, while I was fulfilling peripatetic teaching and research engagements in Poona, Hyderabad, Warangal, Madras, Pondicherry, Mysore, Bandipur, Colombo, Kandy, Periyar, Udaipur, Jaipur, Srinagar, Delhi, Isfahan, Persepolis, Shiraz, Kuwait, Cairo, Luxor, Montigny (Jura), and Wootton (Oxfordshire). For special assistance, I am grateful particularly to Meera Marathe, Sarah, Julia, and Beth Bentley, and B. G. Nitsure.

A

A. 707

A., B.C. 707

A., M. 707

Abbey, collection 132

Abbott, Claude, Colleer 707, 791

ABC–TV 5

Abergavenny (Earl of), ship 613–14

Abernathy & Walker, printers 653

Abott, dealer 340

Abraham, prophet 514, 588, 590

'Abraham & Isaac', drawing 904

Abrams, Lois no. A769

Abrams, M. H. 707, 765, 810, 818

abstracts 4

Abukh, S.B. no. A770

Academy (1874) 728, 884, 904, (1875) 890, 914, (1876) 904, 913, (1893) 843, (1897) 947, (1901) 730, (1906) 783, 903, (1909) 861, (1960) 729

Academy Editions 438

Academy of Natural Sciences (Philadelphia) 535

accounts, Blake's 741

'Accusers' 7 n. 1, 57–8, 61, 66, 69, 71, 76–8, 100, 106–7, 156–7, 204, 210, 267, 269, 298, 339–41, 357–9, 361–2, 802

Achilles 562–3

Ackermann, R., publisher 452, 526, 533–4, 596, 698

Acta Academiae Aboensis series no. A2126

Actes Congrès Londres (1939) 939

Adam 316, 326

'Adam and Eve', drawing (?1809) 212

Adamah 218

Adams, A. K. 504

Adams, Eric no. B770

Adams, Frederick B., Jr. 707–8

Adams, Hazard 45, 47, 708, 901, 937, no. C771, 1218, A1583, A2349

Adams, Marion no. A1512, A2862

Adams, R. B., collection 277, 284, 429, 430

— catalogue (1921) 277, 667, (1929) 277, 667

Adams, R. B., Jr., collection 284

A-Dayot, Magdeleine 708

Adcock, A. St. John 708

Addison, Joseph 352

Adelaide University Graduates' Union Monthly Newsletter and Gazette (1968) 930

Adelaide University Library 517, 636

Adelphi (1925) 760, (1934) 872, (1935) 927

Aders, Mrs. Charles, collection 282, 355, 384, 425

Adhémar, Jean 708

Adlard, John 708–9, 749, 751, 753, 755, 758, no. A787, A791, A792

Adler, E. N., collection 643

Adler, Jacob H. 709

AE, poet 843

Aeschylus 556, 563, 894

— *Tragedies* (1779), Blake's copy 682

Aesop 566

'Africa' in *Song of Los* 359–60

Afro-American no. A2462

Agatha, ship 614

Agnew, picture dealers (London) 109, 184, 216, 267

Agrippa, General to Augustus 629

Agrippa, Cornelius 894, no. A789

'Ah! Sun-Flower' 762, 810, 826, 857, 877, 915, 925

Ahania, woman 873

Ahania; see *Book of Ahania*

Aichi Prefectural University 840

Aiguille, P.d', engraver 532

Ainger, Alfred 856

Aitken, Charles 709, 738

Akesson, Elof. 709

Akhalgazrda Stalineli (1957) 845–6

Albani, Maria 709

Alberta (University of) Library 526, 643, 755

Albertina Museum exhibition (1937) 670, 858, (1947) 945

Johnson, Joseph, publisher 15, 37, 50, 185, 187, 205, 451, 452 n. 1, 512, 526, 534–5, 537, 539, 546, 555, 564, 579–80, 591–2, 606–10, 617–18, 621–4, 635–6, 684, 688–90, 760, 852
Johnson, Lee 859
Johnson, Lionel 843
Johnson, Miss Mary Barham, collection 576
Johnson, Mary C. 646 n. 2
Johnson, Mary Lynn 750, 755, 762, 843, no. A1437 8, A1963
Johnson, Maurice 352 n. 1
Johnson, Richard, collection 185
Johnson, Samuel 384, 611, 667, 709, 824, 861, 941, no. 482, A2076
Johnston, Elizabeth 677, 938
Johnston, Kenneth R. 804
Johnstone, William 844
Jonah 516–17
Jones 381 n. 4
Jones, Ben no. A1964, A2824
Jones, Harold, decorator 435
Jones, Herschel V., collection 105, 126, 160, 184, 192, 349, 405, 644, 666
Jones, Myrddin 844
Jones, P., engraver 633, 940
Jones, Miss Tessie, collection 184, 276, 405
Jones, Warren no. A1965
Jones, William Powell 844
Jones & Co. 633
Jones and Pontifex, copperplate makers 145
Jongh, Nicholas de, collection 844
Jordan, John E. 811, no. A1478
Jordan River 517
Joseph, designer 678
Joseph of Bible 514
'Joseph making himself known to his brethren', drawing 210, 649
Joseph of Arimathea, legend no. A1721
'Joseph of Arimathea Preaching', engraving 7 n. 1, 58, 61–2, 65–6, 68, 73, 77 & n. 1, 100, 106–7, 156–7, 210, 266–9, 357, 358–9, 361–2, 763, 802, 865
'Joseph ordering Simeon to be bound', drawing 211, 649
'Joseph's brethren bowing before him' (1785), drawing 211, 649
Josephus, Flavius, Works 585–7
Joshua 514, 588, 590
Journal des Débats (1913) 816, (1923) 736, (1942) 764
Journal of Aesthetic Education (1972) no. A2176
Journal of Aesthetics and Art Criticism (1951) 769, 772, 811, (1953) no. 1849, (1954) 708, (1956) 817, (1957) 940, (1964) 900, (1969) 785

Journal of Botany, British and Foreign (1896) 603–4
Journal of English and Germanic Philology (1955) 826, (1959) 807, (1970) 843, (1971) no. A1932
Journal of Hokusei Fakuen Women's Junior College (1959) 948
Journal of Koyasan University (1968) 846
Journal of Mental Sciences (1915) 874
Journal of Natural Philosophy (1811) 786
Journal of Psychological Medicine and Mental Pathology (1880) 726
Journal of the Faculty of Literature of Chuo University (1955) 855, (1956) 855
Journal of the History of Medicine and Applied Sciences (1946) 878
Journal of the Royal Society of Arts (1940) 765, (1958) 886
Journal of the Society of English and American Literature, Kwanseigakuin University (1961) 946
Journal of the Toyo University (1958) 877
Journal of the Warburg and Courtauld Institutes (1938) 766, (1943) 766, (1947) 873, (1950) 916, (1952) 802, 872, (1971) no. A1658
'Journey of Life', drawing 58, 257
Jouve, Pierre Jean 896
Joy 865, 896
Joyce, James 44, 767, 782, 811, 817–18, 844, 853, 875, 880, 922, no. B1469
'Judgement of Paris', design 786
'Judgment of Solomon', design (not by Blake) 830
Judith 517
Juel-Jensen, Dr. B. E., collection 61, 140, 430 & n. 2, 432
Jugaku, Bunsho 13 n. 2, 14, 33 n. 1, 133, 185, 433, 435, 667–9, 763–4, 798–9, 844–5, 849, 922, 925, no. A1971, A1975, A1976, A1977
Juliet 616
Julius, Dr. Nikolaus Heinrich 899
Jung, C. G. 48, 797, 893, 915, 935, 938, 942, no. A2275
Juninus no. A1980
Justin, Howard 768, 845, no. 1587 5, 1981B
Juszczek, W. no. A1981
Juvenile Library series 608

K

Kabbala 30, 36, 51, 758, 797, 806, 834, 842, 873, 883, 902, no. A1405
Kachru, Braj B. no. A1556
Kagoshina, University of; see Kenkyu Kiyo
Kahoe, Dr. Walter 432
Kain, Mrs. Louise, collection 61, 448

Sussex County Magazine (1927) 718, 823, 889–90, (1929) 890, (1947) 869
Sussex County Record Office; *see* West Sussex Record Office
Sussex Weekly Advertiser (1803) 711, (1804) 711
Sutherland, Graham 922
Sutherland, John H. 5, 50 n. 1, 804, 868, 922, no. A2782
Suttaby, Evance, and Fox, publishers 603, 721
Sutton, Denys 922
Sutton, Eric A. 922
Suzuki, Teiji 923
Suzuran (1923) 909
Swainson, W. P. 923
swan in *Jerusalem* 846
Swann, Mrs. John Butler, collection 125
Swansea city 107, 163, 264, 597, 599–600, 634, 749
Swarthmore College Library 518
Swayne, dealer? 282
Swedenborg, Emmanuel 44, 48, 51, 285, 288, 727, 731, 741, 776, 791, 797, 801–2, 808, 812, 832, 864, 870, 892, 895, 900, 912–13, 918, 922, 930, no. A789; *see also* New Jerusalem Church
— *Divine Love and Divine Wisdom* (1788) 58, 696, 764, 800, 832
— *Divine Providence* (1790) 61, 696–7, 895
— *Heaven and Hell* (1784) 60, 695, 741, 837
— *Worship and Love of God* 930
Swedish 709
Sweeney, John L. 923
Sweeting, A. 728
Swift, Jonathan 922
— *Gulliver's Travels* 598–600
Swinburne, Algernon Charles 24, 27, 28 & n. 1, 32, 114 n. 1, 164, 166 n. 1, 224 n. 1, 464, 716, 731, 757, 768, 814, 819, 827, 839, 863, 875, 878, 886, 903, 923, no. A1113
Swingle, L. J. 924
Swingler, Randall 924
Swiss Studies in English series 737, 884
Switzerland 864
Syamken, Georg no. C710
Sydney (Australia), view of engraved by W. S. Blake 794
Sydney Public Library (Australia) 585
Sydsvenska nagbladet Snallposten (1957) 709
Sykes, Alexander, collection 161
Sykes, Sir Mark Masterman (1771–1823) 416
Sykes, R., collection 416
Sylvan (1955) 804
symbolism 795, 833, 852, no. C770, A2280, A2759

Symons, Arthur 31–2, 596, 626, 727, 734, 768, 775, 838, 878, 898, 916–17, 924
Symposium (1966) 709
syntax no. A2675
Syracuse University Library 64, 410, 517, 526, 561, 564, 595, 636
Szerb, Antal 925

T

T., M. 585
T., S. 946
T.P.'s Weekly (1904) 775
Tabarde Inn (Southwark) 879
Tachikawa College English Literary Society 840; see *Eibungaku Kenkyu*
Tai, Liu-ling 925
Taidehistoriallisia Tutkimuksis—Konsthistoriska Studier 1 (1974) no. B2126
Taipeh 14
Tait, W. and C. B., publishers (Edinburgh) 654
Tait's Edinburgh Magazine (1840) no. A1478
Takemori, Osamu 925–6, no. A2811
Takeshima, Yasushi 799
Taketomo, Sofu 798
Takeyuki, So 926
Talfourd, Thomas Noon 856
Tanabé, R. 830
Tandon, Jagdish Narain no. A2817
Taniguchi, Shigeru 926
Tannenbaum, Leslie Warren 726, no. A2821
Taoist 808
tape recordings 5
Tarr, Rodger L. 760
Tartt, W. M. 926
Tasso 207, 709; *see also* 'Genesis, The Seven Days of the Created World'
Tate Central Library (Brixton) 774
Tate Gallery (London) 5, 42, 64, 93, 143–4, 151, 152, 169, 174, 183, 211, 214–15, 220, 430, 467, 508, 518, 531, 544, 546, 574, 652, 707, 718, 720, 723, 737–8, 775, 791, 841, 857, 934; *see also* National Gallery, British Art (London)
— catalogue (1940) 671, (1947) 110, 215, 259, 264, 672, 724, 784, 883, 887, (1953) 673, (1957) 248, 674, (1964) 715, (1971) 183 n. 1, 211 n. 1, 214 n. 2, 244, 249, 292, 297, 448 n. 2, 531, 674, 679, no. A1278, C1593, A1594, C2692
Tate Gallery Little Book series 508
Tatham, Charles Heathcote 91, 100, 684 n. 2
— *Etchings* (1799) 697
— *Three Designs for the National Monument* (1802) 697–8
Tatham, Frederick 20, 23 n. 1, 24, 31, 43,

Wedgwood catalogue (?1816–43) 511, *631–2*, 819, 838, 848, 851
Wedgwood Museum (Barlaston, Stoke-on-Trent, Staffordshire) 65, 272, 274, 281, 631
Wedmore, Frederick 937
Weekly News [Auckland] (1962) no. A1721
Wei, Chao-chi 937
Weintraub, Stanley no. A1960
Weisbuch, Claude 304
Weisinger, Nina Lee 937
Weinstein, Ulrich 937
Welch, Dennis Martin 754, no. A–B2942
Weld, F. M., Jr., collection 158
Welford, Charles 659
Wellek, René 937
Weller, friend of Blake 571
Wellesley College Library (Wellesley, Mass.) 65, 344, 349, 405, 518, 526, 544, 565, 571, 576, 593, 595, 606, 611, 621, 628, 630, 634–6, 691
— catalogue (1923) 667
Wells, Dr. Gabriel, dealer 101, 103–4, 106–7, 157, 181, 203, 207, 282, 300, 348, 404, 409, 418 n. 2, 644, 682
— collection 184
Wells, William 190, 411, 677, 937–8
Welsh and Wales 918, 944; *see also* Druid
Welty, Eudora 933
Wenger, A. Grace 938
Wen-hsueh Chou-k'an (19) 889
Wen-hsueh Chou-pao (1927) 780
Wen-hsueh Yen-chiu (1957) 849
Wen-i Yueh-k'an (19) 860
Werblowsky, R. J. Zwi 938
Werk (1947) 919, 945
Wesley, Charles and John 632, 800, 812, 817, 847
West, Sir Benjamin 91 n. 1, 103 n. 2, 776–7
West Sussex Record Office 512–13, 526, 564–5, 570–1, 575, 577–8, 595, 610, 635, 711
West's juvenile theatre 927
West's New Theatrical Characters 918, 921
Westbrook, Mike, musician no. A–B2232
Western Gate (1970) no. A2663
Western Ontario (University of) Library 556, 561, no. 260
Western Reserve Historical Society 536
Westminster Abbey 566–8, 626–7, 719, 733, 859, 865, 868
Westminster Public Library 66, 271, 276, 344, 352, 355, 512–13, 526, 538, 542, 546, 561, 564–5, 571–2, 577–8, 580, 593, 595, 607, 610–11, 621, 628, 634–6
— catalogue (1969) 678, (1972) 678
Westminster Review (1834) 713
Weston, Alexander C., collection 165, 204, 279, 281

Weston, Col. Gould, collection 163, 263 & n. 2, 674, 891
Wetherton, Sir Thomas, collection 404
Weyhe, dealer 276, 420
— catalogue (1938) 144, 341, 374, 429
Wharton (T. G.), Martin & Co., auction (1882) 334
WHATMAN, JAMES, watermark 8, 71 n. 1, 3, 72 & n. 2, 73, 82 n. 3, 87–9, 121, 128, 142–3, 146, 168–9, 194, 204, 207, 211, 212 n. 5, 216, 221 n. 1, 226–7, 259, 266, 268 n. 2, 286, 305, 339, 365–7, 372–3, 409, 424, 428, 453 n. 1, 455 n. 2, 457, 466, 519, 530, 536, 566–7, 615, 637, 646
wheatsheaf binding of R. M. Milnes 299, 433
wheel imagery no. 2561
Wheeler, Charles Henry 615, 617
'When Klopstock England defied' 747
Whistler, Laurence 938
Whitaker, John, *The Seraph* (?1818–28) *632–3*, 640, 940
Whitall, W. Van R., collection 128
White, dealer 424, 543
White, engraver 589
White, A. M. 422
White, Alfred T., collection 219, 282, 410
White, B., publisher 537
White, Emily de F. (Mrs. H. T. White), collection 422
White, F. M., collection 158 n. 2
White, Hal Saunders 938
White, Harold T., collection 158, 422
White, Helen C. 35, 938
White, Henry 132
White, Henry Kirke 632
White, J., publisher 451, 452 n. 1, 526, 617, 684
White (J) and Co., publishers 618
White, James 514
White, Mary Elizabeth no. A2950
White, Newman Ivey 720
White, Wayne 938
White, William 676
White, William A., collection 77, 101, 104, 109, 114, 126, 138–9, 158 & n. 1, 161, 163, 182, 192, 202, 205, 209, 215, 219, 261, 263, 267, 281–2, 299, 323, 334, 343, 352, 362, 406, 410, 422, 424, 443–4, 637, 644–6, 664
White Birch Society 666
White (Andrew Dickson) Museum of Art (Cornell University) 676
Whitefield, preacher 812
Whiteley, W., publisher 721
Whitesell, J. Edwin 735, 938, no. A1587 7
Whiteside, E., publisher 603
Whitley, A. E. 669